SECOND EDITION

National Forest Camping

Directory of 4,108 Designated Camping Areas at 141 Forests in 42 States

Published by:

Roundabout Publications
PO Box 569
LaCygne, KS 66040

Phone: 800-455-2207
Internet: www.RoundaboutPublications.com

Library of Congress Control Number: 2023940158

ISBN-10: 1-885464-85-1
ISBN-13: 978-1-885464-85-9

Table of Contents

Introduction

Huge portions of public lands, managed by a variety of government agencies, are available to the general public for recreational use. This book will guide you to 4,108 select camping areas available from the U.S. Forest Service at 141 forests in 42 states.

U.S. Forest Service

The U.S. Forest Service manages nearly 193 million acres of public land in 154 national forest and 20 national grasslands providing some of the best camping experiences in the United States. While this guide focusses on the areas with designated camping sites the Forest Services does offer numerous dispersed camping areas. These areas are generally more remote with open camping, many are hike-in or boat-in only. To learn more about these dispersed camping areas and the U.S. Forest Service, visit their website: www.fs.usda.gov.

Using This Guide

The guide is especially helpful when used along with Google Maps, Windows Maps, or a GPS device for locating and navigating to each camping area.

State Maps

A state map is provided to aid you in locating the camping areas. A grid overlay on each map is used when cross-referencing with each camping area.

Map Grid Chart & Alphabetical List

Following the state map is a chart showing the camping area ID number(s) located within a map grid. Following this chart is an alphabetical list of each camping area, which is especially helpful when you already know the name of an area. This list provides each location's ID number and map grid location.

Camping Area Details

Camping area details include information about each public camping area within the state. Preceding each location's name is the ID number and map grid location, which is used when referencing the state map.

Details for each camping area generally include the following information:

- Total number of sites or dispersed camping
- Number of RV sites
- Sites with electric hookups
- Full hookup sites, if available
- Water (central location or spigots at site)
- Showers
- RV dump station
- Toilets (flush, pit/vault, or none)
- Laundry facilities
- Camp store
- Maximum RV size limits (if any)
- Reservation information (accepted, not accepted, recommended or required)
- Generator use and hours (if limited)
- Operating season
- Camping fees charged
- Miscellaneous notes
- Length of stay limit
- Elevation in feet and meters
- Telephone number
- Nearby city or town
- GPS coordinates

The Ultimate Public Campground Project

Data for this publication is from The Ultimate Public Campground Project, which was established in 2008 to provide a consolidated and comprehensive source for public campgrounds of all types. Please note that despite our best efforts, there will always be errors to be found in the data. With over 45,000 records in our database, it is impossible to ensure that each one is always up-to-date.

Update: In 2022 The Ultimate Public Campground Project database was acquired by a GPS manufacture. As a result, updated information for this book will no longer be available - this is the last edition.

Happy Camping!

Common Abbreviations Used

ATV	All Terrain Vehicle
BMU	Basin Management Unit
CG	Campground
NF	National Forest
NG	National Grassland
NRA	National Recreation Area
NSA	National Scenic Area
OHV	Off Highway Vehicle
ORV	Off Road Vehicle
RA	Recreation Area
TC	Trail Camp
TH	Trail Head

Alabama

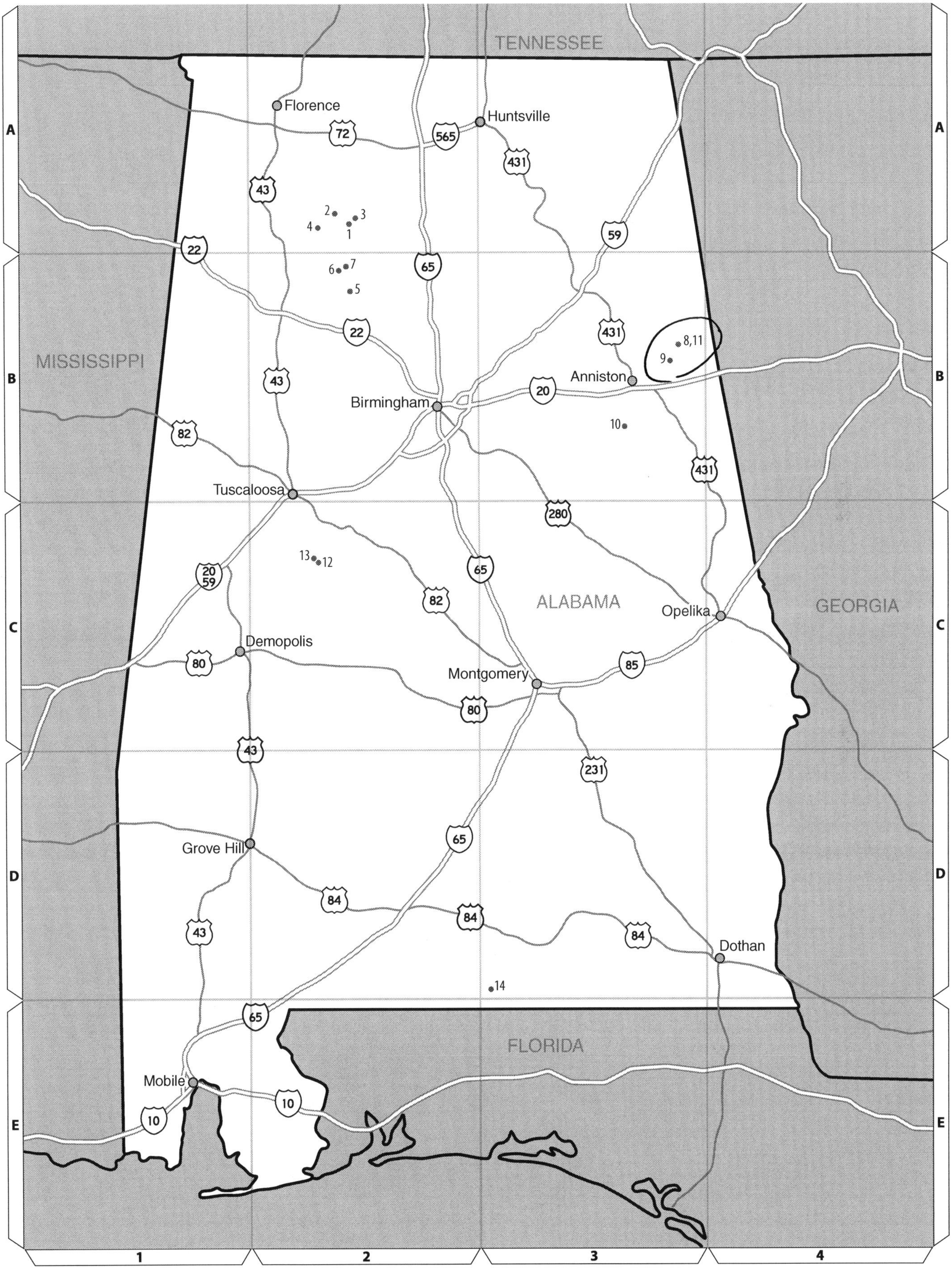
TENNESSEE
MISSISSIPPI
ALABAMA
GEORGIA
FLORIDA
Florence
Huntsville
Birmingham
Anniston
Tuscaloosa
Opelika
Demopolis
Montgomery
Grove Hill
Dothan
Mobile
1 2 3 4 5 6 7 8,11 9 10 12 13 14
A B C D E
1 2 3 4

Map	ID	Map	ID
A2	1-4	C2	12-13
B2	5-7	D3	14
B3	8-11		

Alphabetical List of Camping Areas

1 • A2 | Brushy Lake (Bankhead NF)

Total sites: 13, RV sites: 13, Central water, Flush toilet, Free showers, No RV dump, Tent & RV camping: $5, Open all year, Max Length: 18ft, Reservations not accepted, Elev: 682ft/208m, Tel: 205-489-5111, Nearest town: Moulton. GPS: 34.297225, -87.272131

2 • A2 | McDougle Hunt Camp (Bankhead NF)

Total sites: 10, RV sites: 10, Central water, Vault/pit toilet, No showers, No RV dump, Tent & RV camping: Free, Open all year, Max Length: 22ft, Elev: 945ft/288m, Tel: 205-489-5111, Nearest town: Moulton. GPS: 34.338000, -87.346000

3 • A2 | Owl Creek Horse Camp (Bankhead NF)

Total sites: 6, RV sites: 6, Central water, Vault/pit toilet, No showers, No RV dump, Tent & RV camping: $5, Open all year, Max Length: 22ft, Reservations not accepted, Elev: 899ft/274m, Tel: 205-489-5111, Nearest town: Moulton. GPS: 34.323625, -87.238683

4 • A2 | Wolf Pen Hunters Camp (Bankhead NF)

Total sites: 9, RV sites: 9, Central water, Vault/pit toilet, No showers, No RV dump, Tent & RV camping: Free, Elev: 902ft/275m, Tel: 205-489-5111, Nearest town: Haleyville. GPS: 34.281641, -87.435219

5 • B2 | Clear Creek (Bankhead NF)

Total sites: 102, RV sites: 102, Elec sites: 18, Water at site, Flush toilet, Free showers, RV dump, Tent & RV camping: $30, Group site: $50, Open Mar-Oct, Reservations accepted, Elev: 725ft/221m, Tel: 205-384-4792, Nearest town: Jasper. GPS: 34.014404, -87.265625

6 • B2 | Corinth (Bankhead NF)

Total sites: 52, RV sites: 52, Elec sites: 52, Water at site, Flush toilet, Free showers, RV dump, Tents: $17/RVs: $28, 52 Full hookup sites, Open Mar-Oct, Reservations not accepted, Elev: 630ft/192m, Tel: 205-489-3165, Nearest town: Double Springs. GPS: 34.101279, -87.320193

7 • B2 | Houston (Bankhead NF)

Total sites: 76, RV sites: 76, Central water, Flush toilet, Free showers, RV dump, Tent & RV camping: $13, Open Mar-Oct, Max Length: 30ft, Reservations not accepted, Elev: 676ft/206m, Tel: 205-489-2941, Nearest town: Houston. GPS: 34.122792, -87.290457

8 • B3 | Coleman Lake (Talladega NF)

Total sites: 39, RV sites: 39, Elec sites: 39, Water at site, Flush toilet, Free showers, RV dump, Tents: $8/RVs: $16, Open Mar-Dec, Max Length: 35ft, Reservations not accepted, Elev: 1220ft/372m, Tel: 256-463-2272, Nearest town: Jacksonville. GPS: 33.784180, -85.557617

9 • B3 | Pine Glen (Talladega NF)

Total sites: 21, RV sites: 21, No water, Vault/pit toilet, Tent & RV camping: $3, Open all year, Reservations not accepted, Elev: 1037ft/316m, Tel: 256-463-2272, Nearest town: Heflin. GPS: 33.724609, -85.603271

10 • B3 | Turnipseed (Talladega NF)

Total sites: 8, RV sites: 8, No water, Vault/pit toilet, Tent & RV camping: $5, Open Mar-Nov, Reservations not accepted, Elev: 1184ft/361m, Tel: 256-362-2909, Nearest town: Oxford. GPS: 33.444041, -85.841401

11 • B3 | Warden Station Horse Camp (Talladega NF)

Total sites: 45, RV sites: 45, Central water, Vault/pit toilet, No showers, No RV dump, Tent & RV camping: $6, Open all year, Reservations not accepted, Elev: 1211ft/369m, Tel: 256-463-2272, Nearest town: Heflin. GPS: 33.786967, -85.560387

12 • C2 | Payne Lake Eastside (Talladega NF)

Total sites: 30, RV sites: 30, Central water, Vault/pit toilet, No showers, No RV dump, Tents: $5/RVs: $12, Open all year, Reservations not accepted, Elev: 351ft/107m, Tel: 205-926-9765, Nearest town: Duncanville. GPS: 32.885577, -87.440597

13 • C2 | Payne Lake West (Talladega NF)

Total sites: 18, RV sites: 18, Elec sites: 7, Water at site, Flush toilet, Free showers, RV dump, Tents: $5/RVs: $12-18, Open all year, Reservations not accepted, Elev: 299ft/91m, Tel: 205-926-9765, Nearest town: Duncanville. GPS: 32.888498, -87.443565

14 • D3 | Open Pond (Conecuh NF)

Total sites: 74, RV sites: 65, Elec sites: 65, Water at site, Flush toilet, Free showers, RV dump, Tents: $8/RVs: $16, Open all year, Reservations not accepted, Elev: 236ft/72m, Tel: 334-222-2555, Nearest town: Lockhart. GPS: 31.089101, -86.549068

Alaska

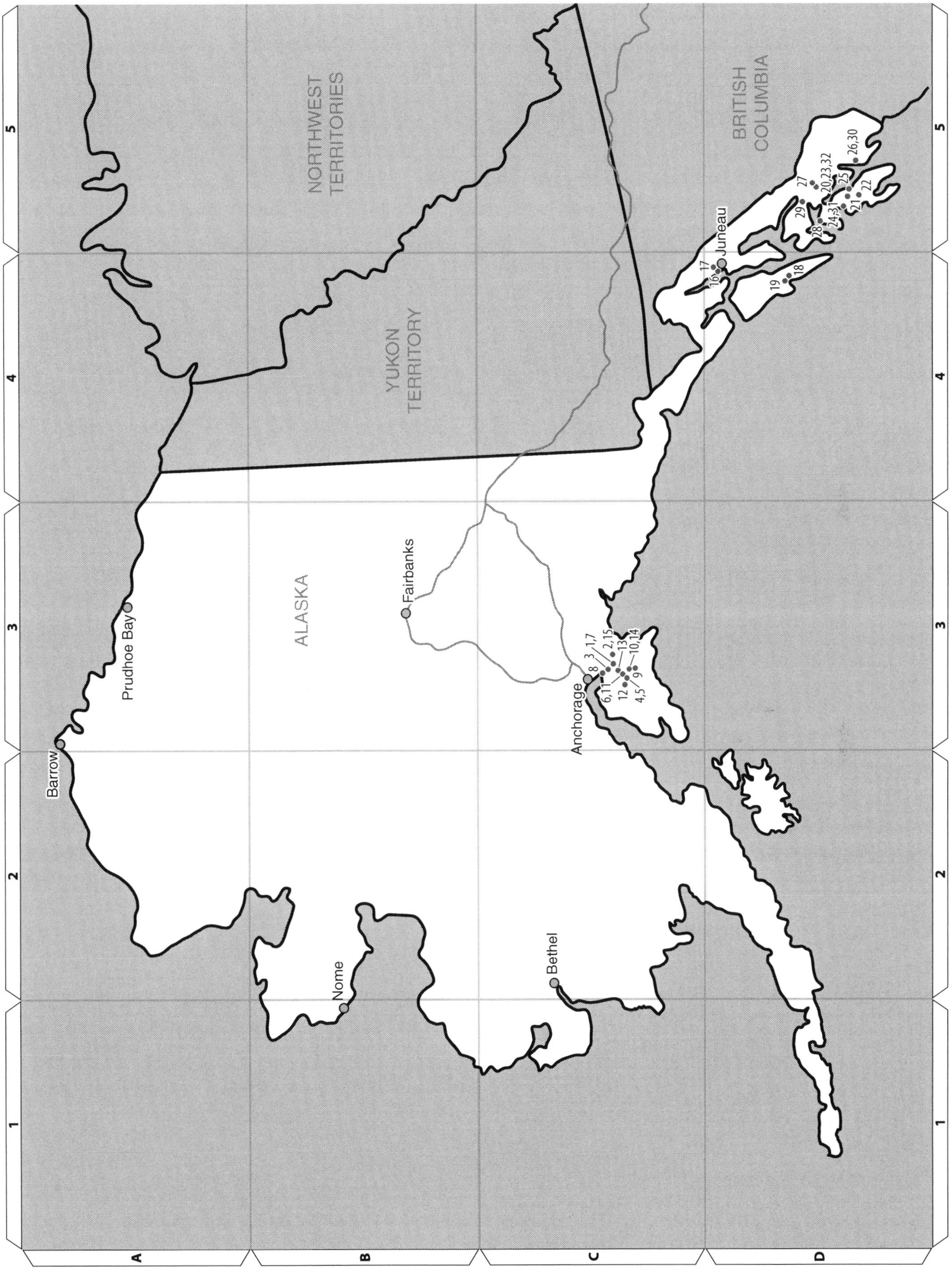
NORTHWEST TERRITORIES
YUKON TERRITORY
BRITISH COLUMBIA
ALASKA
Fairbanks
Prudhoe Bay
Barrow
Anchorage
Juneau
Nome
Bethel
A
B
C
D
1
2
3
4
5

Map	ID	Map	ID
C3	1-15	D5	20-32
D4	16-19		

Alphabetical List of Camping Areas

1 • C3 | Bertha Creek (Chugach NF)

Total sites: 12, RV sites: 12, Central water, Vault/pit toilet, No showers, No RV dump, Tent & RV camping: $14, Max Length: 20ft, Reservations not accepted, Elev: 776ft/237m, Tel: 907-783-3242, Nearest town: Girdwood. GPS: 60.750862, -149.254651

2 • C3 | Black Bear (Chugach NF)

Total sites: 13, RV sites: 13, Central water, Vault/pit toilet, No showers, No RV dump, Tent & RV camping: $14, Nothing larger than van/PU, Open May-Sep, Reservations not accepted, Elev: 74ft/23m, Tel: 907-783-3242, Nearest town: Girdwood. GPS: 60.788948, -148.889305

3 • C3 | Coeur D'Alene (Chugach NF)

Total sites: 6, RV sites: 0, No water, Vault/pit toilet, Tents only: Fee unk, Walk-to sites, Reservations not accepted, Elev: 1404ft/428m, Nearest town: Hope. GPS: 60.849873, -149.533421

4 • C3 | Cooper Creek North (Chugach NF)

Total sites: 8, RV sites: 4, Central water, Vault/pit toilet, Tent & RV camping: $18, RV dump at Quartz Creek, Open May-Sep, Reservations not accepted, Elev: 475ft/145m, Nearest town: Cooper Landing. GPS: 60.483722, -149.887739

5 • C3 | Cooper Creek South (Chugach NF)

Total sites: 20, RV sites: 20, Central water, Vault/pit toilet, Tent & RV camping: $18, RV dump at Quartz Creek, Open May-Sep, Max Length: 45ft, Reservations accepted, Elev: 431ft/131m, Nearest town: Cooper Landing. GPS: 60.483251, -149.882238

6 • C3 | Crescent Creek (Chugach NF)

Total sites: 9, RV sites: 9, Vault/pit toilet, Tent & RV camping: $14, Reservations not accepted, Elev: 562ft/171m, Nearest town: Quartz Creek. GPS: 60.496862, -149.680119

7 • C3 | Granite Creek (Chugach NF)

Total sites: 19, RV sites: 19, Central water, Vault/pit toilet, No showers, No RV dump, Tent & RV camping: $14, Open May-Sep, Max Length: 54ft, Reservations accepted, Elev: 648ft/198m, Nearest town: Girdwood. GPS: 60.724602, -149.293942

8 • C3 | Porcupine (Chugach NF)

Total sites: 34, RV sites: 34, Central water, Vault/pit toilet, No showers, No RV dump, Tent & RV camping: $18, Max Length: 46ft, Reservations accepted, Elev: 85ft/26m. GPS: 60.929462, -149.661324

9 • C3 | Primrose (Chugach NF)

Total sites: 8, RV sites: 8, Central water, Vault/pit toilet, Tent & RV camping: Fee unk, Max Length: 38ft, Reservations not accepted, Elev: 441ft/134m, Nearest town: Seward. GPS: 60.340848, -149.368861

10 • C3 | Ptarmigan (Chugach NF)

Total sites: 16, RV sites: 16, Central water, Vault/pit toilet, Tent & RV camping: $14, Open May-Sep, Reservations accepted, Elev: 511ft/156m, Tel: 907-522-8368, Nearest town: Seward. GPS: 60.406795, -149.362131

11 • C3 | Quartz Creek (Chugach NF)

Total sites: 45, RV sites: 45, Central water, Flush toilet, No showers, RV dump, Tent & RV camping: $18, Open May-Sep, Max Length: 120ft, Reservations accepted, Elev: 454ft/138m, Nearest town: Cooper Landing. GPS: 60.478839, -149.728038

12 • C3 | Russian River (Chugach NF)

Total sites: 83, RV sites: 83, Central water, Flush toilet, Tent & RV camping: $18, Open May-Sep, Max Length: 100ft, Reservations accepted, Elev: 344ft/105m, Tel: 907-288-7756, Nearest town: Sterling. GPS: 60.483244, -149.972313

13 • C3 | Tenderfoot Creek (Chugach NF)

Total sites: 35, RV sites: 35, Central water, Vault/pit toilet, No showers, No RV dump, Tent & RV camping: $18, Open May-Sep, Max Length: 100ft, Reservations accepted, Elev: 1346ft/410m, Tel: 907-288-3178, Nearest town: Coopr Landing. GPS: 60.637047, -149.496248

14 • C3 | Trail River (Chugach NF)

Total sites: 91, RV sites: 91, Central water, Vault/pit toilet, Tent & RV camping: $18, 1 group site $150, Open May-Sep, Max Length: 88ft, Reservations accepted, Elev: 437ft/133m, Tel: 907-288-3178, Nearest town: Seward. GPS: 60.413327, -149.381801

15 • C3 | Williwaw (Chugach NF)

Total sites: 60, RV sites: 60, Central water, Vault/pit toilet, No showers, No RV dump, Tent & RV camping: $18, Open May-Sep, Max Length: 145ft, Reservations accepted, Elev: 112ft/34m, Tel: 907-783-3242, Nearest town: Girdwood. GPS: 60.786825, -148.878515

16 • D4 | Auk Village (Tongass NF)

Total sites: 11, RV sites: 11, Central water, Vault/pit toilet, No showers, No RV dump, Tent & RV camping: $10, Open May-Sep, Max Length: 35ft, Reservations accepted, Elev: 99ft/30m, Tel: 907-586-8800, Nearest town: Juneau. GPS: 58.375773, -134.728408

17 • D4 | Mendenhall Lake (Tongass NF)

Total sites: 76, RV sites: 69, Elec sites: 18, Central water, Flush toilet, No showers, No RV dump, Tents: $10/RVs: $25-28, Also walk-to sites, 9 Full hookup sites, 7 , $5 Senior Pass discount, Open May-Sep, Max Length: 50ft, Reservations accepted, Elev: 75ft/23m, Tel: 907-586-8800, Nearest town: Juneau. GPS: 58.412505, -134.590077

18 • D4 | Sawmill Creek (Tongass NF)

Total sites: 9, RV sites: 9, No water, Vault/pit toilet, Tent & RV camping: Fee unk, Open May-Sep, Reservations not accepted, Elev: 181ft/55m, Tel: 907-747-6671, Nearest town: Sitka. GPS: 57.061604, -135.209649

19 • D4 | Starrigavan Rec Area (Tongass NF)

Total sites: 34, RV sites: 34, Central water, Vault/pit toilet, Tent & RV camping: $12-16, Max Length: 38ft, Reservations accepted, Elev: 64ft/20m, Tel: 907-747-6671, Nearest town: Sitka. GPS: 57.132318, -135.365037

20 • D5 | Anita Bay Overlook (Tongass NF)

Total sites: 2, RV sites: 2, No water, Vault/pit toilet, Tent & RV camping: Free, Reservations not accepted, Elev: 490ft/149m, Tel: 907-874-2323, Nearest town: Wrangell. GPS: 56.285895, -132.346619

21 • D5 | Eagles Nest (Tongass NF)

Total sites: 12, RV sites: 10, Central water, Vault/pit toilet, No showers, No RV dump, Tent & RV camping: $8, 2 walk-to sites, Reservations accepted, Elev: 385ft/117m, Tel: 907-826-3271, Nearest town: Thorne Bay. GPS: 55.703687, -132.846213

22 • D5 | Harris River (Tongass NF)

Total sites: 14, RV sites: 14, Central water, Vault/pit toilet, No showers, No RV dump, Tent & RV camping: $8, Stay limit: 14 days, Max Length: 89ft, Reservations accepted, Elev: 258ft/79m, Tel: 907-826-3271, Nearest town: Hollis. GPS: 55.467047, -132.857195

23 • D5 | Highline (Tongass NF)

Total sites: 2, RV sites: 2, No water, Vault/pit toilet, Tent & RV camping: Free, Max Length: 18ft, Reservations not accepted, Elev: 886ft/270m, Nearest town: Wrangell. GPS: 56.278153, -132.318294

24 • D5 | Horseshoe Hole (Tongass NF)

Total sites: 2, RV sites: 2, No water, No toilets, Tent & RV camping: Free, Stay limit: 14 days, Reservations not accepted, Elev: 37ft/11m, Tel: 907-826-3271. GPS: 55.809085, -133.124509

25 • D5 | Lake No. 3 (Tongass NF)

Total sites: 2, RV sites: 2, No water, No toilets, Tent & RV camping: Free, Reservations not accepted, Elev: 39ft/12m, Tel: 907-826-3271, Nearest town: Thorne Bay. GPS: 55.641079, -132.577914

26 • D5 | Last Chance (Tongass NF)

Total sites: 19, RV sites: 19, Central water, Vault/pit toilet, No showers, No RV dump, Tent & RV camping: $10, Open May-Sep, Reservations not accepted, Elev: 204ft/62m, Tel: 907-225-2148. GPS: 55.431843, -131.686065

27 • D5 | Lower Salamander Creek (Tongass NF)

Total sites: 2, RV sites: 2, No water, Vault/pit toilet, Tent & RV camping: Free, Creek water available, Reservations not accepted, Elev: 172ft/52m, Tel: 907-874-2323, Nearest town: Wrangell. GPS: 56.341132, -132.198893

28 • D5 | Memorial Beach (Tongass NF)

Total sites: 3, No water, Vault/pit toilet, Tents only: Free, Walk-to sites, 1000ft, Open May-Sep, Reservations not accepted, Elev: 59ft/18m, Tel: 907-826-1630, Nearest town: Point Baker. GPS: 56.349334, -133.564303

29 • D5 | Ohmer Creek (Tongass NF)

Total sites: 10, RV sites: 10, Central water, Vault/pit toilet, No showers, No RV dump, Tent & RV camping: $6, Open May-Sep, Max Length: 18ft, Reservations not accepted, Elev: 31ft/9m, Tel: 907-772-3871, Nearest town: Petersburg. GPS: 56.577323, -132.740881

30 • D5 | Signal Creek (Tongass NF)

Total sites: 24, RV sites: 24, Central water, Vault/pit toilet, No showers, No RV dump, Tent & RV camping: $10, Open May-Sep, Max Length: 45ft, Reservations accepted, Elev: 122ft/37m, Tel: 907-225-2148. GPS: 55.409427, -131.695858

31 • D5 | Staney Bridge (Tongass NF)

Total sites: 2, RV sites: 2, No water, No toilets, Tent & RV camping: Free, Reservations not accepted, Elev: 118ft/36m, Tel: 907-826-3271. GPS: 55.797755, -133.119224

32 • D5 | Yunshookuh Loop (Tongass NF)

Total sites: 3, RV sites: 3, No water, Vault/pit toilet, Tent & RV camping: Free, Reservations not accepted, Elev: 242ft/74m, Tel: 907-874-2323, Nearest town: Wrangell. GPS: 56.308256, -132.337534

Arizona

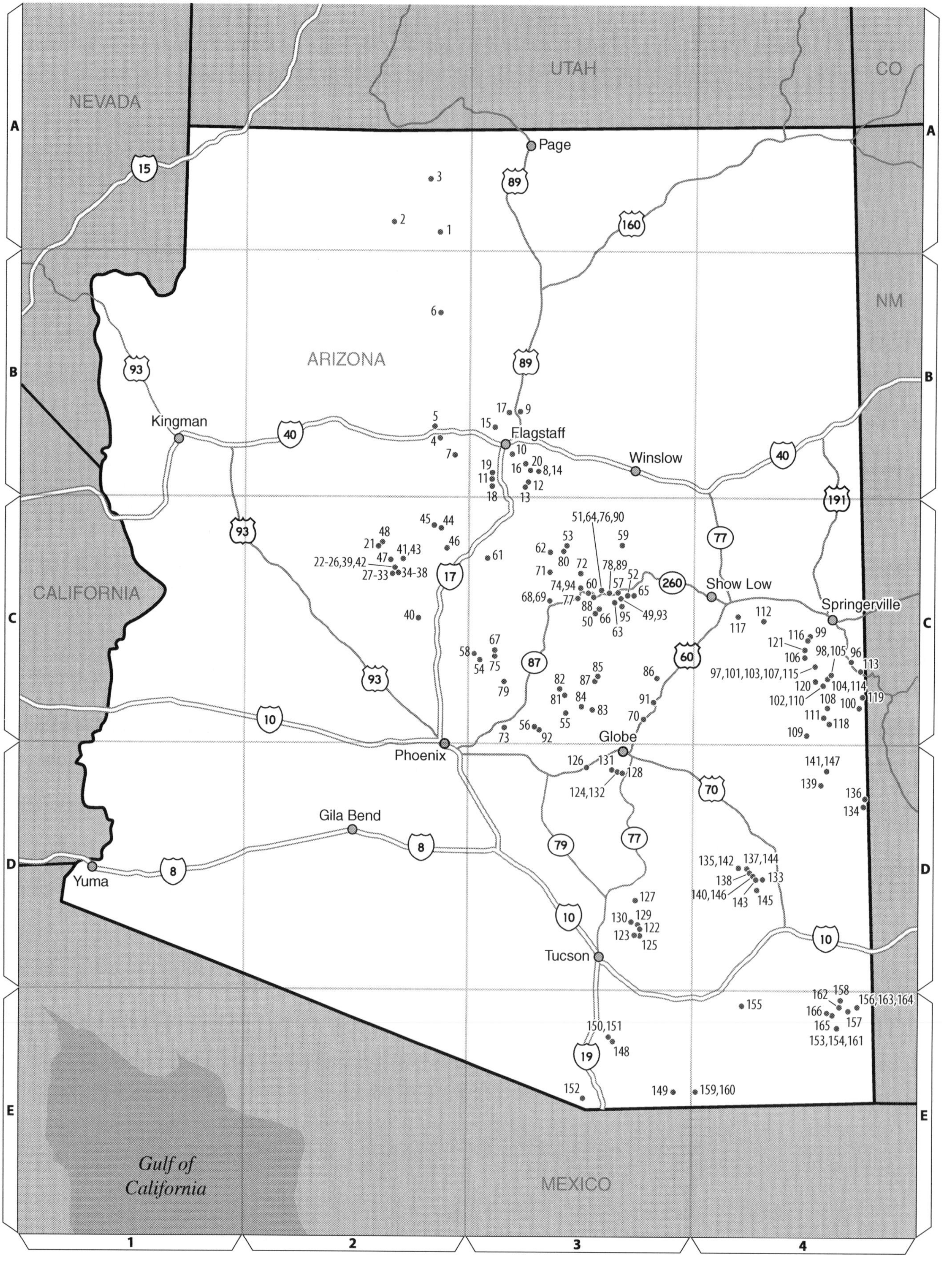
NEVADA
UTAH
CO
NM
ARIZONA
CALIFORNIA
MEXICO
Gulf of California
Page
Kingman
Flagstaff
Winslow
Show Low
Springerville
Phoenix
Globe
Gila Bend
Yuma
Tucson
15
89
160
93
40
191
77
17
260
87
60
10
70
8
79
19
A
B
C
D
E
1
2
3
4
1
2
3
4
5
6
7
8,14
9
10
11
12
13
15
16
17
18
19
20
21
22-26,39,42
27-33
34-38
40
41,43
44
45
46
47
48
49,93
50
51,64,76,90
52
53
54
55
56
57
58
59
60
61
62
63
65
66
67
68,69
70
71
72
73
74,94
75
77
78,89
79
80
81
82
83
84
85
86
87
88
91
92
95
96
97,101,103,107,115
98,105
99
100
102,110
104,114
106
108
109
111
112
113
116
117
118
119
120
121
122
123
124,132
125
126
127
128
129
130
131
133
134
135,142
136
137,144
138
139
140,146
141,147
143
145
148
149
150,151
152
153,154,161
155
156,163,164
157
158
159,160
162
165
166

Map	ID	Map	ID
A2	1-3	C4	96-121
B2	4-7	D3	122-132
B3	8-20	D4	133-147
C2	21-48	E3	148-152
C3	49-95	E4	153-166

Alphabetical List of Camping Areas

Name	ID	Map
Airplane Flat (Tonto NF)	49	C3
Alderwood (Tonto NF)	50	C3
Alpine Divide (Apache-Sitgreaves NF)	96	C4
Alto Pit OHV (Prescott NF)	21	C2
Apache Trout (Apache-Sitgreaves NF)	97	C4
Arcadia (Coronado NF)	133	D4
Ashurst Lake (Coconino NF)	8	B3
Aspen (Apache-Sitgreaves NF)	51	C3
Aspen (Apache-Sitgreaves NF)	98	C4
Bathtub (Coronado NF)	153	E4
Benny Creek (Apache-Sitgreaves NF)	99	C4
Black Canyon Rim (Apache-Sitgreaves NF)	52	C3
Blackjack (Apache-Sitgreaves NF)	134	D4
Blue Crossing (Apache-Sitgreaves NF)	100	C4
Blue Ridge (Coconino NF)	53	C3
Bog Springs (Coronado NF)	148	E3
Bonito (Coconino NF)	9	B3
Bronco Trailhead (Tonto NF)	54	C3
Brookchar (Apache-Sitgreaves NF)	101	C4
Buffalo Crossing (Apache-Sitgreaves NF)	102	C4
Burnt Corral Main (Tonto NF)	55	C3
Camp Rucker Group (Coronado NF)	154	E4
Canyon Lake Marina (Tonto NF)	56	C3
Canyon Point (Apache-Sitgreaves NF)	57	C3
Canyon Vista (Coconino NF)	10	B3
Cave Springs (Coconino NF)	11	B3
CCC (Tonto NF)	58	C3
Chevelon Crossing (Apache-Sitgreaves NF)	59	C3
Christopher Creek (Tonto NF)	60	C3
Clark Creek Corrals Horse Camp (Coronado NF)	135	D4
Clear Creek (Coconino NF)	61	C3
Clint's Well (Coconino NF)	62	C3
Coal Creek (Apache-Sitgreaves NF)	136	D4
Cochise Stronghold (Coronado NF)	155	E4
Colcord Ridge (Tonto NF)	63	C3
Columbine Corrals Horse Camp (Coronado NF)	137	D4
Crook (Apache-Sitgreaves NF)	64	C3
Cunningham (Coronado NF)	138	D4
Cutthroat (Apache-Sitgreaves NF)	103	C4
Dairy Springs (Coconino NF)	12	B3
Deer Creek (East Fork Black River) (Apache-Sitgreaves NF)	104	C4
Demotte (Kaibab NF)	1	A2
Diamond Rock (Apache-Sitgreaves NF)	105	C4
Dogtown Lake (Kaibab NF)	4	B2
Double Springs (Coconino NF)	13	B3
Forked Pine (Coconino NF)	14	B3
Freidlein Prairie Dispersed (Coconino NF)	15	B3
FSR 707 Dispersed 1 (Prescott NF)	22	C2
FSR 707 Dispersed 2 (Prescott NF)	23	C2
FSR 707 Dispersed 3 (Prescott NF)	24	C2
FSR 707 Dispersed 4 (Prescott NF)	25	C2
FSR 707 Dispersed 5 (Prescott NF)	26	C2
FSR 79 Dispersed 1-4 (Prescott NF)	27	C2
FSR 79 Dispersed 10-11 (Prescott NF)	28	C2
FSR 79 Dispersed 12-14 (Prescott NF)	29	C2
FSR 79 Dispersed 5 (Prescott NF)	30	C2
FSR 79 Dispersed 6 (Prescott NF)	31	C2
FSR 79 Dispersed 7 (Prescott NF)	32	C2
FSR 79 Dispersed 8-9 (Prescott NF)	33	C2
FSR 80 Dispersed 1-2 (Prescott NF)	34	C2
FSR 80 Dispersed 3 (Prescott NF)	35	C2
FSR 80 Dispersed 4 (Prescott NF)	36	C2
FSR 80 Dispersed 5 (Prescott NF)	37	C2
FSR 80 Dispersed 6 (Prescott NF)	38	C2
Gabaldon Horse Camp (Apache-Sitgreaves NF)	106	C4
General Hitchcock (Coronado NF)	122	D3
Gentry (Apache-Sitgreaves NF)	65	C3
Gordon Hirabayashi (Coronado NF)	123	D3
Granville (Apache-Sitgreaves NF)	139	D4
Grayling (Apache-Sitgreaves NF)	107	C4
Groom Creek Equestrian (Prescott NF)	39	C2
Haigler Canyon (Tonto NF)	66	C3
Hannagan (Apache-Sitgreaves NF)	108	C4
Hazlett Hollow (Prescott NF)	40	C2
Hilltop (Prescott NF)	41	C2
Honeymoon (Apache-Sitgreaves NF)	109	C4
Horse Springs (Apache-Sitgreaves NF)	110	C4
Horseshoe (Tonto NF)	67	C3
Hospital Flat (Coronado NF)	140	D4
Houston Mesa (Tonto NF)	68	C3
Houston Mesa Horse Camp (Tonto NF)	69	C3
Idlewilde (Coronado NF)	156	E4
Indian Hollow (Kaibab NF)	2	A2
Jacob Lake (Kaibab NF)	3	A2
John Hands (Coronado NF)	157	E4
Jones Water (Tonto NF)	70	C3
Kaibab Lake (Kaibab NF)	5	B2
Kehl Springs Camp (Coconino NF)	71	C3
Knoll Lake (Coconino NF)	72	C3
KP Cienega (Apache-Sitgreaves NF)	111	C4
Lakeview (Coronado NF)	149	E3
Lakeview (Coconino NF)	16	B3
Lockett Meadow (Coconino NF)	17	B3
Los Burros (Apache-Sitgreaves NF)	112	C4
Lower Juan Miller (Apache-Sitgreaves NF)	141	D4
Lower Pinal (Tonto NF)	124	D3
Lower Salt River RA - Coon Bluff (Tonto NF)	73	C3
Lower Tonto Creek (Tonto NF)	74	C3
Lower Wolf Creek (Prescott NF)	42	C2
Luna Lake (Apache-Sitgreaves NF)	113	C4
Lynx Lake (Prescott NF)	43	C2
Manzanita (Tonto NF)	18	B3
Mesquite (Tonto NF)	75	C3
Mingus Mountain (Prescott NF)	44	C2
Mogollon (Apache-Sitgreaves NF)	76	C3
Molino Basin (Coronado NF)	125	D3
Oak Flat (Tonto NF)	126	D3
Peppersauce (Coronado NF)	127	D3
Pine Flat (Coconino NF)	19	B3
Pinegrove (Coconino NF)	20	B3

1 • A2 | Demotte (Kaibab NF)

Total sites: 38, RV sites: 38, Central water, Vault/pit toilet, No showers, No RV dump, Tent & RV camping: $22, Open May-Oct, Max Length: 40ft, Reservations accepted, Elev: 8806ft/2684m, Tel: 520-643-7395, Nearest town: Jacob Lake. GPS: 36.410465, -112.134742

2 • A2 | Indian Hollow (Kaibab NF)

Total sites: 3, RV sites: 3, No water, Vault/pit toilet, Tent & RV camping: Free, Not suitable for large RVs, Open all year, Reservations not accepted, Elev: 6332ft/1930m, Tel: 928 643-7395, Nearest town: Grand Canyon. GPS: 36.461789, -112.484467

3 • A2 | Jacob Lake (Kaibab NF)

Total sites: 51, RV sites: 51, Central water, Vault/pit toilet, No showers, No RV dump, Tent & RV camping: $22, Open May-Oct, Max Length: 45ft, Reservations accepted, Elev: 7936ft/2419m, Tel: 928-643-7395, Nearest town: Jacob Lake. GPS: 36.716112, -112.214947

4 • B2 | Dogtown Lake (Kaibab NF)

Total sites: 54, RV sites: 54, Central water, Vault/pit toilet, No showers, No RV dump, Tent & RV camping: $26, Group site: $276, Open May-Sep, Max Length: 40ft, Reservations accepted, Elev: 7096ft/2163m, Tel: 928-699-1239, Nearest town: Williams. GPS: 35.211545, -112.123084

5 • B2 | Kaibab Lake (Kaibab NF)

Total sites: 63, RV sites: 63, Central water, Vault/pit toilet, No showers, RV dump, Tent & RV camping: $26, 3 group sites $80-$204, Open May-Sep, Max Length: 45ft, Reservations accepted, Elev: 6841ft/2085m, Tel: 928-635-5600, Nearest town: Williams. GPS: 35.281498, -112.157068

6 • B2 | Ten X (Kaibab NF)

Total sites: 70, RV sites: 70, Central water, Vault/pit toilet, No showers, No RV dump, Tent & RV camping: $20, 2 group sites $125-$175, Open May-Oct, Max Length: 50ft, Reservations accepted, Elev: 6670ft/2033m, Tel: 928-638-2443, Nearest town: Tusayan. GPS: 35.937012, -112.123047

7 • B2 | White Horse Lake (Kaibab NF)

Total sites: 94, RV sites: 94, Central water, Vault/pit toilet, No showers, RV dump, Tent & RV camping: $26, Group site: $168, Dump fee: $10, Stay limit: 14 days, Open May-Sep, Max Length: 50ft, Reservations accepted, Elev: 6565ft/2001m, Tel: 928-635-5600, Nearest town: Williams. GPS: 35.115825, -112.017024

8 • B3 | Ashurst Lake (Coconino NF)

Total sites: 25, RV sites: 25, Central water, Vault/pit toilet, No showers, No RV dump, Tent & RV camping: $20, Open fee-free w/ no amenities Nov-Apr when road is open, Stay limit: 14 days, Generator hours: 0600-2200, Open May-Oct, Max Length: 35ft, Reservations not accepted, Elev: 7136ft/2175m, Tel: 928-774-1147, Nearest town: Flagstaff. GPS: 35.019377, -111.408529

9 • B3 | Bonito (Coconino NF)

Total sites: 44, RV sites: 44, Central water, Flush toilet, No showers, No RV dump, Tent & RV camping: $26, Concession, Stay limit: 14 days, Generator hours: 0600-2200, Open May-Oct, Reservations not accepted, Elev: 6952ft/2119m, Tel: 928-526-0866, Nearest town: Flagstaff. GPS: 35.369513, -111.541524

10 • B3 | Canyon Vista (Coconino NF)

Total sites: 11, RV sites: 11, Central water, Vault/pit toilet, No showers, No RV dump, Tent & RV camping: $22, Concession, Stay limit: 14 days, Open May-Oct, Max Length: 22ft, Reservations not accepted, Elev: 6841ft/2085m, Tel: 928-774-1147, Nearest town: Flagstaff. GPS: 35.123901, -111.598352

11 • B3 | Cave Springs (Coconino NF)

Total sites: 82, RV sites: 82, Central water, Flush toilet, Pay showers, No RV dump, Tent & RV camping: $22, Concession, Stay limit: 14 days, Open Apr-Oct, Max Length: 36ft, Reservations accepted, Elev: 5472ft/1668m, Tel: 928-282-1629, Nearest town: Safford. GPS: 34.996437, -111.739522

12 • B3 | Dairy Springs (Coconino NF)

Total sites: 30, RV sites: 30, Central water, Vault/pit toilet, No showers, No RV dump, Tent & RV camping: $22, Group fee: $120, Open May-Oct, Max Length: 40ft, Reservations accepted, Elev: 7162ft/2183m, Tel: 928-226-0493, Nearest town: Flagstaff. GPS: 34.955878, -111.484565

13 • B3 | Double Springs (Coconino NF)

Total sites: 15, RV sites: 15, Central water, Vault/pit toilet, No showers, No RV dump, Tent & RV camping: $20, Open May-Oct, Max Length: 35ft, Reservations not accepted, Elev: 7208ft/2197m, Tel: 928-774-1147, Nearest town: Flagstaff. GPS: 34.942117, -111.493817

14 • B3 | Forked Pine (Coconino NF)

Total sites: 25, RV sites: 25, Central water, Vault/pit toilet, No showers, No RV dump, Tent & RV camping: $20, No water in winter, Stay limit: 14 days, Open Jun-Oct, Max Length: 35ft, Reservations not accepted, Elev: 7129ft/2173m, Tel: 928-774-1147, Nearest town: Flagstaff. GPS: 35.021240, -111.398926

15 • B3 | Freidlein Prairie Dispersed (Coconino NF)

Total sites: 14, RV sites: 14, No water, No toilets, Tent & RV camping: Free, Camp only in 14 designated sites, Small RVs/Tents, No fires, Sites 10-14 closed Mar-Aug, Stay limit: 14 days, Open all year, Reservations not accepted, Elev: 7552ft/2302m, Tel: 928-526-0866, Nearest town: Flagstaff. GPS: 35.282792, -111.718957

16 • B3 | Lakeview (Coconino NF)

Total sites: 30, RV sites: 30, Central water, Vault/pit toilet, No showers, No RV dump, Tent & RV camping: $24, Generator hours: 0600-2200, Open May-Oct, Max Length: 28ft, Reservations not accepted, Elev: 6992ft/2131m, Tel: 928-774-1147, Nearest town: Flagstaff. GPS: 35.066959, -111.496548

17 • B3 | Lockett Meadow (Coconino NF)

Total sites: 17, RV sites: 19, No water, Vault/pit toilet, Tent & RV camping: $18, Stay limit: 14 days, Generator hours: 0600-2200, Open Jun-Oct, Max Length: 18ft, Reservations not accepted, Elev: 8563ft/2610m, Tel: 928-774-1147, Nearest town: Flagstaff. GPS: 35.358046, -111.620580

18 • B3 | Manzanita (Tonto NF)

Total sites: 19, RV sites: 0, Central water, Vault/pit toilet, No showers, No RV dump, Tents only: $22, Small sleep-in vehicles only - no trailers or RVs allowed, Open all year, Reservations accepted, Elev: 4801ft/1463m, Tel: 928-204-2034, Nearest town: Red Rock. GPS: 34.936279, -111.744873

19 • B3 | Pine Flat (Coconino NF)

Total sites: 56, RV sites: 56, Central water, Vault/pit toilet, No showers, No RV dump, Tent & RV camping: $22, Open Apr-Oct, Max Length: 35ft, Reservations accepted, Elev: 5722ft/1744m, Tel: 928-282-3233, Nearest town: Sedona. GPS: 35.012575, -111.737288

20 • B3 | Pinegrove (Coconino NF)

Total sites: 46, RV sites: 46, Central water, Flush toilet, Pay showers, RV dump, Tent & RV camping: $26, Generator hours: 0600-2200, Open May-Oct, Max Length: 42ft, Reservations accepted, Elev: 6939ft/2115m, Tel: 928-226-0493, Nearest town: Flagstaff. GPS: 35.027479, -111.462044

21 • C2 | Alto Pit OHV (Prescott NF)

Total sites: 11, RV sites: 11, No toilets, No showers, No RV dump, Tent & RV camping: $14, Open all year, Max Length: 38ft, Reservations accepted, Elev: 6089ft/1856m, Tel: 928-443-8000, Nearest town: Prescott. GPS: 34.588819, -112.561023

22 • C2 | FSR 707 Dispersed 1 (Prescott NF)

Total sites: 3, RV sites: 3, No water, No toilets, Tent & RV camping: Free, Stay limit: 7 days, Open all year, Elev: 6207ft/1892m, Tel: 928-443-8000, Nearest town: Prescott. GPS: 34.455919, -112.450943

23 • C2 | FSR 707 Dispersed 2 (Prescott NF)

Total sites: 3, RV sites: 3, No water, No toilets, Tent & RV camping: Free, Stay limit: 7 days, Open all year, Elev: 6216ft/1895m, Tel: 928-443-8000, Nearest town: Prescott. GPS: 34.457219, -112.452178

24 • C2 | FSR 707 Dispersed 3 (Prescott NF)

Total sites: 3, RV sites: 3, No water, No toilets, Tent & RV camping: Free, Stay limit: 7 days, Open all year, Elev: 6185ft/1885m, Tel: 928-443-8000, Nearest town: Prescott. GPS: 34.457253, -112.453093

25 • C2 | FSR 707 Dispersed 4 (Prescott NF)

Total sites: 3, RV sites: 3, No water, No toilets, Tent & RV camping: Free, Stay limit: 7 days, Open all year, Elev: 6188ft/1886m, Tel: 928-443-8000, Nearest town: Prescott. GPS: 34.458504, -112.453295

26 • C2 | FSR 707 Dispersed 5 (Prescott NF)

Total sites: 3, RV sites: 3, No water, No toilets, Tent & RV camping: Free, Stay limit: 7 days, Open all year, Elev: 6190ft/1887m, Tel: 928-443-8000, Nearest town: Prescott. GPS: 34.458583, -112.453602

27 • C2 | FSR 79 Dispersed 1-4 (Prescott NF)

Total sites: 2, RV sites: 2, No water, No toilets, Tent & RV camping: Free, 4 sites, Stay limit: 7 days, Open all year, Elev: 6298ft/1920m, Tel: 928-443-8000, Nearest town: Prescott. GPS: 34.450076, -112.444483

28 • C2 | FSR 79 Dispersed 10-11 (Prescott NF)

Total sites: 2, RV sites: 2, No water, No toilets, Tent & RV camping: Free, 2 sites, Stay limit: 7 days, Open all year, Elev: 6056ft/1846m, Tel: 928-443-8000, Nearest town: Prescott. GPS: 34.442177, -112.446591

29 • C2 | FSR 79 Dispersed 12-14 (Prescott NF)

Total sites: 2, RV sites: 2, No water, No toilets, Tent & RV camping: Free, 3 sites, Stay limit: 7 days, Open all year, Elev: 6047ft/1843m, Tel: 928-443-8000, Nearest town: Prescott. GPS: 34.437438, -112.447312

30 • C2 | FSR 79 Dispersed 5 (Prescott NF)

Total sites: 2, RV sites: 2, No water, No toilets, Tent & RV camping: Free, Stay limit: 7 days, Open all year, Elev: 6271ft/1911m, Tel: 928-443-8000, Nearest town: Prescott. GPS: 34.449746, -112.446289

31 • C2 | FSR 79 Dispersed 6 (Prescott NF)

Total sites: 2, RV sites: 2, No water, No toilets, Tent & RV camping: Free, Stay limit: 7 days, Open all year, Elev: 6258ft/1907m, Tel: 928-443-8000, Nearest town: Prescott. GPS: 34.449006, -112.446145

32 • C2 | FSR 79 Dispersed 7 (Prescott NF)

Total sites: 2, RV sites: 2, No water, No toilets, Tent & RV camping: Free, Stay limit: 7 days, Open all year, Elev: 6234ft/1900m, Tel: 928-443-8000, Nearest town: Prescott. GPS: 34.449083, -112.447982

33 • C2 | FSR 79 Dispersed 8-9 (Prescott NF)

Total sites: 2, RV sites: 2, No water, No toilets, Tent & RV camping: Free, 2 sites, Stay limit: 7 days, Open all year, Elev: 6238ft/1901m, Tel: 928-443-8000, Nearest town: Prescott. GPS: 34.448342, -112.447803

34 • C2 | FSR 80 Dispersed 1-2 (Prescott NF)

Total sites: 6, RV sites: 6, No water, No toilets, Tent & RV camping: Free, 2 sites, Stay limit: 7 days, Open all year, Elev: 6398ft/1950m, Tel: 928-443-8000, Nearest town: Prescott. GPS: 34.448313, -112.437269

35 • C2 | FSR 80 Dispersed 3 (Prescott NF)

Total sites: 6, RV sites: 6, No water, No toilets, Tent & RV camping: Free, Stay limit: 7 days, Open all year, Elev: 6406ft/1953m, Tel: 928-443-8000, Nearest town: Prescott. GPS: 34.447728, -112.436342

36 • C2 | FSR 80 Dispersed 4 (Prescott NF)

Total sites: 6, RV sites: 6, No water, No toilets, Tent & RV camping: Free, Stay limit: 7 days, Open all year, Elev: 6395ft/1949m, Tel: 928-443-8000, Nearest town: Prescott. GPS: 34.447099, -112.436627

37 • C2 | FSR 80 Dispersed 5 (Prescott NF)

Total sites: 6, RV sites: 6, No water, No toilets, Tent & RV camping: Free, Stay limit: 7 days, Open all year, Elev: 6349ft/1935m, Tel: 928-443-8000, Nearest town: Prescott. GPS: 34.444693, -112.437603

38 • C2 | FSR 80 Dispersed 6 (Prescott NF)

Total sites: 6, RV sites: 6, No water, No toilets, Tent & RV camping: Free, Stay limit: 7 days, Open all year, Elev: 6383ft/1946m, Tel: 928-443-8000, Nearest town: Prescott. GPS: 34.443433, -112.437778

39 • C2 | Groom Creek Equestrian (Prescott NF)

Total sites: 37, RV sites: 37, Central water, Vault/pit toilet, No showers, No RV dump, Tent & RV camping: $18, Open May-Oct, Max Length: 35ft, Reservations accepted, Elev: 6388ft/1947m, Tel: 928-443-8000, Nearest town: Prescott. GPS: 34.464953, -112.444103

40 • C2 | Hazlett Hollow (Prescott NF)

Total sites: 15, RV sites: 0, Central water, Vault/pit toilet, No showers, No RV dump, Tent & RV camping: $10, Shelters available, High clearance vehicle recommended, No large RVs, Stay limit: 14 days, Generator hours: 0600-2200, Open May-Sep, Reservations not accepted, Elev: 6047ft/1843m, Tel: 928-443-8000, Nearest town: Crown King. GPS: 34.175399, -112.276664

41 • C2 | Hilltop (Prescott NF)

Total sites: 38, RV sites: 38, Central water, Vault/pit toilet, No showers, No RV dump, Tent & RV camping: $18, Stay limit: 14 days, Generator hours: 0600-2200, Open Apr-Oct, Max Length: 40ft, Reservations not accepted, Elev: 5627ft/1715m, Tel: 928-443-8000, Nearest town: Prescott. GPS: 34.510464, -112.380867

42 • C2 | Lower Wolf Creek (Prescott NF)

Total sites: 20, RV sites: 20, No water, Vault/pit toilet, Tent & RV camping: $10, Stay limit: 14 days, Generator hours: 0600-2200, Open May-Oct, Max Length: 32ft, Reservations not accepted, Elev: 6165ft/1879m, Tel: 928-443-8000, Nearest town: Prescott. GPS: 34.454839, -112.454613

43 • C2 | Lynx Lake (Prescott NF)

Total sites: 36, RV sites: 36, Central water, Flush toilet, Tent & RV camping: $18, Open Apr-Oct, Max Length: 35ft, Reservations accepted, Elev: 5620ft/1713m, Tel: 928-443-8000, Nearest town: Prescott. GPS: 34.517308, -112.389036

44 • C2 | Mingus Mountain (Prescott NF)

Total sites: 30, RV sites: 19, Elec sites: 19, No water, Vault/pit toilet, Tents: $10/RVs: $14, Stay limit: 14 days, Generator hours: 0600-2200, Open May-Oct, Max Length: 24ft, Reservations not accepted, Elev: 7477ft/2279m, Tel: 928-567-4121, Nearest town: Clarkdale. GPS: 34.691942, -112.117915

45 • C2 | Potato Patch (Prescott NF)

Total sites: 40, RV sites: 40, Elec sites: 12, Central water, Vault/pit toilet, No showers, No RV dump, Tents: $14/RVs: $14-18, May not fill RV water tanks, Stay limit: 14 days, Generator hours: 0600-2200, Open May-Oct, Max Length: 40ft, Reservations accepted, Elev: 7011ft/2137m, Tel: 928-567-4121, Nearest town: Clarkdale. GPS: 34.709264, -112.155644

46 • C2 | Powell Springs (Prescott NF)

Total sites: 11, RV sites: 11, No water, Vault/pit toilet, Tent & RV camping: Free, Stay limit: 14 days, Generator hours: 0600-2200, Open all year, Max Length: 40ft, Reservations not accepted, Elev: 5331ft/1625m, Tel: 928-567-4121, Nearest town: Camp Verde. GPS: 34.578051, -112.068914

47 • C2 | White Spar (Prescott NF)

Total sites: 56, RV sites: 56, Central water, Vault/pit toilet, No showers, No RV dump, Tent & RV camping: $14, 12 sites open all year - $10 Nov-Mar, Generator hours: 0600-2200, Open all year, Max Length: 60ft, Reservations accepted, Elev: 5656ft/1724m, Tel: 928-443-8000, Nearest town: Prescott. GPS: 34.509334, -112.476753

48 • C2 | Yavapai (Prescott NF)

Total sites: 21, RV sites: 21, Elec sites: 1, Central water, Vault/pit toilet, No showers, No RV dump, Tent & RV camping: $18, Open all year, Max Length: 40ft, Reservations accepted, Elev: 5827ft/1776m, Tel: 928-443-8000, Nearest town: Prescott. GPS: 34.602181, -112.539569

49 • C3 | Airplane Flat (Tonto NF)

Total sites: 12, RV sites: 12, No water, Vault/pit toilet, Tent & RV camping: Free, Stay limit: 14 days, Open May-Oct, Max Length: 16ft, Reservations not accepted, Elev: 6608ft/2014m, Tel: 928-462-4300, Nearest town: Young. GPS: 34.283375, -110.809621

50 • C3 | Alderwood (Tonto NF)

Total sites: 5, RV sites: 5, No water, Vault/pit toilet, Tent & RV camping: Free, 4x4 advised after storms, Stay limit: 14 days, Open all year, Max Length: 16ft, Reservations not accepted, Elev: 5243ft/1598m, Tel: 928-474-7900, Nearest town: Young. GPS: 34.205825, -110.980587

51 • C3 | Aspen (Apache-Sitgreaves NF)

Total sites: 148, RV sites: 148, Central water, Vault/pit toilet, No showers, RV dump, Tent & RV camping: $25-27, Open Apr-Oct, Max Length: 69ft, Reservations accepted, Elev: 7628ft/2325m, Tel: 928-535-9233, Nearest town: Payson. GPS: 34.327085, -110.945989

52 • C3 | Black Canyon Rim (Apache-Sitgreaves NF)

Total sites: 21, RV sites: 21, Central water, Vault/pit toilet, No showers, No RV dump, Tent & RV camping: $20, Open May-Oct, Max Length: 45ft, Reservations accepted, Elev: 7572ft/2308m, Tel: 928-535-7300, Nearest town: Forest Lakes. GPS: 34.304365, -110.743654

53 • C3 | Blue Ridge (Coconino NF)

Total sites: 10, RV sites: 10, Central water, Vault/pit toilet, No showers, No RV dump, Tent & RV camping: $16, Generator hours: 0600-2200, Open May-Sep, Max Length: 22ft, Reservations not accepted, Elev: 6962ft/2122m, Tel: 928-477-2255, Nearest town: Winslow. GPS: 34.591574, -111.200928

54 • C3 | Bronco Trailhead (Tonto NF)

Total sites: 40, RV sites: 40, No water, Vault/pit toilet, Tent & RV camping: Free, Horse corrals, stock water, Max Length: 32ft, Elev: 3707ft/1130m, Tel: 480-595-3300, Nearest town: Carefree. GPS: 33.934822, -111.820501

55 • C3 | Burnt Corral Main (Tonto NF)

Total sites: 82, RV sites: 82, Central water, Vault/pit toilet, No showers, No RV dump, Tent & RV camping: $20, Not recommended for trailers over 22ft, Stay limit: 14 days, Open all year, Max Length: 22ft, Reservations not accepted, Elev: 1959ft/597m, Tel: 602-225-5395, Nearest town: Roosevelt. GPS: 33.626573, -111.204764

56 • C3 | Canyon Lake Marina (Tonto NF)

Total sites: 46, RV sites: 28, Elec sites: 28, Water at site, Flush toilet, Free showers, No RV dump, Tents: $35-40/RVs: $60-65, Concessionaire, RV pump-out available - $20, Open all year, Reservations accepted, Elev: 1670ft/509m, Tel: 480-610-3300, Nearest town: Apache Jct. GPS: 33.534424, -111.422119

57 • C3 | Canyon Point (Apache-Sitgreaves NF)

Total sites: 113, RV sites: 113, Elec sites: 32, Central water, Flush toilet, Pay showers, RV dump, Tents: $28/RVs: $33-37, Dump fee $7, Group sites $200-$265, Open Apr-Oct, Max Length: 99ft, Reservations accepted, Elev: 7703ft/2348m, Tel: 928-535-9233, Nearest town: Greer. GPS: 34.323288, -110.825644

58 • C3 | CCC (Tonto NF)

Total sites: 10, RV sites: 10, No water, No toilets, Tent & RV camping: $16, Stay limit: 14 days, Open all year, Max Length: 16ft, Elev: 3373ft/1028m, Tel: 480-595-3300, Nearest town: Carefree. GPS: 33.970625, -111.865476

59 • C3 | Chevelon Crossing (Apache-Sitgreaves NF)

Total sites: 6, RV sites: 0, No water, Vault/pit toilet, Tents only: Free, Stay limit: 14 days, Open all year, Max Length: 16ft, Reservations not accepted, Elev: 6224ft/1897m, Tel: 928-535-7300, Nearest town: Heber. GPS: 34.590746, -110.787833

60 • C3 | Christopher Creek (Tonto NF)

Total sites: 43, RV sites: 43, Central water, Vault/pit toilet, No showers, No RV dump, Tent & RV camping: $22, Group site: $80, Open Apr-Oct, Max Length: 22ft, Reservations accepted, Elev: 5715ft/1742m, Tel: 928-474-7900, Nearest town: Payson. GPS: 34.307747, -111.035638

61 • C3 | Clear Creek (Coconino NF)

Total sites: 18, RV sites: 18, Central water, Vault/pit toilet, No showers, No RV dump, Tent & RV camping: $18, Open all year, Max Length: 32ft, Reservations not accepted, Elev: 3240ft/988m, Tel: 928-204-0028, Nearest town: Camp Verde. GPS: 34.516072, -111.767313

62 • C3 | Clint's Well (Coconino NF)

Total sites: 7, RV sites: 7, No water, Vault/pit toilet, Tent & RV camping: $8, Generator hours: 0600-2200, Open all year, Max Length: 22ft, Reservations not accepted, Elev: 6900ft/2103m, Tel: 928-477-2255, Nearest town: Flagstaff. GPS: 34.554162, -111.311846

63 • C3 | Colcord Ridge (Tonto NF)

Total sites: 8, RV sites: 8, No water, Vault/pit toilet, Tent & RV camping: Free, Stay limit: 14 days, Open May-Oct, Max Length: 32ft, Reservations not accepted, Elev: 7615ft/2321m, Tel: 928-462-4300, Nearest town: Young. GPS: 34.262172, -110.843822

64 • C3 | Crook (Apache-Sitgreaves NF)

Total sites: 26, RV sites: 26, Central water, Vault/pit toilet, No showers, No RV dump, Tent & RV camping: $20, 2 reservable group sites $270, Single sites available if not in use by group, Open Apr-Nov, Max Length: 32ft, Reservations not accepted, Elev: 7631ft/2326m, Tel: 928-535-7300, Nearest town: Forest Lakes. GPS: 34.317763, -110.942401

65 • C3 | Gentry (Apache-Sitgreaves NF)

Total sites: 5, RV sites: 5, No water, Vault/pit toilet, Tent & RV camping: $18, Reservable as 1 group site: $90, Stay limit: 14 days, Open all year, Max Length: 15ft, Reservations accepted, Elev: 7694ft/2345m, Tel: 928-535-7300, Nearest town: Payson. GPS: 34.301271, -110.713246

66 • C3 | Haigler Canyon (Tonto NF)

Total sites: 14, RV sites: 14, No water, Vault/pit toilet, RV dump, Tent & RV camping: $16, Tonto Pass required: $8/day or $80/year, Dump fee (Ponderosa CG): $5, Stay limit: 14 days, Open May-Oct, Max Length: 20ft, Reservations not accepted, Elev: 5325ft/1623m, Tel: 928-462-4300, Nearest town: Young. GPS: 34.219551, -110.963584

67 • C3 | Horseshoe (Tonto NF)

Total sites: 12, RV sites: 12, No water, Vault/pit toilet, Tent & RV camping: $16, Stay limit: 14 days, Open all year, Max Length: 16ft, Reservations not accepted, Elev: 1916ft/584m, Tel: 480-595-3300, Nearest town: Carefree. GPS: 33.977571, -111.716941

68 • C3 | Houston Mesa (Tonto NF)

Total sites: 47, RV sites: 30, Central water, Flush toilet, Pay showers, RV dump, Tent & RV camping: $27, 2 group sites: $125-$165, RV water: $2, Dump fee: $3, Open all year, Max Length: 99ft, Reservations accepted, Elev: 5056ft/1541m, Tel: 928-468-7135, Nearest town: Payson. GPS: 34.270706, -111.319481

69 • C3 | Houston Mesa Horse Camp (Tonto NF)

Total sites: 28, RV sites: 28, Central water, Flush toilet, Pay showers, RV dump, Tent & RV camping: $20, Open all year, Max Length: 40ft, Reservations accepted, Elev: 5066ft/1544m, Tel: 928-468-7135, Nearest town: Payson. GPS: 34.269521, -111.314412

70 • C3 | Jones Water (Tonto NF)

Total sites: 12, RV sites: 12, No water, Vault/pit toilet, Tent & RV camping: Free, Stay limit: 14 days, Open all year, Max Length: 20ft, Reservations not accepted, Elev: 4193ft/1278m, Tel: 928-402-6200, Nearest town: Globe. GPS: 33.592046, -110.642811

71 • C3 | Kehl Springs Camp (Coconino NF)

Total sites: 8, RV sites: 8, No water, Vault/pit toilet, Tent & RV camping: Free, Generator hours: 0600-2200, Open all year, Max Length: 22ft, Reservations not accepted, Elev: 7477ft/2279m, Tel: 928-477-2255, Nearest town: Clints Well. GPS: 34.435053, -111.317574

72 • C3 | Knoll Lake (Coconino NF)

Total sites: 33, RV sites: 33, Central water, Vault/pit toilet, No showers, No RV dump, Tent & RV camping: $20, Generator hours: 0600-2200, Open May-Sep, Max Length: 32ft, Reservations not accepted, Elev: 7503ft/2287m, Tel: 928-477-2255, Nearest town: Blue Ridge. GPS: 34.426539, -111.093542

73 • C3 | Lower Salt River RA - Coon Bluff (Tonto NF)

Total sites: 5, RV sites: 5, No water, Vault/pit toilet, Tent & RV camping: $8, Overnight camping allowed Oct-Apr on Friday and Saturday nights and Sunday nights before holidays, Requires a Tonto pass - $8/day, Open Oct-Apr, Max Length: 40ft, Reservations not accepted, Elev: 1332ft/406m, Tel: 602-225-5200, Nearest town: Mesa. GPS: 33.547274, -111.646137

74 • C3 | Lower Tonto Creek (Tonto NF)

Total sites: 9, RV sites: 9, Central water, Vault/pit toilet, No showers, No RV dump, Tent & RV camping: $20, Stay limit: 14 days, Open Apr-Oct, Max Length: 16ft, Reservations not accepted, Elev: 5473ft/1668m, Tel: 928 474-7900, Nearest town: Payson. GPS: 34.338524, -111.096145

75 • C3 | Mesquite (Tonto NF)

Total sites: 12, RV sites: 6, No water, Vault/pit toilet, Tent & RV camping: $16, Trailers not recommended, Stay limit: 14 days, Open all year, Reservations not accepted, Elev: 1890ft/576m, Tel: 480-595-3300, Nearest town: Carefree. GPS: 33.964174, -111.716373

76 • C3 | Mogollon (Apache-Sitgreaves NF)

Total sites: 26, RV sites: 26, Central water, Vault/pit toilet, No showers, No RV dump, Tent & RV camping: $18, Open May-Oct, Max Length: 32ft, Reservations accepted, Elev: 7658ft/2334m, Tel: 928-535-7300, Nearest town: Forest Lakes. GPS: 34.321425, -110.956745

77 • C3 | Ponderosa (Tonto NF)

Total sites: 48, RV sites: 48, Central water, Vault/pit toilet, No showers, No RV dump, Tent & RV camping: $20, 2 group sites: $100, Open Apr-Oct, Max Length: 40ft, Reservations accepted, Elev: 5728ft/1746m, Tel: 928-468-7135, Nearest town: Payson. GPS: 34.298919, -111.114209

78 • C3 | Rim (Apache-Sitgreaves NF)

Total sites: 26, RV sites: 26, Elec sites: 32, No water, Vault/pit toilet, Tent & RV camping: $18, Open Apr-Oct, Max Length: 40ft, Reservations accepted, Elev: 7576ft/2309m, Tel: 928-535-7300, Nearest town: Forest Lakes. GPS: 34.304711, -110.908293

79 • C3 | Riverside (Tonto NF)

Total sites: 12, RV sites: 12, No water, Vault/pit toilet, Tent & RV camping: $16, Stay limit: 14 days, Open all year, Max Length: 16ft, Reservations not accepted, Elev: 1604ft/489m, Tel: 480-595-3300, Nearest town: Carefree. GPS: 33.809098, -111.647379

80 • C3 | Rock Crossing (Coconino NF)

Total sites: 36, RV sites: 36, Central water, Vault/pit toilet, No showers, No RV dump, Tent & RV camping: $16, Generator hours: 0600-2200, Open May-Oct, Max Length: 32ft, Reservations not accepted, Elev: 7323ft/2232m, Tel: 928-477-2255, Nearest town: Blue Ridge. GPS: 34.562585, -111.218878

81 • C3 | Roosevelt Lake - Cholla (Tonto NF)

Total sites: 206, RV sites: 194, Central water, Flush toilet, Free showers, No RV dump, Tent & RV camping: $25, Dump station open Thurs. & Fri. from 12pm - 2pm, Stay limit: 14 days, Open all year, Max Length: 32ft, Reservations not accepted, Elev: 2198ft/670m, Tel: 928-467-3200, Nearest town: Roosevelt. GPS: 33.729631, -111.204619

82 • C3 | Roosevelt Lake - Indian Point (Tonto NF)

Total sites: 54, RV sites: 54, Central water, Vault/pit toilet, No

showers, No RV dump, Tent & RV camping: Free, Stay limit: 14 days, Open all year, Max Length: 16ft, Reservations not accepted, Elev: 2185ft/666m, Tel: 928-467-3200, Nearest town: Roosevelt. GPS: 33.767051, -111.239973

83 • C3 | Roosevelt Lake - Schoolhouse (Tonto NF)

Total sites: 211, RV sites: 211, Central water, Vault/pit toilet, No showers, No RV dump, Tent & RV camping: $20, Stay limit: 14 days, Open all year, Max Length: 50ft, Reservations accepted, Elev: 2159ft/658m, Tel: 928-467-3200, Nearest town: Roosevelt. GPS: 33.648392, -111.011187

84 • C3 | Roosevelt Lake - Windy Hill (Tonto NF)

Total sites: 147, RV sites: 147, Central water, Flush toilet, Free showers, RV dump, Tent & RV camping: $25, Stay limit: 14 days, Open all year, Max Length: 45ft, Reservations accepted, Elev: 2206ft/672m, Tel: 928-467-3200, Nearest town: Roosevelt. GPS: 33.663223, -111.090631

85 • C3 | Rose Creek (Tonto NF)

Total sites: 5, RV sites: 5, No water, Vault/pit toilet, Tent & RV camping: Free, Stay limit: 14 days, Open May-Oct, Max Length: 16ft, Reservations not accepted, Elev: 5472ft/1668m, Tel: 928-462-4300, Nearest town: Young. GPS: 33.829667, -110.979623

86 • C3 | Salt River Canyon - Second CG (Tonto NF)

Total sites: 25, RV sites: 25, No water, No toilets, Tent & RV camping: Fee unk, Also boat-in sites, $125 permit per group, Elev: 3337ft/1017m, Tel: 928-402-6200. GPS: 33.826566, -110.546043

87 • C3 | Sawmill Flats (Tonto NF)

Total sites: 5, RV sites: 5, Vault/pit toilet, Tent & RV camping: Free, Stay limit: 14 days, Open May-Oct, Max Length: 16ft, Reservations not accepted, Elev: 5817ft/1773m, Tel: 928-462-4300, Nearest town: Young. GPS: 33.813672, -110.983472

88 • C3 | Sharp Creek (Tonto NF)

Total sites: 28, RV sites: 28, Central water, Vault/pit toilet, No showers, No RV dump, Tent & RV camping: $27, Group site: $150, Stay limit: 14 days, Open Apr-Oct, Max Length: 120ft, Reservations accepted, Elev: 5971ft/1820m, Tel: 928-468-7135, Nearest town: Payson. GPS: 34.300952, -110.998056

89 • C3 | Sinkhole (Apache-Sitgreaves NF)

Total sites: 26, RV sites: 26, Central water, Vault/pit toilet, No showers, No RV dump, Tent & RV camping: $22, Stay limit: 14 days, Open Apr-Oct, Max Length: 35ft, Reservations accepted, Elev: 7572ft/2308m, Tel: 928-535-7300, Nearest town: Forest Lakes. GPS: 34.305158, -110.885495

90 • C3 | Spillway (Apache-Sitgreaves NF)

Total sites: 26, RV sites: 26, Central water, Flush toilet, No showers, No RV dump, Tent & RV camping: $30, Group fee: $124, Open Apr-Oct, Max Length: 42ft, Reservations accepted, Elev: 7513ft/2290m, Tel: 928-535-7300, Nearest town: Heber. GPS: 34.332424, -110.937214

91 • C3 | Timber Camp Rec Area (Tonto NF)

Total sites: 13, RV sites: 13, No water, Vault/pit toilet, Tent & RV camping: $16, 2 group sites (1 equestrian): $75-$150, Stay limit: 14 days, Max Length: 45ft, Reservations accepted, Elev: 5699ft/1737m, Tel: 928-402-6200, Nearest town: Globe. GPS: 33.687924, -110.571446

92 • C3 | Tortilla (Tonto NF)

Total sites: 76, RV sites: 76, Water at site, No showers, RV dump, Tent & RV camping: $20, Narrow road with sharp curves, Stay limit: 14 days, Open Oct-Mar, Max Length: 30ft, Reservations accepted, Elev: 1706ft/520m, Tel: 480-610-3300, Nearest town: Apache Junction. GPS: 33.529232, -111.397548

93 • C3 | Upper Canyon Creek (Tonto NF)

Total sites: 10, RV sites: 10, No water, Vault/pit toilet, Tent & RV camping: Free, Stay limit: 14 days, Open May-Oct, Max Length: 16ft, Reservations not accepted, Elev: 6591ft/2009m, Tel: 928-462-4300, Nearest town: Young. GPS: 34.288308, -110.803339

94 • C3 | Upper Tonto Creek (Tonto NF)

Total sites: 9, RV sites: 9, Central water, Vault/pit toilet, No showers, No RV dump, Tent & RV camping: $20, Stay limit: 14 days, Open Apr-Oct, Reservations not accepted, Elev: 5505ft/1678m, Tel: 928-474-7900, Nearest town: Payson. GPS: 34.340016, -111.095469

95 • C3 | Valentine Ridge (Tonto NF)

Total sites: 10, RV sites: 10, No water, No toilets, Tent & RV camping: Free, Stay limit: 14 days, Open May-Oct, Max Length: 16ft, Reservations not accepted, Elev: 6647ft/2026m, Tel: 928-462-4300, Nearest town: Heber. GPS: 34.244005, -110.798245

96 • C4 | Alpine Divide (Apache-Sitgreaves NF)

Total sites: 12, RV sites: 12, No water, Vault/pit toilet, Tent & RV camping: $10, Open May-Sep, Max Length: 12ft, Reservations not accepted, Elev: 8550ft/2606m, Tel: 928-339-5000, Nearest town: Alpine. GPS: 33.893311, -109.153320

97 • C4 | Apache Trout (Apache-Sitgreaves NF)

Total sites: 124, RV sites: 44, Elec sites: 44, Water at site, Flush toilet, Free showers, RV dump, Tents: $26/RVs: $42, 44 Full hookup sites, Group sites $200-$375, Open May-Oct, Max Length: 70ft, Reservations accepted, Elev: 9147ft/2788m, Tel: 928-333-6200, Nearest town: Eagar. GPS: 33.868887, -109.416307

98 • C4 | Aspen (Apache-Sitgreaves NF)

Total sites: 6, RV sites: 6, Central water, Vault/pit toilet, No showers, No RV dump, Tent & RV camping: $14, Reservations not accepted, Elev: 7858ft/2395m, Tel: 928-339-5000, Nearest town: Heber. GPS: 33.807617, -109.314573

99 • C4 | Benny Creek (Apache-Sitgreaves NF)

Total sites: 24, RV sites: 24, Central water, Vault/pit toilet, No showers, RV dump, Tent & RV camping: $12, Reservable group sites $40-$50, Stay limit: 14 days, Open May-Sep, Max Length: 24ft, Reservations not accepted, Elev: 8274ft/2522m, Tel: 928-735-7313, Nearest town: Greer. GPS: 34.044379, -109.449777

100 • C4 | Blue Crossing (Apache-Sitgreaves NF)

Total sites: 4, RV sites: 4, No water, Vault/pit toilet, Tent & RV camping: Free, Shelters available, 2 sites w/ Adirondack shelters, Stay limit: 14 days, Open Apr-Nov, Max Length: 16ft, Reservations not accepted, Elev: 5824ft/1775m, Tel: 928-339-5000, Nearest town: Alpine. GPS: 33.627892, -109.098102

101 • C4 | Brookchar (Apache-Sitgreaves NF)

Total sites: 13, RV sites: 0, Central water, Flush toilet, No showers, RV dump, Tents only: $16, Walk-to sites, Open May-Oct, Reservations accepted, Elev: 9012ft/2747m, Tel: 928-735-7313, Nearest town: Eagar. GPS: 33.875303, -109.414358

102 • C4 | Buffalo Crossing (Apache-Sitgreaves NF)

Total sites: 16, RV sites: 16, No water, Vault/pit toilet, Tent & RV camping: $14, Stay limit: 14 days, Open May-Oct, Reservations not accepted, Elev: 7648ft/2331m, Tel: 928-339-5000, Nearest town: Alpine. GPS: 33.767822, -109.355225

103 • C4 | Cutthroat (Apache-Sitgreaves NF)

Total sites: 18, RV sites: 0, Central water, Flush toilet, Free showers, RV dump, Tents only: $16, Open May-Oct, Reservations accepted, Elev: 9094ft/2772m, Tel: 928-735-7313, Nearest town: Eagar. GPS: 33.873049, -109.418091

104 • C4 | Deer Creek (East Fork Black River) (Apache-Sitgreaves NF)

Total sites: 6, RV sites: 0, Central water, Vault/pit toilet, No showers, No RV dump, Tents only: $14, Stay limit: 14 days, Open May-Sep, Reservations not accepted, Elev: 7864ft/2397m, Tel: 928-339-5000, Nearest town: Alpine. GPS: 33.805526, -109.319258

105 • C4 | Diamond Rock (Apache-Sitgreaves NF)

Total sites: 12, RV sites: 12, Central water, Vault/pit toilet, No showers, No RV dump, Tent & RV camping: $14, 3 sites with shelters, Open May-Oct, Max Length: 12ft, Reservations not accepted, Elev: 7930ft/2417m, Tel: 928-339-5000, Nearest town: Alpine. GPS: 33.818843, -109.300594

106 • C4 | Gabaldon Horse Camp (Apache-Sitgreaves NF)

Total sites: 5, RV sites: 5, No water, Vault/pit toilet, Tent & RV camping: Free, Horses only, Stay limit: 14 days, Open Jun-Sep, Max Length: 16ft, Reservations not accepted, Elev: 9419ft/2871m, Tel: 928 333-4301, Nearest town: Eager. GPS: 33.929199, -109.487469

107 • C4 | Grayling (Apache-Sitgreaves NF)

Total sites: 23, RV sites: 23, Central water, Flush toilet, Free showers, RV dump, Tent & RV camping: $20, Open May-Oct, Max Length: 45ft, Reservations accepted, Elev: 9068ft/2764m, Tel: 928-537-8888, Nearest town: Eagar. GPS: 33.872859, -109.413159

108 • C4 | Hannagan (Apache-Sitgreaves NF)

Total sites: 8, RV sites: 8, Central water, Vault/pit toilet, No showers, No RV dump, Tent & RV camping: Donation, Stay limit: 14 days, Open May-Sep, Max Length: 16ft, Reservations not accepted, Elev: 9262ft/2823m, Tel: 928-339-5000, Nearest town: Alpine. GPS: 33.635859, -109.322315

109 • C4 | Honeymoon (Apache-Sitgreaves NF)

Total sites: 4, RV sites: 4, No water, Vault/pit toilet, Tent & RV camping: Free, Stay limit: 14 days, Open all year, Max Length: 16ft, Reservations not accepted, Elev: 5456ft/1663m, Tel: 928-687-8600, Nearest town: Clifton. GPS: 33.475351, -109.481205

110 • C4 | Horse Springs (Apache-Sitgreaves NF)

Total sites: 27, RV sites: 27, Central water, Vault/pit toilet, No showers, No RV dump, Tent & RV camping: $16, Stay limit: 14 days, Open May-Oct, Reservations not accepted, Elev: 7664ft/2336m, Tel: 928-339-5000, Nearest town: Alpine. GPS: 33.787814, -109.345291

111 • C4 | KP Cienega (Apache-Sitgreaves NF)

Total sites: 5, RV sites: 5, Central water, Vault/pit toilet, No showers, No RV dump, Tent & RV camping: Free, Stay limit: 14 days, Open May-Sep, Max Length: 16ft, Reservations not accepted, Elev: 8986ft/2739m, Tel: 928-339-5000, Nearest town: Alpine. GPS: 33.576183, -109.355957

112 • C4 | Los Burros (Apache-Sitgreaves NF)

Total sites: 10, RV sites: 10, No water, Vault/pit toilet, Tent & RV camping: Free, Stay limit: 14 days, Open May-Oct, Max Length: 22ft, Reservations not accepted, Elev: 7890ft/2405m, Tel: 928-368-2100, Nearest town: Lakeside. GPS: 34.140878, -109.777324

113 • C4 | Luna Lake (Apache-Sitgreaves NF)

Total sites: 50, RV sites: 50, Central water, Vault/pit toilet, No showers, No RV dump, Tent & RV camping: $16, Group site: $50-$125, Open May-Oct, Max Length: 192ft, Reservations accepted, Elev: 8038ft/2450m, Tel: 928-537-8888, Nearest town: Alpine. GPS: 33.835957, -109.081978

114 • C4 | Raccoon (Apache-Sitgreaves NF)

Total sites: 10, RV sites: 0, Central water, Vault/pit toilet, No showers, No RV dump, Tents only: $14, Stay limit: 14 days, Open May-Oct, Reservations not accepted, Elev: 7785ft/2373m, Tel: 928-339-5000, Nearest town: Alpine. GPS: 33.798679, -109.329398

115 • C4 | Rainbow (Apache-Sitgreaves NF)

Total sites: 161, RV sites: 161, Elec sites: 180, Central water, Flush toilet, Free showers, RV dump, Tent & RV camping: $20-22, Group site: $80, Open May-Oct, Max Length: 32ft, Reservations accepted, Elev: 9157ft/2791m, Tel: 928-333-6200, Nearest town: Greer. GPS: 33.875583, -109.402529

116 • C4 | Rolfe C. Hoyer (Apache-Sitgreaves NF)

Total sites: 91, RV sites: 91, Elec sites: 45, Central water, Vault/pit toilet, Pay showers, No RV dump, Tent & RV camping: $24, Open May-Oct, Max Length: 32ft, Reservations accepted, Elev: 8324ft/2537m, Tel: 928-333-6200, Nearest town: Greer. GPS: 34.033936, -109.453857

117 • C4 | Scott Reservoir (Apache-Sitgreaves NF)

Total sites: 12, RV sites: 12, No water, Vault/pit toilet, Tent & RV camping: Free, Rough access road, Stay limit: 5 days, Open Apr-Oct, Reservations not accepted, Elev: 6742ft/2055m, Tel: 928-368-2100, Nearest town: Lakeside. GPS: 34.176715, -109.961051

118 • C4 | Strayhorse (Apache-Sitgreaves NF)

Total sites: 7, RV sites: 7, Central water, Vault/pit toilet, No showers, No RV dump, Tent & RV camping: Free, Winter access may be limited, Open all year, Max Length: 16ft, Reservations not accepted, Elev: 7802ft/2378m, Tel: 928-687-8600, Nearest town: Alpine. GPS: 33.550321, -109.318093

119 • C4 | Upper Blue (Apache-Sitgreaves NF)

Total sites: 3, RV sites: 3, No water, Vault/pit toilet, Tent & RV camping: Free, Stay limit: 14 days, Open Apr-Nov, Max Length: 16ft, Reservations not accepted, Elev: 6335ft/1931m, Tel: 928-339-5000, Nearest town: Alpine. GPS: 33.694001, -109.071863

120 • C4 | West Fork (Apache-Sitgreaves NF)

Total sites: 70, RV sites: 0, No water, Vault/pit toilet, Tents only: Free, Dispersed sites, Open May-Oct, Elev: 7818ft/2383m, Tel: 928-339-5000, Nearest town: Alpine. GPS: 33.790059, -109.413187

121 • C4 | Winn (Apache-Sitgreaves NF)

Total sites: 63, RV sites: 63, Central water, Vault/pit toilet, No showers, No RV dump, Tent & RV camping: $14, 2 group sites: $125, Stay limit: 14 days, Open May-Oct, Max Length: 45ft, Reservations accepted, Elev: 9350ft/2850m, Tel: 928-333-6200, Nearest town: Greer. GPS: 33.965653, -109.485118

122 • D3 | General Hitchcock (Coronado NF)

Total sites: 11, RV sites: 0, No water, Vault/pit toilet, Tents only: $20, Stay limit: 14 days, Open May-Oct, Reservations not accepted, Elev: 6037ft/1840m, Tel: 520-749-8700, Nearest town: Tucson. GPS: 32.377408, -110.686011

123 • D3 | Gordon Hirabayashi (Coronado NF)

Total sites: 12, RV sites: 12, No water, Vault/pit toilet, Tent & RV camping: $20, Horse corral, Stay limit: 14 days, Open Nov-Apr, Max Length: 22ft, Reservations not accepted, Elev: 4872ft/1485m, Tel: 520-749-8700, Nearest town: Tucson. GPS: 32.338069, -110.718719

124 • D3 | Lower Pinal (Tonto NF)

Total sites: 16, RV sites: 16, Central water, Vault/pit toilet, No showers, No RV dump, Tent & RV camping: Free, Narrow winding mountain gravel road, Stay limit: 14 days, Open May-Nov, Max Length: 20ft, Reservations not accepted, Elev: 7539ft/2298m, Tel: 928-402-6200, Nearest town: Globe. GPS: 33.287354, -110.830322

125 • D3 | Molino Basin (Coronado NF)

Total sites: 37, RV sites: 37, No water, Vault/pit toilet, Tent & RV camping: $20, Open Oct-Apr, Max Length: 22ft, Reservations not accepted, Elev: 4396ft/1340m, Tel: 520-749-8700, Nearest town: Tucson. GPS: 32.337091, -110.693196

126 • D3 | Oak Flat (Tonto NF)

Total sites: 16, RV sites: 16, Vault/pit toilet, Tent & RV camping: Free, Stay limit: 14 days, Open all year, Max Length: 30ft, Reservations not accepted, Elev: 3934ft/1199m, Tel: 928-402-6200, Nearest town: Superior. GPS: 33.307879, -111.050359

127 • D3 | Peppersauce (Coronado NF)

Total sites: 17, RV sites: 17, Central water, Vault/pit toilet, No showers, No RV dump, Tent & RV camping: $15, Stay limit: 14 days, Open all year, Max Length: 22ft, Reservations not accepted, Elev: 4626ft/1410m, Tel: 520-749-8700, Nearest town: Oracle. GPS: 32.538424, -110.716501

128 • D3 | Pioneer Pass (Tonto NF)

Total sites: 23, RV sites: 23, No water, Vault/pit toilet, Tent & RV camping: Free, Stay limit: 14 days, Open May-Nov, Max Length: 18ft, Reservations not accepted, Elev: 5886ft/1794m, Tel: 928-4-2-6200, Nearest town: Globe. GPS: 33.279701, -110.796712

129 • D3 | Rose Canyon (Coronado NF)

Total sites: 73, RV sites: 73, Central water, Vault/pit toilet, No showers, No RV dump, Tent & RV camping: $24, Reservable group site: $39, Open Apr-Oct, Max Length: 22ft, Reservations not accepted, Elev: 7159ft/2182m, Tel: 520-749-8700, Nearest town: Tucson. GPS: 32.394584, -110.697445

130 • D3 | Spencer Canyon (Coronado NF)

Total sites: 60, RV sites: 60, Central water, Vault/pit toilet, No showers, No RV dump, Tent & RV camping: $22, Open Apr-Oct, Max Length: 22ft, Reservations not accepted, Elev: 7923ft/2415m, Tel: 520-576-1492, Nearest town: Tucson. GPS: 32.414339, -110.739034

131 • D3 | Sulphide Del Ray (Tonto NF)

Total sites: 10, RV sites: 10, No water, Vault/pit toilet, Tent & RV camping: Free, Stay limit: 14 days, Open all year, Max Length: 20ft, Elev: 6024ft/1836m, Tel: 928-402-6200, Nearest town: Globe. GPS: 33.292725, -110.867920

132 • D3 | Upper Pinal (Tonto NF)

Total sites: 3, RV sites: 3, Tent & RV camping: Free, Narrow winding mountain gravel road, Stay limit: 14 days, Open May-Nov, Max Length: 20ft, Reservations not accepted, Elev: 7687ft/2343m, Tel: 928-402-6200, Nearest town: Globe. GPS: 33.284227, -110.821267

133 • D4 | Arcadia (Coronado NF)

Total sites: 19, RV sites: 19, No water, Vault/pit toilet, Tent & RV camping: $20, Reservable group site, Stay limit: 14 days, Open all year, Max Length: 22ft, Reservations not accepted, Elev: 6673ft/2034m, Tel: 928-428-4150, Nearest town: Safford. GPS: 32.648247, -109.819429

134 • D4 | Blackjack (Apache-Sitgreaves NF)

Total sites: 10, RV sites: 10, No water, Vault/pit toilet, Tent & RV camping: Free, Stay limit: 14 days, Open all year, Reservations not accepted, Elev: 6276ft/1913m, Tel: 928-687-8600, Nearest town: Clifton. GPS: 33.056422, -109.080427

135 • D4 | Clark Creek Corrals Horse Camp (Coronado NF)

Total sites: 2, RV sites: 2, No water, Tent & RV camping: Free, Open Apr-Nov, Max Length: 22ft, Reservations not accepted, Elev: 8901ft/2713m, Tel: 928-428-4150, Nearest town: Safford. GPS: 32.717116, -109.977026

136 • D4 | Coal Creek (Apache-Sitgreaves NF)

Total sites: 5, RV sites: 5, No water, Vault/pit toilet, Tent & RV camping: Free, Stay limit: 14 days, Open all year, Max Length: 16ft, Reservations not accepted, Elev: 5814ft/1772m, Tel: 928-687-8600, Nearest town: Clifton. GPS: 33.103033, -109.060386

137 • D4 | Columbine Corrals Horse Camp (Coronado NF)

Total sites: 6, RV sites: 6, Central water, Tent & RV camping: $10, Open Apr-Nov, Max Length: 22ft, Reservations not accepted, Elev: 9492ft/2893m, Tel: 928-428-4150. GPS: 32.706549, -109.913616

138 • D4 | Cunningham (Coronado NF)

Total sites: 10, RV sites: 10, No water, Vault/pit toilet, Tent & RV camping: $15, Stay limit: 14 days, Open Apr-Nov, Max Length: 22ft, Reservations not accepted, Elev: 8884ft/2708m, Tel: 928-428-4150, Nearest town: Safford. GPS: 32.678151, -109.894197

139 • D4 | Granville (Apache-Sitgreaves NF)

Total sites: 11, RV sites: 11, Central water, Vault/pit toilet, No showers, No RV dump, Tent & RV camping: Free, Stay limit: 14 days, Open Apr-Nov, Max Length: 16ft, Reservations not accepted, Elev: 6713ft/2046m, Tel: 928-687-8600, Nearest town: Clifton. GPS: 33.188315, -109.383288

140 • D4 | Hospital Flat (Coronado NF)

Total sites: 10, RV sites: 0, Vault/pit toilet, Tents only: $10, Group site: $25, Stay limit: 14 days, Open Apr-Nov, Reservations not accepted, Elev: 9042ft/2756m, Tel: 928-428-4150, Nearest town: Safford. GPS: 32.665624, -109.874801

141 • D4 | Lower Juan Miller (Apache-Sitgreaves NF)

Total sites: 4, RV sites: 4, No water, Vault/pit toilet, Tent & RV camping: Free, Stay limit: 14 days, Open all year, Max Length: 16ft, Reservations not accepted, Elev: 5718ft/1743m, Tel: 928-687-8600, Nearest town: Clifton. GPS: 33.267362, -109.340611

142 • D4 | Riggs Flat (Coronado NF)

Total sites: 31, RV sites: 31, No water, Vault/pit toilet, Tent & RV camping: $20, Stay limit: 14 days, Open Apr-Nov, Max Length: 22ft, Reservations not accepted, Elev: 8832ft/2692m, Tel: 928-428-4150, Nearest town: Safford. GPS: 32.708013, -109.962759

143 • D4 | Shannon (Coronado NF)

Total sites: 11, RV sites: 11, No water, Vault/pit toilet, Tent & RV camping: $15, 2 Adirondack shelters, Stay limit: 14 days, Open Apr-Nov, Max Length: Trlr-22'/RV-16ft, Reservations not accepted, Elev: 9052ft/2759m, Tel: 928-428-4150, Nearest town: Safford. GPS: 32.658379, -109.857961

144 • D4 | Soldier Creek (Coronado NF)

Total sites: 12, RV sites: 12, No water, Vault/pit toilet, Tent & RV camping: $20, Stay limit: 14 days, Open Apr-Nov, Max Length: 22ft, Reservations not accepted, Elev: 9386ft/2861m, Tel: 928-428-4150, Nearest town: Safford. GPS: 32.698958, -109.920357

145 • D4 | Stockton Pass (Coronado NF)

Total sites: 7, RV sites: 7, No water, Vault/pit toilet, Tent & RV camping: $15, Group site, Stay limit: 14 days, Open all year, Max Length: 22ft, Reservations not accepted, Elev: 5705ft/1739m, Tel: 928-428-4150, Nearest town: Safford. GPS: 32.591697, -109.850151

146 • D4 | Upper Hospital Flat Group (Coronado NF)

Total sites: 1, No water, Vault/pit toilet, Tents only: Free, Group site: Free, Individual sites available, High clearance vehicles needed, Open Apr-Nov, Reservations accepted, Elev: 9176ft/2797m, Tel: 928-428-4150, Nearest town: Safford. GPS: 32.669078, -109.872965

147 • D4 | Upper Juan Miller (Apache-Sitgreaves NF)

Total sites: 4, RV sites: 0, No water, Vault/pit toilet, Tents only: Free, Open all year, Reservations not accepted, Elev: 5889ft/1795m, Tel: 928-687-8600, Nearest town: Clifton. GPS: 33.268996, -109.348063

148 • E3 | Bog Springs (Coronado NF)

Total sites: 13, RV sites: 13, Water available, Vault/pit toilet, No showers, No RV dump, Tent & RV camping: $20, Stay limit: 14 days, Generator hours: 0600-2200, Open all year, Max Length: 22ft, Reservations not accepted, Elev: 5121ft/1561m, Tel: 520-281-2296, Nearest town: Green Valley. GPS: 31.726807, -110.875000

149 • E3 | Lakeview (Coronado NF)

Total sites: 65, RV sites: 23, Central water, Vault/pit toilet, No showers, No RV dump, Tent & RV camping: $20, Open all year, Max Length: 36ft, Reservations not accepted, Elev: 5489ft/1673m, Tel: 520-378-0311, Nearest town: Sonoita. GPS: 31.427734, -110.450684

150 • E3 | Proctor Road Dispersed 1 (Coronado NF)

Total sites: 10, RV sites: 10, No water, No toilets, Tent & RV camping: Free, Beware of cattle that may cause damage, Max Length: 18ft, Elev: 4288ft/1307m, Nearest town: Green Valley. GPS: 31.740823, -110.895345

151 • E3 | Proctor Road Dispersed 2 (Coronado NF)

Total sites: 10, RV sites: 10, No water, No toilets, Tent & RV camping: Free, Very rough road, Beware of cattle that may cause damage, Max Length: 18ft, Elev: 4401ft/1341m, Tel: Proctor Rd, Nearest town: Green Valley. GPS: 31.739249, -110.890053

152 • E3 | White Rock (Coronado NF)

Total sites: 15, RV sites: 15, Central water, Vault/pit toilet, No showers, No RV dump, Tent & RV camping: $15, Stay limit: 14 days, Open all year, Max Length: 22ft, Reservations not accepted, Elev: 3930ft/1198m, Tel: 520-281-2296, Nearest town: Nogales. GPS: 31.394631, -111.089591

153 • E4 | Bathtub (Coronado NF)

Total sites: 11, RV sites: 0, Central water, Vault/pit toilet, No showers, No RV dump, Tents only: Free, Walk-to sites, Open all year, Reservations not accepted, Elev: 6112ft/1863m, Nearest town: Elfrida. GPS: 31.780029, -109.309570

154 • E4 | Camp Rucker Group (Coronado NF)

Total sites: 8, RV sites: 8, No water, Vault/pit toilet, Tent & RV camping: $10, 4x4 and/or high-clearance vehicle recommended, Single sites may be used if no group use, Stay limit: 14 days, Max Length: 16ft, Reservations not accepted, Elev: 6145ft/1873m, Tel: 520-364-3468, Nearest town: Douglas. GPS: 31.781598, -109.307316

155 • E4 | Cochise Stronghold (Coronado NF)

Total sites: 10, RV sites: 10, No water, Vault/pit toilet, Tent & RV camping: $10, Stay limit: 14 days, Open Sep-May, Max Length:

22ft, Reservations not accepted, Elev: 4934ft/1504m, Tel: 520-364-3468, Nearest town: Sunsites. GPS: 31.922616, -109.967567

156 • E4 | Idlewilde (Coronado NF)

Total sites: 9, RV sites: 9, No water, Vault/pit toilet, Tent & RV camping: $20, No water in winter, Stay limit: 14 days, Open all year, Max Length: 16ft, Reservations not accepted, Elev: 4944ft/1507m, Tel: 520-364-3468, Nearest town: Portal. GPS: 31.898233, -109.161968

157 • E4 | John Hands (Coronado NF)

Total sites: 6, RV sites: 0, No water, Vault/pit toilet, Tents only: Free, Open all year, Reservations not accepted, Elev: 5610ft/1710m, Tel: 520-364-3468, Nearest town: Rodeo, NM. GPS: 31.878000, -109.222000

158 • E4 | Pinery Canyon (Coronado NF)

Total sites: 4, RV sites: 4, No water, Vault/pit toilet, Tent & RV camping: $15, 4x4 or high-clearance vehicle recommended, Open Apr-Nov, Max Length: 16ft, Reservations not accepted, Elev: 7093ft/2162m, Tel: 520-364-3468, Nearest town: Portal. GPS: 31.933105, -109.272096

159 • E4 | Ramsey Vista (Coronado NF)

Total sites: 8, RV sites: 8, Vault/pit toilet, Tent & RV camping: $15, Difficult access via switchbacks on gravel road, 4x4 recommended, Vehicle length limited to 21ft, Open Apr-Nov, Max Length: 12ft, Reservations not accepted, Elev: 7326ft/2233m, Tel: 520-378-0311, Nearest town: Sierra Vista. GPS: 31.429165, -110.303606

160 • E4 | Reef Townsite (Coronado NF)

Total sites: 14, RV sites: 10, Elec sites: 21, No water, Vault/pit toilet, No showers, No RV dump, Tent & RV camping: $15, Difficult access via switchbacks on gravel road, 4x4 recommended, Stay limit: 14 days, Open Apr-Oct, Max Length: 12ft, Reservations accepted, Elev: 7162ft/2183m, Tel: 520-378-0311, Nearest town: Sierra Vista. GPS: 31.429759, -110.289969

161 • E4 | Rucker Forest Camp (Coronado NF)

Total sites: 14, RV sites: 14, No water, Vault/pit toilet, Tent & RV camping: $15, 4x4 and/or high-clearance vehicle recommended, Stay limit: 14 days, Open all year, Max Length: 16ft, Reservations not accepted, Elev: 6174ft/1882m, Tel: 520-364-3468, Nearest town: Elfrida. GPS: 31.784573, -109.303585

162 • E4 | Rustler Park (Coronado NF)

Total sites: 25, RV sites: 25, No water, Vault/pit toilet, Tent & RV camping: $15, Group site: $5 + $5/car, Stay limit: 14 days, Open Apr-Oct, Max Length: 22ft, Reservations not accepted, Elev: 8478ft/2584m, Tel: 520-364-3468, Nearest town: Rodeo, NM. GPS: 31.905282, -109.280066

163 • E4 | Stewart (Coronado NF)

Total sites: 6, RV sites: 6, Central water, Vault/pit toilet, No showers, No RV dump, Tent & RV camping: $20, No water in winter, Susceptible to flooding, Stay limit: 14 days, Open all year, Max Length: 16ft, Reservations not accepted, Elev: 5102ft/1555m, Tel: 520-364-3468, Nearest town: Portal. GPS: 31.891146, -109.167715

164 • E4 | Sunny Flat (Coronado NF)

Total sites: 14, RV sites: 14, Central water, Vault/pit toilet, No showers, No RV dump, Tent & RV camping: $20, Susceptible to flooding, Stay limit: 14 days, Open all year, Max Length: 28ft, Reservations not accepted, Elev: 5112ft/1558m, Tel: 520-364-3468, Nearest town: Rodeo, NM. GPS: 31.884766, -109.176025

165 • E4 | Sycamore (Coronado NF)

Total sites: 7, RV sites: 7, No water, Vault/pit toilet, No showers, No RV dump, Tent & RV camping: $15, Stay limit: 14 days, Open all year, Max Length: 16ft, Reservations not accepted, Elev: 6355ft/1937m, Tel: 520-364-3468, Nearest town: Douglas. GPS: 31.859799, -109.334303

166 • E4 | West Turkey Creek (Coronado NF)

Total sites: 7, RV sites: 0, No water, No toilets, Tents only: Free, Stay limit: 14 days, Open all year, Reservations not accepted, Elev: 5981ft/1823m, Tel: 520-388-8300, Nearest town: Douglas. GPS: 31.864589, -109.359279

Arkansas

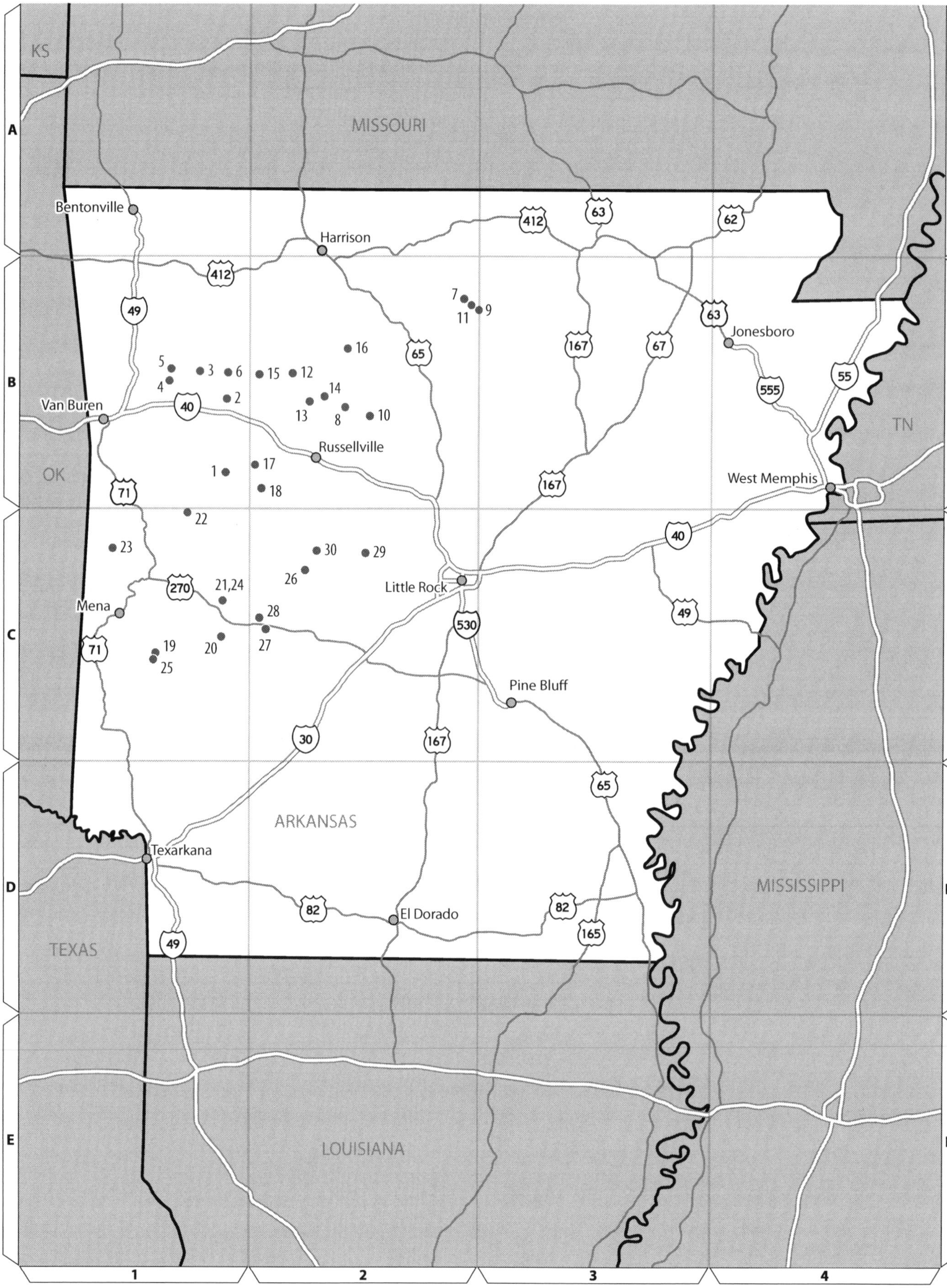
KS
MISSOURI
OK
TN
TEXAS
LOUISIANA
MISSISSIPPI
ARKANSAS
Bentonville
Harrison
Jonesboro
Van Buren
Russellville
West Memphis
Little Rock
Mena
Pine Bluff
Texarkana
El Dorado
412
63
62
49
65
167
67
555
55
40
71
270
530
30
82
165
1
2
3
4
5
6
7
8
9
10
11
12
13
14
15
16
17
18
19
20
21,24
22
23
25
26
27
28
29
30
A
B
C
D
E

Map	ID	Map	ID
B1	1-6	C1	19-25
B2	7-18	C2	26-30

Alphabetical List of Camping Areas

1 • B1 | Cove Lake (Ozark-St Francis NF)

Total sites: 36, RV sites: 36, Central water, Flush toilet, Free showers, No RV dump, Tent & RV camping: $15, Also cabins, Open all year, Max Length: 68ft, Reservations accepted, Elev: 1050ft/320m, Tel: 479-963-6421, Nearest town: Paris. GPS: 35.224778, -93.624113

2 • B1 | Horsehead Lake (Ozark-St Francis NF)

Total sites: 10, RV sites: 10, Central water, Flush toilet, Free showers, No RV dump, Tent & RV camping: $10, Group site $15, Open all year, Max Length: 30ft, Reservations not accepted, Elev: 705ft/215m, Tel: 479-754-2864, Nearest town: Clarksville. GPS: 35.565619, -93.639625

3 • B1 | Redding (Ozark-St Francis NF)

Total sites: 27, RV sites: 27, Central water, Flush toilet, Free showers, No RV dump, Tent & RV camping: $10, Open all year, Reservations not accepted, Elev: 807ft/246m, Tel: 479-754-2864, Nearest town: Ozark. GPS: 35.682129, -93.785645

4 • B1 | Shores Lake (Ozark-St Francis NF)

Total sites: 23, RV sites: 23, Elec sites: Unk, Central water, Flush toilet, Free showers, No RV dump, Tents: $8/RVs: $12, No water Dec-Mar - $6-$10, Open all year, Reservations not accepted, Elev: 712ft/217m, Tel: 479-667-2191, Nearest town: Mulberry. GPS: 35.639648, -93.960205

5 • B1 | White Rock Mt (Ozark-St Francis NF)

Total sites: 8, RV sites: 8, Central water, Vault/pit toilet, No showers, No RV dump, Tent & RV camping: $10, Also cabins, Open all year, Reservations not accepted, Elev: 2342ft/714m, Tel: 479-667-2191, Nearest town: Mulberry. GPS: 35.691434, -93.956608

6 • B1 | Wolf Pen (Ozark-St Francis NF)

Total sites: 6, RV sites: 6, No water, Vault/pit toilet, Tent & RV camping: $10, Open all year, Max Length: 18ft, Reservations not accepted, Elev: 965ft/294m, Tel: 479-754-2864, Nearest town: Oark. GPS: 35.675598, -93.630554

7 • B2 | Barkshed (Ozark-St Francis NF)

Total sites: 5, RV sites: 1, No water, Vault/pit toilet, Tent & RV camping: $3, No large RVs, Open all year, Reservations not accepted, Elev: 548ft/167m, Tel: 870 757 2211, Nearest town: Mountain View. GPS: 36.018687, -92.250417

8 • B2 | Bayou Bluff (Ozark-St Francis NF)

Total sites: 7, RV sites: 7, Central water, Vault/pit toilet, No showers, No RV dump, Tent & RV camping: $7, Shelters available, No large RVs, No water in winter, CCC rock shelters $10, Open Mar-Dec, Reservations not accepted, Elev: 673ft/205m, Tel: 479-284-3150, Nearest town: Jerusalem. GPS: 35.523691, -92.944059

9 • B2 | Blanchard Springs (Ozark-St Francis NF)

Total sites: 32, RV sites: 32, Central water, Flush toilet, Free showers, RV dump, Tent & RV camping: $15, Group sites $35-$60, May be closed during high water, Open all year, Max Length: 25ft, Reservations accepted, Elev: 420ft/128m, Tel: 870-757-2211, Nearest town: Fifty Six. GPS: 35.969104, -92.172821

10 • B2 | Brock Creek Lake (Ozark-St Francis NF)

Total sites: 6, RV sites: 6, No water, Vault/pit toilet, Tent & RV camping: Fee unk, Open all year, Reservations not accepted, Elev: 787ft/240m, Tel: 479-284-3150, Nearest town: Jerusalem. GPS: 35.491575, -92.805673

11 • B2 | Gunner Pool (Ozark-St Francis NF)

Total sites: 27, RV sites: 27, Central water, Vault/pit toilet, No showers, No RV dump, Tent & RV camping: $7, Elev: 486ft/148m, Tel: 870-269-3228, Nearest town: Fifty Six. GPS: 35.994335, -92.212323

12 • B2 | Haw Creek Falls (Ozark-St Francis NF)

Total sites: 9, RV sites: 9, No water, Vault/pit toilet, Tent & RV camping: $4, Closed when heavy rain forecast, Open Mar-Dec, Reservations not accepted, Elev: 892ft/272m, Tel: 479-284-3150, Nearest town: Pelsor. GPS: 35.679235, -93.259637

13 • B2 | Long Pool (Ozark-St Francis NF)

Total sites: 40, RV sites: 40, Elec sites: 20, Water at site, Flush toilet, Free showers, RV dump, Tents: $7/RVs: $7-13, Elev: 568ft/

173m, Tel: 479-284-3150, Nearest town: Dover. GPS: 35.548828, -93.160645

14 • B2 | Moccasin Gap Horse Camp (Ozark-St Francis NF)

Total sites: 17, RV sites: 17, Central water, Vault/pit toilet, No showers, No RV dump, Tent & RV camping: $3, Open all year, Reservations not accepted, Elev: 1411ft/430m, Tel: 479-284-3150, Nearest town: Dover. GPS: 35.573804, -93.068467

15 • B2 | Ozone (Ozark-St Francis NF)

Total sites: 8, RV sites: 8, No water, Vault/pit toilet, Tent & RV camping: $3, Open all year, Elev: 1896ft/578m, Tel: 479-754-2864, Nearest town: Clarksville. GPS: 35.671144, -93.448932

16 • B2 | Richland Creek (Ozark-St Francis NF)

Total sites: 11, No water, Vault/pit toilet, Tents only: $10, Very rough road, Open all year, Reservations not accepted, Elev: 1046ft/319m, Tel: 870-446-5122, Nearest town: Pelsor. GPS: 35.797232, -92.934054

17 • B2 | Sorghum Hollow Horse Camp (Ozark-St Francis NF)

Total sites: 15, RV sites: 15, No water, Vault/pit toilet, Tent & RV camping: Fee unk, Pond water for stock, Elev: 679ft/207m, Tel: 479-963-3076, Nearest town: Paris. GPS: 35.260113, -93.470177

18 • B2 | Spring Lake (Ozark-St Francis NF)

Total sites: 13, RV sites: 13, Central water, Flush toilet, Free showers, No RV dump, Tent & RV camping: $9, Open May-Sep, Reservations not accepted, Elev: 548ft/167m, Tel: 479-963-3076, Nearest town: Belleville. GPS: 35.150574, -93.424561

19 • C1 | Bard Springs (Ouachita NF)

Total sites: 5, RV sites: 0, No water, Vault/pit toilet, Tents only: $8, Adirondack-type shelters, Open all year, Reservations not accepted, Elev: 1326ft/404m, Tel: 501-321-5202, Nearest town: Athens. GPS: 34.391011, -94.010514

20 • C1 | Crystal (Ouachita NF)

Total sites: 9, RV sites: 9, No water, Vault/pit toilet, Tent & RV camping: Free, No large RVs, Open all year, Reservations not accepted, Elev: 1034ft/315m, Tel: 870-356-4186, Nearest town: Norman. GPS: 34.479411, -93.638484

21 • C1 | Dragover Float Camp (Ouachita NF)

Total sites: 7, RV sites: 0, No water, No toilets, Tents only: Free, Also boat-in sites, Elev: 659ft/201m, Tel: 870-867-2101, Nearest town: Mt Ida. GPS: 34.641438, -93.631262

22 • C1 | Jack Creek (Ouachita NF)

Total sites: 5, RV sites: 5, No water, Vault/pit toilet, Tent & RV camping: Free, Open Apr-Nov, Reservations not accepted, Elev: 699ft/213m, Tel: 479-637-4174, Nearest town: Booneville. GPS: 35.033855, -93.845912

23 • C1 | Little Pines (Ouachita NF)

Total sites: 9, RV sites: 9, Elec sites: 9, Water at site, Flush toilet, Free showers, RV dump, Tent & RV camping: $20-25, Open all year, Reservations not accepted, Elev: 833ft/254m, Tel: 479-637-4174, Nearest town: Waldron. GPS: 34.869629, -94.268555

24 • C1 | River Bluff Float Camp (Ouachita NF)

Total sites: 6, RV sites: 0, No water, Vault/pit toilet, Tents only: Free, Also boat-in sites, Reservations not accepted, Elev: 686ft/209m, Tel: 870-867-2101, Nearest town: Mt Ida. GPS: 34.640186, -93.625715

25 • C1 | Shady Lake (Ouachita NF)

Total sites: 65, RV sites: 65, Elec sites: 20, Water at site, Flush toilet, Free showers, RV dump, Tents: $15/RVs: $20-25, Open Mar-Nov, Max Length: 32ft, Reservations not accepted, Elev: 1214ft/370m, Tel: 479-394-2382, Nearest town: Athens. GPS: 34.365234, -94.027832

26 • C2 | Bear Creek Equestrian Camp (Ouachita NF)

Total sites: 3, RV sites: 3, No water, Vault/pit toilet, Tent & RV camping: Free, Small trailers only, Stay limit: 14 days, Open all year, Reservations not accepted, Elev: 1184ft/361m, Tel: 501-984-5313, Nearest town: Jessieville. GPS: 34.785574, -93.160491

27 • C2 | Charlton (Ouachita NF)

Total sites: 58, RV sites: 58, Central water, Flush toilet, Free showers, RV dump, Tents: $15/RVs: $25, Open Apr-Nov, Reservations not accepted, Elev: 705ft/215m, Tel: 870-867-2101, Nearest town: Mt. Ida. GPS: 34.516294, -93.382615

28 • C2 | Hickory Nut Mt (Ouachita NF)

Total sites: 8, RV sites: 8, No water, Vault/pit toilet, Tent & RV camping: Free, Open all year, Elev: 1220ft/372m, Tel: 870-867-2101, Nearest town: Bismarck. GPS: 34.561521, -93.422959

29 • C2 | Lake Sylvia (Ouachita NF)

Total sites: 27, RV sites: 19, Elec sites: 19, Water at site, Flush toilet, Free showers, RV dump, Tents: $15/RVs: $20, 2 group sites $25, Open Apr-Oct, Max Length: 30ft, Reservations not accepted, Elev: 646ft/197m, Tel: 501-984-5313, Nearest town: Perryville. GPS: 34.867894, -92.822738

30 • C2 | South Fourche (Ouachita NF)

Total sites: 6, RV sites: 6, Central water, Vault/pit toilet, No showers, No RV dump, Tent & RV camping: Free, No large RVs, Open all year, Reservations not accepted, Elev: 508ft/155m, Tel: 501-984-5313, Nearest town: Hollis. GPS: 34.869769, -93.109238

California

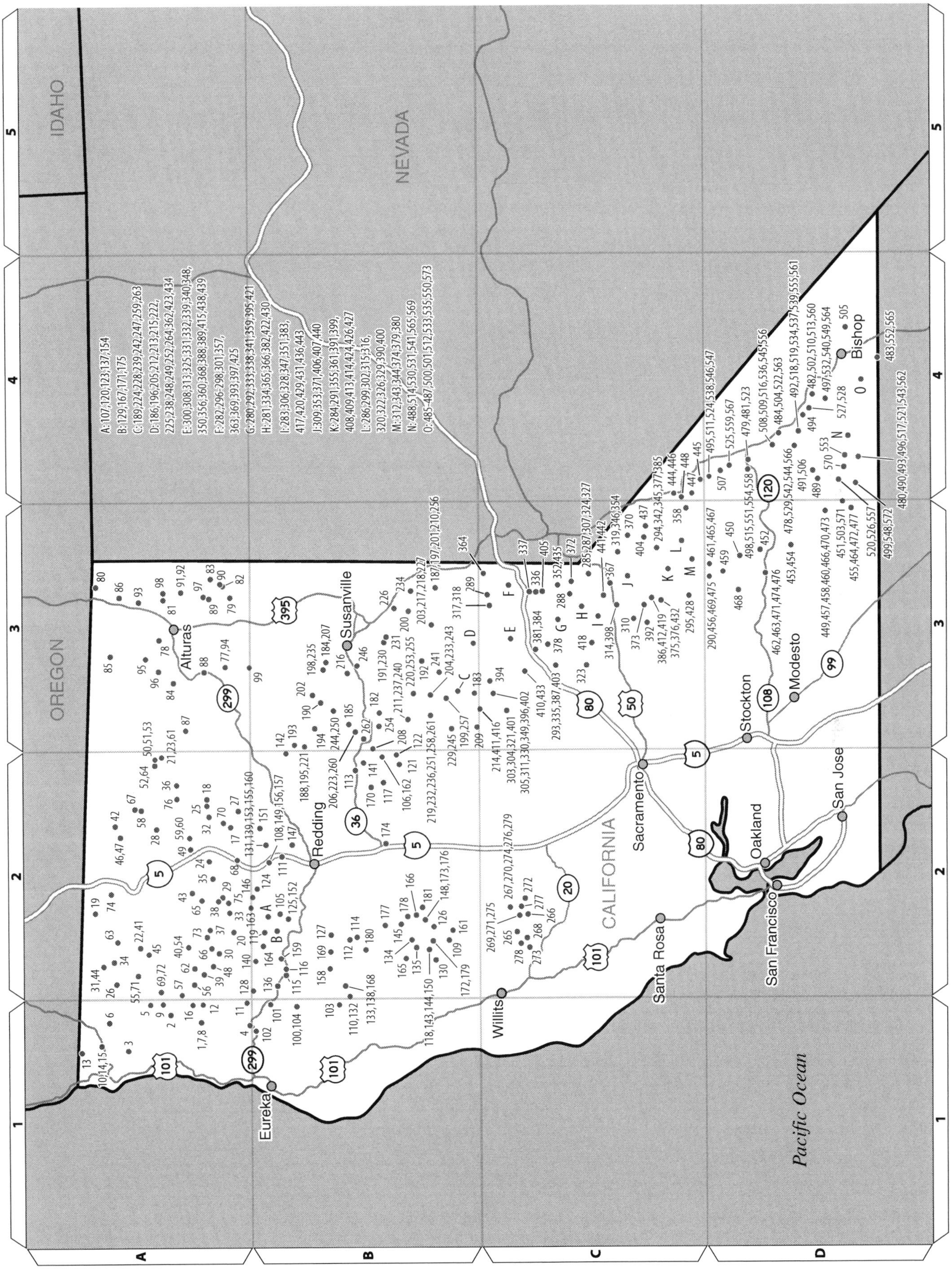
A: 107,120,123,137,154
B: 129,167,171,175
C: 189,224,228,239,242,247,259,263
D: 186,196,205,212,213,215,222, 225,238,248,249,252,264,362,423,434
E: 300,308,313,325,331,332,339,340,348, 350,356,360,368,388,389,415,438,439
F: 282,296-298,301,357, 363,369,393,397,425
G: 280,292,333,338,341,359,395,421
H: 281,334,365,366,382,422,430
I: 283,306,328,347,351,383, 417,420,429,431,436,443
J: 309,353,371,406,407,440
K: 284,291,355,361,391,399, 408,409,413,414,424,426,427
L: 286,299,302,315,316, 320,322,326,329,390,400
M: 312,343,344,374,379,380
N: 488,514,530,531,541,565,569
O: 485-487,500,501,512,533,535,550,573
OREGON
IDAHO
NEVADA
CALIFORNIA
Pacific Ocean
Eureka
Alturas
Redding
Susanville
Willits
Sacramento
Santa Rosa
San Francisco
Oakland
Stockton
Modesto
San Jose
Bishop

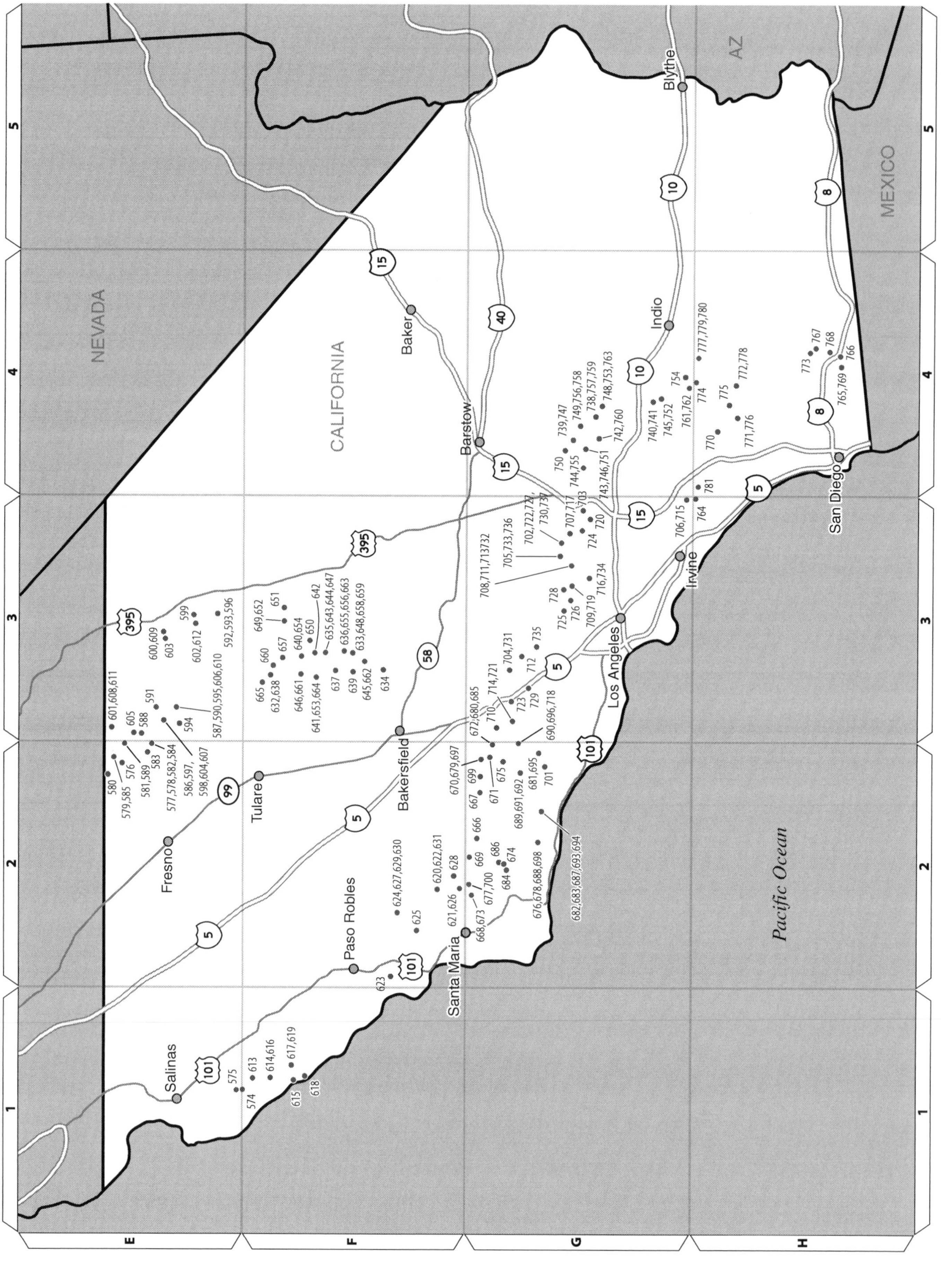
NEVADA
CALIFORNIA
AZ
MEXICO
Pacific Ocean
Salinas
Paso Robles
Santa Maria
Fresno
Tulare
Bakersfield
Baker
Barstow
Los Angeles
Irvine
Indio
Blythe
San Diego
101
5
99
395
58
15
40
10
8
1
2
3
4
5
E
F
G
H

Map	ID	Map	ID
A1	1-16	E1	574-575
A2	17-76	E2	576-585
A3	77-99	E3	586-612
B1	100-104	F1	613-619
B2	105-181	F2	620-631
B3	182-264	F3	632-665
C2	265-279	G2	666-701
C3	280-443	G3	702-737
C4	444-448	G4	738-763
D3	449-477	H3	764
D4	478-573	H4	765-781

Alphabetical List of Camping Areas

Name	ID	Map
Abbott Creek (Sequoia NF)	586	E3
Ackerman (Shasta-Trinity NF)	105	B2
Agnew Meadows (Inyo NF)	478	D4
Ah-Di-Na (Shasta-Trinity NF)	17	A2
Ahart (Tahoe NF)	280	C3
Aikens Creek West (Six Rivers NF)	1	A1
Airport Flat (Eldorado NF)	281	C3
Alder Creek (Lassen) (Lassen NF)	106	B2
Algoma (Shasta-Trinity NF)	18	A2
Aliso (Los Padres NF)	666	G2
Almanor (Lassen NF)	182	B3
Alpine View (Shasta-Trinity NF)	107	B2
American House OHV Camp (Plumas NF)	183	B3
Annie McCloud (Shasta-Trinity NF)	282	C3
Antlers (Shasta-Trinity NF)	108	B2
Appletree (Angeles NF)	702	G3
Applewhite (San Bernadino NF)	703	G3
Arroyo Seco (Los Padres NF)	613	F1
Ash Creek (Modoc NF)	77	A3
Aspen (Inyo NF)	479	D4
Aspen Grove (Lassen NF)	184	B3
Atchison Camp (Mendocino NF)	109	B2
Azalea Cove (Eldorado NF)	283	C3
Backpackers (Stanislaus NF)	284	C3
Badger Flat (Sierra NF)	480	D4
Badger's Den (Lake Tahoe Basin Management Unit)	285	C3
Bailey Canyon (Six Rivers NF)	110	B2
Bailey Cove (Shasta-Trinity NF)	111	B2
Baja (Los Padres NF)	620	F2
Baker (Stanislaus NF)	286	C3
Ballinger (Los Padres NF)	667	G2
Barrel Springs (Los Padres NF)	668	G2
Barton Flats (San Bernadino NF)	738	G4
Basin Gulch (Shasta-Trinity NF)	112	B2
Bates Canyon (Los Padres NF)	669	G2
Battle Creek (Lassen NF)	113	B2
Bayview (Lake Tahoe Basin Management Unit)	287	C3
Beans Camp (Klamath NF)	2	A1
Bear (Angeles NF)	704	G3
Bear Creek (Mendocino NF)	265	C2
Bear Lake (Stanislaus NF)	288	C3
Bear Valley (Tahoe NF)	289	C3
Beardsley Dam (Stanislaus NF)	290	C3
Beaver Creek (Klamath NF)	19	A2
Beegum Gorge (Shasta-Trinity NF)	114	B2
Belknap (Sequoia NF)	632	F3
Benner Creek (Lassen NF)	185	B3
Berger (Tahoe NF)	186	B3
Big Bar (Shasta-Trinity NF)	115	B2
Big Bend (Inyo NF)	481	D4
Big Cove (Plumas NF)	187	B3
Big Flat (Six Rivers NF)	3	A1
Big Flat (Shasta-Trinity NF)	116	B2
Big Flat (Klamath NF)	20	A2
Big Meadow (Stanislaus NF)	291	C3
Big Meadow (Sequoia NF)	587	E3
Big Meadow (Inyo NF)	482	D4
Big Meadows (Eldorado NF)	292	C3
Big Pine (Lassen NF)	188	B3
Big Pine Creek (Inyo NF)	483	D4
Big Pine Flat (San Bernadino NF)	739	G4
Big Reservoir (Tahoe NF)	293	C3
Big Rock (Angeles NF)	705	G3
Big Sage (Modoc NF)	78	A3
Big Sandy (Sierra NF)	449	D3
Big Slide (Shasta-Trinity NF)	100	B1
Big Springs (Inyo NF)	484	D4
Big Trees (Inyo NF)	485	D4
Bishop Park (Inyo NF)	486	D4
Bitterbrush (Inyo NF)	487	D4
Black Mountain Yellow Post (San Bernadino NF)	740	G4
Black Rock (Lassen NF)	117	B2
Black Rock (Plumas NF)	189	B3
Black Rock Reservoir/PGE (Sierra NF)	588	E3
Blanche Lake (Modoc NF)	21	A2
Bloomfield (Stanislaus NF)	294	C3
Blue Jay (Cleveland NF)	706	G3
Blue Lake (Modoc NF)	79	A3
Blue Ridge (Angeles NF)	707	G3
Boardman Camp (Mendocino NF)	118	B2
Boards Crossing (Stanislaus NF)	295	C3
Bobcat Meadow (Cleveland NF)	765	H4
Boca (Tahoe NF)	296	C3
Boca Rest (Tahoe NF)	297	C3
Boca Spring (Tahoe NF)	298	C3
Bogard (Lassen NF)	190	B3
Boise Creek (Six Rivers NF)	4	A1
Bolsillo (Sierra NF)	488	D4
Bootleg (Humboldt-Toiyabe NF)	444	C4
Boulder Basin (San Bernadino NF)	741	G4
Boulder Creek (Plumas NF)	191	B3
Boulder Flat (Stanislaus NF)	299	C3
Boulder Gulch (Sequoia NF)	633	F3
Boulder Oaks Horse Camp (Cleveland NF)	766	H4
Bowler (Sierra NF)	489	D4
Bowman Lake (Tahoe NF)	300	C3
Boyington Mill (Tahoe NF)	301	C3
Bradys Camp (Plumas NF)	192	B3
Breckenridge (Sequoia NF)	634	F3
Bretz Mill (Sierra NF)	576	E2
Bridge (Lassen NF)	193	B3
Bridge Camp (Shasta-Trinity NF)	119	B2

1 • A1 | Aikens Creek West (Six Rivers NF)

Total sites: 10, RV sites: 10, Central water, No toilets, No showers, RV dump, Tent & RV camping: Free, Open May-Sep, Max Length: 35ft, Reservations not accepted, Elev: 312ft/95m, Tel: 530-627-3291, Nearest town: Orleans. GPS: 41.228795, -123.654856

2 • A1 | Beans Camp (Klamath NF)

Total sites: 6, RV sites: 6, No water, Vault/pit toilet, Tent & RV camping: Free, Open May-Oct, Reservations not accepted, Elev: 4324ft/1318m, Tel: 530-627-3291, Nearest town: Orleans. GPS: 41.443717, -123.613089

3 • A1 | Big Flat (Six Rivers NF)

Total sites: 28, RV sites: 28, No water, Vault/pit toilet, Tent & RV camping: $8, Open May-Sep, Reservations not accepted, Elev: 742ft/226m, Tel: 707-457-3131, Nearest town: Crescent City. GPS: 41.687228, -123.909183

4 • A1 | Boise Creek (Six Rivers NF)

Total sites: 17, RV sites: 14, No water, Vault/pit toilet, No showers, No RV dump, Tent & RV camping: $10, Open May-Sep, Max Length: 40ft, Reservations accepted, Elev: 906ft/276m, Tel: 530-629-2118, Nearest town: Willow Creek. GPS: 40.944779, -123.658528

5 • A1 | Dillon Creek (Six Rivers NF)

Total sites: 21, RV sites: 21, No water, Vault/pit toilet, No showers, No RV dump, Tent & RV camping: $10, Food storage lockers, Open May-Sep, Max Length: 35ft, Reservations accepted, Elev: 863ft/263m, Tel: 530-627-3291, Nearest town: Orleans. GPS: 41.573525, -123.542816

6 • A1 | Doe Flat TH (Six Rivers NF)

Total sites: 3, RV sites: 3, No water, Vault/pit toilet, Tent & RV camping: Free, Reservations not accepted, Elev: 4167ft/1270m, Nearest town: Gasquet. GPS: 41.816933, -123.699139

7 • A1 | E-Ne-Nuck (Six Rivers NF)

Total sites: 10, RV sites: 10, Central water, Vault/pit toilet, No showers, No RV dump, Tent & RV camping: $10, Open Jun-Oct, Max Length: 30ft, Reservations not accepted, Elev: 420ft/128m, Tel: 530-627-3291, Nearest town: Orleans. GPS: 41.240357, -123.656291

8 • A1 | Fish Lake (Six Rivers NF)

Total sites: 24, RV sites: 24, No water, Vault/pit toilet, No showers, No RV dump, Tent & RV camping: $10, Open Jun-Sep, Max Length: 28ft, Reservations accepted, Elev: 1752ft/534m, Tel: 530-627-3291, Nearest town: Orleans. GPS: 41.266453, -123.683239

9 • A1 | Frog Pond (Klamath NF)

Total sites: 3, RV sites: 3, No water, Vault/pit toilet, Tent & RV camping: Free, Open May-Oct, Reservations not accepted, Elev: 1932ft/589m, Tel: 530-627-3291, Nearest town: Orleans. GPS: 41.487464, -123.541769

10 • A1 | Grassy Flat (Six Rivers NF)

Total sites: 19, RV sites: 15, No water, Vault/pit toilet, No showers, No RV dump, Tent & RV camping: $10, Also walk-to sites, Open May-Sep, Max Length: 40ft, Reservations accepted, Elev: 718ft/

219m, Tel: 707-457-3131, Nearest town: Crescent City. GPS: 41.856434, -123.888093

11 • A1 | Groves Prairie (Six Rivers NF)

Total sites: 5, RV sites: 5, No water, Vault/pit toilet, Tent & RV camping: Free, Open May-Oct, Reservations not accepted, Elev: 4268ft/1301m, Tel: 530-629-2118, Nearest town: Arcata. GPS: 40.966182, -123.487157

12 • A1 | Le Perron Flat (Six Rivers NF)

Total sites: 4, Tents only: Free, Reservations not accepted, Elev: 2454ft/748m, Tel: 530-627-3291. GPS: 41.241730, -123.521530

13 • A1 | North Fork (Six Rivers) (Six Rivers NF)

Total sites: 6, RV sites: 6, No water, Vault/pit toilet, Tent & RV camping: $8, No large RVs, Open all year, Max Length: 22ft, Reservations not accepted, Elev: 974ft/297m, Tel: 707-442-1721, Nearest town: Gasquet. GPS: 41.981108, -123.960317

14 • A1 | Panther Flat (Six Rivers NF)

Total sites: 38, RV sites: 38, Central water, Flush toilet, Pay showers, No RV dump, Tent & RV camping: $15, Open all year, Max Length: 45ft, Reservations accepted, Elev: 487ft/148m, Tel: 707-457-3131, Nearest town: Gasquet. GPS: 41.843799, -123.928833

15 • A1 | Patrick Creek (Six Rivers NF)

Total sites: 13, RV sites: 13, Central water, Flush toilet, No showers, No RV dump, Tent & RV camping: $14, Open May-Sep, Max Length: 45ft, Reservations accepted, Elev: 925ft/282m, Tel: 707-457-3131, Nearest town: Crescent City. GPS: 41.872252, -123.846282

16 • A1 | Pearch Creek (Six Rivers NF)

Total sites: 10, RV sites: 10, Central water, Vault/pit toilet, No showers, No RV dump, Tent & RV camping: $10, Open all year, Max Length: 40ft, Reservations accepted, Elev: 554ft/169m, Tel: 530-627-3291, Nearest town: Orleans. GPS: 41.308871, -123.520853

17 • A2 | Ah-Di-Na (Shasta-Trinity NF)

Total sites: 16, RV sites: 0, Central water, Flush toilet, No showers, No RV dump, Tents only: $10, 4 miles of very rough rocky roads - trailers/passenger cars not recommended, Open May-Nov, Reservations not accepted, Elev: 2257ft/688m, Tel: 530-964-2184, Nearest town: McCloud. GPS: 41.111328, -122.097900

18 • A2 | Algoma (Shasta-Trinity NF)

Total sites: 8, No water, Vault/pit toilet, Tent & RV camping: Free, Open May-Oct, Max Length: 24ft, Reservations not accepted, Elev: 3848ft/1173m, Tel: 530-964-2184, Nearest town: McCloud. GPS: 41.256047, -121.883773

19 • A2 | Beaver Creek (Klamath NF)

Total sites: 8, RV sites: 8, No water, Vault/pit toilet, Tent & RV camping: Free, Stay limit: 14 days, Open May-Oct, Reservations not accepted, Elev: 2246ft/685m, Tel: 530-493-2243, Nearest town: Happy Camp. GPS: 41.927669, -122.829174

20 • A2 | Big Flat (Klamath NF)

Total sites: 9, RV sites: 9, No water, Vault/pit toilet, Tent & RV camping: Free, Stay limit: 14 days, Open May-Oct, Reservations not accepted, Elev: 5184ft/1580m, Tel: 530-468-5351, Nearest town: Fort Jones. GPS: 41.068035, -122.934505

21 • A2 | Blanche Lake (Modoc NF)

Total sites: 6, RV sites: 6, No water, Vault/pit toilet, Tent & RV camping: Free, Stay limit: 14 days, Open Jul-Oct, Reservations not accepted, Elev: 6818ft/2078m, Tel: 530-667-2246, Nearest town: Bug Station. GPS: 41.557000, -121.570000

22 • A2 | Bridge Flat (Klamath NF)

Total sites: 4, RV sites: 4, No water, Vault/pit toilet, Tent & RV camping: Free, Open May-Oct, Reservations not accepted, Elev: 2205ft/672m, Tel: 530-468-5351, Nearest town: Fort Jones. GPS: 41.650108, -123.113116

23 • A2 | Bullseye Lake (Modoc NF)

Total sites: 10, RV sites: 10, No water, Vault/pit toilet, Tent & RV camping: Free, Stay limit: 14 days, Open May-Oct, Max Length: 22ft, Reservations not accepted, Elev: 6798ft/2072m, Tel: 530-667-2246, Nearest town: McCloud. GPS: 41.554672, -121.573793

24 • A2 | Castle Lake (Shasta-Trinity NF)

Total sites: 6, RV sites: 6, No water, Vault/pit toilet, Tent & RV camping: Free, Not recommended for large RVs, Stay limit: 3 days, Open all year, Reservations not accepted, Elev: 5331ft/1625m, Tel: 530-926-4511, Nearest town: Mt Shasta. GPS: 41.235280, -122.378890

25 • A2 | Cattle Camp (Shasta-Trinity NF)

Total sites: 27, RV sites: 27, No water, Vault/pit toilet, Tent & RV camping: $15, Max Length: 32ft, Reservations not accepted, Elev: 3720ft/1134m, Tel: 530-964-2184, Nearest town: McCloud. GPS: 41.262114, -121.940786

26 • A2 | Curly Jack (Klamath NF)

Total sites: 12, RV sites: 12, Central water, Vault/pit toilet, No showers, No RV dump, Tent & RV camping: $15, Group site: $50, Stay limit: 14 days, Open May-Oct, Max Length: 37ft, Reservations accepted, Elev: 1070ft/326m, Tel: 530-493-2243, Nearest town: Happy Camp. GPS: 41.785682, -123.389859

27 • A2 | Deadlun (Shasta-Trinity NF)

Total sites: 25, RV sites: 25, No water, Vault/pit toilet, Tent & RV camping: Free, Open all year, Max Length: 24ft, Reservations not accepted, Elev: 2746ft/837m, Tel: 530-275-1587, Nearest town: Round Mountain. GPS: 41.061087, -121.975684

28 • A2 | Deer Mt Snowpark (Klamath NF)

Total sites: 8, RV sites: 8, No water, Vault/pit toilet, Tent & RV camping: Free, Winter RV parking in lot, Stay limit: 14 days, Open all year, Max Length: 30ft, Reservations not accepted, Elev: 5763ft/1757m, Tel: 530-398-4391, Nearest town: Weed. GPS: 41.570447, -122.132071

29 • A2 | Eagle Creek (Shasta-Trinity NF)

Total sites: 17, RV sites: 17, Central water, Vault/pit toilet, No showers, No RV dump, Tent & RV camping: $15, Open May-Oct, Max Length: 35ft, Reservations not accepted, Elev: 2799ft/853m,

Tel: 530-623-2121, Nearest town: Trinity Center. GPS: 41.151855, -122.669922

30 • A2 | East Fork (Grasshopper Ridge) (Klamath NF)

Total sites: 6, RV sites: 6, No water, Vault/pit toilet, Tent & RV camping: Free, Stay limit: 14 days, Open May-Oct, Reservations not accepted, Elev: 2461ft/750m, Tel: 530-468-5351, Nearest town: Cecilville. GPS: 41.153992, -123.108632

31 • A2 | Fort Goff (Klamath NF)

Total sites: 5, RV sites: 0, No water, Vault/pit toilet, Tents only: Free, Walk-to sites, Stay limit: 14 days, Open May-Oct, Reservations not accepted, Elev: 1411ft/430m, Tel: 530-493-2243, Nearest town: Seiad. GPS: 41.864979, -123.257371

32 • A2 | Fowlers Camp (Shasta-Trinity NF)

Total sites: 36, RV sites: 36, Central water, Vault/pit toilet, No showers, No RV dump, Tent & RV camping: $15, Stay limit: 14 days, Open May-Oct, Max Length: 59ft, Reservations accepted, Elev: 3376ft/1029m, Tel: 530-964-2184, Nearest town: McCloud. GPS: 41.245361, -122.022949

33 • A2 | Goldfield (Shasta-Trinity NF)

Total sites: 6, RV sites: 6, No water, Vault/pit toilet, Tent & RV camping: Free, Open all year, Max Length: 16ft, Reservations not accepted, Elev: 3032ft/924m, Tel: 530-623-2121, Nearest town: Weaverville. GPS: 41.100000, -122.779000

34 • A2 | Grider Creek (Klamath NF)

Total sites: 10, RV sites: 10, No water, Vault/pit toilet, Tent & RV camping: Free, Stay limit: 14 days, Open May-Oct, Max Length: 16ft, Elev: 1708ft/521m, Tel: 530-493-2243, Nearest town: Seiad Valley. GPS: 41.806631, -123.217908

35 • A2 | Gumboot Lake (Shasta-Trinity NF)

Total sites: 6, RV sites: 4, No water, Vault/pit toilet, Tent & RV camping: Free, No large RVs, Open Jun-Oct, Max Length: 12ft, Reservations not accepted, Elev: 6082ft/1854m, Tel: 530-926-4511, Nearest town: Mount Shasta. GPS: 41.212699, -122.509292

36 • A2 | Harris Spring (Shasta-Trinity NF)

Total sites: 15, RV sites: 15, No water, Vault/pit toilet, Tent & RV camping: Free, Open Aug-Oct, Max Length: 32ft, Reservations not accepted, Elev: 4882ft/1488m, Tel: 530-964-2184, Nearest town: McCloud. GPS: 41.454346, -121.785156

37 • A2 | Hidden Horse Equestrian (Klamath NF)

Total sites: 6, RV sites: 6, Central water, Vault/pit toilet, No showers, No RV dump, Tent & RV camping: $10, Stock facilities, Stay limit: 14 days, Open Jun-Oct, Reservations accepted, Elev: 5325ft/1623m, Tel: 530-468-5351, Nearest town: Callahan. GPS: 41.217500, -122.928889

38 • A2 | Horse Flat (Shasta-Trinity NF)

Total sites: 10, RV sites: 10, No water, Vault/pit toilet, Tent & RV camping: Free, Open May-Oct, Max Length: 16ft, Reservations not accepted, Elev: 3458ft/1054m, Tel: 530-623-2121, Nearest town: Callahan. GPS: 41.165968, -122.691955

39 • A2 | Hotelling (Klamath NF)

Total sites: 4, RV sites: 4, No water, Vault/pit toilet, Tent & RV camping: Free, Stay limit: 14 days, Open May-Oct, Elev: 1401ft/427m, Tel: 530-468-5351, Nearest town: Callahan. GPS: 41.239544, -123.275314

40 • A2 | Idlewild (Klamath NF)

Total sites: 8, RV sites: 8, Central water, Vault/pit toilet, No showers, No RV dump, Tent & RV camping: $10, Stay limit: 14 days, Open May-Oct, Max Length: 24ft, Reservations not accepted, Elev: 2716ft/828m, Tel: 530-468-5351, Nearest town: Etna. GPS: 41.331527, -123.060039

41 • A2 | Indian Scotty (Klamath NF)

Total sites: 27, RV sites: 27, Central water, Vault/pit toilet, No showers, No RV dump, Tent & RV camping: $10, Reservable group site $50, Stay limit: 14 days, Open May-Oct, Max Length: 30ft, Reservations not accepted, Elev: 2503ft/763m, Tel: 530-468-5351, Nearest town: Fort Jones. GPS: 41.634151, -123.079253

42 • A2 | Juanita Lake (Klamath NF)

Total sites: 23, RV sites: 23, Central water, Vault/pit toilet, No showers, No RV dump, Tent & RV camping: $15, Reservable group: $50, Stay limit: 14 days, Open May-Oct, Max Length: 55ft, Reservations not accepted, Elev: 5158ft/1572m, Tel: 530-398-4391, Nearest town: Macdoel. GPS: 41.817139, -122.125488

43 • A2 | Kangaroo Lake (Klamath NF)

Total sites: 18, RV sites: 13, Central water, Vault/pit toilet, No showers, No RV dump, Tent & RV camping: $15, Also walk-to sites, Stay limit: 14 days, Open May-Oct, Reservations not accepted, Elev: 6102ft/1860m, Tel: 530-468-5351, Nearest town: Etna. GPS: 41.334717, -122.640625

44 • A2 | Klamath River - Portuguese Creek Access (Klamath NF)

Total sites: 5, No water, Vault/pit toilet, Tents only: Free, Walk-to sites, Fire permit required, Stay limit: 14 days, Reservations not accepted, Elev: 1319ft/402m, Nearest town: Seiad. GPS: 41.862887, -123.248443

45 • A2 | Lover's Camp (Klamath NF)

Total sites: 8, RV sites: 0, No water, Vault/pit toilet, Tents only: Free, Walk-to sites, Stock facilities - water for horses only, Stay limit: 14 days, Open May-Oct, Reservations not accepted, Elev: 4173ft/1272m, Tel: 530-468-5351, Nearest town: Fort Jones. GPS: 41.594833, -123.142638

46 • A2 | Martins Dairy (Klamath NF)

Total sites: 8, RV sites: 8, Central water, Vault/pit toilet, No showers, No RV dump, Tent & RV camping: $10, No water in winter, Stay limit: 14 days, Reservations not accepted, Elev: 6030ft/1838m, Tel: 530-398-4391, Nearest town: Macdoel. GPS: 41.795897, -122.207735

47 • A2 | Martins Dairy Horse Camp (Klamath NF)

Total sites: 4, RV sites: 4, Tent & RV camping: $10, Stay limit: 14 days, Reservations not accepted, Elev: 6023ft/1836m, Tel: 530-398-4391, Nearest town: Macdoel. GPS: 41.796215, -122.205619

48 • A2 | Matthews Creek (Klamath NF)

Total sites: 12, RV sites: 12, Central water, Vault/pit toilet, No showers, No RV dump, Tent & RV camping: $10, Open May-Oct, Reservations not accepted, Elev: 1795ft/547m, Tel: 530-468-5351, Nearest town: Etna. GPS: 41.186768, -123.213867

49 • A2 | McBride Springs (Shasta-Trinity NF)

Total sites: 10, RV sites: 10, Central water, Vault/pit toilet, No showers, No RV dump, Tent & RV camping: $10, Stay limit: 7 days, Open May-Oct, Max Length: 16ft, Reservations not accepted, Elev: 4938ft/1505m, Tel: 530-926-4511, Nearest town: Mt. Shasta. GPS: 41.352267, -122.283378

50 • A2 | Medicine Lake CG (Modoc NF)

Total sites: 22, RV sites: 22, No water, Vault/pit toilet, Tent & RV camping: $14, Stay limit: 14 days, Open Jul-Sep, Max Length: 60ft, Reservations accepted, Elev: 6732ft/2052m, Tel: 530-233-5811, Nearest town: McCloud. GPS: 41.587175, -121.596541

51 • A2 | Medicine Lake RA - A H Hogue (Modoc NF)

Total sites: 24, RV sites: 24, Central water, Vault/pit toilet, No showers, No RV dump, Tent & RV camping: $14, Stay limit: 14 days, Open Jul-Sep, Max Length: 27ft, Reservations accepted, Elev: 6758ft/2060m, Tel: 530-233-5811, Nearest town: Tionesta. GPS: 41.586282, -121.592038

52 • A2 | Medicine Lake RA - Headquarters (Modoc NF)

Total sites: 22, RV sites: 22, No water, Vault/pit toilet, Tent & RV camping: $14, Stay limit: 14 days, Open May-Oct, Max Length: 22ft, Reservations accepted, Elev: 6745ft/2056m, Tel: 530-667-2246, Nearest town: McCloud. GPS: 41.585738, -121.615343

53 • A2 | Medicine Lake RA - Hemlock (Modoc NF)

Total sites: 19, RV sites: 19, Central water, Vault/pit toilet, No showers, No RV dump, Tent & RV camping: $14, Stay limit: 14 days, Max Length: 22ft, Reservations accepted, Elev: 6772ft/2064m, Tel: 530-233-5811, Nearest town: Tionesta. GPS: 41.585917, -121.589553

54 • A2 | Mulebridge (Klamath NF)

Total sites: 4, RV sites: 4, No water, Vault/pit toilet, Tent & RV camping: Free, Stay limit: 14 days, Open May-Oct, Elev: 2907ft/886m, Tel: 530-468-5351, Nearest town: Etna. GPS: 41.356313, -123.075388

55 • A2 | Norcross (Klamath NF)

Total sites: 6, RV sites: 6, No water, Vault/pit toilet, Tent & RV camping: Free, Stock facilities - non-potable water, Stay limit: 14 days, Open May-Oct, Reservations not accepted, Elev: 2428ft/740m, Tel: 530-493-2243, Nearest town: Happy Camp. GPS: 41.647372, -123.311371

56 • A2 | Nordheimer (Six Rivers NF)

Total sites: 12, RV sites: 12, No water, Vault/pit toilet, No showers, No RV dump, Tent & RV camping: $8, Open Jun-Sep, Reservations not accepted, Elev: 1109ft/338m, Tel: 530-627-3291, Nearest town: Orleans. GPS: 41.298542, -123.362666

57 • A2 | Oak Bottom (Six Rivers NF)

Total sites: 26, RV sites: 26, Central water, Vault/pit toilet, No showers, No RV dump, Tent & RV camping: $10, Open Jun-Oct, Max Length: 40ft, Reservations accepted, Elev: 797ft/243m, Tel: 530-627-3291, Nearest town: Orleans. GPS: 41.376129, -123.452744

58 • A2 | Orr Lake (Klamath NF)

Total sites: 8, RV sites: 8, No water, Vault/pit toilet, No showers, No RV dump, Tent & RV camping: Free, Low-hanging branches, Stay limit: 14 days, Open May-Oct, Reservations not accepted, Elev: 4682ft/1427m, Tel: 530-398-4391, Nearest town: Macdoel. GPS: 41.667571, -121.992377

59 • A2 | Panther Meadows (Shasta-Trinity NF)

Total sites: 10, RV sites: 0, No water, Vault/pit toilet, Tents only: Fee unk, Walk-to sites, Short walk from vehicle, Stay limit: 3 days, Reservations not accepted, Elev: 7451ft/2271m, Tel: 530-926-4511, Nearest town: Mt. Shasta. GPS: 41.354887, -122.203487

60 • A2 | Panther Meadows Trail Overflow Lot (Shasta-Trinity NF)

Total sites: 15, RV sites: 15, No water, No toilets, No tents/RVs: Free, Stay limit: 3 days, Reservations not accepted, Elev: 7725ft/2355m, Tel: 530-926-4511, Nearest town: Mt. Shasta. GPS: 41.359975, -122.202836

61 • A2 | Payne Springs (Modoc NF)

Total sites: 5, RV sites: 5, No water, Vault/pit toilet, Tent & RV camping: Free, Stay limit: 14 days, Open Jul-Oct, Max Length: 20ft, Reservations not accepted, Elev: 6539ft/1993m, Tel: 530-667-2246, Nearest town: McCloud. GPS: 41.555082, -121.562137

62 • A2 | Red Bank (Klamath NF)

Total sites: 5, RV sites: 5, No water, Vault/pit toilet, Tent & RV camping: Free, Stay limit: 14 days, Open May-Oct, Elev: 1752ft/534m, Tel: 530-468-5351, Nearest town: Sawyers Bar. GPS: 41.297842, -123.230272

63 • A2 | Sarah Totten (Klamath NF)

Total sites: 9, RV sites: 9, Central water, Vault/pit toilet, No showers, No RV dump, Tent & RV camping: $10, 2 group sites $50, Stay limit: 14 days, Open May-Oct, Max Length: 24ft, Reservations accepted, Elev: 1568ft/478m, Tel: 530-493-2243, Nearest town: Happy Camp. GPS: 41.786773, -123.053046

64 • A2 | Schonichin Springs (Modoc NF)

Total sites: 10, RV sites: 10, No water, Vault/pit toilet, Tent & RV camping: Free, Stay limit: 14 days, Open Jul-Oct, Max Length: 20ft, Reservations not accepted, Elev: 6782ft/2067m, Tel: 530-667-2246, Nearest town: McCloud. GPS: 41.591564, -121.617552

65 • A2 | Scott Mountan (Shasta-Trinity NF)

Total sites: 7, RV sites: 7, No water, Vault/pit toilet, Tent & RV camping: Free, Open all year, Max Length: 15ft, Reservations not accepted, Elev: 5443ft/1659m, Tel: 530-623-2121, Nearest town: Weaverville. GPS: 41.275000, -122.698000

66 • A2 | Shadow Creek (Klamath NF)

Total sites: 5, RV sites: 5, No water, Vault/pit toilet, Tent & RV camping: Free, Open May-Oct, Reservations not accepted, Elev:

2976ft/907m, Tel: 530-468-5351, Nearest town: Cecilville. GPS: 41.201631, -123.069169

67 • A2 | Shafter (Klamath NF)

Total sites: 10, RV sites: 10, Central water, Vault/pit toilet, No showers, No RV dump, Tent & RV camping: $10, Near RR, no water in winter, Stay limit: 14 days, Reservations not accepted, Elev: 4393ft/1339m, Tel: 530-398-4391, Nearest town: Macdoel. GPS: 41.710225, -121.981279

68 • A2 | Sims Flat (Shasta-Trinity NF)

Total sites: 19, RV sites: 19, Central water, Flush toilet, No showers, No RV dump, Tent & RV camping: $15, Near RR, Open Apr-Nov, Max Length: 16ft, Reservations not accepted, Elev: 1722ft/525m, Tel: 530-926-4511, Nearest town: Dunsmuir. GPS: 41.062012, -122.359619

69 • A2 | Stanshaw Horse Camp (Six Rivers NF)

Total sites: 5, RV sites: 5, Central water, Vault/pit toilet, Tent & RV camping: Free, Stock water, Reservations not accepted, Elev: 4970ft/1515m, Tel: 707-442-1721. GPS: 41.497159, -123.439266

70 • A2 | Star City (Shasta-Trinity NF)

Total sites: 7, No water, No toilets, Tents only: Free, Reservations not accepted, Elev: 2708ft/825m, Tel: 530-964-2184, Nearest town: McCloud. GPS: 41.153805, -122.068762

71 • A2 | Sulphur Springs (Klamath NF)

Total sites: 6, RV sites: 0, No water, Vault/pit toilet, Tents only: Free, Walk-to sites, 50 yds to sites, Stay limit: 14 days, Open May-Oct, Reservations not accepted, Elev: 2342ft/714m, Tel: 530-493-2243, Nearest town: Happy Valley. GPS: 41.659748, -123.318959

72 • A2 | Ten Bear TH (Six Rivers NF)

Total sites: 2, RV sites: 2, No water, Vault/pit toilet, No showers, No RV dump, Tent & RV camping: Free, Stock water, Reservations not accepted, Elev: 4895ft/1492m, Nearest town: Somes Bar. GPS: 41.529463, -123.438368

73 • A2 | Trail Creek (Klamath NF)

Total sites: 12, RV sites: 12, Central water, Vault/pit toilet, No showers, No RV dump, Tent & RV camping: $10, Stay limit: 14 days, Reservations not accepted, Elev: 4869ft/1484m, Tel: 530-468-5351, Nearest town: Etna. GPS: 41.229492, -122.972412

74 • A2 | Tree of Heaven (Klamath NF)

Total sites: 20, RV sites: 20, Central water, Vault/pit toilet, No showers, No RV dump, Tent & RV camping: $15, Group site: $20, Stay limit: 14 days, Open May-Oct, Max Length: 40ft, Reservations accepted, Elev: 2057ft/627m, Tel: 530-493-2243, Nearest town: Yreka. GPS: 41.832147, -122.660438

75 • A2 | Trinity River (Shasta-Trinity NF)

Total sites: 7, RV sites: 7, Central water, Vault/pit toilet, No showers, No RV dump, Tent & RV camping: $10, Open May-Oct, Max Length: 35ft, Reservations not accepted, Elev: 2608ft/795m, Tel: 530-623-2121, Nearest town: Weaverville. GPS: 41.108631, -122.705759

76 • A2 | Trout Creek (Shasta-Trinity NF)

Total sites: 10, RV sites: 10, No water, Vault/pit toilet, Tent & RV camping: Free, Generator hours: 0700-2200, Open Jun-Oct, Max Length: 24ft, Reservations not accepted, Elev: 4941ft/1506m, Tel: 530-964-2184, Nearest town: McCloud. GPS: 41.445285, -121.885922

77 • A3 | Ash Creek (Modoc NF)

Total sites: 5, RV sites: 5, No water, Vault/pit toilet, Tent & RV camping: Free, Rough road, Stay limit: 14 days, Open all year, Max Length: 22ft, Reservations not accepted, Elev: 4895ft/1492m, Tel: 530-299-3215, Nearest town: Adin. GPS: 41.160959, -120.828823

78 • A3 | Big Sage (Modoc NF)

Total sites: 11, RV sites: 11, No water, Vault/pit toilet, Tent & RV camping: Free, Stay limit: 14 days, Open May-Oct, Max Length: 22ft, Reservations not accepted, Elev: 4905ft/1495m, Tel: 530-233-5811, Nearest town: Alturas. GPS: 41.579841, -120.629174

79 • A3 | Blue Lake (Modoc NF)

Total sites: 35, RV sites: 35, Central water, Vault/pit toilet, No showers, No RV dump, Tent & RV camping: $14, Stay limit: 14 days, Open May-Oct, Reservations not accepted, Elev: 6119ft/1865m, Tel: 530-279-6116, Nearest town: Likely. GPS: 41.142129, -120.279564

80 • A3 | Cave Lake (Modoc NF)

Total sites: 3, RV sites: 3, No water, Vault/pit toilet, Tent & RV camping: Free, Stay limit: 14 days, Open Jul-Oct, Reservations not accepted, Elev: 6801ft/2073m, Tel: 530-279-6116, Nearest town: New Pine Creek. GPS: 41.978187, -120.205818

81 • A3 | Cedar Pass (Modoc NF)

Total sites: 17, RV sites: 17, No water, Vault/pit toilet, Tent & RV camping: Free, Stay limit: 14 days, Open May-Oct, Max Length: 17ft, Reservations not accepted, Elev: 5791ft/1765m, Nearest town: Cedarville. GPS: 41.559055, -120.298784

82 • A3 | East Creek Horse Camp (Modoc NF)

Total sites: 5, RV sites: 5, No water, Vault/pit toilet, No showers, No RV dump, Tent & RV camping: Free, Horse corrals, Stay limit: 14 days, Open May-Oct, Max Length: 22ft, Reservations not accepted, Elev: 7119ft/2170m, Tel: 530-279-6116, Nearest town: Likely. GPS: 41.196173, -120.195599

83 • A3 | Emerson (Modoc NF)

Total sites: 4, RV sites: 4, No water, Vault/pit toilet, Tent & RV camping: Free, Narrow, steep, rough, dirt access road, Stay limit: 14 days, Open Jul-Oct, Max Length: 16ft, Reservations not accepted, Elev: 5817ft/1773m, Tel: 530-279-6116, Nearest town: Eagleville. GPS: 41.263166, -120.139048

84 • A3 | Howards Gulch (Modoc NF)

Total sites: 6, RV sites: 6, Central water, Vault/pit toilet, No showers, No RV dump, Tent & RV camping: $12, Stay limit: 14 days, Open May-Oct, Max Length: 27ft, Reservations not accepted, Elev: 4728ft/1441m, Tel: 530-233-5811, Nearest town: Canby. GPS: 41.485407, -120.969315

85 • A3 | Janes Reservoir (Modoc NF)

Total sites: 8, RV sites: 8, No water, Vault/pit toilet, Tent & RV camping: Free, Stay limit: 14 days, Open May-Oct, Max Length: 22ft, Reservations not accepted, Elev: 5121ft/1561m, Tel: 530-233-5811, Nearest town: Alturas. GPS: 41.880000, -120.764000

86 • A3 | Lassen Creek (Modoc NF)

Total sites: 4, RV sites: 4, No water, Vault/pit toilet, Tent & RV camping: Free, Stay limit: 14 days, Open May-Oct, Reservations not accepted, Elev: 5463ft/1665m, Tel: 530-279-6116, Nearest town: Canby. GPS: 41.826733, -120.296228

87 • A3 | Lava Camp (Modoc NF)

Total sites: 12, RV sites: 12, Central water, Vault/pit toilet, No showers, No RV dump, Tent & RV camping: Free, Stay limit: 14 days, Open May-Oct, Max Length: 32ft, Reservations not accepted, Elev: 4426ft/1349m, Tel: 530-299-3215, Nearest town: Adin. GPS: 41.402091, -121.338554

88 • A3 | Lower Rush Creek (Modoc NF)

Total sites: 10, RV sites: 5, No water, Vault/pit toilet, Tent & RV camping: Free, 5 walk-in sites, Inaccessible during inclement weather, Stay limit: 14 days, Open all year, Max Length: 22ft, Reservations not accepted, Elev: 4751ft/1448m, Tel: 530-299-3215, Nearest town: Adin. GPS: 41.292655, -120.878836

89 • A3 | Mill Creek Falls (Modoc NF)

Total sites: 15, RV sites: 8, Central water, Vault/pit toilet, No showers, No RV dump, Tent & RV camping: $12, Stay limit: 14 days, Open Jun-Oct, Max Length: 22ft, Reservations not accepted, Elev: 5725ft/1745m, Tel: 530-279-6116, Nearest town: Likely. GPS: 41.276248, -120.289744

90 • A3 | Patterson (Modoc NF)

Total sites: 6, RV sites: 6, Central water, Vault/pit toilet, No showers, No RV dump, Tent & RV camping: Free, Stay limit: 14 days, Open May-Oct, Max Length: 16ft, Reservations not accepted, Elev: 7274ft/2217m, Tel: 530-279-6116, Nearest town: Eagleville. GPS: 41.197916, -120.186206

91 • A3 | Pepperdine (Modoc NF)

Total sites: 5, RV sites: 5, Central water, Vault/pit toilet, No showers, No RV dump, Tent & RV camping: Free, Not for large RVs, sites are uneven, Stay limit: 14 days, Open Jul-Oct, Reservations not accepted, Elev: 6844ft/2086m, Tel: 530-279-6116, Nearest town: Alturas. GPS: 41.450229, -120.242219

92 • A3 | Pepperdine Horse Camp (Modoc NF)

Total sites: 7, RV sites: 7, No water, Vault/pit toilet, Tent & RV camping: Free, Stay limit: 14 days, Open Jul-Oct, Max Length: 25ft, Reservations not accepted, Elev: 6788ft/2069m, Tel: 530-279-6116, Nearest town: Cedarville. GPS: 41.456011, -120.244147

93 • A3 | Plum Valley (Modoc NF)

Total sites: 7, RV sites: 7, No water, Vault/pit toilet, Tent & RV camping: Free, Stay limit: 14 days, Open Jun-Oct, Max Length: 16ft, Reservations not accepted, Elev: 5748ft/1752m, Tel: 530-279-6116, Nearest town: Davis Creek. GPS: 41.711837, -120.325772

94 • A3 | Red Tail Rim South TH (Modoc NF)

Total sites: 6, RV sites: 6, No water, Vault/pit toilet, Tent & RV camping: Free, Stay limit: 14 days, Open Jun-Oct, Reservations not accepted, Elev: 4938ft/1505m, Tel: 530-233-5811, Nearest town: Adin. GPS: 41.167513, -120.829682

95 • A3 | Reservoir C (Modoc NF)

Total sites: 11, RV sites: 11, No water, Vault/pit toilet, Tent & RV camping: Free, Stay limit: 14 days, Open May-Oct, Max Length: 22ft, Reservations not accepted, Elev: 4954ft/1510m, Tel: 530-233-5811, Nearest town: Alturas. GPS: 41.660135, -120.775258

96 • A3 | Reservoir F (Modoc NF)

Total sites: 9, RV sites: 9, No water, Vault/pit toilet, Tent & RV camping: Free, Stay limit: 14 days, Open May-Oct, Max Length: 22ft, Reservations not accepted, Elev: 4961ft/1512m, Tel: 530-233-5811, Nearest town: Alturas. GPS: 41.580881, -120.874511

97 • A3 | Soup Springs (Modoc NF)

Total sites: 8, RV sites: 8, Central water, Vault/pit toilet, No showers, No RV dump, Tent & RV camping: $12, Stay limit: 14 days, Open Jun-Oct, Max Length: 20ft, Reservations not accepted, Elev: 6854ft/2089m, Tel: 530-279-6116, Nearest town: Likely. GPS: 41.309013, -120.277433

98 • A3 | Stough Reservoir (Modoc NF)

Total sites: 4, RV sites: 4, Central water, Vault/pit toilet, No showers, No RV dump, Tent & RV camping: Free, Stay limit: 14 days, Open May-Oct, Max Length: 22ft, Reservations not accepted, Elev: 6375ft/1943m, Tel: 530-279-6116, Nearest town: Cedar Pass. GPS: 41.562543, -120.255189

99 • A3 | Willow Creek (Modoc NF)

Total sites: 8, RV sites: 8, No water, Vault/pit toilet, No showers, No RV dump, Tent & RV camping: $12, Non-potable water available, Stay limit: 14 days, Open May-Oct, Max Length: 32ft, Reservations not accepted, Elev: 5118ft/1560m, Tel: 530-299-3215, Nearest town: Adin. GPS: 41.013056, -120.828056

100 • B1 | Big Slide (Shasta-Trinity NF)

Total sites: 8, RV sites: 0, No water, Vault/pit toilet, Tents only: Free, Reservations not accepted, Elev: 1213ft/370m, Tel: 530-628-5227, Nearest town: Hyampom. GPS: 40.663444, -123.495538

101 • B1 | Burnt Ranch (Shasta-Trinity NF)

Total sites: 16, RV sites: 16, Central water, Vault/pit toilet, No showers, No RV dump, Tent & RV camping: $12, Max Length: 25ft, Reservations not accepted, Elev: 1257ft/383m, Tel: 530-623-2121, Nearest town: Big Bar. GPS: 40.827414, -123.482634

102 • B1 | East Fork (Six Rivers NF)

Total sites: 10, RV sites: 10, No water, Vault/pit toilet, Tent & RV camping: $8, Open Jun-Sep, Max Length: 22ft, Reservations not accepted, Elev: 1808ft/551m, Tel: 530-629-2118, Nearest town: Willow Creek. GPS: 40.907083, -123.706798

103 • B1 | Mad River (Six Rivers NF)

Total sites: 40, RV sites: 40, Central water, Vault/pit toilet, No showers, No RV dump, Tent & RV camping: $12, Stay limit: 14 days, Open May-Sep, Max Length: 30ft, Reservations not accepted, Elev: 2602ft/793m, Tel: 707-574-6233, Nearest town: Fortuna. GPS: 40.402156, -123.466696

104 • B1 | Slide Creek (Shasta-Trinity NF)

Total sites: 5, RV sites: 0, No water, Vault/pit toilet, Tents only: Free, Reservations not accepted, Elev: 1253ft/382m, Tel: 530-628-5227. GPS: 40.668217, -123.503351

105 • B2 | Ackerman (Shasta-Trinity NF)

Total sites: 51, RV sites: 51, Central water, Flush toilet, No showers, RV dump, Tent & RV camping: $23, Dump station open Apr-Oct, Max Length: 40ft, Reservations accepted, Elev: 1946ft/593m, Tel: 530-623-2121, Nearest town: Lewiston. GPS: 40.785889, -122.771973

106 • B2 | Alder Creek (Lassen) (Lassen NF)

Total sites: 6, RV sites: 0, No water, Vault/pit toilet, Tents only: $10, Open May-Oct, Reservations not accepted, Elev: 3904ft/1190m, Tel: 530-258-2141, Nearest town: Chester. GPS: 40.209134, -121.496721

107 • B2 | Alpine View (Shasta-Trinity NF)

Total sites: 54, RV sites: 54, Central water, Flush toilet, No showers, No RV dump, Tent & RV camping: $23, Open May-Sep, Max Length: 32ft, Reservations accepted, Elev: 2523ft/769m, Tel: 530-623-2121, Nearest town: Trinity Center. GPS: 40.886475, -122.767334

108 • B2 | Antlers (Shasta-Trinity NF)

Total sites: 45, RV sites: 45, Central water, Flush toilet, No showers, No RV dump, Tent & RV camping: $23, Senior Pass cannot be used for double sites, Concessionaire, Open May-Oct, Max Length: 45ft, Reservations accepted, Elev: 1148ft/350m, Tel: 530-275-8113, Nearest town: Lakehead. GPS: 40.887451, -122.378662

109 • B2 | Atchison Camp (Mendocino NF)

Total sites: 6, RV sites: 6, No water, Vault/pit toilet, Tent & RV camping: Free, Open May-Oct, Reservations not accepted, Elev: 4452ft/1357m, Tel: 707-983-6118. GPS: 39.750227, -122.924974

110 • B2 | Bailey Canyon (Six Rivers NF)

Total sites: 25, RV sites: 20, Central water, Vault/pit toilet, No showers, No RV dump, Tent & RV camping: $12, Open May-Sep, Max Length: 22ft, Reservations not accepted, Elev: 2762ft/842m, Tel: 707-574-6233, Nearest town: Mad River. GPS: 40.340597, -123.400673

111 • B2 | Bailey Cove (Shasta-Trinity NF)

Total sites: 7, RV sites: 7, Central water, Flush toilet, No showers, No RV dump, Tent & RV camping: $23, Open all year, Max Length: 45ft, Reservations accepted, Elev: 1105ft/337m, Tel: 530-275-8113, Nearest town: Redding. GPS: 40.799847, -122.318372

112 • B2 | Basin Gulch (Shasta-Trinity NF)

Total sites: 13, RV sites: 13, No water, Vault/pit toilet, Tent & RV camping: Fee unk, Max Length: 20ft, Reservations not accepted, Elev: 2590ft/789m, Tel: 530-352-4211, Nearest town: Platina. GPS: 40.352178, -122.960844

113 • B2 | Battle Creek (Lassen NF)

Total sites: 50, RV sites: 50, Central water, Vault/pit toilet, No showers, No RV dump, Tent & RV camping: $18, Open Apr-Oct, Max Length: 24ft, Reservations not accepted, Elev: 4859ft/1481m, Tel: 530-258-2141, Nearest town: Mineral. GPS: 40.348408, -121.627657

114 • B2 | Beegum Gorge (Shasta-Trinity NF)

Total sites: 2, RV sites: 0, No water, Vault/pit toilet, Tents only: Free, Reservations not accepted, Elev: 2497ft/761m, Tel: 530-352-4211. GPS: 40.313890, -122.933330

115 • B2 | Big Bar (Shasta-Trinity NF)

Total sites: 3, RV sites: 0, No water, Vault/pit toilet, Tents only: Free, Open all year, Reservations not accepted, Elev: 1220ft/372m, Tel: 530-623-2121, Nearest town: Big Bar. GPS: 40.738124, -123.251602

116 • B2 | Big Flat (Shasta-Trinity NF)

Total sites: 10, RV sites: 10, Central water, Vault/pit toilet, No showers, No RV dump, Tent & RV camping: $12, Max Length: 22ft, Reservations not accepted, Elev: 1350ft/411m, Tel: 530-623-2121, Nearest town: Junction City. GPS: 40.739246, -123.204172

117 • B2 | Black Rock (Lassen NF)

Total sites: 6, RV sites: 0, No water, Vault/pit toilet, Tents only: Free, Very poor road - 4x4 recommended, Open all year, Reservations not accepted, Elev: 2172ft/662m, Tel: 530-258-2141, Nearest town: Red Bluff. GPS: 40.183737, -121.713233

118 • B2 | Boardman Camp (Mendocino NF)

Total sites: 3, RV sites: 3, No water, Vault/pit toilet, Tent & RV camping: Free, Reservations not accepted, Elev: 4525ft/1379m, Nearest town: Covelo. GPS: 39.847079, -123.012889

119 • B2 | Bridge Camp (Shasta-Trinity NF)

Total sites: 10, RV sites: 10, No water, Vault/pit toilet, No showers, No RV dump, Tent & RV camping: $10, Limited services Nov-May, Open all year, Max Length: 20ft, Reservations not accepted, Elev: 2936ft/895m, Tel: 530-623-2121, Nearest town: Weaverville. GPS: 40.873535, -122.917969

120 • B2 | Bushytail (Shasta-Trinity NF)

Total sites: 11, RV sites: 11, Elec sites: 9, Central water, Flush toilet, Pay showers, No RV dump, Tent & RV camping: $25, Open May-Sep, Max Length: 99ft, Reservations accepted, Elev: 2441ft/744m, Tel: 530-623-2121, Nearest town: Trinity Center. GPS: 40.851583, -122.813096

121 • B2 | Butte Meadows (Lassen NF)

Total sites: 13, RV sites: 13, Central water, Vault/pit toilet, No showers, No RV dump, Tent & RV camping: $12, Open May-Oct, Reservations not accepted, Elev: 4403ft/1342m, Tel: 530-258-2141, Nearest town: Chester. GPS: 40.079316, -121.558265

122 • B2 | Cherry Hill (Lassen NF)

Total sites: 25, RV sites: 19, Central water, Vault/pit toilet, No showers, No RV dump, Tent & RV camping: $14, Open Apr-Oct, Max Length: 22ft, Reservations not accepted, Elev: 4816ft/1468m,

Tel: 530-258-2141, Nearest town: Chester. GPS: 40.102731, -121.497471

123 • B2 | Clark Springs (Shasta-Trinity NF)

Total sites: 20, RV sites: 20, Central water, No toilets, No showers, No RV dump, Tent & RV camping: $15, Open May-Oct, Reservations not accepted, Elev: 2477ft/755m, Tel: 530-623-2121, Nearest town: Trinity Center. GPS: 40.857561, -122.814652

124 • B2 | Clear Creek (Shasta-Trinity NF)

Total sites: 6, RV sites: 6, No water, Vault/pit toilet, Tent & RV camping: Free, Open all year, Max Length: 22ft, Reservations not accepted, Elev: 3540ft/1079m, Tel: 530-623-2121, Nearest town: Weaverville. GPS: 40.931275, -122.586341

125 • B2 | Cooper Gulch (Shasta-Trinity NF)

Total sites: 5, RV sites: 5, Central water, Vault/pit toilet, No showers, No RV dump, Tent & RV camping: $20, Open Apr-Oct, Max Length: 16ft, Reservations not accepted, Elev: 2018ft/615m, Tel: 530-623-2121, Nearest town: Weaverville. GPS: 40.745848, -122.806377

126 • B2 | Dead Mule (Mendocino NF)

Total sites: 2, RV sites: 2, No water, Vault/pit toilet, Tent & RV camping: Free, Open Jun-Oct, Reservations not accepted, Elev: 5148ft/1569m, Nearest town: Paskenta. GPS: 39.846136, -122.828245

127 • B2 | Deerlick Springs (Shasta-Trinity NF)

Total sites: 13, RV sites: 0, No water, Vault/pit toilet, Tents only: Free, Reservations not accepted, Elev: 3043ft/928m, Tel: 530-352-4211, Nearest town: Platina. GPS: 40.470743, -122.927329

128 • B2 | Denny (Shasta-Trinity NF)

Total sites: 5, RV sites: 5, No water, Vault/pit toilet, Tent & RV camping: Fee unk, Max Length: 22ft, Reservations not accepted, Elev: 1598ft/487m, Tel: 530-623-2121, Nearest town: Denny. GPS: 40.932917, -123.394487

129 • B2 | East Weaver (Shasta-Trinity NF)

Total sites: 11, RV sites: 11, Central water, Vault/pit toilet, No showers, No RV dump, Tent & RV camping: $15, Open all year, Max Length: 25ft, Reservations not accepted, Elev: 2723ft/830m, Tel: 530-623-2121, Nearest town: Weaverville. GPS: 40.772039, -122.922091

130 • B2 | Eel River (Mendocino NF)

Total sites: 15, RV sites: 15, No water, Vault/pit toilet, Tent & RV camping: $8, Open Apr-Nov, Reservations not accepted, Elev: 1519ft/463m, Tel: 707-983-6118, Nearest town: Willits. GPS: 39.824381, -123.085472

131 • B2 | Ellery Creek (Shasta-Trinity NF)

Total sites: 19, RV sites: 19, Central water, Vault/pit toilet, No showers, No RV dump, Tent & RV camping: $23, Food storage lockers, Open May-Sep, Max Length: 40ft, Reservations accepted, Elev: 1073ft/327m, Tel: 530-275-8113, Nearest town: Lakehead. GPS: 40.915334, -122.242636

132 • B2 | Fir Cove (Six Rivers NF)

Total sites: 14, RV sites: 14, Central water, Vault/pit toilet, No showers, No RV dump, Tent & RV camping: $12, Open May-Sep, Max Length: 40ft, Reservations accepted, Elev: 2815ft/858m, Tel: 707-574-6233, Nearest town: Mad River. GPS: 40.342529, -123.404541

133 • B2 | Forest Glen (Shasta-Trinity NF)

Total sites: 15, RV sites: 15, Central water, Vault/pit toilet, No showers, No RV dump, Tent & RV camping: $12, Open May-Sep, Max Length: 16ft, Reservations not accepted, Elev: 2526ft/770m, Tel: 530-628-5227, Nearest town: Hayfork. GPS: 40.376221, -123.327637

134 • B2 | Green Springs Trailhead (Mendocino NF)

Total sites: 6, RV sites: 6, No water, Vault/pit toilet, Tent & RV camping: Free, No large RVs, Sites not level, Open Jun-Nov, Max Length: 22ft, Reservations not accepted, Elev: 6047ft/1843m, Tel: 707-983-6118. GPS: 39.972523, -122.932274

135 • B2 | Hammerhorn Lake (Mendocino NF)

Total sites: 9, RV sites: 9, Central water, Vault/pit toilet, No showers, No RV dump, Tent & RV camping: $8, No large RVs, Open May-Oct, Reservations not accepted, Elev: 3619ft/1103m, Tel: 707-983-6118, Nearest town: Willits. GPS: 39.948853, -122.991495

136 • B2 | Hayden Flat (Shasta-Trinity NF)

Total sites: 35, RV sites: 35, Central water, Vault/pit toilet, No showers, No RV dump, Tent & RV camping: $12, Group site: $40, Open all year, Max Length: 25ft, Reservations not accepted, Elev: 1207ft/368m, Tel: 530-623-2121, Nearest town: Del Loma. GPS: 40.784545, -123.342827

137 • B2 | Haywood Flat (Shasta-Trinity NF)

Total sites: 98, RV sites: 98, Central water, Flush toilet, No showers, No RV dump, Tent & RV camping: $23, Group site $23-$30, Bear boxes, Open May-Sep, Max Length: 45ft, Reservations accepted, Elev: 2388ft/728m, Tel: 530-623-2121, Nearest town: Trinity Center. GPS: 40.872848, -122.767331

138 • B2 | Hell Gate (Shasta-Trinity NF)

Total sites: 17, RV sites: 17, Central water, Vault/pit toilet, No showers, No RV dump, Tent & RV camping: $6, Open May-Sep, Max Length: 16ft, Reservations not accepted, Elev: 2341ft/714m, Tel: 530-628-5227, Nearest town: Hayfork. GPS: 40.370681, -123.313807

139 • B2 | Hirz Bay (Shasta-Trinity NF)

Total sites: 48, RV sites: 48, Central water, Flush toilet, No showers, No RV dump, Tent & RV camping: $23, Open May-Sep, Max Length: 45ft, Reservations accepted, Elev: 1131ft/345m, Tel: 530-275-8113, Nearest town: Lakehead. GPS: 40.865789, -122.256061

140 • B2 | Hobo Gulch (Shasta-Trinity NF)

Total sites: 10, RV sites: 0, No water, Vault/pit toilet, Tents only: Free, Very rough road, Reservations not accepted, Elev: 3182ft/970m, Tel: 530-623-2121, Nearest town: Junction City. GPS: 40.924198, -123.155012

141 • B2 | Hole In The Ground (Lassen NF)

Total sites: 13, RV sites: 5, Central water, Vault/pit toilet, No showers, No RV dump, Tent & RV camping: $12, Not recommended for large RVs, Open May-Oct, Reservations not accepted, Elev: 4266ft/1300m, Tel: 530-258-2141, Nearest town: Mineral. GPS: 40.309482, -121.562485

142 • B2 | Honn Creek (Lassen NF)

Total sites: 6, RV sites: 0, No water, Vault/pit toilet, Tents only: $10, Stay limit: 14 days, Open Apr-Oct, Reservations not accepted, Elev: 3425ft/1044m, Tel: 530-336-5521, Nearest town: Old Station. GPS: 40.779204, -121.503206

143 • B2 | Howard Lake (Mendocino NF)

Total sites: 10, No water, Vault/pit toilet, Tents only: $6, High-clearance vehicles recommended, Open May-Sep, Reservations not accepted, Elev: 3862ft/1177m, Tel: 530-934-3316. GPS: 39.881577, -122.991391

144 • B2 | Howard Meadows (Mendocino NF)

Total sites: 6, RV sites: 6, No water, Vault/pit toilet, Tent & RV camping: $6, High-clearance vehicles required, Open May-Oct, Reservations not accepted, Elev: 3930ft/1198m, Tel: 530-934-3316, Nearest town: Covelo. GPS: 39.877914, -122.992256

145 • B2 | Ides Cove Horsepacker TH (Mendocino NF)

Total sites: 3, RV sites: 3, No water, Vault/pit toilet, No showers, No RV dump, Tent & RV camping: Free, Open Jun-Nov, Max Length: 16ft, Reservations not accepted, Elev: 6634ft/2022m, Tel: 530-934-3316, Nearest town: Paskenta. GPS: 40.037784, -122.818342

146 • B2 | Jackass Spring (Shasta-Trinity NF)

Total sites: 10, RV sites: 10, No water, Vault/pit toilet, Tent & RV camping: Free, Open all year, Max Length: 32ft, Reservations not accepted, Elev: 3501ft/1067m, Tel: 530-623-2121, Nearest town: Trinity Center. GPS: 40.961585, -122.646591

147 • B2 | Jones Valley (Lower) (Shasta-Trinity NF)

Total sites: 9, RV sites: 9, Central water, Vault/pit toilet, No showers, No RV dump, Tent & RV camping: $23, Open all year, Reservations not accepted, Elev: 1125ft/343m, Tel: 530-275-1587. GPS: 40.727558, -122.229083

148 • B2 | Kingsley Glade (Mendocino NF)

Total sites: 6, RV sites: 6, No water, Vault/pit toilet, Tent & RV camping: Free, Horse corral, Open May-Nov, Reservations not accepted, Elev: 4577ft/1395m, Tel: 530-934-3316, Nearest town: Paskenta. GPS: 39.903807, -122.764613

149 • B2 | Lakeshore East (Shasta-Trinity NF)

Total sites: 23, RV sites: 15, Central water, Flush toilet, No showers, No RV dump, Tent & RV camping: $23, Shelters available, Open May-Sep, Max Length: 45ft, Reservations accepted, Elev: 1073ft/327m, Tel: 530-275-1587, Nearest town: Lakehead. GPS: 40.875246, -122.388519

150 • B2 | Little Doe (Mendocino NF)

Total sites: 13, RV sites: 13, No water, Vault/pit toilet, Tent & RV camping: $6, No large RVs, Open May-Oct, Reservations not accepted, Elev: 3842ft/1171m, Tel: 707-983-6118, Nearest town: Covelo. GPS: 39.895575, -122.986747

151 • B2 | Madrone (Shasta-Trinity NF)

Total sites: 10, RV sites: 10, No water, Vault/pit toilet, No showers, No RV dump, Tent & RV camping: Free, Bear boxes, Open all year, Max Length: 16ft, Reservations not accepted, Elev: 1552ft/473m, Tel: 530-275-1587, Nearest town: Redding. GPS: 40.924361, -122.095473

152 • B2 | Mary Smith (Shasta-Trinity NF)

Total sites: 25, RV sites: 0, Central water, Flush toilet, No showers, No RV dump, Tents only: $23, Also walk-to sites, 6 Glamping units - $119, Open May-Oct, Reservations accepted, Elev: 1968ft/600m, Tel: 530-275-8113, Nearest town: Lewiston. GPS: 40.731642, -122.808332

153 • B2 | McCloud Bridge (Shasta-Trinity NF)

Total sites: 14, RV sites: 14, No water, Vault/pit toilet, No showers, No RV dump, Tent & RV camping: $23, Bear boxes, Open Apr-Oct, Max Length: 16ft, Reservations not accepted, Elev: 1171ft/357m, Tel: 530-275-1589, Nearest town: Lakehead. GPS: 40.935515, -122.246044

154 • B2 | Minersville (Shasta-Trinity NF)

Total sites: 14, RV sites: 14, Elec sites: 1, Central water, Flush toilet, No showers, No RV dump, Tents: $15/RVs: $20-25, Also walk-to sites, Open May-Sep, Max Length: 36ft, Reservations accepted, Elev: 2356ft/718m, Tel: 530-623-1203, Nearest town: Trinity Center. GPS: 40.849064, -122.811749

155 • B2 | Moore Creek (Shasta-Trinity NF)

Total sites: 12, RV sites: 12, Central water, Vault/pit toilet, No showers, No RV dump, Tent & RV camping: $20, Reservable group site $150, Bear boxes, Open May-Sep, Max Length: 16ft, Reservations not accepted, Elev: 1112ft/339m, Tel: 530-275-1587, Nearest town: Lakehead. GPS: 40.888478, -122.225007

156 • B2 | Nelson Point (Shasta-Trinity NF)

Total sites: 8, RV sites: 8, No water, Vault/pit toilet, Tent & RV camping: $15, Group site $110, Food storage lockers, primarily a group site but individual FCFS sites may be available, Open Apr-Sep, Max Length: 16ft, Reservations not accepted, Elev: 1171ft/357m, Tel: 530-275-1587, Nearest town: O'Brien. GPS: 40.849249, -122.346455

157 • B2 | Oak Grove (Shasta-Trinity NF)

Total sites: 10, RV sites: 5, No water, No toilets, Tent & RV camping: Free, Reservations not accepted, Elev: 1207ft/368m, Nearest town: Shasta Lake. GPS: 40.849476, -122.353343

158 • B2 | Philpot (Shasta-Trinity NF)

Total sites: 6, RV sites: 0, No water, Vault/pit toilet, Tents only: Free, Reservations not accepted, Elev: 2654ft/809m, Tel: 530-628-5227, Nearest town: Hayfork. GPS: 40.466000, -123.191000

159 • B2 | Pigeon Point (Shasta-Trinity NF)

Total sites: 8, RV sites: 6, No water, Vault/pit toilet, Tent & RV camping: $12, Reservable group site: $75, Non-potable water, Open all year, Max Length: 22ft, Reservations not accepted, Elev:

1545ft/471m, Tel: 530-623-2121, Nearest town: Junction City. GPS: 40.767447, -123.132062

160 • B2 | Pine Point (Shasta-Trinity NF)

Total sites: 14, RV sites: 14, Central water, Vault/pit toilet, No showers, No RV dump, Tent & RV camping: $20, Reservable group site $150, Bear boxes, Open holidays for overflow, Open May-Sep, Max Length: 24ft, Reservations not accepted, Elev: 1089ft/332m, Tel: 530-275-1587, Nearest town: Redding. GPS: 40.927541, -122.247374

161 • B2 | Plaskett Meadows (Mendocino NF)

Total sites: 31, RV sites: 31, Central water, Vault/pit toilet, No showers, No RV dump, Tent & RV camping: $10, Open Jun-Oct, Max Length: 16ft, Reservations not accepted, Elev: 6099ft/1859m, Tel: 530-963-3128, Nearest town: Elk Creek. GPS: 39.728415, -122.846684

162 • B2 | Potato Patch (Lassen NF)

Total sites: 32, RV sites: 32, Central water, Vault/pit toilet, No showers, No RV dump, Tent & RV camping: $14, Open Apr-Sep, Reservations not accepted, Elev: 3534ft/1077m, Tel: 530-258-2141, Nearest town: Chester. GPS: 40.188477, -121.532227

163 • B2 | Preacher Meadow (Shasta-Trinity NF)

Total sites: 45, RV sites: 45, Central water, Vault/pit toilet, No showers, No RV dump, Tent & RV camping: $12, Open Jun-Oct, Max Length: 40ft, Reservations not accepted, Elev: 2989ft/911m, Tel: 530-623-2121, Nearest town: Trinity Center. GPS: 40.963623, -122.731689

164 • B2 | Ripstein (Shasta-Trinity NF)

Total sites: 10, RV sites: 0, No water, Vault/pit toilet, Tents only: Free, Reservations not accepted, Elev: 2825ft/861m, Tel: 530-623-2121, Nearest town: Junction City. GPS: 40.876709, -123.029297

165 • B2 | Rock Cabin Trailhead (Mendocino NF)

Total sites: 3, RV sites: 3, No water, No toilets, Tent & RV camping: Free, No large RVs, Open Apr-Dec, Max Length: 20ft, Reservations not accepted, Elev: 5059ft/1542m, Tel: 707-983-6118. GPS: 40.008229, -123.085231

166 • B2 | Rocky Cabin (Mendocino NF)

Total sites: 3, RV sites: 3, No water, Vault/pit toilet, Tent & RV camping: Free, Open Jun-Oct, Reservations not accepted, Elev: 6246ft/1904m, Nearest town: Paskenta. GPS: 39.954494, -122.739613

167 • B2 | Rush Creek (Shasta-Trinity NF)

Total sites: 10, RV sites: 10, No water, Vault/pit toilet, Tent & RV camping: $10, Open May-Sep, Max Length: 20ft, Reservations not accepted, Elev: 2841ft/866m, Tel: 530-623-2121, Nearest town: Weaverville. GPS: 40.816834, -122.896343

168 • B2 | Scotts Flat (Shasta-Trinity NF)

Total sites: 10, RV sites: 10, No water, Vault/pit toilet, Tent & RV camping: Free, Max Length: 20ft, Reservations not accepted, Elev: 2354ft/717m, Tel: 530-628-5227, Nearest town: Hayfork. GPS: 40.365738, -123.309397

169 • B2 | Shiell Gulch (Shasta-Trinity NF)

Total sites: 5, RV sites: 0, No water, Vault/pit toilet, Tents only: Free, Reservations not accepted, Elev: 2806ft/855m. GPS: 40.470341, -123.060648

170 • B2 | South Antelope (Lassen NF)

Total sites: 4, RV sites: 4, No water, Vault/pit toilet, Tent & RV camping: Free, Reservations not accepted, Elev: 2861ft/872m, Tel: 530-258-2141, Nearest town: Chester. GPS: 40.253027, -121.758434

171 • B2 | Stoney Point (Shasta-Trinity NF)

Total sites: 22, RV sites: 0, Central water, Flush toilet, No showers, No RV dump, Tents only: $13, Walk-to sites, Open May-Oct, Reservations not accepted, Elev: 2470ft/753m, Tel: 530-623-2121, Nearest town: Weaverville. GPS: 40.848818, -122.859339

172 • B2 | Sugar Spring (Mendocino NF)

Total sites: 3, RV sites: 0, No water, Vault/pit toilet, Tents only: Free, Open Jun-Nov, Reservations not accepted, Elev: 5522ft/1683m, Tel: 530-934-3316, Nearest town: Paskenta. GPS: 39.859458, -122.918086

173 • B2 | Sugarfoot Glade (Mendocino NF)

Total sites: 6, RV sites: 6, No water, Vault/pit toilet, Tent & RV camping: Free, Open Jun-Nov, Max Length: 16ft, Reservations not accepted, Elev: 3812ft/1162m, Tel: 530-934-3316, Nearest town: Red Bluff. GPS: 39.885038, -122.777093

174 • B2 | Sycamore Grove (Red Bluff) (Mendocino NF)

Total sites: 30, RV sites: 30, Elec sites: 10, Central water, Flush toilet, Pay showers, No RV dump, Tents: $16/RVs: $16-25, Stay limit: 14 days, Open all year, Max Length: 44ft, Reservations accepted, Elev: 272ft/83m, Tel: 530-934-3316, Nearest town: Red Bluff. GPS: 40.155554, -122.202022

175 • B2 | Tannery Gulch (Shasta-Trinity NF)

Total sites: 82, RV sites: 82, Central water, Flush toilet, No showers, No RV dump, Tent & RV camping: $23, Group site $30, Open May-Sep, Max Length: 45ft, Reservations accepted, Elev: 2513ft/766m, Tel: 530-623-2121, Nearest town: Weaverville. GPS: 40.834683, -122.846859

176 • B2 | Three Prong (Mendocino NF)

Total sites: 6, RV sites: 3, No water, Vault/pit toilet, Tent & RV camping: Free, Open Jun-Dec, Max Length: RV-24'/Trlr-16ft, Reservations not accepted, Elev: 6014ft/1833m, Tel: 530-934-3316, Nearest town: Paskenta. GPS: 39.920713, -122.791721

177 • B2 | Tomhead Saddle (Shasta-Trinity NF)

Total sites: 5, RV sites: 0, No water, Vault/pit toilet, Tents only: Free, Reservations not accepted, Elev: 5686ft/1733m, Tel: 530-352-4211. GPS: 40.140152, -122.830288

178 • B2 | Toomes Camp (Mendocino NF)

Total sites: 2, RV sites: 2, No water, Vault/pit toilet, Tent & RV camping: Free, Open Jun-Oct, Reservations not accepted, Elev: 6001ft/1829m, Nearest town: Red Bluff. GPS: 40.002985, -122.759041

179 • B2 | Wells Cabin (Mendocino NF)

Total sites: 25, RV sites: 15, No water, Vault/pit toilet, Tent & RV camping: Free, Open Jun-Nov, Reservations not accepted, Elev: 6348ft/1935m, Tel: 530-934-3316, Nearest town: Covelo. GPS: 39.837652, -122.949882

180 • B2 | White Rock (Shasta-Trinity NF)

Total sites: 3, RV sites: 0, No water, No toilets, Tents only: Free, Elev: 5000ft/1524m, Tel: 530-352-4211. GPS: 40.253059, -123.023492

181 • B2 | Whitlock (Mendocino NF)

Total sites: 5, RV sites: 5, No water, Vault/pit toilet, Tent & RV camping: Free, Open May-Nov, Reservations not accepted, Elev: 4249ft/1295m, Tel: 530-934-3316, Nearest town: Paskenta. GPS: 39.920028, -122.687032

182 • B3 | Almanor (Lassen NF)

Total sites: 104, RV sites: 104, Central water, Vault/pit toilet, No showers, No RV dump, Tents: $15-18/RVs: $18, 2 group sites: $36-$100, Open May-Sep, Max Length: 40ft, Reservations accepted, Elev: 4619ft/1408m, Tel: 530-258-2141, Nearest town: Chester. GPS: 40.215576, -121.173828

183 • B3 | American House OHV Camp (Plumas NF)

Total sites: 5, RV sites: 0, No water, No toilets, Tents only: Free, Elev: 4534ft/1382m, Nearest town: La Porte. GPS: 39.628499, -121.002283

184 • B3 | Aspen Grove (Lassen NF)

Total sites: 28, RV sites: 0, Central water, Flush toilet, No showers, No RV dump, Tents only: $20, Bear boxes must be used for food storage, No generators, Open May-Oct, Reservations accepted, Elev: 5151ft/1570m, Tel: 530-310-1245, Nearest town: Lee Vining. GPS: 40.556146, -120.772536

185 • B3 | Benner Creek (Lassen NF)

Total sites: 9, RV sites: 9, No water, Vault/pit toilet, Tent & RV camping: Free, Open May-Oct, Reservations not accepted, Elev: 5614ft/1711m, Tel: 530-258-2141, Nearest town: Chester. GPS: 40.395335, -121.268047

186 • B3 | Berger (Tahoe NF)

Total sites: 8, RV sites: 8, Elec sites: 50, No water, Vault/pit toilet, Tent & RV camping: $18, Open May-Oct, Max Length: 18ft, Reservations accepted, Elev: 5928ft/1807m, Tel: 530-862-1368, Nearest town: Bassett. GPS: 39.627930, -120.643555

187 • B3 | Big Cove (Plumas NF)

Total sites: 42, RV sites: 42, Central water, Flush toilet, Free showers, No RV dump, Tent & RV camping: $34, Open May-Sep, Max Length: 70ft, Reservations accepted, Elev: 5633ft/1717m, Tel: 530-258-7606, Nearest town: Chilcoot. GPS: 39.902588, -120.175049

188 • B3 | Big Pine (Lassen NF)

Total sites: 19, RV sites: 19, Central water, Vault/pit toilet, No showers, No RV dump, Tent & RV camping: $12, Open May-Oct, Reservations not accepted, Elev: 4669ft/1423m, Tel: 530-336-5521, Nearest town: Old Station. GPS: 40.633658, -121.466419

189 • B3 | Black Rock (Plumas NF)

Total sites: 20, RV sites: 0, Central water, Vault/pit toilet, No showers, RV dump, Tents only: $23, Walk-to sites, Open May-Oct, Reservations not accepted, Elev: 5164ft/1574m, Tel: 530-534-6500, Nearest town: La Porte. GPS: 39.729016, -121.012059

190 • B3 | Bogard (Lassen NF)

Total sites: 10, RV sites: 10, Central water, Vault/pit toilet, No showers, No RV dump, Tent & RV camping: Free, Not maintained in winter - often inaccessible, Stay limit: 14 days, Open all year, Max Length: 25ft, Reservations not accepted, Elev: 5692ft/1735m, Tel: 530-257-4188, Nearest town: Susanville. GPS: 40.575297, -121.098381

191 • B3 | Boulder Creek (Plumas NF)

Total sites: 42, RV sites: 42, Central water, Vault/pit toilet, No showers, No RV dump, Tent & RV camping: $32, Generator hours: 0600-22000, Open May-Sep, Max Length: 51ft, Reservations accepted, Elev: 5062ft/1543m, Tel: 530-283-0555, Nearest town: Taylorsville. GPS: 40.191650, -120.613037

192 • B3 | Bradys Camp (Plumas NF)

Total sites: 6, RV sites: 0, No water, Vault/pit toilet, Tents only: Free, Uphill gravel road not recommended for RVs or trailers, Open all year, Reservations not accepted, Elev: 7057ft/2151m, Tel: 530-283-0555, Nearest town: Quincey. GPS: 39.956403, -120.753499

193 • B3 | Bridge (Lassen NF)

Total sites: 25, RV sites: 25, No water, Vault/pit toilet, Tent & RV camping: $10, Stay limit: 14 days, Open Apr-Oct, Reservations not accepted, Elev: 3878ft/1182m, Tel: 530-336-5521, Nearest town: Old Station. GPS: 40.730831, -121.438691

194 • B3 | Butte Creek (Lassen NF)

Total sites: 10, RV sites: 0, No water, Vault/pit toilet, Tents only: Free, Open all year, Reservations not accepted, Elev: 5599ft/1707m, Tel: 530-257-4188, Nearest town: Susanville. GPS: 40.611882, -121.297703

195 • B3 | Cave (Lassen NF)

Total sites: 46, RV sites: 46, Central water, Vault/pit toilet, No showers, No RV dump, Tent & RV camping: $16, Stay limit: 14 days, Open Apr-Oct, Max Length: 22ft, Reservations not accepted, Elev: 4354ft/1327m, Tel: 530-336-5521, Nearest town: Old Station. GPS: 40.685053, -121.422711

196 • B3 | Chapman Creek (Tahoe NF)

Total sites: 27, RV sites: 20, Central water, Vault/pit toilet, No showers, No RV dump, Tent & RV camping: $24, Also walk-to sites, Open May-Oct, Max Length: 45ft, Reservations accepted, Elev: 5899ft/1798m, Tel: 530-862-1368, Nearest town: Sierra City. GPS: 39.631104, -120.544678

197 • B3 | Chilcoot (Plumas NF)

Total sites: 40, RV sites: 36, Central water, Flush toilet, Free showers, No RV dump, Tent & RV camping: $34, Open May-Sep, Max Length: 40ft, Reservations accepted, Elev: 5223ft/1592m, Tel: 530-258-7606, Nearest town: Chilcoot. GPS: 39.866455, -120.167480

198 • B3 | Christie (Lassen NF)

Total sites: 69, RV sites: 69, Central water, Flush toilet, No showers, No RV dump, Tent & RV camping: $20, Group sites: $30, Generator hours: 0800-2200, Open May-Sep, Reservations accepted, Elev: 5148ft/1569m, Tel: 530-825-3212, Nearest town: Susanville. GPS: 40.568115, -120.837891

199 • B3 | Cleghorn Bar OHV (Plumas NF)

Total sites: 4, RV sites: 0, No water, Vault/pit toilet, Tents only: Free, 4x4 needed, Stay limit: 14 days, Reservations not accepted, Elev: 3468ft/1057m, Tel: 530-532-1210, Nearest town: Laporte. GPS: 39.820000, -121.013610

200 • B3 | Conklin Park (Plumas NF)

Total sites: 9, RV sites: 9, No water, Vault/pit toilet, Tent & RV camping: Free, Stay limit: 14 days, Open all year, Reservations not accepted, Elev: 5974ft/1821m, Tel: 530-836-2575, Nearest town: Portola. GPS: 40.047000, -120.368000

201 • B3 | Cottonwood Springs (Plumas NF)

Total sites: 12, RV sites: 12, Central water, Flush toilet, Free showers, RV dump, Tent & RV camping: $34, Group sites: $100-$140, Open May-Sep, Max Length: 56ft, Reservations accepted, Elev: 5705ft/1739m, Tel: 530-836-2575, Nearest town: Chilcoot. GPS: 39.890869, -120.211426

202 • B3 | Crater Lake (Lassen NF)

Total sites: 17, RV sites: 17, Central water, Vault/pit toilet, No showers, No RV dump, Tent & RV camping: $10, Generator hours: 0800-2200, Open May-Oct, Max Length: 18ft, Reservations not accepted, Elev: 7024ft/2141m, Tel: 530-257-4188, Nearest town: Susanville. GPS: 40.626664, -121.042071

203 • B3 | Crocker (Plumas NF)

Total sites: 10, RV sites: 10, No water, Vault/pit toilet, Tent & RV camping: Free, Stay limit: 14 days, Open May-Oct, Reservations not accepted, Elev: 5771ft/1759m, Tel: 530-836-2572, Nearest town: Portola. GPS: 39.891000, -120.423000

204 • B3 | Deanes Valley (Plumas NF)

Total sites: 7, RV sites: 7, No water, Vault/pit toilet, Tent & RV camping: Free, Open Apr-Sep, Reservations not accepted, Elev: 4322ft/1317m, Tel: 530-283-0555, Nearest town: Quincy. GPS: 39.889545, -121.024617

205 • B3 | Diablo (Tahoe NF)

Total sites: 19, RV sites: 12, No water, Vault/pit toilet, Tent & RV camping: $18, Open May-Oct, Max Length: 60ft, Reservations accepted, Elev: 5890ft/1795m, Tel: 530-862-1368, Nearest town: Bassett. GPS: 39.631754, -120.638539

206 • B3 | Domingo Springs (Lassen NF)

Total sites: 18, RV sites: 18, Central water, Vault/pit toilet, No showers, No RV dump, Tent & RV camping: $14, Open May-Sep, Reservations not accepted, Elev: 5167ft/1575m, Tel: 530-258-2141, Nearest town: Chester. GPS: 40.360428, -121.347114

207 • B3 | Eagle (Lassen NF)

Total sites: 46, RV sites: 46, Elec sites: 2, Central water, Flush toilet, No showers, No RV dump, Tents: $20/RVs: $20-35, 2 group sites: $30, Additional fee for electric, 1 Full hookup site, Open May-Dec, Max Length: 60ft, Reservations accepted, Elev: 5190ft/1582m, Tel: 530-257-4188, Nearest town: Susanville. GPS: 40.548615, -120.781277

208 • B3 | Elam Creek (Lassen NF)

Total sites: 15, RV sites: 12, Central water, Vault/pit toilet, No showers, No RV dump, Tent & RV camping: $14, Open Apr-Oct, Reservations not accepted, Elev: 4452ft/1357m, Tel: 530-258-2141, Nearest town: Chester. GPS: 40.247559, -121.448486

209 • B3 | Feather Falls Trailhead (Plumas NF)

Total sites: 5, Central water, Vault/pit toilet, No showers, No RV dump, Tents only: Free, Stay limit: 14 days, Open all year, Reservations not accepted, Elev: 2572ft/784m, Tel: 530-534-6500, Nearest town: Feather Falls. GPS: 39.613891, -121.266663

210 • B3 | Frenchman (Plumas NF)

Total sites: 38, RV sites: 38, Central water, Vault/pit toilet, No showers, RV dump, Tent & RV camping: $34, Open Apr-Sep, Max Length: 50ft, Reservations accepted, Elev: 5636ft/1718m, Tel: 530-258-7606, Nearest town: Chilcoot. GPS: 39.900635, -120.187744

211 • B3 | Gansner Bar (Plumas NF)

Total sites: 16, RV sites: 16, Central water, Flush toilet, No showers, No RV dump, Tent & RV camping: $30, Open May-Oct, Reservations not accepted, Elev: 2418ft/737m, Tel: 530-283-0555, Nearest town: Quincy. GPS: 40.019775, -121.222412

212 • B3 | Gold Lake (Plumas NF)

Total sites: 37, RV sites: 37, No water, Vault/pit toilet, Tent & RV camping: $20, Stay limit: 14 days, Open May-Sep, Reservations not accepted, Elev: 6457ft/1968m, Tel: 530-836-2575, Nearest town: Graeagle. GPS: 39.679924, -120.645945

213 • B3 | Gold Lake 4X4 (Plumas NF)

Total sites: 16, RV sites: 16, No water, No toilets, Tent & RV camping: Free, Also boat-in sites, Reservations not accepted, Elev: 6450ft/1966m, Tel: 530-836-2575, Nearest town: Graeagle. GPS: 39.668632, -120.662843

214 • B3 | Golden Trout Crossing (Plumas NF)

Total sites: 15, RV sites: 0, Central water, Vault/pit toilet, No showers, No RV dump, Tents only: $15, Stay limit: 14 days, Reservations not accepted, Elev: 3226ft/983m, Tel: 530-534-6500, Nearest town: Strawberry Valley. GPS: 39.615779, -121.142158

215 • B3 | Goose Lake (Plumas NF)

Total sites: 14, RV sites: 14, No water, Vault/pit toilet, Tent & RV camping: $20, Stay limit: 14 days, Open Jun-Oct, Reservations not accepted, Elev: 6686ft/2038m, Tel: 530-836-2575, Nearest town: Graeagle. GPS: 39.675558, -120.636295

216 • B3 | Goumaz (Lassen NF)

Total sites: 6, RV sites: 6, Central water, Vault/pit toilet, No showers, No RV dump, Tent & RV camping: Free, No water in winter, Open May-Sep, Max Length: 18ft, Reservations not accepted, Elev: 5249ft/1600m, Tel: 530-825-3212, Nearest town: Susanville. GPS: 40.413916, -120.862025

217 • B3 | Grasshopper Flat (Plumas NF)

Total sites: 68, RV sites: 68, Central water, Flush toilet, Pay showers, RV dump, Tent & RV camping: $34, Group site $100, Dump station within 1 mi, Stay limit: 14 days, Open May-Oct, Max Length: 54ft, Reservations accepted, Elev: 5863ft/1787m, Tel: 530-832-1076, Nearest town: Portola. GPS: 39.890381, -120.478027

218 • B3 | Grizzly (Plumas NF)

Total sites: 55, RV sites: 55, Central water, Flush toilet, No showers, RV dump, Tent & RV camping: $30, Stay limit: 14 days, Open May-Sep, Max Length: 32ft, Reservations accepted, Elev: 5909ft/1801m, Tel: 530-832-1076, Nearest town: Portola. GPS: 39.887207, -120.473633

219 • B3 | Grizzly Creek (Plumas NF)

Total sites: 11, RV sites: 8, No water, Vault/pit toilet, Tent & RV camping: $25, Open Apr-Oct, Reservations not accepted, Elev: 5318ft/1621m, Tel: 530-283-0555, Nearest town: Quincy. GPS: 39.867047, -121.206948

220 • B3 | Hallsted (Plumas NF)

Total sites: 20, RV sites: 20, Elec sites: 8, Central water, Flush toilet, Free showers, No RV dump, Tents: $31/RVs: $31-41, Open May-Sep, Max Length: 45ft, Reservations accepted, Elev: 2851ft/869m, Tel: 530-283-0555, Nearest town: Quincy. GPS: 40.017127, -121.073213

221 • B3 | Hat Creek (Lassen NF)

Total sites: 72, RV sites: 72, Central water, Flush toilet, No showers, No RV dump, Tent & RV camping: $16, RV dump in Old Station, Caving nearby, Stay limit: 14 days, Open Apr-Oct, Max Length: 22ft, Reservations not accepted, Elev: 4485ft/1367m, Tel: 530-335-7517, Nearest town: Old Station. GPS: 40.667725, -121.446533

222 • B3 | Haven Lake (Plumas NF)

Total sites: 4, RV sites: 4, No water, Vault/pit toilet, Tent & RV camping: $20, Stay limit: 14 days, Open May-Sep, Reservations not accepted, Elev: 6690ft/2039m, Tel: 530-836-2575, Nearest town: Graeagle. GPS: 39.672723, -120.631198

223 • B3 | High Bridge (Lassen NF)

Total sites: 12, RV sites: 12, No water, Vault/pit toilet, No showers, No RV dump, Tent & RV camping: $12, Generator hours: 0600-2200, Open May-Sep, Reservations not accepted, Elev: 4893ft/1491m, Tel: 530-258-2141, Nearest town: Chester. GPS: 40.337839, -121.308098

224 • B3 | Horse Camp (Plumas NF)

Total sites: 10, RV sites: 10, No water, Vault/pit toilet, Tent & RV camping: $23, Non-potable water, No services/fees Oct-May, Stay limit: 14 days, Open all year, Reservations accepted, Elev: 5118ft/1560m, Tel: 530-534-6500, Nearest town: La Porte. GPS: 39.748294, -120.966319

225 • B3 | Lakes Basin (Plumas NF)

Total sites: 22, RV sites: 19, Central water, Vault/pit toilet, No showers, No RV dump, Tent & RV camping: $32, Group tent site: $80, Stay limit: 14 days, Open May-Oct, Max Length: 30ft, Reservations accepted, Elev: 6332ft/1930m, Tel: 530-836-2575, Nearest town: Graeagle. GPS: 39.703188, -120.661416

226 • B3 | Laufman (Plumas NF)

Total sites: 6, RV sites: 6, No water, Vault/pit toilet, Tent & RV camping: Free, Stay limit: 14 days, Open Apr-Oct, Reservations not accepted, Elev: 5098ft/1554m, Tel: 530-836-2575, Nearest town: Milford. GPS: 40.135000, -120.348000

227 • B3 | Lightning Tree (Plumas NF)

Total sites: 40, RV sites: 40, Central water, Vault/pit toilet, No showers, Tent & RV camping: $34, Stay limit: 14 days, Open Apr-Oct, Max Length: 45ft, Reservations accepted, Elev: 5797ft/1767m, Tel: 530-832-1076, Nearest town: Portola. GPS: 39.931152, -120.508057

228 • B3 | Little Beaver (Plumas NF)

Total sites: 120, RV sites: 120, Central water, Flush toilet, No showers, No RV dump, Tent & RV camping: $23-25, Open May-Oct, Max Length: 50ft, Reservations accepted, Elev: 5115ft/1559m, Tel: 530-534-6500, Nearest town: La Porte. GPS: 39.729861, -120.968331

229 • B3 | Little North Fork (Plumas NF)

Total sites: 8, RV sites: 8, Central water, Vault/pit toilet, No showers, No RV dump, Tent & RV camping: $15, Stay limit: 14 days, Reservations not accepted, Elev: 4032ft/1229m, Tel: 530-534-6500, Nearest town: Berry Creek. GPS: 39.782000, -121.260000

230 • B3 | Lone Rock (Plumas NF)

Total sites: 84, RV sites: 84, Central water, Vault/pit toilet, No showers, No RV dump, Tent & RV camping: $32, Open May-Sep, Max Length: 53ft, Reservations accepted, Elev: 5069ft/1545m, Tel: 530-283-0555, Nearest town: Taylorsville. GPS: 40.195068, -120.618164

231 • B3 | Long Point (Plumas NF)

Total sites: 38, RV sites: 38, Central water, Vault/pit toilet, No showers, No RV dump, Tent & RV camping: $32, 4 group sites: $85, Stay limit: 30 days, Open May-Sep, Max Length: 88ft, Reservations accepted, Elev: 5062ft/1543m, Tel: 530-283-0555, Nearest town: Taylorsville. GPS: 40.178087, -120.578674

232 • B3 | Lower Bucks (Plumas NF)

Total sites: 7, RV sites: 7, No water, Vault/pit toilet, Tent & RV camping: $25, Free w/ no services in winter, Reservations not accepted, Elev: 5164ft/1574m, Tel: 530-283-0555, Nearest town: Quincy. GPS: 39.902000, -121.215000

233 • B3 | Meadow Camp (Plumas NF)

Total sites: 7, RV sites: 7, No water, Vault/pit toilet, Tent & RV camping: $15, Free w/ no services in winter, Open all year, Reservations not accepted, Elev: 3747ft/1142m, Tel: 530-283-0555, Nearest town: Quincy. GPS: 39.930435, -121.041738

234 • B3 | Meadow View Equestrian Camp (Plumas NF)

Total sites: 6, RV sites: 6, No water, Vault/pit toilet, Tent & RV camping: Free, Stay limit: 14 days, Open Apr-Sep, Reservations not accepted, Elev: 6096ft/1858m, Tel: 530-836-2575, Nearest town: Doyle. GPS: 40.036000, -120.213000

235 • B3 | Merrill (Lassen NF)

Total sites: 172, RV sites: 172, Elec sites: 121, Water at site, Flush toilet, No showers, RV dump, Tents: $20/RVs: $30-35, Group sites $60, 57 Full hookup sites, Open May-Oct, Max Length: 172ft, Reservations accepted, Elev: 5151ft/1570m, Tel: 530-825-3450, Nearest town: Susanville. GPS: 40.549072, -120.812256

236 • B3 | Mill Creek (Plumas NF)

Total sites: 10, RV sites: 10, Central water, Vault/pit toilet, No showers, No RV dump, Tent & RV camping: $30, Free w/ no services in winter, Open all year, Reservations not accepted, Elev: 5194ft/1583m, Tel: 530-283-0555, Nearest town: Quincy. GPS: 39.912773, -121.186946

237 • B3 | North Fork (Caribou) (Plumas NF)

Total sites: 21, RV sites: 21, Elec sites: 21, Water at site, Flush toilet, Free showers, Tents: $30/RVs: $30-32, Reservations not accepted, Elev: 2480ft/756m, Tel: 530-283-0555, Nearest town: Quincy. GPS: 40.039886, -121.219921

238 • B3 | Packsaddle (Tahoe NF)

Total sites: 16, RV sites: 16, Central water, Vault/pit toilet, No showers, No RV dump, Tent & RV camping: $24, 2 equestrian sites, Open May-Oct, Max Length: 100ft, Reservations accepted, Elev: 6112ft/1863m, Tel: 530-862-1368, Nearest town: Sierra City. GPS: 39.623788, -120.649662

239 • B3 | Peninsula (Plumas NF)

Total sites: 25, RV sites: 0, Central water, Flush toilet, No showers, No RV dump, Tents only: $23, Walk-to sites, Stay limit: 14 days, Open May-Oct, Reservations not accepted, Elev: 5043ft/1537m, Tel: 530-534-6500, Nearest town: La Porte. GPS: 39.719944, -120.978518

240 • B3 | Queen Lily (Plumas NF)

Total sites: 12, RV sites: 12, Central water, Flush toilet, No showers, No RV dump, Tent & RV camping: $30, Open Apr-Sep, Reservations not accepted, Elev: 2520ft/768m, Tel: 530-283-0555, Nearest town: Quincy. GPS: 40.045718, -121.217863

241 • B3 | Red Bridge (Plumas NF)

Total sites: 5, No water, Vault/pit toilet, Tents only: Free, No services in winter, Open all year, Reservations not accepted, Elev: 5243ft/1598m, Nearest town: Quincy. GPS: 39.850248, -120.837219

242 • B3 | Red Feather (Plumas NF)

Total sites: 59, RV sites: 59, Central water, Flush toilet, No showers, RV dump, Tent & RV camping: $23-25, Stay limit: 14 days, Open May-Sep, Max Length: 48ft, Reservations accepted, Elev: 5148ft/1569m, Tel: 530-534-6500, Nearest town: La Porte. GPS: 39.734456, -120.968909

243 • B3 | Rock Creek (Plumas NF)

Total sites: 3, RV sites: 3, No water, Vault/pit toilet, Tent & RV camping: $15, No services in winter, Open all year, Reservations not accepted, Elev: 4508ft/1374m, Tel: 530-283-0555. GPS: 39.897488, -120.999234

244 • B3 | Rocky Knoll (Lassen NF)

Total sites: 18, RV sites: 18, Central water, Vault/pit toilet, No showers, No RV dump, Tent & RV camping: $12, Open May-Sep, Reservations not accepted, Elev: 6493ft/1979m, Tel: 530-258-2141, Nearest town: Westwood. GPS: 40.498942, -121.155856

245 • B3 | Rogers Cow Camp (Plumas NF)

Total sites: 6, RV sites: 6, Central water, Vault/pit toilet, No showers, No RV dump, Tent & RV camping: $15, Open all year, Reservations not accepted, Elev: 4131ft/1259m, Tel: 530-534-6500, Nearest town: Berry Creek. GPS: 39.766905, -121.312547

246 • B3 | Roxie Peconom (Lassen NF)

Total sites: 10, RV sites: 0, Central water, Vault/pit toilet, No showers, No RV dump, Tents only: Free, Walk-to sites, Stay limit: 14 days, Generator hours: 0800-2200, Open May-Oct, Reservations not accepted, Elev: 5020ft/1530m, Tel: 530-257-4188, Nearest town: Susanville. GPS: 40.354509, -120.809887

247 • B3 | Running Deer (Plumas NF)

Total sites: 40, RV sites: 40, Central water, Flush toilet, No showers, RV dump, Tent & RV camping: $23-25, Open May-Sep, Max Length: 45ft, Reservations accepted, Elev: 5226ft/1593m, Tel: 530-534-6500, Nearest town: La Porte. GPS: 39.738497, -120.967469

248 • B3 | Salmon Creek (Tahoe NF)

Total sites: 31, RV sites: 26, Central water, Vault/pit toilet, No showers, No RV dump, Tent & RV camping: $24, Open May-Oct, Max Length: 45ft, Reservations accepted, Elev: 5810ft/1771m, Tel: 530-862-1368, Nearest town: Sierra City. GPS: 39.623788, -120.613055

249 • B3 | Sardine Lake (Tahoe NF)

Total sites: 27, RV sites: 27, Central water, Vault/pit toilet, No showers, No RV dump, Tent & RV camping: $24, Open May-Oct, Max Length: 42ft, Reservations accepted, Elev: 5751ft/1753m, Tel: 530-862-1368, Nearest town: Sierra City. GPS: 39.618896, -120.617432

250 • B3 | Silver Bowl (Lassen NF)

Total sites: 18, RV sites: 18, Central water, Vault/pit toilet, No showers, No RV dump, Tent & RV camping: $12, Open May-Oct, Reservations not accepted, Elev: 6532ft/1991m, Tel: 530-258-2141, Nearest town: Westwood. GPS: 40.499326, -121.164112

251 • B3 | Silver Lake (Plumas NF)

Total sites: 7, RV sites: 0, No water, Vault/pit toilet, Tents only: $20, Open May-Oct, Elev: 5794ft/1766m, Tel: 530-283-0555, Nearest town: Quincey. GPS: 39.959000, -121.135000

252 • B3 | Snag Lake (Tahoe NF)

Total sites: 12, RV sites: 12, No water, Vault/pit toilet, Tent & RV camping: Free, Open May-Sep, Reservations not accepted, Elev: 6713ft/2046m, Tel: 530-265-4531, Nearest town: Bassetts. GPS: 39.670795, -120.626904

253 • B3 | Snake Lake (Plumas NF)

Total sites: 9, RV sites: 9, No water, Vault/pit toilet, Tent & RV camping: $15, No services in winter, Not plowed, Open all year, Reservations not accepted, Elev: 4010ft/1222m, Tel: 530-283-0555, Nearest town: Quincy. GPS: 39.980787, -121.006064

254 • B3 | Soldier Meadows (Lassen NF)

Total sites: 15, RV sites: 15, No water, Vault/pit toilet, Tent & RV camping: $10, Open May-Oct, Reservations not accepted, Elev: 4829ft/1472m, Tel: 530-258-2141, Nearest town: Chester. GPS: 40.213033, -121.273905

255 • B3 | Spanish Creek (Plumas NF)

Total sites: 24, RV sites: 20, Central water, Vault/pit toilet, No showers, No RV dump, Tent & RV camping: $31, 3 group sites: $80, Near RR, Open May-Sep, Max Length: 99ft, Reservations accepted, Elev: 3089ft/942m, Tel: 530-283-0555, Nearest town: Quincy. GPS: 40.027101, -120.965573

256 • B3 | Spring Creek (Plumas NF)

Total sites: 35, RV sites: 33, Central water, Vault/pit toilet, No showers, RV dump, Tent & RV camping: $34, Stay limit: 14 days, Open May-Sep, Max Length: 49ft, Reservations accepted, Elev: 5627ft/1715m, Tel: 530-258-7606, Nearest town: Chilcoot. GPS: 39.896484, -120.178955

257 • B3 | Stag Point OHV Camp (Plumas NF)

Total sites: 5, RV sites: 0, No water, Vault/pit toilet, Tents only: Free, High clearance 4x4 required, Reservations not accepted, Elev: 2890ft/881m. GPS: 39.791961, -121.079335

258 • B3 | Sundew (Plumas NF)

Total sites: 21, RV sites: 21, Central water, Vault/pit toilet, No showers, No RV dump, Tent & RV camping: $32, Open May-Sep, Reservations accepted, Elev: 5243ft/1598m, Tel: 530-283-0555, Nearest town: Quincy. GPS: 39.900776, -121.200253

259 • B3 | Tooms RV Camp (Plumas NF)

Total sites: 20, RV sites: 20, Central water, Vault/pit toilet, RV dump, No tents/RVs: $23, Stay limit: 14 days, Reservations not accepted, Elev: 5119ft/1560m, Tel: 530-534-6500, Nearest town: La Porte. GPS: 39.723847, -120.981948

260 • B3 | Warner Creek (Lassen NF)

Total sites: 13, RV sites: 13, No water, Vault/pit toilet, Tent & RV camping: $10, Open May-Oct, Reservations not accepted, Elev: 5066ft/1544m, Tel: 530-258-2141. GPS: 40.362235, -121.308075

261 • B3 | Whitehorse (Plumas NF)

Total sites: 19, RV sites: 19, Central water, Vault/pit toilet, No showers, No RV dump, Tent & RV camping: $31, Open May-Sep, Max Length: 39ft, Reservations accepted, Elev: 5305ft/1617m, Tel: 530-283-0555, Nearest town: Quincy. GPS: 39.888486, -121.142624

262 • B3 | Willow Springs (Lassen NF)

Total sites: 14, RV sites: 14, No water, Vault/pit toilet, Tent & RV camping: Free, Open Apr-Oct, Reservations not accepted, Elev: 5184ft/1580m, Tel: 530-258-2141, Nearest town: Chester. GPS: 40.306288, -121.377532

263 • B3 | Wyandotte (Plumas NF)

Total sites: 30, RV sites: 30, Central water, Flush toilet, No showers, No RV dump, Tent & RV camping: $23, Stay limit: 14 days, Open May-Sep, Max Length: 47ft, Reservations accepted, Elev: 5125ft/1562m, Tel: 530-534-6500, Nearest town: La Porte. GPS: 39.726719, -120.984528

264 • B3 | Yuba Pass (Tahoe NF)

Total sites: 20, RV sites: 20, Central water, Vault/pit toilet, No showers, No RV dump, Tent & RV camping: $24, Open May-Oct, Max Length: 60ft, Reservations accepted, Elev: 6717ft/2047m, Tel: 530-862-1368, Nearest town: Sierraville. GPS: 39.615838, -120.490467

265 • C2 | Bear Creek (Mendocino NF)

Total sites: 16, RV sites: 16, No water, Vault/pit toilet, Tent & RV camping: Free, Reservations not accepted, Elev: 2274ft/693m, Tel: 707-275-2361, Nearest town: Upper Lake. GPS: 39.322687, -122.836399

266 • C2 | Cedar Camp (Mendocino NF)

Total sites: 5, RV sites: 0, No water, Vault/pit toilet, Tents only: Free, Open May-Nov, Reservations not accepted, Elev: 4236ft/1291m, Tel: 530-963-3128, Nearest town: Stonyford. GPS: 39.264322, -122.698635

267 • C2 | Davis Flat (Mendocino NF)

Total sites: 20, RV sites: 20, No water, Vault/pit toilet, Tent & RV camping: $5, Open all year, Reservations not accepted, Elev: 1591ft/485m, Tel: 530-963-3128, Nearest town: Stonyford. GPS: 39.362587, -122.654348

268 • C2 | Deer Valley (Mendocino NF)

Total sites: 13, RV sites: 13, No water, Vault/pit toilet, Tent & RV camping: $6, Open all year, Reservations not accepted, Elev: 3553ft/1083m, Tel: 707-275-2361, Nearest town: Upper Lake. GPS: 39.266006, -122.883218

269 • C2 | Dixie Glade (Mendocino NF)

Total sites: 7, RV sites: 7, No water, Vault/pit toilet, Tent & RV camping: $5, Open Apr-Nov, Reservations not accepted, Elev: 3077ft/938m, Tel: 530-963-3128, Nearest town: Stonyford. GPS: 39.335324, -122.703154

270 • C2 | Fouts Springs (Mendocino NF)

Total sites: 11, RV sites: 11, No water, Vault/pit toilet, Tent & RV camping: $5, Open all year, Max Length: 40ft, Reservations not accepted, Elev: 1627ft/496m, Tel: 530-963-3128, Nearest town: Stonyford. GPS: 39.358977, -122.653437

271 • C2 | Letts Lake (Mendocino NF)

Total sites: 42, RV sites: 42, Central water, Vault/pit toilet, No showers, No RV dump, Tent & RV camping: $12, Open May-Oct, Max Length: 24ft, Reservations not accepted, Elev: 4574ft/1394m, Tel: 530-963-3128, Nearest town: Stonyford. GPS: 39.302913, -122.708736

272 • C2 | Little Stony (Mendocino NF)

Total sites: 8, RV sites: 0, No water, Vault/pit toilet, Tents only: $5, Trailers not recommended, Open all year, Reservations not accepted, Elev: 1496ft/456m, Tel: 530-963-3128, Nearest town: Stonyford. GPS: 39.286424, -122.577243

273 • C2 | Middle Creek (Mendocino NF)

Total sites: 23, RV sites: 23, Central water, Vault/pit toilet, No showers, No RV dump, Tent & RV camping: $8, Reservations not accepted, Elev: 1493ft/455m, Tel: 707-275-2361, Nearest town: Upper Lake. GPS: 39.252897, -122.951044

274 • C2 | Mill Creek (Mendocino NF)

Total sites: 6, RV sites: 6, No water, Vault/pit toilet, Tent & RV camping: $5, Open all year, Reservations not accepted, Elev: 1631ft/497m, Tel: 530-963-3128, Nearest town: Stonyford. GPS: 39.355691, -122.655123

275 • C2 | Mill Valley (Mendocino NF)

Total sites: 15, RV sites: 15, No water, Vault/pit toilet, Tent & RV camping: $10, Open May-Oct, Max Length: 32ft, Reservations not accepted, Elev: 4065ft/1239m, Tel: 530-934-3316, Nearest town: Stonyford. GPS: 39.317354, -122.708252

276 • C2 | North Fork (St John) (Mendocino NF)

Total sites: 10, RV sites: 10, No water, Vault/pit toilet, Tent & RV camping: $5, Open May-Nov, Reservations not accepted, Elev: 1535ft/468m, Tel: 530-963-3128, Nearest town: Stonyford. GPS: 39.379101, -122.648233

277 • C2 | Old Mill (Mendocino NF)

Total sites: 10, RV sites: 10, No water, Vault/pit toilet, Tent & RV camping: Free, Road not maintained for passenger cars, Open all year, Max Length: 24ft, Reservations not accepted, Elev: 3632ft/1107m, Tel: 530-963-3128, Nearest town: Stonyford. GPS: 39.308332, -122.645518

278 • C2 | Penny Pines (Mendocino NF)

Total sites: 10, RV sites: 0, No water, Vault/pit toilet, Tents only: $6, Reservations not accepted, Elev: 3665ft/1117m, Nearest town: Upper Lake. GPS: 39.300378, -122.930123

279 • C2 | South Fork (Mendocino NF)

Total sites: 10, RV sites: 10, Central water, Vault/pit toilet, Tent & RV camping: $5, Open all year, Reservations not accepted, Elev: 1667ft/508m, Tel: 530-963-3128, Nearest town: Stonyford. GPS: 39.362311, -122.653389

280 • C3 | Ahart (Tahoe NF)

Total sites: 12, RV sites: 12, No water, Vault/pit toilet, Tent & RV camping: $20, Open May-Oct, Reservations not accepted, Elev: 5387ft/1642m, Tel: 530-265-4531, Nearest town: Foresthill. GPS: 39.145752, -120.407471

281 • C3 | Airport Flat (Eldorado NF)

Total sites: 16, RV sites: 16, No water, Vault/pit toilet, Tent & RV camping: Free, Stay limit: 14 days, Open May-Oct, Reservations not accepted, Elev: 5407ft/1648m, Tel: 530-644-2349, Nearest town: Pollock Pines. GPS: 38.985357, -120.380174

282 • C3 | Annie McCloud (Shasta-Trinity NF)

Total sites: 10, RV sites: 10, No water, Vault/pit toilet, Tent & RV camping: Free, Max Length: 20ft, Elev: 5833ft/1778m, Nearest town: Truckee. GPS: 39.380723, -120.135419

283 • C3 | Azalea Cove (Eldorado NF)

Total sites: 10, RV sites: 0, Central water, Vault/pit toilet, No showers, No RV dump, Tents only: Free, Walk-to/boat-in sites, Stay limit: 14 days, Open May-Oct, Reservations not accepted, Elev: 4980ft/1518m, Tel: 530-647-5415, Nearest town: Pollock Pines. GPS: 38.885559, -120.368174

284 • C3 | Backpackers (Stanislaus NF)

Total sites: 8, RV sites: 0, No water, Vault/pit toilet, Tents only: $26, Walk-to sites, Stay limit: 1 day, Open Jun-Sep, Reservations not accepted, Elev: 7331ft/2234m, Tel: 209-795-1381, Nearest town: Bear Valley. GPS: 38.482351, -119.989826

285 • C3 | Badger's Den (Lake Tahoe Basin Management Unit)

Total sites: 84, RV sites: 0, Central water, Flush toilet, Free showers, No RV dump, Tents only: $45, No pets, Concessionaire, No generators, Open all year, Elev: 6242ft/1903m, Tel: 530-541-1801, Nearest town: South Lake Tahoe. GPS: 38.934102, -120.037878

286 • C3 | Baker (Stanislaus NF)

Total sites: 44, RV sites: 33, Central water, Vault/pit toilet, No showers, No RV dump, Tent & RV camping: $20, Open Apr-Oct, Reservations not accepted, Elev: 6309ft/1923m, Tel: 209-965-3434, Nearest town: Mi-Wuk. GPS: 38.324213, -119.752648

287 • C3 | Bayview (Lake Tahoe Basin Management Unit)

Total sites: 13, RV sites: 13, No water, Vault/pit toilet, Tent & RV camping: $17, Open May-Oct, Max Length: 20ft, Reservations not accepted, Elev: 6850ft/2088m, Tel: 530-543-2600, Nearest town: South Lake Tahoe. GPS: 38.945801, -120.099121

288 • C3 | Bear Lake (Stanislaus NF)

Total sites: 5, RV sites: 0, No water, No toilets, Tents only: Free, Open Jun-Oct, Reservations not accepted, Elev: 7625ft/2324m, Nearest town: Tahoe City. GPS: 39.048626, -120.224918

289 • C3 | Bear Valley (Tahoe NF)

Total sites: 10, RV sites: 5, Central water, Vault/pit toilet, No showers, No RV dump, Tent & RV camping: Free, Reservations not accepted, Elev: 6608ft/2014m, Tel: 530-994-3401, Nearest town: Truckee. GPS: 39.557373, -120.236816

290 • C3 | Beardsley Dam (Stanislaus NF)

Total sites: 16, RV sites: 16, Central water, Vault/pit toilet, No showers, No RV dump, Tent & RV camping: $20, Open May-Oct, Reservations not accepted, Elev: 3350ft/1021m, Tel: 209-965-3434. GPS: 38.210000, -120.075000

291 • C3 | Big Meadow (Stanislaus NF)

Total sites: 20, RV sites: 10, Central water, Vault/pit toilet, No showers, No RV dump, Tent & RV camping: $19, Group fee: $50, Open Jun-Sep, Max Length: 27ft, Reservations not accepted, Elev: 6578ft/2005m, Tel: 209-795-1381, Nearest town: Arnold. GPS: 38.416857, -120.106415

292 • C3 | Big Meadows (Eldorado NF)

Total sites: 54, RV sites: 48, Central water, Vault/pit toilet, No

showers, No RV dump, Tent & RV camping: $10, Water may not be available, Stay limit: 14 days, Open Jun-Oct, Reservations not accepted, Elev: 5417ft/1651m, Tel: 530-333-4312, Nearest town: Foresthill. GPS: 39.074631, -120.428536

293 • C3 | Big Reservoir (Tahoe NF)

Total sites: 100, RV sites: 100, Central water, Flush toilet, Free showers, RV dump, Tent & RV camping: $25-35, Group sites: $100-$160, Pet fee: $5, Reservations through phone number shown, Concessionaire, Reservations accepted, Elev: 4131ft/1259m, Tel: 530-367-2129, Nearest town: Foresthill. GPS: 39.143534, -120.755594

294 • C3 | Bloomfield (Stanislaus NF)

Total sites: 20, RV sites: 10, Central water, Vault/pit toilet, No showers, No RV dump, Tent & RV camping: $12, Trailers not recommended, No services in winter - limited access, Open Jun-Sep, Reservations not accepted, Elev: 7989ft/2435m, Tel: 209-795-1381, Nearest town: Arnold. GPS: 38.537958, -119.825041

295 • C3 | Boards Crossing (Stanislaus NF)

Total sites: 5, RV sites: 0, No water, Vault/pit toilet, Tents only: Free, Narrow steep road, Reservations not accepted, Elev: 3864ft/1178m, Tel: 209-795-1381, Nearest town: Boards Crossing. GPS: 38.301109, -120.235969

296 • C3 | Boca (Tahoe NF)

Total sites: 23, RV sites: 20, No water, Vault/pit toilet, Tent & RV camping: $20, Open May-Oct, Max Length: 44ft, Reservations accepted, Elev: 5646ft/1721m, Tel: 530-587-9281, Nearest town: Truckee. GPS: 39.394461, -120.105268

297 • C3 | Boca Rest (Tahoe NF)

Total sites: 34, RV sites: 34, Central water, Vault/pit toilet, No showers, No RV dump, Tent & RV camping: $20, Open May-Oct, Max Length: 45ft, Reservations accepted, Elev: 5617ft/1712m, Tel: 530-587-9281, Nearest town: Truckee. GPS: 39.418953, -120.087298

298 • C3 | Boca Spring (Tahoe NF)

Total sites: 13, RV sites: 13, Central water, Vault/pit toilet, No showers, No RV dump, Tent & RV camping: $20, Group site: $66, Open May-Oct, Max Length: 20ft, Reservations accepted, Elev: 5961ft/1817m, Tel: 530-587-9281, Nearest town: Truckee. GPS: 39.428179, -120.075184

299 • C3 | Boulder Flat (Stanislaus NF)

Total sites: 20, RV sites: 20, Central water, Vault/pit toilet, No showers, No RV dump, Tent & RV camping: $15, Stay limit: 14 days, Open May-Sep, Reservations not accepted, Elev: 5656ft/1724m, Tel: 209-965-3434, Nearest town: Mi-Wuk. GPS: 38.354321, -119.861582

300 • C3 | Bowman Lake (Tahoe NF)

Total sites: 7, RV sites: 0, No water, Vault/pit toilet, Tents only: Free, Rough road - high-clearance vehicle needed, Open Jun-Oct, Reservations not accepted, Elev: 5607ft/1709m, Tel: 530-265-4531, Nearest town: Nevada City. GPS: 39.458486, -120.612629

301 • C3 | Boyington Mill (Tahoe NF)

Total sites: 12, RV sites: 9, No water, Vault/pit toilet, Tent & RV camping: $20, Open May-Oct, Max Length: 60ft, Reservations accepted, Elev: 5709ft/1740m, Tel: 530-587-9281, Nearest town: Truckee. GPS: 39.437591, -120.090497

302 • C3 | Brightman Flat (Stanislaus NF)

Total sites: 32, RV sites: 32, Central water, Vault/pit toilet, No showers, No RV dump, Tent & RV camping: $19, Stay limit: 14 days, Open May-Oct, Reservations not accepted, Elev: 5725ft/1745m, Tel: 209-965-3434, Nearest town: Mi-Wuk. GPS: 38.352651, -119.848712

303 • C3 | Bullards Lakeshore (Tahoe NF)

Total sites: 60, RV sites: 60, No water, No toilets, Tent & RV camping: $22, Reservations not accepted, Elev: 2198ft/670m, Tel: 530-692-3200, Nearest town: Camptonville. GPS: 39.449196, -121.132965

304 • C3 | Burnt Bridge (Plumas NF)

Total sites: 31, RV sites: 13, Central water, Vault/pit toilet, No showers, No RV dump, Tent & RV camping: Free, Reservations not accepted, Elev: 2264ft/690m, Tel: 530-534-6500, Nearest town: Nevada City. GPS: 39.420342, -121.172944

305 • C3 | Cal-Ida (Tahoe NF)

Total sites: 19, RV sites: 10, Central water, Vault/pit toilet, Tent & RV camping: $24, Open Apr-Oct, Reservations accepted, Elev: 2369ft/722m, Tel: 530-862-1368, Nearest town: Camptonville. GPS: 39.520896, -120.997117

306 • C3 | Camino Cove (Eldorado NF)

Total sites: 32, RV sites: 32, No water, Vault/pit toilet, Tent & RV camping: Free, Stay limit: 14 days, Open Jun-Oct, Elev: 4905ft/1495m, Tel: 530-644-2324, Nearest town: Pollock Pines. GPS: 38.880347, -120.428115

307 • C3 | Camp Richardson RV Park (Lake Tahoe BMU)

Total sites: 103, RV sites: 103, Elec sites: 103, Water at site, Flush toilet, Free showers, RV dump, No tents/RVs: $50, Full hookup sites, No pets, Concessionaire, Open all year, Elev: 6280ft/1914m, Tel: 530-541-1801, Nearest town: South Lake Tahoe. GPS: 38.934171, -120.040136

308 • C3 | Canyon Creek (Tahoe NF)

Total sites: 20, RV sites: 0, No water, Vault/pit toilet, Tents only: Free, Very rough/rocky/narrow road requiring high clearance vehicle, Reservations not accepted, Elev: 6010ft/1832m, Tel: 530-265-4531. GPS: 39.436929, -120.579614

309 • C3 | Caples Lake (Eldorado NF)

Total sites: 34, RV sites: 13, Central water, Vault/pit toilet, No showers, No RV dump, Tent & RV camping: $28, Also walk-to sites, Stay limit: 14 days, Open Jun-Oct, Max Length: 30ft, Reservations not accepted, Elev: 7874ft/2400m, Tel: 209-295-4251, Nearest town: Kit Carson. GPS: 38.705116, -120.053349

310 • C3 | Capps Crossing (Eldorado NF)

Total sites: 11, RV sites: 4, Central water, Vault/pit toilet, No showers, No RV dump, Tent & RV camping: $28, Group site:

$165, Individual sites available if not reserved by group, Stay limit: 14 days, Open May-Sep, Reservations not accepted, Elev: 5154ft/1571m, Tel: 530-644-2324, Nearest town: Pollock Pines. GPS: 38.650969, -120.407095

311 • C3 | Carlton (Tahoe NF)

Total sites: 17, RV sites: 17, Central water, Vault/pit toilet, No showers, No RV dump, Tent & RV camping: $24, Open Apr-Oct, Reservations accepted, Elev: 2359ft/719m, Tel: 530-862-1368, Nearest town: Downieville. GPS: 39.519204, -121.000247

312 • C3 | Cascade Creek (Stanislaus NF)

Total sites: 14, RV sites: 14, No water, Vault/pit toilet, Tent & RV camping: $8, Stay limit: 14 days, Open May-Oct, Reservations not accepted, Elev: 6125ft/1867m, Tel: 209-965-3434, Nearest town: Mi-Wuk. GPS: 38.279871, -119.971522

313 • C3 | Castle Valley (Tahoe NF)

Total sites: 3, RV sites: 0, No water, No toilets, Tents only: Free, Walk-to sites, .25 mi, Reservations not accepted, Elev: 7333ft/2235m, Nearest town: Soda Springs. GPS: 39.344941, -120.352251

314 • C3 | China Flat (Eldorado NF)

Total sites: 18, RV sites: 11, Central water, Vault/pit toilet, No showers, No RV dump, Tent & RV camping: $28, Stay limit: 14 days, Open Jun-Sep, Max Length: 22ft, Reservations not accepted, Elev: 4852ft/1479m, Tel: 530-644-2324, Nearest town: Kyburz. GPS: 38.754267, -120.267991

315 • C3 | Clark Fork (Stanislaus NF)

Total sites: 88, RV sites: 88, Central water, Flush toilet, Free showers, RV dump, Tent & RV camping: $22, Stay limit: 14 days, Open May-Sep, Reservations not accepted, Elev: 6114ft/1864m, Tel: 209-965-3434, Nearest town: Mi-Wuk. GPS: 38.397099, -119.800469

316 • C3 | Clark Fork Horse Camp (Stanislaus NF)

Total sites: 13, RV sites: 13, No water, Vault/pit toilet, Tent & RV camping: $17, Non-potable water, Stay limit: 14 days, Open Apr-Oct, Reservations not accepted, Elev: 6162ft/1878m, Tel: 209-965-3434, Nearest town: Mi-Wuk. GPS: 38.393623, -119.800603

317 • C3 | Cold Creek (Tahoe NF)

Total sites: 13, RV sites: 10, No water, Vault/pit toilet, Tent & RV camping: $16, Open May-Oct, Max Length: 25ft, Reservations accepted, Elev: 5712ft/1741m, Tel: 530-862-1030, Nearest town: Sierraville. GPS: 39.542725, -120.315674

318 • C3 | Cottonwood Creek (Tahoe NF)

Total sites: 48, RV sites: 48, Central water, Vault/pit toilet, No showers, No RV dump, Tent & RV camping: $20, Open May-Oct, Max Length: 45ft, Reservations accepted, Elev: 5659ft/1725m, Tel: 530-862-1030, Nearest town: Sierraville. GPS: 39.548828, -120.318848

319 • C3 | Crystal Springs (Humboldt-Toiyabe NF)

Total sites: 19, RV sites: 19, Central water, Vault/pit toilet, No showers, No RV dump, Tent & RV camping: $18, Stay limit: 14 days, Open Apr-Sep, Reservations not accepted, Elev: 5994ft/1827m, Tel: 775-882-2766, Nearest town: Bridgeport. GPS: 38.765169, -119.845986

320 • C3 | Dardanelle (Stanislaus NF)

Total sites: 28, RV sites: 28, Central water, Vault/pit toilet, No showers, No RV dump, Tent & RV camping: $19, Stay limit: 14 days, Open May-Sep, Max Length: 22ft, Reservations not accepted, Elev: 5771ft/1759m, Tel: 209-965-3434, Nearest town: Dardanelle. GPS: 38.341592, -119.833284

321 • C3 | Dark Day (Tahoe NF)

Total sites: 9, RV sites: 0, Central water, Vault/pit toilet, No showers, No RV dump, Tents only: $22, Open May-Sep, Reservations required, Elev: 2087ft/636m, Tel: 530-692-3200, Nearest town: Camptonville. GPS: 39.428564, -121.109806

322 • C3 | Deadman (Stanislaus NF)

Total sites: 17, RV sites: 15, Central water, Vault/pit toilet, No showers, No RV dump, Tent & RV camping: $20, Also walk-to sites, Stay limit: 14 days, Open Apr-Oct, Reservations not accepted, Elev: 6309ft/1923m, Tel: 209-965-3434, Nearest town: Pinecrest. GPS: 38.317350, -119.748970

323 • C3 | Dru Barner Park (Eldorado NF)

Total sites: 47, RV sites: 47, Central water, Flush toilet, No showers, No RV dump, Tent & RV camping: $8, Access road not plowed in winter, Stay limit: 14 days, Open all year, Reservations not accepted, Elev: 3228ft/984m, Tel: 916-333-4312, Nearest town: Georgetown. GPS: 38.942000, -120.765000

324 • C3 | Eagle's Nest (Lake Tahoe Basin Management Unit)

Total sites: 31, RV sites: 0, Central water, Vault/pit toilet, No showers, No RV dump, Tents only: $45, No pets, Concessionaire, Open all year, Reservations not accepted, Elev: 6259ft/1908m, Tel: 530-541-1801, Nearest town: South Lake Tahoe. GPS: 38.932697, -120.037278

325 • C3 | East Meadow (Tahoe NF)

Total sites: 44, RV sites: 44, Central water, Flush toilet, No showers, Tent & RV camping: $24, Open May-Oct, Max Length: 48ft, Reservations accepted, Elev: 6142ft/1872m, Tel: 530-265-8861, Nearest town: Truckee. GPS: 39.500488, -120.533936

326 • C3 | Eureka Valley (Stanislaus NF)

Total sites: 28, RV sites: 24, Central water, Vault/pit toilet, No showers, No RV dump, Tent & RV camping: $18, Also walk-to sites, Cash only, Stay limit: 14 days, Open Apr-Oct, Max Length: 22ft, Reservations not accepted, Elev: 6142ft/1872m, Tel: 209-965-3434, Nearest town: Dardanelle. GPS: 38.340088, -119.791016

327 • C3 | Fallen Leaf (Lake Tahoe Basin Management Unit)

Total sites: 201, RV sites: 201, Central water, Flush toilet, Pay showers, No RV dump, Tent & RV camping: $36-38, Also cabins, Open May-Oct, Max Length: 45ft, Reservations accepted, Elev: 6391ft/1948m, Tel: 530-544-0426, Nearest town: Lake Tahoe Basin MU. GPS: 38.928605, -120.048461

328 • C3 | Fashoda (Eldorado NF)

Total sites: 30, RV sites: 0, Central water, Flush toilet, Pay showers, RV dump, Tents only: $28, Walk-to sites, Stay limit: 14 days,

Open May-Sep, Reservations accepted, Elev: 4826ft/1471m, Tel: 530-293-0827, Nearest town: Pollock Pines. GPS: 38.868756, -120.396655

329 • C3 | Fence Creek (Stanislaus NF)

Total sites: 38, RV sites: 38, Central water, Vault/pit toilet, No showers, No RV dump, Tent & RV camping: $8, Stay limit: 14 days, Open May-Oct, Reservations not accepted, Elev: 5669ft/1728m, Tel: 209-965-3434, Nearest town: Mi-Wuk. GPS: 38.367000, -119.871000

330 • C3 | Fiddle Creek (Tahoe NF)

Total sites: 15, RV sites: 0, Central water, Vault/pit toilet, No showers, No RV dump, Tents only: $24, Open Apr-Oct, Reservations accepted, Elev: 2276ft/694m, Tel: 530-862-1368, Nearest town: Camptonville. GPS: 39.518234, -120.992443

331 • C3 | Findley (Tahoe NF)

Total sites: 14, RV sites: 14, Central water, Vault/pit toilet, No showers, No RV dump, Tent & RV camping: $24, Open May-Sep, Max Length: 80ft, Reservations accepted, Elev: 6296ft/1919m, Tel: 530-862-1030, Nearest town: Sierraville. GPS: 39.483643, -120.554688

332 • C3 | Fir Top (Tahoe NF)

Total sites: 12, RV sites: 12, Central water, Flush toilet, No showers, No RV dump, Tent & RV camping: $24, Open May-Sep, Max Length: 45ft, Reservations accepted, Elev: 6073ft/1851m, Tel: 530-862-1030, Nearest town: Sierraville. GPS: 39.485697, -120.550015

333 • C3 | French Meadows (Tahoe NF)

Total sites: 73, RV sites: 73, Central water, Flush toilet, No showers, No RV dump, Tent & RV camping: $24, Open May-Oct, Max Length: 45ft, Reservations accepted, Elev: 5354ft/1632m, Tel: 530-478-0248, Nearest town: Foresthill. GPS: 39.113972, -120.421427

334 • C3 | Gerle Creek (Eldorado NF)

Total sites: 50, RV sites: 19, Central water, Vault/pit toilet, No showers, No RV dump, Tent & RV camping: $28, Stay limit: 14 days, Open May-Sep, Max Length: 50ft, Reservations accepted, Elev: 5312ft/1619m, Tel: 530-647-5415, Nearest town: Pollock Pines. GPS: 38.975583, -120.392478

335 • C3 | Giant Gap (Tahoe NF)

Total sites: 28, RV sites: 23, Central water, Vault/pit toilet, No showers, No RV dump, Tent & RV camping: $24, Food storage lockers, Open May-Oct, Max Length: 55ft, Reservations accepted, Elev: 3698ft/1127m, Tel: 530-478-0248, Nearest town: Foresthill. GPS: 39.137672, -120.793366

336 • C3 | Goose Meadow (Tahoe NF)

Total sites: 24, RV sites: 20, Central water, Vault/pit toilet, No showers, No RV dump, Tent & RV camping: $22, Open May-Oct, Max Length: 30ft, Reservations accepted, Elev: 5988ft/1825m, Tel: 530-587-9281, Nearest town: Truckee. GPS: 39.259481, -120.209617

337 • C3 | Granite Flat (Tahoe NF)

Total sites: 73, RV sites: 66, Central water, Vault/pit toilet, No showers, No RV dump, Tent & RV camping: $22, Also walk-to sites, Open May-Oct, Max Length: 65ft, Reservations accepted, Elev: 5892ft/1796m, Tel: 530-587-9281, Nearest town: Truckee. GPS: 39.298628, -120.204732

338 • C3 | Green Valley TC (Angeles NF)

Total sites: 1, RV sites: 0, No water, No toilets, Tents only: Free, Stay limit: 14 days, Reservations not accepted, Elev: 5804ft/1769m, Tel: 661-296-9710. GPS: 39.120439, -120.474091

339 • C3 | Grouse Ridge (Tahoe NF)

Total sites: 9, RV sites: 5, No water, Vault/pit toilet, Tent & RV camping: Free, Rough road, Open May-Sep, Max Length: 16ft, Reservations not accepted, Elev: 7492ft/2284m, Tel: 530-265-4531, Nearest town: Nevada City. GPS: 39.390704, -120.609703

340 • C3 | Hampshire Rocks (Tahoe NF)

Total sites: 31, RV sites: 31, Central water, Vault/pit toilet, No showers, No RV dump, Tent & RV camping: $24, Open May-Oct, Max Length: 45ft, Reservations accepted, Elev: 5928ft/1807m, Tel: 530-478-0248, Nearest town: Big Bend. GPS: 39.310419, -120.497435

341 • C3 | Hell Hole (Eldorado NF)

Total sites: 10, RV sites: 0, No water, Vault/pit toilet, No showers, No RV dump, Tents only: $10, Walk-to sites, Stay limit: 14 days, Open May-Oct, Reservations not accepted, Elev: 5243ft/1598m, Tel: 530-333-4312, Nearest town: Georgetown. GPS: 39.070457, -120.416444

342 • C3 | Hermit Valley (Stanislaus NF)

Total sites: 25, RV sites: 25, No water, Vault/pit toilet, Tent & RV camping: Free, Rough road, Stay limit: 14 days, Open Jun-Oct, Reservations not accepted, Elev: 7136ft/2175m, Tel: 209-795-1381, Nearest town: Bear Valley. GPS: 38.538285, -119.899536

343 • C3 | Herring Creek (Stanislaus NF)

Total sites: 7, RV sites: 7, No water, Vault/pit toilet, Tent & RV camping: Donation, Stay limit: 14 days, Open May-Oct, Reservations not accepted, Elev: 7392ft/2253m, Tel: 209-965-3434, Nearest town: Bumblebee. GPS: 38.244461, -119.932471

344 • C3 | Herring Reservoir (Stanislaus NF)

Total sites: 42, RV sites: 42, No water, Vault/pit toilet, Tent & RV camping: Donation, Stay limit: 14 days, Open May-Sep, Reservations not accepted, Elev: 7448ft/2270m, Tel: 209-965-3434, Nearest town: Bumblebee. GPS: 38.248961, -119.934786

345 • C3 | Highland Lakes (Stanislaus NF)

Total sites: 35, RV sites: 35, Central water, Vault/pit toilet, Tent & RV camping: $12, Stay limit: 14 days, Open Jun-Oct, Reservations not accepted, Elev: 8635ft/2632m, Tel: 209-795-1381, Nearest town: Arnold. GPS: 38.488604, -119.807709

346 • C3 | Hope Valley (Humboldt-Toiyabe NF)

Total sites: 21, RV sites: 18, Central water, Vault/pit toilet, No showers, No RV dump, Tent & RV camping: $22, Stay limit: 14 days, Open May-Sep, Max Length: 45ft, Reservations accepted,

Elev: 7159ft/2182m, Tel: 530-694-1002, Nearest town: Woodfords. GPS: 38.730341, -119.929845

347 • C3 | Ice House (Eldorado NF)

Total sites: 83, RV sites: 61, Central water, Vault/pit toilet, No showers, RV dump, Tent & RV camping: $28, Stay limit: 14 days, Open May-Oct, Max Length: 40ft, Reservations accepted, Elev: 5426ft/1654m, Tel: 530-644-2349, Nearest town: Pollock Pines. GPS: 38.832953, -120.357644

348 • C3 | Indian Springs (Tahoe NF)

Total sites: 35, RV sites: 28, Central water, Vault/pit toilet, No showers, No RV dump, Tent & RV camping: $24, Also walk-to sites, Open May-Oct, Max Length: 35ft, Reservations accepted, Elev: 5577ft/1700m, Tel: 530-478-0248, Nearest town: Big Bend. GPS: 39.327935, -120.568112

349 • C3 | Indian Valley (Tahoe NF)

Total sites: 19, RV sites: 17, Central water, Vault/pit toilet, No showers, No RV dump, Tent & RV camping: $24, Open Apr-Oct, Max Length: 40ft, Reservations accepted, Elev: 2379ft/725m, Tel: 530-862-1368, Nearest town: Camptonville. GPS: 39.512883, -120.980797

350 • C3 | Jackson Creek (Tahoe NF)

Total sites: 14, No water, Vault/pit toilet, Tents only: Free, Very bad road, Bear proof food boxes available, Stream water, Reservations not accepted, Elev: 5718ft/1743m. GPS: 39.457679, -120.601046

351 • C3 | Jones Fork (Eldorado NF)

Total sites: 10, RV sites: 9, No water, Vault/pit toilet, Tent & RV camping: $10, Stay limit: 14 days, Open Jun-Oct, Reservations not accepted, Elev: 5030ft/1533m, Tel: 530-647-5415, Nearest town: Pollock Pines. GPS: 38.859813, -120.384872

352 • C3 | Kaspian (Lake Tahoe Basin Management Unit)

Total sites: 9, RV sites: 0, Central water, Flush toilet, No showers, No RV dump, Tents only: $22-24, Walk-to sites, Open May-Oct, Reservations accepted, Elev: 6184ft/1885m, Tel: 530-583-3642, Nearest town: South Lake Tahoe. GPS: 39.113926, -120.158708

353 • C3 | Kirkwood Lake (Eldorado NF)

Total sites: 12, RV sites: 0, Central water, Vault/pit toilet, No showers, No RV dump, Tents only: $28, Stay limit: 14 days, Open Jun-Sep, Reservations not accepted, Elev: 7769ft/2368m, Tel: 209-295-4251, Nearest town: Pioneer. GPS: 38.707326, -120.087143

354 • C3 | Kit Carson (Humboldt-Toiyabe NF)

Total sites: 12, RV sites: 9, Central water, Vault/pit toilet, No showers, No RV dump, Tent & RV camping: $18, Stay limit: 14 days, Open Apr-Sep, Max Length: 45ft, Reservations accepted, Elev: 7001ft/2134m, Tel: 775-882-2766, Nearest town: Woodfords. GPS: 38.776661, -119.898597

355 • C3 | Lake Alpine (Stanislaus NF)

Total sites: 25, RV sites: 20, Central water, Flush toilet, No showers, No RV dump, Tent & RV camping: $27, Stay limit: 14 days, Open May-Oct, Max Length: 52ft, Reservations accepted, Elev: 7418ft/2261m, Tel: 209-795-1381, Nearest town: Arnold. GPS: 38.477295, -120.006104

356 • C3 | Lake of the Woods (Tahoe NF)

Total sites: 15, RV sites: 0, No water, Vault/pit toilet, Tents only: Free, Reservations not accepted, Elev: 7426ft/2263m, Nearest town: Sierraville. GPS: 39.502925, -120.391289

357 • C3 | Lakeside (Tahoe NF)

Total sites: 42, RV sites: 42, Central water, Vault/pit toilet, No showers, No RV dump, Tent & RV camping: $20, Open May-Oct, Max Length: 50ft, Reservations accepted, Elev: 5725ft/1745m, Tel: 530-587-9281, Nearest town: Truckee. GPS: 39.383846, -120.172139

358 • C3 | Leavitt Meadows (Humboldt-Toiyabe NF)

Total sites: 16, RV sites: 16, Central water, Vault/pit toilet, No showers, No RV dump, Tent & RV camping: $20, Stay limit: 14 days, Open Apr-Sep, Reservations not accepted, Elev: 7231ft/2204m, Tel: 760-932-7070, Nearest town: Walker. GPS: 38.333309, -119.553198

359 • C3 | Lewis (Tahoe NF)

Total sites: 40, RV sites: 40, Central water, Flush toilet, No showers, No RV dump, Tent & RV camping: $20, Open May-Sep, Max Length: 45ft, Reservations accepted, Elev: 5280ft/1609m, Tel: 530-478-0248, Nearest town: Foresthill. GPS: 39.132043, -120.416345

360 • C3 | Little Lasier Meadow Horse Camp (Tahoe NF)

Total sites: 11, RV sites: 11, Central water, Vault/pit toilet, No showers, No RV dump, Tent & RV camping: $24, Open May-Oct, Max Length: 40ft, Reservations accepted, Elev: 6522ft/1988m, Nearest town: Sierraville. GPS: 39.489051, -120.515429

361 • C3 | Lodgepole Overflow (Stanislaus NF)

Total sites: 30, RV sites: 30, Central water, Vault/pit toilet, No showers, No RV dump, Tent & RV camping: $30, Stay limit: 2 days, Open Jun-Sep, Reservations not accepted, Elev: 7408ft/2258m, Tel: 209-795-1381, Nearest town: Bear Valley. GPS: 38.477504, -120.024149

362 • C3 | Loganville (Tahoe NF)

Total sites: 19, RV sites: 0, Central water, Vault/pit toilet, No showers, No RV dump, Tents only: $24, Pan for gold, Open May-Oct, Max Length: 40ft, Reservations accepted, Elev: 4003ft/1220m, Tel: 530-862-1368, Nearest town: Sierra City. GPS: 39.565142, -120.663208

363 • C3 | Logger (Tahoe NF)

Total sites: 251, RV sites: 251, Central water, Vault/pit toilet, No showers, No RV dump, Tent & RV camping: $23, No access via Stampede Dam Road, Open May-Oct, Max Length: 40ft, Reservations accepted, Elev: 6040ft/1841m, Tel: 530-587-9281, Nearest town: Truckee. GPS: 39.465148, -120.123856

364 • C3 | Lookout (Humboldt-Toiyabe NF)

Total sites: 22, RV sites: 22, No water, Vault/pit toilet, Tent & RV camping: $6, Stay limit: 14 days, Open Jun-Sep, Reservations not accepted, Elev: 6801ft/2073m, Tel: 775-882-2766, Nearest town: Reno, NV. GPS: 39.589583, -120.073582

365 • C3 | Loon Lake (Eldorado NF)

Total sites: 53, RV sites: 31, Central water, Vault/pit toilet, No showers, No RV dump, Tent & RV camping: $28, Group sites: $130-$160, Stay limit: 14 days, Open Jun-Aug, Max Length: 40ft, Reservations accepted, Elev: 6450ft/1966m, Tel: 530-293-0827, Nearest town: Pollock Pines. GPS: 38.979194, -120.319174

366 • C3 | Loon Lake Horse Camp (Eldorado NF)

Total sites: 9, RV sites: 9, Central water, Vault/pit toilet, No showers, No RV dump, Tent & RV camping: $28, Stay limit: 14 days, Open Jun-Oct, Reservations accepted, Elev: 6499ft/1981m, Tel: 530-644-2349, Nearest town: Pollock Pines. GPS: 38.982722, -120.314988

367 • C3 | Lover's Leap (Eldorado NF)

Total sites: 21, RV sites: 0, Central water, Vault/pit toilet, No showers, No RV dump, Tents only: $28, Walk-to sites, Stay limit: 14 days, Open Jun-Nov, Reservations not accepted, Elev: 5919ft/1804m, Tel: 530-644-2324, Nearest town: Pollock Pines. GPS: 38.799666, -120.140344

368 • C3 | Lower Lindsey Lake (Tahoe NF)

Total sites: 12, RV sites: 0, No water, Vault/pit toilet, Tents only: $15, Very rough, narrow road, High-clearance vehicles recommended, Operated by PGE, Open Jun-Sep, Reservations not accepted, Elev: 6302ft/1921m, Tel: 530-265-4531, Nearest town: Nevada City. GPS: 39.412654, -120.644323

369 • C3 | Lower Little Truckee (Tahoe NF)

Total sites: 15, RV sites: 15, Central water, Vault/pit toilet, No showers, No RV dump, Tent & RV camping: $20, Open May-Oct, Max Length: 45ft, Reservations accepted, Elev: 6168ft/1880m, Tel: 530-994-3401, Nearest town: Sierraville. GPS: 39.485605, -120.236477

370 • C3 | Markleeville (Humboldt-Toiyabe NF)

Total sites: 10, RV sites: 10, Central water, Vault/pit toilet, No showers, No RV dump, Tent & RV camping: $18, Stay limit: 14 days, Open Apr-Sep, Reservations not accepted, Elev: 5502ft/1677m, Tel: 775-882-2766, Nearest town: Markleeville. GPS: 38.697759, -119.774064

371 • C3 | Martin Meadows (Eldorado NF)

Total sites: 13, RV sites: 13, No water, Vault/pit toilet, No showers, No RV dump, Tent & RV camping: Free, Stay limit: 14 days, Reservations not accepted, Elev: 7641ft/2329m, Nearest town: Kirkwood. GPS: 38.696476, -120.122656

372 • C3 | Meeks Bay (Lake Tahoe Basin Management Unit)

Total sites: 39, RV sites: 21, Central water, Flush toilet, No showers, No RV dump, Tent & RV camping: $33-35, Open May-Oct, Max Length: 38ft, Reservations accepted, Elev: 6240ft/1902m, Tel: 530-525-4733, Nearest town: Meeks Bay. GPS: 39.035889, -120.123535

373 • C3 | Middle Fork Cosumnes (Eldorado NF)

Total sites: 19, No water, Vault/pit toilet, Tents only: $25, Stay limit: 14 days, Open May-Nov, Reservations not accepted, Elev: 5279ft/1609m, Tel: 209-295-4251, Nearest town: Placerville. GPS: 38.583947, -120.301587

374 • C3 | Mill Creek (Stanislaus NF)

Total sites: 17, RV sites: 17, No water, Vault/pit toilet, Tent & RV camping: $8, Stay limit: 14 days, Open May-Oct, Reservations not accepted, Elev: 6312ft/1924m, Tel: 209-965-3434, Nearest town: Mi-Wuk. GPS: 38.301699, -119.938112

375 • C3 | Mokelumne (Eldorado NF)

Total sites: 13, RV sites: 8, No water, Vault/pit toilet, Tent & RV camping: $25, Stay limit: 14 days, Reservations not accepted, Elev: 3343ft/1019m, Tel: 209-295-4251, Nearest town: Jackson. GPS: 38.478221, -120.270822

376 • C3 | Moore Creek (Eldorado NF)

Total sites: 8, RV sites: 0, Central water, Vault/pit toilet, No showers, No RV dump, Tents only: $20, Access blocked - road damage, Stay limit: 14 days, Open all year, Reservations not accepted, Elev: 3297ft/1005m, Tel: 209-295-4251, Nearest town: Pollock Pines. GPS: 38.481588, -120.264961

377 • C3 | Mosquito Lakes (Stanislaus NF)

Total sites: 11, RV sites: 0, No water, Vault/pit toilet, Tents only: $8, Stay limit: 14 days, Open Jun-Oct, Reservations not accepted, Elev: 8114ft/2473m, Tel: 209-795-1381, Nearest town: Bear Valley. GPS: 38.515918, -119.914204

378 • C3 | Mumford Bar CG (Tahoe NF)

Total sites: 4, RV sites: 4, No water, Vault/pit toilet, Tent & RV camping: Free, Hitching posts, Reservations not accepted, Elev: 5330ft/1625m, Tel: 530-367-2224. GPS: 39.181627, -120.614456

379 • C3 | Niagara Creek (Stanislaus NF)

Total sites: 10, RV sites: 10, No water, Vault/pit toilet, Tent & RV camping: $8, Stay limit: 14 days, Open May-Oct, Reservations not accepted, Elev: 6585ft/2007m, Tel: 209-965-3434, Nearest town: Mi-Wuk. GPS: 38.324944, -119.915537

380 • C3 | Niagara OHV (Stanislaus NF)

Total sites: 10, RV sites: 10, No water, Vault/pit toilet, Tent & RV camping: $8, Stay limit: 14 days, Open May-Oct, Reservations not accepted, Elev: 7054ft/2150m, Tel: 209-965-3434, Nearest town: Mi-Wuk. GPS: 38.311284, -119.890882

381 • C3 | North Fork (Blue Canyon) (Tahoe NF)

Total sites: 17, RV sites: 15, Central water, Vault/pit toilet, No showers, No RV dump, Tent & RV camping: $24, Open Apr-Oct, Max Length: 60ft, Reservations accepted, Elev: 4836ft/1474m, Tel: 530-478-0248, Nearest town: Emigrant Gap. GPS: 39.270508, -120.658447

382 • C3 | Northshore (Eldorado NF)

Total sites: 19, RV sites: 15, No water, Vault/pit toilet, Tent & RV camping: $10, Stay limit: 14 days, Open Jun-Oct, Reservations accepted, Elev: 6466ft/1971m, Tel: 530-644-2349, Nearest town: Pollock Pines. GPS: 38.999246, -120.318483

383 • C3 | Northwind (Eldorado NF)

Total sites: 9, RV sites: 8, No water, Vault/pit toilet, Tent & RV camping: $10, Stay limit: 14 days, Open May-Oct, Reservations not accepted, Elev: 5443ft/1659m, Tel: 530-644-2349, Nearest town: Placerville. GPS: 38.831945, -120.347821

384 • C3 | Onion Valley (Tahoe NF)

Total sites: 7, RV sites: 7, No water, Vault/pit toilet, No showers, No RV dump, Tent & RV camping: $18, Open May-Oct, Elev: 4809ft/1466m, Tel: 530-265-4531, Nearest town: Emigrant Gap. GPS: 39.262902, -120.656668

385 • C3 | Pacific Valley (Stanislaus NF)

Total sites: 15, RV sites: 15, No water, Vault/pit toilet, Tent & RV camping: $10, Stay limit: 14 days, Open Jun-Oct, Reservations not accepted, Elev: 7559ft/2304m, Tel: 209-795-1381, Nearest town: Bear Valley. GPS: 38.518541, -119.902269

386 • C3 | Pardoes Point (Eldorado NF)

Total sites: 10, RV sites: 0, Central water, Vault/pit toilet, No showers, No RV dump, Tents only: $28, Stay limit: 14 days, Open May-Nov, Reservations not accepted, Elev: 5837ft/1779m, Tel: 209-295-4251, Nearest town: Pioneer. GPS: 38.537403, -120.240459

387 • C3 | Parker Flat Staging Area (Tahoe NF)

Total sites: 6, RV sites: 6, No water, Vault/pit toilet, Tent & RV camping: Free, Open Apr-Dec, Max Length: 20ft, Reservations not accepted, Elev: 3940ft/1201m, Tel: 530-478-0248, Nearest town: Foresthill. GPS: 39.127425, -120.760353

388 • C3 | Pass Creek (Tahoe NF)

Total sites: 30, RV sites: 30, Central water, Flush toilet, No showers, RV dump, Tent & RV camping: $24, Open May-Oct, Max Length: 50ft, Reservations accepted, Elev: 6198ft/1889m, Tel: 530-265-8861, Nearest town: Truckee. GPS: 39.504971, -120.535096

389 • C3 | Pierce Creek (Tahoe NF)

Total sites: 18, RV sites: 18, No water, Vault/pit toilet, Tent & RV camping: Free, Reservations not accepted, Elev: 5163ft/1574m. GPS: 39.341284, -120.590881

390 • C3 | Pigeon Flat (Stanislaus NF)

Total sites: 7, RV sites: 0, No water, Vault/pit toilet, Tents only: $13, Walk-to sites, Cash only, Stay limit: 14 days, Open May-Oct, Reservations not accepted, Elev: 6070ft/1850m, Tel: 209-965-3434, Nearest town: Bridgeport. GPS: 38.340075, -119.804375

391 • C3 | Pine Marten (Stanislaus NF)

Total sites: 32, RV sites: 32, Central water, Flush toilet, No showers, No RV dump, Tent & RV camping: $27, Stay limit: 14 days, Open Jun-Sep, Max Length: 48ft, Reservations accepted, Elev: 7382ft/2250m, Tel: 209-795-1381, Nearest town: Bear Valley. GPS: 38.481173, -119.988917

392 • C3 | Pipi (Eldorado NF)

Total sites: 51, RV sites: 31, Central water, Vault/pit toilet, No showers, No RV dump, Tent & RV camping: $25, Stay limit: 14 days, Open May-Nov, Reservations not accepted, Elev: 4049ft/1234m, Tel: 209-295-4251, Nearest town: Pioneer. GPS: 38.567543, -120.431592

393 • C3 | Prosser (Tahoe NF)

Total sites: 29, RV sites: 29, Central water, Vault/pit toilet, No showers, No RV dump, Tent & RV camping: $20, Open May-Oct, Max Length: 40ft, Reservations accepted, Elev: 5860ft/1786m, Tel: 530-587-9281, Nearest town: Truckee. GPS: 39.378662, -120.162354

394 • C3 | Ramshorn (Tahoe NF)

Total sites: 16, Central water, Vault/pit toilet, No showers, No RV dump, Tents only: $20, Open Apr-Sep, Max Length: 20ft, Reservations accepted, Elev: 2726ft/831m, Tel: 530-862-1368, Nearest town: Downieville. GPS: 39.539063, -120.909424

395 • C3 | Robinson Flat (Tahoe NF)

Total sites: 14, RV sites: 0, Central water, Vault/pit toilet, No showers, No RV dump, Tents only: Free, 7 equestrian sites, Narro winding road - trailers not recommended, Open all year, Reservations not accepted, Elev: 6699ft/2042m, Nearest town: Foresthill. GPS: 39.156263, -120.502227

396 • C3 | Rocky Rest (Tahoe NF)

Total sites: 10, RV sites: 4, Central water, Vault/pit toilet, No showers, No RV dump, Tent & RV camping: $24, Open Apr-Oct, Max Length: 30ft, Reservations accepted, Elev: 2441ft/744m, Tel: 530-862-1368, Nearest town: Camptonville. GPS: 39.513084, -120.977263

397 • C3 | Sagehen Creek (Tahoe NF)

Total sites: 10, RV sites: 10, No water, Vault/pit toilet, Tent & RV camping: Free, Not suitable for large RVs, Open May-Nov, Max Length: 18ft, Reservations not accepted, Elev: 6526ft/1989m, Tel: 530-994-3401, Nearest town: Truckee. GPS: 39.434371, -120.257461

398 • C3 | Sand Flat (Eldorado NF)

Total sites: 29, RV sites: 27, Central water, Vault/pit toilet, No showers, No RV dump, Tent & RV camping: $28, Stay limit: 14 days, Open May-Sep, Reservations not accepted, Elev: 3960ft/1207m, Tel: 530-644-2324, Nearest town: Placerville. GPS: 38.763516, -120.325835

399 • C3 | Sand Flat (Stanislaus NF)

Total sites: 6, Central water, Vault/pit toilet, No showers, No RV dump, Tents only: Free, High-clearance vehicle recommended, Stay limit: 14 days, Open Jun-Oct, Elev: 5787ft/1764m, Tel: 209-795-1381, Nearest town: Arnold. GPS: 38.410398, -120.081647

400 • C3 | Sand Flat (Stanislaus NF)

Total sites: 68, RV sites: 68, Central water, Vault/pit toilet, No showers, No RV dump, Tent & RV camping: $21, Cash only, May use RV dump at Clark Fork CG, Stay limit: 14 days, Open Apr-Oct, Max Length: 22ft, Reservations not accepted, Elev: 6191ft/1887m, Tel: 209-965-3434, Nearest town: Kyburz. GPS: 38.404219, -119.789774

401 • C3 | Schoolhouse (Tahoe NF)

Total sites: 56, RV sites: 56, Central water, Flush toilet, No showers, No RV dump, Tent & RV camping: $22, Open May-Oct, Max Length: 22ft, Reservations required, Elev: 2310ft/704m, Tel: Info: 530-288-3231/Res: 530-692-3200, Nearest town: Camptonville. GPS: 39.417504, -121.121525

402 • C3 | Shenanigan Flat (Tahoe NF)

Total sites: 8, RV sites: 4, No water, Vault/pit toilet, No showers,

No RV dump, Tent & RV camping: Free, Elev: 2282ft/696m. GPS: 39.507064, -121.022796

403 • C3 | Shirttail Creek (Tahoe NF)

Total sites: 31, RV sites: 29, Central water, Vault/pit toilet, No showers, No RV dump, Tent & RV camping: $24, $6 dump fee, Use food storage lockers, Open May-Oct, Max Length: 50ft, Reservations accepted, Elev: 3766ft/1148m, Tel: 530-478-0248, Nearest town: Foresthill. GPS: 39.142441, -120.785152

404 • C3 | Silver Creek (Hwy 4) (Humboldt-Toiyabe NF)

Total sites: 27, RV sites: 27, No water, Vault/pit toilet, No showers, No RV dump, Tent & RV camping: $18, Stay limit: 14 days, Open Jun-Sep, Max Length: 51ft, Reservations accepted, Elev: 6821ft/2079m, Tel: 530-694-1002, Nearest town: Markleeville. GPS: 38.588057, -119.786696

405 • C3 | Silver Creek (Truckee) (Tahoe NF)

Total sites: 28, RV sites: 15, Central water, Vault/pit toilet, No showers, No RV dump, Tent & RV camping: $20, Also walk-to sites, Open May-Oct, Max Length: 30ft, Reservations accepted, Elev: 6060ft/1847m, Tel: 530-587-9281, Nearest town: Tahoe City. GPS: 39.223389, -120.201904

406 • C3 | Silver Fork (Eldorado NF)

Total sites: 35, RV sites: 22, Central water, Vault/pit toilet, No showers, No RV dump, Tent & RV camping: $28, Stay limit: 14 days, Open Jun-Sep, Max Length: 22ft, Reservations not accepted, Elev: 5587ft/1703m, Tel: 530-644-2324, Nearest town: Pioneer. GPS: 38.699023, -120.207537

407 • C3 | Silver Lake East (Eldorado) (Eldorado NF)

Total sites: 59, RV sites: 48, No water, Vault/pit toilet, No showers, No RV dump, Tent & RV camping: $28, Stay limit: 14 days, Open Jun-Sep, Max Length: 35ft, Reservations accepted, Elev: 7306ft/2227m, Tel: 209-295-4251, Nearest town: Eldorado. GPS: 38.672352, -120.118262

408 • C3 | Silver Valley (Stanislaus NF)

Total sites: 21, RV sites: 21, No water, Flush toilet, No showers, No RV dump, Tent & RV camping: $27, Stay limit: 14 days, Open Jul-Sep, Max Length: 53ft, Reservations accepted, Elev: 7421ft/2262m, Tel: 209-753-6350, Nearest town: Arnold. GPS: 38.479980, -119.987549

409 • C3 | Silvertip (Stanislaus NF)

Total sites: 22, RV sites: 22, No water, Vault/pit toilet, Tent & RV camping: $27, Stay limit: 14 days, Open Jul-Sep, Max Length: 48ft, Reservations not accepted, Elev: 7628ft/2325m, Tel: 209-795-1381, Nearest town: Bear Valley. GPS: 38.481505, -120.017942

410 • C3 | Skillman Horse Camp (Tahoe NF)

Total sites: 17, RV sites: 17, Central water, Vault/pit toilet, No showers, No RV dump, Tent & RV camping: $18, Group site: $110, Corrals and water troughs, 5 equestrian sites, Open May-Sep, Max Length: 35ft, Reservations accepted, Elev: 4567ft/1392m, Tel: 530-478-0248, Nearest town: Nevada City. GPS: 39.318335, -120.793004

411 • C3 | Sly Creek (Plumas NF)

Total sites: 23, RV sites: 23, Central water, Vault/pit toilet, No showers, No RV dump, Tent & RV camping: $20, Stay limit: 14 days, Open May-Oct, Reservations not accepted, Elev: 3524ft/1074m, Tel: 530-534-1221, Nearest town: Strawberry Valley. GPS: 39.584455, -121.117436

412 • C3 | South Shore (Eldorado NF)

Total sites: 22, RV sites: 7, Central water, Vault/pit toilet, No showers, No RV dump, Tent & RV camping: $28, Also walk-to sites, Stay limit: 14 days, Open May-Oct, Reservations not accepted, Elev: 5925ft/1806m, Tel: 209-295-4251, Nearest town: Pioneer. GPS: 38.533779, -120.243501

413 • C3 | Spicer Meadow Reservoir (Stanislaus NF)

Total sites: 43, RV sites: 43, Central water, Vault/pit toilet, No showers, No RV dump, Tent & RV camping: $24, Group site: $140, No camping at boat ramp, Stay limit: 14 days, Open Jun-Oct, Max Length: 50ft, Reservations not accepted, Elev: 6686ft/2038m, Tel: 209-296-8895, Nearest town: Arnold. GPS: 38.407539, -119.998164

414 • C3 | Stanislaus River (Stanislaus NF)

Total sites: 24, RV sites: 10, Central water, Vault/pit toilet, No showers, No RV dump, Tent & RV camping: $12, Stay limit: 14 days, Open Jun-Sep, Reservations not accepted, Elev: 6207ft/1892m, Tel: 209-795-1381, Nearest town: Arnold. GPS: 38.422319, -120.046767

415 • C3 | Sterling lake/PGE (Tahoe NF)

Total sites: 6, No water, Vault/pit toilet, Tents only: $15, Walk-to sites, - 400ft, Steep winding road, Operated by PGandE, Open Jun-Oct, Reservations not accepted, Elev: 6998ft/2133m, Tel: 916-386-5164. GPS: 39.353109, -120.493349

416 • C3 | Strawberry (Plumas NF)

Total sites: 17, RV sites: 17, Central water, Vault/pit toilet, No showers, No RV dump, Tent & RV camping: $20, Stay limit: 14 days, Open May-Sep, Reservations not accepted, Elev: 3711ft/1131m, Tel: 530-534-6500, Nearest town: Strawberry Valley. GPS: 39.588508, -121.090271

417 • C3 | Strawberry Point (Eldorado NF)

Total sites: 10, RV sites: 10, No water, Vault/pit toilet, Tent & RV camping: $10, Stay limit: 14 days, Open May-Oct, Reservations not accepted, Elev: 5515ft/1681m, Tel: 530-644-2349, Nearest town: Placerville. GPS: 38.828635, -120.339103

418 • C3 | Stumpy Meadows (Eldorado NF)

Total sites: 40, RV sites: 30, Central water, Vault/pit toilet, No showers, No RV dump, Tent & RV camping: $28, Stay limit: 14 days, Open May-Oct, Max Length: 35ft, Reservations accepted, Elev: 4501ft/1372m, Tel: 530-333-4312, Nearest town: Georgetown. GPS: 38.904287, -120.591351

419 • C3 | Sugar Pine Point (Eldorado NF)

Total sites: 8, RV sites: 0, No water, Vault/pit toilet, Tents only: $25, Stay limit: 14 days, Open May-Nov, Reservations not accepted, Elev: 5882ft/1793m, Tel: 209-295-4251, Nearest town: Jackson. GPS: 38.544927, -120.241407

420 • C3 | Sunset - Union Valley (Eldorado NF)

Total sites: 121, RV sites: 74, Central water, Vault/pit toilet, No showers, RV dump, Tent & RV camping: $28, Stay limit: 14 days, Open May-Sep, Max Length: 50ft, Reservations accepted, Elev: 4957ft/1511m, Tel: 530-293-0827, Nearest town: Pollock Pines. GPS: 38.866554, -120.406895

421 • C3 | Talbot (Tahoe NF)

Total sites: 5, No water, Vault/pit toilet, Tents only: Free, River water, Reservations not accepted, Elev: 5646ft/1721m, Tel: 530-265-4531, Nearest town: Truckee. GPS: 39.188000, -120.373000

422 • C3 | Tells Creek Horse Camp (Eldorado NF)

Total sites: 5, RV sites: 5, No water, Vault/pit toilet, No showers, No RV dump, Tent & RV camping: Free, Narrow road, Stay limit: 14 days, Reservations not accepted, Elev: 6518ft/1987m, Tel: 530-644-2349, Nearest town: Placerville. GPS: 38.931814, -120.320983

423 • C3 | Union Flat (Tahoe NF)

Total sites: 11, RV sites: 7, Central water, Vault/pit toilet, No showers, No RV dump, Tent & RV camping: $24, Open May-Oct, Max Length: 30ft, Reservations accepted, Elev: 3419ft/1042m, Tel: 530-862-1368, Nearest town: Downieville. GPS: 39.567383, -120.744629

424 • C3 | Union West (Stanislaus NF)

Total sites: 11, RV sites: 11, No water, Vault/pit toilet, Tent & RV camping: $16, Stay limit: 14 days, Max Length: 27ft, Reservations not accepted, Elev: 6906ft/2105m, Tel: 209-795-1381, Nearest town: Bear Valley. GPS: 38.428391, -119.991494

425 • C3 | Upper Little Truckee (Tahoe NF)

Total sites: 18, RV sites: 18, Central water, Vault/pit toilet, No showers, No RV dump, Tent & RV camping: $20, Group site: $66, Open May-Oct, Max Length: 60ft, Reservations accepted, Elev: 6220ft/1896m, Tel: 530-994-3401, Nearest town: Sierraville. GPS: 39.491107, -120.245067

426 • C3 | Utica Reservoir - Rocky Point (Stanislaus NF)

Total sites: 12, No water, Vault/pit toilet, Tents only: $16, Walk-to sites, Stay limit: 14 days, Reservations not accepted, Elev: 6829ft/2081m, Tel: 209-795-1381, Nearest town: Bear Valley. GPS: 38.438693, -120.005285

427 • C3 | Utica Reservoir - Sandy Flat (Stanislaus NF)

Total sites: 11, No water, Vault/pit toilet, Tents only: $16, Walk-to sites, Stay limit: 14 days, Reservations not accepted, Elev: 6824ft/2080m, Tel: 209-795-1381, Nearest town: Bear Valley. GPS: 38.425784, -120.012471

428 • C3 | Wakalu Hep Yo (Stanislaus NF)

Total sites: 49, RV sites: 49, Central water, Flush toilet, No showers, No RV dump, Tent & RV camping: $20, Stay limit: 14 days, Open Jun-Oct, Reservations not accepted, Elev: 4101ft/1250m, Tel: 209-795-1381, Nearest town: Arnold. GPS: 38.322662, -120.217502

429 • C3 | Wench Creek (Eldorado NF)

Total sites: 100, RV sites: 83, Central water, Flush toilet, No showers, No RV dump, Tent & RV camping: $28, Stay limit: 14 days, Open May-Sep, Max Length: 22ft, Reservations not accepted, Elev: 4944ft/1507m, Tel: 530-293-0827, Nearest town: Pollock Pines. GPS: 38.889454, -120.377183

430 • C3 | Wentworth Springs (Eldorado NF)

Total sites: 8, RV sites: 0, No water, Vault/pit toilet, Tents only: Free, Stay limit: 14 days, Open Jun-Oct, Reservations not accepted, Elev: 6207ft/1892m, Tel: 530-644-2349, Nearest town: Placerville. GPS: 39.011553, -120.325248

431 • C3 | West Point (Eldorado NF)

Total sites: 8, RV sites: 8, No water, Vault/pit toilet, Tent & RV camping: $25, Stay limit: 14 days, Open Jun-Oct, Reservations not accepted, Elev: 5016ft/1529m, Tel: 530-647-5415, Nearest town: Pollock Pines. GPS: 38.871111, -120.441168

432 • C3 | White Azelea (Eldorado NF)

Total sites: 6, RV sites: 0, No water, Vault/pit toilet, Tents only: $25, Stay limit: 14 days, Open Jun-Oct, Reservations not accepted, Elev: 3629ft/1106m, Tel: 209-295-4251, Nearest town: Jackson. GPS: 38.489766, -120.261885

433 • C3 | White Cloud (Tahoe NF)

Total sites: 46, RV sites: 38, Central water, Vault/pit toilet, Pay showers, No RV dump, Tent & RV camping: $24, Open May-Oct, Max Length: 40ft, Reservations accepted, Elev: 4334ft/1321m, Tel: 530-478-0248, Nearest town: Nevada City. GPS: 39.319828, -120.845931

434 • C3 | Wild Plum (Tahoe NF)

Total sites: 47, RV sites: 24, Central water, Vault/pit toilet, No showers, No RV dump, Tent & RV camping: $24, Gold panning, Open May-Oct, Max Length: 43ft, Reservations accepted, Elev: 4495ft/1370m, Tel: 530-862-1368, Nearest town: Sierra City. GPS: 39.566406, -120.599121

435 • C3 | William Kent (Lake Tahoe Basin Management Unit)

Total sites: 86, RV sites: 86, Central water, Flush toilet, No showers, RV dump, Tent & RV camping: $31-33, Open May-Oct, Max Length: 57ft, Reservations accepted, Elev: 6302ft/1921m, Tel: 530-583-3642, Nearest town: Tahoe City. GPS: 39.139464, -120.156863

436 • C3 | Wolf Creek (Eldorado NF)

Total sites: 42, RV sites: 10, Central water, Vault/pit toilet, No showers, No RV dump, Tent & RV camping: $28, 3 group sites: $140-$170, Bear boxes must be used for food storage, Stay limit: 14 days, Open May-Sep, Max Length: 50ft, Reservations accepted, Elev: 4928ft/1502m, Tel: 530-293-0827, Nearest town: Placerville. GPS: 38.883836, -120.397768

437 • C3 | Wolf Creek (Humboldt-Toiyabe NF)

Total sites: 6, RV sites: 6, No water, Vault/pit toilet, Tent & RV camping: Free, Reservations not accepted, Elev: 6535ft/1992m. GPS: 38.576713, -119.697261

438 • C3 | Woodcamp (Tahoe NF)

Total sites: 20, RV sites: 20, Central water, Flush toilet, No showers, No RV dump, Tent & RV camping: $24, Open May-Oct, Max Length: 42ft, Reservations accepted, Elev: 6112ft/1863m,

Tel: 530-265-8861, Nearest town: Sierraville. GPS: 39.486905, -120.547642

439 • C3 | Woodchuck (Tahoe NF)

Total sites: 8, RV sites: 8, No water, Vault/pit toilet, Tent & RV camping: Free, Open May-Sep, Reservations not accepted, Elev: 6299ft/1920m, Tel: 530-265-4531, Nearest town: Truckee. GPS: 39.332913, -120.519406

440 • C3 | Woods Lake (Eldorado NF)

Total sites: 25, RV sites: 0, Central water, Vault/pit toilet, No showers, No RV dump, Tents only: $28, Stay limit: 14 days, Open Jul-Oct, Max Length: 16ft, Reservations not accepted, Elev: 8245ft/2513m, Tel: 209-295-4251, Nearest town: Kit Carson. GPS: 38.685451, -120.009233

441 • C3 | Wrights Lake (Eldorado NF)

Total sites: 67, RV sites: 24, Central water, Vault/pit toilet, No showers, No RV dump, Tent & RV camping: $25, Stay limit: 14 days, Open Jun-Oct, Max Length: 22ft, Reservations accepted, Elev: 6998ft/2133m, Tel: 530-647-5415, Nearest town: Kyburz. GPS: 38.845828, -120.237113

442 • C3 | Wrights Lake Equestrian (Eldorado NF)

Total sites: 15, RV sites: 15, Central water, Vault/pit toilet, No showers, No RV dump, Tent & RV camping: $28, Horse campers only, Stay limit: 14 days, Open Jul-Sep, Max Length: 35ft, Reservations accepted, Elev: 6995ft/2132m, Tel: 530-647-5415, Nearest town: Placerville. GPS: 38.843418, -120.232652

443 • C3 | Yellowjacket (Eldorado NF)

Total sites: 40, RV sites: 29, Central water, Flush toilet, No showers, RV dump, Tent & RV camping: $28, Stay limit: 14 days, Open May-Sep, Max Length: 25ft, Reservations accepted, Elev: 4974ft/1516m, Tel: 530-293-0827, Nearest town: Pollock Pines. GPS: 38.889728, -120.386388

444 • C4 | Bootleg (Humboldt-Toiyabe NF)

Total sites: 63, RV sites: 63, Central water, Flush toilet, No showers, No RV dump, Tent & RV camping: $22, Stay limit: 14 days, Open May-Sep, Max Length: 35ft, Reservations not accepted, Elev: 6437ft/1962m, Tel: 760-932-7070, Nearest town: Coleville. GPS: 38.416602, -119.450095

445 • C4 | Buckeye (Humboldt-Toiyabe NF)

Total sites: 65, RV sites: 65, No water, Flush toilet, No showers, No RV dump, Tent & RV camping: $20, Non-potable water, Hot springs nearby, Stay limit: 14 days, Open May-Nov, Max Length: 22ft, Reservations not accepted, Elev: 7205ft/2196m, Tel: 760-932-7070, Nearest town: Bridgeport. GPS: 38.236665, -119.346065

446 • C4 | Chris Flat (Humboldt-Toiyabe NF)

Total sites: 15, RV sites: 15, Central water, Vault/pit toilet, No showers, No RV dump, Tent & RV camping: $20, Stay limit: 14 days, Open Apr-Oct, Reservations not accepted, Elev: 6555ft/1998m, Tel: 760-932-7070, Nearest town: Walker. GPS: 38.394511, -119.452009

447 • C4 | Obsidian (Humboldt-Toiyabe NF)

Total sites: 11, RV sites: 11, No water, Vault/pit toilet, Tent & RV camping: $12, Stay limit: 14 days, Open May-Oct, Reservations not accepted, Elev: 7759ft/2365m, Tel: 760-932-7070, Nearest town: Walker. GPS: 38.297126, -119.447301

448 • C4 | Sonora Bridge (Humboldt-Toiyabe NF)

Total sites: 23, RV sites: 23, Central water, Vault/pit toilet, No showers, No RV dump, Tent & RV camping: $20, Stay limit: 14 days, Open Apr-Oct, Max Length: 35ft, Reservations not accepted, Elev: 6736ft/2053m, Tel: 760-932-7070, Nearest town: Walker. GPS: 38.364368, -119.476963

449 • D3 | Big Sandy (Sierra NF)

Total sites: 18, RV sites: 18, No water, Vault/pit toilet, Tent & RV camping: $24-27, Stay limit: 14 days, Open May-Sep, Max Length: 20ft, Reservations not accepted, Elev: 5856ft/1785m, Tel: 559-877-2218, Nearest town: Fresno. GPS: 37.467395, -119.582956

450 • D3 | Cherry Valley (Stanislaus NF)

Total sites: 45, RV sites: 45, Central water, Vault/pit toilet, No showers, No RV dump, Tent & RV camping: $24, Water source unreliable, Stay limit: 14 days, Open Apr-Sep, Max Length: 24ft, Reservations accepted, Elev: 4997ft/1523m, Tel: 209-962-7825, Nearest town: Groveland. GPS: 37.986286, -119.920279

451 • D3 | Chilkoot (Sierra NF)

Total sites: 14, RV sites: 14, No water, Vault/pit toilet, Tent & RV camping: $30, Stay limit: 14 days, Open May-Nov, Reservations accepted, Elev: 4767ft/1453m, Tel: 559-642-3212, Nearest town: Oakhurst. GPS: 37.367705, -119.538104

452 • D3 | Dimond 'O' (Stanislaus NF)

Total sites: 26, RV sites: 22, Central water, Vault/pit toilet, No showers, No RV dump, Tent & RV camping: $26, Stay limit: 14 days, Open Apr-Oct, Max Length: 48ft, Reservations accepted, Elev: 4482ft/1366m, Tel: 209-379-2258, Nearest town: Groveland. GPS: 37.863233, -119.870422

453 • D3 | Dirt Flat (Sierra NF)

Total sites: 2, RV sites: 0, Central water, Vault/pit toilet, No showers, No RV dump, Tents only: $30-32, Walk-to sites, Stay limit: 14 days, Open all year, Reservations accepted, Elev: 1618ft/493m, Tel: 559-642-3212, Nearest town: El Portal. GPS: 37.671011, -119.836545

454 • D3 | Dry Gulch (Sierra NF)

Total sites: 4, RV sites: 0, No water, Vault/pit toilet, Tents only: $30-32, Walk-to sites, Stay limit: 14 days, Open all year, Reservations accepted, Elev: 1629ft/497m, Tel: 559-642-3212, Nearest town: Mariposa. GPS: 37.673125, -119.833957

455 • D3 | Forks (Bass Lake) (Sierra NF)

Total sites: 27, RV sites: 22, Central water, Flush toilet, No showers, No RV dump, Tent & RV camping: $36-38, Open Apr-Sep, Max Length: 40ft, Reservations accepted, Elev: 3461ft/1055m, Tel: 559-642-3212, Nearest town: Oakhurst. GPS: 37.313111, -119.568991

456 • D3 | Fraser Flat (Stanislaus NF)

Total sites: 38, RV sites: 38, Central water, Vault/pit toilet, No showers, RV dump, Tent & RV camping: $19, Stay limit: 14 days, Open Apr-Oct, Reservations not accepted, Elev: 4869ft/1484m,

Tel: 209-586-3234, Nearest town: Cold Springs. GPS: 38.169814, -120.071219

457 • D3 | Fresno Dome (Sierra NF)

Total sites: 15, RV sites: 0, No water, Vault/pit toilet, Tents only: $27, Stay limit: 14 days, Open May-Oct, Reservations not accepted, Elev: 6542ft/1994m, Tel: 559-877-2218, Nearest town: Oakhurst. GPS: 37.455248, -119.549334

458 • D3 | Greys Mountain (Sierra NF)

Total sites: 26, RV sites: 26, No water, Vault/pit toilet, Tent & RV camping: $30, Open May-Sep, Max Length: 20ft, Reservations not accepted, Elev: 5318ft/1621m, Tel: 559-877-2218, Nearest town: Oakhurst. GPS: 37.397079, -119.564989

459 • D3 | Hull Creek (Stanislaus NF)

Total sites: 18, RV sites: 18, Central water, Vault/pit toilet, No showers, No RV dump, Tent & RV camping: $12, Stay limit: 14 days, Open Apr-Oct, Reservations not accepted, Elev: 5523ft/1683m, Tel: 209-586-3234, Nearest town: Mi-Wuk. GPS: 38.094169, -120.042896

460 • D3 | Kelty Meadow (Sierra NF)

Total sites: 11, RV sites: 11, No water, Vault/pit toilet, No showers, No RV dump, Tent & RV camping: $27-29, Stock facilities - water for horses only, Stay limit: 14 days, Open May-Sep, Max Length: 30ft, Reservations accepted, Elev: 5886ft/1794m, Tel: 559-642-3212, Nearest town: Oakhurst. GPS: 37.440404, -119.544557

461 • D3 | Kerrick Corral Horse Camp (Stanislaus NF)

Total sites: 9, RV sites: 9, No water, Vault/pit toilet, Tent & RV camping: Free, Free fire permit required, Stay limit: 14 days, Open May-Dec, Reservations not accepted, Elev: 7050ft/2149m, Tel: 209-965-3434, Nearest town: Cold Springs. GPS: 38.174292, -119.956079

462 • D3 | Lost Claim (Stanislaus NF)

Total sites: 10, RV sites: 3, No water, Vault/pit toilet, No showers, No RV dump, Tent & RV camping: $21, Not recommended for trailers or RVs, Stay limit: 14 days, Open Apr-Oct, Max Length: 15ft, Reservations accepted, Elev: 3064ft/934m, Tel: 209-962-7825, Nearest town: Groveland. GPS: 37.821045, -120.048584

463 • D3 | Lumsden (Stanislaus NF)

Total sites: 10, RV sites: 0, No water, Vault/pit toilet, Tents only: Free, Stay limit: 14 days, Open all year, Elev: 1460ft/445m, Tel: 209-962-7825, Nearest town: Groveland. GPS: 37.838096, -120.051586

464 • D3 | Lupine (Sierra NF)

Total sites: 51, RV sites: 39, Central water, Flush toilet, No showers, No RV dump, Tent & RV camping: $36-38, Open all year, Max Length: 40ft, Reservations accepted, Elev: 3402ft/1037m, Tel: 559-642-3212, Nearest town: Yosemite. GPS: 37.307655, -119.544244

465 • D3 | Meadowview (Stanislaus NF)

Total sites: 100, RV sites: 100, Central water, Flush toilet, No showers, No RV dump, Tent & RV camping: $30, Cash only, Stay limit: 14 days, Open May-Oct, Max Length: 22ft, Reservations not accepted, Elev: 5588ft/1703m, Tel: 209-965-3434, Nearest town: Mi-Wuk. GPS: 38.186608, -120.004193

466 • D3 | Nelder Grove (Sierra NF)

Total sites: 7, RV sites: 7, No water, Vault/pit toilet, Tent & RV camping: Free, Open May-Dec, Max Length: 20ft, Reservations not accepted, Elev: 5430ft/1655m, Tel: 559-877-2218, Nearest town: Fresno. GPS: 37.431043, -119.583468

467 • D3 | Pinecrest (Stanislaus NF)

Total sites: 200, RV sites: 200, Central water, Flush toilet, Pay showers, RV dump, Tent & RV camping: $32, Stay limit: 14 days, Open May-Oct, Max Length: 40ft, Reservations accepted, Elev: 5682ft/1732m, Tel: 209-965 3434, Nearest town: Mi-Wuk. GPS: 38.191162, -119.993896

468 • D3 | River Ranch (Stanislaus NF)

Total sites: 38, RV sites: 38, Central water, Vault/pit toilet, No showers, No RV dump, Tent & RV camping: $28, Part public/part private, Stay limit: 14 days, Open Mar-Sep, Reservations not accepted, Elev: 2518ft/767m, Tel: 209-586-3234, Nearest town: Tuolumne City. GPS: 37.993645, -120.181522

469 • D3 | Sand Bar Flat (Stanislaus NF)

Total sites: 10, RV sites: 10, Central water, Vault/pit toilet, No showers, No RV dump, Tent & RV camping: $12, Road not suitable for large RVs, Stay limit: 14 days, Open Apr-Nov, Max Length: 35ft, Reservations not accepted, Elev: 2772ft/845m, Tel: 209-586-3234, Nearest town: Mi-Wuk. GPS: 38.184277, -120.155807

470 • D3 | Soquel (Sierra NF)

Total sites: 11, RV sites: 11, No water, Vault/pit toilet, Tent & RV camping: $27-29, Stay limit: 14 days, Open May-Sep, Max Length: 30ft, Reservations accepted, Elev: 5308ft/1618m, Tel: 559-642-3212, Nearest town: Oakhurst. GPS: 37.407226, -119.563106

471 • D3 | South Fork (Stanislaus NF)

Total sites: 9, RV sites: 0, No water, Vault/pit toilet, Tents only: Free, Burn area - use caution, Stay limit: 14 days, Open all year, Reservations not accepted, Elev: 1545ft/471m, Tel: 209-962-7825, Nearest town: Groveland. GPS: 37.838865, -120.045299

472 • D3 | Spring Cove (Sierra NF)

Total sites: 63, RV sites: 63, Central water, Flush toilet, No showers, No RV dump, Tents: $36-36/RVs: $36-38, Open May-Sep, Max Length: 36ft, Reservations accepted, Elev: 3471ft/1058m, Tel: 559-642-3212, Nearest town: Bass Lake. GPS: 37.301423, -119.542812

473 • D3 | Summerdale (Sierra NF)

Total sites: 32, RV sites: 32, Central water, Vault/pit toilet, No showers, No RV dump, Tent & RV camping: $34-36, Water must be boiled, Stay limit: 14 days, Open May-Sep, Max Length: 30ft, Reservations accepted, Elev: 5023ft/1531m, Tel: 559-642-3212, Nearest town: Oakhurst. GPS: 37.490253, -119.632865

474 • D3 | Sweetwater (Stanislaus NF)

Total sites: 12, RV sites: 12, Elec sites: 32, Central water, Vault/pit toilet, No showers, No RV dump, Tent & RV camping: $24, Filling RV water tank not allowed, No services in winter, Stay limit: 14

days, Open all year, Max Length: 18ft, Reservations not accepted, Elev: 3028ft/923m, Tel: 209-962-7825, Nearest town: Groveland. GPS: 37.824179, -120.004424

475 • D3 | TeleLi puLaya (Black Oak) (Stanislaus NF)

Total sites: 20, RV sites: 20, No water, Vault/pit toilet, No showers, No RV dump, Tent & RV camping: $20, 2 group sites: $25, New in 2014, Stay limit: 14 days, Open Apr-Oct, Reservations not accepted, Elev: 5112ft/1558m, Tel: 209-965-3434. GPS: 38.186861, -120.057997

476 • D3 | The Pines (Stanislaus NF)

Total sites: 9, RV sites: 9, Central water, Vault/pit toilet, No showers, No RV dump, Tent & RV camping: $21, Reservable group site $90, No water in winter, Stay limit: 14 days, Open all year, Reservations not accepted, Elev: 3281ft/1000m, Tel: 209-379-2258, Nearest town: Groveland. GPS: 37.818337, -120.095545

477 • D3 | Wishon Point (Sierra NF)

Total sites: 47, RV sites: 38, Central water, Flush toilet, No showers, No RV dump, Tent & RV camping: $36-38, Stay limit: 14 days, Open Apr-Sep, Max Length: 24ft, Reservations accepted, Elev: 3428ft/1045m, Tel: 559-642-3212, Nearest town: Oakhurst. GPS: 37.297161, -119.534812

478 • D4 | Agnew Meadows (Inyo NF)

Total sites: 20, RV sites: 14, Central water, Vault/pit toilet, No showers, No RV dump, Tent & RV camping: $23-25, Reservable group site: $75, Narrow, single lane road, 3 equestrian sites, Must use bear boxes, Stay limit: 14 days, Open Jun-Sep, Reservations not accepted, Elev: 8376ft/2553m, Tel: 760-924-5500, Nearest town: Mammoth Lakes. GPS: 37.682056, -119.086593

479 • D4 | Aspen (Inyo NF)

Total sites: 56, RV sites: 56, Central water, Vault/pit toilet, No showers, No RV dump, Tent & RV camping: $14, Bear boxes must be used for food storage, Stay limit: 14 days, Max Length: 40ft, Reservations not accepted, Elev: 7536ft/2297m, Tel: 760-873-2400, Nearest town: Lee Vining. GPS: 37.939000, -119.188000

480 • D4 | Badger Flat (Sierra NF)

Total sites: 15, RV sites: 15, No water, Vault/pit toilet, Tent & RV camping: $22, Stay limit: 14 days, Open Jun-Oct, Max Length: 25ft, Reservations not accepted, Elev: 8294ft/2528m, Tel: 559-855-5355, Nearest town: Lakeshore. GPS: 37.270598, -119.115989

481 • D4 | Big Bend (Inyo NF)

Total sites: 17, RV sites: 17, Central water, Vault/pit toilet, No showers, No RV dump, Tent & RV camping: $24, Bear boxes must be used for food storage, Stay limit: 14 days, Open May-Oct, Max Length: 30ft, Reservations not accepted, Elev: 7936ft/2419m, Tel: 760-647-3044, Nearest town: Lee Vining. GPS: 37.945451, -119.203181

482 • D4 | Big Meadow (Inyo NF)

Total sites: 11, RV sites: 11, Central water, Flush toilet, No showers, No RV dump, Tent & RV camping: $25, Stay limit: 14 days, Open Jun-Sep, Reservations not accepted, Elev: 8537ft/2602m, Tel: 760-873-2500, Nearest town: Mammoth Lakes. GPS: 37.509824, -118.714269

483 • D4 | Big Pine Creek (Inyo NF)

Total sites: 30, RV sites: 26, No water, Vault/pit toilet, No showers, No RV dump, Tent & RV camping: $23, Stay limit: 14 days, Open Apr-Oct, Max Length: 45ft, Reservations accepted, Elev: 7759ft/2365m, Tel: 760-872-7018, Nearest town: Big Pine. GPS: 37.125683, -118.433418

484 • D4 | Big Springs (Inyo NF)

Total sites: 26, RV sites: 26, No water, Vault/pit toilet, Tent & RV camping: Free, Bear boxes must be used for food storage, Stay limit: 21 days, Open Jun-Oct, Reservations not accepted, Elev: 7290ft/2222m, Tel: 760-647-3044, Nearest town: Mammoth Lakes. GPS: 37.748779, -118.940918

485 • D4 | Big Trees (Inyo NF)

Total sites: 16, RV sites: 10, Central water, Flush toilet, No showers, No RV dump, Tent & RV camping: $26, Bear boxes must be used for food storage, Stay limit: 7 days, Open May-Sep, Reservations not accepted, Elev: 7451ft/2271m, Tel: 760-873-2500, Nearest town: Bishop. GPS: 37.264893, -118.578857

486 • D4 | Bishop Park (Inyo NF)

Total sites: 21, RV sites: 21, Central water, Flush toilet, No showers, No RV dump, Tent & RV camping: $26, Small RVs only, Bear boxes must be used for food storage, Stay limit: 14 days, Open May-Sep, Reservations not accepted, Elev: 8360ft/2548m, Tel: 760-873-2500, Nearest town: Bishop. GPS: 37.243941, -118.597241

487 • D4 | Bitterbrush (Inyo NF)

Total sites: 30, RV sites: 30, Central water, Vault/pit toilet, No showers, No RV dump, Tent & RV camping: $23, Use bear boxes for food storage, Free in winter - no services, Stay limit: 14 days, Open all year, Reservations not accepted, Elev: 6795ft/2071m, Tel: 760-873-2400, Nearest town: Bishop. GPS: 37.286722, -118.558207

488 • D4 | Bolsillo (Sierra NF)

Total sites: 3, RV sites: 3, Central water, Vault/pit toilet, No showers, No RV dump, Tent & RV camping: Free, Large RVs or motorhomes not recommended for travel on the Kaiser Pass Road, Open Jun-Oct, Reservations not accepted, Elev: 7461ft/2274m, Tel: 559-855-5355, Nearest town: Clovis. GPS: 37.315273, -119.042126

489 • D4 | Bowler (Sierra NF)

Total sites: 12, RV sites: 12, No water, Vault/pit toilet, Tent & RV camping: Free, Stay limit: 14 days, Open Jul-Oct, Max Length: 20ft, Reservations not accepted, Elev: 7110ft/2167m, Tel: 559-877-2218, Nearest town: Oakhurst. GPS: 37.509257, -119.328103

490 • D4 | Catavee (Sierra NF)

Total sites: 23, RV sites: 23, Central water, Flush toilet, No showers, No RV dump, Tent & RV camping: $34-36, Stay limit: 14 days, Open May-Sep, Max Length: 30ft, Reservations accepted, Elev: 7103ft/2165m, Tel: 559-893-2111, Nearest town: Lakeshore. GPS: 37.252695, -119.180675

491 • D4 | Clover Meadow (Sierra NF)

Total sites: 7, RV sites: 7, Central water, Vault/pit toilet, No showers, No RV dump, Tent & RV camping: Free, Stay limit: 14

days, Open Jun-Oct, Max Length: 20ft, Reservations not accepted, Elev: 7047ft/2148m, Tel: 209-966-3638, Nearest town: Fresno. GPS: 37.527022, -119.277625

492 • D4 | Coldwater (Inyo NF)

Total sites: 72, RV sites: 72, Central water, Flush toilet, No showers, No RV dump, Tent & RV camping: $23-25, Bear boxes must be used for food storage, Stay limit: 14 days, Open May-Sep, Max Length: 43ft, Reservations accepted, Elev: 9006ft/2745m, Tel: 760-924-5500, Nearest town: Mammoth Lakes. GPS: 37.598445, -118.995575

493 • D4 | College (Sierra NF)

Total sites: 10, Central water, Flush toilet, No showers, No RV dump, Tents only: $34-36, Stay limit: 14 days, Open May-Sep, Reservations accepted, Elev: 7014ft/2138m, Tel: 559-893-2308, Nearest town: Lakeshore. GPS: 37.251872, -119.169828

494 • D4 | Convict Lake (Inyo NF)

Total sites: 86, RV sites: 86, Central water, Flush toilet, No showers, RV dump, Tent & RV camping: $29, Bear boxes must be used for food storage, Stay limit: 14 days, Open Apr-Oct, Max Length: 55ft, Reservations accepted, Elev: 7552ft/2302m, Tel: 760-924-5500, Nearest town: Mammoth Lakes. GPS: 37.595459, -118.848633

495 • D4 | Crags (Humboldt-Toiyabe NF)

Total sites: 27, RV sites: 27, Central water, Flush toilet, No showers, No RV dump, Tent & RV camping: $23, Group site: $125, Stay limit: 14 days, Open Apr-Oct, Max Length: 45ft, Reservations accepted, Elev: 7113ft/2168m, Tel: 760-932-7070, Nearest town: Bridgeport. GPS: 38.172225, -119.321468

496 • D4 | Deer Creek (Sierra NF)

Total sites: 28, RV sites: 28, Central water, Flush toilet, No showers, No RV dump, Tent & RV camping: $34-38, Stay limit: 14 days, Open May-Sep, Max Length: 40ft, Reservations accepted, Elev: 7047ft/2148m, Tel: 559-893-2111, Nearest town: Clovis. GPS: 37.251807, -119.177016

497 • D4 | East Fork (Mount Morgan) (Inyo NF)

Total sites: 71, RV sites: 46, Central water, Flush toilet, No showers, RV dump, Tent & RV camping: $29, Stay limit: 21 days, Open May-Oct, Max Length: 38ft, Reservations accepted, Elev: 8917ft/2718m, Tel: 760-935-4339, Nearest town: Bishop. GPS: 37.487604, -118.719779

498 • D4 | Ellery Lake (Inyo NF)

Total sites: 12, RV sites: 12, Central water, Vault/pit toilet, No showers, No RV dump, Tent & RV camping: $22-24, Bear boxes must be used for food storage, Stay limit: 14 days, Open Jun-Oct, Max Length: 30ft, Reservations not accepted, Elev: 9564ft/2915m, Tel: 760-647-3044, Nearest town: Lee Vining. GPS: 37.937073, -119.243189

499 • D4 | Fish Creek (Mammoth Pool) (Sierra NF)

Total sites: 3, RV sites: 2, No water, Vault/pit toilet, Tent & RV camping: $27-29, Stay limit: 14 days, Open Jun-Nov, Max Length: 20ft, Reservations accepted, Elev: 4645ft/1416m, Tel: 559-642-3212, Nearest town: North Fork. GPS: 37.261192, -119.355292

500 • D4 | Forks (Tungsten Hills) (Inyo NF)

Total sites: 21, RV sites: 21, Central water, Flush toilet, No showers, No RV dump, Tent & RV camping: $26, Bear boxes must be used for food storage, Stay limit: 14 days, Open May-Sep, Reservations not accepted, Elev: 7858ft/2395m, Tel: 760-873-2500, Nearest town: Bishop. GPS: 37.253226, -118.578598

501 • D4 | Four Jeffrey (Inyo NF)

Total sites: 106, RV sites: 102, Central water, Flush toilet, No showers, RV dump, Tent & RV camping: $30, Bear boxes must be used for food storage, Stay limit: 14 days, Open Apr-Oct, Max Length: 40ft, Reservations accepted, Elev: 8143ft/2482m, Tel: 760-935-4339, Nearest town: Bishop. GPS: 37.248772, -118.570709

502 • D4 | French Camp (Inyo NF)

Total sites: 83, RV sites: 62, Central water, Flush toilet, No showers, RV dump, Tent & RV camping: $29, Bear boxes must be used for food storage, Stay limit: 21 days, Open Apr-Oct, Max Length: 35ft, Reservations accepted, Elev: 7333ft/2235m, Tel: 760-935-4339, Nearest town: Bishop. GPS: 37.551987, -118.683793

503 • D4 | Gaggs Camp (Sierra NF)

Total sites: 11, RV sites: 11, No water, Vault/pit toilet, Tent & RV camping: $26, Open Jun-Nov, Max Length: 22ft, Reservations not accepted, Elev: 5902ft/1799m, Tel: 559-877-2218, Nearest town: Oakhurst. GPS: 37.361452, -119.468405

504 • D4 | Glass Creek (Inyo NF)

Total sites: 50, RV sites: 50, No water, Vault/pit toilet, Tent & RV camping: Free, Open Jun-Oct, Max Length: 45ft, Reservations not accepted, Elev: 7546ft/2300m, Tel: 760-647-3044, Nearest town: June Lake. GPS: 37.752693, -118.990749

505 • D4 | Grandview (Inyo NF)

Total sites: 26, RV sites: 26, No water, Vault/pit toilet, Tent & RV camping: $5, Popular star-gazing spot, may be closed by snow, Stay limit: 14 days, Open all year, Max Length: 35ft, Reservations not accepted, Elev: 8537ft/2602m, Tel: 760-873-2500, Nearest town: Big Pine. GPS: 37.332602, -118.189632

506 • D4 | Granite Creek (Sierra NF)

Total sites: 20, RV sites: 20, No water, Vault/pit toilet, Tent & RV camping: Free, Open Jun-Sep, Max Length: 20ft, Reservations not accepted, Elev: 6982ft/2128m, Tel: 559-877-2218, Nearest town: Fresno. GPS: 37.538647, -119.263963

507 • D4 | Green Creek (Humboldt-Toiyabe NF)

Total sites: 11, RV sites: 11, Central water, Vault/pit toilet, No showers, No RV dump, Tent & RV camping: $20, Group sites: $60-$75, Stay limit: 14 days, Open May-Oct, Reservations not accepted, Elev: 7979ft/2432m, Tel: 760-932-7070, Nearest town: Bridgeport. GPS: 38.111457, -119.275508

508 • D4 | Gull Lake (Inyo NF)

Total sites: 11, RV sites: 11, Water available, Flush toilet, No showers, No RV dump, Tent & RV camping: $23, Bear boxes must be used for food storage, Open Jun-Oct, Max Length: 30ft, Reservations not accepted, Elev: 7638ft/2328m, Tel: 760-647-3044, Nearest town: June Lake. GPS: 37.773193, -119.081543

509 • D4 | Hartley Springs (Inyo NF)

Total sites: 25, RV sites: 25, No water, Vault/pit toilet, Tent & RV camping: $10, Bear lockers available, $10 donation requested, Stay limit: 14 days, Open May-Oct, Reservations not accepted, Elev: 8448ft/2575m, Tel: 760-647-3044, Nearest town: Mammoth Lakes. GPS: 37.771921, -119.037386

510 • D4 | Holiday (Inyo NF)

Total sites: 35, RV sites: 35, Central water, Vault/pit toilet, No showers, No RV dump, Tent & RV camping: $25, Used as overflow only, Free in winter - no services, Bear boxes must be used for food storage, Open all year, Reservations not accepted, Elev: 7192ft/2192m, Tel: 760-873-2500, Nearest town: Mammoth Lakes. GPS: 37.552641, -118.675952

511 • D4 | Honeymoon Flat (Humboldt-Toiyabe NF)

Total sites: 35, RV sites: 26, Central water, Vault/pit toilet, No showers, No RV dump, Tent & RV camping: $20, Stay limit: 14 days, Open May-Sep, Max Length: 45ft, Reservations accepted, Elev: 6932ft/2113m, Tel: 760-932-7070, Nearest town: Bridgeport. GPS: 38.198782, -119.320436

512 • D4 | Intake 2 (Inyo NF)

Total sites: 8, RV sites: 8, Central water, Flush toilet, No showers, No RV dump, Tent & RV camping: $26, Bear boxes must be used for food storage, Open all year, Reservations not accepted, Elev: 8192ft/2497m, Tel: 760-873-2500, Nearest town: Bishop. GPS: 37.245428, -118.589856

513 • D4 | Iris Meadow (Inyo NF)

Total sites: 14, RV sites: 14, Central water, Flush toilet, No showers, No RV dump, Tent & RV camping: $25, Stay limit: 21 days, Open May-Sep, Reservations not accepted, Elev: 8396ft/2559m, Tel: 760-873-2500, Nearest town: Mammoth Lakes. GPS: 37.518316, -118.712366

514 • D4 | Jackass Meadow (Sierra NF)

Total sites: 44, RV sites: 44, No water, Vault/pit toilet, Tent & RV camping: $28-30, Stay limit: 14 days, Open May-Sep, Max Length: 46ft, Reservations accepted, Elev: 7195ft/2193m, Tel: 559-893-2308, Nearest town: Lakeshore. GPS: 37.277105, -118.964304

515 • D4 | Junction (Inyo NF)

Total sites: 13, RV sites: 5, No water, Vault/pit toilet, No showers, No RV dump, Tent & RV camping: $19-21, Bear boxes must be used for food storage, Open Jun-Oct, Max Length: 40ft, Reservations not accepted, Elev: 9550ft/2911m, Tel: 760-647-3044, Nearest town: Lee Vining. GPS: 37.937858, -119.251219

516 • D4 | June Lake (Inyo NF)

Total sites: 28, RV sites: 22, Central water, Flush toilet, No showers, No RV dump, Tent & RV camping: $23-25, Stay limit: 14 days, Open Apr-Oct, Max Length: 60ft, Reservations accepted, Elev: 7658ft/2334m, Tel: 760-647-3044, Nearest town: June Lake. GPS: 37.782227, -119.075928

517 • D4 | Kinnikinnick (Sierra NF)

Total sites: 27, RV sites: 27, Central water, Flush toilet, No showers, No RV dump, Tent & RV camping: $34-36, Stay limit: 14 days, Open May-Sep, Max Length: 40ft, Reservations accepted, Elev: 7103ft/2165m, Tel: 559-893-2111, Nearest town: Lakeshore. GPS: 37.253231, -119.177800

518 • D4 | Lake George (Inyo NF)

Total sites: 15, RV sites: 15, Central water, Flush toilet, No showers, No RV dump, Tent & RV camping: $24, Bear boxes must be used for food storage, Open May-Sep, Reservations not accepted, Elev: 9058ft/2761m, Tel: 760-924-5500, Nearest town: Mammoth Lakes. GPS: 37.602051, -119.010254

519 • D4 | Lake Mary (Inyo NF)

Total sites: 48, RV sites: 48, Central water, Flush toilet, No showers, No RV dump, Tent & RV camping: $23-25, Open May-Sep, Max Length: 21ft, Reservations accepted, Elev: 8976ft/2736m, Tel: 650-322-1181, Nearest town: Mammoth Lakes. GPS: 37.606934, -119.007080

520 • D4 | Little Jackass (Sierra NF)

Total sites: 5, No water, Vault/pit toilet, Tents only: Free, Open Jun-Sep, Max Length: 20ft, Elev: 4944ft/1507m, Tel: 559-877-2218, Nearest town: Fresno. GPS: 37.399069, -119.337111

521 • D4 | Lower Billy Creek (Sierra NF)

Total sites: 15, RV sites: 15, Central water, Vault/pit toilet, No showers, No RV dump, Tent & RV camping: $34-38, Open May-Sep, Max Length: 35ft, Reservations accepted, Elev: 7064ft/2153m, Tel: 559-893-2111, Nearest town: Lakeshore. GPS: 37.237726, -119.228551

522 • D4 | Lower Deadman (Inyo NF)

Total sites: 15, RV sites: 15, No water, Vault/pit toilet, Tent & RV camping: Free, Stay limit: 14 days, Reservations not accepted, Elev: 7818ft/2383m, Nearest town: Mammoth Lakes. GPS: 37.720485, -119.009028

523 • D4 | Lower Lee Vining (Inyo NF)

Total sites: 60, RV sites: 60, No water, Vault/pit toilet, Tent & RV camping: $14, Bear boxes must be used for food storage, Stay limit: 14 days, Reservations not accepted, Elev: 7317ft/2230m, Nearest town: Lee Vining. GPS: 37.928875, -119.153332

524 • D4 | Lower Twin Lakes (Humboldt-Toiyabe NF)

Total sites: 14, RV sites: 11, Central water, Flush toilet, No showers, No RV dump, Tent & RV camping: $26, Stay limit: 14 days, Open Apr-Oct, Max Length: 35ft, Reservations accepted, Elev: 7119ft/2170m, Tel: 760-932-7070, Nearest town: Bridgeport. GPS: 38.170205, -119.323546

525 • D4 | Lower Virginia Creek Dispersed (Humboldt-Toiyabe NF)

Total sites: 22, RV sites: 22, No water, Vault/pit toilet, Tent & RV camping: Free, Stay limit: 14 days, Reservations not accepted, Elev: 9055ft/2760m, Tel: 760-932-7070, Nearest town: Lee Vining. GPS: 38.067599, -119.221573

526 • D4 | Mammoth Pool (Sierra NF)

Total sites: 47, RV sites: 47, Central water, Vault/pit toilet, No showers, No RV dump, Tent & RV camping: $28-30, CG closed 2021-22 seasons - fire damage, Stay limit: 14 days, Open May-Sep, Max Length: 30ft, Reservations accepted, Elev: 3691ft/1125m,

Tel: 559-642-3212, Nearest town: North Fork. GPS: 37.344157, -119.333965

527 • D4 | McGee Creek (Inyo NF)

Total sites: 28, RV sites: 28, Central water, Flush toilet, No showers, No RV dump, Tent & RV camping: $27, Bear boxes must be used for food storage, Stay limit: 14 days, Open Apr-Oct, Max Length: 35ft, Reservations accepted, Elev: 7536ft/2297m, Tel: 760-935-4213, Nearest town: Mammoth Lakes. GPS: 37.563965, -118.785400

528 • D4 | McGee Pass TH (Inyo NF)

Total sites: 2, RV sites: 0, No water, Vault/pit toilet, No showers, No RV dump, Tents only: Free, 1 night stay for backpackers, Bear boxes must be used for food storage, Reservations not accepted, Elev: 7843ft/2391m, Tel: 760-935-4213, Nearest town: Mammoth Lakes. GPS: 37.551454, -118.802098

529 • D4 | Minaret Falls (Inyo NF)

Total sites: 27, RV sites: 0, Central water, Vault/pit toilet, No showers, No RV dump, Tents only: $23, Narrow single lane road, Bear boxes must be used for food storage, Open Jun-Sep, Reservations not accepted, Elev: 7690ft/2344m, Tel: 760-924-5500, Nearest town: Mammoth Lakes. GPS: 37.639648, -119.083252

530 • D4 | Mono Creek (Sierra NF)

Total sites: 14, RV sites: 14, No water, Vault/pit toilet, No showers, No RV dump, Tent & RV camping: $28-30, Stay limit: 14 days, Open May-Sep, Max Length: 25ft, Reservations accepted, Elev: 7444ft/2269m, Tel: 559-893-2111, Nearest town: Lakeshore. GPS: 37.357131, -118.995552

531 • D4 | Mono Hot Springs (Sierra NF)

Total sites: 31, RV sites: 31, No water, Vault/pit toilet, Tent & RV camping: $28-30, Stay limit: 14 days, Open May-Sep, Max Length: 25ft, Reservations accepted, Elev: 6572ft/2003m, Tel: 559-893-2111, Nearest town: Lakeshore. GPS: 37.326181, -119.018758

532 • D4 | Mosquito Flat (Inyo NF)

Total sites: 10, RV sites: 0, No water, Vault/pit toilet, Tents only: Free, Walk-to sites, Intended for backpackers, Bear boxes must be used for food storage, Stay limit: 1 day, Open May-Sep, Reservations not accepted, Elev: 10282ft/3134m, Tel: 760-873-2500, Nearest town: Mammoth Lakes. GPS: 37.435722, -118.746799

533 • D4 | Mountain Glen (Inyo NF)

Total sites: 5, RV sites: 0, No water, Vault/pit toilet, Tents only: $24, Bear boxes must be used for food storage, Stay limit: 7 days, Open May-Sep, Reservations not accepted, Elev: 8534ft/2601m, Tel: 760-873-2500, Nearest town: Bishop. GPS: 37.223776, -118.566568

534 • D4 | New Shady Rest (Inyo NF)

Total sites: 92, RV sites: 92, Central water, Flush toilet, No showers, RV dump, Tent & RV camping: $23-25, Bear boxes must be used for food storage, Open May-Oct, Max Length: 38ft, Reservations accepted, Elev: 7825ft/2385m, Tel: 760-924-5500, Nearest town: Mammoth Lakes. GPS: 37.648174, -118.961229

535 • D4 | North Lake (Inyo NF)

Total sites: 11, RV sites: 0, Central water, Vault/pit toilet, No showers, No RV dump, Tents only: $23, Bear boxes must be used for food storage, Stay limit: 7 days, Open Jun-Sep, Reservations not accepted, Elev: 9377ft/2858m, Tel: 760-873-2500, Nearest town: Bishop. GPS: 37.227404, -118.627367

536 • D4 | Oh Ridge (Inyo NF)

Total sites: 140, RV sites: 135, Central water, Flush toilet, No showers, No RV dump, Tent & RV camping: $27-29, Bear boxes must be used for food storage, Stay limit: 14 days, Open Apr-Oct, Max Length: 50ft, Reservations accepted, Elev: 7713ft/2351m, Tel: 760-647-3044, Nearest town: June Lake. GPS: 37.799136, -119.071392

537 • D4 | Old Shady Rest (Inyo NF)

Total sites: 47, RV sites: 47, Central water, Flush toilet, No showers, RV dump, Tent & RV camping: $23-25, Fee for RV dump, Bear boxes must be used for food storage, Open May-Sep, Max Length: 58ft, Reservations accepted, Elev: 7851ft/2393m, Tel: 760-924-5500, Nearest town: Mammoth Lakes. GPS: 37.650167, -118.962926

538 • D4 | Paha (Humboldt-Toiyabe NF)

Total sites: 21, RV sites: 21, Central water, Flush toilet, No showers, No RV dump, Tent & RV camping: $23, Stay limit: 14 days, Open May-Sep, Max Length: 45ft, Reservations accepted, Elev: 7060ft/2152m, Tel: 760-932-7070, Nearest town: Bridgeport. GPS: 38.179632, -119.322969

539 • D4 | Pine City (Inyo NF)

Total sites: 10, RV sites: 10, Central water, Flush toilet, No showers, No RV dump, Tent & RV camping: $24, Bear boxes must be used for food storage, Open May-Sep, Reservations not accepted, Elev: 9022ft/2750m, Tel: 760-924-5500, Nearest town: Mammoth Lakes. GPS: 37.604235, -119.000323

540 • D4 | Pine Grove (Inyo NF)

Total sites: 11, RV sites: 11, Central water, Vault/pit toilet, No showers, No RV dump, Tent & RV camping: $29, Bear boxes must be used for food storage, Stay limit: 21 days, Open May-Sep, Max Length: 14ft, Reservations not accepted, Elev: 9386ft/2861m, Tel: 760-873-2400, Nearest town: Bishop. GPS: 37.470807, -118.724565

541 • D4 | Portal Forebay (Sierra NF)

Total sites: 11, RV sites: 11, No water, Vault/pit toilet, Tent & RV camping: $22, Large RVs not recommended, Open Jun-Sep, Reservations not accepted, Elev: 7195ft/2193m, Tel: 559-855-5355, Nearest town: Lakeshore. GPS: 37.320217, -119.067034

542 • D4 | Pumice Flat (Inyo NF)

Total sites: 16, RV sites: 16, Central water, Flush toilet, No showers, No RV dump, Tent & RV camping: $23, Narrow single lane road, Open Jun-Sep, Reservations not accepted, Elev: 7785ft/2373m, Tel: 760-924-5500, Nearest town: Mammoth Lakes. GPS: 37.648529, -119.074577

543 • D4 | Rancheria (Sierra NF)

Total sites: 149, RV sites: 86, Central water, Flush toilet, No showers, No RV dump, Tent & RV camping: $34-36, 3 group sites: $94, Open May-Oct, Max Length: 71ft, Reservations accepted, Elev: 7103ft/2165m, Tel: 559-893-2111, Nearest town: Lakeshore. GPS: 37.247079, -119.162667

544 • D4 | Reds Meadow (Inyo NF)

Total sites: 56, RV sites: 56, Central water, Flush toilet, No showers, No RV dump, Tent & RV camping: $23, Narrow single lane road, Bear boxes must be used for food storage, Campers may drive into area - shuttle fee applies, Open Jun-Sep, Reservations not accepted, Elev: 7710ft/2350m, Tel: 760-924-5500, Nearest town: Mammoth Lakes. GPS: 37.618896, -119.073242

545 • D4 | Reversed Creek (Inyo NF)

Total sites: 16, RV sites: 16, Central water, Flush toilet, No showers, No RV dump, Tent & RV camping: $23-25, Bear boxes must be used for food storage, Stay limit: 14 days, Open May-Oct, Max Length: 45ft, Reservations accepted, Elev: 7615ft/2321m, Tel: 760-647-3044, Nearest town: June Lake. GPS: 37.770315, -119.084611

546 • D4 | Robinson Creek North (Humboldt-Toiyabe NF)

Total sites: 30, RV sites: 30, Central water, Vault/pit toilet, No showers, No RV dump, Tent & RV camping: $23, Stay limit: 14 days, Open Apr-Sep, Max Length: 40ft, Reservations accepted, Elev: 7041ft/2146m, Tel: 760-932-7070, Nearest town: Bridgeport. GPS: 38.185216, -119.320946

547 • D4 | Robinson Creek South (Humboldt-Toiyabe NF)

Total sites: 25, RV sites: 14, Central water, Vault/pit toilet, No showers, No RV dump, Tent & RV camping: $23, Stay limit: 14 days, Open May-Sep, Max Length: 40ft, Reservations accepted, Elev: 7044ft/2147m, Tel: 760-932-7092, Nearest town: Bridgeport. GPS: 38.183628, -119.321706

548 • D4 | Rock Creek (Sierra NF)

Total sites: 18, RV sites: 18, Central water, Vault/pit toilet, No showers, No RV dump, Tent & RV camping: $26, CG closed 2021-2022 seasons - massive tree hazard removal, No services in winter, Stay limit: 14 days, Open May-Sep, Max Length: 30ft, Reservations accepted, Elev: 4436ft/1352m, Tel: 559-642-3212, Nearest town: North Fork. GPS: 37.291583, -119.361515

549 • D4 | Rock Creek Lake (Inyo NF)

Total sites: 26, RV sites: 7, Central water, Flush toilet, Free showers, No RV dump, Tent & RV camping: $29, Bear boxes must be used for food storage, Stay limit: 7 days, Open May-Oct, Reservations accepted, Elev: 9733ft/2967m, Tel: 760-873-2500, Nearest town: Toms Place. GPS: 37.450816, -118.735682

550 • D4 | Sabrina (Inyo NF)

Total sites: 18, RV sites: 18, Central water, Vault/pit toilet, No showers, No RV dump, Tent & RV camping: $28, Bear boxes must be used for food storage, Stay limit: 7 days, Open May-Sep, Max Length: 16ft, Reservations not accepted, Elev: 8980ft/2737m, Tel: 760-873-2500, Nearest town: Bishop. GPS: 37.219463, -118.606592

551 • D4 | Saddlebag Lake (Inyo NF)

Total sites: 20, RV sites: 20, Central water, Vault/pit toilet, No showers, No RV dump, Tent & RV camping: $24, Group site: $90, Last 2 miles one-lane windy dirt road, Bear boxes must be used for food storage, No large RVs, Open Jun-Oct, Max Length: 16ft, Reservations not accepted, Elev: 10202ft/3110m, Tel: 760-647-3044, Nearest town: Lee Vining. GPS: 37.964357, -119.270883

552 • D4 | Sage Flat (Inyo NF)

Total sites: 28, RV sites: 28, Central water, Vault/pit toilet, No showers, No RV dump, Tent & RV camping: $23, Bear boxes must be used for food storage, Stay limit: 14 days, Open Apr-Oct, Reservations not accepted, Elev: 7619ft/2322m, Tel: 760-873-2400, Nearest town: Big Pine. GPS: 37.130068, -118.412321

553 • D4 | Sample Meadow (Sierra NF)

Total sites: 16, RV sites: 16, No water, Vault/pit toilet, Tent & RV camping: Free, Not recommended for large RVs or motorhomes, Stay limit: 14 days, Open Jun-Oct, Max Length: 20ft, Reservations not accepted, Elev: 7897ft/2407m, Tel: 559-855-5355, Nearest town: Lakeshore. GPS: 37.335862, -119.156009

554 • D4 | Sawmill (Inyo NF)

Total sites: 12, RV sites: 0, No water, Vault/pit toilet, Tents only: $17, Walk-to sites, .25 mi, Bear boxes must be used for food storage, Open Jun-Oct, Elev: 9749ft/2971m, Tel: 760-647-3044, Nearest town: Lee Vining. GPS: 37.957621, -119.270162

555 • D4 | Sherwin Creek (Inyo NF)

Total sites: 85, RV sites: 70, Central water, Vault/pit toilet, No showers, No RV dump, Tent & RV camping: $23-25, Also walk-to sites, Bear boxes must be used for food storage, Open May-Sep, Max Length: 60ft, Reservations accepted, Elev: 7585ft/2312m, Tel: 760-924-5500, Nearest town: Mammoth Lakes. GPS: 37.630127, -118.937500

556 • D4 | Silver Lake (Inyo NF)

Total sites: 63, RV sites: 63, Central water, Flush toilet, No showers, No RV dump, Tent & RV camping: $23-25, Bear boxes must be used for food storage, Open Apr-Oct, Max Length: 38ft, Reservations accepted, Elev: 7244ft/2208m, Tel: 760-647-3044, Nearest town: June Lake. GPS: 37.783165, -119.125897

557 • D4 | Sweetwater (Coarsegold) (Sierra NF)

Total sites: 7, RV sites: 7, No water, Vault/pit toilet, Tent & RV camping: $27-29, Stay limit: 14 days, Open May-Sep, Max Length: 20ft, Reservations accepted, Elev: 3835ft/1169m, Tel: 559-642-3212, Nearest town: Coarsegold. GPS: 37.364525, -119.352583

558 • D4 | Tioga Lake (Inyo NF)

Total sites: 13, RV sites: 13, Central water, Vault/pit toilet, No showers, No RV dump, Tent & RV camping: $22, Bear boxes must be used for food storage, Open Jun-Oct, Max Length: 16ft, Reservations not accepted, Elev: 9659ft/2944m, Tel: 760-647-3044, Nearest town: Lee Vining. GPS: 37.927207, -119.255054

559 • D4 | Trumbull Lake (Humboldt-Toiyabe NF)

Total sites: 32, RV sites: 32, Central water, Vault/pit toilet, No showers, No RV dump, Tent & RV camping: $23, Stay limit: 14 days, Open Jun-Oct, Max Length: 82ft, Reservations accepted, Elev: 9688ft/2953m, Tel: 760-932-7070, Nearest town: Bridgeport. GPS: 38.051724, -119.256892

560 • D4 | Tuff (Inyo NF)

Total sites: 34, RV sites: 34, Central water, Vault/pit toilet, No showers, RV dump, Tent & RV camping: $27, Bear boxes must be used for food storage, Stay limit: 21 days, Open Apr-Oct, Max Length: 45ft, Reservations accepted, Elev: 7021ft/2140m, Tel: 760-935-4026, Nearest town: Bishop. GPS: 37.562341, -118.668409

561 • D4 | Twin Lakes (Inyo NF)

Total sites: 94, RV sites: 94, Central water, Flush toilet, Free showers, No RV dump, Tent & RV camping: $23-25, Bear boxes must be used for food storage, Open May-Oct, Max Length: 55ft, Reservations accepted, Elev: 8661ft/2640m, Tel: 760-924-5500, Nearest town: Mammoth Lakes. GPS: 37.615885, -119.006694

562 • D4 | Upper Billy Creek (Sierra NF)

Total sites: 44, RV sites: 44, Central water, Flush toilet, No showers, No RV dump, Tent & RV camping: $33-35, Group site: $99, Stay limit: 14 days, Open May-Sep, Max Length: 30ft, Reservations accepted, Elev: 7100ft/2164m, Tel: 559-893-2111, Nearest town: Eastwood. GPS: 37.238287, -119.227248

563 • D4 | Upper Deadman (Inyo NF)

Total sites: 15, RV sites: 15, No water, No toilets, Tent & RV camping: Free, No bear lockers available, Stay limit: 14 days, Max Length: 45ft, Reservations not accepted, Elev: 7802ft/2378m, Tel: 760-873-2400, Nearest town: June Lake. GPS: 37.721182, -119.011747

564 • D4 | Upper Pine Grove (Inyo NF)

Total sites: 8, RV sites: 8, Central water, Vault/pit toilet, No showers, No RV dump, Tent & RV camping: $29, Small RVs only, Bear boxes must be used for food storage, Stay limit: 7 days, Open May-Sep, Reservations not accepted, Elev: 9412ft/2869m, Tel: 760-873-2500, Nearest town: Crowley Lake. GPS: 37.469195, -118.725567

565 • D4 | Upper Sage (Inyo NF)

Total sites: 20, RV sites: 20, Central water, Flush toilet, No showers, No RV dump, Tent & RV camping: $27, Bear boxes must be used for food storage, Stay limit: 14 days, Open Apr-Oct, Max Length: 35ft, Reservations accepted, Elev: 7515ft/2291m, Tel: 760-872-7018, Nearest town: Big Pine. GPS: 37.128852, -118.421355

566 • D4 | Upper Soda Springs (Inyo NF)

Total sites: 28, RV sites: 28, Central water, Vault/pit toilet, No showers, No RV dump, Tent & RV camping: $23, Narrow single lane road, Bear boxes must be used for food storage, Campers may drive into area - shuttle fee applies, Open Jun-Sep, Reservations not accepted, Elev: 7779ft/2371m, Tel: 760-924-5500, Nearest town: Mammoth Lakes. GPS: 37.653322, -119.077692

567 • D4 | Upper Virginia Creek (Humboldt-Toiyabe NF)

Total sites: 15, RV sites: 15, No water, Vault/pit toilet, Tent & RV camping: Free, Bear boxes, Stay limit: 14 days, Max Length: 25ft, Reservations not accepted, Elev: 9373ft/2857m, Tel: 760-932-7070, Nearest town: Lee Vining. GPS: 38.059815, -119.236567

568 • D4 | Vermillion (Sierra NF)

Total sites: 34, RV sites: 34, Central water, Vault/pit toilet, No showers, No RV dump, Tent & RV camping: $28-30, Water should be boiled, Stay limit: 14 days, Open May-Sep, Max Length: 30ft, Reservations accepted, Elev: 7835ft/2388m, Tel: 559-893-2111, Nearest town: Lakeshore. GPS: 37.380937, -119.013317

569 • D4 | Ward Lake (Sierra NF)

Total sites: 17, RV sites: 0, No water, Vault/pit toilet, Tents only: $22-24, Open Jun-Oct, Max Length: 25ft, Reservations not accepted, Elev: 7388ft/2252m, Tel: 559-855-5355, Nearest town: Lakeshore. GPS: 37.301068, -118.986093

570 • D4 | West Kaiser (Sierra NF)

Total sites: 8, RV sites: 8, No water, Vault/pit toilet, Tent & RV camping: Free, Open Jun-Dec, Max Length: 25ft, Reservations not accepted, Elev: 5564ft/1696m, Tel: 559-855-5355, Nearest town: Shaver Lake. GPS: 37.344842, -119.240181

571 • D4 | Whiskers (Sierra NF)

Total sites: 8, RV sites: 8, No water, Vault/pit toilet, Tent & RV camping: $27, Road not maintained for passenger cars, Open Jun-Nov, Max Length: 20ft, Reservations not accepted, Elev: 5374ft/1638m, Tel: 559-877-2218, Nearest town: Oakhurst. GPS: 37.333804, -119.492372

572 • D4 | Whiskey Falls (Sierra NF)

Total sites: 14, RV sites: 14, No water, Vault/pit toilet, Tent & RV camping: Free, Open Jun-Nov, Reservations not accepted, Elev: 5902ft/1799m, Tel: 559-877-2218, Nearest town: North Fork. GPS: 37.285756, -119.441554

573 • D4 | Willow (Inyo NF)

Total sites: 8, RV sites: 0, No water, Vault/pit toilet, Tents only: $23, Bear boxes must be used for food storage, Stay limit: 7 days, Open May-Sep, Reservations not accepted, Elev: 9354ft/2851m, Tel: 760-873-2500, Nearest town: Bishop. GPS: 37.194000, -118.561000

574 • E1 | China Camp (Los Padres NF)

Total sites: 9, RV sites: 9, No water, Vault/pit toilet, Tent & RV camping: $20, Stay limit: 14 days, Generator hours: 0800-2200, Open May-Oct, Max Length: 20ft, Reservations accepted, Elev: 4557ft/1389m, Tel: 831-385-5434, Nearest town: Carmel. GPS: 36.295503, -121.566901

575 • E1 | White Oaks (Los Padres NF)

Total sites: 8, RV sites: 8, No water, Vault/pit toilet, No showers, No RV dump, Tent & RV camping: $20, Generator hours: 0600-2200, Open May-Oct, Max Length: 30ft, Reservations accepted, Elev: 4114ft/1254m, Tel: 831-385-5434, Nearest town: Greenfield. GPS: 36.325959, -121.574882

576 • E2 | Bretz Mill (Sierra NF)

Total sites: 10, RV sites: 10, No water, Vault/pit toilet, Tent & RV camping: Free, Stay limit: 14 days, Open all year, Max Length: 24ft, Reservations not accepted, Elev: 3356ft/1023m, Tel: 559-855-5355, Nearest town: Shaver Lake. GPS: 37.037897, -119.240066

577 • E2 | Camp 4 (Sequoia NF)

Total sites: 5, RV sites: 5, No water, Vault/pit toilet, Tent & RV camping: Free, Unsuitable for trailers, Open all year, Max Length:

25ft, Reservations not accepted, Elev: 1129ft/344m, Tel: 559-338-2251, Nearest town: Fresno. GPS: 36.856728, -119.107775

578 • E2 | Camp 4 1/2 (Sequoia NF)

Total sites: 4, RV sites: 4, No water, Vault/pit toilet, Tent & RV camping: Free, Open all year, Max Length: 25ft, Reservations not accepted, Elev: 1027ft/313m, Tel: 559-338-2251, Nearest town: Fresno. GPS: 36.861834, -119.122033

579 • E2 | Dinkey Creek (Sierra NF)

Total sites: 123, RV sites: 70, Central water, Flush toilet, Pay showers, No RV dump, Tent & RV camping: $34-36, Group site: $202, Open May-Oct, Max Length: 50ft, Reservations accepted, Elev: 5876ft/1791m, Tel: 559-841-2705, Nearest town: Dinkey Creek. GPS: 37.072703, -119.155741

580 • E2 | Dorabelle (Sierra NF)

Total sites: 64, RV sites: 42, Central water, Vault/pit toilet, No showers, No RV dump, Tent & RV camping: $35-37, Stay limit: 14 days, Open May-Oct, Max Length: 35ft, Reservations accepted, Elev: 5430ft/1655m, Tel: 559-841-3533, Nearest town: Shaver Lake. GPS: 37.113016, -119.309746

581 • E2 | Gigantea (Sierra NF)

Total sites: 10, RV sites: 10, No water, Vault/pit toilet, Tent & RV camping: $24, Stay limit: 14 days, Open May-Oct, Max Length: 35ft, Reservations not accepted, Elev: 6404ft/1952m, Tel: 559-855-5355, Nearest town: Shaver Lake. GPS: 37.015739, -119.106713

582 • E2 | Green Cabin Flat (Sequoia NF)

Total sites: 5, RV sites: 5, No water, Vault/pit toilet, Tent & RV camping: Free, Max Length: 25ft, Reservations not accepted, Elev: 1063ft/324m, Tel: 559-338-2251, Nearest town: Fresno. GPS: 36.859925, -119.102895

583 • E2 | Kirch Flat (Sierra NF)

Total sites: 17, RV sites: 17, No water, Vault/pit toilet, Tent & RV camping: Free, Stay limit: 14 days, Open all year, Max Length: 30ft, Elev: 1047ft/319m, Tel: 559-885-5355, Nearest town: Prather. GPS: 36.879737, -119.150459

584 • E2 | Mill Flat (Sequoia NF)

Total sites: 5, RV sites: 5, No water, Vault/pit toilet, Tent & RV camping: Free, Open all year, Max Length: 25ft, Reservations not accepted, Elev: 1083ft/330m, Tel: 559-338-2251, Nearest town: Fresno. GPS: 36.856581, -119.096994

585 • E2 | Summit (Sierra NF)

Total sites: 6, RV sites: 0, No water, Vault/pit toilet, Tents only: Free, High-clearance vehicle required, Open Jun-Oct, Reservations not accepted, Elev: 6618ft/2017m, Tel: 559-877-2218, Nearest town: Oakhurst. GPS: 37.082000, -119.199000

586 • E3 | Abbott Creek (Sequoia NF)

Total sites: 2, RV sites: 2, No water, No toilets, Tent & RV camping: Free, Reservations not accepted, Elev: 6004ft/1830m, Nearest town: Miramonte. GPS: 36.768003, -118.974786

587 • E3 | Big Meadow (Sequoia NF)

Total sites: 38, RV sites: 38, No water, Vault/pit toilet, Tent & RV camping: $23, Bear boxes must be used for food storage, Reservations accepted, Elev: 7598ft/2316m, Tel: 559-338-2251, Nearest town: Cedarbrook. GPS: 36.721027, -118.820668

588 • E3 | Black Rock Reservoir/PGE (Sierra NF)

Total sites: 10, RV sites: 0, No water, Vault/pit toilet, Tents only: $14, Pet fee: $2/night, Stay limit: 14 days, Open all year, Reservations not accepted, Elev: 4190ft/1277m, Tel: 559-855-5355. GPS: 36.921428, -119.021229

589 • E3 | Buck Meadow (Sierra NF)

Total sites: 10, RV sites: 10, No water, Vault/pit toilet, Tent & RV camping: $22, Stay limit: 14 days, Open May-Sep, Max Length: 35ft, Reservations not accepted, Elev: 6837ft/2084m, Tel: 559-855-5355, Nearest town: Shaver Lake. GPS: 37.010791, -119.063861

590 • E3 | Buck Rock (Sequoia NF)

Total sites: 8, RV sites: 8, No water, Vault/pit toilet, Tent & RV camping: Free, Max Length: 16ft, Reservations not accepted, Elev: 7779ft/2371m, Tel: 559-338-2251, Nearest town: Grant Grove. GPS: 36.722406, -118.850873

591 • E3 | Convict Flat (Sequoia NF)

Total sites: 5, RV sites: 5, No water, Vault/pit toilet, Tent & RV camping: Free, Open May-Nov, Max Length: 24ft, Reservations not accepted, Elev: 3225ft/983m, Tel: 559-338-2251, Nearest town: Grant Grove Village. GPS: 36.818497, -118.832174

592 • E3 | Cottonwood Lakes TH (Inyo NF)

Total sites: 12, RV sites: 0, Central water, Vault/pit toilet, No showers, No RV dump, Tents only: $6, Walk-to sites, Bear boxes must be used for food storage, Stay limit: 1 day, Open May-Oct, Reservations not accepted, Elev: 10042ft/3061m, Tel: 760-876-6200, Nearest town: Lone Pine. GPS: 36.453343, -118.169283

593 • E3 | Cottonwood Pass TH (Inyo NF)

Total sites: 18, RV sites: 0, Central water, Vault/pit toilet, No showers, No RV dump, Tents only: $6, Walk-to sites, Bear boxes must be used for food storage, Stay limit: 1 day, Open May-Oct, Reservations not accepted, Elev: 9967ft/3038m, Tel: 760-876-6200, Nearest town: Lone Pine. GPS: 36.448314, -118.168828

594 • E3 | Eshom (Sequoia NF)

Total sites: 17, RV sites: 14, Central water, Vault/pit toilet, No showers, No RV dump, Tent & RV camping: $27-29, 7 double sites, Open May-Sep, Max Length: 75ft, Reservations accepted, Elev: 4915ft/1498m, Tel: 559-338-2251, Nearest town: Woodlake. GPS: 36.689143, -118.950277

595 • E3 | Horse Camp (Sequoia NF)

Total sites: 5, RV sites: 5, No water, Vault/pit toilet, Tent & RV camping: Free, Horse corrals, Open Jun-Oct, Reservations not accepted, Elev: 7648ft/2331m, Tel: 559-338-2251, Nearest town: Grant Grove. GPS: 36.716919, -118.849716

596 • E3 | Horseshoe Meadows Horse Camp (Inyo NF)

Total sites: 10, RV sites: 10, Central water, Vault/pit toilet, No showers, No RV dump, Tent & RV camping: $12, Bear boxes must be used for food storage, Open May-Oct, Reservations not accepted, Elev: 10060ft/3066m, Tel: 760-876-6200, Nearest town: Lone Pine. GPS: 36.452151, -118.169866

597 • E3 | Hume Lake (Sequoia NF)

Total sites: 74, RV sites: 50, Central water, Flush toilet, No showers, No RV dump, Tent & RV camping: $29-31, Open May-Sep, Max Length: 35ft, Reservations accepted, Elev: 5328ft/1624m, Tel: 559-338-2251, Nearest town: Hume. GPS: 36.794506, -118.907969

598 • E3 | Landslide (Sequoia NF)

Total sites: 9, RV sites: 3, No water, Vault/pit toilet, Tent & RV camping: $25, Open May-Sep, Max Length: 16ft, Reservations not accepted, Elev: 5840ft/1780m, Tel: 559-338-2251, Nearest town: Grant Grove. GPS: 36.763554, -118.882883

599 • E3 | Lone Pine (Inyo NF)

Total sites: 44, RV sites: 37, Central water, Vault/pit toilet, No showers, No RV dump, Tent & RV camping: $26, Group fee: $60, Bear boxes must be used for food storage, Open Apr-Oct, Max Length: 50ft, Reservations accepted, Elev: 5846ft/1782m, Tel: 760-937-6070, Nearest town: Lone Pine. GPS: 36.597704, -118.184667

600 • E3 | Lower Grays Meadow (Inyo NF)

Total sites: 31, RV sites: 31, Central water, Vault/pit toilet, No showers, No RV dump, Tent & RV camping: $25, Bear boxes must be used for food storage, Open Apr-Oct, Max Length: 40ft, Reservations accepted, Elev: 5968ft/1819m, Tel: 760-937-6070, Nearest town: Independence. GPS: 36.781531, -118.284712

601 • E3 | Marmot Rock/PGE (Sierra NF)

Total sites: 15, No water, Vault/pit toilet, Tents only: $24, Walk-to sites, $18 when no water, $2/night pet fee, Stay limit: 14 days, Open May-Sep, Reservations accepted, Elev: 8179ft/2493m, Tel: 559-855-5355, Nearest town: Shaver Lake. GPS: 37.077445, -118.976501

602 • E3 | Mt. Whitney Trailhead (Inyo NF)

Total sites: 25, RV sites: 0, Central water, Vault/pit toilet, No showers, No RV dump, Tents only: $15, Walk-to sites, Camping not allowed in parking lot, Stay limit: 1 day, Reservations not accepted, Elev: 8340ft/2542m, Tel: 760-876-6200, Nearest town: Lone Pine. GPS: 36.586788, -118.239658

603 • E3 | Onion Valley (Inyo NF)

Total sites: 29, RV sites: 12, No water, Vault/pit toilet, No showers, No RV dump, Tent & RV camping: $22-25, Trailers not recommended - tent trailers OK, Bear boxes must be used for food storage, Open Apr-Oct, Max Length: 25ft, Reservations accepted, Elev: 9173ft/2796m, Tel: 760-876-6200, Nearest town: Independence. GPS: 36.771729, -118.340576

604 • E3 | Princess (Sequoia NF)

Total sites: 82, RV sites: 64, Central water, Vault/pit toilet, No showers, RV dump, Tent & RV camping: $29-31, Open May-Sep, Max Length: 50ft, Reservations accepted, Elev: 5948ft/1813m, Tel: 559-338-2251, Nearest town: Hume. GPS: 36.804237, -118.940967

605 • E3 | Sawmill Flat (Sierra NF)

Total sites: 15, RV sites: 0, No water, Vault/pit toilet, Tents only: Free, Stay limit: 14 days, Open Jun-Dec, Reservations not accepted, Elev: 6811ft/2076m, Tel: 559-855-5355, Nearest town: Fresno. GPS: 36.969583, -119.017023

606 • E3 | Stony Creek (Sequoia NF)

Total sites: 49, RV sites: 31, Central water, Flush toilet, No showers, No RV dump, Tent & RV camping: $29-31, Open May-Sep, Max Length: 30ft, Reservations accepted, Elev: 6522ft/1988m, Tel: 559-335-2232, Nearest town: Wilsonia. GPS: 36.665135, -118.833456

607 • E3 | Tenmile (Sequoia NF)

Total sites: 13, RV sites: 13, No water, Vault/pit toilet, Tent & RV camping: $25-27, No fees/services in winter, Open May-Sep, Max Length: 22ft, Reservations accepted, Elev: 5938ft/1810m, Tel: 559-338-2251, Nearest town: Dunlap. GPS: 36.754000, -118.892000

608 • E3 | Trapper Springs (Sierra NF)

Total sites: 75, RV sites: 75, No water, Vault/pit toilet, Tent & RV camping: $24, Stay limit: 14 days, Open May-Oct, Max Length: 35ft, Reservations not accepted, Elev: 8209ft/2502m, Tel: 559-855-5355, Nearest town: Clovis. GPS: 37.092337, -118.982691

609 • E3 | Upper Grays Meadow (Inyo NF)

Total sites: 35, RV sites: 35, Central water, Flush toilet, No showers, No RV dump, Tent & RV camping: $25, Bear boxes must be used for food storage, Open Apr-Oct, Max Length: 40ft, Reservations accepted, Elev: 6125ft/1867m, Tel: 760-937-6070, Nearest town: Independence. GPS: 36.783591, -118.293652

610 • E3 | Upper Stony Creek (Sequoia NF)

Total sites: 17, RV sites: 17, Central water, Vault/pit toilet, No showers, No RV dump, Tent & RV camping: $25-27, Open May-Sep, Max Length: 40ft, Reservations accepted, Elev: 6572ft/2003m, Tel: 559-338-2251, Nearest town: Dunlap. GPS: 36.667549, -118.831489

611 • E3 | Voyager Rock (Sierra NF)

Total sites: 14, RV sites: 0, No water, No toilets, Tents only: Free, Accessible only by Off Highway Vehicles., Stay limit: 14 days, Open Aug-Nov, Reservations not accepted, Elev: 8274ft/2522m, Tel: 559-855-5355, Nearest town: Clovis. GPS: 37.108724, -118.966556

612 • E3 | Whitney Portal (Inyo NF)

Total sites: 46, RV sites: 26, Central water, Vault/pit toilet, No showers, No RV dump, Tent & RV camping: $28, Also walk-to & group sites, Group site $80, Bear boxes must be used for food storage, Open May-Oct, Max Length: 35ft, Reservations accepted, Elev: 8058ft/2456m, Tel: 760-937-6070, Nearest town: Lone Pine. GPS: 36.588887, -118.231704

613 • F1 | Arroyo Seco (Los Padres NF)

Total sites: 39, RV sites: 24, Central water, Flush toilet, Pay showers, No RV dump, Tents: $25-30/RVs: $30, Group site: $125, Open all year, Max Length: 50ft, Reservations accepted, Elev: 932ft/284m, Tel: 831-674-5726, Nearest town: Greenfield. GPS: 36.233207, -121.484963

614 • F1 | Escondido (Los Padres NF)

Total sites: 9, RV sites: 9, No water, Vault/pit toilet, Tent & RV camping: $20, Stay limit: 14 days, Generator hours: 0800-2200, Open May-Oct, Max Length: 50ft, Reservations accepted, Elev: 2176ft/663m, Tel: 831-385-5434, Nearest town: Tassajara Hot Springs. GPS: 36.141337, -121.493933

615 • F1 | Kirk Creek (Los Padres NF)

Total sites: 40, RV sites: 40, No water, Vault/pit toilet, No showers, No RV dump, Tent & RV camping: $35, Stay limit: 14 days, Generator hours: 0600-2200, Open all year, Max Length: 56ft, Reservations accepted, Elev: 253ft/77m, Tel: 805-434-1996, Nearest town: Lucia. GPS: 35.989807, -121.495666

616 • F1 | Memorial Park (Los Padres NF)

Total sites: 8, RV sites: 8, No water, Vault/pit toilet, Tent & RV camping: $20, Generator hours: 0600-2200, Open Apr-Oct, Max Length: 80ft, Reservations accepted, Elev: 2136ft/651m, Tel: 831-385-5434. GPS: 36.117845, -121.465255

617 • F1 | Nacimiento (Los Padres NF)

Total sites: 9, RV sites: 9, No water, Vault/pit toilet, Tent & RV camping: $20, Stay limit: 14 days, Generator hours: 0600-2200, Open all year, Max Length: 25ft, Reservations not accepted, Elev: 1619ft/493m, Tel: 831-385-5434. GPS: 36.007518, -121.400767

618 • F1 | Plaskett Creek (Los Padres NF)

Total sites: 44, RV sites: 44, Central water, Flush toilet, No showers, No RV dump, Tent & RV camping: $35, 1 group site $150, Open all year, Max Length: 50ft, Reservations accepted, Elev: 233ft/71m, Tel: 805-434-1996, Nearest town: Lucia. GPS: 35.917992, -121.466878

619 • F1 | Ponderosa (Los Padres NF)

Total sites: 22, RV sites: 22, Central water, Vault/pit toilet, No showers, No RV dump, Tent & RV camping: $25, Generator hours: 0600-2200, Open May-Sep, Max Length: 40ft, Reservations accepted, Elev: 1549ft/472m, Tel: 805-434-1996, Nearest town: Pacific Valley. GPS: 35.997889, -121.383145

620 • F2 | Baja (Los Padres NF)

Total sites: 1, RV sites: 1, No water, Vault/pit toilet, Tent & RV camping: Free, Reservations not accepted, Elev: 1411ft/430m, Tel: 805-925-9538, Nearest town: Santa Maria. GPS: 35.139186, -120.137827

621 • F2 | Brookshire (Los Padres NF)

Total sites: 2, RV sites: 2, No water, Vault/pit toilet, Tent & RV camping: $5, Adventure Pass required ($5/day or $30/year) or Interagency Pass, Reservations not accepted, Elev: 1379ft/420m, Tel: 805-925-9538, Nearest town: Santa Maria. GPS: 34.997757, -120.125571

622 • F2 | Buck Springs (Los Padres NF)

Total sites: 1, RV sites: 1, No water, Vault/pit toilet, Tent & RV camping: $5, Adventure Pass required ($5/day or $30/year) or Interagency Pass, Stay limit: 14 days, Open all year, Reservations not accepted, Elev: 1621ft/494m, Tel: 805-925-9538. GPS: 35.134989, -120.117716

623 • F2 | Cerro Alto (Los Padres NF)

Total sites: 22, RV sites: 9, Central water, Vault/pit toilet, No showers, No RV dump, Tent & RV camping: $25, Also walk-to sites, Generator hours: 0600-2200, Open all year, Max Length: 35ft, Reservations accepted, Elev: 1083ft/330m, Tel: 805-434-1996, Nearest town: Atascadero. GPS: 35.424881, -120.740302

624 • F2 | Friis (Los Padres NF)

Total sites: 3, RV sites: 3, No water, Vault/pit toilet, Tent & RV camping: $5, Adventure Pass required ($5/day or $30/year) or Interagency Pass, Stay limit: 14 days, Generator hours: 0600-2200, Reservations not accepted, Elev: 2280ft/695m, Tel: 805-925-9538, Nearest town: Pozo. GPS: 35.380795, -120.326748

625 • F2 | Hi Mountain (Los Padres NF)

Total sites: 11, RV sites: 11, No water, Vault/pit toilet, Tent & RV camping: $5, Adventure Pass required ($5/day or $30/year) or Interagency Pass, Generator hours: 0600-2200, Max Length: 16ft, Reservations not accepted, Elev: 2224ft/678m, Tel: 805-025-9538, Nearest town: San Luis Obispo. GPS: 35.261475, -120.413818

626 • F2 | Horseshoe Springs (Los Padres NF)

Total sites: 3, RV sites: 3, No water, Vault/pit toilet, Tent & RV camping: $5, Adventure Pass required ($5/day or $30/year) or Interagency Pass, Stay limit: 14 days, Generator hours: 0600-2200, Open all year, Reservations not accepted, Elev: 1521ft/464m, Tel: 805-925-9538, Nearest town: Santa Maria. GPS: 35.021076, -120.114467

627 • F2 | La Panza (Los Padres NF)

Total sites: 9, RV sites: 9, No water, Vault/pit toilet, Tent & RV camping: $20, Generator hours: 0600-2200, Open all year, Max Length: 16ft, Reservations accepted, Elev: 2195ft/669m, Tel: 805-925-9538, Nearest town: Santa Maria. GPS: 35.353748, -120.262715

628 • F2 | Miranda Pine (Los Padres NF)

Total sites: 3, RV sites: 3, No water, Vault/pit toilet, Tent & RV camping: $5, Adventure Pass required ($5/day or $30/year) or Interagency Pass, Generator hours: 0600-2200, Reservations not accepted, Elev: 4006ft/1221m, Tel: 805-925-9538, Nearest town: Santa Maria. GPS: 35.035071, -120.037374

629 • F2 | Navajo (Los Padres NF)

Total sites: 2, RV sites: 2, No water, Vault/pit toilet, Tent & RV camping: Free, Reservations not accepted, Elev: 2221ft/677m, Tel: 805-925-9538, Nearest town: Pozo. GPS: 35.368674, -120.312399

630 • F2 | Navajo Flat (Los Padres NF)

Total sites: 6, RV sites: 6, No water, Vault/pit toilet, Tent & RV camping: $20, Stay limit: 14 days, Generator hours: 0600-2200, Reservations accepted, Elev: 1863ft/568m, Tel: 805-925-9538, Nearest town: Santa Margarita. GPS: 35.379157, -120.283997

631 • F2 | Paradise Spring (Los Padres NF)

Total sites: 3, RV sites: 0, No water, Vault/pit toilet, Tents only: Free, Stay limit: 14 days, Reservations not accepted, Elev: 1604ft/489m, Tel: 805-925-9538, Nearest town: Santa Maria. GPS: 35.152542, -120.144622

632 • F3 | Belknap (Sequoia NF)

Total sites: 15, RV sites: 0, Central water, Vault/pit toilet, Tents only: $28-30, Open May-Oct, Reservations accepted, Elev: 5059ft/1542m, Tel: 559-539-2607, Nearest town: Springville. GPS: 36.141699, -118.599704

633 • F3 | Boulder Gulch (Sequoia NF)

Total sites: 78, RV sites: 78, Water available, Flush toilet, Free showers, No RV dump, Tent & RV camping: $28-30, Open Jan-Sep, Max Length: 45ft, Reservations accepted, Elev: 2618ft/798m, Tel: 760-376-3781, Nearest town: Lake Isabella. GPS: 35.672363, -118.470215

634 • F3 | Breckenridge (Sequoia NF)

Total sites: 8, RV sites: 0, No water, Vault/pit toilet, Tents only: Free, Open May-Nov, Reservations not accepted, Elev: 6616ft/2017m, Tel: 760-376-3781, Nearest town: Lake Isabella. GPS: 35.468132, -118.582102

635 • F3 | Camp 3 (Sequoia NF)

Total sites: 49, RV sites: 48, Central water, Vault/pit toilet, No showers, No RV dump, Tent & RV camping: $30-32, Group site: $122, Open May-Sep, Max Length: 40ft, Reservations accepted, Elev: 2920ft/890m, Tel: 760-376-3781, Nearest town: Kernville. GPS: 35.809926, -118.454458

636 • F3 | Camp 9 (Sequoia NF)

Total sites: 109, RV sites: 103, Central water, Flush toilet, No showers, RV dump, Tent & RV camping: $17, Dump fee: $10, 11 reservable group sites: $90-$160, Open all year, Max Length: 40ft, Reservations accepted, Elev: 2618ft/798m, Tel: 760-376-3781, Nearest town: Kernville. GPS: 35.695409, -118.431927

637 • F3 | Cedar Creek (Sequoia NF)

Total sites: 11, RV sites: 0, No water, Vault/pit toilet, No showers, No RV dump, Tents only: Free, Not suitable for trailers, Open all year, Reservations not accepted, Elev: 4944ft/1507m, Tel: 760-376-3781, Nearest town: Kernville. GPS: 35.748978, -118.582784

638 • F3 | Coy Flat (Sequoia NF)

Total sites: 20, RV sites: 20, No water, Vault/pit toilet, Tent & RV camping: $28-30, Open May-Oct, Max Length: 22ft, Reservations accepted, Elev: 4764ft/1452m, Tel: 559-539-2607, Nearest town: Springville. GPS: 36.126955, -118.619043

639 • F3 | Evans Flat (Sequoia NF)

Total sites: 20, RV sites: 20, No water, Vault/pit toilet, Tent & RV camping: Free, 4 horse sites, Max Length: 20ft, Reservations not accepted, Elev: 6145ft/1873m, Tel: 760-379-5646, Nearest town: Wofford Heights. GPS: 35.642804, -118.589455

640 • F3 | Fairview (Sequoia NF)

Total sites: 48, RV sites: 35, Central water, Vault/pit toilet, No showers, RV dump, Tent & RV camping: $30-32, Open Apr-Nov, Max Length: 40ft, Reservations accepted, Elev: 3560ft/1085m, Tel: 760-376-3781, Nearest town: Kernville. GPS: 35.929188, -118.490697

641 • F3 | Frog Meadow (Sequoia NF)

Total sites: 10, RV sites: 10, No water, Vault/pit toilet, Tent & RV camping: Free, Also cabins, Cabin can be reserved, Open Jun-Oct, Max Length: 16ft, Reservations not accepted, Elev: 7710ft/2350m, Tel: 559-539-2607, Nearest town: Glenville. GPS: 35.874118, -118.575265

642 • F3 | Goldledge (Sequoia NF)

Total sites: 37, RV sites: 28, Central water, Vault/pit toilet, No showers, No RV dump, Tent & RV camping: $30-32, Also walk-to sites, Open May-Sep, Max Length: 30ft, Reservations accepted, Elev: 3238ft/987m, Tel: 760-376-3781, Nearest town: Kernville. GPS: 35.874317, -118.457273

643 • F3 | Halfway Group (Sequoia NF)

Total sites: 5, RV sites: 0, No water, Vault/pit toilet, Tent & RV camping: Fee unk, Group sites: $42-$174, Reservations not accepted, Elev: 2825ft/861m, Tel: 760-379-1815, Nearest town: Kernville. GPS: 35.802563, -118.451971

644 • F3 | Headquarters (Sequoia NF)

Total sites: 44, RV sites: 31, Central water, Vault/pit toilet, No showers, No RV dump, Tent & RV camping: $30-32, Open all year, Max Length: 30ft, Reservations accepted, Elev: 2930ft/893m, Tel: 760-376-3781, Nearest town: Kernville. GPS: 35.797084, -118.451221

645 • F3 | Hobo (Sequoia NF)

Total sites: 35, RV sites: 25, No water, Vault/pit toilet, Tent & RV camping: $23-25, Unsuitable for trailers, Open Apr-Sep, Max Length: 22ft, Reservations not accepted, Elev: 2326ft/709m, Tel: 760-376-3781, Nearest town: Lake Isabella. GPS: 35.574285, -118.529196

646 • F3 | Holey Meadow (Sequoia NF)

Total sites: 10, RV sites: 0, No water, Vault/pit toilet, Tents only: $26-28, Open May-Oct, Max Length: 20ft, Reservations accepted, Elev: 6483ft/1976m, Tel: 559-539-5230, Nearest town: California Hot Springs. GPS: 35.953817, -118.618639

647 • F3 | Hospital Flat (Sequoia NF)

Total sites: 40, RV sites: 29, Central water, Vault/pit toilet, No showers, No RV dump, Tent & RV camping: $30-32, Also walk-to sites, Open May-Sep, Max Length: 30ft, Reservations accepted, Elev: 2979ft/908m, Tel: 760-376-3781, Nearest town: Kernville. GPS: 35.828383, -118.458453

648 • F3 | Hungry Gulch (Sequoia NF)

Total sites: 74, RV sites: 74, Central water, Flush toilet, No showers, No RV dump, Tent & RV camping: $30-32, Add $2 summer holiday weekends, Open May-Sep, Max Length: 30ft, Reservations accepted, Elev: 2658ft/810m, Tel: 760-376-3781, Nearest town: Lake Isabella. GPS: 35.671875, -118.473145

649 • F3 | Kern Plateau - Fish Creek (Sequoia NF)

Total sites: 40, RV sites: 40, No water, Vault/pit toilet, Tent & RV camping: $17, Open May-Oct, Max Length: 27ft, Reservations not accepted, Elev: 7418ft/2261m, Tel: 760-376-3781, Nearest town: Inyokern. GPS: 36.059294, -118.219149

650 • F3 | Kern Plateau - Horse Meadow (Sequoia NF)

Total sites: 33, RV sites: 15, No water, Vault/pit toilet, Tent & RV

camping: $17, Open May-Nov, Max Length: 22ft, Reservations not accepted, Elev: 7451ft/2271m, Tel: 760-376-3781, Nearest town: Kernville. GPS: 35.902173, -118.371284

651 • F3 | Kern Plateau - Kennedy Meadows (Inyo NF)

Total sites: 38, RV sites: 38, No water, No toilets, No showers, No RV dump, Tent & RV camping: Free, Stay limit: 14 days, Open all year, Max Length: 30ft, Reservations not accepted, Elev: 6142ft/1872m, Tel: 760-376-3781, Nearest town: Pearsonville. GPS: 36.052734, -118.131348

652 • F3 | Kern Plateau - Troy Meadow (Sequoia NF)

Total sites: 73, RV sites: 73, No water, Vault/pit toilet, Tent & RV camping: $17, Open May-Nov, Max Length: 24ft, Reservations not accepted, Elev: 7792ft/2375m, Tel: 760-376-3781, Nearest town: Inyokern. GPS: 36.064675, -118.237255

653 • F3 | Leavis Flat (Sequoia NF)

Total sites: 9, RV sites: 9, No water, Vault/pit toilet, No showers, No RV dump, Tent & RV camping: $23, Fire permit required, Open all year, Max Length: 16ft, Reservations not accepted, Elev: 3143ft/958m, Tel: 559-539-2607, Nearest town: CA Hot Springs. GPS: 35.879632, -118.676738

654 • F3 | Limestone (Sequoia NF)

Total sites: 22, RV sites: 0, No water, Vault/pit toilet, Tents only: $26-28, Open May-Oct, Max Length: 40ft, Reservations accepted, Elev: 3875ft/1181m, Tel: 760-376-3781, Nearest town: Kernville. GPS: 35.963371, -118.479203

655 • F3 | Live Oak North (Sequoia NF)

Total sites: 60, RV sites: 60, Central water, Flush toilet, Free showers, No RV dump, Tent & RV camping: $24-26, Open May-Sep, Max Length: 30ft, Reservations not accepted, Elev: 2710ft/826m, Tel: 760-376-3781, Nearest town: Wofford Heights. GPS: 35.702892, -118.460908

656 • F3 | Live Oak South (Sequoia NF)

Total sites: 90, Central water, Flush toilet, Free showers, No RV dump, Tents only: $24, Open May-Sep, Reservations not accepted, Elev: 2700ft/823m, Tel: 760-376-3781, Nearest town: Wofford Heights. GPS: 35.701501, -118.461421

657 • F3 | Lower Peppermint (Sequoia NF)

Total sites: 17, RV sites: 10, Central water, Vault/pit toilet, No showers, No RV dump, Tent & RV camping: $17, Open May-Nov, Max Length: 16ft, Reservations not accepted, Elev: 5292ft/1613m, Tel: 559-539-2607, Nearest town: Kernville. GPS: 36.065994, -118.491243

658 • F3 | Paradise Cove (Sequoia NF)

Total sites: 138, RV sites: 138, Central water, Flush toilet, No showers, RV dump, Tent & RV camping: $30-32, $10 dump fee, Open May-Oct, Max Length: 40ft, Reservations accepted, Elev: 2595ft/791m, Tel: 760-379-5646, Nearest town: Lake Isabella. GPS: 35.649817, -118.426828

659 • F3 | Pioneer Point (Sequoia NF)

Total sites: 78, RV sites: 78, Central water, Flush toilet, No showers, No RV dump, Tent & RV camping: $30, Open May-Sep, Max Length: 30ft, Reservations accepted, Elev: 2625ft/800m, Tel: 760-379-5646, Nearest town: Lake Isabella. GPS: 35.651611, -118.487061

660 • F3 | Quaking Aspen (Sequoia NF)

Total sites: 31, RV sites: 27, Central water, Vault/pit toilet, No showers, No RV dump, Tent & RV camping: $28-30, Group sites $55-$203, Open May-Oct, Max Length: 35ft, Reservations accepted, Elev: 7070ft/2155m, Tel: 559-539-2607, Nearest town: Camp Nelson. GPS: 36.121342, -118.544539

661 • F3 | Redwood Meadow (Sequoia NF)

Total sites: 15, RV sites: 14, No water, Vault/pit toilet, Tent & RV camping: $30-32, Open May-Oct, Max Length: 20ft, Reservations accepted, Elev: 6158ft/1877m, Tel: 559-539-2607, Nearest town: Ducor. GPS: 35.977000, -118.592000

662 • F3 | Sandy Flat (Sequoia NF)

Total sites: 35, RV sites: 29, Central water, Vault/pit toilet, No showers, No RV dump, Tent & RV camping: $28-30, 6 walk-in sites, Open May-Oct, Max Length: 50ft, Reservations accepted, Elev: 2362ft/720m, Tel: 760-379-5646, Nearest town: Lake Isabella. GPS: 35.582526, -118.524877

663 • F3 | Tillie Creek (Sequoia NF)

Total sites: 159, RV sites: 159, Central water, Flush toilet, No showers, RV dump, Tent & RV camping: $30, Group sites $243-$608, Open May-Nov, Max Length: 45ft, Reservations accepted, Elev: 2638ft/804m, Tel: 760-379-5646, Nearest town: Wofford Heights. GPS: 35.701572, -118.456129

664 • F3 | White River (Sequoia NF)

Total sites: 12, RV sites: 0, Central water, Vault/pit toilet, No showers, No RV dump, Tents only: $26, Open May-Oct, Max Length: 50ft, Reservations accepted, Elev: 4206ft/1282m, Tel: 559-539-2607, Nearest town: Wofford Heights. GPS: 35.844395, -118.635921

665 • F3 | Wishon (Sequoia NF)

Total sites: 35, RV sites: 35, Central water, Vault/pit toilet, No showers, No RV dump, Tent & RV camping: $28-30, Open all year, Max Length: 30ft, Reservations accepted, Elev: 3947ft/1203m, Tel: 559-539-2607, Nearest town: Springville. GPS: 36.189388, -118.663885

666 • G2 | Aliso (Los Padres NF)

Total sites: 10, RV sites: 10, No water, Vault/pit toilet, Tent & RV camping: $5, Adventure Pass required ($5/day or $30/year) or Interagency Pass, Generator hours: 0600-2200, Open all year, Max Length: 28ft, Reservations not accepted, Elev: 2884ft/879m, Tel: 661-245-3731, Nearest town: New Cuyama. GPS: 34.907715, -119.768555

667 • G2 | Ballinger (Los Padres NF)

Total sites: 13, RV sites: 13, No water, Vault/pit toilet, Tent & RV camping: $20, Generator hours: 0600-2200, Open all year, Max Length: 70ft, Reservations accepted, Elev: 3123ft/952m, Tel: 661-245-3731. GPS: 34.884078, -119.445027

668 • G2 | Barrel Springs (Los Padres NF)

Total sites: 6, RV sites: 6, No water, Vault/pit toilet, Tent & RV camping: $5, Adventure Pass required ($5/day or $30/year) or Interagency Pass, Reservations not accepted, Elev: 1034ft/315m, Tel: 805-925-9538, Nearest town: Santa Maria. GPS: 34.901276, -120.142303

669 • G2 | Bates Canyon (Los Padres NF)

Total sites: 6, RV sites: 6, No water, Vault/pit toilet, Tent & RV camping: $5, Adventure Pass required ($5/day or $30/year) or Interagency Pass, Open all year, Reservations not accepted, Elev: 2858ft/871m, Tel: 805-925-9538, Nearest town: Santa Maria. GPS: 34.953642, -119.907721

670 • G2 | Caballo (Los Padres NF)

Total sites: 5, RV sites: 0, No water, Vault/pit toilet, Tents only: Free, High Clearance vehicles recommended, Generator hours: 0600-2200, Reservations not accepted, Elev: 6092ft/1857m, Tel: 661-245-3731. GPS: 34.868783, -119.226375

671 • G2 | Campo Alto (Los Padres NF)

Total sites: 17, RV sites: 171, Elec sites: ., No water, Vault/pit toilet, Tent & RV camping: $20, 2 group sites: $100, Generator hours: 0600-2200, Open May-Oct, Max Length: 40ft, Reservations accepted, Elev: 8209ft/2502m, Tel: 661-245-3731, Nearest town: Pine Mountain Club. GPS: 34.831393, -119.209368

672 • G2 | Chula Vista (Los Padres NF)

Total sites: 12, RV sites: 12, No water, Vault/pit toilet, Tent & RV camping: Free, 500 yard walk-in to tent CG, Self-contained vehicles only in parking lot, favored star-gazing spot, Generator hours: 0600-2200, Reservations not accepted, Elev: 8324ft/2537m, Tel: 661-245-3731, Nearest town: Frazier Park. GPS: 34.813591, -119.123699

673 • G2 | Colson (Los Padres NF)

Total sites: 5, RV sites: 5, No water, No toilets, Tent & RV camping: Free, Generator hours: 0600-2200, Reservations not accepted, Elev: 2067ft/630m, Tel: 805-925-9538, Nearest town: Santa Maria. GPS: 34.940000, -120.170000

674 • G2 | Davy Brown (Los Padres NF)

Total sites: 13, RV sites: 13, No water, Vault/pit toilet, Tent & RV camping: $20, Stay limit: 14 days, Generator hours: 0600-2200, Max Length: 25ft, Reservations accepted, Elev: 2087ft/636m, Tel: 805-925-9538, Nearest town: Santa Ynez. GPS: 34.757969, -119.953501

675 • G2 | Dome Springs (Los Padres NF)

Total sites: 4, RV sites: 4, No water, Vault/pit toilet, Tent & RV camping: Free, 4x4 may be required, Generator hours: 0600-2200, Open all year, Reservations not accepted, Elev: 4616ft/1407m, Tel: 661-245-3731, Nearest town: Lake of the Woods. GPS: 34.752463, -119.235489

676 • G2 | Fremont (Los Padres NF)

Total sites: 14, RV sites: 7, Central water, Flush toilet, No showers, No RV dump, Tent & RV camping: $30, Walk-to sites, Generator hours: 0600-2200, Open all year, Max Length: 34ft, Reservations accepted, Elev: 955ft/291m, Tel: 805-967-8766, Nearest town: Santa Barbar. GPS: 34.543213, -119.821289

677 • G2 | Lazy (Los Padres NF)

Total sites: 2, RV sites: 2, No water, Vault/pit toilet, Tent & RV camping: Free, High-clearance vehicle required, Reservations not accepted, Elev: 1700ft/518m, Tel: 805-925-9538, Nearest town: Santa Maria. GPS: 34.962444, -120.087572

678 • G2 | Los Prietos (Los Padres NF)

Total sites: 38, RV sites: 30, Central water, Flush toilet, No showers, No RV dump, Tent & RV camping: $30, Generator hours: 0600-2200, Open all year, Max Length: 35ft, Reservations accepted, Elev: 1010ft/308m, Tel: 805-967-8766, Nearest town: Santa Barbara. GPS: 34.540527, -119.802002

679 • G2 | Marian (Los Padres NF)

Total sites: 5, RV sites: 0, No water, Vault/pit toilet, Tents only: Free, High-clearance vehicle recommended, Generator hours: 0600-2200, Open May-Dec, Reservations not accepted, Elev: 6519ft/1987m, Tel: 661-245-3731, Nearest town: Pine Mt Club. GPS: 34.880841, -119.216561

680 • G2 | McGill (Los Padres NF)

Total sites: 73, RV sites: 73, No water, Vault/pit toilet, Tent & RV camping: $20, 2 Group sites: $100-$120, Generator hours: 0600-2200, Open May-Oct, Max Length: 27ft, Reservations accepted, Elev: 7480ft/2280m, Tel: 661-245-3731, Nearest town: Frazier Park. GPS: 34.813965, -119.101807

681 • G2 | Middle Lion (Los Padres NF)

Total sites: 8, RV sites: 8, No water, Vault/pit toilet, Tent & RV camping: $20, Generator hours: 0600-2200, Open all year, Max Length: 20ft, Reservations accepted, Elev: 3161ft/963m, Tel: 805-646-4348, Nearest town: Ojai. GPS: 34.549426, -119.166232

682 • G2 | Middle Santa Ynez (Los Padres NF)

Total sites: 13, RV sites: 0, No water, Vault/pit toilet, Tents only: $5, Walk-to sites, High-clearance vehicle recommended, Adventure Pass required ($5/day or $30/year) or Interagency Pass, Stay limit: 14 days, Generator hours: 0600-2200, Reservations not accepted, Elev: 1600ft/488m, Tel: 805-967-3481, Nearest town: Summerland. GPS: 34.509978, -119.579485

683 • G2 | Mono (Los Padres NF)

Total sites: 3, RV sites: 0, No water, Vault/pit toilet, Tents only: $5, Walk-to sites, Adventure Pass required ($5/day or $30/year) or Interagency Pass, Generator hours: 0600-2200, Reservations not accepted, Elev: 1450ft/442m, Tel: 805-967-3481, Nearest town: Santa Barbara. GPS: 34.528107, -119.627811

684 • G2 | Mt Figueroa (Los Padres NF)

Total sites: 32, RV sites: 32, No water, Vault/pit toilet, No showers, No RV dump, Tent & RV camping: $20, Stay limit: 14 days, Generator hours: 0600-2200, Open all year, Max Length: 25ft, Reservations not accepted, Elev: 3547ft/1081m, Tel: 805-925-9538, Nearest town: Los Olivos. GPS: 34.734447, -119.986548

685 • G2 | Mt. Pinos (Los Padres NF)

Total sites: 19, RV sites: 19, No water, Vault/pit toilet, Tent & RV

camping: $20, Good star-gazing, Generator hours: 0600-2200, Open May-Oct, Max Length: 40ft, Reservations accepted, Elev: 7822ft/2384m, Tel: 661-245-3731, Nearest town: Frazier Park. GPS: 34.810304, -119.108957

686 • G2 | Nira (Los Padres NF)

Total sites: 12, RV sites: 9, No water, Vault/pit toilet, Tent & RV camping: $20, Generator hours: 0600-2200, Max Length: 24ft, Reservations accepted, Elev: 2005ft/611m, Tel: 805-925-9538, Nearest town: Santa Ynez. GPS: 34.770508, -119.937744

687 • G2 | P-Bar Flat (Los Padres NF)

Total sites: 4, RV sites: 4, No water, Vault/pit toilet, Tent & RV camping: $5, High clearance vehicle recommended, Adventure Pass required ($5/day or $30/year) or Interagency Pass, Generator hours: 0600-2200, Reservations not accepted, Elev: 1686ft/514m, Tel: 805-967-3481, Nearest town: Santa Barbara. GPS: 34.514995, -119.591085

688 • G2 | Paradise (Los Padres NF)

Total sites: 15, RV sites: 15, Central water, Flush toilet, No showers, No RV dump, Tent & RV camping: $30, Generator hours: 0600-2200, Open all year, Max Length: 40ft, Reservations accepted, Elev: 938ft/286m, Tel: 805-967-3481, Nearest town: Santa Barbara. GPS: 34.542166, -119.811844

689 • G2 | Pine Mountain (Los Padres NF)

Total sites: 7, RV sites: 0, No water, Vault/pit toilet, Tents only: $20, Generator hours: 0600-2200, Open May-Dec, Reservations accepted, Elev: 6739ft/2054m, Tel: 805-646-4348, Nearest town: Ojai. GPS: 34.638806, -119.326731

690 • G2 | Pine Springs (Los Padres NF)

Total sites: 12, RV sites: 12, No water, Vault/pit toilet, Tent & RV camping: $5, Adventure Pass required ($5/day or $30/year) or Interagency Pass, Generator hours: 0600-2200, Reservations not accepted, Elev: 5812ft/1771m, Tel: 661-245-3731, Nearest town: Frazier Park. GPS: 34.691505, -119.132692

691 • G2 | Reyes Creek (Los Padres NF)

Total sites: 27, RV sites: 18, No water, Vault/pit toilet, Tent & RV camping: $20, Group site: $100, Generator hours: 0600-2200, Open all year, Max Length: 30ft, Reservations accepted, Elev: 3983ft/1214m, Tel: 661-245-3731, Nearest town: Frazier Park. GPS: 34.679024, -119.308428

692 • G2 | Reyes Peak (Los Padres NF)

Total sites: 6, RV sites: 6, No water, Vault/pit toilet, Tent & RV camping: $20, Generator hours: 0600-2200, Open May-Dec, Reservations accepted, Elev: 7132ft/2174m, Tel: 661-245-3731, Nearest town: Ojai. GPS: 34.636939, -119.314442

693 • G2 | Rock (Los Padres NF)

Total sites: 2, No water, No toilets, Tents only: Free, High-clearance vehicle recommended, Reservations not accepted, Elev: 1847ft/563m, Tel: 805-967-3481. GPS: 34.535498, -119.563255

694 • G2 | Rock Camp (Los Padres NF)

Total sites: 2, Tents only: $5, Walk-to sites, Adventure Pass required ($5/day or $30/year) or Interagency Pass, Stay limit: 14 days, Generator hours: 0600-2200, Reservations not accepted, Elev: 2093ft/638m, Tel: 805-967-3481, Nearest town: Santa Barbara. GPS: 34.544299, -119.560614

695 • G2 | Rose Valley (Los Padres NF)

Total sites: 9, RV sites: 9, No water, Vault/pit toilet, Tent & RV camping: $20, Generator hours: 0600-2200, Open all year, Max Length: 20ft, Reservations accepted, Elev: 3425ft/1044m, Tel: 805-646-4348, Nearest town: Ojai. GPS: 34.531889, -119.182671

696 • G2 | Thorn Meadows (Los Padres NF)

Total sites: 5, RV sites: 0, No water, Vault/pit toilet, Tents only: Free, Requires high clearance vehicles due to water crossings, 1 Pipe corral, Open May-Dec, Reservations not accepted, Elev: 5007ft/1526m, Tel: 661-245-3731. GPS: 34.626996, -119.114117

697 • G2 | Toad Springs (Los Padres NF)

Total sites: 5, RV sites: 0, Central water, Vault/pit toilet, No showers, No RV dump, Tents only: Free, Reservations not accepted, Elev: 5676ft/1730m, Tel: 661-245-3731, Nearest town: Pine Mountain Club. GPS: 34.860721, -119.228178

698 • G2 | Upper Oso (Los Padres NF)

Total sites: 25, RV sites: 25, Central water, Flush toilet, No showers, No RV dump, Tents: $30/RVs: $30-35, 10 equestrian sites, Generator hours: 0600-2200, Open all year, Max Length: 40ft, Reservations accepted, Elev: 1247ft/380m, Tel: 805-967-3481, Nearest town: Santa Barbara. GPS: 34.556621, -119.771756

699 • G2 | Valle Vista (Los Padres NF)

Total sites: 7, RV sites: 7, Central water, Vault/pit toilet, No showers, No RV dump, Tent & RV camping: $5, Steep rutted sharply-curved entrance road, Adventure Pass required ($5/day or $30/year) or Interagency Pass, Stay limit: 14 days, Generator hours: 0600-2200, Open all year, Reservations not accepted, Elev: 4678ft/1426m, Tel: 661-245-3731, Nearest town: Frazier Park. GPS: 34.878183, -119.341584

700 • G2 | Wagon Flat (Los Padres NF)

Total sites: 3, RV sites: 3, No water, Vault/pit toilet, Tent & RV camping: $5, Adventure Pass required ($5/day or $30/year) or Interagency Pass, Generator hours: 0600-2200, Reservations not accepted, Elev: 1466ft/447m, Tel: 805-925-9538, Nearest town: Santa Margarita. GPS: 34.956645, -120.097924

701 • G2 | Wheeler Gorge (Los Padres NF)

Total sites: 88, RV sites: 88, No water, Vault/pit toilet, Tent & RV camping: $25, Generator hours: 0600-2200, Open all year, Max Length: 45ft, Reservations accepted, Elev: 1857ft/566m, Tel: 805-640-1977, Nearest town: Ojai. GPS: 34.512939, -119.273438

702 • G3 | Appletree (Angeles NF)

Total sites: 8, RV sites: 0, Central water, Vault/pit toilet, No showers, No RV dump, Tents only: $5, Adventure Pass required ($5/day or $30/year) or Interagency Pass, Stay limit: 14 days, Open all year, Reservations not accepted, Elev: 6214ft/1894m, Tel: 619-249-3483, Nearest town: Big Pines. GPS: 34.386334, -117.713723

703 • G3 | Applewhite (San Bernadino NF)

Total sites: 44, RV sites: 44, Central water, Flush toilet, No showers, No RV dump, Tent & RV camping: $10, No wood or charcoal fires, Open all year, Max Length: 30ft, Reservations not accepted, Elev: 3369ft/1027m, Tel: 909-382-2851, Nearest town: Lytle Creek. GPS: 34.259975, -117.493207

704 • G3 | Bear (Angeles NF)

Total sites: 7, RV sites: 0, No water, No toilets, Tents only: $5, Walk-to sites, Adventure Pass required ($5/day or $30/year) or Interagency Pass, Stay limit: 14 days, Open all year, Reservations not accepted, Elev: 5436ft/1657m, Tel: 661-269-2808, Nearest town: Lake Hughes. GPS: 34.712652, -118.632448

705 • G3 | Big Rock (Angeles NF)

Total sites: 8, RV sites: 8, No water, Vault/pit toilet, Tent & RV camping: $5, Hike-in-only in winter, Adventure Pass required ($5/day or $30/year) or Interagency Pass, Stay limit: 14 days, Open all year, Max Length: 20ft, Reservations not accepted, Elev: 5433ft/1656m, Tel: 805-944-2187, Nearest town: Pearblossom. GPS: 34.388000, -117.777000

706 • G3 | Blue Jay (Cleveland NF)

Total sites: 50, RV sites: 50, Central water, Vault/pit toilet, No showers, No RV dump, Tent & RV camping: $20, Stay limit: 14 days, Open all year, Max Length: 20ft, Reservations not accepted, Elev: 3373ft/1028m, Tel: 619-673-6180, Nearest town: Lake Elsinore. GPS: 33.651741, -117.453185

707 • G3 | Blue Ridge (Angeles NF)

Total sites: 8, RV sites: 8, No water, Vault/pit toilet, Tent & RV camping: $5, No winter road access, Adventure Pass required ($5/day or $30/year) or Interagency Pass, Stay limit: 14 days, Open all year, Max Length: 20ft, Reservations not accepted, Elev: 7950ft/2423m, Tel: 805-944-2187, Nearest town: Wrightwood. GPS: 34.359426, -117.686751

708 • G3 | Buckhorn (Angeles NF)

Total sites: 38, RV sites: 38, Central water, Vault/pit toilet, No showers, No RV dump, Tent & RV camping: $12, Stay limit: 14 days, Generator hours: 0600-2200, Open Apr-Nov, Max Length: 18ft, Reservations not accepted, Elev: 6466ft/1971m, Tel: 818-899-1900, Nearest town: La Canada. GPS: 34.346158, -117.912838

709 • G3 | Chilao (Angeles NF)

Total sites: 83, RV sites: 83, Central water, Vault/pit toilet, No showers, No RV dump, Tent & RV camping: $12, Stay limit: 14 days, Open Apr-Sep, Max Length: 40ft, Reservations not accepted, Elev: 5328ft/1624m, Tel: 626-574-1613, Nearest town: La Canada. GPS: 34.322023, -118.017209

710 • G3 | Chuchupate (Los Padres NF)

Total sites: 30, RV sites: 30, No water, Vault/pit toilet, Tent & RV camping: $20, Generator hours: 0800-2200, Open May-Oct, Max Length: 24ft, Reservations accepted, Elev: 6230ft/1899m, Tel: 661-245-3731, Nearest town: Frazier Park. GPS: 34.786171, -119.001228

711 • G3 | Coldbrook (Angeles NF)

Total sites: 20, RV sites: 20, No water, Vault/pit toilet, Tent & RV camping: $12, Stay limit: 14 days, Max Length: 22ft, Reservations not accepted, Elev: 3350ft/1021m, Tel: 818-335-1251, Nearest town: Big Bear City. GPS: 34.291889, -117.840607

712 • G3 | Cottonwood (Angeles NF)

Total sites: 22, RV sites: 22, No water, Vault/pit toilet, Tent & RV camping: $5, Adventure Pass required ($5/day or $30/year) or Interagency Pass, Stay limit: 14 days, Open all year, Max Length: 22ft, Reservations not accepted, Elev: 2736ft/834m, Tel: 661-269-2808, Nearest town: Lake Hughes. GPS: 34.640025, -118.503028

713 • G3 | Crystal Lake (Angeles NF)

Total sites: 50, RV sites: 50, Central water, Vault/pit toilet, No showers, No RV dump, Tent & RV camping: $12, Walk-in access in winter, Stay limit: 14 days, Open all year, Max Length: 35ft, Reservations not accepted, Elev: 5725ft/1745m, Tel: 626-335-1251, Nearest town: Azusa. GPS: 34.321846, -117.845689

714 • G3 | Dutchman (Los Padres NF)

Total sites: 8, No water, Vault/pit toilet, Tents only: $5, High Clearance vehicles recommended, Adventure Pass required ($5/day or $30/year) or Interagency Pass, Generator hours: 0600-2200, Reservations not accepted, Elev: 6752ft/2058m, Tel: 661-245-3731. GPS: 34.674162, -118.977229

715 • G3 | El Cariso (Cleveland NF)

Total sites: 24, RV sites: 24, Central water, Vault/pit toilet, No showers, No RV dump, Tent & RV camping: $15, Stay limit: 14 days, Open all year, Max Length: 22ft, Reservations not accepted, Elev: 2641ft/805m, Tel: 619-673-6180, Nearest town: Lake Elsinore. GPS: 33.652474, -117.410197

716 • G3 | Glenn Camp (Angeles NF)

Total sites: 10, RV sites: 0, No water, Vault/pit toilet, Tents only: $5, Walk-to sites, Walk or bike in only except for physically challenged groups who may obtain a permit to drive in, Stay limit: 14 days, Open all year, Reservations not accepted, Elev: 2103ft/641m, Nearest town: Azusa. GPS: 34.241000, -117.952000

717 • G3 | Guffy (Angeles NF)

Total sites: 6, RV sites: 0, No water, Vault/pit toilet, Tents only: $5, Rough road, Gate at Inspiration Point closed to vehicles during the winter months, Adventure Pass required ($5/day or $30/year) or Interagency Pass, Stay limit: 14 days, Open all year, Reservations not accepted, Elev: 8225ft/2507m, Tel: 661-269-2808, Nearest town: Big Pines. GPS: 34.341126, -117.655404

718 • G3 | Halfmoon (Los Padres NF)

Total sites: 10, RV sites: 10, No water, Vault/pit toilet, Tent & RV camping: $5, Adventure Pass required ($5/day or $30/year) or Interagency Pass, Generator hours: 0600-2200, Reservations not accepted, Elev: 4731ft/1442m, Tel: 661-245-3731, Nearest town: Frazier Park. GPS: 34.651000, -119.068000

719 • G3 | Horse Flats (Angeles NF)

Total sites: 26, RV sites: 26, No water, Vault/pit toilet, No showers, No RV dump, Tent & RV camping: $12, Stay limit: 14 days, Generator hours: 0600-2200, Open Apr-Nov, Max Length: 20ft, Reservations not accepted, Elev: 5709ft/1740m, Tel: 818-899-1900, Nearest town: La Canada. GPS: 34.342445, -118.010042

720 • G3 | Joe Elliot (San Bernadino NF)

Total sites: 2, RV sites: 0, No water, No toilets, Tents only: Free, High-clearance vehicle needed, Elev: 5830ft/1777m, Tel: 909-887-2576, Nearest town: Rancho Cucamonga. GPS: 34.219193, -117.552789

721 • G3 | Kings Camp (Los Padres NF)

Total sites: 7, RV sites: 7, Vault/pit toilet, Tent & RV camping: $5, Adventure Pass required ($5/day or $30/year) or Interagency Pass, Generator hours: 0600-2200, Open all year, Reservations not accepted, Elev: 4344ft/1324m, Tel: 661-245-3731. GPS: 34.716072, -118.929554

722 • G3 | Lake (Angeles NF)

Total sites: 8, RV sites: 8, Central water, Vault/pit toilet, No showers, No RV dump, Tent & RV camping: $23, Stay limit: 14 days, Open May-Oct, Max Length: 48ft, Reservations accepted, Elev: 6106ft/1861m, Tel: 760-249-3526, Nearest town: Wrightwood. GPS: 34.391161, -117.722882

723 • G3 | Los Alamos (Angeles NF)

Total sites: 93, RV sites: 93, Central water, Vault/pit toilet, No showers, RV dump, Tent & RV camping: $20-35, Group sites: $85-$125, Stay limit: 14 days, Open all year, Max Length: 35ft, Reservations accepted, Elev: 2894ft/882m, Tel: 805-434-1996, Nearest town: Gorman. GPS: 34.702705, -118.810545

724 • G3 | Manker (Angeles NF)

Total sites: 21, RV sites: 21, Central water, Vault/pit toilet, No showers, No RV dump, Tent & RV camping: $14, Stay limit: 14 days, Open all year, Max Length: 16ft, Reservations not accepted, Elev: 6092ft/1857m, Tel: 818-335-1251, Nearest town: Claremont. GPS: 34.264972, -117.630937

725 • G3 | Messenger Flats (Angeles NF)

Total sites: 10, RV sites: 10, No water, Vault/pit toilet, Tent & RV camping: $12, 2 corrals, Hike in only until FSR 3N17 opens, Road not maintained for passenger cars, Stay limit: 14 days, Open all year, Reservations not accepted, Elev: 5853ft/1784m, Tel: 818-899-1900, Nearest town: La Canada. GPS: 34.380861, -118.191086

726 • G3 | Monte Cristo (Angeles NF)

Total sites: 19, RV sites: 19, No water, Vault/pit toilet, Tent & RV camping: $12, Stay limit: 14 days, Open all year, Max Length: 30ft, Reservations not accepted, Elev: 3619ft/1103m, Tel: 818-899-1900, Nearest town: La Canada. GPS: 34.341018, -118.109526

727 • G3 | Mountain Oak (Angeles NF)

Total sites: 17, RV sites: 17, Central water, Flush toilet, No showers, No RV dump, Tent & RV camping: $23, Stay limit: 14 days, Open May-Oct, Max Length: 38ft, Reservations accepted, Elev: 6194ft/1888m, Tel: 661-269-2808, Nearest town: Wrightwood. GPS: 34.394748, -117.729488

728 • G3 | Mt. Pacifico (Angeles NF)

Total sites: 8, RV sites: 8, No water, Vault/pit toilet, Tent & RV camping: $5, Adventure Pass required ($5/day or $30/year) or Interagency Pass, Road not maintained for passenger cars, Stay limit: 14 days, Open May-Sep, Reservations not accepted, Elev: 6982ft/2128m, Tel: 818-899-1900, Nearest town: Pasadena. GPS: 34.379407, -118.034394

729 • G3 | Oak Flat (Whitaker Peak) (Angeles NF)

Total sites: 27, RV sites: 27, Central water, Vault/pit toilet, No showers, No RV dump, Tent & RV camping: $5, Adventure Pass required ($5/day or $30/year) or Interagency Pass, Stay limit: 14 days, Open all year, Max Length: 18ft, Reservations not accepted, Elev: 2782ft/848m, Tel: 661-269-2808, Nearest town: Castaic. GPS: 34.599941, -118.722024

730 • G3 | Peavine (Angeles NF)

Total sites: 4, RV sites: 0, Central water, Vault/pit toilet, No showers, No RV dump, Tents only: $5, Often inaccessible in winter, Adventure Pass required ($5/day or $30/year) or Interagency Pass, Stay limit: 14 days, Open all year, Reservations not accepted, Elev: 6040ft/1841m, Tel: 661-269-2808, Nearest town: Big Pines. GPS: 34.389619, -117.718724

731 • G3 | Sawmill (Angeles NF)

Total sites: 8, RV sites: 8, No water, Vault/pit toilet, Tent & RV camping: $5, Adventure Pass required ($5/day or $30/year) or Interagency Pass, Stay limit: 14 days, Max Length: 16ft, Reservations not accepted, Elev: 5187ft/1581m, Tel: 661-269-2808, Nearest town: Lake Hughes. GPS: 34.701083, -118.572056

732 • G3 | Snowslide Canyon (Angeles NF)

Total sites: 20, RV sites: 20, No water, Vault/pit toilet, Tent & RV camping: Free, Stay limit: 14 days, Reservations not accepted, Elev: 5693ft/1735m, Nearest town: Azusa. GPS: 34.325396, -117.837086

733 • G3 | Southfork (Angeles NF)

Total sites: 21, RV sites: 21, No water, Vault/pit toilet, Tent & RV camping: $5, Group site available, Adventure Pass required ($5/day or $30/year) or Interagency Pass, Stay limit: 14 days, Max Length: 16ft, Reservations not accepted, Elev: 4646ft/1416m, Tel: 661-269-2808, Nearest town: Palmdale. GPS: 34.395621, -117.820716

734 • G3 | Spring Camp (Angeles NF)

Total sites: 3, RV sites: 3, No water, Vault/pit toilet, Tent & RV camping: $5, Rough roads, Permit is required to use the Rincon Shortcut OHV route along which this campground is located, Adventure Pass required ($5/day or $30/year) or Interagency Pass, Stay limit: 14 days, Open all year, Reservations not accepted, Elev: 4695ft/1431m, Tel: 818-899-1900, Nearest town: Monrovia. GPS: 34.215824, -117.977593

735 • G3 | Streamside (Angeles NF)

Total sites: 9, RV sites: 0, No water, Vault/pit toilet, Tents only: $5, Stay limit: 14 days, Open all year, Reservations not accepted, Elev: 2356ft/718m, Tel: 661-269-2808. GPS: 34.549421, -118.431984

736 • G3 | Sycamore Flats (Angeles NF)

Total sites: 12, RV sites: 12, Central water, Vault/pit toilet, No showers, No RV dump, Tent & RV camping: $5, Adventure Pass required ($5/day or $30/year) or Interagency Pass, Stay limit: 14 days, Open all year, Max Length: 18ft, Reservations not accepted, Elev: 4429ft/1350m, Tel: 818-899-1900, Nearest town: Wrightwood. GPS: 34.413463, -117.825285

737 • G3 | Table Mountain (Angeles) (Angeles NF)

Total sites: 41, RV sites: 41, Central water, Vault/pit toilet, No showers, No RV dump, Tent & RV camping: $23, Group fee: $92, Stay limit: 14 days, Open May-Oct, Max Length: 60ft, Reservations accepted, Elev: 7313ft/2229m, Tel: 760-249-3526, Nearest town: Wrightwood. GPS: 34.386471, -117.689954

738 • G4 | Barton Flats (San Bernadino NF)

Total sites: 52, RV sites: 52, Central water, Flush toilet, Free showers, RV dump, Tent & RV camping: $33-35, Open May-Oct, Max Length: 35ft, Reservations accepted, Elev: 6391ft/1948m, Tel: 909-866-8550, Nearest town: Angelus Oaks. GPS: 34.171288, -116.875518

739 • G4 | Big Pine Flat (San Bernadino NF)

Total sites: 19, RV sites: 19, Central water, Vault/pit toilet, Tent & RV camping: $26, Water is limited/please fill up trailers/RVs before arriving, Open May-Oct, Max Length: 30ft, Reservations not accepted, Elev: 6857ft/2090m, Tel: 909-382-2790, Nearest town: Big Bear Lake. GPS: 34.320086, -117.011653

740 • G4 | Black Mountain Yellow Post (San Bernadino NF)

Total sites: 6, RV sites: 0, No water, No toilets, Tents only: Free, High clearance vehicles recommended, No vehicle access in winter, Reservations not accepted, Elev: 7467ft/2276m, Tel: 909-382-2921. GPS: 33.827712, -116.744819

741 • G4 | Boulder Basin (San Bernadino NF)

Total sites: 16, RV sites: 7, No water, Vault/pit toilet, Tent & RV camping: $10, High clearance vehicles are recommended, Open May-Oct, Max Length: 20ft, Reservations accepted, Elev: 7513ft/2290m, Tel: 909-382-2922, Nearest town: Idyllwild. GPS: 33.826395, -116.755803

742 • G4 | Clark's Ranch Yellow Post Site (San Bernadino NF)

Total sites: 1, RV sites: 0, No water, No toilets, Tents only: Free, High-clearance vehicle recommended, Reservations not accepted, Elev: 5059ft/1542m, Tel: 909-382-2882, Nearest town: Big Bear Lake. GPS: 34.183998, -116.977290

743 • G4 | Crab Flats (San Bernadino NF)

Total sites: 27, RV sites: 27, Central water, Vault/pit toilet, No showers, No RV dump, Tent & RV camping: $24-26, Due to washouts (potholes) access road to the campground is very narrow and may not accept large RVs, Open Apr-Oct, Max Length: 26ft, Reservations accepted, Elev: 5961ft/1817m, Tel: 909-867-2165, Nearest town: Lake Arrowhead. GPS: 34.263372, -117.086402

744 • G4 | Dogwood (San Bernadino NF)

Total sites: 89, RV sites: 53, Elec sites: 19, Central water, Flush toilet, Free showers, RV dump, Tents: $37-39/RVs: $37-49, Open Apr-Oct, Max Length: 40ft, Reservations accepted, Elev: 5673ft/1729m, Tel: 909-336-6717, Nearest town: Rimforest. GPS: 34.235575, -117.213083

745 • G4 | Fern Basin (San Bernadino NF)

Total sites: 15, RV sites: 15, Central water, Vault/pit toilet, No showers, No RV dump, Tent & RV camping: $10, Open May-Nov, Max Length: 20ft, Reservations accepted, Elev: 6322ft/1927m, Tel: 909-382-2922, Nearest town: Idyllwild. GPS: 33.789195, -116.736757

746 • G4 | Green Valley (San Bernadino NF)

Total sites: 37, RV sites: 9, Central water, Flush toilet, No showers, No RV dump, Tent & RV camping: $26-28, Open Apr-Oct, Max Length: 25ft, Reservations accepted, Elev: 7159ft/2182m, Tel: 909-867-2165, Nearest town: Lake Arrowhead. GPS: 34.244727, -117.062757

747 • G4 | Hanna Flat (San Bernadino NF)

Total sites: 85, RV sites: 55, Central water, Vault/pit toilet, No showers, No RV dump, Tent & RV camping: $30-32, Open Apr-Oct, Max Length: 28ft, Reservations accepted, Elev: 7159ft/2182m, Tel: 909-382-2790, Nearest town: Fawnskin. GPS: 34.287801, -116.974538

748 • G4 | Heart Bar (San Bernadino NF)

Total sites: 89, RV sites: 89, Central water, Vault/pit toilet, No showers, No RV dump, Tent & RV camping: $26-28, Open Apr-Nov, Max Length: 45ft, Reservations accepted, Elev: 6926ft/2111m, Tel: 909-866-8550, Nearest town: Angelus Oaks. GPS: 34.158919, -116.786185

749 • G4 | Holcomb Valley (San Bernadino NF)

Total sites: 19, RV sites: 19, No water, Vault/pit toilet, Tent & RV camping: $24-26, Open all year, Reservations not accepted, Elev: 7385ft/2251m, Tel: 909-382-2790, Nearest town: Big Bear City. GPS: 34.302573, -116.896108

750 • G4 | Horse Springs (San Bernadino NF)

Total sites: 11, RV sites: 11, No water, Vault/pit toilet, Tent & RV camping: $10, Road conditions may prevent or hinder access during winter/spring, Open all year, Reservations not accepted, Elev: 5732ft/1747m, Tel: 909-382-2790, Nearest town: Fawnskin. GPS: 34.352124, -117.070488

751 • G4 | Keller Peak Yellow Post 3 (San Bernadino NF)

Total sites: 9, RV sites: 0, No water, No toilets, Tents only: Free, Stay limit: 14 days, Elev: 6578ft/2005m, Tel: 909-382-2790, Nearest town: Running Springs. GPS: 34.208772, -117.065052

752 • G4 | Marion Mountain (San Bernadino NF)

Total sites: 25, RV sites: 25, Central water, Vault/pit toilet, No showers, No RV dump, Tent & RV camping: $10, Open May-Nov, Max Length: 20ft, Reservations accepted, Elev: 6453ft/1967m, Tel: 909-382-2922, Nearest town: Idyllwild. GPS: 33.792174, -116.732121

753 • G4 | Mission Springs TC (San Bernadino NF)

Total sites: 2, RV sites: 0, No water, No toilets, Tents only: Free, Elev: 7930ft/2417m, Tel: 909-382-2882, Nearest town: Angelus Oaks. GPS: 34.125608, -116.758241

754 • G4 | Morris Ranch RD Yellow Post (San Bernadino NF)

Total sites: 6, RV sites: 6, No water, No toilets, Tent & RV camping: Free, 1/2 mile past gate, Elev: 5359ft/1633m, Nearest town: Idyllwild. GPS: 33.639480, -116.592490

755 • G4 | North Shore (San Bernadino NF)

Total sites: 28, RV sites: 25, Central water, Flush toilet, No showers, No RV dump, Tent & RV camping: $26-28, Open Apr-Sep, Max Length: 25ft, Reservations accepted, Elev: 5328ft/1624m, Tel: 909-866-8550, Nearest town: Running Springs. GPS: 34.267225, -117.164201

756 • G4 | Pineknot (San Bernadino NF)

Total sites: 47, RV sites: 47, Central water, Flush toilet, No showers, No RV dump, Tent & RV camping: $31-33, Open Apr-Oct, Max Length: 26ft, Reservations accepted, Elev: 6965ft/2123m, Tel: 909-866-8550, Nearest town: Big Bear City. GPS: 34.235772, -116.883829

757 • G4 | San Gorgonio (San Bernadino NF)

Total sites: 51, RV sites: 51, Central water, Flush toilet, Free showers, No RV dump, Tent & RV camping: $31-33, 3 group sites $62-$66, Open Apr-Sep, Max Length: 40ft, Reservations accepted, Elev: 6545ft/1995m, Tel: 909-866-8550, Nearest town: Angelus Oaks. GPS: 34.174437, -116.867463

758 • G4 | Serrano (San Bernadino NF)

Total sites: 108, RV sites: 108, Elec sites: 29, Central water, Flush toilet, Free showers, RV dump, Tents: $37-39/RVs: $37-49, Open Mar-Nov, Reservations accepted, Elev: 6844ft/2086m, Tel: 909-866-8021, Nearest town: Big Bear Lake. GPS: 34.263555, -116.917463

759 • G4 | South Fork (San Bernadino NF)

Total sites: 24, RV sites: 24, Central water, Vault/pit toilet, No showers, No RV dump, Tent & RV camping: $26, Open May-Sep, Max Length: 30ft, Reservations not accepted, Elev: 6339ft/1932m, Tel: 909-382-2790, Nearest town: Angelus Oaks. GPS: 34.168616, -116.825184

760 • G4 | Thomas Yellow Post Sites (San Bernadino NF)

Total sites: 5, RV sites: 0, No water, No toilets, Tents only: Free, High-clearance vehicle recommended, Reservations not accepted, Elev: 5751ft/1753m, Tel: 909-382-2882. GPS: 34.128422, -117.005479

761 • G4 | Tool Box Springs (San Bernadino NF)

Total sites: 6, RV sites: 6, No water, Vault/pit toilet, Tent & RV camping: Free, Open all year, Reservations not accepted, Elev: 6122ft/1866m, Nearest town: Azusa. GPS: 33.611682, -116.661558

762 • G4 | Tool Box Springs Yellow Post (San Bernadino NF)

Total sites: 6, RV sites: 0, No water, No toilets, Tents only: Free, Reservations not accepted, Elev: 6014ft/1833m, Tel: 909-382-2922. GPS: 33.616043, -116.660679

763 • G4 | Wildhorse Equestrian Camp (San Bernadino NF)

Total sites: 11, RV sites: 11, Central water, Flush toilet, Free showers, No RV dump, Tent & RV camping: $32-34, Open May-Sep, Max Length: 30ft, Reservations accepted, Elev: 6955ft/2120m, Tel: 909-866-8550, Nearest town: Redlands. GPS: 34.155908, -116.780423

764 • H3 | Upper San Juan (Cleveland NF)

Total sites: 18, RV sites: 18, Central water, Vault/pit toilet, No showers, No RV dump, Tent & RV camping: $18, Stay limit: 14 days, Open Jun-Sep, Max Length: 32ft, Reservations not accepted, Elev: 1795ft/547m, Tel: 858-673-6180, Nearest town: Lake Elsinore. GPS: 33.607242, -117.432236

765 • H4 | Bobcat Meadow (Cleveland NF)

Total sites: 20, RV sites: 20, No water, Vault/pit toilet, Tent & RV camping: $5, Rough road - high-clearance vehicle required, Adventure Pass required ($5/day or $30/year) or Interagency Pass, Stay limit: 14 days, Open all year, Max Length: 27ft, Reservations not accepted, Elev: 3806ft/1160m, Tel: 619-445-6235, Nearest town: Pine Valley. GPS: 32.711449, -116.556922

766 • H4 | Boulder Oaks Horse Camp (Cleveland NF)

Total sites: 30, RV sites: 30, Central water, Vault/pit toilet, No showers, No RV dump, Tent & RV camping: $14-16, One loop has 17 equestrian sites and corrals - the other loop has family campsites, Stay limit: 14 days, Open all year, Max Length: 40ft, Reservations accepted, Elev: 3182ft/970m, Tel: 619-445-6235, Nearest town: Pine Valley. GPS: 32.729064, -116.483295

767 • H4 | Burnt Rancheria (Cleveland NF)

Total sites: 109, RV sites: 69, Central water, Flush toilet, Pay showers, No RV dump, Tent & RV camping: $28, Stay limit: 14 days, Open Mar-Oct, Max Length: 50ft, Reservations accepted, Elev: 5948ft/1813m, Tel: 619-473-0120, Nearest town: Pine Valley. GPS: 32.859995, -116.417898

768 • H4 | Cibbets Flat (Cleveland NF)

Total sites: 25, RV sites: 25, Central water, Vault/pit toilet, No showers, No RV dump, Tent & RV camping: $14, Stay limit: 14 days, Max Length: 27ft, Reservations not accepted, Elev: 4167ft/1270m, Tel: 858-673-6180, Nearest town: Pine Valley. GPS: 32.777217, -116.446916

769 • H4 | Corral Canyon (Cleveland NF)

Total sites: 20, RV sites: 20, Central water, Vault/pit toilet, No showers, No RV dump, Tent & RV camping: $5, Adventure Pass required ($5/day or $30/year) or Interagency Pass, Stay limit: 14 days, Max Length: 27ft, Reservations not accepted, Elev: 3474ft/1059m, Tel: 619-445-6235, Nearest town: Pine Valley. GPS: 32.712442, -116.572208

770 • H4 | Dripping Springs (Cleveland NF)

Total sites: 33, RV sites: 31, Central water, Vault/pit toilet, No showers, No RV dump, Tent & RV camping: $15, 9 equestrian sites - 20' trailer limit, Stay limit: 14 days, Open all year, Max Length: 25ft, Reservations accepted, Elev: 1673ft/510m, Tel: 760-788-0250, Nearest town: Aguanga. GPS: 33.460689, -116.970862

771 • H4 | Fry Creek (Cleveland NF)

Total sites: 20, RV sites: 20, Central water, Vault/pit toilet, No showers, No RV dump, Tent & RV camping: $15, No trailers, Stay limit: 14 days, Open Apr-Nov, Max Length: 12ft, Reservations accepted, Elev: 4997ft/1523m, Tel: 760-788-0250, Nearest town: Santa Ysabel. GPS: 33.344087, -116.882092

772 • H4 | Indian Flats (Cleveland NF)

Total sites: 17, RV sites: 17, No water, Vault/pit toilet, Tent & RV camping: $12, Group site available, Stay limit: 14 days, Open Jun-

Mar, Max Length: 15ft, Reservations not accepted, Elev: 3648ft/1112m, Tel: 858-673-6180, Nearest town: Warner Springs. GPS: 33.349515, -116.659726

773 • H4 | Laguna (Cleveland NF)

Total sites: 104, RV sites: 95, Central water, Flush toilet, Pay showers, No RV dump, Tent & RV camping: $28, Star-gazing parties, Stay limit: 14 days, Open all year, Max Length: 50ft, Reservations accepted, Elev: 5545ft/1690m, Tel: 619-473-2082, Nearest town: Pine Valley. GPS: 32.888638, -116.448821

774 • H4 | Little Thomas Mt - Yellow Post #1 (San Bernadino NF)

Total sites: 5, RV sites: 5, No water, No toilets, Tent & RV camping: Free, More sites up mountain - 4x4 required, Elev: 5064ft/1544m, Nearest town: Idyllwild. GPS: 33.579653, -116.624299

775 • H4 | Oak Grove (Cleveland NF)

Total sites: 64, RV sites: 64, Central water, Flush toilet, No showers, No RV dump, Tent & RV camping: $15, Stay limit: 14 days, Open all year, Max Length: 25ft, Reservations accepted, Elev: 2772ft/845m, Tel: 760-788-0250, Nearest town: Warner Springs. GPS: 33.386925, -116.790428

776 • H4 | Observatory (Cleveland NF)

Total sites: 43, RV sites: 43, Central water, Flush toilet, Pay showers, No RV dump, Tent & RV camping: $15, Some sites have level cement pads for telescopes, Stay limit: 14 days, Open all year, Max Length: 35ft, Reservations accepted, Elev: 4954ft/1510m, Tel: 760-788-0250, Nearest town: Palomar Mountain. GPS: 33.343002, -116.877867

777 • H4 | Pinyon Flat (San Bernadino NF)

Total sites: 18, RV sites: 18, Central water, Vault/pit toilet, No showers, No RV dump, Tent & RV camping: $8, Open all year, Reservations not accepted, Elev: 4032ft/1229m, Tel: 909-659-2117, Nearest town: Palm Desert. GPS: 33.584877, -116.456766

778 • H4 | Puerta La Cruz (Cleveland NF)

Total sites: 5, RV sites: 5, No water, No toilets, Tent & RV camping: Fee unk, No fires, Adventure Pass and Dispersed Permit required, Stay limit: 14 days, Max Length: 35ft, Elev: 4022ft/1226m, Tel: 760-788-0250, Nearest town: Warner Springs. GPS: 33.334833, -116.641095

779 • H4 | Ribbonwood Horse Camp (San Bernadino NF)

Total sites: 8, RV sites: 8, Central water, Flush toilet, Free showers, No RV dump, Tent & RV camping: $15, Open all year, Reservations accepted, Elev: 4058ft/1237m, Tel: 909-382-2922, Nearest town: Pinyon. GPS: 33.577589, -116.453747

780 • H4 | Santa Rosa Yellow Post (San Bernadino NF)

Total sites: 14, RV sites: 0, No water, No toilets, Tents only: Fee unk, Reservations not accepted, Elev: 7999ft/2438m, Tel: 909-382-2922, Nearest town: Palm Springs. GPS: 33.536915, -116.461755

781 • H4 | Wildomar (Cleveland NF)

Total sites: 11, RV sites: 11, No water, Vault/pit toilet, No showers, No RV dump, Tent & RV camping: $15, Stay limit: 14 days, Max Length: 22ft, Reservations not accepted, Elev: 2487ft/758m, Tel: 858-673-6180, Nearest town: Lake Elsinore. GPS: 33.581419, -117.341497

Colorado

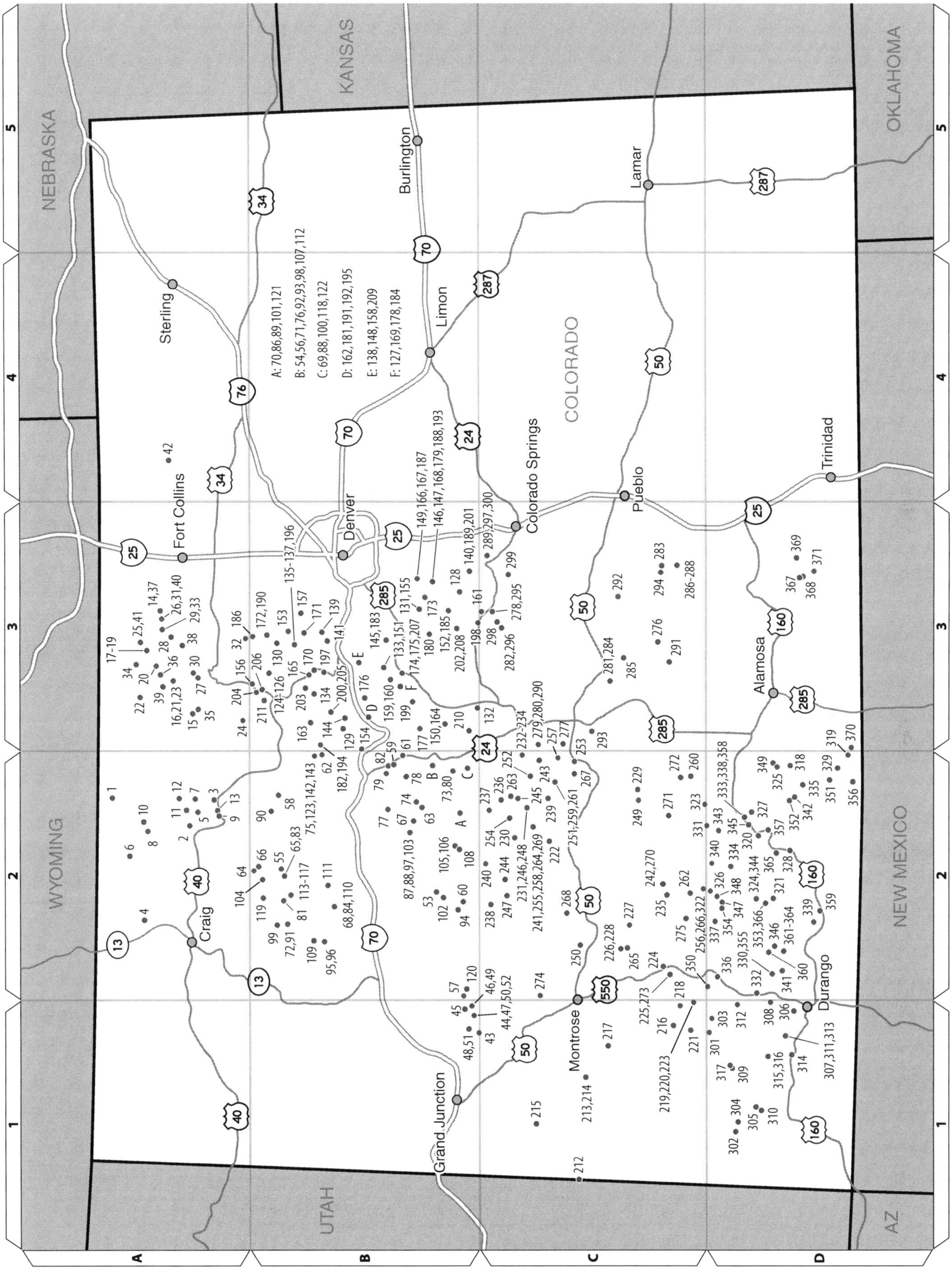
NEBRASKA
WYOMING
KANSAS
OKLAHOMA
NEW MEXICO
UTAH
AZ
COLORADO
Sterling
Fort Collins
Denver
Burlington
Limon
Lamar
Colorado Springs
Pueblo
Trinidad
Alamosa
Durango
Montrose
Grand Junction
Craig
A: 70,86,89,101,121
B: 54,56,71,76,92,93,98,107,112
C: 69,88,100,118,122
D: 162,181,191,192,195
E: 138,148,158,209
F: 127,169,178,184
A
B
C
D
1
2
3
4
5

Map	ID	Map	ID
A2	1-13	C1	212-221
A3	14-41	C2	222-275
A4	42	C3	276-300
B1	43-52	D1	301-317
B2	53-123	D2	318-366
B3	124-211	D3	367-371

Alphabetical List of Camping Areas

1 • A2 | Big Creek Lake (Medicine Bow-Routt NF)

Total sites: 54, RV sites: 54, No water, Vault/pit toilet, No showers, No RV dump, Tent & RV camping: $10, Open Jun-Sep, Max Length: 50ft, Reservations accepted, Elev: 9035ft/2754m, Tel: 970-723-2700, Nearest town: Collbran. GPS: 40.935932, -106.610545

2 • A2 | Dry Lake (Medicine Bow-Routt NF)

Total sites: 8, RV sites: 8, No water, Vault/pit toilet, Tent & RV camping: $10, Open Jun-Oct, Max Length: 20ft, Reservations not accepted, Elev: 8324ft/2537m, Tel: 307-745-2300, Nearest town: Steamboat Springs. GPS: 40.536264, -106.781954

3 • A2 | Dumont Lake (Medicine Bow-Routt NF)

Total sites: 22, RV sites: 22, Water available, Vault/pit toilet, No showers, No RV dump, Tent & RV camping: $12, Open Jun-Oct, Max Length: 40ft, Reservations accepted, Elev: 9537ft/2907m, Tel: 970-870-2299, Nearest town: Steamboat Springs. GPS: 40.401855, -106.624268

4 • A2 | Freeman Reservoir (Medicine Bow-Routt NF)

Total sites: 18, RV sites: 18, Water available, Vault/pit toilet, No showers, No RV dump, Tent & RV camping: $12, Max Length: 25ft, Reservations not accepted, Elev: 8865ft/2702m, Tel: 307-745-2300, Nearest town: Craig. GPS: 40.762395, -107.421546

5 • A2 | Granite (Medicine Bow-Routt NF)

Total sites: 8, RV sites: 8, No water, Vault/pit toilet, Tent & RV camping: $10, Open Jul-Oct, Max Length: 22ft, Reservations not accepted, Elev: 9944ft/3031m, Tel: 307-745-2300, Nearest town: Steamboat Springs. GPS: 40.495512, -106.691759

6 • A2 | Hahns Peak Lake (Medicine Bow-Routt NF)

Total sites: 26, RV sites: 26, No water, Vault/pit toilet, Tent & RV camping: $10, Open Jun-Oct, Max Length: 60ft, Reservations accepted, Elev: 8432ft/2570m, Tel: 970-870-2299, Nearest town: Steamboat Springs. GPS: 40.839433, -106.996528

7 • A2 | Hidden Lakes (Medicine Bow-Routt NF)

Total sites: 9, RV sites: 9, Water available, Vault/pit toilet, No showers, No RV dump, Tent & RV camping: $10, Open all year, Max Length: 20ft, Reservations not accepted, Elev: 8947ft/2727m, Tel: 307-745-2300, Nearest town: Walden. GPS: 40.506609, -106.608701

8 • A2 | Hinman (Medicine Bow-Routt NF)

Total sites: 13, RV sites: 13, Water available, Vault/pit toilet, No showers, No RV dump, Tent & RV camping: $12, Open Jun-Oct, Max Length: 22ft, Reservations not accepted, Elev: 7723ft/2354m, Tel: 307-745-2300, Nearest town: Steamboat Springs. GPS: 40.748584, -106.834213

9 • A2 | Meadows (Medicine Bow-Routt NF)

Total sites: 30, RV sites: 20, No water, Vault/pit toilet, Tent & RV camping: $10, Open Jun-Oct, Reservations not accepted, Elev: 9331ft/2844m, Tel: 970-870-2299, Nearest town: Steamboat Springs. GPS: 40.373791, -106.723288

10 • A2 | Seedhouse (Medicine Bow-Routt NF)

Total sites: 23, RV sites: 23, Central water, Vault/pit toilet, Tent & RV camping: $12, Open May-Oct, Max Length: 22ft, Reservations accepted, Elev: 8054ft/2455m, Tel: 970-870-2299, Nearest town: Steamboat Springs. GPS: 40.771809, -106.771771

11 • A2 | Summit Lake (Medicine Bow-Routt NF)

Total sites: 15, RV sites: 9, No water, Vault/pit toilet, Tent & RV camping: $10, Open Jul-Oct, Max Length: 18ft, Reservations not accepted, Elev: 10397ft/3169m, Tel: 307-745-2300, Nearest town: Walden. GPS: 40.546701, -106.683168

12 • A2 | Teal Lake (Medicine Bow-Routt NF)

Total sites: 17, RV sites: 17, No water, Vault/pit toilet, Tent & RV camping: $10, Open Jun-Sep, Max Length: 25ft, Reservations not accepted, Elev: 8865ft/2702m, Tel: 307-745-2300, Nearest town: Walden. GPS: 40.585059, -106.607064

13 • A2 | Walton Creek (Medicine Bow-Routt NF)

Total sites: 14, RV sites: 14, No toilets, Tent & RV camping: $12, Open Jun-Sep, Max Length: 22ft, Reservations not accepted, Elev: 9384ft/2860m, Tel: 970-870-2299, Nearest town: Steamboat Spring. GPS: 40.381896, -106.684823

14 • A3 | Ansel Watrous (Arapaho & Roosevelt NF)

Total sites: 16, RV sites: 16, Central water, Vault/pit toilet, No showers, No RV dump, Tent & RV camping: $23, Open all year, Max Length: 40ft, Reservations accepted, Elev: 5876ft/1791m, Tel: 970-295-6700, Nearest town: Rustic. GPS: 40.690042, -105.348751

15 • A3 | Aspen (Gould) (Medicine Bow-Routt NF)

Total sites: 7, No water, Vault/pit toilet, Tents only: $10, Open May-Oct, Reservations not accepted, Elev: 8976ft/2736m, Tel: 719-539-7289, Nearest town: Gould. GPS: 40.516383, -106.033441

16 • A3 | Aspen Glen (Arapaho & Roosevelt NF)

Total sites: 9, RV sites: 9, Central water, Vault/pit toilet, No showers, No RV dump, Tent & RV camping: $19, Open May-Sep, Max Length: 35ft, Reservations not accepted, Elev: 8707ft/2654m,

Tel: 970-295-6700, Nearest town: Fort Collins. GPS: 40.619398, -105.818094

17 • A3 | Bellaire Lake (Arapaho & Roosevelt NF)

Total sites: 26, RV sites: 26, Elec sites: 21, Central water, No toilets, No showers, No RV dump, Tents: $24/RVs: $24-32, Open May-Sep, Max Length: 60ft, Reservations accepted, Elev: 8717ft/2657m, Tel: 970-295-6700, Nearest town: Red Feather Lakes. GPS: 40.768556, -105.622389

18 • A3 | Bellaire Lake Dispersed Sites 1-5 (Arapaho & Roosevelt NF)

Total sites: 5, No water, No toilets, Tent & RV camping: Free, Not for larger RVs, Elev: 8467ft/2581m. GPS: 40.777671, -105.602582

19 • A3 | Bellaire Lake Dispersed Sites 6-12 (Arapaho & Roosevelt NF)

Total sites: 7, No water, No toilets, Tent & RV camping: Free, Not for larger RVs, Elev: 8574ft/2613m. GPS: 40.768154, -105.609871

20 • A3 | Big Bend (Arapaho & Roosevelt NF)

Total sites: 8, RV sites: 5, Central water, Vault/pit toilet, No showers, No RV dump, Tent & RV camping: $19, Open May-Dec, Max Length: 20ft, Reservations not accepted, Elev: 7720ft/2353m, Tel: 970-295-6700, Nearest town: Fort Collins. GPS: 40.707476, -105.724763

21 • A3 | Big South (Arapaho & Roosevelt NF)

Total sites: 4, RV sites: 4, No water, Vault/pit toilet, Tent & RV camping: $19, Open Jun-Sep, Max Length: 25ft, Reservations not accepted, Elev: 8560ft/2609m, Tel: 970-295-6700, Nearest town: Fort Collins. GPS: 40.632885, -105.807331

22 • A3 | Browns Park (Arapaho & Roosevelt NF)

Total sites: 28, RV sites: 28, No water, Vault/pit toilet, Tent & RV camping: $18, Open Jun-Sep, Max Length: 30ft, Reservations not accepted, Elev: 8488ft/2587m, Tel: 970-295-6700, Nearest town: Gould. GPS: 40.796143, -105.927246

23 • A3 | Chambers Lake (Arapaho & Roosevelt NF)

Total sites: 51, RV sites: 44, Central water, Vault/pit toilet, No showers, No RV dump, Tent & RV camping: $24, Open Jun-Sep, Max Length: 35ft, Reservations accepted, Elev: 9215ft/2809m, Tel: 970-295-6700, Nearest town: Rustic. GPS: 40.594014, -105.849422

24 • A3 | Denver Creek (Arapaho & Roosevelt NF)

Total sites: 22, RV sites: 22, Central water, Vault/pit toilet, No showers, No RV dump, Tent & RV camping: $21, Open May-Sep, Max Length: 45ft, Reservations not accepted, Elev: 8635ft/2632m, Tel: 970-887-4100, Nearest town: Granby. GPS: 40.254975, -106.079463

25 • A3 | Dowdy Lake (Arapaho & Roosevelt NF)

Total sites: 70, RV sites: 60, Elec sites: 60, Central water, Vault/pit toilet, No showers, No RV dump, Tents: $24/RVs: $24-32, Open all year, Max Length: 84ft, Reservations accepted, Elev: 8163ft/2488m, Tel: 970-295-6700, Nearest town: Fort Collins. GPS: 40.792425, -105.554924

26 • A3 | Dutch George Flats (Arapaho & Roosevelt NF)

Total sites: 20, RV sites: 20, Central water, Vault/pit toilet, No showers, No RV dump, Tent & RV camping: $23, Open Jun-Sep, Max Length: 33ft, Reservations not accepted, Elev: 6526ft/1989m, Tel: 970-295-6700, Nearest town: Fort Collins. GPS: 40.695965, -105.445352

27 • A3 | Grandview (Arapaho & Roosevelt NF)

Total sites: 9, RV sites: 0, Central water, Vault/pit toilet, No showers, No RV dump, Tents only: $20, Walk-to sites, Open Jul-Sep, Reservations not accepted, Elev: 10171ft/3100m, Tel: 970-295-6700, Nearest town: Fort Collins. GPS: 40.493818, -105.802292

28 • A3 | Jacks Gulch (Arapaho & Roosevelt NF)

Total sites: 56, RV sites: 56, Elec sites: 27, Central water, Vault/pit toilet, No showers, No RV dump, Tents: $24/RVs: $24-37, Group site (reservable): $187, 5 equestrian sites, Open May-Nov, Max Length: 80ft, Reservations not accepted, Elev: 8199ft/2499m, Tel: 970-295-6700, Nearest town: Rustic. GPS: 40.636618, -105.527367

29 • A3 | Kelly Flats (Arapaho & Roosevelt NF)

Total sites: 29, RV sites: 25, Central water, Vault/pit toilet, No showers, No RV dump, Tent & RV camping: $24, Open Jun-Sep, Max Length: 40ft, Reservations not accepted, Elev: 6811ft/2076m, Tel: 970-295-6700, Nearest town: Rustic. GPS: 40.682376, -105.483854

30 • A3 | Long Draw (Arapaho & Roosevelt NF)

Total sites: 25, RV sites: 25, Central water, Vault/pit toilet, No showers, No RV dump, Tent & RV camping: $20, Open Jul-Sep, Max Length: 30ft, Reservations not accepted, Elev: 10026ft/3056m, Tel: 970-295-6700, Nearest town: Gould. GPS: 40.515554, -105.767083

31 • A3 | Lower Narrows (Arapaho & Roosevelt NF)

Total sites: 15, RV sites: 7, Central water, Vault/pit toilet, No showers, No RV dump, Tent & RV camping: $23, Open May-Sep, Max Length: 60ft, Reservations accepted, Elev: 6463ft/1970m, Tel: 970-295-6700, Nearest town: Fort Collins. GPS: 40.688848, -105.432473

32 • A3 | Meeker Park Overflow (Arapaho & Roosevelt NF)

Total sites: 29, RV sites: 29, No water, Vault/pit toilet, Tent & RV camping: $13, Better suited for tents - unpaved roads-steep hills-short pull-ins, Open May-Sep, Max Length: 25ft, Reservations not accepted, Elev: 8638ft/2633m, Tel: 303-541-2500, Nearest town: Estes Park. GPS: 40.242525, -105.534311

33 • A3 | Mountain Park (Arapaho & Roosevelt NF)

Total sites: 55, RV sites: 55, Elec sites: 32, Central water, Flush toilet, Pay showers, No RV dump, Tents: $24/RVs: $24-32, Group fee: $145, Open May-Sep, Max Length: 45ft, Reservations accepted, Elev: 6676ft/2035m, Tel: 970-295-6700, Nearest town: Rustic. GPS: 40.682251, -105.466636

34 • A3 | North Fork Poudre (Arapaho & Roosevelt NF)

Total sites: 9, RV sites: 9, No water, Vault/pit toilet, Tent & RV camping: $15, Open Jun-Sep, Max Length: 30ft, Reservations not accepted, Elev: 9190ft/2801m, Tel: 970-295-6700, Nearest town: Livermore. GPS: 40.814232, -105.710238

35 • A3 | Pines (Medicine Bow-Routt NF)

Total sites: 11, RV sites: 11, Central water, Vault/pit toilet, No showers, No RV dump, Tent & RV camping: $10, Snowmobile/ski access in winter, Open all year, Max Length: 20ft, Reservations not accepted, Elev: 9236ft/2815m, Tel: 307-745-2300, Nearest town: Rustic. GPS: 40.491213, -106.007064

36 • A3 | Sleeping Elephant (Arapaho & Roosevelt NF)

Total sites: 15, RV sites: 15, No water, Vault/pit toilet, Tent & RV camping: $19, Open Jun-Sep, Max Length: 20ft, Reservations not accepted, Elev: 7871ft/2399m, Tel: 970-295-6700, Nearest town: Rustic. GPS: 40.682821, -105.773218

37 • A3 | Stove Prairie (Arapaho & Roosevelt NF)

Total sites: 9, RV sites: 5, Central water, Vault/pit toilet, No showers, No RV dump, Tent & RV camping: $23, Also walk-to sites, Open May-Oct, Max Length: 40ft, Reservations accepted, Elev: 6240ft/1902m, Tel: 970-295-6700, Nearest town: Fort Collins. GPS: 40.683851, -105.396935

38 • A3 | Tom Bennett (Arapaho & Roosevelt NF)

Total sites: 10, RV sites: 10, No water, Vault/pit toilet, Tent & RV camping: $15, Open May-Oct, Max Length: 20ft, Reservations not accepted, Elev: 8931ft/2722m, Tel: 970-295-6700, Nearest town: Rustic. GPS: 40.575715, -105.584243

39 • A3 | Tunnel (Arapaho & Roosevelt NF)

Total sites: 49, RV sites: 49, Central water, Vault/pit toilet, No showers, No RV dump, Tent & RV camping: $22, Open Jun-Sep, Max Length: 40ft, Reservations not accepted, Elev: 8606ft/2623m, Tel: 970-295-6700, Nearest town: Rustic. GPS: 40.673695, -105.855942

40 • A3 | Upper Narrows (Arapaho & Roosevelt NF)

Total sites: 7, RV sites: 7, Central water, Vault/pit toilet, No showers, No RV dump, Tent & RV camping: $23, Open May-Sep, Max Length: 60ft, Reservations accepted, Elev: 6539ft/1993m, Tel: 970-295-6700, Nearest town: Fort Collins. GPS: 40.691295, -105.432298

41 • A3 | West Lake (Arapaho & Roosevelt NF)

Total sites: 36, RV sites: 31, Elec sites: 31, Central water, Vault/pit toilet, No showers, No RV dump, Tents: $24/RVs: $24-32, Open May-Sep, Max Length: 40ft, Reservations accepted, Elev: 8238ft/2511m, Tel: 970-295-6700, Nearest town: Red Feather Lakes. GPS: 40.789795, -105.567627

42 • A4 | Crow Valley (Pawnee NG)

Total sites: 10, RV sites: 10, Central water, Vault/pit toilet, No showers, No RV dump, Tent & RV camping: $11-15, 4 group sites: $46-$109, Open Apr-Nov, Max Length: 81ft, Reservations accepted, Elev: 4846ft/1477m, Tel: 970-346-5000, Nearest town: Fort Collins. GPS: 40.644021, -104.336561

43 • B1 | Carson Lake (Grand Mesa-Uncompahgre-Gunnison NF)

Total sites: 4, RV sites: 4, No water, Vault/pit toilet, Tent & RV camping: Free, Open Jul-Sep, Reservations not accepted, Elev: 9915ft/3022m, Tel: 970-874-6600, Nearest town: Grand Junction. GPS: 38.997025, -108.111435

44 • B1 | Cobbett Lake (Grand Mesa-Uncompahgre-Gunnison NF)

Total sites: 20, RV sites: 20, No water, Vault/pit toilet, No showers, No RV dump, Tent & RV camping: $16, Open Jun-Sep, Max Length: 45ft, Reservations accepted, Elev: 10279ft/3133m, Tel: 970-874-6600, Nearest town: Cedaredge. GPS: 39.041491, -107.983347

45 • B1 | Cottonwood Lake (Grand Mesa-Uncompahgre-Gunnison NF)

Total sites: 36, RV sites: 36, No water, Vault/pit toilet, No showers, No RV dump, Tent & RV camping: $14, Open Jul-Sep, Max Length: 40ft, Reservations not accepted, Elev: 10240ft/3121m, Tel: 970-242-8211, Nearest town: Collbran. GPS: 39.072525, -107.962775

46 • B1 | Crag Crest (Grand Mesa-Uncompahgre-Gunnison NF)

Total sites: 11, RV sites: 8, No water, Vault/pit toilet, No showers, No RV dump, Tent & RV camping: $12, Open Jun-Sep, Max Length: 25ft, Reservations not accepted, Elev: 10187ft/3105m, Nearest town: Grand Mesa. GPS: 39.048999, -107.937543

47 • B1 | Island Lake (Grand Mesa-Uncompahgre-Gunnison NF)

Total sites: 41, RV sites: 41, Elec sites: 8, Central water, Vault/pit toilet, No showers, No RV dump, Tents: $22/RVs: $22-30, Open Jun-Sep, Max Length: 100ft, Reservations accepted, Elev: 10321ft/3146m, Tel: 970-874-6600, Nearest town: Cedaredge. GPS: 39.030651, -108.008983

48 • B1 | Jumbo (Grand Mesa-Uncompahgre-Gunnison NF)

Total sites: 26, RV sites: 22, Elec sites: 15, Central water, Vault/pit toilet, No showers, No RV dump, Tents: $22/RVs: $30, Open Jun-Sep, Max Length: 45ft, Reservations accepted, Elev: 9792ft/2985m, Tel: 970-874-6600, Nearest town: Mesa. GPS: 39.053226, -108.093569

49 • B1 | Kiser Creek (Grand Mesa-Uncompahgre-Gunnison NF)

Total sites: 12, RV sites: 12, Vault/pit toilet, Tent & RV camping: Free, Open Jul-Sep, Max Length: 16ft, Elev: 10121ft/3085m, Nearest town: Grand Mesa. GPS: 39.037473, -107.948123

50 • B1 | Little Bear (Grand Mesa-Uncompahgre-Gunnison NF)

Total sites: 36, RV sites: 36, Central water, Flush toilet, No showers, No RV dump, Tent & RV camping: $20, Open Jun-Sep, Max Length: 45ft, Reservations not accepted, Elev: 10312ft/3143m, Tel: 970-874-6600, Nearest town: Delta. GPS: 39.035327, -107.997032

51 • B1 | Spruce Grove (Mesa Lakes) (Grand Mesa-Uncompahgre-Gunnison NF)

Total sites: 16, RV sites: 16, Central water, Vault/pit toilet, No

showers, No RV dump, Tent & RV camping: $12, Open May-Sep, Max Length: 45ft, Reservations not accepted, Elev: 10033ft/3058m, Tel: 970-874-6600, Nearest town: Mesa. GPS: 39.049064, -108.079269

52 • B1 | Ward Lake (Grand Mesa-Uncompahgre-Gunnison NF)

Total sites: 27, RV sites: 27, Central water, Vault/pit toilet, No showers, No RV dump, Tent & RV camping: $16, Food storage order, Open May-Sep, Max Length: 45ft, Reservations not accepted, Elev: 10143ft/3092m, Tel: 970-874-6600, Nearest town: Cedaredge. GPS: 39.036837, -107.984478

53 • B2 | Avalanche (White River NF)

Total sites: 13, RV sites: 13, Central water, Vault/pit toilet, Tent & RV camping: Donation, Open May-Sep, Max Length: 25ft, Reservations not accepted, Elev: 7507ft/2288m, Tel: 970-945-2521, Nearest town: Redstone. GPS: 39.235855, -107.202797

54 • B2 | Baby Doe (Pike & San Isabel NF)

Total sites: 47, RV sites: 47, Central water, No toilets, No showers, No RV dump, Tent & RV camping: $24-26, Open May-Sep, Max Length: 45ft, Reservations accepted, Elev: 9970ft/3039m, Tel: 719-486-0749, Nearest town: Leadville. GPS: 39.271396, -106.352558

55 • B2 | Bear Lake (Medicine Bow-Routt NF)

Total sites: 43, RV sites: 43, Water available, Vault/pit toilet, No showers, No RV dump, Tent & RV camping: $10, Stay limit: 14 days, Open May-Oct, Reservations not accepted, Elev: 9780ft/2981m, Tel: 307-745-2300, Nearest town: Yampa. GPS: 40.046432, -107.068698

56 • B2 | Belle of Colorado (Pike & San Isabel NF)

Total sites: 19, RV sites: 0, Central water, Vault/pit toilet, No showers, No RV dump, Tents only: $24, Open Jun-Sep, Reservations not accepted, Elev: 9944ft/3031m, Tel: 719-553-1400, Nearest town: Leadville. GPS: 39.268071, -106.351983

57 • B2 | Big Creek (Grand Mesa) (Grand Mesa-Uncompahgre-Gunnison NF)

Total sites: 26, RV sites: 26, Central water, Vault/pit toilet, No showers, No RV dump, Tent & RV camping: $16, Open Jun-Sep, Max Length: 30ft, Reservations not accepted, Elev: 10144ft/3092m, Tel: 970-242-8211, Nearest town: Collbran. GPS: 39.078435, -107.882846

58 • B2 | Blacktail Creek (Medicine Bow-Routt NF)

Total sites: 8, RV sites: 8, Central water, Vault/pit toilet, No showers, No RV dump, Tent & RV camping: $10, Open May-Oct, Max Length: 18ft, Reservations not accepted, Elev: 9127ft/2782m, Tel: 970-638-4516, Nearest town: Yampa. GPS: 40.067752, -106.579776

59 • B2 | Blodgett (White River NF)

Total sites: 6, RV sites: 6, Central water, Vault/pit toilet, Tent & RV camping: Fee unk, Max Length: 30ft, Elev: 8855ft/2699m, Nearest town: Vail. GPS: 39.472238, -106.366498

60 • B2 | Bogan Flats (White River NF)

Total sites: 36, RV sites: 36, Central water, Vault/pit toilet, No showers, No RV dump, Tent & RV camping: $27-29, Open May-Oct, Max Length: 80ft, Reservations accepted, Elev: 7605ft/2318m, Tel: 970-927-0107, Nearest town: Marble. GPS: 39.100262, -107.261518

61 • B2 | Camp Hale (White River NF)

Total sites: 21, RV sites: 21, No water, Vault/pit toilet, No showers, No RV dump, Tent & RV camping: $22-24, Open May-Oct, Max Length: 35ft, Reservations accepted, Elev: 9308ft/2837m, Tel: 970-945-2521, Nearest town: Minturn. GPS: 39.420041, -106.314438

62 • B2 | Cataract Creek (White River NF)

Total sites: 5, RV sites: 5, No water, Vault/pit toilet, Tent & RV camping: $18, Open May-Oct, Max Length: 25ft, Reservations not accepted, Elev: 8579ft/2615m, Tel: 970-945-2521, Nearest town: Silverthorne. GPS: 39.838441, -106.307417

63 • B2 | Chapman (White River NF)

Total sites: 84, RV sites: 73, Central water, Vault/pit toilet, No showers, No RV dump, Tent & RV camping: $26-28, Open May-Oct, Max Length: 99ft, Reservations accepted, Elev: 8553ft/2607m, Tel: 970-927-0107, Nearest town: Basalt. GPS: 39.315657, -106.642786

64 • B2 | Chapman Reservoir (Medicine Bow-Routt NF)

Total sites: 12, RV sites: 12, No water, Vault/pit toilet, Tent & RV camping: $10, Open May-Oct, Reservations not accepted, Elev: 9360ft/2853m, Nearest town: Yampa. GPS: 40.187198, -107.086844

65 • B2 | Cold Springs (Orno Peak) (Medicine Bow-Routt NF)

Total sites: 5, RV sites: 5, Water available, Vault/pit toilet, No showers, No RV dump, Tent & RV camping: $10, Open May-Oct, Reservations not accepted, Elev: 10266ft/3129m, Nearest town: Yampa. GPS: 40.030262, -107.119496

66 • B2 | Crosho Lake (Medicine Bow-Routt NF)

Total sites: 10, RV sites: 10, No water, Vault/pit toilet, Tent & RV camping: Free, Open May-Nov, Reservations not accepted, Elev: 8914ft/2717m, Tel: 307-745-2300, Nearest town: Yampa. GPS: 40.170000, -107.052000

67 • B2 | Dearhamer (White River NF)

Total sites: 13, RV sites: 13, Central water, Vault/pit toilet, No showers, No RV dump, Tent & RV camping: $25-27, Open May-Oct, Max Length: 69ft, Reservations accepted, Elev: 7812ft/2381m, Tel: 970-945-2521, Nearest town: Basalt. GPS: 39.360596, -106.737793

68 • B2 | Deep Lake (White River NF)

Total sites: 35, RV sites: 35, No water, Vault/pit toilet, Tent & RV camping: $6, Open Jul-Oct, Max Length: 35ft, Reservations not accepted, Elev: 10505ft/3202m, Tel: 970-945-2521, Nearest town: Gypsum. GPS: 39.772168, -107.295248

69 • B2 | Dexter (Pike & San Isabel NF)

Total sites: 24, RV sites: 24, No water, Vault/pit toilet, No showers, No RV dump, Tent & RV camping: $20, Open May-Sep, Max Length: 37ft, Reservations not accepted, Elev: 9291ft/2832m, Tel: 719-486-0749, Nearest town: Twin Lakes. GPS: 39.088436, -106.367351

70 • B2 | Difficult (White River NF)

Total sites: 47, RV sites: 47, Central water, Vault/pit toilet, No showers, No RV dump, Tent & RV camping: $28-30, Group site $100, Campground roads are tight for large RVs, Vehicles over 35' prohibited over Independence Pass but can access CG via Aspen, Open May-Oct, Max Length: 60ft, Reservations accepted, Elev: 8202ft/2500m, Tel: 970-945-2521, Nearest town: Aspen. GPS: 39.141701, -106.772787

71 • B2 | Dunn Ditch (Pike & San Isabel NF)

Total sites: 3, RV sites: 0, No water, No toilets, Tents only: Free, Elev: 9690ft/2954m, Nearest town: Leadville. GPS: 39.249374, -106.376933

72 • B2 | East Marvine (White River NF)

Total sites: 7, RV sites: 7, No water, Vault/pit toilet, Tent & RV camping: $20, Corral fee: $5, Open May-Nov, Reservations not accepted, Elev: 8225ft/2507m, Tel: 970-945-2521, Nearest town: Meeker. GPS: 40.011581, -107.427279

73 • B2 | Elbert Creek (Pike & San Isabel NF)

Total sites: 17, RV sites: 17, Central water, Vault/pit toilet, No showers, No RV dump, Tent & RV camping: $20, No water 2021 season, Generator hours: 0600-2200, Open May-Sep, Max Length: 16ft, Reservations not accepted, Elev: 10076ft/3071m, Nearest town: Leadville. GPS: 39.152512, -106.413376

74 • B2 | Elk Wallow (White River NF)

Total sites: 7, RV sites: 7, No water, Vault/pit toilet, Tent & RV camping: $17, Open May-Oct, Max Length: 20ft, Reservations not accepted, Elev: 8924ft/2720m, Tel: 970-945-2521, Nearest town: Basalt. GPS: 39.344215, -106.613768

75 • B2 | Elliot Creek (White River NF)

Total sites: 15, RV sites: 15, No water, Vault/pit toilet, Tent & RV camping: $18, Open May-Oct, Reservations not accepted, Elev: 7940ft/2420m, Tel: 970-945-2521, Nearest town: Silverthorne. GPS: 39.874958, -106.325289

76 • B2 | Father Dyer (Pike & San Isabel NF)

Total sites: 26, RV sites: 26, Central water, No toilets, No showers, No RV dump, Tent & RV camping: $24, Open May-Sep, Max Length: 35ft, Reservations accepted, Elev: 9993ft/3046m, Tel: 719-486-0749, Nearest town: Leadville. GPS: 39.274617, -106.350874

77 • B2 | Fulford Cave (White River NF)

Total sites: 7, RV sites: 7, Vault/pit toilet, Tent & RV camping: $8, Narrow and rough rocky road, Open Jun-Sep, Max Length: 25ft, Reservations not accepted, Elev: 9482ft/2890m, Tel: 970-945-2521, Nearest town: Eagle. GPS: 39.491638, -106.658953

78 • B2 | Gold Park (White River NF)

Total sites: 11, RV sites: 11, No water, Vault/pit toilet, Tent & RV camping: $22, Open May-Oct, Max Length: 40ft, Reservations not accepted, Elev: 9350ft/2850m, Tel: 970-945-2521, Nearest town: Red Cliff. GPS: 39.403320, -106.440674

79 • B2 | Halfmoon (White River NF)

Total sites: 7, RV sites: 7, No water, Vault/pit toilet, Tent & RV camping: $15, Food storage order, Open Jun-Oct, Max Length: 16ft, Reservations not accepted, Elev: 10315ft/3144m, Tel: 970-945-2521, Nearest town: Leadville. GPS: 39.500697, -106.432557

80 • B2 | Halfmoon West (Pike & San Isabel NF)

Total sites: 10, RV sites: 10, No water, Vault/pit toilet, Tent & RV camping: $20, Open May-Sep, Reservations not accepted, Elev: 9967ft/3038m, Tel: 719-486-0749, Nearest town: Leadville. GPS: 39.156744, -106.398192

81 • B2 | Himes Peak (White River NF)

Total sites: 11, RV sites: 11, No water, Vault/pit toilet, Tent & RV camping: $20, Open May-Oct, Reservations not accepted, Elev: 8871ft/2704m, Tel: 970-945-2521, Nearest town: Buford. GPS: 40.028195, -107.272591

82 • B2 | Hornsilver (White River NF)

Total sites: 7, RV sites: 7, No water, Vault/pit toilet, Tent & RV camping: $20, Food storage order, Open May-Oct, Max Length: 30ft, Reservations not accepted, Elev: 8812ft/2686m, Tel: 970-945-2521, Nearest town: Minturn. GPS: 39.489077, -106.367731

83 • B2 | Horseshoe (Omo Peak) (Medicine Bow-Routt NF)

Total sites: 7, RV sites: 7, Central water, Vault/pit toilet, No showers, No RV dump, Tent & RV camping: $10, Open Jun-Sep, Reservations not accepted, Elev: 10194ft/3107m, Tel: 970-620-2399, Nearest town: Yampa. GPS: 40.034667, -107.112924

84 • B2 | Klines Folly (White River NF)

Total sites: 4, RV sites: 0, No water, Vault/pit toilet, Tents only: Free, Open Jun-Nov, Reservations not accepted, Elev: 10742ft/3274m, Tel: 970-328-6388, Nearest town: Eagle. GPS: 39.759584, -107.310712

85 • B2 | Lakeview (Pike) (Pike & San Isabel NF)

Total sites: 33, RV sites: 33, Central water, Vault/pit toilet, No showers, No RV dump, Tent & RV camping: $21, Open May-Sep, Max Length: 60ft, Reservations accepted, Elev: 9534ft/2906m, Tel: 719-486-0749, Nearest town: Leadville. GPS: 39.097911, -106.365233

86 • B2 | Lincoln Gulch (White River NF)

Total sites: 7, RV sites: 7, Central water, Vault/pit toilet, Tent & RV camping: $25, Open May-Oct, Max Length: 35ft, Reservations not accepted, Elev: 9692ft/2954m, Tel: 970-945-2521, Nearest town: Aspen. GPS: 39.117184, -106.695913

87 • B2 | Little Mattie (White River NF)

Total sites: 20, RV sites: 20, Central water, Vault/pit toilet, No showers, No RV dump, Tent & RV camping: $26, Open May-Oct, Max Length: 30ft, Reservations not accepted, Elev: 7910ft/2411m, Tel: 970-945-2521, Nearest town: Basalt. GPS: 39.376577, -106.807379

88 • B2 | Little Maud (White River NF)

Total sites: 22, RV sites: 22, Central water, Vault/pit toilet, No showers, No RV dump, Tent & RV camping: $28-30, Open May-Sep, Max Length: 82ft, Reservations accepted, Elev: 7953ft/2424m, Tel: 970-945-2521, Nearest town: Basalt. GPS: 39.377119, -106.814947

89 • B2 | Lost Man (White River NF)

Total sites: 10, RV sites: 10, Central water, Vault/pit toilet, Tent & RV camping: $25, Open May-Sep, Max Length: 30ft, Reservations not accepted, Elev: 10535ft/3211m, Tel: 970-945-2521, Nearest town: Aspen. GPS: 39.121595, -106.625098

90 • B2 | Lynx Pass (Medicine Bow-Routt NF)

Total sites: 11, RV sites: 11, Water available, Vault/pit toilet, No showers, No RV dump, Tent & RV camping: $10, Open May-Oct, Max Length: 18ft, Reservations not accepted, Elev: 8976ft/2736m, Tel: 307-745-2300, Nearest town: Toponas. GPS: 40.105713, -106.683105

91 • B2 | Marvine (White River NF)

Total sites: 23, RV sites: 23, No water, Vault/pit toilet, Tent & RV camping: $23-25, 6 sites w/ corrals: $5 extra, Open May-Sep, Max Length: 40ft, Reservations accepted, Elev: 8148ft/2484m, Tel: 970-945-2521, Nearest town: Buford. GPS: 40.008762, -107.426031

92 • B2 | Matchless (Pike & San Isabel NF)

Total sites: 50, RV sites: 35, Central water, Vault/pit toilet, No showers, No RV dump, Tent & RV camping: $24, A large parking lot, No filling RV water tanks, Generator hours: 0600-2200, Open May-Sep, Reservations not accepted, Elev: 9909ft/3020m, Tel: 719-553-1404, Nearest town: Leadville. GPS: 39.257317, -106.360397

93 • B2 | May Queen (Pike & San Isabel NF)

Total sites: 27, RV sites: 23, Central water, Vault/pit toilet, No showers, No RV dump, Tent & RV camping: $21, Open May-Sep, Max Length: 40ft, Reservations accepted, Elev: 10046ft/3062m, Tel: 719-486-0749, Nearest town: Leadville. GPS: 39.278016, -106.431886

94 • B2 | McClure (Grand Mesa-Uncompahgre-Gunnison NF)

Total sites: 10, RV sites: 10, No water, Vault/pit toilet, Tent & RV camping: Free, Open May-Nov, Max Length: 35ft, Reservations not accepted, Elev: 8205ft/2501m, Tel: 970-527-4131, Nearest town: Redstone. GPS: 39.123713, -107.313118

95 • B2 | Meadow Lake (White River NF)

Total sites: 20, RV sites: 20, No water, Vault/pit toilet, Tent & RV camping: $20, Open May-Oct, Max Length: 16ft, Reservations not accepted, Elev: 9626ft/2934m, Tel: 970-945-2521, Nearest town: New Castle. GPS: 39.817866, -107.542701

96 • B2 | Meadow Ridge (White River NF)

Total sites: 20, RV sites: 20, No water, Vault/pit toilet, Tent & RV camping: $20, Open Jun-Oct, Max Length: 50ft, Reservations not accepted, Elev: 9639ft/2938m, Tel: 970-945-2521, Nearest town: Buford. GPS: 39.810648, -107.536772

97 • B2 | Mollie B (White River NF)

Total sites: 26, RV sites: 26, Central water, Vault/pit toilet, No showers, No RV dump, Tent & RV camping: $28-30, Open May-Sep, Max Length: 55ft, Reservations accepted, Elev: 7868ft/2398m, Tel: 970-945-2521, Nearest town: Basalt. GPS: 39.375330, -106.812678

98 • B2 | Molly Brown (Pike & San Isabel NF)

Total sites: 49, RV sites: 47, Central water, No toilets, No showers, RV dump, Tents: $24/RVs: $24-26, Open May-Sep, Max Length: 40ft, Reservations accepted, Elev: 9957ft/3035m, Tel: 719-486-0749, Nearest town: Leadville. GPS: 39.263737, -106.353162

99 • B2 | North Fork (White River NF)

Total sites: 28, RV sites: 28, Central water, Vault/pit toilet, No showers, No RV dump, Tent & RV camping: $24-26, Open May-Sep, Max Length: 40ft, Reservations accepted, Elev: 7874ft/2400m, Tel: 970-945-2521, Nearest town: Buford. GPS: 40.058752, -107.434534

100 • B2 | Parry Peak (Pike & San Isabel NF)

Total sites: 26, RV sites: 26, No water, Vault/pit toilet, No showers, No RV dump, Tent & RV camping: $22, Generator hours: 0600-2200, Open May-Sep, Max Length: 32ft, Reservations not accepted, Elev: 9514ft/2900m, Tel: 719-553-1400, Nearest town: Twin Lakes. GPS: 39.068115, -106.409912

101 • B2 | Portal (White River NF)

Total sites: 5, RV sites: 0, No water, Vault/pit toilet, Tents only: Donation, High clearance vehicles required - 4x4 recommended, Elev: 10610ft/3234m, Tel: 970-945-2521, Nearest town: Aspen. GPS: 39.076351, -106.612582

102 • B2 | Redstone (White River NF)

Total sites: 37, RV sites: 37, Elec sites: 19, Central water, Flush toilet, Free showers, No RV dump, Tents: $32-34/RVs: $32-43, Open May-Oct, Max Length: 60ft, Reservations accepted, Elev: 7192ft/2192m, Tel: 970-945-2521, Nearest town: Redstone. GPS: 39.200642, -107.231527

103 • B2 | Ruedi Marina (White River NF)

Total sites: 8, RV sites: 8, Central water, Vault/pit toilet, No showers, No RV dump, Tent & RV camping: $25-27, Open May-Sep, Max Length: 45ft, Reservations accepted, Elev: 7805ft/2379m, Tel: 970-945-2521, Nearest town: Basalt. GPS: 39.373831, -106.813506

104 • B2 | Sheriff Reservoir (Medicine Bow-Routt NF)

Total sites: 6, RV sites: 6, No water, Vault/pit toilet, Tent & RV camping: $10, Numerous dispersed sites located along access road suitble for larger RVs, Open Jun-Oct, Max Length: 18ft, Reservations not accepted, Elev: 9797ft/2986m, Tel: 307-745-2300, Nearest town: Yampa. GPS: 40.143685, -107.138939

105 • B2 | Silver Bar (White River NF)

Total sites: 4, RV sites: 0, Central water, Vault/pit toilet, No showers, No RV dump, Tents only: $15, Walk-to sites, Open May-Sep, Max Length: 25ft, Reservations accepted, Elev: 8465ft/2580m, Tel: 970-963-2266, Nearest town: Aspen. GPS: 39.146248, -106.893182

106 • B2 | Silver Bell (White River NF)

Total sites: 14, RV sites: 2, Central water, Vault/pit toilet, No showers, No RV dump, Tent & RV camping: $15, Also walk-to sites, Call for water status, Open May-Oct, Max Length: 30ft, Reservations accepted, Elev: 8507ft/2593m, Tel: 970-925-3445, Nearest town: Aspen. GPS: 39.142579, -106.895261

107 • B2 | Silver Dollar (Pike & San Isabel NF)

Total sites: 43, RV sites: 43, No toilets, RV dump, Tent & RV camping: $24, Open May-Sep, Max Length: 30ft, Reservations accepted, Elev: 9928ft/3026m, Tel: 719-553-1400, Nearest town: Leadville. GPS: 39.259328, -106.352091

108 • B2 | Silver Queen (White River NF)

Total sites: 6, RV sites: 6, Central water, Vault/pit toilet, No showers, No RV dump, Tent & RV camping: $15, Call for water status, Open Jun-Oct, Max Length: 30ft, Reservations accepted, Elev: 8727ft/2660m, Tel: 970-925-3445, Nearest town: Aspen. GPS: 39.129071, -106.901885

109 • B2 | South Fork (Meadow Creek Lake) (White River NF)

Total sites: 18, RV sites: 18, No water, No toilets, Tent & RV camping: $20, Open May-Oct, Reservations not accepted, Elev: 7753ft/2363m, Tel: 970-945-2521, Nearest town: Meeker. GPS: 39.866699, -107.533936

110 • B2 | Supply Basin Dispersed (White River NF)

Total sites: 7, RV sites: 2, No water, Vault/pit toilet, Tent & RV camping: Free, Open Jun-Nov, Max Length: 25ft, Reservations not accepted, Elev: 10785ft/3287m, Tel: 970-328-6388, Nearest town: Dotsero. GPS: 39.759836, -107.320689

111 • B2 | Sweetwater Lake (White River NF)

Total sites: 9, RV sites: 9, No water, Vault/pit toilet, Tent & RV camping: $8, Open May-Sep, Max Length: 30ft, Reservations not accepted, Elev: 7776ft/2370m, Tel: 970-945-2521, Nearest town: Dotsero. GPS: 39.797000, -107.161000

112 • B2 | Tabor (Pike & San Isabel NF)

Total sites: 44, RV sites: 44, Central water, Vault/pit toilet, RV dump, Tent & RV camping: $24, No filling RV tanks, Open May-Sep, Max Length: 37ft, Reservations not accepted, Elev: 9948ft/3032m, Tel: 719-553-1400, Nearest town: Leadville. GPS: 39.273561, -106.354795

113 • B2 | Trappers Lake - Bucks (White River NF)

Total sites: 10, RV sites: 10, Central water, Vault/pit toilet, No showers, RV dump, Tent & RV camping: $20, Open May-Sep, Max Length: 36ft, Reservations not accepted, Elev: 9721ft/2963m, Tel: 970-945-2521, Nearest town: Meeker. GPS: 39.993972, -107.239579

114 • B2 | Trappers Lake - Cutthroat (White River NF)

Total sites: 14, RV sites: 14, Central water, Vault/pit toilet, No showers, RV dump, Tent & RV camping: $20, Open May-Oct, Max Length: 36ft, Reservations not accepted, Elev: 9787ft/2983m, Tel: 970-945-2521, Nearest town: Meeker. GPS: 39.992656, -107.241705

115 • B2 | Trappers Lake - Horse Thief (White River NF)

Total sites: 7, RV sites: 7, Central water, Vault/pit toilet, No showers, RV dump, Tent & RV camping: $20-25, Horse corrals, Open May-Oct, Max Length: 60ft, Reservations not accepted, Elev: 9784ft/2982m, Tel: 970-945-2521, Nearest town: Meeker. GPS: 39.995335, -107.237913

116 • B2 | Trappers Lake - Shepherds Rim (White River NF)

Total sites: 16, RV sites: 15, Central water, Vault/pit toilet, No showers, RV dump, Tent & RV camping: $20-22, Open Jun-Oct, Max Length: 36ft, Reservations accepted, Elev: 9741ft/2969m, Tel: 970-945-2521, Nearest town: Meeker. GPS: 39.994695, -107.242843

117 • B2 | Trappers Lake - Trapline (White River NF)

Total sites: 12, RV sites: 12, Central water, Vault/pit toilet, No showers, RV dump, Tent & RV camping: $20, Open May-Sep, Max Length: 36ft, Reservations not accepted, Elev: 9767ft/2977m, Tel: 970-945-2521, Nearest town: Meeker. GPS: 39.993389, -107.240825

118 • B2 | Twin Peaks (Pike & San Isabel NF)

Total sites: 39, RV sites: 39, Central water, Vault/pit toilet, Tent & RV camping: $23, No water 2021 season, No filling of RV water tanks allowed, Generator hours: 0600-2200, Open May-Sep, Max Length: 32ft, Reservations not accepted, Elev: 9682ft/2951m, Tel: 719-553-1400, Nearest town: Twin Lakes. GPS: 39.067871, -106.421387

119 • B2 | Vaughn Lake (Medicine Bow-Routt NF)

Total sites: 6, RV sites: 6, No water, Vault/pit toilet, Tent & RV camping: $10, Reachable only by snowmobile in winter, Open all year, Max Length: 18ft, Reservations not accepted, Elev: 9518ft/2901m, Tel: 970-638-4516, Nearest town: Yampa. GPS: 40.134055, -107.261397

120 • B2 | Weir and Johnson (Grand Mesa-Uncompahgre-Gunnison NF)

Total sites: 12, RV sites: 12, No water, Vault/pit toilet, Tent & RV camping: $14, Open May-Sep, Max Length: 22ft, Reservations not accepted, Elev: 10508ft/3203m, Tel: 970-874-6600, Nearest town: Collbran. GPS: 39.066162, -107.831787

121 • B2 | Weller (White River NF)

Total sites: 11, RV sites: 11, Central water, Vault/pit toilet, No showers, No RV dump, Tent & RV camping: $25, Open May-Oct, Max Length: 14ft, Reservations not accepted, Elev: 9485ft/2891m, Tel: 970-945-2521, Nearest town: Aspen. GPS: 39.121205, -106.720218

122 • B2 | Whitestar (Pike & San Isabel NF)

Total sites: 68, RV sites: 65, Central water, No toilets, No showers, No RV dump, Tent & RV camping: $21, Open May-Sep, Max Length: 50ft, Reservations accepted, Elev: 9258ft/2822m, Tel: 719-486-0749, Nearest town: Twin Lakes. GPS: 39.090031, -106.366723

123 • B2 | Willows (White River NF)

Total sites: 25, RV sites: 25, Central water, Vault/pit toilet, No showers, No RV dump, Tent & RV camping: $17-19, Open May-Oct, Max Length: 20ft, Reservations accepted, Elev: 7966ft/2428m, Tel: 970-945-2521, Nearest town: Silverthorne. GPS: 39.889284, -106.309259

124 • B3 | Arapaho Bay - Main (Arapaho & Roosevelt NF)

Total sites: 22, RV sites: 22, Central water, Vault/pit toilet, No showers, No RV dump, Tent & RV camping: $23, Open May-Oct,

Max Length: 40ft, Reservations accepted, Elev: 8350ft/2545m, Tel: 970-887-4100, Nearest town: Granby. GPS: 40.119791, -105.756530

125 • B3 | Arapaho Bay - Moraine (Arapaho & Roosevelt NF)

Total sites: 29, RV sites: 29, Central water, Vault/pit toilet, No showers, No RV dump, Tent & RV camping: $23, Open May-Oct, Max Length: 42ft, Reservations accepted, Elev: 8356ft/2547m, Tel: 970-887-4100, Nearest town: Granby. GPS: 40.124204, -105.762226

126 • B3 | Arapaho Bay - Roaring Fork (Arapaho & Roosevelt NF)

Total sites: 34, RV sites: 25, Central water, Vault/pit toilet, No showers, No RV dump, Tent & RV camping: $23, Open May-Oct, Max Length: 40ft, Reservations accepted, Elev: 8320ft/2536m, Tel: 970-887-4100, Nearest town: Granby. GPS: 40.129192, -105.767739

127 • B3 | Aspen (Jefferson) (Pike & San Isabel NF)

Total sites: 12, RV sites: 6, Central water, Vault/pit toilet, No showers, No RV dump, Tent & RV camping: $17, Open May-Oct, Max Length: 27ft, Reservations accepted, Elev: 9955ft/3034m, Tel: 719-836-2031, Nearest town: Jefferson. GPS: 39.425518, -105.841832

128 • B3 | Big Turkey (Pike & San Isabel NF)

Total sites: 10, RV sites: 10, Central water, Vault/pit toilet, No showers, No RV dump, Tent & RV camping: Free, Elev: 8032ft/2448m, Tel: 303-275-5610, Nearest town: West Creek. GPS: 39.119992, -105.227175

129 • B3 | Blue River (White River NF)

Total sites: 24, RV sites: 21, Vault/pit toilet, Tent & RV camping: $21-23, Open May-Sep, Reservations accepted, Elev: 8471ft/2582m, Tel: 970-945-2521, Nearest town: Silverthorne. GPS: 39.726532, -106.131032

130 • B3 | Brainard Lake RA - Pawnee (Arapaho & Roosevelt NF)

Total sites: 47, RV sites: 39, Central water, Vault/pit toilet, No showers, No RV dump, Tent & RV camping: $23, Open Jun-Sep, Max Length: 100ft, Reservations accepted, Elev: 10368ft/3160m, Tel: 303-541-2500, Nearest town: Nederland. GPS: 40.078374, -105.569124

131 • B3 | Buffalo (Pike & San Isabel NF)

Total sites: 37, RV sites: 35, No water, Vault/pit toilet, No showers, No RV dump, Tent & RV camping: $22, Open May-Sep, Max Length: 40ft, Reservations accepted, Elev: 7333ft/2235m, Tel: 303-275-5610, Nearest town: Buffalo Creek. GPS: 39.340687, -105.329825

132 • B3 | Buffalo Springs (Pike & San Isabel NF)

Total sites: 21, RV sites: 20, Central water, Vault/pit toilet, No showers, No RV dump, Tent & RV camping: $17, Also walk-to sites, Open May-Sep, Max Length: 40ft, Reservations accepted, Elev: 9176ft/2797m, Tel: 719 836-2031, Nearest town: Fairplay. GPS: 39.032548, -105.985595

133 • B3 | Burning Bear (Pike & San Isabel NF)

Total sites: 14, RV sites: 13, Central water, Vault/pit toilet, No showers, No RV dump, Tent & RV camping: $22, Stay limit: 14 days, Open May-Dec, Max Length: 50ft, Reservations accepted, Elev: 9718ft/2962m, Tel: 303-275-5610, Nearest town: Jefferson. GPS: 39.513429, -105.710692

134 • B3 | Byers Creek (Arapaho & Roosevelt NF)

Total sites: 6, RV sites: 6, Central water, Vault/pit toilet, No showers, No RV dump, Tent & RV camping: $14, Stay limit: 14 days, Max Length: 32ft, Reservations not accepted, Elev: 9360ft/2853m, Tel: 970-887-4100, Nearest town: Fraser. GPS: 39.878346, -105.896403

135 • B3 | Caribou Ghost Town Sites 1-5 (Arapaho & Roosevelt NF)

Total sites: 11, RV sites: 11, No water, No toilets, Tent & RV camping: Free, Dispersed sites along road, Reservations not accepted, Elev: 10041ft/3060m, Tel: 303-541-2500, Nearest town: Nederland. GPS: 39.980942, -105.579375

136 • B3 | Caribou Ghost Town Sites 6-7 (Arapaho & Roosevelt NF)

Total sites: 2, RV sites: 2, No water, No toilets, Tent & RV camping: Free, Dispersed sites along road, Reservations not accepted, Elev: 9973ft/3040m, Tel: 303-541-2500, Nearest town: Nederland. GPS: 39.992163, -105.578343

137 • B3 | Caribou Ghost Town Sites 8-11 (Arapaho & Roosevelt NF)

Total sites: 4, RV sites: 4, No water, No toilets, Tent & RV camping: Free, Dispersed sites along road, Reservations not accepted, Elev: 10058ft/3066m, Tel: 303-541-2500, Nearest town: Nederland. GPS: 39.995318, -105.568592

138 • B3 | Clear Lake (Arapaho & Roosevelt NF)

Total sites: 8, RV sites: 8, Central water, Vault/pit toilet, No showers, No RV dump, Tent & RV camping: $19, Open Jun-Sep, Max Length: 15ft, Reservations not accepted, Elev: 10039ft/3060m, Tel: 303-567-3000, Nearest town: Georgetown. GPS: 39.651053, -105.708443

139 • B3 | Cold Springs (Black Hawk) (Arapaho & Roosevelt NF)

Total sites: 38, RV sites: 31, Central water, Vault/pit toilet, No showers, No RV dump, Tent & RV camping: $22, Open May-Sep, Max Length: 45ft, Reservations accepted, Elev: 9396ft/2864m, Tel: 303-567-3000, Nearest town: Black Hawk. GPS: 39.841958, -105.495678

140 • B3 | Colorado (Pike & San Isabel NF)

Total sites: 81, RV sites: 81, Water available, No toilets, No showers, No RV dump, Tent & RV camping: $23, Open May-Sep, Max Length: 100ft, Reservations accepted, Elev: 7854ft/2394m, Tel: 719-636-1602, Nearest town: Woodland Park. GPS: 39.080255, -105.093878

141 • B3 | Columbine (Central City) (Arapaho & Roosevelt NF)

Total sites: 46, RV sites: 41, Central water, Vault/pit toilet, No showers, No RV dump, Tent & RV camping: $21, Also walk-to sites, Open May-Sep, Max Length: 55ft, Reservations accepted,

Elev: 9039ft/2755m, Tel: 303-567-3000, Nearest town: Central City. GPS: 39.816895, -105.549072

142 • B3 | Cow Creek North (White River NF)

Total sites: 15, RV sites: 15, No water, Vault/pit toilet, No showers, No RV dump, Tent & RV camping: $18, Open May-Sep, Reservations not accepted, Elev: 7992ft/2436m, Tel: 970-945-2521, Nearest town: Silverthorne. GPS: 39.883384, -106.288359

143 • B3 | Cow Creek South (White River NF)

Total sites: 43, RV sites: 43, No water, Vault/pit toilet, No showers, No RV dump, Tent & RV camping: $17-19, Open May-Oct, Max Length: 90ft, Reservations accepted, Elev: 8005ft/2440m, Tel: 970-945-2521, Nearest town: Silverthorne. GPS: 39.877377, -106.284952

144 • B3 | Crown Point (White River NF)

Total sites: 10, RV sites: 10, No water, Vault/pit toilet, Tent & RV camping: Free, Elev: 9088ft/2770m, Tel: 970-468-5400. GPS: 39.726532, -106.061482

145 • B3 | Deer Creek (Pike & San Isabel NF)

Total sites: 13, RV sites: 13, No water, Vault/pit toilet, Tent & RV camping: $22, Open all year, Max Length: 30ft, Reservations not accepted, Elev: 9272ft/2826m, Tel: 303-275-5610, Nearest town: Bailey. GPS: 39.508057, -105.553711

146 • B3 | Devils Head (Pike & San Isabel NF)

Total sites: 21, RV sites: 21, No water, Vault/pit toilet, Tent & RV camping: $22, Open May-Nov, Max Length: 30ft, Reservations not accepted, Elev: 8883ft/2708m, Tel: 303-275-5610, Nearest town: Sedalia. GPS: 39.271822, -105.102558

147 • B3 | Dutch Fred (Pike & San Isabel NF)

Total sites: 11, RV sites: 11, No water, Vault/pit toilet, Tent & RV camping: Free, Open May-Sep, Reservations not accepted, Elev: 8501ft/2591m, Nearest town: Sedalia. GPS: 39.290192, -105.092383

148 • B3 | Echo Lake (Arapaho & Roosevelt NF)

Total sites: 17, RV sites: 11, Central water, Vault/pit toilet, No showers, No RV dump, Tent & RV camping: $21, Open Jun-Sep, Max Length: 55ft, Reservations accepted, Elev: 10718ft/3267m, Tel: 801-226-3564, Nearest town: Idaho Springs. GPS: 39.656787, -105.594636

149 • B3 | Flat Rocks (Pike & San Isabel NF)

Total sites: 19, RV sites: 19, Central water, Vault/pit toilet, No showers, No RV dump, Tent & RV camping: $22, Open May-Sep, Max Length: 30ft, Reservations not accepted, Elev: 8136ft/2480m, Nearest town: Sedalia. GPS: 39.327944, -105.094008

150 • B3 | Fourmile (Pike & San Isabel NF)

Total sites: 14, RV sites: 14, Central water, Vault/pit toilet, No showers, No RV dump, Tent & RV camping: $17, Open May-Sep, Max Length: 22ft, Reservations not accepted, Elev: 10889ft/3319m, Tel: 719-836-2031, Nearest town: Leavick. GPS: 39.208966, -106.104361

151 • B3 | Geneva Park (Pike & San Isabel NF)

Total sites: 26, RV sites: 25, Central water, Vault/pit toilet, No showers, No RV dump, Tent & RV camping: $22, Open May-Sep, Max Length: 32ft, Reservations accepted, Elev: 9810ft/2990m, Tel: 303-275-5610, Nearest town: Jefferson. GPS: 39.531126, -105.736681

152 • B3 | Goose Creek (Pike & San Isabel NF)

Total sites: 10, RV sites: 0, Central water, Vault/pit toilet, No showers, No RV dump, Tents only: $22, Open May-Sep, Max Length: 20ft, Reservations not accepted, Elev: 7776ft/2370m, Tel: 303-275-5610, Nearest town: Woodland Park. GPS: 39.170187, -105.358562

153 • B3 | Gordon Gulch (Arapaho & Roosevelt NF)

Total sites: 15, RV sites: 15, No water, No toilets, Tent & RV camping: Free, Dispersed sites along 1.5 miles, Road not maintained for passenger cars, Stay limit: 14 days, Elev: 8819ft/2688m, Tel: 303-541-2500, Nearest town: Nederland. GPS: 40.015602, -105.494924

154 • B3 | Gore Creek (White River NF)

Total sites: 25, RV sites: 16, No water, Vault/pit toilet, Tent & RV camping: $25-27, Also walk-to sites, Open May-Oct, Max Length: 35ft, Reservations accepted, Elev: 8822ft/2689m, Tel: 970-945-2521, Nearest town: Vail. GPS: 39.627231, -106.272103

155 • B3 | Green Mountain (Pike & San Isabel NF)

Total sites: 8, RV sites: 0, Central water, Vault/pit toilet, No showers, No RV dump, Tents only: $18, Walk-to sites, Open May-Sep, Reservations not accepted, Elev: 7634ft/2327m, Tel: 303-275-5610, Nearest town: Deckers. GPS: 39.326476, -105.355755

156 • B3 | Green Ridge (Arapaho & Roosevelt NF)

Total sites: 78, RV sites: 78, Central water, Vault/pit toilet, No showers, RV dump, Tent & RV camping: $23, Late season: $18, Open May-Oct, Max Length: 51ft, Reservations accepted, Elev: 8399ft/2560m, Tel: 970-887-4100, Nearest town: Granby. GPS: 40.206196, -105.844369

157 • B3 | Gross Reservoir Dispersed (Arapaho & Roosevelt NF)

Total sites: 6, RV sites: 0, No water, No toilets, Tents only: Free, Walk-to sites, Reservations not accepted, Elev: 7430ft/2265m, Tel: 303-541-2500, Nearest town: Pinecliffe. GPS: 39.949023, -105.372515

158 • B3 | Guanella Pass (Arapaho & Roosevelt NF)

Total sites: 18, RV sites: 11, Central water, Vault/pit toilet, No showers, No RV dump, Tent & RV camping: $21, Open Jun-Sep, Max Length: 45ft, Reservations accepted, Elev: 10784ft/3287m, Tel: 303-567-3000, Nearest town: Georgetown. GPS: 39.611816, -105.717665

159 • B3 | Hall Valley (Pike & San Isabel NF)

Total sites: 9, RV sites: 9, No water, Vault/pit toilet, Tent & RV camping: $22, Open May-Sep, Max Length: 20ft, Reservations not accepted, Elev: 9828ft/2996m, Tel: 303-275-5610, Nearest town: Webster. GPS: 39.482264, -105.804858

160 • B3 | Handcart (Pike & San Isabel NF)

Total sites: 10, RV sites: 0, Central water, Vault/pit toilet, No showers, No RV dump, Tents only: $22, Walk-to sites, Generator hours: 0600-2200, Open May-Sep, Reservations not accepted, Elev: 9789ft/2984m, Tel: 303-275-5610, Nearest town: Jefferson. GPS: 39.482382, -105.800396

161 • B3 | Happy Meadows (Pike & San Isabel NF)

Total sites: 8, RV sites: 8, Central water, Vault/pit toilet, No showers, No RV dump, Tent & RV camping: $17-21, Open May-Oct, Max Length: 30ft, Reservations accepted, Elev: 7897ft/2407m, Tel: 719-748-3619, Nearest town: Woodland Park. GPS: 39.014104, -105.362831

162 • B3 | Heaton Bay (White River NF)

Total sites: 84, RV sites: 65, Elec sites: 14, Central water, Vault/pit toilet, No showers, No RV dump, Tents: $25-27/RVs: $25-32, Open May-Oct, Max Length: 99ft, Reservations accepted, Elev: 9068ft/2764m, Tel: 970-945-2521, Nearest town: Frisco. GPS: 39.602231, -106.077442

163 • B3 | Horseshoe (Arapaho & Roosevelt NF)

Total sites: 7, RV sites: 7, No water, Vault/pit toilet, Tent & RV camping: $18, Open Jun-Oct, Max Length: 50ft, Reservations not accepted, Elev: 8497ft/2590m, Tel: 970-887-4100, Nearest town: Parshall. GPS: 39.900129, -106.095786

164 • B3 | Horseshoe (Fairplay West) (Pike & San Isabel NF)

Total sites: 18, RV sites: 16, Central water, Vault/pit toilet, No showers, No RV dump, Tent & RV camping: $17, Open May-Oct, Max Length: 25ft, Reservations accepted, Elev: 10533ft/3210m, Tel: 719-836-2031, Nearest town: Fairplay. GPS: 39.199557, -106.084121

165 • B3 | Idlewild (Arapaho & Roosevelt NF)

Total sites: 24, RV sites: 24, Central water, Vault/pit toilet, No showers, No RV dump, Tent & RV camping: $22, Open May-Sep, Max Length: 30ft, Reservations not accepted, Elev: 8934ft/2723m, Tel: 970-887-4100, Nearest town: Winter Park. GPS: 39.903764, -105.779307

166 • B3 | Indian Creek (Pike & San Isabel NF)

Total sites: 18, RV sites: 18, Central water, Vault/pit toilet, No showers, No RV dump, Tent & RV camping: $22, Generator hours: 0600-2200, Open May-Sep, Max Length: 20ft, Reservations not accepted, Elev: 7571ft/2308m, Tel: 303-275-5610, Nearest town: Sedalia. GPS: 39.381372, -105.097065

167 • B3 | Indian Creek Equestrian Camp (Pike & San Isabel NF)

Total sites: 7, RV sites: 7, No water, Vault/pit toilet, Tent & RV camping: $22, Open May-Sep, Max Length: 30ft, Reservations accepted, Elev: 7401ft/2256m, Tel: 303-275-5610. GPS: 39.378577, -105.104627

168 • B3 | Jackson Creek (Pike & San Isabel NF)

Total sites: 9, RV sites: 9, No toilets, Tent & RV camping: Free, Trailers not recommended, Max Length: 16ft, Reservations not accepted, Elev: 8212ft/2503m, Tel: 303-275-5610, Nearest town: Denver. GPS: 39.251000, -105.089000

169 • B3 | Jefferson Creek (Pike & San Isabel NF)

Total sites: 17, RV sites: 16, Central water, Vault/pit toilet, No showers, No RV dump, Tent & RV camping: $17, Open May-Oct, Max Length: 40ft, Reservations accepted, Elev: 10037ft/3059m, Tel: 719-836-2031, Nearest town: Jefferson. GPS: 39.434182, -105.853026

170 • B3 | Jim Creek (Arapaho & Roosevelt NF)

Total sites: 7, RV sites: 0, Central water, Vault/pit toilet, Tents only: Free, 7 platform sites, Operated by National Sports Center for the Disabled featuring facilities for persons with disabilities, Open Jun-Sep, Reservations required, Elev: 9293ft/2833m, Tel: 970-726-1518, Nearest town: Winter Park. GPS: 39.881636, -105.748765

171 • B3 | Kelly Dahl (Arapaho & Roosevelt NF)

Total sites: 46, RV sites: 46, Central water, Vault/pit toilet, No showers, No RV dump, Tent & RV camping: $23, Open May-Oct, Max Length: 40ft, Reservations accepted, Elev: 8632ft/2631m, Tel: 303-541-2500, Nearest town: Nederland. GPS: 39.932373, -105.497803

172 • B3 | kelly-Dahl (Arapaho & Roosevelt NF)

Total sites: 41, RV sites: 41, Central water, Vault/pit toilet, No showers, No RV dump, Tent & RV camping: $23, Open Jun-Nov, Max Length: 45ft, Reservations accepted, Elev: 8681ft/2646m, Tel: 303-541-2500, Nearest town: Ward. GPS: 40.128913, -105.519664

173 • B3 | Kelsey (Pike & San Isabel NF)

Total sites: 17, RV sites: 15, No water, Vault/pit toilet, Tent & RV camping: $22, Open May-Sep, Max Length: 60ft, Reservations accepted, Elev: 8081ft/2463m, Tel: 303-275-5610, Nearest town: Pine. GPS: 39.305628, -105.265721

174 • B3 | Kenosha Pass (Pike & San Isabel NF)

Total sites: 24, RV sites: 24, Central water, Vault/pit toilet, No showers, No RV dump, Tent & RV camping: $22, Open May-Sep, Max Length: 55ft, Reservations accepted, Elev: 10016ft/3053m, Tel: 303-275-5610, Nearest town: Jefferson. GPS: 39.413894, -105.761112

175 • B3 | Kenosha Pass East (Pike & San Isabel NF)

Total sites: 12, RV sites: 12, No water, Vault/pit toilet, Tent & RV camping: $20, Open May-Nov, Reservations not accepted, Elev: 10036ft/3059m, Tel: 303-275-5610, Nearest town: Jefferson. GPS: 39.415312, -105.755481

176 • B3 | Keystone/Loveland Pass (Arapaho & Roosevelt NF)

Total sites: 6, RV sites: 6, No water, No toilets, Tent & RV camping: Free, Max Length: 25ft, Elev: 9670ft/2947m, Nearest town: Keystone. GPS: 39.616912, -105.929926

177 • B3 | Kite Lake (Pike & San Isabel NF)

Total sites: 5, RV sites: 0, No water, Vault/pit toilet, Tents only: $15, Open May-Sep, Reservations not accepted, Elev: 12083ft/3683m, Tel: 719-836-2031, Nearest town: Alma. GPS: 39.329425, -106.128549

178 • B3 | Lodgepole (Pike) (Pike & San Isabel NF)

Total sites: 34, RV sites: 26, Central water, Vault/pit toilet, No showers, No RV dump, Tent & RV camping: $17, Open May-Oct, Max Length: 35ft, Reservations accepted, Elev: 9964ft/3037m, Tel: 719-836-2031, Nearest town: Jefferson. GPS: 39.422187, -105.842612

179 • B3 | Lone Rock (Pike & San Isabel NF)

Total sites: 18, RV sites: 15, Central water, Vault/pit toilet, No showers, No RV dump, Tent & RV camping: $22, No services in winter, Open all year, Max Length: 40ft, Reservations accepted, Elev: 6444ft/1964m, Tel: 303-275-5610, Nearest town: Woodland Park. GPS: 39.252188, -105.235733

180 • B3 | Lost Park (Pike & San Isabel NF)

Total sites: 12, RV sites: 12, No water, Vault/pit toilet, Tent & RV camping: $15, Open May-Sep, Max Length: 22ft, Reservations not accepted, Elev: 9984ft/3043m, Tel: 719 836-2031, Nearest town: Jefferson. GPS: 39.284927, -105.507396

181 • B3 | Lowry (White River NF)

Total sites: 30, RV sites: 27, Elec sites: 23, No water, Vault/pit toilet, Tents: $23-25/RVs: $23-31, Open May-Sep, Max Length: 55ft, Reservations accepted, Elev: 9360ft/2853m, Tel: 970-945-2521, Nearest town: Dillon. GPS: 39.597113, -106.026813

182 • B3 | McDonald Flats (White River NF)

Total sites: 13, RV sites: 13, No water, Vault/pit toilet, Tent & RV camping: $18, Open May-Oct, Max Length: 21ft, Reservations not accepted, Elev: 7933ft/2418m, Tel: 970-945-2521, Nearest town: Silverthorne. GPS: 39.850084, -106.237011

183 • B3 | Meridian (Pike & San Isabel NF)

Total sites: 18, RV sites: 18, Central water, Vault/pit toilet, No showers, No RV dump, Tent & RV camping: $22, Open May-Sep, Reservations not accepted, Elev: 9026ft/2751m, Tel: 303-275-5610, Nearest town: Bailey. GPS: 39.511242, -105.535159

184 • B3 | Michigan Creek (Pike & San Isabel NF)

Total sites: 12, RV sites: 12, Central water, Vault/pit toilet, No showers, No RV dump, Tent & RV camping: $15, Open May-Oct, Max Length: 25ft, Reservations not accepted, Elev: 10131ft/3088m, Tel: 719 836-2031, Nearest town: Jefferson. GPS: 39.410514, -105.882698

185 • B3 | Molly Gulch (Pike & San Isabel NF)

Total sites: 15, RV sites: 0, Central water, Vault/pit toilet, No showers, No RV dump, Tents only: Free, Rough road, Reservations not accepted, Elev: 7551ft/2302m, Tel: 303-275-5610, Nearest town: Deckers. GPS: 39.194985, -105.344668

186 • B3 | Olive Ridge (Arapaho & Roosevelt NF)

Total sites: 56, RV sites: 54, No water, Vault/pit toilet, No showers, No RV dump, Tent & RV camping: $18, Stay limit: 14 days, Open May-Sep, Max Length: 50ft, Reservations accepted, Elev: 8350ft/2545m, Tel: 303-541-2500, Nearest town: Estes Park. GPS: 40.208394, -105.523728

187 • B3 | Osprey (Pike & San Isabel NF)

Total sites: 13, RV sites: 0, No water, Vault/pit toilet, Tents only: $18, No services in winter, Generator hours: 0600-2200, Open all year, Reservations not accepted, Elev: 6223ft/1897m, Tel: 719-553-1400, Nearest town: Woodland Park. GPS: 39.349000, -105.177000

188 • B3 | Ouzel (Pike & San Isabel NF)

Total sites: 13, RV sites: 0, No water, Vault/pit toilet, Tents only: $18, Stay limit: 14 days, Generator hours: 0600-2200, Open all year, Reservations not accepted, Elev: 6306ft/1922m, Tel: 719-553-1400, Nearest town: Woodland Park. GPS: 39.320000, -105.188000

189 • B3 | Painted Rocks (Pike & San Isabel NF)

Total sites: 18, RV sites: 13, Water available, Vault/pit toilet, No showers, No RV dump, Tent & RV camping: $23, Generator hours: 0600-2200, Open May-Sep, Max Length: 59ft, Reservations accepted, Elev: 7868ft/2398m, Tel: 719-553-1400, Nearest town: Woodland Park . GPS: 39.084473, -105.105957

190 • B3 | Peaceful Valley (Arapaho & Roosevelt NF)

Total sites: 17, RV sites: 17, Central water, Vault/pit toilet, No showers, No RV dump, Tent & RV camping: $23, Open May-Nov, Max Length: 45ft, Reservations accepted, Elev: 8573ft/2613m, Tel: 303-541-2500, Nearest town: Nederland. GPS: 40.131546, -105.506674

191 • B3 | Peak One (White River NF)

Total sites: 77, RV sites: 77, Central water, Vault/pit toilet, No showers, No RV dump, Tent & RV camping: $24-26, Open May-Sep, Max Length: 99ft, Reservations accepted, Elev: 9043ft/2756m, Tel: 970-945-2521, Nearest town: Frisco. GPS: 39.584199, -106.071483

192 • B3 | Pine Cove (White River NF)

Total sites: 56, RV sites: 56, Central water, Vault/pit toilet, No showers, No RV dump, Tent & RV camping: $24, Open May-Sep, Max Length: 35ft, Reservations not accepted, Elev: 9036ft/2754m, Tel: 970-945-2521, Nearest town: Frisco. GPS: 39.588008, -106.068794

193 • B3 | Platte River (Pike & San Isabel NF)

Total sites: 10, RV sites: 0, No water, Vault/pit toilet, Tents only: $20, Walk-to sites, Generator hours: 0600-2200, Open all year, Reservations not accepted, Elev: 6375ft/1943m, Tel: 719-553-1400, Nearest town: Woodland Park. GPS: 39.294196, -105.204106

194 • B3 | Prairie Point (White River NF)

Total sites: 33, RV sites: 33, No water, Vault/pit toilet, No showers, No RV dump, Tent & RV camping: $17-19, Open May-Sep, Max Length: 20ft, Reservations accepted, Elev: 8035ft/2449m, Tel: 970-945-2521, Nearest town: Dillon. GPS: 39.843380, -106.232020

195 • B3 | Prospector (White River NF)

Total sites: 106, RV sites: 106, No water, No toilets, No showers, No RV dump, Tent & RV camping: $23-25, Open May-Sep, Max Length: 70ft, Reservations accepted, Elev: 9137ft/2785m, Tel: 970-945-2521, Nearest town: Dillon. GPS: 39.600101, -106.042848

196 • B3 | Rainbow Lakes (Arapaho & Roosevelt NF)

Total sites: 16, RV sites: 16, No water, Vault/pit toilet, Tent &

RV camping: $17, High-clearance vehicle recommended, Open Jun-Sep, Max Length: 50ft, Reservations not accepted, Elev: 10066ft/3068m, Tel: 303-541-2500, Nearest town: Nederland. GPS: 40.010712, -105.571016

197 • B3 | Robbers Roost (Arapaho & Roosevelt NF)

Total sites: 11, RV sites: 11, No water, Vault/pit toilet, Tent & RV camping: $22, Max Length: 25ft, Reservations not accepted, Elev: 9797ft/2986m, Tel: 970-887-4100, Nearest town: Winter Park. GPS: 39.831377, -105.756656

198 • B3 | Round Mountain (Pike & San Isabel NF)

Total sites: 15, RV sites: 15, Central water, Vault/pit toilet, No showers, No RV dump, Tent & RV camping: $17, Open May-Oct, Max Length: 30ft, Reservations accepted, Elev: 8573ft/2613m, Nearest town: Florissant. GPS: 39.030735, -105.431971

199 • B3 | Selkirk (Pike & San Isabel NF)

Total sites: 15, RV sites: 15, No water, Vault/pit toilet, Tent & RV camping: $15, Open May-Sep, Max Length: 25ft, Reservations not accepted, Elev: 10522ft/3207m, Tel: 719-836-2031, Nearest town: Fairplay. GPS: 39.371985, -105.951096

200 • B3 | South Fork (Ute Peak) (Arapaho & Roosevelt NF)

Total sites: 21, RV sites: 21, Central water, Vault/pit toilet, No showers, No RV dump, Tent & RV camping: $19, Group site $55, Small corral, Open Jun-Oct, Max Length: 23ft, Reservations not accepted, Elev: 8983ft/2738m, Tel: 970-887-4100, Nearest town: Parshall. GPS: 39.795382, -106.029779

201 • B3 | South Meadows (Pike & San Isabel NF)

Total sites: 64, RV sites: 62, Central water, Vault/pit toilet, No showers, No RV dump, Tent & RV camping: $23, Reduced services in winter, Open May-Oct, Max Length: 84ft, Reservations accepted, Elev: 7907ft/2410m, Tel: 719-686-8816, Nearest town: Woodland Park. GPS: 39.064711, -105.094156

202 • B3 | Spruce Grove (McCurdy Mt) (Pike & San Isabel NF)

Total sites: 27, RV sites: 11, Central water, Vault/pit toilet, No showers, No RV dump, Tent & RV camping: $17, Open May-Oct, Max Length: 36ft, Reservations accepted, Elev: 8534ft/2601m, Tel: 719-836-2031, Nearest town: Florissant. GPS: 39.137829, -105.462068

203 • B3 | St Louis Creek (Arapaho & Roosevelt NF)

Total sites: 16, RV sites: 16, Central water, Vault/pit toilet, No showers, No RV dump, Tent & RV camping: $22, Open May-Oct, Max Length: 25ft, Reservations not accepted, Elev: 8871ft/2704m, Tel: 970-887-4100, Nearest town: Fraser. GPS: 39.924001, -105.859081

204 • B3 | Stillwater (Arapaho & Roosevelt NF)

Total sites: 129, RV sites: 99, Elec sites: 21, Water at site, Flush toilet, Free showers, RV dump, Tents: $26/RVs: $26-39, Open May-Oct, Max Length: 40ft, Reservations accepted, Elev: 8340ft/2542m, Tel: 970-887-4100, Nearest town: Granby. GPS: 40.179856, -105.888521

205 • B3 | Sugarloaf (Arapaho & Roosevelt NF)

Total sites: 11, RV sites: 11, No water, Vault/pit toilet, Tent & RV camping: $19, Open Jun-Oct, Max Length: 35ft, Reservations not accepted, Elev: 8993ft/2741m, Tel: 970-887-4100, Nearest town: Hot Sulphur Springs. GPS: 39.788574, -106.023438

206 • B3 | Sunset Point (Arapaho & Roosevelt NF)

Total sites: 25, RV sites: 25, Central water, Vault/pit toilet, No showers, No RV dump, Tent & RV camping: $26, Open May-Sep, Max Length: 50ft, Reservations not accepted, Elev: 8284ft/2525m, Tel: 970-887-4100, Nearest town: Granby. GPS: 40.153827, -105.873874

207 • B3 | Timberline (Pike & San Isabel NF)

Total sites: 24, RV sites: 24, No water, Vault/pit toilet, No showers, No RV dump, Tent & RV camping: $22, Open May-Dec, Max Length: 45ft, Reservations accepted, Elev: 9854ft/3003m, Tel: 303-275-5610, Nearest town: Denver. GPS: 39.437253, -105.763363

208 • B3 | Twin Eagles (Pike & San Isabel NF)

Total sites: 9, RV sites: 5, No water, Vault/pit toilet, Tent & RV camping: $15, Reduced services in winter, Open all year, Max Length: 22ft, Reservations not accepted, Elev: 8579ft/2615m, Tel: 719 836-2031, Nearest town: Lake George. GPS: 39.152446, -105.478753

209 • B3 | West Chicago Creek (Arapaho & Roosevelt NF)

Total sites: 15, RV sites: 13, Central water, Vault/pit toilet, No showers, No RV dump, Tent & RV camping: $15, Open May-Sep, Max Length: 40ft, Reservations accepted, Elev: 9629ft/2935m, Tel: 303-567-3000, Nearest town: Idaho Springs. GPS: 39.678708, -105.657846

210 • B3 | Weston Pass (Pike & San Isabel NF)

Total sites: 14, RV sites: 12, Central water, Vault/pit toilet, No showers, No RV dump, Tent & RV camping: $15, Open May-Sep, Max Length: 25ft, Reservations not accepted, Elev: 10302ft/3140m, Tel: 719 836-2031, Nearest town: Fairplay. GPS: 39.078119, -106.136385

211 • B3 | Willow Creek (Arapaho & Roosevelt NF)

Total sites: 35, RV sites: 35, Central water, Vault/pit toilet, No showers, No RV dump, Tent & RV camping: $23, Arapaho NRA fee: $5/day, Open May-Oct, Max Length: 25ft, Reservations not accepted, Elev: 8173ft/2491m, Tel: 970-887-4100, Nearest town: Granby. GPS: 40.143308, -105.952198

212 • C1 | Buckeye (Manti-La Sal NF)

Total sites: 48, RV sites: 48, No water, Vault/pit toilet, Tent & RV camping: $15, Group site: $50 - available for single use if no group, 18 sites are dispersed around lake, Open all year, Max Length: 74ft, Reservations accepted, Elev: 7640ft/2329m, Tel: 435-636-3360, Nearest town: Paradox. GPS: 38.446779, -109.045501

213 • C1 | Columbine Pass (New) (Uncompahgre NF)

Total sites: 16, RV sites: 16, No water, Vault/pit toilet, Tent & RV camping: Fee unk, Elev: 9104ft/2775m, Nearest town: Montrose. GPS: 38.427473, -108.374749

214 • C1 | Columbine Pass (Old) (Uncompahgre NF)

Total sites: 6, No water, Vault/pit toilet, Tents only: Free, Open Jun-

Sep, Reservations not accepted, Elev: 9101ft/2774m, Tel: 970-874-6600, Nearest town: Montrose. GPS: 38.424939, -108.381813

215 • C1 | Divide Fork (Uncompahgre NF)

Total sites: 11, RV sites: 11, No water, Vault/pit toilet, Tent & RV camping: Free, Open Apr-Nov, Max Length: 20ft, Reservations not accepted, Elev: 8740ft/2664m, Tel: 970-874-6600, Nearest town: Grand Junction. GPS: 38.684429, -108.689542

216 • C1 | Fall Creek (Uncompahgre NF)

Total sites: 2, RV sites: 2, No water, Vault/pit toilet, Tent & RV camping: Fee unk, Max Length: 25ft, Elev: 7721ft/2353m, Nearest town: Placerville. GPS: 37.979311, -108.030513

217 • C1 | Iron Springs (Grand Mesa-Uncompahgre-Gunnison NF)

Total sites: 8, RV sites: 8, No water, Vault/pit toilet, Tent & RV camping: Free, Small RVs only, Open Jun-Oct, Reservations not accepted, Elev: 9606ft/2928m, Tel: 970-240-5300, Nearest town: Montrose. GPS: 38.316744, -108.164465

218 • C1 | Mary E (Grand Mesa-Uncompahgre-Gunnison NF)

Total sites: 15, RV sites: 15, No water, Vault/pit toilet, No showers, No RV dump, Tent & RV camping: Free, No fires, Max Length: 22ft, Reservations not accepted, Elev: 8061ft/2457m, Nearest town: Telluride. GPS: 37.940273, -107.897701

219 • C1 | Matterhorn (Uncompahgre NF)

Total sites: 28, RV sites: 28, Elec sites: 4, Central water, Flush toilet, Free showers, No RV dump, Tents: $24/RVs: $24-36, Open May-Sep, Max Length: 40ft, Reservations accepted, Elev: 9498ft/2895m, Tel: 970-249-4552, Nearest town: Telluride. GPS: 37.844941, -107.881359

220 • C1 | Sunshine (Grand Mesa-Uncompahgre-Gunnison NF)

Total sites: 15, RV sites: 15, Central water, Vault/pit toilet, No showers, No RV dump, Tent & RV camping: $18, Open May-Sep, Max Length: 35ft, Reservations not accepted, Elev: 9600ft/2926m, Tel: 970-874-6600, Nearest town: Telluride. GPS: 37.889404, -107.890137

221 • C1 | Woods Lake (Grand Mesa-Uncompahgre-Gunnison NF)

Total sites: 41, RV sites: 41, Central water, Vault/pit toilet, No showers, No RV dump, Tent & RV camping: $16-18, 5 horse sites, Open May-Oct, Reservations not accepted, Elev: 9403ft/2866m, Tel: 970-874-6600, Nearest town: Placerville. GPS: 37.886284, -108.055604

222 • C2 | Almont (Grand Mesa-Uncompahgre-Gunnison NF)

Total sites: 10, RV sites: 10, Central water, Vault/pit toilet, No showers, No RV dump, Tent & RV camping: $10, Open May-Sep, Reservations not accepted, Elev: 8045ft/2452m, Nearest town: Almont. GPS: 38.653809, -106.858154

223 • C2 | Alta Lakes Dispersed (Grand Mesa-Uncompahgre-Gunnison NF)

Total sites: 16, RV sites: 0, No water, Vault/pit toilet, Tents only: Free, 1-lane road not well-maintained - high-clearance vehicles only, Open May-Sep, Elev: 11217ft/3419m, Nearest town: Telluride. GPS: 37.885047, -107.847087

224 • C2 | Amphitheater (Uncompahgre NF)

Total sites: 35, RV sites: 17, Central water, Vault/pit toilet, No showers, No RV dump, Tent & RV camping: $26, Open May-Sep, Max Length: 35ft, Reservations accepted, Elev: 8566ft/2611m, Tel: 970-874-6600, Nearest town: Ouray. GPS: 38.022802, -107.661376

225 • C2 | Angel Creek (Grand Mesa-Uncompahgre-Gunnison NF)

Total sites: 8, RV sites: 0, No water, Vault/pit toilet, Tents only: $10, High-clearance vehicles only, Open May-Sep, Reservations not accepted, Elev: 8563ft/2610m, Tel: 970-240-5300, Nearest town: Ouray. GPS: 38.002214, -107.694099

226 • C2 | Beaver Lake (Grand Mesa-Uncompahgre-Gunnison NF)

Total sites: 11, RV sites: 11, No water, Vault/pit toilet, Tent & RV camping: $12, Open May-Sep, Max Length: 20ft, Reservations not accepted, Elev: 8784ft/2677m, Tel: 970-240-5300, Nearest town: Cimarron. GPS: 38.250411, -107.543546

227 • C2 | Big Blue (Grand Mesa-Uncompahgre-Gunnison NF)

Total sites: 11, RV sites: 11, No water, Vault/pit toilet, Tent & RV camping: Free, Open Jun-Sep, Reservations not accepted, Elev: 9652ft/2942m, Nearest town: Sapeniro. GPS: 38.217285, -107.385498

228 • C2 | Big Cimarron (Grand Mesa-Uncompahgre-Gunnison NF)

Total sites: 10, RV sites: 10, No water, Vault/pit toilet, Tent & RV camping: $12, Open Jun-Sep, Reservations not accepted, Elev: 8717ft/2657m, Tel: 970-240-5300, Nearest town: Cimarron. GPS: 38.257568, -107.545166

229 • C2 | Buffalo Pass (Rio Grande NF)

Total sites: 19, RV sites: 19, No water, Vault/pit toilet, Tent & RV camping: $5, Open May-Nov, Max Length: 60ft, Reservations not accepted, Elev: 9140ft/2786m, Tel: 719 655-2547, Nearest town: Saguache. GPS: 38.184814, -106.517090

230 • C2 | Cement Creek (Grand Mesa-Uncompahgre-Gunnison NF)

Total sites: 13, RV sites: 13, Central water, Vault/pit toilet, No showers, No RV dump, Tent & RV camping: $14, Open May-Oct, Reservations not accepted, Elev: 9006ft/2745m, Tel: 970-874-6600, Nearest town: Crested Butte. GPS: 38.827881, -106.836914

231 • C2 | Cold Spring (Taylor Canyon) (Grand Mesa-Uncompahgre-Gunnison NF)

Total sites: 6, RV sites: 6, No water, Vault/pit toilet, Tent & RV camping: $10, Open May-Sep, Reservations not accepted, Elev: 8966ft/2733m, Tel: 970-874-6600, Nearest town: Almont. GPS: 38.767216, -106.643087

232 • C2 | Collegiate Peaks (Pike & San Isabel NF)

Total sites: 56, RV sites: 56, Water available, Vault/pit toilet, No showers, No RV dump, Tent & RV camping: $22, Open May-Sep,

Max Length: 50ft, Reservations accepted, Elev: 9820ft/2993m, Tel: 719-539-3591, Nearest town: Buena Vista. GPS: 38.811241, -106.319324

233 • C2 | Colorado Pass (Pike & San Isabel NF)

Total sites: 10, RV sites: 10, No water, No toilets, Tent & RV camping: Free, Elev: 9364ft/2854m, Nearest town: Buena Vista. GPS: 38.813189, -106.283709

234 • C2 | Cottonwood Lake (Pike & San Isabel NF)

Total sites: 24, RV sites: 24, Central water, Vault/pit toilet, No showers, No RV dump, Tent & RV camping: $11, No water for RV tanks, Generator hours: 0600-2200, Max Length: 35ft, Reservations not accepted, Elev: 9613ft/2930m, Tel: 719-539-3591, Nearest town: Buena Vista. GPS: 38.782629, -106.291934

235 • C2 | Deer Lakes (Grand Mesa-Uncompahgre-Gunnison NF)

Total sites: 15, RV sites: 15, Central water, Vault/pit toilet, No showers, No RV dump, Tent & RV camping: $12, Open May-Sep, Max Length: 30ft, Reservations not accepted, Elev: 10496ft/3199m, Tel: 970-641-0471, Nearest town: Lake City. GPS: 38.020649, -107.187411

236 • C2 | Dinner Station (Grand Mesa-Uncompahgre-Gunnison NF)

Total sites: 22, RV sites: 22, Central water, Vault/pit toilet, No showers, No RV dump, Tent & RV camping: $18, Open May-Sep, Max Length: 99ft, Reservations accepted, Elev: 9616ft/2931m, Tel: 970-642-0566, Nearest town: Almont. GPS: 38.906172, -106.586152

237 • C2 | Dorchester (Grand Mesa-Uncompahgre-Gunnison NF)

Total sites: 10, RV sites: 10, No water, Vault/pit toilet, Tent & RV camping: Donation, Open May-Oct, Reservations not accepted, Elev: 9933ft/3028m, Tel: 970-874-6600, Nearest town: Almont. GPS: 38.965683, -106.660955

238 • C2 | Erickson Springs (Grand Mesa-Uncompahgre-Gunnison NF)

Total sites: 18, RV sites: 18, No water, Vault/pit toilet, No showers, No RV dump, Tent & RV camping: $14, Open May-Sep, Max Length: 35ft, Reservations not accepted, Elev: 6811ft/2076m, Nearest town: Paonia. GPS: 38.954778, -107.270283

239 • C2 | Gold Creek (Grand Mesa-Uncompahgre-Gunnison NF)

Total sites: 6, RV sites: 6, No water, Vault/pit toilet, Tent & RV camping: Donation, Campers are required to store food and other items in a hard sided vehicle or camping unit constructed of solid non-pliable material, Open May-Oct, Max Length: 25ft, Reservations not accepted, Elev: 10069ft/3069m, Tel: 970-874-6600, Nearest town: Gunnison. GPS: 38.655175, -106.574499

240 • C2 | Gothic (Uncompahgre NF)

Total sites: 4, RV sites: 4, No water, Vault/pit toilet, Tent & RV camping: $12, Open Jun-Oct, Reservations not accepted, Elev: 9626ft/2934m, Tel: 970-874-6600, Nearest town: Crested Butte. GPS: 38.982000, -107.006000

241 • C2 | Granite (Taylor Canyon) (Grand Mesa-Uncompahgre-Gunnison NF)

Total sites: 7, RV sites: 0, No water, Vault/pit toilet, Tents only: $12, Open May-Sep, Reservations not accepted, Elev: 8406ft/2562m, Tel: 970-874-6600, Nearest town: Almont. GPS: 38.726061, -106.768228

242 • C2 | Hidden Valley (Grand Mesa-Uncompahgre-Gunnison NF)

Total sites: 4, RV sites: 0, No water, Vault/pit toilet, Tents only: Donation, Open Jun-Sep, Reservations not accepted, Elev: 9692ft/2954m, Tel: 970-641-0471, Nearest town: Lake City. GPS: 38.040979, -107.132788

243 • C2 | Iron City (Pike & San Isabel NF)

Total sites: 15, RV sites: 15, Water available, Vault/pit toilet, No showers, No RV dump, Tent & RV camping: $20, Generator hours: 0600-2200, Max Length: 25ft, Reservations not accepted, Elev: 9954ft/3034m, Tel: 719-539-3591, Nearest town: Nathrop. GPS: 38.708564, -106.336335

244 • C2 | Lake Irwin (Grand Mesa-Uncompahgre-Gunnison NF)

Total sites: 25, RV sites: 10, Central water, Vault/pit toilet, No showers, No RV dump, Tent & RV camping: $20, Open Jul-Sep, Max Length: 99ft, Reservations accepted, Elev: 10417ft/3175m, Tel: 970-641-0471, Nearest town: Crested Butte. GPS: 38.881104, -107.107666

245 • C2 | Lakeview (Gunnison) (Grand Mesa-Uncompahgre-Gunnison NF)

Total sites: 64, RV sites: 64, Elec sites: 9, Central water, Vault/pit toilet, No showers, RV dump, Tents: $22/RVs: $22-30, Open Jun-Sep, Max Length: 45ft, Reservations accepted, Elev: 9511ft/2899m, Tel: 970-642-0566, Nearest town: Almont. GPS: 38.818498, -106.579836

246 • C2 | Lodgepole (Gunnison) (Grand Mesa-Uncompahgre-Gunnison NF)

Total sites: 16, RV sites: 16, Central water, Vault/pit toilet, No showers, No RV dump, Tent & RV camping: $18, Open May-Sep, Max Length: 30ft, Reservations accepted, Elev: 8901ft/2713m, Tel: 970-642-0566, Nearest town: Almont. GPS: 38.761230, -106.661865

247 • C2 | Lost Lake (Grand Mesa-Uncompahgre-Gunnison NF)

Total sites: 19, RV sites: 19, Central water, Vault/pit toilet, No showers, No RV dump, Tent & RV camping: $20, 5 equestrian sites, Open Jun-Sep, Max Length: 28ft, Reservations not accepted, Elev: 9656ft/2943m, Tel: 970-527-4131, Nearest town: Paonia. GPS: 38.869873, -107.208496

248 • C2 | Lottis Creek (Grand Mesa-Uncompahgre-Gunnison NF)

Total sites: 47, RV sites: 47, Elec sites: 41, Central water, Vault/pit toilet, No showers, No RV dump, Tents: $22/RVs: $22-30, Open May-Sep, Max Length: 100ft, Reservations accepted, Elev: 9094ft/2772m, Tel: 970-874-6600, Nearest town: Almont. GPS: 38.775811, -106.628221

249 • C2 | Luders Creek (Rio Grande NF)

Total sites: 6, RV sites: 6, No water, Vault/pit toilet, Tent & RV camping: $5, Stock facilities, Open May-Nov, Max Length: 25ft, Reservations not accepted, Elev: 10056ft/3065m, Tel: 719 655-2547, Nearest town: Saguache. GPS: 38.181194, -106.583802

250 • C2 | Mesa Creek (Grand Mesa-Uncompahgre-Gunnison NF)

Total sites: 4, RV sites: 4, No toilets, Tent & RV camping: Free, Reservations not accepted, Elev: 8995ft/2742m, Nearest town: Crawford. GPS: 38.475338, -107.523574

251 • C2 | Middle Quartz (Grand Mesa-Uncompahgre-Gunnison NF)

Total sites: 7, RV sites: 7, No water, Vault/pit toilet, Tent & RV camping: Donation, Open May-Sep, Reservations not accepted, Elev: 10348ft/3154m, Tel: 970-641-0471, Nearest town: Monarch. GPS: 38.623000, -106.425000

252 • C2 | Mirror Lake (Grand Mesa-Uncompahgre-Gunnison NF)

Total sites: 10, RV sites: 10, No water, Vault/pit toilet, Tent & RV camping: $12, Open May-Sep, Reservations not accepted, Elev: 10988ft/3349m, Tel: 970-641-0471, Nearest town: Almont. GPS: 38.747559, -106.432129

253 • C2 | Monarch Park (Pike & San Isabel NF)

Total sites: 37, RV sites: 35, Water available, Vault/pit toilet, No showers, No RV dump, Tent & RV camping: $20, Open Jun-Sep, Max Length: 40ft, Reservations accepted, Elev: 10492ft/3198m, Tel: 719-539-3591, Nearest town: Poncha Springs. GPS: 38.516258, -106.325131

254 • C2 | Mosca (Grand Mesa-Uncompahgre-Gunnison NF)

Total sites: 16, RV sites: 16, No water, Vault/pit toilet, Tent & RV camping: $14, Open May-Oct, Max Length: 45ft, Reservations not accepted, Elev: 9993ft/3046m, Tel: 970-641-0471, Nearest town: Almont. GPS: 38.860107, -106.710205

255 • C2 | North Bank (Grand Mesa-Uncompahgre-Gunnison NF)

Total sites: 17, RV sites: 17, Central water, Vault/pit toilet, No showers, No RV dump, Tent & RV camping: $14, Open May-Sep, Reservations not accepted, Elev: 8530ft/2600m, Tel: 970-641-0471, Nearest town: Almont. GPS: 38.730182, -106.757965

256 • C2 | North Clear Creek (Rio Grande NF)

Total sites: 21, RV sites: 21, Central water, Vault/pit toilet, No showers, No RV dump, Tent & RV camping: $19, Open May-Sep, Max Length: 30ft, Reservations not accepted, Elev: 9569ft/2917m, Tel: 719-657-3321, Nearest town: Creede. GPS: 37.835217, -107.139025

257 • C2 | North Fork Reservoir (Pike & San Isabel NF)

Total sites: 9, RV sites: 0, No water, Vault/pit toilet, Tent & RV camping: $16, Rough road - high clearance vehicle required, Trailers not recommended, Open May-Sep, Reservations not accepted, Elev: 11503ft/3506m, Tel: 719-539-3591, Nearest town: Salidas. GPS: 38.611941, -106.320024

258 • C2 | One Mile (Grand Mesa-Uncompahgre-Gunnison NF)

Total sites: 25, RV sites: 25, Elec sites: 18, Central water, Vault/pit toilet, No showers, No RV dump, Tent & RV camping: $30, Open May-Sep, Max Length: 99ft, Reservations accepted, Elev: 8444ft/2574m, Tel: 970-642-0566, Nearest town: Almont. GPS: 38.730168, -106.754684

259 • C2 | Pitkin (Grand Mesa-Uncompahgre-Gunnison NF)

Total sites: 21, RV sites: 21, Central water, Vault/pit toilet, No showers, No RV dump, Tent & RV camping: $20, Open Jun-Oct, Max Length: 30ft, Reservations not accepted, Elev: 9400ft/2865m, Tel: 970-641-0471, Nearest town: Pitkin. GPS: 38.610596, -106.501221

260 • C2 | Poso (Rio Grande NF)

Total sites: 11, RV sites: 11, No water, Vault/pit toilet, Tent & RV camping: $5, Open May-Nov, Max Length: 25ft, Reservations not accepted, Elev: 8917ft/2718m, Tel: 719-655-2547, Nearest town: Saguache. GPS: 37.908051, -106.427505

261 • C2 | Quartz (Grand Mesa-Uncompahgre-Gunnison NF)

Total sites: 10, RV sites: 10, Central water, Vault/pit toilet, No showers, No RV dump, Tent & RV camping: $10, Open Jun-Sep, Reservations not accepted, Elev: 9888ft/3014m, Tel: 970-641-0471, Nearest town: Pitkin. GPS: 38.638696, -106.468909

262 • C2 | Rito Hondo (Rio Grande NF)

Total sites: 30, RV sites: 30, No water, Vault/pit toilet, Tent & RV camping: Free, Open all year, Reservations not accepted, Elev: 10253ft/3125m, Tel: 719-852-5941, Nearest town: Creede. GPS: 37.892353, -107.178379

263 • C2 | Rivers End (Grand Mesa-Uncompahgre-Gunnison NF)

Total sites: 15, RV sites: 15, Central water, Vault/pit toilet, No showers, No RV dump, Tent & RV camping: $14, Open May-Sep, Reservations not accepted, Elev: 9360ft/2853m, Tel: 970-641-0471, Nearest town: Almont. GPS: 38.857422, -106.569092

264 • C2 | Rosy Lane (Grand Mesa-Uncompahgre-Gunnison NF)

Total sites: 20, RV sites: 20, Elec sites: 1, Central water, Vault/pit toilet, No showers, No RV dump, Tents: $18/RVs: $18-24, Open May-Sep, Reservations accepted, Elev: 8478ft/2584m, Tel: 970-641-0471, Nearest town: Almont. GPS: 38.730671, -106.747618

265 • C2 | Silver Jack (Grand Mesa-Uncompahgre-Gunnison NF)

Total sites: 60, RV sites: 60, Central water, Vault/pit toilet, No showers, No RV dump, Tent & RV camping: $14, Open Jun-Sep, Max Length: 30ft, Reservations not accepted, Elev: 9121ft/2780m, Tel: 970-874-6600, Nearest town: Cimarron. GPS: 38.236075, -107.537647

266 • C2 | Silver Thread (Rio Grande NF)

Total sites: 10, RV sites: 10, Central water, Vault/pit toilet, No showers, No RV dump, Tent & RV camping: $23, Open all year, Max Length: 30ft, Reservations not accepted, Elev: 9739ft/2968m, Tel: 719-657-3321, Nearest town: Creede. GPS: 37.827616, -107.156227

267 • C2 | Snowblind (Grand Mesa-Uncompahgre-Gunnison NF)

Total sites: 23, RV sites: 23, Central water, Vault/pit toilet, No showers, No RV dump, Tent & RV camping: $12, Open May-Sep, Max Length: 35ft, Reservations not accepted, Elev: 9311ft/2838m, Tel: 970-874-6600, Nearest town: Sargents. GPS: 38.520752, -106.415283

268 • C2 | Soap Creek (Grand Mesa-Uncompahgre-Gunnison NF)

Total sites: 21, RV sites: 21, Central water, Vault/pit toilet, No showers, No RV dump, Tent & RV camping: $12, Open May-Sep, Reservations not accepted, Elev: 7733ft/2357m, Tel: 970-641-0471, Nearest town: Sapeniro. GPS: 38.548103, -107.317784

269 • C2 | Spring Creek (Grand Mesa-Uncompahgre-Gunnison NF)

Total sites: 12, RV sites: 12, Central water, Vault/pit toilet, No showers, No RV dump, Tent & RV camping: $14, Open May-Sep, Reservations not accepted, Elev: 8592ft/2619m, Tel: 970-874-6600, Nearest town: Almont. GPS: 38.749756, -106.767090

270 • C2 | Spruce (Grand Mesa-Uncompahgre-Gunnison NF)

Total sites: 9, RV sites: 9, Central water, Vault/pit toilet, No showers, No RV dump, Tent & RV camping: Free, Open Jun-Oct, Max Length: 15ft, Reservations not accepted, Elev: 9346ft/2849m, Tel: 970-641-0471, Nearest town: Lake City. GPS: 38.047277, -107.117029

271 • C2 | Stone Cellar (Rio Grande NF)

Total sites: 6, RV sites: 6, Central water, Vault/pit toilet, No showers, No RV dump, Tent & RV camping: $5, Open May-Nov, Max Length: 25ft, Reservations not accepted, Elev: 9498ft/2895m, Tel: 719-655-2547, Nearest town: Saguache. GPS: 38.019018, -106.677487

272 • C2 | Storm King (Rio Grande NF)

Total sites: 6, RV sites: 6, No water, Vault/pit toilet, Tent & RV camping: $5, Open May-Nov, Max Length: 25ft, Reservations not accepted, Elev: 9406ft/2867m, Tel: 719-655-2547, Nearest town: Saguache. GPS: 37.959229, -106.431152

273 • C2 | Thistledown (Lincoln NF)

Total sites: 9, RV sites: 0, No water, Vault/pit toilet, Tents only: Free, Nothing larger than van/PU, Food storage order, Open May-Oct, Elev: 8775ft/2675m, Nearest town: Ouray. GPS: 37.993402, -107.700366

274 • C2 | Ute TH (San Juan NF)

Total sites: 2, RV sites: 0, No water, Vault/pit toilet, Tents only: Free, Elev: 6562ft/2000m, Nearest town: Delta. GPS: 38.682509, -107.864016

275 • C2 | Williams Creek (Mesa) (Grand Mesa-Uncompahgre-Gunnison NF)

Total sites: 23, RV sites: 23, Central water, Vault/pit toilet, No showers, RV dump, Tent & RV camping: $14, Open May-Oct, Max Length: 32ft, Reservations not accepted, Elev: 9219ft/2810m, Nearest town: Pagosa Springs. GPS: 37.921942, -107.335923

276 • C3 | Alvarado (Pike & San Isabel NF)

Total sites: 51, RV sites: 46, Central water, Vault/pit toilet, No showers, No RV dump, Tent & RV camping: $22, Open May-Sep, Max Length: 45ft, Reservations accepted, Elev: 9036ft/2754m, Tel: 719-269-8500, Nearest town: Westcliffe. GPS: 38.079278, -105.563324

277 • C3 | Angel of Shavano (Pike & San Isabel NF)

Total sites: 20, RV sites: 20, Central water, Vault/pit toilet, Tent & RV camping: $20, Group site: $125, Stay limit: 14 days, Open Jun-Sep, Max Length: 30ft, Reservations not accepted, Elev: 9200ft/2804m, Tel: 719-553-1400, Nearest town: Maysville. GPS: 38.583008, -106.220703

278 • C3 | Blue Mountain (Pike & San Isabel NF)

Total sites: 20, RV sites: 18, No water, Vault/pit toilet, Tent & RV camping: $17, Open May-Oct, Max Length: 35ft, Reservations accepted, Elev: 8130ft/2478m, Tel: 719-836-2031, Nearest town: Florissant. GPS: 38.959156, -105.362002

279 • C3 | Cascade (Pike & San Isabel NF)

Total sites: 21, RV sites: 21, Central water, Vault/pit toilet, No showers, No RV dump, Tent & RV camping: $22, Open May-Oct, Max Length: 73ft, Reservations accepted, Elev: 9111ft/2777m, Tel: 719-539-3591, Nearest town: Nathrop. GPS: 38.710449, -106.244629

280 • C3 | Chalk Lake (Pike & San Isabel NF)

Total sites: 19, RV sites: 12, No water, Vault/pit toilet, Tent & RV camping: $22, Open May-Sep, Max Length: 30ft, Reservations accepted, Elev: 8721ft/2658m, Tel: 719-539-3591, Nearest town: Nathrop. GPS: 38.712731, -106.233744

281 • C3 | Coaldale (Pike & San Isabel NF)

Total sites: 11, RV sites: 5, No water, Vault/pit toilet, Tent & RV camping: $15, Also walk-to sites, Generator hours: 0600-2200, Open May-Sep, Max Length: 25ft, Reservations not accepted, Elev: 7375ft/2248m, Tel: 719-553-1400, Nearest town: Salida. GPS: 38.333970, -105.804262

282 • C3 | Cove (Pike & San Isabel NF)

Total sites: 4, RV sites: 2, Central water, Vault/pit toilet, No showers, No RV dump, Tent & RV camping: $17, Open May-Oct, Max Length: 30ft, Reservations accepted, Elev: 8586ft/2617m, Tel: 719-836-2031, Nearest town: Lake George. GPS: 38.910017, -105.460614

283 • C3 | Davenport (Pike & San Isabel NF)

Total sites: 12, RV sites: 0, Central water, Vault/pit toilet, No showers, No RV dump, Tents only: $22, Walk-to sites, 3 sites have shelters, Open May-Sep, Reservations accepted, Elev: 8464ft/2580m, Tel: 719-553-1400, Nearest town: Colorado City. GPS: 38.055141, -105.068218

284 • C3 | Hayden Creek (Pike & San Isabel NF)

Total sites: 11, RV sites: 11, Central water, Vault/pit toilet, No showers, No RV dump, Tent & RV camping: $20, Open May-Oct, Max Length: 25ft, Reservations not accepted, Elev: 7831ft/2387m, Tel: 719-539-3591, Nearest town: Salida. GPS: 38.329771, -105.823903

285 • C3 | Lake Creek (Pike & San Isabel NF)

Total sites: 11, RV sites: 11, Central water, Vault/pit toilet, No showers, No RV dump, Tent & RV camping: $21, Open May-Sep, Max Length: 29ft, Reservations not accepted, Elev: 8261ft/2518m, Tel: 719-553-1400, Nearest town: Westcliffe. GPS: 38.264367, -105.661113

286 • C3 | Lake Isabel - La Vista (Pike & San Isabel NF)

Total sites: 29, RV sites: 19, Elec sites: 19, Central water, Vault/pit toilet, No showers, No RV dump, Tents: $24/RVs: $24-28, Open May-Oct, Max Length: 45ft, Reservations accepted, Elev: 8609ft/2624m, Tel: 719-269-8500, Nearest town: Canon City. GPS: 37.984556, -105.060025

287 • C3 | Lake Isabel - Southside (Pike & San Isabel NF)

Total sites: 8, RV sites: 8, Central water, Vault/pit toilet, No showers, No RV dump, Tent & RV camping: $20, Tents not recommended, Open May-Sep, Max Length: 30ft, Reservations accepted, Elev: 8497ft/2590m, Tel: 719-269-8500, Nearest town: Canon City. GPS: 37.983106, -105.056316

288 • C3 | Lake Isabel - St Charles (Pike & San Isabel NF)

Total sites: 15, RV sites: 14, Central water, No toilets, No showers, No RV dump, Tent & RV camping: $22, Open May-Oct, Max Length: 45ft, Reservations accepted, Elev: 8701ft/2652m, Tel: 719-269-8500, Nearest town: Canon City. GPS: 37.981028, -105.067415

289 • C3 | Meadow Ridge (Pike & San Isabel NF)

Total sites: 19, RV sites: 19, Water available, Vault/pit toilet, No showers, No RV dump, Tent & RV camping: $23, Open May-Sep, Max Length: 70ft, Reservations accepted, Elev: 9203ft/2805m, Tel: 970-945-2521, Nearest town: Woodland Park. GPS: 38.977554, -104.986877

290 • C3 | Mt Princeton (Pike & San Isabel NF)

Total sites: 19, RV sites: 19, No water, Vault/pit toilet, Tent & RV camping: $22, Open May-Sep, Max Length: 45ft, Reservations accepted, Elev: 8625ft/2629m, Tel: 719-539-3591, Nearest town: Nathrop. GPS: 38.713911, -106.223672

291 • C3 | North Crestone Creek (Rio Grande NF)

Total sites: 13, RV sites: 13, No water, Vault/pit toilet, Tent & RV camping: $7, Open May-Nov, Max Length: 25ft, Reservations not accepted, Elev: 8573ft/2613m, Tel: 719-655-2547, Nearest town: Crestone. GPS: 38.018539, -105.686026

292 • C3 | Oak Creek (Pike & San Isabel NF)

Total sites: 15, RV sites: 15, No water, Vault/pit toilet, Tent & RV camping: Free, Open all year, Reservations not accepted, Elev: 7680ft/2341m, Tel: 719-553-1400, Nearest town: Canon City. GPS: 38.296335, -105.267209

293 • C3 | Ohaver Lake (Pike & San Isabel NF)

Total sites: 30, RV sites: 30, Water available, Vault/pit toilet, No showers, No RV dump, Tent & RV camping: $22, Open May-Oct, Max Length: 45ft, Reservations accepted, Elev: 9216ft/2809m, Tel: 719-539-3591, Nearest town: Poncha Springs. GPS: 38.426495, -106.143914

294 • C3 | Ophir Creek (Pike & San Isabel NF)

Total sites: 31, RV sites: 12, Central water, Vault/pit toilet, No showers, No RV dump, Tent & RV camping: $21, Open May-Sep, Max Length: 40ft, Reservations accepted, Elev: 8924ft/2720m, Tel: 719-553-1400, Nearest town: Colorado City. GPS: 38.060059, -105.107422

295 • C3 | Riverside (Pike & San Isabel NF)

Total sites: 18, RV sites: 7, Central water, Vault/pit toilet, No showers, No RV dump, Tent & RV camping: $17, Water may not be available, Open May-Oct, Max Length: 70ft, Reservations accepted, Elev: 8064ft/2458m, Tel: 719-836-2031, Nearest town: Florissant. GPS: 38.960181, -105.375222

296 • C3 | Spillway (Pike & San Isabel NF)

Total sites: 23, RV sites: 13, Central water, Vault/pit toilet, No showers, No RV dump, Tent & RV camping: $17, Open May-Oct, Max Length: 35ft, Reservations accepted, Elev: 8563ft/2610m, Tel: 719-836-2031, Nearest town: Lake George. GPS: 38.906635, -105.469217

297 • C3 | Springdale (Pike & San Isabel NF)

Total sites: 12, RV sites: 11, No water, Vault/pit toilet, Tent & RV camping: $18, Generator hours: 0600-2200, Open May-Sep, Max Length: 25ft, Reservations not accepted, Elev: 9309ft/2837m, Nearest town: Woodland Park. GPS: 38.997422, -105.023611

298 • C3 | Springer Gulch (Pike & San Isabel NF)

Total sites: 15, RV sites: 11, Central water, Vault/pit toilet, No showers, No RV dump, Tent & RV camping: $17, Open May-Oct, Max Length: 28ft, Reservations accepted, Elev: 8304ft/2531m, Tel: 719 836-2031, Nearest town: Lake George. GPS: 38.927216, -105.425345

299 • C3 | The Crags (Pike & San Isabel NF)

Total sites: 17, RV sites: 17, Water available, Vault/pit toilet, No showers, No RV dump, Tent & RV camping: $18, Small RVs only, Generator hours: 0600-2200, Open May-Sep, Max Length: 20ft, Reservations not accepted, Elev: 10141ft/3091m, Tel: 719-636-1602, Nearest town: Divide. GPS: 38.871049, -105.121673

300 • C3 | Thunder Ridge (Pike & San Isabel NF)

Total sites: 21, RV sites: 21, Water available, Vault/pit toilet, No showers, No RV dump, Tent & RV camping: $23, Open May-Oct, Max Length: 60ft, Reservations accepted, Elev: 9226ft/2812m, Tel: 719-553-1400, Nearest town: Woodland Park. GPS: 38.977201, -104.982588

301 • D1 | Burro Bridge (San Juan NF)

Total sites: 12, RV sites: 12, Central water, Vault/pit toilet, No showers, No RV dump, Tent & RV camping: $16, No services in winter, Steep road, Horse corral, Open all year, Max Length: 35ft, Reservations not accepted, Elev: 9137ft/2785m, Tel: 970-882-7296, Nearest town: Dolores. GPS: 37.787329, -108.067456

302 • D1 | Cabin Canyon (San Juan NF)

Total sites: 11, RV sites: 11, Central water, No toilets, No showers, RV dump, Tent & RV camping: Free, Max Length: 45ft, Reservations not accepted, Elev: 6555ft/1998m, Nearest town: Cortez. GPS: 37.628199, -108.692988

303 • D1 | Cayton (San Juan NF)

Total sites: 27, RV sites: 27, Elec sites: 16, Central water, Vault/pit toilet, No showers, RV dump, Tents: $24/RVs: $24-30, Open May-Sep, Max Length: 70ft, Reservations accepted, Elev: 9413ft/2869m, Tel: 970-882-7296, Nearest town: Rico. GPS: 37.771256, -107.977195

304 • D1 | Ferris Canyon (San Juan NF)

Total sites: 7, RV sites: 7, No water, Vault/pit toilet, No showers, No RV dump, Tent & RV camping: Free, Open all year, Max Length: 45ft, Reservations not accepted, Elev: 6604ft/2013m, Nearest town: Cortez. GPS: 37.615246, -108.635597

305 • D1 | House Creek (San Juan NF)

Total sites: 22, RV sites: 22, Elec sites: 12, Central water, Vault/pit toilet, No showers, RV dump, Tents: $24/RVs: $24-32, Group site: $80, Dump fee: $15, No services in winter, Open all year, Max Length: 50ft, Reservations accepted, Elev: 6975ft/2126m, Nearest town: Dolores. GPS: 37.516252, -108.535274

306 • D1 | Junction Creek (San Juan NF)

Total sites: 44, RV sites: 44, Elec sites: 14, Central water, Vault/pit toilet, No showers, No RV dump, Tents: $24/RVs: $24-35, Group site: $100, Water at nearby Idlewild CG, Open May-Sep, Max Length: 65ft, Reservations accepted, Elev: 7431ft/2265m, Tel: 970-884-2512, Nearest town: Durango. GPS: 37.339469, -107.917407

307 • D1 | Kroeger (San Juan NF)

Total sites: 10, RV sites: 10, Central water, Vault/pit toilet, No showers, No RV dump, Tent & RV camping: $20, Only 1 site for larger RV, Open May-Sep, Max Length: 35ft, Reservations not accepted, Elev: 8927ft/2721m, Tel: 970-247-4874, Nearest town: Durango. GPS: 37.376231, -108.077104

308 • D1 | Lower Hermosa (San Juan NF)

Total sites: 20, RV sites: 20, No water, Vault/pit toilet, Tent & RV camping: $18, Some sites for horse use only, Reservations not accepted, Elev: 7779ft/2371m, Tel: 970-247-4874, Nearest town: Durango. GPS: 37.454503, -107.856779

309 • D1 | Mavreeso (San Juan NF)

Total sites: 19, RV sites: 19, Elec sites: 4, Central water, Vault/pit toilet, No showers, No RV dump, Tents: $24/RVs: $24-32, Group site $80, Open May-Sep, Max Length: 60ft, Reservations accepted, Elev: 7733ft/2357m, Tel: 970-882-7296, Nearest town: Dolores. GPS: 37.650827, -108.297028

310 • D1 | McPhee (San Juan NF)

Total sites: 71, RV sites: 59, Elec sites: 24, Central water, Flush toilet, No showers, No RV dump, Tents: $24/RVs: $24-32, Also walk-to & group sites, Group site: $80, Open May-Sep, Max Length: 50ft, Reservations accepted, Elev: 7192ft/2192m, Tel: 970-247-4874, Nearest town: Dolores. GPS: 37.497071, -108.552896

311 • D1 | Miners Cabin (San Juan NF)

Total sites: 7, RV sites: 7, No water, Vault/pit toilet, Tent & RV camping: Free, Elev: 8959ft/2731m, Nearest town: Mayday. GPS: 37.381294, -108.076952

312 • D1 | Sig Creek (San Juan NF)

Total sites: 9, RV sites: 9, Central water, Vault/pit toilet, No showers, No RV dump, Tent & RV camping: Free, Reservations not accepted, Elev: 9331ft/2844m, Tel: 970-247-4874, Nearest town: Durango. GPS: 37.633704, -107.883662

313 • D1 | Snowslide (San Juan NF)

Total sites: 13, RV sites: 13, No water, Vault/pit toilet, Tent & RV camping: $16, Max Length: 35ft, Reservations not accepted, Elev: 8846ft/2696m, Tel: 970-247-4874, Nearest town: Durango. GPS: 37.370908, -108.078197

314 • D1 | Target Tree (San Juan NF)

Total sites: 25, RV sites: 25, Central water, Vault/pit toilet, No showers, No RV dump, Tent & RV camping: $20, 5 sites for horse users, 1 group site, Max Length: 35ft, Reservations not accepted, Elev: 7805ft/2379m, Tel: 970-882-6800, Nearest town: Mancos. GPS: 37.340781, -108.188129

315 • D1 | Transfer (San Juan NF)

Total sites: 12, RV sites: 12, Central water, Vault/pit toilet, No showers, No RV dump, Tent & RV camping: $20, Open May-Sep, Max Length: 35ft, Reservations not accepted, Elev: 8937ft/2724m, Nearest town: Mancos. GPS: 37.467396, -108.209666

316 • D1 | Transfer Horse Camp (San Juan NF)

Total sites: 5, RV sites: 5, Central water, Vault/pit toilet, No showers, No RV dump, Tent & RV camping: Fee unk, Horse corral, Reservations not accepted, Elev: 8929ft/2722m, Nearest town: Mancos. GPS: 37.468606, -108.210668

317 • D1 | West Dolores (San Juan NF)

Total sites: 18, RV sites: 18, Elec sites: 7, Central water, Vault/pit toilet, No showers, No RV dump, Tents: $24/RVs: $24-32, Open May-Sep, Max Length: 65ft, Reservations accepted, Elev: 7825ft/2385m, Tel: 970-882-7296, Nearest town: Dolores. GPS: 37.659668, -108.275635

318 • D2 | Alamosa (Rio Grande NF)

Total sites: 5, RV sites: 5, No water, No toilets, Tent & RV camping: Free, Open May-Sep, Max Length: 25ft, Reservations not accepted, Elev: 8684ft/2647m, Tel: 719-274-8971, Nearest town: La Jara. GPS: 37.379395, -106.345215

319 • D2 | Aspen Glade (Rio Grande NF)

Total sites: 32, RV sites: 32, Central water, Vault/pit toilet, No showers, No RV dump, Tent & RV camping: $26, Open May-Sep, Max Length: 75ft, Reservations accepted, Elev: 8586ft/2617m, Tel: 719-376-2535, Nearest town: Antonito. GPS: 37.072998, -106.274658

320 • D2 | Big Meadows (Rio Grande NF)

Total sites: 54, RV sites: 54, Central water, Vault/pit toilet, No showers, No RV dump, Tent & RV camping: $26, Group site: $87, Open May-Sep, Max Length: 50ft, Reservations accepted, Elev: 9380ft/2859m, Tel: 719-657-3321, Nearest town: South Fork. GPS: 37.539795, -106.795410

321 • D2 | Bridge (San Juan NF)

Total sites: 19, RV sites: 19, Central water, Vault/pit toilet, No

showers, No RV dump, Tent & RV camping: Fee unk, Open May-Sep, Max Length: 50ft, Reservations not accepted, Elev: 7930ft/2417m, Tel: 970-247-4874, Nearest town: Pagosa Springs. GPS: 37.465465, -107.196945

322 • D2 | Bristol Head (Rio Grande NF)

Total sites: 15, RV sites: 15, Central water, Vault/pit toilet, No showers, No RV dump, Tent & RV camping: $19-23, Open May-Sep, Max Length: 45ft, Reservations not accepted, Elev: 9508ft/2898m, Tel: 719-657-3321, Nearest town: Creede. GPS: 37.818115, -107.144287

323 • D2 | Cathedral (Rio Grande NF)

Total sites: 22, RV sites: 22, No water, Vault/pit toilet, Tent & RV camping: Free, Open Apr-Dec, Max Length: 45ft, Reservations not accepted, Elev: 9475ft/2888m, Tel: 719-657-3321, Nearest town: Del Norte. GPS: 37.822266, -106.604980

324 • D2 | Cimarrona (San Juan NF)

Total sites: 21, RV sites: 21, Central water, Vault/pit toilet, No showers, No RV dump, Tent & RV camping: Fee unk, Max Length: 35ft, Reservations not accepted, Elev: 8425ft/2568m, Nearest town: Pagosa Springs. GPS: 37.538955, -107.210274

325 • D2 | Comstock (Rio Grande NF)

Total sites: 7, RV sites: 7, No water, Vault/pit toilet, Tent & RV camping: Free, Winter access may be limited, Open all year, Max Length: 35ft, Reservations not accepted, Elev: 9718ft/2962m, Tel: 719-657-3321, Nearest town: Monte Vista. GPS: 37.445309, -106.362832

326 • D2 | Crooked Creek Dispersed (Rio Grande NF)

Total sites: 4, RV sites: 4, No water, Vault/pit toilet, Tent & RV camping: Free, Not plowed in winter, Open all year, Reservations not accepted, Elev: 9163ft/2793m, Tel: 719-852-5941. GPS: 37.791612, -107.162063

327 • D2 | Cross Creek (Rio Grande NF)

Total sites: 12, RV sites: 5, Central water, Vault/pit toilet, No showers, No RV dump, Tents: $24/RVs: $24-29, Very unlevel sites, No water in winter, Open all year, Max Length: 20ft, Reservations not accepted, Elev: 8901ft/2713m, Tel: 719-657-3321, Nearest town: South Fork. GPS: 37.581055, -106.650146

328 • D2 | East Fork (San Juan NF)

Total sites: 26, RV sites: 26, Central water, Vault/pit toilet, No showers, No RV dump, Tent & RV camping: $22, Open May-Sep, Max Length: 40ft, Reservations accepted, Elev: 7776ft/2370m, Tel: 661-702-1420, Nearest town: Pagosa Springs. GPS: 37.374442, -106.887304

329 • D2 | Elk Creek (Rio Grande NF)

Total sites: 38, RV sites: 38, Central water, Vault/pit toilet, No showers, No RV dump, Tent & RV camping: $26, Open May-Sep, Max Length: 60ft, Reservations accepted, Elev: 8704ft/2653m, Tel: 719-274-8971, Nearest town: Antonito. GPS: 37.125465, -106.367577

330 • D2 | Florida (San Juan NF)

Total sites: 20, RV sites: 20, Central water, Vault/pit toilet, No showers, No RV dump, Tent & RV camping: $24, Generator hours: 0600-2200, Open May-Sep, Max Length: 35ft, Reservations not accepted, Elev: 8369ft/2551m, Tel: 970-884-2512, Nearest town: Bayfield. GPS: 37.452655, -107.682091

331 • D2 | Hansons Mill (Rio Grande NF)

Total sites: 3, RV sites: 3, No water, Vault/pit toilet, Tent & RV camping: Free, Reservations not accepted, Elev: 10935ft/3333m, Tel: 719-658-2556, Nearest town: Creede. GPS: 37.813000, -106.737000

332 • D2 | Haviland Lake (San Juan NF)

Total sites: 43, RV sites: 43, Elec sites: 17, Central water, Vault/pit toilet, No showers, No RV dump, Tents: $24/RVs: $24-32, Open Jun-Sep, Max Length: 48ft, Reservations accepted, Elev: 8178ft/2493m, Tel: 970-884-2512, Nearest town: Durango. GPS: 37.533804, -107.806769

333 • D2 | Highway Springs (Rio Grande NF)

Total sites: 13, RV sites: 13, No water, Vault/pit toilet, Tent & RV camping: $20, Open May-Sep, Max Length: 35ft, Reservations not accepted, Elev: 8415ft/2565m, Tel: 719-657-3321, Nearest town: South Fork. GPS: 37.621826, -106.685059

334 • D2 | Ivy Creek (Rio Grande NF)

Total sites: 4, RV sites: 2, No water, Vault/pit toilet, Tent & RV camping: Free, Winter access may be limited, Open all year, Max Length: 25ft, Reservations not accepted, Elev: 9264ft/2824m, Tel: 719-657-3321, Nearest town: Creede. GPS: 37.682097, -106.999589

335 • D2 | Lake Fork (Red Mt) (Rio Grande NF)

Total sites: 19, RV sites: 19, No water, Vault/pit toilet, Tent & RV camping: $23, Open May-Sep, Max Length: 70ft, Reservations accepted, Elev: 9550ft/2911m, Tel: 719-852-5941, Nearest town: Antonito. GPS: 37.309326, -106.477295

336 • D2 | Little Molas Lake (San Juan NF)

Total sites: 10, RV sites: 5, No water, Vault/pit toilet, Tent & RV camping: Free, Reservations not accepted, Elev: 11004ft/3354m, Nearest town: Silverton. GPS: 37.744656, -107.709869

337 • D2 | Lost Trail (Rio Grande NF)

Total sites: 7, RV sites: 7, Central water, Vault/pit toilet, No showers, No RV dump, Tent & RV camping: Free, Max Length: 20ft, Reservations not accepted, Elev: 9619ft/2932m, Tel: 719-657-3321, Nearest town: Creede. GPS: 37.768619, -107.349813

338 • D2 | Lower Beaver Creek (Rio Grande NF)

Total sites: 18, RV sites: 18, Central water, Vault/pit toilet, No showers, No RV dump, Tent & RV camping: $18-24, No services in winter, Open all year, Reservations not accepted, Elev: 8481ft/2585m, Tel: 719-657-3321, Nearest town: South Fork. GPS: 37.616251, -106.676569

339 • D2 | Lower Piedra (San Juan NF)

Total sites: 17, RV sites: 17, Central water, Vault/pit toilet, No showers, No RV dump, Tent & RV camping: $22, Open May-Sep, Max Length: 35ft, Reservations not accepted, Elev: 6627ft/

2020m, Tel: 970-247-4874, Nearest town: Pagosa Springs. GPS: 37.241943, -107.342773

340 • D2 | Marshall Park (Rio Grande NF)

Total sites: 15, RV sites: 14, Central water, Vault/pit toilet, No showers, No RV dump, Tent & RV camping: $23, Open May-Sep, Max Length: 103ft, Reservations accepted, Elev: 8766ft/2672m, Tel: 719-658-0829, Nearest town: Creede. GPS: 37.790499, -106.981491

341 • D2 | Miller Creek (San Juan NF)

Total sites: 12, RV sites: 12, Central water, Vault/pit toilet, No showers, No RV dump, Tent & RV camping: $22, Open May-Sep, Max Length: 35ft, Reservations not accepted, Elev: 8264ft/2519m, Tel: 970-247-4874, Nearest town: Bayfield. GPS: 37.405029, -107.661133

342 • D2 | Mix Lake (Rio Grande NF)

Total sites: 22, RV sites: 22, No water, Vault/pit toilet, Tent & RV camping: $23, Open Jun-Sep, Max Length: 25ft, Reservations not accepted, Elev: 10076ft/3071m, Tel: 719-274-8971, Nearest town: Antonito. GPS: 37.358544, -106.546835

343 • D2 | Palisade (Rio Grande NF)

Total sites: 12, RV sites: 12, Central water, Vault/pit toilet, No showers, No RV dump, Tent & RV camping: $22-26, Open May-Sep, Max Length: 32ft, Reservations not accepted, Elev: 8399ft/2560m, Tel: 719-657-3321, Nearest town: South Fork. GPS: 37.750732, -106.764648

344 • D2 | Palisades Horse Camp (San Juan NF)

Total sites: 12, RV sites: 12, Central water, Vault/pit toilet, No showers, No RV dump, Tent & RV camping: $24, Open May-Sep, Max Length: 45ft, Reservations accepted, Elev: 8504ft/2592m, Tel: 661-702-1420, Nearest town: Pagosa Springs. GPS: 37.541355, -107.199857

345 • D2 | Park Creek (Rio Grande NF)

Total sites: 13, RV sites: 13, Central water, Vault/pit toilet, No showers, No RV dump, Tent & RV camping: $24, Open May-Sep, Max Length: 35ft, Reservations not accepted, Elev: 8547ft/2605m, Tel: 719-657-3321, Nearest town: South Fork. GPS: 37.591553, -106.729248

346 • D2 | Pine River (San Juan NF)

Total sites: 6, RV sites: 6, No water, No toilets, Tent & RV camping: Free, No large RVs, Max Length: 20ft, Reservations not accepted, Elev: 7946ft/2422m, Tel: 970-247-4874, Nearest town: Durango. GPS: 37.447224, -107.505056

347 • D2 | River Hill (Rio Grande NF)

Total sites: 20, RV sites: 20, Central water, Vault/pit toilet, No showers, No RV dump, Tent & RV camping: $26, Open May-Sep, Max Length: 125ft, Reservations accepted, Elev: 9256ft/2821m, Tel: 719-657-3321, Nearest town: Creede. GPS: 37.730036, -107.228105

348 • D2 | Road Canyon (Rio Grande NF)

Total sites: 6, RV sites: 6, No water, Vault/pit toilet, Tent & RV camping: Free, Max Length: 25ft, Elev: 9318ft/2840m, Tel: 719-657-3321, Nearest town: Creede. GPS: 37.754996, -107.192111

349 • D2 | Rock Creek (Greenie Mt) (Rio Grande NF)

Total sites: 10, RV sites: 10, No water, Vault/pit toilet, Tent & RV camping: Free, Open Apr-Dec, Max Length: 40ft, Reservations not accepted, Elev: 9219ft/2810m, Tel: 719-657-3321, Nearest town: Monte Vista. GPS: 37.468506, -106.332275

350 • D2 | South Mineral (San Juan NF)

Total sites: 26, RV sites: 26, Central water, Vault/pit toilet, No showers, No RV dump, Tent & RV camping: Fee unk, Max Length: 25ft, Reservations not accepted, Elev: 9856ft/3004m, Nearest town: Silverton. GPS: 37.804958, -107.775231

351 • D2 | Spectacle Lake (Rio Grande NF)

Total sites: 24, RV sites: 24, Central water, Vault/pit toilet, No showers, No RV dump, Tent & RV camping: $19-23, Open May-Sep, Max Length: 25ft, Reservations not accepted, Elev: 8796ft/2681m, Tel: 719-274-8971, Nearest town: Antonito. GPS: 37.167097, -106.438893

352 • D2 | Stunner (Rio Grande NF)

Total sites: 5, No water, Vault/pit toilet, Tents only: Free, Open May-Sep, Max Length: 25ft, Reservations not accepted, Elev: 9866ft/3007m, Tel: 719-274-8971, Nearest town: La Jara. GPS: 37.377803, -106.574129

353 • D2 | Teal (San Juan NF)

Total sites: 16, RV sites: 16, Central water, Vault/pit toilet, No showers, No RV dump, Tent & RV camping: Fee unk, Max Length: 35ft, Reservations not accepted, Elev: 8304ft/2531m, Tel: 970-247-4874, Nearest town: Pagosa Springs. GPS: 37.510010, -107.229736

354 • D2 | Thirty Mile (Rio Grande NF)

Total sites: 39, RV sites: 39, Central water, Vault/pit toilet, No showers, No RV dump, Tent & RV camping: $26, Open May-Sep, Max Length: 90ft, Reservations accepted, Elev: 9334ft/2845m, Tel: 719-852-5941, Nearest town: Creede. GPS: 37.723389, -107.258057

355 • D2 | Transfer Park (San Juan NF)

Total sites: 25, RV sites: 25, Central water, Vault/pit toilet, No showers, No RV dump, Tent & RV camping: Fee unk, Max Length: 35ft, Elev: 8500ft/2591m, Nearest town: Bayfield. GPS: 37.462908, -107.681508

356 • D2 | Trujillo Meadows (Rio Grande NF)

Total sites: 50, RV sites: 50, Central water, Vault/pit toilet, No showers, No RV dump, Tent & RV camping: $26, Open Jun-Sep, Max Length: 25ft, Reservations not accepted, Elev: 10134ft/3089m, Tel: 719-274-8971, Nearest town: Chama. GPS: 37.046387, -106.449219

357 • D2 | Tucker Ponds (Rio Grande NF)

Total sites: 16, RV sites: 16, Central water, Vault/pit toilet, No showers, No RV dump, Tent & RV camping: $19-23, Open Jun-Sep, Max Length: 35ft, Reservations not accepted, Elev: 9685ft/

2952m, Tel: 719-657-3321, Nearest town: South Fork. GPS: 37.494141, -106.761719

358 • D2 | Upper Beaver Creek (Rio Grande NF)

Total sites: 14, RV sites: 14, Central water, Vault/pit toilet, No showers, No RV dump, Tent & RV camping: $20-24, Open May-Sep, Max Length: 35ft, Reservations not accepted, Elev: 8632ft/2631m, Tel: 719-657-3321, Nearest town: South Fork. GPS: 37.606235, -106.676941

359 • D2 | Ute (San Juan NF)

Total sites: 26, RV sites: 26, Central water, Vault/pit toilet, No showers, No RV dump, Tent & RV camping: $20, Open May-Sep, Max Length: 42ft, Reservations accepted, Elev: 6870ft/2094m, Nearest town: Pagosa Springs. GPS: 37.215000, -107.273000

360 • D2 | Vallecito (San Juan NF)

Total sites: 80, RV sites: 80, Elec sites: 3, Central water, Vault/pit toilet, No showers, No RV dump, Tents: $24-25/RVs: $24-32, Generator hours: 0600-2200, Open May-Sep, Max Length: 50ft, Reservations accepted, Elev: 7972ft/2430m, Tel: 970-247-4874, Nearest town: Vallecito. GPS: 37.476391, -107.547461

361 • D2 | Vallecito Reservoir - Graham Creek (San Juan NF)

Total sites: 25, RV sites: 25, Central water, No toilets, No showers, No RV dump, Tent & RV camping: $22, Steep entrance/exit roads, Open May-Nov, Max Length: 60ft, Reservations accepted, Elev: 7782ft/2372m, Tel: 970-884-2512, Nearest town: Bayfield. GPS: 37.390017, -107.539944

362 • D2 | Vallecito Reservoir - Middle Mountain (San Juan NF)

Total sites: 24, RV sites: 24, Central water, Vault/pit toilet, No showers, No RV dump, Tent & RV camping: Fee unk, Max Length: 22ft, Reservations not accepted, Elev: 7812ft/2381m, Tel: 970-884-2512, Nearest town: Bayfield. GPS: 37.409041, -107.536211

363 • D2 | Vallecito Reservoir - North Canyon (San Juan NF)

Total sites: 21, RV sites: 21, No water, Vault/pit toilet, Tent & RV camping: $20, Open May-Sep, Max Length: 45ft, Reservations accepted, Elev: 7772ft/2369m, Tel: 970-884-2512, Nearest town: Bayfield. GPS: 37.394158, -107.539195

364 • D2 | Vallecito Reservoir - Pine Point (San Juan NF)

Total sites: 28, RV sites: 28, Central water, Vault/pit toilet, No showers, No RV dump, Tent & RV camping: $22-25, Open May-Sep, Max Length: 45ft, Reservations accepted, Elev: 7772ft/2369m, Tel: 970-884-2512, Nearest town: Bayfield. GPS: 37.400009, -107.535291

365 • D2 | West Fork (San Juan NF)

Total sites: 28, RV sites: 28, Central water, Vault/pit toilet, No showers, No RV dump, Tent & RV camping: $22, Open May-Sep, Max Length: 40ft, Reservations accepted, Elev: 7930ft/2417m, Tel: 661-702-1420, Nearest town: Pagosa Springs. GPS: 37.446045, -106.908447

366 • D2 | Williams Creek (San Juan) (San Juan NF)

Total sites: 61, RV sites: 58, Central water, Vault/pit toilet, No showers, RV dump, Tents: $25/RVs: $25-32, Open May-Sep, Max Length: 45ft, Reservations accepted, Elev: 8228ft/2508m, Tel: 970-585-1200, Nearest town: Pagosa Springs. GPS: 37.495559, -107.226359

367 • D3 | Bear Lake (Trinchera Peak) (Pike & San Isabel NF)

Total sites: 14, RV sites: 14, Central water, Vault/pit toilet, No showers, No RV dump, Tent & RV camping: $14, Open May-Sep, Max Length: 30ft, Elev: 10482ft/3195m, Nearest town: La Veta. GPS: 37.326172, -105.143311

368 • D3 | Blue Lake (Pike & San Isabel NF)

Total sites: 15, RV sites: 15, Central water, Vault/pit toilet, No showers, No RV dump, Tent & RV camping: $21, Open May-Oct, Max Length: 56ft, Reservations accepted, Elev: 10554ft/3217m, Tel: 719-269-9719, Nearest town: La Veta. GPS: 37.313232, -105.138672

369 • D3 | Cordova Pass (Pike & San Isabel NF)

Total sites: 3, No water, Vault/pit toilet, Tents only: $12, Open May-Sep, Reservations not accepted, Elev: 11276ft/3437m, Tel: 719-269-8500, Nearest town: La Veta. GPS: 37.348612, -105.025088

370 • D3 | Mogote (Rio Grande NF)

Total sites: 41, RV sites: 41, Central water, Vault/pit toilet, No showers, No RV dump, Tent & RV camping: $26, Group site $85-$150, Open May-Sep, Max Length: 60ft, Reservations accepted, Elev: 8428ft/2569m, Tel: 719-376-2535, Nearest town: Antonito. GPS: 37.065649, -106.231882

371 • D3 | Purgatoire (Pike & San Isabel NF)

Total sites: 23, RV sites: 13, Central water, Vault/pit toilet, No showers, No RV dump, Tent & RV camping: $21, 6 equestrian sites, Open May-Oct, Max Length: 45ft, Reservations accepted, Elev: 9741ft/2969m, Tel: 719-269-8500, Nearest town: La Veta. GPS: 37.253372, -105.109783

Florida

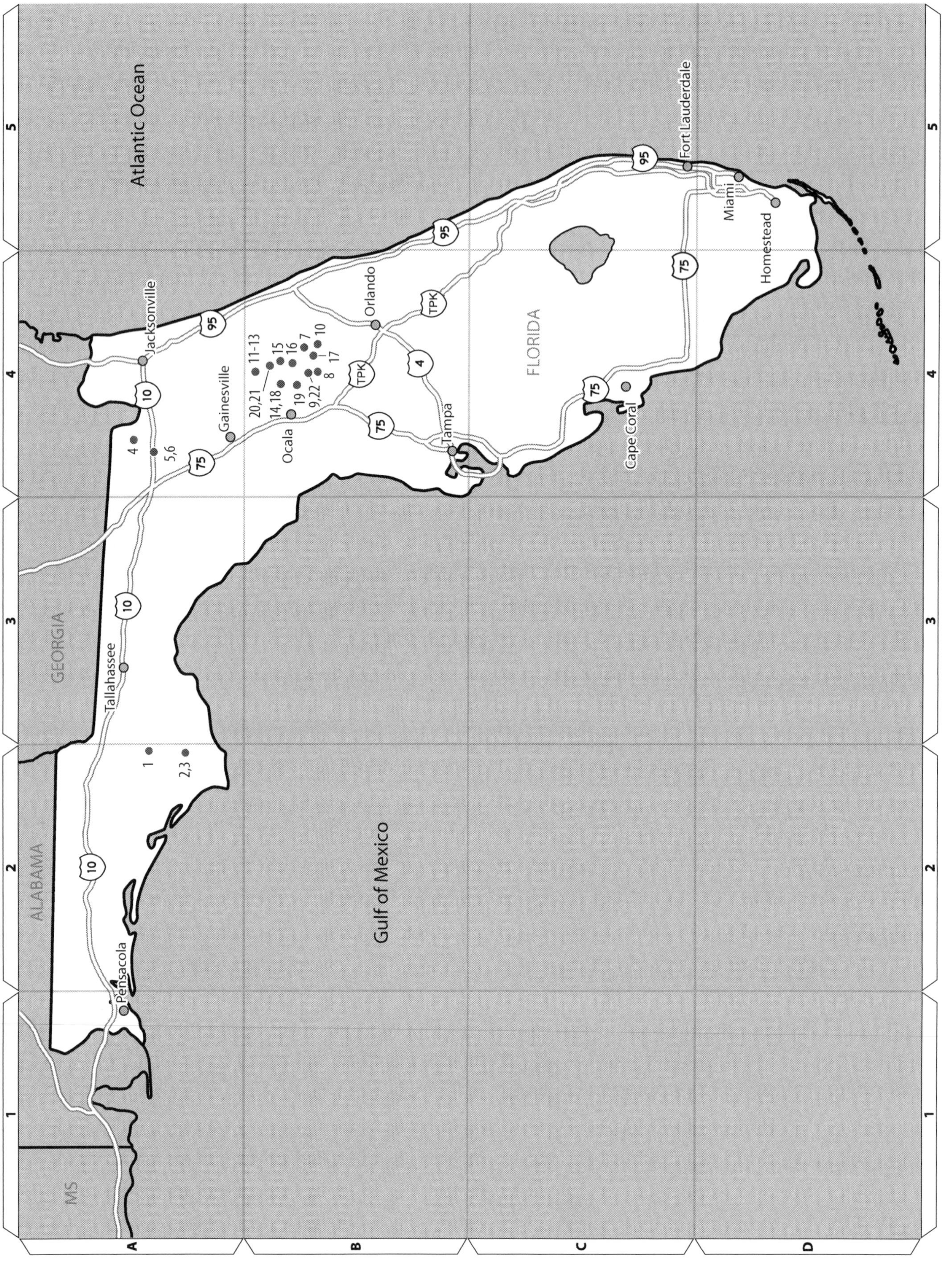

Atlantic Ocean
Gulf of Mexico
GEORGIA
ALABAMA
MS
FLORIDA
Jacksonville
Gainesville
Ocala
Orlando
Tampa
Cape Coral
Fort Lauderdale
Miami
Homestead
Tallahassee
Pensacola
10
75
95
4
TPK
1
2,3
4
5,6
7
8
9,22
10
11-13
14,18
15
16
17
19
20,21
A
B
C
D
1
2
3
4
5

Map	ID	Map	ID
A2	1-3	B4	7-22
A4	4-6		

Alphabetical List of Camping Areas

1 • A2 | Camel Lake (Apalachicola NF)

Total sites: 10, RV sites: 3, Elec sites: 5, Water at site, Flush toilet, Free showers, No RV dump, Tents: $20/RVs: $20-30, Open all year, Max Length: 60ft, Reservations accepted, Elev: 102ft/31m, Tel: 850-643-2282, Nearest town: Bristol. GPS: 30.276629, -84.987302

2 • A2 | Hickory Landing Hunt Camp (Apalachicola NF)

Total sites: 10, RV sites: 10, Central water, Vault/pit toilet, No showers, No RV dump, Tent & RV camping: $10, Generator hours: 0600-2200, Open all year, Reservations not accepted, Elev: 30ft/9m, Nearest town: Sumatra. GPS: 29.988825, -85.012969

3 • A2 | Wright Lake (Apalachicola NF)

Total sites: 20, RV sites: 20, Elec sites: 1, Central water, Flush toilet, Free showers, RV dump, Tents: $20/RVs: $20-30, Stay limit: 14 days, Open all year, Max Length: 60ft, Elev: 33ft/10m, Nearest town: Bristol. GPS: 30.000359, -85.002318

4 • A4 | East Tower Hunt Camp (Osceola NF)

Total sites: 15, RV sites: 0, Central water, Vault/pit toilet, No showers, No RV dump, Tents only: Free, Open all year, Elev: 112ft/34m, Tel: 386-752-2577, Nearest town: Sanderson. GPS: 30.382955, -82.330369

5 • A4 | Hog Pen Landing (Osceola NF)

Total sites: 8, RV sites: 8, No water, Vault/pit toilet, Tent & RV camping: $10, Open all year, Max Length: 24ft, Reservations not accepted, Elev: 131ft/40m, Tel: 386-752-2577, Nearest town: Olustee. GPS: 30.237888, -82.449417

6 • A4 | Ocean Pond (Osceola NF)

Total sites: 67, RV sites: 67, Elec sites: 19, Water at site, Flush toilet, Free showers, RV dump, Tents: $12-20/RVs: $20-30, Open all year, Reservations not accepted, Elev: 131ft/40m, Nearest town: Lake City. GPS: 30.239326, -82.433856

7 • B4 | Alexander Springs (Ocala NF)

Total sites: 66, RV sites: 66, Central water, Flush toilet, Free showers, RV dump, Tent & RV camping: $28, Open all year, Max Length: 44ft, Reservations accepted, Elev: 59ft/18m, Tel: 352-669-3522, Nearest town: Altoona. GPS: 29.080078, -81.578125

8 • B4 | Big Bass Lake Rec Area (Ocala NF)

Total sites: 34, RV sites: 34, Central water, Vault/pit toilet, No showers, RV dump, Tent & RV camping: $15, Stay limit: 14 days, Open Oct-Apr, Reservations not accepted, Elev: 97ft/30m, Nearest town: Altoona. GPS: 28.985894, -81.784419

9 • B4 | Big Scrub (Ocala NF)

Total sites: 48, RV sites: 38, Elec sites: 2, Central water, Flush toilet, Free showers, No RV dump, Tents: $20/RVs: $20-30, Stay limit: 14 days, Open all year, Max Length: 40ft, Reservations accepted, Elev: 171ft/52m, Tel: 352-625-2520, Nearest town: Umatilla. GPS: 29.050537, -81.755615

10 • B4 | Clearwater Lake (Ocala NF)

Total sites: 42, RV sites: 42, Central water, Flush toilet, Free showers, RV dump, Tent & RV camping: $25, Open all year, Max Length: 40ft, Reservations accepted, Elev: 131ft/40m, Tel: 352-669-0078, Nearest town: Paisley. GPS: 28.979611, -81.553523

11 • B4 | Davenport Landing (Ocala NF)

Total sites: 3, RV sites: 0, No water, No toilets, Tents only: Free, Stay limit: 14 days, Open all year, Elev: 62ft/19m, Nearest town: Possum Bluff. GPS: 29.472265, -81.773457

12 • B4 | Delancey East (Ocala NF)

Total sites: 29, RV sites: 0, Central water, Vault/pit toilet, No showers, No RV dump, Tents only: $15, Stay limit: 14 days, Open Oct-Apr, Reservations not accepted, Elev: 33ft/10m, Nearest town: Salt Springs. GPS: 29.430317, -81.786039

13 • B4 | Delancey West (Ocala NF)

Total sites: 30, RV sites: 30, No water, Vault/pit toilet, Tent & RV camping: $5, Stay limit: 14 days, Open all year, Reservations not accepted, Elev: 29ft/9m, Nearest town: Salt Springs. GPS: 29.428051, -81.788953

14 • B4 | Fore Lake (Ocala NF)

Total sites: 30, RV sites: 30, Central water, Flush toilet, Free showers, RV dump, Tent & RV camping: $20, Stay limit: 14 days, Open all year, Elev: 105ft/32m, Nearest town: Ocala. GPS: 29.270508, -81.917969

15 • B4 | Hopkins Prairie (Ocala NF)

Total sites: 21, RV sites: 21, Central water, Vault/pit toilet, No

showers, No RV dump, Tent & RV camping: $15, Stay limit: 14 days, Open Oct-May, Reservations not accepted, Elev: 56ft/17m, Nearest town: Ocala. GPS: 29.275500, -81.693700

16 • B4 | Juniper Springs (Ocala NF)

Total sites: 78, RV sites: 59, Central water, Flush toilet, Free showers, RV dump, Tent & RV camping: $28, Generator hours: 0600-2200, Open all year, Max Length: 45ft, Reservations accepted, Elev: 69ft/21m, Tel: 352-625-3147, Nearest town: Salt Springs. GPS: 29.182373, -81.712402

17 • B4 | Lake Dorr (Ocala NF)

Total sites: 34, RV sites: 32, Central water, Flush toilet, Free showers, No RV dump, Tent & RV camping: $20, Stay limit: 14 days, Open all year, Reservations not accepted, Elev: 62ft/19m, Nearest town: Umatilla. GPS: 29.012927, -81.635559

18 • B4 | Lake Eaton (Ocala NF)

Total sites: 14, RV sites: 14, No water, Vault/pit toilet, Tent & RV camping: $10, Stay limit: 14 days, Open Oct-May, Reservations not accepted, Elev: 43ft/13m, Nearest town: Ocala. GPS: 29.254187, -81.865303

19 • B4 | Little Lake Bryant (Ocala NF)

Total sites: 6, RV sites: 0, No water, No toilets, Tents only: Free, Elev: 62ft/19m, Nearest town: Silver Springs. GPS: 29.143658, -81.898461

20 • B4 | Salt Springs RV Area (Ocala NF)

Total sites: 98, RV sites: 98, Elec sites: 98, Water at site, Flush toilet, Free showers, RV dump, No tents/RVs: $50, 98 Full hookup sites, Open all year, Max Length: 40ft, Reservations accepted, Elev: 69ft/21m, Tel: 352-685-2048, Nearest town: Ocala. GPS: 29.357342, -81.732211

21 • B4 | Salt Springs Tent Area (Ocala NF)

Total sites: 52, RV sites: 0, Tents only: $31, Open all year, Reservations accepted, Elev: 15ft/5m, Tel: 352-685-2048, Nearest town: Ocala. GPS: 29.354063, -81.731572

22 • B4 | Trout Pond (Ocala NF)

Total sites: 2, RV sites: 0, No water, No toilets, Tents only: Free, Stay limit: 14 days, Elev: 65ft/20m, Tel: 352-236-0288, Nearest town: Altoona. GPS: 29.051768, -81.828456

Georgia

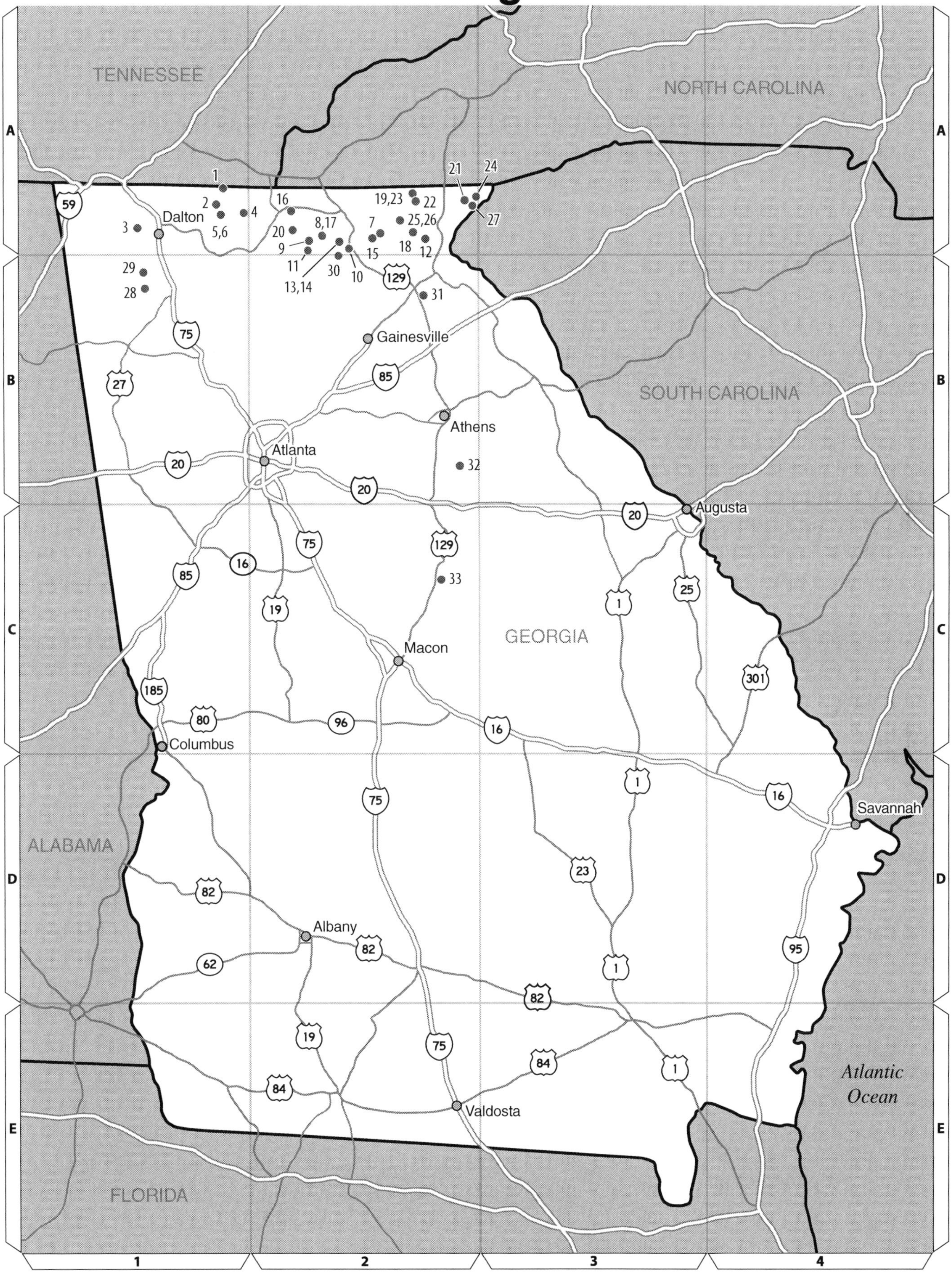
TENNESSEE
NORTH CAROLINA
SOUTH CAROLINA
ALABAMA
FLORIDA
GEORGIA
Atlantic Ocean
Dalton
Gainesville
Athens
Atlanta
Augusta
Macon
Columbus
Savannah
Albany
Valdosta
A
B
C
D
E
1
2
3
4

Map	ID	Map	ID
A1	1-6	B2	30-32
A2	7-27	C2	33
B1	28-29		

Alphabetical List of Camping Areas

1 • A1 | Cottonwood Patch Horse Camp (Chattahoochee-Oconee NF)

Total sites: 8, RV sites: 8, Central water, Vault/pit toilet, No showers, No RV dump, Tent & RV camping: $8, No water in winter, Generator hours: 0600-2200, Open all year, Reservations not accepted, Elev: 1040ft/317m, Tel: 706-695-6736, Nearest town: Chatsworth. GPS: 34.980415, -84.637686

2 • A1 | Hickey Gap (Chattahoochee-Oconee NF)

Total sites: 5, RV sites: 5, No water, Vault/pit toilet, Tent & RV camping: Free, Generator hours: 0600-2200, Open all year, Max Length: 24ft, Reservations not accepted, Elev: 1919ft/585m, Tel: 706-695-6736, Nearest town: Chatsworth. GPS: 34.894086, -84.672397

3 • A1 | Houston Valley OHV (Chattahoochee-Oconee NF)

Total sites: 3, RV sites: 3, No water, Vault/pit toilet, Tent & RV camping: Free, Open Apr-Dec, Reservations not accepted, Elev: 988ft/301m, Tel: 706-695-6736, Nearest town: Dalton. GPS: 34.788855, -85.129528

4 • A1 | Jacks River Fields (Chattahoochee-Oconee NF)

Total sites: 7, RV sites: 7, No water, Vault/pit toilet, Tent & RV camping: $5, Jan-Mar accessible only from Blue Ridge GA, Generator hours: 0600-2200, Open all year, Max Length: 24ft, Reservations not accepted, Elev: 2756ft/840m, Tel: 706-695-6736, Nearest town: Blue Ridge. GPS: 34.863374, -84.519984

5 • A1 | Lake Conasauga (Chattahoochee-Oconee NF)

Total sites: 31, RV sites: 31, Central water, Flush toilet, No showers, No RV dump, Tent & RV camping: $15, Stay limit: 14 days, Open Apr-Oct, Reservations not accepted, Elev: 3205ft/977m, Tel: 706-695-6736, Nearest town: Crandall. GPS: 34.860644, -84.649885

6 • A1 | Lake Conasauga Overflow (Chattahoochee-Oconee NF)

Total sites: 6, RV sites: 0, No water, Vault/pit toilet, Tents only: $8, Open Mar-Dec, Reservations not accepted, Elev: 3266ft/995m, Tel: 706-695-6736, Nearest town: Chatsworth. GPS: 34.853937, -84.649466

7 • A2 | Andrews Cove (Chattahoochee-Oconee NF)

Total sites: 10, RV sites: 10, Central water, Vault/pit toilet, No showers, No RV dump, Tent & RV camping: $12, Stay limit: 14 days, Open Mar-Oct, Reservations not accepted, Elev: 2136ft/651m, Tel: 770-297-3000, Nearest town: Helen. GPS: 34.777993, -83.737357

8 • A2 | Cooper Creek (Chattahoochee-Oconee NF)

Total sites: 15, RV sites: 15, Central water, Vault/pit toilet, No showers, No RV dump, Tent & RV camping: $15, 1/2 off mid-Nov to mid-Mar - no water, Stay limit: 14 days, Generator hours: 0600-2200, Open Mar-Dec, Reservations not accepted, Elev: 2171ft/662m, Tel: 706-745-6928, Nearest town: Blairsville. GPS: 34.762852, -84.068016

9 • A2 | Deep Hole (Chattahoochee-Oconee NF)

Total sites: 8, RV sites: 8, No water, Vault/pit toilet, No showers, No RV dump, Tents: $15/RVs: $16, Stay limit: 14 days, Open all year, Reservations not accepted, Elev: 1996ft/608m, Tel: 706-745-6928, Nearest town: Suches. GPS: 34.739741, -84.140595

10 • A2 | Desoto Falls (Chattahoochee-Oconee NF)

Total sites: 24, RV sites: 24, Central water, Flush toilet, Free showers, No RV dump, Tent & RV camping: $20, 1/2 off mid-Nov to mid-Mar - no water, Stay limit: 14 days, Open all year, Elev: 2083ft/635m, Tel: 706-745-6928, Nearest town: Cleveland. GPS: 34.707266, -83.915153

11 • A2 | Frank Gross (Chattahoochee-Oconee NF)

Total sites: 9, RV sites: 9, No water, Vault/pit toilet, Tent & RV camping: $8, Stay limit: 14 days, Open Mar-Nov, Reservations not accepted, Elev: 2248ft/685m, Tel: 706-745-6928, Nearest town: Blue Ridge. GPS: 34.701251, -84.149148

12 • A2 | Lake Rabun Beach (Chattahoochee-Oconee NF)

Total sites: 80, RV sites: 80, Elec sites: 21, Water at site, Flush toilet, Free showers, RV dump, Tents: $24/RVs: $35, Stay limit: 14 days, Open Apr-Oct, Reservations accepted, Elev: 1775ft/541m, Tel: 706-754-6221, Nearest town: Clarkesville. GPS: 34.755182, -83.480393

13 • A2 | Lake Winfield Scott - North Loop (Chattahoochee-Oconee NF)

Total sites: 17, RV sites: 17, Central water, Flush toilet, Free showers, No RV dump, Tents: $24/RVs: $24-25, No services Nov-Apr: $12, Open all year, Max Length: 40ft, Reservations not accepted, Elev: 2995ft/913m, Tel: 706-455-0342, Nearest town: Suches. GPS: 34.742490, -83.968310

14 • A2 | Lake Winfield Scott - South Loop (Chattahoochee-Oconee NF)

Total sites: 14, RV sites: 14, Central water, Flush toilet, Free showers, No RV dump, Tents: $24/RVs: $24-33, Also group sites & cabins, Group site: $75, Open Apr-Oct, Max Length: 40ft, Reservations required, Elev: 2905ft/885m, Tel: 706-455-0342, Nearest town: Suches. GPS: 34.734549, -83.972994

15 • A2 | Low Gap (Chattahoochee-Oconee NF)

Total sites: 13, RV sites: 13, Central water, Vault/pit toilet, No showers, No RV dump, Tent & RV camping: $12, Narrow steep winding access road, Stay limit: 14 days, Generator hours: 0700-2200, Open Mar-Oct, Max Length: 28ft, Reservations not accepted, Elev: 1815ft/553m, Tel: 706-754-6221, Nearest town: Helen. GPS: 34.752102, -83.785691

16 • A2 | Morganton Point (Chattahoochee-Oconee NF)

Total sites: 41, RV sites: 33, Elec sites: 28, Central water, Flush toilet, Free showers, No RV dump, Tents: $24/RVs: $24-33, Outdoor showers, Stay limit: 14 days, Generator hours: 0700-2200, Open all year, Max Length: 30ft, Reservations accepted, Elev: 1758ft/536m, Tel: 706-455-0342, Nearest town: Morganton. GPS: 34.869214, -84.248256

17 • A2 | Mulky (Chattahoochee-Oconee NF)

Total sites: 11, RV sites: 11, Central water, Vault/pit toilet, No showers, No RV dump, Tent & RV camping: $15, Half price mid-Nov to mid-Mar/no water, Stay limit: 14 days, Open all year, Reservations not accepted, Elev: 2160ft/658m, Tel: 706-745-6928, Nearest town: Morganton. GPS: 34.761802, -84.073087

18 • A2 | Oakey Mountain (Chattahoochee-Oconee NF)

Total sites: 6, RV sites: 6, Central water, Vault/pit toilet, No showers, No RV dump, Tent & RV camping: $10, Steep narrow road - no large RVs, Open Mar-Dec, Reservations not accepted, Elev: 2320ft/707m, Tel: 770-297-3000, Nearest town: Clayton. GPS: 34.784117, -83.554331

19 • A2 | Sandy Bottoms (Chattahoochee-Oconee NF)

Total sites: 14, RV sites: 14, Central water, Vault/pit toilet, No showers, No RV dump, Tent & RV camping: $15, Stay limit: 14 days, Generator hours: 0700-2200, Open Mar-Oct, Reservations not accepted, Elev: 2480ft/756m, Tel: 706-754-6221, Nearest town: Clayton. GPS: 34.960809, -83.557585

20 • A2 | Sandy Bottoms (Toccoa River) (Chattahoochee-Oconee NF)

Total sites: 4, RV sites: 0, No water, Vault/pit toilet, Tents only: $8, Walk-to sites, Stay limit: 14 days, Generator hours: 0600-2200, Open all year, Reservations not accepted, Elev: 1841ft/561m, Tel: 706-745-6928, Nearest town: Blue Ridge. GPS: 34.786292, -84.239739

21 • A2 | Sarahs Creek (Chattahoochee-Oconee NF)

Total sites: 26, RV sites: 26, No water, Vault/pit toilet, Tent & RV camping: $10, Stay limit: 14 days, Generator hours: 0700-2200, Open all year, Reservations not accepted, Elev: 2093ft/638m, Tel: 706-754-6221, Nearest town: Clayton. GPS: 34.925877, -83.262862

22 • A2 | Tallulah River (Chattahoochee-Oconee NF)

Total sites: 17, RV sites: 17, Central water, Vault/pit toilet, No showers, No RV dump, Tent & RV camping: $15, Stay limit: 14 days, Open all year, Reservations not accepted, Elev: 2119ft/646m, Tel: 770-297-3000, Nearest town: Clayton. GPS: 34.927395, -83.544111

23 • A2 | Tate Branch (Chattahoochee-Oconee NF)

Total sites: 19, RV sites: 19, Central water, Vault/pit toilet, No showers, No RV dump, Tent & RV camping: $15, Stay limit: 14 days, Open Mar-Oct, Reservations not accepted, Elev: 2385ft/727m, Tel: 706-754-6221, Nearest town: Clayton. GPS: 34.955176, -83.552405

24 • A2 | West Fork (Chattahoochee-Oconee NF)

Total sites: 5, RV sites: 0, No water, Vault/pit toilet, Tents only: $8, Walk-to sites, Stay limit: 14 days, Generator hours: 0700-2200, Reservations not accepted, Elev: 1847ft/563m, Tel: 706-754-6221, Nearest town: Clayton. GPS: 34.948078, -83.203729

25 • A2 | Wildcat 1 (Chattahoochee-Oconee NF)

Total sites: 16, RV sites: 0, No water, Vault/pit toilet, Tents only: $10, Road closed by landslide - walk-in OK, Stay limit: 14 days, Open all year, Elev: 2387ft/728m, Tel: 706-754-6221, Nearest town: Clayton. GPS: 34.830433, -83.614907

26 • A2 | Wildcat 2 (Chattahoochee-Oconee NF)

Total sites: 16, RV sites: 0, No water, Vault/pit toilet, Tents only: $10, Road closed by landslide - walk-in OK, Stay limit: 14 days, Open all year, Elev: 2649ft/807m, Tel: 706-754-6221, Nearest town: Clayton. GPS: 34.832868, -83.632482

27 • A2 | Willis Knob Horse Camp (Chattahoochee-Oconee NF)

Total sites: 9, RV sites: 9, Elec sites: 9, Water at site, Flush toilet, No showers, No RV dump, Tent & RV camping: $20, Group site: $30-$60, Stay limit: 14 days, Open all year, Max Length: 60ft, Reservations accepted, Elev: 1755ft/535m, Tel: 706-754-6221, Nearest town: Clayton. GPS: 34.900418, -83.222944

28 • B1 | Hidden Creek (Chattahoochee-Oconee NF)

Total sites: 15, RV sites: 15, No water, No toilets, Tent & RV camping: Free, Open May-Oct, Elev: 938ft/286m, Tel: 706-397-2265, Nearest town: Calhoun. GPS: 34.514997, -85.074019

29 • B1 | The Pocket (Chattahoochee-Oconee NF)

Total sites: 26, RV sites: 26, Central water, No toilets, No showers, No RV dump, Tent & RV camping: $15, Stay limit: 14 days, Open Apr-Oct, Reservations not accepted, Elev: 935ft/285m, Tel: 706-695-6736, Nearest town: Dalton. GPS: 34.585532, -85.083369

30 • B2 | Dockery Lake (Chattahoochee-Oconee NF)

Total sites: 11, RV sites: 11, Central water, Flush toilet, No showers, No RV dump, Tent & RV camping: $8, 1/2 off mid-Nov through Dec - no water, Stay limit: 14 days, Generator hours: 0600-2200, Open Mar-Dec, Reservations not accepted, Elev: 2461ft/750m, Tel: 706-745-6928, Nearest town: Dahlonega. GPS: 34.675224, -83.974102

31 • B2 | Lake Russell (Chattahoochee-Oconee NF)

Total sites: 41, RV sites: 32, Central water, Flush toilet, Free showers, RV dump, Tent & RV camping: $24, Jan-mid-Apr: $18, Open all year, Max Length: 67ft, Elev: 1109ft/338m, Tel: 706-754-6221, Nearest town: Mount Airy. GPS: 34.493261, -83.495074

32 • B2 | Oconee River (Chattahoochee-Oconee NF)

Total sites: 5, RV sites: 0, No water, Vault/pit toilet, Tents only: $5, No generators, Open all year, Reservations not accepted, Elev: 452ft/138m, Tel: 706-485-7110, Nearest town: Greensboro. GPS: 33.721501, -83.290675

33 • C2 | Lake Sinclair (Chattahoochee-Oconee NF)

Total sites: 44, RV sites: 44, Elec sites: 6, Water at site, Flush toilet, Free showers, RV dump, Tents: $9/RVs: $9-15, Group site: $80, No generators, Open all year, Reservations not accepted, Elev: 407ft/124m, Tel: 706-485-7110, Nearest town: Eatonton. GPS: 33.206635, -83.398261

Idaho

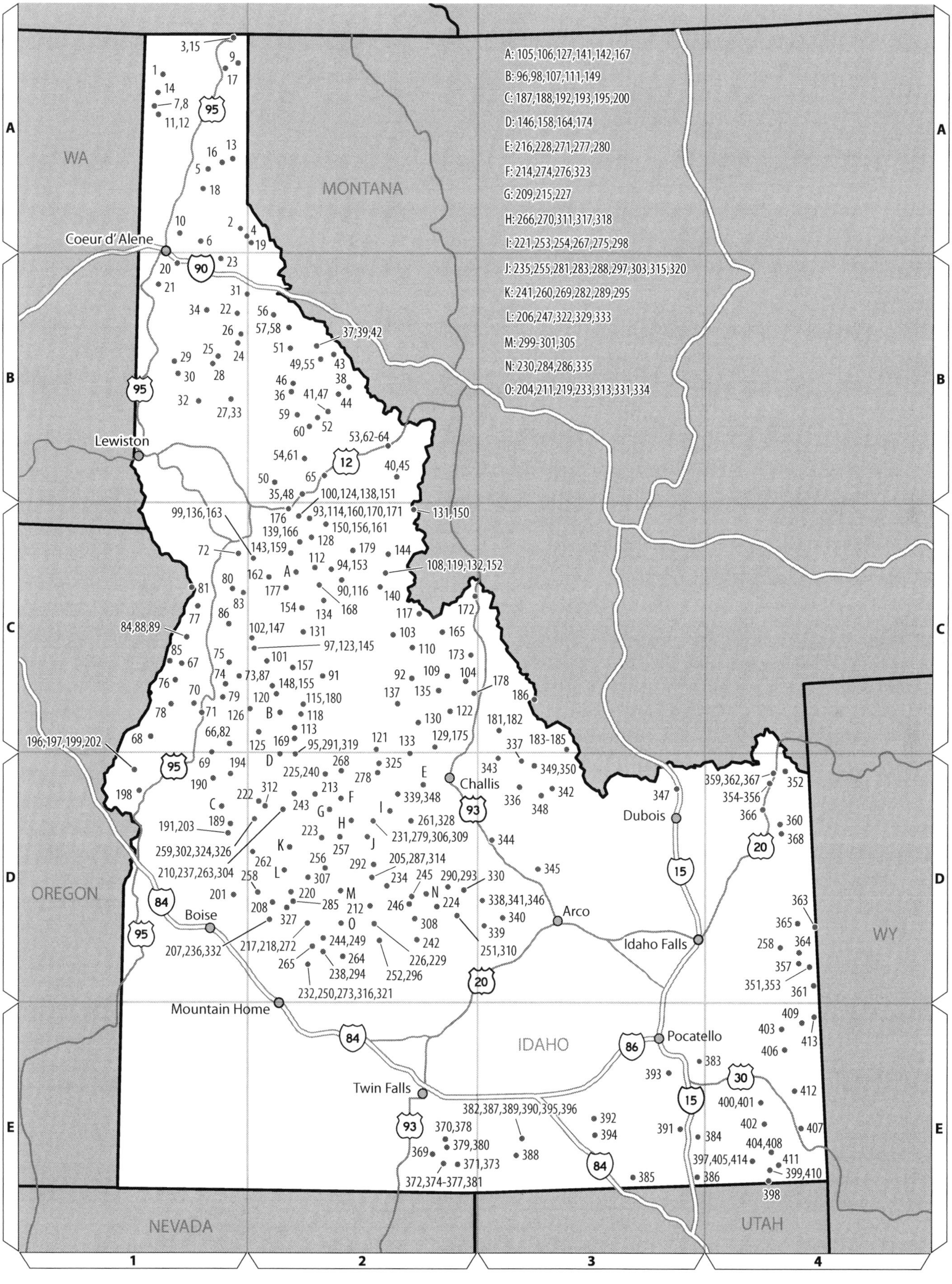
A: 105,106,127,141,142,167
B: 96,98,107,111,149
C: 187,188,192,193,195,200
D: 146,158,164,174
E: 216,228,271,277,280
F: 214,274,276,323
G: 209,215,227
H: 266,270,311,317,318
I: 221,253,254,267,275,298
J: 235,255,281,283,288,297,303,315,320
K: 241,260,269,282,289,295
L: 206,247,322,329,333
M: 299-301,305
N: 230,284,286,335
O: 204,211,219,233,313,331,334
WA
MONTANA
OREGON
NEVADA
UTAH
WY
IDAHO
Coeur d'Alene
Lewiston
Challis
Dubois
Arco
Idaho Falls
Boise
Mountain Home
Pocatello
Twin Falls
A
B
C
D
E
1
2
3
4

Map	ID	Map	ID
A1	1-18	D1	187-203
A2	19	D2	204-335
B1	20-34	D3	336-350
B2	35-65	D4	351-368
C1	66-89	E2	369-381
C2	90-180	E3	382-396
C3	181-186	E4	397-414

Alphabetical List of Camping Areas

Name	ID	Map
14 Mile TH (Nez Perce-Clearwater NF)	90	C2
Abbott (Sawtooth NF)	204	D2
Albert Moser (Caribou-Targhee NF)	397	E4
Alturas Inlet (Sawtooth NF)	205	D2
Amanita (Boise NF)	66	C1
Antelope (Boise NF)	187	D1
Antelope Annex (Boise NF)	188	D1
Apgar (Nez Perce-Clearwater NF)	35	B2
Aquarius (Nez Perce-Clearwater NF)	36	B2
Bad Bear (Boise NF)	206	D2
Badger Creek (Boise NF)	207	D2
Bald Mountain (Boise NF)	208	D2
Banner Creek (Salmon-Challis NF)	209	D2
Barney's (Boise NF)	210	D2
Baumgartner (Sawtooth NF)	211	D2
Bear Creek Transfer Camp (Sawtooth NF)	212	D2
Bear Gulch (Hopper Gulch) (Sawtooth NF)	369	E2
Bear Valley (Boise NF)	213	D2
Bear Valley Horse Camp (Salmon-Challis NF)	181	C3
Bear Valley TH Upper CG (Salmon-Challis NF)	182	C3
Beauty Creek (Idaho Panhandle NF)	20	B1
Beaver Creek (Cape Horn) (Salmon-Challis NF)	214	D2
Beaver Creek (Egan Basin) (Caribou-Targhee NF)	398	E4
Beaver Creek (Priest Lake) (Idaho Panhandle NF)	1	A1
Beaver Creek (Red Ives) (Idaho Panhandle NF)	37	B2
Bell Bay (Idaho Panhandle NF)	21	B1
Bench Creek (Salmon-Challis NF)	215	D2
Bennett Springs (Sawtooth NF)	382	E3
Big Bayhorse (Salmon-Challis NF)	216	D2
Big Bluff (Sawtooth NF)	370	E2
Big Creek (Big Creek Peak) (Salmon-Challis NF)	336	D3
Big Creek (Marble Creek) (Idaho Panhandle NF)	22	B1
Big Creek Airstrip (Payette NF)	91	C2
Big Eddy (Boise NF)	189	D1
Big Eightmile (Salmon-Challis NF)	337	D3
Big Elk (Caribou-Targhee NF)	351	D4
Big Flat (Payette NF)	190	D1
Big Hank (Idaho Panhandle NF)	2	A1
Big Roaring River Lake (Boise NF)	217	D2
Big Springs (Caribou-Targhee NF)	352	D4
Big Springs (Caribou) (Caribou-Targhee NF)	383	E3
Big Trinity Lake (Boise NF)	218	D2
Bighorn Crags (Salmon-Challis NF)	92	C2
Bird Creek (Sawtooth NF)	219	D2
Black Lake (Payette NF)	67	C1
Black Rock (Boise NF)	220	D2
Blind Creek (Salmon-Challis NF)	221	D2
Blowout (Caribou-Targhee NF)	353	D4
Boiling Springs (Boise NF)	222	D2
Bonneville (Boise NF)	223	D2
Bostetter (Sawtooth NF)	371	E2
Boundary (Sun Valley) (Sawtooth NF)	224	D2
Boundary Creek (Salmon-Challis NF)	225	D2
Bowns (Sawtooth NF)	226	D2
Box Canyon (Caribou-Targhee NF)	354	D4
Boyd Creek (Nez Perce-Clearwater NF)	93	C2
Bridge Creek (Nez Perce-Clearwater NF)	94	C2
Broad Canyon (Salmon-Challis NF)	338	D3
Brownlee (Payette NF)	68	C1
Buck Mountain (Boise NF)	95	C2
Buckhorn Bar (Payette NF)	96	C2
Buffalo (Caribou-Targhee NF)	355	D4
Bull Trout Lake (Boise NF)	227	D2
Bumblebee (Idaho Panhandle NF)	23	B1
Burgdorf (Payette NF)	97	C2
Buster Lake TH (Salmon-Challis NF)	228	D2
Buttermilk (Caribou-Targhee NF)	356	D4
Cabin Creek (Payette NF)	69	C1
Calamity (Caribou-Targhee NF)	357	D4
Camp 3 (Idaho Panhandle NF)	24	B1
Camp Creek (Payette NF)	98	C2
Canyon (Boise NF)	191	D1
Canyon Transfer (Sawtooth NF)	229	D2
Caribou (Sawtooth NF)	230	D2
Cartwright Ridge (Boise NF)	192	D1
Casino Creek (Sawtooth NF)	231	D2
Castle Creek (Nez Perce-Clearwater NF)	99	C2
Castle Creek (Boise NF)	232	D2
CCC (Nez Perce-Clearwater NF)	100	C2
Cedar Creek (Idaho Panhandle NF)	25	B1
Cedars (Clearwater NF)	38	B2
Chaparral (Sawtooth NF)	233	D2
Chemeketan (Sawtooth NRA)	234	D2
Cherry Creek (Caribou-Targhee NF)	384	E3
Chinook (Payette NF)	101	C2
Chinook Bay (Sawtooth NF)	235	D2
Cloverleaf (Caribou-Targhee NF)	399	E4
Cold Springs (Banks) (Caribou-Targhee NF)	400	E4
Cold Springs (New Meadows) (Payette NF)	70	C1
Conrad Crossing (Idaho Panhandle NF)	39	B2
Copper Creek (Idaho Panhandle NF)	3	A1
Copper Creek (Sawtooth NF)	339	D3
Corduroy Meadows (Payette NF)	102	C2
Corn Creek (Salmon-Challis NF)	103	C2
Cottonwood (Boise NF)	236	D2
Cougar Point (Salmon-Challis NF)	104	C2
Cozy Cove (Boise NF)	237	D2
Crooked River #3 (Nez Perce-Clearwater NF)	105	C2
Crooked River #4 (Nez Perce-Clearwater NF)	106	C2
Curlew (Curlew NG)	385	E3
Curlew Creek (Boise NF)	238	D2
Custer #1 (Salmon-Challis NF)	239	D2
Dagger Falls (Salmon-Challis NF)	240	D2
Deadman Bar (Payette NF)	107	C2
Deadwood (Boise NF)	241	D2
Deep Creek (Bitterroot NF)	108	C2
Deep Creek (Beaver Jack) (Salmon-Challis NF)	109	C2
Deer Creek (Sawtooth NF)	242	D2

1 • A1 | Beaver Creek (Priest Lake) (Idaho Panhandle NF)

Total sites: 42, RV sites: 42, Central water, Vault/pit toilet, No showers, No RV dump, Tent & RV camping: $23, Group site: $75, Open May-Sep, Max Length: 60ft, Reservations accepted, Elev: 2507ft/764m, Tel: 208-443-1801, Nearest town: Priest Lake. GPS: 48.734845, -116.860511

2 • A1 | Big Hank (Idaho Panhandle NF)

Total sites: 30, RV sites: 30, Central water, Vault/pit toilet, No showers, No RV dump, Tent & RV camping: $21, Stay limit: 14 days, Open May-Sep, Max Length: 40ft, Reservations accepted, Elev: 2759ft/841m, Tel: 208-664-2318, Nearest town: Kingston. GPS: 47.824038, -116.101334

3 • A1 | Copper Creek (Idaho Panhandle NF)

Total sites: 16, RV sites: 16, Central water, Vault/pit toilet, No showers, No RV dump, Tent & RV camping: $15, No fee Sep-May - no water, Open all year, Max Length: 30ft, Reservations not accepted, Elev: 2664ft/812m, Nearest town: Bonners Ferry. GPS: 48.985577, -116.167975

4 • A1 | Devils Elbow (Idaho Panhandle NF)

Total sites: 20, RV sites: 20, Central water, Vault/pit toilet, No showers, No RV dump, Tent & RV camping: $21, Group site: $80, Open May-Sep, Max Length: 100ft, Reservations accepted, Elev: 2621ft/799m, Tel: 208-664-2318, Nearest town: Kingston. GPS: 47.770996, -116.032471

5 • A1 | Green Bay (Idaho Panhandle NF)

Total sites: 11, RV sites: 0, Central water, Vault/pit toilet, Tents only: Free, Open May-Oct, Reservations not accepted, Elev: 2274ft/693m, Tel: 208-765-7223, Nearest town: Sandpoint. GPS: 48.178068, -116.408008

6 • A1 | Honeysuckle (Idaho Panhandle NF)

Total sites: 7, RV sites: 7, Central water, Vault/pit toilet, No showers, No RV dump, Tent & RV camping: $16, Open May-Sep, Reservations not accepted, Elev: 2776ft/846m, Nearest town: Coeur d'Alene. GPS: 47.739245, -116.474743

7 • A1 | Luby Bay Lower (Idaho Panhandle NF)

Total sites: 25, RV sites: 25, Central water, Flush toilet, No showers, RV dump, Tent & RV camping: $21-23, Open May-Sep, Max Length: 65ft, Reservations accepted, Elev: 2530ft/771m, Tel: 208-443-1801, Nearest town: Nordman. GPS: 48.549561, -116.924561

8 • A1 | Luby Bay Upper (Idaho Panhandle NF)

Total sites: 33, RV sites: 33, Central water, Flush toilet, No showers, RV dump, Tent & RV camping: $21-23, Open May-Sep, Max Length: 65ft, Reservations accepted, Elev: 2577ft/785m, Tel: 208-443-1801, Nearest town: Nordman. GPS: 48.550954, -116.927976

9 • A1 | Meadow Creek (Meadow Creek) (Idaho Panhandle NF)

Total sites: 22, RV sites: 22, Central water, Vault/pit toilet, No showers, No RV dump, Tent & RV camping: Fee unk, Open May-Sep, Reservations not accepted, Elev: 2323ft/708m, Nearest town: Bonners Ferry. GPS: 48.819276, -116.148063

10 • A1 | Mokins Bay (Idaho Panhandle NF)

Total sites: 15, RV sites: 15, Central water, Vault/pit toilet, No showers, No RV dump, Tent & RV camping: $21, Open May-Sep, Max Length: 40ft, Reservations accepted, Elev: 2346ft/715m, Tel: 208-762-7444, Nearest town: Coeur d'Alene. GPS: 47.784424, -116.665527

11 • A1 | Osprey (Idaho Panhandle NF)

Total sites: 16, RV sites: 16, Central water, Flush toilet, No showers, No RV dump, Tent & RV camping: $21-23, Open May-Sep, Max Length: 64ft, Reservations accepted, Elev: 2503ft/763m, Tel: 208-443-1801, Nearest town: Priest River. GPS: 48.506104, -116.888672

12 • A1 | Outlet (Priest Lake) (Idaho Panhandle NF)

Total sites: 27, RV sites: 27, Central water, Flush toilet, No showers, No RV dump, Tent & RV camping: $21-23, Open May-Sep, Max Length: 70ft, Reservations accepted, Elev: 2549ft/777m, Tel: 208-443-8053, Nearest town: Lamb Creek. GPS: 48.498779, -116.893311

13 • A1 | Porcupine Lake (Idaho Panhandle NF)

Total sites: 5, RV sites: 5, Central water, Vault/pit toilet, No showers, No RV dump, Tent & RV camping: Free, Rough road, Open May-Sep, Reservations not accepted, Elev: 4774ft/1455m, Tel: 208-263-5111, Nearest town: Clark Fork. GPS: 48.243986, -116.184989

14 • A1 | Reeder Bay (Idaho Panhandle NF)

Total sites: 24, RV sites: 24, Central water, Vault/pit toilet, No showers, No RV dump, Tent & RV camping: $21-23, Open May-Sep, Max Length: 55ft, Reservations accepted, Elev: 2490ft/759m, Tel: 208-443-1801, Nearest town: Priest River. GPS: 48.625244, -116.891846

15 • A1 | Robinson Lake (Idaho Panhandle NF)

Total sites: 10, RV sites: 10, Central water, Vault/pit toilet, No showers, No RV dump, Tent & RV camping: $15, No fee in off-season w/ no water, Open all year, Max Length: 27ft, Reservations not accepted, Elev: 2667ft/813m, Tel: 208-267-5561, Nearest town: Eastport. GPS: 48.970074, -116.217665

16 • A1 | Sam Owen (Idaho Panhandle NF)

Total sites: 80, RV sites: 59, Central water, Vault/pit toilet, No showers, RV dump, Tent & RV camping: $23-25, Dump fee - $7, Open May-Sep, Max Length: 60ft, Reservations accepted, Elev: 2165ft/660m, Tel: 208-264-0209, Nearest town: Hope. GPS: 48.218994, -116.287842

17 • A1 | Smith Lake (Idaho Panhandle NF)

Total sites: 7, RV sites: 7, Central water, Vault/pit toilet, No showers, No RV dump, Tent & RV camping: Free, Open May-Sep, Max Length: 16ft, Reservations not accepted, Elev: 3032ft/924m, Nearest town: Bonners Ferry. GPS: 48.778823, -116.263806

18 • A1 | Whiskey Rock Bay (Idaho Panhandle NF)

Total sites: 9, RV sites: 9, Central water, Vault/pit toilet, No showers, No RV dump, Tent & RV camping: Free, Open May-Sep, Reservations not accepted, Elev: 2123ft/647m, Nearest town: Clark Fork. GPS: 48.050677, -116.452781

19 • A2 | Kit Price (Idaho Panhandle NF)

Total sites: 53, RV sites: 53, Central water, Vault/pit toilet, No showers, No RV dump, Tent & RV camping: $21, Stay limit: 14 days, Open May-Sep, Max Length: 45ft, Reservations accepted, Elev: 2602ft/793m, Tel: 208-664-2318, Nearest town: Prichard. GPS: 47.739990, -116.006592

20 • B1 | Beauty Creek (Idaho Panhandle NF)

Total sites: 19, RV sites: 11, Central water, Vault/pit toilet, No showers, No RV dump, Tent & RV camping: $23, Open May-Sep, Max Length: 40ft, Reservations accepted, Elev: 2398ft/731m, Tel: 208-664-2318, Nearest town: Coeur d'Alene. GPS: 47.606364, -116.667582

21 • B1 | Bell Bay (Idaho Panhandle NF)

Total sites: 26, RV sites: 26, Central water, Vault/pit toilet, No showers, No RV dump, Tent & RV camping: $21, Group site: $98, Stay limit: 14 days, Open May-Sep, Max Length: 40ft, Reservations accepted, Elev: 2369ft/722m, Tel: 208-689-9636, Nearest town: Coeur D'Alene. GPS: 47.474067, -116.845317

22 • B1 | Big Creek (Marble Creek) (Idaho Panhandle NF)

Total sites: 9, RV sites: 9, Central water, Vault/pit toilet, No showers, No RV dump, Tent & RV camping: Free, Open May-Sep, Reservations not accepted, Elev: 2444ft/745m, Nearest town: St. Maries. GPS: 47.303456, -116.120193

23 • B1 | Bumblebee (Idaho Panhandle NF)

Total sites: 25, RV sites: 25, Central water, Vault/pit toilet, No showers, No RV dump, Tent & RV camping: $21, Group site: $167, Stay limit: 14 days, Open May-Sep, Max Length: 80ft, Reservations accepted, Elev: 2246ft/685m, Tel: 208-664-2318, Nearest town: Pinehurst. GPS: 47.634394, -116.277392

24 • B1 | Camp 3 (Idaho Panhandle NF)

Total sites: 4, RV sites: 4, No water, Vault/pit toilet, Tent & RV camping: Free, Open May-Sep, Reservations not accepted, Elev: 3222ft/982m, Nearest town: St. Maries. GPS: 47.129986, -116.103074

25 • B1 | Cedar Creek (Idaho Panhandle NF)

Total sites: 3, RV sites: 3, No water, Vault/pit toilet, Tent & RV camping: $10, Open May-Sep, Reservations not accepted, Elev: 2779ft/847m, Nearest town: Clarkia. GPS: 47.050956, -116.289101

26 • B1 | Donkey Creek (Idaho Panhandle NF)

Total sites: 5, RV sites: 4, No water, No toilets, Tent & RV camping: Free, Elev: 2930ft/893m, Nearest town: St Maries. GPS: 47.185119, -116.080703

27 • B1 | Elk Creek (Nez Perce-Clearwater NF)

Total sites: 14, RV sites: 14, Elec sites: 14, Central water, Vault/pit toilet, No showers, No RV dump, Tent & RV camping: $20, Open May-Oct, Max Length: 40ft, Reservations accepted, Elev: 2843ft/867m, Tel: 208-875-1131, Nearest town: Elk River. GPS: 46.793569, -116.171648

28 • B1 | Emerald Creek (Idaho Panhandle NF)

Total sites: 18, RV sites: 18, Central water, Vault/pit toilet, No

showers, No RV dump, Tent & RV camping: $10, Open May-Sep, Reservations not accepted, Elev: 2900ft/884m, Nearest town: Fernwood. GPS: 47.006973, -116.326698

29 • B1 | Giant White Pine (Nez Perce-Clearwater NF)

Total sites: 14, RV sites: 14, Central water, Vault/pit toilet, No showers, No RV dump, Tent & RV camping: $12, Open May-Sep, Max Length: 30ft, Reservations not accepted, Elev: 2910ft/887m, Tel: 208-875-1131, Nearest town: Princeton. GPS: 47.008875, -116.676841

30 • B1 | Laird Park (Nez Perce-Clearwater NF)

Total sites: 35, RV sites: 31, Central water, Vault/pit toilet, No showers, No RV dump, Tent & RV camping: $12, Open May-Sep, Max Length: 30ft, Reservations not accepted, Elev: 2713ft/827m, Tel: 208-875-1131, Nearest town: Harvard. GPS: 46.942871, -116.649902

31 • B1 | Lake Elsie (Idaho Panhandle NF)

Total sites: 7, RV sites: 3, No water, Vault/pit toilet, Tent & RV camping: Free, Reservations not accepted, Elev: 5138ft/1566m, Tel: 208-783-2363, Nearest town: Osburn. GPS: 47.428208, -116.022835

32 • B1 | Little Boulder (Nez Perce-Clearwater NF)

Total sites: 16, RV sites: 16, Central water, Vault/pit toilet, No showers, No RV dump, Tent & RV camping: $12, No water in Oct, Open May-Oct, Max Length: 30ft, Reservations not accepted, Elev: 2620ft/799m, Tel: 208-875-1131, Nearest town: Deary. GPS: 46.772561, -116.457662

33 • B1 | Partridge Creek (Nez Perce-Clearwater NF)

Total sites: 10, RV sites: 10, No water, Vault/pit toilet, Tent & RV camping: Free, Open May-Oct, Reservations not accepted, Elev: 3022ft/921m, Tel: 208-875-1131, Nearest town: Elk River. GPS: 46.784317, -116.148461

34 • B1 | Shadowy St. Joe (Idaho Panhandle NF)

Total sites: 14, RV sites: 14, Central water, Vault/pit toilet, No showers, No RV dump, Tent & RV camping: $20, Open May-Nov, Reservations not accepted, Elev: 2316ft/706m, Nearest town: St. Maries. GPS: 47.325668, -116.393254

35 • B2 | Apgar (Nez Perce-Clearwater NF)

Total sites: 7, RV sites: 7, Central water, Vault/pit toilet, No showers, No RV dump, Tent & RV camping: $14, Open May-Sep, Max Length: 24ft, Reservations not accepted, Elev: 1618ft/493m, Tel: 208-926-4274, Nearest town: Lowell. GPS: 46.213729, -115.536871

36 • B2 | Aquarius (Nez Perce-Clearwater NF)

Total sites: 7, RV sites: 7, No water, Vault/pit toilet, Tent & RV camping: $10, 2 group sites (Purple Beach), Open May-Oct, Max Length: 22ft, Reservations not accepted, Elev: 1850ft/564m, Tel: 208-476-4541, Nearest town: Headquarters. GPS: 46.840911, -115.617109

37 • B2 | Beaver Creek (Red Ives) (Idaho Panhandle NF)

Total sites: 2, RV sites: 2, No water, Vault/pit toilet, Tent & RV camping: Fee unk, Elev: 3635ft/1108m. GPS: 47.083039, -115.355303

38 • B2 | Cedars (Clearwater NF)

Total sites: 5, RV sites: 0, No water, Vault/pit toilet, Tents only: Free, Limited winter access, Open all year, Reservations not accepted, Elev: 3707ft/1130m, Tel: 208-476-4541, Nearest town: Pierce. GPS: 46.869589, -115.080037

39 • B2 | Conrad Crossing (Idaho Panhandle NF)

Total sites: 8, RV sites: 8, Central water, Vault/pit toilet, No showers, No RV dump, Tent & RV camping: $15, $12 when water turned off, Open May-Sep, Reservations not accepted, Elev: 3432ft/1046m, Nearest town: Avery. GPS: 47.158448, -115.416833

40 • B2 | Elk Summit (Nez Perce-Clearwater NF)

Total sites: 15, RV sites: 15, No water, Vault/pit toilet, Tent & RV camping: Free, Stock facilities, Limited winter access, Stay limit: 14 days, Open all year, Reservations not accepted, Elev: 5781ft/1762m, Tel: 208-942-3113, Nearest town: Lowell. GPS: 46.327986, -114.647344

41 • B2 | Flat Creek (Nez Perce-Clearwater NF)

Total sites: 11, RV sites: 11, No water, Vault/pit toilet, Tent & RV camping: Free, Reservations not accepted, Elev: 2708ft/825m, Nearest town: Pierce. GPS: 46.721051, -115.292398

42 • B2 | Fly Flat (Idaho Panhandle NF)

Total sites: 14, RV sites: 14, Central water, Vault/pit toilet, No showers, No RV dump, Tent & RV camping: $15, $12 when water turned off, Open May-Oct, Reservations not accepted, Elev: 3507ft/1069m, Nearest town: Avery. GPS: 47.112793, -115.390869

43 • B2 | Heller Creek (Idaho Panhandle NF)

Total sites: 4, RV sites: 4, No water, Vault/pit toilet, Tent & RV camping: Free, Road not maintained for passenger car travel, Open Jul-Oct, Reservations not accepted, Elev: 4774ft/1455m, Nearest town: Superior, MT. GPS: 47.064873, -115.218772

44 • B2 | Hidden Creek (Nez Perce-Clearwater NF)

Total sites: 13, RV sites: 13, Central water, Vault/pit toilet, No showers, No RV dump, Tent & RV camping: $10, Open May-Sep, Reservations not accepted, Elev: 3333ft/1016m, Tel: 208-476-4541, Nearest town: Pierce. GPS: 46.831719, -115.178566

45 • B2 | Hoodoo Lake (Nez Perce-Clearwater NF)

Total sites: 7, RV sites: 7, No water, No toilets, Tent & RV camping: Free, 4x4 recommended, Not suitable for large RVs, Reservations not accepted, Elev: 5800ft/1768m, Tel: 208-842-2245, Nearest town: Harlem. GPS: 46.321226, -114.651967

46 • B2 | Isabella Point (Nez Perce-Clearwater NF)

Total sites: 2, RV sites: 0, No water, Vault/pit toilet, Tents only: Free, Open Jun-Oct, Reservations not accepted, Elev: 2421ft/738m, Tel: 208-476-4541, Nearest town: Headquarters. GPS: 46.892041, -115.597432

47 • B2 | Kelly Forks (Nez Perce-Clearwater NF)

Total sites: 13, RV sites: 13, Central water, Vault/pit toilet, No

showers, No RV dump, Tent & RV camping: $10, Open May-Oct, Reservations not accepted, Elev: 2802ft/854m, Tel: 208-476-4541, Nearest town: Pierce. GPS: 46.717041, -115.255859

48 • B2 | Knife Edge (Nez Perce-Clearwater NF)

Total sites: 5, RV sites: 5, No water, Vault/pit toilet, Tent & RV camping: Free, Limited winter access, Open all year, Reservations not accepted, Elev: 1788ft/545m, Tel: 208-926-4274, Nearest town: Lowell. GPS: 46.227242, -115.474474

49 • B2 | Line Creek Stock Camp (Idaho Panhandle NF)

Total sites: 9, RV sites: 9, No water, Vault/pit toilet, Tent & RV camping: Free, Open May-Nov, Reservations not accepted, Elev: 3743ft/1141m, Nearest town: Avery. GPS: 47.043923, -115.349783

50 • B2 | Lolo Creek (Nez Perce-Clearwater NF)

Total sites: 8, RV sites: 6, No toilets, Tent & RV camping: Free, Open May-Oct, Reservations not accepted, Elev: 2878ft/877m, Tel: 208-926-4274, Nearest town: Kamiah. GPS: 46.293437, -115.752283

51 • B2 | Mammoth Springs (Idaho Panhandle NF)

Total sites: 8, RV sites: 8, Central water, Vault/pit toilet, No showers, No RV dump, Tent & RV camping: $15, $12 when water turned off, Open Jun-Oct, Reservations not accepted, Elev: 5633ft/1717m, Nearest town: Avery. GPS: 47.103929, -115.629608

52 • B2 | Noe Creek (Nez Perce-Clearwater NF)

Total sites: 6, RV sites: 6, Central water, Vault/pit toilet, No showers, No RV dump, Tent & RV camping: $10, Open May-Oct, Max Length: 22ft, Reservations not accepted, Elev: 2533ft/772m, Tel: 208-476-4541, Nearest town: Pierce. GPS: 46.684376, -115.366523

53 • B2 | Powell (Nez Perce-Clearwater NF)

Total sites: 34, RV sites: 34, Elec sites: 22, Central water, No toilets, No showers, No RV dump, Tents: $14/RVs: $14-20, Open May-Oct, Max Length: 200ft, Reservations accepted, Elev: 3478ft/1060m, Tel: 208-942-3113, Nearest town: Powell. GPS: 46.512207, -114.722656

54 • B2 | Rocky Ridge Lake (Nez Perce-Clearwater NF)

Total sites: 6, RV sites: 6, No water, No toilets, Tent & RV camping: Free, Open Jun-Sep, Reservations not accepted, Elev: 5671ft/1729m, Tel: 208-926-4274, Nearest town: Pierce. GPS: 46.441078, -115.491879

55 • B2 | Spruce Tree (Idaho Panhandle NF)

Total sites: 9, RV sites: 9, Central water, Vault/pit toilet, No showers, No RV dump, Tent & RV camping: $15, $12 when no water, Open May-Oct, Reservations not accepted, Elev: 3786ft/1154m, Nearest town: Avery. GPS: 47.037994, -115.347921

56 • B2 | Telichpah (Idaho Panhandle NF)

Total sites: 5, RV sites: 5, No water, Vault/pit toilet, Tent & RV camping: Free, Nothing bigger than truck campers, Open May-Sep, Reservations not accepted, Elev: 2762ft/842m, Nearest town: Avery. GPS: 47.295484, -115.774753

57 • B2 | Tin Can Flat (Idaho Panhandle NF)

Total sites: 11, RV sites: 11, Central water, Vault/pit toilet, No showers, No RV dump, Tent & RV camping: Fee unk, Open May-Oct, Reservations not accepted, Elev: 2910ft/887m, Nearest town: Avery. GPS: 47.229980, -115.621094

58 • B2 | Turner Flat (Idaho Panhandle NF)

Total sites: 10, RV sites: 10, Central water, Vault/pit toilet, No showers, No RV dump, Tent & RV camping: $12-15, Open May-Nov, Reservations not accepted, Elev: 2822ft/860m, Nearest town: Avery. GPS: 47.236816, -115.654297

59 • B2 | Washington Creek (Nez Perce-Clearwater NF)

Total sites: 23, RV sites: 23, Central water, Vault/pit toilet, No showers, No RV dump, Tent & RV camping: $10, Open May-Oct, Reservations not accepted, Elev: 2139ft/652m, Tel: 208-476-4541, Nearest town: Pierce. GPS: 46.703984, -115.555859

60 • B2 | Weitas Creek (Nez Perce-Clearwater NF)

Total sites: 6, Vault/pit toilet, Tents only: Free, Limited winter access, Open all year, Reservations not accepted, Elev: 2371ft/723m, Tel: 208-476-4541, Nearest town: Orofino. GPS: 46.637658, -115.433586

61 • B2 | Weitas Meadow Camp (Nez Perce-Clearwater NF)

Total sites: 6, RV sites: 6, No water, Vault/pit toilet, Tent & RV camping: Fee unk, No trailers, Reservations not accepted, Elev: 5432ft/1656m, Nearest town: New Meadows. GPS: 46.435007, -115.482798

62 • B2 | Wendover (Nez Perce-Clearwater NF)

Total sites: 26, RV sites: 26, Central water, Vault/pit toilet, No showers, No RV dump, Tent & RV camping: $14, Open May-Sep, Max Length: 40ft, Reservations not accepted, Elev: 3343ft/1019m, Tel: 208-942-3113, Nearest town: Lowell. GPS: 46.510010, -114.784668

63 • B2 | White Sand (Nez Perce-Clearwater NF)

Total sites: 7, RV sites: 7, Central water, Vault/pit toilet, No showers, No RV dump, Tent & RV camping: $14, Open May-Oct, Max Length: 30ft, Reservations not accepted, Elev: 3439ft/1048m, Tel: 208-942-3113, Nearest town: Powell. GPS: 46.507291, -114.686584

64 • B2 | Whitehouse (Nez Perce-Clearwater NF)

Total sites: 11, RV sites: 11, Central water, Vault/pit toilet, No showers, No RV dump, Tent & RV camping: $14, Open May-Sep, Max Length: 30ft, Reservations not accepted, Elev: 3327ft/1014m, Tel: 208-942-3113, Nearest town: Lowell. GPS: 46.506838, -114.774632

65 • B2 | Wilderness Gateway (Nez Perce-Clearwater NF)

Total sites: 85, RV sites: 85, Central water, Vault/pit toilet, No showers, RV dump, Tent & RV camping: $14, Group site: $280, Open May-Oct, Max Length: 99ft, Reservations accepted, Elev: 2116ft/645m, Tel: 208-926-4274, Nearest town: Lowell. GPS: 46.340129, -115.309191

66 • C1 | Amanita (Boise NF)

Total sites: 10, RV sites: 10, Central water, Vault/pit toilet, No

showers, No RV dump, Tent & RV camping: $15, Open May-Sep, Max Length: 40ft, Reservations accepted, Elev: 4836ft/1474m, Tel: 208-382-7400, Nearest town: Donnelly. GPS: 44.701811, -116.131199

67 • C1 | Black Lake (Payette NF)

Total sites: 4, RV sites: 0, No water, Vault/pit toilet, Tents only: Free, Open Jun-Sep, Reservations not accepted, Elev: 7228ft/2203m, Tel: 541-426-5546, Nearest town: Council. GPS: 45.189535, -116.561543

68 • C1 | Brownlee (Payette NF)

Total sites: 11, RV sites: 11, Central water, Vault/pit toilet, No showers, No RV dump, Tent & RV camping: $10, Max Length: 16ft, Reservations not accepted, Elev: 4282ft/1305m, Tel: 208-549-4200, Nearest town: Cambridge. GPS: 44.738605, -116.819723

69 • C1 | Cabin Creek (Payette NF)

Total sites: 12, RV sites: 12, Central water, Vault/pit toilet, No showers, No RV dump, Tent & RV camping: $10, Reservations not accepted, Elev: 4226ft/1288m, Tel: 208-253-0100, Nearest town: Council. GPS: 44.655152, -116.272523

70 • C1 | Cold Springs (New Meadows) (Payette NF)

Total sites: 30, RV sites: 30, Central water, Vault/pit toilet, No showers, RV dump, Tent & RV camping: $10-15, Open Jun-Sep, Max Length: 24ft, Reservations accepted, Elev: 4829ft/1472m, Tel: 208-347-0300, Nearest town: New Meadows. GPS: 44.949228, -116.440353

71 • C1 | Evergreen (Payette NF)

Total sites: 12, RV sites: 12, Central water, Vault/pit toilet, No showers, No RV dump, Tent & RV camping: $10, Reservations not accepted, Elev: 3947ft/1203m, Tel: 208-253-0100, Nearest town: New Meadows. GPS: 44.893184, -116.388566

72 • C1 | Fish Creek (Nez Perce-Clearwater NF)

Total sites: 10, RV sites: 10, Central water, Vault/pit toilet, No showers, No RV dump, Tent & RV camping: $12, Limited winter access, Open all year, Reservations not accepted, Elev: 5115ft/1559m, Tel: 208-839-2211, Nearest town: Grangeville. GPS: 45.857666, -116.082275

73 • C1 | Granite Lake (Payette NF)

Total sites: 7, RV sites: 7, No water, Vault/pit toilet, Tent & RV camping: Free, 4x4 recommended, Not suitable for large RVs, Open Jul-Sep, Reservations not accepted, Elev: 6762ft/2061m, Tel: 208-634-0400, Nearest town: McCall. GPS: 45.102472, -116.083695

74 • C1 | Grouse (Payette NF)

Total sites: 22, RV sites: 22, Central water, Vault/pit toilet, No showers, No RV dump, Tent & RV camping: $10-15, Open Jul-Sep, Max Length: 35ft, Reservations accepted, Elev: 6381ft/1945m, Tel: 208-347-0300, Nearest town: McCall. GPS: 45.068183, -116.167956

75 • C1 | Hazard Lake (Payette NF)

Total sites: 13, RV sites: 13, Central water, Vault/pit toilet, No showers, No RV dump, Tent & RV camping: $10, Open Jul-Sep, Reservations not accepted, Elev: 7067ft/2154m, Tel: 208-347-0300, Nearest town: McCall. GPS: 45.201492, -116.143287

76 • C1 | Huckleberry (Payette NF)

Total sites: 8, RV sites: 8, Central water, Vault/pit toilet, No showers, No RV dump, Tent & RV camping: $10, Reservations not accepted, Elev: 4911ft/1497m, Tel: 208-253-0100, Nearest town: Council. GPS: 45.084022, -116.614705

77 • C1 | Iron Phone Junction (Nez Perce-Clearwater NF)

Total sites: 4, RV sites: 4, No water, Vault/pit toilet, Tent & RV camping: Free, Limited winter access, Open all year, Reservations not accepted, Elev: 5340ft/1628m, Tel: 208-839-2211, Nearest town: Riggins. GPS: 45.533566, -116.420873

78 • C1 | Lafferty (Payette NF)

Total sites: 8, RV sites: 8, No water, Vault/pit toilet, Tent & RV camping: $10, Reservations not accepted, Elev: 4311ft/1314m, Tel: 208-253-0100, Nearest town: McCall. GPS: 44.939851, -116.655186

79 • C1 | Last Chance (Payette NF)

Total sites: 23, RV sites: 23, Central water, Vault/pit toilet, No showers, No RV dump, Tent & RV camping: $10, Open May-Sep, Reservations not accepted, Elev: 4767ft/1453m, Tel: 208-347-0300, Nearest town: McCall. GPS: 44.989258, -116.190674

80 • C1 | North Fork (Slate Creek) (Nez Perce-Clearwater NF)

Total sites: 5, RV sites: 5, No water, Vault/pit toilet, Tent & RV camping: Free, Limited winter access, Open all year, Max Length: 22ft, Reservations not accepted, Elev: 2986ft/910m, Tel: 208-839-2211, Nearest town: White Bird. GPS: 45.639956, -116.119606

81 • C1 | Pittsburgh Landing (Wallowa-Whitman NF)

Total sites: 28, RV sites: 28, Central water, Vault/pit toilet, No showers, No RV dump, Tent & RV camping: $8, Reservations not accepted, Elev: 1250ft/381m, Nearest town: White Bird. GPS: 45.635727, -116.478202

82 • C1 | Rainbow Point (Boise NF)

Total sites: 12, RV sites: 12, Central water, Vault/pit toilet, No showers, No RV dump, Tent & RV camping: $15, Open May-Sep, Max Length: 45ft, Reservations accepted, Elev: 4846ft/1477m, Tel: 208-382-7400, Nearest town: Donnelly. GPS: 44.703388, -116.131643

83 • C1 | Rocky Bluff (Nez Perce-Clearwater NF)

Total sites: 5, RV sites: 3, No water, No toilets, Tent & RV camping: Free, Limited winter access, Open all year, Max Length: 15ft, Reservations not accepted, Elev: 5253ft/1601m, Tel: 208-839-2211, Nearest town: White Bird. GPS: 45.632316, -116.010984

84 • C1 | Seven Devils (Wallowa-Whitman NF)

Total sites: 10, RV sites: 0, No water, Vault/pit toilet, Tents only: Free, Very steep and narrow road - low clearance vehicles/RVs/trailers are not recommended, Open Jun-Oct, Reservations not accepted, Elev: 7559ft/2304m, Tel: 541-426-5546, Nearest town: Riggins. GPS: 45.347062, -116.517467

85 • C1 | Sheep Rock (Payette NF)

Total sites: 2, No water, Vault/pit toilet, Tent & RV camping: Free, Reservations not accepted, Elev: 6598ft/2011m, Tel: 208-253-0100, Nearest town: Council. GPS: 45.191573, -116.669156

86 • C1 | Spring Bar (Nez Perce-Clearwater NF)

Total sites: 18, RV sites: 0, Central water, Vault/pit toilet, No showers, No RV dump, Tents only: $12, Limited winter access, Open all year, Max Length: 20ft, Reservations not accepted, Elev: 1942ft/592m, Tel: 208-839-2211, Nearest town: Riggins. GPS: 45.426514, -116.153076

87 • C1 | Upper Payette Lake (Payette NF)

Total sites: 24, RV sites: 24, Central water, Vault/pit toilet, No showers, No RV dump, Tent & RV camping: $10-15, Group site $20-$30, Open Jun-Sep, Max Length: 50ft, Reservations accepted, Elev: 5584ft/1702m, Tel: 208-634-0400, Nearest town: McCall. GPS: 45.125844, -116.027232

88 • C1 | Windy Saddle Horse Camp (Wallowa-Whitman NF)

Total sites: 4, RV sites: 4, No water, Vault/pit toilet, Tent & RV camping: Free, Very steep and narrow road - low clearance vehicles/RVs/trailers are not recommended, Open Jun-Sep, Reservations not accepted, Elev: 7687ft/2343m, Tel: 541-426-5546, Nearest town: Riggins. GPS: 45.350815, -116.509681

89 • C1 | Windy Saddle TH (Wallowa-Whitman NF)

Total sites: 4, RV sites: 0, No water, Vault/pit toilet, Tents only: Free, Very steep and narrow road - low clearance vehicles/RVs/trailers are not recommended, Open Jun-Oct, Reservations not accepted, Elev: 7559ft/2304m, Tel: 541-426-5546, Nearest town: Riggins. GPS: 45.349682, -116.512312

90 • C2 | 14 Mile TH (Nez Perce-Clearwater NF)

Total sites: 2, RV sites: 2, No water, Vault/pit toilet, Tent & RV camping: Free, Open May-Oct, Reservations not accepted, Elev: 6982ft/2128m, Nearest town: Elk City. GPS: 45.688711, -115.168916

91 • C2 | Big Creek Airstrip (Payette NF)

Total sites: 4, RV sites: 4, No water, Vault/pit toilet, Tent & RV camping: $10, Reservations not accepted, Elev: 5718ft/1743m, Tel: 208-634-0600, Nearest town: Yellow Pine. GPS: 45.127987, -115.322785

92 • C2 | Bighorn Crags (Salmon-Challis NF)

Total sites: 14, RV sites: 14, Central water, Vault/pit toilet, No showers, No RV dump, Tent & RV camping: $4, Open Jul-Oct, Reservations not accepted, Elev: 8474ft/2583m, Tel: 208-756-5200, Nearest town: Cobalt. GPS: 45.103516, -114.522831

93 • C2 | Boyd Creek (Nez Perce-Clearwater NF)

Total sites: 6, RV sites: 6, No water, Vault/pit toilet, Tent & RV camping: $8, Limited winter access, Open all year, Reservations not accepted, Elev: 1716ft/523m, Tel: 208-926-4258, Nearest town: Lowell. GPS: 46.080953, -115.442696

94 • C2 | Bridge Creek (Nez Perce-Clearwater NF)

Total sites: 5, RV sites: 5, No water, Vault/pit toilet, Tent & RV camping: Free, Limited winter access, Open all year, Max Length: 20ft, Reservations not accepted, Elev: 4847ft/1477m, Tel: 208-842-2245, Nearest town: Elk City. GPS: 45.783055, -115.206529

95 • C2 | Buck Mountain (Boise NF)

Total sites: 4, RV sites: 4, No water, Vault/pit toilet, Tent & RV camping: Free, Open May-Sep, Reservations not accepted, Elev: 6686ft/2038m, Tel: 208-382-7400, Nearest town: Landmark. GPS: 44.681788, -115.539819

96 • C2 | Buckhorn Bar (Payette NF)

Total sites: 13, RV sites: 5, Central water, Vault/pit toilet, No showers, No RV dump, Tent & RV camping: $10, Also walk-to sites, 4, Reservations not accepted, Elev: 3888ft/1185m, Tel: 208-634-0600, Nearest town: Cascade. GPS: 44.937161, -115.739133

97 • C2 | Burgdorf (Payette NF)

Total sites: 5, RV sites: 5, Central water, Vault/pit toilet, No showers, No RV dump, Tent & RV camping: $10, Reservations not accepted, Elev: 6083ft/1854m, Tel: 208-634-0400, Nearest town: McCall. GPS: 45.269086, -115.914251

98 • C2 | Camp Creek (Payette NF)

Total sites: 4, RV sites: 4, No water, Vault/pit toilet, Tent & RV camping: $10, Reservations not accepted, Elev: 4144ft/1263m, Tel: 208-634-0600, Nearest town: Yellow Pine. GPS: 44.890565, -115.707389

99 • C2 | Castle Creek (Nez Perce-Clearwater NF)

Total sites: 8, RV sites: 8, Central water, Vault/pit toilet, No showers, No RV dump, Tent & RV camping: $12, Winter access may be limited, Open all year, Reservations not accepted, Elev: 2336ft/712m, Tel: 208-839-2211, Nearest town: Grangeville. GPS: 45.828155, -115.968432

100 • C2 | CCC (Nez Perce-Clearwater NF)

Total sites: 3, RV sites: 1, No water, Vault/pit toilet, Tent & RV camping: Free, Limited winter access, Open all year, Reservations not accepted, Elev: 1576ft/480m, Tel: 208-926-4258, Nearest town: Kooskia. GPS: 46.090691, -115.520092

101 • C2 | Chinook (Payette NF)

Total sites: 11, RV sites: 11, Central water, Vault/pit toilet, No showers, No RV dump, Tent & RV camping: $10, Open May-Oct, Reservations not accepted, Elev: 5709ft/1740m, Tel: 208-634-0400, Nearest town: McCall. GPS: 45.212235, -115.809857

102 • C2 | Corduroy Meadows (Payette NF)

Total sites: 1, RV sites: 1, No water, No toilets, Tent & RV camping: Free, Reservations not accepted, Elev: 6406ft/1953m, Nearest town: Burgdorf. GPS: 45.343204, -115.946772

103 • C2 | Corn Creek (Salmon-Challis NF)

Total sites: 10, RV sites: 10, Central water, Vault/pit toilet, No showers, No RV dump, Tent & RV camping: $10, Open Mar-Oct, Reservations not accepted, Elev: 3094ft/943m, Tel: 208-865-2700, Nearest town: North Fork. GPS: 45.369929, -114.685717

104 • C2 | Cougar Point (Salmon-Challis NF)

Total sites: 18, RV sites: 18, No water, Vault/pit toilet, Tent & RV camping: Free, Open May-Oct, Reservations not accepted, Elev:

6581ft/2006m, Tel: 208-756-5200, Nearest town: Salmon. GPS: 45.082567, -114.054335

105 • C2 | Crooked River #3 (Nez Perce-Clearwater NF)

Total sites: 1, RV sites: 1, No water, Vault/pit toilet, Tent & RV camping: Free, Limited winter access, Open all year, Reservations not accepted, Elev: 3976ft/1212m, Tel: 208-842-2245, Nearest town: Elk City. GPS: 45.798037, -115.530274

106 • C2 | Crooked River #4 (Nez Perce-Clearwater NF)

Total sites: 1, Vault/pit toilet, Tents only: Free, Open all year, Elev: 3958ft/1206m, Tel: 208-842-2245, Nearest town: Elk City. GPS: 45.793615, -115.530946

107 • C2 | Deadman Bar (Payette NF)

Total sites: 3, RV sites: 0, No water, Vault/pit toilet, Tents only: Free, Walk-to sites, Close to road - can be noisy and dusty, Reservations not accepted, Elev: 4140ft/1262m, Tel: 208-634-0600, Nearest town: Yellow Pine. GPS: 44.963441, -115.662048

108 • C2 | Deep Creek (Bitterroot NF)

Total sites: 3, RV sites: 3, No water, Vault/pit toilet, Tent & RV camping: Free, Horses allowed, Stay limit: 16 days, Max Length: 30ft, Reservations not accepted, Elev: 4337ft/1322m, Tel: 406-821-3269, Nearest town: Darby (MT). GPS: 45.714061, -114.709281

109 • C2 | Deep Creek (Beaver Jack) (Salmon-Challis NF)

Total sites: 3, RV sites: 3, No water, Vault/pit toilet, Tent & RV camping: Fee unk, Open Jun-Oct, Reservations not accepted, Elev: 5039ft/1536m, Tel: 208-756-5200, Nearest town: North Fork. GPS: 45.126023, -114.215059

110 • C2 | Ebenezer (Salmon-Challis NF)

Total sites: 11, RV sites: 11, Central water, Vault/pit toilet, No showers, No RV dump, Tent & RV camping: $5, Open May-Oct, Reservations not accepted, Elev: 3110ft/948m, Tel: 208-865-2700, Nearest town: North Fork. GPS: 45.304896, -114.515601

111 • C2 | Four Mile (White Rock Peak) (Payette NF)

Total sites: 4, RV sites: 4, No water, Vault/pit toilet, Tent & RV camping: $10, Reservations not accepted, Elev: 4183ft/1275m, Tel: 208-634-0600, Nearest town: Cascade. GPS: 44.862835, -115.692063

112 • C2 | French Gulch (Nez Perce-Clearwater NF)

Total sites: 2, RV sites: 2, No water, Vault/pit toilet, Tent & RV camping: Free, Limited winter access, Open all year, Reservations not accepted, Elev: 4199ft/1280m, Tel: 208-842-2245, Nearest town: Elk City. GPS: 45.779331, -115.385365

113 • C2 | FSR 410 Dispersed (Boise NF)

Total sites: 5, RV sites: 3, No water, Vault/pit toilet, Tent & RV camping: Free, At end of road, Reservations not accepted, Elev: 7523ft/2293m, Nearest town: Yellow Pine. GPS: 44.814293, -115.558898

114 • C2 | Glover (Nez Perce-Clearwater NF)

Total sites: 7, RV sites: 7, No water, Vault/pit toilet, Tent & RV camping: $8, Winter access may be limited, Free Oct-Apr, Reservations not accepted, Elev: 1808ft/551m, Tel: 208-926-4258, Nearest town: Lowell. GPS: 46.068971, -115.363253

115 • C2 | Golden Gate (Boise NF)

Total sites: 9, RV sites: 9, No water, Vault/pit toilet, Tent & RV camping: Free, Non-potable water, Open May-Sep, Reservations not accepted, Elev: 4875ft/1486m, Tel: 208-382-7400, Nearest town: Yellow Pine. GPS: 44.935345, -115.485407

116 • C2 | Granite Springs (Nez Perce-Clearwater NF)

Total sites: 4, RV sites: 4, Central water, Vault/pit toilet, No showers, No RV dump, Tent & RV camping: Free, Spring water, Not recommended for low-clearance vehicles or motor homes, Horse facilities, Limited winter access, Open all year, Reservations not accepted, Elev: 6683ft/2037m, Tel: 208-842-2245, Nearest town: Dixie. GPS: 45.725046, -115.129192

117 • C2 | Horse Creek Hot Springs (Salmon-Challis NF)

Total sites: 9, RV sites: 7, No water, Vault/pit toilet, Tent & RV camping: Free, Open Jun-Oct, Reservations not accepted, Elev: 6072ft/1851m, Tel: 208-865-2700, Nearest town: Shoup. GPS: 45.504021, -114.459792

118 • C2 | Ice Hole (Boise NF)

Total sites: 10, RV sites: 10, Central water, Vault/pit toilet, No showers, No RV dump, Tent & RV camping: Free, Open May-Oct, Reservations not accepted, Elev: 5092ft/1552m, Tel: 208-382-7400, Nearest town: Cascade. GPS: 44.887939, -115.499512

119 • C2 | Indian Creek (Spot Mt) (Bitterroot NF)

Total sites: 2, RV sites: 2, No water, Vault/pit toilet, Tent & RV camping: Free, Max Length: 25ft, Reservations not accepted, Elev: 3406ft/1038m, Tel: 406-821-3269, Nearest town: Darby, MT. GPS: 45.789032, -114.763769

120 • C2 | Indian Point (Payette NF)

Total sites: 3, RV sites: 0, No water, No toilets, Tents only: Free, Walk-to sites, Next to road - can be noisy and dusty, Open May-Sep, Reservations not accepted, Elev: 3691ft/1125m, Tel: 208-634-0600, Nearest town: Yellow Pine. GPS: 45.013375, -115.716068

121 • C2 | Indian Springs (Salmon-Challis NF)

Total sites: 2, RV sites: 0, No water, Vault/pit toilet, Tents only: Free, High clearance vehicles are recommended, Open Jul-Oct, Reservations not accepted, Elev: 7703ft/2348m, Tel: 208-879-4101, Nearest town: Stanley. GPS: 44.675211, -114.837718

122 • C2 | Iron Lake (Salmon-Challis NF)

Total sites: 8, RV sites: 0, Central water, Vault/pit toilet, No showers, No RV dump, Tents only: $4, Narrow rough mountain road requiring slow and careful driving, Open Jul-Oct, Max Length: 16ft, Reservations not accepted, Elev: 8865ft/2702m, Tel: 208-756-5200, Nearest town: Salmon. GPS: 44.905786, -114.193567

123 • C2 | Jeanette (Payette NF)

Total sites: 6, RV sites: 6, No water, Vault/pit toilet, Tent & RV camping: $10, Reservations not accepted, Elev: 6247ft/1904m, Tel: 208-634-0400, Nearest town: McCall. GPS: 45.279643, -115.913952

124 • C2 | Johnson Bar (Nez Perce-Clearwater NF)

Total sites: 9, RV sites: 3, Central water, Vault/pit toilet, No showers, No RV dump, Tent & RV camping: $8, Reservable group site $40, Limited winter access, Open all year, Reservations not accepted, Elev: 1637ft/499m, Tel: 208-926-4258, Nearest town: Lowell. GPS: 46.102551, -115.558696

125 • C2 | Kennally Creek (Payette NF)

Total sites: 11, RV sites: 9, Central water, Vault/pit toilet, No showers, No RV dump, Tent & RV camping: $10, Reservations not accepted, Elev: 5709ft/1740m, Tel: 208-634-0400, Nearest town: Donnelly. GPS: 44.781957, -115.875404

126 • C2 | Lake Fork (Payette NF)

Total sites: 9, RV sites: 9, Central water, Vault/pit toilet, No showers, No RV dump, Tent & RV camping: $10, Reservations not accepted, Elev: 5394ft/1644m, Tel: 208-634-0400, Nearest town: McCall. GPS: 44.922953, -115.945956

127 • C2 | Leggett Creek (Nez Perce-Clearwater NF)

Total sites: 5, RV sites: 5, No water, Vault/pit toilet, Tent & RV camping: Free, Limited winter access, Open all year, Reservations not accepted, Elev: 3730ft/1137m, Tel: 208-842-2245, Nearest town: Grangeville. GPS: 45.827803, -115.628908

128 • C2 | Limber Luke (Nez Perce-Clearwater NF)

Total sites: 5, RV sites: 5, No water, Vault/pit toilet, Tent & RV camping: Free, Reservations not accepted, Elev: 5389ft/1643m, Tel: 208-842-2245, Nearest town: Elk City. GPS: 45.963589, -115.424007

129 • C2 | Little West Fork (Salmon-Challis NF)

Total sites: 1, RV sites: 1, No water, No toilets, Tent & RV camping: Free, Reservations not accepted, Elev: 7592ft/2314m, Tel: 208-879-4100, Nearest town: Challis. GPS: 44.684726, -114.342465

130 • C2 | Lost Spring (Salmon-Challis NF)

Total sites: 6, RV sites: 6, No water, Vault/pit toilet, Tent & RV camping: Free, Open Jul-Oct, Reservations not accepted, Elev: 5344ft/1629m, Tel: 208-756-5200, Nearest town: Cobalt. GPS: 44.842999, -114.466441

131 • C2 | MacKay Bar (Nez Perce-Clearwater NF)

Total sites: 3, RV sites: 0, No water, Vault/pit toilet, Tents only: Free, 4x4 recommended, Limited winter access, Open all year, Reservations not accepted, Elev: 2264ft/690m, Tel: 208-842-2245, Nearest town: Elk City. GPS: 45.392305, -115.494507

132 • C2 | Magruder Crossing (Bitterroot NF)

Total sites: 6, RV sites: 6, No water, Vault/pit toilet, Tent & RV camping: Free, Horses accommodated, Stay limit: 16 days, Max Length: 30ft, Reservations not accepted, Elev: 3832ft/1168m, Tel: 406-821-3269, Nearest town: Darby, MT. GPS: 45.736291, -114.759174

133 • C2 | Mahoney Springs (Salmon-Challis NF)

Total sites: 6, RV sites: 0, No water, Vault/pit toilet, Tents only: Free, Open Jul-Oct, Reservations not accepted, Elev: 8448ft/2575m, Nearest town: Challis. GPS: 44.660398, -114.542309

134 • C2 | Mallad Creek (Nez Perce-Clearwater NF)

Total sites: 5, RV sites: 5, No water, Vault/pit toilet, Tent & RV camping: Free, Limited winter access, Open all year, Reservations not accepted, Elev: 5108ft/1557m, Tel: 208-842-2245, Nearest town: Elk City. GPS: 45.579256, -115.308627

135 • C2 | McDonald Flat (Salmon-Challis NF)

Total sites: 6, RV sites: 6, Central water, Vault/pit toilet, No showers, No RV dump, Tent & RV camping: Fee unk, Open May-Oct, Max Length: 20ft, Elev: 5420ft/1652m, Tel: 208-756-5200, Nearest town: Salmon. GPS: 45.034704, -114.296561

136 • C2 | Meadow Creek (Hungry Ridge) (Nez Perce-Clearwater NF)

Total sites: 3, RV sites: 3, No water, Vault/pit toilet, Tent & RV camping: Free, Limited winter access, Not for larger RVs, Open all year, Reservations not accepted, Elev: 2464ft/751m, Tel: 208-839-2211, Nearest town: Harpster. GPS: 45.828974, -115.928205

137 • C2 | Middle Fork Peak (Salmon-Challis NF)

Total sites: 3, RV sites: 3, No water, Vault/pit toilet, Tent & RV camping: Free, Open Jul-Oct, Reservations not accepted, Elev: 7812ft/2381m, Tel: 208-756-5200, Nearest town: Cobalt. GPS: 44.961855, -114.643602

138 • C2 | O'hara Bar (Nez Perce-Clearwater NF)

Total sites: 32, RV sites: 32, Central water, Vault/pit toilet, No showers, No RV dump, Tent & RV camping: $14, Open May-Sep, Max Length: 45ft, Reservations accepted, Elev: 1552ft/473m, Tel: 208-926-4258, Nearest town: Lowell. GPS: 46.085523, -115.513397

139 • C2 | O'Hara Saddle (Nez Perce-Clearwater NF)

Total sites: 2, RV sites: 2, No water, No toilets, Tent & RV camping: Free, Limited winter access, Open all year, Reservations not accepted, Elev: 5184ft/1580m, Tel: 208-842-2245, Nearest town: Elk City. GPS: 45.952271, -115.517223

140 • C2 | Observation Point (Bitterroot NF)

Total sites: 4, RV sites: 4, No water, Vault/pit toilet, Tent & RV camping: Free, Reservations not accepted, Elev: 7598ft/2316m, Tel: 406-821-3269, Nearest town: Darby. GPS: 45.665376, -114.809505

141 • C2 | Orogrande #1 and #2 (Nez Perce-Clearwater NF)

Total sites: 3, RV sites: 3, No water, Vault/pit toilet, Tent & RV camping: Free, Limited winter access, Open all year, Reservations not accepted, Elev: 4603ft/1403m, Tel: 208-842-2245, Nearest town: Boise. GPS: 45.702093, -115.544483

142 • C2 | Orogrande #3 and #4 (Nez Perce-Clearwater NF)

Total sites: 6, RV sites: 6, No water, Vault/pit toilet, Tent & RV camping: Free, Limited winter access, Open all year, Reservations not accepted, Elev: 4646ft/1416m, Tel: 208-842-2245, Nearest town: Boise. GPS: 45.698336, -115.546177

143 • C2 | Oxbow (Nez Perce-Clearwater NF)

Total sites: 1, RV sites: 1, No water, Vault/pit toilet, Tent & RV camping: Free, Limited winter access, Open all year, Reservations not accepted, Elev: 3878ft/1182m, Tel: 208-842-2245, Nearest town: Elk City. GPS: 45.856541, -115.618058

144 • C2 | Paradise (Burnt Strip Mt) (Bitterroot NF)

Total sites: 11, RV sites: 11, Central water, Vault/pit toilet, No showers, No RV dump, Tent & RV camping: Fee unk, Max Length: 25ft, Reservations not accepted, Elev: 3120ft/951m, Tel: 406-821-3269, Nearest town: Darby,MT. GPS: 45.860959, -114.738000

145 • C2 | Pete Creek (Payette NF)

Total sites: 11, RV sites: 11, No water, Vault/pit toilet, Tent & RV camping: Free, Reservations not accepted, Elev: 6288ft/1917m, Nearest town: Burgdorf. GPS: 45.305872, -115.931774

146 • C2 | Picnic Point (Boise NF)

Total sites: 8, RV sites: 0, Central water, Vault/pit toilet, No showers, No RV dump, Tents only: $15, Walk-to sites, Open May-Sep, Reservations accepted, Elev: 5338ft/1627m, Tel: 208-382-7400, Nearest town: Cascade. GPS: 44.653291, -115.670653

147 • C2 | Pond Camp (Payette NF)

Total sites: 9, RV sites: 9, No water, Vault/pit toilet, Tent & RV camping: Free, Elev: 6423ft/1958m, Nearest town: Burgdorf. GPS: 45.339552, -115.945335

148 • C2 | Ponderosa (Payette NF)

Total sites: 10, RV sites: 10, Central water, Vault/pit toilet, No showers, No RV dump, Tent & RV camping: $10, Max Length: 20ft, Reservations not accepted, Elev: 4114ft/1254m, Tel: 208-634-0600, Nearest town: Cascade. GPS: 45.062012, -115.759521

149 • C2 | Poverty Flat (Payette NF)

Total sites: 10, RV sites: 6, Central water, Vault/pit toilet, No showers, No RV dump, Tent & RV camping: $10, Reservations not accepted, Elev: 4278ft/1304m, Tel: 208-634-0600, Nearest town: Cascade. GPS: 44.822897, -115.703721

150 • C2 | Race Creek (Nez Perce-Clearwater NF)

Total sites: 3, RV sites: 3, No water, Vault/pit toilet, Tent & RV camping: Free, Limited winter access, Open all year, Reservations not accepted, Elev: 1893ft/577m, Tel: 208-926-4258, Nearest town: Lowell. GPS: 46.044038, -115.284032

151 • C2 | Rackliff (Nez Perce-Clearwater NF)

Total sites: 6, RV sites: 6, No water, Vault/pit toilet, Tent & RV camping: $8, Limited winter access - free Oct-Apr, Open all year, Reservations not accepted, Elev: 1696ft/517m, Tel: 208-926-4258, Nearest town: Lowell. GPS: 46.085081, -115.494346

152 • C2 | Raven Creek (Bitterroot NF)

Total sites: 2, RV sites: 2, No water, Vault/pit toilet, Tent & RV camping: Free, Max Length: 25ft, Reservations not accepted, Elev: 3711ft/1131m, Tel: 406-821-3269, Nearest town: Red River Hot Springs. GPS: 45.761995, -114.783556

153 • C2 | Red River (Nez Perce-Clearwater NF)

Total sites: 40, RV sites: 31, No water, Vault/pit toilet, Tent & RV camping: $12, Limited access for large RVs, Limited winter access, Open all year, Reservations not accepted, Elev: 4665ft/1422m, Tel: 208-842-2245, Nearest town: Elk City. GPS: 45.750366, -115.269932

154 • C2 | Sam's Creek (Nez Perce-Clearwater NF)

Total sites: 3, RV sites: 3, No water, Vault/pit toilet, Tent & RV camping: Free, Limited winter access, Open all year, Max Length: 22ft, Reservations not accepted, Elev: 5423ft/1653m, Tel: 208-842-2245, Nearest town: Dixie. GPS: 45.536287, -115.495845

155 • C2 | Secesh Horse Camp (Payette NF)

Total sites: 5, RV sites: 5, No water, Vault/pit toilet, Tent & RV camping: $10, Water available across road, Stay limit: 18 days, Reservations not accepted, Elev: 4051ft/1235m, Nearest town: McCall. GPS: 45.063768, -115.760156

156 • C2 | Selway Falls (Nez Perce-Clearwater NF)

Total sites: 7, RV sites: 7, No water, Vault/pit toilet, Tent & RV camping: $6, Limited winter access, Free Oct-Apr), Reservations not accepted, Elev: 1770ft/539m, Tel: 208-926-4258, Nearest town: Lowell. GPS: 46.040224, -115.295183

157 • C2 | Shiefer (Payette NF)

Total sites: 5, RV sites: 5, No water, Vault/pit toilet, Tent & RV camping: Free, Reservations not accepted, Elev: 2979ft/908m, Tel: 208-634-0400, Nearest town: Warren. GPS: 45.173472, -115.579919

158 • C2 | Shoreline (Boise NF)

Total sites: 30, RV sites: 30, Central water, Vault/pit toilet, No showers, No RV dump, Tent & RV camping: $15, Group site $100, Open May-Sep, Max Length: 30ft, Reservations accepted, Elev: 5312ft/1619m, Tel: 208-382-7400, Nearest town: Cascade. GPS: 44.654768, -115.665227

159 • C2 | Sing Lee (Nez Perce-Clearwater NF)

Total sites: 4, RV sites: 4, Central water, Vault/pit toilet, No showers, No RV dump, Tent & RV camping: Free, Limited winter access, Open all year, Reservations not accepted, Elev: 3996ft/1218m, Tel: 208-842-2245, Nearest town: Elk City. GPS: 45.885108, -115.625228

160 • C2 | Slide Creek (Nez Perce-Clearwater NF)

Total sites: 3, RV sites: 3, No water, Vault/pit toilet, Tent & RV camping: Free, Limited winter access, Open all year, Reservations not accepted, Elev: 1906ft/581m, Tel: 208-926-4258, Nearest town: Lowell. GPS: 46.084831, -115.452568

161 • C2 | Slims Camp (Nez Perce-Clearwater NF)

Total sites: 2, RV sites: 2, No water, Vault/pit toilet, Tent & RV camping: Free, Open all year, Reservations not accepted, Elev: 1796ft/547m, Tel: 208-926-4258, Nearest town: Lowell. GPS: 46.030311, -115.289988

162 • C2 | Sourdough Saddle (Nez Perce-Clearwater NF)

Total sites: 4, RV sites: 4, No water, Vault/pit toilet, Tent & RV camping: Free, Corrals & hitching rails, Reservations not accepted, Elev: 6095ft/1858m, Tel: 208-842-2245, Nearest town: Grangeville. GPS: 45.722563, -115.805756

163 • C2 | South Fork (Hungry Ridge) (Nez Perce-Clearwater NF)

Total sites: 9, RV sites: 9, Central water, Vault/pit toilet, No showers, No RV dump, Tent & RV camping: $12, Limited winter access, Open all year, Max Length: 30ft, Reservations not accepted, Elev: 2284ft/696m, Tel: 208-983-1950, Nearest town: Grangeville. GPS: 45.826228, -115.961588

164 • C2 | South Fork Salmon River (Boise NF)

Total sites: 11, RV sites: 11, Central water, Vault/pit toilet, No showers, No RV dump, Tent & RV camping: $15, Open May-Sep, Reservations not accepted, Elev: 5128ft/1563m, Tel: 208-382-7400, Nearest town: Cascade. GPS: 44.653021, -115.702094

165 • C2 | Spring Creek (North Fork) (Salmon-Challis NF)

Total sites: 5, RV sites: 5, Central water, Vault/pit toilet, No showers, No RV dump, Tent & RV camping: $10, Open May-Oct, Reservations not accepted, Elev: 3409ft/1039m, Tel: 208-865-2700, Nearest town: North Fork. GPS: 45.390991, -114.254967

166 • C2 | Table Meadows (Nez Perce-Clearwater NF)

Total sites: 6, RV sites: 6, No water, Vault/pit toilet, Tent & RV camping: Free, Limited winter access, Open all year, Reservations not accepted, Elev: 4895ft/1492m, Tel: 208-842-2245, Nearest town: Elk City. GPS: 45.934253, -115.511608

167 • C2 | Ten Mile (Nez Perce-Clearwater NF)

Total sites: 2, RV sites: 2, No water, No toilets, Tent & RV camping: Free, Limited winter access, Open all year, Reservations not accepted, Elev: 4094ft/1248m, Tel: 208-842-2245, Nearest town: Elk City. GPS: 45.761216, -115.658993

168 • C2 | Trapper Creek (Nez Perce-Clearwater NF)

Total sites: 1, RV sites: 1, No water, Vault/pit toilet, Tent & RV camping: Free, Limted winter access, Open all year, Reservations not accepted, Elev: 4680ft/1426m, Tel: 208-842-2245, Nearest town: Elk City. GPS: 45.674178, -115.344016

169 • C2 | Trout Creek (Boise NF)

Total sites: 8, RV sites: 8, No water, Vault/pit toilet, Tent & RV camping: Free, Open May-Sep, Reservations not accepted, Elev: 6348ft/1935m, Tel: 208-382-7400, Nearest town: Landmark. GPS: 44.747081, -115.555146

170 • C2 | Twenty Mile Bar (Nez Perce-Clearwater NF)

Total sites: 2, RV sites: 2, No water, Vault/pit toilet, Tent & RV camping: Free, Limited winter access, Open all year, Reservations not accepted, Elev: 1886ft/575m, Tel: 208-926-4258, Nearest town: Elk City. GPS: 46.073011, -115.376516

171 • C2 | Twenty-five Mile Bar (Nez Perce-Clearwater NF)

Total sites: 3, RV sites: 3, No water, Vault/pit toilet, Tent & RV camping: Free, Open all year, Reservations not accepted, Elev: 1745ft/532m, Tel: 208-926-4258, Nearest town: Elk city. GPS: 46.076114, -115.412178

172 • C2 | Twin Creek (Gibbonsville) (Salmon-Challis NF)

Total sites: 40, RV sites: 40, Central water, Vault/pit toilet, No showers, No RV dump, Tent & RV camping: $10, Open Jun-Sep, Max Length: 22ft, Reservations not accepted, Elev: 5299ft/1615m, Tel: 208-865-2700, Nearest town: Gibbonsville. GPS: 45.608238, -113.969836

173 • C2 | Wallace Lake (Salmon-Challis NF)

Total sites: 12, RV sites: 0, Central water, Vault/pit toilet, No showers, No RV dump, Tents only: $4, RVs/trailers not recommended, Open Jul-Oct, Reservations not accepted, Elev: 8159ft/2487m, Tel: 208-756-5200, Nearest town: Salmon. GPS: 45.247037, -114.003965

174 • C2 | Warm Lake (Boise NF)

Total sites: 12, RV sites: 12, Central water, Vault/pit toilet, No showers, No RV dump, Tent & RV camping: $15, Open May-Sep, Max Length: 60ft, Reservations accepted, Elev: 5377ft/1639m, Tel: 208-382-7400, Nearest town: Cascade. GPS: 44.651674, -115.656918

175 • C2 | West Fork Morgan Creek (Salmon-Challis NF)

Total sites: 1, RV sites: 1, No water, Vault/pit toilet, Tent & RV camping: Free, Open Jul-Oct, Reservations not accepted, Elev: 6453ft/1967m, Tel: 208-879-4100, Nearest town: Challis. GPS: 44.702738, -114.315662

176 • C2 | Wild Goose (Nez Perce-Clearwater NF)

Total sites: 8, RV sites: 8, Central water, Vault/pit toilet, No showers, No RV dump, Tent & RV camping: $14, Open May-Sep, Max Length: 24ft, Reservations not accepted, Elev: 1604ft/489m, Tel: 208-926-4274, Nearest town: Lowell. GPS: 46.135726, -115.626239

177 • C2 | Wildhorse Lake (Nez Perce-Clearwater NF)

Total sites: 8, RV sites: 0, No water, Vault/pit toilet, Tents only: Free, Primitive road, Reservations not accepted, Elev: 7552ft/2302m, Tel: 208-842-2245, Nearest town: Elk City. GPS: 45.655736, -115.650964

178 • C2 | Williams Lake (Salmon-Challis NF)

Total sites: 2, RV sites: 0, No water, Vault/pit toilet, Tents only: Free, Walk-to/boat-in sites, Open May-Oct, Reservations not accepted, Elev: 5430ft/1655m, Tel: 208-756-5200, Nearest town: Salmon. GPS: 45.017168, -113.983985

179 • C2 | Windy Saddle (Nez Perce-Clearwater NF)

Total sites: 6, RV sites: 3, No water, Vault/pit toilet, Tent & RV camping: Free, Reservations not accepted, Elev: 6549ft/1996m, Nearest town: Elk City. GPS: 45.882187, -115.042773

180 • C2 | Yellow Pine (Boise NF)

Total sites: 14, RV sites: 14, Central water, Vault/pit toilet, No showers, No RV dump, Tent & RV camping: Free, Open May-Sep, Reservations not accepted, Elev: 4734ft/1443m, Tel: 208-382-7400, Nearest town: Cascade. GPS: 44.954590, -115.496582

181 • C3 | Bear Valley Horse Camp (Salmon-Challis NF)

Total sites: 6, RV sites: 6, No water, Vault/pit toilet, Tent & RV camping: Free, Open May-Sep, Elev: 6676ft/2035m, Tel: 208-768-2500, Nearest town: Leadore. GPS: 44.785566, -113.766192

182 • C3 | Bear Valley TH Upper CG (Salmon-Challis NF)

Total sites: 6, RV sites: 6, No water, Vault/pit toilet, Tent & RV

camping: Free, Open May-Oct, Reservations not accepted, Elev: 6845ft/2086m, Nearest town: Lemhi. GPS: 44.792799, -113.779858

183 • C3 | Hawley Creek (Lower) (Salmon-Challis NF)

Total sites: 4, RV sites: 4, No water, Vault/pit toilet, Tent & RV camping: Free, Open May-Sep, Reservations not accepted, Elev: 6722ft/2049m, Tel: 208-768-2500, Nearest town: Leadore. GPS: 44.667474, -113.190627

184 • C3 | Hawley Creek (Upper) (Salmon-Challis NF)

Total sites: 6, RV sites: 6, No water, Vault/pit toilet, Tent & RV camping: Free, Open May-Sep, Reservations not accepted, Elev: 6791ft/2070m, Tel: 208-768-2500, Nearest town: Leadore. GPS: 44.671810, -113.181507

185 • C3 | Reservoir Creek TH (Salmon-Challis NF)

Total sites: 2, RV sites: 2, No water, Vault/pit toilet, Tent & RV camping: Free, Open May-Sep, Elev: 6903ft/2104m, Tel: 208-768-2500, Nearest town: Leadore. GPS: 44.676682, -113.158234

186 • C3 | Sacajawea Memorial (Salmon-Challis NF)

Total sites: 6, RV sites: 2, No water, Vault/pit toilet, Tent & RV camping: Free, Open Jun-Oct, Max Length: 18ft, Reservations not accepted, Elev: 7279ft/2219m. GPS: 44.969891, -113.443482

187 • D1 | Antelope (Boise NF)

Total sites: 20, RV sites: 20, Central water, Vault/pit toilet, No showers, No RV dump, Tent & RV camping: $15, Group site: $65, Open May-Sep, Max Length: 40ft, Reservations accepted, Elev: 5082ft/1549m, Tel: 208-365-7000, Nearest town: Cascade. GPS: 44.335232, -116.186181

188 • D1 | Antelope Annex (Boise NF)

Total sites: 8, RV sites: 8, No water, Vault/pit toilet, Tent & RV camping: $15, Open May-Sep, Max Length: 20ft, Reservations not accepted, Elev: 5001ft/1524m, Tel: 208-365-7000, Nearest town: Emmett. GPS: 44.337534, -116.188409

189 • D1 | Big Eddy (Boise NF)

Total sites: 4, RV sites: 4, No water, Vault/pit toilet, Tent & RV camping: $15, Open May-Oct, Max Length: 30ft, Reservations not accepted, Elev: 4134ft/1260m, Tel: 208-365-7000, Nearest town: Banks. GPS: 44.220378, -116.106772

190 • D1 | Big Flat (Payette NF)

Total sites: 12, RV sites: 12, Central water, Vault/pit toilet, No showers, No RV dump, Tent & RV camping: $10, Windy narrow gravel road, Reservations not accepted, Elev: 4154ft/1266m, Tel: 208 253-0100, Nearest town: Cambridge. GPS: 44.500841, -116.259733

191 • D1 | Canyon (Boise NF)

Total sites: 6, RV sites: 6, Central water, Vault/pit toilet, No showers, No RV dump, Tent & RV camping: $12, Open May-Sep, Max Length: 13ft, Reservations not accepted, Elev: 3855ft/1175m, Tel: 208-365-7000, Nearest town: Banks. GPS: 44.187871, -116.115344

192 • D1 | Cartwright Ridge (Boise NF)

Total sites: 6, RV sites: 6, No water, Vault/pit toilet, Tent & RV camping: $15, Open May-Sep, Max Length: 10ft, Reservations not accepted, Elev: 5092ft/1552m, Tel: 208-365-7000, Nearest town: Emmett. GPS: 44.333952, -116.191647

193 • D1 | Eastside Group (Boise NF)

Total sites: 6, RV sites: 6, Central water, Vault/pit toilet, No showers, No RV dump, Tent & RV camping: $16, Reservable group site: $100, Individual sites available if not reserved for group use, Open Apr-Oct, Max Length: 30ft, Reservations not accepted, Elev: 5000ft/1524m, Tel: 208-365-7000, Nearest town: Ola. GPS: 44.332123, -116.175187

194 • D1 | French Creek (Boise NF)

Total sites: 21, RV sites: 21, Central water, Vault/pit toilet, No RV dump, Tent & RV camping: $15, Open May-Oct, Max Length: 45ft, Reservations accepted, Elev: 4879ft/1487m, Tel: 208-382-7400, Nearest town: Cascade. GPS: 44.527566, -116.107995

195 • D1 | Hollywood (Boise NF)

Total sites: 6, RV sites: 6, Central water, Vault/pit toilet, No showers, No RV dump, Tent & RV camping: $16, Open May-Sep, Max Length: 22ft, Reservations not accepted, Elev: 4993ft/1522m, Tel: 208-365-7000, Nearest town: Emmett. GPS: 44.326954, -116.179038

196 • D1 | Justrite (Payette NF)

Total sites: 4, RV sites: 4, No water, Vault/pit toilet, Tent & RV camping: Free, Reservations not accepted, Elev: 4341ft/1323m, Tel: 208-549-4200, Nearest town: Weiser. GPS: 44.540918, -116.953046

197 • D1 | Kiwanis (Payette NF)

Total sites: 1, RV sites: 1, No water, Vault/pit toilet, Tent & RV camping: Free, Can be dusty and noisy, Reservations not accepted, Elev: 3881ft/1183m, Tel: 208-549-4200, Nearest town: Weiser. GPS: 44.512715, -116.953094

198 • D1 | Mann Creek (Payette NF)

Total sites: 13, RV sites: 13, Central water, Vault/pit toilet, No showers, No RV dump, Tent & RV camping: $10, Open Apr-Sep, Max Length: 55ft, Reservations accepted, Elev: 2943ft/897m, Tel: 208-549-4200, Nearest town: Weiser. GPS: 44.412354, -116.906738

199 • D1 | Paradise (Payette NF)

Total sites: 2, RV sites: 0, Central water, Vault/pit toilet, No showers, No RV dump, Tents only: Free, Reservations not accepted, Elev: 4282ft/1305m, Tel: 208-549-4200, Nearest town: Weiser. GPS: 44.544188, -116.952183

200 • D1 | Sagehen Creek (Boise NF)

Total sites: 15, RV sites: 15, Central water, Vault/pit toilet, No showers, No RV dump, Tent & RV camping: $15, Open May-Sep, Max Length: 35ft, Reservations accepted, Elev: 5049ft/1539m, Tel: 208-365-7000, Nearest town: Cascade. GPS: 44.334859, -116.174724

201 • D1 | Shafer Butte (Boise NF)

Total sites: 7, RV sites: 0, No water, Vault/pit toilet, No showers, No RV dump, Tents only: $10, Walk-to sites, Open May-Sep, Reservations accepted, Elev: 6680ft/2036m, Tel: 208-587-7961, Nearest town: Boise. GPS: 43.782524, -116.085066

202 • D1 | Spring Creek (Weiser) (Payette NF)

Total sites: 14, RV sites: 14, Central water, Vault/pit toilet, No showers, No RV dump, Tent & RV camping: $10-15, Open May-Sep, Max Length: 32ft, Reservations accepted, Elev: 4928ft/1502m, Tel: 208-549-4200, Nearest town: Weiser. GPS: 44.569824, -116.946533

203 • D1 | Swinging Bridge (Boise NF)

Total sites: 11, RV sites: 11, Central water, Vault/pit toilet, No showers, No RV dump, Tent & RV camping: $14, Open May-Sep, Max Length: 35ft, Reservations accepted, Elev: 3681ft/1122m, Tel: 208-365-7000, Nearest town: Horseshoe Bend. GPS: 44.171598, -116.120888

204 • D2 | Abbott (Sawtooth NF)

Total sites: 7, RV sites: 7, No water, Vault/pit toilet, Tent & RV camping: $6, Open May-Oct, Reservations not accepted, Elev: 4701ft/1433m, Tel: 208-764-3202, Nearest town: Featherville. GPS: 43.607925, -115.217813

205 • D2 | Alturas Inlet (Sawtooth NF)

Total sites: 28, RV sites: 28, Central water, Vault/pit toilet, No showers, No RV dump, Tent & RV camping: $20, Stay limit: 10 days, Open Jun-Sep, Max Length: 40ft, Reservations accepted, Elev: 7050ft/2149m, Tel: 208-727-5000, Nearest town: Obsidian. GPS: 43.905057, -114.880569

206 • D2 | Bad Bear (Boise NF)

Total sites: 6, RV sites: 6, Central water, Vault/pit toilet, No showers, No RV dump, Tent & RV camping: $15, Open May-Sep, Max Length: 40ft, Reservations accepted, Elev: 5076ft/1547m, Tel: 208-392-6681, Nearest town: Idaho City. GPS: 43.901323, -115.708278

207 • D2 | Badger Creek (Boise NF)

Total sites: 5, RV sites: 5, No water, Vault/pit toilet, Tent & RV camping: Free, Narrow rough road, Open May-Sep, Reservations not accepted, Elev: 3346ft/1020m, Tel: 208-587-7961, Nearest town: Boise. GPS: 43.661985, -115.711797

208 • D2 | Bald Mountain (Boise NF)

Total sites: 4, RV sites: 4, No water, Vault/pit toilet, Tent & RV camping: Free, Open Jul-Sep, Reservations not accepted, Elev: 6794ft/2071m, Tel: 208-392-6681, Nearest town: Idaho City. GPS: 43.749168, -115.737703

209 • D2 | Banner Creek (Salmon-Challis NF)

Total sites: 5, RV sites: 5, No water, Vault/pit toilet, Tent & RV camping: $5, Open Jun-Oct, Max Length: 16ft, Reservations not accepted, Elev: 6690ft/2039m, Tel: 208-879-4101, Nearest town: Stanley. GPS: 44.353385, -115.214278

210 • D2 | Barney's (Boise NF)

Total sites: 8, RV sites: 8, Central water, Vault/pit toilet, No showers, No RV dump, Tent & RV camping: $12, Open Jun-Sep, Max Length: 50ft, Reservations accepted, Elev: 5354ft/1632m, Tel: 208-259-3361, Nearest town: Lowman. GPS: 44.326147, -115.649221

211 • D2 | Baumgartner (Sawtooth NF)

Total sites: 39, RV sites: 39, Central water, Vault/pit toilet, No showers, No RV dump, Tent & RV camping: $10, Group site $40-$100, Open May-Oct, Max Length: 76ft, Reservations accepted, Elev: 4931ft/1503m, Tel: 208-764-3202, Nearest town: Featherville. GPS: 43.605734, -115.076137

212 • D2 | Bear Creek Transfer Camp (Sawtooth NF)

Total sites: 6, RV sites: 6, No water, Vault/pit toilet, Tent & RV camping: Free, Open May-Oct, Reservations not accepted, Elev: 6083ft/1854m, Nearest town: Fairfield. GPS: 43.726289, -114.904914

213 • D2 | Bear Valley (Boise NF)

Total sites: 6, RV sites: 6, No water, Vault/pit toilet, Tent & RV camping: Free, Open Jun-Sep, Reservations not accepted, Elev: 6414ft/1955m, Tel: 208-259-3361, Nearest town: Stanley. GPS: 44.410971, -115.369787

214 • D2 | Beaver Creek (Cape Horn) (Salmon-Challis NF)

Total sites: 8, RV sites: 8, Central water, Vault/pit toilet, No showers, No RV dump, Tent & RV camping: $10, Open Jun-Sep, Max Length: 32ft, Reservations not accepted, Elev: 6568ft/2002m, Tel: 208-879-4101, Nearest town: Stanley. GPS: 44.414254, -115.146931

215 • D2 | Bench Creek (Salmon-Challis NF)

Total sites: 5, RV sites: 5, No water, Vault/pit toilet, Tent & RV camping: $5, Open Jun-Sep, Max Length: 16ft, Reservations not accepted, Elev: 6965ft/2123m, Tel: 208-879-4101, Nearest town: Stanley. GPS: 44.319549, -115.235385

216 • D2 | Big Bayhorse (Salmon-Challis NF)

Total sites: 10, RV sites: 10, No water, Vault/pit toilet, Tent & RV camping: Free, Narrow steep dirt road, Open Jul-Oct, Max Length: 32ft, Reservations not accepted, Elev: 8665ft/2641m, Tel: 208-879-4100, Nearest town: Stanley. GPS: 44.410177, -114.398127

217 • D2 | Big Roaring River Lake (Boise NF)

Total sites: 12, RV sites: 12, Central water, Vault/pit toilet, No showers, No RV dump, Tent & RV camping: $10, Reservations not accepted, Elev: 8107ft/2471m, Tel: 208-587-7961, Nearest town: Pine. GPS: 43.620629, -115.444039

218 • D2 | Big Trinity Lake (Boise NF)

Total sites: 17, RV sites: 17, Central water, Vault/pit toilet, No showers, No RV dump, Tent & RV camping: $10, Open Jul-Sep, Max Length: 22ft, Reservations not accepted, Elev: 7848ft/2392m, Tel: 208-587-7961, Nearest town: Mountain Home. GPS: 43.624188, -115.432192

219 • D2 | Bird Creek (Sawtooth NF)

Total sites: 5, RV sites: 5, No water, Vault/pit toilet, Tent & RV camping: $6, Free w/ no services in winter, Open May-Oct,

Reservations not accepted, Elev: 4754ft/1449m, Tel: 208-764-3202, Nearest town: Featherville. GPS: 43.620832, -115.175204

220 • D2 | Black Rock (Boise NF)

Total sites: 11, RV sites: 11, Central water, Vault/pit toilet, No showers, No RV dump, Tent & RV camping: $15, Open May-Sep, Max Length: 45ft, Reservations accepted, Elev: 4045ft/1233m, Tel: 208-392-6681, Nearest town: Idaho City. GPS: 43.795769, -115.588883

221 • D2 | Blind Creek (Salmon-Challis NF)

Total sites: 5, RV sites: 5, No water, Vault/pit toilet, Tent & RV camping: $5, Open May-Sep, Max Length: 32ft, Reservations not accepted, Elev: 6037ft/1840m, Tel: 208-879-4100, Nearest town: Stanley. GPS: 44.280646, -114.732802

222 • D2 | Boiling Springs (Boise NF)

Total sites: 9, RV sites: 9, Central water, Vault/pit toilet, No showers, No RV dump, Tent & RV camping: $15, Open May-Oct, Max Length: 30ft, Reservations not accepted, Elev: 4091ft/1247m, Tel: 208-365-7000, Nearest town: Smiths Ferry. GPS: 44.359874, -115.858043

223 • D2 | Bonneville (Boise NF)

Total sites: 22, RV sites: 18, Central water, Vault/pit toilet, No showers, No RV dump, Tent & RV camping: $15, Open May-Sep, Max Length: 100ft, Reservations accepted, Elev: 4767ft/1453m, Tel: 208-259-3361, Nearest town: Lowman. GPS: 44.150962, -115.310909

224 • D2 | Boundary (Sun Valley) (Sawtooth NF)

Total sites: 9, RV sites: 9, Central water, Vault/pit toilet, No showers, No RV dump, Tent & RV camping: $10, Stay limit: 7 days, Open May-Sep, Reservations not accepted, Elev: 6070ft/1850m, Tel: 208-622-5371, Nearest town: Sun Valley. GPS: 43.721863, -114.326665

225 • D2 | Boundary Creek (Salmon-Challis NF)

Total sites: 15, RV sites: 15, Central water, Vault/pit toilet, No showers, No RV dump, Tent & RV camping: $10, Narrow rough road, Open Jun-Aug, Reservations accepted, Elev: 5732ft/1747m, Tel: 208-879-4101, Nearest town: Stanley. GPS: 44.529396, -115.293015

226 • D2 | Bowns (Sawtooth NF)

Total sites: 12, RV sites: 12, No toilets, No showers, No RV dump, Tent & RV camping: $6, Free w/ no services in winter, Open Jun-Oct, Reservations not accepted, Elev: 5568ft/1697m, Tel: 208-764-3202, Nearest town: Fairfield. GPS: 43.607122, -114.880934

227 • D2 | Bull Trout Lake (Boise NF)

Total sites: 38, RV sites: 38, No water, Vault/pit toilet, Tent & RV camping: $15, Group site: $75, Open Jun-Sep, Max Length: 85ft, Reservations accepted, Elev: 6962ft/2122m, Tel: 208-259-3361, Nearest town: Stanley. GPS: 44.302801, -115.258827

228 • D2 | Buster Lake TH (Salmon-Challis NF)

Total sites: 1, No water, No toilets, Tents only: Free, 4x4 recommended, Reservations not accepted, Elev: 8536ft/2602m, Nearest town: Challis. GPS: 44.440274, -114.416956

229 • D2 | Canyon Transfer (Sawtooth NF)

Total sites: 6, RV sites: 6, Central water, Vault/pit toilet, No showers, No RV dump, Tent & RV camping: $6, Free w/ no services in winter, Open May-Oct, Reservations not accepted, Elev: 5599ft/1707m, Tel: 208-764-3202, Nearest town: Fairfield. GPS: 43.628264, -114.858755

230 • D2 | Caribou (Sawtooth NF)

Total sites: 7, RV sites: 0, Central water, Vault/pit toilet, No showers, No RV dump, Tents only: $16, Stay limit: 10 days, Reservations not accepted, Elev: 6478ft/1974m, Tel: 208-678-0439, Nearest town: Ketchum. GPS: 43.814678, -114.424957

231 • D2 | Casino Creek (Sawtooth NF)

Total sites: 19, RV sites: 17, Central water, Vault/pit toilet, No showers, No RV dump, Tent & RV camping: $16, Stay limit: 10 days, Open Mar-Nov, Reservations not accepted, Elev: 6171ft/1881m, Tel: 208-678-0439, Nearest town: Stanley. GPS: 44.256592, -114.855228

232 • D2 | Castle Creek (Boise NF)

Total sites: 2, RV sites: 2, No water, Vault/pit toilet, Tent & RV camping: Free, Open May-Sep, Max Length: 25ft, Reservations not accepted, Elev: 4268ft/1301m, Tel: 208-587-7961, Nearest town: Mountain Home. GPS: 43.410805, -115.395014

233 • D2 | Chaparral (Sawtooth NF)

Total sites: 9, RV sites: 9, No water, Vault/pit toilet, Tent & RV camping: $6, Free w/ no services in winter, Open all year, Reservations not accepted, Elev: 4633ft/1412m, Tel: 208-764-3202, Nearest town: Featherville. GPS: 43.613417, -115.201751

234 • D2 | Chemeketan (Sawtooth NRA)

Total sites: 13, RV sites: 13, Central water, Vault/pit toilet, No showers, No RV dump, Tent & RV camping: $12, Reservable group site ($75-$175) available as single sites when not reserved, Stay limit: 10 days, Open Jun-Sep, Max Length: 30ft, Reservations not accepted, Elev: 7559ft/2304m, Tel: 928-537-8888, Nearest town: Stanley. GPS: 43.847764, -114.753942

235 • D2 | Chinook Bay (Sawtooth NF)

Total sites: 13, RV sites: 0, Central water, Flush toilet, No showers, No RV dump, Tents only: $20, Stay limit: 10 days, Open May-Sep, Reservations not accepted, Elev: 6519ft/1987m, Tel: 208-727-5000, Nearest town: Stanley. GPS: 44.163991, -114.905512

236 • D2 | Cottonwood (Boise NF)

Total sites: 3, RV sites: 3, No water, Vault/pit toilet, Tent & RV camping: Free, Open May-Sep, Reservations not accepted, Elev: 3300ft/1006m, Tel: 208-587-7961, Nearest town: Boise. GPS: 43.632278, -115.825072

237 • D2 | Cozy Cove (Boise NF)

Total sites: 16, RV sites: 16, Central water, Vault/pit toilet, No showers, No RV dump, Tent & RV camping: $12, Open Jun-Oct, Max Length: 100ft, Reservations accepted, Elev: 5351ft/1631m, Tel: 208-259-3361, Nearest town: Garden Valley. GPS: 44.290644, -115.653193

238 • D2 | Curlew Creek (Boise NF)

Total sites: 9, RV sites: 9, Central water, Vault/pit toilet, No showers, No RV dump, Tent & RV camping: $5, Open May-Sep, Reservations not accepted, Elev: 4232ft/1290m, Tel: 208-587-7961, Nearest town: Mountain Home. GPS: 43.436209, -115.288575

239 • D2 | Custer #1 (Salmon-Challis NF)

Total sites: 6, RV sites: 6, No water, Vault/pit toilet, Tent & RV camping: $5, Open Jun-Sep, Max Length: 32ft, Reservations not accepted, Elev: 6726ft/2050m, Tel: 208-879-4100, Nearest town: Stanley. GPS: 44.399295, -114.663673

240 • D2 | Dagger Falls (Salmon-Challis NF)

Total sites: 8, RV sites: 8, Central water, Vault/pit toilet, No showers, No RV dump, Tent & RV camping: $10, Narrow rough road, Open Jun-Oct, Max Length: 16ft, Reservations not accepted, Elev: 5843ft/1781m, Tel: 208-879-4101, Nearest town: Stanley. GPS: 44.529063, -115.285744

241 • D2 | Deadwood (Boise NF)

Total sites: 6, RV sites: 6, Central water, Vault/pit toilet, No showers, No RV dump, Tent & RV camping: $15, Open May-Sep, Max Length: 15ft, Reservations not accepted, Elev: 3724ft/1135m, Tel: 208-259-3361, Nearest town: Boise. GPS: 44.080895, -115.658707

242 • D2 | Deer Creek (Sawtooth NF)

Total sites: 3, RV sites: 3, No water, Vault/pit toilet, Tent & RV camping: Free, Numerous other dispersed sites along creek, Stay limit: 16 days, Open May-Sep, Max Length: 16ft, Reservations not accepted, Elev: 6112ft/1863m, Tel: 208-622-5371, Nearest town: Hailey. GPS: 43.528683, -114.504669

243 • D2 | Deer Flat (Boise NF)

Total sites: 5, RV sites: 5, No water, Vault/pit toilet, Tent & RV camping: Free, Open Jun-Sep, Max Length: 22ft, Reservations not accepted, Elev: 6283ft/1915m, Tel: 208-259-3361, Nearest town: Boise. GPS: 44.408713, -115.553703

244 • D2 | Dog Creek (Boise NF)

Total sites: 13, RV sites: 13, Central water, Vault/pit toilet, No showers, No RV dump, Tent & RV camping: $10, 2 group sites: $20, Open May-Sep, Max Length: 40ft, Reservations accepted, Elev: 4446ft/1355m, Tel: 208-587-7961, Nearest town: Pine. GPS: 43.527344, -115.306641

245 • D2 | Easley (Sawtooth NF)

Total sites: 10, RV sites: 10, Vault/pit toilet, Tent & RV camping: $16, Open Jun-Sep, Max Length: 70ft, Reservations accepted, Elev: 6627ft/2020m, Tel: 208-678-0439, Nearest town: Ketchum. GPS: 43.781264, -114.538375

246 • D2 | East Fork Baker Creek (Sawtooth NF)

Total sites: 7, RV sites: 7, No water, Vault/pit toilet, Tent & RV camping: Free, Open Jun-Nov, Reservations not accepted, Elev: 6926ft/2111m, Tel: 208-622-5371, Nearest town: Ketchum. GPS: 43.744618, -114.565129

247 • D2 | Edna Creek (Boise NF)

Total sites: 9, RV sites: 9, Central water, Vault/pit toilet, No showers, No RV dump, Tent & RV camping: $15, Open May-Sep, Max Length: 40ft, Reservations accepted, Elev: 5249ft/1600m, Tel: 208-392-6681, Nearest town: Idaho City. GPS: 43.962552, -115.622362

248 • D2 | Eightmile (Salmon-Challis NF)

Total sites: 4, RV sites: 4, No water, Vault/pit toilet, Tent & RV camping: Free, Meadow across the road can accomodate larger camp trailers, Open May-Sep, Max Length: 16ft, Reservations not accepted, Elev: 6850ft/2088m, Tel: 208-879-4100, Nearest town: Stanley. GPS: 44.426304, -114.621188

249 • D2 | Elks Flat (Boise NF)

Total sites: 36, RV sites: 36, Central water, Vault/pit toilet, No showers, No RV dump, Tent & RV camping: $10, Reservable group site $100, Open May-Sep, Reservations not accepted, Elev: 4339ft/1323m, Tel: 208-587-7961, Nearest town: Mountain Home. GPS: 43.537894, -115.294592

250 • D2 | Evans Creek (Boise NF)

Total sites: 10, RV sites: 10, No water, Vault/pit toilet, Tent & RV camping: Free, Hairpin turns may be difficult for longer rigs, Stay limit: 14 days, Generator hours: 0600-2200, Open May-Sep, Reservations not accepted, Elev: 4222ft/1287m, Tel: 208-587-7961, Nearest town: Mountain Home. GPS: 43.400146, -115.414244

251 • D2 | Federal Gulch (Sawtooth NF)

Total sites: 3, RV sites: 3, No water, Vault/pit toilet, Tent & RV camping: Free, Stay limit: 16 days, Open Jun-Sep, Max Length: 18ft, Reservations not accepted, Elev: 6801ft/2073m, Tel: 208-622-5371, Nearest town: Hailey. GPS: 43.668589, -114.153456

252 • D2 | Five Points (Sawtooth NF)

Total sites: 5, RV sites: 5, No water, Vault/pit toilet, Tent & RV camping: Free, Reservations not accepted, Elev: 5892ft/1796m, Tel: 208-764-3202, Nearest town: Fairfield. GPS: 43.542478, -114.818662

253 • D2 | Flat Rock (Stanley) (Salmon-Challis NF)

Total sites: 6, RV sites: 6, Central water, Vault/pit toilet, No showers, No RV dump, Tent & RV camping: $10, Open May-Sep, Max Length: 32ft, Reservations not accepted, Elev: 6119ft/1865m, Tel: 208-879-4100, Nearest town: Stanley. GPS: 44.290607, -114.718274

254 • D2 | Flat Rock Extension (Salmon-Challis NF)

Total sites: 3, RV sites: 3, No water, Vault/pit toilet, Tent & RV camping: $5, Open May-Sep, Max Length: 16ft, Reservations not accepted, Elev: 6227ft/1898m, Tel: 208-879-4100, Nearest town: Stanley. GPS: 44.293341, -114.715837

255 • D2 | Glacier View (Sawtooth NF)

Total sites: 64, RV sites: 64, Central water, Flush toilet, No showers, RV dump, Tent & RV camping: $22, Stay limit: 10 days, Open May-Sep, Max Length: 67ft, Reservations accepted, Elev: 6571ft/2003m, Tel: 208-678-0439, Nearest town: Stanley. GPS: 44.146452, -114.915103

256 • D2 | Graham Bridge (Boise NF)

Total sites: 3, RV sites: 3, No water, Vault/pit toilet, Tent & RV

camping: Free, Reservations not accepted, Elev: 5695ft/1736m, Tel: 208-392-6681, Nearest town: Idaho City. GPS: 43.963886, -115.274778

257 • D2 | Grandjean (Sawtooth NF)

Total sites: 34, RV sites: 34, Central water, Vault/pit toilet, No showers, No RV dump, Tent & RV camping: $16, 10 equestrian sites, Max Length: 22ft, Reservations not accepted, Elev: 5203ft/1586m, Tel: 208-774-3000, Nearest town: Lowman. GPS: 44.148291, -115.151975

258 • D2 | Grayback (Boise NF)

Total sites: 20, RV sites: 20, Central water, Vault/pit toilet, No showers, No RV dump, Tent & RV camping: $15, Group site: $100, Open May-Sep, Max Length: 50ft, Reservations accepted, Elev: 3893ft/1187m, Tel: 208-392-6681, Nearest town: Idaho City. GPS: 43.807042, -115.866452

259 • D2 | Hardscrabble (Boise NF)

Total sites: 6, RV sites: 6, No water, Vault/pit toilet, Tent & RV camping: $12, Open May-Sep, Max Length: 30ft, Reservations not accepted, Elev: 3284ft/1001m, Tel: 208-365-7000, Nearest town: Garden Valley. GPS: 44.239013, -115.899204

260 • D2 | Helende (Boise NF)

Total sites: 15, RV sites: 15, Central water, Vault/pit toilet, No showers, No RV dump, Tent & RV camping: $12, Open May-Sep, Max Length: 65ft, Reservations accepted, Elev: 4185ft/1276m, Tel: 208-259-3361, Nearest town: Boise. GPS: 44.092938, -115.475806

261 • D2 | Holman Creek (Sawtooth NF)

Total sites: 10, RV sites: 0, Central water, Vault/pit toilet, No showers, No RV dump, Tents only: $10, Stay limit: 10 days, Reservations not accepted, Elev: 5636ft/1718m, Tel: 208-774-3000, Nearest town: Clayton. GPS: 44.249023, -114.529785

262 • D2 | Hot Springs (Boise NF)

Total sites: 8, RV sites: 8, Central water, Vault/pit toilet, No showers, No RV dump, Tent & RV camping: $16, Reservable group site $115-$230, Open May-Oct, Max Length: 35ft, Reservations not accepted, Elev: 3186ft/971m, Tel: 208-365-7000, Nearest town: Emmett. GPS: 44.055508, -115.908447

263 • D2 | Howers (Boise NF)

Total sites: 10, RV sites: 10, Central water, Vault/pit toilet, No showers, No RV dump, Tent & RV camping: $12, Open Jun-Sep, Max Length: 45ft, Reservations accepted, Elev: 5364ft/1635m, Tel: 208-259-3361, Nearest town: Garden Valley. GPS: 44.322303, -115.648745

264 • D2 | Hunter Creek Transfer Camp (Sawtooth NF)

Total sites: 4, RV sites: 4, No water, Vault/pit toilet, Tent & RV camping: Free, No services in winter, Open May-Oct, Reservations not accepted, Elev: 5455ft/1663m, Tel: 208-764-3202, Nearest town: Fairfield. GPS: 43.424222, -115.132442

265 • D2 | Ice Springs (Boise NF)

Total sites: 4, RV sites: 4, No water, Vault/pit toilet, Tent & RV camping: Free, Open May-Sep, Reservations not accepted, Elev: 4993ft/1522m, Tel: 208-587-7961, Nearest town: Mountain Home. GPS: 43.482909, -115.396997

266 • D2 | Iron Creek (Sawtooth NF)

Total sites: 9, RV sites: 0, Central water, Vault/pit toilet, No showers, No RV dump, Tents only: $16, Stay limit: 10 days, Reservations not accepted, Elev: 6719ft/2048m, Tel: 208-727-5000, Nearest town: Stanley. GPS: 44.198730, -115.009766

267 • D2 | Jerrys Creek (Salmon-Challis NF)

Total sites: 3, RV sites: 0, No water, Vault/pit toilet, Tents only: Free, Rough road - high clearance vehicle recommended, Reservations not accepted, Elev: 6230ft/1899m. GPS: 44.329313, -114.719986

268 • D2 | Josephus Lake (Salmon-Challis NF)

Total sites: 3, RV sites: 3, No water, Vault/pit toilet, Tent & RV camping: Free, Open Jul-Oct, Reservations not accepted, Elev: 7072ft/2156m, Tel: 208-879-4101, Nearest town: Stanley. GPS: 44.548894, -115.143553

269 • D2 | Kirkham (Boise NF)

Total sites: 15, RV sites: 15, Central water, Vault/pit toilet, No showers, No RV dump, Tent & RV camping: $15, Hot springs, Open Apr-Oct, Max Length: 80ft, Reservations accepted, Elev: 3973ft/1211m, Tel: 208-259-3361, Nearest town: Lowman. GPS: 44.072021, -115.542969

270 • D2 | Lake View (Sawtooth NF)

Total sites: 6, RV sites: 6, Central water, Vault/pit toilet, No showers, No RV dump, Tent & RV camping: $18, Stay limit: 10 days, Reservations not accepted, Elev: 6545ft/1995m, Tel: 208-727-5000, Nearest town: Stanley. GPS: 44.248209, -115.057813

271 • D2 | Little Bayhorse Lake (Salmon-Challis NF)

Total sites: 3, RV sites: 3, No water, Vault/pit toilet, Tent & RV camping: Free, Steep narrow road extremely hazardous when wet - RVs/trailers not recommended, Open Jul-Sep, Reservations not accepted, Elev: 8399ft/2560m, Tel: 208-879-4100, Nearest town: Stanley. GPS: 44.413088, -114.386868

272 • D2 | Little Roaring River Lake (Boise NF)

Total sites: 4, RV sites: 4, No water, Vault/pit toilet, Tent & RV camping: Free, Open Jul-Sep, Reservations not accepted, Elev: 7858ft/2395m, Tel: 208-587-7961, Nearest town: Mountain Home. GPS: 43.629575, -115.443523

273 • D2 | Little Wilson Creek (Boise NF)

Total sites: 2, RV sites: 2, No water, Vault/pit toilet, Tent & RV camping: Free, Open May-Oct, Reservations not accepted, Elev: 4255ft/1297m, Tel: 208-587-7961, Nearest town: Mountain Home. GPS: 43.377474, -115.434413

274 • D2 | Lola Creek (Salmon-Challis NF)

Total sites: 21, RV sites: 21, Central water, Vault/pit toilet, No showers, No RV dump, Tent & RV camping: $10, Open May-Oct, Max Length: 35ft, Reservations not accepted, Elev: 6482ft/1976m, Tel: 208-879-4101, Nearest town: Stanley. GPS: 44.407908, -115.178069

275 • D2 | Lower O'Brien (Sawtooth NF)

Total sites: 10, RV sites: 10, Central water, Vault/pit toilet, No showers, No RV dump, Tent & RV camping: $16, Stay limit: 10 days, Open Jun-Sep, Reservations not accepted, Elev: 5899ft/1798m, Tel: 208-774-3000, Nearest town: Clayton. GPS: 44.257404, -114.695143

276 • D2 | Marsh Creek (Sawtooth NF)

Total sites: 3, RV sites: 3, No water, Vault/pit toilet, Tent & RV camping: Free, Reservations not accepted, Elev: 6486ft/1977m, Nearest town: Stanley. GPS: 44.410575, -115.184298

277 • D2 | Mill Creek (Bayhorse) (Salmon-Challis NF)

Total sites: 8, RV sites: 8, Central water, Vault/pit toilet, No showers, No RV dump, Tent & RV camping: $10, Open Jun-Sep, Reservations not accepted, Elev: 7546ft/2300m, Tel: 208-879-4100, Nearest town: Challis. GPS: 44.472412, -114.441162

278 • D2 | Monte Cristo (Salmon-Challis NF)

Total sites: 1, RV sites: 0, No water, Vault/pit toilet, Tents only: Free, High clearance vehicles recommended, Open Jul-Oct, Reservations not accepted, Elev: 5991ft/1826m, Tel: 208-879-4101, Nearest town: Stanley. GPS: 44.542638, -114.830037

279 • D2 | Mormon Bend (Sawtooth NF)

Total sites: 15, RV sites: 15, Central water, Vault/pit toilet, No showers, No RV dump, Tent & RV camping: $16, Stay limit: 10 days, Reservations not accepted, Elev: 6142ft/1872m, Tel: 208-774-3000, Nearest town: Stanley. GPS: 44.261475, -114.842041

280 • D2 | Mosquito Flat (Salmon-Challis NF)

Total sites: 11, RV sites: 11, Central water, Vault/pit toilet, No showers, No RV dump, Tent & RV camping: Free, Open Jun-Oct, Max Length: 32ft, Reservations not accepted, Elev: 7024ft/2141m, Tel: 208-879-4100, Nearest town: Challis. GPS: 44.519616, -114.433212

281 • D2 | Mount Heyburn (Sawtooth NF)

Total sites: 20, RV sites: 20, Central water, Vault/pit toilet, No showers, RV dump, Tent & RV camping: $18, Dump station nearby, Stay limit: 10 days, Open May-Sep, Reservations not accepted, Elev: 6581ft/2006m, Tel: 208-727-5000, Nearest town: Stanley. GPS: 44.135010, -114.915527

282 • D2 | Mountain View (Lowman) (Boise NF)

Total sites: 14, RV sites: 14, Central water, Vault/pit toilet, No showers, No RV dump, Tent & RV camping: $15, Open Apr-Dec, Max Length: 70ft, Reservations accepted, Elev: 3921ft/1195m, Tel: 208-259-3361, Nearest town: Lowman. GPS: 44.078857, -115.604004

283 • D2 | Mountain View (Stanley) (Sawtooth NRA)

Total sites: 6, RV sites: 6, Central water, No toilets, No showers, No RV dump, Tent & RV camping: $18, Stay limit: 10 days, Reservations not accepted, Elev: 6526ft/1989m, Tel: 208-737-3200, Nearest town: Stanley. GPS: 44.161874, -114.904244

284 • D2 | Murdock (Sawtooth NF)

Total sites: 11, RV sites: 11, Central water, Vault/pit toilet, No showers, No RV dump, Tent & RV camping: $16, Stay limit: 10 days, Reservations not accepted, Elev: 6388ft/1947m, Tel: 208-727-5000, Nearest town: Ketchum. GPS: 43.803467, -114.420410

285 • D2 | Ninemeyer (Boise NF)

Total sites: 8, RV sites: 8, No water, Vault/pit toilet, Tent & RV camping: Free, Open Jun-Oct, Reservations not accepted, Elev: 3855ft/1175m, Tel: 208-392-6681, Nearest town: Atlanta. GPS: 43.755774, -115.567925

286 • D2 | North Fork (Ketchum) (Sawtooth NF)

Total sites: 29, RV sites: 29, Central water, Vault/pit toilet, No showers, No RV dump, Tent & RV camping: $18, Open May-Sep, Max Length: 45ft, Reservations accepted, Elev: 6250ft/1905m, Tel: 208-727-5000, Nearest town: Ketchum. GPS: 43.787598, -114.425537

287 • D2 | North Shore (Sawtooth NF)

Total sites: 14, RV sites: 14, Central water, Vault/pit toilet, No showers, No RV dump, Tent & RV camping: $18, Stay limit: 10 days, Open Jun-Sep, Reservations not accepted, Elev: 7064ft/2153m, Tel: 208-774-3000, Nearest town: Stanley. GPS: 43.918701, -114.866699

288 • D2 | Outlet (Sawtooth NF)

Total sites: 18, RV sites: 18, Central water, Vault/pit toilet, No showers, No RV dump, Tent & RV camping: $22, Stay limit: 10 days, Open May-Sep, Max Length: 50ft, Reservations accepted, Elev: 6585ft/2007m, Tel: 928-537-8888, Nearest town: Stanley. GPS: 44.141087, -114.911644

289 • D2 | Park Creek (Lowman) (Boise NF)

Total sites: 24, RV sites: 24, Central water, Vault/pit toilet, No showers, No RV dump, Tent & RV camping: $12, 2 group sites: $100, Individual sites available FC/FS when no group use, Open Jun-Sep, Max Length: 32ft, Reservations accepted, Elev: 4383ft/1336m, Tel: 208-259-3361, Nearest town: Lowman. GPS: 44.116943, -115.581299

290 • D2 | Park Creek (Sun Valley) (Salmon-Challis NF)

Total sites: 12, RV sites: 12, Central water, Vault/pit toilet, No showers, No RV dump, Tent & RV camping: $10, 1 group site, Open Jun-Sep, Reservations not accepted, Elev: 7674ft/2339m, Tel: 208-588-3400, Nearest town: Ketchum. GPS: 43.835938, -114.258789

291 • D2 | Penn Basin (Boise NF)

Total sites: 6, RV sites: 6, No water, Vault/pit toilet, Tent & RV camping: Free, Open May-Sep, Reservations not accepted, Elev: 6683ft/2037m, Tel: 208-382-7400, Nearest town: Landmark. GPS: 44.624417, -115.524476

292 • D2 | Pettit Lake (Sawtooth NF)

Total sites: 12, RV sites: 12, Central water, Vault/pit toilet, No showers, No RV dump, Tent & RV camping: $16, Stay limit: 14 days, Open Jun-Nov, Max Length: 22ft, Reservations not accepted, Elev: 7050ft/2149m, Tel: 208-678-0439, Nearest town: Stanley. GPS: 43.984648, -114.869254

293 • D2 | Phi Kappa (Salmon-Challis NF)

Total sites: 21, RV sites: 21, Central water, Vault/pit toilet, No

showers, No RV dump, Tent & RV camping: $10, Open May-Sep, Max Length: 32ft, Reservations not accepted, Elev: 7467ft/2276m, Tel: 208-588-3400, Nearest town: Ketchum. GPS: 43.858643, -114.218994

294 • D2 | Pine (Boise NF)

Total sites: 7, RV sites: 7, No water, Vault/pit toilet, Tent & RV camping: $10, Open May-Sep, Reservations not accepted, Elev: 4200ft/1280m, Tel: 208-587-7961, Nearest town: Mountain Home. GPS: 43.458002, -115.312239

295 • D2 | Pine Flats (Boise NF)

Total sites: 26, RV sites: 26, Central water, Vault/pit toilet, No showers, No RV dump, Tent & RV camping: $15, Open May-Sep, Max Length: 130ft, Reservations accepted, Elev: 3695ft/1126m, Tel: 208-259-3361, Nearest town: Lowman. GPS: 44.063286, -115.682234

296 • D2 | Pioneer (Sawtooth NF)

Total sites: 5, RV sites: 5, Central water, Vault/pit toilet, No showers, No RV dump, Tent & RV camping: Free, No services in winter, Open May-Sep, Reservations not accepted, Elev: 5846ft/1782m, Tel: 208-764-3202, Nearest town: Fairfield. GPS: 43.489571, -114.831383

297 • D2 | Point (Sawtooth NF)

Total sites: 17, RV sites: 9, Central water, Flush toilet, No showers, No RV dump, Tent & RV camping: $22, Nothing larger than vans/truck campers, Stay limit: 10 days, Open May-Sep, Max Length: 20ft, Reservations accepted, Elev: 6581ft/2006m, Tel: 208-678-0439, Nearest town: Stanley. GPS: 44.138971, -114.925496

298 • D2 | Pole Flat (Salmon-Challis NF)

Total sites: 10, RV sites: 10, Central water, Vault/pit toilet, No showers, No RV dump, Tent & RV camping: $10, 1 group site, Open May-Sep, Max Length: 32ft, Reservations not accepted, Elev: 6171ft/1881m, Tel: 208-879-4100, Nearest town: Stanley. GPS: 44.303467, -114.719727

299 • D2 | Power Plant (Boise NF)

Total sites: 24, RV sites: 24, Central water, Vault/pit toilet, No showers, No RV dump, Tent & RV camping: $15, Narrow rough road, Open May-Sep, Reservations not accepted, Elev: 5443ft/1659m, Tel: 208-392-6681, Nearest town: Lowman. GPS: 43.813988, -115.104677

300 • D2 | Queen's River (Boise NF)

Total sites: 4, RV sites: 4, No water, Vault/pit toilet, Tent & RV camping: Free, Narrow rough road, Open Jun-Sep, Reservations not accepted, Elev: 4987ft/1520m, Tel: 208-392-6681, Nearest town: Atlanta. GPS: 43.820994, -115.210097

301 • D2 | Queens River Transfer Camp (Boise NF)

Total sites: 6, RV sites: 6, No water, Vault/pit toilet, Tent & RV camping: Free, Reservations not accepted, Elev: 5250ft/1600m, Tel: 208-392-6681, Nearest town: Atlanta. GPS: 43.843162, -115.183984

302 • D2 | Rattlesnake (Sixmile Point) (Boise NF)

Total sites: 11, RV sites: 11, Central water, Vault/pit toilet, Tent & RV camping: $15, Reservable group site $125, Open May-Oct, Reservations not accepted, Elev: 3674ft/1120m, Tel: 435-245-6521, Nearest town: Crouch. GPS: 44.266865, -115.880157

303 • D2 | Redfish Outlet (Sawtooth NF)

Total sites: 5, RV sites: 5, No water, Vault/pit toilet, Tent & RV camping: Fee unk, Max Length: 22ft, Reservations not accepted, Elev: 6611ft/2015m, Nearest town: Stanley. GPS: 44.145256, -114.911093

304 • D2 | River Side (Deadwood Reservoir) (Boise NF)

Total sites: 8, RV sites: 8, Central water, Vault/pit toilet, No showers, No RV dump, Tent & RV camping: $12, Open Jun-Sep, Max Length: 100ft, Reservations accepted, Elev: 5377ft/1639m, Tel: 208-259-3361, Nearest town: Lowman. GPS: 44.341236, -115.657573

305 • D2 | Riverside (Idaho City) (Boise NF)

Total sites: 11, RV sites: 11, Central water, Vault/pit toilet, No showers, No RV dump, Tent & RV camping: $15, Narrow rough road, Open May-Sep, Reservations not accepted, Elev: 5325ft/1623m, Tel: 208-392-6681, Nearest town: Lowman. GPS: 43.808789, -115.130637

306 • D2 | Riverside (Stanley) (Sawtooth NF)

Total sites: 17, RV sites: 17, Central water, Vault/pit toilet, No showers, No RV dump, Tent & RV camping: $14, Stay limit: 10 days, Reservations not accepted, Elev: 6126ft/1867m, Tel: 208-774-3000, Nearest town: Stanley. GPS: 44.265922, -114.850719

307 • D2 | Robert E Lee (Boise NF)

Total sites: 8, RV sites: 4, No water, No toilets, Tent & RV camping: Free, No large RVs, Reservations not accepted, Elev: 4705ft/1434m, Nearest town: Boise. GPS: 43.905798, -115.434609

308 • D2 | Rooks Creek (Sawtooth NF)

Total sites: 5, RV sites: 5, No water, Vault/pit toilet, Tent & RV camping: Free, Reservations not accepted, Elev: 6460ft/1969m, Nearest town: Ketchum. GPS: 43.649749, -114.522937

309 • D2 | Salmon River (Sawtooth NF)

Total sites: 30, RV sites: 30, Central water, Vault/pit toilet, No showers, No RV dump, Tent & RV camping: $16, Stay limit: 10 days, Open all year, Reservations not accepted, Elev: 6148ft/1874m, Tel: 208-727-5000, Nearest town: Stanley. GPS: 44.248535, -114.870117

310 • D2 | Sawmill (Sawtooth NF)

Total sites: 3, RV sites: 3, No water, Vault/pit toilet, Tent & RV camping: Free, Stay limit: 16 days, Open May-Sep, Max Length: 16ft, Reservations not accepted, Elev: 6762ft/2061m, Tel: 208-622-5371, Nearest town: Sun Valley. GPS: 43.666556, -114.163628

311 • D2 | Sheep Trail (Sawtooth NRA)

Total sites: 3, RV sites: 3, Central water, Vault/pit toilet, No showers, No RV dump, Tent & RV camping: $14, Group site: $47, Single sites available if not in use as group site, Open May-Sep, Reservations not accepted, Elev: 6588ft/2008m, Tel: 208-678-0439, Nearest town: Stanley. GPS: 44.305658, -115.056445

312 • D2 | Silver Creek (Boise NF)

Total sites: 55, RV sites: 51, Central water, Vault/pit toilet, No showers, No RV dump, Tent & RV camping: $15, Group site $150, Open May-Oct, Max Length: 50ft, Reservations accepted, Elev: 4941ft/1506m, Tel: 208-739-3400, Nearest town: Garden Valley. GPS: 44.332218, -115.803352

313 • D2 | Skeleton (Sawtooth NF)

Total sites: 5, RV sites: 5, No water, Vault/pit toilet, Tent & RV camping: Free, Reservations not accepted, Elev: 5095ft/1553m, Nearest town: Fairfield. GPS: 43.590082, -115.018428

314 • D2 | Smokey Bear (Sawtooth NF)

Total sites: 12, RV sites: 12, Central water, Vault/pit toilet, No showers, No RV dump, Tent & RV camping: $16, Stay limit: 10 days, Reservations not accepted, Elev: 7044ft/2147m, Tel: 208-774-3000, Nearest town: Stanley. GPS: 43.920166, -114.862061

315 • D2 | Sockeye (Sawtooth NF)

Total sites: 23, RV sites: 23, Central water, Vault/pit toilet, No showers, RV dump, Tent & RV camping: $20, Dump station nearby, Stay limit: 10 days, Open May-Sep, Reservations not accepted, Elev: 6601ft/2012m, Tel: 208-678-0439, Nearest town: Stanley. GPS: 44.132519, -114.917355

316 • D2 | Spillway (Boise NF)

Total sites: 3, RV sites: 3, No water, Vault/pit toilet, Tent & RV camping: Free, Open May-Sep, Reservations not accepted, Elev: 4203ft/1281m, Tel: 208-587-7961, Nearest town: Mountain Home. GPS: 43.357214, -115.447505

317 • D2 | Stanley Lake (Sawtooth NF)

Total sites: 34, RV sites: 34, Central water, Vault/pit toilet, No showers, No RV dump, Tent & RV camping: $20, Open May-Sep, Max Length: 52ft, Reservations accepted, Elev: 6555ft/1998m, Tel: 208-678-0439, Nearest town: Stanley. GPS: 44.248747, -115.054425

318 • D2 | Stanley Lake Inlet (Sawtooth NF)

Total sites: 14, RV sites: 0, Central water, Vault/pit toilet, No showers, No RV dump, Tents only: $18, Stay limit: 10 days, Elev: 6530ft/1990m, Tel: 208-727-5000, Nearest town: Stanley. GPS: 44.246405, -115.064801

319 • D2 | Summit Lake (Boise NF)

Total sites: 3, RV sites: 3, No water, Vault/pit toilet, Tent & RV camping: Free, Open May-Sep, Reservations not accepted, Elev: 7313ft/2229m, Tel: 208-382-7400, Nearest town: Cascade. GPS: 44.644943, -115.585514

320 • D2 | Sunny Gulch (Sawtooth NF)

Total sites: 45, RV sites: 45, Central water, Vault/pit toilet, No showers, No RV dump, Tent & RV camping: $20, Stay limit: 10 days, Open May-Sep, Max Length: 35ft, Reservations accepted, Elev: 6453ft/1967m, Tel: 208-678-0439, Nearest town: Stanley. GPS: 44.175045, -114.909738

321 • D2 | Tailwaters (Boise NF)

Total sites: 3, RV sites: 3, No water, Vault/pit toilet, Tent & RV camping: Free, Reservations not accepted, Elev: 3983ft/1214m, Tel: 208-587-7961, Nearest town: Mountain Home. GPS: 43.355917, -115.455304

322 • D2 | Ten Mile (Boise NF)

Total sites: 16, RV sites: 16, Central water, Vault/pit toilet, No showers, No RV dump, Tent & RV camping: $15, Open May-Sep, Reservations not accepted, Elev: 4875ft/1486m, Tel: 208-392-6681, Nearest town: Idaho City. GPS: 43.898566, -115.712541

323 • D2 | Thatcher (Salmon-Challis NF)

Total sites: 5, RV sites: 5, Central water, Vault/pit toilet, No showers, No RV dump, Tent & RV camping: $10, Open May-Oct, Max Length: 32ft, Reservations not accepted, Elev: 6601ft/2012m, Tel: 208-879-4101, Nearest town: Stanley. GPS: 44.367658, -115.145382

324 • D2 | Tie Creek (Boise NF)

Total sites: 8, RV sites: 8, Central water, Vault/pit toilet, No showers, No RV dump, Tent & RV camping: $15, Open May-Oct, Reservations not accepted, Elev: 3120ft/951m, Tel: 208-365-7000, Nearest town: Crouch. GPS: 44.208281, -115.925726

325 • D2 | Tin Cup (Salmon-Challis NF)

Total sites: 13, RV sites: 13, No water, Vault/pit toilet, Tent & RV camping: Free, High clearance vehicles recommended, Open Jul-Oct, Reservations not accepted, Elev: 5466ft/1666m, Tel: 208-879-4101, Nearest town: Challis. GPS: 44.597168, -114.813477

326 • D2 | Trail Creek (Garden Valley) (Boise NF)

Total sites: 11, RV sites: 11, Central water, Vault/pit toilet, No showers, No RV dump, Tent & RV camping: $12, Open May-Sep, Max Length: 35ft, Reservations not accepted, Elev: 3766ft/1148m, Tel: 208-365-7000, Nearest town: Garden Valley. GPS: 44.276552, -115.875152

327 • D2 | Troutdale (Boise NF)

Total sites: 5, RV sites: 5, No water, Vault/pit toilet, Tent & RV camping: Free, Open Apr-Oct, Reservations not accepted, Elev: 3566ft/1087m, Tel: 208-587-7961, Nearest town: Boise. GPS: 43.716272, -115.625111

328 • D2 | Whiskey Flat (Sawtooth NF)

Total sites: 6, RV sites: 4, Central water, Vault/pit toilet, No showers, No RV dump, Tent & RV camping: $10, Stay limit: 10 days, Reservations not accepted, Elev: 5659ft/1725m, Tel: 208-774-3000, Nearest town: Clayton. GPS: 44.254864, -114.552384

329 • D2 | Whoop-Um-Up Horse Camp (Boise NF)

Total sites: 6, RV sites: 6, No water, Vault/pit toilet, Tent & RV camping: $15, Open May-Sep, Reservations not accepted, Elev: 5348ft/1630m, Tel: 208-392-6681, Nearest town: Idaho City. GPS: 43.966444, -115.627658

330 • D2 | Wildhorse (Salmon-Challis NF)

Total sites: 13, RV sites: 13, Central water, Vault/pit toilet, No showers, No RV dump, Tent & RV camping: $10, Limited winter access, Open Jun-Sep, Reservations not accepted, Elev: 7356ft/2242m, Tel: 208-588-3400, Nearest town: Mackay. GPS: 43.822510, -114.095947

331 • D2 | Willow Creek (Sawtooth NF)

Total sites: 3, RV sites: 3, No water, Vault/pit toilet, Tent & RV camping: $6, Open May-Oct, Reservations not accepted, Elev: 4813ft/1467m, Tel: 208-764-3202, Nearest town: Featherville. GPS: 43.606105, -115.142189

332 • D2 | Willow Creek (Arrowrock) (Boise NF)

Total sites: 9, RV sites: 9, Central water, Vault/pit toilet, No showers, No RV dump, Tent & RV camping: Free, Open Apr-Oct, Reservations not accepted, Elev: 3307ft/1008m, Tel: 208-587-7961, Nearest town: Boise. GPS: 43.644043, -115.752686

333 • D2 | Willow Creek (Idaho City) (Boise NF)

Total sites: 4, RV sites: 4, No water, Vault/pit toilet, Tent & RV camping: Free, Reservations not accepted, Elev: 5426ft/1654m, Tel: 208-392-6681, Nearest town: Idaho City. GPS: 43.959142, -115.532166

334 • D2 | Willow Creek Transfer Camp (Sawtooth NF)

Total sites: 3, RV sites: 3, No water, Vault/pit toilet, Tent & RV camping: Donation, Corrals, Open May-Oct, Reservations not accepted, Elev: 5118ft/1560m, Tel: 208-764-3202, Nearest town: Featherville. GPS: 43.626408, -115.134416

335 • D2 | Wood River (Sawtooth NF)

Total sites: 30, RV sites: 30, Central water, Flush toilet, No showers, No RV dump, Tent & RV camping: $16, Reservable group site: $42-$116, Open May-Sep, Max Length: 22ft, Reservations not accepted, Elev: 6368ft/1941m, Tel: 208-678-0439, Nearest town: Ketchum. GPS: 43.792969, -114.459473

336 • D3 | Big Creek (Big Creek Peak) (Salmon-Challis NF)

Total sites: 3, RV sites: 3, No water, Vault/pit toilet, Tent & RV camping: Free, Open May-Sep, Max Length: 16ft, Reservations not accepted, Elev: 6657ft/2029m, Tel: 208-879-4100, Nearest town: Challis. GPS: 44.441716, -113.598972

337 • D3 | Big Eightmile (Salmon-Challis NF)

Total sites: 10, RV sites: 10, Central water, Vault/pit toilet, No showers, No RV dump, Tent & RV camping: Free, Open May-Sep, Reservations not accepted, Elev: 7546ft/2300m, Tel: 208-768-2500, Nearest town: Leadore. GPS: 44.608583, -113.577099

338 • D3 | Broad Canyon (Salmon-Challis NF)

Total sites: 8, RV sites: 8, No water, Vault/pit toilet, Tent & RV camping: Free, Open Jul-Sep, Max Length: 35ft, Reservations not accepted, Elev: 7825ft/2385m, Nearest town: Mackay. GPS: 43.768363, -113.943128

339 • D3 | Copper Creek (Sawtooth NF)

Total sites: 8, RV sites: 8, No water, Vault/pit toilet, Tent & RV camping: Free, Open May-Oct, Reservations not accepted, Elev: 6604ft/2013m, Tel: 208-622-5371, Nearest town: Bellevue. GPS: 43.607146, -113.929486

340 • D3 | Iron Bog (Salmon-Challis NF)

Total sites: 21, RV sites: 21, Central water, Vault/pit toilet, No showers, No RV dump, Tent & RV camping: $10, Max Length: 35ft, Reservations not accepted, Elev: 7162ft/2183m, Tel: 208-588-3400, Nearest town: Mackay. GPS: 43.649892, -113.765254

341 • D3 | Lake Creek (Salmon-Challis NF)

Total sites: 4, RV sites: 4, Central water, Vault/pit toilet, No showers, No RV dump, Tent & RV camping: $5, Open May-Sep, Max Length: 35ft, Reservations not accepted, Elev: 8080ft/2463m. GPS: 43.765196, -113.897029

342 • D3 | Meadow Lake (Salmon-Challis NF)

Total sites: 17, RV sites: 17, No water, Vault/pit toilet, No showers, No RV dump, Tent & RV camping: $10, Open Jul-Sep, Max Length: 28ft, Reservations accepted, Elev: 9163ft/2793m, Tel: 208-768-2500, Nearest town: Leadore. GPS: 44.432715, -113.317259

343 • D3 | Morse Creek (Salmon-Challis NF)

Total sites: 3, RV sites: 3, No water, Vault/pit toilet, Tent & RV camping: Free, Open May-Sep, Max Length: 16ft, Reservations not accepted, Elev: 6332ft/1930m, Tel: 208-879-4100, Nearest town: Ellis. GPS: 44.630867, -113.790528

344 • D3 | Mt Borah TH (Salmon-Challis NF)

Total sites: 5, RV sites: 0, No water, Vault/pit toilet, Tents only: $5, Open May-Oct, Reservations not accepted, Elev: 7399ft/2255m, Nearest town: MacKay. GPS: 44.132528, -113.835457

345 • D3 | Pass Creek Narrows (Salmon-Challis NF)

Total sites: 7, RV sites: 7, No water, Vault/pit toilet, Tent & RV camping: Free, Open May-Sep, Reservations not accepted, Elev: 6376ft/1943m, Nearest town: Mackay. GPS: 43.950649, -113.444765

346 • D3 | Star Hope (Salmon-Challis NF)

Total sites: 21, RV sites: 21, Central water, Vault/pit toilet, No showers, No RV dump, Tent & RV camping: $10, Open May-Sep, Reservations not accepted, Elev: 7913ft/2412m, Tel: 208-588-3400, Nearest town: Mackay. GPS: 43.743645, -113.942588

347 • D3 | Stoddard Creek (Caribou-Targhee NF)

Total sites: 20, RV sites: 20, Central water, Vault/pit toilet, No showers, No RV dump, Tent & RV camping: $13, Group site $75-$150, Open May-Sep, Max Length: 32ft, Reservations accepted, Elev: 6263ft/1909m, Tel: 208-374-5422, Nearest town: Dubois. GPS: 44.417969, -112.216797

348 • D3 | Timber Creek (Salmon-Challis NF)

Total sites: 12, RV sites: 12, Central water, Vault/pit toilet, No showers, No RV dump, Tent & RV camping: $5, Open May-Sep, Reservations not accepted, Elev: 7274ft/2217m, Tel: 208-588-3400, Nearest town: Howe. GPS: 44.395793, -113.409203

349 • D3 | Timber Creek Reservoir (Lower) (Salmon-Challis NF)

Total sites: 2, RV sites: 2, No water, Vault/pit toilet, Tent & RV camping: Free, Open May-Sep, Reservations not accepted, Elev: 7589ft/2313m, Tel: 208-768-2500, Nearest town: Leadore. GPS: 44.581076, -113.466366

350 • D3 | Timber Creek Reservoir (Upper) (Salmon-Challis NF)

Total sites: 5, RV sites: 5, No water, Vault/pit toilet, Tent & RV camping: Free, Open May-Sep, Reservations not accepted, Elev: 7592ft/2314m, Tel: 208-768-2500, Nearest town: Mackay. GPS: 44.576867, -113.470996

351 • D4 | Big Elk (Caribou-Targhee NF)

Total sites: 15, RV sites: 15, Central water, Vault/pit toilet, No showers, No RV dump, Tent & RV camping: $12, Reservable group site: $60-$100, Open May-Sep, Reservations not accepted, Elev: 5676ft/1730m, Tel: 208-523-1412, Nearest town: Irwin. GPS: 43.322344, -111.117521

352 • D4 | Big Springs (Caribou-Targhee NF)

Total sites: 15, RV sites: 15, Water available, Vault/pit toilet, No showers, No RV dump, Tent & RV camping: $15, Reservable group site $50-$100, Open Jun-Sep, Reservations not accepted, Elev: 6430ft/1960m, Tel: 208-558-7658, Nearest town: Island Park. GPS: 44.497446, -111.254743

353 • D4 | Blowout (Caribou-Targhee NF)

Total sites: 15, RV sites: 15, Central water, Vault/pit toilet, No showers, No RV dump, Tent & RV camping: $12, Open May-Sep, Reservations not accepted, Elev: 5718ft/1743m, Tel: 208-523-1412, Nearest town: Alpine (WY). GPS: 43.284948, -111.122132

354 • D4 | Box Canyon (Caribou-Targhee NF)

Total sites: 18, RV sites: 18, Central water, Vault/pit toilet, No showers, No RV dump, Tent & RV camping: $15, Open May-Sep, Reservations not accepted, Elev: 6297ft/1919m, Tel: 208-558-7301, Nearest town: Island Park. GPS: 44.409805, -111.396596

355 • D4 | Buffalo (Caribou-Targhee NF)

Total sites: 126, RV sites: 126, Elec sites: 19, Central water, Flush toilet, No showers, No RV dump, Tents: $20/RVs: $20-26, Group site: $80-$160, Open May-Sep, Max Length: 60ft, Reservations accepted, Elev: 6306ft/1922m, Tel: 208-558-7112, Nearest town: Island Park. GPS: 44.426264, -111.368546

356 • D4 | Buttermilk (Caribou-Targhee NF)

Total sites: 53, RV sites: 53, Elec sites: 1, Central water, Vault/pit toilet, No showers, No RV dump, Tents: $20/RVs: $20-27, Group site: $65-$130, Open May-Sep, Max Length: 50ft, Reservations accepted, Elev: 6329ft/1929m, Tel: 208-558-7301, Nearest town: Island Park. GPS: 44.432125, -111.425953

357 • D4 | Calamity (Caribou-Targhee NF)

Total sites: 41, RV sites: 38, Central water, Vault/pit toilet, No showers, No RV dump, Tent & RV camping: $17, Open May-Sep, Max Length: 99ft, Reservations accepted, Elev: 5646ft/1721m, Tel: 208-523-1412, Nearest town: Irwin. GPS: 43.326332, -111.214626

358 • D4 | Falls (Caribou-Targhee NF)

Total sites: 24, RV sites: 24, Central water, Vault/pit toilet, No showers, No RV dump, Tent & RV camping: $17, Group site: $60, Open May-Sep, Max Length: 120ft, Reservations accepted, Elev: 5289ft/1612m, Tel: 208-523-1412, Nearest town: Swan Valley. GPS: 43.432802, -111.361261

359 • D4 | Flat Rock (Island Park) (Caribou-Targhee NF)

Total sites: 38, RV sites: 38, Elec sites: 8, Central water, Vault/pit toilet, No showers, No RV dump, Tents: $20/RVs: $20-26, Open May-Sep, Max Length: 65ft, Reservations accepted, Elev: 6388ft/1947m, Tel: 208-652-7442, Nearest town: Island Park. GPS: 44.498796, -111.340193

360 • D4 | Grandview (Caribou-Targhee NF)

Total sites: 8, RV sites: 8, Elec sites: 8, Central water, Vault/pit toilet, No showers, No RV dump, Tent & RV camping: $20, Open May-Sep, Reservations not accepted, Elev: 5928ft/1807m, Tel: 208-652-7442, Nearest town: Ashton. GPS: 44.175298, -111.313552

361 • D4 | McCoy Creek (Caribou-Targhee NF)

Total sites: 17, RV sites: 17, Central water, Vault/pit toilet, No showers, No RV dump, Tent & RV camping: $10, Reservations not accepted, Elev: 5617ft/1712m, Tel: 208-523-1412, Nearest town: Alpine. GPS: 43.183793, -111.100767

362 • D4 | McCrea's Bridge (Caribou-Targhee NF)

Total sites: 23, RV sites: 23, Water available, Vault/pit toilet, No showers, No RV dump, Tent & RV camping: $20, Open May-Sep, Max Length: 99ft, Reservations accepted, Elev: 6348ft/1935m, Tel: 208-652-7442, Nearest town: Island Park. GPS: 44.462402, -111.399902

363 • D4 | Mike Harris (Caribou-Targhee NF)

Total sites: 12, RV sites: 12, Central water, Vault/pit toilet, No showers, No RV dump, Tent & RV camping: $17, Open May-Sep, Max Length: 40ft, Reservations accepted, Elev: 6529ft/1990m, Tel: 208-354-2312, Nearest town: Victor. GPS: 43.556399, -111.069352

364 • D4 | Palisades Creek (Caribou-Targhee NF)

Total sites: 7, RV sites: 7, Central water, Vault/pit toilet, No showers, No RV dump, Tent & RV camping: $12, Open May-Sep, Max Length: 22ft, Reservations not accepted, Elev: 5555ft/1693m, Tel: 208-523-1412, Nearest town: Swan Valley. GPS: 43.396866, -111.214193

365 • D4 | Pine Creek (Fourth of July Peak) (Caribou-Targhee NF)

Total sites: 10, RV sites: 10, No water, Vault/pit toilet, Tent & RV camping: $10, Open May-Sep, Max Length: 30ft, Reservations not accepted, Elev: 6627ft/2020m, Tel: 208-354-2312, Nearest town: Swan Valley. GPS: 43.573132, -111.207142

366 • D4 | Riverside Park (Caribou-Targhee NF)

Total sites: 56, RV sites: 56, Central water, Vault/pit toilet, No showers, No RV dump, Tent & RV camping: $20, Group site: $50, Open May-Sep, Max Length: 40ft, Reservations accepted, Elev: 6088ft/1856m, Tel: 208-523-1412, Nearest town: Ashton. GPS: 44.265744, -111.456602

367 • D4 | Upper Coffee Pot (Caribou-Targhee NF)

Total sites: 15, RV sites: 15, Elec sites: 8, Central water, Vault/pit toilet, No showers, No RV dump, Tents: $20/RVs: $20-26, Open May-Sep, Max Length: 66ft, Reservations accepted, Elev: 6394ft/1949m, Tel: 208-652-7442, Nearest town: Island Park. GPS: 44.490913, -111.366123

368 • D4 | Warm River (Caribou-Targhee NF)

Total sites: 28, RV sites: 15, Water at site, Vault/pit toilet, No showers, No RV dump, Tents: $20/RVs: $20-26, Group site $75-$150, Open May-Sep, Max Length: 45ft, Reservations accepted, Elev: 5315ft/1620m, Tel: 208-652-7442, Nearest town: Ashton. GPS: 44.120154, -111.311145

369 • E2 | Bear Gulch (Hopper Gulch) (Sawtooth NF)

Total sites: 8, RV sites: 8, No water, Vault/pit toilet, Tent & RV camping: Free, Stay limit: 14 days, Open May-Oct, Reservations not accepted, Elev: 6017ft/1834m, Tel: 208-678-0439, Nearest town: Burley. GPS: 42.227454, -114.378672

370 • E2 | Big Bluff (Sawtooth NF)

Total sites: 3, RV sites: 0, No water, No toilets, Tents only: Free, Stay limit: 14 days, Reservations not accepted, Elev: 4921ft/1500m, Tel: 208-678-0430, Nearest town: Steer Basin. GPS: 42.310438, -114.260199

371 • E2 | Bostetter (Sawtooth NF)

Total sites: 10, RV sites: 10, Central water, Vault/pit toilet, No showers, No RV dump, Tent & RV camping: Fee unk, Group site, Stay limit: 14 days, Reservations not accepted, Elev: 7188ft/2191m, Tel: 208-678-0430, Nearest town: Oakley. GPS: 42.165771, -114.168945

372 • E2 | Diamondfield Jack (Sawtooth NF)

Total sites: 12, RV sites: 12, Central water, Vault/pit toilet, No showers, No RV dump, Tent & RV camping: Fee unk, Stay limit: 14 days, Open all year, Reservations not accepted, Elev: 7001ft/2134m, Tel: 208-678-0439, Nearest town: Oakley. GPS: 42.171875, -114.279565

373 • E2 | Father And Sons (Sawtooth NF)

Total sites: 12, RV sites: 12, Central water, Vault/pit toilet, No showers, No RV dump, Tent & RV camping: Fee unk, Group site available, Stay limit: 14 days, Open Jun-Sep, Reservations not accepted, Elev: 7284ft/2220m, Tel: 208-678-0430, Nearest town: Oakley. GPS: 42.163086, -114.185547

374 • E2 | FS Flats (Sawtooth NF)

Total sites: 19, RV sites: 19, No water, Vault/pit toilet, Tent & RV camping: Free, 2 group sites, Stay limit: 14 days, Reservations not accepted, Elev: 6971ft/2125m, Tel: 208-678-0430, Nearest town: Hansen. GPS: 42.154118, -114.258898

375 • E2 | Lower Penstemon (Sawtooth NF)

Total sites: 5, RV sites: 5, Central water, Vault/pit toilet, No showers, No RV dump, Tent & RV camping: $8, Stay limit: 14 days, Open May-Sep, Max Length: 30ft, Reservations accepted, Elev: 6637ft/2023m, Tel: 208-678-0439, Nearest town: Burley. GPS: 42.196553, -114.283356

376 • E2 | Pettit (Sawtooth NF)

Total sites: 8, RV sites: 8, Central water, Vault/pit toilet, No showers, No RV dump, Tent & RV camping: Fee unk, Stay limit: 14 days, Open Jun-Sep, Reservations not accepted, Elev: 6834ft/2083m, Tel: 208-678-0439, Nearest town: Hansen. GPS: 42.183774, -114.283264

377 • E2 | Porcupine Springs (Sawtooth NF)

Total sites: 18, RV sites: 18, Water available, Vault/pit toilet, No showers, No RV dump, Tent & RV camping: $10, 3 reservable group sites $75, Stay limit: 14 days, Open May-Sep, Max Length: 30ft, Reservations accepted, Elev: 6926ft/2111m, Tel: 208-678-0439, Nearest town: Burley. GPS: 42.167462, -114.261091

378 • E2 | Schipper (Sawtooth NF)

Total sites: 5, RV sites: 5, No water, Vault/pit toilet, Tent & RV camping: $5, Stay limit: 14 days, Open May-Oct, Reservations not accepted, Elev: 4698ft/1432m, Tel: 208-678-0439, Nearest town: Hansen. GPS: 42.322495, -114.268247

379 • E2 | Steer Basin (Sawtooth NF)

Total sites: 4, RV sites: 4, No water, No toilets, Tent & RV camping: $5, Open May-Oct, Max Length: 20ft, Reservations not accepted, Elev: 5256ft/1602m, Nearest town: Burley. GPS: 42.279611, -114.260306

380 • E2 | Third Fork (Sawtooth NF)

Total sites: 5, RV sites: 5, No water, Vault/pit toilet, Tent & RV camping: Free, Stay limit: 14 days, Open May-Sep, Reservations not accepted, Elev: 5197ft/1584m, Tel: 208-678-0439, Nearest town: Twin Falls. GPS: 42.252024, -114.248199

381 • E2 | Upper Penstemon (Sawtooth NF)

Total sites: 8, RV sites: 8, Central water, Vault/pit toilet, No showers, No RV dump, Tent & RV camping: $8, Stay limit: 14 days, Open Jun-Sep, Reservations not accepted, Elev: 6660ft/2030m, Tel: 208-678-0439, Nearest town: Burley. GPS: 42.194331, -114.285882

382 • E3 | Bennett Springs (Sawtooth NF)

Total sites: 6, RV sites: 6, No water, Vault/pit toilet, Tent & RV camping: Free, Stay limit: 14 days, Open Jun-Oct, Reservations not accepted, Elev: 7421ft/2262m, Tel: 208-678-0439, Nearest town: Burley. GPS: 42.326496, -113.601639

383 • E3 | Big Springs (Caribou) (Caribou-Targhee NF)

Total sites: 15, RV sites: 15, Central water, Vault/pit toilet, No showers, No RV dump, Tent & RV camping: $15, Group site: $50-$100, Open May-Sep, Max Length: 70ft, Reservations accepted, Elev: 6358ft/1938m, Tel: 208-652-7442, Nearest town: Lava Hot Springs. GPS: 42.765636, -112.095479

384 • E3 | Cherry Creek (Caribou-Targhee NF)

Total sites: 5, RV sites: 5, No water, No toilets, Tent & RV camping: Free, Reservations not accepted, Elev: 5839ft/1780m, Nearest town: Downey. GPS: 42.304463, -112.135386

385 • E3 | Curlew (Curlew NG)

Total sites: 13, RV sites: 13, Central water, Vault/pit toilet, No showers, No RV dump, Tent & RV camping: $15, Group site: $60-$100, Stay limit: 14 days, Open May-Sep, Max Length: 35ft, Reservations accepted, Elev: 4619ft/1408m, Tel: 208-236-7500, Nearest town: Holbrook. GPS: 42.070646, -112.691329

386 • E3 | Dry Canyon (Caribou-Targhee NF)

Total sites: 3, RV sites: 3, No water, Vault/pit toilet, Tent & RV camping: Free, Open Jun-Sep, Reservations not accepted, Elev: 6355ft/1937m, Tel: 208-236-7500, Nearest town: Weston. GPS: 42.057849, -112.143917

387 • E3 | Howell Canyon Sno-Park (Sawtooth NF)

Total sites: 2, RV sites: 2, No water, Vault/pit toilet, Tent & RV camping: Free, Elev: 7614ft/2321m, Nearest town: Malta. GPS: 42.327564, -113.608842

388 • E3 | Independence Lakes (Sawtooth NF)

Total sites: 9, RV sites: 9, No water, Vault/pit toilet, Tent & RV camping: Free, Stay limit: 14 days, Open Jul-Oct, Reservations not accepted, Elev: 7707ft/2349m, Tel: 208-678-0439, Nearest town: Oakley. GPS: 42.218924, -113.673615

389 • E3 | Lake Cleveland - East (Sawtooth NF)

Total sites: 17, RV sites: 17, Central water, Vault/pit toilet, No showers, No RV dump, Tent & RV camping: $10, Stay limit: 14 days, Open Jul-Sep, Max Length: 60ft, Reservations accepted, Elev: 8235ft/2510m, Tel: 208-678-0430, Nearest town: Albion. GPS: 42.324146, -113.646827

390 • E3 | Lake Cleveland - West (Sawtooth NF)

Total sites: 9, RV sites: 9, Central water, Vault/pit toilet, No showers, No RV dump, Tent & RV camping: $10, No trailers - narrow road, Stay limit: 14 days, Open Jul-Oct, Reservations not accepted, Elev: 8248ft/2514m, Tel: 208-678-0430, Nearest town: Albion. GPS: 42.319573, -113.652053

391 • E3 | Malad Summit (Caribou-Targhee NF)

Total sites: 11, RV sites: 11, Central water, Vault/pit toilet, No showers, No RV dump, Tent & RV camping: $15, Group site: $60-$100, Open May-Sep, Max Length: 60ft, Reservations accepted, Elev: 6207ft/1892m, Tel: 208-236-7500, Nearest town: Malad. GPS: 42.350137, -112.275445

392 • E3 | Mill Flat (Sawtooth NF)

Total sites: 7, RV sites: 7, No water, Vault/pit toilet, Tent & RV camping: Free, Stay limit: 14 days, Open Jun-Oct, Reservations not accepted, Elev: 5938ft/1810m, Tel: 208-678-0439, Nearest town: Rockland. GPS: 42.432009, -113.015975

393 • E3 | Scout Mountain (Caribou-Targhee NF)

Total sites: 28, RV sites: 28, Central water, Vault/pit toilet, No showers, No RV dump, Tent & RV camping: $15, Group site: $60, Open May-Sep, Max Length: 70ft, Reservations accepted, Elev: 6529ft/1990m, Tel: 208-236-7500, Nearest town: Pocatello. GPS: 42.693604, -112.358887

394 • E3 | Sublett (Sawtooth NF)

Total sites: 9, RV sites: 9, No water, Vault/pit toilet, Tent & RV camping: Free, Stay limit: 14 days, Open Jun-Nov, Reservations not accepted, Elev: 5430ft/1655m, Tel: 208-678-0439, Nearest town: Burley. GPS: 42.327704, -113.003233

395 • E3 | Thompson Flat (Sawtooth NF)

Total sites: 20, RV sites: 20, Vault/pit toilet, Tent & RV camping: $8, Reservable group site $50, Stay limit: 14 days, Open Jul-Oct, Reservations not accepted, Elev: 8051ft/2454m, Tel: 208-678-0439, Nearest town: Albion. GPS: 42.324951, -113.623779

396 • E3 | Twin Lakes (Sawtooth NF)

Total sites: 12, RV sites: 12, No water, Vault/pit toilet, Tent & RV camping: Fee unk, Stay limit: 14 days, Open Jul-Oct, Reservations not accepted, Elev: 8205ft/2501m, Tel: 208-678-0430. GPS: 42.317651, -113.625334

397 • E4 | Albert Moser (Caribou-Targhee NF)

Total sites: 9, RV sites: 9, Central water, Vault/pit toilet, No showers, No RV dump, Tent & RV camping: $14, Open May-Sep, Max Length: 25ft, Reservations accepted, Elev: 5328ft/1624m, Tel: 208-847-0375, Nearest town: Preston. GPS: 42.138463, -111.694053

398 • E4 | Beaver Creek (Egan Basin) (Caribou-Targhee NF)

Total sites: 5, RV sites: 5, No water, Vault/pit toilet, Tent & RV camping: $8, Open Jun-Sep, Reservations not accepted, Elev: 7812ft/2381m, Tel: 208-847-0375, Nearest town: Fish Haven. GPS: 42.020719, -111.529289

399 • E4 | Cloverleaf (Caribou-Targhee NF)

Total sites: 19, RV sites: 19, Central water, Flush toilet, No showers, No RV dump, Tent & RV camping: $16, Group site: $64-$130, Open Jun-Sep, Max Length: 40ft, Reservations accepted, Elev: 6923ft/2110m, Tel: 208-847-0375, Nearest town: St. Charles. GPS: 42.094418, -111.531587

400 • E4 | Cold Springs (Banks) (Caribou-Targhee NF)

Total sites: 6, RV sites: 6, No water, Vault/pit toilet, Tent & RV camping: Free, Open May-Sep, Reservations not accepted, Elev: 6371ft/1942m, Tel: 208-847-0375, Nearest town: Soda Springs. GPS: 42.510625, -111.582985

401 • E4 | Eightmile (Caribou-Targhee NF)

Total sites: 5, RV sites: 5, No water, Vault/pit toilet, Tent & RV camping: Free, Open May-Sep, Reservations not accepted, Elev: 6749ft/2057m, Tel: 208-847-0375, Nearest town: Soda Springs. GPS: 42.487631, -111.584482

402 • E4 | Emigration (Caribou-Targhee NF)

Total sites: 23, RV sites: 23, Central water, Flush toilet, No showers, No RV dump, Tent & RV camping: $17, 2 group sites: $67-$87, Open Jun-Sep, Max Length: 58ft, Reservations accepted, Elev: 7234ft/2205m, Tel: 208-847-0375, Nearest town: Montpelier. GPS: 42.369629, -111.556885

403 • E4 | Gravel Creek (Caribou-Targhee NF)

Total sites: 12, RV sites: 12, No water, Vault/pit toilet, Tent & RV camping: Fee unk, Open May-Sep, Reservations not accepted, Elev: 6667ft/2032m, Tel: 208-547-4356, Nearest town: Soda Springs. GPS: 42.936574, -111.379461

404 • E4 | Harrys Hollow (Caribou-Targhee NF)

Total sites: 3, RV sites: 3, No water, Vault/pit toilet, Tent & RV camping: Free, Reservations not accepted, Elev: 6742ft/2055m, Nearest town: Bloomington. GPS: 42.190296, -111.508191

405 • E4 | Marijuana Flat (Caribou-Targhee NF)

Total sites: 10, RV sites: 10, No water, Vault/pit toilet, Tent & RV camping: Fee unk, Open May-Sep, Reservations not accepted, Elev: 5487ft/1672m, Tel: 208-524-7500, Nearest town: Preston. GPS: 42.138678, -111.670233

406 • E4 | Mill Canyon (Caribou-Targhee NF)

Total sites: 10, RV sites: 10, No water, Vault/pit toilet, Tent & RV camping: Fee unk, Open May-Sep, Reservations not accepted, Elev: 6519ft/1987m, Tel: 208-547-4356, Nearest town: Soda Springs. GPS: 42.810565, -111.360043

407 • E4 | Montpelier Canyon (Caribou-Targhee NF)

Total sites: 15, RV sites: 13, No water, Vault/pit toilet, Tent & RV camping: $10, Larger RVs and trailers may have difficulty maneuvering through the campground, Open May-Sep, Max Length: 30ft, Reservations accepted, Elev: 6250ft/1905m, Tel: 208-847-0375, Nearest town: Montpelier. GPS: 42.331216, -111.232747

408 • E4 | Paris Springs (Caribou-Targhee NF)

Total sites: 9, RV sites: 9, Central water, Vault/pit toilet, No showers, No RV dump, Tent & RV camping: $14, 3 group sites : $87, Open May-Sep, Max Length: 50ft, Reservations accepted, Elev: 6578ft/2005m, Tel: 208-847-0375, Nearest town: Paris. GPS: 42.207322, -111.494793

409 • E4 | Pine Bar (Caribou-Targhee NF)

Total sites: 5, RV sites: 5, No water, Vault/pit toilet, Tent & RV camping: Free, Reservations not accepted, Elev: 6424ft/1958m, Tel: 208-547-4356, Nearest town: Freedom. GPS: 42.972455, -111.210285

410 • E4 | Porcupine (Caribou-Targhee NF)

Total sites: 13, RV sites: 13, Central water, No toilets, No showers, No RV dump, Tent & RV camping: $16, Group site: $32, Open May-Sep, Max Length: 32ft, Reservations accepted, Elev: 6804ft/2074m, Tel: 208-847-0375, Nearest town: Bear Lake. GPS: 42.095459, -111.518311

411 • E4 | St Charles (Caribou-Targhee NF)

Total sites: 6, RV sites: 6, Central water, No toilets, No showers, No RV dump, Tent & RV camping: $16, Reservable group site $37, Open May-Sep, Max Length: 32ft, Reservations not accepted, Elev: 6125ft/1867m, Tel: 435-245-6521, Nearest town: St. Charles. GPS: 42.113041, -111.446759

412 • E4 | Summit View (Georgetown) (Caribou-Targhee NF)

Total sites: 18, RV sites: 18, Central water, Vault/pit toilet, No showers, No RV dump, Tent & RV camping: $14, 3 group sites: $56-$67, Open Jun-Sep, Max Length: 60ft, Reservations accepted, Elev: 7238ft/2206m, Tel: 208-847-0375, Nearest town: Montpelier. GPS: 42.558601, -111.296052

413 • E4 | Tin Cup (Caribou-Targhee NF)

Total sites: 5, RV sites: 5, No water, Vault/pit toilet, Tent & RV camping: Free, Open May-Sep, Reservations not accepted, Elev: 5863ft/1787m, Tel: 208-547-4356, Nearest town: Freedom. GPS: 43.004643, -111.102652

414 • E4 | Willow Flat (Caribou-Targhee NF)

Total sites: 55, RV sites: 45, Central water, No toilets, No showers, No RV dump, Tent & RV camping: $17, 6 group sites: $28-$87, Open May-Sep, Max Length: 75ft, Reservations accepted, Elev: 6119ft/1865m, Tel: 208-847-0375, Nearest town: Preston. GPS: 42.138677, -111.625128

Illinois

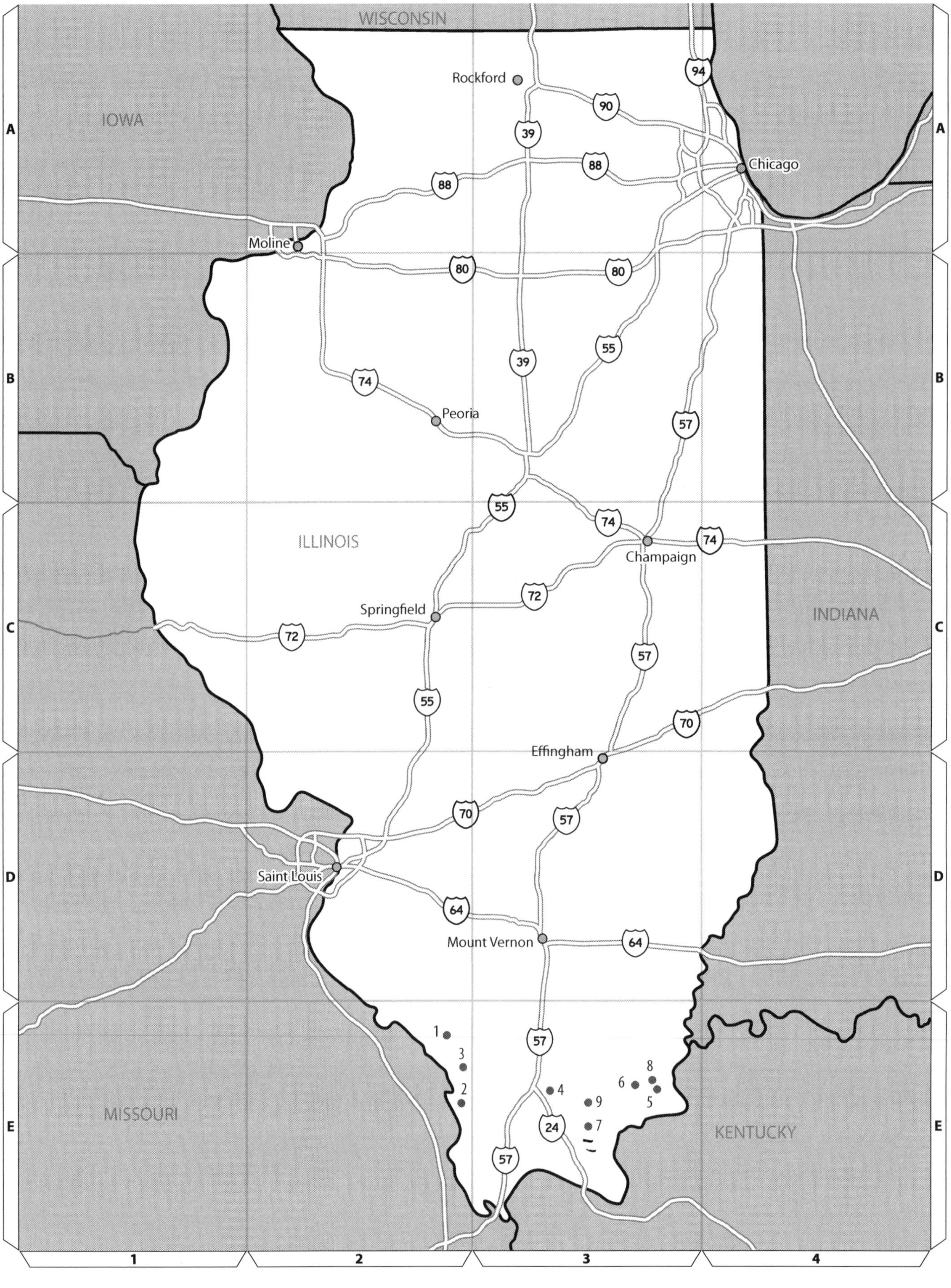
WISCONSIN
IOWA
ILLINOIS
INDIANA
MISSOURI
KENTUCKY
Rockford
Chicago
Moline
Peoria
Champaign
Springfield
Effingham
Saint Louis
Mount Vernon
94
90
39
88
80
74
55
57
72
70
64
24
1
2
3
4
5
6
7
8
9
A
B
C
D
E

Map	ID	Map	ID
E2	1-3	E3	4-9

Alphabetical List of Camping Areas

1 • E2 | Johnson Creek (Shawnee NF)

Total sites: 20, RV sites: 20, No water, No toilets, Tent & RV camping: $10, Open Mar-Dec, Reservations not accepted, Elev: 617ft/188m, Tel: 618-833-8576, Nearest town: Murphysboro. GPS: 37.834581, -89.520042

2 • E2 | Pine Hills (Shawnee NF)

Total sites: 13, RV sites: 13, No water, Vault/pit toilet, Tent & RV camping: $10, Open Mar-Dec, Reservations not accepted, Elev: 456ft/139m, Tel: 618-833-8576, Nearest town: Jonesboro. GPS: 37.514893, -89.423096

3 • E2 | Turkey Bayou (Shawnee NF)

Total sites: 16, RV sites: 16, No water, No toilets, No showers, No RV dump, Tent & RV camping: Free, Open all year, Reservations not accepted, Elev: 371ft/113m, Tel: 618-833-8576, Nearest town: Murphysboro. GPS: 37.684798, -89.411678

4 • E3 | Buck Ridge (Shawnee NF)

Total sites: 37, RV sites: 37, Central water, Vault/pit toilet, Tent & RV camping: $5, Open Mar-Dec, Elev: 574ft/175m, Tel: 618-253-7114, Nearest town: Creal Springs. GPS: 37.579346, -88.883057

5 • E3 | Camp Cadiz (Shawnee NF)

Total sites: 8, RV sites: 8, No water, Vault/pit toilet, Tent & RV camping: $10, Generator hours: 0600-2200, Open all year, Max Length: 18ft, Reservations not accepted, Elev: 591ft/180m, Tel: 618-658-2111, Nearest town: Karber's Ridge. GPS: 37.578296, -88.244672

6 • E3 | Garden of the Gods (Shawnee NF)

Total sites: 12, RV sites: 12, Central water, Vault/pit toilet, No showers, No RV dump, Tent & RV camping: $10, Open all year, Reservations not accepted, Elev: 817ft/249m, Tel: 618-253-7114, Nearest town: Karbers Ridge. GPS: 37.602539, -88.380615

7 • E3 | Lake Glendale Rec Area - Oak Point (Shawnee NF)

K

Total sites: 59, RV sites: 59, Elec sites: 34, Central water, Flush toilet, Free showers, RV dump, Tent & RV camping: $12-22, Open all year, Reservations not accepted, Elev: 459ft/140m, Tel: 618-638-3246, Nearest town: Vienna. GPS: 37.409379, -88.662301

8 • E3 | Pine Ridge-Pounds Hollow (Shawnee NF)

Total sites: 35, RV sites: 35, Central water, Vault/pit toilet, No showers, No RV dump, Tent & RV camping: $10, Open Mar-Dec, Max Length: 40ft, Reservations not accepted, Elev: 636ft/194m, Tel: 618-658-2111, Nearest town: Karber's Ridge. GPS: 37.615511, -88.268439

9 • E3 | Redbud - Bell Smith Springs (Shawnee NF)

Total sites: 21, RV sites: 21, Central water, Vault/pit toilet, No showers, No RV dump, Tent & RV camping: $10, Open Mar-Dec, Reservations not accepted, Elev: 673ft/205m, Tel: 618-253-7114, Nearest town: Vienna. GPS: 37.523142, -88.656819

Indiana

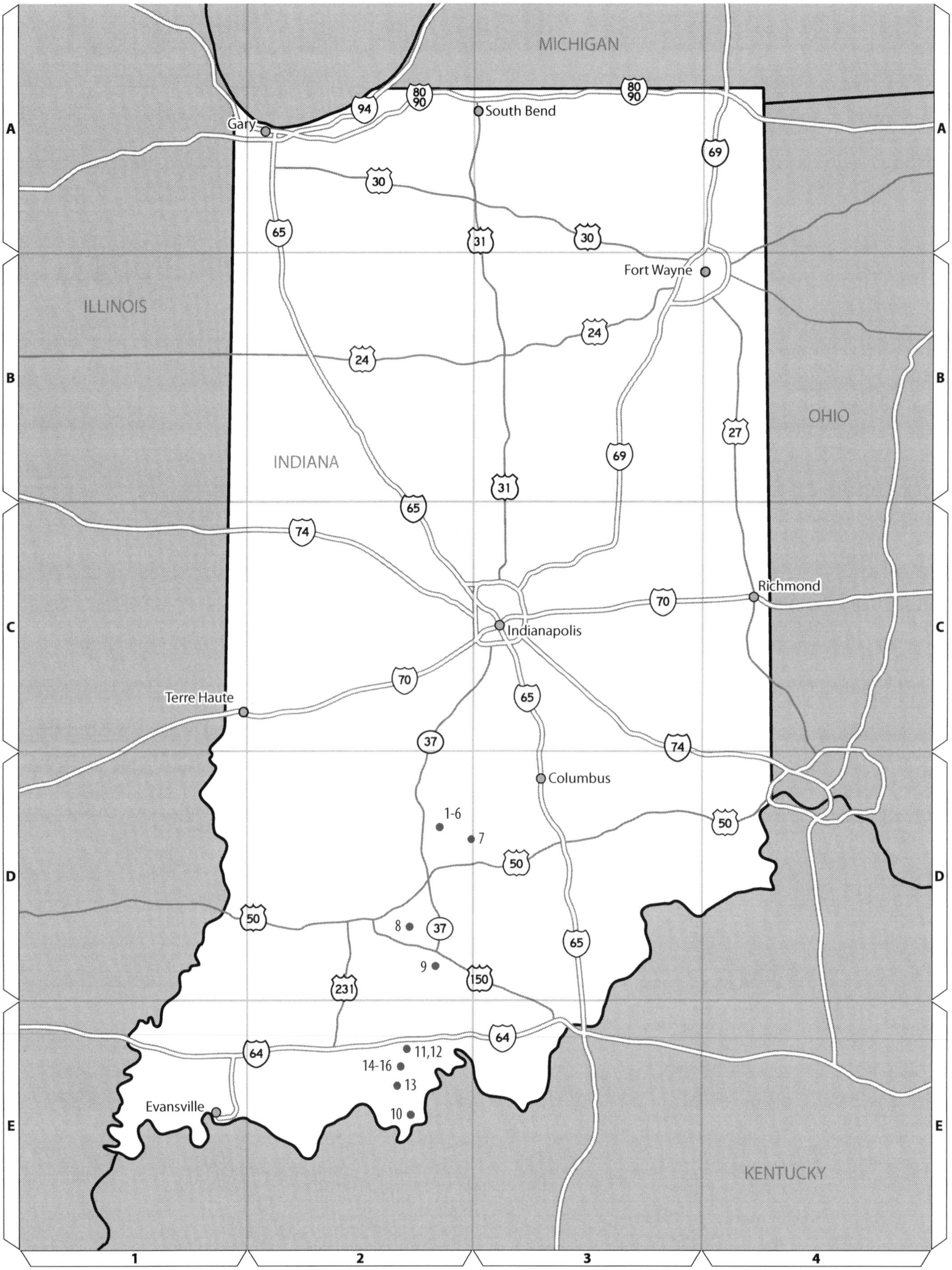
MICHIGAN
ILLINOIS
INDIANA
OHIO
KENTUCKY
Gary
South Bend
Fort Wayne
Richmond
Indianapolis
Terre Haute
Columbus
Evansville
94
80 90
69
30
65
31
24
27
74
70
37
50
74
150
231
64
1-6
7
8
9
10
11,12
13
14-16
A
B
C
D
E
1
2
3
4

Map	ID	Map	ID
D2	1-9	E2	10-16

Alphabetical List of Camping Areas

1 • D2 | Hardin Ridge - Blue Gill (Hoosier NF)

Total sites: 51, RV sites: 35, Elec sites: 17, Water at site, Flush toilet, Free showers, RV dump, Tent & RV camping: $20-27, Generator hours: 0600-2200, Open May-Sep, Reservations not accepted, Elev: 745ft/227m, Tel: 812-837-9453, Nearest town: Bloomington. GPS: 39.022143, -86.440976

2 • D2 | Hardin Ridge - Eads (Hoosier NF)

Total sites: 23, RV sites: 23, Central water, Vault/pit toilet, No showers, No RV dump, Tent & RV camping: $20, Generator hours: 0600-2200, Open Apr-Sep, Reservations not accepted, Elev: 728ft/222m, Tel: 812-837-9453, Nearest town: Bloomington. GPS: 39.014715, -86.431189

3 • D2 | Hardin Ridge - Holland (Hoosier NF)

Total sites: 13, RV sites: 13, Elec sites: 13, Central water, Flush toilet, Free showers, RV dump, Tent & RV camping: $27, Generator hours: 0600-2200, Reservations not accepted, Elev: 784ft/239m, Tel: 812-837-9453, Nearest town: Bloomington. GPS: 39.017743, -86.436279

4 • D2 | Hardin Ridge - Pine (Hoosier NF)

Total sites: 40, RV sites: 40, Elec sites: 20, Central water, RV dump, Tent & RV camping: $20-27, Generator hours: 0600-2200, Reservations not accepted, Elev: 696ft/212m, Tel: 812-837-9453, Nearest town: Bloomington. GPS: 39.026558, -86.451816

5 • D2 | Hardin Ridge - Southern Point (Hoosier NF)

Total sites: 60, RV sites: 46, Central water, No toilets, No showers, RV dump, Tent & RV camping: $20, Generator hours: 0600-2200, Open all year, Reservations not accepted, Elev: 774ft/236m, Tel: 812-837-9453, Nearest town: Bloomington. GPS: 39.014525, -86.445091

6 • D2 | Hardin Ridge - White Oak (Hoosier NF)

Total sites: 17, RV sites: 17, Elec sites: 17, Central water, No toilets, No showers, RV dump, Tent & RV camping: $30, Generator hours: 0600-2200, Open May-Sep, Elev: 771ft/235m, Tel: 812-837-9453, Nearest town: Bloomington. GPS: 39.021584, -86.444933

7 • D2 | Hickory Ridge Horse Camp (Hoosier NF)

Total sites: 20, RV sites: 20, No water, Vault/pit toilet, Tent & RV camping: Free, Water for stock, Open all year, Reservations not accepted, Elev: 899ft/274m, Tel: 812-275-5987, Nearest town: Norman. GPS: 38.976651, -86.294657

8 • D2 | Shirley Creek Horse Camp (Hoosier NF)

Total sites: 19, RV sites: 19, No water, Vault/pit toilet, Tent & RV camping: Free, Water for stock, Open all year, Reservations not accepted, Elev: 768ft/234m, Tel: 812-275-5987, Nearest town: French Lick. GPS: 38.649489, -86.597465

9 • D2 | Young's Creek Horse Camp (Hoosier NF)

Total sites: 50, RV sites: 50, No water, Vault/pit toilet, Tent & RV camping: Free, Generator hours: 0600-2200, Open all year, Reservations not accepted, Elev: 820ft/250m, Tel: 812-547-7051, Nearest town: Paoli. GPS: 38.504112, -86.465459

10 • E2 | German Ridge (Hoosier NF)

Total sites: 20, RV sites: 20, No water, Vault/pit toilet, Tent & RV camping: $8, Non-potable stock water available, Open all year, Reservations not accepted, Elev: 745ft/227m, Tel: 812-547-7051, Nearest town: Cannelton. GPS: 37.951525, -86.588828

11 • E2 | Indian-Celina - North Face (Hoosier NF)

Total sites: 36, RV sites: 36, Elec sites: 3, Central water, Flush toilet, Free showers, RV dump, Tent & RV camping: $20-27, Open all year, Reservations not accepted, Elev: 732ft/223m, Tel: 812-843-4880, Nearest town: St Croix. GPS: 38.197192, -86.605512

12 • E2 | Indian-Celina - South Slope (Hoosier NF)

Total sites: 27, RV sites: 27, Elec sites: 27, Central water, Flush toilet, Free showers, Tent & RV camping: $27, Open Apr-Nov, Reservations not accepted, Elev: 755ft/230m, Tel: 812-843-4880, Nearest town: St Croix. GPS: 38.192722, -86.608235

13 • E2 | Saddle Lake (Hoosier NF)

Total sites: 13, RV sites: 13, No water, Vault/pit toilet, Tent & RV camping: $5, Open all year, Max Length: 21ft, Reservations not accepted, Elev: 656ft/200m, Tel: 812-547-7051, Nearest town: Tell City. GPS: 38.060245, -86.657067

14 • E2 | Tipsaw Lake - Catbrier (Hoosier NF)

Total sites: 10, RV sites: 10, Elec sites: 5, Flush toilet, Free showers, No RV dump, Tent & RV camping: $20-27, Max Length: 65ft, Elev: 617ft/188m, Nearest town: Tell City. GPS: 38.135497, -86.636889

15 • E2 | Tipsaw Lake - Dogwood (Hoosier NF)

Total sites: 14, RV sites: 12, Elec sites: 4, Central water, No RV dump, Tent & RV camping: $20-27, Open Apr-Oct, Elev: 597ft/182m, Nearest town: Tell City. GPS: 38.133608, -86.642724

16 • E2 | Tipsaw Lake - Jackpine (Hoosier NF)

Total sites: 21, RV sites: 21, Elec sites: 8, Central water, No RV dump, Tent & RV camping: $20-27, Open Apr-Oct, Max Length: 55ft, Reservations accepted, Elev: 614ft/187m, Tel: 812-843-4890, Nearest town: Tell City. GPS: 38.135136, -86.642415

Kansas

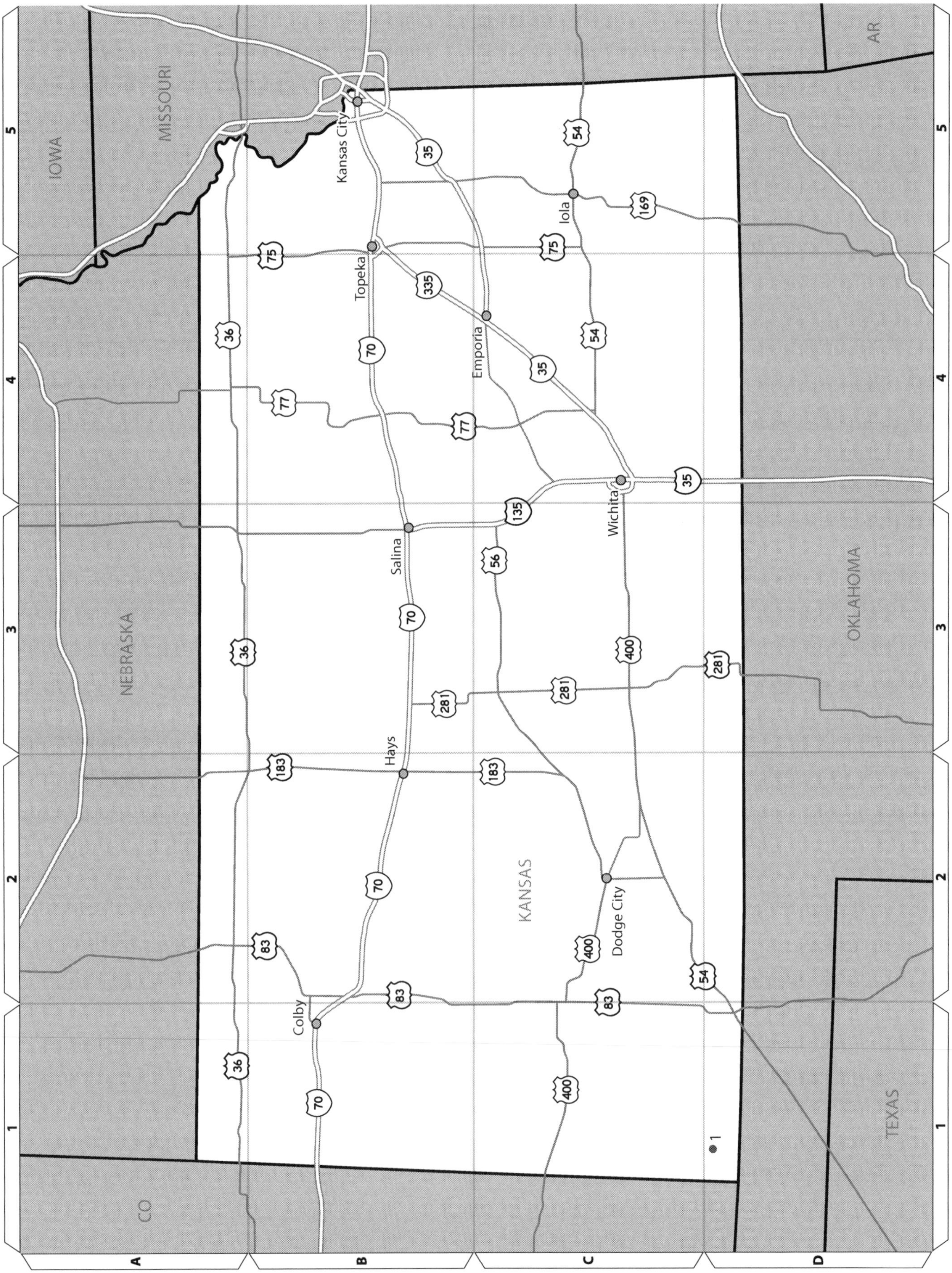
IOWA
MISSOURI
NEBRASKA
KANSAS
OKLAHOMA
TEXAS
CO
AR
Kansas City
Topeka
Emporia
Iola
Wichita
Salina
Hays
Dodge City
Colby
1
35
54
169
75
335
36
70
77
135
56
400
281
183
83
A
B
C
D
1
2
3
4
5

Map	ID	Map	ID
D1	1		

Alphabetical List of Camping Areas

1 • D1 | Cimarron Recreation Area (Cimarron NG)

Total sites: 12, RV sites: 12, Central water, Vault/pit toilet, No showers, No RV dump, Tent & RV camping: $7, No water Dec-Mar, No open fires, Group site $38, Open all year, Reservations not accepted, Elev: 3345ft/1020m, Nearest town: Elkhart. GPS: 37.135591, -101.824756

Kentucky

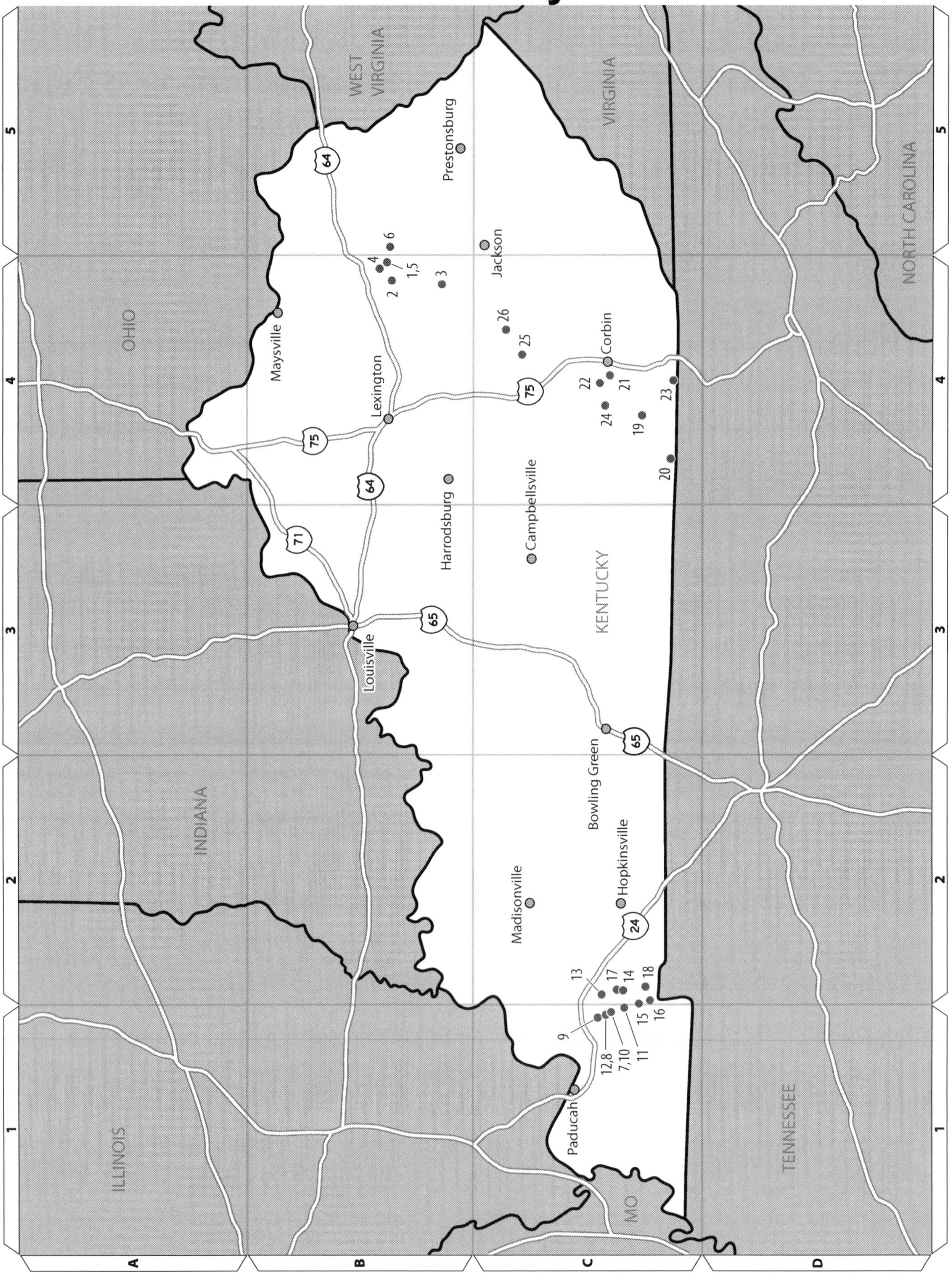

WEST VIRGINIA
VIRGINIA
NORTH CAROLINA
OHIO
INDIANA
ILLINOIS
MO
TENNESSEE
KENTUCKY
Prestonsburg
Jackson
Maysville
Lexington
Corbin
Harrodsburg
Campbellsville
Louisville
Bowling Green
Hopkinsville
Madisonville
Paducah
64
75
71
65
24
1
2
3
4
5
A
B
C
D

Map	ID	Map	ID
B4	1-5	C2	13-18
B5	6	C4	19-26
C1	7-12		

Alphabetical List of Camping Areas

1 • B4 | Claylick (Daniel Boone NF)

Total sites: 13, RV sites: 0, Central water, Vault/pit toilet, No showers, No RV dump, Tents only: $10-15, Walk-to/boat-in sites, Open all year, Reservations not accepted, Elev: 740ft/226m, Tel: 606-784-6428, Nearest town: Morehead. GPS: 38.059349, -83.471608

2 • B4 | Clear Creek (Daniel Boone NF)

Total sites: 21, RV sites: 21, Central water, Vault/pit toilet, No showers, No RV dump, Tent & RV camping: $10-15, Open Apr-Dec, Max Length: 30ft, Reservations not accepted, Elev: 817ft/249m, Tel: 606-768-2722, Nearest town: Salt Lick. GPS: 38.044316, -83.585544

3 • B4 | Koomer Ridge (Daniel Boone NF)

Total sites: 54, RV sites: 19, Central water, Flush toilet, Free showers, No RV dump, Tents: $20/RVs: $25, Nov-Mar: $10, Stay limit: 14 days, Generator hours: 0600-2200, Open all year, Reservations not accepted, Elev: 1299ft/396m, Tel: 606-663-8100, Nearest town: Stanton. GPS: 37.784264, -83.633136

4 • B4 | Twin Knobs (Daniel Boone NF)

Total sites: 216, RV sites: 216, Elec sites: 116, Water at site, Flush toilet, Free showers, RV dump, Tents: $25-30/RVs: $35-40, 2 Full hookup sites, Group site: $70, Dump fee: $6, Open Mar-Nov, Max Length: 70ft, Reservations accepted, Elev: 879ft/268m, Tel: 606-784-8816, Nearest town: Lexington. GPS: 38.091735, -83.508153

5 • B4 | Zilpo (Daniel Boone NF)

Total sites: 172, RV sites: 172, Elec sites: 40, Water at site, Flush toilet, Free showers, RV dump, Tents: $22-27/RVs: $30-41, Also cabins, 4 Full hookup sites, Open Mar-Oct, Max Length: 65ft, Reservations accepted, Elev: 761ft/232m, Tel: 606-768-2722, Nearest town: Salt Lick. GPS: 38.070557, -83.484375

6 • B5 | Paragon (Daniel Boone NF)

Total sites: 7, RV sites: 7, No water, Vault/pit toilet, Tent & RV camping: Free, Open all year, Reservations not accepted, Elev: 722ft/220m, Tel: 606-784-6428, Nearest town: Morehead. GPS: 38.048095, -83.394986

7 • C1 | LBL NRA - Birmingham Ferry (Land Between The Lakes NRA)

Total sites: 26, RV sites: 16, Central water, Vault/pit toilet, No showers, No RV dump, Tent & RV camping: $10, 3-day permit: $10, Stay limit: 14 days, Open all year, Reservations not accepted, Elev: 433ft/132m, Nearest town: Grand Rivers. GPS: 36.923038, -88.162656

8 • C1 | LBL NRA - Hillman Ferry (Land Between The Lakes NRA)

Total sites: 302, RV sites: 238, Elec sites: 267, Water at site, Flush toilet, Free showers, RV dump, Tents: $16/RVs: $34-42, Also cabins, Full hookup sites, Stay limit: 14 days, Open Mar-Nov, Reservations accepted, Elev: 404ft/123m, Tel: 270-924-2181, Nearest town: Grand Rivers. GPS: 36.947287, -88.178188

9 • C1 | LBL NRA - Nickell Branch (Land Between The Lakes NRA)

Total sites: 13, RV sites: 4, No water, Vault/pit toilet, Tent & RV camping: $10, 3-day permit: $10, Stay limit: 14 days, Open all year, Reservations not accepted, Elev: 351ft/107m, Tel: 270-924-2000, Nearest town: Grand Rivers. GPS: 36.988025, -88.199979

10 • C1 | LBL NRA - Smith Bay (Land Between The Lakes NRA)

Total sites: 16, RV sites: 14, No water, Vault/pit toilet, Tent & RV camping: $10, Stay limit: 14 days, Open all year, Elev: 364ft/111m, Nearest town: Grand Rivers. GPS: 36.909075, -88.147868

11 • C1 | LBL NRA - Sugar Bay (Land Between The Lakes NRA)

Total sites: 16, RV sites: 10, No water, Vault/pit toilet, Tent & RV camping: $10, 3-day permit: $10, Stay limit: 14 days, Open all year, Reservations not accepted, Elev: 407ft/124m, Nearest town: Aurora. GPS: 36.856339, -88.126283

12 • C1 | LBL NRA - Twin Lakes (Land Between The Lakes NRA)

Total sites: 14, RV sites: 7, No water, Vault/pit toilet, Tent & RV camping: $10, 3-day permit: $10, rough road, Stay limit: 14 days, Open all year, Elev: 450ft/137m, Nearest town: Eddyville. GPS: 36.964951, -88.198443

13 • C2 | LBL NRA - Cravens Bay (Land Between The Lakes NRA)

Total sites: 30, RV sites: 27, Central water, No toilets, No showers, No RV dump, Tent & RV camping: $12, Stay limit: 14 days, Open all year, Elev: 446ft/136m, Nearest town: Grand Rivers. GPS: 36.960641, -88.053177

14 • C2 | LBL NRA - Energy lake (Land Between The Lakes NRA)

Total sites: 48, RV sites: 43, Elec sites: 35, Central water, Flush toilet, Free showers, No RV dump, Tents: $16/RVs: $28, Also cabins, Stay limit: 14 days, Open Mar-Nov, Reservations accepted, Elev: 423ft/129m, Tel: 270-924-2270, Nearest town: Canton. GPS: 36.855645, -88.020201

15 • C2 | LBL NRA - Fenton Lake (Land Between The Lakes NRA)

Total sites: 12, RV sites: 12, Elec sites: 12, Central water, Vault/pit toilet, No showers, No RV dump, Tent & RV camping: $22, Stay limit: 14 days, Open all year, Reservations not accepted, Elev: 407ft/124m, Nearest town: Aurora. GPS: 36.775703, -88.103585

16 • C2 | LBL NRA - Redd Hollow (Land Between The Lakes NRA)

Total sites: 39, RV sites: 33, No water, Vault/pit toilet, No showers, No RV dump, Tent & RV camping: $10, 3-day permit: $10, Stay limit: 14 days, Open all year, Reservations not accepted, Elev: 423ft/129m, Nearest town: Canton. GPS: 36.713419, -88.073739

17 • C2 | LBL NRA - Taylor Bay (Land Between The Lakes NRA)

Total sites: 35, RV sites: 35, No water, Vault/pit toilet, Tent & RV camping: $10, 3-day permit: $10, Stay limit: 14 days, Open all year, Reservations not accepted, Elev: 407ft/124m, Nearest town: Canton. GPS: 36.883902, -88.020205

18 • C2 | LBL NRA - Wrangler's Horse Camp (Land Between The Lakes NRA)

Total sites: 168, RV sites: 168, Elec sites: 145, Water at site, Flush toilet, Free showers, RV dump, Tents: $16/RVs: $26-40, Also cabins, Full hookup sites, Open all year, Reservations accepted, Elev: 377ft/115m, Tel: 270-924-2201, Nearest town: Canton. GPS: 36.736822, -87.998949

19 • C4 | Barren Fork Horse Camp (Daniel Boone NF)

Total sites: 41, RV sites: 41, Central water, Vault/pit toilet, No showers, No RV dump, Tent & RV camping: $8, Open Apr-Nov, Max Length: 35ft, Reservations not accepted, Elev: 1301ft/397m, Tel: 606-376-5323, Nearest town: Whitley City. GPS: 36.773764, -84.465945

20 • C4 | Great Meadow (Daniel Boone NF)

Total sites: 18, RV sites: 18, Central water, Vault/pit toilet, No showers, No RV dump, Tent & RV camping: Free, Open all year, Reservations not accepted, Elev: 1020ft/311m, Tel: 606-376-5323, Nearest town: Stearns. GPS: 36.628971, -84.725843

21 • C4 | Grove (Daniel Boone NF)

Total sites: 56, RV sites: 52, Elec sites: 52, Central water, Flush toilet, Free showers, RV dump, Tents: $20/RVs: $32-38, Open Apr-Oct, Max Length: 50ft, Reservations accepted, Elev: 1171ft/357m, Tel: 606-528-6156, Nearest town: Corbin. GPS: 36.943604, -84.215332

22 • C4 | Holly Bay (Daniel Boone NF)

Total sites: 94, RV sites: 75, Elec sites: 29, Water at site, Flush toilet, Free showers, RV dump, Tent & RV camping: $32-38, Open Apr-Oct, Max Length: 90ft, Reservations accepted, Elev: 1073ft/327m, Tel: 606-528-6156, Nearest town: London. GPS: 36.981201, -84.261230

23 • C4 | Jellico Creek (Daniel Boone NF)

Total sites: 2, RV sites: 2, No water, No toilets, Tent & RV camping: Fee unk, Elev: 1086ft/331m. GPS: 36.601145, -84.248238

24 • C4 | Little Lick Horse Camp (Daniel Boone NF)

Total sites: 8, RV sites: 0, No water, Vault/pit toilet, Tents only: Free, Stay limit: 14 days, Open all year, Reservations not accepted, Elev: 1119ft/341m, Tel: 606-864-4163, Nearest town: Somerset. GPS: 36.963276, -84.398361

25 • C4 | S-Tree (Daniel Boone NF)

Total sites: 20, RV sites: 20, No water, Vault/pit toilet, Tent & RV camping: Free, Open all year, Max Length: 25ft, Reservations not accepted, Elev: 1426ft/435m, Tel: 606-864-4163, Nearest town: McKee. GPS: 37.386719, -84.074219

26 • C4 | Turkey Foot (Daniel Boone NF)

Total sites: 20, RV sites: 20, No water, Vault/pit toilet, Tent & RV camping: Free, Steep road, Open all year, Reservations not accepted, Elev: 879ft/268m, Tel: 606-864-4163, Nearest town: McKee. GPS: 37.466496, -83.917419

Louisiana

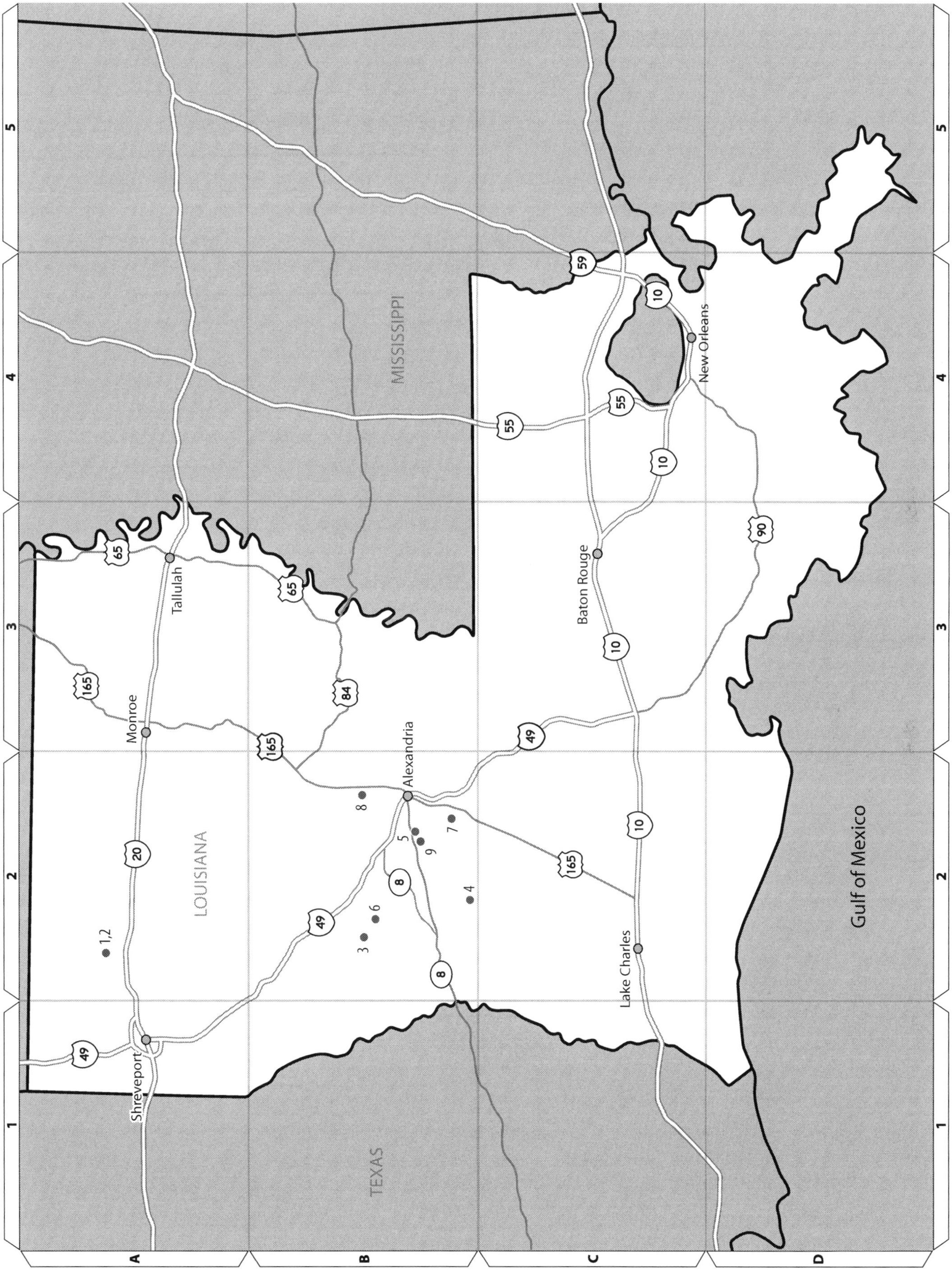
MISSISSIPPI
LOUISIANA
TEXAS
Gulf of Mexico
New Orleans
Baton Rouge
Tallulah
Monroe
Alexandria
Shreveport
Lake Charles
59
10
55
90
65
165
84
49
20
8
1,2
3
4
5
6
7
8
9
A
B
C
D
1
2
3
4
5

Map	ID	Map	ID
A2	1-2	B2	3-9

Alphabetical List of Camping Areas

1 • A2 | Beaver Dam (Kisatchie NF)

Total sites: 29, RV sites: 29, Elec sites: 29, Water at site, Flush toilet, Free showers, RV dump, Tent & RV camping: $25, Open all year, Max Length: 114ft, Reservations accepted, Elev: 236ft/72m, Tel: 318-473-7160, Nearest town: Minden. GPS: 32.673392, -93.292061

2 • A2 | Turtle Slide (Kisatchie NF)

Total sites: 20, RV sites: 20, Central water, Flush toilet, No showers, RV dump, Tent & RV camping: $10, Reservations not accepted, Elev: 220ft/67m, Tel: 318-473-7160, Nearest town: Minden. GPS: 32.672852, -93.297678

3 • B2 | Dogwood (Kisatchie NF)

Total sites: 16, RV sites: 16, Central water, Flush toilet, No showers, No RV dump, Tent & RV camping: Free, Open all year, Max Length: 20ft, Reservations not accepted, Elev: 213ft/65m, Tel: 318-473-7160, Nearest town: Natchitoches. GPS: 31.493239, -93.193046

4 • B2 | Fullerton Lake (Kisatchie NF)

Total sites: 15, RV sites: 15, Central water, Flush toilet, No showers, No RV dump, Tent & RV camping: $15, Open all year, Reservations not accepted, Elev: 236ft/72m, Tel: 318-473-7160, Nearest town: Cravens. GPS: 31.010628, -92.986239

5 • B2 | Kincaid Lake (Kisatchie NF)

Total sites: 41, RV sites: 41, Elec sites: 41, Water at site, Flush toilet, Free showers, RV dump, Tents: $10/RVs: $25, Reservations not accepted, Elev: 121ft/37m, Tel: 318-743-7160, Nearest town: Gardner. GPS: 31.262939, -92.633301

6 • B2 | Kisatchie Bayou (Kisatchie NF)

Total sites: 18, RV sites: 0, No water, Vault/pit toilet, Tents only: $2, Also walk-to sites, Open all year, Reservations not accepted, Elev: 223ft/68m, Tel: 318-473-7160, Nearest town: Provencal. GPS: 31.445071, -93.093061

7 • B2 | Loran/Claiborne Camp (Kisatchie NF)

Total sites: 39, RV sites: 39, No water, Vault/pit toilet, Tent & RV camping: $10, Reservations not accepted, Elev: 249ft/76m, Tel: 318-473-7160, Nearest town: Woodworth. GPS: 31.097801, -92.566609

8 • B2 | Stuart Lake (Kisatchie NF)

Total sites: 8, RV sites: 8, Central water, No toilets, No showers, No RV dump, Tent & RV camping: $15, Reservable group site: $35-$75, Open all year, Reservations not accepted, Elev: 230ft/70m, Tel: 318-473-7160, Nearest town: Alexandria. GPS: 31.508578, -92.444018

9 • B2 | Valentine Lake Northshore (Kisatchie NF)

Total sites: 14, RV sites: 14, Central water, Vault/pit toilet, No showers, No RV dump, Tent & RV camping: $10, Reservations not accepted, Elev: 220ft/67m, Tel: 318-473-7160, Nearest town: Gardner. GPS: 31.243408, -92.681396

Maine

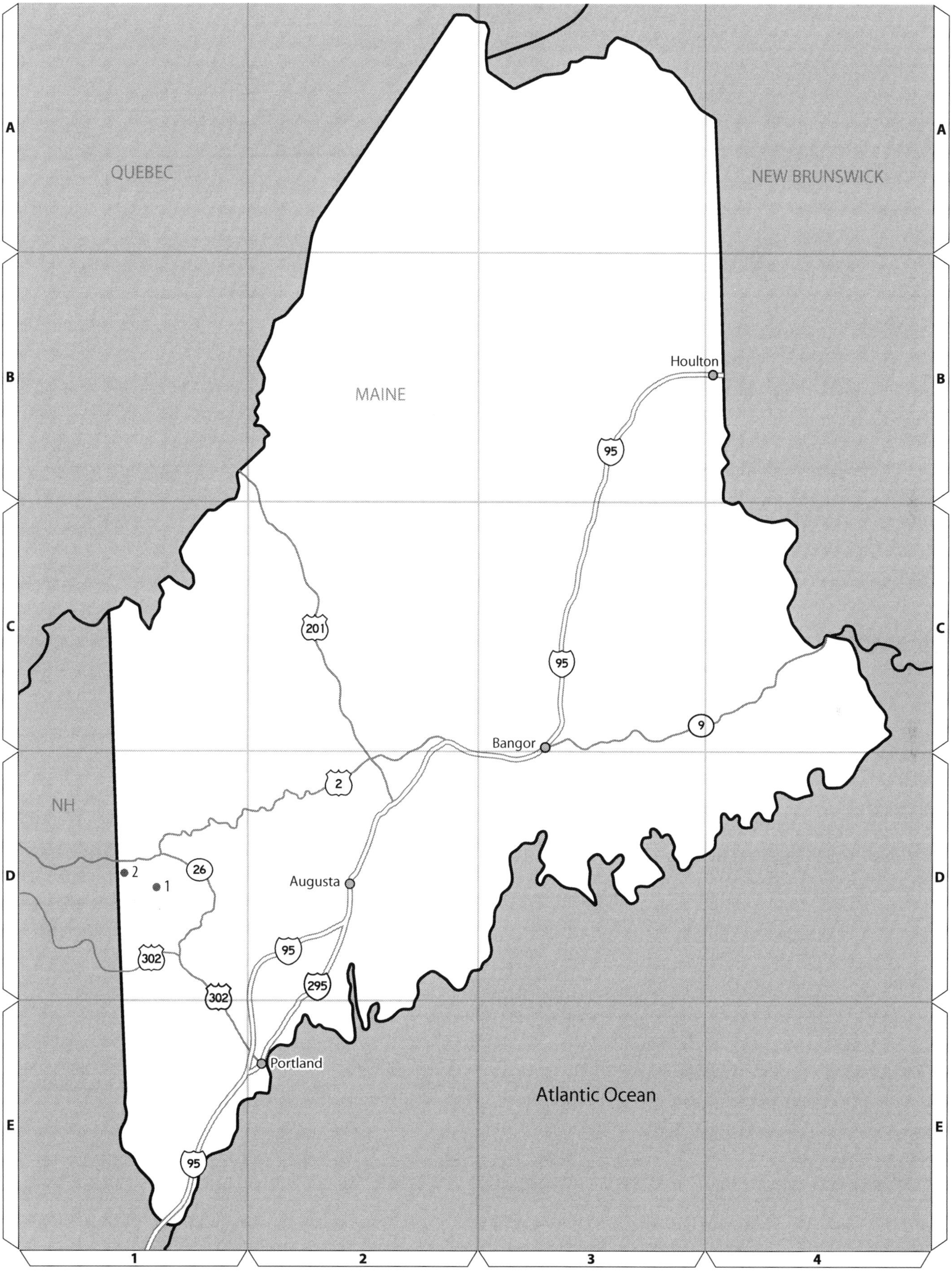
QUEBEC
NEW BRUNSWICK
MAINE
Houlton
95
201
95
9
Bangor
2
NH
26
2
1
Augusta
302
95
295
302
Portland
Atlantic Ocean
95
A
B
C
D
E
1
2
3
4

Map	ID	Map	ID
D1	1-2		

Alphabetical List of Camping Areas

1 • D1 | Crocker Pond (White Mountain NF)

Total sites: 7, RV sites: 7, Central water, Vault/pit toilet, No showers, No RV dump, Tent & RV camping: $18, Open May-Oct, Reservations not accepted, Elev: 879ft/268m, Nearest town: Bethel. GPS: 44.310000, -70.824000

2 • D1 | Hastings (White Mountain NF)

Total sites: 24, RV sites: 23, Central water, Vault/pit toilet, No showers, No RV dump, Tent & RV camping: $20, Open May-Oct, Max Length: 35ft, Reservations accepted, Elev: 863ft/263m, Tel: 603-466-2713, Nearest town: Gilead. GPS: 44.352328, -70.983656

Michigan

Lake Superior
ONTARIO
WISCONSIN
Lake Huron
Lake Michigan
MICHIGAN
ILLINOIS
INDIANA
OHIO
Marquette
Sault Ste. Marie
Grand Rapids
Flint
Lansing
Detroit
A
B
C
D
E
1
2
3
4
28
41
2
75
31
10
131
127
69
94
96
196
12
1
2
4
21
20
5
19
24
10,15,17
7
11,14,18
22
6
3,16
9
8,12,13,23
27
25
34-36,39,43,45,46,54,55,58,59,62
26,33,37,38,44,50,56,57,60,61
42
40
51,52
28-32,41,47-49,53
63
67
69
68
65
64,66
104,112,115
106
107
108
119
105
101
84
110
114
86,88
111
109
113
116,118
117
92
78,95
96
87
72
93
79
85
91
70
94
90
99,100
73,74
103
76
77,80,98,102
81,82
75
121
120
122
71,83,89,97

Map	ID	Map	ID
A1	1	C3	70-103
B1	2-24	C4	104-119
B2	25-62	D3	120-122
B3	63-69		

Alphabetical List of Camping Areas

1 • A1 | Courtney Lake (Ottawa NF)

Total sites: 21, RV sites: 19, Central water, Vault/pit toilet, No showers, No RV dump, Tent & RV camping: $14, 2 walk-to sites, Open May-Oct, Reservations not accepted, Elev: 1161ft/354m, Tel: 906-884-2085, Nearest town: Ontonagon. GPS: 46.753662, -88.940674

2 • B1 | Black River Harbor (Ottawa NF)

Total sites: 40, RV sites: 40, Central water, Vault/pit toilet, No showers, No RV dump, Tent & RV camping: $16, Stay limit: 14 days, Open May-Sep, Reservations accepted, Elev: 722ft/220m, Tel: 218-310-1954, Nearest town: Bessemer. GPS: 46.664382, -90.051884

3 • B1 | Blockhouse (Ottawa NF)

Total sites: 4, RV sites: 4, No water, No toilets, Tent & RV camping: Free, Open all year, Reservations not accepted, Elev: 1493ft/455m, Tel: 906-932-1330, Nearest town: Iron River. GPS: 46.242096, -88.633329

4 • B1 | Bob Lake (Ottawa NF)

Total sites: 17, RV sites: 17, Central water, Vault/pit toilet, No showers, No RV dump, Tent & RV camping: $14, Open May-Oct, Reservations not accepted, Elev: 1191ft/363m, Tel: 906-852-3232, Nearest town: Ontonagon. GPS: 46.661865, -88.914551

5 • B1 | Bobcat Lake (Ottawa NF)

Total sites: 11, RV sites: 11, Central water, Vault/pit toilet, No showers, No RV dump, Tent & RV camping: $13, Stay limit: 14 days, Open May-Sep, Reservations not accepted, Elev: 1591ft/485m, Tel: 218-310-1954, Nearest town: Bessemer. GPS: 46.359131, -89.673096

6 • B1 | Golden Lake (Ottawa NF)

Total sites: 22, RV sites: 22, Central water, Vault/pit toilet, No showers, No RV dump, Tent & RV camping: $16, Stay limit: 14 days, Open May-Sep, Reservations not accepted, Elev: 1660ft/506m, Tel: 906-358-4724, Nearest town: Iron River. GPS: 46.171201, -88.883485

7 • B1 | Henry Lake (Ottawa NF)

Total sites: 11, RV sites: 11, Central water, Vault/pit toilet, No showers, No RV dump, Tent & RV camping: $13, Stay limit: 14 days, Open May-Sep, Reservations not accepted, Elev: 1611ft/491m, Tel: 218-310-1954, Nearest town: Marenisco. GPS: 46.330465, -89.792184

8 • B1 | Imp Lake (Ottawa NF)

Total sites: 22, RV sites: 22, Central water, Vault/pit toilet, No showers, No RV dump, Tent & RV camping: $16, Stay limit: 14 days, Open May-Sep, Reservations not accepted, Elev: 1706ft/520m, Tel: 906-265-5420, Nearest town: Watersmeet. GPS: 46.217899, -89.070991

9 • B1 | Lake Ottawa (Ottawa NF)

Total sites: 32, RV sites: 32, Central water, No toilets, No showers, RV dump, Tent & RV camping: $18, Open May-Sep, Reservations not accepted, Elev: 1608ft/490m, Tel: 906-396-5428, Nearest town: Iron River. GPS: 46.078445, -88.761411

10 • B1 | Lake Sainte Kathryn (Ottawa NF)

Total sites: 24, RV sites: 24, Central water, Vault/pit toilet, No showers, No RV dump, Tent & RV camping: $14, Stay limit: 14 days, Open May-Oct, Reservations not accepted, Elev: 1601ft/488m, Tel: 906-852-3232, Nearest town: Sidnaw. GPS: 46.393078, -88.722501

11 • B1 | Langford Lake (Ottawa NF)

Total sites: 11, RV sites: 11, Central water, Vault/pit toilet, No showers, No RV dump, Tent & RV camping: $13, Stay limit: 14 days, Reservations not accepted, Elev: 1686ft/514m, Tel: 218-310-1954, Nearest town: Marenisco. GPS: 46.272686, -89.492335

12 • B1 | Marion Lake East (Ottawa NF)

Total sites: 40, RV sites: 40, Central water, Vault/pit toilet, No showers, No RV dump, Tent & RV camping: $16, Open all year, Reservations not accepted, Elev: 1670ft/509m, Tel: 906-396-5428, Nearest town: Watersmeet. GPS: 46.267477, -89.083501

13 • B1 | Marion Lake West (Ottawa NF)

Total sites: 15, RV sites: 15, Central water, Vault/pit toilet, No showers, No RV dump, Tent & RV camping: $16, Open all year, Reservations not accepted, Elev: 1641ft/500m, Tel: 906-396-5428, Nearest town: Watersmeet. GPS: 46.269505, -89.093077

14 • B1 | Moosehead Lake (Ottawa NF)

Total sites: 13, RV sites: 13, Central water, Vault/pit toilet, No showers, No RV dump, Tent & RV camping: $13, Stay limit: 14 days, Open May-Sep, Reservations not accepted, Elev: 1693ft/516m, Tel: 906-265-5420, Nearest town: Marenisco. GPS: 46.240479, -89.605469

15 • B1 | Norway Lake (Ottawa NF)

Total sites: 27, RV sites: 27, Central water, Vault/pit toilet, No showers, No RV dump, Tent & RV camping: $14, Stay limit: 14 days, Open May-Oct, Reservations not accepted, Elev: 1552ft/473m, Tel: 906-852-3232, Nearest town: Sidnaw. GPS: 46.417480, -88.684326

16 • B1 | Paint River Forks (Ottawa NF)

Total sites: 4, RV sites: 4, No water, Vault/pit toilet, Tent & RV camping: Free, Open May-Sep, Reservations not accepted, Elev: 1466ft/447m, Tel: 906-932-1330, Nearest town: Iron River. GPS: 46.232722, -88.718654

17 • B1 | Perch Lake (Ottawa NF)

Total sites: 20, RV sites: 20, Central water, Vault/pit toilet, No

showers, No RV dump, Tent & RV camping: $14, Stay limit: 14 days, Open May-Oct, Reservations not accepted, Elev: 1539ft/469m, Tel: 906-852-3232, Nearest town: Sidnaw. GPS: 46.364746, -88.674561

18 • B1 | Pomeroy Lake (Ottawa NF)

Total sites: 17, RV sites: 17, Central water, Vault/pit toilet, No showers, No RV dump, Tent & RV camping: $13, Stay limit: 14 days, Open May-Sep, Reservations not accepted, Elev: 1663ft/507m, Tel: 218-310-1954, Nearest town: Marenisco. GPS: 46.282022, -89.573775

19 • B1 | Robbins Pond (Ottawa NF)

Total sites: 3, RV sites: 3, No water, Vault/pit toilet, No showers, No RV dump, Tent & RV camping: Free, Open May-Sep, Reservations not accepted, Elev: 1307ft/398m, Tel: 906-358-4551, Nearest town: Watersmeet. GPS: 46.381058, -89.228336

20 • B1 | Sparrow Rapids (Ottawa NF)

Total sites: 6, RV sites: 6, No water, Vault/pit toilet, Tent & RV camping: Free, Open May-Sep, Reservations not accepted, Elev: 1158ft/353m, Tel: 906-932-1330, Nearest town: Kenton. GPS: 46.504416, -88.947039

21 • B1 | Sturgeon River (Ottawa NF)

Total sites: 9, RV sites: 9, No water, Vault/pit toilet, Tent & RV camping: Free, Open May-Sep, Reservations not accepted, Elev: 1089ft/332m, Tel: 906-932-1330, Nearest town: Baraga. GPS: 46.570499, -88.656194

22 • B1 | Sylvania (Clark Lake) (Ottawa NF)

Total sites: 48, RV sites: 48, Elec sites: 10, Central water, Flush toilet, Free showers, RV dump, Tents: $18/RVs: $23, Open May-Sep, Max Length: 88ft, Reservations not accepted, Elev: 1844ft/562m, Tel: 906-396-5428, Nearest town: Watersmeet. GPS: 46.240682, -89.321216

23 • B1 | Taylor Lake (Ottawa NF)

Total sites: 10, RV sites: 10, Central water, Vault/pit toilet, No showers, No RV dump, Tent & RV camping: Fee unk, Stay limit: 14 days, Open May-Nov, Elev: 1687ft/514m, Tel: 906-358-4724, Nearest town: Watersmeet. GPS: 46.248146, -89.049122

24 • B1 | Tepee Lake (Ottawa NF)

Total sites: 17, RV sites: 17, Central water, Vault/pit toilet, No showers, No RV dump, Tent & RV camping: Fee unk, Stay limit: 14 days, Open May-Nov, Max Length: 60ft, Elev: 1657ft/505m, Tel: 906-932-1330, Nearest town: Sidnaw. GPS: 46.388606, -88.881607

25 • B2 | Au Train Lake (Hiawatha NF)

Total sites: 37, RV sites: 37, Central water, Vault/pit toilet, No showers, No RV dump, Tent & RV camping: $22, Open May-Sep, Max Length: 60ft, Reservations accepted, Elev: 617ft/188m, Tel: 906-387-2512, Nearest town: AuTrain. GPS: 46.393126, -86.836706

26 • B2 | Bass Lake Dispersed (Hiawatha NF)

Total sites: 1, RV sites: 1, No water, Vault/pit toilet, Tent & RV camping: $8, Stay limit: 14 days, Open May-Oct, Max Length: 16ft, Reservations required, Elev: 743ft/226m, Tel: 906-474-6442, Nearest town: Manistique. GPS: 46.169421, -86.479771

27 • B2 | Bay Furnace (Hiawatha NF)

Total sites: 50, RV sites: 50, Central water, Vault/pit toilet, No showers, RV dump, Tent & RV camping: $22, Open May-Oct, Max Length: 65ft, Reservations accepted, Elev: 614ft/187m, Tel: 906-387-2512, Nearest town: Munising. GPS: 46.441406, -86.708252

28 • B2 | Bear Lake Dispersed (Hiawatha NF)

Total sites: 1, RV sites: 1, No water, Tent & RV camping: $8, Tent or small RV, Stay limit: 14 days, Open May-Oct, Max Length: 24ft, Reservations required, Elev: 696ft/212m, Tel: 906-474-6442, Nearest town: Cooks. GPS: 46.072081, -86.501649

29 • B2 | Camp Cook (Hiawatha NF)

Total sites: 4, RV sites: 3, Central water, Vault/pit toilet, No showers, No RV dump, Tent & RV camping: $8, Open May-Oct, Max Length: 40ft, Reservations required, Elev: 771ft/235m, Tel: 906-387-2512, Nearest town: Rapid River. GPS: 46.038867, -86.581558

30 • B2 | Camp Seven Lake (Hiawatha NF)

Total sites: 41, RV sites: 41, Elec sites: 10, Central water, Vault/pit toilet, No showers, No RV dump, Tents: $22/RVs: $26, Group site: $72, Open May-Oct, Max Length: 60ft, Reservations accepted, Elev: 778ft/237m, Tel: 906-428-5800, Nearest town: Rapid River. GPS: 46.057112, -86.548643

31 • B2 | Carr Lake Dispersed (Hiawatha NF)

Total sites: 1, RV sites: 1, No water, No toilets, Tent & RV camping: $8, Stay limit: 14 days, Open May-Oct, Max Length: 32ft, Reservations required, Elev: 682ft/208m, Tel: 906-387-2512, Nearest town: Cooks. GPS: 46.077802, -86.508005

32 • B2 | Chicago Lake (Hiawatha NF)

Total sites: 4, RV sites: 3, No water, Vault/pit toilet, Tent & RV camping: $8, 4x4 recommended, Reservations required, Elev: 784ft/239m, Tel: 906-474-6442, Nearest town: Rapid River. GPS: 46.041351, -86.602312

33 • B2 | Colwell Lake (Hiawatha NF)

Total sites: 39, RV sites: 37, Elec sites: 7, Water available, Vault/pit toilet, No showers, RV dump, Tents: $20-22/RVs: $22-26, Dump Fee: $4, Group site $60, Open May-Oct, Max Length: 60ft, Reservations accepted, Elev: 774ft/236m, Tel: 906-428-5800, Nearest town: Munising. GPS: 46.222168, -86.436279

34 • B2 | Cookson Lake (Hiawatha NF)

Total sites: 5, RV sites: 5, No water, Vault/pit toilet, Tent & RV camping: $8, Open May-Oct, Reservations accepted, Elev: 764ft/233m, Tel: 906-387-3700, Nearest town: Munising. GPS: 46.195305, -86.561425

35 • B2 | Corner Lake (Hiawatha NF)

Total sites: 9, RV sites: 9, Water available, Vault/pit toilet, No showers, No RV dump, Tent & RV camping: $20, Open May-Sep, Reservations not accepted, Elev: 758ft/231m, Tel: 906-428-5800, Nearest town: Munising. GPS: 46.152975, -86.609299

36 • B2 | Council Lake Dispersed (Hiawatha NF)

Total sites: 4, RV sites: 4, No water, Vault/pit toilet, Tent & RV camping: $8, No large RVs, Open May-Oct, Reservations accepted, Elev: 843ft/257m, Tel: 906-387-3700, Nearest town: Munising. GPS: 46.241935, -86.646889

37 • B2 | Crooked Lake Dispersed (Hiawatha NF)

Total sites: 1, RV sites: 1, No water, No toilets, Tent & RV camping: $8, Stay limit: 14 days, Open May-Oct, Max Length: 24ft, Reservations required, Elev: 738ft/225m, Tel: 906-474-6442, Nearest town: Manistique. GPS: 46.216895, -86.431549

38 • B2 | East Lake Dispersed Sites #2 and #3 (Hiawatha NF)

Total sites: 2, RV sites: 1, No water, Vault/pit toilet, Tent & RV camping: $8, Tents or small RVs. Site #3, Stay limit: 14 days, Open May-Oct, Max Length: 24ft, Reservations accepted, Elev: 705ft/215m, Nearest town: Manistique. GPS: 46.181400, -86.422283

39 • B2 | Ewing Point Dispersed (Hiawatha NF)

Total sites: 1, RV sites: 0, No water, Vault/pit toilet, Tents only: $8, Walk-to sites, Open May-Oct, Reservations required, Elev: 804ft/245m, Tel: 906-387-3700, Nearest town: Munising. GPS: 46.217506, -86.590908

40 • B2 | Flowing Well (Hiawatha NF)

Total sites: 10, RV sites: 10, Central water, Vault/pit toilet, No showers, No RV dump, Tent & RV camping: $22, Water has a heavy iron and sulfur content but is safe to consume, Open May-Oct, Max Length: 25ft, Reservations accepted, Elev: 630ft/192m, Tel: 906-341-5666, Nearest town: Rapid River. GPS: 45.936827, -86.706979

41 • B2 | Gooseneck Lake Dispersed (Hiawatha NF)

Total sites: 4, RV sites: 1, No water, Vault/pit toilet, Tent & RV camping: $8, Small RVs only, Stay limit: 14 days, Open May-Oct, Reservations required, Elev: 784ft/239m, Tel: 906-474-6442, Nearest town: Rapid River. GPS: 46.071868, -86.545166

42 • B2 | Haymeadow Creek Dispersed (Hiawatha NF)

Total sites: 5, RV sites: 5, Water available, Vault/pit toilet, No showers, No RV dump, Tent & RV camping: Free, Open May-Oct, Reservations not accepted, Elev: 738ft/225m, Nearest town: Rapid River. GPS: 46.021671, -86.856812

43 • B2 | Hovey Lake Dispersed (Hiawatha NF)

Total sites: 5, RV sites: 5, No water, Vault/pit toilet, No showers, No RV dump, Tent & RV camping: Free, Open May-Oct, Reservations not accepted, Elev: 892ft/272m, Tel: 906-786-4062, Nearest town: Munising. GPS: 46.289343, -86.700959

44 • B2 | Indian River (Hiawatha NF)

Total sites: 5, RV sites: 5, Water available, Vault/pit toilet, No showers, No RV dump, Tent & RV camping: $20, Open May-Oct, Reservations not accepted, Elev: 718ft/219m, Tel: 906-428-5800, Nearest town: Manistique. GPS: 46.154755, -86.403878

45 • B2 | Ironjaw Lake (Hiawatha NF)

Total sites: 1, RV sites: 1, No water, Vault/pit toilet, No showers, No RV dump, Tent & RV camping: $8, Tent or small RV, Horses OK., Stay limit: 14 days, Open May-Oct, Max Length: 24ft, Reservations required, Elev: 791ft/241m, Nearest town: Rapid River. GPS: 46.171497, -86.548521

46 • B2 | Island Lake (Hiawatha NF)

Total sites: 23, RV sites: 23, Central water, Vault/pit toilet, No showers, No RV dump, Tent & RV camping: $22, Group site: $50, Open May-Sep, Max Length: 45ft, Reservations accepted, Elev: 860ft/262m, Tel: 906-387-2512, Nearest town: Munising. GPS: 46.270020, -86.650635

47 • B2 | Jackpine Lake Dispersed (Hiawatha NF)

Total sites: 2, RV sites: 1, No water, Vault/pit toilet, Tent & RV camping: $8, Stay limit: 14 days, Open May-Oct, Reservations accepted, Elev: 728ft/222m, Tel: 906-341-5666, Nearest town: Cooks. GPS: 46.115965, -86.524789

48 • B2 | Leg Lake Site #1 (Hiawatha NF)

Total sites: 1, RV sites: 1, No water, Vault/pit toilet, Tent & RV camping: $8, Stay limit: 14 days, Open May-Oct, Reservations required, Elev: 702ft/214m, Tel: 906-387-2512, Nearest town: Manistique. GPS: 46.128326, -86.485941

49 • B2 | Leg Lake Site #2 (Hiawatha NF)

Total sites: 1, RV sites: 0, No water, Vault/pit toilet, Tents only: $8, Stay limit: 14 days, Open May-Oct, Reservations required, Elev: 718ft/219m, Tel: 906-387-2512, Nearest town: Manistique. GPS: 46.130153, -86.481258

50 • B2 | Little Bass Lake (Hiawatha NF)

Total sites: 12, RV sites: 12, Central water, Vault/pit toilet, No showers, No RV dump, Tent & RV camping: $8, Stay limit: 14 days, Open May-Oct, Max Length: 24ft, Reservations required, Elev: 794ft/242m, Tel: 906-428-5800, Nearest town: Manistique. GPS: 46.162973, -86.449885

51 • B2 | Little Bay de Noc - Maywood Loop (Hiawatha NF)

Total sites: 14, RV sites: 14, Central water, Vault/pit toilet, No showers, No RV dump, Tent & RV camping: $22, Open May-Oct, Max Length: 60ft, Reservations accepted, Elev: 597ft/182m, Tel: 906-428-5800, Nearest town: Rapid River. GPS: 45.841134, -86.984074

52 • B2 | Little Bay de Noc - Twin Springs/Oaks Loops (Hiawatha NF)

Total sites: 22, RV sites: 22, Central water, Vault/pit toilet, No showers, No RV dump, Tent & RV camping: $22, 2 group sites: $60, Open May-Oct, Max Length: 60ft, Reservations accepted, Elev: 594ft/181m, Tel: 906-428-5800, Nearest town: Rapid River. GPS: 45.833336, -86.992321

53 • B2 | Lyman Lake Dispersed (Hiawatha NF)

Total sites: 10, RV sites: 7, No water, Vault/pit toilet, Tent & RV camping: $8, Stay limit: 14 days, Open May-Oct, Reservations required, Elev: 768ft/234m, Tel: 906-474-6442, Nearest town: Rapid River. GPS: 46.069695, -86.530468

54 • B2 | Mowe Lake Dispersed (Hiawatha NF)

Total sites: 2, RV sites: 2, No water, Vault/pit toilet, Tent & RV camping: $8, Stay limit: 14 days, Open May-Oct, Reservations accepted, Elev: 810ft/247m, Tel: 906-341-5666, Nearest town: Rapid River. GPS: 46.144645, -86.577165

55 • B2 | Pete's Lake (Hiawatha NF)

Total sites: 46, RV sites: 46, Central water, Vault/pit toilet, No showers, No RV dump, Tent & RV camping: $22-24, Open May-Sep, Max Length: 75ft, Reservations accepted, Elev: 837ft/255m, Tel: 906-387-2512, Nearest town: Munising. GPS: 46.229511, -86.598265

56 • B2 | Steuben Lake Dispersed Site #1 (Hiawatha NF)

Total sites: 1, RV sites: 1, No water, Vault/pit toilet, Tent & RV camping: $8, Stay limit: 14 days, Open May-Oct, Reservations required, Elev: 718ft/219m, Tel: 906-474-6442, Nearest town: Manistique. GPS: 46.196763, -86.425825

57 • B2 | Steuben Lake Dispersed Site #2 (Hiawatha NF)

Total sites: 1, RV sites: 1, No water, Vault/pit toilet, Tent & RV camping: $8, Stay limit: 14 days, Open May-Oct, Reservations required, Elev: 738ft/225m, Tel: 906-474-6442, Nearest town: Manistique. GPS: 46.199945, -86.428459

58 • B2 | Swan Lake Dispersed Site #1 (Hiawatha NF)

Total sites: 1, RV sites: 0, No water, Vault/pit toilet, Tents only: $8, Horses OK, Stay limit: 14 days, Open May-Oct, Reservations required, Elev: 768ft/234m, Tel: 906-474-6442, Nearest town: Rapid River. GPS: 46.165324, -86.578451

59 • B2 | Swan Lake Dispersed Sites #2,3,4 (Hiawatha NF)

Total sites: 3, RV sites: 3, No water, Vault/pit toilet, Tent & RV camping: $8, Tent or small RV. Horses OK, Stay limit: 14 days, Open May-Oct, Reservations required, Elev: 774ft/236m, Tel: 906-474-6442, Nearest town: Rapid River. GPS: 46.162495, -86.573411

60 • B2 | Triangle Lake Dispersed Site #1 (Hiawatha NF)

Total sites: 1, RV sites: 1, No water, Vault/pit toilet, Tent & RV camping: $8, Horses OK, Stay limit: 14 days, Open May-Oct, Max Length: 32ft, Reservations required, Elev: 824ft/251m, Tel: 906-474-6442, Nearest town: Manistique. GPS: 46.167124, -86.496967

61 • B2 | Triangle Lake Dispersed Site #2 (Hiawatha NF)

Total sites: 1, RV sites: 0, No water, No toilets, Tents only: $8, Stay limit: 14 days, Open May-Oct, Reservations required, Elev: 800ft/244m, Tel: 906-474-6442. GPS: 46.174328, -86.503428

62 • B2 | Widewaters (Hiawatha NF)

Total sites: 34, RV sites: 34, Water available, Vault/pit toilet, No showers, No RV dump, Tent & RV camping: $22, Open May-Sep, Max Length: 58ft, Reservations accepted, Elev: 804ft/245m, Tel: 906-387-2512, Nearest town: Munising. GPS: 46.217285, -86.627197

63 • B3 | Bay View (Hiawatha NF)

Total sites: 24, RV sites: 24, Central water, Vault/pit toilet, No showers, No RV dump, Tent & RV camping: $18, Open May-Oct, Max Length: 50ft, Reservations accepted, Elev: 594ft/181m, Tel: 906-203-9872, Nearest town: Raco. GPS: 46.449661, -84.781185

64 • B3 | Brevoort Lake (Hiawatha NF)

Total sites: 70, RV sites: 70, Central water, Flush toilet, No showers, RV dump, Tent & RV camping: $20, Dump Fee, Open May-Oct, Max Length: 45ft, Reservations accepted, Elev: 633ft/193m, Tel: 906-203-9872, Nearest town: Brevort. GPS: 46.007719, -84.972433

65 • B3 | Carp River (Hiawatha NF)

Total sites: 38, RV sites: 38, Water available, Vault/pit toilet, No showers, No RV dump, Tent & RV camping: $18, Open May-Oct, Max Length: 35ft, Reservations accepted, Elev: 646ft/197m, Tel: 906-203-9872, Nearest town: St. Ignace. GPS: 46.031941, -84.721499

66 • B3 | Lake Michigan (St Ignace) (Hiawatha NF)

Total sites: 34, RV sites: 34, Central water, Flush toilet, No showers, No RV dump, Tent & RV camping: $20, Open May-Oct, Max Length: 45ft, Reservations accepted, Elev: 606ft/185m, Tel: 906-203-9872, Nearest town: St. Ignace. GPS: 45.985685, -84.971857

67 • B3 | Monocle Lake (Hiawatha NF)

Total sites: 42, RV sites: 42, Central water, Vault/pit toilet, No showers, No RV dump, Tent & RV camping: $18, Open May-Sep, Max Length: 80ft, Reservations accepted, Elev: 666ft/203m, Tel: 906-203-9872, Nearest town: Bay Mills. GPS: 46.472168, -84.639404

68 • B3 | Soldier Lake (Hiawatha NF)

Total sites: 43, RV sites: 43, Central water, Vault/pit toilet, No showers, No RV dump, Tent & RV camping: $18, Open May-Sep, Max Length: 75ft, Reservations accepted, Elev: 902ft/275m, Tel: 906-203-9872, Nearest town: Raco. GPS: 46.348674, -84.864005

69 • B3 | Three Lakes (Hiawatha NF)

Total sites: 28, RV sites: 28, Water available, Vault/pit toilet, No showers, No RV dump, Tent & RV camping: $16, Open May-Oct, Max Length: 20ft, Reservations not accepted, Elev: 879ft/268m, Tel: 906-643-7900, Nearest town: Sault Ste Marie. GPS: 46.319824, -84.981689

70 • C3 | Bear Track (Huron-Manistee NF)

Total sites: 20, RV sites: 15, Central water, Vault/pit toilet, No showers, No RV dump, Tent & RV camping: $18, Open May-Sep, Reservations not accepted, Elev: 751ft/229m, Tel: 231-723-2211, Nearest town: Irons. GPS: 44.147657, -86.031859

71 • C3 | Benton Lake (Huron-Manistee NF)

Total sites: 25, RV sites: 25, Central water, Vault/pit toilet, No showers, No RV dump, Tent & RV camping: $18, Open May-Sep, Reservations not accepted, Elev: 804ft/245m, Tel: 231-745-4631, Nearest town: Brohman. GPS: 43.669678, -85.890381

72 • C3 | Blacksmith Bayou Access (Huron-Manistee NF)

Total sites: 6, RV sites: 6, No water, Vault/pit toilet, Tent & RV camping: $5, Open Apr-Nov, Reservations not accepted, Elev: 614ft/187m, Tel: 231-723-2211, Nearest town: Brethren. GPS: 44.261574, -86.034838

73 • C3 | Bowman Bridge (Huron-Manistee NF)

Total sites: 20, RV sites: 16, Central water, Vault/pit toilet, No

showers, No RV dump, Tent & RV camping: $22, Group site: $80, Open May-Oct, Max Length: 50ft, Reservations accepted, Elev: 758ft/231m, Tel: 231-745-4631, Nearest town: Baldwin. GPS: 43.888228, -85.941584

74 • C3 | Bowman Lake (Huron-Manistee NF)

Total sites: 4, Central water, Vault/pit toilet, No showers, No RV dump, Tents only: Free, Walk-to sites, Open all year, Reservations not accepted, Elev: 804ft/245m, Tel: 801-226-3564, Nearest town: Baldwin. GPS: 43.891336, -85.967527

75 • C3 | Brush Lake (Huron-Manistee NF)

Total sites: 7, RV sites: 7, No water, Vault/pit toilet, Tent & RV camping: $10, Open all year, Max Length: 35ft, Reservations not accepted, Elev: 1014ft/309m, Tel: 231-745-4631, Nearest town: Woodville. GPS: 43.639086, -85.689831

76 • C3 | Claybanks (Huron-Manistee NF)

Total sites: 9, RV sites: 9, Central water, Vault/pit toilet, No showers, No RV dump, Tent & RV camping: $10, Open May-Sep, Max Length: 25ft, Reservations not accepted, Elev: 843ft/257m, Tel: 231-745-4631, Nearest town: Baldwin. GPS: 43.868354, -85.881645

77 • C3 | Condon Lake (Huron-Manistee NF)

Total sites: 6, RV sites: 6, No water, Vault/pit toilet, No showers, No RV dump, Tent & RV camping: Free, Open all year, Reservations not accepted, Elev: 879ft/268m, Tel: 231-745-4631, Nearest town: Baldwin. GPS: 43.738838, -85.890756

78 • C3 | Government Landing (Huron-Manistee NF)

Total sites: 3, RV sites: 0, No water, Vault/pit toilet, Tents only: Free, Open Apr-Nov, Reservations not accepted, Elev: 745ft/227m, Tel: 231-723-2211, Nearest town: Brethren. GPS: 44.264847, -85.936138

79 • C3 | Hemlock (Huron-Manistee NF)

Total sites: 18, RV sites: 18, Central water, Vault/pit toilet, No showers, No RV dump, Tent & RV camping: $18, Open May-Sep, Reservations not accepted, Elev: 1326ft/404m, Tel: 231-723-2211, Nearest town: Cadillac. GPS: 44.231464, -85.503312

80 • C3 | Highbank Lake (Huron-Manistee NF)

Total sites: 9, RV sites: 9, Central water, Vault/pit toilet, No showers, No RV dump, Tent & RV camping: $18, Open May-Sep, Max Length: 20ft, Reservations not accepted, Elev: 928ft/283m, Tel: 231-745-4631, Nearest town: Bitely. GPS: 43.770904, -85.888797

81 • C3 | Hungerford Lake (Huron-Manistee NF)

Total sites: 2, RV sites: 2, No water, Vault/pit toilet, No showers, No RV dump, Tent & RV camping: Free, Open May-Oct, Reservations not accepted, Elev: 1087ft/331m, Tel: 231-745-4631, Nearest town: Big Rapids. GPS: 43.695657, -85.618769

82 • C3 | Hungerford Trail Camp (Huron-Manistee NF)

Total sites: 48, RV sites: 48, Central water, Vault/pit toilet, Tent & RV camping: $15, Group site: $75, Open May-Oct, Reservations not accepted, Elev: 1131ft/345m, Tel: 231-745-4631, Nearest town: Big Rapids. GPS: 43.701425, -85.621094

83 • C3 | Indian Lake (Huron-Manistee NF)

Total sites: 6, RV sites: 6, No water, Vault/pit toilet, Tent & RV camping: $10, Open all year, Reservations not accepted, Elev: 974ft/297m, Tel: 231-745-4631, Nearest town: Brohman. GPS: 43.670189, -85.829379

84 • C3 | Kneff Lake (Huron-Manistee NF)

Total sites: 27, RV sites: 27, Central water, Vault/pit toilet, No showers, No RV dump, Tent & RV camping: $15, Open May-Sep, Max Length: 25ft, Reservations not accepted, Elev: 1201ft/366m, Tel: 989-826-3252, Nearest town: Grayling. GPS: 44.636963, -84.579102

85 • C3 | Lake Michigan (Manistee) (Huron-Manistee NF)

Total sites: 99, RV sites: 99, Central water, Vault/pit toilet, No showers, No RV dump, Tent & RV camping: $29, Group sites: $60-$79, Open May-Oct, Max Length: 54ft, Reservations accepted, Elev: 659ft/201m, Tel: 231-723-2211, Nearest town: Manistee. GPS: 44.115537, -86.423471

86 • C3 | Luzerne Horse Camp (Huron-Manistee NF)

Total sites: 10, RV sites: 10, No water, Vault/pit toilet, Tent & RV camping: Free, Open all year, Reservations not accepted, Elev: 1296ft/395m, Tel: 989-826-3252, Nearest town: Luzerne. GPS: 44.586531, -84.288383

87 • C3 | Marzinski Horse Camp (Huron-Manistee NF)

Total sites: 21, RV sites: 21, Central water, Vault/pit toilet, No showers, No RV dump, Tent & RV camping: Free, Open May-Nov, Reservations not accepted, Elev: 712ft/217m, Tel: 231-723-2211, Nearest town: Wellston. GPS: 44.225735, -86.161871

88 • C3 | Meadows ORV (Huron-Manistee NF)

Total sites: 16, RV sites: 16, Central water, Vault/pit toilet, No showers, No RV dump, Tent & RV camping: $10, Not plowed in winter, Open all year, Max Length: 25ft, Reservations not accepted, Elev: 1161ft/354m, Tel: 989-826-3252, Nearest town: Luzerne. GPS: 44.559948, -84.311133

89 • C3 | Minnie Pond (Huron-Manistee NF)

Total sites: 11, RV sites: 11, No water, Vault/pit toilet, Tent & RV camping: $10, Open all year, Max Length: 25ft, Reservations not accepted, Elev: 830ft/253m, Tel: 231-745-4631, Nearest town: White Cloud. GPS: 43.627076, -85.898939

90 • C3 | Old Grade (Huron-Manistee NF)

Total sites: 20, RV sites: 20, Central water, Vault/pit toilet, No showers, No RV dump, Tent & RV camping: $18, Open Apr-Sep, Reservations not accepted, Elev: 882ft/269m, Tel: 231-745-4631, Nearest town: Baldwin. GPS: 44.060791, -85.849365

91 • C3 | Peterson Bridge (Huron-Manistee NF)

Total sites: 30, RV sites: 17, Central water, Vault/pit toilet, No showers, No RV dump, Tent & RV camping: $23-25, Open Apr-Oct, Max Length: 64ft, Reservations accepted, Elev: 817ft/249m, Tel: 231-745-4631, Nearest town: Baldwin. GPS: 44.201917, -85.798837

92 • C3 | Pine Lake (Huron-Manistee NF)

Total sites: 12, RV sites: 12, Central water, Vault/pit toilet, No showers, No RV dump, Tent & RV camping: $18, Open May-Sep, Reservations not accepted, Elev: 755ft/230m, Tel: 231-723-2211, Nearest town: Wellston. GPS: 44.195567, -86.009457

93 • C3 | Red Bridge Access (Huron-Manistee NF)

Total sites: 4, RV sites: 4, Central water, Vault/pit toilet, No showers, No RV dump, Tent & RV camping: Free, Reservations not accepted, Elev: 709ft/216m, Tel: 231-723-2211, Nearest town: Brethren. GPS: 44.283925, -85.861524

94 • C3 | Sand Lake (Huron-Manistee NF)

Total sites: 47, RV sites: 47, Central water, Flush toilet, Free showers, No RV dump, Tent & RV camping: $25, Group site: $61, Open May-Sep, Max Length: 40ft, Reservations accepted, Elev: 863ft/263m, Tel: 231-723-2211, Nearest town: Wellston. GPS: 44.165814, -85.936383

95 • C3 | Sawdust Hole Access (Huron-Manistee NF)

Total sites: 8, RV sites: 8, No water, Vault/pit toilet, Tent & RV camping: $5, Open Apr-Nov, Reservations not accepted, Elev: 696ft/212m, Tel: 231-723-2211, Nearest town: Brethren. GPS: 44.268511, -85.952483

96 • C3 | Seaton Creek (Huron-Manistee NF)

Total sites: 17, RV sites: 17, Central water, Vault/pit toilet, No showers, No RV dump, Tent & RV camping: $22, 2 group site $44, Open May-Sep, Reservations accepted, Elev: 873ft/266m, Tel: 231-723-2211, Nearest town: Mesick. GPS: 44.358046, -85.809591

97 • C3 | Shelley Lake (Huron-Manistee NF)

Total sites: 8, RV sites: 8, No water, Vault/pit toilet, Tent & RV camping: $10, Max Length: 22ft, Reservations not accepted, Elev: 975ft/297m, Tel: 231-745-4631, Nearest town: Brohman. GPS: 43.711566, -85.816976

98 • C3 | South Nichols Lake (Huron-Manistee NF)

Total sites: 30, RV sites: 30, Central water, No toilets, No showers, No RV dump, Tent & RV camping: $20-22, Open May-Sep, Max Length: 65ft, Reservations accepted, Elev: 824ft/251m, Tel: 231-745-4631, Nearest town: Brohman. GPS: 43.723877, -85.903564

99 • C3 | Sulak (Huron-Manistee NF)

Total sites: 12, RV sites: 12, No water, Vault/pit toilet, Tent & RV camping: Free, Open May-Oct, Max Length: 25ft, Reservations not accepted, Elev: 791ft/241m, Tel: 231-745-4631, Nearest town: Baldwin. GPS: 43.924342, -86.011379

100 • C3 | Timber Creek (Huron-Manistee NF)

Total sites: 9, RV sites: 9, Central water, Vault/pit toilet, No showers, No RV dump, Tent & RV camping: $10, Open all year, Max Length: 50ft, Reservations not accepted, Elev: 830ft/253m, Tel: 231-745-4631, Nearest town: Branch. GPS: 43.948292, -85.995896

101 • C3 | Wakeley Lake (Huron-Manistee NF)

Total sites: 5, RV sites: 5, No water, Vault/pit toilet, Tent & RV camping: $10, Parking lot plowed in winter, Reservations not accepted, Elev: 1116ft/340m, Tel: 989-826-3252, Nearest town: Grayling. GPS: 44.633281, -84.508971

102 • C3 | Walkup Lake (Huron-Manistee NF)

Total sites: 12, RV sites: 12, Central water, Vault/pit toilet, No showers, No RV dump, Tent & RV camping: $10, Not plowed in winter, Open all year, Max Length: 35ft, Reservations not accepted, Elev: 863ft/263m, Tel: 231-745-4631, Nearest town: Bitely. GPS: 43.733822, -85.904996

103 • C3 | Whelan Lake (Huron-Manistee NF)

Total sites: 6, RV sites: 0, No water, No toilets, Tents only: Free, Not plowed in winter, Reservations not accepted, Elev: 650ft/198m, Tel: 231-745-4631, Nearest town: Walhalla. GPS: 43.910743, -86.152935

104 • C4 | Au Sable Loop (Huron-Manistee NF)

Total sites: 5, RV sites: 5, Central water, Vault/pit toilet, No showers, No RV dump, Tent & RV camping: $10, Max Length: 25ft, Reservations not accepted, Elev: 938ft/286m, Tel: 989-826-3252, Nearest town: Mio. GPS: 44.651868, -84.099871

105 • C4 | Buttercup (Huron-Manistee NF)

Total sites: 3, RV sites: 3, No water, Vault/pit toilet, Tent & RV camping: Free, Not plowed in winter, Reservations not accepted, Elev: 899ft/274m, Tel: 989-826-3252, Nearest town: Mio. GPS: 44.641338, -83.913507

106 • C4 | Cathedral Pines (Huron-Manistee NF)

Total sites: 1, RV sites: 0, No water, Vault/pit toilet, Tents only: Free, Walk-to sites, .25 mi, Reservations not accepted, Elev: 892ft/272m, Tel: 989-826-3252, Nearest town: Mio. GPS: 44.655521, -84.007291

107 • C4 | Gabions (Huron-Manistee NF)

Total sites: 4, RV sites: 4, No water, Vault/pit toilet, Tent & RV camping: $10, Not plowed in winter, Open all year, Max Length: 25ft, Reservations not accepted, Elev: 846ft/258m, Tel: 989-826-3252, Nearest town: Glennie. GPS: 44.620952, -83.846278

108 • C4 | Horseshoe Lake (Huron-Manistee NF)

Total sites: 9, RV sites: 9, Central water, Vault/pit toilet, No showers, No RV dump, Tent & RV camping: $10, Open May-Nov, Max Length: 25ft, Reservations not accepted, Elev: 984ft/300m, Tel: 989-739-0728, Nearest town: Curran. GPS: 44.600795, -83.765459

109 • C4 | Island Lake (Hiawatha NF)

Total sites: 17, RV sites: 17, Water available, Vault/pit toilet, No showers, No RV dump, Tent & RV camping: $15, Open May-Sep, Max Length: 25ft, Reservations not accepted, Elev: 1310ft/399m, Tel: 989-826-3252, Nearest town: Mio. GPS: 44.508723, -84.141476

110 • C4 | Jewell Lake (Huron-Manistee NF)

Total sites: 32, RV sites: 32, Central water, Vault/pit toilet, No showers, No RV dump, Tent & RV camping: $15, Open May-Oct, Max Length: 25ft, Reservations not accepted, Elev: 846ft/258m, Tel: 989-739-0728, Nearest town: Harrisville. GPS: 44.677979, -83.599121

111 • C4 | Mack Lake ORV (Huron-Manistee NF)

Total sites: 42, RV sites: 42, Central water, Vault/pit toilet, No showers, No RV dump, Tent & RV camping: $15, Open May-Nov, Max Length: 50ft, Reservations not accepted, Elev: 1184ft/361m, Tel: 989-826-3252, Nearest town: Mio. GPS: 44.577637, -84.064453

112 • C4 | Meadow Springs (Huron-Manistee NF)

Total sites: 2, RV sites: 0, No water, Vault/pit toilet, Tents only: Free, Walk-to/boat-in sites, Open all year, Reservations not accepted, Elev: 942ft/287m, Tel: 989-826-3252, Nearest town: Mio. GPS: 44.656779, -84.075887

113 • C4 | Monument (Huron-Manistee NF)

Total sites: 19, RV sites: 19, Central water, Vault/pit toilet, No showers, No RV dump, Tent & RV camping: $15, Open May-Oct, Max Length: 50ft, Reservations accepted, Elev: 846ft/258m, Tel: 989-739-0728, Nearest town: Oscoda. GPS: 44.434149, -83.620150

114 • C4 | Pine River (Huron-Manistee NF)

Total sites: 11, RV sites: 11, Central water, Vault/pit toilet, No showers, No RV dump, Tent & RV camping: $15, Open May-Nov, Max Length: 25ft, Reservations not accepted, Elev: 761ft/232m, Tel: 989-739-0728, Nearest town: Mikado. GPS: 44.563721, -83.599609

115 • C4 | River Dunes (Huron-Manistee NF)

Total sites: 1, RV sites: 0, No water, Vault/pit toilet, Tents only: Free, Walk-to sites, Not plowed in winter, Reservations not accepted, Elev: 928ft/283m, Tel: 989-826-3252, Nearest town: Mio. GPS: 44.648563, -84.094221

116 • C4 | Rollways (Huron-Manistee NF)

Total sites: 19, RV sites: 19, Central water, Vault/pit toilet, No showers, No RV dump, Tent & RV camping: $15, Open May-Sep, Max Length: 55ft, Reservations accepted, Elev: 864ft/263m, Tel: 989-739-0728, Nearest town: Hale. GPS: 44.459557, -83.773463

117 • C4 | Round Lake (Huron-Manistee NF)

Total sites: 33, RV sites: 33, Central water, Vault/pit toilet, No showers, No RV dump, Tent & RV camping: $14, Open May-Sep, Max Length: 40ft, Reservations accepted, Elev: 800ft/244m, Tel: 989-739-0728, Nearest town: Hale. GPS: 44.341029, -83.663457

118 • C4 | South Branch Trail Camp (Huron-Manistee NF)

Total sites: 21, RV sites: 21, Central water, Vault/pit toilet, No showers, No RV dump, Tent & RV camping: $15, Reservable group site - free, Open May-Nov, Reservations not accepted, Elev: 863ft/263m, Tel: 989-739-0728, Nearest town: Hale. GPS: 44.485438, -83.796343

119 • C4 | Wagner Lake (Huron-Manistee NF)

Total sites: 12, RV sites: 12, Central water, Vault/pit toilet, No showers, No RV dump, Tent & RV camping: $15, 3 group sites, Open May-Sep, Max Length: 50ft, Reservations not accepted, Elev: 1158ft/353m, Tel: 989-826-3252, Nearest town: Mio. GPS: 44.553223, -84.147217

120 • D3 | Diamond Point (Huron-Manistee NF)

Total sites: 2, RV sites: 2, No water, Vault/pit toilet, Tent & RV camping: $10, Open May-Nov, Max Length: 20ft, Reservations not accepted, Elev: 617ft/188m, Tel: 231-745-4631, Nearest town: Muskegon. GPS: 43.474614, -86.212343

121 • D3 | Pines Point (Huron-Manistee NF)

Total sites: 29, RV sites: 29, Central water, Vault/pit toilet, No showers, No RV dump, Tent & RV camping: $18, Reservable group site $66, Open May-Oct, Max Length: 40ft, Reservations not accepted, Elev: 663ft/202m, Tel: 231-745-4631, Nearest town: Hesperia. GPS: 43.527786, -86.119390

122 • D3 | Twinwood Lake (Huron-Manistee NF)

Total sites: 5, RV sites: 5, No water, Vault/pit toilet, Tent & RV camping: $10, Not plowed in winter, Open all year, Reservations not accepted, Elev: 755ft/230m, Tel: 231-745-4631, Nearest town: White Cloud. GPS: 43.476112, -85.767567

Minnesota

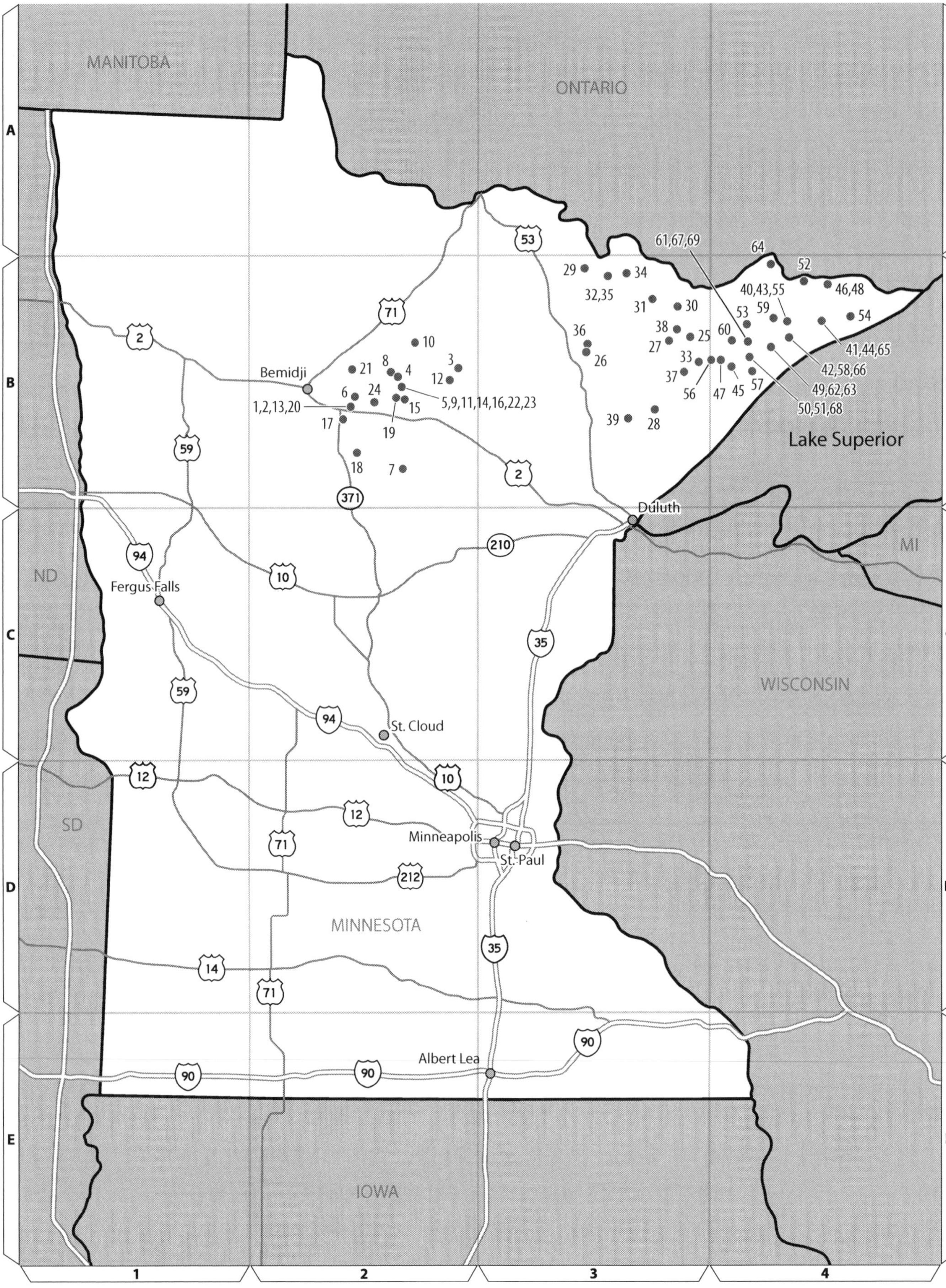
MANITOBA
ONTARIO
A
B
C
D
E
1
2
3
4
61,67,69
64
52
29
34
32,35
40,43,55
46,48
31
30
53
59
54
36
38
25
60
27
41,44,65
10
33
26
3
8
21
4
37
56
47
45
57
42,58,66
Bemidji
12
6
24
5,9,11,14,16,22,23
49,62,63
1,2,13,20
15
50,51,68
17
19
39
28
Lake Superior
18
7
Duluth
MI
ND
Fergus Falls
WISCONSIN
St. Cloud
SD
Minneapolis
St. Paul
MINNESOTA
Albert Lea
IOWA
53
71
2
59
371
210
94
10
35
12
212
14
90

Map	ID	Map	ID
B2	1-24	B4	40-69
B3	25-39		

Alphabetical List of Camping Areas

1 • B2 | Cass Lake (Chippewa NF)

Total sites: 23, RV sites: 23, Central water, Flush toilet, Free showers, RV dump, Tent & RV camping: $21, Open May-Sep, Max Length: 60ft, Reservations accepted, Elev: 1289ft/393m, Tel: 218-335-8600, Nearest town: Cass Lake. GPS: 47.379944, -94.529361

2 • B2 | Chippewa (Chippewa NF)

Total sites: 46, RV sites: 46, Elec sites: 46, Central water, Flush toilet, Free showers, RV dump, Tent & RV camping: $26, Open May-Sep, Max Length: 64ft, Reservations accepted, Elev: 1358ft/414m, Tel: 218-335-8600, Nearest town: Bemidji. GPS: 47.382888, -94.510472

3 • B2 | Clubhouse Lake (Chippewa NF)

Total sites: 47, RV sites: 47, Central water, Vault/pit toilet, No showers, No RV dump, Tent & RV camping: $16, Open May-Nov, Reservations not accepted, Elev: 1411ft/430m, Tel: 218-335-8600, Nearest town: Marcell. GPS: 47.610350, -93.577150

4 • B2 | Cut Foot Horse Camp (Chippewa NF)

Total sites: 34, RV sites: 34, Central water, Vault/pit toilet, No showers, No RV dump, Tent & RV camping: $16, Open Apr-Oct, Max Length: 45ft, Reservations accepted, Elev: 1408ft/429m, Tel: 218-335-8600, Nearest town: Deer River. GPS: 47.559298, -94.110275

5 • B2 | East Seelye Bay (Chippewa NF)

Total sites: 13, RV sites: 13, Central water, Vault/pit toilet, No showers, No RV dump, Tent & RV camping: $16, Open May-Oct, Reservations not accepted, Elev: 1316ft/401m, Tel: 218-335-8600, Nearest town: Deer River. GPS: 47.524227, -94.095952

6 • B2 | Knutson Dam (Chippewa NF)

Total sites: 14, RV sites: 14, Central water, Vault/pit toilet, No showers, No RV dump, Tent & RV camping: $16, Open May-Sep, Reservations not accepted, Elev: 1293ft/394m, Tel: 218-835-4291, Nearest town: Cass Lake. GPS: 47.450684, -94.483154

7 • B2 | Mabel Lake (Chippewa NF)

Total sites: 22, RV sites: 22, Central water, Vault/pit toilet, No showers, No RV dump, Tent & RV camping: $14, Open May-Sep,

Elev: 1348ft/411m, Tel: 218-335-8600, Nearest town: Remer. GPS: 47.049686, -94.072044

8 • B2 | Middle Pigeon Lake (Chippewa NF)

Total sites: 4, RV sites: 0, Central water, Vault/pit toilet, No showers, No RV dump, Tents only: Free, Elev: 1355ft/413m, Tel: 218-246-2123, Nearest town: Squaw Lake. GPS: 47.586730, -94.166130

9 • B2 | Mosomo Point (Chippewa NF)

Total sites: 23, RV sites: 23, Central water, Vault/pit toilet, No showers, No RV dump, Tent & RV camping: $16, Open May-Sep, Max Length: 45ft, Reservations accepted, Elev: 1335ft/407m, Tel: 218-335-8600, Nearest town: Deer River. GPS: 47.517817, -94.048071

10 • B2 | Noma Lake (Chippewa NF)

Total sites: 14, RV sites: 14, Central water, Vault/pit toilet, No showers, No RV dump, Tent & RV camping: $14, Open May-Sep, Reservations not accepted, Elev: 1332ft/406m, Tel: 218-335-8600, Nearest town: Wirt. GPS: 47.756274, -93.966107

11 • B2 | North Deer Lake (Chippewa NF)

Total sites: 17, RV sites: 17, Central water, Vault/pit toilet, No showers, No RV dump, Tent & RV camping: $16, Open May-Oct, Max Length: 45ft, Reservations accepted, Elev: 1365ft/416m, Tel: 218-335-8600, Nearest town: Deer River. GPS: 47.517761, -94.101456

12 • B2 | North Star (Chippewa NF)

Total sites: 38, RV sites: 38, Central water, Vault/pit toilet, No showers, No RV dump, Tent & RV camping: $14, Open May-Oct, Reservations not accepted, Elev: 1398ft/426m, Tel: 218-335-8600, Nearest town: Marcell. GPS: 47.556925, -93.652379

13 • B2 | Norway Beach (Chippewa NF)

Total sites: 55, RV sites: 55, Central water, Flush toilet, Free showers, No RV dump, Tent & RV camping: $21, Open May-Sep, Max Length: 75ft, Reservations accepted, Elev: 1329ft/405m, Tel: 218-335-8600, Nearest town: Cass Lake. GPS: 47.379662, -94.517959

14 • B2 | O-Ne-Gum-E (Chippewa NF)

Total sites: 48, RV sites: 48, Elec sites: 42, Central water, Vault/pit toilet, No showers, No RV dump, Tents: $16/RVs: $23, Electric extra $, Open May-Oct, Max Length: 45ft, Reservations accepted, Elev: 1312ft/400m, Tel: 218-335-8600, Nearest town: Deer River. GPS: 47.510964, -94.043215

15 • B2 | Plug Hat Point (Chippewa NF)

Total sites: 13, RV sites: 13, Vault/pit toilet, Tent & RV camping: Fee unk, Elev: 1345ft/410m, Nearest town: Deer River. GPS: 47.437062, -94.054675

16 • B2 | South Deer Lake (Chippewa NF)

Total sites: 31, RV sites: 31, Central water, Vault/pit toilet, No showers, No RV dump, Tent & RV camping: $16, Open May-Oct, Max Length: 45ft, Reservations accepted, Elev: 1326ft/404m, Tel: 218-335-8600, Nearest town: Deer River. GPS: 47.514730, -94.105550

17 • B2 | South Pike Bay (Chippewa NF)

Total sites: 24, RV sites: 24, No water, Vault/pit toilet, Tent & RV camping: $16, Open May-Sep, Reservations not accepted, Elev: 1302ft/397m, Tel: 218-335-8600, Nearest town: Cass Lake. GPS: 47.328806, -94.582578

18 • B2 | Stony Point (Chippewa NF)

Total sites: 44, RV sites: 44, Elec sites: 44, Central water, Flush toilet, Free showers, RV dump, Tent & RV camping: $26, Elec fee extra, Open May-Sep, Max Length: 45ft, Reservations accepted, Elev: 1312ft/400m, Tel: 218-335-8600, Nearest town: Walker. GPS: 47.136891, -94.455805

19 • B2 | Tamarack Point (Chippewa NF)

Total sites: 32, RV sites: 32, Central water, Vault/pit toilet, No showers, No RV dump, Tent & RV camping: $14, Open May-Jul, Reservations not accepted, Elev: 1319ft/402m, Tel: 218-335-8600, Nearest town: Bena. GPS: 47.444092, -94.120605

20 • B2 | Wanaki Loop (Chippewa NF)

Total sites: 46, RV sites: 46, Central water, Flush toilet, Free showers, RV dump, Tent & RV camping: $21, Open May-Sep, Max Length: 70ft, Elev: 1319ft/402m, Tel: 218-335-8600, Nearest town: Bemidji. GPS: 47.386963, -94.507568

21 • B2 | Webster Lake (Chippewa NF)

Total sites: 15, RV sites: 15, Central water, Vault/pit toilet, No showers, No RV dump, Tent & RV camping: $14, Open May-Oct, Reservations not accepted, Elev: 1388ft/423m, Tel: 218-335-8600, Nearest town: Blackduck. GPS: 47.604980, -94.506836

22 • B2 | West Seelye Bay (Chippewa NF)

Total sites: 22, RV sites: 22, Central water, Vault/pit toilet, No showers, No RV dump, Tent & RV camping: $14, Open May-Jul, Reservations not accepted, Elev: 1329ft/405m, Tel: 218-335-8600, Nearest town: Deer River. GPS: 47.524108, -94.101543

23 • B2 | Williams Narrows (Chippewa NF)

Total sites: 17, RV sites: 17, Central water, Vault/pit toilet, No showers, No RV dump, Tent & RV camping: $16, Open May-Sep, Max Length: 45ft, Reservations accepted, Elev: 1309ft/399m, Tel: 218-335-8600, Nearest town: Bena. GPS: 47.503882, -94.063261

24 • B2 | Winnie (Chippewa NF)

Total sites: 35, RV sites: 35, Central water, Vault/pit toilet, No showers, No RV dump, Tent & RV camping: $16, Open May-Sep, Max Length: 70ft, Reservations accepted, Elev: 1358ft/414m, Tel: 218-335-8600, Nearest town: Cass Lake. GPS: 47.425322, -94.320031

25 • B3 | August Lake (Superior NF)

Total sites: 1, No water, Vault/pit toilet, Tents only: Free, Reservations not accepted, Elev: 1565ft/477m, Tel: 218-365-7600, Nearest town: Ely. GPS: 47.768502, -91.606948

26 • B3 | Big Rice Lake (Superior NF)

Total sites: 3, RV sites: 3, No water, Vault/pit toilet, Tent & RV camping: Free, Max Length: 20ft, Reservations not accepted, Elev: 1466ft/447m, Tel: 218-229-8800, Nearest town: Virginia. GPS: 47.704199, -92.498842

27 • B3 | Birch Lake (Superior NF)

Total sites: 29, RV sites: 29, Central water, Vault/pit toilet, No showers, No RV dump, Tent & RV camping: $17, Group site: $55, Open May-Sep, Max Length: 66ft, Reservations accepted, Elev: 1460ft/445m, Tel: 218-365-7600, Nearest town: Ely. GPS: 47.758632, -91.785303

28 • B3 | Cadotte Lake (Superior NF)

Total sites: 27, RV sites: 27, Central water, Vault/pit toilet, No showers, No RV dump, Tent & RV camping: $20-22, Open May-Sep, Max Length: 45ft, Reservations accepted, Elev: 1637ft/499m, Tel: 218-229-8800, Nearest town: Hoyt Lakes. GPS: 47.380410, -91.917040

29 • B3 | Echo Lake (Superior NF)

Total sites: 24, RV sites: 24, Central water, Vault/pit toilet, No showers, No RV dump, Tent & RV camping: $12, Group site: $20, Open May-Sep, Max Length: 45ft, Reservations accepted, Elev: 1214ft/370m, Tel: 218-666-0020, Nearest town: Orr. GPS: 48.170698, -92.490649

30 • B3 | Fall Lake (Superior NF)

Total sites: 60, RV sites: 50, Elec sites: 50, Central water, Flush toilet, Free showers, No RV dump, Tents: $24/RVs: $24-28, Group sites: $90-$110, Open May-Oct, Max Length: 40ft, Elev: 1339ft/408m, Tel: 218-365-7600, Nearest town: Ely. GPS: 47.951828, -91.719153

31 • B3 | Fenske Lake (Superior NF)

Total sites: 15, RV sites: 10, Elec sites: 80, Central water, Vault/pit toilet, No showers, No RV dump, Tent & RV camping: $17, Also walk-to & group sites, Group site: $50, Open May-Sep, Max Length: 20ft, Elev: 1486ft/453m, Tel: 218-365-7600, Nearest town: Ely. GPS: 47.994873, -91.915527

32 • B3 | Lake Jeanette (Superior NF)

Total sites: 12, RV sites: 10, Central water, Vault/pit toilet, No showers, No RV dump, Tent & RV camping: $12, Open May-Sep, Max Length: 45ft, Reservations accepted, Elev: 1352ft/412m, Tel: 218-666-0020, Nearest town: Orr. GPS: 48.131517, -92.296745

33 • B3 | McDougal Lake (Superior NF)

Total sites: 21, RV sites: 21, Central water, Vault/pit toilet, No showers, No RV dump, Tent & RV camping: $15, Open May-Sep, Reservations not accepted, Elev: 1798ft/548m, Tel: 218-323-7722, Nearest town: Isabella. GPS: 47.639160, -91.534912

34 • B3 | Meander Lake (Superior NF)

Total sites: 2, RV sites: 0, No water, Vault/pit toilet, Tents only: Free, Walk-to sites, Elev: 1394ft/425m, Tel: 218-666-0020, Nearest town: Orr. GPS: 48.133651, -92.145885

35 • B3 | Pauline Lake (Superior NF)

Total sites: 1, RV sites: 0, No water, Vault/pit toilet, Tents only: Free, Elev: 1411ft/430m, Tel: 218-666-0020, Nearest town: Orr. GPS: 48.127621, -92.332795

36 • B3 | Pfeiffer Lake (Superior NF)

Total sites: 16, RV sites: 16, Central water, Vault/pit toilet, No showers, No RV dump, Tent & RV camping: $12, Open May-Sep, Max Length: 45ft, Reservations accepted, Elev: 1470ft/448m, Tel: 218-229-8800, Nearest town: Tower. GPS: 47.751293, -92.473474

37 • B3 | Sand Lake (Superior NF)

Total sites: 2, RV sites: 0, No water, Vault/pit toilet, Tents only: Free, Reservations not accepted, Elev: 1693ft/516m, Tel: 218-323-7722, Nearest town: Isabella. GPS: 47.581409, -91.663755

38 • B3 | South Kawishiwi River (Superior NF)

Total sites: 31, RV sites: 31, Elec sites: 24, Central water, Vault/pit toilet, No showers, No RV dump, Tents: $17/RVs: $21-23, Open May-Sep, Max Length: 107ft, Elev: 1470ft/448m, Tel: 218-365-7600, Nearest town: Ely. GPS: 47.815844, -91.731616

39 • B3 | Whiteface Reservoir (Superior NF)

Total sites: 52, RV sites: 52, Elec sites: 21, Central water, Vault/pit toilet, No showers, No RV dump, Tents: $22/RVs: $22-27, Group Site: $125, Open May-Sep, Max Length: 50ft, Reservations accepted, Elev: 1483ft/452m, Tel: 218-229-8800, Nearest town: Hoyt Lakes. GPS: 47.334557, -92.145631

40 • B4 | Baker Lake (Superior NF)

Total sites: 5, RV sites: 5, Central water, Vault/pit toilet, No showers, No RV dump, Tent & RV camping: Free, Elev: 1749ft/533m, Tel: 218-663-8060, Nearest town: Tofte. GPS: 47.844528, -90.817046

41 • B4 | Cascade River (Superior NF)

Total sites: 4, RV sites: 1, No water, Vault/pit toilet, Tent & RV camping: Free, Elev: 1631ft/497m, Tel: 218-387-1750, Nearest town: Tofte. GPS: 47.833646, -90.530676

42 • B4 | Clara Lake (Superior NF)

Total sites: 3, RV sites: 1, No water, Vault/pit toilet, Tent & RV camping: Free, Elev: 1726ft/526m, Tel: 218-663-8060, Nearest town: Lutsen. GPS: 47.774354, -90.752134

43 • B4 | Crescent Lake (Superior NF)

Total sites: 32, RV sites: 29, Central water, Vault/pit toilet, No showers, No RV dump, Tent & RV camping: $18, Group site: $36, Open May-Sep, Max Length: 45ft, Reservations accepted, Elev: 1788ft/545m, Tel: 218-663-8060, Nearest town: Tofte. GPS: 47.834562, -90.771574

44 • B4 | Devil Track Lake (Superior NF)

Total sites: 16, RV sites: 8, Central water, Vault/pit toilet, No showers, No RV dump, Tent & RV camping: $16-18, Elev: 1670ft/509m, Tel: 218-387-1750, Nearest town: Grand Marais. GPS: 47.830197, -90.466931

45 • B4 | Divide Lake (Superior NF)

Total sites: 3, RV sites: 3, Central water, Vault/pit toilet, No showers, No RV dump, Tent & RV camping: $15, Reservations not accepted, Elev: 1949ft/594m, Tel: 218-323-7722, Nearest town: Isabella. GPS: 47.609981, -91.256365

46 • B4 | East Bearskin Lake (Superior NF)

Total sites: 29, RV sites: 27, Central water, Vault/pit toilet, No showers, No RV dump, Tent & RV camping: $20, Open May-Oct,

Reservations accepted, Elev: 1729ft/527m, Tel: 218-387-1750, Nearest town: Grand Marais. GPS: 48.037109, -90.394043

47 • B4 | Eighteen Lake (Superior NF)

Total sites: 3, RV sites: 3, No water, Vault/pit toilet, Tent & RV camping: Free, Elev: 1926ft/587m, Tel: 218-323-7722, Nearest town: Isabella. GPS: 47.643759, -91.344178

48 • B4 | Flour Lake (Superior NF)

Total sites: 37, RV sites: 30, Central water, Vault/pit toilet, No showers, No RV dump, Tent & RV camping: $20, Open May-Oct, Max Length: 85ft, Reservations accepted, Elev: 1775ft/541m, Tel: 218-387-1750, Nearest town: Grand Marais. GPS: 48.052490, -90.408447

49 • B4 | Fourmile Lake (Superior NF)

Total sites: 4, RV sites: 2, No water, Vault/pit toilet, Tent & RV camping: Free, Reservations not accepted, Elev: 1670ft/509m, Tel: 218-663-8060, Nearest town: Tofte. GPS: 47.702262, -90.963536

50 • B4 | Harriet Lake (Superior NF)

Total sites: 4, RV sites: 2, No water, Vault/pit toilet, Tent & RV camping: Free, Elev: 1772ft/540m, Tel: 218-663-8060, Nearest town: Tofte. GPS: 47.656881, -91.115144

51 • B4 | Hogback Lake (Superior NF)

Total sites: 3, RV sites: 3, No water, Vault/pit toilet, Tent & RV camping: Free, access to 5 back-country sites, Reservations not accepted, Elev: 1775ft/541m, Tel: 218-323-7722, Nearest town: Isabella. GPS: 47.644385, -91.136046

52 • B4 | Iron Lake (Superior NF)

Total sites: 7, RV sites: 7, Central water, Vault/pit toilet, No showers, No RV dump, Tent & RV camping: $22, Open Apr-Oct, Reservations accepted, Elev: 1886ft/575m, Tel: 218-387-1750, Nearest town: Grand Marais. GPS: 48.067485, -90.615216

53 • B4 | Kawishiwi Lake Rustic (Superior NF)

Total sites: 5, RV sites: 5, No water, Vault/pit toilet, No showers, No RV dump, Tent & RV camping: Free, Max Length: 25ft, Reservations not accepted, Elev: 1656ft/505m, Tel: 218-663-8060, Nearest town: Tofte. GPS: 47.838663, -91.102413

54 • B4 | Kimball Lake (Superior NF)

Total sites: 10, RV sites: 10, Central water, Vault/pit toilet, No showers, No RV dump, Tent & RV camping: $16-18, Elev: 1709ft/521m, Tel: 218-387-1750, Nearest town: Grand Marais. GPS: 47.863994, -90.227176

55 • B4 | Lichen Lake Canoe Camp (Superior NF)

Total sites: 1, RV sites: 1, No water, Vault/pit toilet, Tent & RV camping: Free, Open Apr-Sep, Elev: 1808ft/551m, Tel: 218-663-8060, Nearest town: Tofte. GPS: 47.850391, -90.712627

56 • B4 | Little Isabella River (Superior NF)

Total sites: 11, RV sites: 11, Central water, Vault/pit toilet, No showers, No RV dump, Tent & RV camping: $15, Open May-Sep, Reservations not accepted, Elev: 1821ft/555m, Tel: 218-323-7722, Nearest town: Isabella. GPS: 47.647217, -91.423828

57 • B4 | Ninemile Lake (Superior NF)

Total sites: 24, RV sites: 18, Central water, Vault/pit toilet, No showers, No RV dump, Tent & RV camping: $15, Reservations not accepted, Elev: 1624ft/495m, Tel: 218-663-8060, Nearest town: Schroeder. GPS: 47.579031, -91.073808

58 • B4 | Poplar River (Superior NF)

Total sites: 4, RV sites: 2, No water, Vault/pit toilet, Tent & RV camping: Free, Max Length: 20ft, Elev: 1572ft/479m, Tel: 218-663-8060, Nearest town: Lutsen. GPS: 47.738693, -90.777797

59 • B4 | Sawbill Lake (Superior NF)

Total sites: 51, RV sites: 51, Central water, Vault/pit toilet, Pay showers, RV dump, Tent & RV camping: $18, Open May-Sep, Max Length: 45ft, Reservations accepted, Elev: 1842ft/561m, Tel: 218-663-8060, Nearest town: Tofte. GPS: 47.863561, -90.886004

60 • B4 | Section 29 Lake (Superior NF)

Total sites: 3, RV sites: 3, No water, Vault/pit toilet, Tent & RV camping: Free, Reservations not accepted, Elev: 1627ft/496m, Tel: 218-323-7722, Nearest town: Isabella. GPS: 47.741338, -91.241822

61 • B4 | Silver Island Lake (Superior NF)

Total sites: 8, RV sites: 8, No water, Vault/pit toilet, Tent & RV camping: Free, Elev: 1640ft/500m, Tel: 218-323-7722, Nearest town: Isabella. GPS: 47.727398, -91.149167

62 • B4 | Temperance River (Superior NF)

Total sites: 9, RV sites: 9, Central water, Vault/pit toilet, No showers, No RV dump, Tent & RV camping: $18, Reservations not accepted, Elev: 1532ft/467m, Tel: 218-663-8060, Nearest town: Tofte. GPS: 47.718279, -90.879572

63 • B4 | Toohey Lake (Superior NF)

Total sites: 5, RV sites: 3, No water, Vault/pit toilet, Tent & RV camping: Free, Elev: 1690ft/515m, Tel: 218-663-8060, Nearest town: Tofte. GPS: 47.712827, -90.953511

64 • B4 | Trail's End (Superior NF)

Total sites: 33, RV sites: 18, Central water, Vault/pit toilet, No showers, No RV dump, Tent & RV camping: $22-24, Open May-Oct, Max Length: 40ft, Reservations accepted, Elev: 1466ft/447m, Tel: 218-387-1750, Nearest town: Grand Marais. GPS: 48.158975, -90.893034

65 • B4 | Two Island Lake (Superior NF)

Total sites: 36, RV sites: 30, Central water, Vault/pit toilet, No showers, No RV dump, Tent & RV camping: $16-18, Elev: 1785ft/544m, Tel: 218-387-1750, Nearest town: Grand Marais. GPS: 47.879347, -90.445628

66 • B4 | White Pine Lake (Superior NF)

Total sites: 3, RV sites: 2, No water, Vault/pit toilet, Tent & RV camping: Free, Max Length: 20ft, Elev: 1618ft/493m, Tel: 218-663-8060, Nearest town: Lutsen. GPS: 47.738251, -90.752428

67 • B4 | Whitefish Lake (Superior NF)

Total sites: 3, RV sites: 2, No water, Vault/pit toilet, Tent & RV

camping: Free, Elev: 1700ft/518m, Tel: 218-663-8060, Nearest town: Tofte. GPS: 47.719106, -91.045364

68 • B4 | Wilson Lake (Superior NF)

Total sites: 4, RV sites: 3, No water, Vault/pit toilet, Tent & RV camping: Free, Elev: 1713ft/522m, Tel: 218-663-8060, Nearest town: Tofte. GPS: 47.660068, -91.062459

69 • B4 | Windy Lake (Superior NF)

Total sites: 1, RV sites: 1, No water, Vault/pit toilet, Tent & RV camping: Free, Elev: 1680ft/512m, Tel: 218-663-8060, Nearest town: Tofte. GPS: 47.743903, -91.087007

Mississippi

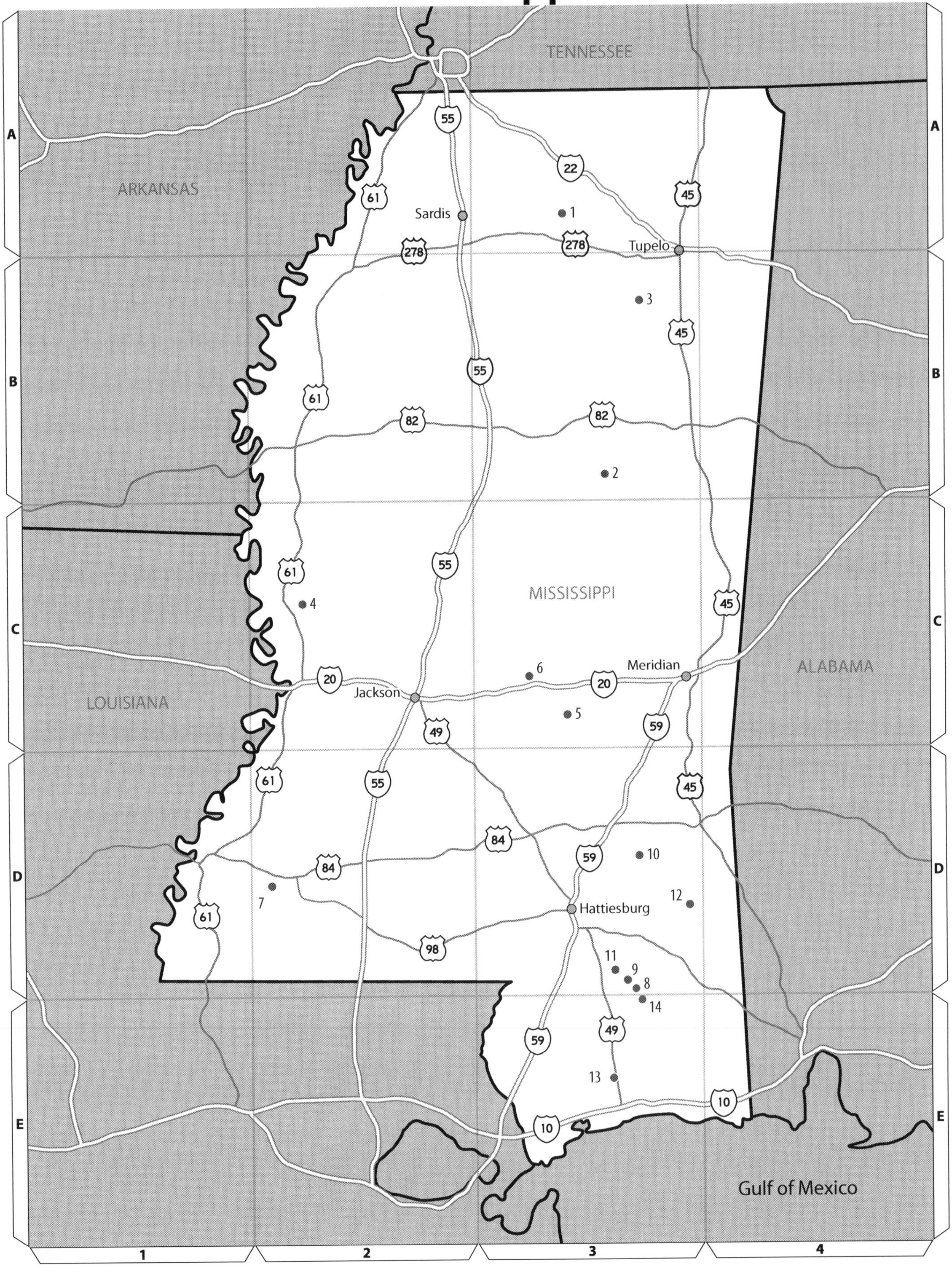

Map	ID	Map	ID
A3	1	D2	7
B3	2-3	D3	8-12
C2	4	E3	13-14
C3	5-6		

Alphabetical List of Camping Areas

1 • A3 | Puskus Lake (Holly Springs NF)

Total sites: 19, RV sites: 19, Vault/pit toilet, Tent & RV camping: $7, Open all year, Reservations not accepted, Elev: 371ft/113m, Tel: 601-965-1600, Nearest town: Oxford. GPS: 34.438141, -89.351275

2 • B3 | Choctaw Lake (Tombigbee NF)

Total sites: 21, RV sites: 21, Elec sites: 21, Water at site, Flush toilet, Free showers, RV dump, Tent & RV camping: $20, Open Mar-Nov, Max Length: 55ft, Reservations accepted, Elev: 499ft/152m, Tel: 662-285-3264, Nearest town: Ackerman. GPS: 33.272949, -89.145508

3 • B3 | Davis Lake (Tombigbee NF)

Total sites: 27, RV sites: 27, Elec sites: 27, Water at site, Flush toilet, Free showers, RV dump, Tent & RV camping: $20, Open all year, Max Length: 45ft, Reservations accepted, Elev: 400ft/122m, Tel: 662-285-3264, Nearest town: Ackerman. GPS: 34.046802, -88.940141

4 • C2 | Little Sunflower River (Delta NF)

Total sites: 3, RV sites: 3, No water, Vault/pit toilet, Tent & RV camping: $7, Call district office for reservations, Open all year, Reservations required, Elev: 125ft/38m, Tel: 662-873-6256, Nearest town: Onward. GPS: 32.695336, -90.817248

5 • C3 | Marathon Lake (Bienville NF)

Total sites: 34, RV sites: 34, Elec sites: 34, Water at site, Flush toilet, Free showers, RV dump, Tent & RV camping: $20, Stay limit: 14 days, Open Mar-Dec, Reservations not accepted, Elev: 450ft/137m, Tel: 601-965-1600, Nearest town: Forest. GPS: 32.200928, -89.360352

6 • C3 | Shockaloe Base Camp I (Bienville NF)

Total sites: 10, RV sites: 10, Central water, Vault/pit toilet, No showers, No RV dump, Tent & RV camping: $7, Stay limit: 14 days, Open Mar-Dec, Reservations not accepted, Elev: 564ft/172m, Nearest town: Forest. GPS: 32.366612, -89.562469

7 • D2 | Clear Springs (Homochitto NF)

Total sites: 44, RV sites: 44, Elec sites: 22, Central water, Flush toilet, Free showers, RV dump, Tents: $7/RVs: $20, Open all year, Reservations not accepted, Elev: 348ft/106m, Tel: 601-384-5876, Nearest town: Meadville. GPS: 31.425326, -90.988256

8 • D3 | Cypress Creek Landing (Desoto NF)

Total sites: 14, RV sites: 14, Central water, Flush toilet, Free showers, No RV dump, Tents only: $7, Stay limit: 14 days, Open all year, Reservations not accepted, Elev: 164ft/50m, Tel: 601-965-1791, Nearest town: Wiggins. GPS: 30.965954, -89.004636

9 • D3 | Janice Landing (Desoto NF)

Total sites: 5, RV sites: 0, Central water, Vault/pit toilet, No showers, No RV dump, Tents only: Free, Stay limit: 14 days, Elev: 158ft/48m, Tel: 601-965-1791, Nearest town: Brooklyn. GPS: 30.995052, -89.050385

10 • D3 | Long Leaf Horse Camp (Desoto NF)

Total sites: 6, RV sites: 6, No water, Vault/pit toilet, Tent & RV camping: $3, Open all year, Reservations not accepted, Elev: 360ft/110m, Tel: 601-428-0594, Nearest town: Laurel. GPS: 31.567066, -88.987473

11 • D3 | Moody's Landing (Desoto NF)

Total sites: 4, Central water, Vault/pit toilet, No showers, No RV dump, Tents only: Free, Also boat-in sites, Stay limit: 14 days, Open all year, Reservations not accepted, Elev: 125ft/38m, Nearest town: Brooklyn. GPS: 31.051328, -89.116989

12 • D3 | Turkey Fork (Desoto NF)

Total sites: 28, RV sites: 20, Elec sites: 20, Water at site, Flush toilet, Free showers, RV dump, Tents: $7/RVs: $20, Generator hours: 0600-2200, Open all year, Elev: 230ft/70m, Tel: 601-428-0594, Nearest town: Richton. GPS: 31.339407, -88.703506

13 • E3 | Big Biloxi (Desoto NF)

Total sites: 25, RV sites: 25, Elec sites: 25, Water at site, Flush toilet, Free showers, RV dump, Tent & RV camping: $20, $13 w/Golden Age Pass, Stay limit: 14-30 days, Generator hours: 0600-2200, Open all year, Reservations not accepted, Elev: 82ft/25m, Nearest town: Saucier. GPS: 30.568873, -89.129295

14 • E3 | Fairley Bridge Landing (Desoto NF)

Total sites: 3, RV sites: 3, No water, Vault/pit toilet, Tent & RV camping: Free, Stay limit: 14 days, Open all year, Reservations not accepted, Elev: 108ft/33m, Tel: 601-965-1600, Nearest town: Wiggins. GPS: 30.918153, -88.966392

Missouri

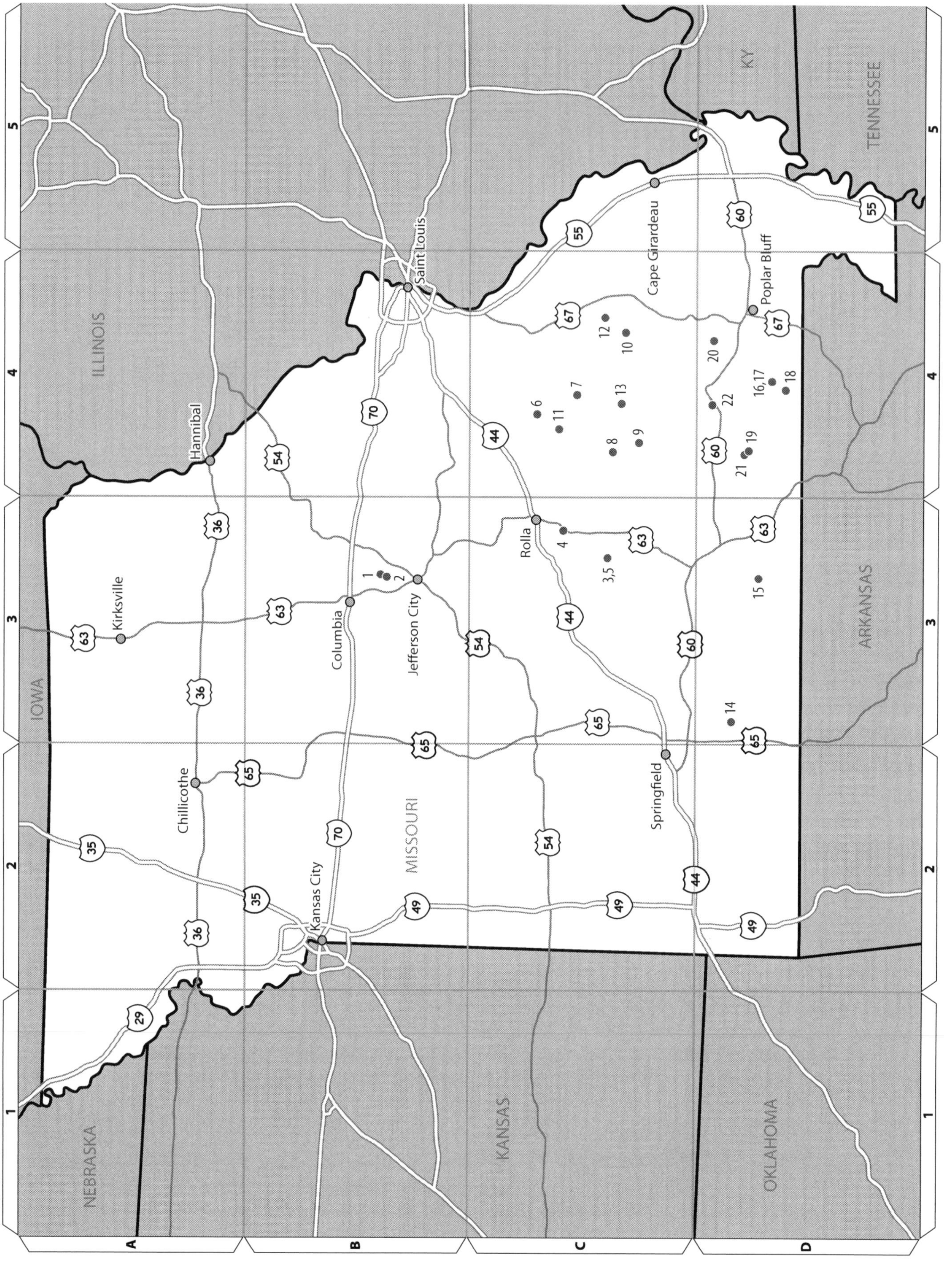
IOWA
ILLINOIS
KY
TENNESSEE
ARKANSAS
OKLAHOMA
KANSAS
NEBRASKA
MISSOURI
Saint Louis
Hannibal
Kirksville
Chillicothe
Kansas City
Columbia
Jefferson City
Rolla
Springfield
Cape Girardeau
Poplar Bluff
1
2
3,5
4
6
7
8
9
10
11
12
13
14
15
16,17
18
19
20
21
22
29
35
36
44
49
54
55
60
63
65
67
70
A
B
C
D
1
2
3
4
5

Map	ID	Map	ID
B3	1-2	D3	14-15
C3	3-5	D4	16-22
C4	6-13		

Alphabetical List of Camping Areas

1 • B3 | Dry Fork (Mark Twain NF)

Total sites: 8, RV sites: 8, Central water, Vault/pit toilet, No showers, No RV dump, Tent & RV camping: Donation, Open Apr-Nov, Max Length: 30ft, Reservations not accepted, Elev: 781ft/238m, Tel: 573-364-4621, Nearest town: Fulton. GPS: 38.783924, -92.125471

2 • B3 | Pine Ridge Rec. Area (Mark Twain NF)

Total sites: 8, RV sites: 8, Central water, Vault/pit toilet, No showers, No RV dump, Tent & RV camping: Free, Max Length: 34ft, Elev: 787ft/240m, Nearest town: Ashland. GPS: 38.758900, -92.144390

3 • C3 | Big Piney Trail Camp (Mark Twain NF)

Total sites: 2, RV sites: 2, No water, Vault/pit toilet, Tent & RV camping: Free, Elev: 1130ft/344m, Nearest town: Licking. GPS: 37.560908, -92.012028

4 • C3 | Lane Spring (Mark Twain NF)

Total sites: 18, RV sites: 18, Elec sites: 6, Central water, Vault/pit toilet, No showers, No RV dump, Tents: $8/RVs: $8-15, Group site: $16, Generator hours: 0600-2200, Open Apr-Oct, Max Length: 34ft, Elev: 863ft/263m, Nearest town: Vida. GPS: 37.797258, -91.836485

5 • C3 | Paddy Creek (Mark Twain NF)

Total sites: 23, RV sites: 23, No water, Vault/pit toilet, Tent & RV camping: Donation, Max Length: 34ft, Reservations not accepted, Elev: 890ft/271m, Nearest town: Licking. GPS: 37.555656, -92.042308

6 • C4 | Berryman (Mark Twain NF)

Total sites: 8, RV sites: 8, No water, Vault/pit toilet, Tent & RV camping: Free, Max Length: 34ft, Elev: 1053ft/321m, Nearest town: Potosi. GPS: 37.929903, -91.062986

7 • C4 | Council Bluff RA - Wild Boar CG (Mark Twain NF)

Total sites: 51, RV sites: 43, Central water, Vault/pit toilet, No showers, No RV dump, Tent & RV camping: $11, Group site: $25-$100, Open May-Oct, Max Length: 40ft, Reservations accepted, Elev: 1312ft/400m, Tel: 573-766-5765, Nearest town: Belgrade. GPS: 37.722634, -90.937009

8 • C4 | Little Scotia Pond (Mark Twain NF)

Total sites: 14, RV sites: 14, Central water, Vault/pit toilet, No showers, No RV dump, Tent & RV camping: Free, Reservations not accepted, Elev: 1371ft/418m, Nearest town: Bunker. GPS: 37.529541, -91.330078

9 • C4 | Loggers Lake (Mark Twain NF)

Total sites: 14, RV sites: 14, Central water, Vault/pit toilet, No showers, No RV dump, Tent & RV camping: $10, Also walk-to sites, Walk-in in winter, Open all year, Max Length: 34ft, Elev: 1073ft/327m, Nearest town: Bunker. GPS: 37.388184, -91.260498

10 • C4 | Marble Creek (Mark Twain NF)

Total sites: 26, RV sites: 26, No water, Vault/pit toilet, Tent & RV camping: $10, Open Apr-Nov, Reservations not accepted, Elev: 682ft/208m, Tel: 573-783-3769, Nearest town: Arcadia. GPS: 37.451172, -90.540771

11 • C4 | Red Bluff (Mark Twain NF)

Total sites: 41, RV sites: 41, Elec sites: 6, Central water, Vault/pit toilet, No showers, No RV dump, Tents: $11/RVs: $18, Open May-Oct, Max Length: 45ft, Reservations accepted, Elev: 827ft/252m, Tel: 573-743-6042, Nearest town: Viburnum. GPS: 37.812988, -91.169189

12 • C4 | Silver Mines (Mark Twain NF)

Total sites: 86, RV sites: 72, Elec sites: 11, Central water, Vault/pit toilet, No showers, No RV dump, Tents: $15/RVs: $25, Group site: $50-$100, Open Mar-Oct, Max Length: 60ft, Reservations accepted, Elev: 764ft/233m, Tel: 573-783-3769, Nearest town: Fredericktown. GPS: 37.560716, -90.438814

13 • C4 | Sutton Bluff (Mark Twain NF)

Total sites: 33, RV sites: 33, Elec sites: 12, Central water, Flush toilet, Free showers, No RV dump, Tents: $10/RVs: $30, Group site: $40, Open Mar-Nov, Max Length: 76ft, Reservations accepted, Elev: 860ft/262m, Tel: 573-729-6656, Nearest town: Centerville. GPS: 37.475586, -91.006592

14 • D3 | Cobb Ridge (Mark Twain NF)

Total sites: 43, RV sites: 38, Elec sites: 25, Central water, Flush toilet, Free showers, No RV dump, Tents: $10/RVs: $10-15, Open all year, Max Length: 34ft, Elev: 1342ft/409m, Tel: 417-683-4428, Nearest town: Chadwick. GPS: 36.889901, -93.100946

15 • D3 | North Fork (Mark Twain NF)

Total sites: 20, RV sites: 20, Elec sites: 2, Central water, Vault/pit toilet, No showers, No RV dump, Tents: $10/RVs: $10-15, Generator hours: 0600-2200, Open May-Nov, Max Length: 34ft, Reservations not accepted, Elev: 814ft/248m, Tel: 417-683-4428, Nearest town: Dora. GPS: 36.755217, -92.151948

16 • D4 | Deer Leap (Mark Twain NF)

Total sites: 10, RV sites: 10, Central water, Vault/pit toilet, No showers, No RV dump, Tent & RV camping: $12, Open May-Sep, Max Length: 34ft, Reservations not accepted, Elev: 374ft/114m, Nearest town: Doniphan. GPS: 36.676399, -90.885546

17 • D4 | Float Camp (Mark Twain NF)

Total sites: 20, RV sites: 20, Elec sites: 8, Central water, Vault/pit toilet, No showers, No RV dump, Tents: $12/RVs: $12-20, Open May-Sep, Elev: 413ft/126m, Nearest town: Doniphan. GPS: 36.665362, -90.871496

18 • D4 | Fourche Lake RA (Mark Twain NF)

Total sites: 6, RV sites: 6, Central water, Vault/pit toilet, No showers, No RV dump, Tent & RV camping: Free, Elev: 568ft/173m, Nearest town: Doniphan. GPS: 36.599501, -90.930136

19 • D4 | Greer Crossing (Mark Twain NF)

Total sites: 19, RV sites: 19, Central water, Vault/pit toilet, No showers, No RV dump, Tent & RV camping: $10, No water/services in winter, Open all year, Reservations not accepted, Elev: 600ft/183m, Nearest town: Alton. GPS: 36.795410, -91.329834

20 • D4 | Markham Spring (Mark Twain NF)

Total sites: 12, RV sites: 12, Elec sites: 12, Central water, Flush toilet, Free showers, No RV dump, Tents: $10/RVs: $17, Open May-Sep, Max Length: 34ft, Reservations accepted, Elev: 420ft/128m, Tel: 573-785-1475, Nearest town: Williamsville. GPS: 36.981434, -90.604934

21 • D4 | McCormack Lake RA (Mark Twain NF)

Total sites: 8, RV sites: 8, Central water, Vault/pit toilet, No showers, No RV dump, Tent & RV camping: Free, Reservations not accepted, Elev: 607ft/185m, Nearest town: Alton. GPS: 36.821904, -91.352333

22 • D4 | Watercress Spring (Mark Twain NF)

Total sites: 17, RV sites: 17, Central water, Flush toilet, No showers, No RV dump, Tent & RV camping: $10-20, Open May-Sep, Max Length: 50ft, Reservations not accepted, Elev: 515ft/157m, Tel: 573-996-2153, Nearest town: Van Buren. GPS: 36.999512, -91.018799

Montana

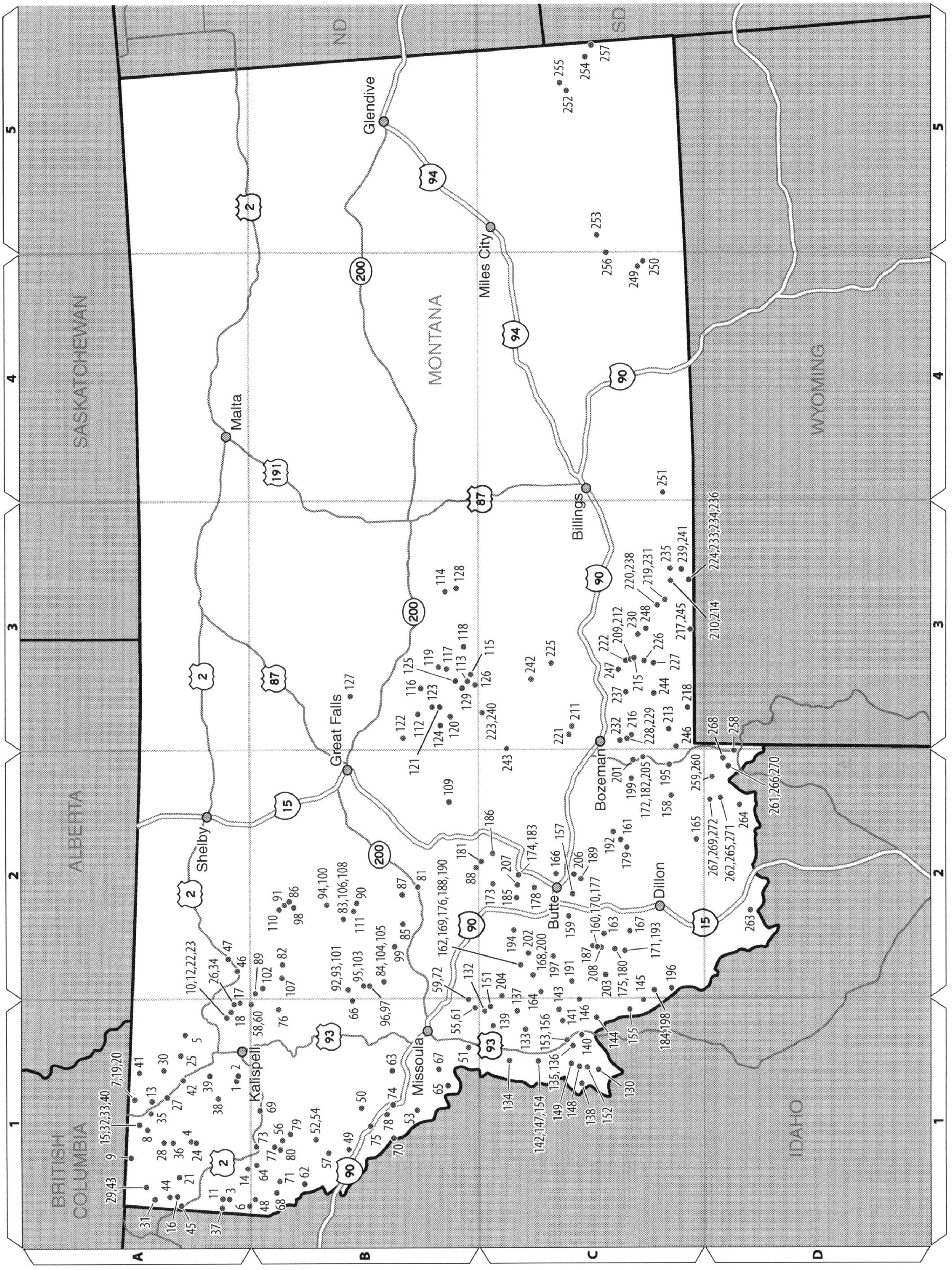
SASKATCHEWAN
ALBERTA
BRITISH COLUMBIA
ND
SD
MONTANA
WYOMING
IDAHO
Glendive
Miles City
Malta
Billings
Great Falls
Shelby
Bozeman
Butte
Dillon
Missoula
Kalispell
A
B
C
D
1
2
3
4
5

Map	ID	Map	ID
A1	1-45	C2	157-208
A2	46-47	C3	209-248
B1	48-80	C4	249-251
B2	81-111	C5	252-257
B3	112-129	D2	258-272
C1	130-156		

Alphabetical List of Camping Areas

1 • A1 | Ashley Lake North (Flathead NF)

Total sites: 5, RV sites: 5, No water, Vault/pit toilet, Tent & RV camping: Free, Stay limit: 5 days, Generator hours: 0600-2200, Open May-Sep, Max Length: 12ft, Reservations not accepted, Elev: 4032ft/1229m, Tel: 406-758-5208, Nearest town: Whitefish. GPS: 48.213724, -114.616946

2 • A1 | Ashley Lake South (Flathead NF)

Total sites: 2, RV sites: 2, No water, Vault/pit toilet, Tents only: Free, Access road has sharp hairpin corner - RVs not reccomended, Stay limit: 5 days, Generator hours: 0600-2200, Open May-Sep, Elev: 3993ft/1217m, Tel: 406-758-5208, Nearest town: Whitefish. GPS: 48.211719, -114.569071

3 • A1 | Bad Medicine (Kootenai NF)

Total sites: 18, RV sites: 18, Central water, Vault/pit toilet, No showers, No RV dump, Tent & RV camping: $16, Limited winter access, Stay limit: 16 days, Open all year, Max Length: 32ft, Reservations not accepted, Elev: 2395ft/730m, Tel: 406-295-4693, Nearest town: Troy. GPS: 48.221005, -115.856651

4 • A1 | Barron Creek (Kootenai NF)

Total sites: 7, RV sites: 7, No water, Vault/pit toilet, Tent & RV camping: Free, Winter access may be limited, Stay limit: 14 days, Open May-Oct, Max Length: 40ft, Reservations not accepted, Elev: 2549ft/777m, Tel: 406-293-7773, Nearest town: Libby. GPS: 48.516000, -115.291000

5 • A1 | Big Creek (Flathead NF)

Total sites: 23, RV sites: 23, Central water, Vault/pit toilet, No showers, No RV dump, Tent & RV camping: $18, Group site: $50-$200, Stay limit: 16 days, Open May-Sep, Max Length: 58ft, Reservations accepted, Elev: 3330ft/1015m, Tel: 406-387-3800, Nearest town: Columbia Falls. GPS: 48.600586, -114.163086

6 • A1 | Big Eddy (Kootenai NF)

Total sites: 5, RV sites: 5, No water, Vault/pit toilet, Tent & RV camping: Free, Limited winter access, Stay limit: 16 days, Open all year, Max Length: 30ft, Reservations not accepted, Elev: 2297ft/700m, Tel: 406-827-3533, Nearest town: Heron. GPS: 48.067000, -115.923000

7 • A1 | Big Therriault Lake (Kootenai NF)

Total sites: 10, RV sites: 10, Central water, Vault/pit toilet, No showers, No RV dump, Tent & RV camping: $10, Access may be limited in winter, Stay limit: 14 days, Open all year, Max Length: 32ft, Reservations not accepted, Elev: 5548ft/1691m, Tel: 406-882-4451, Nearest town: Eureka. GPS: 48.936523, -114.878906

8 • A1 | Camp 32 (Kootenai NF)

Total sites: 8, RV sites: 8, Central water, Vault/pit toilet, No showers, No RV dump, Tent & RV camping: Free, Stay limit: 14 days, Open all year, Max Length: 20ft, Elev: 2779ft/847m, Tel: 406-296-2536, Nearest town: Rexford. GPS: 48.837000, -115.190000

9 • A1 | Caribou (Kootenai NF)

Total sites: 3, RV sites: 3, No water, Vault/pit toilet, Tent & RV camping: Free, Stay limit: 14 days, Open all year, Max Length: 32ft, Reservations not accepted, Elev: 3770ft/1149m, Tel: 406-295-4693, Nearest town: Troy. GPS: 48.948806, -115.503202

10 • A1 | Doris Creek (Flathead NF)

Total sites: 10, RV sites: 10, No water, Vault/pit toilet, Tent & RV camping: $16, Open May-Sep, Max Length: 60ft, Reservations accepted, Elev: 3579ft/1091m, Tel: 406-387-3800, Nearest town: Columbia Falls. GPS: 48.305000, -113.981000

11 • A1 | Dorr Skeels (Kootenai NF)

Total sites: 8, RV sites: 2, Central water, Vault/pit toilet, No showers, No RV dump, Tent & RV camping: $16, Limited winter access, Stay limit: 16 days, Open all year, Max Length: 32ft, Reservations not accepted, Elev: 2339ft/713m, Tel: 406-295-4693, Nearest town: Troy. GPS: 48.267648, -115.854925

12 • A1 | Emery Bay (Flathead NF)

Total sites: 28, RV sites: 28, Central water, Vault/pit toilet, No showers, No RV dump, Tent & RV camping: $18, 2 group sites: $90-$200, Open May-Sep, Max Length: 60ft, Reservations accepted, Elev: 3596ft/1096m, Tel: 406-387-3800, Nearest town: Hungry Horse. GPS: 48.334147, -113.950346

13 • A1 | Grave Creek (Kootenai NF)

Total sites: 4, RV sites: 4, No water, Vault/pit toilet, Tent & RV camping: Free, Access may be limited in winter, Stay limit: 14 days, Open all year, Max Length: 20ft, Reservations not accepted, Elev: 3030ft/924m, Tel: 406-882-4451, Nearest town: Fortine. GPS: 48.819282, -114.886547

14 • A1 | Howard Lake (Kootenai NF)

Total sites: 10, RV sites: 10, Central water, Vault/pit toilet, No showers, No RV dump, Tent & RV camping: $10, Stay limit: 14 days, Open May-Nov, Reservations not accepted, Elev: 4154ft/1266m, Tel: 406-293-7773, Nearest town: Libby. GPS: 48.101318, -115.530518

15 • A1 | Kamloops Terrace (Kootenai NF)

Total sites: 20, RV sites: 20, Central water, Flush toilet, No showers, RV dump, Tent & RV camping: $24, Dump station: $5, Stay limit: 14 days, Open May-Sep, Max Length: 32ft, Reservations not accepted, Elev: 2500ft/762m, Tel: 406-296-2536, Nearest town: Rexford. GPS: 48.902836, -115.159892

16 • A1 | Kilbrennan Lake (Kootenai NF)

Total sites: 7, RV sites: 7, No water, Vault/pit toilet, Tent & RV camping: $10, Stay limit: 14 days, Open all year, Max Length: 24ft, Reservations not accepted, Elev: 2946ft/898m, Nearest town: Troy. GPS: 48.596611, -115.888234

17 • A1 | Lakeview (Flathead NF)

Total sites: 5, RV sites: 5, No water, Vault/pit toilet, Tent & RV camping: Free, Reservations not accepted, Elev: 3530ft/1076m, Tel: 406-387-3800, Nearest town: Hungry Horse. GPS: 48.219127, -113.805384

18 • A1 | Lid Creek (Flathead NF)

Total sites: 23, RV sites: 23, No water, Vault/pit toilet, Tent & RV camping: $16, Stay limit: 16 days, Open May-Sep, Max Length: 55ft, Reservations accepted, Elev: 3596ft/1096m, Tel: 406-387-3800, Nearest town: Hungry Horse. GPS: 48.286516, -113.910682

19 • A1 | Little Therriault Horse Camp (Kootenai NF)

Total sites: 2, RV sites: 2, Central water, Vault/pit toilet, No showers, No RV dump, Tent & RV camping: Free, Stay limit: 16 days, Open all year, Max Length: 32ft, Reservations not accepted, Elev: 5518ft/1682m, Tel: 406-882-4451, Nearest town: Eureka. GPS: 48.944102, -114.892285

20 • A1 | Little Therriault Lake (Kootenai NF)

Total sites: 6, RV sites: 6, Central water, Vault/pit toilet, No showers, No RV dump, Tent & RV camping: $10, Stay limit: 14 days, Open all year, Max Length: 32ft, Reservations not accepted, Elev: 5554ft/1693m, Tel: 406-882-4451, Nearest town: Eureka. GPS: 48.943399, -114.890434

21 • A1 | Loon Lake (Kootenai NF)

Total sites: 4, RV sites: 4, No water, Vault/pit toilet, Tent & RV camping: Free, Stay limit: 14 days, Open all year, Max Length: 20ft, Reservations not accepted, Elev: 3698ft/1127m, Tel: 406-293-7773, Nearest town: Libby. GPS: 48.597851, -115.671557

22 • A1 | Lost Johnny (Flathead NF)

Total sites: 5, RV sites: 5, Central water, Vault/pit toilet, No showers, No RV dump, Tent & RV camping: $16, Stay limit: 16 days, Open May-Sep, Max Length: 24ft, Reservations not accepted, Elev: 3566ft/1087m, Tel: 406-387-3800, Nearest town: Hungry Horse. GPS: 48.306125, -113.969631

23 • A1 | Lost Johnny Point (Flathead NF)

Total sites: 21, RV sites: 21, Central water, Vault/pit toilet, No showers, No RV dump, Tent & RV camping: $18, Open May-Sep, Max Length: 49ft, Reservations accepted, Elev: 3592ft/1095m, Tel: 406-387-3800, Nearest town: Hungry Horse. GPS: 48.310241, -113.963725

24 • A1 | McGillivray (Kootenai NF)

Total sites: 33, RV sites: 33, Central water, Vault/pit toilet, No showers, No RV dump, Tent & RV camping: $16, Group sites (2): $30-$60, Stay limit: 14 days, Open May-Oct, Max Length: 40ft, Reservations accepted, Elev: 2592ft/790m, Tel: 406-293-7773, Nearest town: Libby. GPS: 48.487943, -115.300718

25 • A1 | Moose Lake (Flathead NF)

Total sites: 3, RV sites: 3, No water, Vault/pit toilet, Tent & RV camping: Free, Stay limit: 14 days, Reservations not accepted, Elev: 5728ft/1746m, Tel: 406-387-3800, Nearest town: Columbia Falls. GPS: 48.628775, -114.388784

26 • A1 | Murray Bay (Complex III) (Flathead NF)

Total sites: 20, RV sites: 20, Central water, Vault/pit toilet, No showers, No RV dump, Tent & RV camping: $16, Stay limit: 16 days, Open May-Sep, Max Length: 60ft, Reservations accepted, Elev: 3632ft/1107m, Tel: 406-387-3800, Nearest town: Martin City. GPS: 48.265434, -113.813581

27 • A1 | North Dickey Lake (Kootenai NF)

Total sites: 25, RV sites: 25, Central water, Vault/pit toilet, No showers, No RV dump, Tent & RV camping: $16, Stay limit: 14 days, Open May-Sep, Max Length: 50ft, Reservations accepted, Elev: 3163ft/964m, Tel: 406-882-4451, Nearest town: Eureka. GPS: 48.718506, -114.833496

28 • A1 | Peck Gulch (Kootenai NF)

Total sites: 22, RV sites: 22, Central water, Vault/pit toilet, No showers, No RV dump, Tent & RV camping: $16, Narrow, steep access road, Stay limit: 14 days, Open all year, Max Length: 32ft, Reservations not accepted, Elev: 2513ft/766m, Tel: 406-296-2536, Nearest town: Eureka. GPS: 48.724062, -115.307511

29 • A1 | Pete Creek (Kootenai NF)

Total sites: 13, RV sites: 13, Central water, Vault/pit toilet, No showers, No RV dump, Tent & RV camping: $12, Winter access may be limited, Stay limit: 14 days, Open all year, Reservations not accepted, Elev: 2972ft/906m, Tel: 406-295-4693, Nearest town: Yaak. GPS: 48.830811, -115.766602

30 • A1 | Red Meadow Lake (Flathead NF)

Total sites: 6, RV sites: 6, No water, Vault/pit toilet, Tent & RV

camping: Free, Stay limit: 14 days, Reservations not accepted, Elev: 5562ft/1695m, Tel: 406-387-3800, Nearest town: Columbia Falls. GPS: 48.753736, -114.563547

31 • A1 | Red Top (Kootenai NF)

Total sites: 3, RV sites: 3, No water, Vault/pit toilet, Tent & RV camping: Free, Limited winter access, Stay limit: 14 days, Open all year, Elev: 2825ft/861m, Tel: 406-295-4693, Nearest town: Troy. GPS: 48.760935, -115.918299

32 • A1 | Rexford Bench - Boat Site (Kootenai NF)

Total sites: 30, RV sites: 30, Central water, Vault/pit toilet, No showers, No RV dump, No tents/RVs: $8, Stay limit: 14 days, Elev: 2462ft/750m, Tel: 406-296-2536, Nearest town: Rexford. GPS: 48.903949, -115.162726

33 • A1 | Rexford Bench (Kootenai NF)

Total sites: 54, RV sites: 54, Central water, Flush toilet, No showers, RV dump, Tent & RV camping: $24, Dump station: $5, Stay limit: 14 days, Open Apr-Sep, Max Length: 50ft, Reservations accepted, Elev: 2562ft/781m, Tel: 406-296-2536, Nearest town: Eureka. GPS: 48.899702, -115.157247

34 • A1 | Riverside Boating Site (Flathead NF)

Total sites: 3, RV sites: 3, No water, Vault/pit toilet, No showers, No RV dump, Tent & RV camping: $16, 2 sites are double - $28, Open May-Sep, Max Length: 50ft, Reservations accepted, Elev: 3578ft/1091m, Tel: 406-646-1012, Nearest town: Hungry Horse. GPS: 48.272008, -113.816511

35 • A1 | Rock Lake (Kootenai NF)

Total sites: 5, RV sites: 5, No water, Vault/pit toilet, Tent & RV camping: Free, Stay limit: 14 days, Max Length: 20ft, Elev: 2890ft/881m, Tel: 406-882-4451, Nearest town: Eureka. GPS: 48.823787, -115.010269

36 • A1 | Rocky Gorge (Kootenai NF)

Total sites: 60, RV sites: 60, Central water, Vault/pit toilet, No showers, No RV dump, Tent & RV camping: $16, Stay limit: 14 days, Open all year, Max Length: 32ft, Reservations not accepted, Elev: 2502ft/763m, Nearest town: Eureka. GPS: 48.652234, -115.311173

37 • A1 | Spar Lake (Kootenai NF)

Total sites: 13, RV sites: 13, Central water, Vault/pit toilet, No showers, No RV dump, Tent & RV camping: $12, Limited access and services in winter, Stay limit: 16 days, Open all year, Max Length: 28ft, Reservations not accepted, Elev: 3356ft/1023m, Tel: 406-295-4693, Nearest town: Troy. GPS: 48.269662, -115.953219

38 • A1 | Sylvia Lake (Flathead NF)

Total sites: 3, RV sites: 3, No water, Vault/pit toilet, Tent & RV camping: Free, Generator hours: 0600-2200, Open May-Nov, Max Length: 12ft, Reservations not accepted, Elev: 5056ft/1541m, Tel: 406-758-5208, Nearest town: Kalispell. GPS: 48.344423, -114.818601

39 • A1 | Tally Lake (Flathead NF)

Total sites: 40, RV sites: 40, Central water, Vault/pit toilet, No showers, RV dump, Tent & RV camping: $20, Generator hours: 0600-2200, Open May-Sep, Max Length: 60ft, Reservations accepted, Elev: 3366ft/1026m, Tel: 406-758-5208, Nearest town: Whitefish. GPS: 48.413818, -114.584473

40 • A1 | Tobacco River (Kootenai NF)

Total sites: 6, RV sites: 6, No water, Vault/pit toilet, Tent & RV camping: Free, Winter access may be limited, Stay limit: 14 days, Open all year, Max Length: 20ft, Reservations not accepted, Elev: 2457ft/749m, Tel: 406-296-2536, Nearest town: Eureka. GPS: 48.894411, -115.134981

41 • A1 | Tuchuck (Flathead NF)

Total sites: 7, RV sites: 7, No water, Vault/pit toilet, Tent & RV camping: Free, Horse facilities, Stay limit: 14 days, Open Jun-Sep, Max Length: 22ft, Reservations not accepted, Elev: 4629ft/1411m, Tel: 406-387-3800, Nearest town: Columbia Falls. GPS: 48.922626, -114.599057

42 • A1 | Upper Stillwater Lake (Flathead NF)

Total sites: 5, RV sites: 5, No water, Vault/pit toilet, Tent & RV camping: Free, Generator hours: 0600-2200, Open May-Nov, Reservations not accepted, Elev: 3205ft/977m, Tel: 406-758-5208, Nearest town: Whitefish. GPS: 48.603516, -114.656307

43 • A1 | Whitetail (Kootenai NF)

Total sites: 12, RV sites: 12, Central water, Vault/pit toilet, No showers, No RV dump, Tent & RV camping: $12, Limited access and services in winter, Stay limit: 14 days, Open all year, Reservations not accepted, Elev: 2976ft/907m, Tel: 406-295-4693, Nearest town: Troy. GPS: 48.827637, -115.814453

44 • A1 | Yaak Falls (Kootenai NF)

Total sites: 7, RV sites: 7, No water, Vault/pit toilet, Tent & RV camping: $10, Limited winter access, Stay limit: 14 days, Open all year, Max Length: 24ft, Reservations not accepted, Elev: 2444ft/745m, Tel: 406-295-4693, Nearest town: Troy. GPS: 48.645021, -115.885458

45 • A1 | Yaak River (Kootenai NF)

Total sites: 44, RV sites: 44, Central water, Vault/pit toilet, No showers, No RV dump, Tent & RV camping: $16, Limited access and services in winter, Stay limit: 14 days, Open all year, Max Length: 32ft, Reservations not accepted, Elev: 1855ft/565m, Tel: 406-295-4693, Nearest town: Troy. GPS: 48.561822, -115.972106

46 • A2 | Devil Creek (Flathead NF)

Total sites: 14, RV sites: 14, Central water, Vault/pit toilet, No showers, No RV dump, Tent & RV camping: $16, Open May-Sep, Max Length: 44ft, Reservations accepted, Elev: 4459ft/1359m, Tel: 406-387-3800, Nearest town: East Glacier Park. GPS: 48.251141, -113.463589

47 • A2 | Summit (Helena-Lewis & Clark NF)

Total sites: 17, RV sites: 17, Central water, Vault/pit toilet, No showers, No RV dump, Tent & RV camping: $20, May be reserved as group site, Near RR, Mandatory food storage, Open May-Nov, Reservations not accepted, Elev: 5249ft/1600m, Tel: 406-466-5341, Nearest town: East Glacier Park. GPS: 48.318978, -113.351053

48 • B1 | Bull River (Kootenai NF)

Total sites: 26, RV sites: 26, Central water, Vault/pit toilet, No showers, No RV dump, Tent & RV camping: $16, Reservable group site $30, Stay limit: 16 days, Open May-Nov, Max Length: 40ft, Reservations not accepted, Elev: 2313ft/705m, Tel: 406-827-3533, Nearest town: Noxon. GPS: 48.030233, -115.842666

49 • B1 | Cabin City (Lolo NF)

Total sites: 24, RV sites: 24, Central water, Vault/pit toilet, No showers, No RV dump, Tent & RV camping: $15, Open May-Sep, Reservations not accepted, Elev: 3165ft/965m, Tel: 406-822-4233, Nearest town: De Borgia. GPS: 47.374415, -115.262408

50 • B1 | Cascade (Lolo NF)

Total sites: 10, RV sites: 10, Central water, Vault/pit toilet, No showers, No RV dump, Tent & RV camping: $15, Group site: $20, Open May-Oct, Reservations not accepted, Elev: 2516ft/767m, Tel: 406-826-3821, Nearest town: Plains. GPS: 47.306644, -114.825312

51 • B1 | Charles Waters (Bitterroot NF)

Total sites: 27, RV sites: 27, Central water, Vault/pit toilet, No showers, No RV dump, Tent & RV camping: $15, Stay limit: 16 days, Open May-Sep, Max Length: 70ft, Reservations not accepted, Elev: 3740ft/1140m, Tel: 406-777-5461, Nearest town: Stevensville. GPS: 46.575439, -114.140625

52 • B1 | Clark Memorial (Lolo NF)

Total sites: 5, RV sites: 0, No water, Vault/pit toilet, Tents only: Free, Reservations not accepted, Elev: 2585ft/788m, Tel: 406-826-3821, Nearest town: Thompson Falls. GPS: 47.631795, -115.174211

53 • B1 | Clearwater Crossing (Lolo NF)

Total sites: 3, RV sites: 3, Central water, Vault/pit toilet, No showers, No RV dump, Tent & RV camping: Free, Reservations not accepted, Elev: 3493ft/1065m, Tel: 406-626-5201, Nearest town: Alberton. GPS: 46.908889, -114.803115

54 • B1 | Copper King (Lolo NF)

Total sites: 4, RV sites: 0, No water, Vault/pit toilet, Tents only: Free, Open Jun-Oct, Reservations not accepted, Elev: 2556ft/779m, Tel: 406-826-3821, Nearest town: Thompson Falls. GPS: 47.619478, -115.188245

55 • B1 | Dalles (Lolo NF)

Total sites: 10, RV sites: 0, Central water, Vault/pit toilet, No showers, No RV dump, Tents only: $15, Limited services and no fees Sep - Apr, Open May-Oct, Reservations not accepted, Elev: 4058ft/1237m, Tel: 406-329-3814, Nearest town: Clinton. GPS: 46.557257, -113.710092

56 • B1 | Fishtrap Lake (Lolo NF)

Total sites: 13, RV sites: 4, Central water, Vault/pit toilet, No showers, No RV dump, Tent & RV camping: $10, No water Oct-May, Open all year, Max Length: 28ft, Reservations not accepted, Elev: 4131ft/1259m, Tel: 406-329-3750, Nearest town: Thompson Falls. GPS: 47.861395, -115.202918

57 • B1 | Gold Rush (Lolo NF)

Total sites: 7, RV sites: 7, Central water, Vault/pit toilet, No showers, No RV dump, Tent & RV camping: Free, No water Oct-May, Open Jun-Oct, Reservations not accepted, Elev: 3573ft/1089m, Tel: 406-826-3821, Nearest town: Thompson Falls. GPS: 47.522820, -115.311470

58 • B1 | Graves Bay (Flathead NF)

Total sites: 10, RV sites: 10, Tent & RV camping: Free, Elev: 3547ft/1081m, Nearest town: Hungry Horse. GPS: 48.126689, -113.809421

59 • B1 | Grizzly (Lolo NF)

Total sites: 9, RV sites: 0, Central water, Vault/pit toilet, No showers, No RV dump, Tents only: $15, RVs not recommended due to narrow and rough road, Open May-Sep, Reservations not accepted, Elev: 4056ft/1236m, Tel: 406-329-3814, Nearest town: Clinton. GPS: 46.574239, -113.660637

60 • B1 | Handkerchief Lake (Flathead NF)

Total sites: 3, RV sites: 0, No water, Vault/pit toilet, Tents only: Free, Walk-to sites, Stay limit: 14 days, Open Jun-Sep, Reservations not accepted, Elev: 4134ft/1260m, Tel: 406-387-3800, Nearest town: Hungry Horse. GPS: 48.143803, -113.826242

61 • B1 | Harry's Flat (Lolo NF)

Total sites: 15, RV sites: 0, Central water, Vault/pit toilet, No showers, No RV dump, Tents only: $15, Limited services and no fees Oct - Apr, Open all year, Reservations not accepted, Elev: 4110ft/1253m, Tel: 406-329-3814, Nearest town: Clinton. GPS: 46.535255, -113.752288

62 • B1 | Jack Pine Flats (Kootenai NF)

Total sites: 1, RV sites: 1, No water, Vault/pit toilet, Tent & RV camping: Free, Nothing larger than van/pu, Limited winter access, Stay limit: 14 days, Open all year, Max Length: 16ft, Reservations not accepted, Elev: 2999ft/914m, Nearest town: Trout Creek. GPS: 47.685647, -115.645898

63 • B1 | Kreis Pond (Lolo NF)

Total sites: 7, RV sites: 7, No water, Vault/pit toilet, Tent & RV camping: $10, Open Apr-Nov, Reservations not accepted, Elev: 3711ft/1131m, Tel: 406-626-5201, Nearest town: Alberton. GPS: 47.099820, -114.426330

64 • B1 | Lake Creek (Kootenai NF)

Total sites: 4, RV sites: 4, Central water, Vault/pit toilet, No showers, No RV dump, Tent & RV camping: Free, Limited winter access, Stay limit: 14 days, Open all year, Max Length: 32ft, Reservations not accepted, Elev: 3412ft/1040m, Tel: 406-293-7773, Nearest town: Libby. GPS: 48.038909, -115.489955

65 • B1 | Lee Creek (Lolo NF)

Total sites: 22, RV sites: 22, Central water, Vault/pit toilet, No showers, No RV dump, Tent & RV camping: $15, Open May-Sep, Reservations not accepted, Elev: 4245ft/1294m, Tel: 406-329-3814, Nearest town: Lolo. GPS: 46.705233, -114.537089

66 • B1 | Lindberg Lake (Flathead NF)

Total sites: 11, RV sites: 11, No water, Vault/pit toilet, Tent & RV camping: $10, Stay limit: 16 days, Generator hours: 0600-2200, Max Length: 20ft, Reservations not accepted, Elev: 4393ft/1339m,

Tel: 406-837-7500, Nearest town: Seeley Lake. GPS: 47.407645, -113.721879

67 • B1 | Lolo Creek (Lolo NF)

Total sites: 17, RV sites: 17, Central water, Vault/pit toilet, No showers, No RV dump, Tent & RV camping: $15, Open May-Sep, Reservations not accepted, Elev: 3783ft/1153m, Tel: 406-329-3814, Nearest town: Lolo. GPS: 46.775829, -114.383892

68 • B1 | Marten Creek (Kootenai NF)

Total sites: 6, RV sites: 6, No water, Vault/pit toilet, Tent & RV camping: Free, 1 group site, Stay limit: 14 days, Open all year, Max Length: 32ft, Reservations not accepted, Elev: 2418ft/737m, Tel: 406-827-3533, Nearest town: Trout Creek. GPS: 47.882121, -115.747711

69 • B1 | McGregor Lake (Kootenai NF)

Total sites: 27, RV sites: 27, Central water, Vault/pit toilet, No showers, No RV dump, Tent & RV camping: $20, Reservable group site: $30, Stay limit: 14 days, Open May-Sep, Max Length: 32ft, Reservations not accepted, Elev: 3909ft/1191m, Tel: 406-293-7773, Nearest town: Libby. GPS: 48.032139, -114.902378

70 • B1 | Missoula Lake (Bitterroot NF)

Total sites: 5, RV sites: 5, No water, Vault/pit toilet, Tent & RV camping: Free, Reservations not accepted, Elev: 6319ft/1926m, Nearest town: Superior. GPS: 47.060302, -115.116204

71 • B1 | North Shore (Kootenai NF)

Total sites: 16, RV sites: 16, Central water, Vault/pit toilet, No showers, No RV dump, Tent & RV camping: $16, Stay limit: 14 days, Open May-Nov, Max Length: 40ft, Reservations not accepted, Elev: 2361ft/720m, Tel: 406-827-3533, Nearest town: Trout Creek. GPS: 47.861806, -115.631149

72 • B1 | Norton (Lolo NF)

Total sites: 13, RV sites: 0, Central water, Vault/pit toilet, No showers, No RV dump, Tents only: $15, Open May-Sep, Reservations not accepted, Elev: 3947ft/1203m, Tel: 406-329-3814, Nearest town: Clinton. GPS: 46.587703, -113.668702

73 • B1 | Pleasant Valley (Kootenai NF)

Total sites: 7, RV sites: 7, No water, Vault/pit toilet, No showers, No RV dump, Tent & RV camping: Free, Limted winter access, Stay limit: 14 days, Open all year, Max Length: 32ft, Reservations not accepted, Elev: 3067ft/935m, Nearest town: Libby. GPS: 48.042314, -115.290626

74 • B1 | Quartz Flat (Lolo NF)

Total sites: 77, RV sites: 35, Central water, Flush toilet, No showers, RV dump, Tent & RV camping: $15, Open May-Sep, Reservations accepted, Elev: 2868ft/874m, Tel: 406-822-4233, Nearest town: Superior. GPS: 47.075819, -114.767481

75 • B1 | Sloway (Lolo NF)

Total sites: 27, RV sites: 27, Central water, Vault/pit toilet, No showers, No RV dump, Tent & RV camping: $15, Open May-Sep, Reservations not accepted, Elev: 2671ft/814m, Tel: 406-822-4233, Nearest town: Superior. GPS: 47.232718, -115.021814

76 • B1 | Swan Lake (Flathead NF)

Total sites: 33, RV sites: 33, Central water, Vault/pit toilet, No showers, No RV dump, Tent & RV camping: $20, Group site $100-$325, Open May-Sep, Max Length: 75ft, Reservations accepted, Elev: 3173ft/967m, Tel: 406-837-7500, Nearest town: Swan Lake. GPS: 47.936559, -113.847533

77 • B1 | Sylvan Lake (Kootenai NF)

Total sites: 5, RV sites: 5, No water, Vault/pit toilet, Tent & RV camping: Free, Limited winter access, Stay limit: 16 days, Open all year, Reservations not accepted, Elev: 3627ft/1106m, Tel: 406-293-7773, Nearest town: Kalispell. GPS: 47.916343, -115.278677

78 • B1 | Trout Creek (Lozeau) (Lolo NF)

Total sites: 12, RV sites: 12, Central water, Vault/pit toilet, No showers, No RV dump, Tent & RV camping: $15, Open all year, Max Length: 18ft, Reservations not accepted, Elev: 2923ft/891m, Tel: 406-822-4233, Nearest town: Superior. GPS: 47.116943, -114.868652

79 • B1 | West Fork Fishtrap Creek (Lolo NF)

Total sites: 4, RV sites: 4, Central water, Vault/pit toilet, No showers, No RV dump, Tent & RV camping: Free, No water Oct-May, Open May-Sep, Reservations not accepted, Elev: 3596ft/1096m, Tel: 406-826-3821, Nearest town: Thompson Falls. GPS: 47.816600, -115.149220

80 • B1 | Willow Creek (Vermilion Peak) (Kootenai NF)

Total sites: 6, RV sites: 6, No water, Vault/pit toilet, Tent & RV camping: Free, High-clearance vehicle recommended, Limited winter access, Stay limit: 14 days, Open all year, Max Length: 40ft, Reservations not accepted, Elev: 3593ft/1095m, Tel: 406-827-3533, Nearest town: Trout Creek. GPS: 47.870963, -115.310572

81 • B2 | Aspen Grove (Helena-Lewis & Clark NF)

Total sites: 19, RV sites: 19, Central water, Vault/pit toilet, No showers, No RV dump, Tent & RV camping: $8, Stay limit: 14 days, Open May-Oct, Max Length: 20ft, Reservations not accepted, Elev: 4787ft/1459m, Tel: 406-362-7000, Nearest town: Lincoln. GPS: 46.978516, -112.531494

82 • B2 | Beaver Creek (Flathead NF)

Total sites: 4, RV sites: 4, No water, Vault/pit toilet, Tent & RV camping: Free, Stay limit: 14 days, Open May-Nov, Max Length: 32ft, Reservations not accepted, Elev: 4150ft/1265m, Tel: 406-758-5376, Nearest town: Hungry Horse. GPS: 47.923596, -113.373361

83 • B2 | Benchmark (Helena-Lewis & Clark NF)

Total sites: 25, RV sites: 25, Central water, Vault/pit toilet, No showers, No RV dump, Tent & RV camping: $10, Open Jun-Sep, Max Length: 22ft, Reservations not accepted, Elev: 5318ft/1621m, Nearest town: Augusta. GPS: 47.486572, -112.881104

84 • B2 | Big Larch (Lolo NF)

Total sites: 48, RV sites: 48, Central water, Vault/pit toilet, No showers, No RV dump, Tent & RV camping: $20, Reservable group sites $35, Open all year, Max Length: 32ft, Reservations not accepted, Elev: 4065ft/1239m, Tel: 406-677-2233, Nearest town: Seeley Lake. GPS: 47.184326, -113.492676

85 • B2 | Big Nelson (Lolo NF)

Total sites: 4, No water, Vault/pit toilet, Tents only: Free, Walk-to sites, Reservations not accepted, Elev: 4583ft/1397m, Tel: 406-677-2233, Nearest town: Ovando. GPS: 47.072084, -112.916024

86 • B2 | Cave Mountain (Helena-Lewis & Clark NF)

Total sites: 14, RV sites: 14, Central water, Vault/pit toilet, No showers, No RV dump, Tent & RV camping: $10, Open May-Sep, Max Length: 30ft, Reservations not accepted, Elev: 5131ft/1564m, Tel: 406-466-5341, Nearest town: Choteau. GPS: 47.890137, -112.726563

87 • B2 | Copper Creek (Silver King Mt) (Helena-Lewis & Clark NF)

Total sites: 17, RV sites: 17, Central water, Vault/pit toilet, No showers, No RV dump, Tent & RV camping: $15, Stay limit: 14 days, Open May-Aug, Reservations not accepted, Elev: 5322ft/1622m, Tel: 406-362-7000, Nearest town: Lincoln. GPS: 47.078369, -112.619385

88 • B2 | Cromwell-Dixon (Helena-Lewis & Clark NF)

Total sites: 15, RV sites: 15, Central water, Vault/pit toilet, No showers, No RV dump, Tent & RV camping: $15, Open Jun-Sep, Reservations not accepted, Elev: 6250ft/1905m, Tel: 406-449-5490, Nearest town: Helena. GPS: 46.556303, -112.315633

89 • B2 | Devils Corkscrew (Flathead NF)

Total sites: 4, RV sites: 4, No water, Vault/pit toilet, Tent & RV camping: Free, Stay limit: 16 days, Max Length: 32ft, Reservations not accepted, Elev: 3648ft/1112m, Tel: 406-387-3800, Nearest town: Martin City. GPS: 48.110029, -113.696335

90 • B2 | Double Falls (Helena-Lewis & Clark NF)

Total sites: 4, RV sites: 4, No water, Vault/pit toilet, Tent & RV camping: Free, Mandatory food storage, Reservations not accepted, Elev: 5282ft/1610m, Tel: 406-466-5341, Nearest town: Augusta. GPS: 47.407334, -112.722084

91 • B2 | Elko (Helena-Lewis & Clark NF)

Total sites: 3, RV sites: 3, No water, Vault/pit toilet, Tent & RV camping: Free, Mandatory food storage, Reservations not accepted, Elev: 5349ft/1630m, Tel: 406-466-5341, Nearest town: Choteau. GPS: 47.924348, -112.763595

92 • B2 | Holland Lake - Bay Loop (Flathead NF)

Total sites: 22, RV sites: 22, Central water, Flush toilet, No showers, RV dump, Tent & RV camping: $18, Dump fee, Open May-Sep, Max Length: 48ft, Reservations accepted, Elev: 4078ft/1243m, Tel: 406-837-7500, Nearest town: Seeley Lake. GPS: 47.451098, -113.607858

93 • B2 | Holland Lake - Larch Loop (Flathead NF)

Total sites: 15, RV sites: 15, Central water, Flush toilet, No showers, RV dump, Tent & RV camping: $18, Dump fee, Group site $100-$325, Open May-Sep, Max Length: 48ft, Reservations accepted, Elev: 4065ft/1239m, Tel: 406-837-7500, Nearest town: Seeley Lake. GPS: 47.445358, -113.616815

94 • B2 | Home Gulch (Helena-Lewis & Clark NF)

Total sites: 15, RV sites: 15, Central water, Vault/pit toilet, No showers, No RV dump, Tent & RV camping: $6, May be reserved for larger groups, Open Jun-Sep, Reservations not accepted, Elev: 4488ft/1368m, Tel: 406-466-5341, Nearest town: Augusta. GPS: 47.616012, -112.726167

95 • B2 | Lake Alva (Lolo NF)

Total sites: 39, RV sites: 39, Central water, Vault/pit toilet, No showers, No RV dump, Tent & RV camping: $20, Group sites (2)(Closed 2022): $45-$50, No winter fee, Open all year, Max Length: 27ft, Reservations not accepted, Elev: 4127ft/1258m, Tel: 406-677-2233, Nearest town: Seeley Lake. GPS: 47.324754, -113.583819

96 • B2 | Lake Inez (Lolo NF)

Total sites: 5, RV sites: 5, No water, Vault/pit toilet, Tent & RV camping: $10, Group site: $50, Open all year, Reservations not accepted, Elev: 4209ft/1283m, Tel: 406-677-2233, Nearest town: Seeley Lake. GPS: 47.294099, -113.567813

97 • B2 | Lakeside (Old Alva) (Lolo NF)

Total sites: 4, RV sites: 4, No water, Vault/pit toilet, Tent & RV camping: $15, Reservable group site $14-$28, Open May-Sep, Reservations accepted, Elev: 4176ft/1273m, Tel: 406-677-2233, Nearest town: Seeley Lake. GPS: 47.307000, -113.576000

98 • B2 | Mill Falls (Helena-Lewis & Clark NF)

Total sites: 4, RV sites: 4, No water, Vault/pit toilet, Tent & RV camping: Free, Mandatory food storage, Reservations not accepted, Elev: 5682ft/1732m, Tel: 406-466-5341, Nearest town: Choteau. GPS: 47.859049, -112.772458

99 • B2 | Monture Creek (Lolo NF)

Total sites: 5, RV sites: 5, No water, Vault/pit toilet, Tent & RV camping: Free, Open May-Sep, Reservations not accepted, Elev: 4203ft/1281m, Tel: 406-677-2233, Nearest town: Ovando. GPS: 47.123893, -113.145456

100 • B2 | Mortimer Gulch (Helena-Lewis & Clark NF)

Total sites: 26, RV sites: 26, Central water, Vault/pit toilet, No showers, No RV dump, Tent & RV camping: $15, Reservable group site, Open Jun-Sep, Max Length: 22ft, Reservations not accepted, Elev: 4993ft/1522m, Tel: 406-466-5341, Nearest town: Augusta. GPS: 47.609583, -112.770733

101 • B2 | Owl Creek Packer Camp (Flathead NF)

Total sites: 8, RV sites: 8, Central water, Vault/pit toilet, Tent & RV camping: Fee unk, Open all year, Reservations not accepted, Elev: 4069ft/1240m, Tel: 406-309-2018, Nearest town: Seeley Lake. GPS: 47.440315, -113.607721

102 • B2 | Peters Creek (Flathead NF)

Total sites: 6, RV sites: 6, No water, Vault/pit toilet, Tent & RV camping: Free, Mandatory food storage, Stay limit: 14 days, Open May-Sep, Max Length: 30ft, Reservations not accepted, Elev: 3691ft/1125m, Tel: 406-758-5376, Nearest town: Hungry Horse. GPS: 48.057377, -113.644569

103 • B2 | Rainy Lake (Lolo NF)

Total sites: 5, RV sites: 2, No water, Vault/pit toilet, Tent & RV camping: Free, Reservations not accepted, Elev: 4157ft/1267m,

Tel: 406-677-2233, Nearest town: Seeley Lake. GPS: 47.336831, -113.593337

104 • B2 | River Point (Lolo NF)

Total sites: 26, RV sites: 26, Central water, Vault/pit toilet, No showers, No RV dump, Tent & RV camping: $20, Open May-Sep, Max Length: 22ft, Reservations required, Elev: 3996ft/1218m, Tel: 406-677-2233, Nearest town: Seeley Lake. GPS: 47.187256, -113.514404

105 • B2 | Seeley Lake (Lolo NF)

Total sites: 29, RV sites: 29, Central water, Vault/pit toilet, No showers, No RV dump, Tent & RV camping: $20, Open May-Sep, Max Length: 32ft, Reservations not accepted, Elev: 4042ft/1232m, Tel: 406-677-2233, Nearest town: Seeley Lake. GPS: 47.191650, -113.518555

106 • B2 | South Fork (Helena-Lewis & Clark NF)

Total sites: 7, RV sites: 7, Central water, Vault/pit toilet, No showers, No RV dump, Tent & RV camping: $10, Open Jun-Sep, Reservations not accepted, Elev: 5325ft/1623m, Tel: 406-466-5341, Nearest town: Augusta. GPS: 47.501821, -112.887862

107 • B2 | Spotted Bear (Flathead NF)

Total sites: 13, RV sites: 13, Central water, Vault/pit toilet, No showers, No RV dump, Tent & RV camping: $13, No fee 9/30 - 5/15, Stay limit: 14 days, Open all year, Max Length: 32ft, Reservations not accepted, Elev: 3747ft/1142m, Tel: 406-758-5376, Nearest town: Hungry Horse. GPS: 47.926321, -113.527434

108 • B2 | Straight Creek Packer Horse Camp (Helena-Lewis & Clark NF)

Total sites: 6, RV sites: 6, Central water, Vault/pit toilet, No showers, No RV dump, Tent & RV camping: Fee unk, Reservations not accepted, Elev: 5276ft/1608m, Nearest town: Augusta. GPS: 47.496345, -112.889552

109 • B2 | Vigilante (Helena-Lewis & Clark NF)

Total sites: 14, RV sites: 14, Central water, Vault/pit toilet, No showers, No RV dump, Tent & RV camping: $15, Open May-Oct, Max Length: 16ft, Reservations not accepted, Elev: 4485ft/1367m, Tel: 406-449-5490, Nearest town: Helena. GPS: 46.766846, -111.650635

110 • B2 | West Fork Teton (Helena-Lewis & Clark NF)

Total sites: 6, RV sites: 0, Central water, Vault/pit toilet, No showers, No RV dump, Tents only: $6, Mandatory food storage, Reservations not accepted, Elev: 5640ft/1719m, Nearest town: Choteau. GPS: 47.961182, -112.806931

111 • B2 | Wood Lake (Helena-Lewis & Clark NF)

Total sites: 9, RV sites: 9, Central water, Vault/pit toilet, No showers, No RV dump, Tent & RV camping: $10, Stay limit: 14 days, Open Jun-Sep, Max Length: 22ft, Reservations not accepted, Elev: 5896ft/1797m, Nearest town: Augusta. GPS: 47.427762, -112.793671

112 • B3 | Aspen (Belt Park Butte) (Helena-Lewis & Clark NF)

Total sites: 6, RV sites: 6, Central water, Vault/pit toilet, No showers, No RV dump, Tent & RV camping: $15, Open May-Sep, Reservations not accepted, Elev: 5141ft/1567m, Tel: 406-236-5100, Nearest town: Neihart. GPS: 46.992981, -110.768313

113 • B3 | Basin Creek (Helena-Lewis & Clark NF)

Total sites: 4, RV sites: 4, No water, Vault/pit toilet, Tent & RV camping: Free, Reservations not accepted, Elev: 5669ft/1728m, Nearest town: Checkerboard. GPS: 46.642202, -110.430243

114 • B3 | Crystal Lake (Helena-Lewis & Clark NF)

Total sites: 23, RV sites: 23, Central water, Vault/pit toilet, No showers, No RV dump, Tent & RV camping: $20, Stay limit: 16 days, Open Jun-Sep, Max Length: 22ft, Reservations not accepted, Elev: 6056ft/1846m, Tel: 406-566-2292, Nearest town: Lewistown. GPS: 46.794678, -109.511475

115 • B3 | Daisy Dean (Helena-Lewis & Clark NF)

Total sites: 10, RV sites: 10, No water, Vault/pit toilet, Tent & RV camping: Free, Reservations not accepted, Elev: 6099ft/1859m, Nearest town: Martinsdale. GPS: 46.623207, -110.358729

116 • B3 | Dry Wolf (Helena-Lewis & Clark NF)

Total sites: 25, RV sites: 25, Central water, Vault/pit toilet, No showers, No RV dump, Tent & RV camping: $15, Mandatory food storage, Max Length: 32ft, Reservations not accepted, Elev: 5915ft/1803m, Nearest town: Stanford. GPS: 46.979004, -110.518311

117 • B3 | Hay Canyon (Helena-Lewis & Clark NF)

Total sites: 9, RV sites: 9, No water, Vault/pit toilet, Tent & RV camping: $10, Mandatory food storage, Max Length: 30ft, Reservations not accepted, Elev: 5178ft/1578m, Nearest town: Utica. GPS: 46.798738, -110.300043

118 • B3 | Jellison Place (Helena-Lewis & Clark NF)

Total sites: 10, RV sites: 10, No water, Vault/pit toilet, Tent & RV camping: Free, Mandatory food storage, Reservations not accepted, Elev: 5853ft/1784m, Tel: 406-632-4391, Nearest town: Harlowton. GPS: 46.673281, -110.072132

119 • B3 | Judith Station (Helena-Lewis & Clark NF)

Total sites: 6, RV sites: 6, Central water, Vault/pit toilet, No showers, No RV dump, Tent & RV camping: Fee unk, Stay limit: 16 days, Max Length: 30ft, Reservations not accepted, Elev: 5072ft/1546m, Nearest town: Utica. GPS: 46.848313, -110.289512

120 • B3 | Jumping Creek (Helena-Lewis & Clark NF)

Total sites: 10, RV sites: 10, Central water, Vault/pit toilet, No showers, No RV dump, Tent & RV camping: $15, Open Jun-Sep, Reservations not accepted, Elev: 5922ft/1805m, Tel: 406-547-3361, Nearest town: Neihart. GPS: 46.763916, -110.785400

121 • B3 | Kings Hill (Helena-Lewis & Clark NF)

Total sites: 18, RV sites: 18, Central water, Vault/pit toilet, No showers, No RV dump, Tent & RV camping: $15, Open May-Sep, Reservations not accepted, Elev: 7444ft/2269m, Nearest town: Neihart. GPS: 46.841628, -110.696879

122 • B3 | Logging Creek (Helena-Lewis & Clark NF)

Total sites: 25, RV sites: 25, Central water, Vault/pit toilet, No showers, No RV dump, Tent & RV camping: $10, Open May-Sep,

Reservations not accepted, Elev: 4610ft/1405m, Nearest town: Monarch. GPS: 47.100359, -111.010023

123 • B3 | Many Pines (Helena-Lewis & Clark NF)

Total sites: 22, RV sites: 22, Central water, Vault/pit toilet, No showers, No RV dump, Tent & RV camping: $15, Open May-Sep, Reservations not accepted, Elev: 6050ft/1844m, Nearest town: Neihart. GPS: 46.898665, -110.690765

124 • B3 | Moose Creek (Moose Mt) (Helena-Lewis & Clark NF)

Total sites: 6, RV sites: 6, Central water, Vault/pit toilet, No showers, No RV dump, Tent & RV camping: $10, Open Jun-Sep, Elev: 5879ft/1792m, Nearest town: White Sulphur Springs. GPS: 46.835789, -110.874981

125 • B3 | Russian Flat (Helena-Lewis & Clark NF)

Total sites: 2, RV sites: 2, No water, Vault/pit toilet, Tent & RV camping: Free, Mandatory food storage, Reservations not accepted, Elev: 6346ft/1934m, Nearest town: Checkerboard. GPS: 46.725368, -110.423697

126 • B3 | Spring Creek (Mount Howe) (Helena-Lewis & Clark NF)

Total sites: 10, RV sites: 10, Central water, Vault/pit toilet, No showers, No RV dump, Tent & RV camping: $10, Open May-Sep, Reservations not accepted, Elev: 5305ft/1617m, Nearest town: White Sulphur Springs. GPS: 46.586426, -110.467529

127 • B3 | Thain Creek (Helena-Lewis & Clark NF)

Total sites: 16, RV sites: 16, Central water, Vault/pit toilet, Tent & RV camping: $7, Reservations not accepted, Elev: 4596ft/1401m, Tel: 406-566-2292, Nearest town: Great Falls. GPS: 47.475586, -110.584229

128 • B3 | Timber Creek Dispersed (Helena-Lewis & Clark NF)

Total sites: 4, RV sites: 4, No water, Vault/pit toilet, Tent & RV camping: Free, Max Length: 16ft, Reservations not accepted, Elev: 5804ft/1769m, Nearest town: Lewis and Clark NF. GPS: 46.725361, -109.485475

129 • B3 | Whitetail Camp (Helena-Lewis & Clark NF)

Total sites: 12, RV sites: 12, No water, Vault/pit toilet, Tent & RV camping: Free, Mandatory food storage, Reservations not accepted, Elev: 6375ft/1943m, Nearest town: Checkerboard. GPS: 46.682363, -110.502753

130 • C1 | Alta (Bitterroot NF)

Total sites: 9, RV sites: 9, Central water, Vault/pit toilet, No showers, No RV dump, Tent & RV camping: $15, Open May-Sep, Max Length: 40ft, Reservations accepted, Elev: 4970ft/1515m, Tel: 406-821-3269, Nearest town: Darby. GPS: 45.624432, -114.302107

131 • C1 | Bear Creek Pass Horse Camp (Bitterroot NF)

Total sites: 7, RV sites: 7, No water, Vault/pit toilet, Tent & RV camping: Fee unk, High clearance vehicles recommended, Max Length: 32ft, Reservations not accepted, Elev: 6211ft/1893m, Tel: 406-821-3913, Nearest town: Darby. GPS: 46.115605, -114.494196

132 • C1 | Bitterroot Flat (Lolo NF)

Total sites: 15, RV sites: 0, Central water, Vault/pit toilet, No showers, No RV dump, Tents only: $6, Rough road, Limited services and no fees Sep-Apr, Open all year, Reservations not accepted, Elev: 4429ft/1350m, Tel: 406-329-3814, Nearest town: Clinton. GPS: 46.467568, -113.777049

133 • C1 | Black Bear (Bitterroot NF)

Total sites: 6, RV sites: 6, No water, Vault/pit toilet, Tent & RV camping: Free, Stay limit: 16 days, Generator hours: 0600-2200, Open Jun-Sep, Max Length: 50ft, Reservations not accepted, Elev: 4626ft/1410m, Tel: 406-821-3913, Nearest town: Hamilton. GPS: 46.166026, -113.924677

134 • C1 | Blodgett (Bitterroot NF)

Total sites: 6, RV sites: 5, Central water, Vault/pit toilet, No showers, No RV dump, Tent & RV camping: Fee unk, Open May-Sep, Max Length: 45ft, Reservations not accepted, Elev: 4304ft/1312m, Tel: 406-777-5461, Nearest town: Hamilton. GPS: 46.269529, -114.243869

135 • C1 | Crazy Creek (Bitterroot NF)

Total sites: 7, RV sites: 7, Central water, Vault/pit toilet, No showers, No RV dump, Tent & RV camping: $12, Generator hours: 0600-2200, Open Jun-Nov, Max Length: 26ft, Reservations not accepted, Elev: 4927ft/1502m, Tel: 406-821-3201, Nearest town: Sula. GPS: 45.810623, -114.068587

136 • C1 | Crazy Creek Horse Camp (Bitterroot NF)

Total sites: 5, RV sites: 5, No water, Vault/pit toilet, No showers, No RV dump, Tent & RV camping: Free, Stream water available, Generator hours: 0600-2200, Open Jun-Nov, Max Length: 26ft, Reservations not accepted, Elev: 4815ft/1468m, Tel: 406-821-3201, Nearest town: Sula. GPS: 45.815412, -114.070763

137 • C1 | Crystal Creek (Beaverhead-Deerlodge NF)

Total sites: 3, RV sites: 3, No water, Vault/pit toilet, Tent & RV camping: Free, Open Jul-Sep, Max Length: 16ft, Reservations not accepted, Elev: 6972ft/2125m, Tel: 406-859-3211, Nearest town: Philipsburg. GPS: 46.232615, -113.745901

138 • C1 | Fales Flat Group (Bitterroot NF)

Total sites: 1, No water, Vault/pit toilet, Tent & RV camping: $15, Group sites: $30, Some individual sites available first-come/first-served, Open May-Sep, Reservations accepted, Elev: 5151ft/1570m, Tel: 406-821-3269, Nearest town: Conner. GPS: 45.746043, -114.443457

139 • C1 | Gold Creek (Bitterroot NF)

Total sites: 4, RV sites: 4, No water, Vault/pit toilet, Tent & RV camping: Free, Rough road, Max Length: 25ft, Reservations not accepted, Elev: 4951ft/1509m, Tel: 406-777-5461, Nearest town: Stevensville. GPS: 46.397539, -113.902325

140 • C1 | Indian Trees (Bitterroot NF)

Total sites: 15, RV sites: 14, Central water, Vault/pit toilet, No showers, No RV dump, Tent & RV camping: $15, Generator hours: 0600-2200, Open May-Sep, Max Length: 100ft, Reservations accepted, Elev: 5144ft/1568m, Tel: 406-821-3201, Nearest town: Sula. GPS: 45.755859, -113.954346

141 • C1 | Jennings Camp (Bitterroot NF)

Total sites: 4, RV sites: 4, No water, Vault/pit toilet, Tent & RV camping: Free, Generator hours: 0600-2200, Open May-Nov, Max Length: 20ft, Reservations not accepted, Elev: 4895ft/1492m, Tel: 406-821-3201, Nearest town: Sula. GPS: 45.896241, -113.819515

142 • C1 | Lake Como (Bitterroot NF)

Total sites: 10, RV sites: 10, Elec sites: 10, Water at site, Vault/pit toilet, No showers, No RV dump, Tent & RV camping: $25, Stay limit: 7 days, Open Jun-Sep, Reservations not accepted, Elev: 4285ft/1306m, Tel: 406-821-3913, Nearest town: Darby. GPS: 46.068276, -114.235772

143 • C1 | Martin Creek (Bitterroot NF)

Total sites: 7, RV sites: 7, Central water, Vault/pit toilet, No showers, No RV dump, Tent & RV camping: $12, Generator hours: 0600-2200, Open May-Nov, Max Length: 50ft, Reservations not accepted, Elev: 5315ft/1620m, Tel: 406-821-3201, Nearest town: Sula. GPS: 45.931801, -113.722608

144 • C1 | May Creek (Beaverhead-Deerlodge NF)

Total sites: 21, RV sites: 21, Central water, Vault/pit toilet, No showers, No RV dump, Tent & RV camping: $7, Stay limit: 16 days, Open Jun-Sep, Max Length: 30ft, Reservations not accepted, Elev: 6384ft/1946m, Tel: 406-689-3243, Nearest town: Wisdom. GPS: 45.651556, -113.781353

145 • C1 | Miner Lake (Beaverhead-Deerlodge NF)

Total sites: 18, RV sites: 18, Central water, Vault/pit toilet, No showers, No RV dump, Tent & RV camping: $7, Open Jun-Sep, Max Length: 20ft, Reservations not accepted, Elev: 7034ft/2144m, Tel: 406-689-3243, Nearest town: Jackson. GPS: 45.322943, -113.578941

146 • C1 | Mussigbrod (Beaverhead-Deerlodge NF)

Total sites: 10, RV sites: 10, Central water, Vault/pit toilet, No showers, No RV dump, Tent & RV camping: $7, Open Jun-Sep, Max Length: 30ft, Reservations not accepted, Elev: 6549ft/1996m, Tel: 406-689-3243, Nearest town: Wisdom. GPS: 45.789696, -113.609238

147 • C1 | Rock Creek Horse Camp (Bitterroot NF)

Total sites: 11, RV sites: 11, No water, Vault/pit toilet, Tent & RV camping: $12, Stay limit: 14 days, Generator hours: 0600-2200, Open May-Sep, Reservations not accepted, Elev: 4219ft/1286m, Tel: 406-821-3913, Nearest town: Darby. GPS: 46.063674, -114.229909

148 • C1 | Rombo (Bitterroot NF)

Total sites: 15, RV sites: 15, Central water, Vault/pit toilet, No showers, No RV dump, Tent & RV camping: $15, No services Sep-May, Open all year, Max Length: 50ft, Reservations accepted, Elev: 4521ft/1378m, Tel: 406-821-3269, Nearest town: Darby. GPS: 45.763896, -114.281992

149 • C1 | Sam Billings Memorial (Bitterroot NF)

Total sites: 11, RV sites: 11, No water, Vault/pit toilet, Tent & RV camping: Fee unk, Open May-Nov, Max Length: 30ft, Reservations not accepted, Elev: 4524ft/1379m, Tel: 406-821-3269, Nearest town: Darby. GPS: 45.825741, -114.250667

150 • C1 | Schumaker (Bitterroot NF)

Total sites: 14, RV sites: 14, No water, Vault/pit toilet, Tent & RV camping: Free, Stay limit: 16 days, Generator hours: 0600-2200, Open Jul-Sep, Reservations not accepted, Elev: 6549ft/1996m, Tel: 406-821-3913, Nearest town: Darby. GPS: 46.151268, -114.496812

151 • C1 | Siria (Lolo NF)

Total sites: 4, RV sites: 0, No water, Vault/pit toilet, Tents only: Free, Open all year, Elev: 4477ft/1365m, Tel: 406-329-3814, Nearest town: Philipsburg. GPS: 46.422936, -113.719738

152 • C1 | Slate Creek (Bitterroot NF)

Total sites: 4, RV sites: 4, No water, Vault/pit toilet, Tent & RV camping: Free, Open May-Nov, Max Length: 25ft, Reservations not accepted, Elev: 4820ft/1469m, Tel: 406-821-3269, Nearest town: Darby. GPS: 45.697908, -114.281373

153 • C1 | Spring Gulch (Bitterroot NF)

Total sites: 9, RV sites: 8, Central water, Vault/pit toilet, No showers, No RV dump, Tent & RV camping: $15, Open May-Sep, Max Length: 99ft, Reservations accepted, Elev: 4386ft/1337m, Tel: 406-821-3201, Nearest town: Sula. GPS: 45.858467, -114.022254

154 • C1 | Three Frogs (Bitterroot NF)

Total sites: 20, RV sites: 16, Central water, Vault/pit toilet, No showers, No RV dump, Tent & RV camping: $15, Stay limit: 16 days, Generator hours: 0600-2200, Open May-Sep, Max Length: 30ft, Reservations not accepted, Elev: 4383ft/1336m, Tel: 406-821-3913, Nearest town: Darby. GPS: 46.066601, -114.244992

155 • C1 | Twin Lakes Camp (Beaverhead-Deerlodge NF)

Total sites: 21, RV sites: 21, Central water, Vault/pit toilet, No showers, No RV dump, Tent & RV camping: $7, Open Jun-Sep, Max Length: 25ft, Reservations not accepted, Elev: 7287ft/2221m, Tel: 406-689-3243, Nearest town: Wisdom. GPS: 45.411133, -113.688721

156 • C1 | Warm Springs (Bitterroot NF)

Total sites: 13, RV sites: 13, Central water, Vault/pit toilet, No showers, No RV dump, Tent & RV camping: $12, Generator hours: 0600-2200, Open May-Sep, Reservations not accepted, Elev: 4495ft/1370m, Tel: 406-821-3201, Nearest town: Sula. GPS: 45.843018, -114.040039

157 • C2 | Basin Canyon (Beaverhead-Deerlodge NF)

Total sites: 2, RV sites: 2, No water, Vault/pit toilet, Tent & RV camping: Free, Max Length: 16ft, Reservations not accepted, Elev: 5828ft/1776m, Tel: 406-287-3223, Nearest town: Butte. GPS: 45.855608, -112.546106

158 • C2 | Bear Creek (Beaverhead-Deerlodge NF)

Total sites: 12, RV sites: 12, Central water, Vault/pit toilet, No showers, No RV dump, Tent & RV camping: Free, Stay limit: 16 days, Open Jun-Oct, Max Length: 28ft, Reservations not accepted, Elev: 6365ft/1940m, Tel: 406-682-4253, Nearest town: Cameron. GPS: 45.156557, -111.553688

159 • C2 | Beaver Dam (Beaverhead-Deerlodge NF)

Total sites: 15, RV sites: 15, Central water, Vault/pit toilet, No

showers, No RV dump, Tent & RV camping: $5, Stay limit: 16 days, Open May-Sep, Max Length: 50ft, Elev: 6490ft/1978m, Tel: 406-494-2147, Nearest town: Butte. GPS: 45.884332, -112.782974

160 • C2 | Boulder Creek (Beaverhead-Deerlodge NF)

Total sites: 13, RV sites: 13, Central water, Vault/pit toilet, No showers, No RV dump, Tent & RV camping: $8, Open Jun-Sep, Max Length: 30ft, Reservations not accepted, Elev: 6457ft/1968m, Tel: 406-832-3178, Nearest town: Wise River. GPS: 45.651812, -113.066888

161 • C2 | Branham Lakes (Beaverhead-Deerlodge NF)

Total sites: 6, RV sites: 0, No water, Vault/pit toilet, Tents only: Free, Stay limit: 16 days, Open Jul-Sep, Reservations not accepted, Elev: 8884ft/2708m, Tel: 406-682-4253, Nearest town: West Yellowstone. GPS: 45.516491, -111.989771

162 • C2 | Cable Mountain (Beaverhead-Deerlodge NF)

Total sites: 11, RV sites: 11, Central water, Vault/pit toilet, No showers, No RV dump, Tent & RV camping: $13, Open May-Sep, Max Length: 22ft, Reservations not accepted, Elev: 6627ft/2020m, Tel: 406-859-3211, Nearest town: Philipsburg. GPS: 46.221436, -113.246826

163 • C2 | Canyon Creek (Vipond Park) (Beaverhead-Deerlodge NF)

Total sites: 3, RV sites: 3, No water, Vault/pit toilet, Tent & RV camping: Free, Max Length: 18ft, Elev: 7323ft/2232m, Tel: 406-832-3178, Nearest town: Melrose. GPS: 45.626110, -112.941390

164 • C2 | Copper Creek (Moose Lake) (Beaverhead-Deerlodge NF)

Total sites: 7, RV sites: 7, Central water, Vault/pit toilet, No showers, No RV dump, Tent & RV camping: Free, Stay limit: 16 days, Open May-Nov, Reservations not accepted, Elev: 5981ft/1823m, Tel: 406-859-3211, Nearest town: Philipsburg. GPS: 46.066272, -113.543706

165 • C2 | Cottonwood (Beaverhead-Deerlodge NF)

Total sites: 10, RV sites: 10, No toilets, Tent & RV camping: Free, Stay limit: 16 days, Max Length: 28ft, Reservations not accepted, Elev: 6335ft/1931m, Tel: 406-682-4253, Nearest town: Sheridan. GPS: 44.973933, -111.976399

166 • C2 | Delmoe Lake (Beaverhead-Deerlodge NF)

Total sites: 25, RV sites: 25, Central water, Vault/pit toilet, No showers, No RV dump, Tent & RV camping: $8, Stay limit: 16 days, Open May-Sep, Max Length: 32ft, Reservations not accepted, Elev: 6102ft/1860m, Tel: 406-287-3223, Nearest town: Butte. GPS: 45.986047, -112.353668

167 • C2 | Dinner Station (Beaverhead-Deerlodge NF)

Total sites: 8, RV sites: 8, Central water, Vault/pit toilet, No showers, No RV dump, Tent & RV camping: Fee unk, Stay limit: 16 days, Open May-Sep, Max Length: 16ft, Reservations not accepted, Elev: 7142ft/2177m, Tel: 406-683-3900, Nearest town: Dillon. GPS: 45.428976, -112.903551

168 • C2 | East Fork (Beaverhead-Deerlodge NF)

Total sites: 7, RV sites: 7, Central water, Vault/pit toilet, No showers, No RV dump, Tent & RV camping: Free, Stay limit: 16 days, Open May-Nov, Max Length: 22ft, Reservations not accepted, Elev: 6096ft/1858m, Tel: 406-859-3211, Nearest town: Butte. GPS: 46.134885, -113.387323

169 • C2 | Flint Creek (Beaverhead-Deerlodge NF)

Total sites: 16, RV sites: 16, No water, Vault/pit toilet, Tent & RV camping: Free, Open May-Oct, Max Length: 22ft, Reservations not accepted, Elev: 5620ft/1713m, Tel: 406-859-3211, Nearest town: Philipsburg. GPS: 46.233448, -113.300439

170 • C2 | Fourth of July (Beaverhead-Deerlodge NF)

Total sites: 5, RV sites: 5, Central water, Vault/pit toilet, No showers, No RV dump, Tent & RV camping: $8, Stay limit: 16 days, Open Jun-Sep, Max Length: 30ft, Elev: 6401ft/1951m, Tel: 406-832-3178, Nearest town: Wise River. GPS: 45.662372, -113.064284

171 • C2 | Grasshopper (Elkhorn Hot Springs) (Beaverhead-Deerlodge NF)

Total sites: 24, RV sites: 24, Central water, Vault/pit toilet, No showers, No RV dump, Tent & RV camping: $8, Stay limit: 16 days, Open Jun-Sep, Max Length: 30ft, Elev: 7050ft/2149m, Tel: 406-683-3900, Nearest town: Dillon. GPS: 45.452542, -113.120816

172 • C2 | Greek Creek (Custer Gallatin NF)

Total sites: 14, RV sites: 14, Central water, Vault/pit toilet, No showers, No RV dump, Tent & RV camping: $20, Open May-Sep, Max Length: 60ft, Reservations accepted, Elev: 5768ft/1758m, Tel: 406-522-2520, Nearest town: Big Sky. GPS: 45.380606, -111.181799

173 • C2 | Kading (Helena-Lewis & Clark NF)

Total sites: 11, RV sites: 11, Central water, Vault/pit toilet, No showers, No RV dump, Tent & RV camping: $10, Open Jun-Sep, Max Length: 16ft, Reservations not accepted, Elev: 6125ft/1867m, Tel: 406-449-5490, Nearest town: Elliston. GPS: 46.428069, -112.482357

174 • C2 | Ladysmith (Beaverhead-Deerlodge NF)

Total sites: 6, RV sites: 0, No water, Vault/pit toilet, Tents only: Free, Open May-Sep, Elev: 5797ft/1767m, Tel: 406-287-3223, Nearest town: Butte. GPS: 46.251268, -112.403687

175 • C2 | Little Joe (Beaverhead-Deerlodge NF)

Total sites: 5, RV sites: 5, Central water, Vault/pit toilet, No showers, No RV dump, Tent & RV camping: $8, Open May-Sep, Max Length: 28ft, Reservations not accepted, Elev: 6821ft/2079m, Tel: 406-832-3178, Nearest town: Wise River. GPS: 45.554635, -113.091505

176 • C2 | Lodgepole (Georgetown Lake) (Beaverhead-Deerlodge NF)

Total sites: 31, RV sites: 31, Central water, Vault/pit toilet, No showers, No RV dump, Tent & RV camping: $15, Open May-Sep, Max Length: 35ft, Reservations accepted, Elev: 6457ft/1968m, Tel: 406-859-3211, Nearest town: Philipsburg. GPS: 46.211654, -113.273937

177 • C2 | Lodgepole (Stine Mt) (Beaverhead-Deerlodge NF)

Total sites: 10, RV sites: 10, Central water, Vault/pit toilet, No showers, No RV dump, Tent & RV camping: $8, Open May-Sep, Max Length: 30ft, Reservations not accepted, Elev: 6450ft/1966m, Tel: 406-832-3178, Nearest town: Wise River. GPS: 45.648696, -113.070888

178 • C2 | Lowland (Beaverhead-Deerlodge NF)

Total sites: 11, RV sites: 11, Central water, Vault/pit toilet, No showers, No RV dump, Tent & RV camping: $5, Stay limit: 16 days, Open May-Sep, Max Length: 22ft, Reservations not accepted, Elev: 6562ft/2000m, Tel: 406-494-2147, Nearest town: Butte. GPS: 46.139188, -112.504444

179 • C2 | Mill Creek (Copper Mt) (Beaverhead-Deerlodge NF)

Total sites: 10, RV sites: 10, Central water, Vault/pit toilet, No showers, No RV dump, Tent & RV camping: Free, Open Jun-Oct, Max Length: 22ft, Reservations not accepted, Elev: 6539ft/1993m, Tel: 406-682-4253, Nearest town: Sheridan. GPS: 45.477391, -112.069183

180 • C2 | Mono Creek (Beaverhead-Deerlodge NF)

Total sites: 5, RV sites: 5, Central water, Vault/pit toilet, No showers, No RV dump, Tent & RV camping: $8, Open Jun-Sep, Max Length: 18ft, Reservations not accepted, Elev: 7001ft/2134m, Tel: 406-832-3178, Nearest town: Wise River. GPS: 45.534977, -113.078945

181 • C2 | Moose Creek (MacDonald Pass) (Helena-Lewis & Clark NF)

Total sites: 9, RV sites: 9, Central water, Vault/pit toilet, No showers, No RV dump, Tent & RV camping: $15, Open Jun-Sep, Reservations not accepted, Elev: 4859ft/1481m, Tel: 406-449-5490, Nearest town: Helena. GPS: 46.525061, -112.256927

182 • C2 | Moose Creek Flat (Custer Gallatin NF)

Total sites: 13, RV sites: 13, Central water, Vault/pit toilet, No showers, No RV dump, Tent & RV camping: $20, Open May-Sep, Reservations accepted, Elev: 5699ft/1737m, Tel: 406-522-2520, Nearest town: Big Sky. GPS: 45.355545, -111.172396

183 • C2 | Mormon Gulch (Beaverhead-Deerlodge NF)

Total sites: 16, RV sites: 16, No water, Vault/pit toilet, Tent & RV camping: Free, Open May-Nov, Max Length: 16ft, Reservations not accepted, Elev: 5824ft/1775m, Tel: 406-287-3223, Nearest town: Butte. GPS: 46.256792, -112.362653

184 • C2 | North Van Houten (Beaverhead-Deerlodge NF)

Total sites: 3, RV sites: 3, Central water, Vault/pit toilet, No showers, No RV dump, Tent & RV camping: Free, Stay limit: 16 days, Open Jun-Sep, Max Length: 20ft, Reservations not accepted, Elev: 7057ft/2151m, Tel: 406-689-3243, Nearest town: Jackson. GPS: 45.246561, -113.478182

185 • C2 | Orofino (Beaverhead-Deerlodge NF)

Total sites: 10, RV sites: 10, Central water, Vault/pit toilet, No showers, No RV dump, Tent & RV camping: Free, Stay limit: 16 days, Open May-Sep, Max Length: 22ft, Reservations not accepted, Elev: 6463ft/1970m, Tel: 406-859-3211, Nearest town: Deer Lodge. GPS: 46.259372, -112.608902

186 • C2 | Park Lake (Helena-Lewis & Clark NF)

Total sites: 22, RV sites: 22, Central water, Vault/pit toilet, No showers, No RV dump, Tent & RV camping: $15, Open Jun-Sep, Reservations not accepted, Elev: 6384ft/1946m, Tel: 406-449-5490, Nearest town: Clancy. GPS: 46.442273, -112.169016

187 • C2 | Pettengill (Beaverhead-Deerlodge NF)

Total sites: 3, RV sites: 3, No water, Vault/pit toilet, Tent & RV camping: $6, Max Length: 24ft, Reservations not accepted, Elev: 6286ft/1916m, Tel: 406-832-3178, Nearest town: Wise River. GPS: 45.681421, -113.060971

188 • C2 | Philipsburg Bay (Beaverhead-Deerlodge NF)

Total sites: 69, RV sites: 69, Elec sites: 1, Central water, Vault/pit toilet, No showers, No RV dump, Tents: $16/RVs: $25, Open May-Sep, Max Length: 60ft, Reservations accepted, Elev: 6401ft/1951m, Tel: 406-859-3211, Nearest town: Philipsburg. GPS: 46.206778, -113.290954

189 • C2 | Pigeon Creek (Beaverhead-Deerlodge NF)

Total sites: 6, RV sites: 0, Central water, Vault/pit toilet, No showers, No RV dump, Tents only: Free, Narrow access road w/ sharp turns, Mandatory food storage, Stay limit: 16 days, Open May-Sep, Reservations not accepted, Elev: 6155ft/1876m, Tel: 406-287-3223, Nearest town: Butte. GPS: 45.800717, -112.399795

190 • C2 | Piney (Beaverhead-Deerlodge NF)

Total sites: 48, RV sites: 32, Central water, Vault/pit toilet, No showers, No RV dump, Tent & RV camping: $16, Stay limit: 16 days, Open May-Sep, Max Length: 45ft, Reservations accepted, Elev: 6394ft/1949m, Tel: 406-859-3211, Nearest town: Philipsburg. GPS: 46.196045, -113.302246

191 • C2 | Pintler (Beaverhead-Deerlodge NF)

Total sites: 2, RV sites: 2, Central water, Vault/pit toilet, No showers, No RV dump, Tent & RV camping: Free, Stay limit: 16 days, Max Length: 18ft, Reservations not accepted, Elev: 6365ft/1940m, Tel: 406-832-3178, Nearest town: Wise River. GPS: 45.838743, -113.436441

192 • C2 | Potosi (Beaverhead-Deerlodge NF)

Total sites: 15, RV sites: 15, Central water, Vault/pit toilet, No showers, No RV dump, Tent & RV camping: Free, Open Jun-Sep, Max Length: 22ft, Reservations not accepted, Elev: 6240ft/1902m, Tel: 406-682-4253, Nearest town: Harrison. GPS: 45.572359, -111.913602

193 • C2 | Price Creek (Beaverhead-Deerlodge NF)

Total sites: 28, RV sites: 28, Central water, Vault/pit toilet, No showers, No RV dump, Tent & RV camping: Fee unk, Open Jun-Nov, Max Length: 30ft, Reservations not accepted, Elev: 7877ft/2401m, Tel: 406-683-3900, Nearest town: Dillon. GPS: 45.480019, -113.083201

194 • C2 | Racetrack (Beaverhead-Deerlodge NF)

Total sites: 13, RV sites: 13, Central water, Vault/pit toilet, No showers, No RV dump, Tent & RV camping: Free, Open May-Sep, Max Length: 22ft, Reservations not accepted, Elev: 5381ft/1640m, Tel: 406-859-3211, Nearest town: Butte. GPS: 46.280272, -112.938662

195 • C2 | Red Cliff (Custer Gallatin NF)

Total sites: 65, RV sites: 65, Elec sites: 27, Central water, Vault/pit toilet, No showers, No RV dump, Tents: $20/RVs: $20-28, Open May-Sep, Reservations accepted, Elev: 6289ft/1917m, Tel: 406-522-2520, Nearest town: Big Sky. GPS: 45.174115, -111.241582

196 • C2 | Reservoir Lake (Beaverhead-Deerlodge NF)

Total sites: 16, RV sites: 16, Central water, Vault/pit toilet, No showers, No RV dump, Tent & RV camping: $8, Group site: $25, Stay limit: 16 days, Open Jun-Sep, Max Length: 16ft, Elev: 7070ft/2155m, Tel: 406-683-3900, Nearest town: Dillon. GPS: 45.121849, -113.453644

197 • C2 | Seymour Creek (Beaverhead-Deerlodge NF)

Total sites: 17, RV sites: 17, Central water, Vault/pit toilet, No showers, No RV dump, Tent & RV camping: Free, Stay limit: 16 days, Open May-Sep, Max Length: 18ft, Reservations not accepted, Elev: 6824ft/2080m, Tel: 406-832-3178, Nearest town: Wise River. GPS: 45.988162, -113.184851

198 • C2 | South Van Houten (Beaverhead-Deerlodge NF)

Total sites: 3, RV sites: 3, Central water, Vault/pit toilet, No showers, No RV dump, Tent & RV camping: Free, Stay limit: 16 days, Open Jun-Sep, Max Length: 30ft, Reservations not accepted, Elev: 7024ft/2141m, Tel: 406-689-3243, Nearest town: Jackson. GPS: 45.243839, -113.478157

199 • C2 | Spanish Creek (Custer Gallatin NF)

Total sites: 5, Central water, Vault/pit toilet, No showers, No RV dump, Tent & RV camping: Free, Open May-Sep, Elev: 6109ft/1862m, Nearest town: Big Sky. GPS: 45.447388, -111.377289

200 • C2 | Spillway (Beaverhead-Deerlodge NF)

Total sites: 13, RV sites: 13, Central water, Vault/pit toilet, No showers, No RV dump, Tent & RV camping: Free, Open May-Nov, Max Length: 22ft, Elev: 6056ft/1846m, Tel: 406-859-3211, Nearest town: Philipsburg. GPS: 46.127441, -113.383301

201 • C2 | Spire Rock (Custer Gallatin NF)

Total sites: 19, RV sites: 19, No water, Vault/pit toilet, Tent & RV camping: $16, Group site: $30-$60, Open May-Sep, Reservations accepted, Elev: 5663ft/1726m, Tel: 406-522-2520, Nearest town: Big Sky. GPS: 45.439546, -111.192903

202 • C2 | Spring Hill (Beaverhead-Deerlodge NF)

Total sites: 15, RV sites: 15, Central water, Vault/pit toilet, No showers, No RV dump, Tent & RV camping: $14, Open May-Sep, Max Length: 40ft, Reservations accepted, Elev: 6178ft/1883m, Tel: 406-859-3211, Nearest town: Anaconda. GPS: 46.171631, -113.164795

203 • C2 | Steel Creek (Beaverhead-Deerlodge NF)

Total sites: 9, RV sites: 9, Central water, Vault/pit toilet, No showers, No RV dump, Tent & RV camping: $7, Open Jun-Sep, Max Length: 22ft, Reservations not accepted, Elev: 6378ft/1944m, Tel: 406-689-3243, Nearest town: Dillon. GPS: 45.600845, -113.343496

204 • C2 | Stony (Beaverhead-Deerlodge NF)

Total sites: 10, RV sites: 10, Central water, Vault/pit toilet, No showers, No RV dump, Tent & RV camping: Free, Open Apr-Oct, Max Length: 32ft, Reservations not accepted, Elev: 4806ft/1465m, Tel: 406-859-3211, Nearest town: Philipsburg. GPS: 46.348739, -113.607499

205 • C2 | Swan Creek (Custer Gallatin NF)

Total sites: 13, RV sites: 13, Central water, Vault/pit toilet, No showers, No RV dump, Tent & RV camping: $20, Open May-Sep, Reservations accepted, Elev: 5892ft/1796m, Tel: 406-522-2520, Nearest town: Big Sky. GPS: 45.372464, -111.163764

206 • C2 | Toll Mountain (Beaverhead-Deerlodge NF)

Total sites: 5, RV sites: 5, No water, Vault/pit toilet, Tent & RV camping: Free, Stay limit: 16 days, Open May-Sep, Max Length: 22ft, Reservations not accepted, Elev: 5909ft/1801m, Tel: 406-287-3223, Nearest town: Whitehall. GPS: 45.847955, -112.366663

207 • C2 | Whitehouse (Beaverhead-Deerlodge NF)

Total sites: 5, RV sites: 5, Central water, Vault/pit toilet, No showers, No RV dump, Tent & RV camping: Free, Stay limit: 16 days, Open May-Nov, Max Length: 22ft, Reservations not accepted, Elev: 6086ft/1855m, Tel: 406-494-2147, Nearest town: Butte. GPS: 46.258166, -112.478539

208 • C2 | Willow (Beaverhead-Deerlodge NF)

Total sites: 5, RV sites: 5, Central water, Vault/pit toilet, No showers, No RV dump, Tent & RV camping: $8, Open Jun-Sep, Max Length: 26ft, Reservations not accepted, Elev: 6532ft/1991m, Tel: 406-832-3178, Nearest town: Dillon. GPS: 45.636246, -113.076866

209 • C3 | Aspen (Chrome Mt) (Custer Gallatin NF)

Total sites: 8, RV sites: 8, Central water, Vault/pit toilet, No showers, No RV dump, Tent & RV camping: $12, Limited access/no water in winter, Open all year, Reservations not accepted, Elev: 5433ft/1656m, Tel: 406-932-5155, Nearest town: Big Timber. GPS: 45.456575, -110.197144

210 • C3 | Basin (Custer Gallatin NF)

Total sites: 30, RV sites: 30, No water, Vault/pit toilet, Tent & RV camping: $18, Open May-Sep, Max Length: 45ft, Reservations accepted, Elev: 6923ft/2110m, Tel: 406-446-2103, Nearest town: Red Lodge. GPS: 45.163014, -109.392697

211 • C3 | Battle Ridge (Custer Gallatin NF)

Total sites: 13, RV sites: 13, No water, Vault/pit toilet, No showers, No RV dump, Tent & RV camping: Free, Open May-Sep, Reservations not accepted, Elev: 6390ft/1948m, Tel: 406-522-2520, Nearest town: Bozeman. GPS: 45.882487, -110.879923

212 • C3 | Big Beaver (Custer Gallatin NF)

Total sites: 5, RV sites: 5, No water, Vault/pit toilet, Tent & RV camping: Free, Limited winter access, Open all year, Max Length: 32ft, Reservations not accepted, Elev: 5348ft/1630m, Tel: 406-932-5155, Nearest town: Big Timber. GPS: 45.463875, -110.199043

213 • C3 | Canyon (Custer Gallatin NF)

Total sites: 17, RV sites: 17, No water, Vault/pit toilet, Tent & RV camping: $10, Open all year, Max Length: 48ft, Reservations not accepted, Elev: 5112ft/1558m, Tel: 406-848-7375, Nearest town: Gardiner. GPS: 45.182857, -110.887965

214 • C3 | Cascade (Custer Gallatin NF)

Total sites: 30, RV sites: 30, Central water, Vault/pit toilet, No showers, No RV dump, Tent & RV camping: $15, Stay limit: 16 days, Open Jun-Sep, Max Length: 40ft, Reservations accepted, Elev: 7602ft/2317m, Tel: 406-446-2103, Nearest town: Red Lodge. GPS: 45.173096, -109.450928

215 • C3 | Chippy Park (Custer Gallatin NF)

Total sites: 7, RV sites: 7, Central water, Vault/pit toilet, No showers, No RV dump, Tent & RV camping: $12, Limited winter access, Open all year, Max Length: 42ft, Reservations not accepted, Elev: 5607ft/1709m, Tel: 406-932-5155, Nearest town: Big Timber. GPS: 45.437377, -110.189457

216 • C3 | Chisholm (Custer Gallatin NF)

Total sites: 10, RV sites: 10, Central water, Vault/pit toilet, No showers, No RV dump, Tent & RV camping: $20, Open May-Sep, Max Length: 35ft, Reservations accepted, Elev: 6778ft/2066m, Tel: 406-522-2520, Nearest town: Bozeman. GPS: 45.474644, -110.956458

217 • C3 | Colter (Custer Gallatin NF)

Total sites: 23, RV sites: 23, Central water, Vault/pit toilet, No showers, No RV dump, Tent & RV camping: $20, Open Jul-Sep, Max Length: 32ft, Reservations not accepted, Elev: 8044ft/2452m, Tel: 406-848-7375, Nearest town: Cooke City. GPS: 45.028033, -109.894038

218 • C3 | Eagle Creek (Custer Gallatin NF)

Total sites: 16, RV sites: 16, No water, Vault/pit toilet, Tent & RV camping: $15, Open all year, Max Length: 48ft, Reservations accepted, Elev: 6145ft/1873m, Tel: 406-848-7375, Nearest town: Gardiner. GPS: 45.045609, -110.679758

219 • C3 | East Rosebud Lake (Custer Gallatin NF)

Total sites: 14, RV sites: 14, Central water, Vault/pit toilet, No showers, No RV dump, Tent & RV camping: $15, No services in winter, Open all year, Max Length: 20ft, Reservations not accepted, Elev: 6375ft/1943m, Tel: 406-446-2103, Nearest town: Absarokee. GPS: 45.198973, -109.634409

220 • C3 | Emerald Lake (Custer Gallatin NF)

Total sites: 32, RV sites: 32, Central water, Vault/pit toilet, No showers, No RV dump, Tent & RV camping: $15, No services in winter, Open all year, Max Length: 30ft, Reservations not accepted, Elev: 6342ft/1933m, Tel: 406-446-2103, Nearest town: Fishtail. GPS: 45.254883, -109.699707

221 • C3 | Fairy Lake (Custer Gallatin NF)

Total sites: 9, RV sites: 0, Central water, Vault/pit toilet, No showers, No RV dump, Tents only: Free, High clearance vehicle recommended, Steep gravel road slippery when wet - not suitable for RV or towed unit travel, Open Jul-Sep, Reservations not accepted, Elev: 7658ft/2334m, Tel: 406-522-2520, Nearest town: Bozeman. GPS: 45.906741, -110.961021

222 • C3 | Falls Creek (Custer Gallatin NF)

Total sites: 8, RV sites: 0, Central water, Vault/pit toilet, No showers, No RV dump, Tents only: Free, Open all year, Reservations not accepted, Elev: 5254ft/1601m, Tel: 406-932-5155, Nearest town: Big Timber. GPS: 45.490236, -110.219095

223 • C3 | Grasshopper (Fourmile Spring) Creek (Helena-Lewis & Clark NF)

Total sites: 12, RV sites: 12, Central water, Vault/pit toilet, No showers, No RV dump, Tent & RV camping: $10, Open Jun-Sep, Reservations not accepted, Elev: 5833ft/1778m, Nearest town: White Sulphur Springs. GPS: 46.544149, -110.747806

224 • C3 | Greenough Lake (Custer Gallatin NF)

Total sites: 18, RV sites: 18, Central water, Vault/pit toilet, No showers, No RV dump, Tent & RV camping: $18, Open May-Sep, Max Length: 60ft, Reservations accepted, Elev: 7201ft/2195m, Tel: 406-446-2103, Nearest town: Red Lodge. GPS: 45.056111, -109.412967

225 • C3 | Half Moon (Custer Gallatin NF)

Total sites: 12, RV sites: 12, Central water, Vault/pit toilet, No showers, No RV dump, Tent & RV camping: $12, Limited winter access, Open all year, Max Length: 32ft, Reservations not accepted, Elev: 6486ft/1977m, Tel: 406-932-5155, Nearest town: Big Timber. GPS: 46.041437, -110.239562

226 • C3 | Hells Canyon (Custer Gallatin NF)

Total sites: 11, RV sites: 11, No water, Vault/pit toilet, Tent & RV camping: Free, Limited winter access, Open all year, Max Length: 20ft, Reservations not accepted, Elev: 6132ft/1869m, Tel: 406-932-5155, Nearest town: Big Timber. GPS: 45.361892, -110.215052

227 • C3 | Hicks Park (Custer Gallatin NF)

Total sites: 16, RV sites: 16, Central water, Vault/pit toilet, No showers, No RV dump, Tent & RV camping: $12, Limited winter access, Open all year, Max Length: 32ft, Reservations not accepted, Elev: 6430ft/1960m, Tel: 406-932-5155, Nearest town: Big Timber. GPS: 45.297993, -110.239914

228 • C3 | Hood Creek (Custer Gallatin NF)

Total sites: 25, RV sites: 25, Central water, Vault/pit toilet, No showers, No RV dump, Tent & RV camping: $20, Open May-Sep, Reservations accepted, Elev: 6827ft/2081m, Tel: 406-522-2520, Nearest town: Bozeman. GPS: 45.484152, -110.967554

229 • C3 | Hyalite Below Dam (Custer Gallatin NF)

Total sites: 11, RV sites: 11, No water, Vault/pit toilet, No showers, No RV dump, Tent & RV camping: Free, Water at nearby day-use area, Reservations not accepted, Elev: 6670ft/2033m, Nearest town: Bozeman. GPS: 45.488645, -110.981294

230 • C3 | Initial Creek (Custer Gallatin NF)

Total sites: 6, RV sites: 6, No water, Vault/pit toilet, Tent & RV camping: Free, No services in winter, Stay limit: 16 days, Open all year, Max Length: 20ft, Reservations not accepted, Elev: 6214ft/1894m, Tel: 406-446-2103, Nearest town: Nye. GPS: 45.404000, -109.954000

231 • C3 | Jimmy Joe (Custer Gallatin NF)

Total sites: 12, RV sites: 12, No water, Vault/pit toilet, Tent & RV camping: Free, Stay limit: 16 days, Open May-Sep, Max Length: 30ft, Reservations not accepted, Elev: 5597ft/1706m, Tel: 406-446-2103, Nearest town: Roscoe. GPS: 45.232034, -109.603149

232 • C3 | Langohr (Custer Gallatin NF)

Total sites: 19, RV sites: 19, Central water, Vault/pit toilet, No showers, No RV dump, Tent & RV camping: $20, Open May-Sep, Max Length: 32ft, Reservations accepted, Elev: 6174ft/1882m, Tel: 406-522-2520, Nearest town: Bozeman. GPS: 45.532853, -111.015097

233 • C3 | Limber Pine (Custer Gallatin NF)

Total sites: 13, RV sites: 13, Central water, Vault/pit toilet, No showers, No RV dump, Tent & RV camping: $18, Open May-Sep, Max Length: 60ft, Reservations accepted, Elev: 7164ft/2184m, Tel: 406-446-2103, Nearest town: Red Lodge. GPS: 45.059695, -109.408583

234 • C3 | M-K Campground (Custer Gallatin NF)

Total sites: 10, RV sites: 7, No water, Vault/pit toilet, Tent & RV camping: Free, No services in winter, Stay limit: 16 days, Open May-Sep, Max Length: 20ft, Reservations not accepted, Elev: 7408ft/2258m, Tel: 406-446-2103, Nearest town: Red Lodge. GPS: 45.038323, -109.429648

235 • C3 | Palisades (Custer Gallatin NF)

Total sites: 6, RV sites: 6, No water, Vault/pit toilet, Tent & RV camping: Free, Open May-Sep, Max Length: 16ft, Reservations not accepted, Elev: 6378ft/1944m, Tel: 406-446-2103, Nearest town: Red Lodge. GPS: 45.171578, -109.308995

236 • C3 | Parkside (Custer Gallatin NF)

Total sites: 28, RV sites: 28, Central water, Vault/pit toilet, No showers, No RV dump, Tent & RV camping: $18, Group sites $75-$95, Stay limit: 16 days, Open May-Sep, Max Length: 50ft, Reservations accepted, Elev: 7132ft/2174m, Tel: 406-446-2103, Nearest town: Red Lodge. GPS: 45.060652, -109.405341

237 • C3 | Pine Creek (Custer Gallatin NF)

Total sites: 25, RV sites: 25, Central water, Vault/pit toilet, No showers, No RV dump, Tent & RV camping: $20, Group site: $35-$75, Narrow winding road, Open May-Sep, Max Length: 50ft, Reservations accepted, Elev: 5653ft/1723m, Tel: 406-222-1892, Nearest town: Livingston. GPS: 45.498534, -110.522397

238 • C3 | Pine Grove (Custer Gallatin NF)

Total sites: 46, RV sites: 46, Central water, Vault/pit toilet, No showers, No RV dump, Tent & RV camping: $15, Stay limit: 16 days, Open May-Sep, Max Length: 30ft, Reservations not accepted, Elev: 5892ft/1796m, Tel: 406-446-2103, Nearest town: Fishtail. GPS: 45.275661, -109.643163

239 • C3 | Rattin (Custer Gallatin NF)

Total sites: 6, RV sites: 6, Central water, Vault/pit toilet, No showers, No RV dump, Tent & RV camping: $17, Stay limit: 16 days, Open May-Sep, Max Length: 30ft, Reservations accepted, Elev: 6371ft/1942m, Tel: 406-446-2103, Nearest town: Red Lodge. GPS: 45.087717, -109.322796

240 • C3 | Richardson Creek (Helena-Lewis & Clark NF)

Total sites: 3, RV sites: 3, No water, Vault/pit toilet, Tent & RV camping: Fee unk, Mandatory food storage, Stay limit: 16 days, Open Jun-Sep, Max Length: 16ft, Reservations not accepted, Elev: 5902ft/1799m, Nearest town: White Sulphur Springs. GPS: 46.540448, -110.730859

241 • C3 | Sheridan (Custer Gallatin NF)

Total sites: 9, RV sites: 9, Central water, Vault/pit toilet, No showers, No RV dump, Tent & RV camping: $17, 2 group sites: $34, Stay limit: 16 days, Open May-Sep, Max Length: 33ft, Reservations accepted, Elev: 6299ft/1920m, Tel: 406-446-2103, Nearest town: Red Lodge. GPS: 45.100831, -109.307426

242 • C3 | Shields River (Custer Gallatin NF)

Total sites: 6, RV sites: 6, No water, Vault/pit toilet, Tent & RV camping: Free, Open Jun-Nov, Max Length: 22ft, Reservations not accepted, Elev: 6417ft/1956m, Tel: 406-222-1892, Nearest town: Livingston. GPS: 46.184327, -110.405053

243 • C3 | Skidway (Helena-Lewis & Clark NF)

Total sites: 14, RV sites: 14, Central water, Vault/pit toilet, No showers, No RV dump, Tent & RV camping: $15, Stay limit: 14 days, Open May-Sep, Max Length: 16ft, Reservations not accepted, Elev: 5804ft/1769m, Tel: 406-266-3425, Nearest town: Townsend. GPS: 46.354492, -111.097168

244 • C3 | Snowbank (Custer Gallatin NF)

Total sites: 10, RV sites: 10, Central water, Vault/pit toilet, No showers, No RV dump, Tent & RV camping: $20, Group site: $35-$50, Narrow winding road, Open May-Sep, Max Length: 30ft, Reservations accepted, Elev: 5774ft/1760m, Tel: 406-222-1892, Nearest town: Livingston. GPS: 45.288273, -110.544128

245 • C3 | Soda Butte (Custer Gallatin NF)

Total sites: 27, RV sites: 27, Central water, Vault/pit toilet, No showers, No RV dump, No tents/RVs: $20, Hardside units only, Open Jun-Sep, Max Length: 48ft, Reservations not accepted, Elev: 7874ft/2400m, Tel: 406-848-7375, Nearest town: Cooke City. GPS: 45.024126, -109.912052

246 • C3 | Tom Miner (Custer Gallatin NF)

Total sites: 16, RV sites: 16, Central water, Vault/pit toilet, No showers, No RV dump, Tent & RV camping: $12, Open Jun-Oct, Reservations not accepted, Elev: 7244ft/2208m, Tel: 406-848-7375, Nearest town: Gardiner. GPS: 45.129705, -111.063281

247 • C3 | West Boulder (Custer Gallatin NF)

Total sites: 10, RV sites: 10, Central water, Vault/pit toilet, No showers, No RV dump, Tent & RV camping: $12, Limited winter access - no fee, Open all year, Max Length: 20ft, Reservations not accepted, Elev: 5538ft/1688m, Tel: 406-932-5155, Nearest town: Big Timber. GPS: 45.548901, -110.307702

248 • C3 | Woodbine (Custer Gallatin NF)

Total sites: 44, RV sites: 44, Central water, Vault/pit toilet, No showers, No RV dump, Tent & RV camping: $19, Stay limit: 16 days, Open May-Sep, Max Length: 90ft, Reservations accepted, Elev: 5223ft/1592m, Tel: 406-446-2103, Nearest town: Nye. GPS: 45.352701, -109.896774

249 • C4 | Blacks Pond (Custer Gallatin NF)

Total sites: 2, RV sites: 2, No water, No toilets, Tent & RV camping: Free, Open all year, Reservations not accepted, Elev: 3678ft/1121m, Tel: 406-784-2344, Nearest town: Ashland. GPS: 45.346975, -106.286373

250 • C4 | Cow Creek (Custer Gallatin NF)

Total sites: 4, RV sites: 4, No water, Vault/pit toilet, Tent & RV camping: Free, Stay limit: 10 days, Open all year, Max Length: 32ft, Reservations not accepted, Elev: 3888ft/1185m, Tel: 406-784-2344, Nearest town: Ashland. GPS: 45.310201, -106.244534

251 • C4 | Sage Creek (Custer Gallatin NF)

Total sites: 12, RV sites: 12, Central water, Vault/pit toilet, No showers, No RV dump, Tent & RV camping: $10, RVs/trailers should access from the south via the Crooked Creek Road, No services in winter - free, Stay limit: 16 days, Open May-Sep, Max Length: 30ft, Reservations not accepted, Elev: 5564ft/1696m, Tel: 406-446-2103, Nearest town: Bridger. GPS: 45.213479, -108.554408

252 • C5 | Ekalaka Park (Custer Gallatin NF)

Total sites: 8, RV sites: 8, Central water, Vault/pit toilet, No showers, No RV dump, Tent & RV camping: Free, Stay limit: 14 days, Open May-Nov, Max Length: 30ft, Reservations not accepted, Elev: 3780ft/1152m, Tel: 605-797-4432, Nearest town: Ekalaka. GPS: 45.798633, -104.511426

253 • C5 | Holiday Spring (Custer Gallatin NF)

Total sites: 6, RV sites: 6, No water, Vault/pit toilet, Tent & RV camping: Free, Stay limit: 10 days, Open Apr-Nov, Reservations not accepted, Elev: 4009ft/1222m, Tel: 406-784-2344, Nearest town: Ashland. GPS: 45.638499, -105.974276

254 • C5 | Lantis Spring (Custer Gallatin NF)

Total sites: 4, RV sites: 4, Central water, Vault/pit toilet, No showers, No RV dump, Tent & RV camping: Free, Stay limit: 14 days, Open May-Nov, Max Length: 16ft, Reservations not accepted, Elev: 3914ft/1193m, Tel: 605-797-4432, Nearest town: Camp Crook (SD). GPS: 45.630606, -104.177136

255 • C5 | Macnab Pond (Custer Gallatin NF)

Total sites: 2, RV sites: 2, No water, Vault/pit toilet, Tent & RV camping: Free, Open May-Nov, Max Length: 30ft, Reservations not accepted, Elev: 3474ft/1059m, Tel: 605-797-4432, Nearest town: Ekalaka. GPS: 45.835842, -104.432014

256 • C5 | Red Shale (Custer Gallatin NF)

Total sites: 14, RV sites: 14, No water, Vault/pit toilet, Tent & RV camping: Free, Stay limit: 10 days, Open Apr-Dec, Max Length: 32ft, Reservations not accepted, Elev: 3209ft/978m, Tel: 406-784-2344, Nearest town: Ashland. GPS: 45.568933, -106.146433

257 • C5 | Wickham Gulch (Custer Gallatin NF)

Total sites: 2, RV sites: 2, Central water, Vault/pit toilet, No showers, No RV dump, Tent & RV camping: Free, Stay limit: 14 days, Open all year, Max Length: 16ft, Reservations not accepted, Elev: 3520ft/1073m, Tel: 605-797-4432, Nearest town: Camp Crook (SD). GPS: 45.580109, -104.070973

258 • D2 | Baker's Hole (Custer Gallatin NF)

Total sites: 73, RV sites: 73, Elec sites: 33, Central water, Vault/pit toilet, No showers, No RV dump, Tents: $20/RVs: $20-28, Open May-Sep, Max Length: 32ft, Reservations not accepted, Elev: 6578ft/2005m, Tel: 406-823-6961, Nearest town: West Yellowstone. GPS: 44.704102, -111.101563

259 • D2 | Beaver Creek (Custer Gallatin NF)

Total sites: 65, RV sites: 65, Central water, Vault/pit toilet, No showers, No RV dump, Tent & RV camping: $20, Open May-Sep, Max Length: 56ft, Reservations accepted, Elev: 6575ft/2004m, Tel: 406-823-6961, Nearest town: West Yellowstone. GPS: 44.855733, -111.373557

260 • D2 | Cabin Creek (Custer Gallatin NF)

Total sites: 15, RV sites: 15, Central water, Vault/pit toilet, No showers, No RV dump, Tent & RV camping: $20, Open May-Sep, Reservations accepted, Elev: 6532ft/1991m, Tel: 406-823-6961, Nearest town: West Yellowstone. GPS: 44.871571, -111.343822

261 • D2 | Cherry Creek (Custer Gallatin NF)

Total sites: 7, RV sites: 7, No water, Vault/pit toilet, Tent & RV camping: Free, Open May-Oct, Reservations not accepted, Elev: 6545ft/1995m, Tel: 406-823-6961, Nearest town: West Yellowstone. GPS: 44.751044, -111.263946

262 • D2 | Cliff Point (Beaverhead-Deerlodge NF)

Total sites: 6, RV sites: 6, Central water, Vault/pit toilet, No showers, No RV dump, Tent & RV camping: $15, Stay limit: 16 days, Open May-Sep, Max Length: 16ft, Reservations not accepted, Elev: 6345ft/1934m, Tel: 406-682-4253, Nearest town: West Yellowstone. GPS: 44.792000, -111.562000

263 • D2 | East Creek (Beaverhead-Deerlodge NF)

Total sites: 4, RV sites: 4, Central water, Vault/pit toilet, No showers, No RV dump, Tent & RV camping: Free, Stay limit: 16 days, Open May-Sep, Max Length: 16ft, Reservations not accepted, Elev: 7031ft/2143m, Tel: 406-683-3900, Nearest town: Dillon. GPS: 44.564000, -112.661000

264 • D2 | Elk Lake (Beaverhead-Deerlodge NF)

Total sites: 2, RV sites: 0, No water, Vault/pit toilet, Tents only: Free, Stay limit: 16 days, Reservations not accepted, Elev: 6686ft/2038m, Tel: 406-682-4253, Nearest town: Monida (ID). GPS: 44.669922, -111.631286

265 • D2 | Hilltop (Beaverhead-Deerlodge NF)

Total sites: 18, RV sites: 18, Central water, Vault/pit toilet, No showers, No RV dump, Tent & RV camping: $15, Stay limit: 16 days, Open Jun-Sep, Max Length: 22ft, Reservations not accepted, Elev: 6588ft/2008m, Tel: 4060682-4253, Nearest town: West Yellowstone. GPS: 44.796657, -111.561075

266 • D2 | Lonesomehurst (Custer Gallatin NF)

Total sites: 27, RV sites: 27, Elec sites: 5, Central water, Vault/pit toilet, No showers, No RV dump, Tents: $20/RVs: $20-28, Open May-Sep, Max Length: 32ft, Reservations accepted, Elev: 6545ft/1995m, Tel: 406-823-6961, Nearest town: West Yellowstone. GPS: 44.735481, -111.231338

267 • D2 | Madison River (Beaverhead-Deerlodge NF)

Total sites: 10, RV sites: 10, Central water, Vault/pit toilet, No showers, No RV dump, Tent & RV camping: $15, Stay limit: 16 days, Open May-Nov, Max Length: 30ft, Reservations accepted, Elev: 5899ft/1798m, Tel: 406-682-4253, Nearest town: Ennis. GPS: 44.878722, -111.572474

268 • D2 | Rainbow Point (Custer Gallatin NF)

Total sites: 85, RV sites: 85, Elec sites: 46, Central water, Vault/pit toilet, No showers, No RV dump, Tents: $20/RVs: $20-28, Open May-Sep, Max Length: 52ft, Reservations accepted, Elev: 6558ft/1999m, Tel: 406-823-6961, Nearest town: West Yellowstone. GPS: 44.778682, -111.177063

269 • D2 | Riverview (Beaverhead-Deerlodge NF)

Total sites: 24, RV sites: 24, Central water, Vault/pit toilet, No showers, No RV dump, Tent & RV camping: $15, Stay limit: 16 days, Max Length: 30ft, Reservations not accepted, Elev: 5945ft/1812m, Tel: 406-682-4253, Nearest town: Ennis. GPS: 44.882035, -111.577385

270 • D2 | Spring Creek (Custer Gallatin NF)

Total sites: 15, RV sites: 15, No water, Vault/pit toilet, No showers, No RV dump, Tent & RV camping: $16, Open May-Oct, Reservations not accepted, Elev: 6532ft/1991m, Tel: 406-823-6961, Nearest town: West Yellowstone. GPS: 44.784569, -111.275196

271 • D2 | Wade Lake (Beaverhead-Deerlodge NF)

Total sites: 30, RV sites: 30, Central water, Vault/pit toilet, No showers, No RV dump, Tent & RV camping: $15, Group sites (2): $30, Stay limit: 16 days, Open Apr-Nov, Max Length: 30ft, Reservations accepted, Elev: 6224ft/1897m, Tel: 406-682-4253, Nearest town: West Yellowstone. GPS: 44.807682, -111.566885

272 • D2 | West Fork Madison (Beaverhead-Deerlodge NF)

Total sites: 7, RV sites: 0, Central water, Vault/pit toilet, No showers, No RV dump, Tents only: $12, Stay limit: 16 days, Open Jun-Sep, Reservations not accepted, Elev: 5886ft/1794m, Tel: 406-682-4253, Nearest town: Ennis. GPS: 44.886906, -111.582661

Nebraska

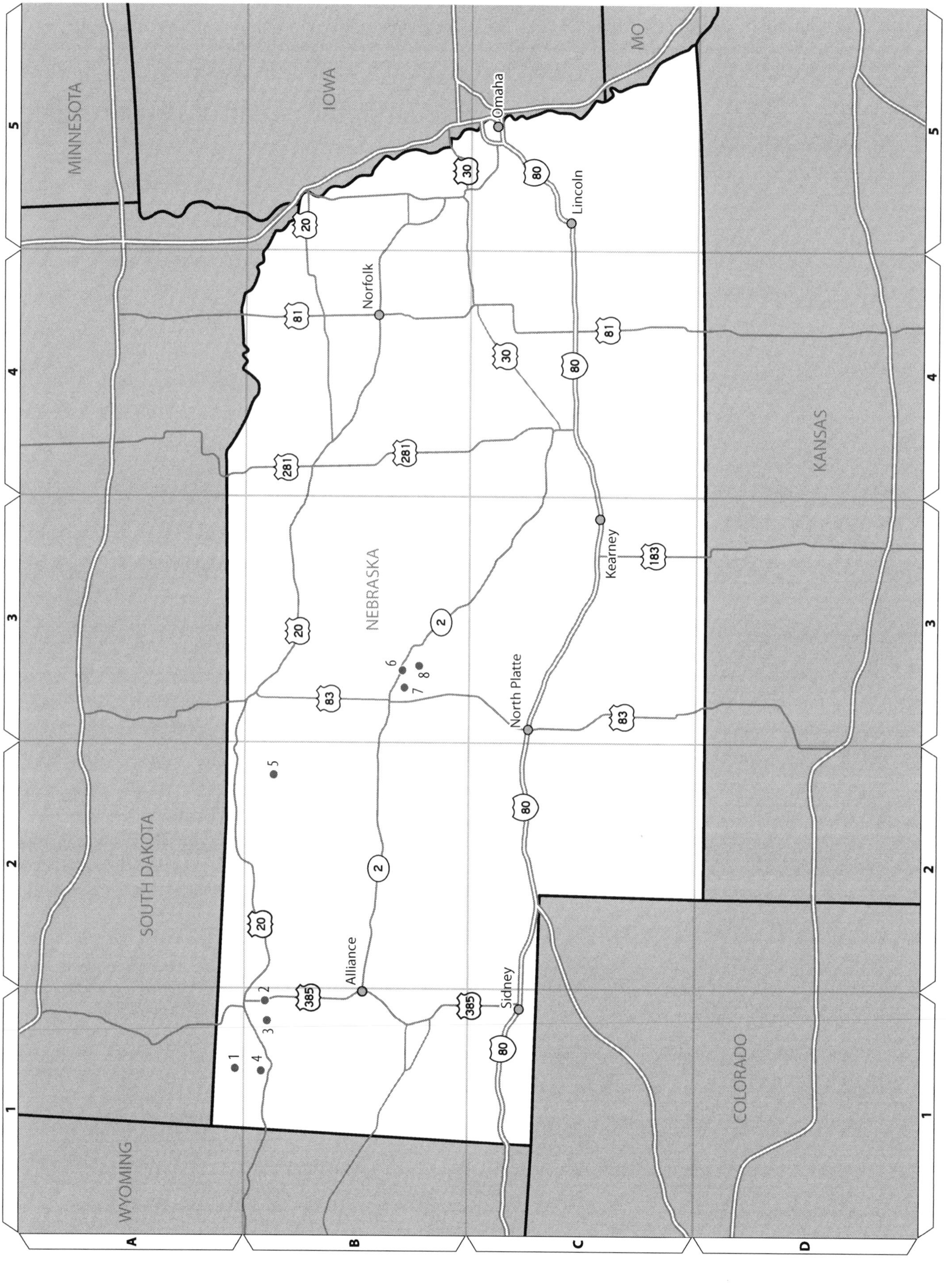
MINNESOTA
IOWA
MO
SOUTH DAKOTA
NEBRASKA
KANSAS
WYOMING
COLORADO
Omaha
Lincoln
Norfolk
Kearney
North Platte
Alliance
Sidney
20
30
80
81
281
183
83
2
385
1
2
3
4
5
6
7
8
A
B
C
D

Map	ID	Map	ID
A1	1	B2	5
B1	2-4	B3	6-8

Alphabetical List of Camping Areas

1 • A1 | Toadstool Geological Park (Nebraska NF)

Total sites: 6, RV sites: 6, Central water, Vault/pit toilet, No showers, No RV dump, Tent & RV camping: $5, Free in winter, Open all year, Reservations not accepted, Elev: 3780ft/1152m, Tel: 308-432-0300, Nearest town: Crawford. GPS: 42.857956, -103.584193

2 • B1 | Red Cloud (Nebraska NF)

Total sites: 13, RV sites: 0, No water, Vault/pit toilet, Tents only: $5, Free mid-Nov to mid-Apr, Open all year, Reservations not accepted, Elev: 3884ft/1184m, Nearest town: Chadron. GPS: 42.696774, -103.005046

3 • B1 | Roberts Tract (Nebraska NF)

Total sites: 4, RV sites: 1, No toilets, No showers, No RV dump, Tent & RV camping: $8, Stock water available mid-May to mid-Oct, Free mid-Nov to early May, Open all year, Reservations not accepted, Elev: 3960ft/1207m, Tel: 308-432-0300, Nearest town: Chadron. GPS: 42.678746, -103.151260

4 • B1 | Soldier Creek (Nebraska NF)

Total sites: 4, RV sites: 4, Central water, Vault/pit toilet, No showers, No RV dump, Tent & RV camping: $8, Free mid-Nov to mid-May, Open all year, Elev: 4104ft/1251m, Tel: 308-432-0300, Nearest town: Crawford. GPS: 42.697811, -103.570514

5 • B2 | Steer Creek (Nebraska NF)

Total sites: 23, RV sites: 23, Central water, Vault/pit toilet, No showers, No RV dump, Tent & RV camping: $5, Open all year, Reservations not accepted, Elev: 3064ft/934m, Nearest town: Nenzel. GPS: 42.688524, -101.152975

6 • B3 | Bessey Rec Area (Nebraska NF)

Total sites: 40, RV sites: 40, Elec sites: 28, Central water, Flush toilet, Free showers, RV dump, Tents: $15/RVs: $20, Group site: $75, No water in winter, Open all year, Max Length: 50ft, Reservations accepted, Elev: 2743ft/836m, Tel: 308-533-2257, Nearest town: Halsey. GPS: 41.898881, -100.297357

7 • B3 | Natick Horse Camp (Nebraska NF)

Total sites: 7, RV sites: 7, Central water, Vault/pit toilet, No showers, No RV dump, Tent & RV camping: $8, Rough road, Reservations not accepted, Elev: 2868ft/874m, Nearest town: Halsey. GPS: 41.882202, -100.413447

8 • B3 | Whitetail (Nebraska NF)

Total sites: 10, RV sites: 10, Central water, Vault/pit toilet, No showers, No RV dump, Tent & RV camping: $8, Open all year, Reservations not accepted, Elev: 2703ft/824m, Tel: 308-533-2257, Nearest town: Halsey. GPS: 41.796088, -100.264495

Nevada

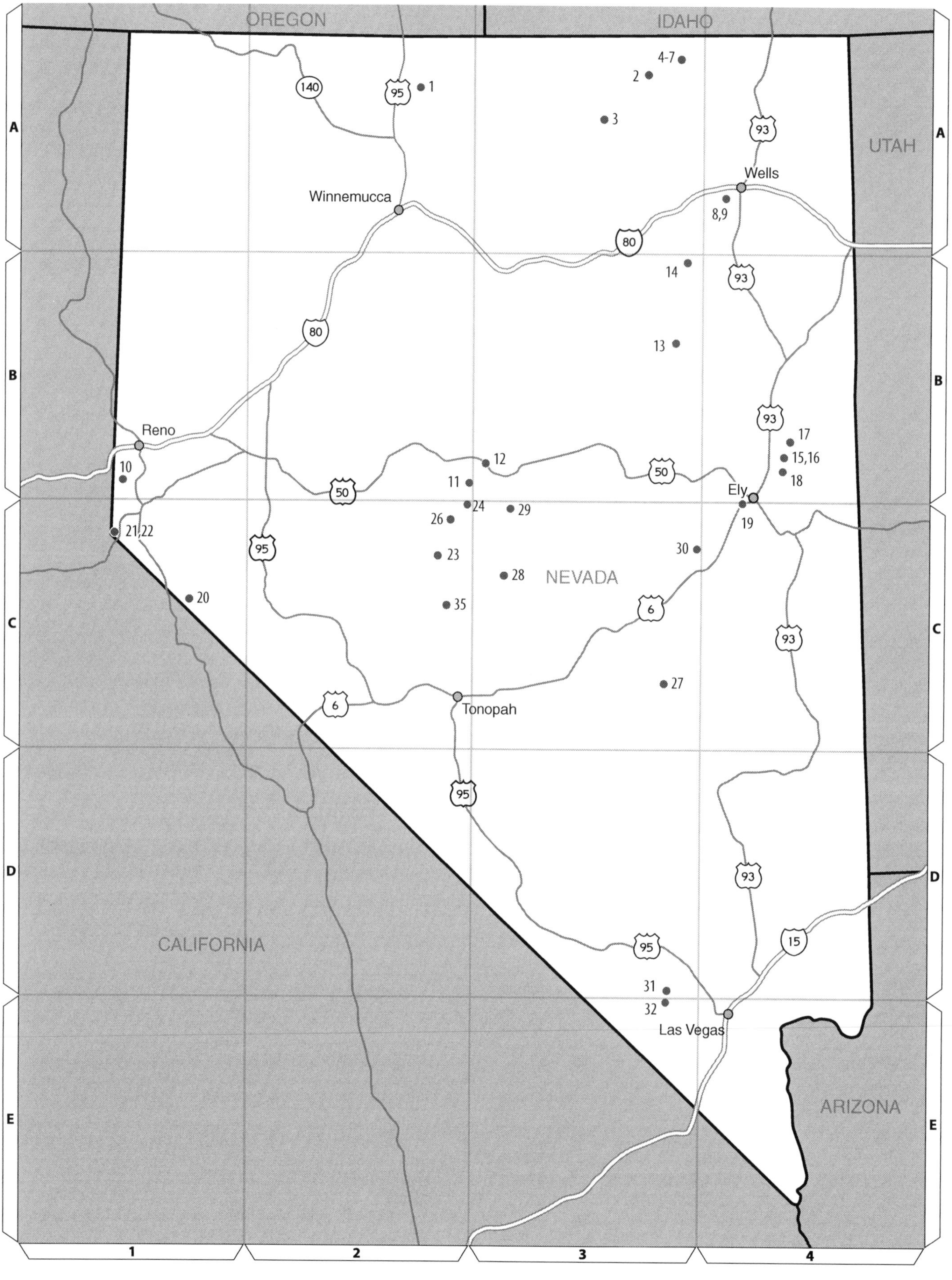
OREGON
IDAHO
UTAH
NEVADA
CALIFORNIA
ARIZONA
Winnemucca
Wells
Reno
Ely
Tonopah
Las Vegas
140
95
93
80
50
6
15
A
B
C
D
E
1
2
3
4
1
2
3
4-7
8,9
10
11
12
13
14
15,16
17
18
19
20
21,22
23
24
26
27
28
29
30
31
32
35

Map	ID	Map	ID
A2	1	B4	15-19
A3	2-7	C1	20-22
A4	8-9	C2	23-26
B1	10	C3	27-30
B2	11	D3	31
B3	12-14	E3	32

Alphabetical List of Camping Areas

1 • A2 | Lye Creek (Humboldt-Toiyabe NF)

Total sites: 18, RV sites: 5, Central water, Vault/pit toilet, No showers, No RV dump, Tent & RV camping: $8, Open Jun-Oct, Max Length: 24ft, Reservations not accepted, Elev: 7309ft/2228m, Tel: 775-623-5025 x4, Nearest town: Winnemucca. GPS: 41.685415, -117.557312

2 • A3 | Big Bend (Humboldt-Toiyabe NF)

Total sites: 19, RV sites: 19, No water, Vault/pit toilet, Tent & RV camping: $8, Open May-Nov, Max Length: 25ft, Reservations not accepted, Elev: 6978ft/2127m, Tel: 775-738-5171, Nearest town: Mountain City. GPS: 41.765869, -115.700195

3 • A3 | Jack Creek (Humboldt-Toiyabe NF)

Total sites: 3, RV sites: 3, No water, Vault/pit toilet, Tent & RV camping: Free, May be inaccessible in winter, Open all year, Max Length: 30ft, Reservations not accepted, Elev: 6519ft/1987m, Tel: 775-738-5171, Nearest town: Mountain City. GPS: 41.513491, -116.063984

4 • A3 | Jarbridge (Humboldt-Toiyabe NF)

Total sites: 5, RV sites: 5, No water, No toilets, Tent & RV camping: Fee unk, Open May-Sep, Max Length: 16ft, Elev: 6470ft/1972m, Nearest town: Jarbridge. GPS: 41.863348, -115.429145

5 • A3 | Lower Bluster (Humboldt-Toiyabe NF)

Total sites: 2, RV sites: 2, No water, Vault/pit toilet, Tent & RV camping: Free, Stay limit: 14 days, Open Jun-Sep, Max Length: 25ft, Reservations not accepted, Elev: 6696ft/2041m, Tel: 775-331-6444, Nearest town: Jarbridge. GPS: 41.838215, -115.426697

6 • A3 | Pine Creek (Jarbridge) (Humboldt-Toiyabe NF)

Total sites: 5, RV sites: 5, No water, Vault/pit toilet, Tent & RV camping: Free, May be inaccessible in winter, Stay limit: 14 days, Open all year, Max Length: 25ft, Reservations not accepted, Elev: 6782ft/2067m, Tel: 775-331-6444, Nearest town: Jarbridge. GPS: 41.835688, -115.426141

7 • A3 | Sawmill (Humboldt-Toiyabe NF)

Total sites: 5, RV sites: 5, No water, Vault/pit toilet, Tent & RV camping: Free, May be inaccessible in winter, Open all year, Reservations not accepted, Elev: 6116ft/1864m, Tel: 775-752-3357, Nearest town: Jarbridge. GPS: 41.885462, -115.429515

8 • A4 | Angel Creek (Humboldt-Toiyabe NF)

Total sites: 12, RV sites: 12, Central water, Vault/pit toilet, No showers, No RV dump, Tent & RV camping: $17, Group site: $71, Open May-Sep, Max Length: 45ft, Reservations accepted, Elev: 6621ft/2018m, Tel: 775-752-3357, Nearest town: Wells. GPS: 41.027344, -115.050293

9 • A4 | Angel Lake (Humboldt-Toiyabe NF)

Total sites: 26, RV sites: 26, Central water, Vault/pit toilet, No showers, No RV dump, Tent & RV camping: $18, Open Jun-Sep, Max Length: 35ft, Reservations accepted, Elev: 8379ft/2554m, Tel: 775-752-3357, Nearest town: Wells. GPS: 41.026988, -115.083439

10 • B1 | Mount Rose (Humboldt-Toiyabe NF)

Total sites: 26, RV sites: 26, Central water, Vault/pit toilet, No showers, No RV dump, Tent & RV camping: $22, Open Jun-Sep, Max Length: 55ft, Reservations accepted, Elev: 8966ft/2733m, Tel: 775-882-2766, Nearest town: Reno. GPS: 39.313232, -119.892334

11 • B2 | Big Creek (Humboldt-Toiyabe NF)

Total sites: 5, RV sites: 5, Central water, Vault/pit toilet, No showers, No RV dump, Tent & RV camping: Free, Trailers prohibited from crossing the top of FSR 002, Open May-Oct, Max Length: 35ft, Reservations not accepted, Elev: 6942ft/2116m, Tel: 775-964-2671, Nearest town: Austin. GPS: 39.345493, -117.136112

12 • B3 | Bob Scott (Humboldt-Toiyabe NF)

Total sites: 9, RV sites: 9, Central water, Vault/pit toilet, No showers, No RV dump, Tent & RV camping: $10, Open May-Oct, Max Length: 35ft, Reservations not accepted, Elev: 7260ft/2213m, Tel: 775-964-2671, Nearest town: Austin. GPS: 39.457631, -116.995003

13 • B3 | South Ruby (Humboldt-Toiyabe NF)

Total sites: 35, RV sites: 35, Central water, Vault/pit toilet, No showers, No RV dump, Tent & RV camping: $17, Open May-Sep, Max Length: 50ft, Reservations accepted, Elev: 6092ft/1857m, Tel: 775-752-3357, Nearest town: Elko. GPS: 40.175929, -115.494557

14 • B3 | Thomas Canyon (Humboldt-Toiyabe NF)

Total sites: 40, RV sites: 40, Central water, Vault/pit toilet, No showers, No RV dump, Tent & RV camping: $19, Open May-Oct, Max Length: 50ft, Reservations accepted, Elev: 7634ft/2327m, Tel: 775-752-3357, Nearest town: Spring Creek. GPS: 40.649902, -115.404541

15 • B4 | Bird Creek (Humboldt-Toiyabe NF)

Total sites: 4, RV sites: 4, Central water, Vault/pit toilet, No showers, No RV dump, Tent & RV camping: $8, Open May-Oct, Max Length: 30ft, Reservations accepted, Elev: 7426ft/2263m, Tel: 775-289-3031, Nearest town: McGill. GPS: 39.463316, -114.652932

16 • B4 | East Creek (Humboldt-Toiyabe NF)

Total sites: 6, RV sites: 6, No water, Vault/pit toilet, Tent & RV camping: $4, Open May-Sep, Max Length: 20ft, Reservations not accepted, Elev: 7625ft/2324m, Tel: 775-289-3031, Nearest town: McGill. GPS: 39.497021, -114.639096

17 • B4 | Kalamazoo (Humboldt-Toiyabe NF)

Total sites: 5, RV sites: 5, No water, No toilets, Tent & RV camping: Free, Open May-Nov, Elev: 7032ft/2143m, Tel: 775-289-3031, Nearest town: Ely. GPS: 39.565337, -114.597821

18 • B4 | Timber Creek (Humboldt-Toiyabe NF)

Total sites: 6, RV sites: 6, Central water, Vault/pit toilet, No showers, No RV dump, Tent & RV camping: $8, 5 group sites: $35-$50, Open May-Oct, Max Length: 34ft, Reservations accepted, Elev: 8472ft/2582m, Tel: 775-289-3031, Nearest town: Ely. GPS: 39.401944, -114.638452

19 • B4 | Ward Mountain (Humboldt-Toiyabe NF)

Total sites: 29, RV sites: 29, Central water, Vault/pit toilet, No showers, No RV dump, Tent & RV camping: $8, Open May-Sep, Max Length: 40ft, Reservations accepted, Elev: 7356ft/2242m, Tel: 775-289-3031, Nearest town: Ely. GPS: 39.211914, -114.968018

20 • C1 | Desert Creek (Humboldt-Toiyabe NF)

Total sites: 19, RV sites: 6, No water, Vault/pit toilet, Tent & RV camping: Free, Creek crossing rqd, Open all year, Max Length: 18ft, Reservations not accepted, Elev: 6398ft/1950m, Tel: 760-932-7070, Nearest town: Bridgeport, CA. GPS: 38.620677, -119.340101

21 • C1 | Nevada Beach (Humboldt-Toiyabe NF)

Total sites: 54, RV sites: 54, Central water, Flush toilet, No showers, No RV dump, Tents: $36-40/RVs: $36-42, Stay limit: 14 days, Open May-Oct, Max Length: 60ft, Reservations accepted, Elev: 6296ft/1919m, Tel: 530-543-2600, Nearest town: Stateline. GPS: 38.980957, -119.952637

22 • C1 | Zephyr Cove (Lake Tahoe Basin Management Unit)

Total sites: 150, RV sites: 93, Elec sites: 93, Water at site, Flush toilet, Free showers, RV dump, Tents: $30/RVs: $30-40, Also walk-to sites/cabins, 93 Full hookup sites, Concessionaire, Max Length: 45ft, Elev: 6270ft/1911m, Tel: 775-589-4906, Nearest town: Lake Tahoe. GPS: 39.006444, -119.946467

23 • C2 | Columbine (Humboldt-Toiyabe NF)

Total sites: 5, RV sites: 5, No water, Vault/pit toilet, Tent & RV camping: Free, Open May-Oct, Max Length: 35ft, Reservations not accepted, Elev: 8661ft/2640m, Tel: 775-964-2671, Nearest town: Austin. GPS: 38.900342, -117.376796

24 • C2 | Kingston (Humboldt-Toiyabe NF)

Total sites: 11, RV sites: 11, No water, Vault/pit toilet, Tent & RV camping: Fee unk, Group site also, Open May-Oct, Max Length: 35ft, Reservations not accepted, Elev: 7195ft/2193m, Tel: 775-964-2671, Nearest town: Austin. GPS: 39.225185, -117.139586

25 • C2 | Peavine (Humboldt-Toiyabe NF)

Total sites: 15, RV sites: 15, No water, Vault/pit toilet, Tent & RV camping: Free, Open May-Oct, Max Length: 35ft, Reservations not accepted, Elev: 6391ft/1948m, Tel: 775-482-6286, Nearest town: Austin. GPS: 38.616291, -117.302569

26 • C2 | San Juan Creek (Humboldt-Toiyabe NF)

Total sites: 10, RV sites: 10, No water, Vault/pit toilet, Tent & RV camping: Free, Open May-Oct, Reservations not accepted, Elev: 7282ft/2220m, Tel: 775-964-2671, Nearest town: Austin. GPS: 39.121823, -117.275517

27 • C3 | Cherry Creek (Humboldt-Toiyabe NF)

Total sites: 4, RV sites: 4, No water, Vault/pit toilet, Tent & RV camping: Free, Open May-Sep, Max Length: 20ft, Reservations not accepted, Elev: 6932ft/2113m, Tel: 775-289-3031, Nearest town: Ely. GPS: 38.153799, -115.624325

28 • C3 | Pine Creek (Humboldt-Toiyabe NF)

Total sites: 21, RV sites: 21, No water, Vault/pit toilet, Tent & RV camping: Free, Group site available, Open May-Oct, Reservations not accepted, Elev: 7493ft/2284m, Tel: 775-482-6286, Nearest town: Tonopah. GPS: 38.795619, -116.850387

29 • C3 | Toquima Caves (Humboldt-Toiyabe NF)

Total sites: 5, RV sites: 1, No water, Vault/pit toilet, Tent & RV camping: Free, Available group site, Open May-Oct, Max Length: 25ft, Reservations not accepted, Elev: 7972ft/2430m, Tel: 775-482-6286, Nearest town: Tonopah. GPS: 39.187411, -116.787364

30 • C3 | White River (Humboldt-Toiyabe NF)

Total sites: 10, RV sites: 10, No toilets, Tent & RV camping: $4, Open May-Nov, Reservations not accepted, Elev: 6986ft/2129m, Tel: 775-289-3031, Nearest town: Ely. GPS: 38.943647, -115.341326

31 • D3 | Hilltop (Humboldt-Toiyabe NF)

Total sites: 35, RV sites: 34, No water, Vault/pit toilet, No showers, No RV dump, Tents: $19/RVs: $23, Open May-Oct, Max Length: 35ft, Reservations accepted, Elev: 8360ft/2548m, Tel: 702-515-5400, Nearest town: Las Vegas. GPS: 36.311388, -115.607056

32 • E3 | Fletcher View (Humboldt-Toiyabe NF)

Total sites: 11, RV sites: 11, Elec sites: 11, Central water, Flush toilet, Free showers, No RV dump, Tent & RV camping: $33, Open all year, Max Length: 40ft, Reservations accepted, Elev: 7054ft/2150m, Tel: 702-515-5400, Nearest town: Las Vegas. GPS: 36.262442, -115.617812

New Hampshire

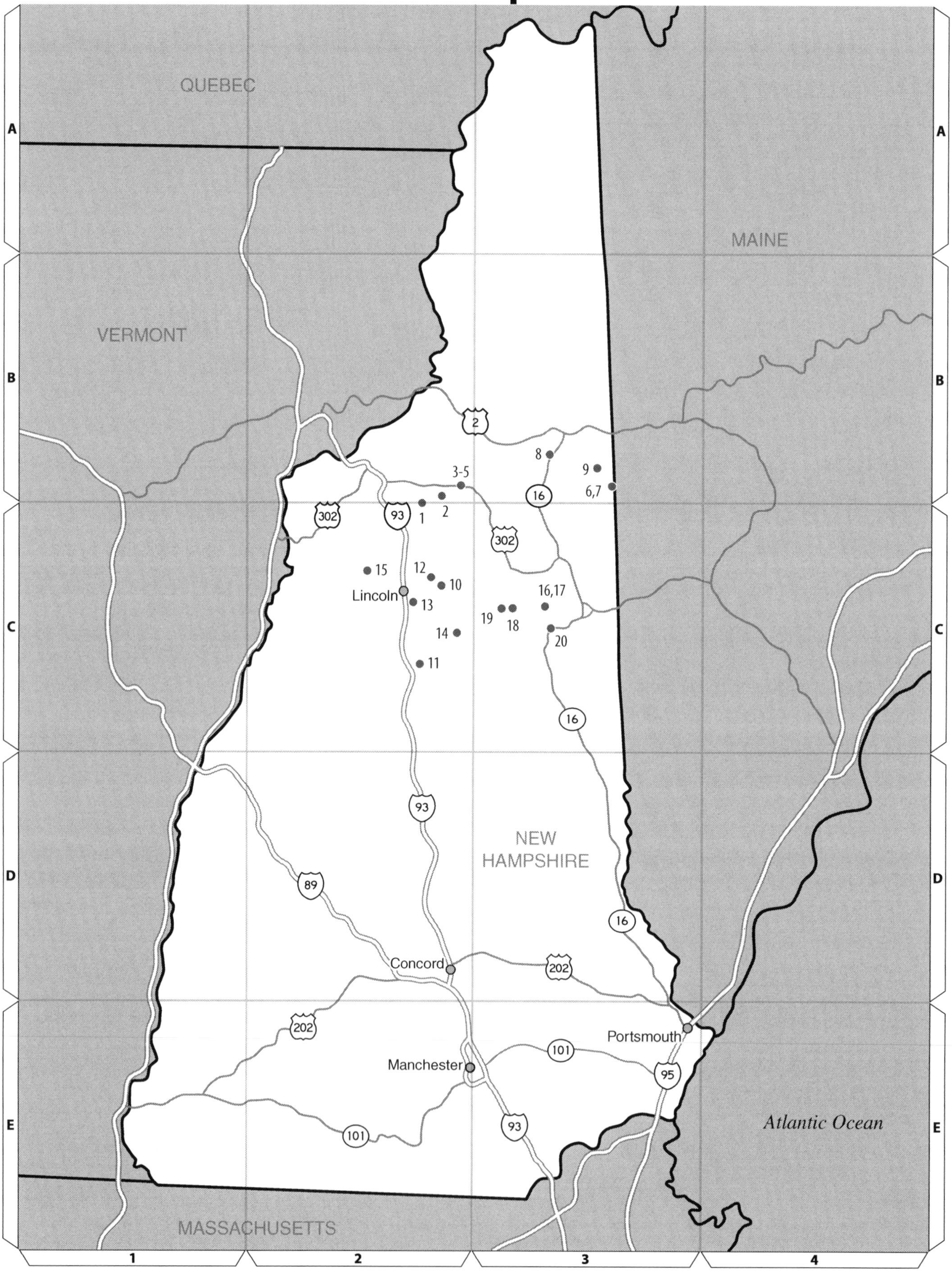

Map	ID	Map	ID
B2	1-5	C2	10-15
B3	6-9	C3	16-20

Alphabetical List of Camping Areas

1 • B2 | Gale River Road Dispersed (White Mountain NF)

Total sites: 10, No water, No toilets, Tent & RV camping: $5, 10 dispersed sites along road mostly for smaller rigs, Free for Interagency, Golden Age, or Golden Access pass holders, Elev: 1683ft/513m, Nearest town: Twin Mountain. GPS: 44.226483, -71.618913

2 • B2 | Haystack Road Dispersed (White Mountain NF)

Total sites: 11, No water, No toilets, Tent & RV camping: $5, 11 dispersed sites along road, Free for Interagency, Golden Age, or Golden Access pass holders, Reservations not accepted, Elev: 1736ft/529m, Nearest town: Twin Mountain. GPS: 44.242754, -71.557976

3 • B2 | Sugarloaf Area I (White Mountain NF)

Total sites: 29, RV sites: 29, Central water, Vault/pit toilet, No showers, No RV dump, Tent & RV camping: $20, Open May-Oct, Reservations accepted, Elev: 1657ft/505m, Tel: 603-536-6100, Nearest town: Twin Mountain. GPS: 44.258057, -71.503662

4 • B2 | Sugarloaf Area II (White Mountain NF)

Total sites: 32, RV sites: 32, Central water, Vault/pit toilet, No showers, No RV dump, Tent & RV camping: $20, Open May-Oct, Reservations accepted, Elev: 1631ft/497m, Tel: 603-536-6100, Nearest town: Twin Mountain. GPS: 44.260742, -71.504150

5 • B2 | Zealand (White Mountain NF)

Total sites: 11, RV sites: 11, Central water, Vault/pit toilet, No showers, No RV dump, Tent & RV camping: $20, Open May-Oct, Reservations not accepted, Elev: 1506ft/459m, Tel: 603-536-1310, Nearest town: Twin Mountain. GPS: 44.264925, -71.499242

6 • B3 | Basin Pond (White Mountain NF)

Total sites: 21, RV sites: 14, Central water, Vault/pit toilet, No showers, No RV dump, Tent & RV camping: $20, Open May-Oct, Max Length: 40ft, Reservations accepted, Elev: 712ft/217m, Tel: 603-447-5448, Nearest town: Gilead, ME. GPS: 44.267900, -71.022000

7 • B3 | Cold River (White Mountain NF)

Total sites: 14, RV sites: 12, Central water, Vault/pit toilet, No showers, No RV dump, Tent & RV camping: $20, Open May-Oct, Reservations accepted, Elev: 627ft/191m, Tel: 603-447-5448, Nearest town: North Chatham. GPS: 44.265194, -71.012469

8 • B3 | Dolly Copp - Big Meadow (White Mountain NF)

Total sites: 177, RV sites: 177, Elec sites: 30, Central water, Flush toilet, No showers, No RV dump, Tents: $25/RVs: $25-37, Open May-Oct, Reservations not accepted, Elev: 1273ft/388m, Tel: 603-466-2713, Nearest town: Gorham. GPS: 44.332648, -71.218862

9 • B3 | Wild River (White Mountain NF)

Total sites: 12, RV sites: 3, Central water, Vault/pit toilet, No showers, No RV dump, Tent & RV camping: $20, Open May-Sep, Reservations not accepted, Elev: 1178ft/359m, Tel: 603-466-2713, Nearest town: Gilead. GPS: 44.305000, -71.065000

10 • C2 | Big Rock (White Mountain NF)

Total sites: 28, RV sites: 20, Central water, Vault/pit toilet, No showers, No RV dump, Tent & RV camping: $25, Open May-Oct, Max Length: 40ft, Reservations accepted, Elev: 1637ft/499m, Tel: 603-536-6100, Nearest town: Lincoln. GPS: 44.048340, -71.559570

11 • C2 | Campton (White Mountain NF)

Total sites: 58, RV sites: 58, Central water, Flush toilet, Pay showers, No RV dump, Tent & RV camping: $25, Open May-Oct, Max Length: 50ft, Reservations accepted, Elev: 718ft/219m, Tel: 603-536-6100, Nearest town: Campton. GPS: 43.873779, -71.626953

12 • C2 | Hancock (White Mountain NF)

Total sites: 56, RV sites: 35, Central water, Vault/pit toilet, No showers, No RV dump, Tent & RV camping: $25, Open all year, Reservations not accepted, Elev: 1198ft/365m, Tel: 603-536-6100, Nearest town: Lincoln. GPS: 44.064453, -71.593750

13 • C2 | Russell Pond (White Mountain NF)

Total sites: 84, RV sites: 15, Central water, Flush toilet, Pay showers, No RV dump, Tent & RV camping: $25, Open May-Oct, Reservations not accepted, Elev: 1732ft/528m, Tel: 603-536-6100, Nearest town: Lincoln. GPS: 44.011963, -71.650635

14 • C2 | Waterville Valley (White Mountain NF)

Total sites: 26, RV sites: 19, Central water, Vault/pit toilet, No showers, No RV dump, Tent & RV camping: $20, Open May-Oct, Reservations accepted, Elev: 1466ft/447m, Tel: 603-536-6100, Nearest town: Waterville Valley. GPS: 43.942954, -71.509827

15 • C2 | Wildwood (White Mountain NF)

Total sites: 26, RV sites: 26, Central water, Vault/pit toilet, No showers, No RV dump, Tent & RV camping: $20, Open May-Oct, Reservations accepted, Elev: 1375ft/419m, Tel: 603-536-6100, Nearest town: North Woodstock. GPS: 44.076172, -71.793457

16 • C3 | Blackberry Crossing (White Mountain NF)

Total sites: 26, RV sites: 26, Central water, Vault/pit toilet, No showers, No RV dump, Tent & RV camping: $25, Open Apr-Oct, Reservations not accepted, Elev: 909ft/277m, Tel: 603-447-5448, Nearest town: Conway. GPS: 44.006967, -71.244546

17 • C3 | Covered Bridge (White Mountain NF)

Total sites: 49, RV sites: 41, Central water, Vault/pit toilet, No showers, No RV dump, Tent & RV camping: $25, 7' 9" height limit from west, Open May-Oct, Max Length: 35ft, Reservations accepted, Elev: 899ft/274m, Tel: 603-447-5448, Nearest town: Conway. GPS: 44.004024, -71.233154

18 • C3 | Jigger Johnson (White Mountain NF)

Total sites: 74, RV sites: 50, Central water, Flush toilet, Pay showers, No RV dump, Tent & RV camping: $25, Open May-Oct, Reservations not accepted, Elev: 1257ft/383m, Tel: 603-447-5448, Nearest town: Conway. GPS: 43.996094, -71.333496

19 • C3 | Passaconway (White Mountain NF)

Total sites: 33, RV sites: 33, Central water, Vault/pit toilet, No showers, No RV dump, Tent & RV camping: $25, Open May-Oct, Reservations not accepted, Elev: 1263ft/385m, Tel: 603-447-5448, Nearest town: Conway. GPS: 43.997094, -71.369482

20 • C3 | White Ledge (White Mountain NF)

Total sites: 28, RV sites: 28, Central water, Vault/pit toilet, No showers, No RV dump, Tent & RV camping: $20, Generator hours: 0800--1000/1700-1900, Open May-Oct, Max Length: 35ft, Reservations accepted, Elev: 761ft/232m, Tel: 603-447-5448, Nearest town: Conway. GPS: 43.954327, -71.214093

New Mexico

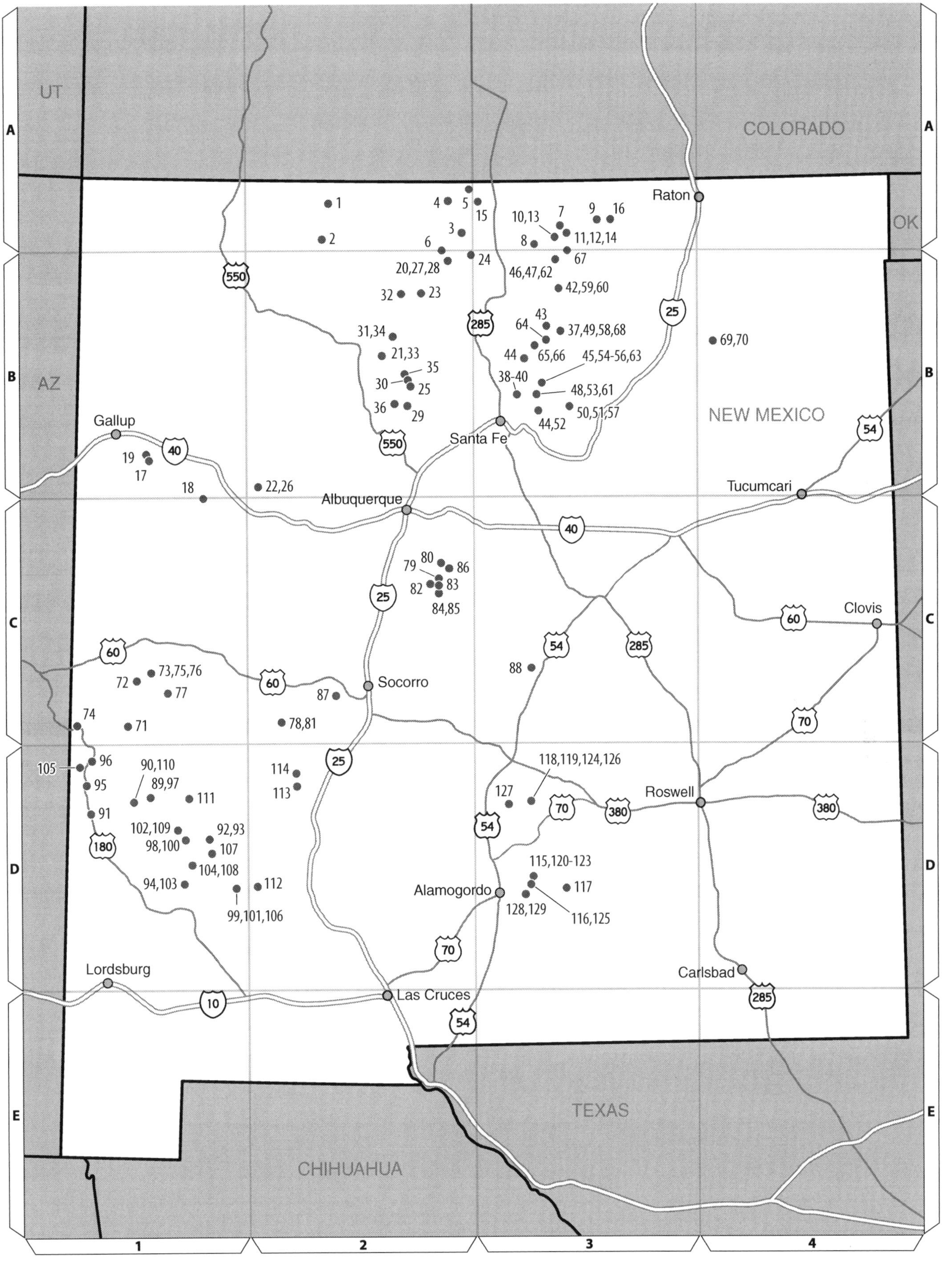
UT
COLORADO
OK
AZ
NEW MEXICO
TEXAS
CHIHUAHUA
A
B
C
D
E
1
2
3
4
Raton
Gallup
Santa Fe
Albuquerque
Tucumcari
Clovis
Socorro
Roswell
Alamogordo
Carlsbad
Lordsburg
Las Cruces
550
285
25
40
54
60
70
380
180
10
1
2
3
4
5
6
7
8
9
10,13
11,12,14
15
16
20,27,28
24
67
46,47,62
42,59,60
32
23
31,34
21,33
35
30
25
36
29
43
64
37,49,58,68
44
65,66
45,54-56,63
38-40
48,53,61
50,51,57
44,52
69,70
19
17
18
22,26
80
79
86
82
83
84,85
73,75,76
72
77
87
88
74
71
78,81
105
96
95
91
90,110
89,97
111
114
113
102,109
92,93
98,100
107
104,108
94,103
112
99,101,106
118,119,124,126
127
115,120-123
117
128,129
116,125

Map	ID	Map	ID
A2	1-6	C1	71-77
A3	7-16	C2	78-87
B1	17-19	C3	88
B2	20-36	D1	89-111
B3	37-68	D2	112-114
B4	69-70	D3	115-129

Alphabetical List of Camping Areas

Name	ID	Map
Aeroplane Mesa (Gila NF)	89	D1
Agua Piedra (Carson NF)	37	B3
Apache (Lincoln NF)	115	D3
Apache Creek (Gila NF)	71	C1
Armijo Springs (Gila NF)	72	C1
Aspen Basin (Santa Fe NF)	38	B3
Bear Trap (Cibola NF)	78	C2
Ben Lilly (Gila NF)	90	D1
Big Tesuque (Santa Fe NF)	39	B3
Bighorn (Gila NF)	91	D1
Black Canyon (Santa Fe NF)	40	B3
Black Canyon Lower (Gila NF)	92	D1
Black Canyon Upper (Gila NF)	93	D1
Borrego Mesa (Santa Fe NF)	41	B3
Buzzard Park (Carson NF)	1	A2
Cabresto Lake (Carson NF)	7	A3
Canjilon Creek (Carson NF)	20	B2
Capilla Peak (Cibola NF)	79	C2
Capulin (Carson NF)	42	B3
Cebolla Mesa (Carson NF)	8	A3
Cedar Springs (Carson NF)	2	A2
Cherry Creek (Gila NF)	94	D1
Cimarron (Carson NF)	9	A3
Clear Creek (Santa Fe NF)	21	B2
Coal Mine (Cibola NF)	22	B2
Columbine (Carson NF)	10	A3
Comales (Carson NF)	43	B3
Cosmic (Gila NF)	95	D1
Cottonwood (Gila NF)	96	D1
Cow Creek (Santa Fe NF)	44	B3
Cowles (Santa Fe NF)	45	B3
Cuchilla (Carson NF)	46	B3
Cuchilla del Medio (Carson NF)	47	B3
Davis Willow (Santa Fe NF)	48	B3
Deerhead (Lincoln NF)	116	D3
Dipping Vat (Gila NF)	97	D1
Duran Canyon (Carson NF)	49	B3
E.V. Long (Santa Fe NF)	50	B3
Echo Amphitheater (Carson NF)	23	B2
El Caso (Gila NF)	73	C1
El Porvenir (Santa Fe NF)	51	B3
El Rito Creek (Carson NF)	24	B2
Elephant Rock (Carson NF)	11	A3
Fawn Lakes (Carson NF)	12	A3
Field Tract (Santa Fe NF)	52	B3
Forks (Gila NF)	98	D1
Fourth of July TH (Cibola NF)	80	C2
Gallinas Upper (Gila NF)	99	D1
Goat Hill (Carson NF)	13	A3
Grapevine (Gila NF)	100	D1
Head Of the Ditch (Apache NF)	74	C1
Holy Ghost (Santa Fe NF)	53	B3
Hopewell Lake (Carson NF)	3	A2
Hughes Mill (Cibola NF)	81	C2
Iron Creek (Gila NF)	101	D1
Iron Gate (Santa Fe NF)	54	B3
Jacks Creek (Santa Fe NF)	55	B3
Jacks Creek Horse Camp (Santa Fe NF)	56	B3
James Canyon (Lincoln NF)	117	D3
Jemez Falls (Santa Fe NF)	25	B2
John F Kennedy (Cibola NF)	82	C2
Johnson Mesa (Santa Fe NF)	57	B3
Junebug (Carson NF)	14	A3
Juniper (Gila NF)	75	C1
Kingston (Gila NF)	112	D2
La Junta Canyon (Carson NF)	58	B3
La Sombra (Carson NF)	59	B3
Laguna Larga (Carson NF)	15	A3
Lagunitas (Carson NF)	4	A2
Las Petacas (Carson NF)	60	B3
Links Tract (Santa Fe NF)	61	B3
Lobo Canyon (Cibola NF)	26	B2
Lower Canjilon Lake (Carson NF)	27	B2
Lower Hondo (Carson NF)	62	B3
Lower Scorpion (Gila NF)	102	D1
Luna Park (Cibola NF)	113	D2
McCrystal Creek (Carson NF)	16	A3
McGaffey (Cibola NF)	17	B1
McMillan (Gila NF)	103	D1
Mesa (Gila NF)	104	D1
Middle Canjilon Lake (Carson NF)	28	B2
Mills Canyon (Cibola NF)	69	B4
Mills Canyon Rim (Cibola NF)	70	B4
Monjeau (Lincoln NF)	118	D3
New Canyon (Cibola NF)	83	C2
Oak Grove (Lincoln NF)	119	D3
Ojo Redondo (Cibola NF)	18	B1
Paliza (Santa Fe NF)	29	B2
Panchuela (Santa Fe NF)	63	B3
Pines (Lincoln NF)	120	D3
Pinon (Gila NF)	76	C1
Pueblo Park (Gila NF)	105	D1
Quaking Aspen (Cibola NF)	19	B1
Railroad Canyon (Gila NF)	106	D1
Red Canyon Horse Camp (Cibola NF)	84	C2
Red Canyon Lower (Cibola NF)	85	C2
Red Cloud (Cibola NF)	88	C3
Redondo (Santa Fe NF)	30	B2
Resumidero (Santa Fe NF)	31	B2
Rio Chama (Santa Fe NF)	32	B2
Rio de Las Vacas (Santa Fe NF)	33	B2
Rio de Los Pinos (Carson NF)	5	A2
Rio Puerco (Santa Fe NF)	34	B2
Rocky Canyon (Gila NF)	107	D1
Saddle (Lincoln NF)	121	D3
San Antonio (Santa Fe NF)	35	B2
Santa Barbara (Carson NF)	64	B3
Silver (Lincoln NF)	122	D3
Silver Overflow (Lincoln NF)	123	D3

1 • A2 | Buzzard Park (Carson NF)

Total sites: 4, RV sites: 4, No water, Vault/pit toilet, Tent & RV camping: Free, No large RVs, Open May-Nov, Reservations not accepted, Elev: 6975ft/2126m, Tel: 505-632-2956, Nearest town: Dulce. GPS: 36.881061, -107.216887

2 • A2 | Cedar Springs (Carson NF)

Total sites: 4, RV sites: 0, No water, No toilets, Tents only: Free, Open May-Nov, Reservations not accepted, Elev: 7461ft/2274m, Tel: 505-632-2956, Nearest town: Gobernador. GPS: 36.671958, -107.253189

3 • A2 | Hopewell Lake (Carson NF)

Total sites: 21, RV sites: 21, Central water, Vault/pit toilet, No showers, No RV dump, Tent & RV camping: $20, Open May-Sep, Max Length: 45ft, Reservations accepted, Elev: 9754ft/2973m, Tel: 505-758-8678, Nearest town: Tres Piedras. GPS: 36.704448, -106.235506

4 • A2 | Lagunitas (Carson NF)

Total sites: 12, RV sites: 12, No water, Vault/pit toilet, Tent & RV camping: Fee unk, 4x4 recommended, Open Jun-Oct, Max Length: 16ft, Reservations not accepted, Elev: 10545ft/3214m, Tel: 575-758-8678, Nearest town: Penasco. GPS: 36.886232, -106.320596

5 • A2 | Rio de Los Pinos (Carson NF)

Total sites: 4, RV sites: 4, No water, Vault/pit toilet, Tent & RV camping: Free, Open Jun-Sep, Max Length: 16ft, Reservations not accepted, Elev: 8290ft/2527m, Tel: 575-758-8678, Nearest town: Tres Piedras. GPS: 36.955753, -106.178232

6 • A2 | Trout Lakes (Carson NF)

Total sites: 12, RV sites: 12, No water, Vault/pit toilet, Tent & RV camping: Free, High-clearance vehicle needed, Open May-Sep, Max Length: 16ft, Reservations not accepted, Elev: 9229ft/2813m, Tel: 505-684-2486, Nearest town: Canjilon. GPS: 36.608215, -106.382244

7 • A3 | Cabresto Lake (Carson NF)

Total sites: 9, RV sites: 0, No water, Vault/pit toilet, Tent & RV camping: Free, Nothing larger than van/pickup, Open May-Sep, Reservations not accepted, Elev: 9160ft/2792m, Tel: 575-586-0520, Nearest town: Questa. GPS: 36.746685, -105.499292

8 • A3 | Cebolla Mesa (Carson NF)

Total sites: 5, RV sites: 5, No water, No toilets, Tent & RV camping: Fee unk, Road is dirt/gravel and hazardous in muddy conditions, Open May-Sep, Max Length: 32ft, Reservations not accepted, Elev: 7375ft/2248m, Tel: 575-586-0520, Nearest town: Questa. GPS: 36.640308, -105.689195

9 • A3 | Cimarron (Carson NF)

Total sites: 36, RV sites: 36, No water, Vault/pit toilet, Tent & RV camping: $20, Horse facilities, Open May-Sep, Max Length: 180ft, Reservations accepted, Elev: 9485ft/2891m, Tel: 505-586-0520, Nearest town: Costilla. GPS: 36.769433, -105.204977

10 • A3 | Columbine (Carson NF)

Total sites: 27, RV sites: 27, Central water, Vault/pit toilet, No showers, No RV dump, Tent & RV camping: $20, Open May-Sep, Max Length: 70ft, Reservations accepted, Elev: 7900ft/2408m, Tel: 505-586-0520, Nearest town: Questa. GPS: 36.679199, -105.515625

11 • A3 | Elephant Rock (Carson NF)

Total sites: 22, RV sites: 22, Central water, Vault/pit toilet, No showers, No RV dump, Tent & RV camping: $20, Open May-Sep, Max Length: 44ft, Reservations accepted, Elev: 8556ft/2608m, Tel: 505-586-0520, Nearest town: Red River. GPS: 36.707333, -105.448790

12 • A3 | Fawn Lakes (Carson NF)

Total sites: 22, RV sites: 22, Central water, Vault/pit toilet, No showers, No RV dump, Tent & RV camping: $20, Open May-Oct, Max Length: 45ft, Reservations accepted, Elev: 8488ft/2587m, Tel: 505-586-0520, Nearest town: Red River. GPS: 36.705811, -105.456543

13 • A3 | Goat Hill (Carson NF)

Total sites: 6, RV sites: 6, No water, Vault/pit toilet, Tent & RV camping: $8, Open May-Oct, Max Length: 32ft, Reservations not accepted, Elev: 7716ft/2352m, Tel: 575-586-0520, Nearest town: Questa. GPS: 36.688141, -105.540516

14 • A3 | Junebug (Carson NF)

Total sites: 20, RV sites: 20, Central water, Vault/pit toilet, No showers, No RV dump, Tent & RV camping: $18, Open May-Sep, Max Length: 22ft, Reservations not accepted, Elev: 8606ft/2623m, Tel: 505-586-0520, Nearest town: Red River. GPS: 36.707764, -105.434814

15 • A3 | Laguna Larga (Carson NF)

Total sites: 4, RV sites: 4, No water, No toilets, Tent & RV camping: Free, Open May-Oct, Reservations not accepted, Elev: 9003ft/2744m, Tel: 575-758-8678, Nearest town: Tres Piedras. GPS: 36.884181, -106.108633

16 • A3 | McCrystal Creek (Carson NF)

Total sites: 60, RV sites: 60, No water, Vault/pit toilet, Tent & RV camping: $13, 6 sites for horse campers, Open May-Sep, Max Length: 32ft, Reservations not accepted, Elev: 8140ft/2481m, Tel: 505-586-0520, Nearest town: Costilla. GPS: 36.776981, -105.113884

17 • B1 | McGaffey (Cibola NF)

Total sites: 29, RV sites: 29, Central water, No toilets, No showers, No RV dump, Tents: $10/RVs: $10-15, Stay limit: 14 days, Open May-Sep, Max Length: 22ft, Reservations not accepted, Elev: 7813ft/2381m, Tel: 505-287-8833, Nearest town: Fort Wingate. GPS: 35.368302, -108.522008

18 • B1 | Ojo Redondo (Cibola NF)

Total sites: 15, RV sites: 15, No water, Vault/pit toilet, Tent & RV camping: Free, Stay limit: 14 days, Open May-Sep, Max Length: 22ft, Reservations not accepted, Elev: 8835ft/2693m, Tel: 505-287-8833, Nearest town: Thoreau. GPS: 35.158849, -108.107332

19 • B1 | Quaking Aspen (Cibola NF)

Total sites: 20, RV sites: 20, No water, Vault/pit toilet, Tent & RV camping: $5, Stay limit: 14 days, Open May-Sep, Max Length: 22ft, Reservations not accepted, Elev: 7579ft/2310m, Tel: 505-287-8833, Nearest town: Wingate. GPS: 35.407179, -108.539472

20 • B2 | Canjilon Creek (Carson NF)

Total sites: 4, RV sites: 4, No water, Vault/pit toilet, Tent & RV camping: Free, Open Jun-Sep, Max Length: 16ft, Reservations not accepted, Elev: 9452ft/2881m, Nearest town: Canjilon. GPS: 36.543352, -106.317422

21 • B2 | Clear Creek (Santa Fe NF)

Total sites: 15, RV sites: 15, Central water, Vault/pit toilet, Tent & RV camping: $10, Group area $35, Generator hours: 0600-2200, Open May-Nov, Max Length: 47ft, Reservations accepted, Elev: 8428ft/2569m, Tel: 505-289-3265, Nearest town: Cuba. GPS: 35.996835, -106.826928

22 • B2 | Coal Mine (Cibola NF)

Total sites: 15, RV sites: 15, No water, Vault/pit toilet, Tent & RV camping: $5, Open May-Sep, Max Length: 45ft, Reservations accepted, Elev: 7484ft/2281m, Tel: 505-287-8833, Nearest town: Grants. GPS: 35.234371, -107.701862

23 • B2 | Echo Amphitheater (Carson NF)

Total sites: 9, RV sites: 9, Central water, Flush toilet, No showers, No RV dump, Tent & RV camping: $10, No water in winter, Open all year, Elev: 6624ft/2019m, Tel: 505-684-2486, Nearest town: Abiquiu. GPS: 36.359703, -106.523562

24 • B2 | El Rito Creek (Carson NF)

Total sites: 9, RV sites: 9, No water, Vault/pit toilet, Tent & RV camping: Free, Open Apr-Nov, Reservations not accepted, Elev: 8091ft/2466m, Tel: 575-581-4554, Nearest town: El Rito. GPS: 36.579414, -106.168605

25 • B2 | Jemez Falls (Santa Fe NF)

Total sites: 52, RV sites: 52, Central water, Vault/pit toilet, No showers, No RV dump, Tent & RV camping: $10, Open May-Oct, Max Length: 47ft, Reservations required, Elev: 8008ft/2441m, Tel: 505-829-3535, Nearest town: Jemez Springs. GPS: 35.824173, -106.606912

26 • B2 | Lobo Canyon (Cibola NF)

Total sites: 9, RV sites: 0, No water, Vault/pit toilet, Tents only: Free, Stay limit: 14 days, Open May-Sep, Reservations not accepted, Elev: 7487ft/2282m, Tel: 505-287-8833, Nearest town: Grants. GPS: 35.203738, -107.715035

27 • B2 | Lower Canjilon Lake (Carson NF)

Total sites: 48, RV sites: 48, No water, Vault/pit toilet, Tent & RV camping: $5, Stay limit: 14 days, Max Length: 22ft, Reservations not accepted, Elev: 9859ft/3005m, Tel: 575-684-2489, Nearest town: Cebolla. GPS: 36.549461, -106.344159

28 • B2 | Middle Canjilon Lake (Carson NF)

Total sites: 22, RV sites: 22, Vault/pit toilet, Tent & RV camping: $5, Stay limit: 14 days, Reservations not accepted, Elev: 10023ft/3055m, Tel: 575-684-2489, Nearest town: Cebolla. GPS: 36.554733, -106.332348

29 • B2 | Paliza (Santa Fe NF)

Total sites: 30, RV sites: 30, No water, Vault/pit toilet, Tent & RV camping: $8, High clearance vehicle recommended, Stay limit: 14 days, Open May-Oct, Max Length: 16ft, Reservations not accepted, Elev: 6860ft/2091m, Tel: 575-829-3535, Nearest town: San Ysidra. GPS: 35.704385, -106.627059

30 • B2 | Redondo (Santa Fe NF)

Total sites: 60, RV sites: 60, No water, Vault/pit toilet, Tent & RV camping: $10, Open May-Oct, Max Length: 30ft, Reservations not accepted, Elev: 8140ft/2481m, Tel: 505-829-3535, Nearest town: Jemez Springs. GPS: 35.861606, -106.626933

31 • B2 | Resumidero (Santa Fe NF)

Total sites: 15, RV sites: 6, No water, Vault/pit toilet, Tent & RV camping: Free, Open May-Sep, Max Length: 16ft, Reservations not accepted, Elev: 8976ft/2736m, Tel: 575-638-5526, Nearest town: Coyote. GPS: 36.113076, -106.745846

32 • B2 | Rio Chama (Santa Fe NF)

Total sites: 18, RV sites: 18, No water, Vault/pit toilet, Tent & RV camping: Free, Open Apr-Oct, Max Length: 20ft, Reservations not accepted, Elev: 6427ft/1959m, Tel: 575-638-5526, Nearest town: Abiquiu. GPS: 36.355248, -106.673673

33 • B2 | Rio de Las Vacas (Santa Fe NF)

Total sites: 15, RV sites: 15, Central water, Vault/pit toilet, No showers, No RV dump, Tent & RV camping: $10, Open May-Sep, Max Length: 42ft, Reservations accepted, Elev: 8353ft/2546m, Tel: 505-289-3265, Nearest town: Cuba. GPS: 35.997017, -106.806788

34 • B2 | Rio Puerco (Santa Fe NF)

Total sites: 5, RV sites: 5, No water, Vault/pit toilet, Tent & RV camping: Free, Very tight turn around loop, Open May-Sep, Max Length: 20ft, Reservations not accepted, Elev: 8271ft/2521m, Tel: 575-638-5526, Nearest town: Coyote. GPS: 36.100641, -106.723683

35 • B2 | San Antonio (Santa Fe NF)

Total sites: 21, RV sites: 21, Elec sites: 6, Water at site, Vault/pit toilet, No showers, No RV dump, Tents: $10/RVs: $10-15, Group site: $150, Open May-Sep, Max Length: 52ft, Reservations accepted, Elev: 7812ft/2381m, Tel: 575-829-3535, Nearest town: Jemez Springs. GPS: 35.886613, -106.646995

36 • B2 | Vista Linda (Santa Fe NF)

Total sites: 13, RV sites: 13, Central water, Vault/pit toilet, No showers, No RV dump, Tent & RV camping: $10, Stay limit: 14 days, Generator hours: 0700-2100, Open Mar-Oct, Max Length: 40ft, Reservations not accepted, Elev: 5860ft/1786m, Tel: 575-829-3535, Nearest town: San Ysidro. GPS: 35.717363, -106.721290

37 • B3 | Agua Piedra (Carson NF)

Total sites: 44, RV sites: 44, Central water, Vault/pit toilet, No showers, No RV dump, Tent & RV camping: $20, Horse Corral, Group sites $65-$115, Water in lower loop has strong sulphur smell - but is potable, Loops A and B have no water, Open May-Sep, Max Length: 40ft, Reservations accepted, Elev: 8415ft/2565m, Nearest town: Penasco. GPS: 36.135254, -105.529053

38 • B3 | Aspen Basin (Santa Fe NF)

Total sites: 10, RV sites: 10, No water, Vault/pit toilet, Tent & RV camping: Free, Severe winter conditions, Open all year, Reservations not accepted, Elev: 10358ft/3157m, Tel: 505-753-7331, Nearest town: Santa Fe. GPS: 35.795966, -105.805287

39 • B3 | Big Tesuque (Santa Fe NF)

Total sites: 10, RV sites: 0, No water, Vault/pit toilet, Tents only: Free, Walk-to sites, Open all year, Reservations not accepted, Elev: 9767ft/2977m, Tel: 505-753-7331, Nearest town: Santa Fe. GPS: 35.769396, -105.809089

40 • B3 | Black Canyon (Santa Fe NF)

Total sites: 42, RV sites: 36, No water, Vault/pit toilet, No showers, No RV dump, Tent & RV camping: $10, Also walk-to sites, Open May-Oct, Max Length: 61ft, Reservations accepted, Elev: 8448ft/2575m, Tel: 575-536-2250, Nearest town: Santa Fe. GPS: 35.725889, -105.836607

41 • B3 | Borrego Mesa (Santa Fe NF)

Total sites: 8, RV sites: 8, No water, No toilets, Tent & RV camping: Free, Small horse corrals at each site, Vault toilets vandalized, Open all year, Max Length: 14ft, Reservations not accepted, Elev: 8802ft/2683m, Tel: 505-753-7331, Nearest town: Espanola. GPS: 35.979192, -105.772525

42 • B3 | Capulin (Carson NF)

Total sites: 11, RV sites: 11, No water, Vault/pit toilet, Tent & RV camping: $10, Open May-Oct, Max Length: 16ft, Reservations not accepted, Elev: 7868ft/2398m, Tel: 575-587-2255, Nearest town: Taos. GPS: 36.370707, -105.483165

43 • B3 | Comales (Carson NF)

Total sites: 2, RV sites: 2, No water, Vault/pit toilet, Tent & RV camping: $12, Open May-Sep, Max Length: 22ft, Reservations not accepted, Elev: 7936ft/2419m, Tel: 575-587-2255, Nearest town: Penasco. GPS: 36.160028, -105.596415

44 • B3 | Cow Creek (Santa Fe NF)

Total sites: 5, RV sites: 0, No water, No toilets, Tents only: Free, Open Apr-Nov, Reservations not accepted, Elev: 8540ft/2603m, Tel: 505-757-6121, Nearest town: Pecos. GPS: 35.671000, -105.640000

45 • B3 | Cowles (Santa Fe NF)

Total sites: 9, RV sites: 0, No water, Vault/pit toilet, Tents only: $6, Open Apr-Nov, Reservations not accepted, Elev: 8360ft/2548m, Tel: 505-757-6121, Nearest town: Pecos. GPS: 35.812344, -105.663428

46 • B3 | Cuchilla (Carson NF)

Total sites: 3, RV sites: 3, No water, Vault/pit toilet, Tent & RV camping: Free, Open May-Sep, Max Length: 22ft, Reservations not accepted, Elev: 8240ft/2512m, Nearest town: Taos. GPS: 36.569361, -105.518488

47 • B3 | Cuchilla del Medio (Carson NF)

Total sites: 3, RV sites: 3, No water, Vault/pit toilet, Tent & RV camping: Free, Open May-Sep, Max Length: 16ft, Reservations not accepted, Elev: 8064ft/2458m, Tel: 575-586-0520, Nearest town: Taos. GPS: 36.559253, -105.535424

48 • B3 | Davis Willow (Santa Fe NF)

Total sites: 15, RV sites: 15, No water, Vault/pit toilet, Tent & RV camping: Free, Open Apr-Nov, Reservations not accepted, Elev: 8114ft/2473m, Tel: 505-757-6121, Nearest town: Pecos. GPS: 35.757409, -105.663266

49 • B3 | Duran Canyon (Carson NF)

Total sites: 12, RV sites: 12, No water, Vault/pit toilet, Tent & RV camping: $11, Stay limit: 14 days, Open May-Oct, Reservations not accepted, Elev: 8842ft/2695m, Tel: 575-587-2255, Nearest town: Penasco. GPS: 36.134033, -105.477295

50 • B3 | E.V. Long (Santa Fe NF)

Total sites: 14, RV sites: 14, No water, Vault/pit toilet, No showers, No RV dump, Tent & RV camping: $8, Generator hours: 0700-2200, Open Apr-Nov, Max Length: 16ft, Reservations not accepted, Elev: 7493ft/2284m, Tel: 505-757-6121, Nearest town: Las Vegas. GPS: 35.698386, -105.422791

51 • B3 | El Porvenir (Santa Fe NF)

Total sites: 13, RV sites: 13, Central water, Vault/pit toilet, No showers, No RV dump, Tent & RV camping: $8, Open Apr-Nov, Max Length: 32ft, Reservations not accepted, Elev: 7556ft/2303m, Tel: 505-757-6121, Nearest town: Las Vegas. GPS: 35.710205, -105.412109

52 • B3 | Field Tract (Santa Fe NF)

Total sites: 15, RV sites: 15, Central water, Flush toilet, No showers, No RV dump, Tent & RV camping: $8, 6 sites have shelters, Open May-Oct, Max Length: 62ft, Reservations accepted, Elev: 7382ft/2250m, Tel: 505-757-6121, Nearest town: Pecos. GPS: 35.686768, -105.693115

53 • B3 | Holy Ghost (Santa Fe NF)

Total sites: 23, No water, Vault/pit toilet, No showers, No RV dump, Tents only: $8, Generator hours: 0700-2200, Open

Apr-Nov, Max Length: 32ft, Reservations not accepted, Elev: 8379ft/2554m, Tel: 505-757-6121, Nearest town: Santa Fe. GPS: 35.773000, -105.701000

54 • B3 | Iron Gate (Santa Fe NF)

Total sites: 14, RV sites: 14, No water, Vault/pit toilet, Tent & RV camping: $4, 4 horse corrals, Rough road - high-clearance vehicle required, Open Apr-Nov, Max Length: 30ft, Reservations not accepted, Elev: 9383ft/2860m, Tel: 505-757-6121, Nearest town: Pecos. GPS: 35.839844, -105.621338

55 • B3 | Jacks Creek (Santa Fe NF)

Total sites: 39, RV sites: 39, Central water, Vault/pit toilet, No showers, No RV dump, Tent & RV camping: $10, Open Apr-Nov, Max Length: 32ft, Reservations not accepted, Elev: 9006ft/2745m, Tel: 505-757-6121, Nearest town: Pecos. GPS: 35.841372, -105.654891

56 • B3 | Jacks Creek Horse Camp (Santa Fe NF)

Total sites: 8, RV sites: 8, Central water, Vault/pit toilet, No showers, No RV dump, Tent & RV camping: $10, Corrals and highlines, Open May-Oct, Reservations not accepted, Elev: 9022ft/2750m, Tel: 505-757-6121, Nearest town: Pecos. GPS: 35.834637, -105.655387

57 • B3 | Johnson Mesa (Santa Fe NF)

Total sites: 17, RV sites: 17, No water, Vault/pit toilet, Tent & RV camping: Free, Open Apr-Nov, Max Length: 30ft, Reservations not accepted, Elev: 9465ft/2885m, Tel: 505-757-6121, Nearest town: Las Vegas. GPS: 35.703394, -105.468662

58 • B3 | La Junta Canyon (Carson NF)

Total sites: 30, RV sites: 30, Central water, Vault/pit toilet, No showers, No RV dump, Tent & RV camping: $6, Open Jun, Max Length: 16ft, Reservations not accepted, Elev: 8707ft/2654m, Tel: 575-587-2255, Nearest town: Taos. GPS: 36.127856, -105.497767

59 • B3 | La Sombra (Carson NF)

Total sites: 13, RV sites: 0, No water, Vault/pit toilet, Tents only: $6, Open May-Oct, Max Length: 16ft, Reservations not accepted, Elev: 8008ft/2441m, Tel: 575-587-2255, Nearest town: Taos. GPS: 36.369141, -105.473389

60 • B3 | Las Petacas (Carson NF)

Total sites: 9, RV sites: 9, No water, Vault/pit toilet, Tent & RV camping: $10, Open May-Oct, Max Length: 16ft, Reservations not accepted, Elev: 7438ft/2267m, Tel: 575-587-2255, Nearest town: Taos. GPS: 36.381683, -105.521949

61 • B3 | Links Tract (Santa Fe NF)

Total sites: 12, RV sites: 12, No water, Vault/pit toilet, Tent & RV camping: Free, Generator hours: 0700-2200, Max Length: 32ft, Reservations not accepted, Elev: 8176ft/2492m, Nearest town: Pecos. GPS: 35.757152, -105.662069

62 • B3 | Lower Hondo (Carson NF)

Total sites: 5, RV sites: 4, No water, Vault/pit toilet, Tent & RV camping: Free, Open May-Oct, Max Length: 16ft, Reservations not accepted, Elev: 7861ft/2396m, Tel: 575-586-0520, Nearest town: Taos. GPS: 36.548528, -105.549558

63 • B3 | Panchuela (Santa Fe NF)

Total sites: 5, RV sites: 0, Central water, Vault/pit toilet, No showers, No RV dump, Tents only: $5, Generator hours: 0700-2200, Open Apr-Nov, Reservations not accepted, Elev: 8432ft/2570m, Tel: 505-757-6121, Nearest town: Pecos. GPS: 35.831094, -105.665007

64 • B3 | Santa Barbara (Carson NF)

Total sites: 22, RV sites: 22, Central water, Vault/pit toilet, No showers, No RV dump, Tent & RV camping: $20, Open May-Sep, Max Length: 65ft, Reservations accepted, Elev: 8921ft/2719m, Tel: 505-587-2255, Nearest town: Penasco. GPS: 36.086576, -105.609551

65 • B3 | Trampas Diamante (Carson NF)

Total sites: 5, RV sites: 5, No water, Vault/pit toilet, Tent & RV camping: Fee unk, Open May-Sep, Max Length: 16ft, Elev: 8491ft/2588m, Nearest town: Penasco. GPS: 36.067077, -105.708816

66 • B3 | Trampas Trailhead (Carson NF)

Total sites: 4, RV sites: 4, No water, Vault/pit toilet, Tent & RV camping: Free, Open all year, Elev: 9035ft/2754m, Nearest town: Penasco. GPS: 36.044556, -105.673089

67 • B3 | Twining (Carson NF)

Total sites: 4, RV sites: 4, No water, Vault/pit toilet, Tent & RV camping: Free, Self-contained units only, Open May-Oct, Max Length: 16ft, Elev: 9438ft/2877m, Tel: 575-586-0520, Nearest town: Taos. GPS: 36.596731, -105.449569

68 • B3 | Upper La Junta (Carson NF)

Total sites: 8, RV sites: 8, Central water, Vault/pit toilet, No showers, No RV dump, Tent & RV camping: $11, Open Jun-Oct, Reservations not accepted, Elev: 9203ft/2805m, Tel: 575-587-2255, Nearest town: Penasco. GPS: 36.147822, -105.455297

69 • B4 | Mills Canyon (Cibola NF)

Total sites: 12, RV sites: 0, No water, Vault/pit toilet, Tents only: Free, High clearance vehicles recommended, Stay limit: 14 days, Open all year, Reservations not accepted, Elev: 5154ft/1571m, Tel: 505-374-9652, Nearest town: Roy. GPS: 36.048109, -104.377551

70 • B4 | Mills Canyon Rim (Cibola NF)

Total sites: 6, RV sites: 6, No water, Vault/pit toilet, Tent & RV camping: Free, Stay limit: 14 days, Reservations not accepted, Elev: 5738ft/1749m, Tel: 505-374-9652, Nearest town: Roy. GPS: 36.071977, -104.350478

71 • C1 | Apache Creek (Gila NF)

Total sites: 20, RV sites: 20, No water, Vault/pit toilet, Tent & RV camping: Free, Stay limit: 14 days, Open May-Nov, Elev: 6460ft/1969m, Tel: 575-533-6231, Nearest town: Reserve. GPS: 33.828564, -108.627903

72 • C1 | Armijo Springs (Gila NF)

Total sites: 5, RV sites: 5, No water, Vault/pit toilet, Tent & RV camping: Free, Stay limit: 14 days, Open all year, Max Length: 40ft, Reservations not accepted, Elev: 7959ft/2426m, Tel: 575-773-4678, Nearest town: Quemado. GPS: 34.096528, -108.569956

73 • C1 | El Caso (Gila NF)

Total sites: 22, RV sites: 22, No water, Vault/pit toilet, Tent & RV camping: Free, Stay limit: 14 days, Open May-Sep, Max Length: 20ft, Elev: 7695ft/2345m, Tel: 505-773-4678, Nearest town: Quemado. GPS: 34.137404, -108.471583

74 • C1 | Head Of the Ditch (Apache NF)

Total sites: 12, RV sites: 4, No water, Vault/pit toilet, Tent & RV camping: Free, Open all year, Max Length: 40ft, Reservations not accepted, Elev: 7244ft/2208m, Tel: 505-547-2612, Nearest town: Alpine, AZ. GPS: 33.818745, -108.990777

75 • C1 | Juniper (Gila NF)

Total sites: 34, RV sites: 17, Elec sites: 17, Central water, Vault/pit toilet, No showers, No RV dump, Tents: $10/RVs: $15, Stay limit: 14 days, Open May-Sep, Max Length: 30ft, Reservations not accepted, Elev: 7720ft/2353m, Tel: 575-773-4678, Nearest town: Quemado. GPS: 34.137674, -108.488936

76 • C1 | Pinon (Gila NF)

Total sites: 23, RV sites: 0, Central water, Vault/pit toilet, No showers, RV dump, Tents only: $10, 2 reservable group sites: $35-$55, Dump fee: $5, Stay limit: 14 days, Open May-Sep, Reservations not accepted, Elev: 7877ft/2401m, Tel: 575-773-4678, Nearest town: Quemado. GPS: 34.137918, -108.483035

77 • C1 | Valle Tio Vinces (Gila NF)

Total sites: 4, RV sites: 4, No water, Vault/pit toilet, Tent & RV camping: Free, Stay limit: 14 days, Open all year, Max Length: 40ft, Reservations not accepted, Elev: 8120ft/2475m, Tel: 575-773-4678, Nearest town: Aragon. GPS: 34.029903, -108.350778

78 • C2 | Bear Trap (Cibola NF)

Total sites: 4, RV sites: 4, No water, Vault/pit toilet, Tent & RV camping: Free, Open May-Sep, Max Length: 20ft, Elev: 8606ft/2623m, Tel: 505-854-2281, Nearest town: Magdalena. GPS: 33.883174, -107.514862

79 • C2 | Capilla Peak (Cibola NF)

Total sites: 8, RV sites: 8, No water, Vault/pit toilet, Tents only: $5, Open May-Sep, Max Length: 16ft, Reservations not accepted, Elev: 9304ft/2836m, Nearest town: Manzano. GPS: 34.699729, -106.402676

80 • C2 | Fourth of July TH (Cibola NF)

Total sites: 25, RV sites: 0, Central water, Vault/pit toilet, No showers, No RV dump, Tents only: $7, Stay limit: 14 days, Open Apr-Nov, Reservations not accepted, Elev: 7644ft/2330m, Tel: 505-847-2990, Nearest town: Tajique. GPS: 34.792844, -106.383062

81 • C2 | Hughes Mill (Cibola NF)

Total sites: 2, RV sites: 2, No water, Vault/pit toilet, Tent & RV camping: Free, Also dispersed sites, Stay limit: 14 days, Open May-Oct, Max Length: 20ft, Reservations not accepted, Elev: 8274ft/2522m, Tel: 575-854-2281, Nearest town: Magdalena. GPS: 33.857247, -107.540276

82 • C2 | John F Kennedy (Cibola NF)

Total sites: 14, RV sites: 14, No water, No toilets, Tent & RV camping: Fee unk, Stay limit: 14 days, Open all year, Reservations not accepted, Elev: 6201ft/1890m, Tel: 505-847-2990, Nearest town: Belen. GPS: 34.671448, -106.468076

83 • C2 | New Canyon (Cibola NF)

Total sites: 3, RV sites: 3, No water, Vault/pit toilet, Tent & RV camping: Free, Stay limit: 14 days, Open all year, Max Length: 18ft, Reservations not accepted, Elev: 7904ft/2409m, Nearest town: Tajique. GPS: 34.671133, -106.410193

84 • C2 | Red Canyon Horse Camp (Cibola NF)

Total sites: 10, RV sites: 10, No water, Vault/pit toilet, Tent & RV camping: $7, Stay limit: 14 days, Open Apr-Oct, Max Length: 22ft, Reservations not accepted, Elev: 8025ft/2446m, Nearest town: Tajique. GPS: 34.622103, -106.412279

85 • C2 | Red Canyon Lower (Cibola NF)

Total sites: 38, RV sites: 38, No water, Vault/pit toilet, Tent & RV camping: $7, Stay limit: 14 days, Open Apr-Oct, Max Length: 22ft, Reservations not accepted, Elev: 7723ft/2354m, Nearest town: Tajique. GPS: 34.616876, -106.403317

86 • C2 | Tajique (Cibola NF)

Total sites: 6, RV sites: 0, No water, Vault/pit toilet, Tents only: Free, Stay limit: 14 days, Open all year, Reservations not accepted, Elev: 7018ft/2139m, Nearest town: Tajique. GPS: 34.765894, -106.327772

87 • C2 | Water Canyon (Cibola NF)

Total sites: 16, RV sites: 16, No water, Vault/pit toilet, Tent & RV camping: Free, Rough twisting road, Stay limit: 14 days, Open Mar-Nov, Max Length: 20ft, Reservations not accepted, Elev: 6870ft/2094m, Tel: 505-854-2381, Nearest town: Magdalena. GPS: 34.024619, -107.133125

88 • C3 | Red Cloud (Cibola NF)

Total sites: 5, RV sites: 5, No water, Vault/pit toilet, Tent & RV camping: Free, Stay limit: 14 days, Reservations not accepted, Elev: 7264ft/2214m, Nearest town: Corona. GPS: 34.190267, -105.725883

89 • D1 | Aeroplane Mesa (Gila NF)

Total sites: 6, RV sites: 6, No water, Vault/pit toilet, Tent & RV camping: Free, Open all year, Elev: 8022ft/2445m, Tel: 575-533-6231, Nearest town: Reserve. GPS: 33.417495, -108.441222

90 • D1 | Ben Lilly (Gila NF)

Total sites: 7, RV sites: 0, No water, Vault/pit toilet, Tents only: Free, Stay limit: 14 days, Open May-Nov, Max Length: 17ft, Reservations not accepted, Elev: 8087ft/2465m, Tel: 575-533-6231, Nearest town: Reserve. GPS: 33.397586, -108.593641

91 • D1 | Bighorn (Gila NF)

Total sites: 6, RV sites: 6, No water, Vault/pit toilet, Tent & RV camping: Free, Can walk to town, Stay limit: 14 days, Open all year, Max Length: 30ft, Reservations not accepted, Elev: 4833ft/1473m, Tel: 575-539-2481, Nearest town: Glenwood. GPS: 33.324129, -108.882746

92 • D1 | Black Canyon Lower (Gila NF)

Total sites: 3, RV sites: 3, No water, Vault/pit toilet, Tent & RV

camping: Free, Stay limit: 14 days, Open Apr-Nov, Reservations not accepted, Elev: 6765ft/2062m, Tel: 575-536-2250, Nearest town: Mimbres,. GPS: 33.184064, -108.035107

93 • D1 | Black Canyon Upper (Gila NF)

Total sites: 2, RV sites: 0, No water, Vault/pit toilet, Tents only: Free, Stay limit: 14 days, Open Apr-Nov, Max Length: 17ft, Reservations not accepted, Elev: 6772ft/2064m, Tel: 575-536-2250, Nearest town: Mimbres,. GPS: 33.185325, -108.033076

94 • D1 | Cherry Creek (Gila NF)

Total sites: 12, RV sites: 12, No water, Vault/pit toilet, Tent & RV camping: Free, Stay limit: 14 days, Open all year, Max Length: 17ft, Reservations not accepted, Elev: 6864ft/2092m, Tel: 575-388-8201, Nearest town: Silver City. GPS: 32.914239, -108.224214

95 • D1 | Cosmic (Gila NF)

Total sites: 6, RV sites: 6, No water, Vault/pit toilet, Tent & RV camping: Free, First International Dark Sky Sanctuary in North America, Generator hours: 0600-2200, Open all year, Max Length: 36ft, Reservations not accepted, Elev: 5363ft/1635m, Tel: 575-539-2481, Nearest town: Alma. GPS: 33.480066, -108.922918

96 • D1 | Cottonwood (Gila NF)

Total sites: 4, RV sites: 4, No water, Vault/pit toilet, Tent & RV camping: Free, Stay limit: 14 days, Open Apr-Nov, Max Length: 22ft, Reservations not accepted, Elev: 5813ft/1772m, Tel: 575-539-2481, Nearest town: Glenwood. GPS: 33.618849, -108.894143

97 • D1 | Dipping Vat (Gila NF)

Total sites: 40, RV sites: 40, Central water, Vault/pit toilet, No showers, No RV dump, Tent & RV camping: $6, Open Apr-Sep, Max Length: 19ft, Reservations not accepted, Elev: 7379ft/2249m, Tel: 575-533-6231, Nearest town: Reserve. GPS: 33.423045, -108.500849

98 • D1 | Forks (Gila NF)

Total sites: 7, RV sites: 0, No water, Vault/pit toilet, Tents only: Free, Open all year, Reservations not accepted, Elev: 5571ft/1698m, Tel: 575-536-2250, Nearest town: Mimbres,. GPS: 33.183819, -108.205823

99 • D1 | Gallinas Upper (Gila NF)

Total sites: 10, RV sites: 10, No water, Vault/pit toilet, Tent & RV camping: Free, Stay limit: 14 days, Open all year, Reservations not accepted, Elev: 7024ft/2141m, Tel: 575-388-8201, Nearest town: Mimbres,. GPS: 32.898743, -107.823695

100 • D1 | Grapevine (Gila NF)

Total sites: 20, No water, Vault/pit toilet, No showers, No RV dump, Tents only: Free, Open all year, Reservations not accepted, Elev: 5584ft/1702m, Tel: 575-536-2250, Nearest town: Silver City. GPS: 33.179336, -108.204978

101 • D1 | Iron Creek (Gila NF)

Total sites: 15, RV sites: 15, No water, Vault/pit toilet, Tent & RV camping: Free, Stay limit: 14 days, Open Mar-Oct, Max Length: 17ft, Reservations not accepted, Elev: 7260ft/2213m, Tel: 505-536-2250, Nearest town: Mimbres. GPS: 32.909123, -107.805018

102 • D1 | Lower Scorpion (Gila NF)

Total sites: 7, RV sites: 0, No water, Vault/pit toilet, No showers, Tents only: Free, Walk-to sites, Small RVs may overnight in parking lot, Stay limit: 14 days, Open all year, Max Length: 17ft, Reservations not accepted, Elev: 5764ft/1757m, Tel: 575-536-2250, Nearest town: Mimbres. GPS: 33.230254, -108.257616

103 • D1 | McMillan (Gila NF)

Total sites: 3, RV sites: 3, No water, Vault/pit toilet, Tent & RV camping: Free, Stay limit: 14 days, Open Apr-Oct, Max Length: 17ft, Reservations not accepted, Elev: 7034ft/2144m, Tel: 575-388-8201, Nearest town: Silver City. GPS: 32.924001, -108.213686

104 • D1 | Mesa (Gila NF)

Total sites: 36, RV sites: 12, Elec sites: 12, Water at site, No toilets, No showers, RV dump, Tents: $10/RVs: $15, Stay limit: 14 days, Open all year, Reservations not accepted, Elev: 6151ft/1875m, Tel: 505-536-2250, Nearest town: Mimbres. GPS: 33.032886, -108.155379

105 • D1 | Pueblo Park (Gila NF)

Total sites: 10, RV sites: 0, No water, Vault/pit toilet, Tents only: Free, Open Apr-Nov, Reservations not accepted, Elev: 6217ft/1895m, Tel: 505-539-2481, Nearest town: Reserve. GPS: 33.595066, -108.962161

106 • D1 | Railroad Canyon (Gila NF)

Total sites: 6, RV sites: 6, No water, Vault/pit toilet, Tent & RV camping: Free, Open all year, Reservations not accepted, Elev: 7149ft/2179m, Tel: 575-388-8201, Nearest town: Mimbres,. GPS: 32.908974, -107.816725

107 • D1 | Rocky Canyon (Gila NF)

Total sites: 2, RV sites: 2, No water, Vault/pit toilet, Tent & RV camping: Free, Open Apr-Nov, Max Length: 17ft, Elev: 7484ft/2281m, Tel: 575-536-2250, Nearest town: Mimbres,. GPS: 33.100174, -108.013248

108 • D1 | Upper End (Gila NF)

Total sites: 12, RV sites: 12, Central water, Vault/pit toilet, No showers, No RV dump, Tent & RV camping: $10, Stay limit: 14 days, Open all year, Max Length: 32ft, Reservations not accepted, Elev: 6070ft/1850m, Tel: 505-536-2250, Nearest town: Mimbres. GPS: 33.027458, -108.152117

109 • D1 | Upper Scorpion (Gila NF)

Total sites: 10, Central water, Vault/pit toilet, No showers, No RV dump, Tent & RV camping: Free, Water at Visitor Center, Small RVs may overnight in parking lot, Stay limit: 14 days, Open all year, Max Length: 17ft, Reservations not accepted, Elev: 5840ft/1780m, Tel: 575-536-2250, Nearest town: Mimbres. GPS: 33.230679, -108.260772

110 • D1 | Willow Creek (Gila NF)

Total sites: 9, RV sites: 9, No water, Vault/pit toilet, Tent & RV camping: Fee unk, Open Apr-Nov, Max Length: 17ft, Reservations not accepted, Elev: 7956ft/2425m, Tel: 505-773-4678, Nearest town: Reserve. GPS: 33.402367, -108.579565

111 • D1 | Wolf Hollow (Gila NF)

Total sites: 5, RV sites: 0, No water, Vault/pit toilet, Tents only: Free, 4x4 recommended, Stay limit: 14 days, Max Length: 28ft, Reservations not accepted, Elev: 7818ft/2383m. GPS: 33.422955, -108.197131

112 • D2 | Kingston (Gila NF)

Total sites: 2, RV sites: 0, No water, Vault/pit toilet, Tents only: Free, Stay limit: 14 days, Open Sep-Jun, Max Length: 20ft, Reservations not accepted, Elev: 6184ft/1885m, Tel: 575-388-8201, Nearest town: Kingston. GPS: 32.918414, -107.700616

113 • D2 | Luna Park (Cibola NF)

Total sites: 3, RV sites: 3, No water, Vault/pit toilet, Tent & RV camping: Free, Stay limit: 14 days, Open Mar-Nov, Max Length: 20ft, Reservations not accepted, Elev: 6842ft/2085m, Tel: 575-854-2281, Nearest town: Monticello. GPS: 33.496266, -107.416005

114 • D2 | Springtime (Cibola NF)

Total sites: 6, RV sites: 0, No water, Vault/pit toilet, Tents only: Free, Log shelters - trailers must park by entrance, Stay limit: 14 days, Open Mar-Nov, Reservations not accepted, Elev: 7385ft/2251m, Tel: 575-854-2281, Nearest town: Monticello. GPS: 33.575401, -107.404515

115 • D3 | Apache (Lincoln NF)

Total sites: 25, RV sites: 25, Central water, Vault/pit toilet, No showers, No RV dump, Tent & RV camping: $22, Water: $0.25 per gallon after 1st free 5 gallons, Stay limit: 14 days, Open May-Sep, Max Length: 32ft, Reservations not accepted, Elev: 8917ft/2718m, Tel: 575-682-2551, Nearest town: Cloudcroft. GPS: 32.966797, -105.728760

116 • D3 | Deerhead (Lincoln NF)

Total sites: 20, RV sites: 20, Central water, Vault/pit toilet, No showers, No RV dump, Tent & RV camping: $25, Showers at Silver CG, Stay limit: 14 days, Open Apr-Oct, Max Length: 30ft, Reservations not accepted, Elev: 8770ft/2673m, Tel: 575-682-2551, Nearest town: Cloudcroft. GPS: 32.943604, -105.746338

117 • D3 | James Canyon (Lincoln NF)

Total sites: 5, RV sites: 5, No water, Vault/pit toilet, Tent & RV camping: Free, Open all year, Max Length: 16ft, Reservations not accepted, Elev: 6801ft/2073m, Nearest town: Tularosa. GPS: 32.904536, -105.504667

118 • D3 | Monjeau (Lincoln NF)

Total sites: 4, RV sites: 0, No water, Vault/pit toilet, Tents only: Free, Stay limit: 14 days, Open May-Sep, Elev: 9258ft/2822m, Tel: 575-257-4095, Nearest town: Tularosa. GPS: 33.432111, -105.730042

119 • D3 | Oak Grove (Lincoln NF)

Total sites: 30, RV sites: 30, No water, Vault/pit toilet, Tent & RV camping: $6, Stay limit: 14 days, Open May-Sep, Max Length: 18ft, Reservations not accepted, Elev: 8379ft/2554m, Tel: 575-257-4095, Nearest town: Ruidoso. GPS: 33.396176, -105.747131

120 • D3 | Pines (Lincoln NF)

Total sites: 24, RV sites: 24, Central water, Vault/pit toilet, No showers, No RV dump, Tent & RV camping: $22, Open May-Sep, Max Length: 40ft, Reservations not accepted, Elev: 8691ft/2649m, Tel: 575-682-2551, Nearest town: Cloudcroft. GPS: 32.966309, -105.737305

121 • D3 | Saddle (Lincoln NF)

Total sites: 16, RV sites: 16, Central water, Flush toilet, Free showers, RV dump, Tent & RV camping: $25, Fee showers and RV dump available at nearby Silver CG, Open May-Oct, Max Length: 30ft, Reservations not accepted, Elev: 8983ft/2738m, Tel: 575-682-2551, Nearest town: Cloudcroft. GPS: 32.970459, -105.725586

122 • D3 | Silver (Lincoln NF)

Total sites: 30, RV sites: 30, Central water, Flush toilet, Pay showers, RV dump, Tent & RV camping: $22, $5 dump fee, Open Apr-Oct, Max Length: 32ft, Reservations not accepted, Elev: 9003ft/2744m, Tel: 505-682-2551, Nearest town: Cloudcroft. GPS: 32.973389, -105.725342

123 • D3 | Silver Overflow (Lincoln NF)

Total sites: 52, RV sites: 52, Central water, Vault/pit toilet, Free showers, No RV dump, Tent & RV camping: $18, Fee showers and RV available at nearby Silver CG, Open Apr-Oct, Reservations not accepted, Elev: 8990ft/2740m, Tel: 575-682-2551, Nearest town: Cloudcroft. GPS: 32.975605, -105.723941

124 • D3 | Skyline (Lincoln NF)

Total sites: 17, RV sites: 0, No water, Vault/pit toilet, Tents only: Free, Rough road, Stay limit: 14 days, Open all year, Reservations not accepted, Elev: 8953ft/2729m, Tel: 575-257-4095, Nearest town: Ruidoso. GPS: 33.419281, -105.733444

125 • D3 | Sleepy Grass (Lincoln NF)

Total sites: 15, RV sites: 15, Central water, Vault/pit toilet, No showers, No RV dump, Tent & RV camping: $16, 2 double and 3 triple sites, Open May-Sep, Max Length: 16ft, Reservations not accepted, Elev: 8855ft/2699m, Tel: 575-682-2551, Nearest town: Cloudcroft. GPS: 32.943902, -105.725759

126 • D3 | South Fork (Lincoln NF)

Total sites: 60, RV sites: 60, Central water, Vault/pit toilet, No showers, No RV dump, Tent & RV camping: $10, Stay limit: 14 days, Open May-Sep, Max Length: 35ft, Reservations not accepted, Elev: 7612ft/2320m, Tel: 505-257-4095, Nearest town: Ruidoso. GPS: 33.449525, -105.753432

127 • D3 | Three Rivers (Lincoln NF)

Total sites: 12, RV sites: 12, Central water, Vault/pit toilet, No showers, No RV dump, Tent & RV camping: $6, Stay limit: 14 days, Open all year, Max Length: 25ft, Reservations not accepted, Elev: 6408ft/1953m, Tel: 575-257-4095, Nearest town: Tularosa. GPS: 33.401275, -105.884961

128 • D3 | Upper Karr (Lincoln NF)

Total sites: 6, RV sites: 6, No water, Vault/pit toilet, Tent & RV camping: Free, Stay limit: 14 days, Open all year, Max Length: 16ft, Elev: 9341ft/2847m, Tel: 575-682-2551, Nearest town: Cloudcroft. GPS: 32.880363, -105.780001

129 • D3 | Upper Karr Canyon (Lincoln NF)

Total sites: 6, RV sites: 6, No water, Vault/pit toilet, Tent & RV camping: Free, Stay limit: 14 days, Open all year, Max Length: 16ft, Reservations not accepted, Elev: 9400ft/2865m, Tel: 575-434-7200, Nearest town: Cloudcroft. GPS: 32.880557, -105.780365

New York

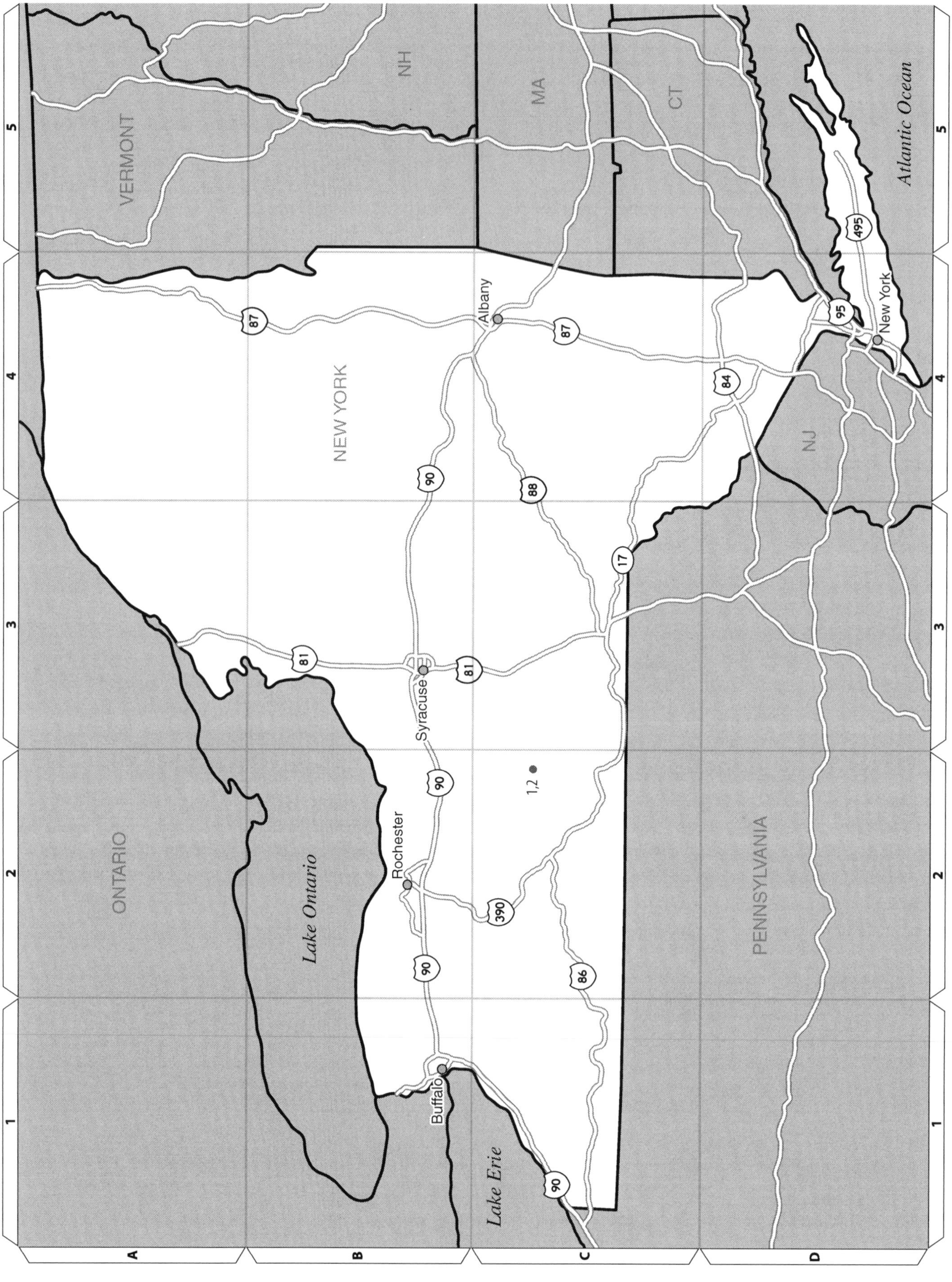
VERMONT
NH
MA
CT
Atlantic Ocean
495
New York
95
Albany
87
87
84
NEW YORK
NJ
90
88
17
81
81
Syracuse
ONTARIO
Lake Ontario
90
1,2
Rochester
390
PENNSYLVANIA
90
86
Buffalo
Lake Erie
90
A
B
C
D
1
2
3
4
5

Map	ID	Map	ID
C2	1-2		

Alphabetical List of Camping Areas

1 • C2 | Backbone Horse Camp (Finger Lakes NF)

Total sites: 11, RV sites: 11, No water, Vault/pit toilet, No showers, No RV dump, Tent & RV camping: $10, Pond water for stock, Open all year, Reservations not accepted, Elev: 1680ft/512m, Tel: 607-546-4470, Nearest town: Logan. GPS: 42.485225, -76.806348

2 • C2 | Blueberry Patch (Finger Lakes NF)

Total sites: 9, RV sites: 9, No water, Vault/pit toilet, No showers, No RV dump, Tent & RV camping: $15, Open May-Oct, Max Length: 24ft, Reservations not accepted, Elev: 1831ft/558m, Tel: 607-546-4470, Nearest town: Logan. GPS: 42.483471, -76.799511

North Carolina

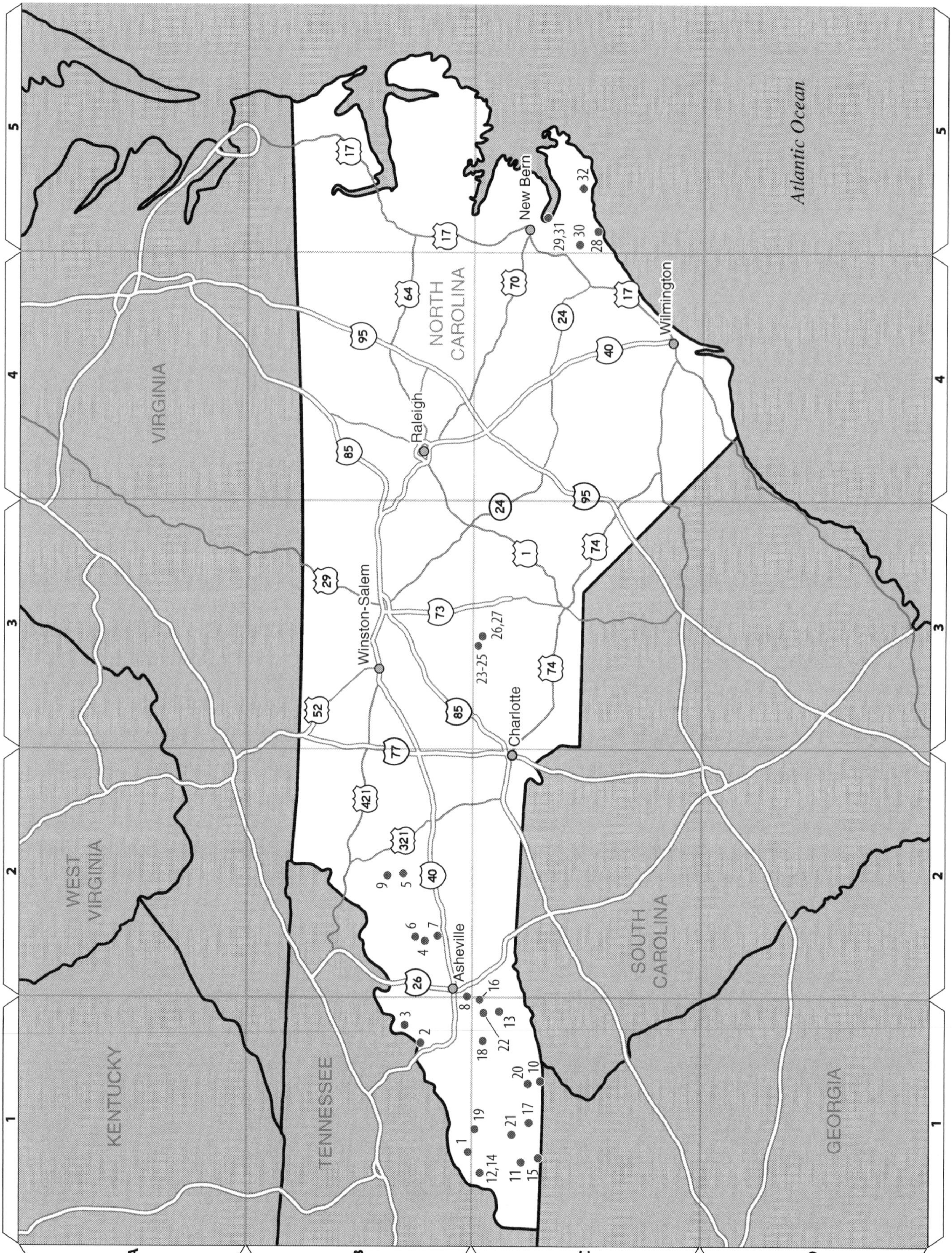

Map	ID	Map	ID
B1	1-3	C3	23-27
B2	4-9	C5	28-32
C1	10-22		

Alphabetical List of Camping Areas

1 • B1 | Cable Cove (Nantahala NF)

Total sites: 26, RV sites: 26, Central water, Vault/pit toilet, No showers, No RV dump, Tent & RV camping: $15, Open Apr-Oct, Reservations not accepted, Elev: 1804ft/550m, Tel: 828-479-6431, Nearest town: Fontana Village. GPS: 35.432332, -83.751514

2 • B1 | Harmon Den Horse Camp (Pisgah NF)

Total sites: 10, RV sites: 10, Central water, Vault/pit toilet, No showers, No RV dump, Tent & RV camping: $15, Open May-Oct, Max Length: 30ft, Reservations required, Elev: 2992ft/912m, Tel: 828-689-9694, Nearest town: Canton. GPS: 35.758071, -82.975744

3 • B1 | Rocky Bluff (Pisgah NF)

Total sites: 15, RV sites: 15, Central water, No toilets, No showers, No RV dump, Tent & RV camping: $15, Stay limit: 14 days, Open May-Sep, Reservations not accepted, Elev: 1798ft/548m, Tel: 828-689-9694, Nearest town: Hot Springs. GPS: 35.861542, -82.846535

4 • B2 | Black Mountain (Pisgah NF)

Total sites: 37, RV sites: 37, Elec sites: 3, Central water, Flush toilet, Free showers, RV dump, Tents: $25/RVs: $25-32, Open Apr-Oct, Reservations not accepted, Elev: 3036ft/925m, Tel: 828-675-5616, Nearest town: Asheville. GPS: 35.748351, -82.225523

5 • B2 | Brown Mt CUA Dispersed (Pisgah NF)

Total sites: 1, RV sites: 1, No water, No toilets, Tent & RV camping: Free, Max Length: 18ft, Reservations not accepted, Elev: 1194ft/364m. GPS: 35.892968, -81.740245

6 • B2 | Carolina Hemlocks (Pisgah NF)

Total sites: 37, RV sites: 34, Central water, Flush toilet, Pay showers, No RV dump, Tent & RV camping: $25, Open Apr-Oct, Max Length: 35ft, Reservations accepted, Elev: 2772ft/845m, Tel: 828-675-5509, Nearest town: Burnsville. GPS: 35.804596, -82.203406

7 • B2 | Curtis Creek (Pisgah NF)

Total sites: 14, RV sites: 8, Central water, Vault/pit toilet, No showers, No RV dump, Tent & RV camping: $10, Generator hours: 0600-2200, Open Apr-Dec, Reservations accepted, Elev: 1690ft/515m, Nearest town: Old Fort. GPS: 35.671691, -82.192913

8 • B2 | Lake Powhatan (Pisgah NF)

Total sites: 85, RV sites: 54, Elec sites: 24, Water at site, Flush toilet, Free showers, RV dump, Tents: $28/RVs: $34-37, 21 Full hookup sites, Open Mar-Dec, Max Length: 50ft, Reservations accepted, Elev: 2182ft/665m, Tel: 828-670-5627, Nearest town: Asheville. GPS: 35.482503, -82.627823

9 • B2 | Mortimer (Pisgah NF)

Total sites: 21, RV sites: 16, Central water, Flush toilet, Free showers, No RV dump, Tent & RV camping: $15, Generator hours: 0600-2200, Open Apr-Nov, Reservations not accepted, Elev: 1631ft/497m, Tel: 828-652-2144, Nearest town: Lenoir. GPS: 35.991595, -81.761015

10 • C1 | Blue Valley (Nantahala NF)

Total sites: 22, RV sites: 22, No water, Vault/pit toilet, Tent & RV camping: Free, Open all year, Reservations not accepted, Elev: 2621ft/799m, Tel: 828-524-6441, Nearest town: Highlands. GPS: 35.009317, -83.227345

11 • C1 | Bristol Fields Horse Camp (Nantahala NF)

Total sites: 9, RV sites: 9, Central water, Vault/pit toilet, Tent & RV camping: $8, Open all year, Reservations not accepted, Elev: 2405ft/733m, Tel: 828-837-5152, Nearest town: Hayesville,. GPS: 35.107673, -83.811172

12 • C1 | Cheoah Point (Nantahala NF)

Total sites: 26, RV sites: 26, Elec sites: 6, Central water, Flush toilet, Free showers, No RV dump, Tents: $20/RVs: $25, Open Apr-Oct, Max Length: 40ft, Reservations accepted, Elev: 1982ft/604m, Tel: 828-479-6431, Nearest town: Robbinsville. GPS: 35.370605, -83.871338

13 • C1 | Davidson River (Pisgah NF)

Total sites: 163, RV sites: 163, Elec sites: 3, Central water, Flush toilet, Free showers, No RV dump, Tents: $28/RVs: $28-34, Full hookup sites, Open all year, Max Length: 67ft, Reservations accepted, Elev: 2201ft/671m, Tel: 828-862-5960, Nearest town: Brevard. GPS: 35.282898, -82.726105

14 • C1 | Horse Cove (Nantahala NF)

Total sites: 18, RV sites: 11, Central water, No toilets, No showers, No RV dump, Tent & RV camping: $15, No water in winter, Open all year, Reservations not accepted, Elev: 2076ft/633m, Tel: 828-479-6431, Nearest town: Robbinsville. GPS: 35.365251, -83.921242

15 • C1 | Jackrabbit Mountain (Nantahala NF)

Total sites: 100, RV sites: 90, Central water, Flush toilet, Free showers, RV dump, Tent & RV camping: $20, Open May-Oct, Max Length: 128ft, Reservations accepted, Elev: 1946ft/593m, Tel: 828-837-5152, Nearest town: Hayesville. GPS: 35.011230, -83.772705

16 • C1 | North Mills River (Pisgah NF)

Total sites: 31, RV sites: 31, Central water, Flush toilet, Free showers, No RV dump, Tent & RV camping: $26, 1 Full hookup site, Jan-Mar: $11 - no water, Open all year, Max Length: 35ft, Reservations accepted, Elev: 2274ft/693m, Tel: 828-890-3284, Nearest town: Mills River. GPS: 35.406250, -82.646240

17 • C1 | Standing Indian (Nantahala NF)

Total sites: 81, RV sites: 81, Central water, Flush toilet, Free showers, RV dump, Tent & RV camping: $20, Group site: $75, Open Apr-Nov, Max Length: 50ft, Reservations accepted, Elev: 3576ft/1090m, Nearest town: Franklin. GPS: 35.076542, -83.528542

18 • C1 | Sunburst (Pisgah NF)

Total sites: 9, RV sites: 9, Central water, Flush toilet, No showers, No RV dump, Tent & RV camping: $15, Open May-Oct, Reservations not accepted, Elev: 3163ft/964m, Tel: 828-648-7841, Nearest town: Canton. GPS: 35.373863, -82.940325

19 • C1 | Tsali (Nantahala NF)

Total sites: 42, RV sites: 29, Central water, Flush toilet, Free showers, No RV dump, Tent & RV camping: $20, Open Apr-Oct, Reservations not accepted, Elev: 1801ft/549m, Nearest town: Bryson City. GPS: 35.407471, -83.587402

20 • C1 | Vanhook Glade (Nantahala NF)

Total sites: 18, RV sites: 14, Central water, Flush toilet, Free showers, No RV dump, Tent & RV camping: $24, Open Apr-Oct, Max Length: 36ft, Reservations accepted, Elev: 3340ft/1018m, Tel: 828-526-5918, Nearest town: Highlands. GPS: 35.077285, -83.248173

21 • C1 | Wine Springs Horse Camp (Nantahala NF)

Total sites: 6, RV sites: 6, No water, Vault/pit toilet, Tent & RV camping: $10, Contact Nantahala RD for reservations, Open all year, Reservations required, Elev: 4013ft/1223m, Tel: 828-524-6441, Nearest town: Franklin. GPS: 35.177604, -83.614074

22 • C1 | Wolf Ford Horse Camp (Pisgah NF)

Total sites: 13, RV sites: 13, No water, No toilets, Tent & RV camping: $10, 6 dispersed locations along road, Reservations not accepted, Elev: 3231ft/985m, Tel: 828-877-3265, Nearest town: Mills River. GPS: 35.377682, -82.739263

23 • C3 | Arrowhead (Uwharrie NF)

Total sites: 48, RV sites: 44, Elec sites: 34, Central water, Flush toilet, Free showers, RV dump, Tent & RV camping: $20-27, Open all year, Max Length: 45ft, Reservations accepted, Elev: 584ft/178m, Tel: 910-576-6391, Nearest town: Uwharrie. GPS: 35.438468, -80.070593

24 • C3 | Badin Lake (Uwharrie NF)

Total sites: 34, RV sites: 33, Central water, Flush toilet, Free showers, No RV dump, Tent & RV camping: $20, Open all year, Max Length: 40ft, Reservations accepted, Elev: 561ft/171m, Tel: 910-576-6391, Nearest town: Troy. GPS: 35.448126, -80.078354

25 • C3 | Canebreak Horse Camp (Uwharrie NF)

Total sites: 28, RV sites: 28, Elec sites: 28, Central water, Flush toilet, Free showers, RV dump, Tent & RV camping: $27, Open all year, Max Length: 85ft, Reservations accepted, Elev: 501ft/153m, Tel: 910-576-6391, Nearest town: Troy. GPS: 35.440296, -80.046978

26 • C3 | Uwharrie Hunt Camp (Uwharrie NF)

Total sites: 8, RV sites: 0, Central water, Vault/pit toilet, No showers, No RV dump, Tents only: $5, Open all year, Reservations not accepted, Elev: 423ft/129m, Tel: 910-576-6391, Nearest town: Troy. GPS: 35.428983, -80.020376

27 • C3 | West Morris Mountain (Uwharrie NF)

Total sites: 14, RV sites: 14, No water, Vault/pit toilet, Tent & RV camping: $5, 2 group sites - $10, Open all year, Elev: 482ft/147m, Tel: 910-576-6391, Nearest town: Troy. GPS: 35.428352, -79.993708

28 • C5 | Cedar Point (Croatan NF)

Total sites: 40, RV sites: 40, Elec sites: 40, Central water, Flush toilet, Free showers, RV dump, Tent & RV camping: $27, Open all year, Max Length: 75ft, Reservations accepted, Elev: 23ft/7m, Tel: 252-393-7642, Nearest town: Cape Carteret. GPS: 34.692527, -77.083597

29 • C5 | Fishers Landing (Croatan NF)

Total sites: 9, RV sites: 0, Central water, Vault/pit toilet, No showers, No RV dump, Tents only: Free, Reservations not accepted, Elev: 10ft/3m, Tel: 252-638-5628, Nearest town: New Bern. GPS: 35.000782, -76.976317

30 • C5 | Long Point (Croatan NF)

Total sites: 3, No water, Vault/pit toilet, Tents only: Free, Open all year, Reservations not accepted, Elev: -10ft/-3m, Tel: 252-638-5628, Nearest town: Maysville. GPS: 34.798185, -77.178128

31 • C5 | Neuse River/Flanners Beach (Croatan NF)

Total sites: 41, RV sites: 41, Elec sites: 22, Central water, Flush toilet, Free showers, RV dump, Tents: $20/RVs: $20-25, Open Mar-Nov, Max Length: 80ft, Reservations accepted, Elev: 10ft/3m, Tel: 252-638-5628, Nearest town: Havelock. GPS: 34.981716, -76.948525

32 • C5 | Oyster Point (Croatan NF)

Total sites: 15, RV sites: 15, Central water, Vault/pit toilet, No showers, No RV dump, Tent & RV camping: $8, Open all year, Reservations not accepted, Elev: 43ft/13m, Tel: 252-638-5628, Nearest town: Morehead City. GPS: 34.760951, -76.761564

North Dakota

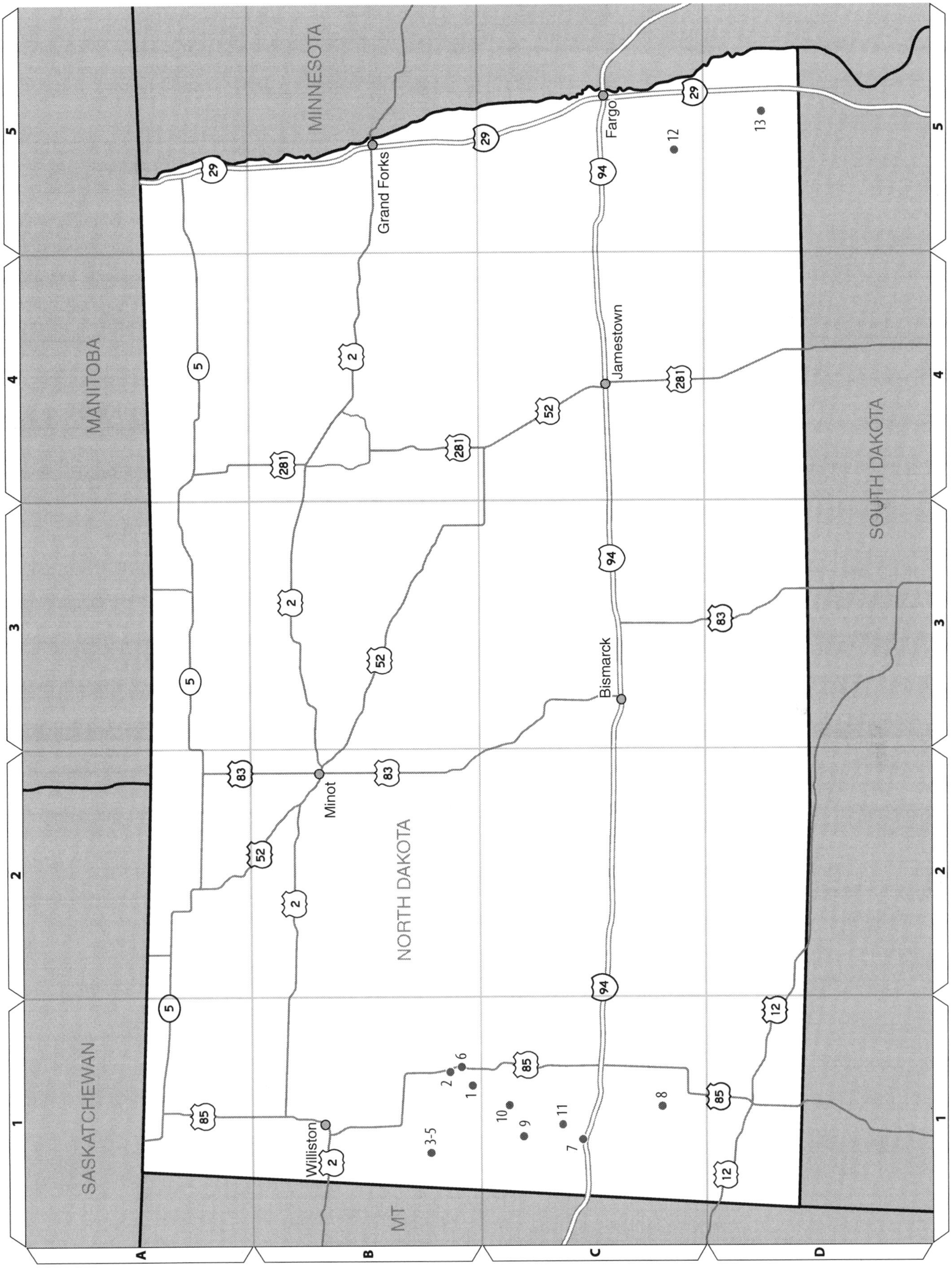

Map	ID	Map	ID
B1	1-6	C5	12
C1	7-11	D5	13

Alphabetical List of Camping Areas

1 • B1 | Bennett Camp (Dakota Prairie Grasslands)

Total sites: 13, RV sites: 13, Central water, Vault/pit toilet, No showers, Tent & RV camping: $6, Steep road, Stay limit: 14 days, Elev: 2188ft/667m, Tel: 701-842-2393, Nearest town: Watford City. GPS: 47.490129, -103.349335

2 • B1 | CCC (Dakota Prairie Grasslands)

Total sites: 38, RV sites: 38, Central water, Vault/pit toilet, No showers, No RV dump, Tent & RV camping: $6, Elev: 1968ft/600m, Tel: 701-842-2393, Nearest town: Watford City. GPS: 47.587159, -103.276698

3 • B1 | Sather Lake - Bass Loop (Dakota Prairie Grasslands)

Total sites: 6, RV sites: 6, No water, Vault/pit toilet, Tent & RV camping: $10, Stay limit: 14 days, Open all year, Reservations not accepted, Elev: 2284ft/696m, Tel: 701-842-8500, Nearest town: Watford City. GPS: 47.672721, -103.805279

4 • B1 | Sather Lake - Perch Loop (Dakota Prairie Grasslands)

Total sites: 6, RV sites: 6, No water, Vault/pit toilet, Tent & RV camping: $10, Stay limit: 14 days, Open all year, Reservations not accepted, Elev: 2274ft/693m, Tel: 701-842-8500, Nearest town: Watford City. GPS: 47.665648, -103.810448

5 • B1 | Sather Lake - Trout Loop (Dakota Prairie Grasslands)

Total sites: 5, RV sites: 5, No water, Vault/pit toilet, Tent & RV camping: $10, Stay limit: 14 days, Open all year, Reservations not accepted, Elev: 2260ft/689m, Tel: 701-842-8500, Nearest town: Watford City. GPS: 47.669241, -103.811099

6 • B1 | Summit (Dakota Prairie Grasslands)

Total sites: 5, RV sites: 3, No water, Vault/pit toilet, Tent & RV camping: Free, Reservations not accepted, Elev: 2518ft/767m, Tel: 701-842-8500, Nearest town: Watford City. GPS: 47.539945, -103.241835

7 • C1 | Buffalo Gap (Dakota Prairie Grasslands)

Total sites: 37, RV sites: 37, Central water, Flush toilet, Pay showers, No RV dump, Tent & RV camping: $6, Limited services in winter, Stay limit: 1 day, Open all year, Reservations not accepted, Elev: 2579ft/786m, Tel: 701-227-7800, Nearest town: Medora. GPS: 46.954550, -103.674660

8 • C1 | Burning Coal Vein (Dakota Prairie Grasslands)

Total sites: 5, RV sites: 5, Central water, Vault/pit toilet, No showers, No RV dump, Tent & RV camping: $10, Stay limit: 14 days, Reservations not accepted, Elev: 2526ft/770m, Tel: 701-227-7800, Nearest town: Belfield. GPS: 46.597091, -103.443322

9 • C1 | Elkhorn (Dakota Prairie Grasslands)

Total sites: 9, RV sites: 9, Central water, Vault/pit toilet, No showers, No RV dump, Tent & RV camping: $6, Stay limit: 14 days, Reservations not accepted, Elev: 2310ft/704m, Tel: 701-227-7800, Nearest town: Beach. GPS: 47.228665, -103.669126

10 • C1 | Magpie Camp (Dakota Prairie Grasslands)

Total sites: 11, RV sites: 11, Central water, Vault/pit toilet, No showers, No RV dump, Tent & RV camping: $6, Stay limit: 14 days, Reservations not accepted, Elev: 2229ft/679m, Tel: 701-227-7800, Nearest town: Watford City. GPS: 47.308468, -103.473431

11 • C1 | Wannagan (Dakota Prairie Grasslands)

Total sites: 10, RV sites: 10, Central water, Vault/pit toilet, No showers, No RV dump, Tent & RV camping: $6, Reservations not accepted, Elev: 2434ft/742m, Tel: 701-227-7800, Nearest town: Beach. GPS: 47.055293, -103.587699

12 • C5 | Jorgen's Hollow (Sheyenne NG)

Total sites: 14, RV sites: 14, Central water, Vault/pit toilet, No showers, No RV dump, Tent & RV camping: Fee unk, 7 horse sites, Reservations not accepted, Elev: 1049ft/320m, Nearest town: Leonard. GPS: 46.524089, -97.202116

13 • D5 | Hankinson Hills (Sheyenne NG)

Total sites: 15, RV sites: 15, Central water, Vault/pit toilet, No showers, No RV dump, Tent & RV camping: $6, 6 equestrian sites, Reservations not accepted, Elev: 1063ft/324m, Tel: 701-683-4342, Nearest town: Hankinson. GPS: 46.118907, -96.967129

Ohio

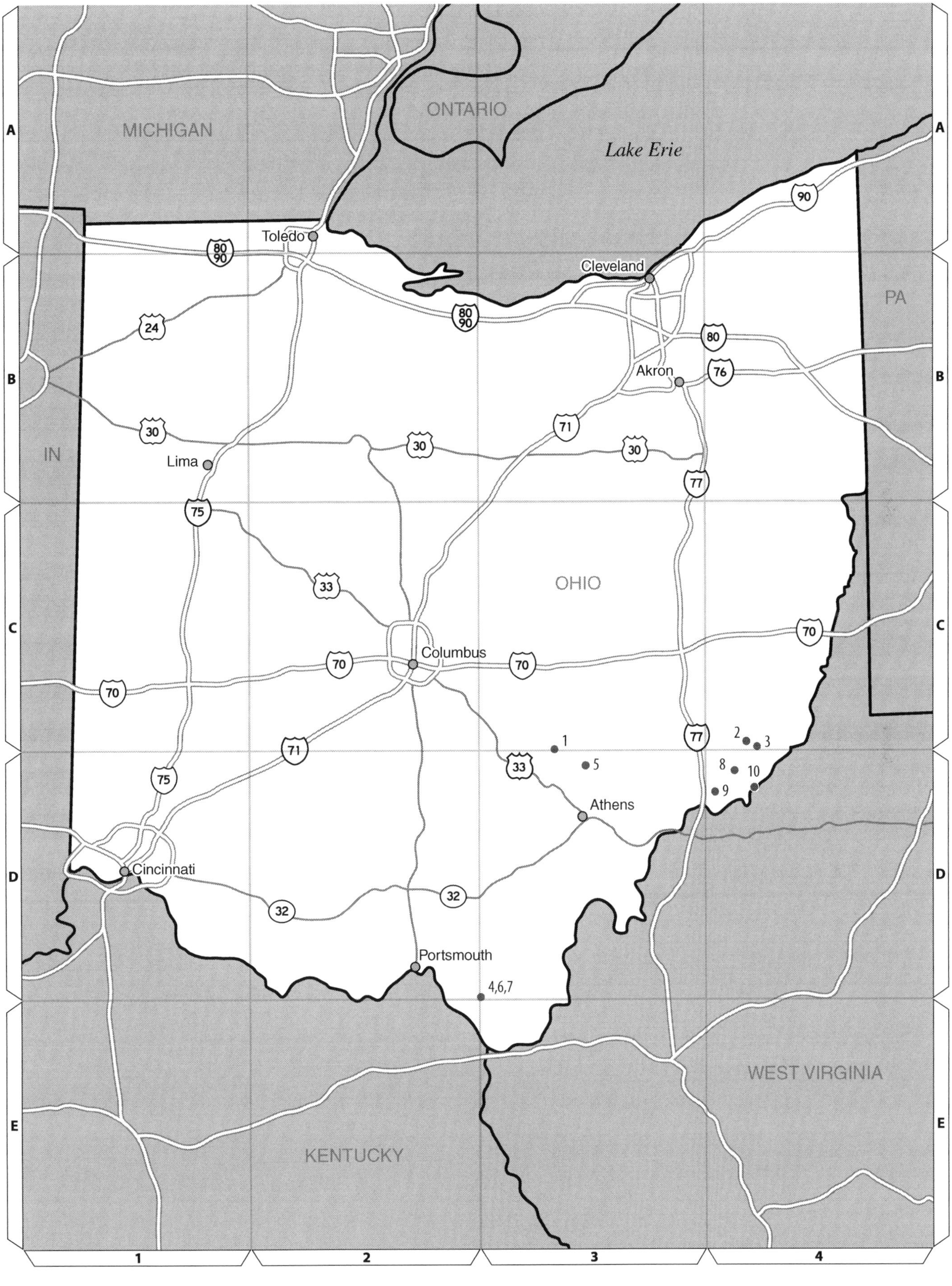
MICHIGAN
ONTARIO
Lake Erie
PA
IN
OHIO
KENTUCKY
WEST VIRGINIA
Toledo
Cleveland
Akron
Lima
Columbus
Athens
Cincinnati
Portsmouth
80
90
24
30
71
76
77
75
33
70
32
1
2
3
4,6,7
5
8
9
10
A
B
C
D
E
1
2
3
4

Map	ID	Map	ID
C3	1	D3	5-7
C4	2-3	D4	8-10
D2	4		

Alphabetical List of Camping Areas

1 • C3 | Stone Church Horse Camp (Wayne NF)

Total sites: 10, RV sites: 10, No water, Vault/pit toilet, Tent & RV camping: $14, Open Apr-Dec, Max Length: 50ft, Elev: 830ft/253m, Tel: 740-753-0101, Nearest town: Shawnee. GPS: 39.609771, -82.241369

2 • C4 | Lamping Homestead (Wayne NF)

Total sites: 6, RV sites: 0, No water, Vault/pit toilet, Tents only: Free, Walk-to sites, Open all year, Elev: 791ft/241m, Tel: 740-373-9055, Nearest town: Woodsfield. GPS: 39.630815, -81.189692

3 • C4 | Ring Mill (Wayne NF)

Total sites: 3, RV sites: 3, No water, Vault/pit toilet, Tent & RV camping: Free, Open all year, Elev: 702ft/214m, Tel: 740-373-9055, Nearest town: Sistersville. GPS: 39.608231, -81.122444

4 • D2 | Pine Knob (Lake Vesuvius) (Wayne NF)

Total sites: 8, RV sites: 0, Central water, Vault/pit toilet, Tents only: $16, Walk-to sites, Open Apr-Oct, Elev: 889ft/271m, Tel: 740-534-6500, Nearest town: Ironton. GPS: 38.620331, -82.635268

5 • D3 | Burr Oak Cove (Wayne NF)

Total sites: 19, RV sites: 15, Central water, Vault/pit toilet, No showers, No RV dump, Tent & RV camping: $44119, Open Apr-Dec, Reservations not accepted, Elev: 853ft/260m, Tel: 740-753-0101, Nearest town: Glouster. GPS: 39.549566, -82.060194

6 • D3 | Iron Ridge at Lake Vesuvius (Wayne NF)

Total sites: 41, RV sites: 19, Elec sites: 22, Central water, Vault/pit toilet, No showers, No RV dump, Tent & RV camping: $15-20, Open Jun-Sep, Max Length: 45ft, Reservations accepted, Elev: 748ft/228m, Tel: 740-534-6500, Nearest town: Ironton. GPS: 38.612635, -82.619392

7 • D3 | Oak Hill (Lake Vesuvius) (Wayne NF)

Total sites: 32, RV sites: 32, Elec sites: 32, Water at site, Flush toilet, Free showers, RV dump, Tent & RV camping: $21, Open Apr-Oct, Elev: 820ft/250m, Tel: 740-534-6500, Nearest town: Ironton. GPS: 38.614414, -82.633615

8 • D4 | Hune Bridge (Wayne NF)

Total sites: 3, RV sites: 3, No water, Vault/pit toilet, Tent & RV camping: Free, Open all year, Elev: 643ft/196m, Tel: 740-373-9055, Nearest town: Marietta. GPS: 39.509969, -81.250889

9 • D4 | Lane Farm (Wayne NF)

Total sites: 4, RV sites: 4, No water, Vault/pit toilet, Tent & RV camping: Free, Open all year, Elev: 610ft/186m, Tel: 740-373-9055, Nearest town: Marietta. GPS: 39.435556, -81.358611

10 • D4 | Leith Run (Wayne NF)

Total sites: 21, RV sites: 18, Elec sites: 18, Central water, Flush toilet, Free showers, RV dump, Tents: $15/RVs: $21, Open Apr-Oct, Elev: 607ft/185m, Tel: 740-373-9055, Nearest town: Newport. GPS: 39.445474, -81.151795

Oklahoma

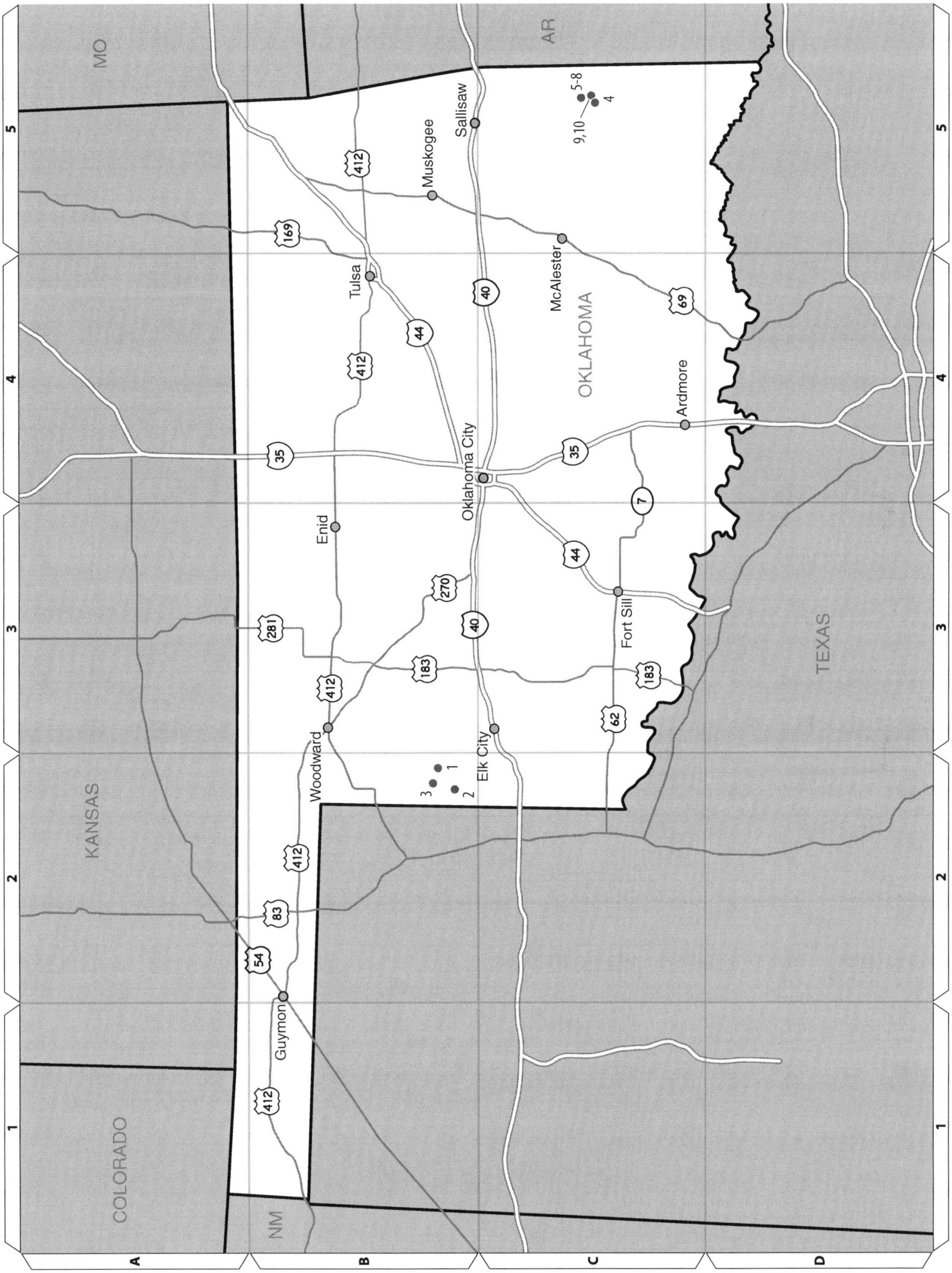
MO
AR
KANSAS
COLORADO
NM
TEXAS
OKLAHOMA
Sallisaw
Muskogee
McAlester
Tulsa
Ardmore
Oklahoma City
Enid
Fort Sill
Woodward
Elk City
Guymon
412
169
40
44
35
7
270
281
183
62
83
54
69
5-8
4
9,10
1
2
3
A
B
C
D
1
2
3
4
5

Map	ID	Map	ID
B2	1-3	C5	4-10

Alphabetical List of Camping Areas

1 • B2 | Black Kettle (Black Kettle NG)

Total sites: 12, RV sites: 12, Central water, Vault/pit toilet, No showers, No RV dump, Tent & RV camping: Free, Open all year, Max Length: 27ft, Reservations not accepted, Elev: 2100ft/640m, Tel: 580-497-2143, Nearest town: Cheyenne. GPS: 35.745318, -99.714557

2 • B2 | Skipout (Cibola NF)

Total sites: 12, RV sites: 12, Central water, Vault/pit toilet, No showers, No RV dump, Tent & RV camping: Free, Stay limit: 14 days, Open all year, Max Length: 27ft, Reservations not accepted, Elev: 2313ft/705m, Tel: 580-497-2143, Nearest town: Cheyenne. GPS: 35.635595, -99.880054

3 • B2 | Spring Creek (Cibola NF)

Total sites: 5, RV sites: 5, Central water, Vault/pit toilet, No showers, No RV dump, Tent & RV camping: Free, Stay limit: 14 days, Open all year, Max Length: 22ft, Reservations not accepted, Elev: 2198ft/670m, Tel: 580-497-2143, Nearest town: Cheyenne. GPS: 35.772811, -99.839531

4 • C5 | Billy Creek (Ouachita NF)

Total sites: 12, RV sites: 0, Central water, Vault/pit toilet, No showers, No RV dump, Tents only: Free, Open all year, Reservations not accepted, Elev: 877ft/267m, Tel: 580-494-6402, Nearest town: Muse. GPS: 34.690822, -94.731482

5 • C5 | Cedar Lake Equestrian (Ouachita NF)

Total sites: 34, RV sites: 34, Elec sites: 25, Water at site, Flush toilet, Free showers, No RV dump, Tents: $15/RVs: $20, Current negative Coggins test required, Open all year, Max Length: 60ft, Reservations accepted, Elev: 899ft/274m, Tel: 918-653-2991, Nearest town: Heavener. GPS: 34.771921, -94.701276

6 • C5 | Cedar Lake North Shore (Ouachita NF)

Total sites: 24, RV sites: 24, Central water, Vault/pit toilet, No showers, RV dump, Tent & RV camping: $15, Open all year, Max Length: 70ft, Reservations accepted, Elev: 830ft/253m, Tel: 918-653-2991, Nearest town: Heavener. GPS: 34.779858, -94.693582

7 • C5 | Cedar Lake Sandy Beach (Ouachita NF)

Total sites: 22, RV sites: 22, Elec sites: 18, Central water, RV dump, Tents: $15/RVs: $20, Group sites (2): $35, Open all year, Reservations accepted, Elev: 715ft/218m, Tel: 918-653-2991, Nearest town: Heavener. GPS: 34.778082, -94.697967

8 • C5 | Cedar Lake Shady Lane (Ouachita NF)

Total sites: 25, RV sites: 25, Elec sites: 25, Water at site, RV dump, Tent & RV camping: $25, 25 Full hookup sites, Open all year, Reservations accepted, Elev: 758ft/231m, Tel: 918-653-2991, Nearest town: Heavener. GPS: 34.774981, -94.695581

9 • C5 | Winding Stair - Backpackers Camp (Ouachita NF)

Total sites: 5, RV sites: 0, Central water, Flush toilet, Free showers, No RV dump, Tents only: $3, Walk-to sites, Open all year, Reservations not accepted, Elev: 1921ft/586m, Tel: 918-653-2991, Nearest town: Heavener. GPS: 34.714955, -94.678691

10 • C5 | Winding Stair (Ouachita NF)

Total sites: 28, RV sites: 23, Central water, Flush toilet, Free showers, No RV dump, Tent & RV camping: $8, 5 backpacker sites ($3) open all year, Generator hours: 0600-2200, Open Mar-Dec, Reservations not accepted, Elev: 1942ft/592m, Tel: 918-653-2991, Nearest town: Heavener. GPS: 34.714508, -94.675571

Oregon

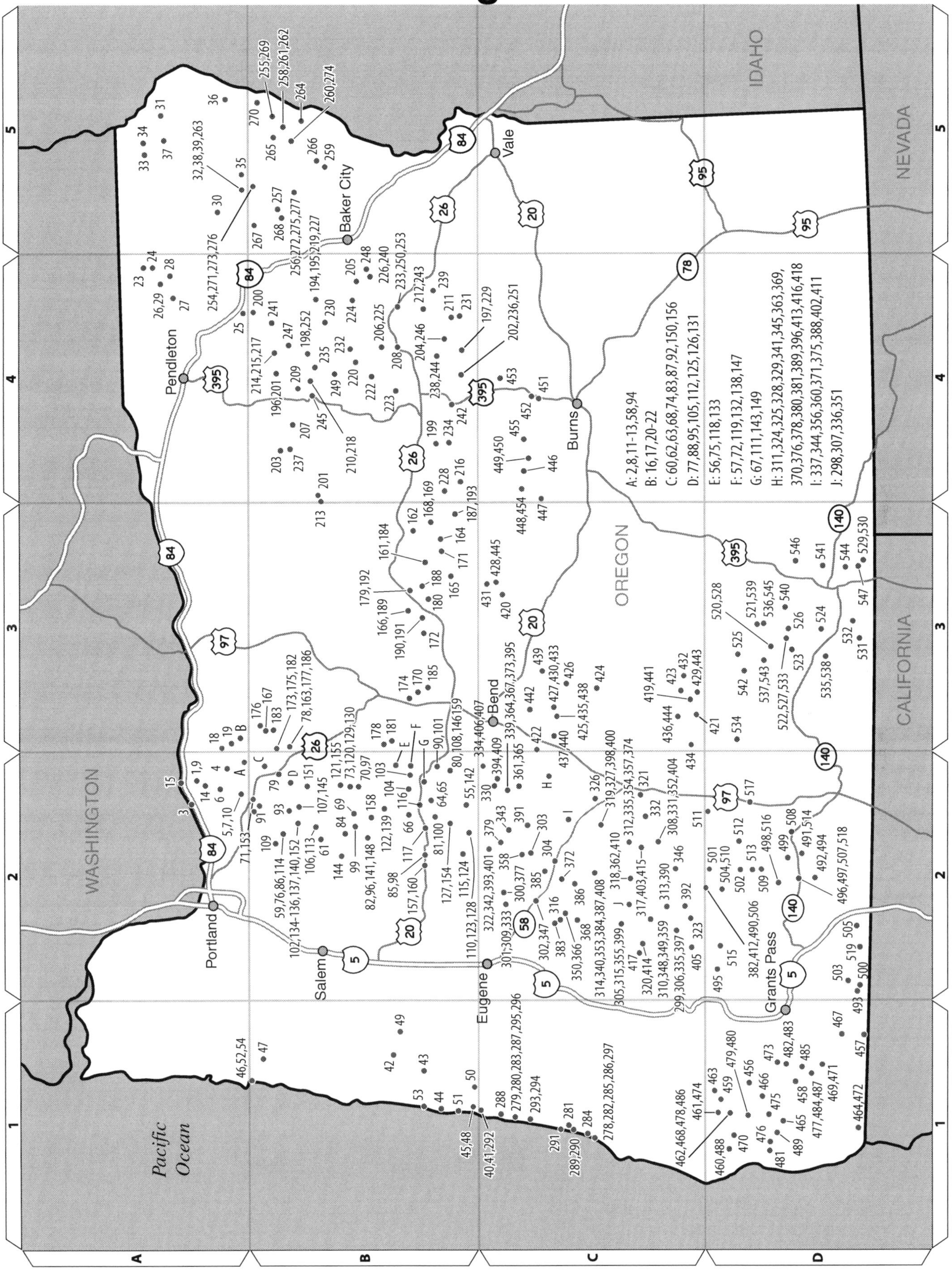
WASHINGTON
IDAHO
NEVADA
CALIFORNIA
OREGON
Pacific Ocean
Portland
Salem
Eugene
Bend
Pendleton
Baker City
Vale
Burns
Grants Pass
A: 2,8,11-13,58,94
B: 16,17,20-22
C: 60,62,63,68,74,83,87,92,150,156
D: 77,88,95,105,112,125,126,131
E: 56,75,118,133
F: 57,72,119,132,138,147
G: 67,111,143,149
H: 311,324,325,328,329,341,345,363,369,
370,376,378,380,381,389,396,413,416,418
I: 337,344,356,360,371,375,388,402,411
J: 298,307,336,351

Map	ID	Map	ID
A2	1-15	B5	254-277
A3	16-22	C1	278-297
A4	23-29	C2	298-418
A5	30-39	C3	419-445
B1	40-54	C4	446-455
B2	55-160	D1	456-489
B3	161-193	D2	490-519
B4	194-253	D3	520-547

Alphabetical List of Camping Areas

1 • A2 | Black Lake (Mt Hood NF)

Total sites: 3, RV sites: 3, No water, No toilets, Tent & RV camping: $19, High-clearance vehicle needed, Reservations not accepted, Elev: 3727ft/1136m, Tel: 503-668 1700, Nearest town: Council. GPS: 45.615193, -121.759763

2 • A2 | Cloud Cap Saddle (Mt Hood NF)

Total sites: 3, RV sites: 3, Central water, Vault/pit toilet, No showers, No RV dump, Tent & RV camping: $21, Reservations not accepted, Elev: 5879ft/1792m, Tel: 503-668 1700, Nearest town: Parkdale. GPS: 45.402195, -121.655298

3 • A2 | Eagle Creek (Bonneville Dam) (Columbia River Gorge NSA)

Total sites: 16, RV sites: 16, Central water, Vault/pit toilet, No showers, No RV dump, Tent & RV camping: $15, Near RR, Stay limit: 14 days, Open May-Sep, Max Length: 30ft, Reservations accepted, Elev: 417ft/127m, Tel: 541-386-2333, Nearest town: Cascade Locks. GPS: 45.640625, -121.924072

4 • A2 | Kinnickinnick (Mt Hood NF)

Total sites: 20, RV sites: 6, No water, Vault/pit toilet, Tent & RV camping: $24, Open May-Sep, Max Length: 26ft, Reservations accepted, Elev: 3000ft/914m, Tel: 503-668 1700, Nearest town: Parkdale. GPS: 45.457657, -121.663632

5 • A2 | Lost Creek (Mt Hood NF)

Total sites: 16, RV sites: 8, Central water, Vault/pit toilet, No showers, No RV dump, Tent & RV camping: $23-25, Open May-Sep, Max Length: 40ft, Reservations accepted, Elev: 2467ft/752m, Tel: 541-328-0909, Nearest town: Zigzag. GPS: 45.381697, -121.836174

6 • A2 | Lost Lake (Mt Hood NF)

Total sites: 129, RV sites: 129, Central water, Vault/pit toilet, No showers, RV dump, Tents: $33-41/RVs: $39-43, Group sites $71-$78, Open May-Sep, Max Length: 105ft, Reservations accepted, Elev: 3261ft/994m, Tel: 503-668 1700, Nearest town: Parkdale. GPS: 45.497501, -121.816337

7 • A2 | McNeil (Mt Hood NF)

Total sites: 34, RV sites: 34, No water, Vault/pit toilet, Tent & RV camping: $17-19, Open May-Sep, Max Length: 22ft, Reservations not accepted, Elev: 2100ft/640m, Tel: 503-668 1700, Nearest town: Welches. GPS: 45.385453, -121.866818

8 • A2 | Nottingham (Mt Hood NF)

Total sites: 23, RV sites: 23, No water, No toilets, Tent & RV camping: $24, Open May-Sep, Max Length: 26ft, Reservations accepted, Elev: 3303ft/1007m, Tel: 503-668 1700, Nearest town: Hood River. GPS: 45.367668, -121.569518

9 • A2 | Rainy Lake (Mt Hood NF)

Total sites: 4, RV sites: 0, No water, Vault/pit toilet, Tents only: $19, Open Jun-Oct, Reservations not accepted, Elev: 4068ft/1240m, Tel: 503-668 1700, Nearest town: Parkdale. GPS: 45.626757, -121.758763

10 • A2 | Riley Horse Camp (Mt Hood NF)

Total sites: 14, RV sites: 14, No water, Vault/pit toilet, Tent & RV camping: $21-23, Horse camp but anyone may use, Open May-Sep, Max Length: 35ft, Reservations accepted, Elev: 2110ft/643m, Tel: 541-328-0909, Nearest town: Welches. GPS: 45.381129, -121.861002

11 • A2 | Robinhood (Mt Hood NF)

Total sites: 24, RV sites: 0, No water, Vault/pit toilet, Tents only: Free, Reservations not accepted, Elev: 3572ft/1089m, Tel: 541-352-6002, Nearest town: Mount Hood Parkdale. GPS: 45.338012, -121.572062

12 • A2 | Sherwood (Mt Hood NF)

Total sites: 14, RV sites: 14, No water, Vault/pit toilet, Tent & RV camping: $15, Open May-Sep, Max Length: 16ft, Reservations not accepted, Elev: 3143ft/958m, Tel: 503-668 1700, Nearest town: Hood River. GPS: 45.394531, -121.571289

13 • A2 | Tilly Jane (Mt Hood NF)

Total sites: 14, RV sites: 0, No water, Vault/pit toilet, Tents only: $21, Narrow winding and may require high-clearance or 4X4, Open Jun-Sep, Reservations not accepted, Elev: 5718ft/1743m, Tel: 541-352-6002, Nearest town: Parkdale. GPS: 45.399902, -121.647705

14 • A2 | Wahtum Lake (Mt Hood NF)

Total sites: 5, RV sites: 5, No water, Vault/pit toilet, Tent & RV camping: $21, Open Jun-Oct, Reservations not accepted, Elev: 4012ft/1223m, Tel: 503-668 1700, Nearest town: Hood River. GPS: 45.577413, -121.792704

15 • A2 | Wyeth (Columbia River Gorge NSA)

Total sites: 14, RV sites: 14, Central water, No toilets, No showers, No RV dump, Tent & RV camping: $20, Stay limit: 14 days, Open May-Sep, Max Length: 30ft, Reservations not accepted, Elev: 138ft/42m, Tel: 541-308-1700, Nearest town: Cascade Locks. GPS: 45.690024, -121.771425

16 • A3 | Eight Mile Crossing (Mt Hood NF)

Total sites: 21, RV sites: 21, No water, Vault/pit toilet, Tent & RV camping: $21, Open May-Oct, Max Length: 30ft, Reservations not accepted, Elev: 3934ft/1199m, Tel: 503-668 1700, Nearest town: Hood River. GPS: 45.406250, -121.456787

17 • A3 | Fifteenmile (Mt Hood NF)

Total sites: 3, RV sites: 3, No water, Vault/pit toilet, Tent & RV camping: Free, Open Jun-Sep, Max Length: 16ft, Reservations not accepted, Elev: 4610ft/1405m, Tel: 503-668 1700, Nearest town: Dufur. GPS: 45.350278, -121.472778

18 • A3 | Gibson Prairie Horse Camp (Mt Hood NF)

Total sites: 4, RV sites: 4, No water, No toilets, Tent & RV camping: $12, Stock water, Open Apr-Oct, Max Length: 56ft, Reservations not accepted, Elev: 4035ft/1230m, Tel: 503-668 1700, Nearest town: Parkdale. GPS: 45.483147, -121.523938

19 • A3 | Knebal Springs (Mt Hood NF)

Total sites: 8, RV sites: 8, No water, Vault/pit toilet, Tent & RV camping: $19, Open May-Sep, Max Length: 22ft, Reservations not accepted, Elev: 3809ft/1161m, Tel: 503-668 1700, Nearest town: Dufur. GPS: 45.434195, -121.478651

20 • A3 | Lower Eightmile Crossing (Mt Hood NF)

Total sites: 3, RV sites: 3, No water, Vault/pit toilet, Tent & RV camping: $21, Open May-Oct, Max Length: 16ft, Reservations not accepted, Elev: 3737ft/1139m, Tel: 503-668 1700, Nearest town: Dufur. GPS: 45.413592, -121.442771

21 • A3 | Pebble Ford (Mt Hood NF)

Total sites: 3, RV sites: 3, No water, Vault/pit toilet, Tent & RV camping: $19, Open May-Sep, Max Length: 16ft, Reservations not accepted, Elev: 4209ft/1283m, Tel: 503-668 1700, Nearest town: Dufur. GPS: 45.400081, -121.463902

22 • A3 | Underhill Site (Mt Hood NF)

Total sites: 2, RV sites: 2, No water, Vault/pit toilet, Tent & RV camping: $5, Open May-Sep, Max Length: 18ft, Reservations not accepted, Elev: 3556ft/1084m, Tel: 503-668 1700, Nearest town: Dufur. GPS: 45.396911, -121.415751

23 • A4 | Jubilee Lake (Umatilla NF)

Total sites: 53, RV sites: 48, Central water, No toilets, No showers, No RV dump, Tent & RV camping: $17, Stay limit: 14 days, Open Jul-Oct, Max Length: 32ft, Reservations not accepted, Elev: 4724ft/1440m, Tel: 541-278-3716, Nearest town: Walla Walla. GPS: 45.829332, -117.966029

24 • A4 | Mottet (Umatilla NF)

Total sites: 6, RV sites: 5, Central water, Vault/pit toilet, No showers, No RV dump, Tent & RV camping: $8, Stay limit: 14 days, Open Jul-Nov, Reservations not accepted, Elev: 5164ft/1574m, Tel: 541-278-3716, Nearest town: Walla Walla. GPS: 45.867916, -117.961325

25 • A4 | Spring Creek (Wallowa-Whitman NF)

Total sites: 4, RV sites: 0, No water, Vault/pit toilet, Tents only: Free, Stay limit: 14 days, Open May-Sep, Reservations not accepted, Elev: 3382ft/1031m, Tel: 541-383-5300, Nearest town: La Grande. GPS: 45.357359, -118.312294

26 • A4 | Target Meadows (Umatilla NF)

Total sites: 18, RV sites: 16, Central water, Vault/pit toilet, No showers, No RV dump, Tent & RV camping: $12, Useable in winter - no services, Stay limit: 14 days, Open Jul-Nov, Reservations not accepted, Elev: 4839ft/1475m, Tel: 541-278-3716, Nearest town: Weston. GPS: 45.806038, -118.076837

27 • A4 | Umatilla Forks (Umatilla NF)

Total sites: 12, RV sites: 6, Central water, Vault/pit toilet, No showers, No RV dump, Tent & RV camping: $10, Stay limit: 14 days, Open Jun-Sep, Reservations not accepted, Elev: 2366ft/721m, Tel: 541-278-3716, Nearest town: Bingham Springs. GPS: 45.722795, -118.186467

28 • A4 | Woodland (Umatilla NF)

Total sites: 6, RV sites: 6, No water, Vault/pit toilet, Tent & RV camping: $8, Stay limit: 14 days, Open Jun-Nov, Reservations not accepted, Elev: 5220ft/1591m, Tel: 541-278-3716, Nearest town: Toll Gate. GPS: 45.734000, -118.030000

29 • A4 | Woodward (Umatilla NF)

Total sites: 15, RV sites: 15, Central water, Vault/pit toilet, No showers, No RV dump, Tent & RV camping: $12, Stay limit: 14 days, Open Jul-Sep, Reservations not accepted, Elev: 4948ft/1508m, Tel: 541-278-3716, Nearest town: Weston. GPS: 45.779053, -118.098389

30 • A5 | Boundary (Wallowa-Whitman NF)

Total sites: 8, RV sites: 0, No water, Vault/pit toilet, Tents only: Free, Stay limit: 14 days, Open Jun-Sep, Elev: 3776ft/1151m, Tel: 541-523-6391, Nearest town: Enterprise. GPS: 45.472012, -117.559108

31 • A5 | Buckhorn (Wallowa-Whitman NF)

Total sites: 5, RV sites: 0, No water, Vault/pit toilet, Tents only: Free, Stay limit: 14 days, Open Jun-Sep, Reservations not accepted, Elev: 5240ft/1597m, Tel: 541-523-6391, Nearest town: Enterprise. GPS: 45.755214, -116.837007

32 • A5 | Canyon Forest (Wallowa-Whitman NF)

Total sites: 4, RV sites: 0, No water, Vault/pit toilet, Tents only: Free, Stay limit: 14 days, Open May-Sep, Reservations not accepted, Elev: 4931ft/1503m, Tel: 541-523-6391, Nearest town: Lostine. GPS: 45.351447, -117.414866

33 • A5 | Coyote (Wallowa-Whitman NF)

Total sites: 29, RV sites: 8, No water, Vault/pit toilet, Tent & RV camping: Free, Stay limit: 14 days, Generator hours: 0600-2200, Open Jun-Sep, Reservations not accepted, Elev: 5085ft/1550m, Tel: 541-523-6391, Nearest town: Enterprise. GPS: 45.842285, -117.113281

34 • A5 | Dougherty Springs (Wallowa-Whitman NF)

Total sites: 12, RV sites: 4, No water, Vault/pit toilet, Tent & RV camping: Free, Stay limit: 14 days, Open Jun-Sep, Reservations not accepted, Elev: 5154ft/1571m, Tel: 541-523-6391, Nearest town: Enterprise. GPS: 45.852295, -117.033203

35 • A5 | Hurricane Creek (Wallowa-Whitman NF)

Total sites: 8, RV sites: 3, No water, Vault/pit toilet, Tent & RV camping: $6, Stay limit: 14 days, Open Jun-Sep, Reservations not accepted, Elev: 4655ft/1419m, Tel: 541-523-6391, Nearest town: Enterprise. GPS: 45.332183, -117.298794

36 • A5 | Saddle Creek (Wallowa-Whitman NF)

Total sites: 7, RV sites: 0, No water, Vault/pit toilet, Tents only: Free, Walk-to sites, Very steep narrow winding gravel road, Stay limit: 14 days, Open Jun-Oct, Reservations not accepted, Elev: 6562ft/2000m, Tel: 541-523-6391, Nearest town: Enterprise. GPS: 45.401373, -116.723733

37 • A5 | Vigne (Wallowa-Whitman NF)

Total sites: 6, RV sites: 6, Central water, Vault/pit toilet, No showers, No RV dump, Tent & RV camping: $6, Stay limit: 14 days, Open Jun-Oct, Max Length: 16ft, Reservations not accepted, Elev: 3806ft/1160m, Tel: 541-523-6391, Nearest town: Enterprise. GPS: 45.745381, -117.021862

38 • A5 | Walla Walla Forest Camp (Wallowa-Whitman NF)

Total sites: 4, RV sites: 4, No water, Vault/pit toilet, Tent & RV camping: $5, Stay limit: 14 days, Open Jun-Sep, Max Length: 18ft, Reservations not accepted, Elev: 5010ft/1527m, Tel: 541-523-6391, Nearest town: Lostine. GPS: 45.316277, -117.402473

39 • A5 | Williamson (Wallowa-Whitman NF)

Total sites: 13, RV sites: 8, No water, Vault/pit toilet, Tent & RV camping: $6, Stay limit: 14 days, Open Jun-Sep, Max Length: 18ft, Reservations not accepted, Elev: 5003ft/1525m, Tel: 541-523-6391, Nearest town: Enterprise. GPS: 45.342432, -117.411691

40 • B1 | Alder Dune (Siuslaw NF)

Total sites: 39, RV sites: 39, Central water, Flush toilet, No showers, No RV dump, Tents: $26/RVs: $25, Stay limit: 14 days, Open all year, Max Length: 75ft, Reservations accepted, Elev: 187ft/57m, Tel: 541-997-2526, Nearest town: Florence. GPS: 44.068894, -124.101891

41 • B1 | Baker Beach Horse Camp (Siuslaw NF)

Total sites: 5, RV sites: 5, No water, Vault/pit toilet, Tent & RV camping: $13, Stay limit: 14 days, Reservations not accepted, Elev: 69ft/21m, Tel: 541-563-8400, Nearest town: Florence. GPS: 44.087517, -124.118097

42 • B1 | Big Elk (Siuslaw NF)

Total sites: 8, RV sites: 8, Central water, No toilets, No showers, No RV dump, Tent & RV camping: $10, Stay limit: 14 days, Open all year, Reservations not accepted, Elev: 459ft/140m, Tel: 541-563-8400, Nearest town: Newport. GPS: 44.543847, -123.722922

43 • B1 | Blackberry (Siuslaw NF)

Total sites: 32, RV sites: 32, Central water, Vault/pit toilet, No showers, No RV dump, Tent & RV camping: $24, Stay limit: 14 days, Open all year, Max Length: 32ft, Reservations accepted, Elev: 112ft/34m, Tel: 541-563-8400, Nearest town: Waldport. GPS: 44.373346, -123.835367

44 • B1 | Cape Perpetua (Siuslaw NF)

Total sites: 38, RV sites: 38, Central water, Flush toilet, No showers, No RV dump, Tent & RV camping: $28, Stay limit: 14 days, Open Mar-Sep, Max Length: 60ft, Reservations accepted, Elev: 158ft/48m, Tel: 541-547-4580, Nearest town: Yachats. GPS: 44.281064, -124.104979

45 • B1 | Dry Lake Horse Camp (Siuslaw NF)

Total sites: 3, RV sites: 3, No water, Vault/pit toilet, Tent & RV camping: Free, Stay limit: 14 days, Open all year, Reservations not accepted, Elev: 1099ft/335m, Tel: 541-563-8400, Nearest town: Florence. GPS: 44.096473, -124.070714

46 • B1 | East Dune (Siuslaw NF)

Total sites: 61, RV sites: 61, Central water, Vault/pit toilet, No showers, No RV dump, No tents/RVs: $25, Stay limit: 14 days, Open all year, Max Length: 40ft, Reservations not accepted, Elev: 33ft/10m, Tel: 503-392-3161, Nearest town: Pacific City. GPS: 45.287307, -123.957833

47 • B1 | Hebo Lake (Siuslaw NF)

Total sites: 12, RV sites: 0, No water, Vault/pit toilet, Tents only: $18, Stay limit: 14 days, Open Apr-Oct, Reservations accepted, Elev: 1685ft/514m, Tel: 503-392-5100, Nearest town: Beaver. GPS: 45.231466, -123.794595

48 • B1 | Horse Creek Horse Camp (Siuslaw NF)

Total sites: 10, RV sites: 10, No water, Vault/pit toilet, Tent & RV camping: $11, Stay limit: 14 days, Open all year, Max Length: 60ft, Reservations not accepted, Elev: 1391ft/424m, Tel: 541-902-6940, Nearest town: Florence. GPS: 44.107327, -124.093947

49 • B1 | Marys Peak (Siuslaw NF)

Total sites: 6, RV sites: 6, No water, Vault/pit toilet, Tent & RV camping: $12, Permit required, Stay limit: 14 days, Open May-Sep, Reservations not accepted, Elev: 3570ft/1088m, Tel: 541-563-8400, Nearest town: Corvallis. GPS: 44.509323, -123.561007

50 • B1 | North Fork Siuslaw (Siuslaw NF)

Total sites: 7, RV sites: 7, No water, Vault/pit toilet, Tent & RV camping: Free, Stay limit: 14 days, Open May-Sep, Reservations not accepted, Elev: 240ft/73m, Tel: 541-563-8400, Nearest town: Florence. GPS: 44.101526, -123.936956

51 • B1 | Rock Creek (Siuslaw) (Siuslaw NF)

Total sites: 15, RV sites: 15, Central water, Vault/pit toilet, No showers, No RV dump, Tent & RV camping: $28, Stay limit: 14 days, Open May-Sep, Max Length: 45ft, Reservations accepted, Elev: 269ft/82m, Tel: 541-563-8400, Nearest town: Yachats. GPS: 44.185644, -124.110748

52 • B1 | Sandbeach (Siuslaw NF)

Total sites: 80, RV sites: 80, Central water, Flush toilet, No showers, RV dump, Tent & RV camping: $25, Stay limit: 14 days, Open all year, Max Length: 40ft, Reservations accepted, Elev: 13ft/4m, Tel: 503-392-5100, Nearest town: Pacific City. GPS: 45.283203, -123.956787

53 • B1 | Tillicum Beach (Siuslaw NF)

Total sites: 59, RV sites: 59, Elec sites: 20, Central water, Flush toilet, No showers, No RV dump, Tents: $28/RVs: $28-36, Stay limit: 14 days, Open all year, Max Length: 66ft, Reservations accepted, Elev: 72ft/22m, Tel: 541-563-8400, Nearest town: Waldport. GPS: 44.366314, -124.091484

54 • B1 | West Winds (Siuslaw NF)

Total sites: 20, RV sites: 20, Central water, Vault/pit toilet, No showers, No RV dump, No tents/RVs: $25, Stay limit: 14 days, Open all year, Max Length: 40ft, Reservations not accepted, Elev: 56ft/17m, Tel: 503-392-3161, Nearest town: Pacific City. GPS: 45.286855, -123.955851

55 • B2 | Alder Springs (Willamette NF)

Total sites: 6, RV sites: 0, No water, Vault/pit toilet, Tents only: Free, Stay limit: 14 days, Open Jun-Oct, Reservations not accepted, Elev: 3724ft/1135m, Tel: 541-822-3381, Nearest town: Silver Lake. GPS: 44.177649, -121.913313

56 • B2 | Allen Springs (Deschutes NF)

Total sites: 16, RV sites: 7, No water, Vault/pit toilet, Tent & RV camping: $18-22, $12 winter rate, Open May-Oct, Max Length: 36ft, Reservations accepted, Elev: 2746ft/837m, Tel: 541-338-7869, Nearest town: Sisters. GPS: 44.528672, -121.629017

57 • B2 | Allingham (Deschutes NF)

Total sites: 10, RV sites: 10, Central water, Vault/pit toilet, No showers, No RV dump, Tent & RV camping: $19-21, Open May-Sep, Max Length: 40ft, Reservations accepted, Elev: 3005ft/916m, Tel: 541-338-7869, Nearest town: Sisters. GPS: 44.472772, -121.637072

58 • B2 | Alpine (Mt Hood NF)

Total sites: 16, RV sites: 0, Central water, Vault/pit toilet, No showers, No RV dump, Tents only: $21, Open Jun-Sep, Max Length: 16ft, Reservations not accepted, Elev: 5476ft/1669m, Tel: 503-668 1700, Nearest town: Government Camp. GPS: 45.319761, -121.706135

59 • B2 | Armstrong (Mt Hood NF)

Total sites: 12, RV sites: 12, Central water, Vault/pit toilet, No showers, No RV dump, Tent & RV camping: $20-22, Generator hours: 0600-2200, Open Apr-Sep, Max Length: 26ft, Reservations accepted, Elev: 896ft/273m, Tel: 503-630-5721, Nearest town: Estacada. GPS: 45.161993, -122.152311

60 • B2 | Badger Lake (Mt Hood NF)

Total sites: 4, RV sites: 0, No water, Vault/pit toilet, Tents only: Free, Rough road - 4x4 or high clearance vehicles recommended, Open Jun-Sep, Reservations not accepted, Elev: 4528ft/1380m, Tel: 503-668 1700, Nearest town: Dufur. GPS: 45.302836, -121.558517

61 • B2 | Bagby (Mt Hood NF)

Total sites: 15, RV sites: 0, No water, Vault/pit toilet, Tents only: $18, Open Apr-Sep, Reservations not accepted, Elev: 2091ft/637m, Tel: 503-668 1700, Nearest town: Estacada. GPS: 44.954369, -122.169159

62 • B2 | Barlow Creek (Mt Hood NF)

Total sites: 3, RV sites: 3, No water, Vault/pit toilet, Tent & RV camping: $12, Open Jun-Sep, Reservations not accepted, Elev: 3084ft/940m, Tel: 503-668 1700, Nearest town: Government Creek. GPS: 45.235156, -121.626947

63 • B2 | Barlow Crossing (Mt Hood NF)

Total sites: 6, RV sites: 6, No water, Vault/pit toilet, Tent & RV camping: $12, Open Jun-Sep, Reservations not accepted, Elev: 3061ft/933m, Tel: 503-668 1700, Nearest town: Parkdale. GPS: 45.216759, -121.614176

64 • B2 | Big Lake (Willamette NF)

Total sites: 49, RV sites: 49, Central water, No toilets, No showers, No RV dump, Tent & RV camping: $23, Stay limit: 14 days, Open May-Sep, Max Length: 65ft, Reservations accepted, Elev: 4669ft/1423m, Tel: 801-226-3564, Nearest town: Sisters. GPS: 44.379639, -121.870117

65 • B2 | Big Lake West (Willamette NF)

Total sites: 11, RV sites: 0, Central water, Vault/pit toilet, Tents only: $43, Stay limit: 14 days, Open May-Sep, Max Length: 20ft, Reservations accepted, Elev: 4682ft/1427m, Tel: 801-226-3564, Nearest town: Sisters. GPS: 44.375395, -121.881832

66 • B2 | Big Meadows Horse Camp (Willamette NF)

Total sites: 9, RV sites: 9, Central water, Vault/pit toilet, No showers, No RV dump, Tent & RV camping: $14, Stay limit: 14 days, Open Jul-Oct, Max Length: 36ft, Reservations not accepted, Elev: 3652ft/1113m, Tel: 503-854-3366, Nearest town: Detroit. GPS: 44.493874, -121.983439

67 • B2 | Blue Bay (Deschutes NF)

Total sites: 25, RV sites: 25, Central water, Vault/pit toilet, No showers, No RV dump, Tent & RV camping: $21-23, Open May-Sep, Max Length: 50ft, Reservations accepted, Elev: 3510ft/1070m, Tel: 541-338-7869, Nearest town: Sisters. GPS: 44.419926, -121.732334

68 • B2 | Bonney Meadows (Mt Hood NF)

Total sites: 6, RV sites: 6, No water, Vault/pit toilet, Tent & RV camping: Free, 4x4 and/or high clearance vehicles recommended, Open Jun-Sep, Max Length: 16ft, Reservations not accepted, Elev: 5259ft/1603m, Tel: 503-668 1700, Nearest town: Dufur. GPS: 45.265536, -121.583139

69 • B2 | Breitenbush (Willamette NF)

Total sites: 29, RV sites: 29, Elec sites: 80, Central water, Vault/pit toilet, No showers, No RV dump, Tent & RV camping: $18, Stay limit: 14 days, Open May-Sep, Max Length: 24ft, Reservations accepted, Elev: 2270ft/692m, Tel: 503-854-3366, Nearest town: Detroit. GPS: 44.780583, -121.991033

70 • B2 | Breitenbush Lake (Mt Hood NF)

Total sites: 20, RV sites: 20, No water, Vault/pit toilet, Tent & RV camping: Free, Elev: 5541ft/1689m, Tel: 541-553-2001, Nearest town: Detroit. GPS: 44.765107, -121.785687

71 • B2 | Camp Creek (Mt Hood NF)

Total sites: 25, RV sites: 25, Central water, Vault/pit toilet, No showers, No RV dump, Tent & RV camping: $21-25, Open May-Sep, Max Length: 30ft, Reservations accepted, Elev: 2228ft/679m, Tel: 541-328-0909, Nearest town: Zigzag. GPS: 45.302979, -121.865967

72 • B2 | Camp Sherman (Deschutes NF)

Total sites: 15, RV sites: 15, Central water, Vault/pit toilet, No showers, No RV dump, Tent & RV camping: $17-19, $14 in winter, no water, Open May-Dec, Max Length: 40ft, Reservations accepted, Elev: 2979ft/908m, Tel: 541-338-7869, Nearest town: Sisters. GPS: 44.463135, -121.639893

73 • B2 | Camp Ten (Mt Hood NF)

Total sites: 10, RV sites: 10, No water, Vault/pit toilet, Tent & RV camping: $15-20, Open May-Nov, Max Length: 16ft, Reservations not accepted, Elev: 4948ft/1508m, Tel: 503-668 1700, Nearest town: Detroit. GPS: 44.803152, -121.788898

74 • B2 | Camp Windy (Mt Hood NF)

Total sites: 3, RV sites: 0, No water, Vault/pit toilet, Tents only: Free, Open May-Sep, Reservations not accepted, Elev: 5407ft/1648m, Tel: 503-668 1700, Nearest town: Dufur. GPS: 45.288707, -121.583394

75 • B2 | Candle Creek (Deschutes NF)

Total sites: 10, RV sites: 10, No water, Vault/pit toilet, Tent & RV camping: $12-14, Open May-Sep, Max Length: 18ft, Reservations accepted, Elev: 2700ft/823m, Tel: 541-338-7869, Nearest town: Sisters. GPS: 44.574981, -121.620231

76 • B2 | Carter Bridge (Mt Hood NF)

Total sites: 15, RV sites: 15, No water, Vault/pit toilet, Tent & RV camping: $17, Open May-Sep, Max Length: 28ft, Reservations not accepted, Elev: 1217ft/371m, Tel: 503-668 1700, Nearest town: Estacada. GPS: 45.168006, -122.156662

77 • B2 | Clackamas Lake (Mt Hood NF)

Total sites: 46, RV sites: 46, Central water, Vault/pit toilet, No showers, No RV dump, Tent & RV camping: $23-25, 11 reservable equestrian sites, Open May-Sep, Max Length: 120ft, Reservations accepted, Elev: 3369ft/1027m, Tel: 541-328-0909, Nearest town: Government Camp. GPS: 45.095642, -121.747536

78 • B2 | Clear Creek Crossing (Mt Hood NF)

Total sites: 7, RV sites: 7, No water, Vault/pit toilet, Tent & RV camping: $12, Open May-Sep, Max Length: 16ft, Reservations not accepted, Elev: 3061ft/933m, Tel: 503-668 1700, Nearest town: Dufur. GPS: 45.144834, -121.578996

79 • B2 | Clear Lake (Mt Hood NF)

Total sites: 32, RV sites: 32, Central water, Vault/pit toilet, No showers, No RV dump, Tent & RV camping: $24-26, Open May-Sep, Max Length: 34ft, Reservations accepted, Elev: 3645ft/1111m, Tel: 541-328-0909, Nearest town: Government Camp. GPS: 45.180893, -121.697515

80 • B2 | Cold Spring (Black Crater) (Deschutes NF)

Total sites: 23, RV sites: 23, Central water, Vault/pit toilet, No showers, No RV dump, Tent & RV camping: $15-17, Open May-Oct, Max Length: 156ft, Reservations accepted, Elev: 3399ft/1036m, Tel: 541-338-7869, Nearest town: Sisters. GPS: 44.309706, -121.630268

81 • B2 | Cold Water Cove (Willamette NF)

Total sites: 35, RV sites: 27, Central water, Vault/pit toilet, No showers, No RV dump, Tent & RV camping: $21, Stay limit: 14 days, Open May-Oct, Max Length: 50ft, Reservations accepted, Elev: 3258ft/993m, Tel: 801-226-3564, Nearest town: McKenzie Bridge. GPS: 44.366281, -121.987521

82 • B2 | Cove Creek (Willamette NF)

Total sites: 65, RV sites: 65, Central water, Flush toilet, Pay showers,

No RV dump, Tent & RV camping: $23, Group site: $217, Stay limit: 14 days, Open May-Sep, Max Length: 60ft, Reservations accepted, Elev: 1696ft/517m, Tel: 801-226-3564, Nearest town: Detroit. GPS: 44.711978, -122.159347

83 • B2 | Devils Half Acre (Mt Hood NF)

Total sites: 2, RV sites: 2, No water, Vault/pit toilet, Tent & RV camping: Free, Open May-Oct, Reservations not accepted, Elev: 3881ft/1183m, Tel: 541-352-6002, Nearest town: Parkdale. GPS: 45.273948, -121.679715

84 • B2 | Elk Lake (Battle Ax) (Willamette NF)

Total sites: 17, RV sites: 0, No water, Vault/pit toilet, Tents only: $10, Stay limit: 14 days, Open Jul-Oct, Reservations not accepted, Elev: 3776ft/1151m, Tel: 503-854-3366, Nearest town: Detroit. GPS: 44.821965, -122.127506

85 • B2 | Fernview (Willamette NF)

Total sites: 11, RV sites: 9, Central water, Vault/pit toilet, No showers, No RV dump, Tent & RV camping: $18, Reservable group site $150, Stay limit: 14 days, Open May-Sep, Max Length: 22ft, Reservations not accepted, Elev: 1411ft/430m, Tel: 541-967-3917, Nearest town: Sweet Home. GPS: 44.402344, -122.299805

86 • B2 | Fish Creek (Mt Hood NF)

Total sites: 24, RV sites: 0, Central water, Vault/pit toilet, No showers, No RV dump, Tents only: $22-24, Open May-Sep, Reservations accepted, Elev: 951ft/290m, Tel: 503-630-6861, Nearest town: Estacada. GPS: 45.159444, -122.152222

87 • B2 | Frog Lake (Mt Hood NF)

Total sites: 33, RV sites: 33, Central water, Vault/pit toilet, No showers, No RV dump, Tent & RV camping: $24-26, Open May-Sep, Max Length: 26ft, Reservations accepted, Elev: 3927ft/1197m, Tel: 541-328-0909, Nearest town: Government Camp. GPS: 45.222244, -121.693725

88 • B2 | Gone Creek (Mt Hood NF)

Total sites: 50, RV sites: 50, Central water, Vault/pit toilet, No showers, No RV dump, Tent & RV camping: $22, Open May-Sep, Max Length: 60ft, Reservations accepted, Elev: 3284ft/1001m, Tel: 503-622-3191, Nearest town: Government Camp. GPS: 45.112872, -121.777546

89 • B2 | Gorge (Deschutes NF)

Total sites: 18, RV sites: 18, No water, Vault/pit toilet, Tent & RV camping: $18-22, Stay limit: 14 days, Open May-Oct, Max Length: 40ft, Reservations accepted, Elev: 2953ft/900m, Tel: 541-338-7869, Nearest town: Sisters. GPS: 44.485840, -121.640137

90 • B2 | Graham Corral Horse Camp (Deschutes NF)

Total sites: 13, RV sites: 13, Central water, Vault/pit toilet, No showers, No RV dump, Tent & RV camping: $15-17, Open May-Oct, Max Length: 40ft, Reservations accepted, Elev: 3343ft/1019m, Tel: 541-338-7869, Nearest town: Sisters. GPS: 44.344806, -121.642498

91 • B2 | Green Canyon (Mt Hood NF)

Total sites: 15, RV sites: 15, No water, Vault/pit toilet, Tent & RV camping: $21, Open May-Sep, Max Length: 22ft, Reservations not accepted, Elev: 1680ft/512m, Tel: 503-668 1700, Nearest town: Zigzag. GPS: 45.283203, -121.942871

92 • B2 | Grindstone (Mt Hood NF)

Total sites: 3, RV sites: 3, No water, Vault/pit toilet, Tent & RV camping: Free, Reservations not accepted, Elev: 3402ft/1037m, Tel: 503-668 1700, Nearest town: Parkdale. GPS: 45.247319, -121.658907

93 • B2 | Hideaway Lake (Mt Hood NF)

Total sites: 9, RV sites: 9, No water, Vault/pit toilet, Tent & RV camping: $19, Open Jun-Sep, Max Length: 16ft, Reservations not accepted, Elev: 4163ft/1269m, Tel: 503-668 1700, Nearest town: Estacada. GPS: 45.123321, -121.967825

94 • B2 | Hood River Meadows (Mt Hood NF)

Total sites: 5, RV sites: 5, No water, No toilets, Tent & RV camping: Free, Max Length: 21ft, Elev: 4520ft/1378m, Tel: 503-668 1700, Nearest town: Mt Hood. GPS: 45.320637, -121.634325

95 • B2 | Hoodview (Mt Hood NF)

Total sites: 43, RV sites: 43, Central water, Vault/pit toilet, No showers, No RV dump, Tents: $18-22/RVs: $22, Open May-Sep, Max Length: 35ft, Reservations accepted, Elev: 3249ft/990m, Tel: 503-622-3191, Nearest town: Government Camp. GPS: 45.107911, -121.791844

96 • B2 | Hoover (Willamette NF)

Total sites: 35, RV sites: 35, Central water, Vault/pit toilet, No showers, No RV dump, Tent & RV camping: $24, Group site: $211, Stay limit: 14 days, Open May-Sep, Max Length: 45ft, Reservations accepted, Elev: 1591ft/485m, Tel: 801-226-3564, Nearest town: Detroit. GPS: 44.713264, -122.124048

97 • B2 | Horseshoe Lake (Mt Hood NF)

Total sites: 6, RV sites: 0, No water, Vault/pit toilet, Tents only: $15-20, Road not maintained for passenger cars, Open May-Sep, Reservations not accepted, Elev: 5394ft/1644m, Tel: 503-668 1700, Nearest town: Estacada. GPS: 44.779555, -121.785134

98 • B2 | House Rock (Willamette NF)

Total sites: 17, RV sites: 12, Central water, Vault/pit toilet, No showers, No RV dump, Tent & RV camping: $20, Stay limit: 14 days, Open May-Sep, Max Length: 65ft, Reservations accepted, Elev: 1768ft/539m, Tel: 541-967-3917, Nearest town: Sweet Home. GPS: 44.392773, -122.245205

99 • B2 | Humbug (Willamette NF)

Total sites: 21, RV sites: 21, Central water, Vault/pit toilet, No showers, No RV dump, Tent & RV camping: $18, Stay limit: 14 days, Open May-Sep, Max Length: 75ft, Reservations accepted, Elev: 1913ft/583m, Tel: 503-854-3366, Nearest town: Detroit. GPS: 44.771973, -122.077881

100 • B2 | Ice Cap Creek (Willamette NF)

Total sites: 22, RV sites: 14, No water, Vault/pit toilet, Tent & RV camping: $18, Stay limit: 14 days, Open May-Sep, Max Length: 30ft, Reservations accepted, Elev: 2815ft/858m, Tel: 801-226-3564, Nearest town: Blue River. GPS: 44.341309, -122.001953

101 • B2 | Indian Ford (Deschutes NF)

Total sites: 25, RV sites: 25, No water, Vault/pit toilet, Tent & RV camping: $11-13, Open May-Oct, Max Length: 50ft, Reservations accepted, Elev: 3287ft/1002m, Tel: 541-338-7869, Nearest town: Sisters. GPS: 44.357432, -121.610434

102 • B2 | Indian Henry (Mt Hood NF)

Total sites: 86, RV sites: 86, Central water, Flush toilet, No showers, RV dump, Tent & RV camping: $23-25, Open May-Sep, Max Length: 30ft, Reservations accepted, Elev: 1348ft/411m, Tel: 503-630-6861, Nearest town: Estacada. GPS: 45.108177, -122.075636

103 • B2 | Jack Creek (Deschutes NF)

Total sites: 19, RV sites: 19, No water, Vault/pit toilet, Tent & RV camping: $12-14, Open May-Oct, Max Length: 40ft, Reservations accepted, Elev: 3110ft/948m, Tel: 541-338-7869, Nearest town: Sisters. GPS: 44.484351, -121.700815

104 • B2 | Jack Lake (Deschutes NF)

Total sites: 2, RV sites: 0, No water, Vault/pit toilet, Tents only: Free, Wilderness Permits required May-Oct, Open May-Oct, Elev: 5161ft/1573m, Tel: 541-549-7700, Nearest town: Sisters. GPS: 44.491898, -121.794484

105 • B2 | Joe Graham Horse Camp (Mt Hood NF)

Total sites: 14, RV sites: 14, Central water, Vault/pit toilet, No showers, No RV dump, Tent & RV camping: $23-25, Open May-Sep, Max Length: 40ft, Reservations accepted, Elev: 3465ft/1056m, Tel: 541-328-0909, Nearest town: Government Camp. GPS: 45.100074, -121.747006

106 • B2 | Kingfisher Camp (Mt Hood NF)

Total sites: 23, RV sites: 6, Central water, Vault/pit toilet, No showers, No RV dump, Tent & RV camping: $24-26, Open May-Sep, Max Length: 20ft, Reservations accepted, Elev: 1864ft/568m, Tel: 503-630-5721, Nearest town: Estacada. GPS: 44.976189, -122.092852

107 • B2 | Lake Harriet (Mt Hood NF)

Total sites: 8, RV sites: 8, Central water, Vault/pit toilet, No showers, No RV dump, Tent & RV camping: $18, Managed by PGE, Open May-Sep, Max Length: 35ft, Reservations accepted, Elev: 2198ft/670m, Tel: 503-630-6861, Nearest town: Estacada. GPS: 45.073291, -121.958426

108 • B2 | Lava Camp Lake (Deschutes NF)

Total sites: 12, RV sites: 12, No water, Vault/pit toilet, Tent & RV camping: Free, Open Jun-Oct, Max Length: 35ft, Reservations not accepted, Elev: 5312ft/1619m, Tel: 541-549-7700, Nearest town: Sisters. GPS: 44.261227, -121.785608

109 • B2 | Lazy Bend (Mt Hood NF)

Total sites: 21, RV sites: 21, Central water, Flush toilet, No showers, No RV dump, Tent & RV camping: $23-25, Open Apr-Sep, Max Length: 23ft, Reservations accepted, Elev: 814ft/248m, Tel: 503-630-4156, Nearest town: Estacada. GPS: 45.190891, -122.207558

110 • B2 | Limberlost (Willamette NF)

Total sites: 12, RV sites: 10, No water, Vault/pit toilet, Tent & RV camping: $13, Stay limit: 14 days, Open May-Sep, Max Length: 36ft, Reservations accepted, Elev: 1762ft/537m, Tel: 801-226-3564, Nearest town: Blue River. GPS: 44.174316, -122.053223

111 • B2 | Link Creek (Deschutes NF)

Total sites: 33, RV sites: 33, Central water, Vault/pit toilet, No showers, No RV dump, Tent & RV camping: $16-20, Open all year, Max Length: 50ft, Reservations accepted, Elev: 3481ft/1061m, Tel: 541-338-7869, Nearest town: Sisters. GPS: 44.416260, -121.755615

112 • B2 | Little Crater Lake (Mt Hood NF)

Total sites: 16, RV sites: 8, Central water, Vault/pit toilet, No showers, No RV dump, Tent & RV camping: $23-25, Open May-Sep, Max Length: 26ft, Reservations accepted, Elev: 3327ft/1014m, Tel: 541-328-0909, Nearest town: Government Camp. GPS: 45.148453, -121.745648

113 • B2 | Little Fan Creek (Mt Hood NF)

Total sites: 4, RV sites: 4, Vault/pit toilet, Tent & RV camping: $14, Reservations not accepted, Elev: 1686ft/514m, Tel: 503-668 1700, Nearest town: Estacada. GPS: 44.991726, -122.063976

114 • B2 | Lockaby (Mt Hood NF)

Total sites: 30, RV sites: 6, Central water, Vault/pit toilet, No showers, No RV dump, Tent & RV camping: $23-25, Open May-Sep, Max Length: 26ft, Reservations accepted, Elev: 945ft/288m, Tel: 503-630-6861, Nearest town: Estacada. GPS: 45.165676, -122.153137

115 • B2 | Lookout (Willamette NF)

Total sites: 20, RV sites: 20, Central water, Vault/pit toilet, No showers, No RV dump, Tent & RV camping: $14, Stay limit: 14 days, Open all year, Max Length: 30ft, Reservations accepted, Elev: 1357ft/414m, Tel: 541-822-3381, Nearest town: Blue River. GPS: 44.202493, -122.260586

116 • B2 | Lost Lake (Willamette NF)

Total sites: 15, RV sites: 15, No water, Vault/pit toilet, Tent & RV camping: $8, Trailers not recommended, Stay limit: 14 days, Open May-Oct, Reservations not accepted, Elev: 4039ft/1231m, Tel: 541-822-3381, Nearest town: McKenzie Bridge. GPS: 44.433216, -121.909772

117 • B2 | Lost Prairie (Willamette NF)

Total sites: 10, RV sites: 2, Central water, Vault/pit toilet, No showers, No RV dump, Tent & RV camping: $18, Can reserve whole park - $125, Stay limit: 14 days, Open May-Oct, Max Length: 24ft, Reservations not accepted, Elev: 3389ft/1033m, Tel: 541-967-3917, Nearest town: Sweet Home. GPS: 44.402588, -122.076172

118 • B2 | Lower Bridge (Deschutes NF)

Total sites: 12, RV sites: 12, Central water, Vault/pit toilet, No showers, No RV dump, Tent & RV camping: $18-20, Open all year, Max Length: 30ft, Reservations accepted, Elev: 2802ft/854m, Tel: 541-338-7869, Nearest town: Sisters. GPS: 44.557461, -121.619857

119 • B2 | Lower Canyon Creek (Deschutes NF)

Total sites: 7, RV sites: 7, No water, Vault/pit toilet, Tent & RV

camping: $12-14, Open May-Sep, Max Length: 40ft, Reservations accepted, Elev: 2877ft/877m, Tel: 541-338-7869, Nearest town: Sisters. GPS: 44.501341, -121.641506

120 • B2 | Lower Lake (Mt Hood NF)

Total sites: 8, RV sites: 8, No water, No toilets, Tent & RV camping: $15-20, Open Jun-Sep, Max Length: 16ft, Reservations not accepted, Elev: 4875ft/1486m, Tel: 503-668 1700, Nearest town: Estacada. GPS: 44.822873, -121.797541

121 • B2 | Lower Olallie Meadow (Mt Hood NF)

Total sites: 7, RV sites: 7, No water, Vault/pit toilet, Tent & RV camping: $15-20, Open Jun-Sep, Reservations not accepted, Elev: 4492ft/1369m, Tel: 503-668 1700, Nearest town: Estacada. GPS: 44.859666, -121.773714

122 • B2 | Marion Forks (Willamette NF)

Total sites: 15, RV sites: 15, No water, Vault/pit toilet, Tent & RV camping: $10, Stay limit: 14 days, Open all year, Max Length: 24ft, Reservations not accepted, Elev: 2566ft/782m, Tel: 503-854-3366, Nearest town: Detroit. GPS: 44.609474, -121.946124

123 • B2 | McKenzie Bridge (Willamette NF)

Total sites: 20, RV sites: 20, Central water, Vault/pit toilet, No showers, No RV dump, Tent & RV camping: $19, Stay limit: 14 days, Open May-Sep, Max Length: 70ft, Reservations accepted, Elev: 1394ft/425m, Tel: 801-226-3564, Nearest town: McKenzie Bridge. GPS: 44.174805, -122.176270

124 • B2 | Mona (Willamette NF)

Total sites: 23, RV sites: 23, Central water, No toilets, No showers, No RV dump, Tent & RV camping: $19, Stay limit: 14 days, Open May-Sep, Max Length: 70ft, Reservations accepted, Elev: 1413ft/431m, Tel: 541-822-3381, Nearest town: Blue River. GPS: 44.203187, -122.263298

125 • B2 | North Arm (Mt Hood NF)

Total sites: 19, RV sites: 15, No water, Vault/pit toilet, Tents: $16/ RVs: $20, Also walk-to sites, Open May-Sep, Max Length: 16ft, Reservations not accepted, Elev: 3284ft/1001m, Tel: 503-668 1700, Nearest town: Sandy. GPS: 45.144315, -121.771605

126 • B2 | Oak Fork (Timothy Lake) (Mt Hood NF)

Total sites: 44, RV sites: 36, Central water, Vault/pit toilet, No showers, No RV dump, Tents: $18/RVs: $22, Also walk-to sites/ cabins, Open May-Sep, Max Length: 60ft, Reservations accepted, Elev: 3268ft/996m, Tel: 503-668-1700, Nearest town: Government Camp. GPS: 45.115058, -121.770519

127 • B2 | Olallie (Willamette) (Willamette NF)

Total sites: 17, RV sites: 17, Central water, Vault/pit toilet, No showers, No RV dump, Tent & RV camping: $18, Stay limit: 14 days, Open Apr-Oct, Max Length: 40ft, Reservations accepted, Elev: 2100ft/640m, Tel: 801-226-3564, Nearest town: Estacada. GPS: 44.256974, -122.039976

128 • B2 | Paradise (Willamette NF)

Total sites: 64, RV sites: 64, Central water, Flush toilet, No showers, No RV dump, Tent & RV camping: $22, Stay limit: 14 days, Open May-Oct, Max Length: 80ft, Reservations accepted, Elev: 1533ft/ 467m, Tel: 541-822-3381, Nearest town: McKenzie Bridge. GPS: 44.185093, -122.091239

129 • B2 | Paul Dennis (Olallie Lake) (Mt Hood NF)

Total sites: 17, RV sites: 17, No water, Vault/pit toilet, Tent & RV camping: $15-20, Open Jun-Sep, Max Length: 16ft, Reservations not accepted, Elev: 4968ft/1514m, Tel: 503-668 1700, Nearest town: Estacada. GPS: 44.811387, -121.786948

130 • B2 | Peninsula (Olallie Lake) (Mt Hood NF)

Total sites: 36, RV sites: 36, No water, Vault/pit toilet, Tent & RV camping: $15-20, Reservations not accepted, Elev: 4984ft/1519m, Tel: 503-630-6861, Nearest town: Detroit. GPS: 44.802547, -121.783142

131 • B2 | Pine Point (Mt Hood NF)

Total sites: 13, RV sites: 13, Central water, Vault/pit toilet, No showers, No RV dump, Tent & RV camping: $22, 5 group sites: $66-$132, Open May-Sep, Max Length: 40ft, Reservations accepted, Elev: 3254ft/992m, Tel: 503-622-3191, Nearest town: Government Camp. GPS: 45.113432, -121.801335

132 • B2 | Pine Rest (Deschutes NF)

Total sites: 7, RV sites: 0, No water, Vault/pit toilet, Tents only: $18-22, Open all year, Max Length: 18-22ft, Reservations not accepted, Elev: 2982ft/909m, Tel: 541-338-7869, Nearest town: Sisters. GPS: 44.481736, -121.638038

133 • B2 | Pioneer Ford (Deschutes NF)

Total sites: 20, RV sites: 18, Central water, Vault/pit toilet, No showers, No RV dump, Tents: $21-23/RVs: $21-25, Open May-Sep, Max Length: 40ft, Reservations accepted, Elev: 2805ft/855m, Tel: 541-338-7869, Nearest town: Sisters. GPS: 44.552156, -121.620839

134 • B2 | Rainbow (Fish Creek Mt) (Mt Hood NF)

Total sites: 19, RV sites: 0, Central water, Vault/pit toilet, Tents only: $20-22, Open Apr-Sep, Max Length: 24ft, Reservations accepted, Elev: 1463ft/446m, Tel: 503-834-2322, Nearest town: Estacada. GPS: 45.076595, -122.045425

135 • B2 | Ripplebrook (Mt Hood NF)

Total sites: 13, RV sites: 13, No water, Vault/pit toilet, No showers, No RV dump, Tent & RV camping: $20-22, Open Apr-Sep, Max Length: 24ft, Reservations accepted, Elev: 1578ft/481m, Tel: 503-834-2322, Nearest town: Estacada. GPS: 45.080197, -122.042118

136 • B2 | Riverford (Mt Hood NF)

Total sites: 10, RV sites: 10, No water, Vault/pit toilet, Tent & RV camping: $19, Open May-Sep, Max Length: 16ft, Reservations not accepted, Elev: 1490ft/454m, Tel: 503-668 1700, Nearest town: Estacada. GPS: 45.032567, -122.058574

137 • B2 | Riverside (Mt Hood NF)

Total sites: 16, RV sites: 2, Central water, Vault/pit toilet, No showers, No RV dump, Tent & RV camping: $20-22, Open May-Sep, Max Length: 24ft, Reservations accepted, Elev: 1624ft/495m, Tel: 503-630-6861, Nearest town: Estacada. GPS: 45.044619, -122.062532

138 • B2 | Riverside (Deschutes NF)

Total sites: 16, RV sites: 0, Central water, Vault/pit toilet, No showers, No RV dump, Tents only: $12-14, Walk-to sites, Open May-Sep, Reservations accepted, Elev: 3041ft/927m, Tel: 541-338-7869, Nearest town: Sisters. GPS: 44.442855, -121.634834

139 • B2 | Riverside at Detroit (Willamette NF)

Total sites: 38, RV sites: 38, No water, Vault/pit toilet, Tent & RV camping: $18, Stay limit: 14 days, Open May-Sep, Max Length: 35ft, Reservations accepted, Elev: 2398ft/731m, Tel: 503-854-3366, Nearest town: Detroit. GPS: 44.641824, -121.945452

140 • B2 | Roaring River (Mt Hood NF)

Total sites: 14, RV sites: 1, Central water, Vault/pit toilet, No showers, No RV dump, Tent & RV camping: $20-22, Open May-Sep, Max Length: 20ft, Reservations accepted, Elev: 1253ft/382m, Tel: 503-630-6861, Nearest town: Estacada. GPS: 45.158203, -122.114258

141 • B2 | Santiam Flats (Willamette NF)

Total sites: 32, RV sites: 32, Central water, Vault/pit toilet, No showers, No RV dump, Tent & RV camping: $18, Stay limit: 14 days, Open Apr-Sep, Max Length: 40ft, Reservations accepted, Elev: 1624ft/495m, Tel: 503-854-3366, Nearest town: Detroit. GPS: 44.711526, -122.115679

142 • B2 | Scott Lake (Willamette NF)

Total sites: 18, RV sites: 0, No water, Vault/pit toilet, Tents only: $5, Walk-to sites, Stay limit: 14 days, Open Jun-Oct, Reservations not accepted, Elev: 4836ft/1474m, Tel: 541-822-3381, Nearest town: Sisters. GPS: 44.211914, -121.889404

143 • B2 | Scout Lake (Deschutes NF)

Total sites: 10, RV sites: 10, Central water, Vault/pit toilet, No showers, No RV dump, Tent & RV camping: $18-20, 1 single site/6 doubles/3 triples, No dogs at beach, Open May-Sep, Max Length: 40ft, Reservations accepted, Elev: 3681ft/1122m, Tel: 541-338-7869, Nearest town: Sisters. GPS: 44.411713, -121.749652

144 • B2 | Shady Cove (Willamette NF)

Total sites: 13, RV sites: 13, No water, Vault/pit toilet, Tent & RV camping: $8, Stay limit: 14 days, Open all year, Max Length: 16ft, Reservations not accepted, Elev: 1565ft/477m, Tel: 503-854-3366, Nearest town: Mill City. GPS: 44.844886, -122.301194

145 • B2 | Shellrock Creek (Mt Hood NF)

Total sites: 8, RV sites: 8, No water, Vault/pit toilet, Tent & RV camping: $19, Open Jun-Sep, Max Length: 16ft, Reservations not accepted, Elev: 2411ft/735m, Tel: 503-668 1700, Nearest town: Estacada. GPS: 45.084558, -121.923683

146 • B2 | Sisters Cow Camp Horse Camp (Deschutes NF)

Total sites: 5, RV sites: 5, No water, Vault/pit toilet, Tent & RV camping: Free, Open Apr-Oct, Max Length: 40ft, Reservations not accepted, Elev: 3432ft/1046m, Tel: 541-383-5300, Nearest town: Sisters. GPS: 44.274196, -121.615078

147 • B2 | Smiling River (Deschutes NF)

Total sites: 36, RV sites: 36, Central water, Flush toilet, No showers, No RV dump, Tent & RV camping: $20-24, Open May-Oct, Max Length: 50ft, Reservations accepted, Elev: 2972ft/906m, Tel: 541-338-7869, Nearest town: Camp Sherman. GPS: 44.474558, -121.636496

148 • B2 | South Shore (Detroit) (Willamette NF)

Total sites: 32, RV sites: 32, Central water, Vault/pit toilet, No showers, No RV dump, Tent & RV camping: $22, Stay limit: 14 days, Open May-Sep, Max Length: 130ft, Reservations accepted, Elev: 1644ft/501m, Tel: 503-854-3366, Nearest town: Detroit. GPS: 44.705817, -122.176186

149 • B2 | South Shore (Suttle Lake) (Deschutes NF)

Total sites: 38, RV sites: 38, Central water, Vault/pit toilet, No showers, No RV dump, Tent & RV camping: $21-23, Open May-Sep, Max Length: 40ft, Reservations accepted, Elev: 3461ft/1055m, Tel: 541-338-7869, Nearest town: Sisters. GPS: 44.417969, -121.741455

150 • B2 | Still Creek (Mt Hood NF)

Total sites: 27, RV sites: 9, Central water, Vault/pit toilet, No showers, No RV dump, Tent & RV camping: $24-26, Open May-Sep, Max Length: 30ft, Reservations accepted, Elev: 3852ft/1174m, Tel: 541-328-0909, Nearest town: Government Camp. GPS: 45.295410, -121.737305

151 • B2 | Summit Lake (Mt Hood NF)

Total sites: 8, RV sites: 8, No water, Vault/pit toilet, Tent & RV camping: $17-19, Open Jun-Sep, Max Length: 16ft, Reservations not accepted, Elev: 4213ft/1284m, Tel: 503-668 1700, Nearest town: Sand. GPS: 45.031808, -121.789967

152 • B2 | Sunstrip (Mt Hood NF)

Total sites: 8, RV sites: 0, No water, Vault/pit toilet, Tents only: $23-25, Open Apr-Sep, Reservations accepted, Elev: 1168ft/356m, Tel: 503-630-4156, Nearest town: Estacada. GPS: 45.150593, -122.106215

153 • B2 | Toll Gate (Mt Hood NF)

Total sites: 15, RV sites: 15, Central water, Vault/pit toilet, No showers, No RV dump, Tent & RV camping: $24-26, Open May-Sep, Max Length: 40ft, Reservations accepted, Elev: 1791ft/546m, Tel: 541-328-0909, Nearest town: Zigzag. GPS: 45.322118, -121.905628

154 • B2 | Trail Bridge (Willamette NF)

Total sites: 46, RV sites: 19, Central water, No toilets, No showers, No RV dump, Tent & RV camping: $10, Stay limit: 14 days, Open May-Oct, Max Length: 45ft, Reservations not accepted, Elev: 2111ft/643m, Tel: 541-822-3381, Nearest town: McKenzie Bridge. GPS: 44.279675, -122.048815

155 • B2 | Triangle Lake Horse Camp (Mt Hood NF)

Total sites: 8, RV sites: 8, No water, Vault/pit toilet, Tent & RV camping: $15-20, Open Jun-Sep, Max Length: 30ft, Reservations not accepted, Elev: 4603ft/1403m, Tel: 503-668 1700, Nearest town: Estacada. GPS: 44.850245, -121.776356

156 • B2 | Trillium Lake (Mt Hood NF)

Total sites: 57, RV sites: 57, Central water, Vault/pit toilet, No showers, No RV dump, Tent & RV camping: $24-26, Group site: $86, Open May-Sep, Max Length: 95ft, Reservations accepted, Elev: 3658ft/1115m, Tel: 503-272-3220, Nearest town: Government Camp. GPS: 45.270508, -121.735596

157 • B2 | Trout Creek (Willamette NF)

Total sites: 23, RV sites: 19, Central water, Vault/pit toilet, No showers, No RV dump, Tent & RV camping: $20, Stay limit: 14 days, Open May-Sep, Max Length: 115ft, Reservations accepted, Elev: 1339ft/408m, Tel: 541-367-5168, Nearest town: Sweet Home. GPS: 44.397606, -122.348613

158 • B2 | Whispering Falls (Willamette NF)

Total sites: 16, RV sites: 16, Central water, Vault/pit toilet, No showers, No RV dump, Tent & RV camping: $18, Stay limit: 14 days, Open May-Sep, Max Length: 80ft, Reservations accepted, Elev: 2060ft/628m, Tel: 503-854-3366, Nearest town: Detroit. GPS: 44.687744, -122.009521

159 • B2 | Whispering Pines Horse Camp (Deschutes NF)

Total sites: 9, RV sites: 9, No water, Vault/pit toilet, Tent & RV camping: $16-18, Open May-Oct, Reservations accepted, Elev: 4432ft/1351m, Tel: 541-338-7869, Nearest town: Sisters. GPS: 44.253452, -121.690573

160 • B2 | Yukwah (Willamette NF)

Total sites: 19, RV sites: 19, Central water, Vault/pit toilet, No showers, No RV dump, Tent & RV camping: $20, Stay limit: 14 days, Open May-Sep, Max Length: 40ft, Reservations accepted, Elev: 1348ft/411m, Tel: 541-367-5168, Nearest town: Sweet Home. GPS: 44.399248, -122.338179

161 • B3 | Allen Creek Horse Camp (Ochoco NF)

Total sites: 11, RV sites: 11, No water, Vault/pit toilet, Tent & RV camping: Free, 16 horse stalls, stock water, Stay limit: 14 days, Open all year, Reservations not accepted, Elev: 4846ft/1477m, Tel: 541-416-6500, Nearest town: Prineville. GPS: 44.398276, -120.171993

162 • B3 | Barnhouse (Ochoco NF)

Total sites: 6, RV sites: 6, No water, Vault/pit toilet, Tent & RV camping: Free, Stay limit: 14 days, Open all year, Max Length: 25ft, Reservations not accepted, Elev: 5076ft/1547m, Tel: 541-416-6500, Nearest town: Paulina. GPS: 44.473809, -119.934569

163 • B3 | Bear Springs (Mt Hood NF)

Total sites: 21, RV sites: 21, Central water, Vault/pit toilet, No showers, No RV dump, Tent & RV camping: $17, Reservable group sites $51-$76, Open May-Sep, Max Length: 32ft, Reservations not accepted, Elev: 3146ft/959m, Tel: 541-467-2291, Nearest town: Government Camp. GPS: 45.116748, -121.531466

164 • B3 | Big Spring (Ochoco NF)

Total sites: 5, RV sites: 5, No water, Vault/pit toilet, Tent & RV camping: Free, Stay limit: 14 days, Open all year, Reservations not accepted, Elev: 5052ft/1540m, Tel: 541-416-6500, Nearest town: Paulina. GPS: 44.331874, -119.991419

165 • B3 | Biggs Springs (Ochoco NF)

Total sites: 3, RV sites: 3, No water, Vault/pit toilet, Tent & RV camping: Free, Stay limit: 14 days, Open all year, Reservations not accepted, Elev: 4898ft/1493m, Tel: 541-416-6500, Nearest town: Post. GPS: 44.272121, -120.259769

166 • B3 | Bingham Spring (Ochoco NF)

Total sites: 4, RV sites: 1, No water, Vault/pit toilet, Tent & RV camping: Free, Stay limit: 14 days, Open all year, Max Length: 18ft, Reservations not accepted, Elev: 5495ft/1675m, Tel: 541-416-6500, Nearest town: Paulina. GPS: 44.514082, -120.529316

167 • B3 | Bonney Crossing (Mt Hood NF)

Total sites: 8, RV sites: 8, No water, Vault/pit toilet, Tent & RV camping: $12, Open May-Sep, Max Length: 16ft, Reservations not accepted, Elev: 2195ft/669m, Tel: 541-467-2291, Nearest town: Dufur. GPS: 45.255917, -121.390567

168 • B3 | Cottonwood (Antone) (Ochoco NF)

Total sites: 6, RV sites: 5, No water, Vault/pit toilet, Tent & RV camping: Free, Stay limit: 14 days, Open all year, Reservations not accepted, Elev: 5745ft/1751m, Tel: 541-416-6500, Nearest town: Paulina. GPS: 44.387618, -119.854969

169 • B3 | Cottonwood Pit (Ochoco NF)

Total sites: 3, RV sites: 3, No water, Vault/pit toilet, Tent & RV camping: Free, Stay limit: 14 days, Open May-Sep, Elev: 5630ft/1716m, Tel: 541-416-6500, Nearest town: Paulina. GPS: 44.368809, -119.869979

170 • B3 | Cyrus Horse Camp (Ochoco NF)

Total sites: 5, RV sites: 5, No water, Vault/pit toilet, Tent & RV camping: Free, Stay limit: 14 days, Reservations not accepted, Elev: 3350ft/1021m, Tel: 541-416-6640, Nearest town: Terrebonne. GPS: 44.447776, -121.103144

171 • B3 | Deep Creek (Ochoco NF)

Total sites: 14, RV sites: 14, Central water, Vault/pit toilet, No showers, No RV dump, Tent & RV camping: $8, Stay limit: 14 days, Open May-Oct, Reservations not accepted, Elev: 4373ft/1333m, Tel: 541-416-6500, Nearest town: Prineville. GPS: 44.327862, -120.077131

172 • B3 | Dry Creek Horse Camp (Ochoco NF)

Total sites: 5, RV sites: 5, No water, Vault/pit toilet, Tent & RV camping: Free, Stay limit: 14 days, Max Length: 20ft, Reservations not accepted, Elev: 3963ft/1208m, Tel: 541-416-6500, Nearest town: Prineville. GPS: 44.417768, -120.669165

173 • B3 | Forest Creek (Mt Hood NF)

Total sites: 8, RV sites: 8, No water, Vault/pit toilet, Tent & RV camping: $12, Open May-Sep, Max Length: 16ft, Reservations not accepted, Elev: 3176ft/968m, Tel: 503-668 1700, Nearest town: Dufur. GPS: 45.179976, -121.524673

174 • B3 | Haystack Reservoir (Ochoco NF)

Total sites: 24, RV sites: 24, Central water, Vault/pit toilet, No showers, No RV dump, Tent & RV camping: $15, Open Apr-Oct, Max Length: 140ft, Reservations accepted, Elev: 2923ft/891m, Tel: 208-270-0094, Nearest town: Madras. GPS: 44.493478, -121.140846

175 • B3 | Keeps Mill (Mt Hood NF)

Total sites: 5, RV sites: 5, No water, Vault/pit toilet, Tent & RV camping: Free, High-clearance vehicle required, Open Jun-Sep, Reservations not accepted, Elev: 2648ft/807m, Tel: 503-668 1700, Nearest town: Dufur. GPS: 45.154543, -121.519807

176 • B3 | Little Badger (Mt Hood NF)

Total sites: 3, RV sites: 3, No water, Vault/pit toilet, Tent & RV camping: Free, Open May-Sep, Max Length: 16ft, Reservations not accepted, Elev: 2077ft/633m, Tel: 503-668 1700, Nearest town: Dufur. GPS: 45.281799, -121.348385

177 • B3 | McCubbins Gulch (Mt Hood NF)

Total sites: 15, RV sites: 15, No water, Vault/pit toilet, Tent & RV camping: $12, Open May-Sep, Max Length: 25ft, Reservations not accepted, Elev: 3025ft/922m, Tel: 503-668 1700, Nearest town: Government Camp. GPS: 45.115286, -121.483065

178 • B3 | Monty (Deschutes NF)

Total sites: 34, RV sites: 34, No water, Vault/pit toilet, Tent & RV camping: $16, Rough access road, Managed by PGE, Open May-Sep, Max Length: 90ft, Reservations accepted, Elev: 2014ft/614m, Tel: 541-338-7869, Nearest town: Culver. GPS: 44.625488, -121.483154

179 • B3 | Ochoco Divide (Ochoco NF)

Total sites: 28, RV sites: 28, No water, Vault/pit toilet, Tent & RV camping: $13, Stay limit: 14 days, Open May-Oct, Reservations not accepted, Elev: 4823ft/1470m, Tel: 208-270-0094, Nearest town: Prineville. GPS: 44.500244, -120.385742

180 • B3 | Ochoco Forest Camp (Ochoco NF)

Total sites: 5, RV sites: 5, Central water, Vault/pit toilet, No showers, No RV dump, Tent & RV camping: $15, Group site: $60-$100, Stay limit: 14 days, Open May-Oct, Reservations accepted, Elev: 4029ft/1228m, Tel: 541-416-3689, Nearest town: Prineville. GPS: 44.395999, -120.422446

181 • B3 | Perry South (Deschutes NF)

Total sites: 64, RV sites: 55, Central water, Flush toilet, No showers, No RV dump, Tent & RV camping: $20, Open May-Sep, Max Length: 50ft, Reservations accepted, Elev: 1998ft/609m, Tel: 541-338-7869, Nearest town: Culver. GPS: 44.584621, -121.448015

182 • B3 | Post Camp (Mt Hood NF)

Total sites: 4, RV sites: 4, No water, Vault/pit toilet, Tent & RV camping: Free, Open May-Sep, Max Length: 16ft, Reservations not accepted, Elev: 4045ft/1233m, Tel: 541-467-2291, Nearest town: Dufur. GPS: 45.216371, -121.520079

183 • B3 | Rock Creek (Mt Hood) (Mt Hood NF)

Total sites: 33, RV sites: 33, Central water, Vault/pit toilet, No showers, No RV dump, Tent & RV camping: $21-22, Open Apr-Oct, Max Length: 35ft, Reservations not accepted, Elev: 2213ft/675m, Tel: 503-668 1700, Nearest town: Dufur. GPS: 45.216783, -121.385783

184 • B3 | Scotts Camp (Ochoco NF)

Total sites: 3, RV sites: 3, No water, Vault/pit toilet, Tent & RV camping: Free, Stay limit: 14 days, Open all year, Reservations not accepted, Elev: 5423ft/1653m, Tel: 541-416-6500, Nearest town: Big Summit Prairie. GPS: 44.424523, -120.145264

185 • B3 | Skull Hollow Camp (Crooked River NG)

Total sites: 28, RV sites: 28, No water, Vault/pit toilet, Tent & RV camping: $10, Open May-Nov, Reservations not accepted, Elev: 3002ft/915m, Tel: 541-416-6640, Nearest town: Terrebonne. GPS: 44.397404, -121.062925

186 • B3 | Spring Drive RV Park (Mt Hood NF)

Total sites: 8, RV sites: 8, Elec sites: 8, Water at site, No toilets, No showers, RV dump, No tents/RVs: $32-34, 8 Full hookup sites, Open Apr-Sep, Max Length: 50ft, Reservations accepted, Elev: 3281ft/1000m, Tel: 541-328-0909, Nearest town: Maupin. GPS: 45.115316, -121.517711

187 • B3 | Sugar Creek (Ochoco NF)

Total sites: 3, RV sites: 3, Central water, Vault/pit toilet, No showers, No RV dump, Tent & RV camping: $8, Stay limit: 14 days, Open May-Oct, Reservations not accepted, Elev: 4042ft/1232m, Tel: 541-416-6500, Nearest town: Paulina. GPS: 44.233944, -119.805076

188 • B3 | Walton Lake (Ochoco NF)

Total sites: 27, RV sites: 21, Central water, Vault/pit toilet, No showers, No RV dump, Tent & RV camping: $15, 2 group sites $60, Stay limit: 14 days, Open May-Oct, Max Length: 40ft, Reservations accepted, Elev: 5194ft/1583m, Tel: 541-416-6500, Nearest town: Prineville. GPS: 44.433535, -120.336334

189 • B3 | Whistler (Ochoco NF)

Total sites: 4, RV sites: 4, No water, Vault/pit toilet, Tent & RV camping: Free, Very rough road, Stay limit: 14 days, Open all year, Reservations not accepted, Elev: 5745ft/1751m, Nearest town: Paulina. GPS: 44.497803, -120.482553

190 • B3 | White Rock (Ochoco NF)

Total sites: 3, RV sites: 1, No water, Vault/pit toilet, Tent & RV camping: Free, Stay limit: 14 days, Open all year, Reservations not accepted, Elev: 5479ft/1670m, Tel: 541-416-6500, Nearest town: Prineville. GPS: 44.423165, -120.543703

191 • B3 | Wildcat (Ochoco NF)

Total sites: 17, RV sites: 17, Central water, Vault/pit toilet, No showers, No RV dump, Tent & RV camping: $15, Stay limit: 14 days, Open May-Sep, Reservations not accepted, Elev: 3802ft/1159m, Tel: 541-416-6500, Nearest town: Prineville. GPS: 44.440303, -120.578431

192 • B3 | Wildwood (Ochoco NF)

Total sites: 5, RV sites: 5, No water, Vault/pit toilet, Tent & RV camping: Free, Stay limit: 14 days, Open all year, Reservations not accepted, Elev: 4869ft/1484m, Tel: 541-416-6500, Nearest town: Prineville. GPS: 44.485000, -120.335000

193 • B3 | Wolf Creek (Ochoco NF)

Total sites: 16, RV sites: 16, No water, Vault/pit toilet, Tent & RV camping: $6, No services in winter, Narrow CG roads with sharp turns, Stay limit: 14 days, Open all year, Max Length: 20ft,

Reservations not accepted, Elev: 4003ft/1220m, Tel: 541-416-6500, Nearest town: Paulina. GPS: 44.252930, -119.825928

194 • B4 | Anthony Lake (Wallowa-Whitman NF)

Total sites: 37, RV sites: 16, Central water, Vault/pit toilet, No showers, No RV dump, Tents: $10/RVs: $14, Stay limit: 14 days, Open Jul-Sep, Max Length: 22ft, Reservations not accepted, Elev: 7198ft/2194m, Tel: 541-523-6391, Nearest town: Haines. GPS: 44.961514, -118.228125

195 • B4 | Anthony Lake Tent CG (Wallowa-Whitman NF)

Total sites: 7, RV sites: 0, Central water, No toilets, No showers, No RV dump, Tents only: $10, Walk-to sites, Stay limit: 14 days, Open Jun-Sep, Reservations not accepted, Elev: 7165ft/2184m, Tel: 541-523-6391, Nearest town: Baker City. GPS: 44.958949, -118.229037

196 • B4 | Bear Wallow Creek (Umatilla NF)

Total sites: 8, RV sites: 8, No water, Vault/pit toilet, Tent & RV camping: $8, Free Nov-May - no services, Stay limit: 14 days, Open all year, Max Length: 25ft, Reservations not accepted, Elev: 3921ft/1195m, Tel: 541-278-3716, Nearest town: Ukiah. GPS: 45.184082, -118.752197

197 • B4 | Big Creek (Malheur NF)

Total sites: 15, RV sites: 15, No water, Vault/pit toilet, Tent & RV camping: $8, Road not plowed in winter, Stay limit: 14 days, Open all year, Reservations not accepted, Elev: 5135ft/1565m, Tel: 541-575-3000, Nearest town: Seneca. GPS: 44.187755, -118.616102

198 • B4 | Big Creek Meadows (Umatilla NF)

Total sites: 3, RV sites: 3, No water, Vault/pit toilet, Tent & RV camping: Free, Rough road, Stay limit: 14 days, Open all year, Reservations not accepted, Elev: 5066ft/1544m, Tel: 541-278-3716, Nearest town: Ukiah. GPS: 45.009755, -118.617112

199 • B4 | Billy Fields Forest Camp (Malheur NF)

Total sites: 4, RV sites: 3, No water, Vault/pit toilet, Tent & RV camping: Free, Stay limit: 14 days, Open Jun-Oct, Reservations not accepted, Elev: 4190ft/1277m, Tel: 541-575-3000, Nearest town: Mount Vernon. GPS: 44.346585, -119.299542

200 • B4 | Birdtrack Springs (Wallowa-Whitman NF)

Total sites: 22, RV sites: 22, No water, Vault/pit toilet, Tent & RV camping: $5, Stay limit: 14 days, Open May-Sep, Reservations not accepted, Elev: 3120ft/951m, Tel: 541-523-6391, Nearest town: La Grande. GPS: 45.300000, -118.306000

201 • B4 | Bull Prairie Lake (Umatilla NF)

Total sites: 59, RV sites: 58, Central water, Vault/pit toilet, No showers, RV dump, Tent & RV camping: $14, Group site: $28, Free - no services Nov-May, Stay limit: 14 days, Open all year, Reservations not accepted, Elev: 4058ft/1237m, Tel: 541-278-3716, Nearest town: Heppner. GPS: 44.972912, -119.663944

202 • B4 | Canyon Meadows (Malheur NF)

Total sites: 5, RV sites: 5, No water, Vault/pit toilet, Tent & RV camping: Free, Stay limit: 14 days, Open May-Sep, Reservations not accepted, Elev: 5197ft/1584m, Tel: 541-575-3000, Nearest town: Canyon City. GPS: 44.238525, -118.771973

203 • B4 | Coalmine Hill (Umatilla NF)

Total sites: 10, RV sites: 10, No water, Vault/pit toilet, Tent & RV camping: $8, Free Nov-May - no services, Stay limit: 14 days, Open all year, Reservations not accepted, Elev: 4856ft/1480m, Tel: 541-278-3716, Nearest town: Heppner. GPS: 45.167000, -119.332000

204 • B4 | Crescent (Malheur NF)

Total sites: 4, RV sites: 4, No water, Vault/pit toilet, Tent & RV camping: Free, Stay limit: 14 days, Open May-Sep, Reservations not accepted, Elev: 5236ft/1596m, Tel: 541-820-3800, Nearest town: Prairie City. GPS: 44.281779, -118.545261

205 • B4 | Deer Creek (Wallowa-Whitman NF)

Total sites: 6, RV sites: 0, No water, Vault/pit toilet, Tents only: Free, 4x4 or high clearance vehicle required, Stay limit: 14 days, Open May-Nov, Reservations not accepted, Elev: 4492ft/1369m, Tel: 541-523-4476, Nearest town: Sumpter. GPS: 44.747339, -118.106271

206 • B4 | Deerhorn Forest Camp (Malheur NF)

Total sites: 5, RV sites: 5, No water, Vault/pit toilet, Tent & RV camping: $8, Stay limit: 14 days, Open May-Sep, Reservations not accepted, Elev: 3993ft/1217m, Tel: 541-575-3000, Nearest town: Prairie City. GPS: 44.622625, -118.581575

207 • B4 | Divide Well (Umatilla NF)

Total sites: 11, RV sites: 11, No water, Vault/pit toilet, Tent & RV camping: Free, Snow-mobile access only Nov-May - no services, Stay limit: 14 days, Open all year, Reservations not accepted, Elev: 4747ft/1447m, Tel: 541-278-3716, Nearest town: Ukiah. GPS: 45.102637, -119.142102

208 • B4 | Dixie (Malheur NF)

Total sites: 10, RV sites: 10, No water, Vault/pit toilet, Tent & RV camping: $8, Stay limit: 14 days, Open May-Sep, Reservations not accepted, Elev: 5181ft/1579m, Tel: 541-820-3800, Nearest town: Prairie City. GPS: 44.538809, -118.589757

209 • B4 | Drift Fence (Umatilla NF)

Total sites: 6, RV sites: 4, No water, Vault/pit toilet, Tent & RV camping: Free, Nov-May - no services, Stay limit: 14 days, Open May-Nov, Reservations not accepted, Elev: 4626ft/1410m, Tel: 541-278-3716, Nearest town: Ukiah. GPS: 45.071777, -118.875732

210 • B4 | Driftwood (Umatilla NF)

Total sites: 6, RV sites: 6, No water, Vault/pit toilet, Tent & RV camping: $8, Free Nov-May - no services, Stay limit: 14 days, Open all year, Reservations not accepted, Elev: 3054ft/931m, Tel: 541-278-3716, Nearest town: Dale. GPS: 45.018687, -118.858867

211 • B4 | Elk Creek (Malheur NF)

Total sites: 5, RV sites: 5, No water, Vault/pit toilet, Tent & RV camping: Free, Stay limit: 14 days, Open May-Sep, Reservations not accepted, Elev: 5062ft/1543m, Tel: 541-820-3800, Nearest town: Prairie City. GPS: 44.245921, -118.398393

212 • B4 | Elk Creek (Rail Gulch) (Wallowa-Whitman NF)

Total sites: 10, RV sites: 6, No water, Vault/pit toilet, Tent & RV

camping: $5, Stay limit: 14 days, Open May-Oct, Reservations not accepted, Elev: 4518ft/1377m, Tel: 541-523-6391, Nearest town: Unity. GPS: 44.400649, -118.329041

213 • B4 | Fairview (Umatilla NF)

Total sites: 5, RV sites: 5, Central water, Vault/pit toilet, No showers, No RV dump, Tent & RV camping: Free, No services Nov-May, Stay limit: 14 days, Open all year, Reservations not accepted, Elev: 4324ft/1318m, Tel: 541-278-3716, Nearest town: Heppner. GPS: 44.955151, -119.712474

214 • B4 | Four Corners Sno-Park (Umatilla NF)

Total sites: 2, RV sites: 2, No water, Vault/pit toilet, Tent & RV camping: Free, Stay limit: 14 days, Elev: 4442ft/1354m, Tel: 541-278-3716, Nearest town: Ukiah. GPS: 45.178511, -118.606898

215 • B4 | Frazier (Umatilla NF)

Total sites: 20, RV sites: 20, Central water, Vault/pit toilet, No showers, No RV dump, Tent & RV camping: $10, Group site: $25, Free Nov-May - no services, Stay limit: 14 days, Open all year, Max Length: 40ft, Reservations not accepted, Elev: 4334ft/1321m, Tel: 541-278-3716, Nearest town: Ukiah. GPS: 45.159668, -118.639893

216 • B4 | Frazier (Ochoco NF)

Total sites: 10, RV sites: 9, No water, Vault/pit toilet, Tent & RV camping: Free, No services in winter, Stay limit: 14 days, Open May-Sep, Reservations not accepted, Elev: 4603ft/1403m, Tel: 541-416-6500, Nearest town: Prineville. GPS: 44.220865, -119.576757

217 • B4 | Frog Heaven Forest Camp (Wallowa-Whitman NF)

Total sites: 6, RV sites: 6, No water, No toilets, Tent & RV camping: Free, Stay limit: 14 days, Open May-Sep, Reservations not accepted, Elev: 4797ft/1462m, Tel: 541-523-6391, Nearest town: La Grande. GPS: 45.212624, -118.601921

218 • B4 | Gold Dredge (Umatilla NF)

Total sites: 7, RV sites: 7, No water, Vault/pit toilet, Tent & RV camping: $8, Free Nov-May - no services, Stay limit: 14 days, Open May-Nov, Max Length: 40ft, Reservations not accepted, Elev: 3110ft/948m, Tel: 541-278-3716, Nearest town: Dale. GPS: 45.001816, -118.819135

219 • B4 | Grande Ronde Lake (Wallowa-Whitman NF)

Total sites: 8, RV sites: 8, Central water, Vault/pit toilet, No showers, No RV dump, Tent & RV camping: $10, Stay limit: 14 days, Open Jul-Oct, Reservations not accepted, Elev: 7172ft/2186m, Tel: 541-523-6391, Nearest town: Baker City. GPS: 44.975441, -118.243155

220 • B4 | Head O Boulder Forest Camp (Malheur NF)

Total sites: 3, RV sites: 3, No water, Vault/pit toilet, Tent & RV camping: Free, Stay limit: 14 days, Reservations not accepted, Elev: 7182ft/2189m, Tel: 541-575-3000, Nearest town: Austin Junction. GPS: 44.755165, -118.692366

221 • B4 | Lane Creek (Umatilla NF)

Total sites: 7, RV sites: 7, No water, Vault/pit toilet, Tent & RV camping: $8, 1 group site $25, Free - no services Nov-May, Stay limit: 14 days, Open all year, Max Length: 20ft, Reservations not accepted, Elev: 3908ft/1191m, Tel: 541-278-3716, Nearest town: Ukiah. GPS: 45.189595, -118.766126

222 • B4 | Lower Camp Creek (Malheur NF)

Total sites: 6, RV sites: 6, No water, Vault/pit toilet, Tent & RV camping: $6, Stay limit: 14 days, Open Jun-Sep, Reservations not accepted, Elev: 3622ft/1104m, Tel: 541-820-3800, Nearest town: Prairie City. GPS: 44.673000, -118.799000

223 • B4 | Magone Lake (Malheur NF)

Total sites: 22, RV sites: 19, Central water, Vault/pit toilet, No showers, No RV dump, Tent & RV camping: $13, Reservable group site: $60, Stay limit: 14 days, Open May-Oct, Max Length: 50ft, Reservations not accepted, Elev: 5052ft/1540m, Tel: 541-820-3800, Nearest town: Mount Vernon. GPS: 44.552464, -118.911023

224 • B4 | McCully Forks (Wallowa-Whitman NF)

Total sites: 7, RV sites: 7, No water, Vault/pit toilet, Tent & RV camping: $6, Stay limit: 14 days, Open Jun-Sep, Reservations not accepted, Elev: 4632ft/1412m, Tel: 541-523-6391, Nearest town: Baker City. GPS: 44.767061, -118.247249

225 • B4 | Middle Fork (Malheur NF)

Total sites: 10, RV sites: 10, No water, Vault/pit toilet, Tent & RV camping: $8, Stay limit: 14 days, Open May-Sep, Max Length: 30ft, Reservations not accepted, Elev: 3917ft/1194m, Tel: 541-575-3000, Nearest town: Prairie City. GPS: 44.630019, -118.605254

226 • B4 | Millers Lane (Wallowa-Whitman NF)

Total sites: 8, RV sites: 4, No water, Vault/pit toilet, Tent & RV camping: $10, Small RVs, Stay limit: 14 days, Open May-Sep, Reservations not accepted, Elev: 4065ft/1239m, Tel: 541-523-6391, Nearest town: Baker City. GPS: 44.673317, -118.068025

227 • B4 | Mud Lake (Wallowa-Whitman NF)

Total sites: 7, RV sites: 7, No water, Vault/pit toilet, Tent & RV camping: $10, Reservable group site: $50, Stay limit: 14 days, Open Jul-Oct, Max Length: 18ft, Reservations not accepted, Elev: 7134ft/2174m, Tel: 541-894-2393, Nearest town: Baker City. GPS: 44.964459, -118.232954

228 • B4 | Mud Springs Horse Camp (Ochoco NF)

Total sites: 6, RV sites: 6, No water, Vault/pit toilet, Tent & RV camping: Free, 9 corrals, Stay limit: 14 days, Reservations not accepted, Elev: 4938ft/1505m, Tel: 541-416-6500, Nearest town: Paulina. GPS: 44.302028, -119.646881

229 • B4 | Murray (Malheur NF)

Total sites: 5, RV sites: 5, No water, Vault/pit toilet, Tent & RV camping: $8, Stay limit: 14 days, Open May-Sep, Reservations not accepted, Elev: 5299ft/1615m, Tel: 541-575-3000, Nearest town: Seneca. GPS: 44.212369, -118.638214

230 • B4 | North Fork John Day (Umatilla NF)

Total sites: 20, RV sites: 15, No water, Vault/pit toilet, Tent & RV camping: $8, Free Nov-May - no services, Stay limit: 14 days, Open all year, Reservations not accepted, Elev: 5236ft/1596m, Tel: 541-278-3716, Nearest town: Granite. GPS: 44.913985, -118.401882

231 • B4 | North Fork Malheur (Malheur NF)

Total sites: 5, RV sites: 5, No water, Vault/pit toilet, Tent & RV camping: Free, Stay limit: 14 days, Open May-Sep, Reservations not accepted, Elev: 4780ft/1457m, Tel: 541-820-3800, Nearest town: Prairie City. GPS: 44.208885, -118.382434

232 • B4 | Olive Lake (Umatilla NF)

Total sites: 23, RV sites: 23, No water, Vault/pit toilet, Tent & RV camping: $12, Free Nov-May - no services, Stay limit: 14 days, Open all year, Max Length: 40ft, Reservations not accepted, Elev: 6061ft/1847m, Tel: 541-278-3716, Nearest town: Granite. GPS: 44.784424, -118.598292

233 • B4 | Oregon (Wallowa-Whitman NF)

Total sites: 8, RV sites: 8, Central water, Vault/pit toilet, No showers, No RV dump, Tent & RV camping: $5, Stay limit: 14 days, Open Jun-Sep, Max Length: 16ft, Reservations not accepted, Elev: 5016ft/1529m, Tel: 541-523-6391, Nearest town: Unity. GPS: 44.546231, -118.341067

234 • B4 | Oregon Mine (Malheur NF)

Total sites: 1, RV sites: 1, No water, Vault/pit toilet, Tent & RV camping: Free, Stay limit: 14 days, Open all year, Reservations not accepted, Elev: 4409ft/1344m, Tel: 541-575-3000, Nearest town: John Day. GPS: 44.276935, -119.296968

235 • B4 | Oriental (Umatilla NF)

Total sites: 7, RV sites: 7, No water, Vault/pit toilet, Tent & RV camping: $8, Free Nov-May - no services, Rough road, Stay limit: 14 days, Open May-Nov, Reservations not accepted, Elev: 3297ft/1005m, Tel: 541-278-3716, Nearest town: Dale. GPS: 44.973976, -118.727448

236 • B4 | Parish Cabin (Malheur NF)

Total sites: 18, RV sites: 18, No water, Vault/pit toilet, Tent & RV camping: $8, Stay limit: 14 days, Open May-Sep, Reservations not accepted, Elev: 4980ft/1518m, Tel: 541-575-3000, Nearest town: Seneca. GPS: 44.179932, -118.765381

237 • B4 | Penland Lake (Umatilla NF)

Total sites: 12, RV sites: 10, No water, Vault/pit toilet, Tent & RV camping: $8, Free Nov-May - no services, Rough road, Stay limit: 14 days, Open all year, Reservations not accepted, Elev: 4951ft/1509m, Tel: 541-278-3716, Nearest town: Heppner. GPS: 45.118641, -119.315989

238 • B4 | Slide Creek (Malheur NF)

Total sites: 3, RV sites: 3, No water, Vault/pit toilet, Tent & RV camping: Free, Stay limit: 14 days, Open May-Sep, Reservations not accepted, Elev: 4934ft/1504m, Tel: 541-820-3800, Nearest town: Prairie City. GPS: 44.342302, -118.657366

239 • B4 | South Fork Camp Creek (Wallowa-Whitman NF)

Total sites: 14, RV sites: 12, Vault/pit toilet, Tent & RV camping: $5, Stay limit: 14 days, Open May-Oct, Reservations not accepted, Elev: 4829ft/1472m, Tel: 541-523-6391, Nearest town: Unity. GPS: 44.343018, -118.201416

240 • B4 | Southwest Shore (Wallowa-Whitman NF)

Total sites: 16, RV sites: 16, No water, Vault/pit toilet, Tent & RV camping: $10, Stay limit: 14 days, Open May-Sep, Reservations not accepted, Elev: 4098ft/1249m, Tel: 541-523-6391, Nearest town: Baker City. GPS: 44.675308, -118.082142

241 • B4 | Spool Cart (Wallowa-Whitman NF)

Total sites: 12, RV sites: 12, No water, Vault/pit toilet, Tent & RV camping: $5, Stay limit: 14 days, Open May-Sep, Max Length: 45ft, Reservations not accepted, Elev: 3550ft/1082m, Tel: 541-523-6391, Nearest town: La Grande. GPS: 45.202634, -118.394946

242 • B4 | Starr (Malheur NF)

Total sites: 10, RV sites: 10, No water, Vault/pit toilet, Tent & RV camping: $6, 1 group site, Stay limit: 14 days, Open May-Sep, Reservations not accepted, Elev: 5143ft/1568m, Tel: 541-575-3000, Nearest town: John Day. GPS: 44.259825, -119.016918

243 • B4 | Stevens Creek (Wallowa-Whitman NF)

Total sites: 7, RV sites: 0, No water, Vault/pit toilet, Tents only: $5, Stay limit: 14 days, Open May-Sep, Reservations not accepted, Elev: 4524ft/1379m, Tel: 541-523-6391, Nearest town: Unity. GPS: 44.400181, -118.320831

244 • B4 | Strawberry (Malheur NF)

Total sites: 10, RV sites: 10, Central water, Vault/pit toilet, Tent & RV camping: $8, Stay limit: 14 days, Open May-Sep, Reservations not accepted, Elev: 5761ft/1756m, Tel: 541-820-3311, Nearest town: Prairie City. GPS: 44.319241, -118.674645

245 • B4 | Toll Bridge (Umatilla NF)

Total sites: 5, RV sites: 5, No water, Vault/pit toilet, Tent & RV camping: $8, Free Nov-May - no services, Rough road, Stay limit: 14 days, Open all year, Reservations not accepted, Elev: 2822ft/860m, Tel: 541-278-3716, Nearest town: Mt Hood. GPS: 44.996787, -118.934915

246 • B4 | Trout Farm (Malheur NF)

Total sites: 6, RV sites: 6, Central water, Vault/pit toilet, No showers, No RV dump, Tent & RV camping: $8, Stay limit: 14 days, Open May-Sep, Reservations not accepted, Elev: 4980ft/1518m, Tel: 541-820-3800, Nearest town: Prairie City. GPS: 44.305178, -118.551941

247 • B4 | Umapine (Wallowa-Whitman NF)

Total sites: 5, RV sites: 5, No water, Vault/pit toilet, Tent & RV camping: Free, Stay limit: 14 days, Open May-Sep, Reservations not accepted, Elev: 5079ft/1548m, Tel: 541-523-6391, Nearest town: Ukiah. GPS: 45.114075, -118.562078

248 • B4 | Union Creek (Wallowa) (Wallowa-Whitman NF)

Total sites: 78, RV sites: 60, Elec sites: 55, Water at site, Flush toilet, No showers, No RV dump, Tent & RV camping: $27-40, 22 Full hookup sites, Group sites: $60, Stay limit: 14 days, Open May-Sep, Max Length: 60ft, Reservations accepted, Elev: 4144ft/1263m, Tel: 541-523-6391, Nearest town: Baker City. GPS: 44.687861, -118.027186

249 • B4 | Welch Creek (Umatilla NF)

Total sites: 7, RV sites: 7, No water, Vault/pit toilet, Tent & RV camping: $8, Free Nov-May - no services – snowmobile access, Stay limit: 14 days, Open May-Nov, Reservations not accepted,

Elev: 4646ft/1416m, Tel: 541-278-3716, Nearest town: Dale. GPS: 44.876896, -118.778417

250 • B4 | Wetmore (Wallowa-Whitman NF)

Total sites: 12, RV sites: 12, Central water, Vault/pit toilet, No showers, No RV dump, Tent & RV camping: $5, Stay limit: 14 days, Open May-Sep, Reservations not accepted, Elev: 4370ft/1332m, Tel: 541-523-6391, Nearest town: Unity. GPS: 44.523835, -118.303948

251 • B4 | Wickiup (Malheur NF)

Total sites: 6, RV sites: 6, No water, Vault/pit toilet, Tent & RV camping: $6, Group site also, Stay limit: 14 days, Open May-Sep, Reservations not accepted, Elev: 4353ft/1327m, Tel: 541-575-3000, Nearest town: John Day. GPS: 44.217596, -118.853663

252 • B4 | Winom Creek (Umatilla NF)

Total sites: 7, RV sites: 7, No water, Vault/pit toilet, Tent & RV camping: $10, Free Nov-May - no services, Stay limit: 14 days, Open May-Nov, Reservations not accepted, Elev: 4944ft/1507m, Tel: 541-278-3716, Nearest town: Ukiah. GPS: 45.012236, -118.641641

253 • B4 | Yellow Pine (Wallowa-Whitman NF)

Total sites: 20, RV sites: 20, Central water, Vault/pit toilet, No showers, No RV dump, Tent & RV camping: $5, Stay limit: 14 days, Open May-Sep, Reservations not accepted, Elev: 4478ft/1365m, Tel: 541-523-6391, Nearest town: Unity. GPS: 44.530272, -118.310439

254 • B5 | Arrow Forest Camp (Wallowa-Whitman NF)

Total sites: 3, RV sites: 0, No water, Vault/pit toilet, Tents only: $5, Stay limit: 14 days, Open Jun-Sep, Reservations not accepted, Elev: 5469ft/1667m, Tel: 541-523-6391, Nearest town: Enterprise. GPS: 45.265666, -117.385674

255 • B5 | Blackhorse (Wallowa-Whitman NF)

Total sites: 16, RV sites: 16, No water, Vault/pit toilet, Tent & RV camping: $8, Stay limit: 14 days, Open Jun-Sep, Reservations not accepted, Elev: 3980ft/1213m, Tel: 541-426-5546, Nearest town: Joseph. GPS: 45.158753, -116.874729

256 • B5 | Boulder Park (Wallowa-Whitman NF)

Total sites: 7, RV sites: 7, No water, Vault/pit toilet, Tent & RV camping: Free, Stay limit: 14 days, Open May-Sep, Elev: 4954ft/1510m, Tel: 541-523-6391, Nearest town: Medical Springs. GPS: 45.068311, -117.406406

257 • B5 | Buck Creek Forest Camp (Wallowa-Whitman NF)

Total sites: 4, RV sites: 4, No water, Vault/pit toilet, Tent & RV camping: $5, Stay limit: 14 days, Open May-Oct, Reservations not accepted, Elev: 5558ft/1694m, Tel: 541-426-5546, Nearest town: Union. GPS: 45.148123, -117.572106

258 • B5 | Coverdale (Wallowa-Whitman NF)

Total sites: 7, RV sites: 2, No water, Vault/pit toilet, Tent & RV camping: $6, Stay limit: 14 days, Open Jun-Sep, Reservations not accepted, Elev: 4318ft/1316m, Tel: 541-523-6391, Nearest town: Enterprise. GPS: 45.108154, -116.923340

259 • B5 | Eagle Forks (Wallowa-Whitman NF)

Total sites: 8, RV sites: 8, Central water, Vault/pit toilet, No showers, No RV dump, Tent & RV camping: $5, Stay limit: 14 days, Open May-Sep, Reservations not accepted, Elev: 3058ft/932m, Tel: 541-523-6391, Nearest town: Richland. GPS: 44.891494, -117.262072

260 • B5 | Fish Lake (Deadman Point) (Wallowa-Whitman NF)

Total sites: 21, RV sites: 21, Central water, Vault/pit toilet, No showers, No RV dump, Tent & RV camping: $6, Stay limit: 14 days, Open Jun-Oct, Max Length: 30ft, Reservations not accepted, Elev: 6722ft/2049m, Tel: 541-523-6391, Nearest town: Halfway. GPS: 45.050381, -117.095487

261 • B5 | Hidden (Wallowa-Whitman NF)

Total sites: 10, RV sites: 10, No water, Vault/pit toilet, Tent & RV camping: $6, Stay limit: 14 days, Open Jun-Sep, Reservations not accepted, Elev: 4537ft/1383m, Tel: 541-523-6391, Nearest town: Joseph. GPS: 45.113770, -116.980225

262 • B5 | Indian Crossing (Wallowa-Whitman NF)

Total sites: 14, RV sites: 14, No water, Vault/pit toilet, Tent & RV camping: $6, Stay limit: 14 days, Open Jun-Oct, Reservations not accepted, Elev: 4606ft/1404m, Tel: 541-523-6391, Nearest town: Joseph. GPS: 45.113214, -117.013494

263 • B5 | Irondyke Forest Camp (Wallowa-Whitman NF)

Total sites: 5, RV sites: 0, No water, Vault/pit toilet, Tents only: $5, Stay limit: 14 days, Open Jun-Sep, Reservations not accepted, Elev: 5213ft/1589m, Tel: 541-523-6391, Nearest town: Lostine. GPS: 45.297648, -117.396855

264 • B5 | Lake Fork (Wallowa-Whitman NF)

Total sites: 10, RV sites: 10, No water, Vault/pit toilet, Tent & RV camping: $6, Stay limit: 14 days, Open May-Oct, Reservations not accepted, Elev: 3242ft/988m, Nearest town: Joseph. GPS: 45.008392, -116.912068

265 • B5 | Lick Creek (Wallowa-Whitman NF)

Total sites: 12, RV sites: 5, No water, Vault/pit toilet, Tent & RV camping: $6, Stay limit: 14 days, Open Jun-Sep, Reservations not accepted, Elev: 5472ft/1668m, Tel: 541-523-6391, Nearest town: Joseph. GPS: 45.158159, -117.034239

266 • B5 | McBride (Wallowa-Whitman NF)

Total sites: 7, RV sites: 7, No water, Vault/pit toilet, Tent & RV camping: Free, Stay limit: 14 days, Open Jul-Sep, Max Length: 30ft, Reservations not accepted, Elev: 4774ft/1455m, Tel: 541-523-6391, Nearest town: Halfway. GPS: 44.934672, -117.222522

267 • B5 | Moss Springs (Wallowa-Whitman NF)

Total sites: 8, RV sites: 8, No water, Vault/pit toilet, Tent & RV camping: $5, Stay limit: 14 days, Open Jun-Sep, Max Length: 18ft, Reservations not accepted, Elev: 5896ft/1797m, Tel: 541-523-6391, Nearest town: Cove. GPS: 45.275204, -117.679141

268 • B5 | North Fork Catherine Creek (Wallowa-Whitman NF)

Total sites: 7, RV sites: 7, No water, No toilets, Tent & RV camping: Free, Campsites are composed of pull-off parking areas and several small campsites along the road, Stay limit: 14 days, Open Jun-Sep, Max Length: 18ft, Reservations not accepted, Elev:

3937ft/1200m, Tel: 541-523-6391, Nearest town: La Grande. GPS: 45.131867, -117.629586

269 • B5 | Ollokot (Wallowa-Whitman NF)

Total sites: 12, RV sites: 12, Central water, Vault/pit toilet, No showers, No RV dump, Tent & RV camping: $8, Stay limit: 14 days, Open Jun-Oct, Reservations not accepted, Elev: 4042ft/1232m, Tel: 541-523-6391, Nearest town: Enterprise. GPS: 45.151436, -116.876775

270 • B5 | PO Saddle Trailhead (Wallowa-Whitman NF)

Total sites: 10, RV sites: 0, No water, Vault/pit toilet, Tents only: $5, Stay limit: 14 days, Reservations not accepted, Elev: 5827ft/1776m, Tel: 541-523-6391, Nearest town: Halfway. GPS: 45.236091, -116.766372

271 • B5 | Shady (Wallowa-Whitman NF)

Total sites: 11, RV sites: 7, No water, Vault/pit toilet, Tent & RV camping: $5, Stay limit: 14 days, Open Jun-Sep, Reservations not accepted, Elev: 5528ft/1685m, Tel: 541-523-6391, Nearest town: Enterprise. GPS: 45.257324, -117.383789

272 • B5 | Tamarack (Wallowa-Whitman NF)

Total sites: 12, RV sites: 12, Central water, Vault/pit toilet, No showers, No RV dump, Tent & RV camping: $6, Stay limit: 14 days, Open Jun-Sep, Reservations not accepted, Elev: 4531ft/1381m, Tel: 541-523-6391, Nearest town: Baker City. GPS: 45.019804, -117.453801

273 • B5 | Turkey Flat Forest Camp (Wallowa-Whitman NF)

Total sites: 4, RV sites: 4, No water, Vault/pit toilet, Tent & RV camping: $5, Stay limit: 14 days, Open Jun-Sep, Max Length: 18ft, Reservations not accepted, Elev: 5440ft/1658m, Tel: 541-523-6391, Nearest town: Lostine. GPS: 45.279683, -117.390693

274 • B5 | Twin Lakes (Wallowa-Whitman NF)

Total sites: 8, RV sites: 0, No water, Vault/pit toilet, Tents only: Free, Stay limit: 14 days, Open Jun-Sep, Reservations not accepted, Elev: 6427ft/1959m, Tel: 541-523-6391, Nearest town: Halfway. GPS: 45.079846, -117.055333

275 • B5 | Two Color (Wallowa-Whitman NF)

Total sites: 11, RV sites: 11, No water, Vault/pit toilet, Tent & RV camping: Free, Stay limit: 14 days, Open Jun-Sep, Reservations not accepted, Elev: 4806ft/1465m, Tel: 541-523-6391, Nearest town: Baker City. GPS: 45.037354, -117.445557

276 • B5 | Two Pan (Wallowa-Whitman NF)

Total sites: 5, RV sites: 5, No water, Vault/pit toilet, Tent & RV camping: $5, Stay limit: 14 days, Open Jun-Sep, Max Length: 18ft, Reservations not accepted, Elev: 5732ft/1747m, Tel: 541-523-6391, Nearest town: Enterprise. GPS: 45.250459, -117.376091

277 • B5 | West Eagle Meadow (Wallowa-Whitman NF)

Total sites: 12, RV sites: 5, No water, Vault/pit toilet, Tent & RV camping: $5, Road extremely rough - not recommended for passenger cars or trailers, Stay limit: 14 days, Open Jul-Sep, Max Length: 18ft, Reservations not accepted, Elev: 5528ft/1685m, Tel: 541-523-6391, Nearest town: La Grande. GPS: 45.079813, -117.476694

278 • C1 | Bluebill Lake (Siuslaw NF)

Total sites: 18, RV sites: 18, Central water, Vault/pit toilet, No showers, No RV dump, Tent & RV camping: $22, Stay limit: 14 days, Open May-Sep, Max Length: 85ft, Reservations accepted, Elev: 36ft/11m, Tel: 541-271-6000, Nearest town: North Bend. GPS: 43.450463, -124.261922

279 • C1 | Carter Lake (Siuslaw NF)

Total sites: 23, RV sites: 23, Central water, Flush toilet, No showers, No RV dump, Tent & RV camping: $22, Stay limit: 14 days, Open May-Sep, Max Length: 30ft, Reservations accepted, Elev: 89ft/27m, Tel: 541-271-6000, Nearest town: Florence. GPS: 43.857229, -124.145963

280 • C1 | Driftwood II OHV (Siuslaw NF)

Total sites: 67, RV sites: 67, Central water, Flush toilet, Pay showers, No RV dump, Tent & RV camping: $25, Stay limit: 14 days, Open all year, Max Length: 61ft, Reservations accepted, Elev: 33ft/10m, Tel: 541-271-3611, Nearest town: Florence. GPS: 43.881121, -124.148414

281 • C1 | Eel Creek (Siuslaw NF)

Total sites: 53, RV sites: 53, Central water, Flush toilet, No showers, No RV dump, Tent & RV camping: $22, Stay limit: 14 days, Open all year, Max Length: 54ft, Reservations accepted, Elev: 95ft/29m, Tel: 541-271-6000, Nearest town: Reedsport. GPS: 43.588447, -124.186566

282 • C1 | Horsfall Beach (Siuslaw NF)

Total sites: 34, RV sites: 34, Central water, Flush toilet, No showers, No RV dump, Tent & RV camping: $25, Stay limit: 14 days, Open all year, Max Length: 61ft, Reservations required, Elev: 13ft/4m, Tel: 541-271-3611, Nearest town: North Bend. GPS: 43.453695, -124.276075

283 • C1 | Lagoon (Siuslaw NF)

Total sites: 39, RV sites: 39, Central water, Flush toilet, No showers, No RV dump, Tent & RV camping: $22, Stay limit: 14 days, Open all year, Max Length: 35ft, Reservations accepted, Elev: 30ft/9m, Tel: 541-271-3611, Nearest town: Florence. GPS: 43.879944, -124.142074

284 • C1 | Oregon Dunes NRA - Hauser Sand Camps (Oregon Dunes NRA)

Total sites: 25, RV sites: 8, No water, No toilets, Tent & RV camping: $10, 2 group sites: $20, 4x4 required, Bring portable toilets, Fire pans required, Max Length: 100ft, Reservations accepted, Elev: 39ft/12m, Tel: 541-271-3611, Nearest town: Florence. GPS: 43.489093, -124.227067

285 • C1 | Oregon Dunes NRA - Horsfall OHV (Siuslaw NF)

Total sites: 70, RV sites: 70, Central water, Flush toilet, Free showers, No RV dump, Tent & RV camping: $25, Stay limit: 14 days, Open all year, Max Length: 52ft, Reservations accepted, Elev: 43ft/13m, Tel: 541-271-3611, Nearest town: North Bend. GPS: 43.441576, -124.246016

286 • C1 | Oregon Dunes NRA - Horsfall Sand Camps (Siuslaw NF)

Total sites: 36, RV sites: 21, No water, No toilets, Tent & RV camping: $10, 3 group sites: $20, 4x4 required, Portable toilet and fire pan required, Stay limit: 14 days, Max Length: 100ft, Reservations accepted, Elev: 24ft/7m, Tel: 541-271-6000, Nearest town: North Bend. GPS: 43.443288, -124.244308

287 • C1 | Oregon Dunes NRA - Siltcoos Sand Camps (Oregon Dunes NRA)

Total sites: 16, RV sites: 16, No water, No toilets, Tent & RV camping: $10, Group site: $20, 4x4 required, Portable toilet and fire pan required, Max Length: 100ft, Reservations accepted, Elev: 23ft/7m, Tel: 541-271-6000, Nearest town: Florence. GPS: 43.890856, -124.145347

288 • C1 | Oregon Dunes NRA - South Jetty Sand Camps (Oregon Dunes NRA)

Total sites: 14, RV sites: 13, No water, No toilets, Tent & RV camping: $10, Group site: $20, 4x4 required, Portable toilet and fire pan required, Max Length: 100ft, Reservations accepted, Elev: 46ft/14m, Tel: 541-271-6000, Nearest town: Florence. GPS: 43.954263, -124.130618

289 • C1 | Oregon Dunes NRA - Spinreel OHV (Siuslaw NF)

Total sites: 36, RV sites: 36, Water at site, Flush toilet, No showers, No RV dump, Tent & RV camping: $25, OHV campground, Stay limit: 14 days, Open all year, Max Length: 61ft, Reservations accepted, Elev: 22ft/7m, Tel: 541-271-3611, Nearest town: Reedsport. GPS: 43.568766, -124.203247

290 • C1 | Oregon Dunes NRA - Spinreel Sand Camps (Siuslaw NF)

Total sites: 10, No water, No toilets, Tents only: $10, Group site: $20, 4x4 required, Portable toilet and fire pan required, Stay limit: 14 days, Reservations accepted, Elev: 27ft/8m, Tel: 541-271-6000, Nearest town: Lakeside. GPS: 43.568399, -124.213182

291 • C1 | Oregon Dunes NRA - Umpqua Sand Camps North (Siuslaw NF)

Total sites: 27, RV sites: 0, No water, No toilets, Tents only: $10, 2 group sites: $20, 4x4 required, Portable toilet and fire pan required, Stay limit: 14 days, Open all year, Reservations accepted, Elev: 22ft/7m, Tel: 541-271-6000, Nearest town: Winchester Bay. GPS: 43.632409, -124.211527

292 • C1 | Sutton (Siuslaw NF)

Total sites: 77, RV sites: 77, Elec sites: 22, Central water, Flush toilet, No showers, No RV dump, Tents: $26/RVs: $26-34, Group sites: $85-$148, Stay limit: 14 days, Open all year, Max Length: 111ft, Reservations accepted, Elev: 44ft/13m, Tel: 541-563-8400, Nearest town: Florence. GPS: 44.053989, -124.106445

293 • C1 | Takhenitch (Siuslaw NF)

Total sites: 34, RV sites: 34, Central water, Flush toilet, No showers, No RV dump, Tent & RV camping: $22, Stay limit: 14 days, Open May-Sep, Max Length: 36ft, Reservations accepted, Elev: 49ft/15m, Tel: 541-271-6000, Nearest town: Reedsport. GPS: 43.795898, -124.148682

294 • C1 | Takhenitch Landing (Siuslaw NF)

Total sites: 27, RV sites: 27, No water, Vault/pit toilet, No showers, No RV dump, Tent & RV camping: $22, Stay limit: 14 days, Open all year, Max Length: 40ft, Reservations accepted, Elev: 92ft/28m, Tel: 541-271-6000, Nearest town: Florence. GPS: 43.800369, -124.145994

295 • C1 | Tyee (Siuslaw NF)

Total sites: 9, RV sites: 9, Central water, Vault/pit toilet, No showers, No RV dump, Tent & RV camping: $22, Stay limit: 14 days, Open May-Sep, Max Length: 20ft, Reservations accepted, Elev: 72ft/22m, Tel: 541-271-6000, Nearest town: Florence. GPS: 43.883461, -124.122236

296 • C1 | Waxmyrtle (Siuslaw NF)

Total sites: 55, RV sites: 55, Central water, Flush toilet, No showers, No RV dump, Tent & RV camping: $22, Stay limit: 14 days, Open May-Sep, Max Length: 85ft, Reservations accepted, Elev: 33ft/10m, Tel: 541-271-3611, Nearest town: Florence. GPS: 43.876487, -124.143307

297 • C1 | Wild Mare Horse Camp (Siuslaw NF)

Total sites: 12, RV sites: 12, Central water, Vault/pit toilet, No showers, No RV dump, Tent & RV camping: $22, Stay limit: 14 days, Open all year, Max Length: 61ft, Reservations accepted, Elev: 26ft/8m, Tel: 541-271-6000, Nearest town: North Bend. GPS: 43.450857, -124.266247

298 • C2 | Apple Creek (Umpqua NF)

Total sites: 8, RV sites: 8, No water, Vault/pit toilet, Tent & RV camping: $10, Stay limit: 14 days, Generator hours: 0600-2200, Open May-Sep, Max Length: 22ft, Reservations not accepted, Elev: 1457ft/444m, Tel: 541-957-3200, Nearest town: North Umpqua. GPS: 43.305406, -122.676727

299 • C2 | Ash Flat Forest Camp (Umpqua NF)

Total sites: 4, RV sites: 4, No water, Vault/pit toilet, Tent & RV camping: $10, Stay limit: 14 days, Generator hours: 0600-2200, Max Length: 35ft, Reservations not accepted, Elev: 1654ft/504m, Tel: 541-825-3100, Nearest town: Tiller. GPS: 43.045037, -122.732246

300 • C2 | Bedrock (Willamette NF)

Total sites: 15, RV sites: 9, No water, Vault/pit toilet, Tent & RV camping: $17, Stay limit: 14 days, Generator hours: 0600-2200, Open Apr-Sep, Max Length: 30ft, Reservations not accepted, Elev: 1263ft/385m, Tel: 541-782-2283, Nearest town: Lowell. GPS: 43.973251, -122.546771

301 • C2 | Big Pool (Willamette NF)

Total sites: 5, RV sites: 1, No water, Vault/pit toilet, Tent & RV camping: $14, Stay limit: 14 days, Generator hours: 0600-2200, Open Apr-Sep, Max Length: 14ft, Reservations not accepted, Elev: 1001ft/305m, Nearest town: Lowell. GPS: 43.966481, -122.598404

302 • C2 | Black Canyon (Willamette NF)

Total sites: 72, RV sites: 59, Central water, Vault/pit toilet, No showers, No RV dump, Tent & RV camping: $21, Stay limit: 14 days, Generator hours: 0600-2200, Open May-Sep, Max Length: 44ft, Reservations accepted, Elev: 1017ft/310m, Tel: 541-782-2283, Nearest town: Oakridge. GPS: 43.806396, -122.566650

303 • C2 | Blair Lake (Willamette NF)

Total sites: 7, RV sites: 0, Central water, Vault/pit toilet, No showers, No RV dump, Tents only: $8, Also walk-to sites, 4, Stay limit: 14 days, Generator hours: 0600-2200, Open Jun-Sep, Reservations not accepted, Elev: 4787ft/1459m, Tel: 541-782-2283, Nearest town: Oakridge. GPS: 43.836113, -122.241594

304 • C2 | Blue Pool (Willamette NF)

Total sites: 24, RV sites: 17, Central water, No toilets, No showers, No RV dump, Tent & RV camping: $19, 7 walk-to sites, Stay limit: 14 days, Generator hours: 0600-2200, Open May-Sep, Max Length: 20ft, Reservations not accepted, Elev: 2031ft/619m, Tel: 541-782-2283, Nearest town: Oakridge. GPS: 43.708984, -122.298584

305 • C2 | Bogus Creek (Umpqua NF)

Total sites: 15, RV sites: 15, Central water, No toilets, No showers, No RV dump, Tent & RV camping: $15, Stay limit: 14 days, Generator hours: 0600-2200, Open May-Oct, Max Length: 35ft, Reservations accepted, Elev: 1266ft/386m, Tel: 541-496-3534, Nearest town: Idleyld Park. GPS: 43.324755, -122.800278

306 • C2 | Boulder Creek (Umpqua NF)

Total sites: 7, RV sites: 7, Central water, Vault/pit toilet, No showers, No RV dump, Tent & RV camping: $10, Stay limit: 14 days, Generator hours: 0600-2200, Open May-Oct, Max Length: 22ft, Reservations not accepted, Elev: 1522ft/464m, Tel: 541-825-3100, Nearest town: Tiller. GPS: 43.053971, -122.777537

307 • C2 | Boulder Flat (Umpqua NF)

Total sites: 9, RV sites: 9, No water, Vault/pit toilet, No showers, No RV dump, Tent & RV camping: $10, Stay limit: 14 days, Generator hours: 0600-2200, Open all year, Max Length: 24ft, Reservations accepted, Elev: 1791ft/546m, Tel: 541-498-2515, Nearest town: Idleyld Park. GPS: 43.303947, -122.526648

308 • C2 | Broken Arrow (Umpqua NF)

Total sites: 128, RV sites: 128, Central water, Flush toilet, Free showers, RV dump, Tent & RV camping: $15, 3 group sites $70-$95, Stay limit: 14 days, Generator hours: 0600-2200, Open Jun-Sep, Max Length: 70ft, Reservations accepted, Elev: 5220ft/1591m, Tel: 541-498-2531, Nearest town: Diamond Lake. GPS: 43.133347, -122.143579

309 • C2 | Broken Bowl (Willamette NF)

Total sites: 16, RV sites: 6, Central water, Flush toilet, No showers, No RV dump, Tent & RV camping: $19, 3 walk-to sites, Stay limit: 14 days, Generator hours: 0600-2200, Open Apr-Sep, Max Length: 20ft, Reservations not accepted, Elev: 1089ft/332m, Tel: 541-782-2283, Nearest town: Lowell. GPS: 43.962058, -122.610583

310 • C2 | Buckhead Mt (Umpqua NF)

Total sites: 3, RV sites: 3, Vault/pit toilet, Tent & RV camping: Free, Stay limit: 14 days, Max Length: 18ft, Elev: 5075ft/1547m, Tel: 541-825-3100, Nearest town: North Umpqua. GPS: 43.177256, -122.625617

311 • C2 | Bull Bend (Deschutes NF)

Total sites: 12, RV sites: 12, No water, Vault/pit toilet, Tent & RV camping: $12, Open May-Oct, Max Length: 30ft, Reservations not accepted, Elev: 4275ft/1303m, Tel: 541-383-4000, Nearest town: La Pine. GPS: 43.725398, -121.628082

312 • C2 | Bunker Hill (Umpqua NF)

Total sites: 5, RV sites: 5, No water, Vault/pit toilet, No showers, No RV dump, Tent & RV camping: $10, Stay limit: 14 days, Generator hours: 0600-2200, Open Jun-Oct, Max Length: 25ft, Reservations accepted, Elev: 4278ft/1304m, Tel: 541-498-2531, Nearest town: Diamond Lake. GPS: 43.319346, -122.187985

313 • C2 | Camp Comfort (Umpqua NF)

Total sites: 5, RV sites: 5, No water, Vault/pit toilet, Tent & RV camping: $10, Stay limit: 14 days, Generator hours: 0600-2200, Open all year, Max Length: 22ft, Reservations not accepted, Elev: 2156ft/657m, Tel: 541-825-3100, Nearest town: Tiller. GPS: 43.105919, -122.593664

314 • C2 | Campers Flat (Willamette NF)

Total sites: 5, RV sites: 5, Central water, Vault/pit toilet, No showers, No RV dump, Tent & RV camping: $14, Stay limit: 14 days, Generator hours: 0600-2200, Open May-Sep, Max Length: 18ft, Reservations not accepted, Elev: 2087ft/636m, Tel: 541-782-2283, Nearest town: Oakridge. GPS: 43.500845, -122.413367

315 • C2 | Canton Creek (Umpqua NF)

Total sites: 5, RV sites: 5, Central water, No toilets, No showers, No RV dump, Tent & RV camping: $10, Stay limit: 14 days, Generator hours: 0600-2200, Open May-Sep, Max Length: 24ft, Reservations accepted, Elev: 1201ft/366m, Tel: 541-496-3532, Nearest town: North Umpqua. GPS: 43.348321, -122.729937

316 • C2 | Cedar Creek (Umpqua NF)

Total sites: 10, RV sites: 10, No water, Vault/pit toilet, Tent & RV camping: $8, Stay limit: 14 days, Generator hours: 0600-2200, Open May-Sep, Max Length: 16ft, Reservations not accepted, Elev: 1693ft/516m, Tel: 541-767-5000, Nearest town: Cottage Grove. GPS: 43.669812, -122.705852

317 • C2 | Clearwater Falls (Umpqua NF)

Total sites: 12, RV sites: 12, No water, Vault/pit toilet, Tent & RV camping: $10, Stay limit: 14 days, Generator hours: 0600-2200, Open Jun-Oct, Max Length: 25ft, Reservations not accepted, Elev: 4318ft/1316m, Tel: 541-957-3200, Nearest town: Diamond Lake. GPS: 43.248356, -122.230595

318 • C2 | Clearwater Forebay (Umpqua NF)

Total sites: 5, RV sites: 5, No water, Vault/pit toilet, Tent & RV camping: Free, Stay limit: 14 days, Reservations not accepted, Elev: 3185ft/971m, Tel: 541-498-2531, Nearest town: Toketee Falls. GPS: 43.261991, -122.404545

319 • C2 | Contorta Flat (Deschutes NF)

Total sites: 19, RV sites: 13, No water, Vault/pit toilet, Tent & RV camping: $11-13, Open May-Oct, Max Length: 40ft, Reservations accepted, Elev: 4855ft/1480m, Tel: 541-338-7869, Nearest town: Crescent. GPS: 43.461356, -122.006782

320 • C2 | Coolwater (Umpqua NF)

Total sites: 7, RV sites: 7, Central water, Vault/pit toilet, No showers, No RV dump, Tent & RV camping: $10, Stay limit: 14

days, Generator hours: 0600-2200, Open Jun-Oct, Max Length: 24ft, Reservations not accepted, Elev: 1512ft/461m, Tel: 541-496-3534, Nearest town: North Umpqua. GPS: 43.232301, -122.872557

321 • C2 | Corral Springs (Fremont-Winema NF)

Total sites: 5, RV sites: 5, No water, Vault/pit toilet, Tent & RV camping: Free, Reduced services 10/15-5/14, Open all year, Max Length: 50ft, Reservations not accepted, Elev: 4878ft/1487m, Tel: 541-365-7001, Nearest town: Chemult. GPS: 43.252518, -121.822121

322 • C2 | Cougar Crossing (Willamette NF)

Total sites: 11, RV sites: 11, No water, Vault/pit toilet, Tent & RV camping: $14, Stay limit: 14 days, Open all year, Max Length: 40ft, Reservations accepted, Elev: 1795ft/547m, Tel: 541-603-8564, Nearest town: Blue River. GPS: 44.057667, -122.219946

323 • C2 | Cover (Umpqua NF)

Total sites: 7, RV sites: 7, Central water, Vault/pit toilet, No showers, No RV dump, Tent & RV camping: $10, Stay limit: 14 days, Generator hours: 0600-2200, Open May-Oct, Max Length: 22ft, Reservations not accepted, Elev: 1795ft/547m, Tel: 541-825-3100, Nearest town: Tiller. GPS: 42.975924, -122.687963

324 • C2 | Cow Meadow (Deschutes NF)

Total sites: 18, RV sites: 18, No water, Vault/pit toilet, Tent & RV camping: $12-14, Open May-Sep, Max Length: 30ft, Reservations accepted, Elev: 4472ft/1363m, Tel: 541-338-7869, Nearest town: Crescent. GPS: 43.812988, -121.776367

325 • C2 | Crane Prairie (Deschutes NF)

Total sites: 146, RV sites: 140, Central water, No toilets, No showers, No RV dump, Tent & RV camping: $17-19, Group site: $247, Open May-Oct, Max Length: 60ft, Reservations accepted, Elev: 4478ft/1365m, Tel: 541-338-7869, Nearest town: Sunriver. GPS: 43.797852, -121.758545

326 • C2 | Crescent Creek (Deschutes NF)

Total sites: 9, RV sites: 9, Central water, Vault/pit toilet, No showers, No RV dump, Tent & RV camping: $14-16, Open May-Sep, Max Length: 40ft, Reservations accepted, Elev: 4544ft/1385m, Tel: 541-338-7869, Nearest town: Crescent. GPS: 43.498949, -121.848129

327 • C2 | Crescent Lake (Deschutes NF)

Total sites: 46, RV sites: 46, Central water, Vault/pit toilet, No showers, No RV dump, Tent & RV camping: $17-21, Open May-Oct, Max Length: 40ft, Reservations accepted, Elev: 4866ft/1483m, Tel: 541-338-7869, Nearest town: Crescent Lake. GPS: 43.502346, -121.974723

328 • C2 | Cultus Corral Horse Camp (Deschutes NF)

Total sites: 11, RV sites: 11, Central water, Vault/pit toilet, No showers, No RV dump, Tent & RV camping: $13-15, Open May-Oct, Max Length: 40ft, Reservations accepted, Elev: 4475ft/1364m, Tel: 541-338-7869, Nearest town: Blue River. GPS: 43.824871, -121.800615

329 • C2 | Cultus Lake (Deschutes NF)

Total sites: 55, RV sites: 55, Central water, Vault/pit toilet, No showers, No RV dump, Tent & RV camping: $21-25, Open May-Sep, Max Length: 40ft, Reservations accepted, Elev: 4747ft/1447m, Tel: 541-338-7869, Nearest town: Bend. GPS: 43.836776, -121.834062

330 • C2 | Devils Lake (Deschutes-Ochoco NF)

Total sites: 10, RV sites: 0, No water, Vault/pit toilet, Tents only: $5, Walk-to sites, Open Jun-Oct, Elev: 5466ft/1666m, Tel: 541-383-5300, Nearest town: Bend. GPS: 44.034523, -121.765456

331 • C2 | Diamond Lake (Umpqua NF)

Total sites: 238, RV sites: 238, Central water, Flush toilet, Free showers, RV dump, Tent & RV camping: $16-22, Stay limit: 14 days, Open Jun-Sep, Max Length: 75ft, Reservations accepted, Elev: 5256ft/1602m, Tel: 541-498-2531, Nearest town: Diamond Lake. GPS: 43.159481, -122.134086

332 • C2 | Digit Point (Fremont-Winema NF)

Total sites: 65, RV sites: 64, Central water, Flush toilet, RV dump, Tent & RV camping: $12, Reduced services 10/15-5/14, Open Jun-Oct, Max Length: 33ft, Reservations not accepted, Elev: 5699ft/1737m, Tel: 541-365-7001, Nearest town: Chemult. GPS: 43.228271, -121.965576

333 • C2 | Dolly Varden (Willamette NF)

Total sites: 5, RV sites: 0, No water, Vault/pit toilet, Tents only: $15, Stay limit: 14 days, Generator hours: 0600-2200, Open Apr-Sep, Reservations not accepted, Elev: 1142ft/348m, Tel: 541-782-2283, Nearest town: Lowell. GPS: 43.963706, -122.616735

334 • C2 | Driftwood (Broken Top) (Deschutes NF)

Total sites: 18, RV sites: 18, No water, Vault/pit toilet, Tent & RV camping: $16-18, Open Jun-Sep, Max Length: 40ft, Reservations accepted, Elev: 6551ft/1997m, Tel: 541-338-7869, Nearest town: Sisters. GPS: 44.102904, -121.626101

335 • C2 | Dumont Creek (Umpqua NF)

Total sites: 3, RV sites: 0, No water, Vault/pit toilet, Tents only: $10, Trailers not recommended, Stay limit: 14 days, Generator hours: 0600-2200, Open May-Oct, Reservations not accepted, Elev: 1457ft/444m, Tel: 541-825-3100, Nearest town: Tiller. GPS: 43.035911, -122.809475

336 • C2 | Eagle Rock (Umpqua NF)

Total sites: 25, RV sites: 25, No water, Vault/pit toilet, Tent & RV camping: $10, Stay limit: 14 days, Open May-Sep, Max Length: 30ft, Reservations accepted, Elev: 1627ft/496m, Tel: 541-496-3532, Nearest town: Steamboat. GPS: 43.295654, -122.553916

337 • C2 | East Davis (Deschutes NF)

Total sites: 20, RV sites: 20, Central water, Vault/pit toilet, No showers, No RV dump, Tent & RV camping: $14-16, Open May-Sep, Max Length: 40ft, Reservations accepted, Elev: 4419ft/1347m, Tel: 541-338-7869, Nearest town: Crescent. GPS: 43.588379, -121.853027

338 • C2 | East Lemolo (Umpqua NF)

Total sites: 15, RV sites: 15, Central water, Vault/pit toilet, No showers, No RV dump, Tent & RV camping: $10, Stay limit: 14 days, Open Jun-Sep, Max Length: 25ft, Reservations accepted,

Elev: 4232ft/1290m, Tel: 541-498-2531, Nearest town: Chemult. GPS: 43.312831, -122.166357

339 • C2 | Elk Lake (Deschutes NF)

Total sites: 26, RV sites: 22, Central water, Vault/pit toilet, No showers, No RV dump, Tent & RV camping: $16-18, Open May-Sep, Max Length: 36ft, Reservations accepted, Elev: 4948ft/1508m, Tel: 541-338-7869, Nearest town: Bend. GPS: 43.978994, -121.808823

340 • C2 | Everage Flat (Willamette NF)

Total sites: 8, RV sites: 6, No water, No toilets, Tent & RV camping: Free, Stay limit: 14 days, Reservations not accepted, Elev: 1942ft/592m, Nearest town: Oakridge. GPS: 43.524096, -122.447401

341 • C2 | Fall River (Deschutes NF)

Total sites: 12, RV sites: 12, No water, Vault/pit toilet, Tent & RV camping: $13-15, Open May-Oct, Max Length: 40ft, Reservations accepted, Elev: 4275ft/1303m, Tel: 541-383-4000, Nearest town: La Pine. GPS: 43.772705, -121.620117

342 • C2 | French Pete (Willamette NF)

Total sites: 17, RV sites: 17, Central water, Vault/pit toilet, No showers, No RV dump, Tent & RV camping: $17, Stay limit: 14 days, Open May-Sep, Max Length: 42ft, Reservations accepted, Elev: 1883ft/574m, Tel: 801-226-3564, Nearest town: Blue River. GPS: 44.041758, -122.208482

343 • C2 | Frissell Crossing (Willamette NF)

Total sites: 12, RV sites: 12, Central water, Vault/pit toilet, No showers, No RV dump, Tent & RV camping: $14, Stay limit: 14 days, Open May-Sep, Max Length: 50ft, Reservations accepted, Elev: 2607ft/795m, Tel: 801-226-3564, Nearest town: Blue River. GPS: 43.958733, -122.085201

344 • C2 | Gold Lake (Willamette NF)

Total sites: 21, RV sites: 21, Central water, Vault/pit toilet, No showers, No RV dump, Tent & RV camping: $21, Stay limit: 14 days, Open May-Oct, Max Length: 24ft, Reservations not accepted, Elev: 4885ft/1489m, Tel: 541-782-2283, Nearest town: Oakridge. GPS: 43.631162, -122.050106

345 • C2 | Gull Point (Deschutes NF)

Total sites: 79, RV sites: 79, Central water, No toilets, No showers, RV dump, Tent & RV camping: $15-19, $10 dump fee, Stay limit: 14 days, Open May-Oct, Max Length: 40ft, Reservations accepted, Elev: 4364ft/1330m, Tel: 541-338-7869, Nearest town: Bend. GPS: 43.704466, -121.762789

346 • C2 | Hamaker (Rogue River-Siskiyou NF)

Total sites: 10, RV sites: 10, No water, Vault/pit toilet, Tent & RV camping: $12, Stay limit: 14 days, Open May-Sep, Reservations not accepted, Elev: 4131ft/1259m, Nearest town: Prospect. GPS: 43.056792, -122.328718

347 • C2 | Hampton (Willamette NF)

Total sites: 4, RV sites: 4, Central water, Vault/pit toilet, No showers, No RV dump, Tent & RV camping: $5, Stay limit: 14 days, Open Apr-Sep, Reservations not accepted, Elev: 919ft/280m, Tel: 541-782-2283, Nearest town: Oakridge. GPS: 43.816011, -122.589591

348 • C2 | Hemlock Lake (Quartz Mt) (Umpqua NF)

Total sites: 13, RV sites: 10, No water, Vault/pit toilet, Tent & RV camping: $10, Stay limit: 14 days, Generator hours: 0600-2200, Open May-Nov, Max Length: 35ft, Reservations not accepted, Elev: 4550ft/1387m, Tel: 541-496-3534, Nearest town: Glide. GPS: 43.191439, -122.703961

349 • C2 | Hemlock Meadows (Umpqua NF)

Total sites: 4, RV sites: 4, No water, Vault/pit toilet, Tent & RV camping: $10, Stay limit: 14 days, Generator hours: 0600-2200, Open Jun-Oct, Max Length: 35ft, Reservations not accepted, Elev: 4541ft/1384m, Tel: 541-496-3534, Nearest town: North Umpqua. GPS: 43.188629, -122.696646

350 • C2 | Hobo Forest Camp (Umpqua NF)

Total sites: 4, RV sites: 4, No water, Vault/pit toilet, Tent & RV camping: Free, No services in winter, Stay limit: 14 days, Generator hours: 0600-2200, Open all year, Max Length: 16ft, Reservations not accepted, Elev: 2113ft/644m, Tel: 541-957-3200, Nearest town: Cottage Grove. GPS: 43.647035, -122.667811

351 • C2 | Horseshoe Bend (Steamboat) (Umpqua NF)

Total sites: 25, RV sites: 25, Central water, Flush toilet, No showers, No RV dump, Tent & RV camping: $15, Stay limit: 14 days, Open May-Sep, Max Length: 35ft, Reservations accepted, Elev: 1424ft/434m, Tel: 541-496-3534, Nearest town: Idleyld Park. GPS: 43.288704, -122.627577

352 • C2 | Howlock Mt. TH (Umpqua NF)

Total sites: 2, RV sites: 0, No water, Vault/pit toilet, Tents only: $5, On site payment not available, Stay limit: 14 days, Reservations not accepted, Elev: 5333ft/1625m, Tel: 541-957-3200, Nearest town: Medford. GPS: 43.183371, -122.134088

353 • C2 | Indigo Springs (Willamette NF)

Total sites: 3, RV sites: 0, No water, Vault/pit toilet, Tents only: Free, Stay limit: 14 days, Generator hours: 0600-2200, Open all year, Reservations not accepted, Elev: 2946ft/898m, Tel: 541-782-2283, Nearest town: Oakridge. GPS: 43.497564, -122.264448

354 • C2 | Inlet (Umpqua NF)

Total sites: 13, RV sites: 13, No water, Vault/pit toilet, Tent & RV camping: $10, Stay limit: 14 days, Open Jun-Sep, Max Length: 25ft, Reservations required, Elev: 4213ft/1284m, Tel: 541-498-2531, Nearest town: Chemult. GPS: 43.311751, -122.150246

355 • C2 | Island (Steamboat) (Umpqua NF)

Total sites: 7, RV sites: 7, No water, Vault/pit toilet, Tent & RV camping: $10, Stay limit: 14 days, Generator hours: 0600-2200, Open all year, Max Length: 24ft, Reservations not accepted, Elev: 1381ft/421m, Tel: 541-957-3200, Nearest town: Powers. GPS: 43.339539, -122.722845

356 • C2 | Islet (Willamette NF)

Total sites: 55, RV sites: 55, Central water, Vault/pit toilet, No showers, No RV dump, Tent & RV camping: $22, Stay limit: 14 days, Open Jun-Sep, Max Length: 43ft, Reservations accepted, Elev: 5502ft/1677m, Tel: 801-226-3564, Nearest town: Oakridge. GPS: 43.748732, -122.006976

357 • C2 | Kelsay Valley Forest Camp (Umpqua NF)

Total sites: 15, RV sites: 15, No water, Vault/pit toilet, Tent & RV camping: $10, 11 sites w/ corral, Stay limit: 14 days, Open Jun-Oct, Max Length: 25ft, Reservations accepted, Elev: 4360ft/1329m, Tel: 541-498-2531, Nearest town: Chemult. GPS: 43.312316, -122.112586

358 • C2 | Kiahanie (Willamette NF)

Total sites: 19, RV sites: 19, Central water, Vault/pit toilet, No showers, No RV dump, Tent & RV camping: $10, Stay limit: 14 days, Open May-Oct, Max Length: 24ft, Reservations not accepted, Elev: 2270ft/692m, Tel: 541-782-2283, Nearest town: Oakridge. GPS: 43.885010, -122.257813

359 • C2 | Lake in the Woods (Umpqua NF)

Total sites: 11, RV sites: 10, Central water, No toilets, No showers, No RV dump, Tent & RV camping: $10, Stay limit: 14 days, Open May-Oct, Max Length: 35ft, Reservations not accepted, Elev: 3032ft/924m, Tel: 541-496-3534, Nearest town: Glide. GPS: 43.216958, -122.722065

360 • C2 | Lava Flow (Deschutes-Ochoco NF)

Total sites: 6, RV sites: 6, No water, Vault/pit toilet, Tent & RV camping: Free, Open Apr-Oct, Max Length: 60ft, Elev: 4475ft/1364m, Nearest town: Crescent. GPS: 43.622943, -121.820543

361 • C2 | Lava Lake (Deschutes NF)

Total sites: 44, RV sites: 38, Central water, Vault/pit toilet, No showers, No RV dump, Tent & RV camping: $19-21, Open May-Oct, Max Length: 40ft, Reservations accepted, Elev: 4751ft/1448m, Tel: 541-338-7869, Nearest town: Bend. GPS: 43.913964, -121.767884

362 • C2 | Lemolo Two Forebay (Umpqua NF)

Total sites: 3, RV sites: 0, No water, Vault/pit toilet, Tents only: Free, Stay limit: 14 days, Open May-Oct, Reservations not accepted, Elev: 3264ft/995m, Tel: 541-498-2531, Nearest town: Roseburg. GPS: 43.293946, -122.402288

363 • C2 | Little Cultus Lake (Deschutes NF)

Total sites: 31, RV sites: 31, Central water, Vault/pit toilet, No showers, No RV dump, Tent & RV camping: $18-22, Open May-Sep, Max Length: 40ft, Reservations accepted, Elev: 4777ft/1456m, Tel: 541-338-7869, Nearest town: Crescent. GPS: 43.799887, -121.867789

364 • C2 | Little Fawn (Deschutes NF)

Total sites: 20, RV sites: 20, No water, Vault/pit toilet, No showers, No RV dump, Tent & RV camping: $18-20, Group site: $225, Open May-Sep, Max Length: 30ft, Reservations accepted, Elev: 4905ft/1495m, Tel: 541-338-7869, Nearest town: Bend. GPS: 43.962662, -121.796447

365 • C2 | Little Lava Lake (Deschutes NF)

Total sites: 13, RV sites: 13, Central water, Flush toilet, No showers, No RV dump, Tent & RV camping: $16-20, Group site: $50-$90, Open May-Oct, Max Length: 40ft, Reservations accepted, Elev: 4751ft/1448m, Tel: 541-338-7869, Nearest town: Bend. GPS: 43.910325, -121.762277

366 • C2 | Lund Park (Umpqua NF)

Total sites: 10, RV sites: 10, No water, Vault/pit toilet, Tent & RV camping: $8, 3 spaces outside gate open year round, Stay limit: 14 days, Generator hours: 0600-2200, Open May-Nov, Max Length: 16ft, Reservations not accepted, Elev: 2057ft/627m, Tel: 541-767-5000, Nearest town: Cottage Grove. GPS: 43.650908, -122.676731

367 • C2 | Mallard Marsh (Deschutes NF)

Total sites: 15, RV sites: 15, No water, Flush toilet, Tent & RV camping: $15-17, Open May-Sep, Max Length: 40ft, Reservations accepted, Elev: 4974ft/1516m, Tel: 541-338-7869, Nearest town: Bend. GPS: 43.963379, -121.782715

368 • C2 | Mineral Forest Camp (Umpqua NF)

Total sites: 3, RV sites: 3, No water, Vault/pit toilet, Tent & RV camping: Free, Reduced services Sep-May, Stay limit: 14 days, Open all year, Reservations not accepted, Elev: 1913ft/583m, Tel: 541-957-3200, Nearest town: Cottage Grove. GPS: 43.582621, -122.713668

369 • C2 | North Davis Creek (Deschutes NF)

Total sites: 14, RV sites: 14, Central water, Vault/pit toilet, No showers, No RV dump, Tent & RV camping: $14-16, Open May-Sep, Max Length: 40ft, Reservations accepted, Elev: 4350ft/1326m, Tel: 541-338-7869, Nearest town: Crescent. GPS: 43.675655, -121.822956

370 • C2 | North Twin Lake (Deschutes NF)

Total sites: 20, RV sites: 20, No water, Vault/pit toilet, Tent & RV camping: $14-16, Open May-Oct, Max Length: 40ft, Reservations accepted, Elev: 4383ft/1336m, Tel: 541-338-7869, Nearest town: Crescent. GPS: 43.732569, -121.764971

371 • C2 | North Waldo (Willamette NF)

Total sites: 58, RV sites: 58, Central water, Vault/pit toilet, No showers, No RV dump, Tent & RV camping: $22, RV dump nearby, Stay limit: 14 days, Open Jun-Sep, Max Length: 50ft, Reservations accepted, Elev: 5495ft/1675m, Tel: 541-782-2283, Nearest town: Oakridge. GPS: 43.758176, -122.003921

372 • C2 | Packard Creek (Willamette NF)

Total sites: 35, RV sites: 35, Central water, Vault/pit toilet, No showers, No RV dump, Tent & RV camping: $19, Stay limit: 14 days, Open Apr-Sep, Max Length: 45ft, Reservations accepted, Elev: 1634ft/498m, Tel: 541-523-6391, Nearest town: Oakridge. GPS: 43.669481, -122.431955

373 • C2 | Point (Deschutes NF)

Total sites: 9, RV sites: 9, No water, Vault/pit toilet, Tent & RV camping: $14-16, Open May-Sep, Max Length: 40ft, Reservations accepted, Elev: 4892ft/1491m, Tel: 541-323-1746, Nearest town: Bend. GPS: 43.966718, -121.808304

374 • C2 | Poole Creek (Umpqua NF)

Total sites: 60, RV sites: 60, Central water, Vault/pit toilet, No showers, No RV dump, Tent & RV camping: $15, Group site: $85, Stay limit: 14 days, Generator hours: 0600-2200, Open Jun-Sep, Max Length: 30ft, Reservations accepted, Elev: 4173ft/1272m, Tel:

541-498-2531, Nearest town: Diamond Lake. GPS: 43.310928, -122.196128

375 • C2 | Princess Creek (Deschutes NF)

Total sites: 32, RV sites: 32, No water, Vault/pit toilet, Tent & RV camping: $14-18, Open May-Oct, Max Length: 32ft, Reservations accepted, Elev: 4931ft/1503m, Tel: 541-338-7869, Nearest town: Crescent Lake. GPS: 43.586426, -122.010498

376 • C2 | Pringle Falls (Deschutes NF)

Total sites: 7, RV sites: 7, Central water, Vault/pit toilet, No showers, No RV dump, Tent & RV camping: $12-14, Open May-Oct, Max Length: 30ft, Reservations accepted, Elev: 4236ft/1291m, Tel: 541-383-4000, Nearest town: La Pine. GPS: 43.747831, -121.603025

377 • C2 | Puma (Willamette NF)

Total sites: 11, RV sites: 8, Central water, Vault/pit toilet, No showers, No RV dump, Tent & RV camping: $15, Stay limit: 14 days, Open Apr-Sep, Max Length: 25ft, Reservations not accepted, Elev: 1220ft/372m, Tel: 541-782-2283, Nearest town: Lowell. GPS: 43.978516, -122.515381

378 • C2 | Quinn River (Deschutes NF)

Total sites: 41, RV sites: 41, Central water, Vault/pit toilet, No showers, No RV dump, Tent & RV camping: $16-18, Open May-Sep, Max Length: 40ft, Reservations accepted, Elev: 4475ft/1364m, Tel: 541-338-7869, Nearest town: Bend. GPS: 43.785156, -121.836426

379 • C2 | Red Diamond (Willamette NF)

Total sites: 6, RV sites: 6, Vault/pit toilet, Tent & RV camping: $18, Reservable as group site: $44, Stay limit: 14 days, Open May-Sep, Max Length: 36ft, Reservations not accepted, Elev: 2047ft/624m, Tel: 541-822-3381, Nearest town: Coburg. GPS: 44.002842, -122.172244

380 • C2 | Reservoir (Deschutes NF)

Total sites: 24, RV sites: 24, No water, Vault/pit toilet, Tent & RV camping: $12-14, Open May-Sep, Max Length: 125ft, Reservations accepted, Elev: 4341ft/1323m, Tel: 541-338-7869, Nearest town: La Pine. GPS: 43.672119, -121.770508

381 • C2 | Rock Creek (Crane Prairie) (Deschutes NF)

Total sites: 30, RV sites: 30, Central water, Vault/pit toilet, No showers, No RV dump, Tent & RV camping: $18-20, Open May-Sep, Max Length: 40ft, Reservations accepted, Elev: 4472ft/1363m, Tel: 541-338-7869, Nearest town: Crescent. GPS: 43.768197, -121.834184

382 • C2 | Rogue River - Farewell Bend (Rogue River-Siskiyou NF)

Total sites: 61, RV sites: 61, Central water, Flush toilet, No showers, No RV dump, Tent & RV camping: $25, Use of fire pans mandatory, Stay limit: 14 days, Generator hours: 0600-2200, Open May-Oct, Max Length: 40ft, Reservations accepted, Elev: 3433ft/1046m, Tel: 541-479-3735, Nearest town: Prospect. GPS: 42.916234, -122.435059

383 • C2 | Rujada (Umpqua NF)

Total sites: 15, RV sites: 15, Central water, Flush toilet, No showers, No RV dump, Tent & RV camping: $12, Stay limit: 14 days, Generator hours: 0600-2200, Open May-Sep, Max Length: 22ft, Reservations accepted, Elev: 1273ft/388m, Tel: 541-767-5000, Nearest town: Cottage Grove. GPS: 43.705924, -122.744463

384 • C2 | Sacandaga (Willamette NF)

Total sites: 17, RV sites: 17, Central water, Vault/pit toilet, No showers, No RV dump, Tent & RV camping: $8, Stay limit: 14 days, Open Jun-Oct, Max Length: 24ft, Reservations not accepted, Elev: 2566ft/782m, Tel: 541-782-2283, Nearest town: Oakridge. GPS: 43.496094, -122.329834

385 • C2 | Salmon Creek Falls (Willamette NF)

Total sites: 15, RV sites: 15, Central water, Vault/pit toilet, No showers, No RV dump, Tent & RV camping: $17, Stay limit: 14 days, Generator hours: 0600-2200, Open Apr-Sep, Max Length: 20ft, Reservations not accepted, Elev: 1558ft/475m, Tel: 541-782-2283, Nearest town: Oakridge. GPS: 43.762623, -122.374212

386 • C2 | Sand Prairie (Willamette NF)

Total sites: 21, RV sites: 21, No water, Vault/pit toilet, Tent & RV camping: $14, Stay limit: 14 days, Open May-Sep, Max Length: 28ft, Reservations not accepted, Elev: 1634ft/498m, Tel: 541-782-2283, Nearest town: Oakridge. GPS: 43.601318, -122.452637

387 • C2 | Secret (Willamette NF)

Total sites: 6, RV sites: 6, No water, Vault/pit toilet, Tent & RV camping: $14, Stay limit: 14 days, Generator hours: 0600-2200, Open May-Sep, Max Length: 24ft, Reservations not accepted, Elev: 1965ft/599m, Tel: 541-782-2283, Nearest town: Oakridge. GPS: 43.514232, -122.441477

388 • C2 | Shadow Bay (Willamette NF)

Total sites: 21, RV sites: 21, Central water, Vault/pit toilet, No showers, No RV dump, Tent & RV camping: $18-22, Group sites: $81-$282, Stay limit: 14 days, Open Jun-Sep, Max Length: 40ft, Reservations accepted, Elev: 5489ft/1673m, Tel: 541-782-2283, Nearest town: Oakridge. GPS: 43.692871, -122.042725

389 • C2 | Sheep Bridge (Deschutes NF)

Total sites: 20, RV sites: 20, Central water, Vault/pit toilet, No showers, No RV dump, Tent & RV camping: $12-14, 3 group sites: $30, Open May-Oct, Max Length: 40ft, Reservations accepted, Elev: 4354ft/1327m, Tel: 541-338-7869, Nearest town: Crescent. GPS: 43.732005, -121.785076

390 • C2 | Skillet Creek (Umpqua NF)

Total sites: 4, RV sites: 4, Vault/pit toilet, Tent & RV camping: Fee unk, Stay limit: 14 days, Reservations not accepted, Elev: 1982ft/604m, Tel: 541-825-3100, Nearest town: Tiller. GPS: 43.091843, -122.620226

391 • C2 | Skookum Creek (Willamette NF)

Total sites: 9, RV sites: 0, Central water, Vault/pit toilet, No showers, No RV dump, Tents only: $5, Walk-to sites, Stay limit: 14 days, Open May-Oct, Reservations not accepted, Elev: 4636ft/1413m, Tel: 541-782-2283, Nearest town: Oakridge. GPS: 43.861129, -122.045123

392 • C2 | Skookum Pond (Umpqua NF)

Total sites: 3, RV sites: 0, No water, No toilets, Tents only: Free, Stay limit: 14 days, Reservations not accepted, Elev: 3502ft/1067m, Tel: 541-825-3100, Nearest town: Tiller. GPS: 43.008725, -122.599581

393 • C2 | Slide Creek (Willamette NF)

Total sites: 16, RV sites: 16, No water, Vault/pit toilet, Tent & RV camping: $17, Stay limit: 14 days, Open Apr-Sep, Max Length: 90ft, Reservations accepted, Elev: 1923ft/586m, Tel: 541-822-3381, Nearest town: Blue River. GPS: 44.076644, -122.224531

394 • C2 | Soda Creek (Deschutes NF)

Total sites: 10, RV sites: 10, No water, Vault/pit toilet, No showers, No RV dump, Tent & RV camping: $15-17, Open May-Sep, Max Length: 40ft, Reservations accepted, Elev: 5463ft/1665m, Tel: 541-338-7869, Nearest town: Bend. GPS: 44.024619, -121.726901

395 • C2 | South (Deschutes NF)

Total sites: 23, RV sites: 23, No water, Vault/pit toilet, Tent & RV camping: $15-17, Open May-Sep, Max Length: 40ft, Reservations accepted, Elev: 5000ft/1524m, Tel: 541-338-7869, Nearest town: Bend. GPS: 43.960361, -121.788116

396 • C2 | South Twin Lake (Deschutes NF)

Total sites: 21, RV sites: 21, Central water, Flush toilet, No showers, No RV dump, Tent & RV camping: $20-24, Open May-Oct, Max Length: 40ft, Reservations accepted, Elev: 4373ft/1333m, Tel: 541-338-7869, Nearest town: Bend. GPS: 43.717059, -121.770587

397 • C2 | South Umpqua Falls (Umpqua NF)

Total sites: 19, RV sites: 19, No water, Vault/pit toilet, Tent & RV camping: $10, Stay limit: 14 days, Open all year, Max Length: 35ft, Reservations not accepted, Elev: 1722ft/525m, Tel: 541-825-3100, Nearest town: Tiller. GPS: 43.055401, -122.689745

398 • C2 | Spring (Deschutes NF)

Total sites: 73, RV sites: 68, Central water, Vault/pit toilet, No showers, No RV dump, Tent & RV camping: $20-24, Group site: $225, Open May-Oct, Max Length: 40ft, Reservations accepted, Elev: 4875ft/1486m, Tel: 541-338-7869, Nearest town: Crescent. GPS: 43.461595, -122.016413

399 • C2 | Steamboat Falls (Umpqua NF)

Total sites: 10, RV sites: 7, No water, Vault/pit toilet, Tent & RV camping: $10, Stay limit: 14 days, Generator hours: 0600-2200, Open all year, Max Length: 20ft, Reservations not accepted, Elev: 1736ft/529m, Tel: 541-957-3200, Nearest town: Steamboat. GPS: 43.374852, -122.642835

400 • C2 | Summit Lake (Deschutes NF)

Total sites: 3, RV sites: 0, No water, Vault/pit toilet, Tents only: Free, Rough road - 4x4 required, Open Jul-Sep, Reservations not accepted, Elev: 5597ft/1706m, Nearest town: Crescent. GPS: 43.462508, -122.133163

401 • C2 | Sunnyside (Willamette NF)

Total sites: 13, RV sites: 5, No water, Vault/pit toilet, Tent & RV camping: $14, Stay limit: 14 days, Open May-Sep, Max Length: 21ft, Reservations accepted, Elev: 1715ft/523m, Tel: 541-822-3381, Nearest town: Blue River. GPS: 44.061697, -122.220903

402 • C2 | Sunset Cove (Deschutes NF)

Total sites: 21, RV sites: 21, Central water, Vault/pit toilet, No showers, No RV dump, Tent & RV camping: $16-18, Open May-Oct, Max Length: 40ft, Reservations accepted, Elev: 4885ft/1489m, Tel: 541-338-7869, Nearest town: Crescent. GPS: 43.562500, -121.964111

403 • C2 | Thielsen Forest Camp (Umpqua NF)

Total sites: 4, RV sites: 4, No water, Vault/pit toilet, Tent & RV camping: Free, Stay limit: 14 days, Max Length: 20ft, Reservations not accepted, Elev: 4531ft/1381m, Tel: 541-498-2531, Nearest town: Diamond Lake. GPS: 43.256028, -122.164725

404 • C2 | Thielsen View (Umpqua NF)

Total sites: 60, RV sites: 60, Central water, Vault/pit toilet, No showers, No RV dump, Tent & RV camping: $22, Stay limit: 14 days, Open Jun-Sep, Max Length: 35ft, Reservations accepted, Elev: 5216ft/1590m, Tel: 541-498-2531, Nearest town: Diamond Lake. GPS: 43.166612, -122.166518

405 • C2 | Three C Rock (Umpqua NF)

Total sites: 5, RV sites: 5, No water, Vault/pit toilet, Tent & RV camping: $10, Stay limit: 14 days, Generator hours: 0600-2200, Open all year, Max Length: 35ft, Reservations not accepted, Elev: 1113ft/339m, Tel: 541-825-3100, Nearest town: Tiller. GPS: 42.964847, -122.887799

406 • C2 | Three Creek Lake (Deschutes NF)

Total sites: 11, RV sites: 11, No water, Vault/pit toilet, Tent & RV camping: $16-18, Open Jun-Sep, Max Length: 40ft, Reservations accepted, Elev: 6539ft/1993m, Tel: 541-338-7869, Nearest town: Sisters. GPS: 44.095703, -121.624756

407 • C2 | Three Creek Meadow Horse Camp (Deschutes NF)

Total sites: 20, RV sites: 20, No water, Vault/pit toilet, Tent & RV camping: $15-19, 9 horse sites, Open May-Sep, Max Length: 30ft, Reservations not accepted, Elev: 6332ft/1930m, Tel: 541-338-7869, Nearest town: Sisters. GPS: 44.115048, -121.625248

408 • C2 | Timpanogas Lake (Willamette NF)

Total sites: 10, RV sites: 10, Central water, Vault/pit toilet, No showers, No RV dump, Tent & RV camping: $8, Stay limit: 14 days, Open Jun-Oct, Max Length: 24ft, Reservations not accepted, Elev: 5279ft/1609m, Tel: 541-782-2283, Nearest town: Oakridge. GPS: 43.410238, -122.114467

409 • C2 | Todd Lake (Deschutes NF)

Total sites: 3, RV sites: 0, No water, Vault/pit toilet, Tents only: Free, Walk-to sites, - 10 minutes, Recreation Fee Area, Open Jun-Oct, Reservations not accepted, Elev: 6273ft/1912m, Tel: 541-383-5300, Nearest town: Bend. GPS: 44.024973, -121.683621

410 • C2 | Toketee Lake (Umpqua NF)

Total sites: 33, RV sites: 33, No water, Vault/pit toilet, Tent & RV camping: $10, Group site: $50, Stay limit: 14 days, Generator hours: 0600-2200, Open Jun-Sep, Max Length: 24ft, Reservations accepted, Elev: 2461ft/750m, Tel: 541-498-2531, Nearest town: Idleyld Park. GPS: 43.273594, -122.406351

411 • C2 | Trapper Creek (Deschutes NF)

Total sites: 29, RV sites: 29, Central water, Vault/pit toilet, No showers, No RV dump, Tent & RV camping: $18-22, Open May-Oct, Max Length: 40ft, Reservations accepted, Elev: 4879ft/1487m, Tel: 541-338-7869, Nearest town: Crescent Lake. GPS: 43.582001, -122.043818

412 • C2 | Union Creek (Rogue River-Siskiyou NF)

Total sites: 74, RV sites: 74, Elec sites: 3, Central water, Vault/pit toilet, No showers, No RV dump, Tents: $22/RVs: $22-35, 3 Full hookup sites, Stay limit: 14 days, Generator hours: 0600-2200, Open May-Oct, Max Length: 40ft, Reservations accepted, Elev: 3386ft/1032m, Tel: 541-560-3400, Nearest town: Prospect. GPS: 42.909011, -122.450656

413 • C2 | West South Twin (Deschutes NF)

Total sites: 24, RV sites: 24, Central water, Flush toilet, No showers, No RV dump, Tent & RV camping: $16-20, Open May-Sep, Max Length: 40ft, Reservations accepted, Elev: 4347ft/1325m, Tel: 541-338-7869, Nearest town: La Pine. GPS: 43.714772, -121.772355

414 • C2 | White Creek (Umpqua NF)

Total sites: 4, RV sites: 0, Central water, Vault/pit toilet, No showers, No RV dump, Tents only: $10, Walk-to sites, Stay limit: 14 days, Open Jun-Sep, Reservations not accepted, Elev: 1506ft/459m, Tel: 541-496-3534, Nearest town: North Umpqua. GPS: 43.227682, -122.861745

415 • C2 | Whitehorse Falls (Umpqua NF)

Total sites: 5, RV sites: 5, No water, Vault/pit toilet, Tent & RV camping: $10, Stay limit: 14 days, Open May-Oct, Max Length: 25ft, Reservations not accepted, Elev: 3773ft/1150m, Tel: 541-957-3200, Nearest town: Diamond Lake. GPS: 43.246698, -122.304341

416 • C2 | Wickiup Butte (Deschutes NF)

Total sites: 8, RV sites: 8, No water, Vault/pit toilet, Tent & RV camping: Free, Open Apr-Sep, Reservations not accepted, Elev: 4356ft/1328m, Tel: 541-383-4000, Nearest town: La Pine. GPS: 43.673562, -121.685304

417 • C2 | Wolf Creek (Umpqua NF)

Total sites: 8, RV sites: 5, Central water, No toilets, No showers, No RV dump, Tent & RV camping: $15, Stay limit: 14 days, Open May-Sep, Max Length: 30ft, Reservations not accepted, Elev: 1145ft/349m, Tel: 541-496-3534, Nearest town: Glide. GPS: 43.240235, -122.933447

418 • C2 | Wyeth (Deschutes-Ochoco NF)

Total sites: 5, RV sites: 5, No water, Vault/pit toilet, Tent & RV camping: $11-13, Open May-Oct, Max Length: 40ft, Reservations accepted, Elev: 4278ft/1304m, Tel: 541-383-4000, Nearest town: Hood River. GPS: 43.738888, -121.614573

419 • C3 | Alder Springs (Fremont-Winema NF)

Total sites: 3, RV sites: 0, No water, Vault/pit toilet, Tents only: Free, Open Jun-Nov, Elev: 5233ft/1595m. GPS: 42.969152, -121.132492

420 • C3 | Antelope Flat Reservoir (Ochoco NF)

Total sites: 24, RV sites: 24, Central water, Vault/pit toilet, No showers, No RV dump, Tent & RV camping: $8, Stay limit: 14 days, Open May-Sep, Reservations not accepted, Elev: 5036ft/1535m, Tel: 541-416-6500, Nearest town: Prineville. GPS: 44.001692, -120.392416

421 • C3 | Antler Horse Camp (Fremont-Winema NF)

Total sites: 5, RV sites: 5, Central water, Vault/pit toilet, No showers, No RV dump, Tent & RV camping: Free, Horse corrals, Reduced services 09/16-06/14, Open all year, Reservations not accepted, Elev: 6416ft/1956m, Tel: 541-576-2107, Nearest town: Silver Lake. GPS: 42.959185, -121.247684

422 • C3 | Big River (Deschutes NF)

Total sites: 10, RV sites: 10, No water, Vault/pit toilet, Tent & RV camping: $13-15, 3 reservable group sites: $69, Open May-Oct, Max Length: 40ft, Reservations accepted, Elev: 4180ft/1274m, Tel: 541-383-4000, Nearest town: La Pine. GPS: 43.816895, -121.497803

423 • C3 | Bunyard Crossing (Fremont-Winema NF)

Total sites: 3, RV sites: 3, No water, Vault/pit toilet, Tent & RV camping: Free, Open May-Nov, Reservations not accepted, Elev: 4530ft/1381m, Tel: 541-576-2107, Nearest town: Silver Lake. GPS: 43.043797, -121.081691

424 • C3 | Cabin Lake (Deschutes NF)

Total sites: 14, RV sites: 14, No water, No toilets, Tent & RV camping: Free, Elev: 4554ft/1388m, Nearest town: Bend. GPS: 43.495064, -121.057634

425 • C3 | Chief Paulina Horse Camp (Deschutes NF)

Total sites: 14, RV sites: 14, No water, Flush toilet, Tent & RV camping: $14-18, Non-potable water, Open Jun-Sep, Max Length: 50ft, Reservations accepted, Elev: 6398ft/1950m, Tel: 541-338-7869, Nearest town: La Pine. GPS: 43.703418, -121.254906

426 • C3 | China Hat (Deschutes NF)

Total sites: 13, RV sites: 13, No water, Vault/pit toilet, Tent & RV camping: Free, Open Apr-Oct, Max Length: 30ft, Elev: 5079ft/1548m, Tel: 541-383-5300, Nearest town: La Pine. GPS: 43.657625, -121.036915

427 • C3 | Cinder Hill (Deschutes NF)

Total sites: 108, RV sites: 108, Central water, Vault/pit toilet, No showers, No RV dump, Tent & RV camping: $18, Open Jun-Sep, Max Length: 65ft, Reservations accepted, Elev: 6394ft/1949m, Tel: 541-338-7869, Nearest town: La Pine. GPS: 43.736683, -121.199299

428 • C3 | Double Cabin (Ochoco NF)

Total sites: 5, RV sites: 5, No water, Vault/pit toilet, Tent & RV camping: Free, Stay limit: 14 days, Open all year, Reservations not accepted, Elev: 5246ft/1599m, Tel: 541-416-6500, Nearest town: Prineville. GPS: 44.029298, -120.320336

429 • C3 | East Bay (Fremont-Winema NF)

Total sites: 17, RV sites: 17, Central water, Vault/pit toilet, No showers, No RV dump, Tent & RV camping: $10, Reduced services 10/15-5/14, Open all year, Reservations not accepted, Elev: 4993ft/1522m, Tel: 541-576-2107, Nearest town: Silver Lake. GPS: 42.942947, -121.065849

430 • C3 | East Lake (Deschutes NF)

Total sites: 29, RV sites: 29, Central water, Flush toilet, No showers, No RV dump, Tent & RV camping: $18, Open Jun-Oct, Max Length: 40ft, Reservations accepted, Elev: 6434ft/1961m, Tel: 541-338-7869, Nearest town: La Pine. GPS: 43.717529, -121.210693

431 • C3 | Elkhorn (Ochoco NF)

Total sites: 4, RV sites: 4, No water, Vault/pit toilet, Tent & RV camping: Free, Stay limit: 14 days, Open all year, Reservations not accepted, Elev: 4452ft/1357m, Tel: 541-416-6500, Nearest town: Prineville. GPS: 44.080509, -120.319147

432 • C3 | Farm Well Horse Camp TH (Fremont-Winema NF)

Total sites: 5, RV sites: 5, No water, Vault/pit toilet, Tent & RV camping: Free, Reduced services Sep-Jun, Open all year, Reservations not accepted, Elev: 5058ft/1542m, Tel: 541-576-2107, Nearest town: Silver Lake. GPS: 43.026758, -120.977777

433 • C3 | Hot Springs (Deschutes NF)

Total sites: 26, RV sites: 26, No toilets, Tent & RV camping: $10, Max Length: 26ft, Reservations not accepted, Elev: 6421ft/1957m, Nearest town: La Pine. GPS: 43.717435, -121.200735

434 • C3 | Jackson Creek (Fremont-Winema NF)

Total sites: 12, No water, Vault/pit toilet, Tents only: Free, Reduced services 10/16-5/14, Open all year, Reservations not accepted, Elev: 4744ft/1446m, Tel: 541-365-7001, Nearest town: Chemult. GPS: 42.983092, -121.457146

435 • C3 | Little Crater Lake (Deschutes NF)

Total sites: 49, RV sites: 49, Central water, Vault/pit toilet, No showers, No RV dump, Tent & RV camping: $18, Open Jun-Oct, Max Length: 40ft, Reservations accepted, Elev: 6371ft/1942m, Tel: 541-338-7869, Nearest town: Bend. GPS: 43.713538, -121.242541

436 • C3 | Lower Buck Creek Forest Camp (Fremont-Winema NF)

Total sites: 5, RV sites: 5, No water, Vault/pit toilet, Tent & RV camping: Free, Reduced services 10/15-5/14, Open all year, Reservations not accepted, Elev: 4917ft/1499m, Tel: 541-576-2107, Nearest town: Silver Lake. GPS: 43.068544, -121.246333

437 • C3 | McKay Crossing (Deschutes NF)

Total sites: 16, RV sites: 16, No water, Vault/pit toilet, Tent & RV camping: $10, Open May-Oct, Max Length: 26ft, Reservations accepted, Elev: 4758ft/1450m, Tel: 541-383-4000, Nearest town: Bend. GPS: 43.716825, -121.377324

438 • C3 | Paulina Lake (Deschutes NF)

Total sites: 69, RV sites: 69, Central water, Flush toilet, No showers, RV dump, Tent & RV camping: $18, Dump fee $10, Open Jun-Sep, Max Length: 90ft, Reservations accepted, Elev: 6329ft/1929m, Tel: 541-338-7869, Nearest town: La Pine. GPS: 43.711914, -121.274902

439 • C3 | Pine Mountain (Deschutes NF)

Total sites: 6, RV sites: 6, No water, Vault/pit toilet, Tent & RV camping: Fee unk, Near observatory, Open May-Sep, Max Length: 30ft, Reservations not accepted, Elev: 6234ft/1900m, Tel: 541-383-5300, Nearest town: Bend. GPS: 43.790879, -120.942974

440 • C3 | Prairie (Deschutes NF)

Total sites: 17, RV sites: 17, Central water, Vault/pit toilet, No showers, RV dump, Tent & RV camping: $14, $10 dump fee, Open May-Oct, Max Length: 40ft, Reservations accepted, Elev: 4318ft/1316m, Tel: 541-383-4000, Nearest town: La Pine. GPS: 43.725071, -121.424191

441 • C3 | Silver Creek Marsh (Fremont-Winema NF)

Total sites: 17, RV sites: 17, Central water, No toilets, No showers, No RV dump, Tent & RV camping: $6, Horse corrals, Reduced services 10/15-5/14, Stay limit: 14 days, Open all year, Reservations not accepted, Elev: 4824ft/1470m, Tel: 541-576-2107, Nearest town: Silver Lake. GPS: 43.006236, -121.134888

442 • C3 | Swamp Wells Horse Camp (Deschutes NF)

Total sites: 5, RV sites: 5, No water, Vault/pit toilet, Tent & RV camping: Free, Rough road, Corrals, Open May-Sep, Max Length: 30ft, Reservations not accepted, Elev: 5427ft/1654m, Tel: 541-383-5300, Nearest town: Bend. GPS: 43.853515, -121.216038

443 • C3 | Thompson Reservoir (Fremont-Winema NF)

Total sites: 19, RV sites: 19, Central water, Vault/pit toilet, No showers, No RV dump, Tent & RV camping: $6, Reduced services 10/15-5/14, Open all year, Reservations not accepted, Elev: 4987ft/1520m, Tel: 541-576-2107, Nearest town: Silver Lake. GPS: 42.959473, -121.091309

444 • C3 | Upper Buck Creek (Fremont-Winema NF)

Total sites: 6, RV sites: 6, No water, Vault/pit toilet, Tent & RV camping: Free, Reduced services 10/15-5/14, Open all year, Reservations not accepted, Elev: 5066ft/1544m, Tel: 541-576-2107, Nearest town: Silver Lake. GPS: 43.053408, -121.266372

445 • C3 | Wiley Flat (Ochoco NF)

Total sites: 5, RV sites: 5, No water, Vault/pit toilet, Tent & RV camping: Free, Stay limit: 14 days, Open all year, Reservations not accepted, Elev: 5364ft/1635m, Tel: 541-416-6500, Nearest town: Prineville. GPS: 44.042271, -120.297644

446 • C4 | Alder Springs Camp (Malheur NF)

Total sites: 3, RV sites: 3, No water, Vault/pit toilet, Tent & RV camping: Free, Stay limit: 14 days, Open May-Sep, Reservations not accepted, Elev: 5489ft/1673m, Tel: 541-575-3000, Nearest town: Burns. GPS: 43.877429, -119.505422

447 • C4 | Buck Spring (Malheur NF)

Total sites: 7, RV sites: 7, No water, Vault/pit toilet, Tent & RV camping: $6, Stay limit: 14 days, Open May-Sep, Max Length: 20ft, Reservations not accepted, Elev: 5033ft/1534m, Tel: 541-575-3000, Nearest town: Burns. GPS: 43.789005, -119.708701

448 • C4 | Delintment Lake (Ochoco NF)

Total sites: 35, RV sites: 29, Central water, Vault/pit toilet, No showers, No RV dump, Tent & RV camping: $10, Stay limit: 14 days, Open May-Sep, Max Length: 20ft, Reservations not accepted, Elev: 5598ft/1706m, Nearest town: Hines. GPS: 43.889639, -119.626504

449 • C4 | Emigrant (Malheur NF)

Total sites: 6, RV sites: 6, No water, Vault/pit toilet, Tent & RV camping: $8, Stay limit: 14 days, Open May-Sep, Max Length: 20ft, Reservations not accepted, Elev: 4905ft/1495m, Tel: 541-575-3000, Nearest town: Burns. GPS: 43.864739, -119.418362

450 • C4 | Falls (Malheur NF)

Total sites: 6, RV sites: 6, Central water, Vault/pit toilet, No showers, No RV dump, Tent & RV camping: $8, Stay limit: 14 days, Open May-Sep, Reservations not accepted, Elev: 4823ft/1470m, Tel: 541-575-3000, Nearest town: Burns. GPS: 43.849786, -119.410735

451 • C4 | Idlewild (Malheur NF)

Total sites: 22, RV sites: 22, Central water, Vault/pit toilet, No showers, No RV dump, Tent & RV camping: $10, Stay limit: 14 days, Open May-Sep, Reservations not accepted, Elev: 5348ft/1630m, Tel: 541-575-3000, Nearest town: Burns. GPS: 43.799561, -118.989990

452 • C4 | Joaquin Miller Horse Camp (Malheur NF)

Total sites: 8, RV sites: 8, Central water, Vault/pit toilet, No showers, No RV dump, Tent & RV camping: $8, Stay limit: 14 days, Open May-Sep, Max Length: 20ft, Reservations not accepted, Elev: 5210ft/1588m, Tel: 541-575-3000, Nearest town: Burns. GPS: 43.826528, -118.971843

453 • C4 | Rock Springs (Malheur NF)

Total sites: 12, RV sites: 12, No water, Vault/pit toilet, Tent & RV camping: $6, Stay limit: 14 days, Open May-Sep, Reservations not accepted, Elev: 5157ft/1572m, Tel: 541-575-3000, Nearest town: Burns. GPS: 43.999224, -118.838921

454 • C4 | Tip Top (Malheur NF)

Total sites: 4, RV sites: 4, No water, Vault/pit toilet, Tent & RV camping: $6, Stay limit: 14 days, Open May-Sep, Reservations not accepted, Elev: 5527ft/1685m, Tel: 541-575-3000, Nearest town: Burns. GPS: 43.896612, -119.642755

455 • C4 | Yellow Jacket (Malheur NF)

Total sites: 20, RV sites: 20, Central water, Vault/pit toilet, No showers, No RV dump, Tent & RV camping: $10, Stay limit: 14 days, Open May-Sep, Reservations not accepted, Elev: 4810ft/1466m, Tel: 541-575-3000, Nearest town: Hines. GPS: 43.876221, -119.272544

456 • D1 | Bear Camp Pasture (Rogue River-Siskiyou NF)

Total sites: 1, RV sites: 1, No water, Vault/pit toilet, Tent & RV camping: Free, Stay limit: 14 days, Generator hours: 0600-2200, Open May-Sep, Reservations not accepted, Elev: 4806ft/1465m, Tel: 541-471 6514, Nearest town: Grants Pass. GPS: 42.627158, -123.830147

457 • D1 | Bolan Lake (Rogue River-Siskiyou NF)

Total sites: 12, RV sites: 12, No water, Vault/pit toilet, Tent & RV camping: $10, Stay limit: 14 days, Generator hours: 0800-2000, Reservations not accepted, Elev: 5558ft/1694m, Tel: 541-592-4000, Nearest town: Cave Junction. GPS: 42.023625, -123.458695

458 • D1 | Briggs Creek (Rogue River-Siskiyou NF)

Total sites: 3, RV sites: 3, No water, Vault/pit toilet, Tent & RV camping: Free, Stay limit: 14 days, Generator hours: 0600-2200, Open May-Oct, Reservations not accepted, Elev: 891ft/272m, Tel: 541-471-6500, Nearest town: Selma. GPS: 42.377761, -123.804198

459 • D1 | Buck Creek (Rogue River-Siskiyou NF)

Total sites: 2, RV sites: 2, No water, Vault/pit toilet, Tent & RV camping: Free, Stay limit: 14 days, Generator hours: 0600-2200, Reservations not accepted, Elev: 2277ft/694m, Tel: 541-439-6200, Nearest town: Powers. GPS: 42.774739, -123.952364

460 • D1 | Butler Bar (Rogue River-Siskiyou NF)

Total sites: 7, RV sites: 7, Central water, Vault/pit toilet, No showers, No RV dump, Tent & RV camping: Free, Stay limit: 14 days, Generator hours: 0600-2200, Open all year, Reservations not accepted, Elev: 626ft/191m, Tel: 541-439-6200, Nearest town: Powers. GPS: 42.725667, -124.270727

461 • D1 | China Flat (Rogue River-Siskiyou NF)

Total sites: 15, RV sites: 15, No water, Vault/pit toilet, Tent & RV camping: Free, Stay limit: 14 days, Generator hours: 0600-2200, Reservations not accepted, Elev: 725ft/221m, Tel: 541-439-6200, Nearest town: Powers. GPS: 42.778692, -124.065509

462 • D1 | Daphne Grove (Rogue River-Siskiyou NF)

Total sites: 14, RV sites: 14, Central water, Vault/pit toilet, No showers, No RV dump, Tent & RV camping: $10, Stay limit: 14 days, Generator hours: 0600-2200, Open all year, Max Length: 30ft, Reservations not accepted, Elev: 1224ft/373m, Tel: 541-439-6200, Nearest town: Powers. GPS: 42.736328, -124.053955

463 • D1 | Eden Valley (Rogue River-Siskiyou NF)

Total sites: 11, RV sites: 11, No water, Vault/pit toilet, Tent & RV camping: Free, Stay limit: 14 days, Generator hours: 0600-2200, Open all year, Reservations not accepted, Elev: 2441ft/744m, Tel: 541-439-6200, Nearest town: Powers. GPS: 42.809014, -123.890941

464 • D1 | First Camp (Rogue River-Siskiyou NF)

Total sites: 3, RV sites: 3, No water, Vault/pit toilet, Tent & RV camping: Free, Dispersed sites along river, Stay limit: 14 days, Generator hours: 0600-2200, Open May-Sep, Max Length: 20ft, Reservations not accepted, Elev: 262ft/80m, Nearest town: Gold Beach. GPS: 42.015218, -124.113084

465 • D1 | Game Lake (Rogue River-Siskiyou NF)

Total sites: 3, RV sites: 3, No water, Vault/pit toilet, Tent & RV camping: Free, Stay limit: 14 days, Generator hours: 0600-2200, Open May-Nov, Reservations not accepted, Elev: 3983ft/1214m, Tel: 541-247-3600, Nearest town: Gold Beach. GPS: 42.432765, -124.087062

466 • D1 | Grassy Flats (Rogue River-Siskiyou NF)

Total sites: 5, RV sites: 5, No water, No toilets, Tent & RV camping: Free, Stay limit: 14 days, Generator hours: 0600-2200, Open May-Oct, Elev: 4429ft/1350m, Tel: 541-471 6514, Nearest town: Agness. GPS: 42.553000, -123.919000

467 • D1 | Grayback (Rogue River-Siskiyou NF)

Total sites: 39, RV sites: 0, Central water, Vault/pit toilet, No showers, No RV dump, Tents only: $15, Stay limit: 14 days, Generator hours: 0600-2200, Open May-Oct, Max Length: 35ft, Reservations not accepted, Elev: 1909ft/582m, Tel: 541-592-4000, Nearest town: Cave Junction. GPS: 42.141628, -123.462913

468 • D1 | Island Camp (Illahe) (Rogue River-Siskiyou NF)

Total sites: 5, RV sites: 5, No water, Vault/pit toilet, Tent & RV camping: $10, Stay limit: 14 days, Open all year, Reservations not accepted, Elev: 1099ft/335m, Tel: 541-439-6200, Nearest town: Powers. GPS: 42.722243, -124.042249

469 • D1 | Josephine (Rogue River-Siskiyou NF)

Total sites: 6, RV sites: 6, No water, Vault/pit toilet, Tent & RV camping: Free, Stay limit: 14 days, Generator hours: 0600-2200, Open all year, Reservations not accepted, Elev: 1204ft/367m, Tel: 541-592-4000, Nearest town: Cave Junction. GPS: 42.242434, -123.686041

470 • D1 | Laird Lake (Rogue River-Siskiyou NF)

Total sites: 4, RV sites: 4, No water, Vault/pit toilet, Tent & RV camping: Free, Winter access limited, Stay limit: 14 days, Generator hours: 0600-2200, Open all year, Reservations not accepted, Elev: 1893ft/577m, Tel: 541-439-6200, Nearest town: Powers. GPS: 42.699259, -124.203098

471 • D1 | Little Falls (Rogue River-Siskiyou NF)

Total sites: 3, RV sites: 3, No water, Vault/pit toilet, Tent & RV camping: $10, Stay limit: 14 days, Generator hours: 0600-2200, Open May-Sep, Reservations not accepted, Elev: 1368ft/417m, Tel: 541-592-4000, Nearest town: Cave Junction. GPS: 42.240779, -123.676284

472 • D1 | Ludlum (Rogue River-Siskiyou NF)

Total sites: 7, RV sites: 7, Central water, No toilets, No showers, No RV dump, Tent & RV camping: $10, Stay limit: 14 days, Generator hours: 0600-2200, Open Apr-Nov, Reservations not accepted, Elev: 233ft/71m, Tel: 541-412-6000, Nearest town: Chetco. GPS: 42.035683, -124.109192

473 • D1 | Meyers Camp (Rogue River-Siskiyou NF)

Total sites: 2, RV sites: 2, No water, Vault/pit toilet, Tent & RV camping: Free, Stay limit: 14 days, Generator hours: 0600-2200, Open May-Sep, Reservations not accepted, Elev: 2497ft/761m, Tel: 541-592-4000, Nearest town: Grants Pass. GPS: 42.472516, -123.670827

474 • D1 | Myrtle Grove (Rogue River-Siskiyou NF)

Total sites: 5, RV sites: 5, No water, Vault/pit toilet, Tent & RV camping: Free, Stay limit: 14 days, Generator hours: 0600-2200, Open all year, Reservations not accepted, Elev: 699ft/213m, Tel: 541-439-6200, Nearest town: Powers. GPS: 42.785651, -124.024461

475 • D1 | Oak Flat/Gravel Bar (Rogue River-Siskiyou NF)

Total sites: 15, RV sites: 15, No water, Vault/pit toilet, Tent & RV camping: Free, Stay limit: 14 days, Generator hours: 0600-2200, Open all year, Max Length: 18ft, Reservations not accepted, Elev: 364ft/111m, Tel: 541-247-3600, Nearest town: Agness. GPS: 42.517147, -124.039712

476 • D1 | Quosatana (Rogue River-Siskiyou NF)

Total sites: 43, RV sites: 43, Central water, Flush toilet, No showers, RV dump, Tent & RV camping: $20, Stay limit: 14 days, Generator hours: 0600-2200, Open all year, Max Length: 30ft, Reservations not accepted, Elev: 216ft/66m, Tel: 541-479-3735, Nearest town: Gold Beach. GPS: 42.497751, -124.232023

477 • D1 | River Bench (Rogue River-Siskiyou NF)

Total sites: 8, RV sites: 0, No water, Vault/pit toilet, Tents only: $10, Walk-to sites, Stay limit: 14 days, Generator hours: 0600-2200, Open May-Sep, Reservations not accepted, Elev: 1118ft/341m, Tel: 541-592-4000, Nearest town: Grants Pass. GPS: 42.294933, -123.739359

478 • D1 | Rock Creek (Coquille) (Rogue River-Siskiyou NF)

Total sites: 7, RV sites: 0, No water, Vault/pit toilet, Tents only: $10, No fee Nov-May, Stay limit: 14 days, Generator hours: 0600-2200, Max Length: 16ft, Reservations not accepted, Elev: 1227ft/374m, Tel: 541-439-6200, Nearest town: Powers. GPS: 42.707905, -124.059248

479 • D1 | Rogue River - Foster Bar (Rogue River-Siskiyou NF)

Total sites: 8, RV sites: 4, Central water, Flush toilet, No showers, No RV dump, Tent & RV camping: $15, Also boat-in sites, Use of fire pans mandatory, Stay limit: 14 days, Generator hours: 0600-2200, Open all year, Reservations not accepted, Elev: 207ft/63m, Tel: 541-479-3735, Nearest town: Illahe. GPS: 42.634255, -124.051978

480 • D1 | Rogue River - Illahe (Rogue River-Siskiyou NF)

Total sites: 14, RV sites: 9, Central water, Flush toilet, No showers, No RV dump, Tent & RV camping: Free, Also boat-in sites, Stay limit: 14 days, Generator hours: 0600-2200, Open May-Sep, Reservations not accepted, Elev: 341ft/104m, Tel: 541-479-3735, Nearest town: Illahe. GPS: 42.626199, -124.057353

481 • D1 | Rogue River - Lobster Creek (Rogue River-Siskiyou NF)

Total sites: 7, RV sites: 4, Central water, Flush toilet, No showers, No RV dump, Tent & RV camping: $15, Stay limit: 14 days, Generator hours: 0600-2200, Open all year, Reservations not accepted, Elev: 49ft/15m, Tel: 541-479-3735, Nearest town: Gold Beach. GPS: 42.502564, -124.295414

482 • D1 | Sam Brown (Rogue River-Siskiyou NF)

Total sites: 19, RV sites: 19, No water, Vault/pit toilet, Tent & RV camping: $10, Stay limit: 14 days, Generator hours: 0600-2200, Open May-Oct, Max Length: 24ft, Reservations not accepted, Elev: 2041ft/622m, Tel: 541-592-4000, Nearest town: Merlin. GPS: 42.441902, -123.686355

483 • D1 | Secret Creek (Rogue River-Siskiyou NF)

Total sites: 4, RV sites: 4, No water, Vault/pit toilet, Tent & RV

camping: Free, Stay limit: 14 days, Generator hours: 0600-2200, Open May-Sep, Reservations not accepted, Elev: 2070ft/631m, Tel: 541-592-4000, Nearest town: Galice. GPS: 42.421799, -123.688916

484 • D1 | Sixmile Camp (Rogue River-Siskiyou NF)

Total sites: 4, RV sites: 0, No water, Vault/pit toilet, Tents only: $10, Walk-to sites, Stay limit: 14 days, Generator hours: 0600-2200, Open May-Sep, Reservations not accepted, Elev: 1227ft/374m, Tel: 541-592-4000, Nearest town: Cave Junction. GPS: 42.297109, -123.730821

485 • D1 | Spalding Pond (Rogue River-Siskiyou NF)

Total sites: 4, RV sites: 4, No water, No toilets, Tent & RV camping: Free, Stay limit: 14 days, Generator hours: 0600-2200, Open May-Oct, Reservations not accepted, Elev: 3402ft/1037m, Tel: 541-592-4000, Nearest town: Galice. GPS: 42.346501, -123.703682

486 • D1 | Sru Lake (Rogue River-Siskiyou NF)

Total sites: 6, RV sites: 6, No water, Vault/pit toilet, Tent & RV camping: Free, Stay limit: 14 days, Generator hours: 0600-2200, Open all year, Reservations not accepted, Elev: 2362ft/720m, Tel: 541-439-6200, Nearest town: Powers. GPS: 42.730834, -124.006088

487 • D1 | Store Gulch (Rogue River-Siskiyou NF)

Total sites: 6, RV sites: 4, No water, Vault/pit toilet, Tent & RV camping: $10, 2 walk-to sites, Stay limit: 14 days, Generator hours: 0600-2200, Open May-Sep, Reservations not accepted, Elev: 1178ft/359m, Tel: 541-592-4000, Nearest town: Galice. GPS: 42.295385, -123.754264

488 • D1 | Sunshine Bar (Rogue River-Siskiyou NF)

Total sites: 6, RV sites: 6, No water, Vault/pit toilet, Tent & RV camping: Free, Stay limit: 14 days, Generator hours: 0600-2200, Open all year, Reservations not accepted, Elev: 594ft/181m, Tel: 541-439-6200, Nearest town: Powers. GPS: 42.712405, -124.311761

489 • D1 | Wildhorse (Rogue River-Siskiyou NF)

Total sites: 3, RV sites: 3, No water, Vault/pit toilet, Tent & RV camping: Free, Stay limit: 14 days, Generator hours: 0600-2200, Open May-Nov, Reservations not accepted, Elev: 3556ft/1084m, Tel: 541-247-3600, Nearest town: Gold Beach. GPS: 42.460766, -124.162819

490 • D2 | Abbott Creek (Abbott Butte) (Rogue River-Siskiyou NF)

Total sites: 25, RV sites: 25, Central water, Vault/pit toilet, No showers, No RV dump, Tent & RV camping: $14, Stay limit: 14 days, Generator hours: 0600-2200, Open May-Oct, Max Length: 20ft, Reservations not accepted, Elev: 3084ft/940m, Tel: 541-865-2795, Nearest town: Prospect. GPS: 42.881095, -122.506241

491 • D2 | Aspen Point (Fremont-Winema NF)

Total sites: 49, RV sites: 43, Central water, Flush toilet, No showers, RV dump, Tent & RV camping: $25, Group site: $125, Open May-Sep, Max Length: 120ft, Reservations accepted, Elev: 5020ft/1530m, Tel: 541-885-3400, Nearest town: Klamath Falls. GPS: 42.384521, -122.213623

492 • D2 | Beaver Dam (Rogue River-Siskiyou NF)

Total sites: 4, RV sites: 2, No water, Vault/pit toilet, Tent & RV camping: $8, Stay limit: 14 days, Generator hours: 0600-2200, Open May-Nov, Max Length: 16ft, Reservations not accepted, Elev: 4550ft/1387m, Tel: 541-560-3400, Nearest town: Butte Falls. GPS: 42.304182, -122.367211

493 • D2 | Carberry (Rogue River-Siskiyou NF)

Total sites: 10, RV sites: 0, No water, Vault/pit toilet, Tents only: $15, No fees in winter, Stay limit: 14 days, Generator hours: 0600-2200, Open all year, Reservations not accepted, Elev: 2293ft/699m, Tel: 541-899-3800, Nearest town: Applegate. GPS: 42.058943, -123.163844

494 • D2 | Daley Creek (Rogue River-Siskiyou NF)

Total sites: 6, RV sites: 3, No water, Vault/pit toilet, Tent & RV camping: $8, Stay limit: 14 days, Generator hours: 0800-2200, Open May-Nov, Reservations not accepted, Elev: 4583ft/1397m, Tel: 541-865-2700, Nearest town: Butte Falls. GPS: 42.306475, -122.367068

495 • D2 | Devil's Flat (Umpqua NF)

Total sites: 3, RV sites: 3, No water, Vault/pit toilet, Tent & RV camping: $10, Stay limit: 14 days, Generator hours: 0600-2200, Open May-Oct, Max Length: 22ft, Reservations not accepted, Elev: 2503ft/763m, Tel: 541-825-3100, Nearest town: Tiller. GPS: 42.817701, -123.026486

496 • D2 | Doe Point (Rogue River-Siskiyou NF)

Total sites: 29, RV sites: 24, Central water, Flush toilet, No showers, RV dump, Tents: $13/RVs: $25, Stay limit: 14 days, Open May-Oct, Max Length: 72ft, Reservations accepted, Elev: 4744ft/1446m, Tel: 541-560-3900, Nearest town: White City. GPS: 42.392634, -122.323913

497 • D2 | Fish Lake (Mt McLoughlin) (Rogue River-Siskiyou NF)

Total sites: 20, RV sites: 17, Central water, No toilets, No showers, No RV dump, Tents: $13/RVs: $25, Also walk-to sites, Stay limit: 14 days, Open May-Sep, Max Length: 60ft, Reservations accepted, Elev: 4816ft/1468m, Tel: 541-560-3900, Nearest town: Klamath Falls. GPS: 42.395055, -122.321433

498 • D2 | Fourbit Ford (Rogue River-Siskiyou NF)

Total sites: 7, RV sites: 7, Central water, Vault/pit toilet, No showers, No RV dump, Tent & RV camping: $14, Stay limit: 14 days, Generator hours: 0600-2200, Open May-Sep, Reservations not accepted, Elev: 3264ft/995m, Tel: 541-560-3400, Nearest town: Butte Falls. GPS: 42.501214, -122.404295

499 • D2 | Fourmile Lake (Fremont-Winema NF)

Total sites: 29, RV sites: 29, No water, Vault/pit toilet, Tent & RV camping: $20, Generator hours: 0700-2200, Open Jul-Sep, Max Length: 88ft, Reservations accepted, Elev: 5758ft/1755m, Tel: 541-885-3400, Nearest town: Klamath Falls. GPS: 42.455322, -122.248291

500 • D2 | Hart-tish Park (Rogue River-Siskiyou NF)

Total sites: 15, RV sites: 8, Central water, Flush toilet, Tent & RV camping: $20, Group site $40, Stay limit: 14 days, Open Apr-Sep,

Max Length: 40ft, Reservations accepted, Elev: 2090ft/637m, Tel: 541-899-9220, Nearest town: Jacksonville. GPS: 42.052041, -123.128651

501 • D2 | Huckleberry Mountain (Rogue River-Siskiyou NF)

Total sites: 25, RV sites: 25, No water, Vault/pit toilet, Tent & RV camping: Free, Stay limit: 14 days, Generator hours: 0600-2200, Open May-Oct, Max Length: 16ft, Reservations not accepted, Elev: 5467ft/1666m, Tel: 541-560-3400, Nearest town: Prospect. GPS: 42.876344, -122.338061

502 • D2 | Imnaha (Rogue River-Siskiyou NF)

Total sites: 5, RV sites: 5, Central water, Vault/pit toilet, No showers, No RV dump, Tent & RV camping: $10, Stay limit: 14 days, Open May-Oct, Reservations not accepted, Elev: 3852ft/1174m, Tel: 541-865-2700, Nearest town: Butte Falls. GPS: 42.702528, -122.334408

503 • D2 | Jackson on Applegate (Rogue River-Siskiyou NF)

Total sites: 11, RV sites: 3, Central water, Flush toilet, No showers, No RV dump, Tent & RV camping: $20, Group site: $40, Tents/small RVs only - no trailers, Stay limit: 14 days, Open all year, Max Length: 25ft, Reservations accepted, Elev: 1673ft/510m, Tel: 541-899-3800, Nearest town: Ruch. GPS: 42.114108, -123.087455

504 • D2 | Mill Creek (Rogue River-Siskiyou NF)

Total sites: 10, RV sites: 10, No water, Vault/pit toilet, Tent & RV camping: $8, Stay limit: 14 days, Generator hours: 0800-2200, Open May-Oct, Reservations not accepted, Elev: 2813ft/857m, Tel: 541-865-2700, Nearest town: Prospect. GPS: 42.795382, -122.467727

505 • D2 | Mt Ashland (Klamath NF)

Total sites: 9, RV sites: 9, No water, Vault/pit toilet, Tent & RV camping: Free, Open May-Oct, Reservations not accepted, Elev: 6795ft/2071m, Tel: 530-493-2243, Nearest town: Ashland. GPS: 42.075548, -122.714284

506 • D2 | Natural Bridge (Rogue River-Siskiyou NF)

Total sites: 17, RV sites: 17, No water, Vault/pit toilet, Tent & RV camping: $15, Stay limit: 14 days, Generator hours: 0600-2200, Open May-Oct, Max Length: 30ft, Reservations not accepted, Elev: 3268ft/996m, Tel: 541-560-3400, Nearest town: Prospect. GPS: 42.889648, -122.463867

507 • D2 | North Fork (Mt McLoughlin) (Rogue River-Siskiyou NF)

Total sites: 6, RV sites: 3, Central water, Vault/pit toilet, No showers, No RV dump, Tent & RV camping: $16, Stay limit: 14 days, Generator hours: 0600-2200, Open May-Oct, Max Length: 50ft, Reservations accepted, Elev: 4675ft/1425m, Tel: 541-865-2700, Nearest town: Butte Falls. GPS: 42.378131, -122.360263

508 • D2 | Odessa (Fremont-Winema NF)

Total sites: 6, RV sites: 6, No water, No toilets, Tent & RV camping: Free, Open all year, Reservations not accepted, Elev: 4190ft/1277m, Tel: 541-885-3400, Nearest town: Odessa. GPS: 42.429045, -122.061419

509 • D2 | Parker Meadows (Rogue River-Siskiyou NF)

Total sites: 8, RV sites: 5, Central water, Vault/pit toilet, No showers, No RV dump, Tent & RV camping: $10, Stay limit: 14 days, Generator hours: 0600-2200, Open Jul-Oct, Reservations not accepted, Elev: 5007ft/1526m, Tel: 541-560-3400, Nearest town: Butte Falls. GPS: 42.600143, -122.323304

510 • D2 | River Bridge (Rogue River-Siskiyou NF)

Total sites: 11, RV sites: 11, No water, Vault/pit toilet, Tent & RV camping: $8, Stay limit: 14 days, Generator hours: 0600-2200, Open May-Oct, Max Length: 25ft, Reservations not accepted, Elev: 2930ft/893m, Tel: 541-560-3400, Nearest town: Prospect. GPS: 42.822012, -122.493674

511 • D2 | Scott Creek (Fremont-Winema NF)

Total sites: 6, RV sites: 6, No water, Vault/pit toilet, Tent & RV camping: Free, Reduced services 10/15-5/14, Open all year, Reservations not accepted, Elev: 4710ft/1436m, Tel: 541-365-7001, Nearest town: Chemult. GPS: 42.885341, -121.924226

512 • D2 | Sevenmile Marsh Horse Camp (Fremont-Winema NF)

Total sites: 8, RV sites: 8, No water, Vault/pit toilet, Tent & RV camping: Free, Open Jun-Sep, Reservations not accepted, Elev: 4833ft/1473m, Tel: 541-883-6714, Nearest town: Fort Klamath. GPS: 42.714375, -122.130955

513 • D2 | South Fork (Rogue River) (Rogue River-Siskiyou NF)

Total sites: 6, RV sites: 6, No water, Vault/pit toilet, Tent & RV camping: $15, Stay limit: 14 days, Generator hours: 0600-2200, Open May-Oct, Reservations not accepted, Elev: 4058ft/1237m, Tel: 541-865-2700, Nearest town: Prospect. GPS: 42.645000, -122.334000

514 • D2 | Sunset (Fremont-Winema NF)

Total sites: 64, RV sites: 64, Elec sites: 4, Central water, Flush toilet, Tents: $25/RVs: $25-30, Open May-Sep, Max Length: 65ft, Reservations accepted, Elev: 5059ft/1542m, Tel: 866-201-4194, Nearest town: Klamath Falls. GPS: 42.370648, -122.205256

515 • D2 | Threehorn (Umpqua NF)

Total sites: 5, RV sites: 5, No water, Vault/pit toilet, Tent & RV camping: $10, Stay limit: 14 days, Generator hours: 0600-2200, Open all year, Max Length: 22ft, Reservations not accepted, Elev: 2743ft/836m, Tel: 541-825-3100, Nearest town: Tiller. GPS: 42.802909, -122.867552

516 • D2 | Whiskey Springs (Rogue River-Siskiyou NF)

Total sites: 34, RV sites: 34, Central water, Vault/pit toilet, No showers, No RV dump, Tent & RV camping: $18, Stay limit: 14 days, Generator hours: 0600-2200, Open May-Sep, Max Length: 40ft, Reservations accepted, Elev: 3182ft/970m, Tel: 541-865-2700, Nearest town: Butte Falls. GPS: 42.496811, -122.419475

517 • D2 | Williamson River (Fremont-Winema NF)

Total sites: 20, RV sites: 20, Central water, Vault/pit toilet, No showers, No RV dump, Tent & RV camping: $15, Reduced services 10/15-5/14, Open all year, Reservations not accepted, Elev: 4236ft/1291m, Tel: 541-783-4009, Nearest town: Chiloquin. GPS: 42.659001, -121.854485

518 • D2 | Willow Prairie Horse Camp (Rogue River-Siskiyou NF)

Total sites: 10, RV sites: 10, Central water, Vault/pit toilet, No showers, No RV dump, Tent & RV camping: $15, Stay limit: 14 days, Generator hours: 0600-2200, Open May-Oct, Max Length: 40ft, Reservations accepted, Elev: 4423ft/1348m, Tel: 541-865-2700, Nearest town: Butte Falls. GPS: 42.405857, -122.389982

519 • D2 | Wrangle (Rogue River-Siskiyou NF)

Total sites: 5, RV sites: 0, No water, Vault/pit toilet, Tents only: Free, Stay limit: 14 days, Generator hours: 0600-2200, Open Jun-Oct, Reservations not accepted, Elev: 6283ft/1915m, Tel: 541-899-3800, Nearest town: Ashland. GPS: 42.050203, -122.856392

520 • D3 | Campbell Lake (Fremont-Winema NF)

Total sites: 16, RV sites: 16, Central water, Vault/pit toilet, No showers, No RV dump, Tent & RV camping: $6, Reduced services 10/15-5/14, Open all year, Elev: 7257ft/2212m, Tel: 541-943-3114, Nearest town: Paisley. GPS: 42.560547, -120.753174

521 • D3 | Chewaucan Crossing TH (Fremont-Winema NF)

Total sites: 5, RV sites: 5, No water, Vault/pit toilet, Tent & RV camping: Free, Reduced services 10/15-5/14, Open all year, Elev: 4806ft/1465m, Tel: 541-943-3114, Nearest town: Paisley. GPS: 42.616626, -120.606173

522 • D3 | Clear Springs (Fremont-Winema NF)

Total sites: 2, RV sites: 2, Central water, Vault/pit toilet, No showers, No RV dump, Tent & RV camping: Free, Reduced services 10/15-5/14, Open all year, Elev: 5466ft/1666m, Tel: 541-943-3114, Nearest town: Paisley. GPS: 42.471846, -120.711657

523 • D3 | Corral Creek (Fremont-Winema NF)

Total sites: 6, RV sites: 6, No water, Vault/pit toilet, Tent & RV camping: Free, Reduced services 10/15-5/14, Open all year, Elev: 5955ft/1815m, Tel: 541-943-3114, Nearest town: Bly. GPS: 42.457116, -120.784746

524 • D3 | Cottonwood (Fremont-Winema NF)

Total sites: 27, RV sites: 23, Central water, Vault/pit toilet, No showers, No RV dump, Tent & RV camping: $6, Reduced services 10/15-5/14, Open all year, Reservations not accepted, Elev: 6204ft/1891m, Tel: 541-943-3114, Nearest town: Lakeview. GPS: 42.285360, -120.639240

525 • D3 | Currier Horse Camp (Fremont-Winema NF)

Total sites: 4, RV sites: 4, No water, No toilets, Tent & RV camping: Free, Open Jun-Sep, Reservations not accepted, Elev: 6900ft/2103m, Tel: 541-943-3114, Nearest town: Paisley. GPS: 42.729426, -120.819381

526 • D3 | Dairy Point (Fremont-Winema NF)

Total sites: 5, RV sites: 5, Central water, Vault/pit toilet, No showers, No RV dump, Tent & RV camping: Free, Reduced services 10/15-5/14, Open all year, Reservations not accepted, Elev: 5201ft/1585m, Tel: 541-943-3114, Nearest town: Lakeview. GPS: 42.467041, -120.640637

527 • D3 | Dead Horse Creek (Fremont-Winema NF)

Total sites: 4, RV sites: 4, No water, Vault/pit toilet, Tent & RV camping: Free, Open Apr-Oct, Elev: 5390ft/1643m, Nearest town: Paisley. GPS: 42.474167, -120.703889

528 • D3 | Dead Horse Lake (Fremont-Winema NF)

Total sites: 9, RV sites: 9, Central water, No toilets, No showers, No RV dump, Tent & RV camping: $6, Reduced services Oct-May, Open all year, Reservations not accepted, Elev: 7429ft/2264m, Tel: 541-943-3114, Nearest town: Paisley. GPS: 42.559752, -120.775017

529 • D3 | Deep Creek (Fremont-Winema NF)

Total sites: 4, RV sites: 4, No water, Vault/pit toilet, Tent & RV camping: Free, Reduced services 10/15-5/14, Open all year, Reservations not accepted, Elev: 5876ft/1791m, Tel: 541-947-6300, Nearest town: Lakeview. GPS: 42.057583, -120.174339

530 • D3 | Dismal Creek (Fremont-Winema NF)

Total sites: 3, RV sites: 3, No water, Vault/pit toilet, Tent & RV camping: Free, Open Jun-Oct, Reservations not accepted, Elev: 5760ft/1756m, Nearest town: Lakeview. GPS: 42.062389, -120.152574

531 • D3 | Dog Lake (Fremont-Winema NF)

Total sites: 15, RV sites: 15, No water, Vault/pit toilet, Tent & RV camping: $6, Reduced services 10/15-5/14, Open all year, Reservations not accepted, Elev: 5257ft/1602m, Tel: 541-947-3334, Nearest town: Lakeview. GPS: 42.085179, -120.706878

532 • D3 | Drews Creek (Fremont-Winema NF)

Total sites: 3, RV sites: 3, Central water, Vault/pit toilet, No showers, No RV dump, Tent & RV camping: Free, 2 group sites, Reduced services 10/15-5/14, Open all year, Reservations not accepted, Elev: 4842ft/1476m, Tel: 541-947-3334, Nearest town: Lakeview. GPS: 42.119277, -120.581392

533 • D3 | Happy Camp (Fremont-Winema NF)

Total sites: 9, RV sites: 9, Central water, Vault/pit toilet, Tent & RV camping: Free, Reduced services 10/15-5/14, Open all year, Reservations not accepted, Elev: 5325ft/1623m, Tel: 541-943-3114, Nearest town: Paisley. GPS: 42.476078, -120.684258

534 • D3 | Head of the River (Fremont-Winema NF)

Total sites: 5, RV sites: 0, No water, Vault/pit toilet, Tents only: Free, Reduced services 10/15-5/14, Open all year, Reservations not accepted, Elev: 4636ft/1413m, Tel: 541-783-4001, Nearest town: Chiloquin. GPS: 42.731532, -121.420563

535 • D3 | Holbrook Reservoir (Fremont-Winema NF)

Total sites: 1, RV sites: 1, No water, Vault/pit toilet, Tent & RV camping: Free, Reduced services 10/15-5/14, Open all year, Reservations not accepted, Elev: 5439ft/1658m, Tel: 541-353-2427, Nearest town: Bly. GPS: 42.265477, -120.853135

536 • D3 | Jones Crossing Forest Camp (Fremont-Winema NF)

Total sites: 8, RV sites: 8, No water, Vault/pit toilet, Tent & RV camping: Free, Reduced services 10/15-5/14, Open all year, Reservations not accepted, Elev: 4829ft/1472m, Tel: 541-943-3114, Nearest town: Paisley. GPS: 42.605851, -120.598874

537 • D3 | Lee Thomas (Fremont-Winema NF)

Total sites: 7, RV sites: 7, Central water, No RV dump, Tent & RV camping: Free, Reduced services 10/15-5/14, Open all year, Reservations not accepted, Elev: 6253ft/1906m, Tel: 541-943-3114, Nearest town: Paisley. GPS: 42.590151, -120.838902

538 • D3 | Lofton Reservoir (Fremont-Winema NF)

Total sites: 26, RV sites: 26, No water, Vault/pit toilet, Tent & RV camping: $6, Reduced services 10/15-5/14, Open May-Oct, Reservations not accepted, Elev: 6174ft/1882m, Tel: 541-353-2750, Nearest town: Bly. GPS: 42.262939, -120.816895

539 • D3 | Marster Spring (Fremont-Winema NF)

Total sites: 10, RV sites: 10, Central water, Vault/pit toilet, No showers, No RV dump, Tent & RV camping: $6, Reduced services 10/15-5/14, Open May-Oct, Reservations not accepted, Elev: 4767ft/1453m, Tel: 541-943-4479, Nearest town: Paisley. GPS: 42.623337, -120.605521

540 • D3 | Moss Meadow Horse Camp (Fremont-Winema NF)

Total sites: 3, RV sites: 3, No water, Vault/pit toilet, Tent & RV camping: Free, Reduced services 9/16-6/14, Open all year, Reservations not accepted, Elev: 5961ft/1817m, Tel: 541-943-3114, Nearest town: Lakeview. GPS: 42.478759, -120.485495

541 • D3 | Mud Creek (Fremont-Winema NF)

Total sites: 7, RV sites: 7, No water, Vault/pit toilet, Tent & RV camping: Free, Reduced services 10/15-5/14, Open all year, Reservations not accepted, Elev: 6486ft/1977m, Tel: 541-947-6300, Nearest town: Lakeview. GPS: 42.281714, -120.204986

542 • D3 | Pike's Crossing (Fremont-Winema NF)

Total sites: 6, RV sites: 6, No water, Vault/pit toilet, Tent & RV camping: Free, Open May-Oct, Reservations not accepted, Elev: 5712ft/1741m, Tel: 541-943-4479, Nearest town: Paisley. GPS: 42.697896, -120.933069

543 • D3 | Sandhill Crossing (Fremont-Winema NF)

Total sites: 5, RV sites: 5, Central water, Vault/pit toilet, No showers, No RV dump, Tent & RV camping: Free, Reduced services 10/15-5/14, Open all year, Reservations not accepted, Elev: 6119ft/1865m, Tel: 541-943-4479, Nearest town: Paisley. GPS: 42.594055, -120.879944

544 • D3 | Twin Springs (Fremont-Winema NF)

Total sites: 3, RV sites: 0, Central water, Vault/pit toilet, No showers, No RV dump, Tents only: Free, Open May-Sep, Reservations not accepted, Elev: 6457ft/1968m, Tel: 541-947-6300, Nearest town: Lakeview. GPS: 42.156855, -120.212942

545 • D3 | Upper Jones (Fremont-Winema NF)

Total sites: 2, RV sites: 2, No water, No toilets, Tent & RV camping: Free, Open Apr-Oct, Reservations not accepted, Elev: 4879ft/1487m, Nearest town: Paisley. GPS: 42.598642, -120.599055

546 • D3 | Vee Lake (Fremont-Winema NF)

Total sites: 2, RV sites: 2, No water, Vault/pit toilet, Tent & RV camping: Free, Reduced services 10/15-5/14, Open all year, Reservations not accepted, Elev: 6132ft/1869m, Tel: 541-947-6300, Nearest town: Lakeview. GPS: 42.422085, -120.161946

547 • D3 | Willow Creek (Fremont-Winema NF)

Total sites: 8, RV sites: 8, No water, Vault/pit toilet, Tent & RV camping: Free, Reduced services 10/15-5/14, Open all year, Reservations not accepted, Elev: 6129ft/1868m, Tel: 541-947-6300, Nearest town: Lakeview. GPS: 42.093062, -120.201818

Pennsylvania

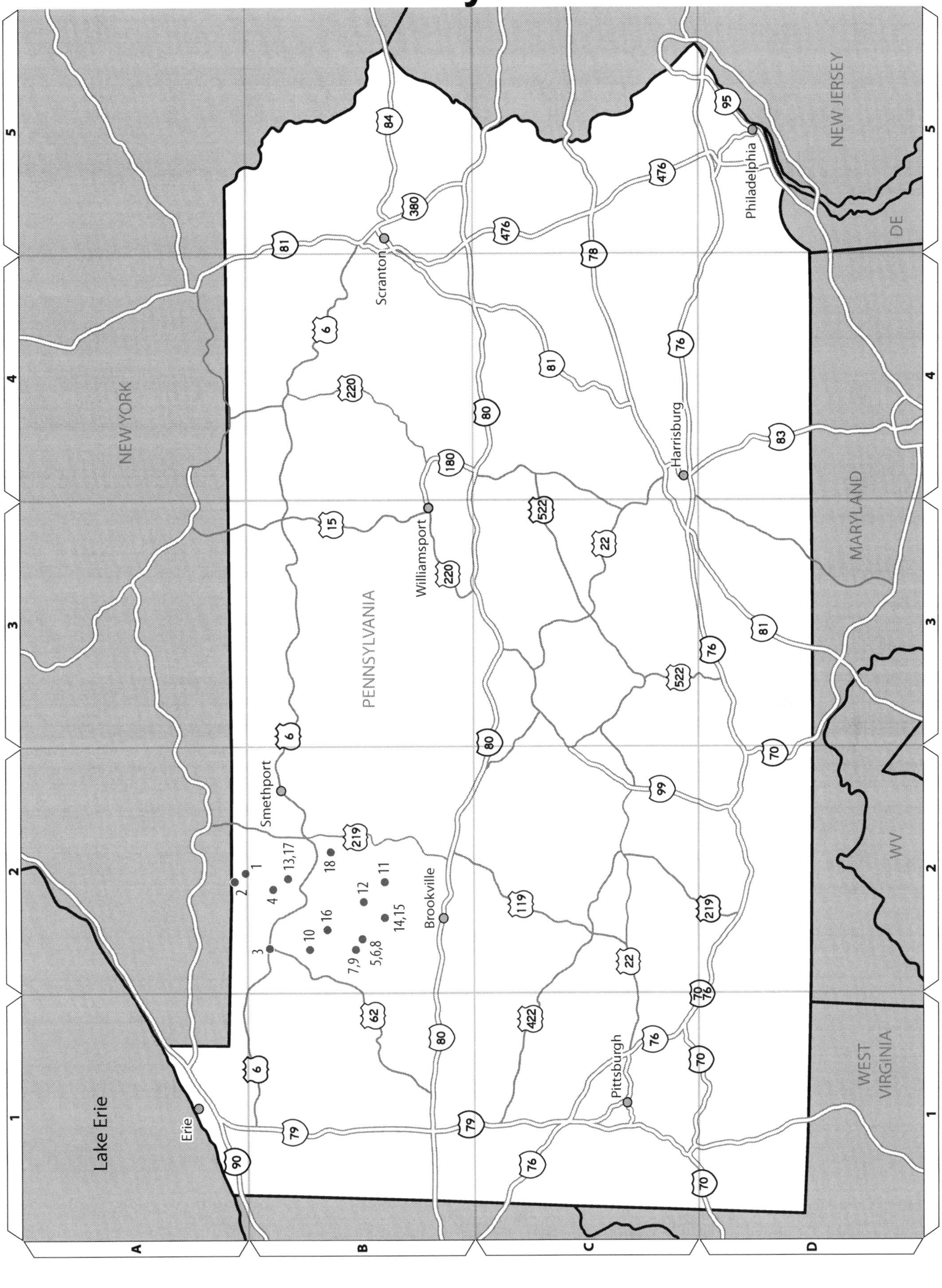

Map	ID	Map	ID
A2	1-2	B2	3-18

Alphabetical List of Camping Areas

1 • A2 | Tracy Ridge (Allegheny NF)

Total sites: 45, RV sites: 45, Central water, Vault/pit toilet, No showers, RV dump, Tent & RV camping: $12, Group sites: $75, Stay limit: 14 days, Open Apr-Dec, Max Length: 60ft, Reservations accepted, Elev: 2257ft/688m, Tel: 814-368-4158, Nearest town: Bradford. GPS: 41.943003, -78.876615

2 • A2 | Willow Bay (Allegheny NF)

Total sites: 101, RV sites: 74, Elec sites: 38, Central water, Flush toilet, Free showers, RV dump, Tents: $20-24/RVs: $20-29, Also cabins, Stay limit: 14 days, Open all year, Max Length: 60ft, Reservations accepted, Elev: 1332ft/406m, Tel: 814-362-4613, Nearest town: Bradford. GPS: 41.988770, -78.917236

3 • B2 | Buckaloons (Allegheny NF)

Total sites: 51, RV sites: 51, Elec sites: 43, Central water, Flush toilet, Free showers, RV dump, Tents: $20/RVs: $20-25, Group site: $20-$60, Stay limit: 14 days, Generator hours: 0600-2200, Open May-Oct, Max Length: 45ft, Reservations accepted, Elev: 1164ft/355m, Tel: 814-362-4613, Nearest town: Warren. GPS: 41.838855, -79.257367

4 • B2 | Dewdrop (Allegheny NF)

Total sites: 74, RV sites: 56, Central water, Flush toilet, Free showers, RV dump, Tent & RV camping: $20-24, Stay limit: 14 days, Generator hours: 0600-2200, Open May-Sep, Max Length: 50ft, Reservations accepted, Elev: 1437ft/438m, Tel: 814-945-6511, Nearest town: Warren. GPS: 41.832031, -78.959229

5 • B2 | FR 145 Site 17 (Allegheny NF)

Total sites: 2, RV sites: 1, No water, No toilets, Tent & RV camping: Free, Stay limit: 14 days, Elev: 1273ft/388m, Tel: 814-728-6100, Nearest town: Marienville. GPS: 41.507126, -79.210917

6 • B2 | FR 145 Site 24 (Allegheny NF)

Total sites: 2, RV sites: 1, No water, No toilets, Tent & RV camping: Free, Stay limit: 14 days, Elev: 1353ft/412m, Tel: 814-728-6100, Nearest town: Marienville. GPS: 41.475287, -79.209062

7 • B2 | FR 145 Sites 13-14 (Allegheny NF)

Total sites: 6, RV sites: 1, No water, No toilets, Tents only: Free, Walk-to sites, Stay limit: 14 days, Elev: 1222ft/372m, Tel: 814-728-6100, Nearest town: Marienville. GPS: 41.517125, -79.231661

8 • B2 | FR 145 Sites 21-22 (Allegheny NF)

Total sites: 5, No water, No toilets, Tents only: Free, Walk-to sites, Stay limit: 14 days, Elev: 1289ft/393m, Tel: 814-728-6100, Nearest town: Marienville. GPS: 41.494156, -79.207703

9 • B2 | FR 210 Site 3 (Allegheny NF)

Total sites: 3, RV sites: 1, No water, No toilets, Tent & RV camping: Free, Stay limit: 14 days, Elev: 1751ft/534m, Tel: 814-728-6100, Nearest town: Marienville. GPS: 41.499857, -79.256063

10 • B2 | Hearts Content (Allegheny NF)

Total sites: 26, RV sites: 26, Central water, Vault/pit toilet, No showers, RV dump, Tent & RV camping: $12-14, Group site: $20-$60, 2 sites with lean-to shelters, Open May-Oct, Reservations accepted, Elev: 1925ft/587m, Tel: 814-368-4158, Nearest town: Warren. GPS: 41.691282, -79.257121

11 • B2 | Irwin Run Canoe Launch (Allegheny NF)

Total sites: 1, RV sites: 0, No water, Vault/pit toilet, Tents only: Free, Walk-to sites, Stay limit: 14 days, Elev: 1278ft/390m, Nearest town: Portland Mills. GPS: 41.400134, -78.905666

12 • B2 | Kelly Pines Equestrian (Allegheny NF)

Total sites: 7, RV sites: 7, No water, Vault/pit toilet, Tent & RV camping: $15, 2 sites are non-equestrian, Stock water available, Stay limit: 14 days, Open Apr-Dec, Max Length: 40ft, Reservations accepted, Elev: 1493ft/455m, Tel: 814-368-4158, Nearest town: Marienville. GPS: 41.483794, -79.009945

13 • B2 | Kiasutha (Allegheny NF)

Total sites: 93, RV sites: 92, Elec sites: 17, Water at site, Flush toilet, Free showers, RV dump, Tents: $20/RVs: $25-35, 12 Full hookup sites, Stay limit: 14 days, Generator hours: 0600-2200, Open May-Sep, Max Length: 45ft, Reservations accepted, Elev: 1348ft/411m, Tel: 814-945-6511, Nearest town: Kane. GPS: 41.785156, -78.902344

14 • B2 | Loleta RV (Allegheny NF)

Total sites: 20, RV sites: 20, Elec sites: 20, Central water, Vault/pit toilet, No showers, No RV dump, Tent & RV camping: $16-25, Showers at beach bathhouse, Stay limit: 14 days, Generator hours: 0600-2200, Open Apr-Sep, Max Length: 90ft, Reservations accepted, Elev: 1344ft/410m, Nearest town: Marienville. GPS: 41.400006, -79.082301

15 • B2 | Loleta Upper (Allegheny NF)

Total sites: 18, RV sites: 18, Central water, Vault/pit toilet, No showers, No RV dump, Tent & RV camping: $16, 2 group sites: $40-$100, Showers at beach bathhouse, Stay limit: 14 days, Generator hours: 0600-2200, Open Apr-Oct, Max Length:

90ft, Reservations accepted, Elev: 1501ft/458m, Nearest town: Marienville. GPS: 41.404424, -79.079684

16 • B2 | Minister Creek (Allegheny NF)

Total sites: 6, RV sites: 6, Central water, Vault/pit toilet, No showers, No RV dump, Tent & RV camping: $12, Stay limit: 14 days, Generator hours: 0600-2200, Open Apr-Dec, Reservations not accepted, Elev: 1371ft/418m, Tel: 814-362-4613, Nearest town: Sheffield. GPS: 41.621406, -79.154023

17 • B2 | Red Bridge (Allegheny NF)

Total sites: 67, RV sites: 57, Elec sites: 25, Central water, Flush toilet, Free showers, RV dump, Tents: $20-24/RVs: $20-39, Also cabins, 12 Full hookup sites, Stay limit: 14 days, Open Apr-Oct, Max Length: 50ft, Reservations accepted, Elev: 1430ft/436m, Tel: 814-945-6511, Nearest town: Kane. GPS: 41.776367, -78.887207

18 • B2 | Twin Lakes (Allegheny NF)

Total sites: 48, RV sites: 48, Elec sites: 19, Central water, Flush toilet, Free showers, RV dump, Tents: $16/RVs: $16-23, 10' height limit - low bridge, Stay limit: 14 days, Open May-Dec, Max Length: 28ft, Reservations accepted, Elev: 1814ft/553m, Tel: 814-389-3019, Nearest town: Wilcox. GPS: 41.613178, -78.759647

South Carolina

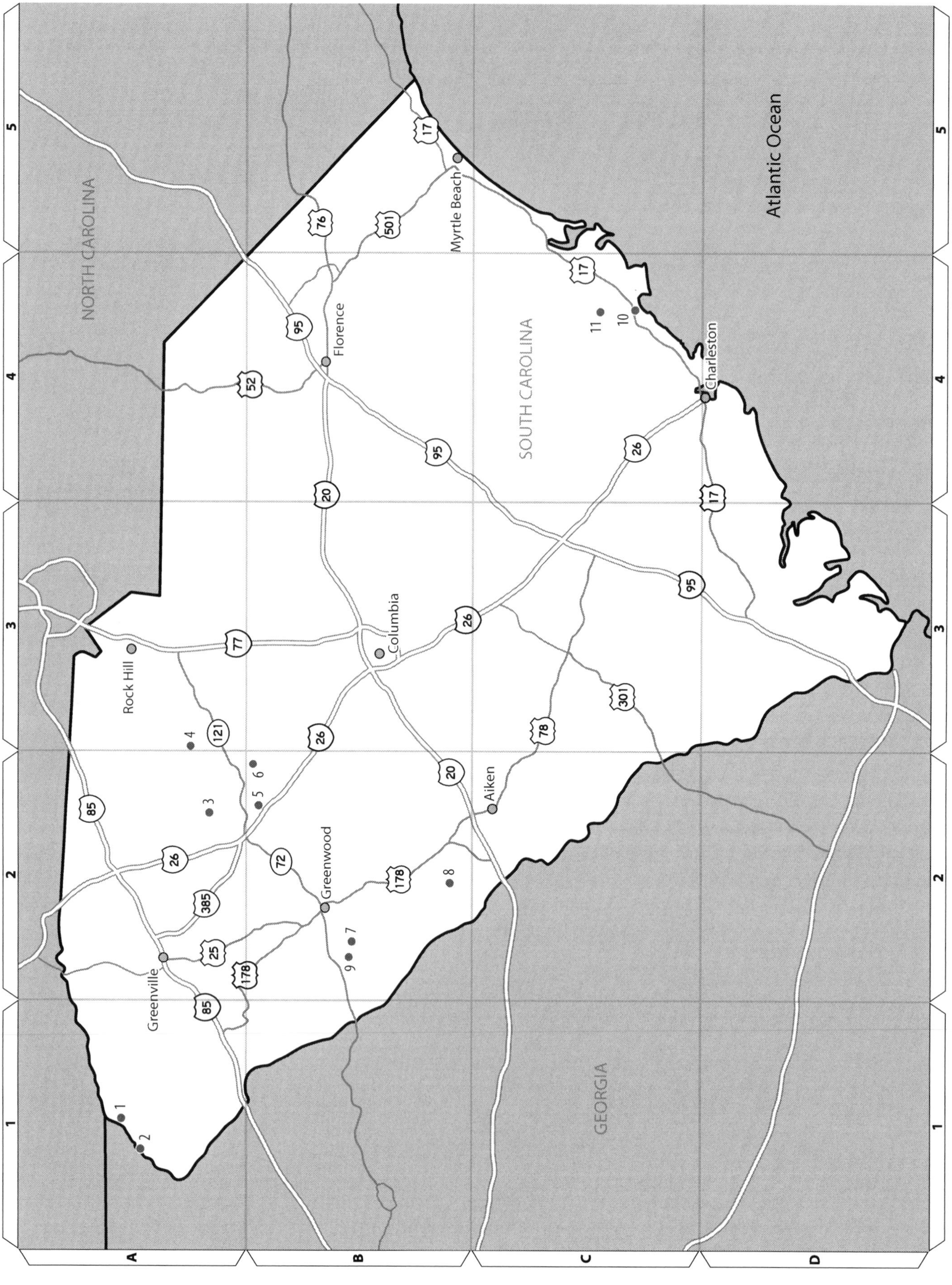

Map	ID	Map	ID
A1	1-2	B2	5-9
A2	3	C4	10-11
A3	4		

Alphabetical List of Camping Areas

1 • A1 | Cherry Hill (Francis Marion & Sumter NF)

Total sites: 29, RV sites: 12, Central water, Flush toilet, Free showers, RV dump, Tent & RV camping: $15, Open Apr-Oct, Max Length: 60ft, Reservations accepted, Elev: 2267ft/691m, Tel: 864-638-9568, Nearest town: Mountain Rest. GPS: 34.941573, -83.087634

2 • A1 | Whetstone Horse Camp (Francis Marion & Sumter NF)

Total sites: 18, RV sites: 18, Central water, Vault/pit toilet, No showers, No RV dump, Tent & RV camping: $15, Open all year, Reservations accepted, Elev: 1706ft/520m, Tel: 864-638-9568, Nearest town: Mountain Rest. GPS: 34.862912, -83.224011

3 • A2 | Sedalia (Francis Marion & Sumter NF)

Total sites: 4, RV sites: 4, Central water, Vault/pit toilet, No showers, No RV dump, Tent & RV camping: $5, Some seasonal hunting sites, Stay limit: 14 days, Open all year, Reservations not accepted, Elev: 614ft/187m, Tel: 803-276-4810, Nearest town: Union. GPS: 34.630848, -81.738211

4 • A3 | Woods Ferry (Francis Marion & Sumter NF)

Total sites: 28, RV sites: 28, Central water, Vault/pit toilet, No showers, No RV dump, Tent & RV camping: $7, 2 group sites: $14, Corrals, Stay limit: 14 days, Open Apr-Oct, Reservations not accepted, Elev: 436ft/133m, Tel: 803-276-4810, Nearest town: Union. GPS: 34.700684, -81.450684

5 • B2 | Brick House (Francis Marion & Sumter NF)

Total sites: 23, RV sites: 23, Central water, Vault/pit toilet, No showers, No RV dump, Tent & RV camping: $5, 8 extended-stay sites, Open all year, Reservations not accepted, Elev: 581ft/177m, Tel: 803-276-4810, Nearest town: Whitmire. GPS: 34.447991, -81.706659

6 • B2 | Collins Creek Seasonal Camp (Francis Marion & Sumter NF)

Total sites: 43, Central water, Vault/pit toilet, Free showers, No RV dump, Tent & RV camping: $5, Check for open dates, Hot outdoor showers, Open all year, Reservations not accepted, Elev: 472ft/144m, Tel: 803-276-4810, Nearest town: Long Branch. GPS: 34.471974, -81.524344

7 • B2 | Fell Camp (Francis Marion & Sumter NF)

Total sites: 66, RV sites: 66, Central water, Vault/pit toilet, Tent & RV camping: $5, Open all year, Reservations not accepted, Elev: 545ft/166m, Tel: 803-637-5396, Nearest town: Greenwood. GPS: 34.093158, -82.292014

8 • B2 | Lick Fork Lake (Francis Marion & Sumter NF)

Total sites: 9, RV sites: 9, Central water, Vault/pit toilet, No showers, No RV dump, Tent & RV camping: $7, Stay limit: 14 days, Open May-Nov, Reservations not accepted, Elev: 469ft/143m, Tel: 803-637-5396, Nearest town: Edgefield. GPS: 33.729736, -82.039795

9 • B2 | Parsons Mountain Lake (Francis Marion & Sumter NF)

Total sites: 23, RV sites: 23, Central water, No toilets, No showers, No RV dump, Tent & RV camping: $7, Stay limit: 14 days, Open May-Nov, Reservations not accepted, Elev: 532ft/162m, Tel: 803-637-5396, Nearest town: Anderson. GPS: 34.099795, -82.354187

10 • C4 | Buck Hall (Francis Marion & Sumter NF)

Total sites: 19, RV sites: 14, Elec sites: 14, Central water, Flush toilet, Free showers, RV dump, Tents: $20/RVs: $28, Open all year, Max Length: 40ft, Reservations accepted, Elev: 7ft/2m, Tel: 843-336-3248, Nearest town: McClellanville. GPS: 33.038086, -79.562256

11 • C4 | Honey Hill (Francis Marion & Sumter NF)

Total sites: 10, Central water, Vault/pit toilet, No showers, No RV dump, Tents only: Free, Open all year, Reservations not accepted, Elev: 49ft/15m, Tel: 843-336-3248, Nearest town: McClellanville. GPS: 33.174365, -79.561842

South Dakota

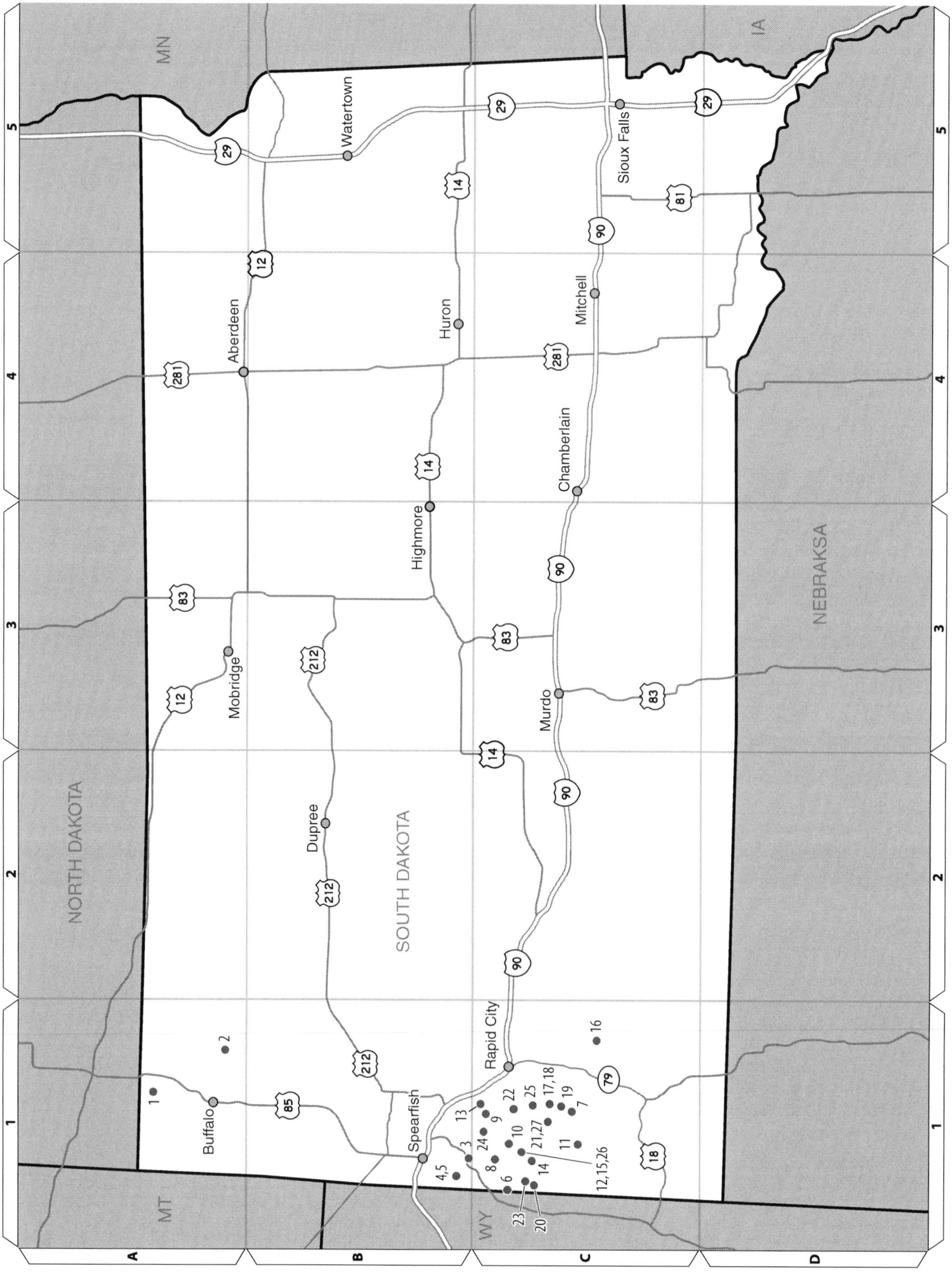

Map	ID	Map	ID
A1	1-2	C1	6-27
B1	3-5		

Alphabetical List of Camping Areas

Name	ID	Map
Beaver Creek (Black Hills NF)	6	C1
Bismarck Lake (Black Hills NF)	7	C1
Black Fox (Black Hills NF)	8	C1
Boxelder Forks (Black Hills NF)	9	C1
Castle Peak (Black Hills NF)	10	C1
Comanche Park (Black Hills NF)	11	C1
Custer Trail (Black Hills NF)	12	C1
Dalton Lake (Black Hills NF)	13	C1
Ditch Creek (Black Hills NF)	14	C1
Dutchman (Black Hills NF)	15	C1
French Creek (Buffalo Gap NG)	16	C1
Grizzly Creek (Black Hills NF)	17	C1
Hanna (Black Hills NF)	3	B1
Horsethief Lake (Black Hills NF)	18	C1
Iron Creek Horse Camp (Black Hills NF)	19	C1
Moon (Black Hills NF)	20	C1
Oreville (Black Hills NF)	21	C1
Pactola (Black Hills NF)	22	C1
Picnic Spring (Custer Gallatin NF)	1	A1
Redbank Spring (Black Hills NF)	23	C1
Reva Gap (Custer Gallatin NF)	2	A1
Rod and Gun (Black Hills NF)	4	B1
Roubaix Lake (Black Hills NF)	24	C1
Sheridan Lake South Shore (Black Hills NF)	25	C1
Timon (Black Hills NF)	5	B1
Whitetail (Black Hills NF)	26	C1
Willow Creek Horse Camp (Black Hills NF)	27	C1

1 • A1 | Picnic Spring (Custer Gallatin NF)

Total sites: 8, RV sites: 8, Central water, Vault/pit toilet, No showers, No RV dump, Tent & RV camping: Free, Open May-Sep, Max Length: 30ft, Reservations not accepted, Elev: 3245ft/989m, Tel: 605-797-4432, Nearest town: Camp Crook. GPS: 45.874398, -103.485574

2 • A1 | Reva Gap (Custer Gallatin NF)

Total sites: 8, RV sites: 8, Central water, Vault/pit toilet, No showers, No RV dump, Tent & RV camping: Free, Max Length: 30ft, Reservations not accepted, Elev: 3284ft/1001m, Tel: 605-797-4432, Nearest town: Camp Crook. GPS: 45.525763, -103.177222

3 • B1 | Hanna (Black Hills NF)

Total sites: 13, RV sites: 6, Central water, Vault/pit toilet, No showers, No RV dump, Tent & RV camping: $18, Walk-to tent sites open year round, Open all year, Reservations not accepted, Elev: 5653ft/1723m, Tel: 605-673-9200, Nearest town: Lead. GPS: 44.274805, -103.851459

4 • B1 | Rod and Gun (Black Hills NF)

Total sites: 7, RV sites: 7, Central water, No toilets, No showers, No RV dump, Tent & RV camping: $18, Reservations not accepted, Elev: 5518ft/1682m, Tel: 605-673-9200, Nearest town: Spearfish. GPS: 44.338543, -103.963657

5 • B1 | Timon (Black Hills NF)

Total sites: 7, RV sites: 7, Central water, Vault/pit toilet, No showers, No RV dump, Tent & RV camping: $18, Reservations not accepted, Elev: 5699ft/1737m, Tel: 605-673-9200, Nearest town: Spearfish. GPS: 44.328046, -103.988151

6 • C1 | Beaver Creek (Black Hills NF)

Total sites: 8, RV sites: 8, Central water, Vault/pit toilet, No showers, No RV dump, Tent & RV camping: $16, Max Length: 45ft, Reservations not accepted, Elev: 6207ft/1892m, Nearest town: Newcastle. GPS: 44.075334, -104.051017

7 • C1 | Bismarck Lake (Black Hills NF)

Total sites: 23, RV sites: 23, Central water, Flush toilet, No showers, No RV dump, Tent & RV camping: $26, Open May-Sep, Reservations not accepted, Elev: 5266ft/1605m, Tel: 605-574 4402, Nearest town: Custer. GPS: 43.774976, -103.510969

8 • C1 | Black Fox (Black Hills NF)

Total sites: 9, RV sites: 9, No water, Vault/pit toilet, Tent & RV camping: $16, Open all year, Reservations not accepted, Elev: 5892ft/1796m, Nearest town: Rochford. GPS: 44.144884, -103.845871

9 • C1 | Boxelder Forks (Black Hills NF)

Total sites: 14, RV sites: 14, Central water, No toilets, No showers, No RV dump, Tent & RV camping: $18, Reservations not accepted, Elev: 4852ft/1479m, Nearest town: Nemo. GPS: 44.198011, -103.535601

10 • C1 | Castle Peak (Black Hills NF)

Total sites: 9, RV sites: 9, No water, Vault/pit toilet, Tent & RV camping: $16, Open all year, Reservations not accepted, Elev: 5420ft/1652m, Nearest town: Hill City. GPS: 44.080118, -103.727335

11 • C1 | Comanche Park (Black Hills NF)

Total sites: 34, RV sites: 34, Central water, Vault/pit toilet, No showers, No RV dump, Tent & RV camping: $16, Open May-Oct, Reservations not accepted, Elev: 5528ft/1685m, Tel: 605-574-4402, Nearest town: Custer. GPS: 43.733831, -103.714427

12 • C1 | Custer Trail (Black Hills NF)

Total sites: 16, RV sites: 16, Central water, Vault/pit toilet, No showers, No RV dump, Tent & RV camping: $16, Reservations not accepted, Elev: 5955ft/1815m, Nearest town: Hill City. GPS: 44.025428, -103.798437

13 • C1 | Dalton Lake (Black Hills NF)

Total sites: 11, RV sites: 11, Central water, Vault/pit toilet, No showers, No RV dump, Tent & RV camping: $18, Reservations not accepted, Elev: 4406ft/1343m, Nearest town: Nemo. GPS: 44.230169, -103.476212

14 • C1 | Ditch Creek (Black Hills NF)

Total sites: 13, RV sites: 13, Central water, Vault/pit toilet, No showers, No RV dump, Tent & RV camping: $20, Reservations not accepted, Elev: 6243ft/1903m, Nearest town: Hill City. GPS: 43.960709, -103.841905

15 • C1 | Dutchman (Black Hills NF)

Total sites: 44, RV sites: 44, Water available, Vault/pit toilet, No showers, No RV dump, Tent & RV camping: $20, Open May-Oct, Max Length: 99ft, Reservations accepted, Elev: 6079ft/1853m, Nearest town: Hill City. GPS: 44.022019, -103.781002

16 • C1 | French Creek (Buffalo Gap NG)

Total sites: 3, RV sites: 3, No water, Vault/pit toilet, Tent & RV camping: Fee unk, Reservations not accepted, Elev: 2897ft/883m, Tel: 605-745-4107, Nearest town: Fairburn. GPS: 43.662331, -103.022473

17 • C1 | Grizzly Creek (Black Hills NF)

Total sites: 20, RV sites: 20, Central water, Vault/pit toilet, No showers, No RV dump, Tent & RV camping: $20, Large trailers not recommended, Max Length: 28ft, Reservations not accepted, Elev: 4544ft/1385m, Nearest town: Keystone. GPS: 43.876898, -103.439542

18 • C1 | Horsethief Lake (Black Hills NF)

Total sites: 36, RV sites: 36, Water available, No toilets, No showers, No RV dump, Tent & RV camping: $26, Open May-Sep, Reservations not accepted, Elev: 5013ft/1528m, Tel: 605-574-4402, Nearest town: Keystone. GPS: 43.895020, -103.483643

19 • C1 | Iron Creek Horse Camp (Black Hills NF)

Total sites: 9, RV sites: 9, No water, Vault/pit toilet, Tent & RV camping: $24, Corrals, stock water available, Open May-Sep, Max Length: 50ft, Reservations accepted, Elev: 5121ft/1561m, Tel: 605-574-4402, Nearest town: Custer. GPS: 43.826716, -103.473447

20 • C1 | Moon (Black Hills NF)

Total sites: 3, RV sites: 3, No water, Vault/pit toilet, Tent & RV camping: Free, Open Jun-Nov, Max Length: 30ft, Elev: 6440ft/1963m, Nearest town: Newcastle, WY. GPS: 43.946136, -104.009197

21 • C1 | Oreville (Black Hills NF)

Total sites: 24, RV sites: 24, Water available, Vault/pit toilet, No showers, No RV dump, Tent & RV camping: $20, Open May-Sep, Max Length: 95ft, Reservations accepted, Elev: 5377ft/1639m, Tel: 605-574-4402, Nearest town: Hill City. GPS: 43.877383, -103.611668

22 • C1 | Pactola (Black Hills NF)

Total sites: 77, RV sites: 77, Central water, Vault/pit toilet, No showers, No RV dump, Tent & RV camping: $26, Open May-Sep, Max Length: 82ft, Reservations accepted, Elev: 4665ft/1422m, Tel: 605-574-4402, Nearest town: Hill City. GPS: 44.068095, -103.506349

23 • C1 | Redbank Spring (Black Hills NF)

Total sites: 4, RV sites: 4, No water, Vault/pit toilet, Tent & RV camping: $16, Open all year, Reservations not accepted, Elev: 6614ft/2016m, Nearest town: Newcastle. GPS: 43.990745, -103.981186

24 • C1 | Roubaix Lake (Black Hills NF)

Total sites: 56, RV sites: 56, Water available, No toilets, No showers, No RV dump, Tent & RV camping: $24, Open all year, Reservations not accepted, Elev: 5548ft/1691m, Tel: 605-574-4402, Nearest town: Deadwood. GPS: 44.198245, -103.664012

25 • C1 | Sheridan Lake South Shore (Black Hills NF)

Total sites: 129, RV sites: 129, Water available, Vault/pit toilet, No showers, No RV dump, Tent & RV camping: $26, Open May-Sep, Reservations not accepted, Elev: 4678ft/1426m, Tel: 605-574-4402, Nearest town: Hill City. GPS: 43.970604, -103.474207

26 • C1 | Whitetail (Black Hills NF)

Total sites: 17, RV sites: 17, Central water, Vault/pit toilet, No showers, No RV dump, Tent & RV camping: $20, Several sites remain open off-season - free, Open May-Sep, Reservations not accepted, Elev: 5938ft/1810m, Tel: 605-673-9200, Nearest town: Hill City. GPS: 44.013049, -103.803456

27 • C1 | Willow Creek Horse Camp (Black Hills NF)

Total sites: 8, RV sites: 8, Central water, Vault/pit toilet, No showers, No RV dump, Tent & RV camping: $24, Reservable group sites $24-$110, Open May-Sep, Max Length: 99ft, Reservations accepted, Elev: 5056ft/1541m, Tel: 605-574-4402, Nearest town: Hill City. GPS: 43.897233, -103.536888

Tennessee

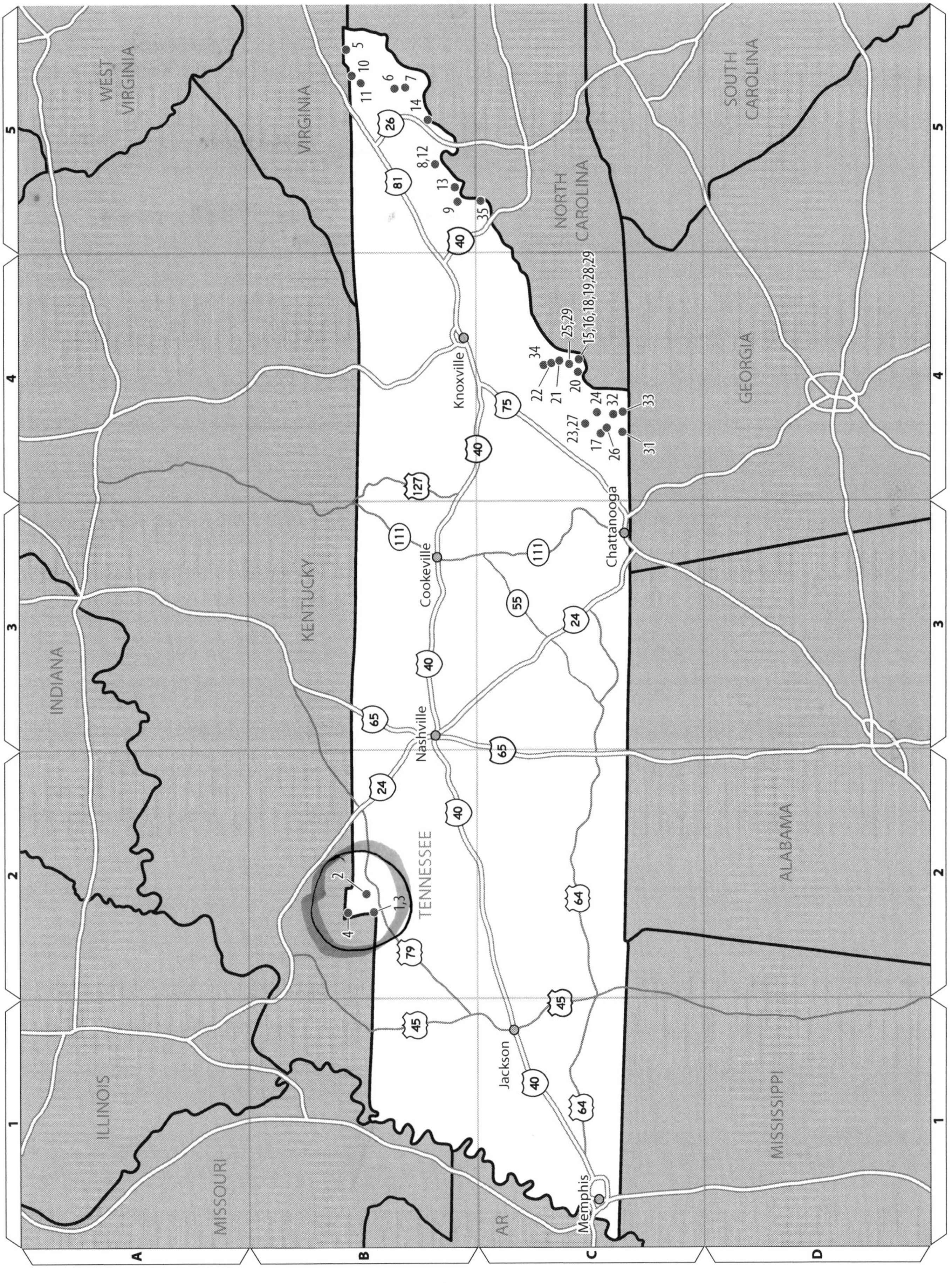

WEST VIRGINIA
VIRGINIA
KENTUCKY
INDIANA
ILLINOIS
MISSOURI
AR
TENNESSEE
NORTH CAROLINA
SOUTH CAROLINA
GEORGIA
ALABAMA
MISSISSIPPI
Knoxville
Cookeville
Nashville
Chattanooga
Jackson
Memphis
A
B
C
D
1
2
3
4
5

Map	ID	Map	ID
B2	1-4	C4	15-34
B5	5-14	C5	35

Alphabetical List of Camping Areas

1 • B2 | LBL NRA - Boswell Landing (Land Between The Lakes NRA)

Total sites: 19, RV sites: 16, No water, Vault/pit toilet, Tent & RV camping: $10, 3-day permit: $10, Stay limit: 14 days, Elev: 364ft/111m, Nearest town: Dover. GPS: 36.519217, -88.024924

2 • B2 | LBL NRA - Gatlin Point (Land Between The Lakes NRA)

Total sites: 19, RV sites: 17, Central water, Vault/pit toilet, No showers, No RV dump, Tent & RV camping: $10, 3-day permit: $10, Stay limit: 14 days, Open all year, Reservations not accepted, Elev: 374ft/114m, Nearest town: Dover. GPS: 36.556641, -87.903809

3 • B2 | LBL NRA - Piney (Land Between The Lakes NRA)

Total sites: 384, RV sites: 384, Elec sites: 327, Central water, Flush toilet, Free showers, RV dump, Tents: $16/RVs: $26-42, Also cabins, 44 Full hookup sites, Stay limit: 14 days, Open all year, Reservations accepted, Elev: 397ft/121m, Tel: 931-232-5331, Nearest town: Dover. GPS: 36.486026, -88.038251

4 • B2 | LBL NRA - Rushing Creek (Land Between The Lakes NRA)

Total sites: 40, RV sites: 40, Central water, Flush toilet, Free showers, No RV dump, Tent & RV camping: $10, 3-day permit: $10, Stay limit: 14 days, Open all year, Reservations not accepted, Elev: 358ft/109m, Tel: 270-924-2000, Nearest town: Canton. GPS: 36.658654, -88.037148

5 • B5 | Backbone Rock (Cherokee NF)

Total sites: 11, RV sites: 11, Central water, Flush toilet, No showers, No RV dump, Tent & RV camping: $10, Open Apr-Oct, Reservations accepted, Elev: 2313ft/705m, Tel: 423-735-1500, Nearest town: Bristol. GPS: 36.594493, -81.814255

6 • B5 | Cardens Bluff (Cherokee NF)

Total sites: 43, RV sites: 3, Central water, Flush toilet, Free showers, No RV dump, Tent & RV camping: $12, Open Apr-Oct, Max Length: 30ft, Reservations accepted, Elev: 2028ft/618m, Tel: 423-735-1500, Nearest town: Elizabethton. GPS: 36.312744, -82.117432

7 • B5 | Dennis Cove (Cherokee NF)

Total sites: 15, RV sites: 15, Central water, Flush toilet, No showers, No RV dump, Tent & RV camping: $10, Open Jul-Oct, Max Length: 30ft, Reservations accepted, Elev: 2703ft/824m, Nearest town: Hampton. GPS: 36.257568, -82.110352

8 • B5 | Horse Creek (Cherokee NF)

Total sites: 15, RV sites: 9, Central water, Flush toilet, Free showers, No RV dump, Tent & RV camping: $10, Open Apr-Nov, Max Length: 24ft, Reservations not accepted, Elev: 1883ft/574m, Tel: 423-638-4109, Nearest town: Greeneville. GPS: 36.108629, -82.656702

9 • B5 | Houston Valley (Cherokee NF)

Total sites: 8, RV sites: 8, Central water, Vault/pit toilet, No showers, No RV dump, Tent & RV camping: $7, Open May-Oct, Reservations accepted, Elev: 1834ft/559m, Nearest town: Greeneville. GPS: 35.964807, -82.942937

10 • B5 | Jacobs Creek (Cherokee NF)

Total sites: 27, RV sites: 27, Central water, Flush toilet, Free showers, RV dump, Tent & RV camping: $12, Open May-Oct, Reservations not accepted, Elev: 1726ft/526m, Nearest town: Bristol. GPS: 36.568115, -82.011963

11 • B5 | Little Oak (Cherokee NF)

Total sites: 68, RV sites: 68, Central water, Flush toilet, Free showers, RV dump, Tent & RV camping: $12, $10 during shoulder seasons with limited facilities, no water, Open Apr-Nov, Reservations accepted, Elev: 1788ft/545m, Tel: 423-735-1500, Nearest town: Bristol. GPS: 36.520264, -82.061279

12 • B5 | Old Forge (Cherokee NF)

Total sites: 10, No water, Vault/pit toilet, Tents only: $7, Walk-to sites, Open Mar-Dec, Reservations not accepted, Elev: 2034ft/620m, Nearest town: Greeneville. GPS: 36.090399, -82.681603

13 • B5 | Paint Creek (Cherokee NF)

Total sites: 20, RV sites: 20, Central water, Vault/pit toilet, No showers, No RV dump, Tent & RV camping: $10, Open May-Oct, Reservations not accepted, Elev: 1883ft/574m, Nearest town: Greeneville. GPS: 35.978027, -82.844482

14 • B5 | Rock Creek (Cherokee NF)

Total sites: 37, RV sites: 32, Elec sites: 32, Central water, Flush toilet, Free showers, RV dump, Tent & RV camping: $20, Also walk-to & group sites, Group site: $50, Open May-Oct, Max Length: 48ft, Reservations accepted, Elev: 2316ft/706m, Tel: 423-638-4109, Nearest town: Erwin. GPS: 36.137647, -82.352559

15 • C4 | Big Oak Cove (Cherokee NF)

Total sites: 11, RV sites: 11, No water, Vault/pit toilet, Tent & RV camping: $10, Open Mar-Dec, Reservations not accepted, Elev: 2602ft/793m, Tel: 423-253-8400, Nearest town: Tellico Plains. GPS: 35.264355, -84.086709

16 • C4 | Birch Branch (Cherokee NF)

Total sites: 5, RV sites: 5, No water, Vault/pit toilet, Tent & RV camping: $10, Open all year, Reservations not accepted, Elev: 2234ft/681m, Tel: 423-253-8400, Nearest town: Tellico Plains. GPS: 35.282325, -84.097144

17 • C4 | Chilhowee (Cherokee NF)

Total sites: 78, RV sites: 71, Elec sites: 36, Central water, Flush toilet, Free showers, RV dump, Tents: $12-15/RVs: $12-20, 16 sites open through winter with limited services, Be Aware: Do not use GPS directions - GPS will direct you up Benton Springs Road (narrow and winding) - recommend use of FSR 77, Open Apr-Oct, Max Length: 90ft, Reservations accepted, Elev: 1926ft/587m, Tel: 423-338-3300, Nearest town: Benton. GPS: 35.149642, -84.612428

18 • C4 | Davis Branch (Cherokee NF)

Total sites: 6, RV sites: 6, No water, Vault/pit toilet, Tent & RV camping: $10, Open all year, Reservations not accepted, Elev: 2424ft/739m, Tel: 423-253-8400, Nearest town: Tellico Plains. GPS: 35.279077, -84.096412

19 • C4 | Holder Cove (Cherokee NF)

Total sites: 7, RV sites: 7, No water, Vault/pit toilet, Tent & RV camping: $10, Open all year, Reservations not accepted, Elev: 2516ft/767m, Tel: 423-253-8400, Nearest town: Tellico Plains. GPS: 35.271096, -84.086348

20 • C4 | Holly Flats (Cherokee NF)

Total sites: 16, RV sites: 16, No water, Vault/pit toilet, Tent & RV camping: $6, Open May-Nov, Reservations not accepted, Elev: 1939ft/591m, Tel: 423-253-8400, Nearest town: Tellico Plains. GPS: 35.285400, -84.177734

21 • C4 | Indian Boundary (Cherokee NF)

Total sites: 87, RV sites: 87, Elec sites: 87, Central water, Flush toilet, Free showers, RV dump, Tent & RV camping: $20, Open Apr-Oct, Max Length: 26ft, Reservations accepted, Elev: 1880ft/573m, Tel: 423-253-8400, Nearest town: Knoxville. GPS: 35.402100, -84.105957

22 • C4 | Jake Best (Cherokee NF)

Total sites: 7, RV sites: 7, No water, Vault/pit toilet, Tent & RV camping: $6, Open Mar-Nov, Reservations not accepted, Elev: 1079ft/329m, Nearest town: Vonore. GPS: 35.445937, -84.109288

23 • C4 | Lost Corral Horse Camp (Cherokee NF)

Total sites: 20, RV sites: 20, Central water, Vault/pit toilet, No showers, No RV dump, Tent & RV camping: $15, Open all year, Reservations not accepted, Elev: 797ft/243m, Tel: 423-338-3300, Nearest town: Delano. GPS: 35.238607, -84.548762

24 • C4 | Lost Creek (Cherokee NF)

Total sites: 15, RV sites: 15, No water, Vault/pit toilet, Tent & RV camping: Free, Open all year, Max Length: 24ft, Reservations not accepted, Elev: 994ft/303m, Nearest town: Benton. GPS: 35.160291, -84.468434

25 • C4 | North River (Cherokee NF)

Total sites: 11, RV sites: 11, No water, Vault/pit toilet, Tent & RV camping: $8, Open May-Nov, Reservations not accepted, Elev: 1982ft/604m, Tel: 423-253-8400, Nearest town: Tellico Plains. GPS: 35.318634, -84.125181

26 • C4 | Parksville Lake (Cherokee NF)

Total sites: 41, RV sites: 17, Elec sites: 17, Central water, Flush toilet, Free showers, RV dump, Tent & RV camping: $20, Open all year, Reservations accepted, Elev: 899ft/274m, Nearest town: Benton. GPS: 35.117385, -84.575472

27 • C4 | Quinn Springs (Cherokee NF)

Total sites: 23, RV sites: 14, Central water, Flush toilet, Free showers, No RV dump, Tent & RV camping: $12, Open all year, Reservations accepted, Elev: 735ft/224m, Tel: 423-338-3300, Nearest town: Delano. GPS: 35.229736, -84.546143

28 • C4 | Rough Ridge (Cherokee NF)

Total sites: 5, RV sites: 5, No water, Vault/pit toilet, Tent & RV camping: $10-20, Open all year, Max Length: 26ft, Reservations not accepted, Elev: 2674ft/815m, Tel: 423-253-8400, Nearest town: Tellico Plains. GPS: 35.261107, -84.084183

29 • C4 | Spivey Cove (Cherokee NF)

Total sites: 16, RV sites: 16, No water, Vault/pit toilet, Tent & RV camping: $6, Open May-Nov, Reservations not accepted, Elev: 1995ft/608m, Tel: 423-253-8400, Nearest town: Tellico Plains. GPS: 35.303759, -84.113611

30 • C4 | State Line (Cherokee NF)

Total sites: 7, RV sites: 7, No water, Vault/pit toilet, Tent & RV camping: $10-20, Group site, Max Length: 26ft, Reservations not accepted, Elev: 2703ft/824m, Tel: 423-253-8400, Nearest town: Tellico Plains. GPS: 35.261567, -84.081259

31 • C4 | Sylco (Cherokee NF)

Total sites: 12, RV sites: 12, No water, No toilets, Tent & RV camping: Free, Open all year, Reservations not accepted, Elev: 1151ft/351m, Nearest town: Ducktown. GPS: 35.028096, -84.602215

32 • C4 | Thunder Rock (Cherokee NF)

Total sites: 38, RV sites: 38, Elec sites: 1, Central water, Flush toilet, Free showers, No RV dump, Tents: $12/RVs: $12-20, 3 sites open all winter, Open all year, Reservations not accepted, Elev: 1148ft/350m, Tel: 423-338-3300, Nearest town: Ducktown. GPS: 35.076357, -84.486237

33 • C4 | Tumbling Creek (Cherokee NF)

Total sites: 8, RV sites: 8, No water, No toilets, Tent & RV camping: Free, Open all year, Reservations not accepted, Elev: 1512ft/461m, Nearest town: Ducktown. GPS: 35.016771, -84.466506

34 • C4 | Young Branch Horse Camp (Cherokee NF)

Total sites: 7, RV sites: 7, No water, Vault/pit toilet, Tent & RV camping: $15, Open all year, Reservations not accepted, Elev: 971ft/296m, Tel: 423-253-8400, Nearest town: Tariffville. GPS: 35.483597, -84.123001

35 • C5 | Round Mountain (Cherokee NF)

Total sites: 14, RV sites: 12, No water, Vault/pit toilet, Tent & RV camping: $7, Open May-Oct, Reservations not accepted, Elev: 3163ft/964m, Nearest town: Greeneville. GPS: 35.838575, -82.955323

Texas

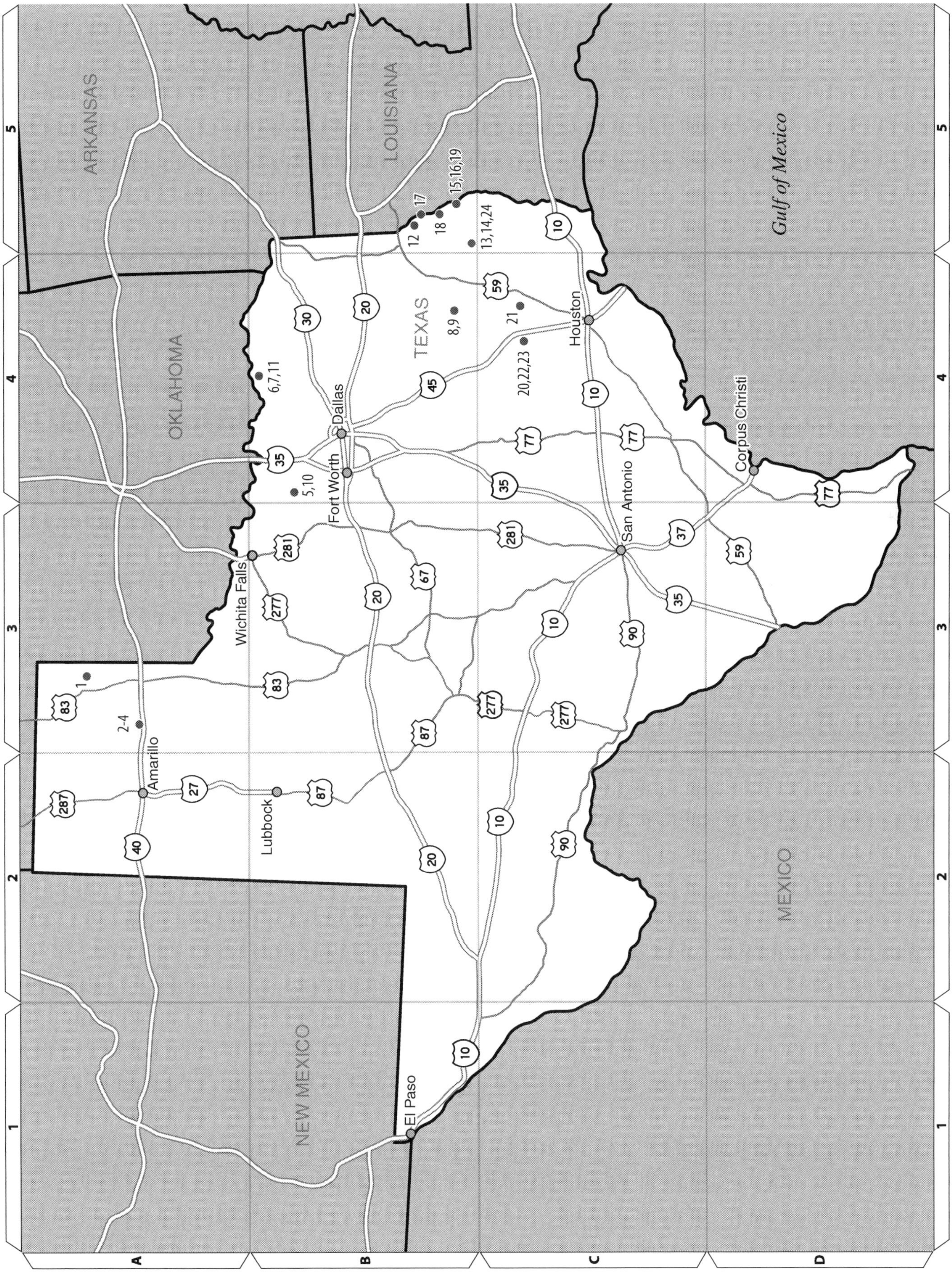
ARKANSAS
LOUISIANA
OKLAHOMA
TEXAS
NEW MEXICO
MEXICO
Gulf of Mexico
Dallas
Fort Worth
Houston
San Antonio
Corpus Christi
Wichita Falls
Amarillo
Lubbock
El Paso
1
2-4
5,10
6,7,11
8,9
12
13,14,24
15,16,19
17
18
20,22,23
21
A
B
C
D
1
2
3
4
5

Map	ID	Map	ID
A3	1-4	C4	20-23
B4	5-11	C5	24
B5	12-19		

Alphabetical List of Camping Areas

1 • A3 | Lake Marvin (Cibola NF)

Total sites: 12, RV sites: 4, Elec sites: 4, Central water, Vault/pit toilet, No showers, No RV dump, Tents: Free/RVs: $20, Stay limit: 14 days, Open all year, Reservations not accepted, Elev: 2297ft/700m, Tel: 580-497-2143, Nearest town: Canadian. GPS: 35.886063, -100.180689

2 • A3 | Lake McClellan - East Bluff #1 (McClellan Creek NG)

Total sites: 7, RV sites: 0, No water, Vault/pit toilet, Tents only: $10, Reservations not accepted, Elev: 2930ft/893m, Tel: 580-497-2143, Nearest town: McLean. GPS: 35.212403, -100.865032

3 • A3 | Lake McClellan (McClellan Creek NG)

Total sites: 23, RV sites: 18, Elec sites: 13, Central water, Vault/pit toilet, No showers, No RV dump, Tents: $10/RVs: $10-15, Open all year, Reservations not accepted, Elev: 2940ft/896m, Tel: 580-497-2143, Nearest town: Groom. GPS: 35.212139, -100.873703

4 • A3 | McDowell (Black Kettle NG)

Total sites: 9, RV sites: 9, Elec sites: 6, Central water, Vault/pit toilet, No showers, No RV dump, Tents: $10/RVs: $15, Open all year, Reservations not accepted, Elev: 2928ft/892m, Tel: 580-497-2143, Nearest town: Groom. GPS: 35.215517, -100.866309

5 • B4 | Black Creek (Lyndom B Johnson NG)

Total sites: 7, RV sites: 0, No water, Vault/pit toilet, No showers, No RV dump, Tents only: $10, Walk-to sites, Reservations not accepted, Elev: 1024ft/312m, Tel: 940-627-5475, Nearest town: Decatur. GPS: 33.345134, -97.595753

6 • B4 | Bois D' Arc (Caddo NG)

Total sites: 20, RV sites: 20, Central water, Vault/pit toilet, Tent & RV camping: $10, Reservations not accepted, Elev: 584ft/178m, Tel: 940-627-5475, Nearest town: Bonham. GPS: 33.745427, -95.990136

7 • B4 | Coffee Mill Lake (Caddo NG)

Total sites: 8, RV sites: 4, Central water, Vault/pit toilet, No showers, No RV dump, Tent & RV camping: $10, Reservations not accepted, Elev: 541ft/165m, Tel: 940-627-5475, Nearest town: Honey Grove. GPS: 33.737091, -95.972987

8 • B4 | Piney Creek Horse Camp (Davy Crockett NF)

Total sites: 15, RV sites: 15, Central water, Vault/pit toilet, No showers, No RV dump, Tent & RV camping: $10, Open all year, Reservations not accepted, Elev: 423ft/129m, Tel: 936-655-2299, Nearest town: Kennard. GPS: 31.316971, -95.186594

9 • B4 | Ratcliff Lake (Davy Crockett NF)

Total sites: 72, RV sites: 72, Elec sites: 25, Central water, Flush toilet, Free showers, RV dump, Tent & RV camping: $15-20, Open all year, Max Length: 60ft, Reservations accepted, Elev: 394ft/120m, Tel: 936-655-2299, Nearest town: Ratcliff. GPS: 31.391956, -95.154438

10 • B4 | Tadra Point Trailhead Camp (Lyndom B Johnson NG)

Total sites: 26, RV sites: 26, No water, Vault/pit toilet, Tent & RV camping: $4, Reservations not accepted, Elev: 909ft/277m, Tel: 940-627-5475, Nearest town: Decatur. GPS: 33.381740, -97.571530

11 • B4 | West Lake Davy Crockett (Caddo NG)

Total sites: 10, RV sites: 10, Central water, Vault/pit toilet, No showers, No RV dump, Tent & RV camping: $4, Reservations not accepted, Elev: 551ft/168m, Tel: 940-627-5475, Nearest town: Caddo. GPS: 33.736987, -95.928651

12 • B5 | Boles Field (Sabine NF)

Total sites: 20, RV sites: 20, Elec sites: 20, Water at site, Flush toilet, Free showers, No RV dump, Tent & RV camping: $6, Open all year, Max Length: 24ft, Reservations not accepted, Elev: 374ft/114m, Tel: 409-625-1940, Nearest town: Shelbyville. GPS: 31.772612, -93.968167

13 • B5 | Boykin Springs (Angelina NF)

Total sites: 24, RV sites: 21, Central water, Flush toilet, Free showers, No RV dump, Tent & RV camping: $10, Open all year, Max Length: 24ft, Reservations not accepted, Elev: 210ft/64m, Tel: 936-897-1068, Nearest town: Zavalla. GPS: 31.059117, -94.274294

14 • B5 | Caney Creek (Angelina NF)

Total sites: 26, RV sites: 26, No water, Vault/pit toilet, No showers, No RV dump, Tents only: $6, Max Length: 24ft, Reservations not accepted, Elev: 226ft/69m, Tel: 936-897-2073, Nearest town: Zavalla. GPS: 31.134033, -94.256104

15 • B5 | Indian Mounds (Sabine NF)

Total sites: 37, RV sites: 37, Central water, Vault/pit toilet, No showers, No RV dump, Tent & RV camping: Fee unk, Open all year, Max Length: 24ft, Reservations not accepted, Elev: 200ft/61m, Tel: 409-625-1940, Nearest town: Hemphill. GPS: 31.309326, -93.695801

16 • B5 | Lakeview (Sabine NF)

Total sites: 10, RV sites: 10, Central water, Vault/pit toilet, No showers, No RV dump, Tent & RV camping: $3, Stay limit: 28 days, Max Length: 24ft, Reservations not accepted, Elev: 220ft/67m, Tel: 409-565-2273, Nearest town: Pineland. GPS: 31.261462, -93.679696

17 • B5 | Ragtown (Sabine NF)

Total sites: 25, RV sites: 25, Central water, Flush toilet, Free showers, RV dump, Tent & RV camping: $5, Max Length: 24ft, Reservations not accepted, Elev: 292ft/89m, Tel: 409-625-1940, Nearest town: Shelbyville. GPS: 31.682129, -93.825684

18 • B5 | Red Hills Lake (Sabine NF)

Total sites: 26, RV sites: 9, Elec sites: 9, Central water, Vault/pit toilet, No showers, RV dump, Tents: $6/RVs: $6-10, Outside showers, Open May-Sep, Max Length: 35ft, Reservations not accepted, Elev: 381ft/116m, Tel: 409-625-1940, Nearest town: Hemphill. GPS: 31.473877, -93.832764

19 • B5 | Willow Oak (Sabine NF)

Total sites: 15, RV sites: 15, Central water, Vault/pit toilet, No showers, No RV dump, Tent & RV camping: $4, Stay limit: 28 days, Reservations not accepted, Elev: 177ft/54m, Tel: 409-565-2273, Nearest town: Fairmount. GPS: 31.210117, -93.733339

20 • C4 | Cagle (Sam Houston NF)

Total sites: 47, RV sites: 47, Elec sites: 47, Water at site, Flush toilet, Free showers, RV dump, Tent & RV camping: $30, 47 Full hookup sites, Open all year, Max Length: 60ft, Reservations accepted, Elev: 295ft/90m, Tel: 936-344-6205, Nearest town: New Waverly. GPS: 30.523001, -95.589109

21 • C4 | Double Lake (Sam Houston NF)

Total sites: 74, RV sites: 73, Elec sites: 41, Water at site, Flush toilet, Free showers, No RV dump, Tents: $20/RVs: $20-32, Group site: $85, 10 Full hookup sites, Open all year, Max Length: 45ft, Reservations accepted, Elev: 331ft/101m, Tel: 936-653-3448, Nearest town: Coldspring. GPS: 30.550631, -95.132224

22 • C4 | Kelley's Pond (Sam Houston NF)

Total sites: 8, No water, Vault/pit toilet, Tents only: Free, Walk-to sites, Reservations not accepted, Elev: 302ft/92m, Tel: 936-344-6205, Nearest town: New Waverly. GPS: 30.510522, -95.661976

23 • C4 | Stubblefield Lake (Sam Houston NF)

Total sites: 30, RV sites: 30, Central water, Flush toilet, Free showers, No RV dump, Tent & RV camping: $15, Max Length: 28ft, Reservations not accepted, Elev: 230ft/70m, Tel: 936-344-6205, Nearest town: New Waverly. GPS: 30.561132, -95.637576

24 • C5 | Bouton Lake Recreation Area (Angelina NF)

Total sites: 7, RV sites: 0, No water, Vault/pit toilet, Tents only: Free, Reservations not accepted, Elev: 151ft/46m, Tel: 936-897-1068, Nearest town: Zavalla. GPS: 31.027309, -94.316954

Utah

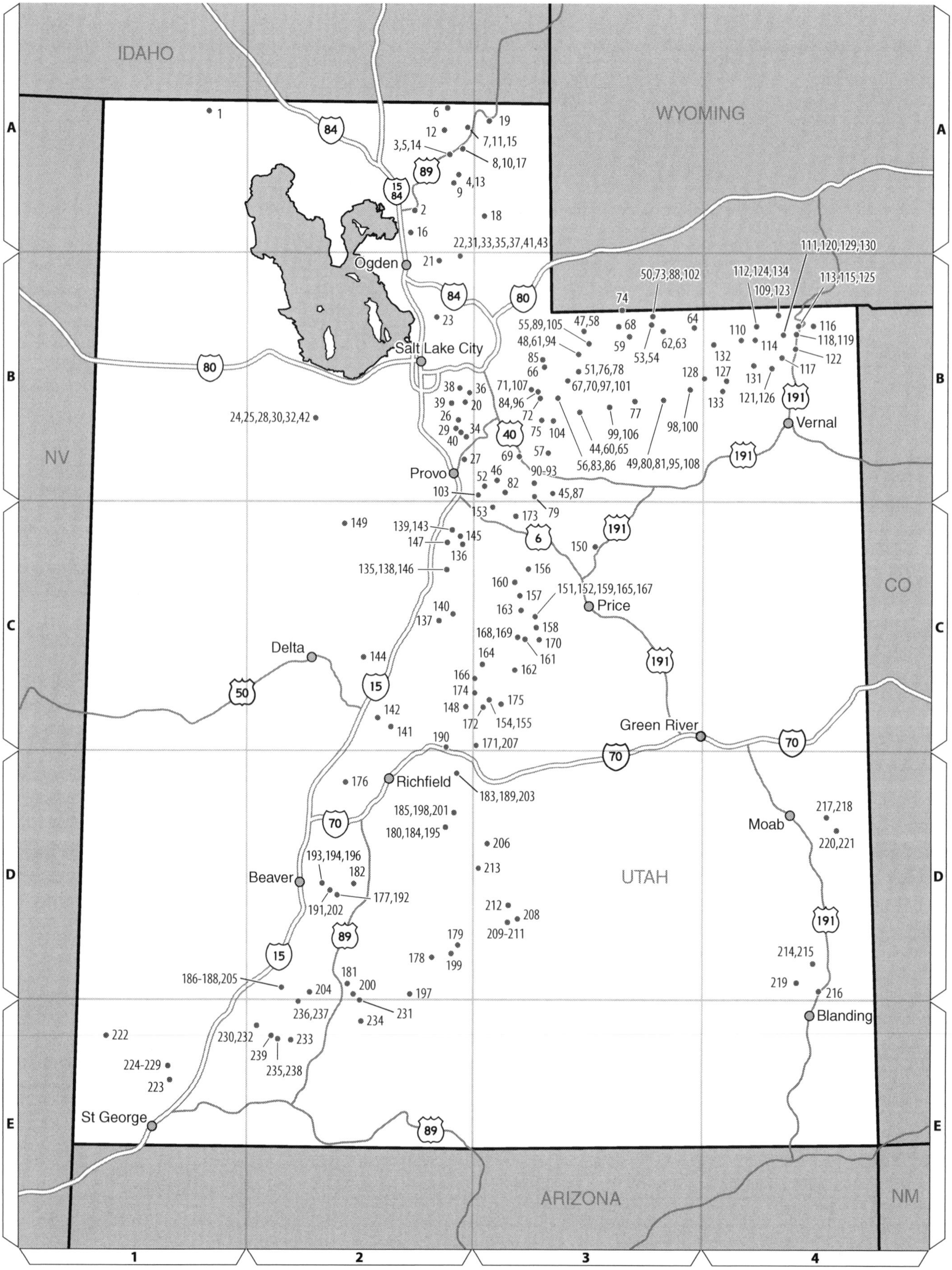
IDAHO
WYOMING
NV
CO
ARIZONA
NM
UTAH
Ogden
Salt Lake City
Provo
Vernal
Price
Delta
Green River
Richfield
Moab
Beaver
Blanding
St George
84
15
89
80
40
191
6
50
70
A
B
C
D
E
1
2
3
4
1
6
12
19
7,11,15
3,5,14
8,10,17
4,13
9
2
18
16
22,31,33,35,37,41,43
21
23
24,25,28,30,32,42
38
36
39
20
26
29
34
40
71,107
84,96
72
75
104
27
69
57
52
46
82
90-93
103
45,87
79
153
173
55,89,105
47,58
74
68
48,61,94
59
85
66
51,76,78
67,70,97,101
44,60,65
56,83,86
99,106
77
49,80,81,95,108
98,100
50,73,88,102
53,54
62,63
64
128
112,124,134
109,123
111,120,129,130
113,115,125
110
114
116
118,119
122
117
132
127
133
131
121,126
149
139,143
147
145
136
135,138,146
150
156
160
157
151,152,159,165,167
163
158
140
137
168,169
170
161
164
162
144
166
174
175
148
172
154,155
142
141
190
171,207
176
183,189,203
185,198,201
180,184,195
206
213
193,194,196
182
177,192
191,202
212
208
209-211
179
178
199
186-188,205
204
181
200
197
236,237
231
234
230,232
233
239
235,238
222
224-229
223
217,218
220,221
214,215
219
216

Map	ID	Map	ID
A1	1	C3	150-175
A2	2-17	D2	176-205
A3	18-19	D3	206-213
B2	20-43	D4	214-221
B3	44-108	E1	222-229
B4	109-134	E2	230-239
C2	135-149		

Alphabetical List of Camping Areas

Name	ID	Map
Adelaide (Fishlake NF)	176	D2
Albion Basin (Uinta-Wasatch-Cache NF)	20	B2
Anderson Cove (Uinta-Wasatch-Cache NF)	21	B2
Anderson Meadow (Fishlake NF)	177	D2
Antelope Flat (Ashley NF)	109	B4
Aspen (Ashley NF)	44	B3
Aspen Grove (Uinta-Wasatch-Cache NF)	45	B3
Avintaquin (Ashley NF)	150	C3
Balsam (Uinta-Wasatch-Cache NF)	46	B3
Barker Reservoir (Dixie NF)	178	D2
Bear Canyon (Uinta-Wasatch-Cache NF)	135	C2
Bear River (Uinta-Wasatch-Cache NF)	47	B3
Beaver View (Uinta-Wasatch-Cache NF)	48	B3
Blackhawk Horse Camp (Uinta-Wasatch-Cache NF)	136	C2
Blue Spruce (Dixie NF)	179	D2
Botts (Uinta-Wasatch-Cache NF)	22	B2
Bountiful Peak (Uinta-Wasatch-Cache NF)	23	B2
Bowery Creek (Fishlake NF)	180	D2
Box Elder (Uinta-Wasatch-Cache NF)	2	A2
Boy Scout (Uinta-Wasatch-Cache NF)	24	B2
Bridge (Ashley NF)	49	B3
Bridger (Uinta-Wasatch-Cache NF)	3	A2
Bridger Lake (Uinta-Wasatch-Cache NF)	50	B3
Bridges - Riverside (Manti-La Sal NF)	151	C3
Bridges (Manti-La Sal NF)	152	C3
Browne Lake (Ashley NF)	110	B4
Buckboard (Manti-La Sal NF)	214	D4
Butterfly Lake (Uinta-Wasatch-Cache NF)	51	B3
Canyon Rim (Ashley NF)	111	B4
Carmel (Ashley NF)	112	B4
Casto Canyon (Dixie NF)	181	D2
Cedar Canyon (Dixie NF)	230	E2
Cedar Springs (Ashley NF)	113	B4
Cherry (Uinta-Wasatch-Cache NF)	52	B3
Chicken Creek (Manti-La Sal NF)	137	C2
China Meadows (Uinta-Wasatch-Cache NF)	53	B3
China Meadows TH (Uinta-Wasatch-Cache NF)	54	B3
Christmas Meadows (Uinta-Wasatch-Cache NF)	55	B3
City Creek (Fishlake NF)	182	D2
Clear Creek (Sawtooth NF)	1	A1
Cobblerest (Uinta-Wasatch-Cache NF)	56	B3
Cold Springs (Fishlake NF)	183	D2
Cottonwood (SFRD) (Uinta-Wasatch-Cache NF)	138	C2
Cottonwood (SLRD) (Uinta-Wasatch-Cache NF)	25	B2
Coyote Hollow Horse Camp (Dixie NF)	231	E2
Currant Creek (Uinta-Wasatch-Cache NF)	57	B3
Dalton Springs (Manti-La Sal NF)	215	D4
Deep Creek (Ashley NF)	114	B4
Deer Haven (Dixie NF)	232	E2
Deer Run (Ashley NF)	115	B4
Devils Canyon (Manti-La Sal NF)	216	D4
Diamond (Uinta-Wasatch-Cache NF)	153	C3
Doctor Creek (Fishlake NF)	184	D2
Dripping Springs (Ashley NF)	116	B4
Duck Creek (Dixie NF)	233	E2
East Fork Bear River (Uinta-Wasatch-Cache NF)	58	B3
East Fork Blacks Fork TH (Uinta-Wasatch-Cache NF)	59	B3
East Park (Ashley NF)	117	B4
Elk Horn (Fishlake NF)	206	D3
Ferron Reservoir South (Manti-La Sal NF)	154	C3
Ferron Reservoir West (Manti-La Sal NF)	155	C3
Firefighter's Memorial (Ashley NF)	118	B4
Fish Creek (Manti-La Sal NF)	156	C3
Flat Canyon (Manti-La Sal NF)	157	C3
Forks of Huntington (Manti-La Sal NF)	158	C3
Friendship (Uinta-Wasatch-Cache NF)	4	A2
Frying Pan (Fishlake NF)	185	D2
FSR 009 (Lazy Mtn) Dispersed 1 (Fishlake NF)	207	D3
FSR 0110 Dispersed 1 (Manti-La Sal NF)	159	C3
FSR 3023 Dispersed 1 (Dixie NF)	186	D2
FSR 3026 Dispersed 1 (Dixie NF)	187	D2
FSR 3027 Dispersed 1 (Dixie NF)	188	D2
Gooseberry (Fishlake) (Fishlake NF)	189	D2
Gooseberry I-70 TH (Fishlake NF)	190	D2
Gooseberry Reservoir (Manti-La Sal NF)	160	C3
Granite Flat (Uinta-Wasatch-Cache NF)	26	B2
Greendale (Ashley NF)	119	B4
Greens Lake (Ashley NF)	120	B4
Guinavah-Malibu (Uinta-Wasatch-Cache NF)	5	A2
Hades (Ashley NF)	60	B3
Hayden Fork (Uinta-Wasatch-Cache NF)	61	B3
Henrys Fork Horse Camp (Uinta-Wasatch-Cache NF)	62	B3
Henrys Fork TH (Uinta-Wasatch-Cache NF)	63	B3
High Creek (Uinta-Wasatch-Cache NF)	6	A2
Honeycomb Rocks (Dixie NF)	222	E1
Hoop Lake (Uinta-Wasatch-Cache NF)	64	B3
Hope (Uinta-Wasatch-Cache NF)	27	B2
Indian Creek Group (Manti-La Sal NF)	161	C3
Intake (Uinta-Wasatch-Cache NF)	28	B2
Iron Mine (Ashley NF)	65	B3
Joe's Valley (Manti-La Sal NF)	162	C3
Kaler Hollow (Ashley NF)	121	B4
Kents Lake (Fishlake NF)	191	D2
King Creek (Dixie NF)	234	E2
Kokopelli's Trail - Porcupine Rim (Manti-La Sal NF)	217	D4
Lake Canyon (Manti-La Sal NF)	163	C3
Lake Hill (Manti-La Sal NF)	164	C3
LeBaron Lake (Fishlake NF)	192	D2
Ledgefork (Uinta-Wasatch-Cache NF)	66	B3
Lewis M Turner (Uinta-Wasatch-Cache NF)	7	A2
Lilly Lake (Uinta-Wasatch-Cache NF)	67	B3
Little Cottonwood (Fishlake NF)	193	D2
Little Lyman Lake (Uinta-Wasatch-Cache NF)	68	B3
Little Mill (Uinta-Wasatch-Cache NF)	29	B2
Little Reservoir (Fishlake NF)	194	D2
Little Rock (Manti-La Sal NF)	165	C3
Lodge (Uinta-Wasatch-Cache NF)	8	A2
Lodgepole (Central) (Uinta-Wasatch-Cache NF)	69	B3

1 • A1 | Clear Creek (Sawtooth NF)

Total sites: 12, RV sites: 12, Central water, Vault/pit toilet, No showers, No RV dump, Tent & RV camping: Free, Stay limit: 14 days, Open Jun-Oct, Reservations not accepted, Elev: 6312ft/1924m, Tel: 208-678-0439, Nearest town: Burley. GPS: 41.953483, -113.321782

2 • A2 | Box Elder (Uinta-Wasatch-Cache NF)

Total sites: 25, RV sites: 20, Central water, Flush toilet, No showers, No RV dump, Tent & RV camping: $24, 4 group sites $81-$208, Stay limit: 7 days, Open Apr-Oct, Max Length: 40ft, Reservations accepted, Elev: 5158ft/1572m, Tel: 435-755-3620, Nearest town: Brigham City. GPS: 41.494325, -111.950222

3 • A2 | Bridger (Uinta-Wasatch-Cache NF)

Total sites: 10, RV sites: 10, Water available, No toilets, No showers, No RV dump, Tent & RV camping: $20, Stay limit: 7 days, Open May-Sep, Reservations not accepted, Elev: 5158ft/1572m, Tel: 435-755-3620, Nearest town: Logan. GPS: 41.748047, -111.735352

4 • A2 | Friendship (Uinta-Wasatch-Cache NF)

Total sites: 5, RV sites: 0, No water, Vault/pit toilet, No showers, No RV dump, Tents only: $16, Group site: $55, Stay limit: 7 days, Open May-Sep, Reservations accepted, Elev: 5459ft/1664m, Tel: 435-755-3620, Nearest town: Logan. GPS: 41.660749, -111.665259

5 • A2 | Guinavah-Malibu (Uinta-Wasatch-Cache NF)

Total sites: 39, RV sites: 39, Central water, Flush toilet, No showers, No RV dump, Tent & RV camping: $24, 2 group sites: $145-$170, Stay limit: 7 days, Open May-Oct, Max Length: 35ft, Reservations accepted, Elev: 5085ft/1550m, Tel: 801-435-3620, Nearest town: Logan. GPS: 41.761963, -111.699463

6 • A2 | High Creek (Uinta-Wasatch-Cache NF)

Total sites: 2, RV sites: 2, No water, Vault/pit toilet, Tent & RV camping: Free, Stay limit: 7 days, Open May-Oct, Reservations not accepted, Elev: 5600ft/1707m, Tel: 435-755-3620, Nearest town: Logan. GPS: 41.976000, -111.735000

7 • A2 | Lewis M Turner (Uinta-Wasatch-Cache NF)

Total sites: 10, RV sites: 10, Central water, Vault/pit toilet, No showers, No RV dump, Tent & RV camping: $20, Stay limit: 7 days, Open Jun-Sep, Reservations not accepted, Elev: 6414ft/1955m, Tel: 435-755-3620, Nearest town: Garden City. GPS: 41.885010, -111.572754

8 • A2 | Lodge (Uinta-Wasatch-Cache NF)

Total sites: 10, RV sites: 10, Central water, Vault/pit toilet, No showers, No RV dump, Tent & RV camping: $20, Stay limit: 7 days, Reservations not accepted, Elev: 5538ft/1688m, Tel: 435-755-3620, Nearest town: Logan. GPS: 41.778564, -111.621826

9 • A2 | Pioneer (Uinta-Wasatch-Cache NF)

Total sites: 18, RV sites: 18, Central water, Vault/pit toilet, No showers, No RV dump, Tent & RV camping: $20, Stay limit: 7 days, Reservations not accepted, Elev: 5230ft/1594m, Tel: 435-755-3620, Nearest town: Hyrum. GPS: 41.628174, -111.693359

10 • A2 | Preston Valley (Uinta-Wasatch-Cache NF)

Total sites: 9, RV sites: 9, Central water, Vault/pit toilet, No showers, No RV dump, Tent & RV camping: $20, Open May-Oct, Reservations not accepted, Elev: 5220ft/1591m, Tel: 435-755-3620, Nearest town: Logan. GPS: 41.773425, -111.654283

11 • A2 | Red Banks (Uinta-Wasatch-Cache NF)

Total sites: 12, RV sites: 12, Central water, Vault/pit toilet, No showers, No RV dump, Tent & RV camping: $20, Stay limit: 7 days, Open Jun-Oct, Reservations not accepted, Elev: 6358ft/1938m, Tel: 435-755-3620, Nearest town: Garden City. GPS: 41.898926, -111.564941

12 • A2 | Smithfield (Uinta-Wasatch-Cache NF)

Total sites: 6, RV sites: 6, Central water, Vault/pit toilet, No showers, No RV dump, Tent & RV camping: $20, Stay limit: 7 days, Open May-Sep, Reservations not accepted, Elev: 5482ft/1671m, Tel: 435-755-3620, Nearest town: Heber City. GPS: 41.870399, -111.753995

13 • A2 | Spring (Uinta-Wasatch-Cache NF)

Total sites: 3, RV sites: 3, Central water, Vault/pit toilet, No showers, No RV dump, Tent & RV camping: $12, Stay limit: 7 days, Reservations not accepted, Elev: 5584ft/1702m, Tel: 435-755-3620, Nearest town: Logan. GPS: 41.661984, -111.653988

14 • A2 | Spring Hollow (Uinta-Wasatch-Cache NF)

Total sites: 12, RV sites: 12, Central water, Vault/pit toilet, No showers, No RV dump, Tent & RV camping: $24, 2 group sites: $70-$140, Stay limit: 7 days, Open May-Sep, Max Length: 25ft, Reservations accepted, Elev: 5033ft/1534m, Tel: 801-226-3564, Nearest town: Logan. GPS: 41.752735, -111.716653

15 • A2 | Tony Grove (Uinta-Wasatch-Cache NF)

Total sites: 33, RV sites: 33, No water, Vault/pit toilet, No showers, No RV dump, Tent & RV camping: $24, Stay limit: 7 days, Open Jul-Oct, Max Length: 35ft, Reservations accepted, Elev: 8081ft/2463m, Tel: 435-755-3620, Nearest town: Logan. GPS: 41.891186, -111.640694

16 • A2 | Willard Basin Dispersed (Uinta-Wasatch-Cache NF)

Total sites: 5, RV sites: 5, Elec sites: 0, No water, No toilets, No showers, No RV dump, Tent & RV camping: Free, Road not maintained for passenger cars, Open Jul-Nov, Reservations not accepted, Elev: 8681ft/2646m, Tel: 801-625-5112, Nearest town: Woodruff. GPS: 41.391842, -111.977999

17 • A2 | Wood Camp (Uinta-Wasatch-Cache NF)

Total sites: 6, RV sites: 6, No water, Vault/pit toilet, No showers, No RV dump, Tent & RV camping: $20, Stay limit: 7 days, Open May-

Oct, Reservations not accepted, Elev: 5377ft/1639m, Tel: 435-755-3620, Nearest town: Logan. GPS: 41.797363, -111.645020

18 • A3 | Monte Cristo (Uinta-Wasatch-Cache NF)

Total sites: 45, RV sites: 45, Central water, Flush toilet, No showers, No RV dump, Tent & RV camping: $24, 2 reservable group sites: $243, Stay limit: 7 days, Open Jul-Sep, Max Length: 60ft, Reservations not accepted, Elev: 8909ft/2715m, Tel: 801-625-5112, Nearest town: Woodruff. GPS: 41.462959, -111.497642

19 • A3 | Sunrise (Uinta-Wasatch-Cache NF)

Total sites: 26, RV sites: 26, Central water, Vault/pit toilet, No showers, No RV dump, Tent & RV camping: $22, Stay limit: 7 days, Open Jul-Oct, Max Length: 36ft, Reservations accepted, Elev: 7615ft/2321m, Tel: 435-755-3620, Nearest town: Garden City. GPS: 41.919605, -111.461689

20 • B2 | Albion Basin (Uinta-Wasatch-Cache NF)

Total sites: 19, RV sites: 19, No water, Vault/pit toilet, No showers, No RV dump, Tent & RV camping: $25, Stay limit: 7 days, Open Jul-Sep, Max Length: 25ft, Reservations accepted, Elev: 9442ft/2878m, Tel: 801-733-2660, Nearest town: Alta . GPS: 40.577881, -111.613525

21 • B2 | Anderson Cove (Uinta-Wasatch-Cache NF)

Total sites: 67, RV sites: 67, Central water, Vault/pit toilet, No showers, RV dump, Tents: $22/RVs: $30, 5 group sites: $295, Dump fee for campers: $12, Stay limit: 7 days, Generator hours: 0600-2200, Open May-Sep, Max Length: 77ft, Reservations accepted, Elev: 4931ft/1503m, Tel: 801-745-3215, Nearest town: Ogden. GPS: 41.250184, -111.787519

22 • B2 | Botts (Uinta-Wasatch-Cache NF)

Total sites: 8, RV sites: 8, Central water, Vault/pit toilet, No showers, No RV dump, Tent & RV camping: $23, Generator hours: 0800-2200, Open May-Dec, Reservations not accepted, Elev: 5282ft/1610m, Tel: 801-226-3564, Nearest town: Ogden. GPS: 41.278549, -111.657137

23 • B2 | Bountiful Peak (Uinta-Wasatch-Cache NF)

Total sites: 43, RV sites: 43, Water available, Vault/pit toilet, No showers, No RV dump, Tent & RV camping: $16, Stay limit: 7 days, Max Length: 24ft, Reservations not accepted, Elev: 7526ft/2294m, Tel: 801-733-2660, Nearest town: Farmington. GPS: 40.979801, -111.804612

24 • B2 | Boy Scout (Uinta-Wasatch-Cache NF)

Total sites: 8, RV sites: 8, No water, No toilets, Tent & RV camping: $14, 1 group site: $45, Stay limit: 7 days, Open May-Oct, Reservations not accepted, Elev: 6532ft/1991m, Tel: 801-733-2660, Nearest town: Salt Lake City. GPS: 40.494091, -112.578581

25 • B2 | Cottonwood (SLRD) (Uinta-Wasatch-Cache NF)

Total sites: 3, RV sites: 3, No toilets, Tent & RV camping: $14, Stay limit: 7 days, Reservations not accepted, Elev: 6119ft/1865m, Tel: 801-733-2660, Nearest town: Salt Lake City. GPS: 40.501555, -112.559697

26 • B2 | Granite Flat (Uinta-Wasatch-Cache NF)

Total sites: 52, RV sites: 52, Central water, Vault/pit toilet, No showers, No RV dump, Tent & RV camping: $26, 3 group sites: $$255-$290, No water-tank filling allowed, Stay limit: 7 days, Open Jun-Oct, Max Length: 69ft, Reservations accepted, Elev: 6745ft/2056m, Tel: 801-785-3563, Nearest town: Cedar Hills. GPS: 40.488505, -111.653123

27 • B2 | Hope (Uinta-Wasatch-Cache NF)

Total sites: 26, RV sites: 26, No water, Vault/pit toilet, Tent & RV camping: $26, Stay limit: 7 days, Open May-Sep, Max Length: 35ft, Reservations accepted, Elev: 6631ft/2021m, Tel: 801-785-3563, Nearest town: Orem. GPS: 40.301854, -111.615214

28 • B2 | Intake (Uinta-Wasatch-Cache NF)

Total sites: 5, RV sites: 5, No water, No toilets, Tent & RV camping: $14, Stay limit: 7 days, Reservations not accepted, Elev: 6378ft/1944m, Tel: 801-733-2660, Nearest town: Salt Lake City. GPS: 40.497694, -112.571421

29 • B2 | Little Mill (Uinta-Wasatch-Cache NF)

Total sites: 36, RV sites: 36, No water, Vault/pit toilet, Tent & RV camping: $26, Group site: $214, Stay limit: 7 days, Open May-Oct, Max Length: 55ft, Reservations accepted, Elev: 6214ft/1894m, Tel: 801-785-3563, Nearest town: American Forks. GPS: 40.450195, -111.670898

30 • B2 | Loop (Uinta-Wasatch-Cache NF)

Total sites: 13, RV sites: 13, No water, Tent & RV camping: $14, Stay limit: 7 days, Reservations not accepted, Elev: 7342ft/2238m, Tel: 801-733-2660, Nearest town: Salt Lake City. GPS: 40.484071, -112.606085

31 • B2 | Lower Meadows (Uinta-Wasatch-Cache NF)

Total sites: 25, RV sites: 25, Central water, Vault/pit toilet, No showers, No RV dump, Tent & RV camping: $23, Generator hours: 0800-2200, Open May-Sep, Reservations accepted, Elev: 5325ft/1623m, Tel: 801-999-2103, Nearest town: Ogden. GPS: 41.286621, -111.645264

32 • B2 | Lower Narrows (Uinta-Wasatch-Cache NF)

Total sites: 3, RV sites: 3, No water, No toilets, Tent & RV camping: $14, Stay limit: 7 days, Reservations not accepted, Elev: 6890ft/2100m, Tel: 801-733-2660, Nearest town: Stockton. GPS: 40.491621, -112.591882

33 • B2 | Magpie (Uinta-Wasatch-Cache NF)

Total sites: 16, RV sites: 16, Central water, Vault/pit toilet, No showers, No RV dump, Tent & RV camping: $20, Generator hours: 0800-2200, Open May-Dec, Reservations not accepted, Elev: 5256ft/1602m, Tel: 801-625-5112, Nearest town: Ogden. GPS: 41.270437, -111.666087

34 • B2 | Mount Timpanogos (Uinta-Wasatch-Cache NF)

Total sites: 27, RV sites: 27, Central water, Flush toilet, No showers, No RV dump, Tent & RV camping: $26, Stay limit: 7 days, Open Jun-Sep, Max Length: 20ft, Reservations accepted, Elev: 6920ft/2109m, Tel: 801-885-7391, Nearest town: Orem. GPS: 40.406083, -111.606289

35 • B2 | Perception Park (Uinta-Wasatch-Cache NF)

Total sites: 14, RV sites: 14, Central water, Vault/pit toilet, No

showers, No RV dump, Tent & RV camping: $24, 3 group sites $272, Designed for physically challenged, Stay limit: 7 days, Generator hours: 0800-2200, Open May-Sep, Max Length: 60ft, Reservations accepted, Elev: 5344ft/1629m, Tel: 801-625-5112, Nearest town: Ogden. GPS: 41.288764, -111.641201

36 • B2 | Redman (Uinta-Wasatch-Cache NF)

Total sites: 39, RV sites: 39, Central water, Flush toilet, No showers, No RV dump, Tent & RV camping: $28, 2 group sites: $174-$203, Stay limit: 7 days, Open Jun-Sep, Max Length: 36ft, Reservations accepted, Elev: 8317ft/2535m, Tel: 801-733-2660, Nearest town: Murray. GPS: 40.615273, -111.588783

37 • B2 | South Fork (Uinta-Wasatch-Cache NF)

Total sites: 43, RV sites: 43, Central water, Vault/pit toilet, No showers, No RV dump, Tent & RV camping: $24, Stay limit: 7 days, Generator hours: 0800-2200, Open May-Sep, Max Length: 50ft, Reservations accepted, Elev: 5295ft/1614m, Tel: 801-625-5112, Nearest town: Huntsville. GPS: 41.281696, -111.654018

38 • B2 | Spruces (Uinta-Wasatch-Cache NF)

Total sites: 93, RV sites: 93, Central water, Flush toilet, No showers, No RV dump, Tent & RV camping: $28, 2 group sites: $209, No pets, Glamping tents, Stay limit: 7 days, Open May-Sep, Max Length: 80ft, Reservations accepted, Elev: 7438ft/2267m, Tel: 435-649-7534, Nearest town: Salt Lake City. GPS: 40.642179, -111.637703

39 • B2 | Tanners Flat (Uinta-Wasatch-Cache NF)

Total sites: 34, RV sites: 34, Central water, Flush toilet, No showers, No RV dump, Tent & RV camping: $28, 4 group sites: $121-$203, Stay limit: 7 days, Open May-Oct, Max Length: 80ft, Reservations accepted, Elev: 7293ft/2223m, Tel: 435-649-7402, Nearest town: Sandy. GPS: 40.572394, -111.699051

40 • B2 | Timpooneke (Uinta-Wasatch-Cache NF)

Total sites: 27, RV sites: 27, Central water, Vault/pit toilet, No showers, No RV dump, Tent & RV camping: $26, Group site $133, 9 equestrian sites, Stay limit: 7 days, Open Jun-Oct, Max Length: 30ft, Reservations accepted, Elev: 7576ft/2309m, Tel: 801-885-7391, Nearest town: American Forks. GPS: 40.431947, -111.645916

41 • B2 | Upper Meadows (Uinta-Wasatch-Cache NF)

Total sites: 9, RV sites: 9, Central water, Vault/pit toilet, No showers, No RV dump, Tent & RV camping: $20, Stay limit: 7 days, Open May-Sep, Reservations not accepted, Elev: 5361ft/1634m, Tel: 801-625-5112, Nearest town: Ogden. GPS: 41.291000, -111.636000

42 • B2 | Upper Narrows (Uinta-Wasatch-Cache NF)

Total sites: 6, RV sites: 6, No water, Vault/pit toilet, Tent & RV camping: $14, Group site $45-$80, Stay limit: 7 days, Open Jun-Oct, Reservations not accepted, Elev: 6965ft/2123m, Tel: 801-733-2660, Nearest town: Salt Lake City. GPS: 40.491541, -112.594503

43 • B2 | Willows (Uinta-Wasatch-Cache NF)

Total sites: 17, RV sites: 17, Central water, Vault/pit toilet, No showers, No RV dump, Tent & RV camping: $20, Stay limit: 7 days, Generator hours: 0800-2200, Open May-Sep, Max Length: 40ft, Reservations not accepted, Elev: 5371ft/1637m, Tel: 801-625-5112, Nearest town: Ogden. GPS: 41.291695, -111.633153

44 • B3 | Aspen (Ashley NF)

Total sites: 29, RV sites: 29, No water, Vault/pit toilet, No showers, No RV dump, Tent & RV camping: $10, Group site: $30, Open May-Sep, Max Length: 60ft, Reservations accepted, Elev: 7169ft/2185m, Tel: 435-738-2482, Nearest town: Hanna. GPS: 40.497070, -110.846436

45 • B3 | Aspen Grove (Uinta-Wasatch-Cache NF)

Total sites: 53, RV sites: 53, Elec sites: 1, Central water, Flush toilet, No showers, No RV dump, Tents: $24/RVs: $24-39, 1 Full hookup site: $36, Stay limit: 7 days, Generator hours: 0600-2200, Open May-Oct, Max Length: 60ft, Reservations accepted, Elev: 7779ft/2371m, Tel: 801-226-3564, Nearest town: Hanna. GPS: 40.120767, -111.036691

46 • B3 | Balsam (Uinta-Wasatch-Cache NF)

Total sites: 25, RV sites: 12, Central water, Vault/pit toilet, No showers, No RV dump, Tent & RV camping: $24, Group site: $65-$220, Stay limit: 16 days, Open May-Sep, Max Length: 35ft, Reservations accepted, Elev: 6020ft/1835m, Tel: 801-226-3564, Nearest town: Springville. GPS: 40.198486, -111.402100

47 • B3 | Bear River (Uinta-Wasatch-Cache NF)

Total sites: 4, RV sites: 4, Central water, Vault/pit toilet, No showers, No RV dump, Tent & RV camping: $18, No water in winter, Stay limit: 14 days, Open all year, Reservations not accepted, Elev: 8360ft/2548m, Tel: 307-789-3194, Nearest town: Evanston. GPS: 40.910239, -110.830246

48 • B3 | Beaver View (Uinta-Wasatch-Cache NF)

Total sites: 17, RV sites: 17, Central water, Vault/pit toilet, No showers, No RV dump, Tent & RV camping: $21, Reservations not accepted, Elev: 8990ft/2740m, Tel: 307-789-3194, Nearest town: Evanston. GPS: 40.823828, -110.863135

49 • B3 | Bridge (Ashley NF)

Total sites: 5, RV sites: 5, Water available, Vault/pit toilet, No showers, No RV dump, Tent & RV camping: $8, Open May-Sep, Max Length: 15ft, Elev: 7680ft/2341m, Nearest town: Altamont. GPS: 40.545594, -110.334169

50 • B3 | Bridger Lake (Uinta-Wasatch-Cache NF)

Total sites: 30, RV sites: 30, No water, Vault/pit toilet, Tent & RV camping: $22, Stay limit: 14 days, Open Jun-Sep, Max Length: 55ft, Reservations accepted, Elev: 9403ft/2866m, Tel: 307-789-3194, Nearest town: Mountain View. GPS: 40.964701, -110.387964

51 • B3 | Butterfly Lake (Uinta-Wasatch-Cache NF)

Total sites: 20, RV sites: 20, Water available, Vault/pit toilet, No showers, No RV dump, Tent & RV camping: $21, Stay limit: 7 days, Open Jul-Sep, Reservations not accepted, Elev: 10354ft/3156m, Tel: 435-654-0470, Nearest town: Kamas. GPS: 40.721436, -110.869141

52 • B3 | Cherry (Uinta-Wasatch-Cache NF)

Total sites: 28, RV sites: 28, Central water, Vault/pit toilet, No showers, No RV dump, Tent & RV camping: $24, 4 group sites:

$115-$155, Open Apr-Oct, Max Length: 48ft, Reservations accepted, Elev: 5282ft/1610m, Tel: 801-226-3564, Nearest town: Springville. GPS: 40.168705, -111.476704

53 • B3 | China Meadows (Uinta-Wasatch-Cache NF)

Total sites: 9, RV sites: 9, No water, Vault/pit toilet, Tent & RV camping: $16, Stay limit: 14 days, Open Jun-Oct, Reservations not accepted, Elev: 9406ft/2867m, Tel: 307-782-6555, Nearest town: Mountain View. GPS: 40.931114, -110.403468

54 • B3 | China Meadows TH (Uinta-Wasatch-Cache NF)

Total sites: 11, RV sites: 11, No water, Vault/pit toilet, Tent & RV camping: $14, Reservations not accepted, Elev: 9484ft/2891m, Tel: 307-782-6555, Nearest town: Mountain View. GPS: 40.924208, -110.405997

55 • B3 | Christmas Meadows (Uinta-Wasatch-Cache NF)

Total sites: 11, RV sites: 11, Central water, Vault/pit toilet, No showers, No RV dump, Tent & RV camping: $22, Stay limit: 14 days, Open Jun-Sep, Max Length: 40ft, Reservations accepted, Elev: 8839ft/2694m, Tel: 307-789-3194, Nearest town: Evanston. GPS: 40.824396, -110.802154

56 • B3 | Cobblerest (Uinta-Wasatch-Cache NF)

Total sites: 18, RV sites: 18, Water available, Vault/pit toilet, No showers, No RV dump, Tent & RV camping: $21, Stay limit: 7 days, Open Jun-Sep, Reservations not accepted, Elev: 8333ft/2540m, Tel: 435-783-4338, Nearest town: Kamas. GPS: 40.594482, -110.975342

57 • B3 | Currant Creek (Uinta-Wasatch-Cache NF)

Total sites: 98, RV sites: 98, Central water, Flush toilet, No showers, RV dump, Tent & RV camping: $24, 4 group sites: $90-$120, Stay limit: 7 days, Open Jun-Sep, Max Length: 55ft, Reservations accepted, Elev: 7848ft/2392m, Tel: 435-654-0470, Nearest town: Heber City. GPS: 40.331399, -111.066636

58 • B3 | East Fork Bear River (Uinta-Wasatch-Cache NF)

Total sites: 7, RV sites: 7, No water, Tent & RV camping: $18, Stay limit: 14 days, Reservations not accepted, Elev: 8309ft/2533m, Tel: 307-789-3194, Nearest town: Evanston. GPS: 40.912889, -110.829167

59 • B3 | East Fork Blacks Fork TH (Uinta-Wasatch-Cache NF)

Total sites: 8, RV sites: 8, No water, Vault/pit toilet, Tent & RV camping: Free, Reservations not accepted, Elev: 9351ft/2850m, Nearest town: Mountain View. GPS: 40.884487, -110.538462

60 • B3 | Hades (Ashley NF)

Total sites: 14, RV sites: 14, No water, Vault/pit toilet, Tent & RV camping: $10, Open May-Sep, Max Length: 30ft, Reservations accepted, Elev: 7434ft/2266m, Tel: 435-738-2482, Nearest town: Hanna. GPS: 40.534180, -110.873535

61 • B3 | Hayden Fork (Uinta-Wasatch-Cache NF)

Total sites: 9, RV sites: 9, Central water, Vault/pit toilet, No showers, No RV dump, Tent & RV camping: $18, Stay limit: 14 days, Reservations not accepted, Elev: 8871ft/2704m, Tel: 307-789-3194, Nearest town: Evanston. GPS: 40.829633, -110.853542

62 • B3 | Henrys Fork Horse Camp (Uinta-Wasatch-Cache NF)

Total sites: 3, RV sites: 3, No water, Vault/pit toilet, Tent & RV camping: Free, Reservations not accepted, Elev: 9389ft/2862m, Tel: 307-782-6555, Nearest town: Mountain View (WY). GPS: 40.912636, -110.327841

63 • B3 | Henrys Fork TH (Uinta-Wasatch-Cache NF)

Total sites: 4, RV sites: 4, No water, Vault/pit toilet, Tent & RV camping: Free, Max Length: 20ft, Reservations not accepted, Elev: 9422ft/2872m, Tel: 307-782-6555, Nearest town: Mountain View (WY). GPS: 40.909777, -110.330552

64 • B3 | Hoop Lake (Uinta-Wasatch-Cache NF)

Total sites: 44, RV sites: 44, Central water, Vault/pit toilet, No showers, No RV dump, Tent & RV camping: $18, Stay limit: 14 days, Open Jun-Nov, Reservations not accepted, Elev: 9218ft/2810m, Tel: 307-789-3194, Nearest town: Mountain View, WY. GPS: 40.924449, -110.124936

65 • B3 | Iron Mine (Ashley NF)

Total sites: 26, RV sites: 26, Central water, Vault/pit toilet, No showers, No RV dump, Tent & RV camping: $10, 1 group site $25, Open May-Sep, Max Length: 60ft, Reservations accepted, Elev: 7552ft/2302m, Tel: 435-738-2482, Nearest town: Hanna. GPS: 40.553575, -110.886683

66 • B3 | Ledgefork (Uinta-Wasatch-Cache NF)

Total sites: 73, RV sites: 73, Central water, Vault/pit toilet, No showers, No RV dump, Tent & RV camping: $26, Stay limit: 7 days, Open May-Oct, Max Length: 99ft, Reservations accepted, Elev: 7740ft/2359m, Tel: 801-226-3564, Nearest town: Oakley. GPS: 40.742491, -111.098815

67 • B3 | Lilly Lake (Uinta-Wasatch-Cache NF)

Total sites: 14, RV sites: 14, Central water, Vault/pit toilet, No showers, No RV dump, Tent & RV camping: $23, Stay limit: 7 days, Reservations not accepted, Elev: 9948ft/3032m, Tel: 435-783-4338, Nearest town: Kamas. GPS: 40.681168, -110.939883

68 • B3 | Little Lyman Lake (Uinta-Wasatch-Cache NF)

Total sites: 10, RV sites: 10, Central water, No showers, No RV dump, Tent & RV camping: $16, Stay limit: 14 days, Reservations not accepted, Elev: 9314ft/2839m, Tel: 307-789-3194, Nearest town: Mountain View, WY. GPS: 40.934409, -110.613921

69 • B3 | Lodgepole (Central) (Uinta-Wasatch-Cache NF)

Total sites: 55, RV sites: 49, Central water, Flush toilet, No showers, RV dump, Tent & RV camping: $24, 2 group sites: $175-$335, Stay limit: 7 days, Open May-Sep, Max Length: 70ft, Reservations accepted, Elev: 7710ft/2350m, Tel: 435-654-0470, Nearest town: Heber City. GPS: 40.312087, -111.259508

70 • B3 | Lost Creek (Uinta-Wasatch-Cache NF)

Total sites: 35, RV sites: 35, Central water, Vault/pit toilet, No showers, No RV dump, Tent & RV camping: $24, Glamping tents: $133, Stay limit: 7 days, Open Jun-Sep, Max Length: 40ft, Reservations accepted, Elev: 9987ft/3044m, Tel: 801-226-3564, Nearest town: Kamas. GPS: 40.680914, -110.933045

71 • B3 | Lower Canyon (Fishlake NF)

Total sites: 6, RV sites: 6, No water, No toilets, Tent & RV camping: Free, Elev: 7128ft/2173m, Tel: 435-783-4338, Nearest town: Kamas. GPS: 40.628795, -111.177702

72 • B3 | Lower Provo River (Uinta-Wasatch-Cache NF)

Total sites: 10, RV sites: 10, Central water, Vault/pit toilet, No showers, No RV dump, Tent & RV camping: $18, Stay limit: 7 days, Open May-Oct, Reservations not accepted, Elev: 7418ft/2261m, Tel: 435-783-4338, Nearest town: Kamas. GPS: 40.593111, -111.116683

73 • B3 | Marsh Lake (Uinta-Wasatch-Cache NF)

Total sites: 28, RV sites: 28, Central water, Vault/pit toilet, Tent & RV camping: $22, Group site: $78, Dump station 1.5 mile at Stateline Reservoir, Stay limit: 14 days, Open Jun-Sep, Max Length: 75ft, Reservations accepted, Elev: 9383ft/2860m, Tel: 307-782-6555, Nearest town: Mountain View. GPS: 40.952145, -110.395835

74 • B3 | Meeks Cabin (Uinta-Wasatch-Cache NF)

Total sites: 24, RV sites: 24, Water available, Vault/pit toilet, No showers, No RV dump, Tent & RV camping: $24, Stay limit: 14 days, Reservations not accepted, Elev: 8714ft/2656m, Tel: 307-789-3194, Nearest town: Mountain View. GPS: 41.006266, -110.584071

75 • B3 | Mill Hollow (Uinta-Wasatch-Cache NF)

Total sites: 26, RV sites: 15, Central water, Vault/pit toilet, No showers, No RV dump, Tent & RV camping: $22, Stay limit: 7 days, Open Jun-Sep, Max Length: 50ft, Reservations accepted, Elev: 8842ft/2695m, Tel: 801-226-3564, Nearest town: Woodland. GPS: 40.490514, -111.103721

76 • B3 | Mirror Lake (Uinta-Wasatch-Cache NF)

Total sites: 78, RV sites: 78, No water, Vault/pit toilet, Tent & RV camping: $24, Stay limit: 7 days, Open Jul-Sep, Max Length: 74ft, Reservations accepted, Elev: 10016ft/3053m, Tel: 435-783-4338, Nearest town: Kamas. GPS: 40.700684, -110.884277

77 • B3 | Moon Lake (Ashley NF)

Total sites: 54, RV sites: 46, Central water, Flush toilet, No showers, No RV dump, Tent & RV camping: $20, Open May-Sep, Max Length: 60ft, Reservations accepted, Elev: 8150ft/2484m, Tel: 435-738-2482, Nearest town: Duchesne. GPS: 40.569092, -110.510254

78 • B3 | Moosehorn (Uinta-Wasatch-Cache NF)

Total sites: 33, RV sites: 33, No water, Vault/pit toilet, No showers, No RV dump, Tent & RV camping: $24, Stay limit: 7 days, Open Jul-Sep, Max Length: 35ft, Reservations accepted, Elev: 10312ft/3143m, Tel: 435-783-4338, Nearest town: Kamas. GPS: 40.697266, -110.891846

79 • B3 | Renegade (Uinta-Wasatch-Cache NF)

Total sites: 62, RV sites: 62, Central water, Flush toilet, No showers, No RV dump, Tent & RV camping: $24, Concessionaire, Stay limit: 7 days, Open May-Sep, Max Length: 30ft, Reservations accepted, Elev: 7658ft/2334m, Tel: 801-226-3564, Nearest town: Heber City. GPS: 40.119491, -111.159597

80 • B3 | Reservoir (Ashley NF)

Total sites: 5, RV sites: 5, Central water, Vault/pit toilet, No showers, No RV dump, Tent & RV camping: $5, Open May-Sep, Max Length: 15ft, Reservations not accepted, Elev: 7950ft/2423m, Tel: 435-722-5018, Nearest town: Roosevelt. GPS: 40.575384, -110.325523

81 • B3 | Riverview (Ashley NF)

Total sites: 19, RV sites: 19, Central water, Vault/pit toilet, No showers, No RV dump, Tent & RV camping: $10, Open May-Sep, Max Length: 20ft, Reservations not accepted, Elev: 8028ft/2447m, Tel: 435-722-5018, Nearest town: Altonah. GPS: 40.590332, -110.336182

82 • B3 | Sawmill Hollow (Uinta-Wasatch-Cache NF)

Total sites: 6, RV sites: 4, No water, Vault/pit toilet, No showers, No RV dump, Tent & RV camping: Free, Max Length: 30ft, Elev: 6207ft/1892m, Tel: 801-798-3571, Nearest town: Mapleton. GPS: 40.141000, -111.341000

83 • B3 | Shady Dell (Uinta-Wasatch-Cache NF)

Total sites: 20, RV sites: 20, Central water, Vault/pit toilet, No showers, No RV dump, Tent & RV camping: $21, Stay limit: 7 days, Open Jun-Oct, Reservations not accepted, Elev: 8074ft/2461m, Tel: 435-654-0470, Nearest town: Kamas. GPS: 40.591797, -111.011963

84 • B3 | Shingle Creek ATV (Uinta-Wasatch-Cache NF)

Total sites: 21, RV sites: 21, Water available, Vault/pit toilet, No showers, No RV dump, Tent & RV camping: $18, Stay limit: 7 days, Open May-Oct, Reservations not accepted, Elev: 7497ft/2285m, Tel: 435-783-4338, Nearest town: Kamas. GPS: 40.615715, -111.132215

85 • B3 | Smith-Morehouse (Uinta-Wasatch-Cache NF)

Total sites: 34, RV sites: 34, Central water, Vault/pit toilet, No showers, No RV dump, Tent & RV camping: $26, Stay limit: 7 days, Open May-Sep, Max Length: 45ft, Reservations accepted, Elev: 7644ft/2330m, Tel: 435-783-4338, Nearest town: Oakley. GPS: 40.768031, -111.107141

86 • B3 | Soapstone (Uinta-Wasatch-Cache NF)

Total sites: 32, RV sites: 32, Central water, Vault/pit toilet, No showers, No RV dump, Tent & RV camping: $24, Stay limit: 7 days, Open May-Sep, Max Length: 86ft, Reservations accepted, Elev: 7920ft/2414m, Tel: 435-783-4338, Nearest town: Kamas. GPS: 40.578369, -111.026611

87 • B3 | Soldier Creek (Uinta-Wasatch-Cache NF)

Total sites: 160, RV sites: 160, Central water, Flush toilet, No showers, RV dump, Tent & RV camping: $24, Group site: $348, Long-term rentals available, Concessionaire, Open May-Oct, Max Length: 90ft, Reservations accepted, Elev: 7674ft/2339m, Tel: 435-654-0470, Nearest town: Heber City. GPS: 40.152733, -111.051206

88 • B3 | Stateline Reservoir (Uinta-Wasatch-Cache NF)

Total sites: 36, RV sites: 36, Central water, Vault/pit toilet, No showers, RV dump, Tent & RV camping: $22, 3 long-term sites, Open May-Sep, Max Length: 99ft, Reservations accepted, Elev:

9252ft/2820m, Tel: 307-782-6555, Nearest town: Mountain View. GPS: 40.981884, -110.384703

89 • B3 | Stillwater (Uinta-Wasatch-Cache NF)

Total sites: 17, RV sites: 17, Central water, Vault/pit toilet, No showers, No RV dump, Tent & RV camping: $22, 4 group sites: $81-$92, Stay limit: 14 days, Open Jun-Sep, Max Length: 50ft, Reservations accepted, Elev: 8510ft/2594m, Tel: 307-789-3194, Nearest town: Evanston. GPS: 40.868896, -110.835449

90 • B3 | Strawberry Bay - Loop F (Uinta-Wasatch-Cache NF)

Total sites: 47, RV sites: 47, Central water, Flush toilet, No showers, Tent & RV camping: $24, Open May-Oct, Max Length: 99ft, Reservations accepted, Elev: 7618ft/2322m, Tel: 801-226-3564, Nearest town: Provo. GPS: 40.185091, -111.158096

91 • B3 | Strawberry Bay - Loop G (Uinta-Wasatch-Cache NF)

Total sites: 59, RV sites: 59, Central water, Flush toilet, No showers, Tent & RV camping: $24, Open May-Oct, Reservations accepted, Elev: 7634ft/2327m, Tel: 801-226-3564, Nearest town: Provo. GPS: 40.181986, -111.156582

92 • B3 | Strawberry Bay - Loops A-E (Uinta-Wasatch-Cache NF)

Total sites: 175, RV sites: 175, Elec sites: 26, Water at site, Flush toilet, No showers, Tents: $24/RVs: $24-39, 23 Full hookup sites/ Loop B, Group site $200, Open May-Oct, Reservations accepted, Elev: 7628ft/2325m, Tel: 801-226-3564, Nearest town: Provo. GPS: 40.175939, -111.171908

93 • B3 | Strawberry Bay - Overflow (Uinta-Wasatch-Cache NF)

Total sites: 72, RV sites: 72, Central water, Flush toilet, No showers, Tent & RV camping: $24, Open May-Oct, Reservations not accepted, Elev: 7697ft/2346m, Tel: 801-226-3564, Nearest town: Provo. GPS: 40.179788, -111.178281

94 • B3 | Sulphur (Uinta-Wasatch-Cache NF)

Total sites: 21, RV sites: 21, Central water, Vault/pit toilet, No showers, No RV dump, Tent & RV camping: $22, Group site: $69, Stay limit: 14 days, Open Jun-Sep, Max Length: 38ft, Reservations accepted, Elev: 9104ft/2775m, Tel: 307-789-3194, Nearest town: Evanston, WY. GPS: 40.788873, -110.884809

95 • B3 | Swift Creek (Ashley NF)

Total sites: 13, RV sites: 13, Central water, Vault/pit toilet, No showers, No RV dump, Tent & RV camping: $8, Reservations not accepted, Elev: 8153ft/2485m, Tel: 435-722-5018, Nearest town: Altamont. GPS: 40.601074, -110.347900

96 • B3 | Taylors Fork ATV (Uinta-Wasatch-Cache NF)

Total sites: 11, RV sites: 11, Central water, Vault/pit toilet, No showers, No RV dump, Tent & RV camping: $14, Stay limit: 7 days, Open May-Oct, Reservations not accepted, Elev: 7418ft/ 2261m, Tel: 435-783-4338, Nearest town: Kamas. GPS: 40.620014, -111.137581

97 • B3 | Trial Lake (Uinta-Wasatch-Cache NF)

Total sites: 60, RV sites: 60, Central water, Vault/pit toilet, No showers, No RV dump, Tent & RV camping: $24, Stay limit: 7 days, Open Jul-Sep, Max Length: 88ft, Reservations accepted, Elev: 9879ft/3011m, Tel: 435-783-4338, Nearest town: Kamas. GPS: 40.681624, -110.950247

98 • B3 | Uinta Canyon (Ashley NF)

Total sites: 24, RV sites: 24, No water, Vault/pit toilet, Tent & RV camping: $5, Max Length: 22ft, Reservations not accepted, Elev: 7634ft/2327m, Nearest town: Roosevelt. GPS: 40.623291, -110.143799

99 • B3 | Upper Stillwater (Ashley NF)

Total sites: 11, RV sites: 11, Central water, Flush toilet, No showers, No RV dump, Tent & RV camping: $10, Group site: $30, Open May-Sep, Max Length: 25ft, Reservations accepted, Elev: 8061ft/ 2457m, Tel: 435-789-1181, Nearest town: Mountain Home. GPS: 40.555894, -110.700582

100 • B3 | Wandin (Ashley NF)

Total sites: 4, RV sites: 4, No water, Vault/pit toilet, Tent & RV camping: $5, Max Length: 15ft, Reservations not accepted, Elev: 7795ft/2376m, Nearest town: Roosevelt. GPS: 40.630702, -110.153772

101 • B3 | Washington Lake (Uinta-Wasatch-Cache NF)

Total sites: 45, RV sites: 45, No water, Vault/pit toilet, No showers, No RV dump, Tent & RV camping: $24, Stay limit: 7 days, Open Jul-Sep, Max Length: 105ft, Reservations accepted, Elev: 10007ft/ 3050m, Tel: 435-654-0470, Nearest town: Kamas. GPS: 40.679014, -110.961644

102 • B3 | West Marsh Lake (Uinta-Wasatch-Cache NF)

Total sites: 17, RV sites: 17, Central water, Vault/pit toilet, Tent & RV camping: $22, Group site: $78, Dump station 1.5 mi at Stateline, Stay limit: 14 days, Open Jun-Sep, Max Length: 75ft, Reservations accepted, Elev: 9354ft/2851m, Tel: 307-782-6555, Nearest town: Mountain View. GPS: 40.955502, -110.396994

103 • B3 | Whiting (Uinta-Wasatch-Cache NF)

Total sites: 26, RV sites: 26, Central water, Flush toilet, No showers, No RV dump, Tent & RV camping: $24, 2 group sites: $255-$510, 3 sites equipped for horses, RVs may NOT fill water tanks, Stay limit: 16 days, Open Apr-Oct, Max Length: 45ft, Reservations accepted, Elev: 5532ft/1686m, Tel: 801-798-3571, Nearest town: Mapleton. GPS: 40.131495, -111.527386

104 • B3 | Wolf Creek (Uinta-Wasatch-Cache NF)

Total sites: 3, RV sites: 3, Central water, Vault/pit toilet, No showers, No RV dump, Tent & RV camping: $22, 2 group sites $133-$232, Stay limit: 7 days, Open Jul-Sep, Max Length: 15ft, Reservations accepted, Elev: 9471ft/2887m, Tel: 435-783-4338, Nearest town: Heber City. GPS: 40.482476, -111.033555

105 • B3 | Wolverine ATV (Uinta-Wasatch-Cache NF)

Total sites: 7, RV sites: 6, No water, Vault/pit toilet, No showers, No RV dump, Tent & RV camping: $16, Reservations not accepted, Elev: 9101ft/2774m, Tel: 801-466-6411, Nearest town: Peoa. GPS: 40.845957, -110.814671

106 • B3 | Yellow Pine (Ashley) (Ashley NF)

Total sites: 11, RV sites: 11, Central water, Flush toilet, No showers, RV dump, Tent & RV camping: $10, 1 group site $30, Open

May-Sep, Max Length: 30ft, Reservations accepted, Elev: 7555ft/2303m, Tel: 435-738-2482, Nearest town: Mountain Home. GPS: 40.536416, -110.639975

107 • B3 | Yellow Pine (Wasatch) (Uinta-Wasatch-Cache NF)

Total sites: 33, RV sites: 33, Central water, Vault/pit toilet, No showers, No RV dump, Tent & RV camping: $18, Stay limit: 7 days, Open May-Oct, Max Length: 25ft, Reservations not accepted, Elev: 7293ft/2223m, Tel: 435-783-4338, Nearest town: Kamas. GPS: 40.630859, -111.173828

108 • B3 | Yellowstone (Ashley NF)

Total sites: 4, RV sites: 4, Central water, Vault/pit toilet, No showers, No RV dump, Tent & RV camping: $10, Reservable group site: $30, Open May-Sep, Max Length: 25ft, Reservations not accepted, Elev: 7661ft/2335m, Tel: 435-722-5018, Nearest town: Mountain Home. GPS: 40.542425, -110.336645

109 • B4 | Antelope Flat (Ashley NF)

Total sites: 46, RV sites: 46, Water available, No toilets, No showers, RV dump, Tent & RV camping: $20, Group sites: $105-$120, Open May-Sep, Max Length: 40ft, Reservations accepted, Elev: 6083ft/1854m, Tel: 435-889-3000, Nearest town: Dutch John. GPS: 40.965164, -109.550618

110 • B4 | Browne Lake (Ashley NF)

Total sites: 20, RV sites: 20, No water, Vault/pit toilet, Tent & RV camping: $14, Reservable group site: $60, Open May-Sep, Reservations not accepted, Elev: 8363ft/2549m, Tel: 435-784-3483, Nearest town: Flaming Gorge. GPS: 40.861164, -109.816312

111 • B4 | Canyon Rim (Ashley NF)

Total sites: 15, RV sites: 7, Water available, Vault/pit toilet, No showers, No RV dump, Tent & RV camping: $22, 7 sites open for pack-in until snow closes, Open May-Sep, Max Length: 65ft, Elev: 7431ft/2265m, Tel: 435-784-3445, Nearest town: Dutch John. GPS: 40.884521, -109.546875

112 • B4 | Carmel (Ashley NF)

Total sites: 15, RV sites: 15, No water, Vault/pit toilet, Tent & RV camping: $12, Open May-Sep, Max Length: 25ft, Reservations not accepted, Elev: 6293ft/1918m, Nearest town: Manila. GPS: 40.931043, -109.731705

113 • B4 | Cedar Springs (Ashley NF)

Total sites: 21, RV sites: 21, Central water, Vault/pit toilet, No showers, RV dump, Tent & RV camping: $28, Open Apr-Sep, Max Length: 62ft, Reservations accepted, Elev: 6129ft/1868m, Tel: 435-889-3000, Nearest town: Dutch John. GPS: 40.908936, -109.450439

114 • B4 | Deep Creek (Ashley NF)

Total sites: 17, RV sites: 17, No water, Vault/pit toilet, Tent & RV camping: $12, Open May-Sep, Max Length: 30ft, Reservations not accepted, Elev: 7730ft/2356m, Nearest town: Manila. GPS: 40.855824, -109.729974

115 • B4 | Deer Run (Ashley NF)

Total sites: 13, RV sites: 13, Central water, Flush toilet, Free showers, RV dump, Tent & RV camping: $28, Open May-Oct, Max Length: 45ft, Reservations accepted, Elev: 6207ft/1892m, Tel: 435-889-3000, Nearest town: Dutch John. GPS: 40.905701, -109.444214

116 • B4 | Dripping Springs (Ashley NF)

Total sites: 23, RV sites: 23, Central water, Flush toilet, No showers, No RV dump, Tent & RV camping: $20, 4 group sites: $95-$115, No water in winter - $5, Open all year, Max Length: 95ft, Reservations accepted, Elev: 6145ft/1873m, Tel: 435-889-3000, Nearest town: Dutch John. GPS: 40.923558, -109.360253

117 • B4 | East Park (Ashley NF)

Total sites: 21, RV sites: 21, Central water, Vault/pit toilet, No showers, No RV dump, Tent & RV camping: $12, Open Jun-Sep, Max Length: 25ft, Reservations not accepted, Elev: 9052ft/2759m, Tel: 435-789-1181, Nearest town: Vernal. GPS: 40.783019, -109.553264

118 • B4 | Firefighter's Memorial (Ashley NF)

Total sites: 94, RV sites: 94, Central water, Flush toilet, No showers, RV dump, Tent & RV camping: $24, Open May-Sep, Max Length: 60ft, Reservations accepted, Elev: 6864ft/2092m, Tel: 435-789-1181, Nearest town: Dutch John. GPS: 40.892653, -109.454951

119 • B4 | Greendale (Ashley NF)

Total sites: 8, RV sites: 8, Central water, Vault/pit toilet, No showers, No RV dump, Tent & RV camping: $20, Open May-Sep, Max Length: 65ft, Reservations accepted, Elev: 7014ft/2138m, Tel: 435-889-3000, Nearest town: Dutch John. GPS: 40.882615, -109.460911

120 • B4 | Greens Lake (Ashley NF)

Total sites: 20, RV sites: 20, Water available, Vault/pit toilet, No showers, No RV dump, Tent & RV camping: $22, 1 group site $77, Open May-Sep, Max Length: 40ft, Reservations accepted, Elev: 7474ft/2278m, Tel: 435-784-3445, Nearest town: Dutch John. GPS: 40.873291, -109.537354

121 • B4 | Kaler Hollow (Ashley NF)

Total sites: 4, RV sites: 0, Central water, Vault/pit toilet, Tents only: Free, No water after Sep 15th, Open May-Sep, Reservations not accepted, Elev: 9022ft/2750m, Tel: 435-789-1181, Nearest town: Vernal. GPS: 40.702112, -109.614724

122 • B4 | Lodgepole at Flaming Gorge (Ashley NF)

Total sites: 35, RV sites: 35, Central water, Flush toilet, No showers, RV dump, Tent & RV camping: $20, Open May-Sep, Max Length: 63ft, Reservations accepted, Elev: 8117ft/2474m, Tel: 435-889-3000, Nearest town: Dutch John. GPS: 40.811634, -109.466297

123 • B4 | Lucerne Valley (Ashley NF)

Total sites: 143, RV sites: 143, Elec sites: 75, Central water, Flush toilet, Free showers, RV dump, Tents: $22/RVs: $31, Group site: $140, Open May-Sep, Max Length: 70ft, Reservations accepted, Elev: 6066ft/1849m, Tel: 435-784-3445, Nearest town: Manila. GPS: 40.983541, -109.591715

124 • B4 | Manns (Ashley NF)

Total sites: 8, RV sites: 8, No water, Vault/pit toilet, Tent & RV camping: $12, Open Apr-Sep, Reservations not accepted, Elev:

6158ft/1877m, Tel: 435-784-3445, Nearest town: Manila. GPS: 40.924857, -109.709071

125 • B4 | Mustang Ridge (Ashley NF)

Total sites: 70, RV sites: 70, Central water, Flush toilet, Free showers, No RV dump, Tent & RV camping: $28, Group site: $154, Open May-Sep, Max Length: 80ft, Reservations accepted, Elev: 6109ft/1862m, Tel: 435-889-3000, Nearest town: Dutch John. GPS: 40.927246, -109.439941

126 • B4 | Oaks Park (Ashley NF)

Total sites: 11, RV sites: 11, Central water, Vault/pit toilet, Tent & RV camping: Free, Open Jun-Sep, Max Length: 20ft, Reservations not accepted, Elev: 9262ft/2823m, Tel: 435-789-1181, Nearest town: Vernal. GPS: 40.742089, -109.623605

127 • B4 | Paradise Park (Ashley NF)

Total sites: 15, RV sites: 15, No water, Vault/pit toilet, Tent & RV camping: $5, Open Jun-Sep, Max Length: 25ft, Reservations not accepted, Elev: 9993ft/3046m, Tel: 435-789-1181, Nearest town: Lapoint. GPS: 40.666323, -109.913874

128 • B4 | Pole Creek Lake (Ashley NF)

Total sites: 19, RV sites: 19, No water, Vault/pit toilet, Tent & RV camping: $5, Open May-Sep, Reservations not accepted, Elev: 10272ft/3131m, Tel: 435-722-5018, Nearest town: Whiterocks. GPS: 40.678467, -110.059814

129 • B4 | Red Canyon (Ashley) (Ashley NF)

Total sites: 8, RV sites: 8, Central water, Vault/pit toilet, No showers, No RV dump, Tent & RV camping: $22, Open May-Sep, Max Length: 40ft, Reservations accepted, Elev: 7395ft/2254m, Tel: 435-784-3445, Nearest town: Dutch John. GPS: 40.889343, -109.559029

130 • B4 | Skull Creek (Ashley NF)

Total sites: 17, RV sites: 17, No water, Vault/pit toilet, No showers, No RV dump, Tent & RV camping: $15, Open May-Sep, Max Length: 80ft, Reservations accepted, Elev: 7434ft/2266m, Tel: 435-784-3445, Nearest town: Dutch John. GPS: 40.864905, -109.526508

131 • B4 | South Fork (Ashley NF)

Total sites: 6, RV sites: 6, No water, Vault/pit toilet, Tent & RV camping: Free, Reservations not accepted, Elev: 9688ft/2953m, Nearest town: Vernal. GPS: 40.734967, -109.739576

132 • B4 | Spirit Lake (Ashley NF)

Total sites: 24, RV sites: 24, No water, Vault/pit toilet, Tent & RV camping: $14, Open May-Sep, Max Length: 30ft, Reservations not accepted, Elev: 10207ft/3111m, Tel: 435-789-1181, Nearest town: Manila. GPS: 40.837438, -110.000379

133 • B4 | Whiterocks (Ashley NF)

Total sites: 21, RV sites: 21, Central water, Vault/pit toilet, No showers, No RV dump, Tent & RV camping: $8, Open May-Sep, Max Length: 25ft, Reservations not accepted, Elev: 7510ft/2289m, Tel: 435-789-1181, Nearest town: Whiterocks. GPS: 40.619388, -109.941458

134 • B4 | Willows (Ashley NF)

Total sites: 8, RV sites: 8, No water, Vault/pit toilet, Tent & RV camping: $12, Open Apr-Sep, Reservations not accepted, Elev: 6165ft/1879m, Tel: 435-784-3445, Nearest town: Manila. GPS: 40.925959, -109.714713

135 • C2 | Bear Canyon (Uinta-Wasatch-Cache NF)

Total sites: 6, RV sites: 6, No water, Flush toilet, Tent & RV camping: $21, Reservable group sites: $87-$121, Non-potable water, Stay limit: 16 days, Open May-Oct, Max Length: 30ft, Reservations not accepted, Elev: 6700ft/2042m, Tel: 801-798-3571, Nearest town: Payson. GPS: 39.787699, -111.731098

136 • C2 | Blackhawk Horse Camp (Uinta-Wasatch-Cache NF)

Total sites: 15, RV sites: 15, Central water, Flush toilet, No showers, RV dump, Tent & RV camping: $23, Stay limit: 16 days, Open May-Sep, Max Length: 45ft, Reservations required, Elev: 7864ft/2397m, Tel: 801-798-3571, Nearest town: Payson. GPS: 39.889477, -111.625858

137 • C2 | Chicken Creek (Manti-La Sal NF)

Total sites: 7, RV sites: 7, No water, Vault/pit toilet, Tent & RV camping: Free, Open May-Nov, Reservations not accepted, Elev: 6125ft/1867m, Nearest town: Levan. GPS: 39.530000, -111.774000

138 • C2 | Cottonwood (SFRD) (Uinta-Wasatch-Cache NF)

Total sites: 18, RV sites: 18, No water, Vault/pit toilet, Tent & RV camping: Free, Stay limit: 7 days, Open Apr-Oct, Reservations not accepted, Elev: 6594ft/2010m, Tel: 801-798-3571, Nearest town: Nephi. GPS: 39.780366, -111.723377

139 • C2 | Maple Bench (Uinta-Wasatch-Cache NF)

Total sites: 10, RV sites: 10, Central water, Vault/pit toilet, No showers, No RV dump, Tent & RV camping: $21, Stay limit: 16 days, Open May-Oct, Reservations not accepted, Elev: 5899ft/1798m, Tel: 801-798-3571, Nearest town: Payson. GPS: 39.962981, -111.691831

140 • C2 | Maple Canyon (Manti-La Sal NF)

Total sites: 12, RV sites: 12, No water, Vault/pit toilet, Tent & RV camping: $10, Also walk-to & group sites, Group site: $40, Open May-Oct, Max Length: 25ft, Reservations accepted, Elev: 7041ft/2146m, Tel: 435-637-2817, Nearest town: Moroni. GPS: 39.556338, -111.686537

141 • C2 | Maple Grove (Fishlake NF)

Total sites: 16, RV sites: 16, Central water, Vault/pit toilet, No showers, No RV dump, Tent & RV camping: $15, Reservable group site: $50-$90, Open May-Sep, Reservations not accepted, Elev: 6499ft/1981m, Tel: 435-743-5721, Nearest town: Scipio. GPS: 39.016557, -112.089458

142 • C2 | Maple Hollow (Fishlake NF)

Total sites: 6, RV sites: 4, Central water, Vault/pit toilet, No showers, No RV dump, Tent & RV camping: Free, Open May-Sep, Reservations not accepted, Elev: 7031ft/2143m, Tel: 435-743-5721, Nearest town: Holden. GPS: 39.061151, -112.170831

143 • C2 | Maple Lake (Uinta-Wasatch-Cache NF)

Total sites: 7, RV sites: 7, No water, Vault/pit toilet, Tent & RV camping: $24, Stay limit: 16 days, Open May-Oct, Reservations not accepted, Elev: 6447ft/1965m, Tel: 801-798-3571, Nearest town: Payson. GPS: 39.957000, -111.693000

144 • C2 | Oak Creek (Fishlake NF)

Total sites: 10, RV sites: 7, Central water, Vault/pit toilet, No showers, No RV dump, Tent & RV camping: $12, 4 group sites: $30-$60, Stay limit: 14 days, Generator hours: 0600-2200, Open May-Sep, Reservations accepted, Elev: 6061ft/1847m, Tel: 435-743-5721, Nearest town: Oak City. GPS: 39.352459, -112.260743

145 • C2 | Payson Lakes (Uinta-Wasatch-Cache NF)

Total sites: 108, RV sites: 108, Central water, Flush toilet, No showers, No RV dump, Tent & RV camping: $24, 2 group sites: $155-$220, Stay limit: 16 days, Open May-Oct, Max Length: 128ft, Reservations accepted, Elev: 7995ft/2437m, Tel: 801-226-3564, Nearest town: Payson. GPS: 39.930322, -111.642672

146 • C2 | Ponderosa (Uinta) (Uinta-Wasatch-Cache NF)

Total sites: 23, RV sites: 23, Central water, Vault/pit toilet, No showers, No RV dump, Tent & RV camping: $22, Stay limit: 16 days, Open Apr-Oct, Max Length: 110ft, Reservations accepted, Elev: 6293ft/1918m, Tel: 801-798-3571, Nearest town: Nephi. GPS: 39.766073, -111.713801

147 • C2 | Tinney Flat (Uinta-Wasatch-Cache NF)

Total sites: 13, RV sites: 13, Central water, Vault/pit toilet, No showers, No RV dump, Tent & RV camping: $24, 3 group sites: $133, Stay limit: 16 days, Open May-Sep, Max Length: 55ft, Reservations accepted, Elev: 7192ft/2192m, Tel: 801-798-3571, Nearest town: Santaquin. GPS: 39.900527, -111.727811

148 • C2 | Twin Lake (Manti-La Sal NF)

Total sites: 21, RV sites: 21, No water, Vault/pit toilet, Tent & RV camping: $10, Group site: $30, Open May-Sep, Max Length: 40ft, Reservations accepted, Elev: 7211ft/2198m, Tel: 435-283-4151, Nearest town: Mayfield. GPS: 39.118654, -111.604125

149 • C2 | Vernon Reservoir (Uinta-Wasatch-Cache NF)

Total sites: 10, RV sites: 10, No water, Vault/pit toilet, Tent & RV camping: Free, Stay limit: 16 days, Open Apr-Dec, Reservations not accepted, Elev: 6191ft/1887m, Tel: 801-798-3571, Nearest town: Vernon. GPS: 39.991743, -112.385556

150 • C3 | Avintaquin (Ashley NF)

Total sites: 17, RV sites: 17, No water, Vault/pit toilet, Tent & RV camping: $5, Group site $20, Open Jun-Sep, Max Length: 48ft, Reservations accepted, Elev: 8983ft/2738m, Tel: 435-738-2482, Nearest town: Duchesne. GPS: 39.884033, -110.775879

151 • C3 | Bridges - Riverside (Manti-La Sal NF)

Total sites: 2, RV sites: 2, No water, Vault/pit toilet, Tent & RV camping: $5, 2 double sites: $5/vehicle, Open May-Oct, Max Length: 30ft, Reservations accepted, Elev: 8086ft/2465m, Tel: 435-384-2372, Nearest town: Huntington. GPS: 39.547749, -111.166941

152 • C3 | Bridges (Manti-La Sal NF)

Total sites: 2, RV sites: 2, No water, Vault/pit toilet, Tent & RV camping: $5, Group site: $40, Open May-Oct, Max Length: 30ft, Reservations accepted, Elev: 8113ft/2473m, Tel: 435-384-2372, Nearest town: Huntington. GPS: 39.561755, -111.174854

153 • C3 | Diamond (Uinta-Wasatch-Cache NF)

Total sites: 50, RV sites: 50, Central water, Vault/pit toilet, No showers, No RV dump, Tent & RV camping: $24, Also walk-to & group sites, 7 group sites: $75-$295, Open Apr-Oct, Max Length: 70ft, Reservations accepted, Elev: 5236ft/1596m, Tel: 385-273-1100, Nearest town: Thistle. GPS: 40.072122, -111.428203

154 • C3 | Ferron Reservoir South (Manti-La Sal NF)

Total sites: 7, RV sites: 7, Central water, Vault/pit toilet, No showers, No RV dump, Tent & RV camping: $10, Open Jun-Oct, Max Length: 22ft, Reservations not accepted, Elev: 9489ft/2892m, Tel: 435-384-2372, Nearest town: Ferron. GPS: 39.138425, -111.453058

155 • C3 | Ferron Reservoir West (Manti-La Sal NF)

Total sites: 14, RV sites: 14, Central water, Vault/pit toilet, No showers, No RV dump, Tent & RV camping: $10, Open Jun-Oct, Max Length: 45ft, Reservations accepted, Elev: 9495ft/2894m, Tel: 435-384-2372, Nearest town: Ferron. GPS: 39.142730, -111.455298

156 • C3 | Fish Creek (Manti-La Sal NF)

Total sites: 7, RV sites: 7, No water, Vault/pit toilet, Tent & RV camping: $7, Open May-Sep, Reservations not accepted, Elev: 7697ft/2346m, Tel: 435-637-2817, Nearest town: Scofield. GPS: 39.774000, -111.203000

157 • C3 | Flat Canyon (Manti-La Sal NF)

Total sites: 12, RV sites: 12, Central water, Vault/pit toilet, No showers, No RV dump, Tent & RV camping: $10, Group site: $50, Open Jun-Sep, Max Length: 35ft, Reservations accepted, Elev: 8884ft/2708m, Tel: 435-384-2372, Nearest town: Fairview. GPS: 39.646201, -111.259767

158 • C3 | Forks of Huntington (Manti-La Sal NF)

Total sites: 2, RV sites: 2, No water, Vault/pit toilet, No showers, No RV dump, Tent & RV camping: $10, Group site: $40, Open Apr-Nov, Max Length: 30ft, Reservations accepted, Elev: 7700ft/2347m, Tel: 435-384-2372, Nearest town: Huntington. GPS: 39.500731, -111.160091

159 • C3 | FSR 0110 Dispersed 1 (Manti-La Sal NF)

Total sites: 3, RV sites: 3, No water, Vault/pit toilet, Tent & RV camping: $3, Open May-Sep, Reservations not accepted, Elev: 8212ft/2503m, Tel: 435-636-3500, Nearest town: Huntington. GPS: 39.534858, -111.140891

160 • C3 | Gooseberry Reservoir (Manti-La Sal NF)

Total sites: 16, RV sites: 16, No water, Vault/pit toilet, Tent & RV camping: $10, Open Jun-Sep, Max Length: 40ft, Reservations accepted, Elev: 8435ft/2571m, Tel: 435-384-2372, Nearest town: Fairview. GPS: 39.711624, -111.293841

161 • C3 | Indian Creek Group (Manti-La Sal NF)

Total sites: 7, RV sites: 7, Central water, Vault/pit toilet, No showers, No RV dump, Tent & RV camping: $3, 7 reservable group sites: $30-$50, Individual sites available if not in use, Open Jun-Oct, Reservations accepted, Elev: 8780ft/2676m, Tel: 801-756-8616, Nearest town: Huntington. GPS: 39.442543, -111.238806

162 • C3 | Joe's Valley (Manti-La Sal NF)

Total sites: 46, RV sites: 46, No water, Vault/pit toilet, Tent & RV camping: $10, Open Apr-Nov, Max Length: 40ft, Reservations accepted, Elev: 7123ft/2171m, Tel: 435-384-2372, Nearest town: Orangeville. GPS: 39.295356, -111.292157

163 • C3 | Lake Canyon (Manti-La Sal NF)

Total sites: 9, RV sites: 9, No water, Vault/pit toilet, Tent & RV camping: $15, 5 group sites: $40-$60, Open Jun-Nov, Max Length: 50ft, Reservations accepted, Elev: 8963ft/2732m, Tel: 435-384-2372, Nearest town: Fairview. GPS: 39.575664, -111.258165

164 • C3 | Lake Hill (Manti-La Sal NF)

Total sites: 10, RV sites: 10, Central water, Vault/pit toilet, No showers, No RV dump, Tent & RV camping: $10, 2 group sites: $30-$40, Open May-Sep, Max Length: 25ft, Reservations accepted, Elev: 8428ft/2569m, Tel: 435-283-4151, Nearest town: Ephraim. GPS: 39.327416, -111.499333

165 • C3 | Little Rock (Manti-La Sal NF)

Total sites: 1, RV sites: 1, No water, No toilets, Tent & RV camping: $5, Open May-Sep, Reservations not accepted, Elev: 8100ft/2469m, Tel: 435-637-2817, Nearest town: Huntington. GPS: 39.547358, -111.168333

166 • C3 | Manti Community (Manti-La Sal NF)

Total sites: 8, RV sites: 8, No water, Vault/pit toilet, No showers, No RV dump, Tent & RV camping: $10, 1 group site $40, Open May-Sep, Max Length: 30ft, Reservations accepted, Elev: 7512ft/2290m, Tel: 435-283-4151, Nearest town: Manti. GPS: 39.253668, -111.541328

167 • C3 | Old Folks Flat (Manti-La Sal NF)

Total sites: 8, RV sites: 8, Central water, Flush toilet, No showers, No RV dump, Tent & RV camping: $10, group sites: $40-$75, Open May-Sep, Max Length: 30ft, Reservations accepted, Elev: 8123ft/2476m, Tel: 801-756-8616, Nearest town: Huntington. GPS: 39.539000, -111.159000

168 • C3 | Potters Pond (Manti-La Sal NF)

Total sites: 19, RV sites: 19, No water, Vault/pit toilet, Tent & RV camping: $10, 2 group sites $210-$280, Open Jun-Oct, Max Length: 50ft, Reservations accepted, Elev: 9005ft/2745m, Tel: 435-384-2372, Nearest town: Huntington. GPS: 39.450753, -111.268867

169 • C3 | Potters Pond Equestrian (Manti-La Sal NF)

Total sites: 4, RV sites: 4, No water, Vault/pit toilet, Tent & RV camping: $15-25, Open Jun-Sep, Max Length: 30ft, Reservations accepted, Elev: 9008ft/2746m, Tel: 435-384-2372, Nearest town: Huntington. GPS: 39.451594, -111.273141

170 • C3 | River Bend (Manti-La Sal NF)

Total sites: 1, RV sites: 1, No water, No toilets, Tent & RV camping: $3, Open May-Sep, Reservations not accepted, Elev: 7126ft/2172m, Tel: 435-636-3500, Nearest town: Huntington. GPS: 39.437756, -111.133604

171 • C3 | Salina Creek Second Crossing (Fishlake NF)

Total sites: 28, RV sites: 22, No water, Vault/pit toilet, No showers, No RV dump, Tent & RV camping: Free, Open Mar-Oct, Reservations not accepted, Elev: 7275ft/2217m, Tel: 435-896-9233, Nearest town: Salina. GPS: 38.937869, -111.543251

172 • C3 | Twelve Mile Flat (Manti-La Sal NF)

Total sites: 14, RV sites: 14, No water, Vault/pit toilet, No showers, No RV dump, Tent & RV camping: $7-12, Group site: $40, Open Jun-Oct, Max Length: 35ft, Reservations accepted, Elev: 10118ft/3084m, Tel: 435-283-4151, Nearest town: Mayfield. GPS: 39.123032, -111.487814

173 • C3 | Unicorn Ridge (Uinta-Wasatch-Cache NF)

Total sites: 5, RV sites: 5, No water, Vault/pit toilet, Tent & RV camping: Free, Open May-Oct, Reservations not accepted, Elev: 7591ft/2314m, Nearest town: Spanish Fork. GPS: 40.029454, -111.281752

174 • C3 | Upper Six Mile Ponds (Manti-La Sal NF)

Total sites: 5, RV sites: 5, No water, Vault/pit toilet, Tent & RV camping: Free, Rough road, 4x4 recommended, Open Jun-Oct, Reservations not accepted, Elev: 8986ft/2739m, Nearest town: Sterling. GPS: 39.188436, -111.540601

175 • C3 | Willow Lake (Manti-La Sal NF)

Total sites: 10, RV sites: 10, No water, Vault/pit toilet, Tent & RV camping: $7-10, Open Jun-Oct, Max Length: 30ft, Reservations accepted, Elev: 9649ft/2941m, Tel: 435-384-2372, Nearest town: Ferron. GPS: 39.134811, -111.381332

176 • D2 | Adelaide (Fishlake NF)

Total sites: 10, RV sites: 10, Central water, Flush toilet, No showers, No RV dump, Tent & RV camping: $16, Reservable group site: $68, Open May-Sep, Max Length: 70ft, Reservations accepted, Elev: 5591ft/1704m, Tel: 435-743-5721, Nearest town: Kanosh. GPS: 38.753946, -112.364498

177 • D2 | Anderson Meadow (Fishlake NF)

Total sites: 10, RV sites: 10, Central water, Vault/pit toilet, No showers, No RV dump, Tent & RV camping: $19, Open Jun-Sep, Max Length: 78ft, Reservations accepted, Elev: 9593ft/2924m, Tel: 435-438-2436, Nearest town: Beaver. GPS: 38.210649, -112.431714

178 • D2 | Barker Reservoir (Dixie NF)

Total sites: 13, RV sites: 13, Central water, Vault/pit toilet, No showers, No RV dump, Tent & RV camping: $14, FSR 149 is steep single-lane with switchbacks and turnouts, Open May-Sep, Max Length: 35ft, Reservations accepted, Elev: 9305ft/2836m, Tel: 435-826-5499, Nearest town: Escalante. GPS: 37.920443, -111.816583

179 • D2 | Blue Spruce (Dixie NF)

Total sites: 6, RV sites: 4, Central water, Vault/pit toilet, No showers,

No RV dump, Tent & RV camping: $9, Stay limit: 14 days, Open all year, Reservations not accepted, Elev: 7979ft/2432m, Tel: 435-826-5499, Nearest town: Escalante. GPS: 37.972745, -111.651841

180 • D2 | Bowery Creek (Fishlake NF)

Total sites: 44, RV sites: 44, Central water, Flush toilet, No showers, RV dump, Tent & RV camping: $20, Group sites: $40-$60, Stay limit: 10 days, Generator hours: 0600-2200, Open May-Sep, Max Length: 125ft, Reservations accepted, Elev: 8924ft/2720m, Tel: 435-638-1069, Nearest town: Loa. GPS: 38.560547, -111.709961

181 • D2 | Casto Canyon (Dixie NF)

Total sites: 5, RV sites: 5, No water, Vault/pit toilet, Tent & RV camping: Free, Max Length: 35ft, Elev: 7028ft/2142m, Tel: 435-676-2676, Nearest town: Panguitch. GPS: 37.785266, -112.339231

182 • D2 | City Creek (Fishlake NF)

Total sites: 5, RV sites: 5, Water available, Vault/pit toilet, No showers, No RV dump, Tent & RV camping: Fee unk, Group sites, Open May-Sep, Max Length: 24ft, Reservations accepted, Elev: 7540ft/2298m, Tel: 435-896-9233, Nearest town: Beaver. GPS: 38.269726, -112.311266

183 • D2 | Cold Springs (Fishlake NF)

Total sites: 9, RV sites: 9, No water, Vault/pit toilet, Tent & RV camping: Free, Reservations not accepted, Elev: 9152ft/2790m, Tel: 435-896-9233, Nearest town: Salina. GPS: 38.782456, -111.643283

184 • D2 | Doctor Creek (Fishlake NF)

Total sites: 30, RV sites: 30, Central water, Flush toilet, No showers, RV dump, Tent & RV camping: $20, 2 reservable group sites: $135, Open May-Oct, Max Length: 50ft, Reservations accepted, Elev: 8924ft/2720m, Tel: 435-638-1069, Nearest town: Loa. GPS: 38.527965, -111.743433

185 • D2 | Frying Pan (Fishlake NF)

Total sites: 11, RV sites: 11, Central water, Flush toilet, No showers, No RV dump, Tent & RV camping: $20, 1 group site $95, Open May-Sep, Max Length: 45ft, Reservations accepted, Elev: 9078ft/2767m, Tel: 435-638-1069, Nearest town: Loa. GPS: 38.608887, -111.679688

186 • D2 | FSR 3023 Dispersed 1 (Dixie NF)

Total sites: 6, RV sites: 6, No water, No toilets, Tent & RV camping: Free, Elev: 8340ft/2542m, Tel: 435-865-3200, Nearest town: Parowan. GPS: 37.772495, -112.746534

187 • D2 | FSR 3026 Dispersed 1 (Dixie NF)

Total sites: 16, RV sites: 16, No water, No toilets, Tent & RV camping: Free, Elev: 8238ft/2511m, Tel: 435-865-3200, Nearest town: Parowan. GPS: 37.769644, -112.753658

188 • D2 | FSR 3027 Dispersed 1 (Dixie NF)

Total sites: 8, RV sites: 8, No water, No toilets, Tent & RV camping: Free, Elev: 8255ft/2516m, Tel: 435-865-3200, Nearest town: Parowan. GPS: 37.769790, -112.750460

189 • D2 | Gooseberry (Fishlake) (Fishlake NF)

Total sites: 13, RV sites: 13, Central water, Vault/pit toilet, No showers, No RV dump, Tent & RV camping: $10, Group site $20, Open Apr-Nov, Reservations not accepted, Elev: 7894ft/2406m, Nearest town: Salina. GPS: 38.802843, -111.685251

190 • D2 | Gooseberry I-70 TH (Fishlake NF)

Total sites: 6, RV sites: 4, No water, Vault/pit toilet, Tent & RV camping: Free, Elev: 5766ft/1757m, Tel: 435-896-9233, Nearest town: Salina. GPS: 38.915284, -111.732219

191 • D2 | Kents Lake (Fishlake NF)

Total sites: 30, RV sites: 30, Central water, Vault/pit toilet, No showers, No RV dump, Tent & RV camping: $20, Open May-Sep, Max Length: 193ft, Reservations accepted, Elev: 8894ft/2711m, Tel: 435-438-2436, Nearest town: Beaver. GPS: 38.236572, -112.459961

192 • D2 | LeBaron Lake (Fishlake NF)

Total sites: 13, RV sites: 13, No water, Vault/pit toilet, Tent & RV camping: $10, Open Jul-Sep, Max Length: 69ft, Reservations accepted, Elev: 9963ft/3037m, Tel: 435-438-2436, Nearest town: Beaver. GPS: 38.224352, -112.402527

193 • D2 | Little Cottonwood (Fishlake NF)

Total sites: 14, RV sites: 14, Central water, Flush toilet, No showers, No RV dump, Tent & RV camping: $20, Open May-Sep, Max Length: 82ft, Reservations accepted, Elev: 6463ft/1970m, Tel: 435-438-2436, Nearest town: Beaver. GPS: 38.256899, -112.543814

194 • D2 | Little Reservoir (Fishlake NF)

Total sites: 8, RV sites: 8, Central water, Vault/pit toilet, No showers, No RV dump, Tent & RV camping: $12, Open May-Sep, Max Length: 40ft, Reservations not accepted, Elev: 7346ft/2239m, Tel: 435-896-9233, Nearest town: Beaver. GPS: 38.260984, -112.489468

195 • D2 | Mackinaw (Fishlake NF)

Total sites: 44, RV sites: 44, Central water, Flush toilet, Free showers, No RV dump, Tent & RV camping: $20, 4 group sites: $40, Stay limit: 10 days, Generator hours: 0600-2200, Open May-Sep, Max Length: 115ft, Reservations accepted, Elev: 8914ft/2717m, Tel: 435-638-1069, Nearest town: Loa. GPS: 38.555420, -111.716797

196 • D2 | Mahogany Cove (Fishlake NF)

Total sites: 7, RV sites: 7, Water available, Vault/pit toilet, No showers, No RV dump, Tent & RV camping: $12, Group site $70, Individual sites available if no group use, Open May-Sep, Reservations not accepted, Elev: 7526ft/2294m, Tel: 435-438-2436, Nearest town: Beaver. GPS: 38.269364, -112.485762

197 • D2 | Pine Lake (Dixie NF)

Total sites: 33, RV sites: 33, Central water, Vault/pit toilet, No showers, No RV dump, Tent & RV camping: $19, 4 group sites: $53-$104, Open May-Sep, Max Length: 30ft, Reservations accepted, Elev: 8255ft/2516m, Tel: 435-826-5499, Nearest town: Bryce Canyon. GPS: 37.744229, -111.950891

198 • D2 | Piute (Fishlake NF)

Total sites: 47, RV sites: 47, Central water, Vault/pit toilet, No showers, RV dump, Tent & RV camping: $10, Open May-Sep, Reservations not accepted, Elev: 8855ft/2699m, Tel: 435-638-1069, Nearest town: Loa. GPS: 38.617854, -111.652737

199 • D2 | Posey Lake (Dixie NF)

Total sites: 21, RV sites: 21, Central water, Vault/pit toilet, No showers, No RV dump, Tents: $14/RVs: $15, Group site: $53, Open May-Sep, Max Length: 35ft, Reservations accepted, Elev: 8688ft/2648m, Tel: 435-826-5499, Nearest town: Escalante. GPS: 37.935394, -111.694205

200 • D2 | Red Canyon (Dixie NF)

Total sites: 37, RV sites: 37, Central water, Flush toilet, Pay showers, RV dump, Tent & RV camping: $21, Stay limit: 14 days, Generator hours: 0600-2200, Open May-Oct, Max Length: 45ft, Reservations not accepted, Elev: 7290ft/2222m, Tel: 435-676-2676, Nearest town: Panguitch. GPS: 37.742676, -112.309082

201 • D2 | Tasha Equestrian (Fishlake NF)

Total sites: 10, RV sites: 10, Central water, Flush toilet, No showers, No RV dump, Tent & RV camping: $14, Group site: $50, Must have horse, Open May-Sep, Reservations accepted, Elev: 9111ft/2777m, Tel: 435-638-1069, Nearest town: Loa. GPS: 38.621591, -111.659449

202 • D2 | Tushar (Fishlake NF)

Total sites: 24, RV sites: 24, Central water, Flush toilet, No showers, No RV dump, Tent & RV camping: $12, Group fee: $50-$160, Open May-Sep, Reservations accepted, Elev: 8691ft/2649m, Tel: 435-438-2436, Nearest town: Beaver. GPS: 38.238026, -112.469397

203 • D2 | Twin Ponds (Fishlake NF)

Total sites: 13, RV sites: 13, No water, Vault/pit toilet, No showers, No RV dump, Tent & RV camping: Free, Reservations not accepted, Elev: 9098ft/2773m, Tel: 435-896-9233, Nearest town: Salina. GPS: 38.786458, -111.640573

204 • D2 | White Bridge (Dixie NF)

Total sites: 29, RV sites: 29, Central water, Flush toilet, No showers, RV dump, Tent & RV camping: $21, Open May-Sep, Max Length: 45ft, Reservations accepted, Elev: 7881ft/2402m, Tel: 435-865-3200, Nearest town: Panguitch. GPS: 37.745827, -112.587909

205 • D2 | Yankee Meadow (Dixie NF)

Total sites: 29, RV sites: 29, Central water, Vault/pit toilet, No showers, No RV dump, Tent & RV camping: $15, Open May-Sep, Reservations not accepted, Elev: 8520ft/2597m, Tel: 435-865-3200, Nearest town: Cedar City. GPS: 37.760232, -112.760014

206 • D3 | Elk Horn (Fishlake NF)

Total sites: 6, RV sites: 6, Central water, Vault/pit toilet, No showers, No RV dump, Tent & RV camping: $12, Group site: $45, Open Jun-Sep, Reservations accepted, Elev: 9820ft/2993m, Tel: 435-836-2811, Nearest town: Loa. GPS: 38.463768, -111.456071

207 • D3 | FSR 009 (Lazy Mtn) Dispersed 1 (Fishlake NF)

Total sites: 13, RV sites: 13, No water, No toilets, Tent & RV camping: Free, Reservations not accepted, Elev: 7093ft/2162m, Tel: 435-896-9233, Nearest town: Salina. GPS: 38.915623, -111.530678

208 • D3 | Lower Bowns (Dixie NF)

Total sites: 4, RV sites: 4, No water, Vault/pit toilet, No showers, No RV dump, Tent & RV camping: $16, Group site $60, Open May-Oct, Reservations required, Elev: 7450ft/2271m, Tel: 435-836-2811, Nearest town: Torrey. GPS: 38.106231, -111.277116

209 • D3 | Oak Creek (Dixie NF)

Total sites: 9, RV sites: 9, Central water, Vault/pit toilet, No showers, No RV dump, Tent & RV camping: $12, Generator hours: 0600-2200, Open May-Sep, Max Length: 25ft, Reservations not accepted, Elev: 8888ft/2709m, Tel: 435-896-9233, Nearest town: Teasdale. GPS: 38.088834, -111.342031

210 • D3 | Pleasant Creek (Dixie NF)

Total sites: 16, RV sites: 16, Central water, Vault/pit toilet, No showers, No RV dump, Tent & RV camping: $12, Open May-Sep, Reservations not accepted, Elev: 8625ft/2629m, Tel: 435-896-9233, Nearest town: Torrey. GPS: 38.102405, -111.336141

211 • D3 | Rosebud ATV (Fishlake NF)

Total sites: 4, RV sites: 4, No water, Vault/pit toilet, Tent & RV camping: $20, 4 double sites, water 1 mile away, Open Jun-Sep, Reservations accepted, Elev: 8534ft/2601m. GPS: 38.100596, -111.326053

212 • D3 | Singletree (Fishlake NF)

Total sites: 31, RV sites: 31, Central water, Flush toilet, No showers, RV dump, Tent & RV camping: $20, 2 group sites: $80, Open May-Oct, Max Length: 40ft, Reservations accepted, Elev: 8255ft/2516m, Tel: 435-896-9233, Nearest town: Torrey. GPS: 38.162434, -111.331178

213 • D3 | Sunglow (Fishlake NF)

Total sites: 6, RV sites: 6, Central water, Flush toilet, No showers, No RV dump, Tent & RV camping: $16, Group site $40, No water in winter, Generator hours: 0600-2200, Open May-Sep, Reservations accepted, Elev: 7287ft/2221m, Tel: 435-836-2811, Nearest town: Bicknell. GPS: 38.342035, -111.519529

214 • D4 | Buckboard (Manti-La Sal NF)

Total sites: 8, RV sites: 8, Central water, Vault/pit toilet, No showers, No RV dump, Tent & RV camping: $20, Group site: $50, Open May-Sep, Max Length: 43ft, Reservations accepted, Elev: 8724ft/2659m, Tel: 435-637-2817, Nearest town: Monticello. GPS: 37.880649, -109.449293

215 • D4 | Dalton Springs (Manti-La Sal NF)

Total sites: 16, RV sites: 16, Central water, Vault/pit toilet, No showers, No RV dump, Tent & RV camping: $10, Open May-Sep, Max Length: 30ft, Reservations not accepted, Elev: 8386ft/2556m, Tel: 435-637-2817, Nearest town: Monticello. GPS: 37.873914, -109.432817

216 • D4 | Devils Canyon (Manti-La Sal NF)

Total sites: 42, RV sites: 42, Central water, Vault/pit toilet, No showers, No RV dump, Tent & RV camping: $20, Open May-Sep,

Max Length: 95ft, Reservations accepted, Elev: 7093ft/2162m, Tel: 435-587-2041, Nearest town: Blanding. GPS: 37.738858, -109.406363

217 • D4 | Kokopelli's Trail - Porcupine Rim (Manti-La Sal NF)

Total sites: 8, RV sites: 0, No water, Vault/pit toilet, Tents only: Free, High-clearance vehicle recommended, Reservations not accepted, Elev: 7418ft/2261m, Tel: 435-259-2100. GPS: 38.575059, -109.347123

218 • D4 | Mason Draw (Manti-La Sal NF)

Total sites: 5, RV sites: 5, No water, Vault/pit toilet, Tent & RV camping: $5, Open May-Sep, Reservations not accepted, Elev: 8268ft/2520m, Tel: 435-637-2817, Nearest town: Moab. GPS: 38.543000, -109.303000

219 • D4 | Nizhoni (Manti-La Sal NF)

Total sites: 25, RV sites: 25, Central water, Vault/pit toilet, No showers, No RV dump, Tent & RV camping: $20, 2 group sites: $50, Open all year, Max Length: 53ft, Reservations accepted, Elev: 7812ft/2381m, Tel: 435-587-2041, Nearest town: Blanding. GPS: 37.781000, -109.539000

220 • D4 | Oowah (Manti-La Sal NF)

Total sites: 11, RV sites: 0, No water, Vault/pit toilet, No showers, No RV dump, Tents only: $5, Open Jun-Sep, Reservations not accepted, Elev: 8842ft/2695m, Nearest town: Moab. GPS: 38.502671, -109.272236

221 • D4 | Warner Lake (Manti-La Sal NF)

Total sites: 20, RV sites: 20, No water, Vault/pit toilet, No showers, No RV dump, Tent & RV camping: $20, Also group sites & cabins, Group site: $50, Open May-Dec, Max Length: 20ft, Reservations accepted, Elev: 9436ft/2876m, Tel: 435-636-3360, Nearest town: Moab. GPS: 38.519524, -109.277145

222 • E1 | Honeycomb Rocks (Dixie NF)

Total sites: 21, RV sites: 21, Central water, Vault/pit toilet, No showers, No RV dump, Tent & RV camping: $13, Open May-Sep, Reservations not accepted, Elev: 5735ft/1748m, Nearest town: Enterprise. GPS: 37.517090, -113.856445

223 • E1 | Oak Grove (Dixie NF)

Total sites: 7, RV sites: 5, No water, Vault/pit toilet, Tent & RV camping: $2-4, Open May-Oct, Reservations not accepted, Elev: 6528ft/1990m, Tel: 435-652-3100, Nearest town: Leeds. GPS: 37.316862, -113.452991

224 • E1 | Pine Valley Rec Area - Crackfoot (Dixie NF)

Total sites: 22, RV sites: 17, Central water, Vault/pit toilet, No showers, No RV dump, Tent & RV camping: $17, Generator hours: 0600-2200, Open May-Sep, Max Length: 50ft, Reservations not accepted, Elev: 6890ft/2100m, Tel: 435-652-3100, Nearest town: Pine Valley. GPS: 37.374185, -113.466044

225 • E1 | Pine Valley Rec Area - Dean Gardner (Dixie NF)

Total sites: 24, RV sites: 24, Central water, Vault/pit toilet, No showers, No RV dump, Tent & RV camping: $17, Generator hours: 0600-2200, Open May-Sep, Max Length: 30ft, Reservations not accepted, Elev: 6775ft/2065m, Tel: 435-652-3100, Nearest town: Pine Valley. GPS: 37.377722, -113.476009

226 • E1 | Pine Valley Rec Area - Ebenezer Bryce (Dixie NF)

Total sites: 19, RV sites: 19, Central water, Vault/pit toilet, No showers, No RV dump, Tent & RV camping: $17, Large, Generator hours: 0600-2200, Open May-Sep, Max Length: 45ft, Reservations not accepted, Elev: 6900ft/2103m, Tel: 435-652-3100, Nearest town: Pine Valley. GPS: 37.373783, -113.461586

227 • E1 | Pine Valley Rec Area - Equestrian (Dixie NF)

Total sites: 18, RV sites: 15, Central water, Vault/pit toilet, No showers, No RV dump, Tent & RV camping: $17, Generator hours: 0600-2200, Open May-Sep, Reservations accepted, Elev: 6736ft/2053m, Tel: 435-652-3100, Nearest town: Pine Valley. GPS: 37.379311, -113.483132

228 • E1 | Pine Valley Rec Area - Mitt Moody (Dixie NF)

Total sites: 8, RV sites: 0, Tents only: $17, Walk-to sites, Reservations not accepted, Elev: 7008ft/2136m, Tel: 435-652-3100, Nearest town: Pine Valley. GPS: 37.375365, -113.455545

229 • E1 | Pine Valley Rec Area - Yellow Pine (Dixie NF)

Total sites: 6, RV sites: 6, Central water, Vault/pit toilet, No showers, No RV dump, Tent & RV camping: $17, Generator hours: 0600-2200, Open May-Sep, Max Length: 25ft, Reservations not accepted, Elev: 6722ft/2049m, Tel: 435-652-3100, Nearest town: Pine Valley. GPS: 37.380242, -113.479862

230 • E2 | Cedar Canyon (Dixie NF)

Total sites: 18, RV sites: 18, Central water, Flush toilet, No showers, No RV dump, Tent & RV camping: $21, Group site: $62, Open May-Sep, Max Length: 40ft, Reservations accepted, Elev: 8547ft/2605m, Tel: 435-865-3200, Nearest town: Cedar City. GPS: 37.591355, -112.903665

231 • E2 | Coyote Hollow Horse Camp (Dixie NF)

Total sites: 4, RV sites: 4, No water, Vault/pit toilet, Tent & RV camping: $10, Reservations not accepted, Elev: 7864ft/2397m, Tel: 435-676-2676, Nearest town: Panguitch. GPS: 37.713993, -112.270952

232 • E2 | Deer Haven (Dixie NF)

Total sites: 10, RV sites: 10, Central water, Flush toilet, No showers, No RV dump, Tent & RV camping: $21, Reservable group site $71-$248, Generator hours: 0600-2200, Open May-Sep, Reservations not accepted, Elev: 9176ft/2797m, Tel: 435-865-3200, Nearest town: Cedar City. GPS: 37.574116, -112.910502

233 • E2 | Duck Creek (Dixie NF)

Total sites: 54, RV sites: 54, Water available, Flush toilet, No showers, RV dump, Tent & RV camping: $21, Group sites: $71-$127, Open May-Oct, Max Length: 60ft, Reservations accepted, Elev: 8638ft/2633m, Tel: 435-865-3200, Nearest town: Cedar City. GPS: 37.520621, -112.698352

234 • E2 | King Creek (Dixie NF)

Total sites: 37, RV sites: 37, Central water, Flush toilet, No showers, RV dump, Tent & RV camping: $17, Stay limit: 14 days, Generator hours: 0600-2200, Open May-Sep, Max Length: 45ft, Reservations not accepted, Elev: 7982ft/2433m, Tel: 435-676-2676, Nearest town: Panguitch. GPS: 37.609131, -112.260498

235 • E2 | Navajo Lake (Dixie NF)

Total sites: 27, RV sites: 16, Central water, Flush toilet, No showers, RV dump, Tent & RV camping: $21, Stay limit: 14 days, Open May-Sep, Max Length: 60ft, Reservations accepted, Elev: 9094ft/2772m, Tel: 435-865-3200, Nearest town: Cedar City. GPS: 37.520709, -112.789445

236 • E2 | Panguitch Lake North (Dixie NF)

Total sites: 47, RV sites: 47, Central water, Flush toilet, No showers, RV dump, Tent & RV camping: $21, Group site: $55, Open May-Sep, Max Length: 40ft, Reservations accepted, Elev: 8389ft/2557m, Tel: 435-865-3200, Nearest town: Panguitch. GPS: 37.702351, -112.656904

237 • E2 | Panguitch Lake South (Dixie NF)

Total sites: 18, RV sites: 0, Water available, Flush toilet, No showers, RV dump, Tents only: $14, Open May-Sep, Reservations not accepted, Elev: 8409ft/2563m, Tel: 435-865-3200, Nearest town: Panguitch. GPS: 37.700151, -112.655196

238 • E2 | Spruces (Navajo Lake) (Dixie NF)

Total sites: 28, RV sites: 25, Central water, Flush toilet, No showers, No RV dump, Tent & RV camping: $17, 3 walk-to sites, Generator hours: 0600-2200, Open May-Sep, Reservations not accepted, Elev: 9075ft/2766m, Tel: 435-865-3200, Nearest town: Cedar City. GPS: 37.518715, -112.774349

239 • E2 | Te-ah (Dixie NF)

Total sites: 42, RV sites: 42, Central water, Flush toilet, No showers, RV dump, Tent & RV camping: $21, 1 group site $48, Open May-Sep, Max Length: 116ft, Reservations accepted, Elev: 9203ft/2805m, Tel: 435-865-3200, Nearest town: Cedar City. GPS: 37.533676, -112.818909

Vermont

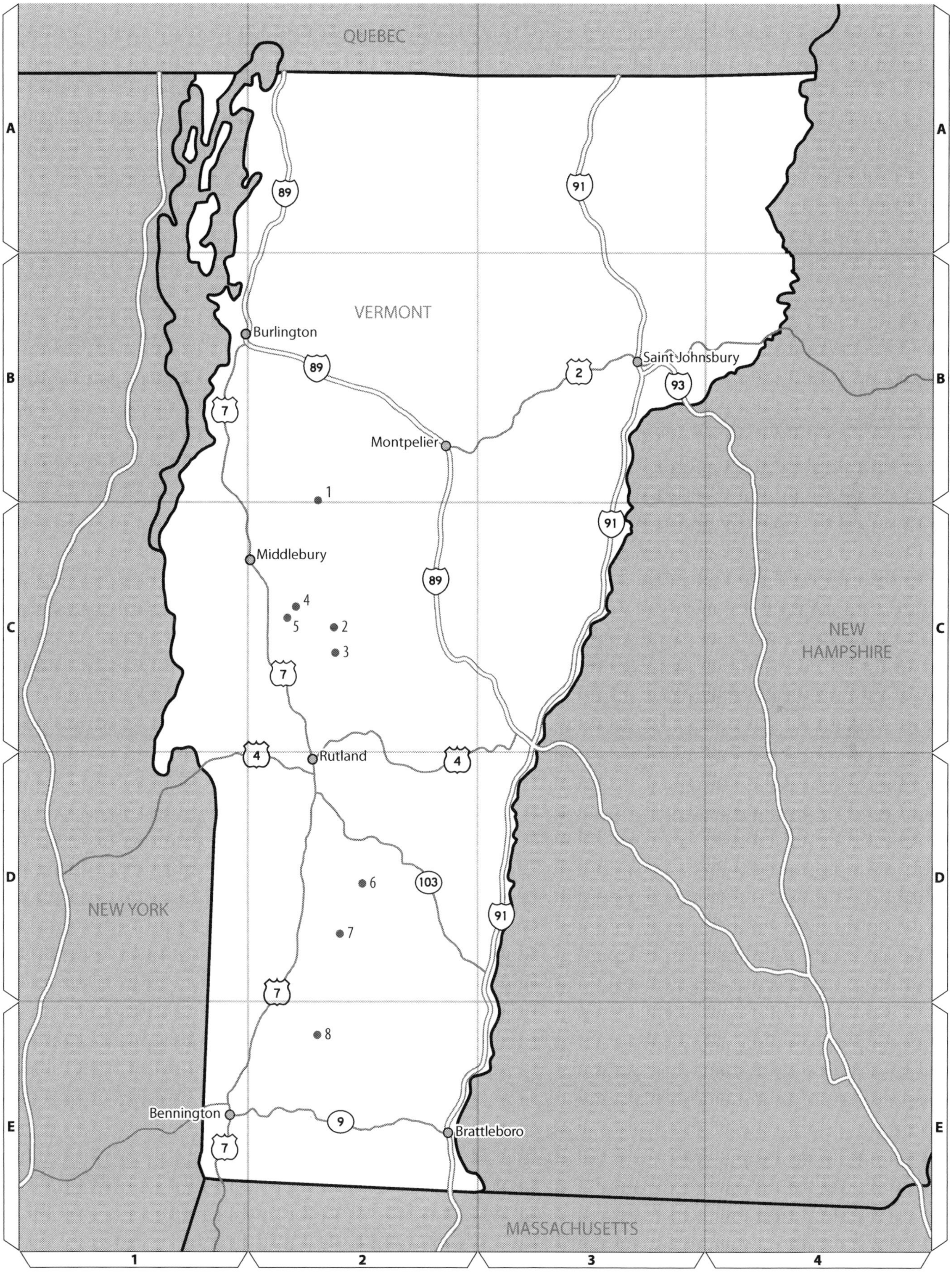
QUEBEC
VERMONT
Burlington
Saint Johnsbury
Montpelier
Middlebury
Rutland
NEW HAMPSHIRE
NEW YORK
Bennington
Brattleboro
MASSACHUSETTS
89
91
2
93
7
4
103
9
1
2
3
4
5
6
7
8
A
B
C
D
E

Map	ID	Map	ID
B2	1	D2	6-7
C2	2-5	E2	8

Alphabetical List of Camping Areas

1 • B2 | Downingville (Green Mountain NF)

Total sites: 1, RV sites: 1, No toilets, Tent & RV camping: Free, Stay limit: 14 days, Elev: 1532ft/467m, Nearest town: Downingville. GPS: 44.137614, -72.966192

2 • C2 | Bingo (Green Mountain NF)

Total sites: 10, RV sites: 10, No toilets, Tent & RV camping: Free, Stay limit: 14 days, Open Apr-Dec, Elev: 1317ft/401m, Tel: 802-388-4362, Nearest town: Robinson. GPS: 43.875324, -72.913288

3 • C2 | Chittenden Brook (Green Mountain NF)

Total sites: 17, RV sites: 0, No water, Vault/pit toilet, No showers, No RV dump, Tents only: $15, Stay limit: 14 days, Generator hours: 0600-2200, Open May-Oct, Max Length: 18ft, Reservations accepted, Elev: 1765ft/538m, Tel: 802-767-4261, Nearest town: Rochester. GPS: 43.825684, -72.909912

4 • C2 | Moosalamoo (Green Mountain NF)

Total sites: 19, RV sites: 19, Central water, Vault/pit toilet, No showers, No RV dump, Tent & RV camping: $15, Stay limit: 14 days, Open May-Oct, Max Length: 20ft, Reservations accepted, Elev: 1585ft/483m, Tel: 802-388-4362, Nearest town: Ripton. GPS: 43.918612, -73.025721

5 • C2 | Silver Lake (Green Mountain NF)

Total sites: 15, No water, Vault/pit toilet, Tents only: $10, Walk-to sites, .6 mi, Stay limit: 14 days, Open May-Oct, Reservations accepted, Elev: 1293ft/394m, Tel: 802-388-4362, Nearest town: East Middlebury. GPS: 43.896254, -73.050657

6 • D2 | Greendale (Green Mountain NF)

Total sites: 11, RV sites: 11, No water, Vault/pit toilet, Tent & RV camping: $10, Stay limit: 14 days, Generator hours: 0600-2200, Open May-Oct, Reservations not accepted, Elev: 1791ft/546m, Tel: 802-362-2307, Nearest town: Weston. GPS: 43.354492, -72.826172

7 • D2 | Hapgood Pond (Green Mountain NF)

Total sites: 28, RV sites: 28, Central water, Vault/pit toilet, No showers, No RV dump, Tent & RV camping: $20, No large RVs, Stay limit: 14 days, Open May-Oct, Max Length: 35ft, Reservations not accepted, Elev: 1535ft/468m, Tel: 802-362-2307, Nearest town: Manchester. GPS: 43.253653, -72.892582

8 • E2 | Grout Pond (Green Mountain NF)

Total sites: 17, RV sites: 6, Central water, Vault/pit toilet, No showers, No RV dump, Tent & RV camping: $16, No large RVs, Road not plowed in winter, Stay limit: 14 days, Open all year, Reservations not accepted, Elev: 2260ft/689m, Tel: 802-362-2307, Nearest town: Stratton. GPS: 43.046074, -72.952078

Virginia

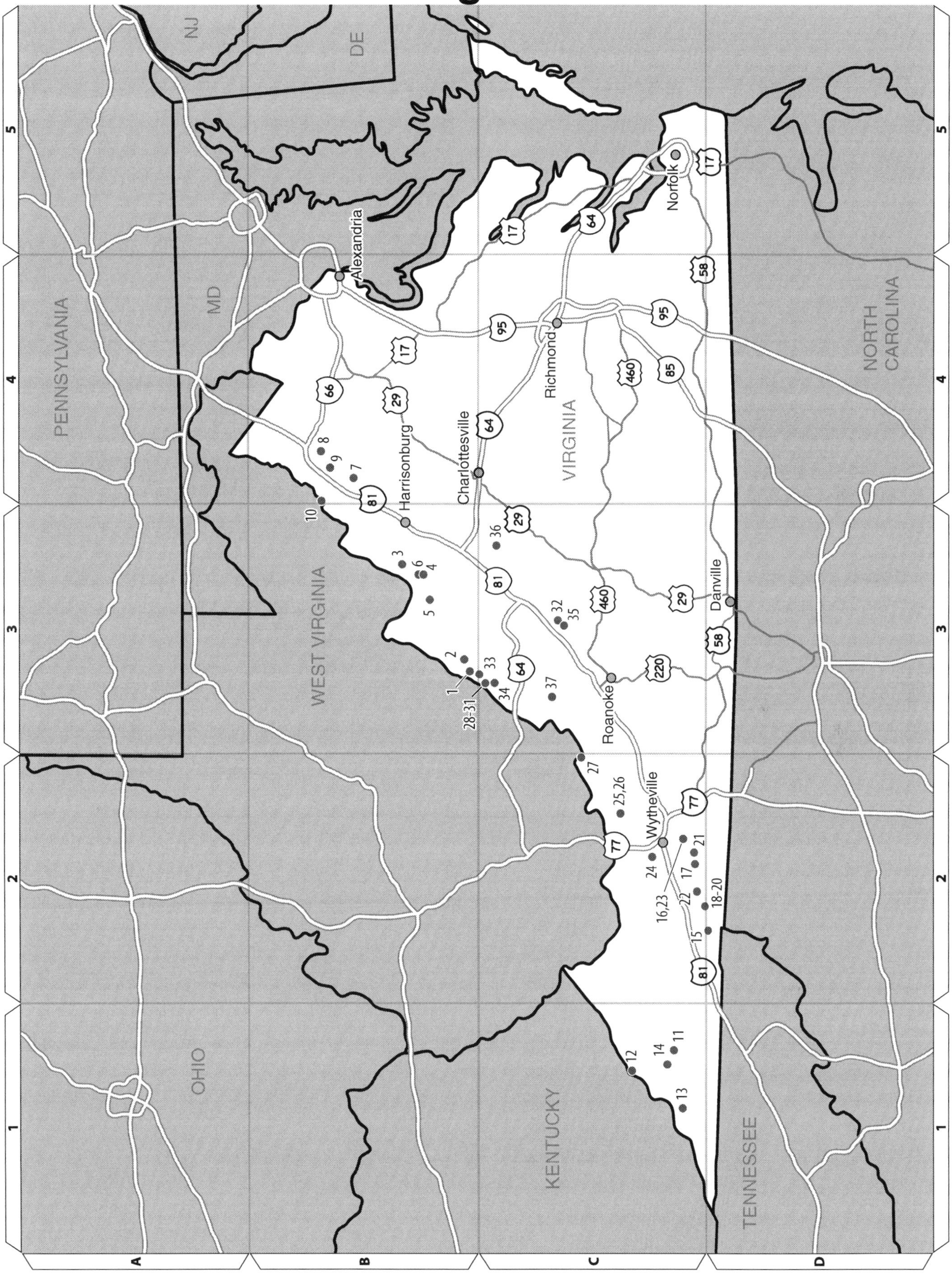

PENNSYLVANIA
NJ
DE
MD
OHIO
WEST VIRGINIA
KENTUCKY
VIRGINIA
TENNESSEE
NORTH CAROLINA
Alexandria
Norfolk
Richmond
Charlottesville
Harrisonburg
Roanoke
Danville
Wytheville
17
64
58
95
66
29
460
85
81
220
77
1
2
3
4
5
6
7
8
9
10
11
12
13
14
15
16,23
17
18-20
21
22
24
25,26
27
28-31
32
33
34
35
36
37
A
B
C
D

Map	ID	Map	ID
B3	1-6	C2	15-27
B4	7-10	C3	28-37
C1	11-14		

Alphabetical List of Camping Areas

1 • B3 | Blowing Springs (George Washington & Jefferson NF)

Total sites: 40, RV sites: 40, Central water, Vault/pit toilet, No showers, RV dump, Tent & RV camping: $12, Open Mar-Sep, Reservations not accepted, Elev: 1811ft/552m, Tel: 540-839-2521, Nearest town: Covington. GPS: 38.069092, -79.884521

2 • B3 | Hidden Valley (George Washington & Jefferson NF)

Total sites: 31, RV sites: 31, Central water, Vault/pit toilet, No showers, No RV dump, Tent & RV camping: $12, Open Mar-Dec, Reservations not accepted, Elev: 1804ft/550m, Tel: 540-839-2521, Nearest town: Warm Springs. GPS: 38.098768, -79.821744

3 • B3 | Hone Quarry (George Washington & Jefferson NF)

Total sites: 26, RV sites: 26, Central water, Vault/pit toilet, No showers, No RV dump, Tent & RV camping: $5, Open all year, Reservations not accepted, Elev: 1946ft/593m, Tel: 540-432-0187, Nearest town: Harrisonburg. GPS: 38.462746, -79.135584

4 • B3 | North River (George Washington & Jefferson NF)

Total sites: 9, RV sites: 9, No water, Vault/pit toilet, Tent & RV camping: $5, Open all year, Reservations not accepted, Elev: 1867ft/569m, Tel: 540-432-0187, Nearest town: Stokesville. GPS: 38.339211, -79.206031

5 • B3 | Shaws Fork Horse Camp (George Washington & Jefferson NF)

Total sites: 5, RV sites: 5, No water, Vault/pit toilet, Tent & RV camping: Free, Open all year, Reservations not accepted, Elev: 2940ft/896m, Tel: 540-432-0187, Nearest town: McDowell. GPS: 38.311186, -79.383575

6 • B3 | Todd Lake (George Washington & Jefferson NF)

Total sites: 36, RV sites: 36, Central water, Flush toilet, Free showers, No RV dump, Tent & RV camping: $18, Open May-Nov, Max Length: 18ft, Reservations not accepted, Elev: 1992ft/607m, Tel: 540-432-0187, Nearest town: Stokesville. GPS: 38.365723, -79.211670

7 • B4 | Camp Roosevelt (George Washington & Jefferson NF)

Total sites: 10, RV sites: 10, Central water, Flush toilet, No showers, RV dump, Tent & RV camping: $10, Open May-Oct, Reservations not accepted, Elev: 1266ft/386m, Tel: 540-984-4101, Nearest town: Luray. GPS: 38.731906, -78.517929

8 • B4 | Elizabeth Furnace - Family (George Washington & Jefferson NF)

Total sites: 35, RV sites: 35, Central water, Flush toilet, Free showers, RV dump, Tent & RV camping: $16, $10 Oct-Apr - limited services, Open all year, Reservations not accepted, Elev: 829ft/253m, Tel: 540-984-4101, Nearest town: Front Royal. GPS: 38.924507, -78.331606

9 • B4 | Little Fort (George Washington & Jefferson NF)

Total sites: 11, No water, Vault/pit toilet, No showers, No RV dump, Tents only: Free, Open all year, Reservations not accepted, Elev: 1365ft/416m, Tel: 540-984-4101, Nearest town: Fort Valley. GPS: 38.867231, -78.444056

10 • B4 | Wolf Gap (George Washington & Jefferson NF)

Total sites: 9, RV sites: 9, Central water, Vault/pit toilet, No showers, No RV dump, Tent & RV camping: Free, Open all year, Elev: 2300ft/701m, Tel: 540-984-4101, Nearest town: Columbia Furnace. GPS: 38.924412, -78.689182

11 • C1 | Bark Camp (George Washington & Jefferson NF)

Total sites: 34, RV sites: 34, Elec sites: 9, Central water, Flush toilet, Free showers, No RV dump, Tent & RV camping: $18-23, Open May-Sep, Reservations not accepted, Elev: 2877ft/877m, Tel: 276-679-8370, Nearest town: Coeburn. GPS: 36.867697, -82.523363

12 • C1 | Cane Patch (George Washington & Jefferson NF)

Total sites: 35, RV sites: 35, Elec sites: 7, Central water, Flush toilet, Free showers, RV dump, Tents: $12/RVs: $12-17, Open May-Sep, Elev: 1690ft/515m, Tel: 276-796-5832, Nearest town: Pound. GPS: 37.100888, -82.677886

13 • C1 | Cave Springs (George Washington & Jefferson NF)

Total sites: 37, RV sites: 37, Elec sites: 9, Central water, Flush toilet, Free showers, RV dump, Tents: $12/RVs: $17, Open May-Sep, Reservations not accepted, Elev: 1627ft/496m, Tel: 276-546-4297, Nearest town: Big Stone Gap. GPS: 36.800537, -82.923474

14 • C1 | High Knob (George Washington & Jefferson NF)

Total sites: 13, RV sites: 13, Central water, Flush toilet, Free showers, No RV dump, Tent & RV camping: $10, Group site: $25, Open May-Sep, Max Length: 16ft, Reservations not accepted, Elev: 3698ft/1127m, Tel: 276-679-1754, Nearest town: Norton. GPS: 36.890306, -82.622992

15 • C2 | Beartree (George Washington & Jefferson NF)

Total sites: 90, RV sites: 90, Central water, Flush toilet, Free showers, RV dump, Tent & RV camping: $24, Group site: $55, Open Apr-Oct, Reservations accepted, Elev: 3143ft/958m, Tel: 276-388-3642, Nearest town: Damascus. GPS: 36.668259, -81.678972

16 • C2 | Collins Cove Horse Camp (George Washington & Jefferson NF)

Total sites: 10, RV sites: 10, No water, Vault/pit toilet, Tent & RV camping: $5, Open Apr-Nov, Reservations not accepted, Elev: 2257ft/688m, Tel: 800-628-7202, Nearest town: Wytheville. GPS: 36.832736, -81.042282

17 • C2 | Comers Rock (George Washington & Jefferson NF)

Total sites: 6, RV sites: 6, Central water, Vault/pit toilet, No showers, No RV dump, Tent & RV camping: $5, Open Apr-Oct, Reservations not accepted, Elev: 3766ft/1148m, Tel: 800-628-7202, Nearest town: Speedwell. GPS: 36.763428, -81.223389

18 • C2 | Fox Creek Horse Camp (George Washington & Jefferson NF)

Total sites: 32, RV sites: 32, No water, Vault/pit toilet, Tent & RV camping: $5, Open Apr-Nov, Reservations not accepted, Elev: 3481ft/1061m, Tel: 800-628-7202, Nearest town: Troutdale. GPS: 36.698702, -81.504108

19 • C2 | Grindstone (George Washington & Jefferson NF)

Total sites: 108, RV sites: 108, Elec sites: 60, Water at site, Flush toilet, Free showers, RV dump, Tents: $24/RVs: $24-32, Open May-Nov, Max Length: 110ft, Reservations accepted, Elev: 3724ft/1135m, Tel: 276-388-3983, Nearest town: Troutdale. GPS: 36.687883, -81.542115

20 • C2 | Hurricane (George Washington & Jefferson NF)

Total sites: 30, RV sites: 30, Central water, Flush toilet, Free showers, No RV dump, Tent & RV camping: $20, Open Apr-Oct, Max Length: 110ft, Reservations accepted, Elev: 2923ft/891m, Tel: 800-628-7202, Nearest town: Sugar Grove. GPS: 36.723094, -81.489375

21 • C2 | Hussy Mountain Horse Camp (George Washington & Jefferson NF)

Total sites: 10, RV sites: 10, Central water, Vault/pit toilet, No showers, No RV dump, Tent & RV camping: $7, Open Apr-Oct, Reservations not accepted, Elev: 2976ft/907m, Tel: 800-628-7202, Nearest town: Speedwell. GPS: 36.771798, -81.143511

22 • C2 | Raccoon Branch (George Washington & Jefferson NF)

Total sites: 20, RV sites: 20, Elec sites: 7, Central water, Flush toilet, No showers, RV dump, Tents: $20/RVs: $27, Open Apr-Nov, Max Length: 60ft, Reservations accepted, Elev: 2769ft/844m, Tel: 800-628-7202, Nearest town: Sugar Grove. GPS: 36.747803, -81.424805

23 • C2 | Raven Cliff (George Washington & Jefferson NF)

Total sites: 20, RV sites: 20, No water, Vault/pit toilet, Tent & RV camping: $5, Open Apr-Oct, Reservations not accepted, Elev: 2254ft/687m, Tel: 800-628-7202, Nearest town: Cripple Creek. GPS: 36.836139, -81.068654

24 • C2 | Stony Fork (George Washington & Jefferson NF)

Total sites: 54, RV sites: 54, Elec sites: 9, Water at site, Flush toilet, Free showers, RV dump, Tents: $20/RVs: $26-30, Open Apr-Nov, Max Length: 132ft, Reservations accepted, Elev: 2434ft/742m, Tel: 800-628-7202, Nearest town: Wytheville. GPS: 37.010056, -81.181408

25 • C2 | Walnut Flats (George Washington & Jefferson NF)

Total sites: 8, RV sites: 8, Central water, Vault/pit toilet, No showers, No RV dump, Tent & RV camping: Free, Open Apr-Dec, Reservations not accepted, Elev: 2457ft/749m, Tel: 540-552-4641, Nearest town: Holly Brook. GPS: 37.198227, -80.886911

26 • C2 | White Cedar Horse Camp (George Washington & Jefferson NF)

Total sites: 16, RV sites: 16, Central water, Vault/pit toilet, Tent & RV camping: $15, Corrals, Open Apr-Nov, Reservations not accepted, Elev: 2562ft/781m, Tel: 540-552-4641, Nearest town: Dublin. GPS: 37.202516, -80.884094

27 • C2 | White Rocks Camp (George Washington & Jefferson NF)

Total sites: 50, RV sites: 50, Central water, Flush toilet, No showers, RV dump, Tent & RV camping: $8, Open Apr-Nov, Reservations not accepted, Elev: 2999ft/914m, Tel: 540-552-4641, Nearest town: Simmonsville. GPS: 37.430107, -80.492676

28 • C3 | Bolar Mountain - #1 (George Washington & Jefferson NF)

Total sites: 42, RV sites: 42, Elec sites: 22, Central water, Flush toilet, Free showers, RV dump, Tents: $21/RVs: $21-30, Open May-Nov, Max Length: 45ft, Reservations accepted, Elev: 1670ft/

509m, Tel: 540-839-2521, Nearest town: Warm Springs. GPS: 37.985352, -79.970459

29 • C3 | Bolar Mountain - #2 (George Washington & Jefferson NF)

Total sites: 16, RV sites: 16, Elec sites: 5, Water at site, Flush toilet, Free showers, RV dump, Tents: $21/RVs: $21-30, Open May-Oct, Max Length: 45ft, Elev: 1575ft/480m, Nearest town: Warm Springs. GPS: 37.979415, -79.986099

30 • C3 | Bolar Mountain - #3 (George Washington & Jefferson NF)

Total sites: 37, RV sites: 37, Elec sites: 7, Water at site, Flush toilet, Free showers, RV dump, Tents: $21/RVs: $21-30, Open May-Sep, Max Length: 45ft, Elev: 1565ft/477m, Nearest town: Warm Springs. GPS: 37.976791, -79.985102

31 • C3 | Bolar Mountain - Sugar Ridge (George Washington & Jefferson NF)

Total sites: 35, RV sites: 30, Central water, Flush toilet, Free showers, RV dump, Tents: $16-18/RVs: $21-30, Group site: $85, Open May-Sep, Max Length: 50ft, Reservations accepted, Elev: 1646ft/502m, Tel: 540-839-2521, Nearest town: Warm Springs. GPS: 37.984053, -79.967817

32 • C3 | Cave Mountain Lake (George Washington & Jefferson NF)

Total sites: 41, RV sites: 41, Central water, Flush toilet, Free showers, RV dump, Tent & RV camping: $20, Open Apr-Oct, Max Length: 80ft, Reservations accepted, Elev: 1270ft/387m, Tel: 540-291-2188, Nearest town: Lexington. GPS: 37.568574, -79.540596

33 • C3 | McClintic Point (George Washington & Jefferson NF)

Total sites: 21, RV sites: 21, No water, Vault/pit toilet, Tent & RV camping: $12, Group site: $165, Open May-Sep, Max Length: 21ft, Elev: 1663ft/507m, Tel: 540-839-2521, Nearest town: Warm Springs. GPS: 38.014631, -79.920428

34 • C3 | Morris Hill (George Washington & Jefferson NF)

Total sites: 58, RV sites: 58, Central water, Flush toilet, Free showers, No RV dump, Tent & RV camping: $18, Open May-Sep, Max Length: 40ft, Reservations accepted, Elev: 2083ft/635m, Tel: 540-962-2214, Nearest town: Covington. GPS: 37.933435, -79.970313

35 • C3 | North Creek (George Washington & Jefferson NF)

Total sites: 16, RV sites: 16, Central water, Vault/pit toilet, No showers, No RV dump, Tent & RV camping: $12, Open Mar-Nov, Max Length: 22ft, Reservations not accepted, Elev: 1201ft/366m, Tel: 540-291-2188, Nearest town: Buchanan. GPS: 37.541793, -79.584499

36 • C3 | Sherando Lake (George Washington & Jefferson NF)

Total sites: 65, RV sites: 29, Elec sites: 29, Central water, Flush toilet, Free showers, RV dump, Tents: $25/RVs: $32, Open Apr-Oct, Max Length: 40ft, Reservations accepted, Elev: 1903ft/580m, Tel: 540-291-2188, Nearest town: Lyndhurst. GPS: 37.919633, -79.008176

37 • C3 | The Pines (George Washington & Jefferson NF)

Total sites: 12, RV sites: 12, Central water, Vault/pit toilet, No showers, No RV dump, Tent & RV camping: Free, Open Apr-Nov, Max Length: 16ft, Reservations not accepted, Elev: 1896ft/578m, Tel: 540-552-4641, Nearest town: New Castle. GPS: 37.605216, -80.076455

Washington

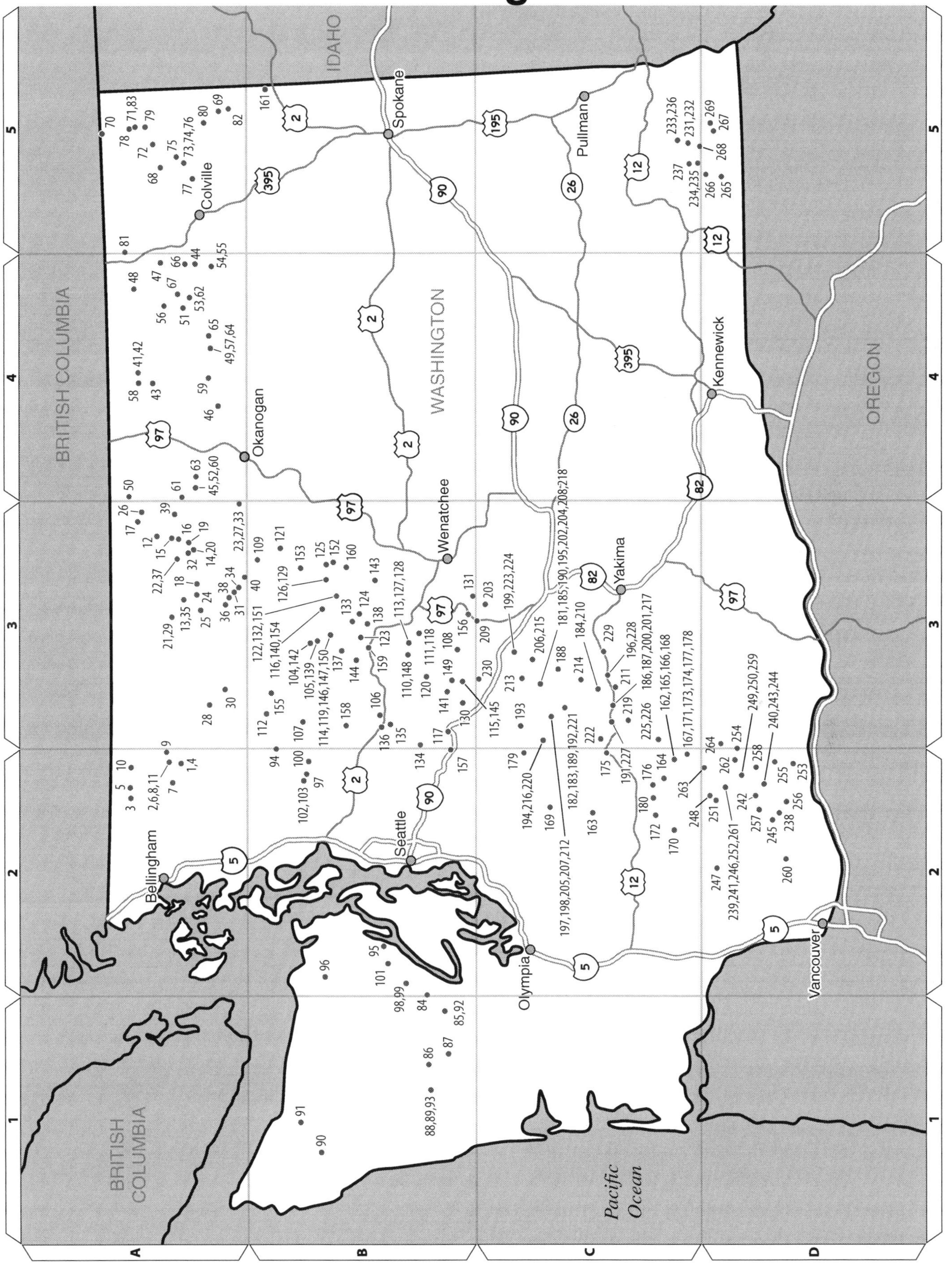
IDAHO
BRITISH COLUMBIA
WASHINGTON
OREGON
BRITISH COLUMBIA
Pacific Ocean
Spokane
Pullman
Colville
Okanogan
Kennewick
Wenatchee
Yakima
Seattle
Bellingham
Olympia
Vancouver

Map	ID	Map	ID
A2	1-11	B5	161
A3	12-40	C2	162-180
A4	41-67	C3	181-230
A5	68-83	C5	231-237
B1	84-93	D2	238-263
B2	94-103	D3	264
B3	104-160	D5	265-269

Alphabetical List of Camping Areas

1 • A2 | Bayview (Mt Baker-Snoqualmie NF)

Total sites: 24, RV sites: 24, No water, Vault/pit toilet, Tent & RV camping: $25-27, Open May-Sep, Max Length: 28ft, Elev: 740ft/226m, Tel: 541-338-7869, Nearest town: Sedro-Woolley. GPS: 48.675587, -121.678141

2 • A2 | Boulder Creek (Mt Baker-Snoqualmie NF)

Total sites: 8, RV sites: 8, No water, Vault/pit toilet, Tent & RV camping: $25-29, Group site: $70, No large RVs, Open May-Sep, Max Length: 25ft, Reservations accepted, Elev: 1020ft/311m, Tel: 360-856-5700. GPS: 48.714355, -121.691895

3 • A2 | Douglas Fir (Mt Baker-Snoqualmie NF)

Total sites: 29, RV sites: 29, Central water, Vault/pit toilet, No showers, No RV dump, Tents: $25-27/RVs: $25-29, Open May-Sep, Max Length: 100ft, Reservations accepted, Elev: 1000ft/305m, Tel: 360-599-2714, Nearest town: Glacier. GPS: 48.901637, -121.916298

4 • A2 | Horseshoe Cove (Mt Baker-Snoqualmie NF)

Total sites: 36, RV sites: 34, Central water, Flush toilet, No showers, No RV dump, Tent & RV camping: $30-34, 3 group sites: $70, Open May-Sep, Max Length: 66ft, Reservations accepted, Elev: 833ft/254m, Tel: 360-856-5700, Nearest town: Burlington. GPS: 48.669739, -121.679071

5 • A2 | Nooksack River (Mt Baker-Snoqualmie NF)

Total sites: 4, RV sites: 4, No water, Vault/pit toilet, Tent & RV camping: Fee unk, Elev: 1272ft/388m, Nearest town: Glacier. GPS: 48.905463, -121.845241

6 • A2 | Panorama Point (Mt Baker-Snoqualmie NF)

Total sites: 15, RV sites: 15, Central water, Vault/pit toilet, No showers, No RV dump, Tent & RV camping: $30-34, Open May-Sep, Max Length: 40ft, Reservations accepted, Elev: 709ft/216m, Tel: 360-856-5700, Nearest town: Concrete. GPS: 48.723409, -121.671084

7 • A2 | Park Butte TH (Schrieber's Meadow) (Mt Baker-Snoqualmie NF)

Total sites: 6, RV sites: 6, No water, Vault/pit toilet, Tent & RV camping: Free, Stay limit: 1 day, Elev: 3419ft/1042m, Tel: 360-856-5700 x515, Nearest town: Sedro-Woolley. GPS: 48.707103, -121.812416

8 • A2 | Park Creek (Mt Baker-Snoqualmie NF)

Total sites: 12, RV sites: 12, No water, Vault/pit toilet, Tent & RV camping: $25-27, Open May-Sep, Max Length: 40ft, Reservations accepted, Elev: 892ft/272m, Tel: 360-856-5700, Nearest town: Concrete. GPS: 48.734863, -121.665771

9 • A2 | Shannon Creek (Mt Baker-Snoqualmie NF)

Total sites: 20, RV sites: 15, Central water, Vault/pit toilet, No showers, No RV dump, Tents: $25-29/RVs: $25-27, Open May-Sep, Max Length: 36ft, Reservations accepted, Elev: 902ft/275m, Tel: 360-856-5700, Nearest town: Burlington. GPS: 48.739789, -121.599784

10 • A2 | Silver Fir (Mt Baker-Snoqualmie NF)

Total sites: 20, RV sites: 20, Central water, Vault/pit toilet, No showers, No RV dump, Tent & RV camping: $23-25, Open May-Sep, Max Length: 77ft, Reservations accepted, Elev: 2008ft/612m, Tel: 360-599-2714, Nearest town: Maple Falls. GPS: 48.905946, -121.700461

11 • A2 | Swift Creek (Mt Baker-Snoqualmie NF)

Total sites: 50, RV sites: 50, Central water, Vault/pit toilet, No showers, No RV dump, Tent & RV camping: $30-32, 2 group sites: $140, Open May-Sep, Max Length: 100ft, Reservations accepted, Elev: 843ft/257m, Tel: 541-338-7869, Nearest town: Concrete. GPS: 48.728214, -121.657684

12 • A3 | Andrews Creek (Okanogan-Wenatchee NF)

Total sites: 4, RV sites: 2, No water, Vault/pit toilet, Tent & RV camping: Free, Reservations not accepted, Elev: 3037ft/926m, Tel: 509-996-4003, Nearest town: Winthrop. GPS: 48.783460, -120.108347

13 • A3 | Ballard (Okanogan-Wenatchee NF)

Total sites: 7, RV sites: 7, No water, Vault/pit toilet, Tent & RV camping: $10, Open May-Sep, Max Length: 28ft, Reservations not accepted, Elev: 2536ft/773m, Tel: 509-996-4003, Nearest town: Winthrop. GPS: 48.658477, -120.544554

14 • A3 | Buck Lake (Okanogan-Wenatchee NF)

Total sites: 9, RV sites: 9, No water, Vault/pit toilet, Tent & RV camping: $10, Stay limit: 14 days, Open May-Sep, Max Length: 25ft, Reservations not accepted, Elev: 3272ft/997m, Tel: 509-996-4003, Nearest town: Carlton. GPS: 48.605942, -120.202005

15 • A3 | Camp 4 (Okanogan-Wenatchee NF)

Total sites: 5, RV sites: 0, No water, Vault/pit toilet, Tents only: $10, Stay limit: 14 days, Max Length: 16ft, Reservations not accepted, Elev: 2424ft/739m, Tel: 509-996-4003, Nearest town: Winthrop. GPS: 48.715106, -120.125036

16 • A3 | Chewuch (Okanogan-Wenatchee NF)

Total sites: 16, RV sites: 16, Central water, Vault/pit toilet, No showers, No RV dump, Tent & RV camping: $20, Stay limit: 14 days, Open May-Oct, Max Length: 35ft, Reservations not accepted, Elev: 2293ft/699m, Tel: 509-996-4003, Nearest town: Winthrop. GPS: 48.677307, -120.129764

17 • A3 | Chewuch TH (Okanogan-Wenatchee NF)

Total sites: 1, No water, Vault/pit toilet, Tents only: Fee unk, Elev: 5725ft/1745m, Tel: 509-486-2186, Nearest town: Tonasket. GPS: 48.872278, -120.003364

18 • A3 | Early Winters (Okanogan-Wenatchee NF)

Total sites: 12, RV sites: 12, Central water, Vault/pit toilet, No showers, No RV dump, Tent & RV camping: $15, Stay limit: 14 days, Open May-Oct, Max Length: 32ft, Reservations not accepted, Elev: 2175ft/663m, Tel: 509-996-4003, Nearest town: Winthrop. GPS: 48.598087, -120.439991

19 • A3 | Falls Creek (Okanogan-Wenatchee NF)

Total sites: 7, RV sites: 7, Central water, Vault/pit toilet, No showers, No RV dump, Tent & RV camping: $15, Stay limit: 14 days, Max Length: 18ft, Reservations not accepted, Elev: 2228ft/679m, Tel: 509-996-4003, Nearest town: Winthrop. GPS: 48.635166, -120.155407

20 • A3 | Flat Camp (Okanogan-Wenatchee NF)

Total sites: 12, RV sites: 12, Central water, Vault/pit toilet, No showers, No RV dump, Tent & RV camping: $15, Stay limit: 14 days, Open May-Oct, Max Length: 36ft, Reservations not accepted, Elev: 2582ft/787m, Tel: 509-996-4003, Nearest town: Carlton. GPS: 48.614746, -120.195801

21 • A3 | Harts Pass (Okanogan-Wenatchee NF)

Total sites: 5, RV sites: 0, No water, Vault/pit toilet, Tents only: $10, Open Jul-Oct, Reservations not accepted, Elev: 6204ft/1891m, Tel: 509-996-4000, Nearest town: Mazama. GPS: 48.720565, -120.670116

22 • A3 | Honeymoon (Okanogan-Wenatchee NF)

Total sites: 5, RV sites: 5, No water, Vault/pit toilet, Tent & RV camping: $10, Stay limit: 14 days, Open May-Oct, Max Length: 22ft, Reservations not accepted, Elev: 3337ft/1017m, Tel: 509-996-4003, Nearest town: Winthrop. GPS: 48.696751, -120.264828

23 • A3 | J-R (Okanogan-Wenatchee NF)

Total sites: 6, RV sites: 6, No water, Vault/pit toilet, Tent & RV camping: $8, Stay limit: 14 days, Open Apr-Sep, Max Length: 25ft, Reservations not accepted, Elev: 3944ft/1202m, Tel: 509-996-4003, Nearest town: Okanogan. GPS: 48.387828, -119.900848

24 • A3 | Klipchuck (Okanogan-Wenatchee NF)

Total sites: 46, RV sites: 46, Central water, Vault/pit toilet, No showers, No RV dump, Tent & RV camping: $20, Stay limit: 14 days, Open May-Oct, Max Length: 34ft, Reservations not accepted, Elev: 2992ft/912m, Tel: 509-996-4003, Nearest town: Mazama. GPS: 48.597866, -120.513455

25 • A3 | Lone Fir (Okanogan-Wenatchee NF)

Total sites: 27, RV sites: 27, Central water, Vault/pit toilet, No showers, No RV dump, Tent & RV camping: $20, Stay limit: 14 days, Open May-Oct, Max Length: 36ft, Reservations not accepted, Elev: 3625ft/1105m, Tel: 509-996-4003, Nearest town: Mazama. GPS: 48.580322, -120.625244

26 • A3 | Long Swamp (Okanogan-Wenatchee NF)

Total sites: 2, RV sites: 2, No water, Vault/pit toilet, Tent & RV camping: $5, Open Jun-Sep, Reservations not accepted, Elev: 5541ft/1689m, Tel: 509-486-2186, Nearest town: Twisp. GPS: 48.854977, -119.946295

27 • A3 | Loup Loup (Okanogan-Wenatchee NF)

Total sites: 25, RV sites: 25, Central water, Vault/pit toilet, No showers, No RV dump, Tent & RV camping: $15, Stay limit: 14 days, Open May-Oct, Max Length: 35ft, Reservations not accepted, Elev: 4134ft/1260m, Tel: 509-996-4003, Nearest town: Trout Lake. GPS: 48.395996, -119.901123

28 • A3 | Marble Creek (Mt Baker-Snoqualmie NF)

Total sites: 23, RV sites: 23, No water, Vault/pit toilet, Tent & RV camping: $23-25, Open May-Sep, Max Length: 40ft, Reservations accepted, Elev: 1234ft/376m, Tel: 360-856-5700, Nearest town: Marblemount. GPS: 48.534418, -121.272404

29 • A3 | Meadows (Okanogan-Wenatchee NF)

Total sites: 14, RV sites: 0, No water, Vault/pit toilet, Tents only: $10, Very narrow road - no trailers, Reservations not accepted, Elev: 6286ft/1916m, Tel: 509-996-4000, Nearest town: Mazama. GPS: 48.708169, -120.674852

30 • A3 | Mineral Park (Mt Baker-Snoqualmie NF)

Total sites: 21, RV sites: 21, No water, Vault/pit toilet, Tent & RV camping: $19-21, Open May-Sep, Max Length: 66ft, Reservations accepted, Elev: 1447ft/441m, Tel: 360-856-5700, Nearest town: Marblemount. GPS: 48.463135, -121.165039

31 • A3 | Mystery (Okanogan-Wenatchee NF)

Total sites: 4, RV sites: 4, No water, Vault/pit toilet, Tent & RV camping: $8, Group site: $40, Stay limit: 14 days, Open Apr-Oct, Max Length: 30ft, Reservations not accepted, Elev: 2897ft/883m, Tel: 509-996-4003, Nearest town: Twisp. GPS: 48.402027, -120.471718

32 • A3 | Nice (Okanogan-Wenatchee NF)

Total sites: 3, RV sites: 3, No water, Vault/pit toilet, Tent & RV camping: $8, Group site: $40, Stay limit: 14 days, Max Length: 30ft, Reservations not accepted, Elev: 2756ft/840m, Tel: 509-996-4003, Nearest town: Winthrop. GPS: 48.632028, -120.221462

33 • A3 | North Summit Horse Camp (Okanogan-Wenatchee NF)

Total sites: 12, RV sites: 12, Central water, Vault/pit toilet, No showers, No RV dump, Tent & RV camping: $10, Elev: 4078ft/1243m, Tel: 509-996-4000, Nearest town: Twisp. GPS: 48.391652, -119.888354

34 • A3 | Poplar Flat (Okanogan-Wenatchee NF)

Total sites: 16, RV sites: 16, Central water, Vault/pit toilet, No showers, No RV dump, Tent & RV camping: $20, Stay limit: 14 days, Open May-Oct, Max Length: 30ft, Reservations not accepted, Elev: 3028ft/923m, Tel: 509-996-4003, Nearest town: Twisp. GPS: 48.421631, -120.498779

35 • A3 | River Bend (Okanogan-Wenatchee NF)

Total sites: 5, RV sites: 5, No water, Vault/pit toilet, Tent & RV camping: $10, Stay limit: 14 days, Open May-Oct, Max Length: 30ft, Reservations not accepted, Elev: 2716ft/828m, Tel: 509-996-4003, Nearest town: Mazama. GPS: 48.652344, -120.553912

36 • A3 | Road's End (Okanogan-Wenatchee NF)

Total sites: 4, RV sites: 4, No water, Vault/pit toilet, Tent & RV camping: $10, Stay limit: 14 days, Open Jun-Oct, Max Length: 16ft, Reservations not accepted, Elev: 3917ft/1194m, Tel: 509-996-4003, Nearest town: Twisp. GPS: 48.461394, -120.577396

37 • A3 | Ruffed Grouse (Okanogan-Wenatchee NF)

Total sites: 4, RV sites: 4, Central water, Vault/pit toilet, No showers, No RV dump, Tent & RV camping: $15, Stay limit: 14 days, Open May-Oct, Max Length: 35ft, Reservations not accepted, Elev: 3196ft/974m, Tel: 509-996-4003, Nearest town: Twisp. GPS: 48.680899, -120.258405

38 • A3 | South Creek (Okanogan-Wenatchee NF)

Total sites: 4, RV sites: 4, No water, Vault/pit toilet, Tent & RV camping: $10, Stay limit: 14 days, Open May-Oct, Max Length: 30ft, Reservations not accepted, Elev: 3186ft/971m, Tel: 509-996-4003, Nearest town: Twisp. GPS: 48.437861, -120.529241

39 • A3 | Tiffany Spring (Okanogan-Wenatchee NF)

Total sites: 6, RV sites: 6, No water, Vault/pit toilet, Tent & RV camping: Free, No trailers, Open Jun-Sep, Reservations not accepted, Elev: 6857ft/2090m, Tel: 509-486-2186, Nearest town: Twisp. GPS: 48.700623, -119.953735

40 • A3 | War Creek (Okanogan-Wenatchee NF)

Total sites: 10, RV sites: 10, Central water, Vault/pit toilet, No showers, No RV dump, Tent & RV camping: $15, Stay limit: 14 days, Open May-Oct, Max Length: 25ft, Reservations not accepted, Elev: 2559ft/780m, Tel: 509-996-4003, Nearest town: Twisp. GPS: 48.367676, -120.398193

41 • A4 | Beaver Lake (Okanogan-Wenatchee NF)

Total sites: 11, RV sites: 11, Central water, Vault/pit toilet, No showers, No RV dump, Tent & RV camping: $8, Open May-Oct, Reservations not accepted, Elev: 2792ft/851m, Tel: 509-486-2186, Nearest town: Wauconda. GPS: 48.849858, -118.968346

42 • A4 | Beth Lake (Colville NF)

Total sites: 14, RV sites: 13, Central water, Vault/pit toilet, No showers, No RV dump, Tent & RV camping: $15, Stay limit: 14 days, Generator hours: 0600-2200, Open May-Oct, Reservations not accepted, Elev: 2868ft/874m, Tel: 509-486-2186, Nearest town: Tonasket. GPS: 48.859269, -118.984619

43 • A4 | Bonaparte Lake (Colville NF)

Total sites: 28, RV sites: 28, Central water, Vault/pit toilet, No showers, No RV dump, Tent & RV camping: $20, Group site: $125, Stay limit: 14 days, Generator hours: 0600-2200, Open May-Oct, Max Length: 48ft, Reservations accepted, Elev: 3620ft/1103m, Tel: 509-486-2186, Nearest town: Tonasket. GPS: 48.794778, -119.057269

44 • A4 | Canyon Creek (Colville NF)

Total sites: 12, RV sites: 12, No water, Vault/pit toilet, Tent & RV camping: $6, No turn-around if miss entrance, Generator hours: 0600-2200, Open May-Oct, Reservations not accepted, Elev: 2234ft/681m, Tel: 509-738-7700, Nearest town: Kettle Falls. GPS: 48.577747, -118.240614

45 • A4 | Cottonwood (Tonasket) (Colville NF)

Total sites: 3, RV sites: 3, Central water, Vault/pit toilet, No showers, No RV dump, Tent & RV camping: $10, Stay limit: 14 days, Generator hours: 0600-2200, Open May-Oct, Reservations not accepted, Elev: 2808ft/856m, Tel: 509-486-2186, Nearest town: Conconully. GPS: 48.586926, -119.763644

46 • A4 | Crawfish Lake (Colville NF)

Total sites: 19, RV sites: 14, No water, Vault/pit toilet, Tent & RV camping: $10, Open May-Sep, Max Length: 18ft, Reservations not accepted, Elev: 4547ft/1386m, Tel: 509-486-2186, Nearest town: Riverside. GPS: 48.484619, -119.216064

47 • A4 | Davis Lake (Colville NF)

Total sites: 4, RV sites: 4, No water, Vault/pit toilet, Tent & RV camping: Free, Stay limit: 14 days, Generator hours: 0600-2200, Open all year, Elev: 4528ft/1380m, Tel: 509-738-7700, Nearest town: Colville. GPS: 48.738738, -118.228761

48 • A4 | Deer Creek Forest Camp (Colville NF)

Total sites: 9, RV sites: 9, No water, Vault/pit toilet, Tent & RV camping: $5, Stay limit: 14 days, Generator hours: 0600-2200, Open all year, Reservations not accepted, Elev: 4728ft/1441m, Tel: 509-775-7400, Nearest town: Orient. GPS: 48.864848, -118.395571

49 • A4 | Ferry Lake (Colville NF)

Total sites: 9, RV sites: 9, No water, Vault/pit toilet, Tent & RV camping: $6, Generator hours: 0600-2200, Open May-Oct, Reservations not accepted, Elev: 3468ft/1057m, Tel: 509-775-7400, Nearest town: Republic. GPS: 48.523062, -118.810748

50 • A4 | Fourteen Mile TH (Okanogan-Wenatchee NF)

Total sites: 6, RV sites: 6, No water, Vault/pit toilet, Tent & RV

camping: Fee unk, Elev: 4770ft/1454m, Tel: 509-486-2186, Nearest town: Tonasket. GPS: 48.908064, -119.831772

51 • A4 | Jungle Hill Horse Camp (Colville NF)

Total sites: 5, RV sites: 5, No water, Vault/pit toilet, Tent & RV camping: Free, Reservations not accepted, Elev: 4118ft/1255m, Nearest town: Colville. GPS: 48.633257, -118.545341

52 • A4 | Kerr (Colville NF)

Total sites: 13, RV sites: 13, No water, Vault/pit toilet, Tent & RV camping: $10, Stay limit: 14 days, Generator hours: 0600-2200, Open May-Sep, Reservations not accepted, Elev: 3182ft/970m, Tel: 509-486-2186, Nearest town: Conconully. GPS: 48.611454, -119.788275

53 • A4 | Kettle Crest (Colville NF)

Total sites: 2, RV sites: 2, No water, Vault/pit toilet, No showers, No RV dump, Tent & RV camping: Free, Suitable for equestrian use, Sno-Park permit required if camping between 11/01 and 05/01, Stay limit: 14 days, Generator hours: 0600-2200, Open all year, Reservations not accepted, Elev: 5467ft/1666m, Tel: 509-447-3129, Nearest town: Kettle Falls. GPS: 48.608652, -118.476856

54 • A4 | Lake Ellen East (Colville NF)

Total sites: 15, RV sites: 15, No water, Vault/pit toilet, Tent & RV camping: $6, Stay limit: 14 days, Generator hours: 0600-2200, Open May-Sep, Reservations not accepted, Elev: 2293ft/699m, Tel: 509-738-7700, Nearest town: Kettle Falls. GPS: 48.502274, -118.247387

55 • A4 | Lake Ellen West (Colville NF)

Total sites: 15, RV sites: 15, No water, Vault/pit toilet, Tent & RV camping: $6, Stay limit: 14 days, Generator hours: 0600-2200, Open May-Sep, Reservations not accepted, Elev: 2234ft/681m, Tel: 509-738-7700, Nearest town: Kettle Falls. GPS: 48.496272, -118.263412

56 • A4 | Lambert Creek Horse Camp (Colville NF)

Total sites: 5, RV sites: 5, No water, Vault/pit toilet, Tent & RV camping: Free, Watering trough, Reservations not accepted, Elev: 3889ft/1185m, Tel: 509-775-7400, Nearest town: Republic. GPS: 48.728711, -118.522669

57 • A4 | Long Lake (Colville NF)

Total sites: 12, RV sites: 12, Central water, Vault/pit toilet, No showers, No RV dump, Tent & RV camping: $8, Stay limit: 14 days, Generator hours: 0600-2200, Open all year, Reservations not accepted, Elev: 3320ft/1012m, Tel: 509-775-7400, Nearest town: Republic. GPS: 48.500838, -118.810169

58 • A4 | Lost Lake (Colville NF)

Total sites: 19, RV sites: 19, Central water, Flush toilet, No showers, No RV dump, Tent & RV camping: $20, Group site: $75, Stay limit: 14 days, Generator hours: 0600-2200, Open May-Oct, Reservations not accepted, Elev: 3875ft/1181m, Tel: 509-486-2186, Nearest town: Wauconda. GPS: 48.852051, -119.052246

59 • A4 | Lyman Lake (Okanogan-Wenatchee NF)

Total sites: 4, RV sites: 4, No water, Vault/pit toilet, Tent & RV camping: Free, Open Jun-Sep, Elev: 2930ft/893m, Tel: 509-486-2186, Nearest town: Tonasket. GPS: 48.526111, -119.024979

60 • A4 | Oriole (Colville NF)

Total sites: 10, RV sites: 8, Central water, Vault/pit toilet, No showers, No RV dump, Tent & RV camping: $10, Stay limit: 14 days, Generator hours: 0600-2200, Open May-Oct, Reservations not accepted, Elev: 2920ft/890m, Tel: 509-486-2186, Nearest town: Conconully. GPS: 48.593983, -119.772278

61 • A4 | Salmon Meadows (Okanogan-Wenatchee NF)

Total sites: 7, RV sites: 7, Central water, Vault/pit toilet, No showers, No RV dump, Tent & RV camping: $10, Stay limit: 14 days, Generator hours: 0600-2200, Open May-Oct, Reservations not accepted, Elev: 4488ft/1368m, Tel: 509-486-2186, Nearest town: Omak. GPS: 48.658531, -119.841833

62 • A4 | Sherman Overlook (Colville NF)

Total sites: 10, RV sites: 10, Central water, Vault/pit toilet, No showers, No RV dump, Tent & RV camping: $6, Stay limit: 14 days, Generator hours: 0600-2200, Open all year, Max Length: 20ft, Reservations not accepted, Elev: 5148ft/1569m, Tel: 509-738-7700, Nearest town: Kettle Falls. GPS: 48.605418, -118.463326

63 • A4 | Sugarloaf (Colville NF)

Total sites: 4, RV sites: 4, No water, Vault/pit toilet, Tent & RV camping: $10, Stay limit: 14 days, Generator hours: 0600-2200, Open May-Sep, Reservations not accepted, Elev: 2424ft/739m, Tel: 509-486-2186, Nearest town: Conconully. GPS: 48.594482, -119.697221

64 • A4 | Swan Lake (Colville NF)

Total sites: 25, RV sites: 21, Central water, Vault/pit toilet, No showers, No RV dump, Tent & RV camping: $10, Stay limit: 14 days, Generator hours: 0600-2200, Reservations not accepted, Elev: 3734ft/1138m, Tel: 509-775-7400, Nearest town: Republic. GPS: 48.513042, -118.834451

65 • A4 | Ten Mile (Colville NF)

Total sites: 5, RV sites: 5, No water, Vault/pit toilet, Tents only: $6, Open May-Sep, Reservations not accepted, Elev: 2112ft/644m, Tel: 509-775-7400, Nearest town: Republic. GPS: 48.517581, -118.738081

66 • A4 | Trout Lake (Colville NF)

Total sites: 5, RV sites: 0, No water, Vault/pit toilet, No showers, No RV dump, Tents only: Free, Reservations not accepted, Elev: 3123ft/952m, Tel: 509-738-7700, Nearest town: Kettle Falls. GPS: 48.624498, -118.240203

67 • A4 | Wapaloosie Horse Camp (Colville NF)

Total sites: 5, RV sites: 5, No water, Vault/pit toilet, Tent & RV camping: Free, No services Labor Day-Memorial Day, Stay limit: 14 days, Generator hours: 0600-2200, Open all year, Reservations not accepted, Elev: 5007ft/1526m, Nearest town: Kettle Falls. GPS: 48.662933, -118.439506

68 • A5 | Big Meadow Lake (Colville NF)

Total sites: 17, RV sites: 17, Central water, Vault/pit toilet, No showers, No RV dump, Tent & RV camping: Free, Stay limit: 14

days, Generator hours: 0600-2200, Open May-Sep, Reservations not accepted, Elev: 3428ft/1045m, Tel: 509-738-7700, Nearest town: Ione. GPS: 48.726164, -117.562668

69 • A5 | Browns Lake (Colville NF)

Total sites: 18, RV sites: 18, No water, Vault/pit toilet, Tent & RV camping: $16, Stay limit: 14 days, Generator hours: 0600-2200, Open all year, Max Length: 20ft, Reservations not accepted, Elev: 3399ft/1036m, Tel: 509-447-7300, Nearest town: Usk. GPS: 48.436523, -117.196045

70 • A5 | Crescent Lake (Colville NF)

Total sites: 3, RV sites: 3, No water, Vault/pit toilet, Tent & RV camping: Free, Stay limit: 14 days, Generator hours: 0600-2200, Open May-Sep, Elev: 2713ft/827m, Tel: 509-446-7500, Nearest town: Metaline Falls. GPS: 48.988564, -117.311432

71 • A5 | East Sullivan (Colville NF)

Total sites: 38, RV sites: 38, Central water, Vault/pit toilet, No showers, No RV dump, Tent & RV camping: $24, Group site: $90, Generator hours: 0600-2200, Open May-Sep, Max Length: 55ft, Reservations accepted, Elev: 2658ft/810m, Tel: 509-446-7500, Nearest town: Metaline. GPS: 48.839781, -117.280981

72 • A5 | Edgewater (Colville NF)

Total sites: 20, RV sites: 20, Central water, Vault/pit toilet, No showers, No RV dump, Tent & RV camping: $24, Generator hours: 0600-2200, Open May-Sep, Max Length: 72ft, Reservations accepted, Elev: 2106ft/642m, Tel: 509-446-7500, Nearest town: Ione. GPS: 48.754483, -117.405590

73 • A5 | Gillette (Colville NF)

Total sites: 30, RV sites: 30, Central water, Vault/pit toilet, No showers, No RV dump, Tent & RV camping: $24, Stay limit: 14 days, Generator hours: 0600-2200, Open May-Sep, Max Length: 55ft, Reservations accepted, Elev: 3173ft/967m, Tel: 509-738-7700, Nearest town: Ione. GPS: 48.612257, -117.535463

74 • A5 | Lake Gillette (Colville NF)

Total sites: 14, RV sites: 14, Central water, Vault/pit toilet, No showers, No RV dump, Tent & RV camping: $18, Stay limit: 14 days, Generator hours: 0600-2200, Open May-Sep, Reservations not accepted, Elev: 3189ft/972m, Tel: 509-738-7700, Nearest town: Ione. GPS: 48.612551, -117.539039

75 • A5 | Lake Leo (Colville NF)

Total sites: 8, RV sites: 8, Central water, Vault/pit toilet, No showers, No RV dump, Tent & RV camping: $18, Stay limit: 14 days, Generator hours: 0600-2200, Open May-Sep, Reservations not accepted, Elev: 3215ft/980m, Tel: 509-738-7700, Nearest town: Colville. GPS: 48.649769, -117.497163

76 • A5 | Lake Thomas (Colville NF)

Total sites: 16, RV sites: 8, Central water, Vault/pit toilet, No showers, No RV dump, Tent & RV camping: $18, Stay limit: 14 days, Open May-Sep, Reservations not accepted, Elev: 3228ft/984m, Tel: 509-738-7700, Nearest town: Ione. GPS: 48.623779, -117.535645

77 • A5 | Little Twin Lakes (Colville NF)

Total sites: 20, RV sites: 20, No water, Vault/pit toilet, Tent & RV camping: Free, Generator hours: 0600-2200, Open May-Sep, Elev: 3750ft/1143m, Tel: 509-738-7700, Nearest town: Colville. GPS: 48.574777, -117.645809

78 • A5 | Mill Pond (Colville NF)

Total sites: 10, RV sites: 10, Central water, Vault/pit toilet, No showers, No RV dump, Tent & RV camping: $24, Generator hours: 0600-2200, Open May-Sep, Max Length: 20ft, Reservations not accepted, Elev: 2661ft/811m, Tel: 509-446-7500, Nearest town: Metaline. GPS: 48.854401, -117.290516

79 • A5 | Noisy Creek (Colville NF)

Total sites: 19, RV sites: 19, Central water, Vault/pit toilet, No showers, No RV dump, Tent & RV camping: $24, Group site: $90, Generator hours: 0600-2200, Open May-Sep, Max Length: 45ft, Reservations accepted, Elev: 2644ft/806m, Tel: 509-446-7500, Nearest town: Metaline. GPS: 48.790355, -117.284428

80 • A5 | Panhandle (Colville NF)

Total sites: 13, RV sites: 13, Central water, Vault/pit toilet, No showers, No RV dump, Tent & RV camping: $24, Generator hours: 0600-2200, Open May-Sep, Max Length: 33ft, Reservations accepted, Elev: 2096ft/639m, Tel: 509-447-7300, Nearest town: Newport. GPS: 48.509692, -117.271344

81 • A5 | Pierre Lake (Colville NF)

Total sites: 16, RV sites: 16, No water, Vault/pit toilet, Tent & RV camping: $6, Stay limit: 14 days, Generator hours: 0600-2200, Open all year, Reservations not accepted, Elev: 2014ft/614m, Tel: 509-738-7700, Nearest town: Orient. GPS: 48.904053, -118.139893

82 • A5 | South Skookum Lake (Colville NF)

Total sites: 25, RV sites: 25, Central water, Vault/pit toilet, No showers, No RV dump, Tent & RV camping: $18, Stay limit: 14 days, Generator hours: 0600-2200, Open May-Sep, Reservations not accepted, Elev: 3547ft/1081m, Tel: 509-447-7300, Nearest town: Usk. GPS: 48.392175, -117.184521

83 • A5 | West Sullivan (Colville NF)

Total sites: 10, RV sites: 10, Central water, Vault/pit toilet, No showers, No RV dump, Tent & RV camping: $24, Generator hours: 0600-2200, Open May-Sep, Max Length: 30ft, Reservations accepted, Elev: 2625ft/800m, Tel: 509-446-7500, Nearest town: Metaline. GPS: 48.839316, -117.285775

84 • B1 | Big Creek (Olympic NF)

Total sites: 23, RV sites: 23, Central water, Vault/pit toilet, No showers, No RV dump, Tent & RV camping: $20, Stay limit: 14 days, Open May-Sep, Max Length: 36ft, Reservations not accepted, Elev: 1001ft/305m, Tel: 360-765-2200, Nearest town: Hoodsport. GPS: 47.494498, -123.211182

85 • B1 | Brown Creek (Olympic NF)

Total sites: 20, RV sites: 12, Central water, Vault/pit toilet, No showers, No RV dump, Tent & RV camping: $14, 6 sites open all winter, Stay limit: 14 days, Open all year, Max Length: 21ft,

Reservations not accepted, Elev: 620ft/189m, Tel: 360-765-2200, Nearest town: Shelton. GPS: 47.413177, -123.318668

86 • B1 | Campbell Tree Grove (Olympic NF)

Total sites: 31, RV sites: 21, No water, Vault/pit toilet, Tent & RV camping: Free, Open May-Sep, Max Length: 16ft, Reservations not accepted, Elev: 1188ft/362m, Tel: 360-288-2525, Nearest town: Humptulips. GPS: 47.480937, -123.688034

87 • B1 | Coho (Olympic NF)

Total sites: 55, RV sites: 46, Central water, Flush toilet, No showers, RV dump, Tents: $25/RVs: $30, Also walk-to & group sites, 2 group sites: $55, Open May-Oct, Max Length: 32ft, Reservations accepted, Elev: 882ft/269m, Tel: 360-765-2200, Nearest town: Montesano. GPS: 47.389648, -123.603760

88 • B1 | Falls Creek (Olympic NF)

Total sites: 31, RV sites: 21, Central water, Flush toilet, No showers, No RV dump, Tent & RV camping: $25, Open May-Sep, Max Length: 16ft, Reservations accepted, Elev: 233ft/71m, Tel: 360-288-2525, Nearest town: Quinault. GPS: 47.469321, -123.845766

89 • B1 | Gatton Creek (Olympic NF)

Total sites: 5, RV sites: 0, No water, Vault/pit toilet, Tents only: $25, Walk-to sites, Open May-Sep, Reservations not accepted, Elev: 190ft/58m, Tel: 360-288-2525, Nearest town: Aberdeen. GPS: 47.473389, -123.837891

90 • B1 | Klahanie (Olympic NF)

Total sites: 20, RV sites: 20, No water, Vault/pit toilet, Tent & RV camping: $10, Open May-Sep, Max Length: 21ft, Reservations not accepted, Elev: 479ft/146m, Tel: 360-374-6522, Nearest town: Klahanie. GPS: 47.963396, -124.305507

91 • B1 | Klahowya (Olympic NF)

Total sites: 56, RV sites: 56, Central water, Vault/pit toilet, No showers, No RV dump, Tent & RV camping: $17, Stay limit: 14 days, Open May-Sep, Max Length: 30ft, Reservations not accepted, Elev: 856ft/261m, Tel: 360-288 2525, Nearest town: Sappho. GPS: 48.065908, -124.113121

92 • B1 | Lebar Horse Camp (Olympic NF)

Total sites: 13, RV sites: 13, No water, Vault/pit toilet, Tent & RV camping: $14, High lines, Stay limit: 14 days, Open May-Sep, Max Length: 28ft, Reservations not accepted, Elev: 646ft/197m, Tel: 360-765 2200, Nearest town: Shelton. GPS: 47.415408, -123.320572

93 • B1 | Willaby (Olympic NF)

Total sites: 21, Central water, Flush toilet, No showers, No RV dump, Tents only: $25, Also walk-to sites, 2 walk-to sites, Open Apr-Oct, Max Length: 30ft, Reservations accepted, Elev: 276ft/84m, Tel: 360-288-2525, Nearest town: Quinault. GPS: 47.460449, -123.861328

94 • B2 | Clear Creek (Mt Baker-Snoqualmie NF)

Total sites: 13, RV sites: 13, No water, Vault/pit toilet, Tent & RV camping: $21-25, Open May-Sep, Max Length: 40ft, Reservations accepted, Elev: 630ft/192m, Tel: 360-436-1155, Nearest town: Darrington. GPS: 48.220215, -121.571777

95 • B2 | Collins (Olympic NF)

Total sites: 16, RV sites: 10, No water, Vault/pit toilet, Tent & RV camping: $14, Open May-Sep, Max Length: 21ft, Reservations not accepted, Elev: 351ft/107m, Tel: 360-765-2200, Nearest town: Brinnon. GPS: 47.682711, -123.019192

96 • B2 | Dungeness Forks (Olympic NF)

Total sites: 10, RV sites: 0, No water, Vault/pit toilet, Tents only: $14, Steep access road, Stay limit: 14 days, Open May-Sep, Elev: 1070ft/326m, Tel: 360-765-2200, Nearest town: Sequim. GPS: 47.971732, -123.111424

97 • B2 | Gold Basin (Mt Baker-Snoqualmie NF)

Total sites: 99, RV sites: 99, Central water, Flush toilet, Free showers, No RV dump, Tent & RV camping: $28-30, Group sites: $225, Open May-Sep, Max Length: 45ft, Reservations accepted, Elev: 1155ft/352m, Tel: 360-436-1155, Nearest town: Granite Falls. GPS: 48.077393, -121.737305

98 • B2 | Hamma Hamma (Olympic NF)

Total sites: 15, RV sites: 15, No water, Vault/pit toilet, Tent & RV camping: $14, Stay limit: 14 days, Open May-Sep, Max Length: 21ft, Reservations not accepted, Elev: 689ft/210m, Tel: 360-765-2200, Nearest town: Lilliwaup. GPS: 47.595657, -123.123072

99 • B2 | Lena Creek (Olympic NF)

Total sites: 13, RV sites: 13, Central water, Vault/pit toilet, No showers, No RV dump, Tent & RV camping: $14, Stay limit: 14 days, Open May-Sep, Max Length: 21ft, Reservations not accepted, Elev: 745ft/227m, Tel: 360-765-2200, Nearest town: Lilliwaup. GPS: 47.599366, -123.151822

100 • B2 | Red Bridge (Mt Baker-Snoqualmie NF)

Total sites: 16, RV sites: 16, No water, Vault/pit toilet, Tent & RV camping: $20-24, Open May-Sep, Max Length: 40ft, Reservations accepted, Elev: 1430ft/436m, Tel: 360-436-1155, Nearest town: Granite Falls. GPS: 48.070601, -121.651781

101 • B2 | Seal Rock (Olympic NF)

Total sites: 41, RV sites: 41, Central water, Vault/pit toilet, No showers, No RV dump, Tent & RV camping: $18, Stay limit: 14 days, Open Apr-Sep, Reservations not accepted, Elev: 115ft/35m, Tel: 360-765-2200, Nearest town: Brinnon. GPS: 47.708963, -122.890311

102 • B2 | Turlo (Mt Baker-Snoqualmie NF)

Total sites: 18, RV sites: 18, Central water, Flush toilet, No showers, No RV dump, Tent & RV camping: $23-27, Open Apr-Sep, Max Length: 40ft, Reservations accepted, Elev: 1034ft/315m, Tel: 360-436-1155, Nearest town: Granite Falls. GPS: 48.091788, -121.783487

103 • B2 | Verlot (Mt Baker-Snoqualmie NF)

Total sites: 26, RV sites: 26, Central water, Flush toilet, No showers, No RV dump, Tent & RV camping: $25-27, Open Apr-Sep, Max Length: 40ft, Reservations accepted, Elev: 1007ft/307m, Tel: 360-436-1155, Nearest town: Granite Falls. GPS: 48.089785, -121.777559

104 • B3 | Alpine Meadows (Okanogan-Wenatchee NF)

Total sites: 4, RV sites: 4, No water, Vault/pit toilet, Tent & RV camping: $14, Very rough road - high-clearance vehicle may be needed, Max Length: 20ft, Reservations not accepted, Elev: 2707ft/825m, Tel: 509-548-2550, Nearest town: Leavenworth. GPS: 48.046578, -120.833922

105 • B3 | Atkinson Flat (Okanogan-Wenatchee NF)

Total sites: 11, RV sites: 4, No water, Vault/pit toilet, Tent & RV camping: $14, Very rough road - high-clearance vehicle may be needed, Open Jun-Sep, Max Length: 20ft, Reservations not accepted, Elev: 2615ft/797m, Tel: 509-548-2550, Nearest town: Leavenworth. GPS: 48.000409, -120.816870

106 • B3 | Beckler River (Mt Baker-Snoqualmie NF)

Total sites: 27, RV sites: 27, Central water, Vault/pit toilet, No showers, No RV dump, Tent & RV camping: $23-27, Open May-Sep, Max Length: 40ft, Reservations accepted, Elev: 1112ft/339m, Tel: 360-677-2414, Nearest town: Skykomish. GPS: 47.734619, -121.332275

107 • B3 | Bedal (Mt Baker-Snoqualmie NF)

Total sites: 21, RV sites: 21, No water, Vault/pit toilet, Tent & RV camping: $18-20, Open May-Sep, Max Length: 32ft, Reservations accepted, Elev: 1272ft/388m, Tel: 360-436-1155, Nearest town: Granite Falls. GPS: 48.096951, -121.387348

108 • B3 | Beverly (Okanogan-Wenatchee NF)

Total sites: 10, RV sites: 10, No water, Vault/pit toilet, Tent & RV camping: $10, No fees 10/1-5/15, Open all year, Reservations not accepted, Elev: 3205ft/977m, Tel: 509-852-1100, Nearest town: Cle Elum. GPS: 47.378174, -120.883789

109 • B3 | Black Pine Lake (Okanogan-Wenatchee NF)

Total sites: 23, RV sites: 23, Central water, Vault/pit toilet, No showers, No RV dump, Tent & RV camping: $20, Stay limit: 14 days, Open Apr-Oct, Max Length: 30ft, Reservations not accepted, Elev: 4137ft/1261m, Tel: 509-996-4003, Nearest town: Twisp. GPS: 48.313477, -120.274414

110 • B3 | Blackpine Creek Horse Camp (Okanogan-Wenatchee NF)

Total sites: 10, RV sites: 10, Central water, Vault/pit toilet, No showers, No RV dump, Tent & RV camping: $16, Max Length: 60ft, Reservations not accepted, Elev: 2854ft/870m, Tel: 509-548-2550, Nearest town: Leavenworth. GPS: 47.610088, -120.945413

111 • B3 | Bridge Creek (Okanogan-Wenatchee NF)

Total sites: 6, RV sites: 6, Central water, Vault/pit toilet, No showers, No RV dump, Tent & RV camping: $19, Reservable group site $100, Max Length: 19ft, Reservations not accepted, Elev: 2102ft/641m, Tel: 509-548-2550, Nearest town: Leavenworth. GPS: 47.562918, -120.782445

112 • B3 | Buck Creek (Mt Baker-Snoqualmie NF)

Total sites: 29, RV sites: 26, No water, Vault/pit toilet, Tent & RV camping: $18-20, Open May-Sep, Max Length: 108ft, Reservations accepted, Elev: 1253ft/382m, Tel: 541-338-7869, Nearest town: Darrington. GPS: 48.267188, -121.332144

113 • B3 | Chatter Creek (Okanogan-Wenatchee NF)

Total sites: 12, RV sites: 12, Central water, Vault/pit toilet, No showers, No RV dump, Tent & RV camping: $18, Group site: $100, Reservations not accepted, Elev: 2743ft/836m, Tel: 509-548-2550, Nearest town: Leavenworth. GPS: 47.608000, -120.886000

114 • B3 | Chiwawa Horse Camp (Okanogan-Wenatchee NF)

Total sites: 21, RV sites: 21, Central water, Vault/pit toilet, No showers, No RV dump, Tent & RV camping: $14, Open May-Oct, Reservations not accepted, Elev: 2566ft/782m, Tel: 509-548-2550, Nearest town: Leavenworth. GPS: 47.972653, -120.791639

115 • B3 | Cle Elum River (Okanogan-Wenatchee NF)

Total sites: 14, RV sites: 14, Central water, Vault/pit toilet, No showers, No RV dump, Tent & RV camping: $18, Reservable group site $115, Open May-Sep, Reservations not accepted, Elev: 2300ft/701m, Tel: 509-852-1100, Nearest town: Cle Elum. GPS: 47.349764, -121.104569

116 • B3 | Cottonwood (Okanogan-Wenatchee NF)

Total sites: 25, RV sites: 25, Central water, Vault/pit toilet, No showers, No RV dump, Tent & RV camping: $15, No fee winter months, Open all year, Max Length: 20ft, Reservations not accepted, Elev: 3150ft/960m, Tel: 509-784-4700, Nearest town: Entiat. GPS: 48.020574, -120.642210

117 • B3 | Denny Creek (Mt Baker-Snoqualmie NF)

Total sites: 23, RV sites: 23, Elec sites: 10, Central water, Flush toilet, No showers, No RV dump, Tents: $28-30/RVs: $31-42, Group site $105, Open May-Sep, Max Length: 40ft, Reservations accepted, Elev: 2297ft/700m, Tel: 425-888-1421, Nearest town: North Bend. GPS: 47.412138, -121.442136

118 • B3 | Eightmile (Okanogan-Wenatchee NF)

Total sites: 45, RV sites: 45, Central water, Vault/pit toilet, No showers, No RV dump, Tent & RV camping: $24, Open May-Oct, Max Length: 47ft, Reservations accepted, Elev: 1923ft/586m, Tel: 509-548-2550, Nearest town: Leavenworth. GPS: 47.550778, -120.764757

119 • B3 | Finner Creek (Okanogan-Wenatchee NF)

Total sites: 3, RV sites: 3, Central water, Vault/pit toilet, No showers, No RV dump, Tent & RV camping: $14, Max Length: 30ft, Reservations not accepted, Elev: 2589ft/789m, Tel: 509-548-2550, Nearest town: Leavenworth. GPS: 47.953383, -120.772385

120 • B3 | Fish Lake (Okanogan-Wenatchee NF)

Total sites: 3, RV sites: 0, No water, No toilets, Tents only: Free, Walk-to sites, Reservations not accepted, Elev: 3484ft/1062m, Tel: 509-852-1100, Nearest town: Cle Elum. GPS: 47.523765, -121.073080

121 • B3 | Foggy Dew (Okanogan-Wenatchee NF)

Total sites: 12, RV sites: 12, No water, Vault/pit toilet, Tent & RV camping: $10, Stay limit: 14 days, Open May-Oct, Max Length: 25ft, Reservations not accepted, Elev: 2251ft/686m, Tel: 509-996-4003, Nearest town: Carlton. GPS: 48.205591, -120.195899

122 • B3 | Fox Creek (Okanogan-Wenatchee NF)

Total sites: 16, RV sites: 16, Central water, Vault/pit toilet, No

showers, No RV dump, Tent & RV camping: $15, Max Length: 28ft, Reservations not accepted, Elev: 2080ft/634m, Tel: 509-784-4700, Nearest town: Ardenvoir. GPS: 47.925293, -120.510986

123 • B3 | Glacier View (Okanogan-Wenatchee NF)

Total sites: 23, RV sites: 23, Central water, Vault/pit toilet, No showers, No RV dump, Tent & RV camping: $20, Max Length: 15ft, Reservations not accepted, Elev: 1903ft/580m, Tel: 509-548-2550, Nearest town: Leavenworth. GPS: 47.824207, -120.808631

124 • B3 | Goose Creek (Okanogan-Wenatchee NF)

Total sites: 29, RV sites: 29, Central water, Vault/pit toilet, No showers, No RV dump, Tent & RV camping: $14, Reservations not accepted, Elev: 2264ft/690m, Tel: 509-548-2550, Nearest town: Leavenworth. GPS: 47.838691, -120.647821

125 • B3 | Grouse Mt (Okanogan-Wenatchee NF)

Total sites: 4, RV sites: 0, No water, Vault/pit toilet, Tents only: Free, Reservations not accepted, Elev: 4459ft/1359m, Tel: 509-682-4900, Nearest town: Chelan. GPS: 47.988683, -120.310512

126 • B3 | Handy Springs (Okanogan-Wenatchee NF)

Total sites: 1, RV sites: 0, No water, Vault/pit toilet, Tents only: Free, Reservations not accepted, Elev: 6348ft/1935m, Tel: 509-682-4900, Nearest town: Chelan. GPS: 47.979177, -120.412465

127 • B3 | Ida Creek (Okanogan-Wenatchee NF)

Total sites: 10, RV sites: 10, Central water, Vault/pit toilet, No showers, No RV dump, Tent & RV camping: $19, Max Length: 30ft, Reservations not accepted, Elev: 2648ft/807m, Tel: 509-548-2550, Nearest town: Leavenworth. GPS: 47.607617, -120.847819

128 • B3 | Johnny Creek (Okanogan-Wenatchee NF)

Total sites: 65, RV sites: 65, Central water, Vault/pit toilet, No showers, No RV dump, Tent & RV camping: $19-22, Max Length: 50ft, Reservations not accepted, Elev: 2464ft/751m, Tel: 509-548-2550, Nearest town: Leavenworth. GPS: 47.599303, -120.817072

129 • B3 | Junior Point (Okanogan-Wenatchee NF)

Total sites: 5, RV sites: 0, No water, Vault/pit toilet, Tents only: Free, Reservations not accepted, Elev: 6424ft/1958m, Tel: 509-682-4900, Nearest town: Chelan. GPS: 47.994379, -120.400309

130 • B3 | Kachess (Okanogan-Wenatchee NF)

Total sites: 152, RV sites: 152, No water, No toilets, Tent & RV camping: $24, Group site: $130, Open Jun-Sep, Max Length: 110ft, Reservations accepted, Elev: 2269ft/692m, Tel: 509-852-1100, Nearest town: Easton. GPS: 47.355196, -121.244578

131 • B3 | Ken Wilcox Horse Camp (Okanogan-Wenatchee NF)

Total sites: 19, RV sites: 19, No water, Vault/pit toilet, Tent & RV camping: $10, Stock water, Open Jun-Nov, Reservations not accepted, Elev: 5537ft/1688m, Tel: 509-852-1100, Nearest town: Cle Elum. GPS: 47.311494, -120.533642

132 • B3 | Lake Creek (Entiat River) (Okanogan-Wenatchee NF)

Total sites: 18, RV sites: 18, Central water, Vault/pit toilet, No showers, No RV dump, Tent & RV camping: $15, Open May-Sep, Max Length: 25ft, Reservations accepted, Elev: 2260ft/689m, Tel: 509-784-4700, Nearest town: Ardenvoir. GPS: 47.936671, -120.516386

133 • B3 | Meadow Creek (Okanogan-Wenatchee NF)

Total sites: 4, RV sites: 4, No water, No toilets, Tent & RV camping: Free, Max Length: 30ft, Reservations not accepted, Elev: 2280ft/695m, Tel: 509-548-2550, Nearest town: Leavenworth. GPS: 47.867438, -120.693655

134 • B3 | Middle Fork (Mt Baker-Snoqualmie NF)

Total sites: 38, RV sites: 38, Central water, Vault/pit toilet, No showers, No RV dump, Tent & RV camping: $23-25, 2 group sites: $75, Open May-Sep, Max Length: 46ft, Reservations accepted, Elev: 1112ft/339m, Tel: 425-888-1421, Nearest town: North Bend. GPS: 47.554000, -121.537000

135 • B3 | Miller River (Mt Baker-Snoqualmie NF)

Total sites: 18, RV sites: 18, Central water, Vault/pit toilet, No showers, No RV dump, Tent & RV camping: $22, Reservable group site $300, 6-ton weight limit on access road, Open May-Sep, Reservations not accepted, Elev: 1099ft/335m, Tel: 541-338-7869, Nearest town: Miller River. GPS: 47.690204, -121.394063

136 • B3 | Money Creek (Mt Baker-Snoqualmie NF)

Total sites: 25, RV sites: 25, Central water, Vault/pit toilet, No showers, No RV dump, Tent & RV camping: $25-30, 6-ton weight limit on access road, Near RR, Open May-Sep, Max Length: 40ft, Reservations accepted, Elev: 915ft/279m, Tel: 541-338-7869, Nearest town: Skykomish. GPS: 47.729004, -121.408203

137 • B3 | Napeequa Crossing (Okanogan-Wenatchee NF)

Total sites: 5, RV sites: 5, No water, Vault/pit toilet, Tent & RV camping: $10, Max Length: 30ft, Reservations not accepted, Elev: 2041ft/622m, Tel: 509-548-2550, Nearest town: Leavenworth. GPS: 47.920462, -120.894839

138 • B3 | Nason Creek (Okanogan-Wenatchee NF)

Total sites: 73, RV sites: 25, Central water, Flush toilet, No showers, No RV dump, Tent & RV camping: $24, Open May-Oct, Max Length: 35ft, Reservations accepted, Elev: 1939ft/591m, Tel: 509-763-7020, Nearest town: Coles Corner. GPS: 47.798943, -120.715262

139 • B3 | Nineteenmile (Okanogan-Wenatchee NF)

Total sites: 4, RV sites: 4, No water, Vault/pit toilet, Tent & RV camping: $14, Very rough road - high-clearance vehicle may be needed, Max Length: 30ft, Reservations not accepted, Elev: 2598ft/792m, Tel: 509-548-2550, Nearest town: Leavenworth. GPS: 48.019666, -120.827204

140 • B3 | North Fork (Okanogan-Wenatchee NF)

Total sites: 8, RV sites: 8, No water, Vault/pit toilet, No showers, No RV dump, Tents only: $10, Group site: $75, Max Length: 28ft, Reservations not accepted, Elev: 2756ft/840m, Tel: 509-784-4700, Nearest town: Entiat. GPS: 47.989023, -120.580696

141 • B3 | Owhi (Okanogan-Wenatchee NF)

Total sites: 22, RV sites: 0, No water, Vault/pit toilet, Tents only: $14, Walk-to sites, Open May-Nov, Reservations not accepted,

Elev: 2926ft/892m, Tel: 509-852-1100, Nearest town: Cle Elum. GPS: 47.424495, -121.170018

142 • B3 | Phelps Creek (Okanogan-Wenatchee NF)

Total sites: 13, RV sites: 13, No water, Vault/pit toilet, Tent & RV camping: $14, Max Length: 30ft, Reservations not accepted, Elev: 2789ft/850m, Tel: 509-548-2550, Nearest town: Leavenworth. GPS: 48.069454, -120.848994

143 • B3 | Pine Flats (Okanogan-Wenatchee NF)

Total sites: 6, RV sites: 6, Central water, Flush toilet, No showers, No RV dump, Tent & RV camping: $15, Reservable group site $75, Open Apr-Oct, Max Length: 28ft, Reservations not accepted, Elev: 1719ft/524m, Tel: 509-784-4700, Nearest town: Entiat. GPS: 47.758628, -120.425108

144 • B3 | Rainy Creek (Okanogan-Wenatchee NF)

Total sites: 10, RV sites: 10, No water, Vault/pit toilet, No showers, No RV dump, Tent & RV camping: $10, Max Length: 30ft, Reservations not accepted, Elev: 2159ft/658m, Tel: 509-548-2550, Nearest town: Leavenworth. GPS: 47.851212, -120.963607

145 • B3 | Red Mountain (Okanogan-Wenatchee NF)

Total sites: 10, RV sites: 10, No water, Vault/pit toilet, Tent & RV camping: $14, Open May-Oct, Reservations not accepted, Elev: 2313ft/705m, Tel: 509-852-1100, Nearest town: Cle Elum. GPS: 47.366455, -121.102539

146 • B3 | Riverbend (Okanogan-Wenatchee NF)

Total sites: 6, RV sites: 6, No water, Vault/pit toilet, Tent & RV camping: $14, Open Jun-Sep, Max Length: 30ft, Reservations not accepted, Elev: 2530ft/771m, Tel: 509-548-2550, Nearest town: Leavenworth. GPS: 47.962417, -120.786351

147 • B3 | Rock Creek (Okanogan-Wenatchee NF)

Total sites: 4, RV sites: 4, No water, Vault/pit toilet, Tent & RV camping: $14, Open Jun-Sep, Max Length: 30ft, Reservations not accepted, Elev: 2536ft/773m, Tel: 509-548-2550, Nearest town: Leavenworth. GPS: 47.970330, -120.789683

148 • B3 | Rock Island (Okanogan-Wenatchee NF)

Total sites: 22, RV sites: 22, Central water, Vault/pit toilet, No showers, No RV dump, Tent & RV camping: $18, Reservations not accepted, Elev: 2815ft/858m, Tel: 509-548-2550, Nearest town: Leavenworth. GPS: 47.608433, -120.917594

149 • B3 | Salmon La Sac (Okanogan-Wenatchee NF)

Total sites: 67, RV sites: 67, Central water, Vault/pit toilet, No showers, No RV dump, Tent & RV camping: $25, Open May-Sep, Max Length: 127ft, Reservations accepted, Elev: 2415ft/736m, Tel: 509-852-1100, Nearest town: Cle Elum. GPS: 47.401580, -121.099234

150 • B3 | Schaefer Creek (Okanogan-Wenatchee NF)

Total sites: 10, RV sites: 10, No water, Vault/pit toilet, Tent & RV camping: $14, Open Jun-Sep, Max Length: 30ft, Reservations not accepted, Elev: 2497ft/761m, Tel: 509-548-2550, Nearest town: Leavenworth. GPS: 47.974000, -120.802000

151 • B3 | Silver Falls (Okanogan-Wenatchee NF)

Total sites: 14, RV sites: 14, Central water, Vault/pit toilet, No showers, No RV dump, Tent & RV camping: $20, Reservable group site $60, Open May-Sep, Max Length: 35ft, Reservations not accepted, Elev: 2480ft/756m, Tel: 509-784-4700, Nearest town: Entiat. GPS: 47.958496, -120.537354

152 • B3 | Snowberry (Okanogan-Wenatchee NF)

Total sites: 7, RV sites: 7, Central water, Vault/pit toilet, No showers, No RV dump, Tent & RV camping: $15, Small group site: $20, Reservations not accepted, Elev: 2030ft/619m, Tel: 509-682-4900, Nearest town: Chelan. GPS: 47.958324, -120.289999

153 • B3 | South Navarre (Okanogan-Wenatchee NF)

Total sites: 4, RV sites: 4, No water, Vault/pit toilet, Tent & RV camping: Free, Reservations not accepted, Elev: 6463ft/1970m, Tel: 509-682-4900, Nearest town: Chelan. GPS: 48.107487, -120.339647

154 • B3 | Spruce Grove (Okanogan-Wenatchee NF)

Total sites: 2, RV sites: 0, No water, Vault/pit toilet, Tents only: Free, Open all year, Reservations not accepted, Elev: 2926ft/892m, Tel: 509-784-4700, Nearest town: Entiat. GPS: 48.004503, -120.604471

155 • B3 | Sulphur Creek (Mt Baker-Snoqualmie NF)

Total sites: 20, RV sites: 20, No water, Vault/pit toilet, Tent & RV camping: $18-20, Group site: $25, Open May-Sep, Max Length: 62ft, Reservations accepted, Elev: 1726ft/526m, Tel: 360-436-1155, Nearest town: Darrington. GPS: 48.248264, -121.193362

156 • B3 | Swauk (Okanogan-Wenatchee NF)

Total sites: 21, RV sites: 21, Central water, Vault/pit toilet, No showers, No RV dump, Tent & RV camping: $18, Open May-Sep, Reservations not accepted, Elev: 3196ft/974m, Tel: 509-852-1100, Nearest town: Cle Elum. GPS: 47.329004, -120.654993

157 • B3 | Tinkham (Mt Baker-Snoqualmie NF)

Total sites: 47, RV sites: 47, Central water, Vault/pit toilet, No showers, No RV dump, Tent & RV camping: $23-27, Open May-Sep, Max Length: 46ft, Reservations accepted, Elev: 1529ft/466m, Tel: 541-338-7869, Nearest town: North Bend. GPS: 47.402832, -121.567871

158 • B3 | Troublesome Creek (Mt Baker-Snoqualmie NF)

Total sites: 25, RV sites: 18, Central water, Vault/pit toilet, No showers, No RV dump, Tent & RV camping: $23-25, Open Jun-Sep, Max Length: 30ft, Reservations accepted, Elev: 1356ft/413m, Tel: 360-677-2414, Nearest town: Index. GPS: 47.898178, -121.402865

159 • B3 | White Pine (Okanogan-Wenatchee NF)

Total sites: 5, RV sites: 5, No water, Vault/pit toilet, Tent & RV camping: Free, Open May-Sep, Elev: 2369ft/722m, Tel: 509-548-2550, Nearest town: Leavenworth. GPS: 47.789091, -120.872694

160 • B3 | Windy Camp (Okanogan-Wenatchee NF)

Total sites: 2, RV sites: 0, Central water, Vault/pit toilet, No showers, No RV dump, Tents only: Free, Elev: 5965ft/1818m, Tel: 509-682-4900, Nearest town: Chelan. GPS: 47.899071, -120.331957

161 • B5 | Pioneer Park (Colville NF)

Total sites: 17, RV sites: 17, Central water, Vault/pit toilet, No showers, No RV dump, Tents: $20-24/RVs: $24, Open May-Sep, Max Length: 40ft, Reservations accepted, Elev: 2132ft/650m, Tel: 509-447-7300, Nearest town: Newport. GPS: 48.213025, -117.053999

162 • C2 | Adams Fork (Gifford Pinchot NF)

Total sites: 22, RV sites: 22, No water, Vault/pit toilet, Tent & RV camping: $22, Group sites: $35-$45, Open May-Sep, Max Length: 42ft, Reservations accepted, Elev: 2697ft/822m, Tel: 360-497-1100, Nearest town: Randle. GPS: 46.339101, -121.646541

163 • C2 | Big Creek (Gifford) (Gifford Pinchot NF)

Total sites: 27, RV sites: 27, Central water, Vault/pit toilet, No showers, No RV dump, Tent & RV camping: $22, Open May-Sep, Max Length: 20ft, Reservations accepted, Elev: 1857ft/566m, Tel: 360-497-1100, Nearest town: Ashford. GPS: 46.735628, -121.970332

164 • C2 | Blue Lake Creek (Gifford Pinchot NF)

Total sites: 11, RV sites: 11, No water, Vault/pit toilet, Tent & RV camping: $18-22, Open May-Sep, Max Length: 48ft, Reservations accepted, Elev: 1949ft/594m, Tel: 360-497-1100, Nearest town: Randle. GPS: 46.403632, -121.736681

165 • C2 | Cat Creek (Gifford Pinchot NF)

Total sites: 5, RV sites: 5, No water, Vault/pit toilet, Tent & RV camping: Free, Open May-Sep, Elev: 2753ft/839m, Tel: 360-497-1100, Nearest town: Randle. GPS: 46.348408, -121.624807

166 • C2 | Cat Creek Chimney Site (Gifford Pinchot NF)

Total sites: 10, RV sites: 10, No water, Vault/pit toilet, Tent & RV camping: Fee unk, Open May-Sep, Max Length: 35ft, Elev: 2874ft/876m, Tel: 360-497-1100, Nearest town: Randle. GPS: 46.353805, -121.618185

167 • C2 | Chain of Lakes TH (Gifford Pinchot NF)

Total sites: 3, RV sites: 3, No water, Vault/pit toilet, Tent & RV camping: Free, Open Jul-Sep, Max Length: 16ft, Elev: 4386ft/1337m, Tel: 360-497-1100, Nearest town: Randle. GPS: 46.293498, -121.595741

168 • C2 | Cody Horse Camp (Gifford Pinchot NF)

Total sites: 16, RV sites: 16, Central water, Vault/pit toilet, No showers, No RV dump, Tent & RV camping: Free, Max Length: 35ft, Elev: 3150ft/960m, Tel: 360-497-1100, Nearest town: Randle. GPS: 46.364328, -121.566356

169 • C2 | Evans Creek ORV (Mt Baker-Snoqualmie NF)

Total sites: 23, RV sites: 23, Central water, Vault/pit toilet, No showers, No RV dump, Tent & RV camping: Fee unk, Generator hours: 0800-2200, Open May-Oct, Reservations not accepted, Elev: 3616ft/1102m, Tel: 360-825-6585, Nearest town: Wilkeson. GPS: 46.940059, -121.940076

170 • C2 | Green River Horse Camp (Gifford Pinchot NF)

Total sites: 8, RV sites: 8, No water, Vault/pit toilet, Tent & RV camping: Free, Max Length: 40ft, Reservations not accepted, Elev: 2887ft/880m, Tel: 360-497-1100, Nearest town: Randle. GPS: 46.349505, -122.084408

171 • C2 | Horseshoe Lake (Gifford Pinchot NF)

Total sites: 11, RV sites: 11, No water, Vault/pit toilet, Tent & RV camping: $12, Open Jul-Sep, Max Length: 16ft, Reservations not accepted, Elev: 4173ft/1272m, Tel: 360-497-1100, Nearest town: Randle. GPS: 46.309814, -121.567139

172 • C2 | Iron Creek (Gifford Pinchot NF)

Total sites: 98, RV sites: 98, Central water, Vault/pit toilet, No showers, No RV dump, Tent & RV camping: $24, Open May-Sep, Max Length: 40ft, Reservations accepted, Elev: 1224ft/373m, Tel: 360-497-1100, Nearest town: Randle. GPS: 46.430664, -121.986084

173 • C2 | Keenes Horse Camp (Gifford Pinchot NF)

Total sites: 13, RV sites: 13, No water, Vault/pit toilet, Tent & RV camping: $14, Stock water, Open Jun-Sep, Reservations not accepted, Elev: 4367ft/1331m, Tel: 360-497-1100, Nearest town: Randle. GPS: 46.309114, -121.547471

174 • C2 | Killen Creek (Gifford Pinchot NF)

Total sites: 9, RV sites: 9, No water, Vault/pit toilet, Tent & RV camping: $12, Open Jul-Sep, Max Length: 22ft, Reservations not accepted, Elev: 4468ft/1362m, Tel: 360-497-1100, Nearest town: Randle. GPS: 46.294801, -121.548949

175 • C2 | La Wis Wis (Gifford Pinchot NF)

Total sites: 122, RV sites: 115, Central water, Flush toilet, No showers, No RV dump, Tent & RV camping: $24, Large RVs not recommended, Open May-Sep, Max Length: 60ft, Reservations accepted, Elev: 1368ft/417m, Tel: 360-497-1100, Nearest town: Packwood. GPS: 46.674843, -121.586464

176 • C2 | North Fork (Gifford Pinchot NF)

Total sites: 32, RV sites: 30, Central water, Vault/pit toilet, No showers, No RV dump, Tent & RV camping: $22, Open May-Sep, Max Length: 40ft, Reservations accepted, Elev: 1503ft/458m, Tel: 360-497-1100, Nearest town: Randle. GPS: 46.451201, -121.787257

177 • C2 | Olallie Lake (Gifford Pinchot NF)

Total sites: 5, RV sites: 5, No water, Vault/pit toilet, Tent & RV camping: $12, Open Jul-Sep, Max Length: 22ft, Reservations not accepted, Elev: 4298ft/1310m, Tel: 360-497-1100, Nearest town: Randle. GPS: 46.289242, -121.619278

178 • C2 | Takhlakh (Gifford Pinchot NF)

Total sites: 54, RV sites: 44, No water, Vault/pit toilet, Tent & RV camping: $22, Open May-Sep, Max Length: 99ft, Reservations accepted, Elev: 4423ft/1348m, Tel: 360-497-1100, Nearest town: Trout Lake. GPS: 46.278267, -121.600266

179 • C2 | The Dalles (Mt Baker-Snoqualmie NF)

Total sites: 41, RV sites: 41, No water, Vault/pit toilet, Tent & RV camping: $23-27, Open May-Sep, Max Length: 45ft, Reservations accepted, Elev: 2293ft/699m, Tel: 541-338-7869, Nearest town: Greenwater. GPS: 47.068335, -121.576783

180 • C2 | Tower Rock (Gifford Pinchot NF)

Total sites: 21, RV sites: 21, Central water, Vault/pit toilet, No showers, No RV dump, Tent & RV camping: $22, Open May-Sep, Max Length: 32ft, Reservations accepted, Elev: 1240ft/378m, Tel: 360-497-1100, Nearest town: Randle. GPS: 46.445557, -121.866943

181 • C3 | American Forks (Okanogan-Wenatchee NF)

Total sites: 12, RV sites: 12, No water, Vault/pit toilet, Tent & RV camping: $15, Open May-Sep, Max Length: 45ft, Reservations accepted, Elev: 2789ft/850m, Tel: 509-653-1401, Nearest town: Cliffdell. GPS: 46.976074, -121.158691

182 • C3 | Bumping Lake Lower (Okanogan-Wenatchee NF)

Total sites: 20, RV sites: 20, Central water, No toilets, No showers, No RV dump, Tent & RV camping: $25, Open May-Oct, Max Length: 154ft, Reservations accepted, Elev: 3451ft/1052m, Tel: 509-653-1401, Nearest town: Yakima. GPS: 46.861387, -121.300921

183 • C3 | Bumping Lake Upper (Okanogan-Wenatchee NF)

Total sites: 45, RV sites: 44, Central water, Vault/pit toilet, No showers, No RV dump, Tent & RV camping: $25, Open May-Oct, Max Length: 55ft, Reservations accepted, Elev: 3478ft/1060m, Tel: 541-338-7869, Nearest town: Cliffdell. GPS: 46.855464, -121.304523

184 • C3 | Cash Prairie TH (Okanogan-Wenatchee NF)

Total sites: 1, No water, No toilets, Tent & RV camping: Free, Elev: 6298ft/1920m, Tel: 509-653-1401, Nearest town: Naches. GPS: 46.716617, -121.164099

185 • C3 | Cedar Springs (Okanogan-Wenatchee NF)

Total sites: 14, RV sites: 14, Central water, Vault/pit toilet, No showers, No RV dump, Tent & RV camping: $18, Open May-Oct, Max Length: 40ft, Reservations accepted, Elev: 2756ft/840m, Tel: 509-653-1401, Nearest town: Cliffdell. GPS: 46.971191, -121.162842

186 • C3 | Clear Lake North (Okanogan-Wenatchee NF)

Total sites: 36, RV sites: 36, No water, Vault/pit toilet, Tent & RV camping: $15, Open May-Sep, Max Length: 22ft, Reservations not accepted, Elev: 3064ft/934m, Tel: 509-653-1401, Nearest town: Naches. GPS: 46.633946, -121.267531

187 • C3 | Clear Lake South (Okanogan-Wenatchee NF)

Total sites: 31, RV sites: 31, Central water, Vault/pit toilet, No showers, No RV dump, Tent & RV camping: $15, Open May-Sep, Max Length: 22ft, Reservations not accepted, Elev: 3064ft/934m, Tel: 509-653-1401, Nearest town: Naches. GPS: 46.627686, -121.267822

188 • C3 | Cottonwood (Naches) (Okanogan-Wenatchee NF)

Total sites: 4, RV sites: 4, Central water, Vault/pit toilet, No showers, No RV dump, Tent & RV camping: $18, Open May-Oct, Max Length: 40ft, Reservations accepted, Elev: 2316ft/706m, Tel: 509-653-1401, Nearest town: Cliffdell. GPS: 46.906982, -121.025879

189 • C3 | Cougar Flat (Okanogan-Wenatchee NF)

Total sites: 12, RV sites: 8, Central water, Vault/pit toilet, No showers, No RV dump, Tent & RV camping: $18, Also walk-to sites, Open May-Oct, Max Length: 40ft, Reservations accepted, Elev: 3140ft/957m, Tel: 509-653-1404, Nearest town: Cliffdell. GPS: 46.916499, -121.231108

190 • C3 | Crow Creek (Okanogan-Wenatchee NF)

Total sites: 15, RV sites: 15, No water, Vault/pit toilet, Tent & RV camping: $10, Discover Pass ($10/day or $30/year) required, Sno-Park permit required if camping between 11/01 and 05/01, Max Length: 30ft, Reservations not accepted, Elev: 2772ft/845m, Tel: 509-653-1401, Nearest town: Naches. GPS: 47.016042, -121.137167

191 • C3 | Dog Lake (Okanogan-Wenatchee NF)

Total sites: 8, RV sites: 8, No water, Vault/pit toilet, Tent & RV camping: $8, Open Jun-Sep, Max Length: Trlr-20ft, RV-24ft, Reservations not accepted, Elev: 4196ft/1279m, Tel: 509-653-1401, Nearest town: Naches. GPS: 46.655000, -121.360000

192 • C3 | Fish Lake Way Horse Camp (Okanogan-Wenatchee NF)

Total sites: 12, RV sites: 12, No water, Vault/pit toilet, Tent & RV camping: Fee unk, Elev: 3904ft/1190m, Tel: 509-653-1401, Nearest town: Naches. GPS: 46.833583, -121.351408

193 • C3 | Government Meadows Horse Camp (Mt Baker-Snoqualmie NF)

Total sites: 5, RV sites: 5, No water, No toilets, Tent & RV camping: Fee unk, Elev: 4800ft/1463m, Tel: 360-825-6585, Nearest town: Enumclaw. GPS: 47.084409, -121.403799

194 • C3 | Half Camp Horse Camp (Mt Baker-Snoqualmie NF)

Total sites: 9, RV sites: 9, No water, Vault/pit toilet, Tent & RV camping: Free, Elev: 3927ft/1197m, Tel: 360-825-6585, Nearest town: Enumclaw. GPS: 46.974083, -121.496039

195 • C3 | Halfway Flat (Okanogan-Wenatchee NF)

Total sites: 8, RV sites: 8, Central water, Vault/pit toilet, No showers, No RV dump, Tent & RV camping: $10-18, Open May-Sep, Max Length: 150ft, Reservations accepted, Elev: 2543ft/775m, Tel: 509-653-1436, Nearest town: Naches. GPS: 46.980112, -121.095801

196 • C3 | Hause Creek (Okanogan-Wenatchee NF)

Total sites: 42, RV sites: 37, No water, Vault/pit toilet, No showers, No RV dump, Tent & RV camping: $22, Open May-Oct, Max Length: 74ft, Reservations accepted, Elev: 2559ft/780m, Tel: 509-653-1401, Nearest town: Naches. GPS: 46.674561, -121.079590

197 • C3 | Hells Crossing East (Okanogan-Wenatchee NF)

Total sites: 10, RV sites: 6, Central water, Vault/pit toilet, No showers, No RV dump, Tent & RV camping: $18, Open May-Oct, Max Length: 40ft, Reservations accepted, Elev: 3287ft/1002m, Tel: 541-338-7869, Nearest town: Cliffdell. GPS: 46.965778, -121.263983

198 • C3 | Hells Crossing West (Okanogan-Wenatchee NF)

Total sites: 8, RV sites: 6, Central water, Vault/pit toilet, No

showers, No RV dump, Tent & RV camping: $18, Open May-Oct, Max Length: 40ft, Reservations accepted, Elev: 3265ft/995m, Tel: 541-338-7869, Nearest town: Cliffdell. GPS: 46.965198, -121.266752

199 • C3 | Icewater Creek (Okanogan-Wenatchee NF)

Total sites: 14, RV sites: 14, No water, Vault/pit toilet, Tent & RV camping: $18, Reservations not accepted, Elev: 2822ft/860m, Tel: 509-852-1100, Nearest town: Cle Elum. GPS: 47.113000, -120.904000

200 • C3 | Indian Creek (Okanogan-Wenatchee NF)

Total sites: 39, RV sites: 39, Central water, Vault/pit toilet, No showers, No RV dump, Tent & RV camping: $22, Open May-Oct, Max Length: 40ft, Reservations accepted, Elev: 3002ft/915m, Tel: 541-338-7869, Nearest town: Naches. GPS: 46.644287, -121.242188

201 • C3 | Indian Creek TH (Okanogan-Wenatchee NF)

Total sites: 6, RV sites: 6, No water, No toilets, Tent & RV camping: Free, Reservations not accepted, Elev: 3360ft/1024m, Nearest town: Naches. GPS: 46.664767, -121.285207

202 • C3 | Kaner Flat (Okanogan-Wenatchee NF)

Total sites: 49, RV sites: 49, Central water, Flush toilet, No showers, No RV dump, Tent & RV camping: $20, Open May-Sep, Max Length: 105ft, Reservations accepted, Elev: 2812ft/857m, Tel: 509-653-1401, Nearest town: American River. GPS: 47.011382, -121.129520

203 • C3 | Lion Rock Spring (Okanogan-Wenatchee NF)

Total sites: 3, RV sites: 3, No water, Vault/pit toilet, Tent & RV camping: Free, Open Jun-Oct, Max Length: 22ft, Reservations not accepted, Elev: 6260ft/1908m, Tel: 509-852-1100, Nearest town: Ellensburg. GPS: 47.251369, -120.581709

204 • C3 | Little Naches (Okanogan-Wenatchee NF)

Total sites: 21, RV sites: 21, Central water, Vault/pit toilet, No showers, No RV dump, Tent & RV camping: $22, Open May-Oct, Max Length: 48ft, Reservations accepted, Elev: 2615ft/797m, Tel: 509-653-1401, Nearest town: Cliffdell. GPS: 46.989985, -121.098032

205 • C3 | Lodgepole (Okanogan-Wenatchee NF)

Total sites: 34, RV sites: 34, Central water, Vault/pit toilet, No showers, No RV dump, Tent & RV camping: $20, Open May-Oct, Max Length: 101ft, Reservations accepted, Elev: 3596ft/1096m, Tel: 541-338-7869, Nearest town: American River. GPS: 46.915978, -121.384016

206 • C3 | Manastash Camp/Sno-Park (Okanogan-Wenatchee NF)

Total sites: 14, RV sites: 14, No water, Vault/pit toilet, Tent & RV camping: $10, Open Jun-Nov, Reservations not accepted, Elev: 4341ft/1323m, Tel: 509-852-1100, Nearest town: Ellensburg. GPS: 47.034743, -120.953608

207 • C3 | Mesatchee Creek Horse Camp (Okanogan-Wenatchee NF)

Total sites: 3, RV sites: 3, No water, Vault/pit toilet, Tent & RV camping: Free, Elev: 3664ft/1117m, Tel: 509-653-1401, Nearest town: Naches. GPS: 46.912788, -121.405879

208 • C3 | Milk Pond (Okanogan-Wenatchee NF)

Total sites: 5, RV sites: 5, No water, Vault/pit toilet, Tent & RV camping: Free, Elev: 2989ft/911m, Tel: 509-653-1401, Nearest town: Cliffdell. GPS: 46.987000, -121.063000

209 • C3 | Mineral Springs (Okanogan-Wenatchee NF)

Total sites: 6, RV sites: 6, No water, Vault/pit toilet, Tent & RV camping: $18, Reservable group site $80, Reservations not accepted, Elev: 2753ft/839m, Tel: 509-852-1100, Nearest town: Cle Elum. GPS: 47.290154, -120.699695

210 • C3 | MJB TH (Okanogan-Wenatchee NF)

Total sites: 2, RV sites: 2, No water, No toilets, Tent & RV camping: Fee unk, Elev: 5335ft/1626m, Tel: 509-653-1401, Nearest town: Naches. GPS: 46.734779, -121.130911

211 • C3 | Peninsula (Okanogan-Wenatchee NF)

Total sites: 60, RV sites: 60, No water, Vault/pit toilet, Tent & RV camping: $10, Reservations not accepted, Elev: 3077ft/938m, Tel: 509-653-1401, Nearest town: Naches. GPS: 46.633862, -121.146835

212 • C3 | Pleasant Valley (Okanogan-Wenatchee NF)

Total sites: 12, RV sites: 12, Central water, Vault/pit toilet, No showers, No RV dump, Tent & RV camping: $20, Open May-Oct, Max Length: 40ft, Reservations accepted, Elev: 3406ft/1038m, Tel: 541-338-7869, Nearest town: Cliffdell. GPS: 46.942627, -121.325439

213 • C3 | Quartz Mt (Okanogan-Wenatchee NF)

Total sites: 3, RV sites: 3, Tent & RV camping: Free, Max Length: 22ft, Elev: 6116ft/1864m, Nearest town: Ellensburg. GPS: 47.076645, -121.079628

214 • C3 | Rattlesnake TH (Okanogan-Wenatchee NF)

Total sites: 3, RV sites: 3, Tent & RV camping: Free, Elev: 3100ft/945m, Tel: 509 996-4000, Nearest town: Naches. GPS: 46.795487, -121.100495

215 • C3 | Riders Camp (Okanogan-Wenatchee NF)

Total sites: 5, RV sites: 5, No water, Vault/pit toilet, Tent & RV camping: $10, Reservations not accepted, Elev: 4206ft/1282m, Tel: 509-852-1100, Nearest town: Ellensburg. GPS: 47.029255, -120.934953

216 • C3 | Sand Flat Horse Camp (Mt Baker-Snoqualmie NF)

Total sites: 6, RV sites: 6, No water, Vault/pit toilet, Tent & RV camping: $5, Stock water, Reservations not accepted, Elev: 4009ft/1222m, Tel: 360-825-6585, Nearest town: Enumclaw. GPS: 46.961135, -121.481126

217 • C3 | Sand Ridge TH (Okanogan-Wenatchee NF)

Total sites: 2, RV sites: 2, No water, Vault/pit toilet, Tent & RV camping: Free, Elev: 3550ft/1082m, Tel: 509-653-1401, Nearest town: Naches. GPS: 46.651026, -121.279787

218 • C3 | Sawmill Flat (Okanogan-Wenatchee NF)

Total sites: 23, RV sites: 15, Central water, Vault/pit toilet, No showers, No RV dump, Tent & RV camping: $20, Open May-Oct, Max Length: 60ft, Reservations accepted, Elev: 2556ft/779m, Tel: 509-653-1401, Nearest town: Naches. GPS: 46.974365, -121.096436

219 • C3 | Scatter Creek TH (Okanogan-Wenatchee NF)

Total sites: 4, RV sites: 4, No water, Vault/pit toilet, Tent & RV camping: Fee unk, Bridge out on road - no vehicle access to site, Elev: 3294ft/1004m, Tel: 509-653-1401, Nearest town: Naches. GPS: 46.577474, -121.357305

220 • C3 | Silver Springs (Mt Baker-Snoqualmie NF)

Total sites: 55, RV sites: 55, Central water, Flush toilet, No showers, No RV dump, Tent & RV camping: $28-32, 5 double sites, Open May-Sep, Max Length: 46ft, Reservations accepted, Elev: 2740ft/835m, Tel: 360-825-6585, Nearest town: Greenwater. GPS: 46.993652, -121.531250

221 • C3 | Soda Springs (Okanogan-Wenatchee NF)

Total sites: 26, RV sites: 26, Central water, Vault/pit toilet, No showers, No RV dump, Tent & RV camping: $20, Open May-Oct, Max Length: 100ft, Reservations accepted, Elev: 3035ft/925m, Tel: 509-653-1401, Nearest town: Cliffdell. GPS: 46.925781, -121.214355

222 • C3 | Soda Springs (Gifford Pinchot NF)

Total sites: 6, RV sites: 6, No water, No toilets, Tent & RV camping: Free, No services in winter, Open all year, Max Length: 18ft, Reservations not accepted, Elev: 3224ft/983m, Tel: 360-497-1100, Nearest town: Packwood. GPS: 46.704269, -121.481736

223 • C3 | Taneum (Okanogan-Wenatchee NF)

Total sites: 13, RV sites: 13, Central water, Vault/pit toilet, No showers, No RV dump, Tent & RV camping: $18, Open May-Sep, Reservations not accepted, Elev: 2556ft/779m, Tel: 509-852-1100, Nearest town: Cle Elum. GPS: 47.108695, -120.856139

224 • C3 | Taneum Junction ORV (Okanogan-Wenatchee NF)

Total sites: 15, RV sites: 15, No water, Vault/pit toilet, Tent & RV camping: $5, Open May-Nov, Reservations not accepted, Elev: 2851ft/869m, Tel: 509-852-1100, Nearest town: Cle Elum. GPS: 47.112000, -120.933000

225 • C3 | Walupt Horse Camp (Gifford Pinchot NF)

Total sites: 9, RV sites: 9, Central water, Vault/pit toilet, No showers, No RV dump, Tent & RV camping: $16, Open Jun-Sep, Max Length: 22ft, Reservations not accepted, Elev: 3839ft/1170m, Tel: 541-338-7869, Nearest town: Randle. GPS: 46.425475, -121.489572

226 • C3 | Walupt Lake (Gifford Pinchot NF)

Total sites: 42, RV sites: 27, Central water, Vault/pit toilet, No showers, No RV dump, Tent & RV camping: $24, Also walk-to sites, on lakeshore, Open Jun-Sep, Max Length: 30ft, Reservations accepted, Elev: 3980ft/1213m, Tel: 541-338-7869, Nearest town: Randle. GPS: 46.423584, -121.473877

227 • C3 | White Pass Lake (Okanogan-Wenatchee NF)

Total sites: 10, RV sites: 10, No water, Vault/pit toilet, Tent & RV camping: $8, Open Jun-Sep, Max Length: 20ft, Reservations not accepted, Elev: 4442ft/1354m, Tel: 509-653-1401, Nearest town: Naches. GPS: 46.644486, -121.380960

228 • C3 | Willows (Okanogan-Wenatchee NF)

Total sites: 16, RV sites: 16, Central water, Vault/pit toilet, No showers, No RV dump, Tent & RV camping: $18, Open May-Oct, Max Length: 35ft, Reservations accepted, Elev: 2474ft/754m, Tel: 509-653-1401, Nearest town: Naches. GPS: 46.672607, -121.039795

229 • C3 | Windy Point (Okanogan-Wenatchee NF)

Total sites: 15, RV sites: 15, Central water, Vault/pit toilet, No showers, No RV dump, Tent & RV camping: $18, Open May-Oct, Max Length: 42ft, Reservations accepted, Elev: 2077ft/633m, Tel: 541-338-7869, Nearest town: Naches. GPS: 46.693060, -120.907220

230 • C3 | Wish Poosh (Okanogan-Wenatchee NF)

Total sites: 34, RV sites: 34, Central water, Flush toilet, No showers, No RV dump, Tent & RV camping: $25, Open May-Sep, Max Length: 54ft, Reservations accepted, Elev: 2284ft/696m, Tel: 509-852-1100, Nearest town: Cle Elum. GPS: 47.279933, -121.088678

231 • C5 | Alder Thicket (Umatilla NF)

Total sites: 5, RV sites: 5, No water, Vault/pit toilet, Tent & RV camping: Free, Open May-Oct, Elev: 5141ft/1567m, Tel: 509-843-1891, Nearest town: Pomeroy. GPS: 46.258932, -117.567041

232 • C5 | Big Springs (Umatilla NF)

Total sites: 10, RV sites: 5, No water, Vault/pit toilet, Tent & RV camping: Free, Open all year, Reservations not accepted, Elev: 5066ft/1544m, Tel: 541-278-3716, Nearest town: Pomeroy. GPS: 46.231099, -117.543764

233 • C5 | Forest Boundary (Umatilla NF)

Total sites: 6, RV sites: 6, No water, Vault/pit toilet, Tent & RV camping: Free, Reservations not accepted, Elev: 4506ft/1373m, Tel: 541-278-3716, Nearest town: Pomeroy. GPS: 46.292971, -117.558402

234 • C5 | Ladybug (Umatilla NF)

Total sites: 7, RV sites: 7, No water, Vault/pit toilet, Tent & RV camping: $8, No fees/services Dec-Mar, Open Apr-Nov, Reservations not accepted, Elev: 3246ft/989m, Tel: 509-843-1891, Nearest town: Pomeroy. GPS: 46.196755, -117.668872

235 • C5 | Panjab (Umatilla NF)

Total sites: 3, RV sites: 0, No water, Vault/pit toilet, Tents only: $8, Open Jun-Nov, Reservations not accepted, Elev: 2991ft/912m, Tel: 509-843-1891, Nearest town: Pomeroy. GPS: 46.204167, -117.706922

236 • C5 | Pataha (Umatilla NF)

Total sites: 3, RV sites: 2, No water, Vault/pit toilet, Tent & RV camping: Free, No services Dec-Mar, Open all year, Reservations not accepted, Elev: 3993ft/1217m, Tel: 509-843-1891, Nearest town: Pomeroy. GPS: 46.292000, -117.514000

237 • C5 | Tucannon (Umatilla NF)

Total sites: 18, RV sites: 15, No water, Vault/pit toilet, Tent & RV camping: $8, No fees/services Nov-Feb, Open all year, Reservations not accepted, Elev: 2694ft/821m, Tel: 509-843-1891, Nearest town: Pomeroy. GPS: 46.242903, -117.688108

238 • D2 | Beaver (Gifford Pinchot NF)

Total sites: 23, RV sites: 23, Central water, Flush toilet, No showers, No RV dump, Tent & RV camping: $24, Group site $125, Open May-Sep, Max Length: 40ft, Reservations accepted, Elev: 1116ft/340m, Tel: 509-395-3400, Nearest town: Carson. GPS: 45.853406, -121.955136

239 • D2 | Cold Spring Indian (Gifford Pinchot NF)

Total sites: 12, RV sites: 12, No water, Vault/pit toilet, Tent & RV camping: Free, Reservations not accepted, Elev: 4185ft/1276m, Tel: 509-395-3400, Nearest town: Trout Lake. GPS: 46.084754, -121.758225

240 • D2 | Crest Camp (Gifford Pinchot NF)

Total sites: 3, RV sites: 1, No water, Vault/pit toilet, Tent & RV camping: Fee unk, On PCT, Elev: 3547ft/1081m, Tel: 509-395-3400, Nearest town: Carson. GPS: 45.909247, -121.802613

241 • D2 | Cultus Creek (Gifford Pinchot NF)

Total sites: 50, RV sites: 50, No water, Vault/pit toilet, Tent & RV camping: $10, Open Jun-Sep, Max Length: 32ft, Reservations not accepted, Elev: 4016ft/1224m, Tel: 509-395-3400, Nearest town: Trout Lake. GPS: 46.047607, -121.755127

242 • D2 | Falls Creek Horse Camp (Gifford Pinchot NF)

Total sites: 4, RV sites: 4, No water, Vault/pit toilet, Tent & RV camping: Free, Large RVs not recommended, Open Jun-Sep, Reservations not accepted, Elev: 3602ft/1098m, Tel: 509-395-3402, Nearest town: Carson. GPS: 45.966551, -121.846105

243 • D2 | Forlorn Lakes (Gifford Pinchot NF)

Total sites: 25, RV sites: 25, No water, Vault/pit toilet, Tent & RV camping: $10, Open Jun-Oct, Max Length: 18ft, Reservations not accepted, Elev: 3766ft/1148m, Tel: 509-395-3400, Nearest town: Trout Lake. GPS: 45.960627, -121.754844

244 • D2 | Goose Lake (Gifford Pinchot NF)

Total sites: 18, RV sites: 0, No water, Vault/pit toilet, Tents only: $10, RVs not recommended, Open Jul-Oct, Reservations not accepted, Elev: 3287ft/1002m, Tel: 509-395-3400, Nearest town: Trout Lake. GPS: 45.939799, -121.758072

245 • D2 | Govt Mineral Springs (Gifford Pinchot NF)

Total sites: 5, RV sites: 5, No water, Vault/pit toilet, Tent & RV camping: $5, Open May-Sep, Max Length: 18ft, Reservations not accepted, Elev: 1280ft/390m, Tel: 509-395-3400, Nearest town: Carson. GPS: 45.882297, -121.995962

246 • D2 | Huckleberry Access (Gifford Pinchot NF)

Total sites: 3, RV sites: 3, Central water, Vault/pit toilet, No showers, No RV dump, Tent & RV camping: Free, Open May-Oct, Max Length: 32ft, Elev: 4216ft/1285m, Tel: 509-395-3400, Nearest town: Trout Lake. GPS: 46.091084, -121.799871

247 • D2 | Kalama Horse Camp (Gifford Pinchot NF)

Total sites: 17, RV sites: 17, No water, Vault/pit toilet, Tent & RV camping: $8-12, Corrals - high lines - stock troughs, Reservations not accepted, Elev: 2106ft/642m, Tel: 360-449-7800, Nearest town: Cougar. GPS: 46.143417, -122.323993

248 • D2 | Lewis River Horse Camp (Gifford Pinchot NF)

Total sites: 9, RV sites: 9, No water, Vault/pit toilet, Tent & RV camping: $5, Not maintained in winter, Open all year, Reservations not accepted, Elev: 1896ft/578m, Tel: 360-449-7800, Nearest town: Northwoods. GPS: 46.184918, -121.851719

249 • D2 | Little Goose (Gifford Pinchot NF)

Total sites: 6, RV sites: 0, No water, Vault/pit toilet, Tents only: Free, Reservations not accepted, Elev: 4049ft/1234m, Tel: 509-395-3400, Nearest town: Trout Lake. GPS: 46.037811, -121.713962

250 • D2 | Little Goose Horse Camp (Gifford Pinchot NF)

Total sites: 7, RV sites: 7, No water, Vault/pit toilet, Tent & RV camping: Free, Max Length: 24ft, Elev: 4088ft/1246m, Tel: 509-395-3400, Nearest town: Trout Lake. GPS: 46.034912, -121.715088

251 • D2 | Lower Falls (Gifford Pinchot NF)

Total sites: 44, RV sites: 44, Central water, Vault/pit toilet, No showers, No RV dump, Tent & RV camping: $15, Open Apr-Oct, Max Length: 36ft, Reservations accepted, Elev: 1640ft/500m, Tel: 360-449-7800, Nearest town: Northwoods. GPS: 46.156286, -121.879205

252 • D2 | Meadow Creek Indian (Gifford Pinchot NF)

Total sites: 3, RV sites: 3, No water, Vault/pit toilet, Tent & RV camping: Free, Elev: 4139ft/1262m, Tel: 509-395-3400, Nearest town: Trout Lake. GPS: 46.069309, -121.756569

253 • D2 | Moss Creek (Gifford Pinchot NF)

Total sites: 17, RV sites: 14, Central water, Vault/pit toilet, No showers, No RV dump, Tent & RV camping: $20, Open May-Sep, Max Length: 40ft, Reservations accepted, Elev: 1444ft/440m, Tel: 509-395-3400, Nearest town: White Salmon. GPS: 45.794247, -121.634552

254 • D2 | Mt Adams Horse Camp (Gifford Pinchot NF)

Total sites: 11, RV sites: 11, No water, Vault/pit toilet, Tent & RV camping: $5, Reservations not accepted, Elev: 2690ft/820m, Tel: 509-395-3400, Nearest town: Trout Lake. GPS: 46.054254, -121.539594

255 • D2 | Oklahoma (Gifford Pinchot NF)

Total sites: 22, RV sites: 20, Central water, Vault/pit toilet, No showers, No RV dump, Tent & RV camping: $20, Open May-Sep, Max Length: 40ft, Reservations accepted, Elev: 1791ft/546m, Tel: 509-395-3400, Nearest town: Cook. GPS: 45.872313, -121.623184

256 • D2 | Panther Creek (Gifford Pinchot NF)

Total sites: 33, RV sites: 33, Central water, Vault/pit toilet, No showers, No RV dump, Tent & RV camping: $22, Open May-Sep, Max Length: 40ft, Reservations accepted, Elev: 988ft/301m,

Tel: 509-395-3400, Nearest town: Carson. GPS: 45.820314, -121.877338

257 • D2 | Paradise Creek (Gifford Pinchot NF)

Total sites: 42, RV sites: 42, Central water, Vault/pit toilet, No showers, No RV dump, Tent & RV camping: $22, Open May-Sep, Max Length: 40ft, Reservations accepted, Elev: 1634ft/498m, Tel: 509-395-3400, Nearest town: Carson. GPS: 45.948893, -121.935065

258 • D2 | Peterson Prairie (Gifford Pinchot NF)

Total sites: 27, RV sites: 27, Central water, Vault/pit toilet, No showers, No RV dump, Tent & RV camping: $20, 2 group sites: $100, Open Jun-Sep, Max Length: 40ft, Reservations accepted, Elev: 3041ft/927m, Tel: 541-338-7869, Nearest town: Trout Lake. GPS: 45.968461, -121.659451

259 • D2 | Smokey Creek (Gifford Pinchot NF)

Total sites: 3, RV sites: 0, No water, Vault/pit toilet, Tents only: Free, Reservations not accepted, Elev: 3668ft/1118m, Tel: 509-395-3400, Nearest town: Trout Lake. GPS: 46.030785, -121.687629

260 • D2 | Sunset Falls (Gifford Pinchot NF)

Total sites: 18, RV sites: 10, No water, Vault/pit toilet, Tent & RV camping: $18, Open all year, Max Length: 40ft, Reservations accepted, Elev: 1073ft/327m, Tel: 360-449-7800, Nearest town: Yacolt. GPS: 45.818302, -122.252246

261 • D2 | Tillicum (Gifford Pinchot NF)

Total sites: 15, RV sites: 15, No water, Vault/pit toilet, Tent & RV camping: $5, Open Jul-Sep, Max Length: 18ft, Reservations not accepted, Elev: 3888ft/1185m, Tel: 360-449-7800, Nearest town: Trout Lake. GPS: 46.123291, -121.779785

262 • D2 | Trout Lake Creek (Gifford Pinchot NF)

Total sites: 17, RV sites: 0, No water, Vault/pit toilet, Tents only: $10, Reservations not accepted, Elev: 2185ft/666m, Tel: 509-395-3400, Nearest town: Trout Lake. GPS: 46.056428, -121.611867

263 • D2 | Twin Falls (Gifford Pinchot NF)

Total sites: 5, RV sites: 0, No water, Vault/pit toilet, Tents only: Free, Walk-to sites, No services off-season, Open all year, Elev: 2776ft/846m, Tel: 509-395-3402, Nearest town: Trout Lake. GPS: 46.215511, -121.669012

264 • D3 | Morrison Creek (Gifford Pinchot NF)

Total sites: 12, No water, Vault/pit toilet, Tents only: Free, Rough road - RVs not recommended, Open Jun-Oct, Reservations not accepted, Elev: 4738ft/1444m, Tel: 509-395-3402, Nearest town: Trout Lake. GPS: 46.129594, -121.516730

265 • D5 | Godman (Umatilla NF)

Total sites: 8, RV sites: 3, No water, Vault/pit toilet, No showers, No RV dump, Tent & RV camping: Free, Open May-Nov, Reservations not accepted, Elev: 5702ft/1738m, Tel: 509-843-1891, Nearest town: Pomeroy. GPS: 46.099644, -117.786664

266 • D5 | Midway (Umatilla NF)

Total sites: 5, RV sites: 5, No water, Vault/pit toilet, Tent & RV camping: $8, No fees/services Dec-Mar, Open all year, Reservations not accepted, Elev: 5149ft/1569m, Tel: 509-843-1891, Nearest town: Pomeroy. GPS: 46.166658, -117.763064

267 • D5 | Misery Spring (Umatilla NF)

Total sites: 5, RV sites: 5, No water, Vault/pit toilet, No showers, No RV dump, Tent & RV camping: Free, No services/Limited access Nov-May, Stay limit: 14 days, Open all year, Reservations not accepted, Elev: 6147ft/1874m, Tel: 541-278-3716, Nearest town: Pomeroy. GPS: 46.120366, -117.484589

268 • D5 | Teal (Umatilla NF)

Total sites: 7, RV sites: 7, No water, Vault/pit toilet, Tent & RV camping: Fee unk, No services Dec-Mar, Open all year, Elev: 5663ft/1726m, Tel: 509-843-1891, Nearest town: Pomeroy. GPS: 46.189066, -117.573111

269 • D5 | Wickiup (Umatilla NF)

Total sites: 7, RV sites: 7, No water, Vault/pit toilet, Tent & RV camping: Free, No services Dec-Mar, Elev: 5968ft/1819m, Tel: 509-843-1891, Nearest town: Pomeroy. GPS: 46.137000, -117.435000

West Virginia

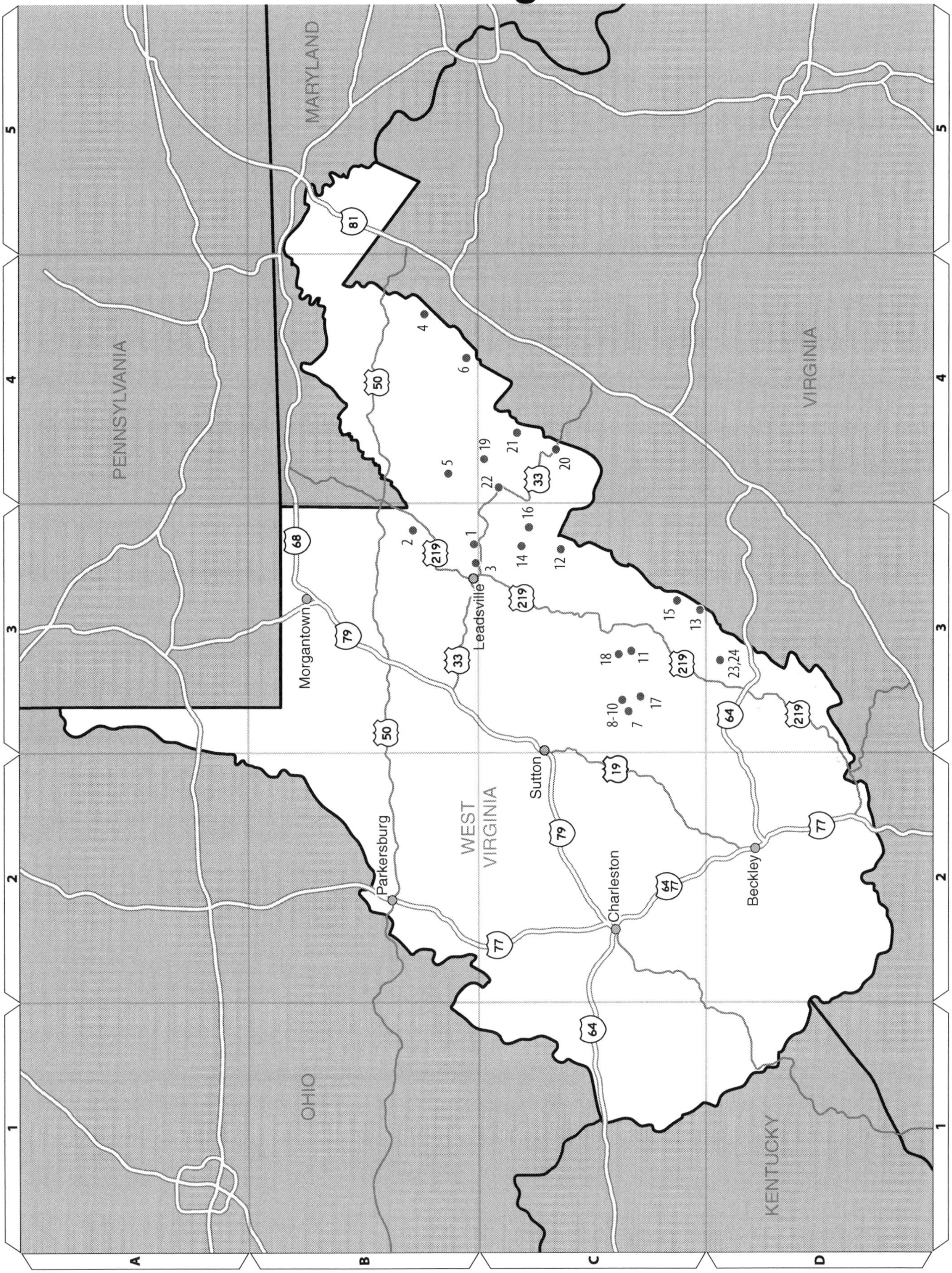

Map	ID	Map	ID
B3	1-3	C4	19-22
B4	4-6	D3	23-24
C3	7-18		

Alphabetical List of Camping Areas

1 • B3 | Bear Heaven (Monongahela NF)

Total sites: 8, RV sites: 0, No water, Vault/pit toilet, Tents only: $10, Stay limit: 14 days, Open Apr-Nov, Reservations not accepted, Elev: 3445ft/1050m, Tel: 304-478-2000, Nearest town: Elkins. GPS: 38.928949, -79.675647

2 • B3 | Horseshoe (Monongahela NF)

Total sites: 21, RV sites: 18, Central water, Vault/pit toilet, No showers, No RV dump, Tent & RV camping: $22, Group sites available - $20-$85, Open May-Sep, Max Length: 35ft, Reservations accepted, Elev: 1768ft/539m, Tel: 304-478-2481, Nearest town: Parsons. GPS: 39.180386, -79.601185

3 • B3 | Stuart (Monongahela NF)

Total sites: 26, RV sites: 26, Elec sites: 26, Central water, Flush toilet, Free showers, RV dump, Tent & RV camping: $30, Group site: $55-$130, Open Apr-Oct, Max Length: 45ft, Reservations accepted, Elev: 2346ft/715m, Tel: 304-636-5070, Nearest town: Elkins. GPS: 38.917480, -79.770996

4 • B4 | Hawk (George Washington & Jefferson NF)

Total sites: 15, RV sites: 15, Central water, Vault/pit toilet, No showers, No RV dump, Tent & RV camping: Free, Open Apr-Dec, Max Length: 16ft, Reservations not accepted, Elev: 1363ft/415m, Tel: 540-984-4101, Nearest town: Intermont. GPS: 39.116244, -78.499712

5 • B4 | Red Creek (Monongahela NF)

Total sites: 12, RV sites: 12, Central water, Vault/pit toilet, No showers, No RV dump, Tent & RV camping: $11, Stay limit: 14 days, Open Apr-Nov, Reservations not accepted, Elev: 3878ft/1182m, Tel: 304-257-4488, Nearest town: Petersburg. GPS: 39.031738, -79.316406

6 • B4 | Trout Pond (George Washington & Jefferson NF)

Total sites: 36, RV sites: 36, Elec sites: 11, Central water, Flush toilet, Free showers, RV dump, Tents: $25/RVs: $32, Open May-Oct, Max Length: 99ft, Reservations accepted, Elev: 1995ft/608m, Tel: 304-897-6450, Nearest town: Wardensville. GPS: 38.953771, -78.733634

7 • C3 | Big Rock (Monongahela NF)

Total sites: 5, RV sites: 5, Central water, Vault/pit toilet, No showers, No RV dump, Tent & RV camping: $10, No large RVs, Stay limit: 14 days, Open Mar-Nov, Reservations not accepted, Elev: 2251ft/686m, Tel: 304-846-2695, Nearest town: Richwood. GPS: 38.296109, -80.523824

8 • C3 | Bishop Knob (Monongahela NF)

Total sites: 54, RV sites: 54, Central water, Vault/pit toilet, No showers, No RV dump, Tent & RV camping: $8, Stay limit: 14 days, Open Apr-Nov, Max Length: 40ft, Reservations not accepted, Elev: 3150ft/960m, Tel: 304-846-2695, Nearest town: Dyer. GPS: 38.337731, -80.489029

9 • C3 | Cranberry (Monongahela NF)

Total sites: 30, RV sites: 30, Central water, Vault/pit toilet, No showers, No RV dump, Tent & RV camping: $10, Stay limit: 14 days, Open Mar-Nov, Max Length: 40ft, Reservations not accepted, Elev: 2598ft/792m, Tel: 304-846-2695, Nearest town: Dyer. GPS: 38.325439, -80.441895

10 • C3 | Cranberry River Dispersed (Monongahela NF)

Total sites: 12, RV sites: 12, No water, Vault/pit toilet, Tent & RV camping: $5, Stay limit: 14 days, Open Mar-Nov, Reservations not accepted, Elev: 2385ft/727m, Tel: 304-846-2695, Nearest town: Richwood. GPS: 38.314442, -80.478049

11 • C3 | Day Run (Monongahela NF)

Total sites: 12, RV sites: 12, Central water, Vault/pit toilet, No showers, No RV dump, Tent & RV camping: $8, Stay limit: 14 days, Open Mar-Nov, Reservations not accepted, Elev: 3117ft/950m, Tel: 304-799-4334, Nearest town: Marlinton. GPS: 38.287618, -80.215737

12 • C3 | Island (Monongahela NF)

Total sites: 12, RV sites: 10, No water, Vault/pit toilet, Tent & RV camping: $10, 2 walk-to sites, Open Apr-Nov, Reservations not accepted, Elev: 2998ft/914m, Tel: 304-456-3335, Nearest town: Bartow. GPS: 38.579109, -79.704029

13 • C3 | Lake Sherwood (Monongahela NF)

Total sites: 153, RV sites: 153, Central water, Flush toilet, Free showers, RV dump, Tents: $16/RVs: $20, Open Apr-Oct, Max

Length: 40ft, Reservations accepted, Elev: 2684ft/818m, Tel: 304-536-2144, Nearest town: White Sulphur Springs. GPS: 38.007259, -80.010093

14 • C3 | Laurel Fork (Monongahela NF)

Total sites: 15, RV sites: 15, Central water, Vault/pit toilet, No showers, No RV dump, Tent & RV camping: $8, Open Apr-Dec, Reservations not accepted, Elev: 3120ft/951m, Tel: 304-456-3335, Nearest town: Elkins. GPS: 38.739990, -79.693359

15 • C3 | Pocahontas (Monongahela NF)

Total sites: 8, RV sites: 8, Central water, Vault/pit toilet, No showers, No RV dump, Tent & RV camping: $8, Stay limit: 14 days, Open Mar-Nov, Reservations not accepted, Elev: 2523ft/769m, Tel: 304-799-4334, Nearest town: Marlinton. GPS: 38.102051, -79.966553

16 • C3 | Spruce Knob Lake (Monongahela NF)

Total sites: 42, RV sites: 29, Central water, Vault/pit toilet, No showers, No RV dump, Tent & RV camping: $16, Stay limit: 14 days, Open Apr-Oct, Max Length: 30ft, Reservations accepted, Elev: 4055ft/1236m, Tel: 304-567-3082, Nearest town: Riverton. GPS: 38.707275, -79.588135

17 • C3 | Summit Lake (Monongahela NF)

Total sites: 33, RV sites: 33, Central water, Vault/pit toilet, No showers, No RV dump, Tent & RV camping: $10, Stay limit: 14 days, Open Apr-Nov, Reservations not accepted, Elev: 3527ft/1075m, Tel: 304-846-2695, Nearest town: Richwood. GPS: 38.248646, -80.444052

18 • C3 | Tea Creek (Monongahela NF)

Total sites: 28, RV sites: 28, Central water, Vault/pit toilet, No showers, No RV dump, Tent & RV camping: $10, Stay limit: 14 days, Open Apr-Nov, Reservations not accepted, Elev: 3028ft/923m, Tel: 304-799-4334, Nearest town: Marlinton. GPS: 38.341872, -80.232626

19 • C4 | Big Bend (Monongahela NF)

Total sites: 46, RV sites: 46, Central water, Flush toilet, No showers, RV dump, Tent & RV camping: $22-23, Stay limit: 14 days, Open Apr-Oct, Max Length: 30ft, Reservations accepted, Elev: 1234ft/376m, Tel: 304-358-3253, Nearest town: Petersburg. GPS: 38.889160, -79.239502

20 • C4 | Brandywine Lake (George Washington & Jefferson NF)

Total sites: 46, RV sites: 46, Central water, Flush toilet, Free showers, RV dump, Tent & RV camping: $18, No large RVs, $8 in off-season, Open May-Nov, Reservations not accepted, Elev: 2034ft/620m, Tel: 540-432-0187, Nearest town: Brandywine. GPS: 38.599609, -79.200928

21 • C4 | Camp Run (George Washington & Jefferson NF)

Total sites: 9, RV sites: 9, No water, Vault/pit toilet, Tent & RV camping: Free, Rough road, Open all year, Reservations not accepted, Elev: 1716ft/523m, Tel: 540-432-0187, Nearest town: Milam. GPS: 38.747117, -79.109119

22 • C4 | Seneca Shadows (Monongahela NF)

Total sites: 78, RV sites: 38, Elec sites: 13, Central water, Flush toilet, Free showers, No RV dump, Tents: $17-22/RVs: $30, Group site: $65, Stay limit: 14 days, Open Apr-Oct, Max Length: 90ft, Reservations accepted, Elev: 1834ft/559m, Tel: 304-567-3082, Nearest town: Riverton. GPS: 38.828154, -79.385544

23 • D3 | Blue Bend (Monongahela NF)

Total sites: 21, RV sites: 21, Central water, Flush toilet, Free showers, No RV dump, Tents: $16/RVs: $16-20, Stay limit: 14 days, Open May-Sep, Max Length: 60ft, Reservations accepted, Elev: 1998ft/609m, Tel: 304-536-2144, Nearest town: White Sulphur Springs. GPS: 37.921365, -80.267422

24 • D3 | Blue Meadow Group (Monongahela NF)

Total sites: 19, RV sites: 15, No water, Vault/pit toilet, Tent & RV camping: Fee unk, Group site: $75, Individual sites available when no group use, Open May-Sep, Max Length: 45ft, Reservations accepted, Elev: 1998ft/609m, Tel: 304-536-2144, Nearest town: White Sulphur Springs. GPS: 37.920654, -80.270752

Wisconsin

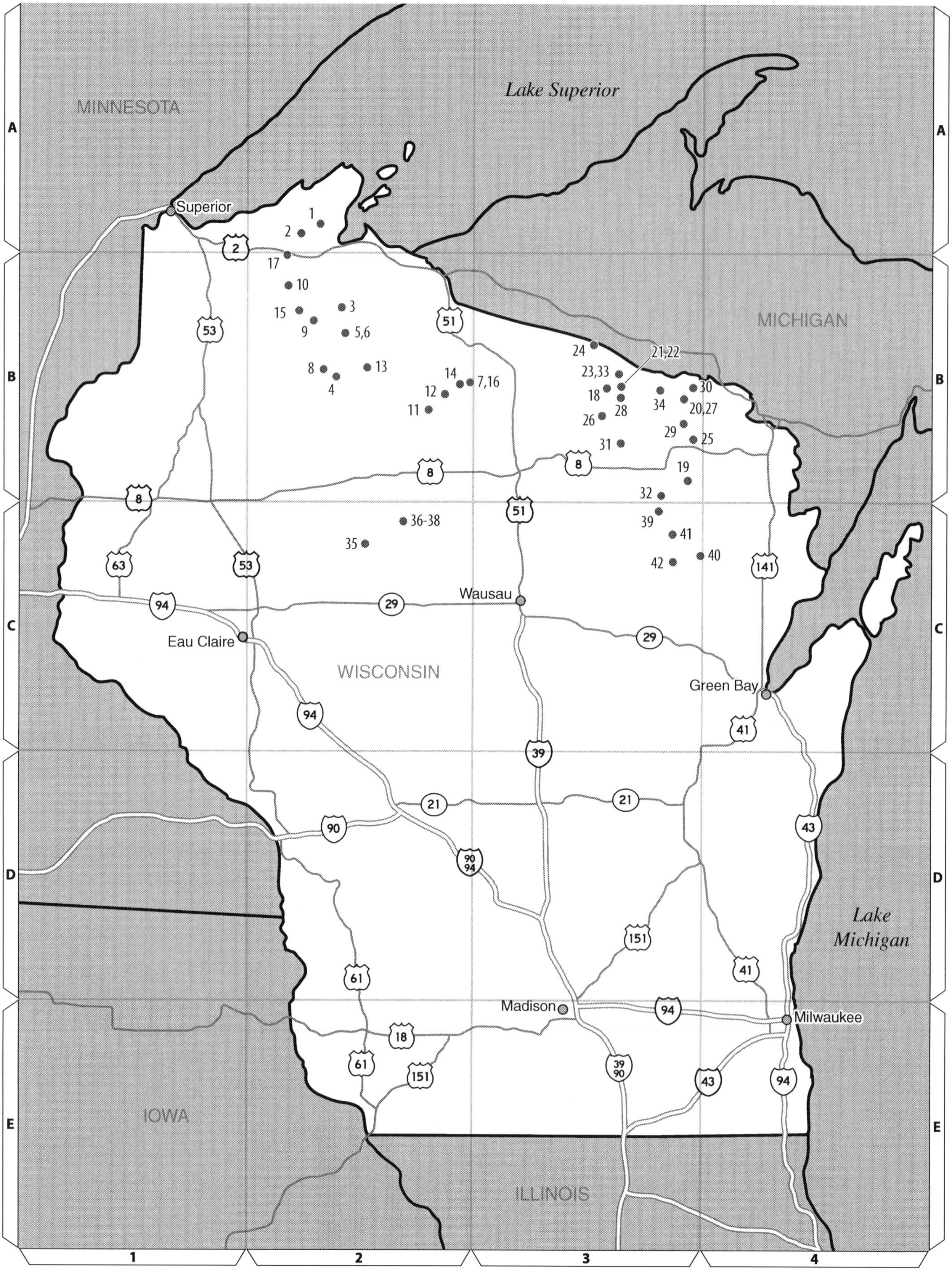

Lake Superior
MINNESOTA
MICHIGAN
WISCONSIN
IOWA
ILLINOIS
Lake Michigan
Superior
Wausau
Eau Claire
Green Bay
Madison
Milwaukee
A
B
C
D
E
1
2
3
4

Map	ID	Map	ID
A2	1-2	C2	35-38
B2	3-17	C3	39-42
B3	18-34		

Alphabetical List of Camping Areas

1 • A2 | Birch Grove (Chequamegon-Nicolet NF)

Total sites: 16, RV sites: 14, Central water, Vault/pit toilet, No showers, No RV dump, Tent & RV camping: $15, Open May-Sep, Max Length: 35ft, Reservations not accepted, Elev: 1135ft/346m, Tel: 715-373-2667, Nearest town: Washburn. GPS: 46.686035, -91.060547

2 • A2 | Horseshoe Lake (Chequamegon-Nicolet NF)

Total sites: 9, RV sites: 9, No water, Vault/pit toilet, Tent & RV camping: $12, Group site: $25, Horse ties, Open Apr-Nov, Reservations not accepted, Elev: 1296ft/395m, Tel: 715-373-2667, Nearest town: Ino. GPS: 46.642391, -91.183953

3 • B2 | Beaver Lake (Chequamegon-Nicolet NF)

Total sites: 10, RV sites: 5, Central water, Vault/pit toilet, No showers, No RV dump, Tent & RV camping: $15, Open May-Oct, Max Length: 35ft, Reservations accepted, Elev: 1460ft/445m, Tel: 715-264-2511, Nearest town: Mellen. GPS: 46.301270, -90.897705

4 • B2 | Black Lake (Chequamegon-Nicolet NF)

Total sites: 29, RV sites: 26, Central water, Vault/pit toilet, No showers, No RV dump, Tent & RV camping: $15, 3 walk-to sites, Open May-Oct, Max Length: 45ft, Reservations accepted, Elev: 1421ft/433m, Tel: 715-264-2511, Nearest town: Hayward. GPS: 45.988525, -90.929199

5 • B2 | Day Lake (Chequamegon-Nicolet NF)

Total sites: 55, RV sites: 52, Central water, Vault/pit toilet, No showers, No RV dump, Tent & RV camping: $18, Blueberry/Heron loops closed, Open May-Oct, Max Length: 60ft, Reservations accepted, Elev: 1466ft/447m, Tel: 715-264-2511, Nearest town: Clam Lake. GPS: 46.181192, -90.903699

6 • B2 | East Twin Lake (Chequamegon-Nicolet NF)

Total sites: 10, RV sites: 8, Central water, Vault/pit toilet, No showers, No RV dump, Tent & RV camping: $15, Open May-Oct, Max Length: 45ft, Reservations accepted, Elev: 1466ft/447m, Tel: 715-264-2511, Nearest town: Clam Lake. GPS: 46.192627, -90.859863

7 • B2 | Emily Lake (Chequamegon-Nicolet NF)

Total sites: 11, RV sites: 8, Central water, Vault/pit toilet, No showers, No RV dump, Tent & RV camping: $15, Open May-Oct, Reservations not accepted, Elev: 1585ft/483m, Tel: 715-762-2461, Nearest town: Park Falls. GPS: 45.964600, -90.010010

8 • B2 | Moose Lake (Chequamegon-Nicolet NF)

Total sites: 15, RV sites: 11, Central water, Vault/pit toilet, No showers, No RV dump, Tent & RV camping: $15, 4 walk-to sites, Open May-Sep, Max Length: 40ft, Reservations accepted, Elev: 1417ft/432m, Tel: 715-264-2511, Nearest town: Hayward. GPS: 46.017578, -91.017090

9 • B2 | Namekagon Lake (Chequamegon-Nicolet NF)

Total sites: 34, RV sites: 34, Central water, Vault/pit toilet, No showers, No RV dump, Tent & RV camping: $18, Open May-Oct, Max Length: 55ft, Reservations accepted, Elev: 1444ft/440m, Tel: 715-264-2511, Nearest town: Cable. GPS: 46.244629, -91.086670

10 • B2 | Perch Lake (Drummond) (Chequamegon-Nicolet NF)

Total sites: 16, RV sites: 15, Central water, Vault/pit toilet, No showers, No RV dump, Tent & RV camping: $15, Open May-Oct, Max Length: 35ft, Reservations not accepted, Elev: 1234ft/376m, Tel: 715-373-2878, Nearest town: Drummond. GPS: 46.404535, -91.268991

11 • B2 | Sailor Lake (Chequamegon-Nicolet NF)

Total sites: 25, RV sites: 22, Central water, Vault/pit toilet, No showers, No RV dump, Tent & RV camping: $15, 3 walk-to sites, Open Apr-Oct, Max Length: 70ft, Reservations accepted, Elev: 1542ft/470m, Tel: 715-762-2461, Nearest town: Park Falls. GPS: 45.841693, -90.275804

12 • B2 | Smith Rapids (Chequamegon-Nicolet NF)

Total sites: 11, RV sites: 11, No water, Vault/pit toilet, No showers, No RV dump, Tent & RV camping: $15, 7 sites for equestrian use, Open Apr-Oct, Max Length: 75ft, Reservations accepted, Elev: 1545ft/471m, Tel: 715-748-4875, Nearest town: Park Falls. GPS: 45.909996, -90.173962

13 • B2 | Stockfarm Bridge (Chequamegon-Nicolet NF)

Total sites: 8, RV sites: 8, Central water, Vault/pit toilet, No showers, No RV dump, Tent & RV camping: $15, Group site: $40, Open May-Oct, Max Length: 40ft, Reservations accepted, Elev: 1483ft/452m, Tel: 715-264-2511, Nearest town: Glidden. GPS: 46.037515, -90.715335

14 • B2 | Twin Lakes (Chequamegon-Nicolet NF)

Total sites: 17, RV sites: 17, Central water, Vault/pit toilet, No showers, No RV dump, Tent & RV camping: $15, Open Apr-Oct, Max Length: 70ft, Reservations accepted, Elev: 1594ft/486m, Tel: 715-762-2461, Nearest town: Park Falls. GPS: 45.955526, -90.071987

15 • B2 | Two Lakes (Chequamegon NF)

Total sites: 94, RV sites: 83, Central water, Vault/pit toilet, No showers, RV dump, Tent & RV camping: $23, 7 walk-to sites, Dump fee: $10/campers/$25 unregistered campers, Open May-Oct, Max Length: 203ft, Reservations accepted, Elev: 1388ft/423m, Tel: 715-739-6334, Nearest town: Washburn. GPS: 46.292132, -91.196771

16 • B2 | Wabasso Lake (Chequamegon-Nicolet NF)

Total sites: 3, RV sites: 0, Central water, Vault/pit toilet, No showers, No RV dump, Tents only: $5, Walk-to/boat-in sites, Open all year, Reservations not accepted, Elev: 1608ft/490m, Tel: 715-748-4875, Nearest town: Lac Du Flambeau. GPS: 45.972665, -89.998063

17 • B2 | Wanoka Lake (Chequamegon-Nicolet NF)

Total sites: 20, RV sites: 19, Central water, Vault/pit toilet, No showers, No RV dump, Tent & RV camping: $15, Open May-Nov, Max Length: 35ft, Reservations not accepted, Elev: 1116ft/340m, Tel: 715-373-2667, Nearest town: Washburn. GPS: 46.543533, -91.283115

18 • B3 | Anvil Lake (Chequamegon-Nicolet NF)

Total sites: 17, RV sites: 13, Central water, Vault/pit toilet, No showers, No RV dump, Tent & RV camping: $15, No generators, Open May-Oct, Elev: 1752ft/534m, Tel: 715-479-2827, Nearest town: Eagle River. GPS: 45.936523, -89.060791

19 • B3 | Bear Lake (Chequamegon-Nicolet NF)

Total sites: 27, RV sites: 21, Central water, Vault/pit toilet, No showers, No RV dump, Tent & RV camping: $15, Open May-Nov, Max Length: 64ft, Reservations accepted, Elev: 1384ft/422m, Tel: 715-674-4481, Nearest town: Laona. GPS: 45.514102, -88.529479

20 • B3 | Chipmunk Rapids (Chequamegon-Nicolet NF)

Total sites: 6, RV sites: 6, Central water, Vault/pit toilet, No showers, No RV dump, Tent & RV camping: $15, Open Apr-Nov, Reservations not accepted, Elev: 1444ft/440m, Tel: 715-479-2827, Nearest town: Florence. GPS: 45.892832, -88.557319

21 • B3 | Franklin Lake North (Chequamegon-Nicolet NF)

Total sites: 37, RV sites: 37, Central water, Vault/pit toilet, No showers, No RV dump, Tents: $15/RVs: $15-18, Open May-Oct, Max Length: 40ft, Reservations accepted, Elev: 1758ft/536m, Tel: 715-479-2827, Nearest town: Eagle River. GPS: 45.940598, -88.985699

22 • B3 | Franklin Lake South (Chequamegon-Nicolet NF)

Total sites: 40, RV sites: 40, Central water, Vault/pit toilet, No showers, No RV dump, Tents: $15/RVs: $15-18, Open May-Oct, Max Length: 40ft, Reservations accepted, Elev: 1736ft/529m, Tel: 715-479-2827, Nearest town: Eagle River. GPS: 45.930416, -88.994124

23 • B3 | Kentuck Lake (Chequamegon-Nicolet NF)

Total sites: 31, RV sites: 31, Central water, Vault/pit toilet, No showers, No RV dump, Tent & RV camping: $15-18, Open May-Nov, Max Length: 40ft, Reservations accepted, Elev: 1742ft/531m, Tel: 715-479-2827, Nearest town: Eagle River. GPS: 45.992920, -88.980469

24 • B3 | Lac Vieux Desert (Chequamegon-Nicolet NF)

Total sites: 31, RV sites: 31, Central water, Vault/pit toilet, No showers, No RV dump, Tent & RV camping: $15, Open May-Oct, Reservations not accepted, Elev: 1693ft/516m, Tel: 715-479-2827, Nearest town: Eagle River. GPS: 46.136031, -89.156127

25 • B3 | Laura Lake (Chequamegon-Nicolet NF)

Total sites: 41, RV sites: 38, Central water, Vault/pit toilet, No showers, No RV dump, Tent & RV camping: $15, Open May-Oct, Max Length: 73ft, Reservations accepted, Elev: 1509ft/460m, Tel: 715-674-4481, Nearest town: Laona. GPS: 45.701746, -88.502792

26 • B3 | Laurel Lake (Chequamegon-Nicolet NF)

Total sites: 12, RV sites: 12, Central water, Vault/pit toilet, No showers, No RV dump, Tent & RV camping: $15, Open May-Oct, Max Length: 40ft, Reservations accepted, Elev: 1670ft/509m, Tel: 715-479-2827, Nearest town: Eagle River. GPS: 45.815918, -89.110596

27 • B3 | Lost Lake (Chequamegon-Nicolet NF)

Total sites: 27, RV sites: 27, Central water, Vault/pit toilet, No showers, No RV dump, Tent & RV camping: $15, Open May-Oct, Max Length: 40ft, Reservations accepted, Elev: 1542ft/470m, Tel: 715-479-2827, Nearest town: Tipler. GPS: 45.883789, -88.558350

28 • B3 | Luna - White Deer (Chequamegon-Nicolet NF)

Total sites: 37, RV sites: 37, Central water, Vault/pit toilet, No showers, No RV dump, Tent & RV camping: $15-18, Open May-Oct, Max Length: 40ft, Reservations accepted, Elev: 1736ft/529m,

Tel: 715-479-2827, Nearest town: Eagle River. GPS: 45.899658, -88.962158

29 • B3 | Morgan Lake (Chequamegon-Nicolet NF)

Total sites: 18, RV sites: 18, Central water, Vault/pit toilet, No showers, No RV dump, Tent & RV camping: $15, Group site: $35, Open May-Oct, Max Length: 40ft, Reservations accepted, Elev: 1470ft/448m, Tel: 715-479-2827, Nearest town: Florence. GPS: 45.772217, -88.543945

30 • B3 | Perch Lake (Florence Co) (Chequamegon-Nicolet NF)

Total sites: 5, RV sites: 0, No water, Vault/pit toilet, Tents only: Free, Walk-to sites, 1/4 mile, Open all year, Elev: 1532ft/467m, Nearest town: Iron Mountain. GPS: 45.933247, -88.494779

31 • B3 | Pine Lake (Chequamegon-Nicolet NF)

Total sites: 12, RV sites: 12, Central water, Vault/pit toilet, No showers, No RV dump, Tent & RV camping: $15, Open May-Sep, Reservations not accepted, Elev: 1654ft/504m, Tel: 715-276-6333, Nearest town: Laona. GPS: 45.685961, -88.991583

32 • B3 | Richardson Lake (Chequamegon-Nicolet NF)

Total sites: 26, RV sites: 25, Central water, Vault/pit toilet, No showers, No RV dump, Tent & RV camping: $15, Open May-Nov, Max Length: 56ft, Reservations accepted, Elev: 1598ft/487m, Tel: 715-276-6333, Nearest town: Laona. GPS: 45.441650, -88.713623

33 • B3 | Spectacle Lake (Chequamegon-Nicolet NF)

Total sites: 33, RV sites: 31, Central water, Vault/pit toilet, No showers, No RV dump, Tent & RV camping: $15-18, Open May-Oct, Max Length: 40ft, Reservations accepted, Elev: 1772ft/540m, Tel: 715-479-2827, Nearest town: Eagle River. GPS: 46.008301, -89.011230

34 • B3 | Stevens Lake (Chequamegon-Nicolet NF)

Total sites: 6, RV sites: 6, No water, Vault/pit toilet, Tent & RV camping: $15, Open May-Oct, Max Length: 40ft, Reservations not accepted, Elev: 1555ft/474m, Tel: 715-479-2827, Nearest town: Florence. GPS: 45.925084, -88.713741

35 • C2 | Chippewa (Chequamegon NF)

Total sites: 78, RV sites: 76, Central water, Flush toilet, Free showers, RV dump, Tent & RV camping: $15-18, Open May-Sep, Max Length: 65ft, Reservations accepted, Elev: 1289ft/393m, Tel: 715-748-4875, Nearest town: Medford. GPS: 45.222457, -90.705954

36 • C2 | Eastwood (Chequamegon-Nicolet NF)

Total sites: 21, RV sites: 21, Central water, Vault/pit toilet, No showers, No RV dump, Tent & RV camping: $15, Open Apr-Oct, Max Length: 65ft, Reservations accepted, Elev: 1470ft/448m, Tel: 715-748-4875, Nearest town: Medford. GPS: 45.332031, -90.444824

37 • C2 | Spearhead Point (Chequamegon-Nicolet NF)

Total sites: 27, RV sites: 24, Central water, Vault/pit toilet, No showers, No RV dump, Tent & RV camping: $15-18, Open Apr-Oct, Max Length: 70ft, Reservations accepted, Elev: 1391ft/424m, Tel: 715-748-4875, Nearest town: Medford. GPS: 45.327637, -90.444824

38 • C2 | West Point (Chequamegon-Nicolet NF)

Total sites: 15, RV sites: 15, Central water, Vault/pit toilet, No showers, No RV dump, Tent & RV camping: $15, Open all year, Reservations not accepted, Elev: 1384ft/422m, Tel: 715-748-4875, Nearest town: Medford. GPS: 45.318191, -90.438158

39 • C3 | Ada Lake (Chequamegon-Nicolet NF)

Total sites: 19, RV sites: 19, Central water, Vault/pit toilet, No showers, No RV dump, Tent & RV camping: $15, Open May-Oct, Reservations not accepted, Elev: 1709ft/521m, Tel: 715-674-4481, Nearest town: Wabeno. GPS: 45.370445, -88.731153

40 • C3 | Bagley Rapids (Chequamegon-Nicolet NF)

Total sites: 30, RV sites: 30, Central water, Vault/pit toilet, No showers, No RV dump, Tent & RV camping: $15, Open May-Oct, Reservations not accepted, Elev: 958ft/292m, Tel: 715-276-6333, Nearest town: Lakewood. GPS: 45.157604, -88.465838

41 • C3 | Boot Lake (Chequamegon-Nicolet NF)

Total sites: 34, RV sites: 26, Central water, Vault/pit toilet, No showers, No RV dump, Tent & RV camping: $18, Open May-Oct, Max Length: 88ft, Reservations accepted, Elev: 1352ft/412m, Tel: 715-276-6333, Nearest town: Mountain. GPS: 45.267012, -88.646001

42 • C3 | Boulder Lake (Chequamegon-Nicolet NF)

Total sites: 89, RV sites: 89, Elec sites: 23, Central water, Flush toilet, Free showers, RV dump, Tent & RV camping: $15-20, Open May-Oct, Max Length: 45ft, Reservations accepted, Elev: 1129ft/344m, Tel: 715-276-6333, Nearest town: Langlade. GPS: 45.141201, -88.635138

Wyoming

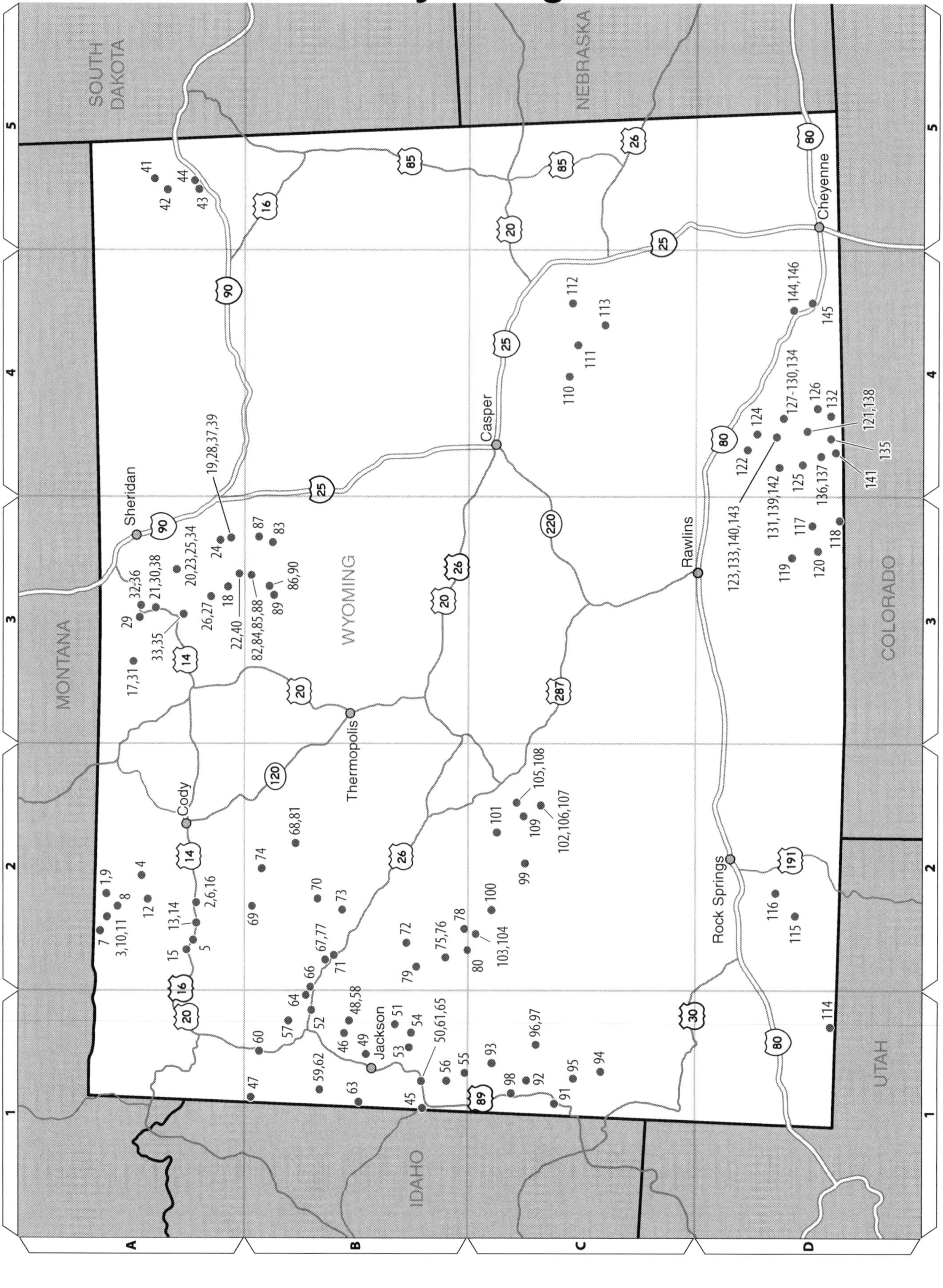

SOUTH DAKOTA
NEBRASKA
MONTANA
WYOMING
COLORADO
IDAHO
UTAH
Sheridan
Casper
Cheyenne
Rawlins
Thermopolis
Cody
Jackson
Rock Springs

Map	ID	Map	ID
A2	1-16	C2	99-109
A3	17-40	C4	110-113
A5	41-44	D1	114
B1	45-65	D2	115-116
B2	66-81	D3	117-120
B3	82-90	D4	121-146
C1	91-98		

Alphabetical List of Camping Areas

Name	ID	Map
Allred Flat (Bridger-Teton NF)	91	C1
Alpine North Loop (Caribou-Targhee NF)	45	B1
Angles (Bridger-Teton NF)	66	B2
Atherton Creek (Bridger-Teton NF)	46	B1
Bald Mountain (Bighorn NF)	17	A3
Battle Park TH (Bighorn NF)	18	A3
Bearlodge (Black Hills NF)	41	A5
Beartooth Lake (Shoshone NF)	1	A2
Big Game (Shoshone NF)	2	A2
Big Sandy (Bridger-Teton NF)	99	C2
Bobbie Thompson (Medicine Bow-Routt NF)	121	D4
Bottle Creek (Medicine Bow-Routt NF)	117	D3
Boulder Lake (Bridger-Teton NF)	100	C2
Boulder Park (Bighorn NF)	82	B3
Bow River (Medicine Bow-Routt NF)	122	D4
Brooklyn Lake (Medicine Bow-Routt NF)	123	D4
Brooks Lake (Shoshone NF)	67	B2
Brown Mountain (Shoshone NF)	68	B2
Buckboard Crossing (Ashley NF)	115	D2
Campbell Creek (Medicine Bow-Routt NF)	110	C4
Cave Falls (Caribou-Targhee NF)	47	B1
Circle Park (Bighorn NF)	19	A3
Cook Lake (Black Hills NF)	42	A5
Cottonwood Lake (Bridger-Teton NF)	92	C1
Crazy Creek (Shoshone NF)	3	A2
Cross Creek (Bighorn NF)	20	A3
Crystal Creek (Bridger-Teton NF)	48	B1
Curtis Canyon (Bridger-Teton NF)	49	B1
Curtis Gulch (Medicine Bow-Routt NF)	111	C4
Dead Indian (Shoshone NF)	4	A2
Dead Swede (Bighorn NF)	21	A3
Deadhorse TH Dispersed (Uinta-Wasatch-Cache NF)	114	D1
Deep Creek (Medicine Bow-Routt NF)	124	D4
Deer Creek (Shoshone NF)	69	B2
Deer Park (Bighorn NF)	22	A3
Dickinson Creek (Shoshone NF)	101	C2
Double Cabin (Shoshone NF)	70	B2
Doyle (Bighorn NF)	83	B3
Eagle Creek (Shoshone NF)	5	A2
East Fork (Bighorn NF)	23	A3
East Table Creek (Bridger-Teton NF)	50	B1
Elk Fork (Shoshone NF)	6	A2
Esterbrook (Medicine Bow-Routt NF)	112	C4
Falls (Shoshone NF)	71	B2
Fiddlers Lake (Shoshone NF)	102	C2
Firehole Canyon (Ashley NF)	116	D2
Forest Park (Bridger-Teton NF)	93	C1
Fox Creek (Shoshone NF)	7	A2
Fremont Lake (Bridger-Teton NF)	103	C2
French Creek (Medicine Bow-Routt NF)	125	D4
Friend Park (Medicine Bow-Routt NF)	113	C4
Granite Creek (Bridger-Teton NF)	51	B1
Green River Lake (Bridger-Teton NF)	72	B2
Half Moon Lake (Bridger-Teton NF)	104	C2
Hams Fork (Bridger-Teton NF)	94	C1
Hatchet (Bridger-Teton NF)	52	B1
Hoback (Bridger-Teton NF)	53	B1
Hobble Creek (Bridger-Teton NF)	95	C1
Hog Park (Medicine Bow-Routt NF)	118	D3
Horse Creek (Shoshone NF)	73	B2
Hugh Otte (Shoshone NF)	105	C2
Hunter Horse Camp (Bighorn NF)	24	A3
Hunter Peak (Shoshone NF)	8	A2
Island Lake (Shoshone NF)	9	A2
Island Park (Bighorn NF)	84	B3
Jack Creek (Shoshone NF)	74	B2
Jack Creek (Medicine Bow-Routt NF)	119	D3
Kozy (Bridger-Teton NF)	54	B1
Lake Creek (Shoshone NF)	10	A2
Lake Owen (Medicine Bow-Routt NF)	126	D4
Lakeview (Bighorn NF)	85	B3
Leigh Creek (Bighorn NF)	86	B3
Libby Creek - Aspen (Medicine Bow-Routt NF)	127	D4
Libby Creek - Pine (Medicine Bow-Routt NF)	128	D4
Libby Creek - Spruce (Medicine Bow-Routt NF)	129	D4
Libby Creek - Willow (Medicine Bow-Routt NF)	130	D4
Lily Lake (Shoshone NF)	11	A2
Lincoln Park (Medicine Bow-Routt NF)	131	D4
Little Goose (Bighorn NF)	25	A3
Little Popo Agie (Shoshone NF)	106	C2
Little Sunlight (Shoshone NF)	12	A2
Lost Cabin (Bighorn NF)	87	B3
Lost Creek (Medicine Bow-Routt NF)	120	D3
Louis Lake (Shoshone NF)	107	C2
Lower Paintrock Lake (Bighorn NF)	26	A3
Medicine Lodge Lake (Bighorn NF)	27	A3
Middle Fork (Bighorn NF)	28	A3
Middle Piney Lake (Bridger-Teton NF)	96	C1
Miller Lake (Medicine Bow-Routt NF)	132	D4
Moose Flat (Bridger-Teton NF)	55	B1
Murphy Creek (Bridger-Teton NF)	56	B1
Narrows (Bridger-Teton NF)	75	B2
Nash Fork (Medicine Bow-Routt NF)	133	D4
New Fork Lake (Bridger-Teton NF)	76	B2
Newton Creek (Shoshone NF)	13	A2
North Fork (Medicine Bow-Routt NF)	134	D4
North Tongue (Bighorn NF)	29	A3
Owen Creek (Bighorn NF)	30	A3
Pacific Creek (Bridger-Teton NF)	57	B1
Pelton Creek (Medicine Bow-Routt NF)	135	D4
Pickaroon (Medicine Bow-Routt NF)	136	D4
Pike Pole (Medicine Bow-Routt NF)	137	D4
Pinnacles (Shoshone NF)	77	B2
Porcupine (Bighorn NF)	31	A3
Prune Creek (Bighorn NF)	32	A3
Ranger Creek (Paintrock) (Bighorn NF)	33	A3
Ranger Creek (Tongue) (Bighorn NF)	34	A3

1 • A2 | Beartooth Lake (Shoshone NF)

Total sites: 21, RV sites: 21, Central water, Vault/pit toilet, No showers, No RV dump, Tent & RV camping: $15, Food storage order 04-00-104, Stay limit: 16 days, Open Jul-Sep, Max Length: 32ft, Reservations not accepted, Elev: 8963ft/2732m, Tel: 307-527-6921, Nearest town: Cody. GPS: 44.943705, -109.590529

2 • A2 | Big Game (Shoshone NF)

Total sites: 16, RV sites: 16, No water, Vault/pit toilet, Tent & RV camping: $10, Food storage order 04-00-104, Open May-Sep, Max Length: 120ft, Reservations accepted, Elev: 5919ft/1804m, Tel: 307-527-6921, Nearest town: Wapiti. GPS: 44.461914, -109.605469

3 • A2 | Crazy Creek (Shoshone NF)

Total sites: 16, RV sites: 16, No water, Vault/pit toilet, No showers, No RV dump, Tent & RV camping: $10, Food Storage Order 04-00-104, Not ADA-accessible, Stay limit: 16 days, Open May-Sep, Max Length: 28ft, Reservations not accepted, Elev: 6939ft/2115m, Tel: 307-527-6921, Nearest town: Cooke City, MT. GPS: 44.942524, -109.775604

4 • A2 | Dead Indian (Shoshone NF)

Total sites: 10, RV sites: 10, No water, Vault/pit toilet, Tent & RV camping: $10, Food storage order 04-00-104, Stay limit: 16 days, Open all year, Max Length: 32ft, Reservations not accepted, Elev: 6014ft/1833m, Tel: 307-527-6921, Nearest town: Cody. GPS: 44.753416, -109.418004

5 • A2 | Eagle Creek (Shoshone NF)

Total sites: 20, RV sites: 20, Central water, Vault/pit toilet, No showers, No RV dump, No tents/RVs: $15, Food storage order 04-00-104, Hard-side units only, Stay limit: 16 days, Open May-Sep, Max Length: 40ft, Reservations not accepted, Elev: 6490ft/1978m, Tel: 307-527-6921, Nearest town: Wapiti. GPS: 44.471680, -109.888672

6 • A2 | Elk Fork (Shoshone NF)

Total sites: 13, RV sites: 13, No water, Vault/pit toilet, Tent & RV camping: $10, Food storage order 04-00-104, No fee/no services Oct-Apr, Stay limit: 16 days, Open all year, Max Length: 22ft, Reservations not accepted, Elev: 5988ft/1825m, Tel: 307-527-6921, Nearest town: Cody. GPS: 44.462891, -109.629395

7 • A2 | Fox Creek (Shoshone NF)

Total sites: 33, RV sites: 33, Elec sites: 27, Water at site, Vault/pit toilet, No showers, No RV dump, Tent & RV camping: $20, Newly remodeled, Stay limit: 16 days, Open Jul-Sep, Max Length: 32ft, Reservations not accepted, Elev: 7090ft/2161m, Tel: 307-527-6921, Nearest town: Cody. GPS: 44.976612, -109.833924

8 • A2 | Hunter Peak (Shoshone NF)

Total sites: 10, RV sites: 10, Central water, Vault/pit toilet, No showers, No RV dump, Tent & RV camping: $15, Food storage order 04-00-104, Open May-Sep, Max Length: 56ft, Reservations accepted, Elev: 6634ft/2022m, Tel: 307-527-6921, Nearest town: Clarks Fork. GPS: 44.885276, -109.655263

9 • A2 | Island Lake (Shoshone NF)

Total sites: 20, RV sites: 20, Central water, Vault/pit toilet, No showers, No RV dump, Tent & RV camping: $15, Food storage order 04-00-104, Stay limit: 16 days, Open Jul-Sep, Max Length: 32ft, Reservations not accepted, Elev: 9541ft/2908m, Tel: 307-527-6921, Nearest town: Cody. GPS: 44.941382, -109.538894

10 • A2 | Lake Creek (Shoshone NF)

Total sites: 6, RV sites: 6, No water, Vault/pit toilet, Tent & RV camping: $10, Food storage order 04-00-104, Stay limit: 16 days, Open Jun-Sep, Max Length: 22ft, Elev: 7008ft/2136m, Tel: 307-527-6921, Nearest town: Clarks Fork. GPS: 44.921356, -109.706989

11 • A2 | Lily Lake (Shoshone NF)

Total sites: 8, RV sites: 8, No water, Vault/pit toilet, Tent & RV camping: Donation, Snow may hamper winter access, Stay limit: 16 days, Open all year, Max Length: 22ft, Reservations not accepted, Elev: 7700ft/2347m, Tel: 307-527-6921, Nearest town: Cooke City (MT). GPS: 44.945000, -109.714000

12 • A2 | Little Sunlight (Shoshone NF)

Total sites: 5, RV sites: 5, No water, Vault/pit toilet, Tent & RV camping: Free, Not ADA-compliant, Food storage order 04-00-104, Stay limit: 16 days, Reservations not accepted, Elev: 6952ft/2119m, Tel: 307-527-6921, Nearest town: Cody. GPS: 44.718000, -109.591000

13 • A2 | Newton Creek (Shoshone NF)

Total sites: 31, RV sites: 31, Central water, Vault/pit toilet, No showers, No RV dump, Tent & RV camping: $15, Food storage order 04-00-104, Hard-side units only, Not ADA compliant, Stay limit: 16 days, Open May-Sep, Max Length: 40ft, Reservations not accepted, Elev: 6266ft/1910m, Tel: 307-527-6921, Nearest town: Cody. GPS: 44.452217, -109.757546

14 • A2 | Rex Hale (Shoshone NF)

Total sites: 30, RV sites: 30, Elec sites: 8, Central water, Vault/pit toilet, No showers, No RV dump, Tents: $15/RVs: $15-20, Food storage order 04-00-104, Open May-Sep, Max Length: 40ft, Reservations accepted, Elev: 6152ft/1875m, Tel: 307-527-6921, Nearest town: Cody. GPS: 44.454352, -109.730896

15 • A2 | Threemile (Shoshone NF)

Total sites: 21, RV sites: 21, Central water, Vault/pit toilet, No showers, No RV dump, No tents/RVs: $15, Hard-side units only, Stay limit: 16 days, Open Jul-Sep, Max Length: 75ft, Reservations accepted, Elev: 6713ft/2046m, Tel: 307-527-6921, Nearest town: Lake Junction. GPS: 44.496338, -109.951172

16 • A2 | Wapiti (Shoshone NF)

Total sites: 41, RV sites: 41, Elec sites: 21, Central water, Vault/pit toilet, No showers, No RV dump, Tents: $15/RVs: $20, Food storage order 04-00-104, $5 Elec fee, Stay limit: 16 days, Open May-Sep, Max Length: 145ft, Reservations accepted, Elev: 5945ft/1812m, Tel: 307-527-6921, Nearest town: Cody. GPS: 44.465978, -109.624538

17 • A3 | Bald Mountain (Bighorn NF)

Total sites: 15, RV sites: 15, Central water, Vault/pit toilet, No showers, No RV dump, Tent & RV camping: $16, Stay limit: 14 days, Open Jun-Sep, Reservations accepted, Elev: 9101ft/2774m, Nearest town: Lovell. GPS: 44.805908, -107.858887

18 • A3 | Battle Park TH (Bighorn NF)

Total sites: 15, RV sites: 15, Central water, Vault/pit toilet, Tent & RV camping: Donation, Camping allowed only across road from the TH parking area, Horse corrals, Stay limit: 14 days, Reservations not accepted, Elev: 9134ft/2784m, Nearest town: Ten Sleep. GPS: 44.306587, -107.310747

19 • A3 | Circle Park (Bighorn NF)

Total sites: 10, RV sites: 10, Central water, Vault/pit toilet, No showers, No RV dump, Tent & RV camping: $16, Stay limit: 14 days, Open Jun-Sep, Max Length: 50ft, Reservations accepted, Elev: 8107ft/2471m, Tel: 406-587-9054, Nearest town: Buffalo. GPS: 44.282764, -106.990528

20 • A3 | Cross Creek (Bighorn NF)

Total sites: 3, RV sites: 3, No water, Vault/pit toilet, Tent & RV camping: Free, 4x4 required, Stay limit: 14 days, Open Jun-Sep, Reservations not accepted, Elev: 8299ft/2530m, Tel: 307-674-2600, Nearest town: Sheridan. GPS: 44.546249, -107.216325

21 • A3 | Dead Swede (Bighorn NF)

Total sites: 22, RV sites: 22, Central water, Vault/pit toilet, No showers, No RV dump, Tent & RV camping: $18, Stay limit: 14 days, Open Jun-Sep, Max Length: 60ft, Reservations accepted, Elev: 8471ft/2582m, Tel: 406-587-9054, Nearest town: Dayton. GPS: 44.688965, -107.447021

22 • A3 | Deer Park (Bighorn NF)

Total sites: 7, RV sites: 7, Central water, Vault/pit toilet, No showers, No RV dump, Tent & RV camping: $16, Stay limit: 14 days, Open Jun-Sep, Reservations not accepted, Elev: 8914ft/2717m, Tel: 307-674-2600, Nearest town: Ten Sleep. GPS: 44.244559, -107.222858

23 • A3 | East Fork (Bighorn NF)

Total sites: 12, RV sites: 12, Central water, Vault/pit toilet, No showers, No RV dump, Tent & RV camping: $14, Stay limit: 14 days, Open Jun-Sep, Reservations not accepted, Elev: 7634ft/2327m, Tel: 307-674-2600, Nearest town: Big Horn. GPS: 44.595931, -107.208718

24 • A3 | Hunter Horse Camp (Bighorn NF)

Total sites: 11, RV sites: 11, Central water, Vault/pit toilet, No showers, No RV dump, Tent & RV camping: $10, Open Jun-Sep, Max Length: 40ft, Reservations accepted, Elev: 8008ft/2441m, Tel: 307-684-7806, Nearest town: Buffalo. GPS: 44.338162, -106.975496

25 • A3 | Little Goose (Bighorn NF)

Total sites: 3, RV sites: 3, No water, Vault/pit toilet, Tent & RV camping: Free, 4x4 required, Stay limit: 14 days, Open Jun-Sep, Reservations not accepted, Elev: 6972ft/2125m, Nearest town: Sheridan. GPS: 44.589575, -107.125142

26 • A3 | Lower Paintrock Lake (Bighorn NF)

Total sites: 15, RV sites: 15, Central water, Vault/pit toilet, No showers, No RV dump, Tent & RV camping: $15, Stay limit: 14 days, Open Jun-Sep, Reservations not accepted, Elev: 9242ft/2817m, Tel: 307-674-2600, Nearest town: Shell. GPS: 44.394382, -107.383872

27 • A3 | Medicine Lodge Lake (Bighorn NF)

Total sites: 13, RV sites: 13, Central water, Vault/pit toilet, No showers, No RV dump, Tent & RV camping: $15, Open Jun-Sep, Reservations not accepted, Elev: 9275ft/2827m, Nearest town: Shell. GPS: 44.400563, -107.387528

28 • A3 | Middle Fork (Bighorn NF)

Total sites: 9, RV sites: 9, Central water, Vault/pit toilet, No showers, No RV dump, Tent & RV camping: $18, Open May-Sep, Max Length: 80ft, Reservations accepted, Elev: 7533ft/2296m, Tel: 406-587-9054, Nearest town: Buffalo. GPS: 44.301555, -106.950974

29 • A3 | North Tongue (Bighorn NF)

Total sites: 12, RV sites: 12, Central water, Vault/pit toilet, No showers, No RV dump, Tent & RV camping: $17, Stay limit: 14 days, Open Jun-Sep, Max Length: 100ft, Reservations accepted,

Elev: 7884ft/2403m, Tel: 406-587-9054, Nearest town: Dayton. GPS: 44.780029, -107.533691

30 • A3 | Owen Creek (Bighorn NF)

Total sites: 7, RV sites: 7, Central water, Vault/pit toilet, No showers, No RV dump, Tent & RV camping: $17, Open Jun-Sep, Max Length: 50ft, Reservations accepted, Elev: 8465ft/2580m, Tel: 406-587-9054, Nearest town: Burgess Jct. GPS: 44.704655, -107.500399

31 • A3 | Porcupine (Bighorn NF)

Total sites: 16, RV sites: 13, Central water, Vault/pit toilet, No showers, No RV dump, Tent & RV camping: $17, Open Jun-Sep, Max Length: 100ft, Reservations accepted, Elev: 8806ft/2684m, Tel: 406-587-9054, Nearest town: Lovell. GPS: 44.831595, -107.858279

32 • A3 | Prune Creek (Bighorn NF)

Total sites: 21, RV sites: 21, Central water, Vault/pit toilet, No showers, No RV dump, Tent & RV camping: $18, Open Jun-Sep, Max Length: 55ft, Reservations accepted, Elev: 7716ft/2352m, Tel: 406-587-9054, Nearest town: Dayton. GPS: 44.769395, -107.469242

33 • A3 | Ranger Creek (Paintrock) (Bighorn NF)

Total sites: 10, RV sites: 10, Central water, Vault/pit toilet, No showers, No RV dump, Tent & RV camping: $17, Reservable group site $75-$145, Open Jun-Sep, Max Length: 75ft, Reservations accepted, Elev: 7707ft/2349m, Tel: 406-587-9054, Nearest town: Big Horn. GPS: 44.545929, -107.500241

34 • A3 | Ranger Creek (Tongue) (Bighorn NF)

Total sites: 11, RV sites: 11, Central water, Vault/pit toilet, No showers, No RV dump, Tent & RV camping: $14, Stay limit: 14 days, Open Jun-Sep, Reservations not accepted, Elev: 7707ft/2349m, Tel: 307-674-2600, Nearest town: Big Horn. GPS: 44.600505, -107.218599

35 • A3 | Shell Creek (Bighorn NF)

Total sites: 15, RV sites: 15, Central water, Vault/pit toilet, No showers, No RV dump, Tent & RV camping: $17, Open May-Sep, Max Length: 75ft, Reservations accepted, Elev: 7618ft/2322m, Tel: 406-587-9054, Nearest town: Greybull. GPS: 44.550654, -107.515246

36 • A3 | Sibley Lake (Bighorn NF)

Total sites: 20, RV sites: 20, Elec sites: 14, Central water, Vault/pit toilet, No showers, No RV dump, Tents: $16/RVs: $16-20, Open Jun-Sep, Reservations accepted, Elev: 8008ft/2441m, Tel: 406-587-9054, Nearest town: Dayton. GPS: 44.759033, -107.438965

37 • A3 | South Fork (Bighorn NF)

Total sites: 14, RV sites: 9, Central water, Vault/pit toilet, No showers, No RV dump, Tent & RV camping: $18, Also walk-to sites, Open May-Sep, Max Length: 65ft, Reservations accepted, Elev: 7690ft/2344m, Tel: 406-587-9054, Nearest town: Buffalo. GPS: 44.277175, -106.947647

38 • A3 | Tie Flume (Bighorn NF)

Total sites: 27, RV sites: 27, Central water, Vault/pit toilet, No showers, No RV dump, Tent & RV camping: $18, Open Jun-Sep, Max Length: 80ft, Reservations accepted, Elev: 8366ft/2550m, Tel: 406-587-9054, Nearest town: Burgess Junction. GPS: 44.715096, -107.450733

39 • A3 | Tie Hack (Bighorn NF)

Total sites: 19, RV sites: 19, Central water, Vault/pit toilet, No showers, No RV dump, Tent & RV camping: $18, Open May-Sep, Max Length: 45ft, Reservations accepted, Elev: 7805ft/2379m, Tel: 406-587-9054, Nearest town: Buffalo. GPS: 44.282825, -106.943389

40 • A3 | West Tensleep (Bighorn NF)

Total sites: 9, RV sites: 8, Central water, Vault/pit toilet, No showers, No RV dump, Tent & RV camping: $17, Stay limit: 14 days, Open Jun-Sep, Max Length: 45ft, Reservations accepted, Elev: 9114ft/2778m, Tel: 406-587-9054, Nearest town: Ten Sleep. GPS: 44.258615, -107.215786

41 • A5 | Bearlodge (Black Hills NF)

Total sites: 8, RV sites: 8, No water, Vault/pit toilet, No showers, No RV dump, Tent & RV camping: $14, Stay limit: 10 days, Open all year, Reservations not accepted, Elev: 4675ft/1425m, Nearest town: Aladdin. GPS: 44.655000, -104.327000

42 • A5 | Cook Lake (Black Hills NF)

Total sites: 32, RV sites: 32, No toilets, Tent & RV camping: $18, $10 mid-Sep to mid-May, Open all year, Reservations not accepted, Elev: 4862ft/1482m, Tel: 605-673-9200, Nearest town: Sundance. GPS: 44.594262, -104.411833

43 • A5 | Reuter Canyon (Black Hills NF)

Total sites: 24, RV sites: 24, Central water, Vault/pit toilet, No showers, No RV dump, Tent & RV camping: $14, Sep-May: $10, Open all year, Max Length: 45ft, Reservations accepted, Elev: 5466ft/1666m, Tel: 605-574-4402, Nearest town: Sundance. GPS: 44.425922, -104.423934

44 • A5 | Sundance Horse Camp (Black Hills NF)

Total sites: 10, RV sites: 10, No water, Vault/pit toilet, Tent & RV camping: $14, $10/night mid-Sept to mid-May, Open all year, Reservations not accepted, Elev: 4810ft/1466m, Tel: 307-283-1361, Nearest town: Sundance. GPS: 44.443057, -104.348538

45 • B1 | Alpine North Loop (Caribou-Targhee NF)

Total sites: 16, RV sites: 16, Central water, Vault/pit toilet, No showers, No RV dump, Tent & RV camping: $17, 3 group sites: $60-$100, Open May-Sep, Max Length: 60ft, Reservations accepted, Elev: 5681ft/1732m, Nearest town: Alpine. GPS: 43.196918, -111.042077

46 • B1 | Atherton Creek (Bridger-Teton NF)

Total sites: 21, RV sites: 21, Central water, Vault/pit toilet, No showers, No RV dump, Tent & RV camping: $15, Open May-Sep, Reservations not accepted, Elev: 6978ft/2127m, Tel: 307-739-5500, Nearest town: Jackson. GPS: 43.636963, -110.523193

47 • B1 | Cave Falls (Caribou-Targhee NF)

Total sites: 23, RV sites: 23, Central water, Vault/pit toilet, No showers, No RV dump, Tent & RV camping: $10, Open Jun-Sep,

Reservations not accepted, Elev: 6207ft/1892m, Tel: 208-557-5900, Nearest town: Ashton, ID. GPS: 44.130843, -111.014876

48 • B1 | Crystal Creek (Bridger-Teton NF)

Total sites: 6, RV sites: 6, Central water, Vault/pit toilet, No showers, No RV dump, Tent & RV camping: $12, 2 overflow sites can take 32' rigs, Open May-Sep, Max Length: 24ft, Reservations not accepted, Elev: 7014ft/2138m, Tel: 307-739-5500, Nearest town: Jackson. GPS: 43.610736, -110.431379

49 • B1 | Curtis Canyon (Bridger-Teton NF)

Total sites: 11, RV sites: 11, Central water, Vault/pit toilet, No showers, No RV dump, Tent & RV camping: $15, Open May-Sep, Max Length: 24ft, Reservations not accepted, Elev: 7041ft/2146m, Tel: 307-739-5500, Nearest town: Jackson. GPS: 43.512451, -110.661377

50 • B1 | East Table Creek (Bridger-Teton NF)

Total sites: 20, RV sites: 20, Central water, Vault/pit toilet, No showers, No RV dump, Tent & RV camping: $15, Open May-Sep, Max Length: 30ft, Reservations not accepted, Elev: 5830ft/1777m, Tel: 307-739-5500, Nearest town: Hoback Junction. GPS: 43.211670, -110.807373

51 • B1 | Granite Creek (Bridger-Teton NF)

Total sites: 51, RV sites: 51, Central water, Vault/pit toilet, No showers, No RV dump, Tent & RV camping: $15, Open May-Sep, Reservations not accepted, Elev: 6831ft/2082m, Nearest town: Hoback Junction. GPS: 43.359131, -110.445313

52 • B1 | Hatchet (Bridger-Teton NF)

Total sites: 9, RV sites: 9, Central water, Vault/pit toilet, Tent & RV camping: $12, No service/no fee in winter, Food storage order 04-00-104, Open all year, Max Length: 24ft, Reservations not accepted, Elev: 6886ft/2099m, Nearest town: Moran Junction. GPS: 43.824103, -110.353564

53 • B1 | Hoback (Bridger-Teton NF)

Total sites: 12, RV sites: 12, Central water, Vault/pit toilet, No showers, No RV dump, Tent & RV camping: $15, Open May-Sep, Max Length: 32ft, Reservations not accepted, Elev: 6230ft/1899m, Tel: 307-739-5400, Nearest town: Hoback Junction. GPS: 43.279704, -110.597651

54 • B1 | Kozy (Bridger-Teton NF)

Total sites: 8, RV sites: 8, No water, Vault/pit toilet, Tent & RV camping: $15, Open May-Sep, Reservations not accepted, Elev: 6401ft/1951m, Tel: 307-739-5400, Nearest town: Bondurant. GPS: 43.270168, -110.513831

55 • B1 | Moose Flat (Bridger-Teton NF)

Total sites: 10, RV sites: 10, Central water, Vault/pit toilet, No showers, No RV dump, Tent & RV camping: $10, Free off-season - no services, Open May-Sep, Max Length: 30ft, Reservations not accepted, Elev: 6427ft/1959m, Tel: 307-654-0249, Nearest town: Alpine. GPS: 42.971714, -110.769273

56 • B1 | Murphy Creek (Bridger-Teton NF)

Total sites: 10, RV sites: 10, Central water, Vault/pit toilet, No showers, No RV dump, Tent & RV camping: $7, 1 70' pull-through, Stay limit: 16 days, Open May-Sep, Max Length: 30ft, Reservations not accepted, Elev: 6237ft/1901m, Tel: 307-886-5300, Nearest town: Alpine. GPS: 43.072266, -110.835938

57 • B1 | Pacific Creek (Bridger-Teton NF)

Total sites: 8, RV sites: 8, No water, Vault/pit toilet, Tent & RV camping: $10, Food storage order 04-00-104, Open May-Oct, Reservations not accepted, Elev: 7034ft/2144m, Tel: 307-739-5500, Nearest town: Jackson. GPS: 43.939921, -110.442754

58 • B1 | Red Hills (Bridger-Teton NF)

Total sites: 5, RV sites: 5, Central water, Vault/pit toilet, No showers, No RV dump, Tent & RV camping: $15, Stay limit: 16 days, Open May-Sep, Max Length: 30ft, Reservations not accepted, Elev: 7034ft/2144m, Tel: 307-739-5400, Nearest town: Jackson. GPS: 43.611408, -110.437492

59 • B1 | Reunion Flat (Caribou-Targhee NF)

Total sites: 4, RV sites: 4, Central water, Vault/pit toilet, No showers, No RV dump, Tent & RV camping: $12, 3 reservable group sites $50, Open May-Sep, Reservations not accepted, Elev: 6909ft/2106m, Nearest town: Driggs. GPS: 43.757307, -110.951781

60 • B1 | Sheffield (Bridger-Teton NF)

Total sites: 5, RV sites: 5, Vault/pit toilet, Tent & RV camping: $10, Must ford creek to reach CG, Not recommended for large RVs, Open May-Sep, Max Length: 25ft, Reservations not accepted, Elev: 6879ft/2097m, Nearest town: Jackson. GPS: 44.093231, -110.663017

61 • B1 | Station Creek (Bridger-Teton NF)

Total sites: 16, RV sites: 16, Central water, Vault/pit toilet, No showers, No RV dump, Tent & RV camping: $15, Open May-Oct, Reservations not accepted, Elev: 5860ft/1786m, Nearest town: Hoback Junction. GPS: 43.204346, -110.834473

62 • B1 | Teton Canyon (Caribou-Targhee NF)

Total sites: 20, RV sites: 20, Central water, Vault/pit toilet, No showers, No RV dump, Tent & RV camping: $17, 2 equestrian sites, Open Jun-Sep, Max Length: 20ft, Reservations accepted, Elev: 6964ft/2123m, Nearest town: Alta. GPS: 43.756576, -110.919724

63 • B1 | Trail Creek (Caribou-Targhee NF)

Total sites: 10, RV sites: 10, Central water, Vault/pit toilet, No showers, No RV dump, Tent & RV camping: $17, Open May-Sep, Max Length: 40ft, Reservations accepted, Elev: 6722ft/2049m, Tel: 208-354-2312, Nearest town: Victor, ID. GPS: 43.538574, -111.037598

64 • B1 | Turpin Meadow (Bridger-Teton NF)

Total sites: 18, RV sites: 18, Central water, Vault/pit toilet, No showers, No RV dump, Tent & RV camping: $12, Food storage order 04-00-104, Open May-Sep, Reservations not accepted, Elev: 6949ft/2118m, Tel: 307-739-5500, Nearest town: Jackson. GPS: 43.854935, -110.262977

65 • B1 | Wolf Creek (Bridger-Teton NF)

Total sites: 20, RV sites: 20, Central water, Vault/pit toilet, No showers, No RV dump, Tent & RV camping: $15, Open May-Sep,

Max Length: 62ft, Reservations not accepted, Elev: 5860ft/1786m, Tel: 307-739-5400, Nearest town: Jackson. GPS: 43.198538, -110.895835

66 • B2 | Angles (Bridger-Teton NF)

Total sites: 4, RV sites: 4, Central water, Vault/pit toilet, No showers, No RV dump, Tent & RV camping: $5, Food storage order 04-00-104, Open Jun-Sep, Elev: 8602ft/2622m, Tel: 307-739-5500, Nearest town: Jackson. GPS: 43.825442, -110.201607

67 • B2 | Brooks Lake (Shoshone NF)

Total sites: 13, RV sites: 13, No water, Vault/pit toilet, No tents/RVs: $10, Hard sided camping only, Open Jun-Sep, Max Length: 32ft, Reservations not accepted, Elev: 9068ft/2764m, Tel: 307-455-2466, Nearest town: Dubois. GPS: 43.751044, -110.004671

68 • B2 | Brown Mountain (Shoshone NF)

Total sites: 7, RV sites: 7, No water, Vault/pit toilet, Tent & RV camping: Donation, Rough road - 4-wheel drive recommended, Food storage order, Open May-Oct, Max Length: 16ft, Reservations not accepted, Elev: 7557ft/2303m, Tel: 307-527-6921, Nearest town: Meeteetse. GPS: 43.935238, -109.179001

69 • B2 | Deer Creek (Shoshone NF)

Total sites: 6, RV sites: 6, No water, Vault/pit toilet, Tent & RV camping: Donation, Food storage order 04-00-104, Not ADA-accessible, Stay limit: 16 days, Open all year, Max Length: 16ft, Reservations not accepted, Elev: 6447ft/1965m, Tel: 307-527-6921, Nearest town: Cody. GPS: 44.158457, -109.619461

70 • B2 | Double Cabin (Shoshone NF)

Total sites: 14, RV sites: 14, Central water, Vault/pit toilet, No showers, No RV dump, Tent & RV camping: $15, Food storage order 04-00-104, Stay limit: 16 days, Open May-Sep, Max Length: 32ft, Reservations not accepted, Elev: 8077ft/2462m, Tel: 307-527-6241, Nearest town: Dubois. GPS: 43.806233, -109.560665

71 • B2 | Falls (Shoshone NF)

Total sites: 54, RV sites: 54, Central water, Vault/pit toilet, No showers, No RV dump, Tent & RV camping: $15-20, Food storage order 04-00-104, Stay limit: 16 days, Open Jun-Sep, Max Length: 32ft, Reservations not accepted, Elev: 8357ft/2547m, Tel: 307-455-2466, Nearest town: Dubois. GPS: 43.706445, -109.971104

72 • B2 | Green River Lake (Bridger-Teton NF)

Total sites: 52, RV sites: 52, Central water, Vault/pit toilet, No showers, No RV dump, Tent & RV camping: $12, Reservable group site $35, Food storage order 04-00-104, Open Jul-Sep, Reservations not accepted, Elev: 8064ft/2458m, Tel: 307-367-4326, Nearest town: Pinedale. GPS: 43.311768, -109.859863

73 • B2 | Horse Creek (Shoshone NF)

Total sites: 9, RV sites: 9, Central water, Vault/pit toilet, No showers, No RV dump, Tent & RV camping: $15, Not ADA-compliant, Food storage order 04-00-104, Stay limit: 16 days, Open May-Sep, Max Length: 32ft, Reservations not accepted, Elev: 7740ft/2359m, Tel: 307-455-2466, Nearest town: Dubois. GPS: 43.666666, -109.635365

74 • B2 | Jack Creek (Shoshone NF)

Total sites: 7, RV sites: 7, No water, Vault/pit toilet, Tent & RV camping: Donation, Very rough road last 3 miles, Not ADA-compliant, Food storage order, Open all year, Max Length: 32ft, Reservations not accepted, Elev: 7572ft/2308m, Tel: 307-527-6921, Nearest town: Meeteetse. GPS: 44.110045, -109.351875

75 • B2 | Narrows (Bridger-Teton NF)

Total sites: 19, RV sites: 19, Central water, Vault/pit toilet, No showers, No RV dump, Tent & RV camping: $12, Food storage order 04-00-104, Open May-Sep, Max Length: 25ft, Reservations accepted, Elev: 7900ft/2408m, Tel: 307-367-4326, Nearest town: Pinedale. GPS: 43.103271, -109.940918

76 • B2 | New Fork Lake (Bridger-Teton NF)

Total sites: 15, RV sites: 15, No water, Vault/pit toilet, Tent & RV camping: $7, Reservable group site $35, Food storage order 04-00-104, Open Jun-Sep, Reservations not accepted, Elev: 7835ft/2388m, Tel: 307-367-4326, Nearest town: Pinedale. GPS: 43.083008, -109.967041

77 • B2 | Pinnacles (Shoshone NF)

Total sites: 21, RV sites: 21, Central water, Vault/pit toilet, No showers, No RV dump, Tent & RV camping: $15, Hard sided campers only, Food storage order, Not ADA compliant, Stay limit: 16 days, Open Jun-Sep, Max Length: 32ft, Reservations not accepted, Elev: 9150ft/2789m, Tel: 307-455-2466, Nearest town: Dubois. GPS: 43.754258, -109.996443

78 • B2 | Trails End (Bridger-Teton NF)

Total sites: 8, RV sites: 8, Central water, Vault/pit toilet, No showers, No RV dump, Tent & RV camping: $12, Open Jun-Sep, Reservations not accepted, Elev: 9314ft/2839m, Nearest town: Pinedale. GPS: 43.006371, -109.753064

79 • B2 | Whiskey Grove (Bridger-Teton NF)

Total sites: 9, RV sites: 9, Central water, Vault/pit toilet, No showers, No RV dump, Tent & RV camping: $7, Food storage order 04-00-104, Open Jun-Sep, Reservations not accepted, Elev: 7746ft/2361m, Tel: 307-367-4326, Nearest town: Pinedale. GPS: 43.255000, -110.026000

80 • B2 | Willow Lake (Bridger-Teton NF)

Total sites: 19, RV sites: 17, No water, Vault/pit toilet, No showers, No RV dump, Tent & RV camping: Free, Food storage order 04-00-104, Open Jun-Sep, Reservations not accepted, Elev: 7707ft/2349m, Tel: 307-739-5500, Nearest town: Pinedale. GPS: 42.990811, -109.900115

81 • B2 | Wood River (Shoshone NF)

Total sites: 5, RV sites: 5, No water, Vault/pit toilet, Tent & RV camping: Donation, Food storage order, Stay limit: 16 days, Open May-Sep, Max Length: 30ft, Reservations not accepted, Elev: 7316ft/2230m, Tel: 307-527-6921, Nearest town: Meeteetse. GPS: 43.931703, -109.132183

82 • B3 | Boulder Park (Bighorn NF)

Total sites: 32, RV sites: 32, Central water, Vault/pit toilet, No showers, RV dump, Tent & RV camping: $17, Open Jun-Sep, Max

Length: 58ft, Reservations accepted, Elev: 7989ft/2435m, Tel: 406-587-9054, Nearest town: Ten Sleep. GPS: 44.163272, -107.253051

83 • B3 | Doyle (Bighorn NF)

Total sites: 19, RV sites: 18, Central water, Vault/pit toilet, No showers, No RV dump, Tent & RV camping: $16, Open Jun-Sep, Max Length: 85ft, Reservations accepted, Elev: 8182ft/2494m, Tel: 406-587-9054, Nearest town: Buffalo. GPS: 44.072585, -106.987182

84 • B3 | Island Park (Bighorn NF)

Total sites: 10, RV sites: 10, Central water, Vault/pit toilet, No showers, No RV dump, Tent & RV camping: $17, Open Jun-Sep, Max Length: 75ft, Reservations accepted, Elev: 8573ft/2613m, Tel: 406-587-9054, Nearest town: Ten Sleep. GPS: 44.205444, -107.236011

85 • B3 | Lakeview (Bighorn NF)

Total sites: 20, RV sites: 11, Central water, Vault/pit toilet, No showers, No RV dump, Tent & RV camping: $18, Open Jun-Sep, Max Length: 70ft, Reservations accepted, Elev: 8556ft/2608m, Tel: 406-587-9054, Nearest town: Ten Sleep. GPS: 44.176941, -107.215965

86 • B3 | Leigh Creek (Bighorn NF)

Total sites: 11, RV sites: 11, Central water, Vault/pit toilet, No showers, No RV dump, Tent & RV camping: $16, Open May-Sep, Max Length: 36ft, Reservations accepted, Elev: 5417ft/1651m, Tel: 406-587-9054, Nearest town: Ten Sleep. GPS: 44.080528, -107.314515

87 • B3 | Lost Cabin (Bighorn NF)

Total sites: 19, RV sites: 19, Central water, Vault/pit toilet, No showers, No RV dump, Tent & RV camping: $17, Open Jun-Sep, Max Length: 90ft, Reservations accepted, Elev: 8218ft/2505m, Tel: 406-587-9054, Nearest town: Buffalo. GPS: 44.146823, -106.953639

88 • B3 | Sitting Bull (Bighorn NF)

Total sites: 41, RV sites: 41, Central water, Vault/pit toilet, No showers, No RV dump, Tent & RV camping: $18, Open all year, Max Length: 60ft, Reservations accepted, Elev: 8674ft/2644m, Tel: 406-587-9054, Nearest town: Ten Sleep. GPS: 44.191647, -107.212079

89 • B3 | Tensleep Canyon (Bighorn NF)

Total sites: 5, RV sites: 5, No water, No toilets, Tent & RV camping: Free, Reservations not accepted, Elev: 4892ft/1491m, Nearest town: Ten Sleep. GPS: 44.068419, -107.368815

90 • B3 | Tensleep Creek (Bighorn NF)

Total sites: 5, RV sites: 5, No water, Vault/pit toilet, No showers, No RV dump, Tent & RV camping: $13, Open Jun-Sep, Elev: 5564ft/1696m, Nearest town: Ten Sleep. GPS: 44.084959, -107.307909

91 • C1 | Allred Flat (Bridger-Teton NF)

Total sites: 32, RV sites: 32, Central water, Vault/pit toilet, No showers, No RV dump, Tent & RV camping: $10, Open May-Sep, Max Length: 22ft, Reservations not accepted, Elev: 6814ft/2077m, Tel: 307-739-5500, Nearest town: Smoot. GPS: 42.489502, -110.962402

92 • C1 | Cottonwood Lake (Bridger-Teton NF)

Total sites: 18, RV sites: 18, Central water, Vault/pit toilet, No showers, No RV dump, Tent & RV camping: $10, Horse corrals, Reservable group site $35, Reservations not accepted, Elev: 7530ft/2295m, Tel: 307-739-5500, Nearest town: Afton. GPS: 42.640229, -110.816899

93 • C1 | Forest Park (Bridger-Teton NF)

Total sites: 13, RV sites: 13, Central water, Vault/pit toilet, No showers, No RV dump, Tent & RV camping: $10, Open May-Sep, Max Length: 30ft, Reservations not accepted, Elev: 6975ft/2126m, Nearest town: Alpine. GPS: 42.831299, -110.689941

94 • C1 | Hams Fork (Bridger-Teton NF)

Total sites: 13, RV sites: 13, Central water, Vault/pit toilet, No showers, No RV dump, Tent & RV camping: $7, Open May-Sep, Reservations not accepted, Elev: 7995ft/2437m, Tel: 307-828-5100, Nearest town: Kemmerer. GPS: 42.250732, -110.730469

95 • C1 | Hobble Creek (Bridger-Teton NF)

Total sites: 18, RV sites: 18, Central water, Vault/pit toilet, No showers, No RV dump, Tent & RV camping: $7, Corrals available, Open Jun-Sep, Max Length: 30ft, Reservations not accepted, Elev: 7369ft/2246m, Tel: 307-828-5100, Nearest town: Kemmerer. GPS: 42.398246, -110.783021

96 • C1 | Middle Piney Lake (Bridger-Teton NF)

Total sites: 5, RV sites: 5, No water, Vault/pit toilet, Tent & RV camping: Free, Rough road, Reservations not accepted, Elev: 8917ft/2718m, Nearest town: Big Piney. GPS: 42.603328, -110.564412

97 • C1 | Sacajawea (Bridger-Teton NF)

Total sites: 17, RV sites: 17, Central water, Vault/pit toilet, No showers, No RV dump, Tent & RV camping: $7, Open Jun-Sep, Max Length: 22ft, Reservations not accepted, Elev: 8386ft/2556m, Tel: 307-276-3375, Nearest town: Big Piney. GPS: 42.617397, -110.533716

98 • C1 | Swift Creek (Bridger-Teton NF)

Total sites: 8, RV sites: 8, Central water, Vault/pit toilet, No showers, No RV dump, Tent & RV camping: $10, Periodic Spring, Open May-Sep, Reservations not accepted, Elev: 6420ft/1957m, Nearest town: Afton. GPS: 42.725058, -110.904915

99 • C2 | Big Sandy (Bridger-Teton NF)

Total sites: 12, RV sites: 12, No water, Vault/pit toilet, Tent & RV camping: $7, Open Jun-Sep, Max Length: 22ft, Reservations not accepted, Elev: 9124ft/2781m, Tel: 307-739-5500, Nearest town: Boulder. GPS: 42.687829, -109.270774

100 • C2 | Boulder Lake (Bridger-Teton NF)

Total sites: 15, RV sites: 15, No water, Vault/pit toilet, Tent & RV camping: $7, Open Jun-Sep, Max Length: 100ft, Reservations not accepted, Elev: 7333ft/2235m, Tel: 307-367-4326, Nearest town: Boulder. GPS: 42.857201, -109.617225

101 • C2 | Dickinson Creek (Shoshone NF)

Total sites: 15, RV sites: 15, No water, Vault/pit toilet, Tent & RV camping: Free, Tribal fishing license required if on nearby reservation land, Stay limit: 16 days, Open Apr-Oct, Max Length: 20ft, Reservations not accepted, Elev: 9354ft/2851m, Tel: 307-332-5460, Nearest town: Ft. Washakie. GPS: 42.835693, -109.057617

102 • C2 | Fiddlers Lake (Shoshone NF)

Total sites: 20, RV sites: 20, Central water, Vault/pit toilet, No showers, No RV dump, Tent & RV camping: $15, Stay limit: 16 days, Max Length: 40ft, Reservations not accepted, Elev: 9416ft/2870m, Tel: 307-332-5460, Nearest town: Lander. GPS: 42.629691, -108.881472

103 • C2 | Fremont Lake (Bridger-Teton NF)

Total sites: 54, RV sites: 54, Water available, Vault/pit toilet, No showers, No RV dump, Tent & RV camping: $15, Group site: $50, Open May-Sep, Max Length: 32ft, Reservations accepted, Elev: 7530ft/2295m, Tel: 307-367-4326, Nearest town: Pinedale. GPS: 42.946149, -109.792327

104 • C2 | Half Moon Lake (Bridger-Teton NF)

Total sites: 17, RV sites: 17, No water, Vault/pit toilet, Tent & RV camping: $12, Food storage order 04-00-104, Open May-Sep, Reservations accepted, Elev: 7648ft/2331m, Tel: 307-367-4326, Nearest town: Pinedale. GPS: 42.936881, -109.761537

105 • C2 | Hugh Otte (Shoshone NF)

Total sites: 8, RV sites: 8, No water, Vault/pit toilet, Tent & RV camping: Free, Horse corral, Stay limit: 16 days, Reservations not accepted, Elev: 7056ft/2151m, Tel: 307-332-5460, Nearest town: Lander. GPS: 42.732432, -108.849298

106 • C2 | Little Popo Agie (Shoshone NF)

Total sites: 4, RV sites: 1, No water, Vault/pit toilet, Tent & RV camping: Free, Stay limit: 16 days, Max Length: 16ft, Reservations not accepted, Elev: 8802ft/2683m, Tel: 307-332-5460, Nearest town: Lander. GPS: 42.607848, -108.857318

107 • C2 | Louis Lake (Shoshone NF)

Total sites: 9, RV sites: 9, No water, Vault/pit toilet, Tent & RV camping: $10, Stay limit: 16 days, Max Length: 24ft, Reservations not accepted, Elev: 8594ft/2619m, Tel: 307-332-5460, Nearest town: Lander. GPS: 42.592449, -108.843566

108 • C2 | Sinks Canyon (Shoshone NF)

Total sites: 14, RV sites: 9, Central water, Vault/pit toilet, No showers, No RV dump, Tent & RV camping: $15, Open May-Sep, Max Length: 20ft, Reservations not accepted, Elev: 6903ft/2104m, Tel: 307-332-5460, Nearest town: Lander. GPS: 42.736683, -108.836672

109 • C2 | Worthen Meadow (Shoshone NF)

Total sites: 28, RV sites: 28, Central water, Vault/pit toilet, No showers, No RV dump, Tent & RV camping: $15, Stay limit: 16 days, Open May-Oct, Max Length: 24ft, Reservations not accepted, Elev: 8826ft/2690m, Tel: 307-332-5460, Nearest town: Lander. GPS: 42.698798, -108.929953

110 • C4 | Campbell Creek (Medicine Bow-Routt NF)

Total sites: 6, RV sites: 6, No water, Vault/pit toilet, Tent & RV camping: $10, Stay limit: 14 days, Open Jun-Aug, Max Length: 22ft, Reservations not accepted, Elev: 8018ft/2444m, Tel: 307-358-4690, Nearest town: Douglas. GPS: 42.455311, -105.835949

111 • C4 | Curtis Gulch (Medicine Bow-Routt NF)

Total sites: 6, RV sites: 6, Central water, Vault/pit toilet, No showers, No RV dump, Tent & RV camping: $10, Open May-Oct, Max Length: 22ft, Reservations not accepted, Elev: 6683ft/2037m, Tel: 307-745-2300, Nearest town: Douglas. GPS: 42.407354, -105.623326

112 • C4 | Esterbrook (Medicine Bow-Routt NF)

Total sites: 12, RV sites: 12, No water, Vault/pit toilet, Tent & RV camping: $10, No fee in winter - no water, Stay limit: 14 days, Open all year, Max Length: 22ft, Reservations not accepted, Elev: 6333ft/1930m, Tel: 307-358-4690, Nearest town: Douglas. GPS: 42.425222, -105.324637

113 • C4 | Friend Park (Medicine Bow-Routt NF)

Total sites: 11, RV sites: 8, No water, Vault/pit toilet, Tent & RV camping: $10, 3 walk-to sites, Max Length: 22ft, Reservations not accepted, Elev: 7556ft/2303m, Tel: 307-358-4690, Nearest town: Douglas. GPS: 42.256138, -105.484929

114 • D1 | Deadhorse TH Dispersed (Uinta-Wasatch-Cache NF)

Total sites: 4, RV sites: 4, No water, No toilets, Tent & RV camping: $14, Reservations not accepted, Elev: 8964ft/2732m, Tel: 307-782-6555, Nearest town: Mountain View. GPS: 41.033829, -110.365901

115 • D2 | Buckboard Crossing (Ashley NF)

Total sites: 46, RV sites: 46, Elec sites: 14, Central water, Flush toilet, Free showers, No RV dump, Tents: $22/RVs: $31, 8 sites with electric, Fee showers, Open May-Sep, Max Length: 45ft, Reservations accepted, Elev: 6112ft/1863m, Tel: 435-784-3445, Nearest town: Green River. GPS: 41.248954, -109.601870

116 • D2 | Firehole Canyon (Ashley NF)

Total sites: 37, RV sites: 37, Water available, Flush toilet, Free showers, RV dump, Tent & RV camping: $22, Open May-Sep, Max Length: 35ft, Reservations accepted, Elev: 6079ft/1853m, Tel: 801-226-3564, Nearest town: Rock Spring. GPS: 41.350596, -109.445167

117 • D3 | Bottle Creek (Medicine Bow-Routt NF)

Total sites: 11, RV sites: 11, Central water, Vault/pit toilet, No showers, No RV dump, Tent & RV camping: $10, Stay limit: 14 days, Open Jun-Oct, Max Length: 16ft, Reservations not accepted, Elev: 8747ft/2666m, Tel: 307-745-2300, Nearest town: Encampment. GPS: 41.174682, -106.900458

118 • D3 | Hog Park (Medicine Bow-Routt NF)

Total sites: 17, RV sites: 17, Central water, Vault/pit toilet, No showers, No RV dump, Tent & RV camping: $10, Stay limit: 14 days, Open Jun-Oct, Max Length: 30ft, Reservations accepted, Elev: 8524ft/2598m, Tel: 307-326-5258, Nearest town: Encampment. GPS: 41.025981, -106.863193

119 • D3 | Jack Creek (Medicine Bow-Routt NF)

Total sites: 16, RV sites: 16, Central water, Vault/pit toilet, No showers, No RV dump, Tent & RV camping: $10, No fees/services Oct-May, Open all year, Max Length: 22ft, Reservations not accepted, Elev: 8433ft/2570m, Tel: 307-326-5258, Nearest town: Saratoga. GPS: 41.283313, -107.120419

120 • D3 | Lost Creek (Medicine Bow-Routt NF)

Total sites: 13, RV sites: 13, Central water, Vault/pit toilet, No showers, No RV dump, Tent & RV camping: $10, No services/no fees Oct-Jun, Open all year, Max Length: 22ft, Reservations not accepted, Elev: 8816ft/2687m, Tel: 307-745-2300, Nearest town: Encampment. GPS: 41.141602, -107.075928

121 • D4 | Bobbie Thompson (Medicine Bow-Routt NF)

Total sites: 16, RV sites: 12, Central water, Vault/pit toilet, No showers, No RV dump, Tent & RV camping: $10, No longer a designated CG but dispersed camping allowed, Reservations not accepted, Elev: 8727ft/2660m, Tel: 307-745-2300, Nearest town: Saratoga. GPS: 41.156892, -106.255284

122 • D4 | Bow River (Medicine Bow-Routt NF)

Total sites: 13, RV sites: 13, Central water, Vault/pit toilet, No showers, No RV dump, Tent & RV camping: $10, Max Length: 32ft, Reservations not accepted, Elev: 8591ft/2619m, Tel: 307-745-2300, Nearest town: Elk Mountain. GPS: 41.513503, -106.371114

123 • D4 | Brooklyn Lake (Medicine Bow-Routt NF)

Total sites: 19, RV sites: 19, No water, Vault/pit toilet, Tent & RV camping: $10, Max Length: 22ft, Elev: 10659ft/3249m, Tel: 307-745-2300, Nearest town: Centennial. GPS: 41.373779, -106.246582

124 • D4 | Deep Creek (Medicine Bow-Routt NF)

Total sites: 12, RV sites: 12, Central water, Vault/pit toilet, No showers, No RV dump, Tent & RV camping: $10, Stay limit: 14 days, Open Jul-Sep, Max Length: 22ft, Reservations not accepted, Elev: 10108ft/3081m, Tel: 307-326-5258, Nearest town: Arlington. GPS: 41.459004, -106.272645

125 • D4 | French Creek (Medicine Bow-Routt NF)

Total sites: 11, RV sites: 11, Central water, Vault/pit toilet, No showers, No RV dump, Tent & RV camping: $10, No fees/services Oct-Apr, Open all year, Max Length: 20ft, Reservations not accepted, Elev: 7792ft/2375m, Tel: 307-326-5258, Nearest town: Saratoga. GPS: 41.226683, -106.480591

126 • D4 | Lake Owen (Medicine Bow-Routt NF)

Total sites: 38, RV sites: 38, Central water, Vault/pit toilet, No showers, No RV dump, Tent & RV camping: $10, Stay limit: 14 days, Max Length: 22ft, Reservations not accepted, Elev: 8999ft/2743m, Tel: 307-745-2300, Nearest town: Foxpark. GPS: 41.146484, -106.100830

127 • D4 | Libby Creek - Aspen (Medicine Bow-Routt NF)

Total sites: 8, RV sites: 8, Water available, Vault/pit toilet, No showers, No RV dump, Tent & RV camping: $10, Open May-Sep, Max Length: 22ft, Reservations not accepted, Elev: 8606ft/2623m, Tel: 307-745-2300, Nearest town: Centennial. GPS: 41.318668, -106.160802

128 • D4 | Libby Creek - Pine (Medicine Bow-Routt NF)

Total sites: 6, RV sites: 6, Water available, Vault/pit toilet, No showers, No RV dump, Tent & RV camping: $10, Open May-Sep, Max Length: 22ft, Reservations not accepted, Elev: 8652ft/2637m, Tel: 307-745-2300, Nearest town: Centennial. GPS: 41.319632, -106.162826

129 • D4 | Libby Creek - Spruce (Medicine Bow-Routt NF)

Total sites: 8, RV sites: 8, Water available, Vault/pit toilet, No showers, No RV dump, Tent & RV camping: $10, Open May-Sep, Max Length: 16ft, Reservations not accepted, Elev: 8573ft/2613m, Tel: 307-745-2300, Nearest town: Centennial. GPS: 41.319306, -106.158437

130 • D4 | Libby Creek - Willow (Medicine Bow-Routt NF)

Total sites: 16, RV sites: 16, No water, Vault/pit toilet, Tent & RV camping: $10, Open May-Sep, Max Length: 22ft, Reservations not accepted, Elev: 8665ft/2641m, Tel: 307-745-2300, Nearest town: Centennial. GPS: 41.320542, -106.166375

131 • D4 | Lincoln Park (Medicine Bow-Routt NF)

Total sites: 12, RV sites: 12, Central water, Vault/pit toilet, No showers, No RV dump, Tent & RV camping: $10, No services/no fees Oct-May, Stay limit: 14 days, Open all year, Max Length: 32ft, Reservations not accepted, Elev: 8114ft/2473m, Tel: 307-326-5258, Nearest town: Saratoga. GPS: 41.373554, -106.514147

132 • D4 | Miller Lake (Medicine Bow-Routt NF)

Total sites: 7, RV sites: 7, Central water, Vault/pit toilet, No showers, No RV dump, Tent & RV camping: $10, Stay limit: 14 days, Max Length: 22ft, Reservations not accepted, Elev: 9094ft/2772m, Tel: 307-745-2300, Nearest town: Laramie. GPS: 41.069348, -106.155917

133 • D4 | Nash Fork (Medicine Bow-Routt NF)

Total sites: 27, RV sites: 27, Central water, Vault/pit toilet, No showers, No RV dump, Tent & RV camping: $10, Max Length: 22ft, Reservations not accepted, Elev: 10230ft/3118m, Tel: 307-745-2300, Nearest town: Centennial. GPS: 41.358643, -106.233643

134 • D4 | North Fork (Medicine Bow-Routt NF)

Total sites: 60, RV sites: 60, Central water, Vault/pit toilet, Tent & RV camping: $10, Open Jun-Oct, Max Length: 45ft, Reservations accepted, Elev: 8547ft/2605m, Tel: 307-745-2300, Nearest town: Centennial. GPS: 41.324463, -106.156738

135 • D4 | Pelton Creek (Medicine Bow-Routt NF)

Total sites: 16, RV sites: 16, Water available, Vault/pit toilet, No showers, No RV dump, Tent & RV camping: $10, Max Length: 16ft, Reservations not accepted, Elev: 8258ft/2517m, Tel: 307-745-2300, Nearest town: Laramie. GPS: 41.073391, -106.303591

136 • D4 | Pickaroon (Medicine Bow-Routt NF)

Total sites: 8, RV sites: 8, No toilets, Tent & RV camping: Free, Stay limit: 14 days, Open Jun-Sep, Max Length: 16ft, Reservations not accepted, Elev: 7448ft/2270m, Tel: 307-745-2300, Nearest town: Laramie. GPS: 41.126000, -106.431000

137 • D4 | Pike Pole (Medicine Bow-Routt NF)

Total sites: 6, No water, No toilets, Tents only: Free, Stay limit: 14

days, Open Jun-Sep, Max Length: 16ft, Reservations not accepted, Elev: 7460ft/2274m, Tel: 307-745-2300, Nearest town: Laramie. GPS: 41.129305, -106.426689

138 • D4 | Rob Roy (Medicine Bow-Routt NF)

Total sites: 65, RV sites: 65, Central water, Vault/pit toilet, No showers, No RV dump, Tent & RV camping: $10, Max Length: 35ft, Reservations not accepted, Elev: 9590ft/2923m, Tel: 307-745-2300, Nearest town: Laramie. GPS: 41.216087, -106.253221

139 • D4 | Ryan Park (Medicine Bow-Routt NF)

Total sites: 42, RV sites: 41, Central water, Vault/pit toilet, No showers, No RV dump, Tent & RV camping: $10, Group site $100, Open Jun-Sep, Max Length: 99ft, Reservations accepted, Elev: 8474ft/2583m, Tel: 307-326-5258, Nearest town: Saratoga. GPS: 41.326008, -106.492299

140 • D4 | Silver Lake (Medicine Bow-Routt NF)

Total sites: 17, RV sites: 17, Central water, Vault/pit toilet, No showers, No RV dump, Tent & RV camping: $10, Open Jul-Sep, Max Length: 32ft, Reservations not accepted, Elev: 10490ft/3197m, Nearest town: Centennial. GPS: 41.311648, -106.359852

141 • D4 | Six Mile Gap (Medicine Bow-Routt NF)

Total sites: 9, RV sites: 9, Central water, Vault/pit toilet, No showers, No RV dump, Tent & RV camping: $10, Open May-Oct, Max Length: 32ft, Reservations not accepted, Elev: 7802ft/2378m, Tel: 307-326-5258, Nearest town: Encampment. GPS: 41.044396, -106.399187

142 • D4 | South Brush Creek (Medicine Bow-Routt NF)

Total sites: 20, RV sites: 20, Central water, Vault/pit toilet, No showers, No RV dump, Tent & RV camping: $10, Open Jun-Oct, Max Length: 32ft, Reservations not accepted, Elev: 8235ft/2510m, Tel: 307-326-5258, Nearest town: Saratoga. GPS: 41.344787, -106.503815

143 • D4 | Sugarloaf (Medicine Bow-Routt NF)

Total sites: 16, RV sites: 16, No water, Vault/pit toilet, Tent & RV camping: $10, Open Jul-Sep, Max Length: 32ft, Reservations not accepted, Elev: 10807ft/3294m, Tel: 307-745-2300, Nearest town: Centennial. GPS: 41.353856, -106.293654

144 • D4 | Tie City (Medicine Bow-Routt NF)

Total sites: 17, RV sites: 17, Central water, Vault/pit toilet, No showers, No RV dump, Tent & RV camping: $10, Max Length: 32ft, Reservations not accepted, Elev: 8606ft/2623m, Tel: 307-745-2300, Nearest town: Laramie. GPS: 41.250141, -105.434753

145 • D4 | Vedauwoo (Medicine Bow-Routt NF)

Total sites: 28, RV sites: 20, Central water, Vault/pit toilet, No showers, No RV dump, Tent & RV camping: $10, Max Length: 32ft, Reservations not accepted, Elev: 8297ft/2529m, Tel: 307-745-2300, Nearest town: Buford. GPS: 41.156839, -105.376952

146 • D4 | Yellow Pine (Medicine Bow-Routt NF)

Total sites: 19, RV sites: 19, No water, Vault/pit toilet, No showers, No RV dump, Tent & RV camping: $10, Horse corrals, Open Jun-Sep, Max Length: 32ft, Reservations not accepted, Elev: 8327ft/2538m, Tel: 307-745-2300, Nearest town: Laramie. GPS: 41.254796, -105.410843

Made in the USA
Monee, IL
07 September 2023

42299465R00179